CRIMINAL LAW & PROCEDURE
Proof, Defences, and Beyond

FOURTH EDITION

JENNIE ABELL
ELIZABETH SHEEHY
NATASHA BAKHT

Faculty of Common Law
University of Ottawa

Captus Press

Criminal Law & Procedure: Proof, Defences, and Beyond, Fourth Edition

The publisher and the editors gratefully acknowledge the authors, publishers and organizations for their permission to reproduce their work in this book. Care has been taken to trace ownership of copyright material contained in this book. The publisher will gladly take any information that will enable the rectification of any reference or credit in subsequent editions and apologizes for any errors or omissions.

Captus Press Inc.
Units 14 & 15, 1600 Steeles Avenue West
Concord, ON L4K 4M2 Canada
Tel.: (416) 736-5537
Fax: (416) 736-5793
Email: info@captus.com
Internet: http://www.captus.com

Canada *We acknowledge the financial support of the Government of Canada through the Canada Book Fund for our publishing activities.*

Library and Archives Canada Cataloguing in Publication Data

Abell, J. (Jennie), 1951–
Criminal law & procedure: proof, defences, and beyond / Jennie Abell, Elizabeth Sheehy, Natasha Bakht. — 4th ed.

Includes bibliographical references and index.
ISBN 978-1-55322-200-2

1. Criminal law — Canada. 2. Criminal procedure — Canada. 3. Sociological jurisprudence. I. Sheehy, Elizabeth A. II. Bakht, Natasha. III. Title. IV. Title: Criminal law and procedure.

KE8809.A38 2008 345.71 C2008-906443-7
KF9220.ZA2A38 2008

0 9 8 7 6 5 4 3 2
Printed in Canada

Table of Contents

Introduction

Criminal Law & Procedure: Proof, Defences, and Beyond is the companion volume to our book, *Criminal Law & Procedure: Cases, Context, Critique* [hereinafter Abell & Sheehy, *Cases, Context, Critique*]. Although we teach and use both volumes in the first year law school course on criminal law, the volumes also stand on their own and can be used alone or in conjunction with other materials.

This book serves legal educators and students who are interested in critical frameworks in their application to criminal law. It shows the impact of the *Canadian Charter of Rights and Freedoms*,[1] the interface between criminal law doctrine and legal practice, and the evolution of Canadian criminal law as it is shaped by the activism and creativity of lawyers, clients, and other affected groups. We believe that this book will also be useful to those who work and teach in law-related disciplines such as criminology or sociology.

Our approach in this book is similar to that used for *Cases, Content, Critique*: we have relied upon a variety of materials to explicate the subjects, including cases, facta, articles, books from inside and outside of law, and statutes. Our materials are primarily Canadian, but include selections from England, the United States, South Africa, Ireland, and Australia. The influence of the *Charter* upon the proof and defence of criminal offences in Canada is explored throughout this book, with particular attention to s. 15 equality arguments and analyses.

Since the publication of the first, second, and third editions in 1995, 1998, and 2004, there have been significant developments in criminal law. In this fourth edition of *Criminal Law & Procedure: Proof, Defences and Beyond*, we update the materials through a consideration of new case law and litigation, legislative developments, and critical analysis. We continue to develop the themes of feminist analysis, inquiry into colonization, colonialism and racism, and a class-based critique of law.

STRUCTURE

In this volume, we turn to the specifics of the prosecution's obligation of **Proving a Case** against an accused in **Part I**. This part includes chapters on subject matters that are typically found in law school course materials: the **Burden of Proof**, proof of the ***Actus Reus*** or physical aspects of a crime, proof of the ***Mens Rea*** or mental aspect of a crime, and **Proof of Inchoate Crimes**.

Part I goes beyond the traditional subject matters, however, by including chapters on **Corporate Homicide**, by way of a case study of the issues of proof that such prosecutions present; **The Trial Process**, which includes discussion of the

Preliminary Inquiry and the Jury and, among other issues, The Media and the Trial Process. This section touches on the diverse interests that are at stake in the law and the practice of publicly identifying the complainant/witness/victim and the accused in sexual assault cases, the role of the media in shaping public opinion and judging those on trial, and the effects of the use of video cameras by reporters on the detection and prosecution of "crime".

Part II, Defending a Case, examines defences, again including all the traditional subjects such as **Mistake of Fact**, **Mistake of Law**, **Incapacity** (in terms of age and mental disorder), **Intoxication and Extreme Intoxication**, **Automatism**, **Provocation**, **Self-Defence and Defence of Others**, **Duress**, **Necessity**, and **Entrapment**.

Part II also moves beyond the usual treatment of defences by developing a **Case Study on Assault**, which introduces the defences of consent, correction, and *de minimis*; examining an emerging defence of **Colour of Right** that crosses legal boundaries, which is used primarily by Aboriginal peoples charged with property offences in relation to efforts to assert land claims, for example, at Ipperwash and on the Secwepemc (Shuswap) First Nation near Kamloops; illuminating the legal treatment of the defence of conscience using the examples of Perry Dunlop, Mordechai Vanunu, Clive Ponting, and Paul Watson; exploring what a reconceptualized defence of necessity might look like if, for example, courts were attentive to violence and abuse within the family; and positing **Broadening the Defences: Necessity, Self-Defence, and Conscience** in light of examples drawn from the Treason Trials in South Africa, the prosecutions of the Suffragettes in England, and the more contemporary prosecutions of the Lubicon Nation, Leonard Peltier, and anti-poverty protesters, among others.

THEMES

Our treatment of the "traditional" chapters outlined above is not a narrow one. While we include the key cases on all of these issues, we have enriched the book by the development of specific themes in relation to each. In addition to the themes of feminism, colonization, racism, and class-based critique, the materials also raise issues about the impact of criminal law and the criminal justice system upon persons with disabilities and upon lesbians and gays.

Feminism

Feminist analysis of criminal law is prolific and has, in certain instances, been profoundly influential in shaping criminal law and policy. This analysis at a general level accepts that women experience inequality vis-à-vis men through Canadian social, legal, political, and economic institutions and seeks to use law, when possible, to challenge that inequality or shift relations of dominance.

Many current issues in Canadian law that are the subject of both criminal litigation and law reform have been raised, developed, and pursued by feminists. These issues are at the core of intense public debates about the meaning of moral responsibility and legal "fault", whose versions of women's lives will be accorded social and legal credibility, and who has the ultimate legal and moral authority on these issues — Canadian judges or elected members of Parliament? The arguments and criticisms raised by feminist analysis also suggest that a uniform body of neutral principles, developed from the point of view of those in power, will inevitably serve women poorly.

Women's experience of battering provides an important context from which to evaluate some of these debates. Thus, under ***Actus Reus*** and, more specifically, responsibility for omissions, this book raises the issue of the legal responsibility of mothers who fail to prevent their partners from assaulting their children, particularly in situations where those women themselves have been subjected to violence. To what degree is it just to punish those women with the same sentence as that imposed upon the offender? Is it appropriate to use the criminal law power against battered mothers of battered children when the law has itself failed to provide protection or assistance to them?

Under **Duress** we look at the successful constitutional challenge in *R. v. Ruzic*[2] to the statutory defence of duress but also how that defence is slowly being re-conceived to benefit women who, in response to threats from violent partners, commit crime to avert harm to themselves and their children. Under **Self-Defence and Defence of Others**, this book asks whether the judicial re-interpretation of this defence for battered women who kill violent men in *R. v. Lavallee*[3] will benefit accused women; and we consider the recommendations of and response to Judge Ratushny's Self-Defence Review.[4] Under **Necessity** and **Broadening the Defences**, the question is raised whether women should be given a defence when they act in defiance of legal rulings by attempting to protect their children. Attention to the context of battering and its social meaning for gender relations also allows for critical questions to be raised about the legal interpretations of the defences of **Intoxication and Extreme Intoxication, Automatism, Provocation, Self-Defence and Defence of Others**, and **Necessity** when used in defence to charges involving femicide. Those legal interpretations have increasingly been the subject of challenge in the wake of such cases as *R. v. Thibert*,[5] *R. v. Parent*,[6] *R. v. Malott*,[7] and *R. v. Graveline*.[8]

Women's experience of sexual assault and the response of the legal system have also prompted feminist engagements with criminal law. We have therefore woven this issue throughout the materials in this book. Specifically, we consider the consequences for the prosecution of sexual assault of the particular judicial interpretation of the requisite ***Mens Rea*** element for sexual assault by individual men and by groups of men. **The Trial Process** discusses the law reform response of Parliament through Bill C-46 to defence efforts to secure disclosure of women's counselling records.[9] Under the section on The Media and The Trial Process we examine the media's failed legal bid to publish the names of complainants/witnesses/victims in rape trials. The defence of **Mistake of Fact** is explored through a sustained analysis of the impact of this defence upon the successful prosecution of sexual assault and, ultimately, upon our social understandings of the degree to which men are permitted to use force and coercion to gain access to women's sexuality. Again, Parliament's response to judicial decision-making in this area, in the form of Bill C-49,[10] is also considered.

The chapter on the defence of **Intoxication and Extreme Intoxication** also raises the issue of the legal treatment of sexual assault, given that the facts on which the Supreme Court of Canada's decision in *R. v. Daviault*[11] was played out involved a serious sexual assault upon an elderly woman who used a wheelchair. Bill C-72,[12] the law enacted in the wake of *Daviault*, is discussed for the issues it raises.

Thus, these chapters consider the relationship between the Supreme Court of Canada and Parliament, as Parliament has intervened legislatively to repair or reaffirm the legal rights of women after the Court has rendered decisions pursuant to the *Charter* that substantially impaired those interests. This constitutionalization of political issues is an important theme that is pursued throughout the book.

Colonization, Colonialism, and Racism

The history of colonization and colonialism were explored in our first book, *Cases, Context, Critique*. Some of the effects were highlighted in terms of the definition of crime, patterns of enforcement of the law, and policing practices. In this volume, the process and impact of colonization surface through examination of the legal doctrine and practice that effectively conceal structural racism. By structural racism we intend to convey those legal, social, and economic structures that may have the appearance of neutrality or even meritocracy, but which reinforce and valorize a standpoint that presumes "whiteness". This means that certain forms of knowledge are credited and others discounted, that particular claims to historical "truth" are accepted and others rejected, and that specific "facts", such as the social reality of racism, may be "relevant" or "irrelevant" to the law of criminal defences.[13] This theme of credibility and power recurs throughout the discussion of criminal law, and is highlighted in the last section of the book where the credibility of victim/witnesses is addressed more directly.

As we explore this theme of the impact of colonization and racism, we focus on the effect of criminal law upon Aboriginal and "racialized"[14] peoples. Our starting point assumption is that "race", like "gender", is a social construct that is used to create and maintain "racial" categories and hierarchies.[15] For example, in Western legal systems and in social "understandings", both of which reflect dominant interests, people are classified as "visible minority", regardless of the complexities of their heritage, if they have any amount of "non-white blood"; on the other hand, to be considered "white", a different set of considerations is invoked.[16]

In the context of Aboriginal peoples, part of the process of colonization was for the state to claim the right to classify Aboriginal peoples racially, through the *Indian Act*. Even though certain legislative changes have been achieved that extend the definition of "Indian" in Bill C-31 in 1985, the state has still reserved to itself the right to define who is an "Indian", using blood lines and quantities as determinants.[17] Therefore, instead of focusing on "race" or "culture" as inherently relevant, we focus upon racism as the social response that requires legal analysis.

In Canadian criminal law, while the "racial" identities of the accused and victim/witness are highly significant for the application and impact of its practice and doctrine, racism is usually hidden and denied by the legal system. For example, as Constance Backhouse demonstrates, historically, prosecutions of racialized people for breaching the informal "law" of segregation were pursued through resort to distorted interpretations of other criminal and regulatory laws such as the *Theatres and Amusements Act*.[18] Similarly, in current Canadian criminal law there is scant legal doctrine that explicitly or specifically targets Aboriginal or racialized peoples, although there is other evidence that suggests that targeting indeed occurs.

In the materials that follow, we attempt to make visible the ways that structural racism shapes the criminal law to the detriment of Aboriginal peoples. For example, the law requiring disclosure by the Crown prosecutor of all "records" of the victim/witness in criminal trials has a profoundly negative impact upon Aboriginal women who attempt to prosecute sexual assault, in part because those "records" include residential school records, child welfare records, and juvenile records, all of which were produced within the context of what Judge Murray Sinclair has described as the ethnocide of Aboriginal peoples,[19] and informed by racist ideologies. As the Aboriginal Women's Council *et al.* argued in their factum intervening in the prosecution of Archbishop Hubert O'Connor, discussed under **The Trial Process**, the utility of these records to the defence for the purpose of intimidating and undermining the credibility of the victim/witness depends upon judicial understandings of "relevance" that contravene the s. 15 equality rights of Aboriginal women under the *Charter*.

Under the heading of **The Trial Process**, we discuss Aboriginal peoples in various contexts: the ways in which the facially neutral language on jury selection in the *Criminal Code* has been used to systematically exclude Aboriginal peoples from jury service is explored under The Jury, as is a legal challenge asserting the right of an Aboriginal accused to challenge prospective jurors about their biases.[20] An article by Adrian Howe on the media's role in the wrongful conviction of Lindy Chamberlain in Australia highlights the manner in which the expertise of an Aboriginal witness was discounted.

The historical legacy of the separation of Aboriginal peoples from their lands through the criminal law has specific consequences for current legal struggles that are played out in the criminal law domain. For example, under the defence **Colour of Right: Mistake of Fact, Mistake of Law, or Affirmative Defence**, we explore the legal argument made by Aboriginal peoples that they cannot be prosecuted for criminal offences in relation to land that they hold claim to. This section includes cases where this defence has been asserted in response to trespass and mischief charges, obstructing a highway at Sun Peaks, and a piece by Daniel Ashini, who describes the legal struggle of the Innu in opposition to low-level flying over their lands. In the chapter, **Self-Defence and Defence of Others**, we consider the successful defence of one of the Ipperwash protesters to charges of dangerous driving and assault of a peace officer for his rescue of a fellow protester: *R. v. N.C.*[21] Finally, in the chapter **Broadening the Defences: Necessity, Self-Defence, and Conscience**, examples of the state's use of the criminal law power to silence political dissent include the collusion of the United States and Canadian governments in the extradition and conviction of Leonard Peltier, and the prosecution of Milton Born With A Tooth, of the Lubicon Nation.

The influence of systemic racism upon other racialized peoples, as victims and as accused, is explored within several chapters. The chapter on ***Actus Reus*** and, more specifically, on the subject of proof of Causation, raises questions about the narrow way in which the law attributes "causality" so as to exclude systemic forces such as racism. The chapter on **The Trial Process** documents two developments: the Supreme Court of Canada decision in *R. v. Williams*[22] that acknowledged racism as a social reality such that the jury selection process must be altered to take it into account, and media involvement in the framing of racialized crime and its prosecution through video evidence. Examples of the media depiction of protest and the legal response to racism are also developed. Finally, the minimization of the influence of racism in *R. v. Ellard*[23] in both the media and the trial process is highlighted.

Under **Mistake of Fact** the specific difficulties faced by racialized women in prosecuting sexual assault are identified and, under **Incapacity**, note is taken of the link between status as a member of a "visible minority" community and the attribution of mental illness. The defence of **Provocation** is explored in reference to the test of the "ordinary person", which historically precluded consideration of the accused's racialized identity. The chapter also takes up current legal debates about whether an accused's "culture", for instance, should be relevant to a provocation defence for example in *R. v. Humaid*.[24] Finally, **Self-Defence and Defence of Others** identifies as significant the successful use of self-defence by police officers who have killed often unarmed racialized men.

Class-Based Critique

This theme focuses upon the role of criminal law in ordering a capitalist state and class relations. It includes attention to the ways in which criminal law reinforces the values that permit class domination through law such as the venerable authority and tradition of the common law, the belief in the objectivity and neutrality of the judiciary, and the assertion that the *Charter* "is there to protect the minority against the majority, the individual against the state."[25]

This book explores the political bias of the criminal law at a number of junctures, and often through specific examples illustrating the use of the criminal law to prosecute corporate crime. The first discussion of this theme occurs under **Burden of Proof**, where the Supreme Court decisions regarding the constitutionality of particular burdens of proof are considered for their impact upon the prosecution of regulatory crimes. Under ***Actus Reus***, Causation, the work of Eric Tucker is discussed for the purpose of illustrating the bias in the law of causation when accounting for workplace accidents. Under ***Mens Rea***, more detailed attention is given to the theoretical structuring of the concept of *mens rea* such that prosecutions of corporations and individual directors and managers become not only legally difficult but also, even if successful, lose the social disapproval reserved for "truly criminal" conduct. The chapter **Case Study on Corporate Homicide** looks at the specific hurdles faced in such prosecutions, referring to the efforts to prosecute Ford for the Pinto deaths, the owners and operators of *The Herald of the Free Enterprise* for the deaths in the Zeebrugge disaster, and, in more detail, the history of the effort to prosecute the Curragh Inc. for the Nova Scotia mine explosion (Westray) in 1992 that killed 26 workers. This chapter also explores the new *Code* provisions, ss. 22.1, 22.2 and s. 217.1, that purport to facilitate prosecution of organizations, including corporations. It asks whether, in light of the failed prosecutions under the previous law with respect to the deaths of a woman and her child and the serious injuries caused to numerous others when a dam released flood waters onto a dry river bed (*R. v. Ontario Power Generation*[26] and *R. v. Tammadge*[27]), any different results would be reached under the reformed law.

The theme of the maintenance of class relations through criminal law is likewise raised by some defences. Under **Mistake of Law**, it appears that the developing exception to the bar on mistake of law arguments, that of "officially induced error of law", will benefit corporations that engage in regulated industries such that they can fulfil the requirements of the defence. The defence of **Necessity**, as narrowly defined by the Supreme Court of Canada, also serves entrenched economic interests: its terms would deny the defence to the poor who make deliberate decisions to commit welfare fraud to feed their children or to commit trespass to seek shelter, but might offer the defence to individuals whose crimes do not threaten the current economic and social ordering, such as drivers, drug smugglers, and men who assault women. Under **Self-Defence and Defence of Others**, we examine the implications for prisoners of an expanded view of self-defence in *R. v. McConnell*[28] and *R. v. Kerr*,[29] for example. Under **Broadening the Defences: Necessity, Self-Defence, and Conscience**, we consider the ways in which private corporations are able to invoke the state's criminal powers against individuals to prevent protest, in the case of MacMillan Bloedel and Clayoquot Sound, for example. We also examine cases where poverty activists attempted to argue necessity.

Compulsory Heterosexuality

The interest of the criminal law in enforcing the gender roles dictated by compulsory heterosexuality is closely linked to the state's interest in maintaining patriarchal authority. The criminal law has been used to police male sexuality by punishing gay men's transgressions from the male gender role through specific criminal offences such as s. 159 of the *Criminal Code* (ruled unconstitutional for violating s. 15 of the *Charter* in *R. v. C.(M.)*[30]), expansive interpretations of police powers, media exposure, and failure to condemn violence against gay men. The criminal law has been less overt in its stance towards lesbians, rarely criminalizing lesbian sexuality in part because it was denied as a possibility.[31] However, the role of criminal law in policing women's expressions of sexuality through the law of juvenile delinquency, prostitution, and the failure to enforce the law of sexual assault, has been as pervasive.

The following specific examples are taken up in this book: under ***Actus Reus***, Act or Omission, we look at the expansive interpretation given to the offence of mischief in order to convict a gay man who donated HIV-positive blood to the Red Cross; and under the defence of **Provocation** we explore in more detail the use of this defence in cases involving hate-motivated violence against gays and lesbians in light of the implicit premise of heterosexuality in the criminal law's construction of the "ordinary person".

Disabilityism

The expression "disabilityism" derives from the work of Dianne Pothier,[32] and signals an understanding of the systemic devaluation of the validity of the experience and the impact of law on persons with mental and physical disabilities. Although we cannot purport to have treated this analytical framework as a theme in these materials, we have attempted to make some links between criminal law and disabilityism. For example, under the chapter **The Trial Process**, The Jury, we note some of the barriers that have excluded persons with disabilities from jury service and we discuss the right under s. 14 of the *Charter* to translation for persons with hearing impairments, as well as the impact of the curtailment of the "right to silence" on those with mental disabilities. Under **Mistake of Fact**, we attend to the barriers that make the successful prosecution of sexual assault by women with disabilities even more remote. The chapters on **Incapacity, Intoxication and Extreme Intoxication**, and **Automatism** raise questions about whether and when offenders with disabilities should be held legally responsible for their offences. Under **Necessity**, we consider the prosecution of Robert Latimer for killing his disabled daughter and the intervenors' arguments that highlight equality rights issues and problematize the defence arguments. Finally, the chapter on **Broadening the Defences** contains reference to the legal treatment by the state of political protest by persons with disabilities.

We hope that this book will prove useful for those who are committed to seeking social justice through law, whether law students, lawyers, or researchers. The materials in this book were current as of July 2008.

Notes

1. Part 1 of the *Constitution Act, 1982*, being Schedule B to the *Canada Act, 1982* (U.K.), 1982, c. 11 [hereinafter *Charter*].
2. *R. v. Ruzic*, [2001] 1 S.C.R. 687.
3. *R. v. Lavallee*, [1990] 1 S.C.R. 852.
4. Judge Lynn Ratushny, *Self-Defence Review: Final Report* (Ottawa: Department of Justice and Solicitor General, 1997).
5. *R. v. Thibert*, [1996] 1 S.C.R. 37.
6. *R. v. Parent*, [2001] 1 S.C.R. 761.
7. *R. v. Malott*, [1998] 1 S.C.R. 123.
8. *R. v. Graveline*, [2006] 1 S.C.R. 609.
9. *An Act to amend the Criminal Code (production of records in sexual assault proceedings)*, S.C. 1997, c. 38, s. 1.
10. *An Act to amend the Criminal Code (sexual assault)*, S.C. 1992, c. 38, s. 1.
11. [1994] 3 S.C.R. 63.
12. *An Act to amend the Criminal Code (self-induced intoxication)*, S.C. 1995, c. 32, s. 1.
13. Linda Carty, "Black Women in Academia: A Statement from the Periphery" in Himani Bannerji *et al. Unsettling Relations. The University as a Site of Feminist Struggle* (Toronto: Women's Press, 1991) 13 at 26.
14. This is the term adopted in Joanne St. Lewis & Sheila Galloway, *Reforming the Law of Provocation* (Toronto: Ontario Women's Directorate, 1994).
15. Carty, *supra* note 12.
16. This issue has been a matter of public debate because of the questions regarding "race" and how the responses will be analyzed in the 1996 Census by Statistics Canada: Dan Gardner, "Statscan's task is not black-and-white" *The [Toronto] Globe and Mail* (18 September 1995) A21; Dan Gardner, "When racial categories make no sense" *The [Toronto] Globe and Mail* (21 October 1995) D8.
17. For a compelling criticism of C-31, see Mary Ellen Turpel, "Discrimination and the 1985 Amendments to the Indian Act: Full of Snares for Women" *Rights and Freedoms* (September 1987) 6.
18. Constance Backhouse, "Racial Segregation in Canadian Legal History: Viola Desmond's Challenge, Nova Scotia, 1946" (1994) 17 Dalhousie L.J. 299.
19. Judge Murray Sinclair, "A Presentation to the Western Workshop of the Western Judicial Education Centre" in Abell & Sheehy, *Cases, Context, Critique* 51 at 52.
20. *R. v. Williams*, [1998] 1 S.C.R. 1128.
21. *R. v. N.C.*, [1997] O.J. No. 2302 (Prov. Div.) (QL).
22. *Supra* note 20.
23. *R. v. Ellard*, [2005] B.C.J. No. 2987 (B.C.S.C.) (QL).
24. *R. v. Humaid* (2006), 81 O.R. (3d) 456 (C.A.).
25. Interestingly, this statement was made by Justice Sopinka, of the Supreme Court of Canada, who went on to say that "naturally many of our decisions would be subject to criticism by the majority." In fact, he was speaking in defence of the decisions from the Court, such as *R. v. Daviault*, which have been criticized by feminist groups as harmful to women, hardly a majoritarian interest: "Do not rule for popularity, judge says" *The [Toronto] Globe and Mail* (29 June 1995) A4.
26. *R. v. Ontario Power Generation*, [2006] O.J. No. 4659 (Ct. J.) (QL).
27. *R. v. Tammadge*, [2006] O.J. No. 5103 (Ct. J.) (QL).
28. *R. v. McConnell* (1995), 32 Alta. L.R. (3d) 1 (C.A.).
29. *R. v. Kerr*, [2004] 2 S.C.R. 371.
30. *R. v. C.(M.)* (1995), 23 O.R. (3d) 629 (C.A.).
31. Katherine Arnup, "'Mothers Just Like Others': Lesbians, Divorce, and Child Custody in Canada" (1989) 3:1 C.J.W.L. 18 at 19.
32. Dianne Pothier, "Miles to Go: Some Personal Reflections on the Social Construction of Disability" (1992) 14 Dalhousie L.J. 526.

I

Proving a Case

1

Burden of Proof

A. INTRODUCTION

Generally, the Crown prosecutor bears a legal or persuasive burden of proof in a criminal trial. A legal or persuasive burden of proof requires that the Crown persuade or convince the trier of fact, whether judge alone or jury, that the ultimate burden of proof has been met so as to warrant a conviction on the charge. In criminal law, this burden has been described as proof "beyond a reasonable doubt" and is constitutionalized as the "presumption of innocence" in s. 11(d) of the *Canadian Charter of Rights and Freedom* [hereinafter *Charter*]. As a matter within the domain of the trier of fact, the question of whether the case has been proven "beyond a reasonable doubt" is a question of fact, although the trial judge's charge to the jury on this standard of proof is a question of law. For example, see *R. v. Lifchus*, [1997] 3 S.C.R. 320, where the Court held that jurors must be instructed on the meaning of "proof beyond a reasonable doubt" and gave examples of acceptable and unacceptable explanations.

Both Crown and defence bear evidential (or evidentiary) burdens throughout a criminal trial. An evidential burden, also referred to as a housekeeping burden, requires that the party who wishes to rely upon a legal rule or defence introduce sufficient evidence to support the proposed argument. Although this burden is less than a persuasive burden, requiring only enough evidence to put the matter at issue, it functions to preclude from consideration arguments for which there is insufficient factual support. For instance, an accused will not be entitled to insist that a judge ask a jury to consider an intoxication defence when the only evidence to support the defence is that the accused consumed two glasses of beer. The question of whether the evidential burden has been met is said to be a question of law and, therefore, rests with the judge for resolution.

The *Criminal Code of Canada* [hereinafter *Code*] and various other statutes contain provisions that describe or vary these burdens of proof in relation to specific offences and defences. For example, some sections of the *Code* impose burdens of proof upon an accused, using language suggesting a persuasive burden ("the proof of which lies upon him" [*sic*]), and other sections indicate an evidential burden ("in the absence of evidence to the contrary"). The issues that have arisen since the advent of the *Charter* include whether the constitutional guarantee of the presumption of innocence, contained in s. 11(d), can be used to challenge these statutory presumptions, as well as whether s. 1 can be invoked to save the *Charter* violation.

B. SECTION 11(D)

R. v. Oakes†

[DICKSON C.J.:]

This appeal concerns the constitutionality of s. 8 of the *Narcotic Control Act*, R.S.C. 1970, C. N-1. The section provides, in brief, that if the Court finds the accused in possession of a narcotic, he is presumed to be in possession for the purpose of trafficking. Unless the accused can establish the contrary, he must be convicted of trafficking. The Ontario Court of Appeal held that this provision constitutes a "reverse onus" clause and is unconstitutional because it violates one of the core values of our criminal justice system, the presumption of innocence, now entrenched in s. 11(d) of the *Canadian Charter of Rights and Freedoms*. The Crown has appealed.

. . . .

FACTS

The respondent, David Edwin Oakes, was charged with unlawful possession of a narcotic for the purpose of trafficking, contrary to s. 4(2) of the *Narcotic Control Act*. He elected trial by magistrate without a jury. At trial, the Crown adduced evidence to establish that Mr. Oakes was found in possession of eight one gram vials of *cannabis* resin in the form of hashish oil. Upon a further search conducted at the police station, $619.45 was located. Mr. Oakes told the police that he had bought ten vials of hashish oil for $150 for his own use, and that the $619.45 was from a workers' compensation cheque. He elected not to call evidence as to possession of the narcotic. Pursuant to the procedural provisions of s. 8 of the *Narcotic Control Act*, the trial judge proceeded to make a finding that it was beyond a reasonable doubt that Mr. Oakes was in possession of the narcotic. [Section 8 of the *Narcotic Control Act* provided that "[i]f the court finds that the accused was in possession of the narcotic ... he shall be given an opportunity of establishing that he was not in possession of the narcotic for the purpose of trafficking ... [I]f the accused established that he was not in possession of the narcotic for the purpose of trafficking, he shall be acquitted of the offence as charged but he shall be convicted of possession ... [I]f the accused fails to establish that he was not in possession for the purpose of trafficking, he shall be convicted and sentenced."]

Following this finding, Mr Oakes brought a motion to challenge the constitutional validity of s. 8 of the *Narcotic Control Act*, which he maintained imposes a burden on an accused to prove that he or she was not in possession for the purpose of trafficking. He argued that s. 8 violates the presumption of innocence contained in s. 11(d) of the *Charter*.

. . . .

THE ISSUES

. . . .

To interpret the meaning of s. 11(d), it is important to adopt a purposive approach. As this Court stated in *R. v. Big M Drug Mart Ltd.*, [1985] 1 S.C.R. 295, at p. 344:

> The meaning of a right or freedom guaranteed by the *Charter* was to be ascertained by an analysis of the *purpose* of such a guarantee; it was to be understood, in other words, in the light of the interests it was meant to protect.
>
> In my view this analysis is to be undertaken, and the purpose of the right or freedom in question is to be sought by reference to the character and the larger objects of the *Charter* itself, to the language chosen to articulate the specific right or freedom, to the historical origins of the concepts enshrined, and where applicable, to the meaning and purpose of the other specific rights and freedoms....

To identify the underlying purpose of the *Charter* right in question, therefore, it is important to begin by understanding the cardinal values it embodies.

The presumption of innocence is a hallowed principle lying at the very heart of criminal law. Although protected expressly in s. 11(d) of the *Charter*, the presumption of innocence is referable and integral to the general protection of life, liberty and security of the person contained in s. 7 of the *Charter* (see *Re B.C. Motor Vehicle Act*, [1985] 2 S.C.R. 486, *per* Lamer J.). The presumption of innocence

† [1986] 1 S.C.R. 103.

protects the fundamental liberty and human dignity of any and every person accused by the State of criminal conduct. An individual charged with a criminal offence faces grave social and personal consequences, including potential loss of physical liberty, subjection to social stigma and ostracism from the community, as well as other social, psychological and economic harms. In light of the gravity of these consequences, the presumption of innocence is crucial. It ensures that until the State proves an accused's guilt beyond all reasonable doubt, he or she is innocent. This is essential in a society committed to fairness and social justice. The presumption of innocence confirms our faith in humankind; it reflects our belief that individuals are decent and law-abiding members of the community until proven otherwise.

The presumption of innocence has enjoyed long-standing recognition at common law. In the leading case, *Woolmington v. Director of Public Prosecutions*, [1935] A.C. 462 (H.L.), Viscount Sankey wrote at pp. 481–82:

> Throughout the web of the English Criminal Law one golden thread is always to be seen, that it is the duty of the prosecution to prove the prisoner's guilt subject to what I have already said as to the defence of insanity and subject also to any statutory exception. If, at the end of and on the whole of the case, there is a reasonable doubt, created by the evidence given by either the prosecution or the prisoner, as to whether the prisoner killed the deceased with a malicious intention, the prosecution has not made out the case and the prisoner is entitled to an acquittal. No matter what the charge or where the trial, the principle that the prosecution must prove the guilt of the prisoner is part of the common law of England and no attempt to whittle it down can be entertained.

Subsequent Canadian cases have cited the *Woolmington* principle with approval (see, for example, *Manchuk v. The King*, [1938] S.C.R. 341, at p. 349; *R. v. City of Sault Ste. Marie*, [1978] 2 S.C.R. 1299, at p. 1316).

Further evidence of the widespread acceptance of the principle of the presumption of innocence is its inclusion in the major international human rights documents. Article 11(1) of the *Universal Declaration of Human Rights*, adopted December 10, 1948 by the General Assembly of the United Nations, provides:

> *Article* 11
> 1. Everyone charged with a penal offence has the right to be presumed innocent until proved guilty according to law in a public trial at which he has had all the guarantees necessary for his defence.

In the *International Covenant on Civil and Political Rights*, 1966, art. 14(2) states:

> *Article* 14
> 2. Everyone charged with a criminal offence shall have the right to be presumed innocent until proved guilty according to law.

Canada acceded to this Covenant, and the Optional Protocol which sets up machinery for implementing the Covenant, on May 19, 1976. Both came into effect on August 19, 1976.

In light of the above, the right to be presumed innocent until proven guilty requires that s. 11(d) have, at a minimum, the following content. First, an individual must be proven guilty beyond a reasonable doubt. Second, it is the State which must bear the burden of proof. As Lamer J. stated in *Dubois v. The Queen*, [1985] 2 S.C.R. 350, at p. 357:

> Section 11(d) imposes upon the Crown the burden of proving the accused's guilt beyond a reasonable doubt as well as that of making out the case against the accused before he or she need respond, either by testifying or calling other evidence.

Third, criminal prosecutions must be carried out in accordance with lawful procedures and fairness. The latter part of s. 11(d), which requires the proof of guilt "according to law in a fair and public hearing by an independent and impartial tribunal," underlines the importance of this procedural requirement.

. . . .

The *Woolmington* case was decided in the context of a legal system with no constitutionally entrenched human rights document. In Canada, we have tempered parliamentary supremacy by entrenching important rights and freedoms in the Constitution. Viscount Sankey's statutory exception proviso is clearly not applicable in this context and would subvert the very purpose of the entrenchment of the presumption of innocence in the *Charter*. I do not, therefore, feel constrained in this case by the interpretation of s. 2(f) of the *Canadian Bill of Rights* presented in the majority judgment in *Appleby*. Section 8 of the *Narcotic Control Act* is not rendered constitutionally valid simply by virtue of the fact that it is a statutory provision.

. . . .

In general one must, I think, conclude that a provision which requires an accused to disprove on a balance of probabilities the existence of a presumed fact, which is an important element of the offence in question, violates the presumption of innocence in s. 11(d). If an accused bears the burden of disproving on a balance of probabilities an essential element of an offence, it would be possible for a conviction to occur despite the existence of a reasonable doubt. This would arise if the accused adduced sufficient evidence to raise a reasonable doubt as to his or her innocence but did not convince the jury on a balance of probabilities that the presumed fact was untrue.

The fact that the standard is only the civil one does not render a reverse onus clause constitutional. As Sir Rupert Cross commented in the *Rede Lectures*, "The Golden Thread of the English Criminal Law: The Burden of Proof," delivered in 1976 at the University of Toronto, at pp. 11–13:

> It is sometimes said that exceptions to the Woolmington rule are acceptable because, whenever the burden of proof on any issue in a criminal case is borne by the accused, he only has to satisfy the jury on the balance of probabilities, whereas on issues on which the Crown bears the burden of proof the jury must be satisfied beyond a reasonable doubt.... The fact that the standard is lower when the accused bears the burden of proof than it is when the burden of proof is borne by the prosecution is no answer to my objection to the existence of exceptions to the Woolmington rule as it does not alter the fact that a jury or bench of magistrates may have to convict the accused although they are far from sure of his guilt.

As we have seen, the potential for a rational connection between the basic fact and the presumed fact to justify a reverse onus provision has been elaborated in some of the cases discussed above and is now known as the "rational connection test." In the context of s. 11(d), however, the following question arises: if we apply the rational connection test to the consideration of whether s. 11(d) has been violated, are we adequately protecting the constitutional principle of the presumption of innocence? As Professors MacKay and Cromwell point out in their article "Oakes: A Bold Initiative Impeded by Old Ghosts" (1983), 32 C.R. (3d) 221, at p. 233:

> The rational connection test approves a provision that *forces* the trier to infer a fact that may be simply rationally connected to the proved fact. Why does it follow that such a provision does not offend the constitutional right to be proved guilty beyond a reasonable doubt?

A basic fact may rationally tend to prove a presumed fact, but not prove its existence beyond a reasonable doubt. An accused person could thereby be convicted despite the presence of a reasonable doubt. This would violate the presumption of innocence.

I should add that this questioning of the constitutionality of the "rational connection test" as a guide to interpreting s. 11(d) does not minimize its importance. The appropriate stage for invoking the rational connection test, however, is under s. 1 of the *Charter*. This consideration did not arise under the *Canadian Bill of Rights* because of the absence of an equivalent to s. 1. At the Court of Appeal level in the present case, Martin J.A. sought to combine the analysis of s. 11(d) and s. 1 to overcome the limitations of the *Canadian Bill of Rights* jurisprudence. To my mind, it is highly desirable to keep s. 1 and s. 11(d) analytically distinct. Separating the analysis into two components is consistent with the approach this Court has taken to the *Charter* to date (see *R. v. Big M Drug Mart Ltd.*, *supra*; *Hunter v. Southam Inc.*, [1984] 2 S.C.R. 145; *Law Society of Upper Canada v. Skapinker*, [1984] 1 S.C.R. 357).

To return to s. 8 of the *Narcotic Control Act*, I am in no doubt whatsoever that it violates s. 11(d) of the *Charter* by requiring the accused to prove on a balance of probabilities that he was not in possession of the narcotic for the purpose of trafficking. Mr. Oakes is compelled by s. 8 to prove he is *not* guilty of the offence of trafficking. He is thus denied his right to be presumed innocent and subjected to the potential penalty of life imprisonment unless he can rebut the presumption. This is radically and fundamentally inconsistent with the societal values of human dignity and liberty which we espouse, and is directly contrary to the presumption of innocence enshrined in s. 11(d). Let us turn now to s. 1 of the *Charter*.

. . . .

It is important to observe at the outset that s. 1 has two functions: first, it constitutionally guarantees the rights and freedoms set out in the provisions which follow; and, second, it states explicitly the exclusive justificatory criteria (outside of s. 33 of the *Constitution Act, 1982*) against which limitations on those rights and freedoms must be measured. Accordingly, any s. 1 inquiry must be premised on an understanding that the impugned limit violates constitutional rights and freedoms — rights and freedoms which are part of the supreme law of Canada. As Wilson J. stated in *Singh v. Minister of Employ-*

ment and Immigration, *supra*, at p. 218: "...it is important to remember that the courts are conducting this inquiry in light of a commitment to uphold the rights and freedoms set out in the other sections of the *Charter*."

A second contextual element of interpretation of s. 1 is provided by the words "free and democratic society." Inclusion of these words as the final standard of justification for limits on rights and freedoms refers the Court to the very purpose for which the *Charter* was originally entrenched in the Constitution: Canadian society is to be free and democratic. The Court must be guided by the values and principles essential to a free and democratic society which I believe embody, to name but a few, respect for the inherent dignity of the human person, commitment to social justice and equality, accommodation of a wide variety of beliefs, respect for cultural and group identity, and faith in social and political institutions which enhance the participation of individuals and groups in society. The underlying values and principles of a free and democratic society are the genesis of the rights and freedoms guaranteed by the *Charter* and the ultimate standard against which a limit on a right or freedom must be shown, despite its effect, to be reasonable and demonstrably justified.

The rights and freedoms guaranteed by the *Charter* are not, however, absolute. It may become necessary to limit rights and freedoms in circumstances where their exercise would be inimical to the realization of collective goals of fundamental importance. For this reason, s. 1 provides criteria of justification for limits on the rights and freedoms guaranteed by the *Charter*. These criteria impose a stringent standard of justification, especially when understood in terms of the two contextual considerations discussed above, namely, the violation of a constitutionally guaranteed right or freedom and the fundamental principles of a free and democratic society.

The onus of proving that a limit on a right or freedom guaranteed by the *Charter* is reasonable and demonstrably justified in a free and democratic society rests upon the party seeking to uphold the limitation. It is clear from the text of s. 1 that limits on the rights and freedoms enumerated in the *Charter* are exceptions to their general guarantee. The presumption is that the rights and freedoms are guaranteed unless the party invoking s. 1 can bring itself within the exceptional criteria which justify their being limited. This is further substantiated by the use of the word "demonstrably" which clearly indicates that the onus of justification is on the party seeking to limit: *Hunter v. Southam Inc.*, *supra*.

The standard of proof under s. 1 is the civil standard, namely, proof by a preponderance of probability. The alternative criminal standard, proof beyond a reasonable doubt, would, in my view, be unduly onerous on the party seeking to limit. Concepts such as "reasonableness," "justifiability" and "free and democratic society" are simply not amenable to such a standard. Nevertheless, the preponderance of probability test must be applied rigorously. Indeed, the phrase "demonstrably justified" in s. 1 of the *Charter* supports this conclusion. Within the broad category of the civil standard, there exist different degrees of probability depending on the nature of the case: see Sopinka and Lederman, *The Law of Evidence in Civil Cases* (Toronto: 1974), at p. 385. As Lord Denning explained in *Bater v. Bater*, [1950] 2 All E.R. 458 (C.A.), at p. 459:

> The case may be proved by a preponderance of probability, but there may be degrees of probability within that standard. The degree depends on the subject-matter. A civil court, when considering a charge of fraud, will naturally require a higher degree of probability than that which it would require if considering whether negligence were established. It does not adopt so high a degree as a criminal court, even when it is considering a charge of a criminal nature, but still it does require a degree of probability which is commensurate with the occasion.

This passage was cited with approval in *Hanes v. Wawanesa Mutual Insurance Co.*, [1963] S.C.R. 154, at p. 161. A similar approach was put forward by Cartwright J. in *Smith v. Smith*, [1952] 2 S.C.R. 312, at pp. 331–32:

> I wish, however, to emphasize that in every civil action before the tribunal can safely find the affirmative of an issue of fact required to be proved it must be reasonably satisfied, and that whether or not it will be so satisfied must depend on the totality of the circumstances on which its judgment is formed including the gravity of the consequences....

Having regard to the fact that s. 1 is being invoked for the purpose of justifying a violation of the constitutional rights and freedoms the *Charter* was designed to protect, a very high degree of probability will be, in the words of Lord Denning, "commensurate with the occasion." Where evidence is required in order to prove the constituent elements of a s. 1 inquiry, and this will generally be the case, it should be cogent and persuasive and make clear to the Court the consequences of imposing or not imposing the limit. See: *Law Society of Upper Can-*

ada v. Skapinker, *supra*, at p. 384; *Singh v. Minister of Employment and Immigration*, *supra*, at p. 217. A court will also need to know what alternative measures for implementing the objective were available to the legislators when they made their decisions. I should add, however, that there may be cases where certain elements of the s. 1 analysis are obvious or self-evident.

To establish that a limit is reasonable and demonstrably justified in a free and democratic society, two central criteria must be satisfied. First, the objective, which the measures responsible for a limit on a *Charter* right or freedom are designed to serve, must be "of sufficient importance to warrant overriding a constitutionally protected right or freedom": *R. v. Big M Drug Mart Ltd.*, *supra*, at p. 352. The standard must be high in order to ensure that objectives which are trivial or discordant with the principles integral to a free and democratic society do not gain s. 1 protection. It is necessary, at a minimum, that an objective relate to concerns which are pressing and substantial in a free and democratic society before it can be characterized as sufficiently important.

Second, once a sufficiently significant objective is recognized, then the party invoking s. 1 must show that the means chosen are reasonable and demonstrably justified. This involves "a form of proportionality test": *R. v. Big M Drug Mart Ltd.*, *supra*, at p. 352. Although the nature of the proportionality test will vary depending on the circumstances, in each case courts will be required to balance the interests of society with those of individuals and groups. There are, in my view, three important components of a proportionality test. First, the measures adopted must be carefully designed to achieve the objective in question. They must not be arbitrary, unfair or based on irrational considerations. In short, they must be rationally connected to the objective. Second, the means, even if rationally connected to the objective in this first sense, should impair "as little as possible" the right or freedom in question: *R. v. Big M Drug Mart Ltd.*, *supra*, at p. 352. Third, there must be a proportionality between the *effects* of the measures which are responsible for limiting the *Charter* right or freedom, and the objective which has been identified as of "sufficient importance."

With respect to the third component, it is clear that the general effect of any measure impugned under s. 1 will be the infringement of a right or freedom guaranteed by the *Charter*; this is the reason why resort to s. 1 is necessary. The inquiry into effects must, however, go further. A wide range of rights and freedoms are guaranteed by the *Charter*, and an almost infinite number of factual situations may arise in respect of these. Some limits on rights and freedoms protected by the *Charter* will be more serious than others in terms of the nature of the right or freedom violated, the extent of the violation, and the degree to which the measures which impose the limit trench upon the integral principles of a free and democratic society. Even if an objective is of sufficient importance, and the first two elements of the proportionality test are satisfied, it is still possible that, because of the severity of the deleterious effects of a measure on individuals or groups, the measure will not be justified by the purposes it is intended to serve. The more severe the deleterious effects of a measure, the more important the objective must be if the measure is to be reasonable and demonstrably justified in a free and democratic society.

Having outlined the general principles of a s. 1 inquiry, we must apply them to s. 8 of the *Narcotic Control Act*. Is the reverse onus provision in s. 8 a reasonable limit on the right to be presumed innocent until proven guilty beyond a reasonable doubt as can be demonstrably justified in a free and democratic society?

The starting point for formulating a response to this question is, as stated above, the nature of Parliament's interest or objective which accounts for the passage of s. 8 of the *Narcotic Control Act*. According to the Crown, s. 8 of the *Narcotic Control Act* is aimed at curbing drug trafficking by facilitating the conviction of drug traffickers. In my opinion, Parliament's concern that drug trafficking be decreased can be characterized as substantial and pressing. The problem of drug trafficking has been increasing since the 1950's at which time there was already considerable concern. (See *Report of the Special Committee on Traffic in Narcotic Drugs*, Appendix to Debates of the Senate, Canada, Session 1955, pp. 690–700; see also *Final Report of the Commission of Inquiry into the Non-Medical Use of Drugs* (Ottawa, 1973).) Throughout this period, numerous measures were adopted by free and democratic societies, at both the international and national levels.

At the international level, on June 23, 1953, the *Protocol for Limiting and Regulating the Cultivation of the Poppy Plant, the Production of, International and Wholesale Trade in, and Use of Opium*, to which Canada is a signatory, was adopted by the United Nations Opium Conference held in New York. The *Single Convention on Narcotic Drugs, 1961*, was acceded to in New York on March 30, 1961. This treaty was signed by Canada on March 30, 1961. It entered into force on December 13, 1964. As stated in the Preamble, "addiction to narcotic drugs constitutes a serious evil for the individual and is fraught with social and economic danger to mankind, ..."

At the national level, statutory provisions have been enacted by numerous countries which, *inter alia*, attempt to deter drug trafficking by imposing criminal sanctions (see, for example, *Misuse of Drugs Act 1975*, 1975 (N.Z.), No. 116; *Misuse of Drugs Act 1971*, 1971 (U.K.), c. 38).

The objective of protecting our society from the grave ills associated with drug trafficking, is, in my view, one of sufficient importance to warrant overriding a constitutionally protected right or freedom in certain cases. Moreover, the degree of seriousness of drug trafficking makes its acknowledgement as a sufficiently important objective for the purposes of s. 1, to a large extent, self-evident. The first criterion of a s. 1 inquiry, therefore, has been satisfied by the Crown.

The next stage of inquiry is a consideration of the means chosen by Parliament to achieve its objective. The means must be reasonable and demonstrably justified in a free and democratic society. As outlined above, this proportionality test should begin with a consideration of the rationality of the provision: is the reverse onus clause in s. 8 rationally related to the objective of curbing drug trafficking? At a minimum, this requires that s. 8 be internally rational; there must be a rational connection between the basic fact of possession and the presumed fact of possession for the purpose of trafficking. Otherwise, the reverse onus clause could give rise to unjustified and erroneous convictions for drug trafficking of persons guilty only of possession of narcotics.

In my view, s. 8 does not survive this rational connection test. As Martin J.A. of the Ontario Court of Appeal concluded, possession of a small or negligible quantity of narcotics does not support the inference of trafficking. In other words, it would be irrational to infer that a person had an intent to traffic on the basis of his or her possession of a very small quantity of narcotics. The presumption required under s. 8 of the *Narcotic Control Act* is overinclusive and could lead to results in certain cases which would defy both rationality and fairness. In light of the seriousness of the offence in question, which carries with it the possibility of imprisonment for life, I am further convinced that the first component of the proportionality test has not been satisfied by the Crown.

Having concluded that s. 8 does not satisfy this first component of proportionality, it is unnecessary to consider the other two components.

CONCLUSION

The Ontario Court of Appeal was correct in holding that s. 8 of the *Narcotic Control Act* violates the *Canadian Charter of Rights and Freedoms* and is therefore of no force or effect. Section 8 imposes a limit on the right guaranteed by s. 11(d) of the *Charter* which is not reasonable and is not demonstrably justified in a free and democratic society for the purpose of s. 1. Accordingly, the constitutional question is answered as follows:

Question:
Is s. 8 of the *Narcotic Control Act* inconsistent with s. 11(d) of the *Canadian Charter of Rights and Freedoms* and thus of no force and effect?

Answer:
Yes.

I would, therefore, dismiss the appeal.

■

Canadian judges have drawn a number of distinctions in analyzing statutory burdens of proof in light of s. 11(d) of the *Charter*. One such distinction is, of course, drawn between **persuasive** and **evidential** burdens, persuasive burdens on accused persons being much more likely to attract a judicial declaration of conflict with s. 11(d), as *Oakes* illustrates.

Even evidential burdens can be declared unconstitutional in light of another distinction between mandatory and permissive presumptions. A second distinction, therefore, asks whether failure of the accused to meet the burden results in a **mandatory** conclusion of guilt and conviction, or merely makes such a conclusion **permissible**, in light of all the evidence. In *Re Boyle and the Queen* (1983), 41 O.R. (2d) 713 (C.A.) the court held that s. 354(2) of the *Code* offended s. 11(d) because the section was said to require conviction if an accused failed to introduce evidence suggesting no knowledge of the fact that a vehicle was obtained by criminal means.

A third distinction has been raised in the cases between burdens imposed upon the accused with respect to proof of the elements of the **offence** itself (the *actus reus* and the *mens rea*) and burdens imposed with respect to **defences** or other matters. In *R. v. Holmes*, [1988] 1 S.C.R. 914, members of the Court disagreed with respect to the proper interpretation of the burden of proof in s. 309(1) of the *Code*, which states that if, "without lawful excuse, the proof of which lies upon him", a person is found in possession of instruments suitable for housebreaking in circumstances giving rise to a reasonable inference of intention to housebreak, then that person is guilty of the offence. While all of the justices agreed that s. 309(1) did not relieve the Crown of its obligation to prove the intent to use the tools for housebreaking beyond a reasonable doubt, they disagreed as to its constitutionality in light of the fact that the accused is not required to disprove an essential element of the offence.

This conflict may have been resolved by *R. v. Chaulk*, discussed below, under **Incapacity**, where the Court ruled that s. 16(4) of the *Code* violates s. 11(d) of the *Charter* by requiring that an accused prove alleged mental disorder on a balance of probabilities. The Court held that such a provision offends the *Charter* by presuming a factor required for guilt — sanity — but went on to rule that it can be justified under s. 1.

Finally, a fourth distinction should be noted: some members of the Supreme Court have given a different contextual interpretation to s. 11(d) for the burden of proof regarding **regulatory** crimes. See *R. v. Wholesale Travel Group Inc.*, below, under ***Mens Rea***. *Wholesale Travel* was applied by the Court to s. 16 of the New Brunswick *Provincial Offences Act*, which allowed recipients of traffic tickets a period of time in which to contest the offence; thereafter, offenders were convicted without a trial and sentenced to a fine. In *R. v. Richard*, [1996] 3 S.C.R. 525, the Court held that s. 11(d) was not offended when, in the regulatory context where imprisonment is not an available punishment, an offender is presumed to have waived s. 11(d) rights by failing to respond to a procedural scheme, such as the New Brunswick act, in which adequate safeguards are in place.

C. SECTION 1

A judicial finding of conflict with s. 11(d) does not necessarily result in a finding of unconstitutionality. Under s. 1 of the *Charter*, the government can "save" the legislation by showing, on a balance of probabilities, that the law is "demonstrably justified, in a free and democratic society." In *R. v. Whyte*, [1988] 2 S.C.R. 3, for example, the justices of the Supreme Court held that *Code* s. 237(1)(a) violated s. 11(d) but was saved under s. 1 due to the significance of the governmental objective of punishing drunk driving and the impracticality of requiring the Crown to prove intention for an offence aimed at intoxicated offenders.

Consider the kinds of evidence and materials that the Crown counsel would have had to put forward in support of the s. 1 argument: law or not law? Section 1 analyses rely upon interdisciplinary materials, including statistics and other research, legislative history, scholarly articles, and public policy. An example of a successful s. 1 argument, where the Crown and the Attorney General assembled multidisciplinary materials, is found in *Downey v. R.*, [1992] 2 S.C.R. 10, where the shifting of the evidential burden to the accused regarding the "pimping presumption" in s. 212(3), with a mandatory conclusion of guilt should the burden not be met, was held to offend s. 11(d). First, Cory J., writing for a four-justice majority, reviewed studies, scholarly articles, and committee reports in reaching the conclusion that prosecuting the violent control by pimps over women and girls was a "sufficiently important governmental objective to warrant overriding a constitutional right": "the section is attempting to deal with a cruel and pervasive social evil" (at 36).

Second, he found that there was a "rational connection" between the fact to be proven to invoke the presumption, that of maintaining close ties to a prostitute, and the presumption, that of living off the avails of prostitution. He noted that since police evidence suggested that prostitutes are afraid to testify against their pimps, it would otherwise be difficult to obtain evidence about the financial relationship between pimp and prostitute.

Third, he found that since Parliament is not required to choose the least intrusive means of pursuing its important objective, and that a similar presumption exists in U.K. and Australian law, this law meets the "minimal impairment of constitutional rights" test by only imposing an evidentiary burden upon the accused. Such a burden can be met without the accused being forced to testify by, for instance, relying on evidence from the Crown's case or through cross-examination of witnesses.

Finally, Cory J. found "proportionality" between the measure and its effects on an accused's constitutional rights, particularly in light of the fact that prostitutes are a vulnerable group in our society.

It must be noted, however, that three justices dissented from this decision on whether s. 1 could justify the legislation. Justices McLachlin and Iacobucci found that the "rational connection test" could not be met because the fact of living with or associating with a woman who works as a prostitute does not make it likely that the person lives off the avails of prostitution; they also suggested that the legislation may work to further isolate prostitutes, thus making them more vulnerable to pimps. La Forest J. agreed, noting that the government had not shown why it needed to cast the net so widely that it might include people who have "legitimate, non-parasitic living arrangements with prostitutes." What does this sort of four-three split among the justices tell you about the judicial function regarding s. 1 of the *Charter*?

Questioning the "Wisdom" of Legislation: R. v. Oakes†

In the *Motor Vehicle Reference*, the Court asserted that Charter adjudication does not require judges to inquire into the "wisdom" of legislation. Nowhere is this assertion put more to the test than in relation to section 11 of the Charter. Under section 1, the court is asked to "balance" the rights protected by the Charter against considerations of general welfare. There is nothing peculiarly legal about the process of balancing individual against collective interests. The legislature would have made just such a calculation when it enacted the statute in question. Thus section 1 appears to be a vehicle for asking the fundamental legislative question: "is this policy worth what it costs?"

Given the overtly political character of such an analysis, we would expect to observe courts experiencing particular difficulty in interpreting and applying section 1. This expectation was confirmed by the first dozen Supreme Court decisions interpreting the Charter. In these early cases, section 1 was usually mentioned only to point out that counsel had failed to address argument as to its application, or that the consideration of section 1 was, for a variety of reasons, "unnecessary." Such techniques of confession and avoidance were abandoned in the Court's recent judgment in *R. v. Oakes*. In *Oakes*, Chief Justice Dickson suggests a general approach for the application of section 1, as well as a framework of analysis to structure its application to particular cases.

. . . .

The opinion of the Chief Justice suggests that the section 1 analysis is determinate and objective. The Court need not be concerned with the wisdom of legislative policy, but only with the separate question of whether it satisfies the two-pronged "test" under section 1. There are a number of features of the analysis that contribute to this sense of objectivity and neutrality. First, the inquiry is framed in terms of the traditional and familiar standard of proof in civil cases, proof on a preponderance of probability. This characterization evokes the imagery of a court deciding a garden-variety dispute between private parties. The court will hear evidence on the section 1 issue and then determine, as it would in any private litigation, whether the civil standard of proof has been satisfied. Of course, the evidence and arguments in a Charter case will often be complex and require the court to exercise considerable discretion. But this is not significantly different from the task of a court in complex civil litigation. Since the court's competence in these complex civil cases is generally accepted, there should be no serious qualms about the judiciary embarking on the task of Charter adjudication.

---

† From Patrick Monahan & Andrew Petter, "Developments in Canadian Law: The 1985–86 Term" (1987) 9 Sup. Ct. L. Rev. 69 at 102–103, 107–108, 112–15, 118–25. [Notes omitted.] Reproduced with permission of the authors.

There is a second feature of the judgment that is even more crucial in terms of bolstering the legitimacy of the Court's role. This is the manner in which the Chief Justice actually applies the section 1 analysis. By purporting to accept the validity of the state's goal in enacting section 8 of the *Narcotic Control Act*, Dickson C.J. is able to strike down the provision on the basis that Parliament has pursued its policy in an "irrational" way. The constitutional objection is not to the state's policy as such, but to the manner in which it has attempted to carry out that policy. The Court's ruling appears wholly instrumentalist, designed to measure the "fit" between the state goal and the means chosen to achieve that goal. Assuming a decidedly deferential posture, the Court is saying to Parliament: "*given* that you have decided to pursue this goal, you have done so in a way that is arbitrary or irrational."

This type of analysis appears to resolve any possible tension between judicial review and democratic values. Under a rationality standard, judges are not purporting to substitute their values for those of legislators. The Court is simply ensuring that legislation accurately reflects the chosen values of the legislators themselves. This could be regarded as the perfection of democracy rather than its negation. Judicial review is promoting precision and care in the drafting of legislation and eliminating needless and arbitrary restrictions of individual liberty. There is nothing undemocratic about requiring the legislature to pursue its goals in a precise and careful fashion.

A similar set of assumptions underlies the "least restrictive means" analysis, the second branch of the proportionality test outlined by the Chief Justice. As with the "rationality" standard, the "least restrictive means" test does not purport to dictate to the state which value choices it must pursue or avoid. Rather, it is a limited attempt to identify inefficient legislation. The "least restrictive means" analysis says to the legislature: "*given* that you have decided to pursue this goal, you have done so inefficiently. There are other legislative devices available that would allow you to pursue the same goal, but in a manner that would be less restrictive of individual liberty." It seems self-evident that the state should never restrict individual liberty needlessly. Given a choice, the state must select the device that is least intrusive in terms of the fundamental values guaranteed by the Charter.

It is hardly a coincidence that the trial court and both appellate courts in *Oakes* resolved the constitutional issue on the basis of the "rationality" standard. Indeed, it seems safe to predict that whenever courts in the future decide to invalidate legislation, they will focus on the "irrationality" of the law or stress the availability of "less restrictive means." This is because these techniques allow the court to overturn legislation without appearing to be a super-legislature. The crucial question is whether these techniques actually enable the court to avoid having to assess the wisdom of legislative policy, or whether they are a subterfuge that permits the court to make such a political judgment in a covert fashion. It is to this important question that we now turn.

. . . .

The Rationality of Reverse Onus Provisions

It remains to apply this analysis to the reverse onus provision considered by the Supreme Court in *Oakes*. As we have seen, section 8 of the *Narcotic Control Act* created a "rebuttable presumption" in favour of the Crown: once the fact of possession had been proven, an intention to traffic would be inferred unless the accused established the absence of such an intention. The Supreme Court ruled the provision unconstitutional since there was no "rational connection" between the predicate fact — possession — and the presumed fact — an intention to traffic. ...

[T]he implication from the judgment of Dickson C.J. is that some lesser degree of fit between predicate fact and presumed fact will be constitutionally satisfactory under the Charter. The Chief Justice strikes down section 8 because of the lack of a "rational connection" between the fact proved and the fact presumed. Although Dickson C.J. did not define what constitutes a "rational connection," Martin J.A. in the Ontario Court of Appeal had concluded that a rational connection exists "where the proved fact raises a probability that the presumed fact exists." This seems to suggest that, although proof of the predicate fact must raise a probability that the presumed fact is true, it need not prove the presumed fact beyond a reasonable doubt. The sum total of Dickson C.J.'s reasoning on the point is as follows:

> [I]s the reverse onus clause in s. 8 rationally related to the objective of curbing drug trafficking? At a minimum, this requires that s. 8 be internally rational; there must be a rational connection between the basic fact of possession and the presumed fact of possession for the purpose of trafficking. Otherwise, the reverse onus clause could give rise to unjustified and erroneous convictions for drug trafficking of persons guilty only of possession of narcotics.

> In my view, s. 8 does not survive this rational connection test. As Martin J.A. of the Ontario Court of Appeal concluded, possession of a small or negligible quantity of narcotics does not support the inference of trafficking. In other words, it would be irrational to infer that a person had an intent to traffic on the basis of his or her possession of a very small quantity of narcotics. The presumption required under s. 8 of the *Narcotic Control Act* is overinclusive and could lead to results in certain cases which would defy both rationality and fairness.

This passage is framed in the classic terminology of instrumental rationality. The argument is deceptively simple and apparently uncontroversial. Dickson C.J. disclaims any desire to substitute his values for those of Parliament; his goal is simply to ascertain whether Parliament has enacted a law which is rationally related to its own goal of "curbing drug trafficking." The next proposition in the argument is equally uncontroversial. In order for a law to satisfy the minimum rationality standard it must be internally rational. Now comes the crucial leap in the argument. The Chief Justice claims that this law is "internally rational" only if there is a "rational connection" between the basic fact of possession and the presumed fact of possession for the purpose of trafficking. Why? The reason seems to be that the existing law "could give rise to unjustified and erroneous convictions for drug trafficking." Unless there is a "rational connection" between mere possession and drug trafficking, the result "in certain cases" would be contrary to "both rationality and fairness."

There are two initial observations that should be made about this argument. First, if the constitutional objection is to the possibility of erroneous convictions "in certain cases," then requiring a "rational connection" between the predicate and presumed facts is no remedy to the problem. The "rational connection" test merely requires that the fact of possession raise a probability that the accused had an intention to traffic; the Crown need not satisfy the "reasonable doubt" standard. The accused is then faced with the burden of disproving an intention to traffic. There will always be "certain cases" in which an accused who is innocent will be unable to discharge such a burden and be wrongly convicted. The possibility of error is inherent in the probabilistic process of drawing inferences from circumstantial evidence. The essential difficulty is in bridging the gap from an aggregate likelihood to a conclusion in a specific case. The reasoning runs as follows: it is *generally* true that, if a defendant has done X, he wanted Y to happen; *this* defendant has done X, therefore, *this* defendant intended Y to occur. But there can never be any guarantee that the aggregate likelihood is actually true with respect to any particular defendant. Thus, the "rational connection" test announced by the Court "could lead to results in certain cases which would defy both rationality and fairness" and must itself be unconstitutional.

The second initial observation about the Chief Justice's argument is really a corollary of the first. It is a *non sequitur* to claim that a law is "irrational" because it produces erroneous results "in certain cases." Taken literally, this form of reasoning would mean that a law which was accurate 99 per cent of the time would nevertheless be deemed irrational because of a one per cent rate of error. The trouble with this reasoning is that it is doubtful whether there are any laws that achieve their purpose 100 per cent of the time. If the Court's reasoning is correct, the result is that most, if not all, existing laws are irrational. But this would be an absurd result, trivializing the "rationality" requirement.

Thus the Court's discovery of "irrationality" in *Oakes* was a foregone conclusion. The Court selected a standard which *no* law could satisfy and then discovered that, indeed, the reverse onus provision fell short of this unattainable standard. There was no serious attempt to assess the rationality of the reverse onus provision in the *Narcotic Control Act*. Had such an inquiry actually been undertaken, the Court would have encountered two overwhelming problems. First, it would have been forced to acknowledge that the reverse onus provision, as drafted, was "internally rational." Second, it would have discovered that the task of determining whether the law was "rationally connected" to the goal of curbing drug trafficking was an empirical question, the answer to which depends upon an assessment of the instrumental impact of the law on drug traffickers. The trouble is that the Court had no information whatsoever on the instrumental effects of the reverse onus provision. In the absence of such data, it is absurd and unintelligible to claim that there is no "rational connection" between the law and Parliament's goal of curbing drug trafficking.

. . . .

This total absence of empirical evidence leads us to the second overwhelming difficulty with the *Oakes* opinion. The Court purported to decide the case on the basis that the law was not "rationally related" to Parliament's goal of curbing drug trafficking. This is an assertion about the instrumental impact of the law on drug traffickers. But it is absurd for the Court to claim that the provision is not "rationally related" to Parliament's goal of curbing drug trafficking; the Court has no idea of the effect of the provision on drug trafficking.

Of course, any attempt to measure impact would have to be done at the margin; the court would have to compare the existing regime against a situation in which the Crown was put to the proof of each of the elements of the offence of trafficking. It is obvious that any such evaluation of costs and benefits would be extraordinarily difficult. The purpose of the reverse onus provision is evidently to make it relatively easy to secure convictions against drug traffickers. But in order to measure the efficiency of the measure, one would have to know how much difficulty the Crown would have in proving an intention to traffic in the absence of the statutory presumption. It could be, for example, that the Crown would be able to prove the relevant intention in most cases relatively easily; if this were so, the statutory presumption would appear superfluous. Alternatively, the Crown might encounter serious difficulties in proving an intention to traffic were it deprived of the assistance of the reverse onus provision in section 8. In these circumstances, the effect of striking down the provision would be to compromise significantly Parliament's goal of curbing drug traffickers. This analysis of the importance of section 8 for law enforcement values would have to be balanced against a consideration of the increased risk of convicting innocent defendants under the provision.

The Court did not even attempt to undertake any such empirical analysis in *Oakes*. But it is possible to attribute responsibility for this omission to Parliament itself rather than the Court. In this view, once there has been a *prima facie* limitation of a right, the burden of adducing empirical evidence to justify the limitation under section 1 rests on Parliament. Until Parliament offers sufficiently compelling evidence, the Court is entitled to refuse to give effect to the impugned law.

The problem is that the Court did not suggest the need for more evidence on the issue. The judgment found that the reverse onus provision was not rationally related to the goal of curbing drug trafficking even though the Court had no evidence on the actual effects of the reverse onus provision. It may turn out that the provision plays no significant role in the enforcement of drug laws. But this is an empirical question and can only be resolved through evidence on the effects of the provision as well as the consequences of eliminating it. The judgment of the Court displays no awareness of the complexity of the calculations that would have to be made in order to find the law "irrational."

THE IMPACT OF THE DECISION

Given the absence of any empirical evidence on the effects of the reverse onus provision, it is difficult to assess the impact of *Oakes* on the enforcement of Canada's drug laws. It may be, for example, that the elimination of the provision will have little or no immediate instrumental impact. In any event, the decision is certain to have important consequences outside the field of drug enforcement. *Oakes* represents the Court's first articulation of the standard under section 1 of the Charter. It also has implications for the use of reverse onus provisions in penal law generally. What assessment can be made of the broader consequences of the decision?

. . . .

... *Oakes* may have important second-order effects on Charter adjudication in general. These second-order effects flow from the way in which the Chief Justice proposes to structure analysis of legislation under section 1 of the Charter. The Court claims that the state must satisfy a "stringent standard of justification" in order to uphold limits on rights pursuant to section 1. Limits on rights can be justified only when there is a "pressing and substantial" governmental goal at stake. Further, in some instances the standard will be set even higher since "[t]he more severe the deleterious effects of a measure, the more important the objective must be if the measure is to be reasonable and demonstrably justified in a free and democratic society."

This is an exacting standard indeed. Just how exacting is revealed by comparing the *Oakes* test to the approach of American courts in considering governmental limits on constitutionally protected rights. Although the U.S. Constitution does not contain any provision comparable to section 1, the American courts do not construe constitutional limits on government in an absolutist fashion. Instead, the judiciary has developed a series of balancing tests that vary according to the context. In certain cases, the burden on the state is so onerous that it is virtually a foregone conclusion that the provision will be struck down; in other instances, judicial scrutiny is so lax that the limit on rights is essentially assumed to be constitutional. In doctrinal terms, state limits on rights are generally permitted as long as there is a "legitimate" state purpose and the law is "rationally" related to fulfilment of that purpose. A higher-order justification is demanded only if there is a "fundamental interest" at stake or if the state utilizes a classification that has been identified as "suspect."

There is nothing magical or compelling about these particular doctrinal categories. The jurisprudence surrounding the Charter should reflect Canadian assumptions and values and Canadian jurists should avoid the temptation to simply mimic their American counterparts. At the same time, our courts will act at their peril if they ignore the important lessons to be learned from a thoughtful examination of the American constitutional experience. Putting the doctrinal details to one side for the moment, the point is that American courts have developed a number of techniques and devices that impose a relatively modest burden of justification on the state. There are very sound reasons for nurturing and applying such techniques. When the state intervenes, it does not necessarily do so for reasons that can be characterized as "compelling" or "pressing." The state may act, not out of a sense of urgency, but simply because it seeks to effect some marginal improvement in the *status quo*. The effect of demanding a "compelling" or "pressing" state interest in these contexts is to deprive the community of the additional net benefits associated with the impugned legislation.

. . . .

The second contextual justification offered by the Court is the fact that section 1 includes the words "free and democratic." This is said to suggest a commitment to values such as the dignity of the human person and social justice. But it is difficult to understand why a commitment to these values cuts in favour of a stringent and rigorous interpretation of section 1. The assumption underlying the analysis must be that expansive readings of constitutional restraints upon government necessarily advance goals of social justice and equality. Conversely, construing constitutional restraints in a narrow or restrictive manner is somehow regarded as antithetical to such values. On this view, expansive interpretations of individual rights are essentially costless; everyone gains because everyone's rights against the state are being protected.

This is an impoverished conception of the nature of state power and of the effect of constitutional constraints upon that power. First, the alleged tension between state intervention, on the one hand, and the goals of social justice and equality, on the other, is illusory. Indeed, the primary means by which goals of social justice and the plight of the disadvantaged have been advanced in the twentieth century has been through state intervention in and regulation of the market. This does not mean that *all* state regulation has necessarily advanced the cause of social justice. The point is simply that, where there has been progress towards this goal, the impetus has, with few exceptions, come in the democratic rather than the judicial arena.

The corollary is that constitutional constraints upon government are far from costless. Because the state often acts to advance the cause of social justice, constitutional constraints upon government may well frustrate rather than further the achievement of that important goal. The costs of the process are not imposed on the state *per se*, but on those individuals who stood to gain from the state policy that has been challenged. Not all citizens can be winners in such a process. Rather than simultaneously increasing the rights of everyone, constitutional constraints serve to advance the interests of some at the expense of the interests of others.

Thus the Court's reading of section 1 stands the section on its head while at the same time fundamentally mistaking the nature of the relationship between state power and the goals of social justice and equality. Despite these difficulties, we do find some aspects of Chief Justice Dickson's analysis suggestive and attractive. Consider the "proportionality" test proposed as the second stage of the section 1 analysis. We have already pointed out the political and value-laden nature of this kind of analysis. The potential danger of the test is the mistaken belief that the process of matching means to ends is neutral or objective. Yet it must be acknowledged that some version of a proportionality test seems inevitable and necessary in Charter adjudication. The virtue of a proportionality test is that it focuses attention directly at the margin. Beginning with the regulation as it stands, it seeks to measure the trade-offs involved in a regulation framed more narrowly or more broadly. By focusing on the actual effects of a law and its various alternatives, courts are likely to be more sensitive to the costs involved when a law is ruled unconstitutional. Further, the judiciary will come to appreciate the terrible complexity in attempting to measure the actual impact of a law on social behaviour.

Such a judicial appreciation would be very healthy. We believe that an awareness of the complex, political character of judicial review reinforces the case for some limits to the legitimacy of the judicial role. This, in turn, suggests that it is unwise for the Court to state a single, all inclusive standard for section 1 analysis, as it did in *Oakes*. It is inappropriate, for example, to demand a "stringent" or "pressing" justification from the state in all contexts. This is not to deny that there may well be occasions on which such a high standard is appropriate.

But there will be other instances in which a much more flexible and deferential standard should be applied, even though there has been a *prima facie* violation of a protected right. The task for the Court is to come to an understanding of when it ought to be either more or less demanding of the state. This task requires attention to the question of legitimacy, and the development of a larger conception of the purposes underlying judicial review and, indeed, of the Charter itself.

■

As an example of Patrick Monahan and Andrew Petter's argument, consider *Whyte*, *supra*, where the Court ruled that s. 237(1)(a) violated s. 11(d) because an accused found intoxicated in the driver's seat could be convicted despite a reasonable doubt as to whether the driver intended to assume control over the vehicle, but upheld the section on the basis of *Charter* s. 1:

> There is every reason to believe the person in the driver's seat has the care or control of the vehicle. The driver's seat is designed to give the occupant access to all the controls of the car, to be able to operate it. It is true that a vehicle can be occupied by one who does not assume care or control, but a person in this state of mind is likely to assume a position in the vehicle intended for a passenger rather than the driver. In my view, the relationship between the proved fact and the presumed fact under s. 237(1)(a) is direct and self-evident, quite unlike that which confronted the Court in *Oakes*. [*per* Dickson C.J.C. at 21–22]

Do you agree? In *R. v. Laba*, [1994] 3 S.C.R. 965, after ruling that the clause in s. 394(1)(b) of the *Code* was unconstitutional in violation of s. 11(d), the Court "read down" the law and substituted an evidential burden for a persuasive burden instead of declaring the provision void. Does this case undermine or further the argument presented by Monahan and Petter?

One might also argue, along the lines of the work of Monahan and Petter, that the s. 11(d) cases are really about the formal requirements for sustaining convictions and do not, in fact, do anything to shift the actual burden of proof of innocence resting upon many persons charged with crimes. Consider, for example, Donald Marshall, Jr.'s prosecution: did he receive the benefit of the presumption of innocence? Could he have successfully invoked s. 11(d) in his defence? Michael Mandel in *The Charter of Rights and the Legalization of Politics in Canada* (Toronto: Wall and Thompson, 1994) argues at 196: "The reasonable doubt standard seems to exist in the same symbolic realm as the Charter itself. It seems aimed at resolving the doubts about the **point** of the system by ensuring that those convicted at least have nothing to complain about on the score of their guilt or innocence" [emphasis in original].

2

Actus Reus

The offence with which the accused is charged will be described in the *Code* or other statute. Each offence has a physical or *actus reus* component that must be proven by the Crown unless the statute indicates otherwise. The *actus reus* will include

- an act or omission;
- a common law voluntariness requirement;
- a causation element, if the *actus reus* includes proof of prohibited consequences, such as death or bodily harm to a victim; and/or
- certain surrounding circumstances or other criteria, such as location, age of victim, or time of day.

As is the case for all aspects of criminal law, the *Charter* also shapes the *actus reus* requirement.

A. ACT OR OMISSION

The *actus reus* may be committed by way of positive act or omission to do something that the accused had a positive legal duty to do. That duty may be specified in the *Code*, in other legislation, or be imported from tort law: *R. v. Coyne* (1958), 31 C.R. 355 (N.B.C.A.). The following cases demonstrate the uncertainty and scope of omissions offences.

R. v. Instan†

[DAY J. (stated the case):]

Kate Instan was tried before me at the last assizes for the county of Worcester upon a charge of feloniously killing one Ann Hunt. The prisoner, who is between thirty and forty years of age and unmarried, had no occupation and no means of her own of living. She was a niece of the deceased.

† [1893] 1 Q.B. 450.

At the time of the committal of the alleged offence, and for some time previous thereto, she had been living with and had been maintained by the deceased. Deceased was a woman of some seventy-three years of age, and until a few weeks before her death was healthy and able to take care of herself. She was possessed of a small life income, and had in the house in which she lived some little furniture, and a few other articles of trifling value. The two women lived together in a house taken by the deceased; no one lived with them or in any way attended to them.

The deceased shortly before her death suffered from gangrene in the leg, which rendered her during the last ten days of her life quite unable to attend to herself or to move about or to do anything to procure assistance. No one but the prisoner had previous to the death any knowledge of the condition in which her aunt thus was. The prisoner continued to live in the house at the cost of the deceased, and took in the food supplied by the tradespeople; but does not appear to have given any to the deceased, and she certainly did not give or procure any medical or nursing attendance to or for her, or give notice to any neighbour of her condition or wants, although she had abundant opportunity and occasion to do so.

The body of the deceased was on August 2, while the prisoner was still living in the house, found much decomposed, partially dressed in her day clothes, and lying partly on the ground and partly prone upon the bed. The death probably occurred from four to seven days before August 3, the date of the post-mortem examination of the body. The cause of death was exhaustion caused by the gangrene, but substantially accelerated by neglect, want of food, of nursing, and of medical attendance during several days previous to the death. All these wants could and would have been supplied if any notice of the condition of the deceased had been given by the prisoner to any of the neighbours, of whom there were several living in adjoining houses, or to the relations of the deceased, who lived within a few miles. It was proved that the prisoner, while the deceased must have been just about dying, had conversations with neighbours about the deceased, but did not avail herself of the opportunities thus afforded of disclosing the condition in which she then was.

At the close of the case it was objected on behalf of the prisoner, that there was no evidence of any legal duty such as would bind the prisoner to give or to procure any food, or nursing, or attendance to or for the deceased, or to give any notice to any one that such was required. I thought it better not to stop the case, but to leave it to the jury to say whether, having regard to the circumstances under which the prisoner lived with the deceased, and continued to occupy the house, and to take the food provided at the expense of the deceased, while the deceased was, as she knew, unable to communicate with any other person and thus to procure necessaries for herself, the prisoner did or did not impliedly undertake with the deceased either to wait upon and attend to her herself, or to communicate to persons outside the house the knowledge of her helpless condition; and I told them that if they came to the conclusion that she did so undertake, and that the death of the deceased was substantially accelerated by her failure to carry out such undertaking, they might find the prisoner guilty of manslaughter, but that otherwise they should acquit her. The jury found the prisoner guilty.

If the facts above stated do not afford evidence of the existence of any such undertaking or duty, then the conviction is to be quashed; if otherwise, it is to stand.

[LORD COLERIDGE C.J.:]

We are all of opinion that this conviction must be affirmed. It would not be correct to say that every moral obligation involves a legal duty; but every legal duty is founded on a moral obligation. A legal common law duty is nothing else than the enforcing by law of that which is a moral obligation without legal enforcement. There can be no question in this case that it was the clear duty of the prisoner to impart to the deceased so much as was necessary to sustain life of the food which she from time to time took in, and which was paid for by the deceased's own money for the purpose of the maintenance of herself and the prisoner; it was only through the instrumentality of the prisoner that the deceased could get the food. There was, therefore, a common law duty imposed upon the prisoner which she did not discharge.

Nor can there be any question that the failure of the prisoner to discharge her legal duty at least accelerated the death of the deceased, if it did not actually cause it. There is no case directly in point; but it would be a slur upon and a discredit to the administration of justice in this country if there were any doubt as to the legal principle, or as to the present case being within it. The prisoner was under a moral obligation to the deceased from which arose a legal duty towards her; that legal duty the prisoner has wilfully and deliberately left unperformed, with the consequence that there has been an acceleration of the death of the deceased owing to the non-performance of that legal duty. It is unnecessary to say more than that upon the evidence this conviction was most properly arrived at.

[Hawkins, Cave, Day, and Collins JJ. concurred.]

Conviction affirmed.

People v. Beardsley†

[McALVAY C.J.:]

Respondent was convicted of manslaughter before the circuit court for Oakland county, and was sentenced to the state prison at Jackson for a minimum term of one year and a maximum term not to exceed five years.

He was a married man living at Pontiac, and at the time the facts herein narrated occurred he was working as a bartender and clerk at the Columbia Hotel. He lived with his wife in Pontiac, occupying two rooms on the ground floor of a house. Other rooms were rented to tenants, as was also one living room in the basement. His wife being temporarily absent from the city, respondent arranged with a woman named Blanche Burns, who at the time was working at another hotel, to go to his apartments with him. He had been acquainted with her for some time. They knew each other's habits and character. They had drunk liquor together, and had on two occasions been in Detroit and spent the night together in houses of assignation. On the evening of Saturday, March 18, 1905, he met her at the place where she worked, and they went together to his place of residence. They at once began to drink, and continued to drink steadily, and remained together, day and night, from that time until the afternoon of the Monday following, except when respondent went to his work on Sunday afternoon. There was liquor at these rooms, and when it was all used they were served with bottles of whisky and beer by a young man who worked at the Columbia Hotel, and who also attended respondent's fires at the house. He was the only person who saw them in the house during the time they were there together. Respondent gave orders for liquor by telephone. On Monday afternoon, about 1 o'clock, the young man went to the house to see if anything was wanted. At this time he heard respondent say they must fix up the rooms, and the woman must not be found there by his wife, who was likely to return at any time. During this visit to the house the woman sent the young man to a drug store to purchase, with money she gave him, camphor and morphine tablets. He procured both articles. There were six grains of morphine in quarter-grain tablets. She concealed the morphine from respondent's notice, and was discovered putting something into her mouth by him and the young man as they were returning from the other room after taking a drink of beer. She in fact was taking morphine. Respondent struck the box from her hand. Some of the tablets fell on the floor, and of these respondent crushed several with his foot. She picked up and swallowed two of them, and the young man put two of them in the spittoon. Altogether it is probable she took from three to four grains of morphine. The young man went away soon after this. Respondent called him by telephone about an hour later, and after he came to the house requested him to take the woman into the room in the basement which was occupied by a Mr. Skoba. She was in a stupor, and did not rouse when spoken to. Respondent was too intoxicated to be of any assistance, and the young man proceeded to take her downstairs. While doing this, Skoba arrived, and together they put her in his room on the bed. Respondent requested Skoba to look after her, and let her out the back way when she [woke] up. Between 9 and 10 o'clock in the evening, Skoba became alarmed at her condition. He at once called the city marshal and a doctor. An examination by them disclosed that she was dead.

Many errors are assigned by respondent, who asks to have his conviction set aside. The principal

† 113 N.W. 1128 (Mich. Sup. Ct. 1907).

assignments of error are based upon the charge of the court and refusal to give certain requests to charge, and are upon the theory that under the undisputed evidence in the case, as claimed by the people and detailed by the people's witnesses, the respondent should have been acquitted and discharged. In the brief of the prosecutor, his position is stated as follows: "It is the theory of the prosecution that the facts and circumstances attending the death of Blanche Burns in the house of respondent were such as to lay upon him a duty to care for her and the duty to take steps for her protection, the failure to take which was sufficient to constitute such an omission as would render him legally responsible for her death.... There is no claim on the part of the people that the respondent was in any way an active agent in bringing about the death of Blanche Burns, but simply that he owed her a duty which he failed to perform, and that in consequence of such failure on his part she came to her death." Upon this theory a conviction was asked and secured.

The law recognizes that under some circumstances the omission of a duty owed by one individual to another, where such omission results in the death of the one to whom the duty is owing, will make the other chargeable with manslaughter. 21 Cyc. p. 770 *et seq.*, and cases cited. This rule of law is always based upon the proposition that the duty neglected must be a legal duty, and not a mere moral obligation. It must be a duty imposed by law or by contract, and the omission to perform the duty must be the immediate and direct cause of death. Bishop's Crim. Law (6th Ed.) vol. 1, § 217; *Id.*, volume 2, § 695; 21 Am. & E. Enc. Law (2d Ed.) 99; 21 Cyc., *supra*; *State v. Noakes*, 70 Vt. 247, 40 Atl. 249; Wharton's Crim. Law (7th Ed.) p. 1011; Clark & M. Crimes (2d Ed.) p. 375 (e) and cases cited. Although the literature upon the subject is quite meager and the cases few, nevertheless the authorities are in harmony as to the relationship which must exist between the parties to create the duty, the omission of which establishes legal responsibility. One authority has briefly and correctly stated the rule, which the prosecution claims should be applied to the case at bar, as follows: "If a person who sustains to another the legal relation of protector, as husband to wife, parent to child, master to seaman, etc., knowing such person to be in peril, willfully and negligently fails to make such reasonable and proper efforts to rescue him as he might have done, without jeopardizing his own life, or the lives of others, he is guilty of manslaughter at least, if by reason of his omission of duty the dependent person dies." "So one who from domestic relationship, public duty, voluntary choice, or otherwise, has the custody and care of a human being, helpless either from imprisonment, infancy, sickness, age, imbecility, or other incapacity of mind or body is bound to execute the charge with proper diligence, and will be held guilty of manslaughter, if by culpable negligence he lets the helpless creature die." 21 Am. & Eng. Enc. of Law (2d Ed.) p. 192, notes and cases cited.

The following brief digest of cases gives the result of our examination of American and English authorities, where the doctrine of criminal liability was involved when death resulted from an omission to perform a claimed duty. We discuss no cases where statutory provisions are involved. In *Territory v. Manton*, 8 Mont. 95, 19 Pac. 387, a husband was convicted of manslaughter for leaving his intoxicated wife one winter's night lying in the snow, from which exposure she died. The conviction was sustained on the ground that a legal duty rested upon him to care for and protect his wife, and that for his neglect to perform that duty, resulting in her death, he was properly convicted. *State v. Smith*, 65 Me. 257, is a similar case. A husband neglected to provide clothing and shelter for his insane wife. He left her in a bare room without fire during severe winter weather. Her death resulted. The charge in the indictment is predicated upon a known legal duty of the husband to furnish his wife with suitable protection. In *State v. Behm*, 72 Iowa 533, 34 N.W. 319, the conviction of a mother of manslaughter for exposing her infant child without protection was affirmed upon the same ground. Also, *Gibson v. Commonwealth*, 106 Ky. 360, 50 S.W. 532, 90 Am. St. Rep. 230. *State v. Noakes*, *supra*, was a prosecution and conviction of a husband and wife for manslaughter. A child of a maid servant was born under their roof. They were charged with neglecting to furnish it with proper care. In addition to announcing the principle in support of which the case is already cited, the court said: "To create a criminal liability for neglect by nonfeasance, the neglect must also be of a personal legal duty, the natural and ordinary consequences of neglect of which would be dangerous to life." In reversing the case for error in the charge — not necessary to here set forth — the court expressly stated that it did not concede that respondents were under a legal duty to care for this child, because it was permitted to be born under their roof, and declined to pass upon that question. In a federal case tried in California before Mr. Justice Field, of the United States Supreme Court, where the master of a vessel was charged with murder in omitting any effort to rescue a sailor who had fallen overboard, the learned justice, in charging the jury, said: "There may be in the omission to do a particular act under some circumstances, as well as in the commission of an act, such a degree of criminality as to render the offender liable to indictment for manslaughter.... In the first place, the duty omitted must be a plain duty.... In the second place, it must be one which the party is bound to perform by law, or by contract, and is not one the performance of which depends simply upon his humanity, or his sense of justice and propriety." *United States v. Knowles*, 4 Sawy. (U. S.) 517, Fed. Cas. No. 15,540.

The following English cases are referred to as in accord with the American cases above cited, and are cases where a clear and known legal duty existed: *Reg. v. Conde*, 10 Cox Crim. Cases, 547; *Reg. v. Rugg*, 12 Cox Crim. Cases, 16. The case of *Reg. v. Nicholls*, 13 Cox Crim. Cases, 75, was a prosecution of a penniless old woman, a grandmother, for neglecting to supply an infant grandchild left in her charge with sufficient food and proper care. The case was tried at Assizes in Stafford, before Brett, J., who said to the jury: "If a grown up person chooses to undertake the charge of a human creature, helpless either from infancy, simplicity, lunacy, or other infirmity, he is bound to execute that charge without, at all events, wicked negligence, and if a person who has chosen to take charge of a helpless creature lets it die by wicked negligence, that person is guilty of manslaughter." The vital question was whether there had been any such negligence in the case designated by the trial judge as wicked negligence. The trial resulted in an acquittal. The charge of this *nisi prius* judge recognizes the principle that a person may voluntarily assume the care of a helpless human being, and, having assumed it, will be held to be under an implied legal duty to care for and protect such person; the duty assumed being that of caretaker and protector to the exclusion of all others. Another English case decided in the Appellate Court, Lord Coleridge, C. J., delivering the opinion, is *Reg. v. Instan*, 17 Cox Crim. Cases, 602. An unmarried woman without means lived with and was maintained by her aged aunt. The aunt suddenly became very sick, and for 10 days before her death was unable to attend to herself, to move about, or to do anything to procure assistance. Before her death no one but the prisoner had any knowledge of her condition. The prisoner continued to live in the house at the cost of the deceased and took in the food supplied by the trades people. The prisoner did not give food to the deceased, or give or procure any medical or nursing attendance for her; nor did she give notice to any neighbor of her condition or wants, although she had abundant opportunity and occasion to do so. In the opinion, Lord Coleridge, speaking for the court, said: "It is not correct to say that every moral obligation is a legal duty; but every legal duty is founded upon a moral obligation. In this case, as in most cases, the legal duty can be nothing else than taking upon one's self the performance of the moral obligation. There is no question whatever that it was this woman's clear duty to impart to the deceased so much of that food, which was taken into the house for both and paid for by the deceased, as was necessary to sustain her life. The deceased could not get it for herself. She could only get it through the prisoner. It was the prisoner's clear duty at the common law, and that duty she did not perform. Nor is there any question that the prisoner's failure to discharge her legal duty, if it did not directly cause, at any rate accelerated the death of the deceased. There is no case directly in point; but it would be a slur and a stigma upon our law if there could be any doubt as to the law to be derived from the principle of decided cases, if cases were necessary. There was a clear moral obligation and a legal duty founded upon it, a duty willfully disregarded, and the death was at least accelerated, if not caused by the nonperformance of the legal duty." The opening sentences of this opinion are so closely connected with the portion material to this discussion that they could not well be omitted. Quotation does not necessarily mean approval. We do not understand from this opinion that the court held that there was a legal duty founded solely upon a moral obligation. The court indicated that the law applied in the case was derived from the principles of decided cases. It was held that the prisoner had omitted to perform that which was a clear duty at the common law. The prisoner had wrongfully appropriated the food of the deceased and withheld it from her. She was the only other person in the house, and had assumed charge of her helpless relative. She was under a clear legal duty to give her the food she withheld, and under an implied legal duty by reason of her assumption of charge and care, within the law as stated in the case of *Reg. v. Nicholls*, *supra*.

These adjudicated cases and all others examined in this investigation we find are in entire harmony with the proposition first stated in this opinion. Seeking for a proper determination of the case at bar by the application of the legal principles involved, we must eliminate from the case all consideration of mere moral obligation, and discover whether respondent was under a legal duty towards Blanche Burns at the time of her death, knowing her to be in peril of her life, which required him to make all reasonable and proper effort to save her, the omission to perform which duty would make him responsible for her death. This is the important and determining question in this case. If we hold that such legal duty rested upon respondent, it must arise by implication from the facts and circumstances already recited. The record in this case discloses that the deceased was a woman past 30 years of age. She had been twice married. She was accustomed to visiting saloons and to the use of intoxicants. She previously had made assignations with this man in Detroit at least twice. There is no evidence or claim from this record that any duress, fraud, or deceit had been practiced upon her. On the contrary, it appears that she went upon this carouse with respondent voluntarily, and so continued to remain with him. Her entire conduct indicates that she had ample experience in such affairs.

It is urged by the prosecutor that the respondent "stood towards this woman for the time being in the place of her natural guardian and protector, and as such owed her a clear legal duty which he completely failed to perform." The cases cited and digested establish that no such legal duty is created based upon a mere moral obligation. The fact that this woman was in his house created no such legal duty as exists in law and is due from a husband towards his wife, as seems to be intimated by the prosecutor's brief. Such an inference would be very repugnant to our moral sense. Respondent had assumed either in fact or by implication no care or control over his companion. Had this been a case where two men under like circumstances had voluntarily gone on a debauch together, and one had attempted suicide, no one would claim that this doctrine of legal duty could be invoked to hold the other criminally responsible for omitting to make effort to rescue his companion. How can the fact that in this case one of the parties was a woman change the principle of law applicable to it? Deriving and applying the law in this case from the principle of decided cases, we do not find that such legal duty as is contended for existed in fact or by implication on the part of respondent towards the deceased, the omission of which involved criminal liability. We find no more apt words to apply to this case than those used by Mr. Justice Field, in *United States v. Knowles*, *supra*: "In the absence of such obligations, it is undoubtedly the moral duty of every person to extend to others assistance when in danger, ... and, if such efforts should be omitted by any one when they could be made without imperilling his own life, he would by his conduct draw upon himself the just censure and reproach of good men; but this is the only punishment to which he would be subjected by society."

Other questions discussed in the briefs need not be considered.

The conviction is set aside, and respondent is ordered discharged.

■

After reading these two cases, consider the legal method at work in each. What was the source of the duty in *Instan*? What would have been the theory of the prosecution in *Beardsley*? Are the characterization of the facts in *Instan* and the distinctions drawn by the judge in *Beardsley* compelling? What role does moral outrage play in the law of omissions? For a recent decision of the Ontario Court of Appeal that is comparable to *Beardsley*, see *R. v. Browne*, discussed below, under ***Mens Rea***. Would legislation such as that enacted in the Northern Territory in Australia, s. 155 of its *Criminal Code*, which provides a sentence of up to seven years imprisonment for persons who are able yet fail callously to provide rescue, medical attention, or aid of any kind to persons urgently in need and whose lives may be endangered by that failure, address the concerns prompted by these cases? See Ian Leader-Elliott, "Case and Comment: Good Samaritan legislation — Appeal against conviction following guilty plea" (1996) 20 Crim. L.J. 102.

Instan and *Beardsley* were prosecuted at common law. The relevant *Code* offences can now be found in s. 215 (failing to provide the necessaries of life), and ss. 220 and 221 (criminal negligence causing death or bodily harm). The case that follows provides an example of the current problems raised by omissions prosecutions.

R. v. Urbanovich†

[MONNIN C.J.M.:]

The two accused separately appeal from their convictions by Lockwood Co. Ct. J. on counts of unlawfully causing death to their four-month-old infant by criminal negligence. They also appeal the term of seven years imposed on each for such crime: see *R. v. Brown and Urbanovich* (1983), 24 Man. R. (2d) 189. We have heard the appeal as to conviction and the matter has been reserved for decision. Depending upon the decisions reached by all three members of this court, the matter of sentence may then have to be addressed. The parties are out on bail pending determination of this appeal.

The child was born out of wedlock.

All events occurred in 1981 and henceforth I shall only use the date and the month to specify various events.

The infant was born on January 24th and died on May 28th. The post-mortem was held on May 29th. Between the date of her birth and the date of her death, the child was taken to a doctor or to Misericordia Hospital on approximately 11 occasions. On May 20th she was taken to the hospital by her mother, apparently suffering from gastroenteritis. She had no visible injuries or bruises on her body. She was discharged two days later and returned to the same hospital on May 27th in a hopeless condition, namely, irreversible coma. She was placed on life-support systems and transported to Children's Hospital. Twenty-four hours later, when the life-support systems were removed, she was pronounced dead. At death there were still not noticeable or external injuries.

While the infant was on the monitors, X-rays were taken of her chest. For the first time these disclosed fractures of the ribs. Further X-rays were taken immediately before the post-mortem and the broken bones were removed for examination. This is what the post-mortem and X-rays shockingly disclosed:

1. a Y-shaped defect in the skull about 5 cm. in length;
2. underneath there was a subdural haematoma about 5 cm. in diameter which contained fresh and old haemorrhages;
3. further subarachnoid haemorrhage in the posterior portion of the brain on both sides — this means haemorrhage situate or occurring beneath the arachnoid;
4. small haemorrhages in the retina;
5. fractures of the 1st, 2nd, 3rd and 11th ribs, being from two to six weeks old; and
6. a twisting fracture of the tibia less than two weeks old.

The degree of force required to fracture the ribs and the tibia was considerable. It also required considerable force to cause the skull fractures.

All these injuries were consistent with the application of external force to different parts of the body. The cause of death was damage to the brain, reduction of oxygen in the body tissues and swelling of the brain with death ensuing.

Neither accused testified. Explanatory statements signed by each prior to being charged were tendered and admitted in evidence.

. . . .

The Accused Urbanovich

Now to the mother, whose situation is different since she did not apply force to the body or skull of this infant.

Can the mother be linked to the actions of the father? She was also less than frank with the investigating officers. Did she omit to carry out what was a plain legal duty of care to her infant in a course of conduct which shows wanton and reckless disregard for the safety of her child?

A mother has a duty of care to an infant; she must provide it with medical aid and the necessities of life. There is no evidence that the mother was present when the father applied force to the infant between May 22nd and 27th. That is consistent with what happened on the prior occasions since it appears from her statement that on all prior occasions she discovered them after the commission of the injuries. What the statement does not disclose is whether she was told of them by the father or whether she discovered them herself. She was obviously aware that prior to the fatal injury some force had been applied to this child by its father. The baby was in her immediate care between May 22nd

† (1985), 19 C.C.C. (3d) 43 (Man. C.A.).

and 27th. Is it possible that under such circumstances she failed to appreciate that the child was at risk? Is it possible that she failed to appreciate the nature of its injuries?

From what we know from the post-mortem and the X-rays, there can be no doubt that the child was in need of medical help and attention at the time in question and that the mother must have been aware that the child's health was in danger if it was not immediately provided with medical assistance[.] The suddenness of the illness as described by the father is totally unrealistic and the events did not occur as we are told they did.

A person or a child does not simply, suddenly become limp and die from a blow to the skull when the autopsy clearly shows that a subdural haematoma had been present for a few days — be it five or seven — to the extent that in that region there was some discoloured blood, namely, old blood, and also red blood or fresh blood. With the amount of blood in the baby's cranium, the injury must have occurred many hours before death and many hours before limpness. It ought to have been plain to the mother that something was drastically and radically wrong with that child. She may not have known immediately the cause of the illness, since she did not see the striking of the blows, but she nevertheless had a duty to inquire and if unable to obtain a satisfactory explanation to immediately seek medical attention.

There are two prongs to the test which need be applied. The first is whether the child was in need of medical care and there can be no doubt that it was in such need. The second test is whether the accused was aware that the child was at risk unless help was quickly provided or else that she did not care that the child's health was at risk. Is it possible that this mother honestly failed to realize that her child was in need of care? I do not think that such a situation in the circumstances of this case is plausible. It must have been plainly visible to both parents that something was amiss since in fact the child was near death. The father certainly knew what had happened, namely, a blow which caused bleeding in the brain. Could the mother be totally ignorant of that fact? There is no evidence indicating that she inquired from her mate or that she investigated the matter herself. I think that a jury could reasonably infer from the circumstances, including the previous mistreatment of the child and the fact that all three persons were living in the same house, that the mother knew that the child was in need of medical attention or that she did not care whether the child was at risk.

The conduct of this mother was criminally negligent by virtue of her omission to take care of the child. It was her duty so to do and by omitting or failing to do so she showed wanton or reckless disregard for the life of her child. Such being the case, her conviction must be affirmed and the appeal dismissed.

In view of this finding, there is no need to discuss s. 21 of the *Criminal Code*, which deals with parties to the offence. The accused Urbanovich is guilty of criminal negligence causing death by omission.

[MATAS J.A.:]

. . . .

Lockwood Co. Ct. J. relied on the definition of criminal negligence in s. 202 of the *Code* and the provisions of s. 197 prescribing the duty to provide necessaries of life, which would include medical treatment: *R. v. Popen* (1981), 60 C.C.C. (2d) 232 at p. 240 (Ont. C.A.). Lockwood Co. Ct. J. found that the infant sustained a series of serious injuries caused by the acts of Mr. Brown and that the inference to be drawn from all the evidence is that the child was a victim of deliberately applied trauma. Lockwood Co. Ct. J. held that Mr. Brown committed all the acts, including the act or acts which resulted in the brain injuries that led to the infant's death, and held as well that Mr. Brown was liable for depriving the child of the opportunity of receiving proper medical treatment.

Lockwood Co. Ct. J. held that Ms. Urbanovich was not directly responsible for the injuries to the infant but that she failed to take reasonable steps to protect the infant from the violence which caused the injuries. Lockwood Co. Ct. J. held as well that Ms. Urbanovich had deprived the infant of necessary medical attention.

. . . .

Medical Visits between March 12th and May 27, 1981

Lee Anna was seen by her paediatrician, Dr. Kowall, six times between March 12th and May 20th. She was usually brought in by her mother. According to Dr. Kowall's recollection, Mr. Brown came in once. He was abusive on that occasion.

At the first appointment Dr. Kowall performed a quite detailed examination. The infant appeared to be essentially well developed and well nourished. The only negative findings were a small conjunctival haemorrhage, *i.e.*, a little bruising to the white part of the eye and a positional deformity of the right leg which had been noted from birth. The head was well formed with no particular deformity. The haemorrhage in the eye was explained by Ms. Urbanovich as having been caused by the infant poking herself. Dr. Kowall accepted the explanation as a reasonable one.

On March 20th, Dr. Kowall saw the infant because Ms. Urbanovich was concerned that the infant might be tongue-tied but it was found that there was no problem. Dr. Kowall saw Lee Anna on April 9th for [inoculation], and again on May 9th for the same purpose. A detailed examination was done on April 9th. Dr. Kowall recommended taking the infant to see an orthopaedic specialist about her foot; apparently this was done. Nothing untoward was noted by Dr. Kowall on any of the visits.

On May 20th, Lee Anna was brought in to see Dr. Kowall. The infant had been at the Misericordia Hospital the day before. She had been vomiting, appeared listless and had diarrhoea. Dr. Kowall said the baby appeared somewhat ill, lethargic and rather pale. Dr. Kowall assumed she had a [gastro-enteritis] or intestinal flu and because of the mother's anxiety and concern, he had the baby admitted to the Misericordia Hospital. He saw the baby once at the hospital where she still appeared rather listless, apathetic and somewhat pale. No external injuries were visible. Dr. Nigam took over her care. The baby was discharged on May 22nd. The next time Dr. Kowall saw the baby was in the intensive care unit at Children's Hospital on May 27th. He was not involved in the treatment at that time.

Dr. Nigam saw the infant, for a minute or two, one morning at the Misericordia Hospital and authorized her discharge. He said she was in the hospital recovering from a diarrhoea problem and was doing quite well. He did not notice any abnormalities or injuries to the infant, or tenderness about the ribs or abdomen, irritability, or that the infant was favouring any limbs, or other disturbing signs. Dr. Nigam was at the Misericordia Hospital when the infant was brought in on May 27th and assisted in her care and her transfer to Children's Hospital.

Mr. Brown said he told Dr. Kowall about one incident involving the infant when her head was injured by a collision with a door but according to Mr. Brown, the doctor said it was not serious. Mr. Brown said that the swelling, which Mr. Brown described in his statements, was gone by the time he told Dr. Kowall of the incident.

Dr. Hwang said, in cross-examination, that he had "phoned up the family physician which I talked with, Dr. Kowall, and he gave me a bit more information about the child having fallen, being hit." Further in cross-examination, Dr. Hwang said: "No, I think — anyway, I think it is the family doctor. It was the family doctor working out of Misericordia Hospital." And later in cross-examination, he said: "As far as I can recollect it was from the family physician." And Dr. Duncan, in looking at an historical basis for his diagnosis when the infant was in intensive care at Children's Hospital, said that Dr. Kowall felt the infant "had previously been reasonably well save faint history of a fall some weeks prior to that earlier hospitalization" (*i.e.*, May 20th). In cross-examination, Dr. Duncan said he could not "with any surety" say the information about a fall came from Dr. Kowall.

It was in evidence that the chart at Children's Hospital contained information about a head injury, although the source of that information is not clear. And Mr. Brown, in his question-and-answer session on June 25th with the police, in reply to a question whether he had told the doctor about what happened or about the line on Lee Anna's head said:

> I didn't tell him about the accident like I just told you. I told him I bumped her head and had a little accident with her but I didn't tell him how it happened and didn't tell him why it happened. I didn't want to tell him I had been drinking. It was a stupid accident.

And Mr. Brown said to the police at the conclusion of the questions by the police that he did not take the infant to Dr. Kowall or for any medical treatment after any of the incidents happened.

The response of Mr. Brown to the questions asked by the police should be considered in the context of Dr. Ferguson's evidence under cross-examination that "[w]e are dealing with a non-witness as a patient" and in the context of the comment made by Dr. Ferguson about difficulties inherent in diagnosing the infant's illnesses in the absence of full and careful explanation by the infant's caretaker. In particular, Dr. Ferguson commented on the reference in the statements to the fact that Dr. Kowall was told about a bump on the head, in this way:

> About a bump on the head and about a line, but those of course are not specific and most babies that you might examine at that age have lines and bumps and they are probably not of significance, although I can't say the details on these particular items.

Dr. Kowall firmly denied that he had been told about any accidents. He said the parents did not point out any injuries to him and said he did not recollect any concern having been expressed about injuries or accidents.

In his first statement Mr. Brown said that he told Mrs. Askew, at the time of admission to Misericordia Hospital on May 20th, that

> ...if she was wondering what the marks on the baby's arm was, it's because when I was bathing her a day or so before and she was squirming in the tub and was going to fall on her face in the water. I grabbed her arm and lifted her up and I later noticed like a bruise on her left arm where I grabbed her.

Mrs. Askew said that Mr. Brown had made a comment about bruises in response to a question she had asked about immunization. She said she examined the infant but did not notice any bruising at all. She commented that Mr. Brown was hostile to her and said that the baby had a surprising reaction. When Mrs. Askew picked her up the infant "just started, and almost jumped out of [her] arms at that point."

. . . .

Ms. Urbanovich's Explanations Taken from Her Statements to the Police

According to Ms. Urbanovich, the appellants lived on Luxton for about two months after the baby was born. Towards the end of March they moved to William Ave. and then about the beginning of May to Langside St.

In her first statement on June 2nd, Ms. Urbanovich mentioned the collision with the door and the collapse of the crib. She said the collision with the door occurred when the infant was a month or month and a half old. Mr. Brown went through the doorway "kind of ... sideways" and the infant bumped her head against the doorway. The baby was sleeping and she woke up. She seemed alright. In the morning they checked again. She had a lump on the top left side of her head and the head swelled up a little on the right side. The swelling went down so she and Mr. Brown did not see the doctor. Ms. Urbanovich did not tell the doctor anything about this injury.

When the infant was about two months old one side of the crib collapsed. The infant rolled and hit the bars on the crib with her head and arm, apparently without injury. On William Ave., when Lee Anna was two months, three weeks old, she fell off the bed onto the floor, possibly hitting the end-table. She cried for a while. In the first week of May the baby fell sideways while in her "jolly jumper." Ms. Urbanovich also mentioned one time when Mr. Brown noticed a bruise on the baby's leg which he said he must have done when he was changing the baby. Ms. Urbanovich then described the events around May 20th and May 27th.

In her second statement on June 25th, Ms. Urbanovich expanded on the description she had given earlier. In describing the collision with the door, she said that it occurred when Lee Anna was about one month old. On the next day she noticed a bump on the back of the infant's head and that the forehead was swollen a bit. It went down in a couple of days so she and Mr. Brown did not worry about it. They took the infant to see the doctor about a month later and Mr. Brown told the doctor about it. In answering questions by the police, Ms. Urbanovich said they took the infant to see the doctor on the next check-up which was two weeks to a month later. She said she did not contact a doctor on any of the other incidents.

In the second statement, Ms. Urbanovich said that the incident with the crib occurred either before or after the visit to the doctor, while still living on Luxton. Ms. Urbanovich did not notice anything wrong with the infant but the baby cried for a little while. The fall off the bed, when the baby was about three months old, was referred to again. Ms. Urbanovich said the child fell off the bed, perhaps hitting an end-table. The baby cried but not for long. Ms. Urbanovich then recounted the events around May 20th and May 27th. Ms. Urbanovich claimed she noticed a difference in personality after the baby's stay in hospital. This change was not mentioned in the first statement.

In the question-and-answer session after the second statement, Ms. Urbanovich said she was not present at all the incidents but she knew about them through Rob (*i.e.*, Mr. Brown).

Lockwood Co. Ct. J. made the following comments in assessing the value of the appellants' statements [at p. 172]:

> In the statements of the two accused, various so-called accidents are described. The mother claimed that she had not been present at all of them. She did, however, admit that her husband told her about them. Having regard to the injuries to the child, it seems clear that the two accused were less than frank in their statements.
>
> ...
>
> According to the medical evidence, the injuries are not consistent with the explanations given by the parents to the police. The inference to be drawn from their lack of frankness, is that they did not want to be found out. The accused

> deliberately misled the pediatrician, Dr. Kowall and the police.
>
> ...
>
> By their lack of frankness, the parents deprived the child of the opportunity of receiving proper medical treatment.

Lockwood Co. Ct. J. had the advantage of seeing and hearing the witnesses and assessing their evidence. He was able to relate this evidence to statements made by each of Mr. Brown and Ms. Urbanovich. It is my respectful view that the conclusion of the learned trial judge with respect to the separate explanations of the appellants is amply supported by the totality of the evidence.

. . . .

Conclusion on Convictions

Taking all the evidence into account, it is my respectful opinion that it amply supports the conclusion of the learned trial judge that there was an "act or acts which resulted in the brain injuries" which in turn led to the child's death. I agree with the conclusion of the learned trial judge that Mr. Brown, as the perpetrator of the acts causing the trauma to the infant, was guilty of causing bodily harm to her by criminal negligence and causing her death by criminal negligence.

With respect to the position of Ms. Urbanovich, it is inconceivable that she would not have known that the infant should have been given medical attention for the injuries she suffered. The visits to the paediatrician do not absolve Ms. Urbanovich from her responsibility to ensure that her medical advisers knew as much as possible about the state of health of the infant. Withholding the vital information from her medical advisers can only be categorized as wilful blindness and wanton and reckless disregard for the infant's safety: *R. v. Caldwell* (1981), 73 Cr. App. R. 13 (H.L.).

. . . .

[HUBAND J.A. (dissenting):]

. . . .

The accused persons, Robin Brown and Tracie Urbanovich, have lived in a common law relationship for several years. Tracie Urbanovich gave birth to a baby girl, Lee Anna, on January 24, 1981. The mother was 17 years old at the time. She turned 18 a month later. Robin Brown was 21. The child died some four months later, on May 28, 1981.

. . . .

There is simply no evidence against the accused Urbanovich that any of the accidents were attributable to her, with the possible exception of the incident where the child fell off the bed. She may have been careless in the way Lee Anna was propped against the pillow on the bed. She may have been careless in her attentiveness, and thus in failing to reach the child before the fall. But the incident is entirely lacking in qualities of wantonness or recklessness which are necessary ingredients to a charge of criminal negligence. Moreover, in the end result, the learned trial judge concluded that accidents involving the accused Brown, and not the accused Urbanovich, were the cause of injury and death, and the accused Urbanovich is entitled to the benefit of that conclusion.

... I think the delay in seeking medical attention can hardly be described as a wanton or reckless disregard for the life of the child. The child seemed to be normal and the symptoms were abating to the point that there were no visible signs of injury at the time of the visit. They say they told Dr. Kowall of a bump or blow to the head, and there is independent evidence to indicate that, despite his denials, Dr. Kowall had knowledge of such trauma. The numerous trips to the paediatrician, plus the admission to hospital, negate elements of wantonness or recklessness. The parents showed obvious concern for the child when it became comatose and had to be rushed to hospital on the morning of May 27th, and their concern is inconsistent with a criminal intention to omit medical treatment in disregard for the life or safety of their daughter.

. . . .

In my opinion, the verdict of guilty should be set aside under s. 613(1)(*a*)(i) [now s. 686(1)(a)(i)] of the *Code* because it is unreasonable and cannot be supported by the evidence. So too, there should be an acquittal entered with respect to the lesser charge of criminal negligence causing bodily harm.

This is not a case for a new trial. A verdict of acquittal should be substituted for the guilty verdicts.

Appeals dismissed.

■

This case raises a number of questions about the law of omissions, as well as criminal practice. For example, might a miscarriage of justice have occurred because both accused were represented by the same counsel? See *R. v. Widdifield* (1995), 25 O.R. (3d) 161 (C.A.), where the court discussed the relevant principles in a case of a husband and wife jointly charged with sexual abuse of their niece. See also the Rules of Professional Responsibility on joint representation, discussed in Gavin Mackenzie, *Lawyers and Ethics*, 3d ed. (Toronto: Carswell, 2001) at 7-15–20.

Was it appropriate, pursuant to the relevant sentencing principles, to punish Brown and Urbanovich with the identical sentence? Is there any evidence or argument in support of a position that Urbanovich should not have been prosecuted at all? Consider the case of Hedda Nussbaum, who was originally indicted along with her partner, Joel Steinberg, for the death of six-year-old Lisa, their adopted daughter, whom Steinberg (a disbarred lawyer) had abused over the years and, finally, beaten to death. At the time of Lisa's death, Ms. Nussbaum was hospitalized with nine fractured ribs, a broken nose, gangrenous sores on her leg, a fractured jaw, a cauliflower ear, and minor brain damage. It took over one year of surgery, rehabilitation, and de-programming to get Ms. Nussbaum even to the stage where she was willing to testify against Steinberg: "'She was physically as badly injured as any battered woman I have ever seen — short of those who have been killed,' said Julie Blackman, a New York psychologist and recognized expert on abused women." Quoted in Sam Ehrlich, *Lisa, Hedda and Joel: The Steinberg Murder Case* (New York: St. Martin's Press, 1989) at 127.

It was reported in "Man sentenced to maximum in child's death" *The [Toronto] Globe and Mail* (25 March 1989) A11 that "[t]he charges were dropped against Ms. Nussbaum when prosecutors said she was 'so physically and mentally incapacitated on the night of the murder that she was not criminally responsible for Lisa's death.' In testimony against Mr. Steinberg, Ms. Nussbaum described an 11-year relationship with him that included beatings, brainwashing, food deprivation, bizarre punishments and drug use."

It is important, however, to put the issue of child abuse in a larger context so as to appreciate the systemic reinforcement that law and society provide for the acts of individuals. For example, authors S.E. Longstaffe, K.N. McRae, and C.A. Ferguson in "Sexual Abuse on Manitoba Indian Reserves — Medical, Social and Legal Issues, and Obstacles to Resolution" (1987) 8 Health Law in Canada 52, document the failures of the criminal justice system regarding sexual abuse of Aboriginal children on reserves, including "[a]n insufficient and disorganized legal input with different lawyers at different hearings, inadequate transmission and enforcement of bail conditions ... failure to prepare victims for court appearances or to prevent victim intimidation" (at 53), "[e]rrors in court servicing", "[i]nstructions by Crown Attorneys to RCMP to stop investigation", "[m]ajor communication breakdown slowing communication", "RCMP disbelief of credible victim", and "[b]lunted RCMP investigation with offender of high status" (at 56).

In light of the statistics on physical and sexual abuse of children such as Jane Gadd, "10,000 child-abuse cases tallied: Toronto police investigated an average of 10 incidents a day in past three years" *The [Toronto] Globe and Mail* (28 March 1997) A1, and in light of the structures that facilitate abuse of children, is it effective or just for the criminal law to focus solely on the fathers and mothers themselves? For example, in British Columbia in 1995, Judge Thomas Gove was appointed to review 69 of 332 deaths between 1986 and 1995, where these children were known to child protection authorities. The death of Matthew Vaudreuil in 1992, who was the subject of at least 60 reports to the Ministry of Social Services concerning his safety and had seen 24 doctors a total of 75 times in his five-year-old life, was a particular focus of the inquiry. Judge Gove's report, released in 1995 and consisting of 118 recommendations, prompted a major overhaul of child protection services in that province and the creation of a new Ministry for Children and Families, with a Children's Commissioner empowered to investigate all child deaths in the province. In Ontario, eight coroner's inquests were instigated with respect to children's deaths (Jane Gadd, "Inquiries put child care on trial" *The [Toronto] Globe and Mail* (1 April 1997) A1), and all child deaths known to the children's aid societies must now be reported to the coroner's office.

Child welfare legislation may raise particular issues for lawyers. For example, the *Child and Family Services Act*, R.S.O. 1990, c. 11, s. 72(2) imposes a duty to report to a society on the part of any person who **believes**, on reasonable grounds, that a child is in need of protection. It places a higher burden in s. 72(3) upon professionals and officials who perform duties with respect to a child to report where they have reasonable grounds to **suspect** that a child is suffering, may be suffering, or may have suffered abuse. Ken Armstrong, in "The Duty of Confidentiality and the Child Beating Client" (1995) 13 C.F.L.Q.

49, argues that comparable provisions in Alberta's legislation, in combination with Alberta's *Code of Professional Conduct* for lawyers (in Ontario, *The Professional Conduct Handbook* (Toronto: Law Society of Upper Canada, 1996) Rule 4, commentaries 10 and 11), require lawyers to protect children by reporting abuse that might be repeated in the future, regardless of whether the information is confidential. He suggests that even information protected by solicitor/client privilege should be disclosed in a manner consistent with that privilege. For an examination of the strain that this legal obligation places on police officers, see the discussion of the Perry Dunlop case, below, under **Broadening the Defences: Necessity, Self-Defence, and Conscience.**

Returning to the role of the *Criminal Code* in the abuse of children, what can child welfare authorities accomplish as long as s. 43 of the *Code* remains in force? The *Code* provides a defence for assaults upon children when characterized as "correction", "if the force does not exceed what is reasonable in the circumstances": s. 43. See **Case Study on Assault**, below.

R. v. Thornton†

[GALLIGAN J.A.:]

The presence in a person's blood of antibodies to Human Immunodeficiency Virus (HIV) indicates that the person is probably infected with Acquired Immune Deficiency Syndrome (AIDS). AIDS is a grave illness which is usually fatal. It is infectious and particularly contagious through the blood.

All of this is now well known. The appellant knew it in November 1987. In fact, he was well informed about AIDS and its means of transmission. He knew as well that he was a member of a group which was highly at risk of contracting AIDS. Moreover, he knew that he had twice tested positive for HIV antibodies and that he was therefore infectious. He knew that the Canadian Red Cross collected blood for transfusion to persons in need of it and that AIDS is transmitted by blood. He also knew that the Red Cross would not knowingly accept donations of blood from persons who had tested positive to HIV antibodies or who were members of his high risk group. Nevertheless, on November 16, 1987, he donated blood to the Red Cross at a clinic in Ottawa. Fortunately, the Red Cross's screening process detected the contaminated blood and it was put aside.

The appellant was charged with an offence contrary to s. 176(1)(*a*) of the *Criminal Code*, R.S.C. 1970, c. C-34. That provision is now s. 180 of the *Criminal Code*, R.S.C. 1985, c. C-46, and in these reasons for judgment reference will be made to the present provision. He was charged that he:

> ...on or about the 16th day of November, 1987, at the City of Ottawa in the said Judicial District did commit a common nuisance endangering the lives or health of the public by donating to the Canadian Red Cross Society a quantity of his blood knowing that his blood had previously been found to contain antibodies to Human Immunodeficiency Virus and intentionally withholding the information from the Canadian Red Cross Society, contrary to Section 176(a) [*sic*] of the *Criminal Code of Canada*.

He was convicted of the charge by Flanigan J., sitting without a jury, and sentenced to a term of 15 months' imprisonment. He appeals both his conviction and his sentence.

Counsel for the appellant attacked the conviction on three grounds:

1. that, reprehensible as the appellant's conduct may have been, it did not amount to an offence known to the law;
2. that it was not proved that his conduct endangered the lives or health of the public or any member of it;
3. that the appellant did not have the necessary *mens rea*.

The provisions of s. 180 of the *Code* are:

> 180.(1) Every one who commits a common nuisance and thereby
> (*a*) endangers the lives, safety or health of the public, or
> (*b*) causes physical injury to any person,

† (1991), 1 O.R. (3d) 480 (C.A.).

> is guilty of an indictable offence and liable to imprisonment for a term not exceeding two years.
>
> (2) For the purposes of this section, every one commits a common nuisance who does an unlawful act or fails to discharge a legal duty and thereby
> (*a*) endangers the lives, safety or health, property or comfort of the public; or
> (*b*) obstructs the public in the exercise or enjoyment of any right that is common to all the subjects of Her Majesty in Canada.

I will deal first with the argument that the appellant's conduct did not amount to an offence known to law. If, in the circumstances, the appellant's act of donating blood which he knew was HIV-contaminated to the Red Cross was neither an unlawful act nor a failure to discharge a legal duty, then the indictment does not allege an offence known to law.

Section 180(2)(*a*) provides that a common nuisance is committed by either the doing of an unlawful act or the failure to discharge a legal duty which endangers the lives or health of the public. For the purposes of this appeal, I am prepared to assume the correctness of Mr. Greenspon's cogent argument that the words "unlawful act" must be taken to mean conduct which is specifically proscribed by legislation. The *Code* does not make it an offence to donate contaminated blood. Counsel were unable to refer the court to any other statutory provision, federal or provincial, which does so. On the assumption, therefore, that the appellant's conduct could not constitute an "unlawful act" I will examine whether it amounted to a failure to discharge a "legal duty."

I am unable to find any provision in the *Code* or any other statute which I can read as specifically imposing a legal duty upon a person to refrain from donating contaminated blood. The immediate issue therefore is twofold. Can a "legal duty" within the meaning of s. 180(2) be one which arises at common law or must it be one found in a statute? Is there a "legal duty" arising at common law the breach of which, assuming the other essential elements of the offence were proved, could be the basis of an offence under s. 180?

There are no cases deciding whether the "legal duty" in s. 180(2) must be a duty imposed by statute or whether it can be a duty according to common law. However, the "duty imposed by law" which forms part of the definition of criminal negligence set out in s. 219 of the *Code* has been held to be either a duty imposed by statute or a duty arising at common law. The provisions of s. 219 are as follows:

> 219.(1) Every one is criminally negligent who
> (*a*) in doing anything, or
> (*b*) in omitting to do anything that it is his duty to do,
> shows wanton or reckless disregard for the lives or safety of other persons.
>
> (2) For the purposes of this section, "duty" means a duty imposed by law.

In *R. v Coyne* (1958), 124 C.C.C. 176, 31 C.R. 335, the New Brunswick Supreme Court Appeal Division considered the criminal negligence provisions of the *Code* in relation to a hunting accident. Speaking for that court, Ritchie J.A. held at pp. 179–80 C.C.C.:

> The "duty imposed by law" may be a duty arising by virtue of either the common law or by statute. Use of a firearm, in the absence of proper caution, may readily endanger the lives or safety of others. Under the common law anyone carrying such a dangerous weapon as a rifle is under the duty to take such precaution in its use as, in the circumstances, would be observed by a reasonably careful man. If he fails in that duty and his behaviour is of such a character as to show or display a wanton or reckless disregard for the lives or safety of other persons, then, by virtue of s. 191, his conduct amounts to criminal negligence....

In *R. v Popen* (1981), 60 C.C.C. (2d) 232, this court also had occasion to consider the nature of the "duty imposed by law" contained in the definition of criminal negligence. It was a child abuse case. In giving the judgment of the court, Martin J.A. said at p. 240 C.C.C.:

> ...a parent is under a legal duty at common law to take reasonable steps to protect his or her child from illegal violence used by the other parent or by a third person towards the child which the parent foresees or ought to foresee.

The effect of that judgment is to hold that the common law duty, which was there described, was a "duty imposed by law" within the meaning of s. 219 because the court held that its breach could amount to criminal negligence.

These decisions lead me to the opinion that it is well settled that, for the purpose of defining criminal negligence, a "duty imposed by law" includes a duty which arises at common law.

While the words "legal duty" in s. 180(2) are not the same as a "duty imposed by law" used in s. 219, they have exactly the same meaning. It follows, therefore, that the meaning given to a "duty imposed by law" in s. 219 should also be given to the "legal duty" contained in s. 180(2). Thus, I am of the opinion that the legal duty referred to in s. 180(2) is a duty which is imposed by statute or which arises at common law. It becomes necessary, then, to decide whether at common law there is a duty which would prohibit the donation of blood known to be HIV-contaminated to the Red Cross.

While this is not a civil case and the principles of tort law are not directly applicable to it, the jurisprudence on that subject is replete with discussions about the legal duties of one person to another which arise at common law. The jurisprudence is constant that those duties are legal ones, that is, they are ones which are imposed by law. Throughout this century and indeed since much earlier times, the common law has recognized a very fundamental duty, which while it has many qualifications, can be summed up as being a duty to refrain from conduct which could cause injury to another person.

This is not the place to make a detailed examination of the jurisprudence on the subject of tort law but a few references to authority are in order. In *Le Lievre v. Gould*, [1893] 1 Q.B. 491, 62 L.J.Q.B. 353, 41 W.R. 468 (C.A.), after a reference to *Heaven v. Pender* (1883), 11 Q.B.D. 503, [1881–5] All E.R. Rep. 35, 52 L.J.Q.B. 702 (C.A.), Lord Esher M.R. said at p. 497 Q.B.:

> That case established that, under certain circumstances, one man may owe a duty to another, even though there is no contract between them. If one man is near to another, or is near to the property of another, a *duty lies upon him not to do that which may cause a personal injury to that other*, or may injure his property. (Emphasis added.)

In the course of his oft quoted speech in the famous case of *Donoghue v. Stevenson*, [1932] A.C. 562, [1932] All E.R. Rep. 1, 101 L.J.P.C. 119 (H.L.), Lord Atkin said at p. 589 A.C.:

> The rule that you are to love your neighbour becomes in law, you must not injure your neighbour....

The editors [William James Byrne and Andrew Dewar Gibb] of the 4th edition of Thomas Beven, *Negligence in Law* (London: Sweet & Maxwell, 1928), vol. 1 at p. 8, have described the fundamental common law duty of one person toward another and the rationale for it:

> Before the law every man is entitled to the enjoyment of unfettered freedom so long as his conduct does not interfere with the equal liberty of all others. Where one man's sphere of activity impinges on another man's, a conflict of interests arises. The [debatable] land where these collisions may occur is taken possession of by the law, which lays down the rules of mutual intercourse. A liberty of action which is allowed therein is called a right, the obligation of restraint a duty, and these terms are purely relative, each implying the other. Duty, then, as a legal term indicates the obligation to limit freedom of action and to conform to a prescribed course of conduct. *The widest generalisation of duty is that each citizen "must do no act to injure another."* (Emphasis added.)

The authority which the editors give for their quoted statement of the duty is the judgment of Bramwell L.J. in *Foulkes v. Metropolitan District Railway Co.* (1880), 5 C.P.D. 157, 49 L.J.Q.B. 361, 28 W.R. 526 (C.A.).

That brief reference to jurisprudence in civil matters shows that there is deeply embedded in the common law a broad fundamental duty which, although subject to many qualifications, requires everyone to refrain from conduct which could injure another. It is not necessary to decide in this case how far that duty extends. At the very least, however, it requires everyone to refrain from conduct which it is reasonably foreseeable could cause serious harm to other persons. Accepting, as I have said, that a "legal duty" within the meaning of that term in s. 180(2) includes a duty arising at common law, I think that the common law duty to refrain from conduct which it is reasonably foreseeable could cause serious harm to other persons is a "legal duty" within the meaning of that term in s. 180(2).

Donating blood which one knows to be HIV-contaminated to an organization whose purpose is to make the blood available for transfusion to other persons clearly constitutes a breach of the common law duty to refrain from conduct which one foresees could cause serious harm to another person. It is thus a failure to discharge a "legal duty" within the contemplation of s. 180(2). It is therefore my conclusion that the indictment which alleges the commission of a nuisance by the donation of blood which the appellant knew to be HIV-contaminated does allege an offence known to law. The first argument made by counsel for the appellant cannot be accepted.

Counsel for the Crown referred to a number of cases where, at common law, the courts held that the exposing of others to the risk of becoming infected by a contagious disease constituted a common nuisance. Those cases are: *R. v. Vantandillo* (1815), 4 M. & S. 73, 105 E.R. 762, *R. v. Burnett*

(1815), 4 M. & S. 272, 105 E.R. 835, and *R. v. Henson* (1852), Dears. C.C. 24, 20 L.T.O.S. 63, 16 J.P. 711. I have not cited them as authority in this case because s. 9(*a*) [rep. & sub. R.S.C. 1985, c. 27 (1st Supp.), s. 6] of the *Code* abolishes common law offences. They are, however, very helpful for two reasons. The first is they seem to be based upon the fundamental duty recognized by the common law to refrain from conduct which one can foresee could cause injury to others. The second reason is perhaps a stronger one. It has been said by the editor of the 6th edition of *Tremeear's Annotated Criminal Code* (Toronto: Carswell, 1964) at p. 241 that the statutory definition of a common nuisance contained in the *Code* "does not differ from a criminal common nuisance at common law." Those cases show that the conduct of donating blood known to be HIV-contaminated, if it exposed others to the risk of infection, is conduct very similar to that which the law has recognized to be a criminal common nuisance for almost 200 years. Finding that conduct to constitute a common nuisance under s. 180 is consistent with the common law position and does not extend it.

. . . .

[With respect to the accused's argument that no one had been "endangered" because the screening process had caught his donation, Galligan J. held that, since screening is 99.3 per cent effective, the public had been endangered even though the risk itself was low in probability. Justice Galligan's conclusions regarding the *mens rea* argument follow.]

In the light of the findings of the trial judge on the issue of credibility and in the light of all of the other evidence, there can be no doubt that this appellant had personal knowledge that he should not donate his blood, that it was possible for it to get through the testing screen and that it could cause serious damage to the life and health of members of the public. It follows that he knew that, by giving his blood to the Red Cross, he was endangering the lives and health of other members of the public. It therefore becomes unnecessary to decide whether some lesser form of *mens rea* could satisfy the requirements of s. 180. This appellant knew personally the danger to which the public was subjected by his donation of blood. He clearly had *mens rea*. Mr. Greenspon's third argument fails.

It is my opinion that the appellant was properly convicted of the offence under s. 180. Accordingly, I would dismiss the appeal from conviction.

With respect to sentence, the trial judge did not impose the maximum sentence prescribed by law. The maximum sentence must be reserved for the worst offender committing the worst category of the offence. The sentence imposed took into account that, because of his prior good record, the appellant would not fall into the category of the worst offender. The offence, however, can certainly be categorized as among the worst offences. The appellant's conduct verges on the unspeakable. It cried out for a sentence which would act as a deterrent to others and which would express society's repudiation of what he did. One must have great compassion for this man. He faces a terrible future. Nevertheless, the sentence demonstrates no error in principle and is one that is eminently fit.

While I would allow the application for leave to appeal sentence, I would dismiss the appeal from sentence.

Appeal dismissed.

■

What specific problems does this omissions prosecution present? Paragraph 9(a) of the *Code* states that no person shall be convicted of an offence at common law (the offence of contempt of court is expressly exempted), and s. 11(g) of the *Charter* says that a person charged must not be found guilty of an offence unless the act was an offence at the time it was committed. Is *Thornton* consistent with these principles?

The Supreme Court of Canada dismissed Thornton's appeal from conviction with the following oral statement, and no further reasoning: "Section 216 imposed upon the appellant a duty of care in giving his blood to the Red Cross. This duty of care was breached by not disclosing that his blood contained HIV antibodies. This common nuisance obviously endangered the life, safety and health of the public." See *R. v. Thornton*, [1993] 2 S.C.R. 445. Does invocation of s. 216 resolve the *Charter* s. 11(g) problem?

In contrast to Thornton, Charles Ssenyonga was discharged at his preliminary inquiry with respect to charges of common nuisance after he had unprotected intercourse with three women to whom he did not disclose his HIV-positive status, and who developed HIV as a result. In *R. v.*

Ssenyonga (1992), 73 C.C.C. (3d) 216 at 224 (Ont. Ct. (Gen. Div.)), Judge Livingstone distinguished *Thornton* on the following grounds:

> The facts in this case are significantly different. I have heard no evidence that Mr. Ssenyonga offered himself to the general public. The evidence before me is of specific relationships with specific individuals with whom the accused had apparently developed an attachment over time.
>
> Certainly the complainants are members of the public but I cannot accept that they, from a legal perspective, represent the community as a whole. The offence of common nuisance, is, in my view, not appropriate based on the evidence presented at this preliminary inquiry.

Sexual assault charges against the accused were also dismissed on the basis of consent: *R. v. Ssenyonga* (1993), 81 C.C.C. (3d) 257 (Ont. Ct. (Gen. Div.)). See now *R. v. Cuerrier*, below, under **Case Study on Assault**. Ssenyonga died before the judge had rendered a verdict on criminal negligence charges, and the trial abated as a result: *R. v. Ssenyonga*, [1993] O.J. No. 3273 (Ct. J. (Gen. Div.)) (QL).

B. VOLUNTARINESS

A common law requirement has been read in by the judges that holds that the *actus reus* or physical act must be voluntary and chosen at a basic level. When a person is said to have acted involuntarily, this state is called "automatism" in law. A state of automatism can result in a finding of no *actus reus* and, of course, no *mens rea*.

The criminal law characterizes the automatism as sane or insane: a finding of sane automatism results in an acquittal; a finding of insane automatism would require a finding under s. 16 of the *Code*, which deals with the defence of mental disorder and its repercussions. Insane automatism or mental disorder will be discussed below, under **Incapacity**.

Some accused have been acquitted using a sane automatism defence on the basis of

- **Intoxication**: see *R. v. King*, [1962] S.C.R. 746 (involuntary intoxication). The legal effect of voluntary intoxication is more complex. See **Intoxication**, below.
- **Physical Blow**: see *R. v. Bartlett* (1983), 33 C.R. (3d) 247 (Ont. H.C.) (witnesses supported the accused's evidence that a police officer had delivered a blow to his head seconds before the accused went into an automatic state); *R. v. Haslam* (1990), 56 C.C.C. (3d) 491 (B.C.C.A.) (acquittal ordered based on evidence that woman who had been violently assaulted by blows to the head had turned on her aggressor).
- **Psychological Blow**: see *R. v. Rabey* (1977), 17 O.R. (2d) 1 (C.A.) affirmed, [1980] 2 S.C.R. 513 (unsuccessful attempt to argue psychological blow based on rejection by a female friend, because courts characterized the accused's automatism as resulting from his own internal frailties rather than the alleged "blow"). See **Automatism**, below.
- **Sleepwalking**: see *R. v. Parks*, [1992] 2 S.C.R. 871. In *Parks*, the accused had driven 23 km in the middle of the night to the home of his in-laws, where he killed the mother of his wife, seriously injured her father, and then took himself to the police station where he told them what he had done. Parks was successful in his non-insane automatism claim at trial, after introducing evidence of the stress he had been under, his good relationship with his in-laws, his patterns of deep sleep, and evidence that members of his family also suffered from sleepwalking and other sleep disorders: see **Automatism**, below.

C. CAUSATION

Only if an offence in the *Code* holds an accused responsible for a particular consequence will the Crown be required to prove, on the criminal standard of proof, both **factual** and **legal causation**. In fact, even in those cases, such as where the accused is charged with "causing death" or "causing bodily harm", it will usually be a simple matter to show that the act of the accused "caused" the harm.

As you read the following materials on causation, consider the work of Eric Tucker, who argues in "The Westray Mining Disaster and its Aftermath: The Politics of Causation" (1995) 10 Can. J. Law & Soc. 91 that "causation" is ultimately a political question:

> Thus, for example, if hazardous working conditions are, in some sense, an inevitable by-product of capitalist relations of production, but capitalism is seen as good or necessary, then the goal of protecting workers will be reformulated. It will be to protect workers within capitalist relations of production. Once the goal is restated in this way, the system of production and its supporting ideology will cease to be seen as causally significant and, therefore, requiring change.

Tucker identifies the legal terrain within which causation analysis is undertaken, including "prevailing political-economic conditions, dominant ideological assumptions and the particular institutional context" (e.g., criminal or civil trial, public inquiry) as also shaping its political content: "Not only do these factors militate against the selection of approaches to causation that emphasize systemic conditions, the opportunity to raise and interrogate the underlying political commitments that inform dominant conceptions of causation is also severely constrained" (at 95).

FACTUAL CAUSATION

R. v. Smithers, [1978] 1 S.C.R. 506, was one of the first Supreme Court decisions to address the issue of causation in any depth. Paul Smithers was the leading player for the Cooksville Midget Team in Mississauga; he was also African-Canadian. The leading player on the opposing team was Barrie Cobby, a white. During their hockey game in February 1973, Cobby and other members of his team subjected Smithers to racial insults and verbal abuse. Cobby and Smithers were both ejected from the game when they exchanged "profanities", whereupon Smithers threatened to "get" Cobby after the game. Smithers caught up with Cobby in the parking lot and, when Cobby attempted to get into a car, he delivered one or two punches to Cobby's head. Cobby's teammates restrained Smithers, but he managed to pull away and kick Cobby, who was already doubled up. The kick was to the stomach area, and Cobby groaned, fell to the ground, and gasped for air. He stopped breathing within five minutes and was pronounced dead on arrival at the hospital. The cause of death was said to be the aspiration of foreign materials present from vomiting. The medical evidence suggested that the vomiting was either spontaneous or caused by fear or the kick, or both. It suggested that aspiration was either spontaneous or caused the deceased's faulty epiglottis or the kick, or both.

Smithers was charged with manslaughter and, thus, provocation was not available as a defence: see **Provocation**, below. At trial, the defence challenged the evidence on causation and argued self-defence to the jury. The accused was convicted.

On appeal to the Supreme Court, the defence focused on what is required for proof of factual causation, suggesting that it was an error for the trial judge to fail to instruct the jury that they could only convict if they found, beyond a reasonable doubt, that the kick caused Cobby's death. The Supreme Court of Canada affirmed the accused's manslaughter conviction, responding that the Crown has "the burden of showing factual causation — that beyond a reasonable doubt the [accused's act] caused the death", and that that act "was at least a contributing cause of death, outside the *de minimis* range" (at 89, 90). Given the above evidence, the Court concluded that there was ample evidence to suggest that the accused's assault was at least a contributing cause of death and dismissed the appeal. Might a different conclusion have been reached if the Crown had been required to prove that "but for" the kick, Cobby would not have died? How does Eric Tucker's analysis help you to understand why *Smithers* has generated debate about whether and how racism is embedded in criminal law doctrine?

In a similar vein, consider the ways in which causation as a factual issue is framed in the AIDS virus nuisance and aggravated assault cases. Recall that in *Thornton* the accused was said to have endangered the lives of others through his donation based on the fact that there was a .7 per cent risk that the Red Cross's screening processes might fail. In contrast, in *R. v. Napora* (1995), 36 Alta. L.R. (3d) 13 (Q.B.) the accused was acquitted of nuisance on the basis that the Crown could not prove beyond a reasonable doubt that the male complainant was not already infected with the HIV virus before unprotected contact with the accused took place. Can you reconcile these cases? In a

Toronto prosecution of a transvestite with HIV for aggravated assault on a police officer by biting, no evidence was tendered in support of the argument that the complainant's life was endangered by the bite because the accused pleaded guilty: *R. v. Thissen*, [1996] O.J. No. 2074 (Ct. J. (Prov. Div.)) (QL). In fact, argue Richard Elliott and several other lawyers who work on behalf of persons with HIV/AIDS in Canada, it is discrimination, rather than either scientific evidence or, indeed, any documented cases of transmission through bites of a few seconds, that provides the causal link: Richard Elliott, "The justice system overreacts to a bite" *The [Toronto] Globe and Mail* (2 July 1996) A17.

A rare example of an acquittal based on lack of adequate proof of factual causation can be found in *R. v. Duncan* (1984), 57 A.R. 362 (C.A.) where the accused had stabbed the deceased after an altercation. The victim had undergone surgery, was in a stable condition, and his wound had been pronounced not life-threatening. Fifty-eight hours after surgery, he died from cardiac arrest due to the wound and severe coronary arteriosclerosis. The accused's acquittal of second degree murder was affirmed on appeal because, on cross-examination, the expert had conceded that the victim's death could possibly have been the result of heart disease unrelated to the stab wound.

More recently, the Supreme Court re-cast the *Smithers* test for factual causation in a 5:4 decision, reproduced below.

R. v. Nette†

[ARBOUR J.:]

I. INTRODUCTION

The present appeal raises the issue of causation in second degree murder. It requires a determination of the threshold test of causation that must be met before an accused may be held legally responsible for causing a victim's death in a charge of second degree murder. We must also examine how the applicable standard of causation should be conveyed to the jury.

II. FACTUAL BACKGROUND

On Monday, August 21, 1995, Mrs. Clara Loski, a 95-year-old widow who lived alone in her house in Kelowna, British Columbia, was found dead in her bedroom. Her house had been robbed. Mrs. Loski was bound with electrical wire in a way that is referred to colloquially as "hog-tying". Her hands were bound behind her back, her legs were brought upwards behind her back and tied, and her hands and feet were bound together. A red garment was tied around her head and neck and entrapped her chin. ...

The appellant was charged with first degree murder on the basis that he had committed murder while committing the offence of unlawfully confining Mrs. Loski. The Crown's position at trial was that the act of causing death and the acts comprising the offence of unlawful confinement all formed part of one continuous sequence of events making up a single transaction, and that the appellant was therefore guilty of first degree murder pursuant to s. 231(5) of the *Criminal Code*, R.S.C. 1985, c. C-46. The appellant was tried before a judge and jury. The jury returned a verdict of second degree murder and the Court of Appeal dismissed the appellant's appeal from that verdict. The only ground of appeal both before the Court of Appeal and before us concerns the test of causation applicable to second degree murder. ...

While the standard of causation for second degree murder has not been raised squarely before this Court until now, it was before the Ontario Court of Appeal in *Cribbin* [(1994), 17 O.R. (3d) 548] and *Meiler* [(1999), 136 C.C.C. (3d) 11]. In both of these cases, the *Smithers* standard of "beyond *de minimis*" was expressly approved of in relation to a charge of second degree murder. ...

The law of causation is in large part judicially developed, but is also expressed, directly or indi-

† [2001] 3 S.C.R. 488.

rectly, in provisions of the *Criminal Code*. For example, s. 225 of the *Code* provides that where a person causes bodily injury that is in itself dangerous and from which death results, that person causes the death notwithstanding that the immediate cause of death is proper or improper treatment ... These statutory provisions and others like them in the *Code* preempt any speculation as to whether the act of the accused would be seen as too remote to have caused the result alleged, or whether the triggering of a chain of events was then interrupted by an intervening cause which serves to distance and exonerate the accused from any responsibility for the consequences. Where the factual situation does not fall within one of the statutory rules of causation in the *Code*, the common law general principles of criminal law apply to resolve any causation issues that may arise. ...

It is clear from a reading of *Harbottle* that the "substantial cause" test expresses the increased degree of moral culpability, as evidenced by the accused person's degree of participation in the killing, that is required before an accused can be found guilty under s. 231(5) of the *Criminal Code* of first degree murder. The increased degree of participation in the killing, coupled with a finding that the accused had the requisite *mens rea* for murder, justifies a verdict of guilty under s. 231(5) of the *Code*.

As I discussed earlier, it is important to distinguish between what the legal standard of causation is and how that standard is conveyed to the jury. The difference between these two concepts has been obscured somewhat in the present case by the parties' focus on the terminology used to describe the standard of causation. I agree with the appellant's submission that there is only one standard of causation for all homicide offences, whether manslaughter or murder. However, I do not agree with the appellant that the standard must be expressed for all homicide offences, including second degree murder, as one of "substantial cause" as stated in *Harbottle*. Nor must the applicable standard be expressed with the terminology of "beyond *de minimis*" used in the *Smithers* standard. ...

The causation standard expressed in *Smithers* is still valid and applicable to all forms of homicide. In addition, in the case of first degree murder under s. 231(5) of the *Code*, *Harbottle* requires additional instructions, to which I will return. The only potential shortcoming with the *Smithers* test is not in its substance, but in its articulation. Even though it causes little difficulty for lawyers and judges, the use of Latin expressions and the formulation of the test in the negative are not particularly useful means of conveying an abstract idea to a jury. In order to explain the standard as clearly as possible to the jury, it may be preferable to phrase the standard of causation in positive terms using a phrase such as "significant contributing cause" rather than using expressions phrased in the negative such as "not a trivial cause" or "not insignificant". Latin terms such as "*de minimis*" are rarely helpful.

The present appeal does not present the classic thin-skull scenario where the victim's death occurred unexpectedly as a result of the victim's unusual and unforeseeable susceptibility to injury. It is clear on the medical evidence that the victim's physical conditions related to her advanced age may have hastened her demise.... A much younger victim, subjected to the same treatment, may also have failed to survive. An example of a true thin-skull situation is *Smithers*, the facts of which are discussed earlier....

As I stated in *Cribbin*, causation is a legal rule based on concepts of moral responsibility and is not a mechanical or mathematical exercise. On the facts of the present appeal, the jury properly found that the appellant caused Mrs. Loski's death and must bear legal responsibility for having done so. ...

In this case, the charge to the jury was entirely satisfactory. The trial judge charged the jury on the elements of manslaughter, second degree murder and first degree murder under s. 231(5) of the *Criminal Code*. With respect to manslaughter and second degree murder, the trial judge told the jurors that they must find that the accused was "more than a trivial cause" of death in order to conclude that the accused caused Mrs. Loski's death. In essence, this reflects the test of causation set out in *Smithers*, and accurately states the correct standard of causation for second degree murder. On two occasions, once in the main charge and once in responding to a question from the jurors, Wilkinson J. misspoke in describing the appropriate test of causation for second degree murder, by contrasting the high standard of causation for first degree murder with the "slight or trivial cause necessary to find second degree murder". In my view, these errors, which reflect the difficulty of expressing a standard in the negative, would not have caused the jury to believe that the applicable standard of causation for second degree murder was lower than the *Smithers* standard of "more than a trivial cause". What the slips in the jury charge do illustrate is the fact that it is easier to express the standard of causation in positive terms, by referring to a "significant" contribution or cause, instead of using the negative phraseology of "beyond *de minimis*" or "more than a slight or trivial cause" in explaining causation to the jury.

[The dissenting judgment (*per* McLachlin C.J. and L'Heureux-Dubé, Gonthier, and Bastarache JJ.) would have held that no legitimate reasons existed to change the test in *Smithers* from "a contributing cause of death, outside the *de minimis* range" to "a significant contributing cause", as the *Smithers* test was an authoritative test of causation that had withstood the test of time. Furthermore, the four justices found that the reformulation of the *Smithers* test by the majority calls for a more direct causal relationship than a "not significant" or "not trivial" test requires, thus raising the threshold for causation for homicide, and drastically changing the substance of the test in a manner that ignores the reasons behind using a double negative. The dissent maintained that the correct test for trial judges in determining causation for all homicide offences, apart from first degree murder, should remain "a contributing cause that is not trivial or insignificant".]

R. v. Johnson, [2002] S.J. No. 603 (Q.B.), applied *Nette*. The accused taxi driver had transported an intoxicated passenger to an address where no one was home. When she was unable to pay her fare, the accused took one of her two jackets as collateral and, after verifying that it was the correct address and helping her check her keys, he left her there. He called the dispatcher three times to request that police be called to check on the woman, but the dispatcher thought the action unnecessary. The woman died of hypothermia as the temperature that night was between minus 9 and minus 12 degrees centigrade. Johnson was acquitted of criminal negligence causing death in part because it could not be proven that the loss of her jacket made a significant contribution to the woman's death.

LEGAL CAUSATION

The issue behind proximate or legal causation is whether it is somehow just to attribute causality to the accused for a particular consequence. Once the Crown has established factual causation beyond a reasonable doubt, legal causation will rarely be a live issue: if the accused is factually responsible for the harm, it is difficult to argue that it was too remote to hold the accused accountable in criminal law. The *Code* itself does not provide a great deal of guidance in ss. 222(5),(6), 224, 225, 226, and 228. What specific limits on legal causation are articulated therein?

The judges, in fact, rarely refer to the *Code* sections on causation, although the common law rules regarding legal causation parallel these sections. For example, the justices in *Smithers* adopted the "thin-skull" rule from *R. v. Blaue*, [1975] 1 W.L.R. 1411 (C.A.), in holding that Smithers legally caused the death, even if the victim had a faulty epiglottis that produced the aspiration. They reached this conclusion without referring to s. 226.

In *Blaue*, the accused had argued that he did not cause his victim's death because she, as a Jehovah's Witness, refused a blood transfusion in treatment for four stab wounds, including one to her lung, that would have saved her life. His argument was rejected at 1415, on terms that reproduce the ideas behind ss. 224 and 225 of our *Code*:

> It has long been the policy of the law that those who use violence on other people must take their victims as they find them. This in our judgment means the whole man [*sic*], not just the physical man [*sic*].... The question for decision is what caused her death. The answer is the stab wound. The fact that the victim refused to stop this end coming about did not break the causal connection between the act and death.

In *Smithers*, the accused also argued that it was unjust to attribute legal causation to him through a manslaughter conviction when death had been an unforeseeable consequence of the kick. The justices rejected this argument as well, stating, "It is no defence to a manslaughter charge that the fatality was not anticipated or that death ordinarily would not result from the unlawful act" (at 90).

The constitutionality of the element of legal causation for the offence of manslaughter was affirmed by the Supreme Court of Canada in *R. v. Creighton*, below, under ***Mens Rea***, where the accused had injected the deceased with cocaine (consensually), and she had died as a result: "the test for the *mens rea* of unlawful act manslaughter in Canada ... is (in addition to the *mens rea* of the underlying offence) objective foreseeability of the risk of bodily harm which is neither trivial nor transitory, in the context of a dangerous act": [1993] 3 S.C.R. 3 at 44. In *R. v. Cribbin* (1994), 17 O.R. (3d) 548 (C.A.) the court held that when the "contributing cause beyond a *de minimis* range" test is combined with the constitutionally required fault element set out in *Creighton*, there is no danger that a "morally innocent" person might be convicted of manslaughter.

However, the Supreme Court in *Harbottle* has held that a more stringent test for legal causation is required in the case of first degree murder. The Crown must prove that the accused participated in the murder in such a manner that he was "a substantial and integral cause of the death" and where "there was no intervening act of another which resulted in the accused's no longer being substantially connected to the death": at 326. More recently, in *Nette, supra*, the Court affirmed that this additional causation burden is limited to first degree murder, by virtue of s. 231(5), and should only be considered after the jury has found the accused guilty of murder: "it is then necessary to consider whether the moral culpability of the accused, as evidenced by his role in the killing, justifies a verdict of first degree murder" (at para 64).

3

Mens Rea

Every criminal offence requires proof beyond a reasonable doubt of not only an *actus reus* element, but also of some form of *mens rea* or fault element. One discerns the nature of the *mens rea* by reference to the language in the relevant section of the *Code*, the common law, actual practice, and, most recently, *Charter* judgments. This part of the materials raises the following questions: How have the judges used the *Charter* to formulate the *mens rea*? What is the real significance and impact of the *mens rea* requirement upon accused persons, upon women who have survived male violence, and upon our social understandings of what is a criminal or blameworthy state of mind? Does the legal formulation of the *mens rea* permit successful prosecution of individuals who act as a group, as in the case of gang rape or through a corporate structure?

One of the main preoccupations of the judges has been to determine whether a given *mens rea* is tested subjectively, by reference to the accused's actual state of mind, or objectively, by reference to what a reasonable person would have thought or intended by those actions. This preoccupation has been reinforced and given constitutional significance through a series of judicial decisions that have interpreted s. 7 of the *Charter* as having implications for the justness and, therefore, legality of the *mens rea* requirement for given offences.

The *mens rea* requirement as shaped by the judiciary cannot be understood without an appreciation of the underlying assumptions and ideologies regarding free market capitalism, economic efficiency, individual responsibility, class bias, the cult of "expert evidence" (most evident in the context of defences), and the male (hetero)sexual prerogative. It is thus instructive to note that the requirement of strict proof of a subjectively tested *mens rea* is taken very seriously for accusations of sexual assault. For example, in their text, *Dimensions of Criminal Law* (Toronto: Emond Montgomery Publications, 1992), Toni Pickard and Phil Goldman argue at 394–395 that

> the subjective standard in sexual assault cases generally protects patriarchal interests by validating and protecting male understandings of the world.... Maintaining the subjective test has as its most important (though not perhaps consciously intended) consequence the ability of the Courts to deal with sexual assault defendants **as if they were aberrations**, as if the important problem ... has to do with individual bad choices rather than social pathologies. [Emphasis in original.]

In contrast, those charged with many property offences are often unable to challenge successfully the ordinary inference that a trier of fact will draw, from the accused's actions, that he or she intended the consequences of those deliberate actions. The class bias of the *mens rea* requirement and the ideology of individualized notions of "moral fault" are discussed by Andrew Hopkins in "Class Bias in the Criminal Law" in Steven Brickey & Elizabeth Comack, *The Social Basis of Law: Critical Readings in the Sociology of Law* (Toronto: Garamond Press, 1986) 127. He compares the legal treatment of the mental element for offences such as insider trading or defrauding shareholders with that of offences such as theft or dealing in stolen goods, and argues that, while in both categories of cases it would be reasonable to infer intention from the actions of the accused, judges are less likely to draw the inference of criminal intent for white-collar crimes.

A. ABSOLUTE LIABILITY

Absolute liability as a fault element requires only that the prosecutor prove the *actus reus* of the offence, with no avenues of defence open to the accused other than *actus reus* defences. Historically, the development of what is now called the absolute liability category of offences (then described frequently as "strict liability") dates from the middle of the nineteenth century in England. In a case called *R. v. Woodrow*, 15 M. & M. 404 (Exch. 1846), a statute prohibiting the possession of adulterated tobacco was held to be violated regardless of whether the accused could prove that he had no knowledge of the adulteration because "the public inconvenience would be much greater, if in every case the officers were obliged to prove knowledge. They would be very seldom able to do so."

This interpretation was soon followed in the reading of other regulatory offences where the public welfare was at stake. Absolute liability prosecutions in Canada that followed *Woodrow* illustrate the role of judicial choice in determining which offences ought to be read as affording no *mens rea* defence to the charge. Consider, for example, *R. v. Ping Yuen* (1921), 36 C.C.C. 269 (Sask. C.A.), where the accused was convicted of violating s. 35 of the *Saskatchewan Temperance Act*, which created an offence when "any person engaged in the business of selling soft drinks ... keeps or has ... on his business premises any liquor...". Some of the soft drink bottles found on his premises contained a percentage of alcohol in excess of the permissible level. Even though the bottles had been purchased wholesale from a drink company that purported to sell soft drinks and the contents could not have been tested by the accused without destroying their resale value, the court said "no doubt hardships must occur through the enforcement of these Acts in particular instances, but ... it is either for the Legislature to alter the law if too great hardships results, or for the department charged with its enforcement to abstain from enforcing in proper cases. But to hold that in each case a guilty knowledge must be proved, would no doubt make the Act of no practical value" (at 280).

See also R. v. Sung Lung (1923), 39 C.C.C. 187 (Que. Dist. Ct.) where the accused was convicted for an offence under the *Opium and Narcotic Drug Act*, S.C. 1991, c. 17: "The defendant pleaded not guilty but admitted that opium pipes, apparatus, etc., were found in his possession, but without his knowledge; that he never used them, and that the house he was occupying was formerly occupied by another Chinaman [*sic*]" (at 188). The court rejected the definition of "possession" found in the *Criminal Code*, which requires knowledge, stating, "we are proceeding under a special penal law, and must take the words as we find them; so when, according to the law, one is accused of having in his possession such and such things, and the fact is proven, there is no necessity of *mens rea*, as there is under the *Crim. Code* ...." "If such a defence could be admitted, it would be very easy to evade the law and as this law must be, in the public welfare and interest, strictly interpreted, I find the defendant guilty."

In contrast, *R. v. Regina Cold Storage & Forwarding* (1923), 41 C.C.C. 21 (Sask. C.A.) distinguished *Ping Yuen* and held that a warehousing company could not be convicted under the same act for storing "temperance" beer that was found, upon analysis, to contain alcohol. This company was charged under s. 49, which provided that "no person shall have, or keep ... liquor in any place whatsoever other than a dwelling house...." Here the court started from the premise that criminal offences require proof of a guilty mind, and held that the prosecution must show that the legislature intended to create an absolute liability offence. In quashing the conviction the court held: "The case at Bar ... is clearly distinguishable from the *Ping Yuen* case, in that the appellants were not dealing in the beer stored, nor did they offer or expose it for sale to the public, and they had no lawful right to examine to ascertain if the bottles contained alcohol.... Under these circumstances, it would ... require much clearer language than is used in the Act to justify the conclusion that the Legislature intended by enacting the section in question that storage companies should be held responsible for the contents of packages stored with them."

A very simplified explanation of the legal development of absolute liability identifies the industrial revolution and the consequent growth of dangerous products, machinery, and workplace accidents as prompting the creation of an expeditious and just way of dealing with the overwhelming numbers of prosecutions: Francis Bowes Sayre, "Public Welfare Offences" (1933) 33 Colum. L. Rev. 55. Upton Sinclair's novel, *The Jungle*, which was published in 1906, is credited with a role in the passage of pure food laws in the United States. It provided graphic descriptions of the working conditions in Chicago's slaughterhouses and the health and criminal issues raised by the practices in the meat packing plants, where the workers in the "spoiled meat industry" "read a new and grim meaning to that old Packington jest — that they use everything of the pig except the squeal" (at 162). Do we have any lesser need for absolute liability offences today? Consider some of the consumer products that create serious health hazards, such as the Dalkon Shield (see Abell & Sheehy, *Cases, Context, Critique*, **Definition of Crime**), the Meme Breast Implants, and numerous drug fiascos: Nicholas Regush, "Health and Welfare's National Disgrace" *Saturday Night* (April 1991) 9.

The case reproduced below, *R. v. Sault Ste. Marie*, transformed the absolute liability category into two distinct categories of offence: absolute and strict liability.

R. v. Sault Ste. Marie†

[DICKSON J.:]

In the present appeal the Court is concerned with offences variously referred to as "statutory," "public welfare," "regulatory," "absolute liability," or "strict responsibility," which are not criminal in any real sense, but are prohibited in the public interest. (*Sherras v. De Rutzen*) Although enforced as penal laws through the utilization of the machinery of the criminal law, the offences are in substance of a civil nature and might well be regarded as a branch of administrative law to which traditional principles of criminal law have but limited application. They relate to such everyday matters as traffic infractions, sales of impure food, violations of liquor laws, and the like. In this appeal we are concerned with pollution.

The doctrine of the guilty mind expressed in terms of intention or recklessness, but not negligence, is at the foundation of the law of crimes. In the case of true crimes there is a presumption that a person should not be held liable for the wrongfulness of his act if that act is without *mens rea*: (*R. v. Prince*; *R. v. Tolson*; *R. v. Rees*; *Beaver v. The Queen*; *R. v. King*). Blackstone made the point over two hundred years ago in words still apt: "...to constitute a crime against human law, there must be first a vicious will, and secondly, an unlawful act consequent upon such vicious will...." 4 Comm. 21. I would emphasise at the outset that nothing in the discussion which follows is intended to dilute or erode that basic principle.

The appeal raises a preliminary issue as to whether the charge, as laid, is duplicitous, and if so, whether ss. 732(1) and 755(4) of the *Criminal Code* preclude the accused City of Sault Ste. Marie from raising the duplicity claim for the first time on appeal. It will be convenient to deal first with this preliminary point and then consider the concept of liability in relation to public welfare offences.

The City of Sault Ste. Marie was charged that it did discharge, or cause to be discharged, or permitted to be discharged, or deposited materials into

† [1978] 2 S.C.R. 1299. [Notes omitted.]

Cannon Creek and Root River, or on the shore or bank thereof, or in such place along the side that might impair the quality of the water in Cannon Creek and Root River, between March 13, 1972 and September 11, 1972. The charge was laid under s. 32(1) of *The Ontario Water Resources Commission Act*, R.S.O. 1970, c. 332, which provides so far as relevant, that every municipality or person that discharges, or deposits, or causes, or permits the discharge or deposit of any material of any kind into any water course, or on any shore or bank thereof, or in any place that may impair the quality of water, is guilty of an offence and, on summary conviction, is liable on first conviction to a fine of not more than $5,000 and on each subsequent conviction to a fine of not more than $10,000 or to imprisonment of a term of not more than one year, or to both fine and imprisonment.

Although the facts do not rise above the routine, the proceedings have to date had the anxious consideration of five courts. The City was acquitted in Provincial Court (Criminal Division), but convicted following a trial *de novo* on a Crown appeal. A further appeal, by the City, to the Divisional Court was allowed and the conviction quashed. The Court of Appeal for Ontario on yet another appeal directed a new trial. Because of the importance of the legal issues, this Court granted leave to the Crown to appeal and leave to the City to cross-appeal.

To relate briefly the facts, the City on November 18, 1970 entered into an agreement with Cherokee Disposal and Construction Co. Ltd., for the disposal of all refuse originating in the City. Under the terms of the agreement, Cherokee became obligated to furnish a site and adequate labour, material and equipment. The site selected bordered Cannon Creek which, it would appear, runs into the Root River. The method of disposal adopted is known as the "area," or "continuous slope" method of sanitary land fill, whereby garbage is compacted in layers which are covered each day by natural sand or gravel.

Prior to 1970, the site had been covered with a number of fresh-water springs that flowed into Cannon Creek. Cherokee dumped material to cover and submerge these springs and then placed garbage and wastes over such material. The garbage and wastes in due course formed a high mound sloping steeply toward, and within twenty feet of, the Creek. Pollution resulted. Cherokee was convicted of a breach of s. 32(1) of *The Ontario Water Resources Commission Act*, the section under which the City has been charged. The question now before the Court is whether the City is also guilty of an offence under that section.

In dismissing the charge at first instance, the judge found that the City had had nothing to do with the actual disposal operations, that Cherokee was an independent contractor and its employees were not employees of the City. On the appeal *de novo* Judge Vannini found the offence to be one of strict liability and he convicted. The Divisional Court in setting aside the judgment found that the charge was duplicitous. As a secondary point, the Divisional Court also held that the charge required *mens rea* with respect to causing or permitting a discharge. When the case reached the Court of Appeal that Court held that the conviction could not be quashed on the ground of duplicity, because there had been no challenge to the information at trial. The Court of Appeal agreed, however, that the charge was one requiring proof of *mens rea*. A majority of the Court (Brooke and Howland JJ. A.) held there was not sufficient evidence to establish *mens rea* and ordered a new trial. In the view of Mr. Justice Lacourciere, dissenting, the inescapable inference to be drawn from the findings of fact of Judge Vannini was that the City had known of the potential impairment of waters of Cannon Creek and Root River and had failed to exercise its clear powers of control.

The divers, and diverse, judicial opinions to date on the points under consideration reflect the dubiety in these branches of the law.

. . . .

The *Mens Rea* Point

The distinction between the true criminal offence and the public welfare offence is one of prime importance. Where the offence is criminal, the Crown must establish a mental element, namely, that the accused who committed the prohibited act did so intentionally or recklessly, with knowledge of the facts constituting the offence, or with wilful blindness toward them. Mere negligence is excluded from the concept of the mental element required for conviction. Within the context of a criminal prosecution a person who fails to make such enquiries as a reasonable and prudent person would make, or who fails to know facts he should have known, is innocent in the eyes of the law.

In sharp contrast, "absolute liability" entails conviction on proof merely that the defendant committed the prohibited act constituting the *actus reus* of the offence. There is no relevant mental element. It is no defence that the accused was entirely without fault. He may be morally innocent in every sense, yet be branded as a malefactor and punished as such.

Public welfare offences obviously lie in a field of conflicting values. It is essential for society to maintain, through effective enforcement, high standards of public health and safety. Potential victims of those who carry on latently pernicious activities have a strong claim to consideration. On the other hand, there is a generally held revulsion against punishment of the morally innocent.

Public welfare offences evolved in mid-nineteenth century Britain: (*R. v. Woodrow* and *R. v. Stephens*) as a means of doing away with the requirement of *mens rea* for petty police offences. The concept was a judicial creation, founded on expediency. That concept is now firmly imbedded in the concrete of Anglo-American and Canadian jurisprudence, its importance heightened by the [ever-increasing] complexities of modern society.

Various arguments are advanced in justification of absolute liability in public welfare offences. Two predominate. Firstly, it is argued that the protection of social interests requires a high standard of care and attention on the part of those who follow certain pursuits and such persons are more likely to be stimulated to maintain those standards if they know that ignorance or mistake will not excuse them. The removal of any possible loophole acts, it is said, as an incentive to take precautionary measures beyond what would otherwise be taken, in order that mistakes and mishaps be avoided. The second main argument is one based on administrative efficiency. Having regard to both the difficulty of proving mental culpability and the number of petty cases which daily come before the Courts, proof of fault is just too great a burden in time and money to place upon the prosecution. To require proof of each person's individual intent would allow almost every violator to escape. This, together with the glut of work entailed in proving *mens rea* in every case would clutter the docket and impede adequate enforcement as virtually to nullify the regulatory statutes. In short, absolute liability, it is contended, is the most efficient and effective way of ensuring compliance with minor regulatory legislation and the social ends to be achieved are of such importance as to override the unfortunate by-product of punishing those who may be free of moral turpitude. In further justification, it is urged that slight penalties are usually imposed and that conviction for breach of a public welfare offence does not carry the stigma associated with conviction for a criminal offence.

Arguments of greater force are advanced against absolute liability. The most telling is that it violates fundamental principles of penal liability. It also rests upon assumptions which have not been, and cannot be, empirically established. There is no evidence that a higher standard of care results from absolute liability. If a person is already taking every reasonable precautionary measure, is he likely to take additional measures, knowing that however much care he takes, it will not serve as a defence in the event of breach? If he has exercised care and skill, will conviction have a deterrent effect upon him or others? Will the injustice of conviction lead to cynicism and disrespect for the law, on his part and on the part of others? These are among the questions asked. The argument that no stigma attaches does not withstand analysis, for the accused will have suffered loss of time, legal costs, exposure to the processes of the criminal law at trial and, however one may downplay it, the opprobrium of conviction. It is not sufficient to say that the public interest is engaged and, therefore, liability may be imposed without fault. In serious crimes, the public interest is involved and *mens rea* must be proven. The administrative argument has little force. In sentencing, evidence of due diligence is admissible and therefore the evidence might just as well be heard when considering guilt. Additionally, it may be noted that s. 198 of *The Highway Traffic Act of Alberta*, R.S.A. 1970, c. 169, provides that upon a person being charged with an offence under this Act, if the judge trying the case is of the opinion that the offence (a) was committed wholly by accident or misadventure and without negligence, and (b) could not by the exercise of reasonable care or precaution have been avoided, the judge may dismiss the case. See also s. 230(2) of the Manitoba *Highway Traffic Act*, R.S.M. 1970, c. H60, which has a similar effect. In these instances at least, the Legislature has indicated that administrative efficiency does not foreclose inquiry as to fault. It is also worthy of note that historically the penalty for breach of statutes enacted for the regulation of individual conduct in the interests of health and safety was minor, \$20 or \$25; today, it may amount to thousands of dollars and entail the possibility of imprisonment for a second conviction. The present case is an example.

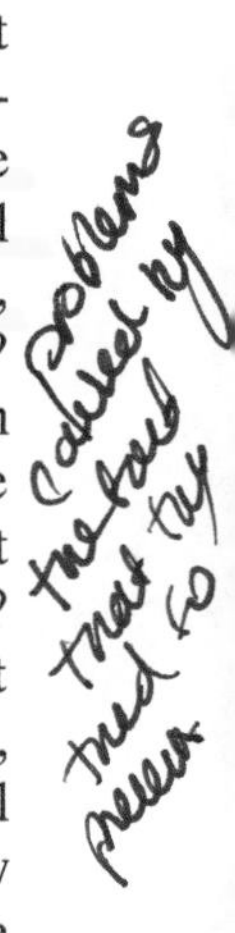

Public welfare offences involve a shift of emphasis from the protection of individual interests to the protection of public and social interests. See Sayre, *Public Welfare Offences* (1933), 33 Colum. L. Rev. 55; Hall, *Principles of Criminal Law*, (1947), ch. 13; Perkins, *The Civil Offence* (1952), 100 U. of Pa. L. Rev. 832; Jobson, *Far From Clear*, 18 Crim. L.Q. 294. The unfortunate tendency in many past cases has been to see the choice as between two stark alternatives; (i) full *mens rea*; or (ii) absolute liability. In respect of public welfare offences (within which category pollution offences fall) where full *mens rea* is not required, absolute liability has often been imposed. English jurisprudence has consistently maintained this dichotomy: see Hals. (4th ed.), Vol. II, *Criminal Law, Evidence and Procedure*, para. 18. There has, however, been an attempt in Australia, in many Canadian courts, and indeed in England, to seek a middle position, fulfilling the goals of public welfare offences while still not punishing the entirely blameless. There is an increasing and impressive stream of authority which holds that where an offence does not require full *mens rea*, it is nevertheless a good defence for the defendant to prove that he was not negligent.

Dr. Glanville Williams has written: "There is a half-way house between *mens rea* and strict responsibility which has not yet been properly utilized, and that is responsibility for negligence," (*Criminal Law (2d ed.): The General Part*, p. 262). Morris and Howard, in *Studies in Criminal Law*, (1964), p. 200, suggest that strict responsibility might with advantage be replaced by a doctrine of responsibility for negligence strengthened by a shift in the burden of proof. The defendant would be allowed to exculpate himself by proving affirmatively that he was not negligent. Professor Howard (*Strict Responsibility in the High Court of Australia*, 76 L.Q.R. 547) offers the comment that English law of strict responsibility in minor statutory offences is distinguished only by its irrationality, and then has this to say in support of the position taken by the Australian High Court, at p. 548:

> Over a period of nearly sixty years since its inception the High Court has adhered with consistency to the principle that there should be no criminal responsibility without fault, however minor the offence. It has done so by utilizing the very half-way house to which Dr. Williams refers, responsibility for negligence.

In his work, *Public Welfare Offences*, at p. 78, Professor Sayre suggests that if the penalty is really slight involving, for instance, a maximum fine of twenty-five dollars, particularly if adequate enforcement depends upon wholesale prosecution, or if the social danger arising from violation is serious, the doctrine of basing liability upon mere activity rather than fault, is sound. He continues, however, at p. 79:

> On the other hand, some public welfare offences involve a possible penalty of imprisonment or heavy fine. In such cases it would seem sounder policy to maintain the orthodox requirement of a guilty mind but to shift the burden of proof to the shoulders of the defendant to establish his lack of a guilty intent if he can. For public welfare offences defendants may be convicted by proof of the mere act of violation; but, if the offence involves a possible prison penalty, the defendant should not be denied the right of bringing forward affirmative evidence to prove that the violation was the result of no fault on his part.

and at p. 82:

> It is fundamentally unsound to convict a defendant for a crime involving a substantial term of imprisonment without giving him the opportunity to prove that his action was due to an honest and reasonable mistake of fact or that he acted without guilty intent. If the public danger is widespread and serious, the practical situation can be met by shifting to the shoulders of the defendant the burden of proving a lack of guilty intent.

The doctrine proceeds on the assumption that the defendant could have avoided the *prima facie* offence through the exercise of reasonable care and he is given the opportunity of establishing, if he can, that he did in fact exercise such care.

The case which gave the lead in this branch of the law is the Australian case of *Proudman v. Dayman* where Dixon J. said, at pp. 540–41:

> It is one thing to deny that a necessary ingredient of the offence is positive knowledge of the fact that the driver holds no subsisting licence. It is another to say that an honest belief founded on reasonable grounds that he is licensed cannot exculpate a person who permits him to drive. As a general rule an honest and reasonable belief in a state of facts which, if they existed, would make the defendant's act innocent affords an excuse for doing what would otherwise be an offence.
>
> . . . .

This case, and several others like it, speak of the defence as being that of reasonable mistake of fact. The reason is that the offences in question have generally turned on the possession by a person or place of an unlawful status, and the accused's defence was that he reasonably did not know of this status: e.g. permitting an unlicensed person to drive, or lacking a valid licence oneself, or being the owner of property in a dangerous condition. In such cases, negligence consists of an unreasonable failure to know the facts which constitute the offence. It is clear, however, that in principle the defence is that all reasonable care was taken. In other circumstances, the issue will be whether the accused's behaviour was negligent in bringing about the forbidden event when he knew the relevant facts. Once the defence of reasonable mistake of fact is accepted, there is no barrier to acceptance of the other constituent part of a defence of due diligence.

. . . .

[The Court then reviewed cases from New Zealand and lower courts in Canada that had adopted this "half-way house" approach.]

It is interesting to note the recommendations made by the Law Reform Commission to the Minister of Justice (*Our Criminal Law*) in March, 1976. The Commission advises (p. 32) that (i) every offence outside the *Criminal Code* be recognized as admitting of a defence of due diligence; (ii) in the case of any such offence for which intent or recklessness is not specifically required the onus of proof should lie on the defendant to establish such defence; (iii) the defendant would have to prove this on the preponderance or balance of probabilities. The recommendation endorsed a working paper (*The Meaning of Guilt — Strict Liability*) in which it was stated that negligence should be the minimum standard of liability in regulatory offences, that such offences were (p. 32), "to promote higher standards of care in business, trade and industry, higher standards of honesty in commerce and advertising, higher standards of respect for the ... environment and [therefore] the ... offence is basically and typically an offence of negligence"; that an accused should never be convicted of a regulatory offence if he establishes that he acted with due diligence, that is, that he was not negligent. In the working paper, the Commission further stated (p. 33), "let us recognize the regulatory offence for what it is — an offence of negligence — and frame the law to ensure that guilt depends upon lack of reasonable care." The view is expressed that in regulatory law, to make the defendant disprove negligence — prove due diligence — would be both justifiable and desirable.

In an interesting article on the matter now under discussion, *Far From Clear, supra*, Professor Jobson refers to a series of recent cases, arising principally under s. 32(1) of *The Ontario Water Resources Commission Act*, the section at issue in the present proceedings, which "openly acknowledged a defence based on lack of fault or neglect; these cases require proof of the *actus reus* but then permit the accused to show that he was without fault or had no opportunity to prevent the harm." The paramount case in the series is *R. v. Industrial Tankers Ltd.* in which Judge Sprague, relying upon *R. v. Hawinda Taverns Ltd.* and *R. v. Bruin Hotel Co. Ltd.*, held that the Crown did not need to prove that the accused had *mens rea*, but it did have to show that the accused had the power and authority to prevent the pollution, and could have prevented it, but did not do so. Liability rests upon control and the opportunity to prevent, i.e. that the accused could have and should have prevented the pollution. In *Industrial Tankers*, the burden was placed on the Crown to prove lack of reasonable care. To that extent *Industrial Tankers* and s. 32(1) cases which followed it, such as *R. v. Sheridan*, differ from other authorities on s. 32(1) which would place upon the accused the burden of showing as a defence that he did not have control or otherwise could not have prevented the impairment: see *R. v. Cherokee Disposals & Construction Limited*; *R. v. Liquid Cargo Lines Ltd.* and *R. v. North Canadian Enterprises Ltd.*

The element of control, particularly by those in charge of business activities which may endanger the public, is vital to promote the observance of regulations designed to avoid that danger. This control may be exercised by "supervision or inspection, by improvement of his business methods or by exhorting those whom he may be expected to influence or control" (Lord Evershed in *Lim Chin Aik v. The Queen*, at p. 174). The purpose, Dean Roscoe Pound has said (*The Spirit of the Common Law* (1906)), is to "put pressure upon the thoughtless and inefficient to do their whole duty in the interest of public health or safety or morale." As Devlin J. noted in *Reynolds v. Austin & Sons Limited*, at p. 139: "...a man may be responsible for the acts of his servants, or even for defects in his business arrangements, because it can fairly be said that by such sanctions citizens are induced to keep themselves and their organizations up to the mark." Devlin J. added, however: "If a man is punished because of an act done by another, whom he cannot reasonably be expected to influence or control, the law is engaged, not in punishing thoughtlessness or inefficiency, and thereby promoting the welfare of the community, but in pouncing on the most convenient victim."

The decision of this Court in *The Queen v. Pierce Fisheries Ltd.* is not inconsistent with the concept of a "half-way house" between *mens rea* and absolute liability. In *Pierce Fisheries* the charge was that of having possession of undersized lobsters contrary to the regulations under the *Fisheries Act*, R.S.C. 1952, c. 119. Two points arise in connection with the judgment of Ritchie J., who wrote for the majority of the Court. First, the adoption of what had been said by the Ontario Court of Appeal in *R. v. Pee-Kay Smallwares, Ltd*:

> If on a prosecution for the offences created by the *Act*, the Crown had to prove the evil intent of the accused, or if the accused could escape by denying such evil intent, the statute, by which it was obviously intended that there should be complete control without the possibility of any leaks, would have so many holes in it that in truth it would be nothing more than a legislative sieve.

Ritchie J. held that the offence was one in which the Crown, for the reason indicated in the *Pee-Kay Smallwares* case, did not have to prove *mens rea* in order to obtain a conviction. This, in my opinion, is the *ratio decidendi* of the case. Second, Ritchie J. did not, however, foreclose the possibility of a defence. The following passage from the judgment (at p. 21) suggests that a defence of reasonable care might have been open to the accused, but that in that case care had not been taken to acquire the knowledge of the facts constituting the offence:

> As employees of the company working on the premises in the shed "where fish is weighed and packed" were taking lobsters from boxes "preparatory for packing" in crates, and as some of the undersized lobsters were found "in crates ready for shipment," it would not appear to have been a difficult matter for some "officer or responsible employee" to acquire knowledge of their presence on the premises.

In a later passage Ritchie J. added (at p. 22):

> In this case the respondent knew that it had upwards of 60,000 pounds of lobsters on its premises; it only lacked knowledge as to the small size of some of them, and I do not think that the failure of any of its responsible employees to acquire this knowledge affords any defence to a charge of violating the provisions of s. 3(1)(*b*) of the *Lobster Fishery Regulations*.

I do not read *Pierce Fisheries* as denying the accused all defences, in particular the defence that the company had done everything possible to acquire knowledge of the undersized lobsters. Ritchie J. concluded merely that the Crown did not have to prove knowledge.

The judgment of this Court in *Hill v. The Queen*, has been interpreted (*R. v. Gillis*) as imposing absolute liability and denying the driver of a motor vehicle the right to plead in defence an honest and reasonable belief in a state of facts which, if true, would have made the act non-culpable. In *Hill*, the appellant was charged under the *Highway Traffic Act* with failing to remain at the scene of an accident. Her car had "touched" the rear of another vehicle. She did not stop, but drove off, believing no damage had been done. This Court affirmed the conviction, holding that the offence was not one requiring *mens rea*. In that case the essential fact was that an accident had occurred, to the knowledge of Mrs. Hill. Any belief that she might have held as to the extent of the damage could not obliterate that fact, or make it appear that she had reasonable grounds for believing in a state of facts which, if true, would have constituted a defence to the charge. The case does not stand in the way of a defence of reasonable care in a proper case.

We have the situation therefore in which many Courts of this country, at all levels, dealing with public welfare offences favour (i) *not* requiring the Crown to prove *mens rea*, (ii) rejecting the notion that liability inexorably follows upon mere proof of the *actus reus*, excluding any possible defence. The Courts are following the lead set in Australia many years ago and tentatively broached by several English courts in recent years.

It may be suggested that the introduction of a defence based on due diligence and the shifting of the burden of proof might better be implemented by legislative act. In answer, it should be recalled that the concept of absolute liability and the creation of a jural category of public welfare offences are both the product of the judiciary and not of the Legislature. The development to date of this defence, in the numerous decisions I have referred to, of courts in this country as well as in Australia and New Zealand, has also been the work of judges. The present case offers the opportunity of consolidating and clarifying the doctrine.

The correct approach, in my opinion, is to relieve the Crown of the burden of proving *mens rea*, having regard to *Pierce Fisheries* and to the virtual impossibility in most regulatory cases of proving wrongful intention. In a normal case, the accused alone will have knowledge of what he has done to avoid the breach and it is not improper to expect him to come forward with the evidence of due diligence. This is particularly so when it is alleged, for example, that pollution was caused by the activities of a large and complex corporation. Equally, there is nothing wrong with rejecting absolute liability and admitting the defence of reasonable care.

In this doctrine it is not up to the prosecution to prove negligence. Instead, it is open to the defendant to prove that all due care has been taken. This burden falls upon the defendant as he is the only one who will generally have the means of proof. This would not seem unfair as the alternative is absolute liability which denies an accused any defence whatsoever. While the prosecution must prove beyond a reasonable doubt that the defendant committed the prohibited act, the defendant must only establish on the balance of probabilities that he has a defence of reasonable care.

I conclude, for the reasons which I have sought to express, that there are compelling grounds for the recognition of three categories of offences rather than the traditional two:

1. Offences in which *mens rea*, consisting of some positive state of mind such as intent, knowledge, or recklessness, must be proved by the prosecution either as an inference from the nature of the act committed, or by additional evidence.
2. Offences in which there is no necessity for the prosecution to prove the existence of *mens rea*; the doing of the prohibited act *prima facie* imports the offence, leaving it open to the accused to avoid liability by proving that he took all reasonable care. This involves consideration of what a reasonable man would have done in the circumstances. The defence will be available if the accused reasonably believed in a mistaken set of facts which, if true, would render the act or omission innocent, or if he took all reasonable steps to avoid the particular event. These offences may properly be called offences of strict liability. Mr. Justice Estey so referred to them in *Hickey's* case.
3. Offences of absolute liability where it is not open to the accused to exculpate himself by showing that he was free of fault.

Offences which are criminal in the true sense fall in the first category. Public welfare offences would *prima facie* be in the second category. They are not subject to the presumption of full *mens rea*. An offence of this type would fall in the first category only if such words as "wilfully," "with intent," "knowingly," or "intentionally" are contained in the statutory provision creating the offence. On the other hand, the principle that punishment should in general not be inflicted on those without fault applies. Offences of absolute liability would be those in respect of which the Legislature had made it clear that guilt would follow proof merely of the proscribed act. The overall regulatory pattern adopted by the Legislature, the subject matter of the legislation, the importance of the penalty, and the precision of the language used will be primary considerations in determining whether the offence falls into the third category.

The *Ontario Water Resources Commission Act*, s. 32(1)

Turning to the subject matter of s. 32(1) — the prevention of pollution of lakes, rivers and streams — it is patent that this is of great public concern. Pollution has always been unlawful and, in itself, a nuisance: *Groat v. City of Edmonton*. A riparian owner has an inherent right to have a stream of water "come to him in its natural state, in flow, quantity and quality": *Chasemore v. Richards*, at p. 382. Natural streams which formerly afforded "pure and healthy" water for drinking or swimming purposes become little more than cesspools when riparian factory owners and municipal corporations discharge into them filth of all descriptions. Pollution offences are undoubtedly public welfare offences enacted in the interests of public health. There is thus no presumption of a full *mens rea*.

There is another reason, however, why this offence is not subject to a presumption of *mens rea*. The presumption applies only to offences which are "criminal in the true sense," as Rithie J. said in *The Queen v. Pierce Fisheries (supra)*, at p. 13. *The Ontario Water Resources Commission Act* is a provincial statute. If it is valid provincial legislation (and no suggestion was made to the contrary), then it cannot possibly create an offence which is criminal in the true sense.

The present case concerns the interpretation of two troublesome words frequently found in public welfare statutes: "cause" and "permit." These two words are troublesome because neither denotes clearly either full *mens rea* nor absolute liability. It is said that a person could not be said to be permitting something unless he knew what he was permitting. This is an over-simplification. There is authority both ways, indicating that the courts are uneasy with the traditional dichotomy. Some authorities favour the position that "permit" does not import *mens rea*: see *Millar v. The Queen*; *R. v. Royal Canadian Legion*; *R. v. Teperman and Sons*; *R. v. Jack Crewe Ltd.*; *Browning v. J.H. Watson Ltd.*; *Lyons v. May*; *Korten v. West Sussex C.C.* For a *mens rea* construction see *James & Son Ltd. v. Smee*; *Somerset v. Hart*; *Grays Haulage Co. Ltd. v. Arnold*; Smith & Hogan, *Criminal Law* (3rd ed.) at p. 87; Edwards, *Mens Rea and Statutory Offences* (1955), at pp. 98–119. The same is true of "cause." For a non-*mens rea* construction, see *R. v. Peconi*; *Alphacell Limited v. Woodward*; *Sopp v. Long*; *Laird v. Dobell*; *Korten v. West Sussex C.C., (supra)*;

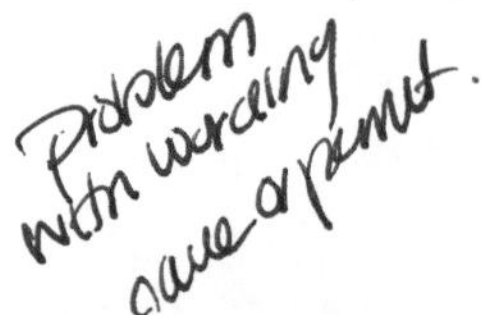

Shave v. Rosner. Others say that "cause" imports a requirement for a *mens rea*: see *Lovelace v. D.P.P.*; *Ross Hillman Ltd. v. Bond, supra*; Smith and Hogan, *Criminal Law* (3rd ed.) at pp. 89–90.

The Divisional Court of Ontario relied on these latter authorities in concluding that s. 32(1) created a *mens rea* offence.

The conflict in the above authorities, however, shows that in themselves the words "cause" and "permit," fit much better into an offence of strict liability than either full *mens rea* or absolute liability. Since s. 32(1) creates a public welfare offence, without a clear indication that liability is absolute, and without any words such as "knowingly" or "wilfully" expressly to import *mens rea*, application of the criteria which I have outlined above undoubtedly places the offence in the category of strict liability.

Proof of the prohibited act *prima facie* imports the offence, but the accused may avoid liability by proving that he took reasonable care. I am strengthened in this view by the recent case of *R. v. Servico Limited, supra*, in which the Appellate Division of the Alberta Supreme Court held that an offence of "permitting" a person under eighteen years to work during prohibited hours was an offence of strict liability in the sense which I have described. It also will be recalled that the decisions of many lower courts which have considered s. 32(1) have rejected absolute liability as the basis for the offence of causing or permitting pollution, and have equally rejected full *mens rea* as an ingredient of the offence.

The Present Case

As I am of the view that a new trial is necessary, it would be inappropriate to discuss at this time the facts of the present case. It may be helpful, however, to consider in a general way the principles to be applied in determining whether a person or municipality has committed the *actus reus* of discharging, causing, or permitting pollution within the terms of s. 32(1), in particular in connection with pollution from garbage disposal. The prohibited act would, in my opinion, be committed by those who undertake the collection and disposal of garbage, who are in a position to exercise continued control of this activity and prevent the pollution from occurring, but fail to do so. The "discharging" aspect of the offence centres on direct acts of pollution. The "causing" aspect centres on the defendant's active undertaking of something which it is in a position to control and which results in pollution. The "permitting" aspect of the offence centres on the defendant's passive lack of interference or, in other words, its failure to prevent an occurrence which it ought to have foreseen. The close interweaving of the meanings of these terms emphasizes again that s. 32(1) deals with only one generic offence.

When the defendant is a municipality, it is of no avail to it in law that it had no duty to pick up the garbage, s. 354(1)(76) of *The Municipal Act*, R.S.O. 1970, c. 284, merely providing that it "may" do so. The law is replete with instances where a person has no duty to act, but where he is subject to certain duties if he does act. The duty here is imposed by s. 32(1) of *The Ontario Water Resources Commission Act*. The position in this respect is no different from that of private persons, corporate or individual, who have no duty to dispose of garbage, but who will incur liability under s. 32(1) if they do so and thereby discharge, cause, or permit pollution.

Nor does liability rest solely on the terms of any agreement by which a defendant arranges for eventual disposal. The test is a factual one, based on an assessment of the defendant's position with respect to the activity which it undertakes and which causes pollution. If it can and should control the activity at the point where pollution occurs, then it is responsible for the pollution. Whether it "discharges," "causes," or "permits" the pollution will be a question of degree, depending on whether it is actively involved at the point where pollution occurs, or whether it merely passively fails to prevent the pollution. In some cases the contract may expressly provide the defendant with the power and authority to control the activity. In such a case the factual assessment will be straightforward. *Prima facie*, liability will be incurred where the defendant could have prevented the impairment by intervening pursuant to its right to do so under the contract, but failed to do so. Where there is no such express provision in the contract, other factors will come into greater prominence. In every instance the question will depend on an assessment of all the circumstances of the case. Whether an "independent contractor" rather than an "employee" is hired will not be decisive. A homeowner who pays a fee for the collection of his garbage by a business which services the area could probably not be said to have caused or permitted the pollution of the collector dumps the garbage in the river. His position would be analogous to a householder in Sault Ste. Marie, who could not be said to have caused or permitted the pollution here. A large corporation which arranges for the nearby disposal of industrial pollutants by a small local independent contractor with no experience in this matter would probably be in an entirely different position.

It must be recognized, however, that a municipality is in a somewhat different position by virtue of the legislative power which it possesses and which others lack. This is important in the assessment of whether the defendant was in a position to control the activity which it undertook and which caused the pollution. A municipality cannot slough off responsibility by contracting out the work. It is in a position to control those whom it hires to carry out garbage disposal operations, and to supervise the activity, either through the provisions of the contract or by municipal by-laws. It fails to do so at its peril.

One comment on the defence of reasonable care in this context should be added. Since the issue is whether the defendant is guilty of an offence, the doctrine of *respondeat superior* has no application. The due diligence which must be established is that of the accused alone. Where an employer is charged in respect of an act committed by an employee acting in the course of employment, the question will be whether the act took place without the accused's direction or approval, thus negating wilful involvement of the accused, and whether the accused exercised all reasonable care by establishing a proper system to prevent commission of the offence and by taking reasonable steps to ensure the effective operation of the system. The availability of the defence to a corporation will depend on whether such due diligence was taken by those who are the directing mind and will of the corporation, whose acts are therefore in law the acts of the corporation itself. For a useful discussion of this matter in the context of a statutory defence of due diligence see *Tesco Supermarkets v. Nattras*.

The majority of the Ontario Court of Appeal directed a new trial as, in the opinion of that court, the findings of the trial judge were not sufficient to establish actual knowledge on the part of the City. I share the view that there should be a new trial, but for a different reason. The City did not lead evidence directed to a defence of due diligence, nor did the trial judge address himself to the availability of such a defence. In these circumstances, it would not be fair for this Court to determine, upon findings of fact directed toward other ends, whether the City was without fault.

I would dismiss the appeal and direct a new trial. I would dismiss the cross-appeal. There should be no costs.

■

At the new trial, the City of Sault Ste. Marie was convicted and fined $1,000: unreported judgment of O'Connell J., Ontario District Court, June 16, 1980. While the conviction in this case took years to obtain and the fine may seem insignificant, it is rare in Ontario for polluters to be charged at all. A report prepared by the Sierra Legal Defence Fund reports that between 1996 and 1999 in Ontario water regulations were broken nearly 10,000 times, but only 11 charges were laid: Martin Mittelstaedt, "Few Ontario polluters charged, study says" *The Globe and Mail* (5 November 2001) A10.

After *Sault Ste. Marie*, the overwhelming majority of regulatory offences would have been characterized as strict liability unless the statute contained clear language indicating an intention to create an absolute liability offence. The *Charter* has provided a means by which lawyers and judges have further marginalized the absolute liability category of offences, as the case below illustrates.

Re B.C. Motor Vehicle Act†

[LAMER J.:]

THE FACTS

On August 16, 1982, the Lieutenant-Governor in Council of British Columbia referred the following question to the Court of Appeal of that province, by virtue of s. 1 of the *Constitutional Question Act*, R.S.B.C. 1979, c. 63:

> Is s. 94(2) of the *Motor Vehicle Act*, R.S.B.C. 1979, as amended by the *Motor Vehicle Amend-*

† [1985] 2 S.C.R. 486.

ment Act, 1982, consistent with the *Canadian Charter of Rights and Freedoms*?

On February 3, 1983, the Court of Appeal handed down reasons in answer to the question in which it stated that s. 94(2) of the Act is inconsistent with the *Canadian Charter of Rights and Freedoms*: (1983), 42 B.C.L.R. 364, 147 D.L.R. (3d) 539, 4 C.C.C. (3d) 243, 33 C.R. (3d) 22, 5 C.R.R. 148, 19 M.V.R. 63, [1983] 3 W.W.R. 756. The Attorney General for British Columbia launched an appeal to this Court.

THE LEGISLATION

Motor Vehicle Act, R.S.B.C. 1979, c. 288, s. 94, as amended by the *Motor Vehicle Amendment Act, 1982*, 1982 (B.C.), c. 36, s. 19:

> **94.**(1) A person who drives a motor vehicle on a highway or industrial road while
>
> (a) he is prohibited from driving a motor vehicle under sections 90, 91, 92 or 92.1, or
>
> (b) his driver's licence or his right to apply for or obtain a driver's licence is suspended under section 82 or 92 as it was before its repeal and replacement came into force pursuant to the *Motor Vehicle Amendment Act, 1982*,
>
> commits an offence and is liable,
>
> (c) on a first conviction, to a fine of not less than $300 and not more than $2000 and to imprisonment for not less than 7 days and not more than 6 months, and
>
> (d) on a subsequent conviction, regardless of when the contravention occurred, to a fine of not less than $300 and not more than $2000 and to imprisonment for not less than 14 days and not more than one year.
>
> (2) Subsection (1) creates an absolute liability offence in which guilt is established by proof of driving, whether or not the defendant knew of the prohibition or suspension.

Canadian Charter of Rights and Freedoms; *Constitution Act, 1982*:

> **1.** The *Canadian Charter of Rights and Freedoms* guarantees the rights and freedoms set out in it subject only to such reasonable limits prescribed by law as can be demonstrably justified in a free and democratic society.
>
> **7.** Everyone has the right to life, liberty and security of the person and the right not to be deprived thereof except in accordance with the principles of fundamental justice.

. . . .

THE JUDGMENT OF THE COURT OF APPEAL OF BRITISH COLUMBIA

The Court was of the view that the phrase "principles of fundamental justice" was not restricted to matters of procedure, but extended to substantive law, and that the courts were "therefore called upon, in construing the provisions of s. 7 of the Charter, to have regard to the content of legislation."

Relying on the decision of this Court in *R. v. City of Sault Ste. Marie*, [1978] 2 S.C.R. 1299, the Court of Appeal found "that s. 94(2) of the Motor Vehicle Act is inconsistent with the principles of fundamental justice." They did not heed the invitation of counsel opposing the validity of s. 94(2) to declare that, as a result of that decision by our Court, all absolute liability offences violated s. 7 of the *Charter* and could not be salvaged under s. 1. Quite the contrary, the Court of Appeal said that "there are, and will remain, certain public welfare offences, e.g. air and water pollution offences, where the public interest requires that the offences be absolute liability offences." Their finding was predicated on the following reasoning:

> The effect of s. 94(2) is to transform the offence from a mens rea offence to an absolute liability offence, hence giving the defendant no opportunity to prove that his action was due to an honest and reasonable mistake of fact or that he acted without guilty intent. Rather than placing the burden to establish such facts on the defendant and thus making the offence a strict liability offence, the legislature has seen fit to make it an absolute liability offence coupled with a mandatory term of imprisonment.

It can therefore be inferred with certainty that, in the Court's view, the combination of mandatory imprisonment and absolute liability was offensive to s. 7. It cannot however be ascertained from their judgment whether the violation was triggered by the requirement of minimum imprisonment or solely by the availability of imprisonment as a sentence.

SECTION 7

. . . .

The concerns with the bounds of constitutional adjudication explain the characterization of the issue in a narrow and restrictive fashion, *i.e.*, whether the term "principles of fundamental justice" has a substantive or merely procedural content. In my view, the characterization of the issue in such fashion preempts an open-minded approach to determining the meaning of "principles of fundamental justice."

The substantive/procedural dichotomy narrows the issue almost to an all-or-nothing proposition. Moreover, it is largely bound up in the American experience with substantive and procedural due process. It imports into the Canadian context American concepts, terminology and jurisprudence, all of which are inextricably linked to problems concerning the nature and legitimacy of adjudication under the U.S. Constitution. That Constitution, it must be remembered, has no s. 52 nor has it the internal checks and balances of ss. 1 and 33. We would, in my view, do our own Constitution a disservice to simply allow the American debate to define the issue for us, all the while ignoring the truly fundamental structural differences between the two constitutions. Finally, the dichotomy creates its own set of difficulties by the attempt to distinguish between two concepts whose outer boundaries are not always clear and often tend to overlap. Such difficulties can and should, when possible, be avoided.

. . . .

The task of the Court is not to choose between substantive or procedural content *per se* but to secure for persons "the full benefit of the *Charter*'s protection" (Dickson J. (as he then was) in *R. v. Big M Drug Mart Ltd.*, [1985] 1 S.C.R. 295, at p. 344), under s. 7, while avoiding adjudication of the merits of public policy. This can only be accomplished by a purposive analysis and the articulation (to use the words in *Curr v. The Queen*, [1972] S.C.R. 889, at p. 899) of "objective and manageable standards" for the operation of the section within such a framework.

. . . .

The main sources of support for the argument that "fundamental justice" is simply synonymous with natural justice have been the Minutes of the Proceedings and Evidence of the Special Joint Committee on the Constitution and the *Canadian Bill of Rights* jurisprudence. In my view, neither the Minutes nor the *Canadian Bill of Rights* jurisprudence are persuasive or of any great force. The historical usage of the term "fundamental justice" is, on the other hand, shrouded in ambiguity. Moreover, not any one of these arguments, taken singly or as a whole, manages to overcome in my respectful view the textual and contextual analyses.

Consequently, my conclusion may be summarized as follows:

The term "principles of fundamental justice" is not a right, but a qualifier of the right not to be deprived of life, liberty and security of the person; its function is to set the parameters of that right.

Sections 8 to 14 address specific deprivations of the "right" to life, liberty and security of the person in breach of the principles of fundamental justice, and as such, violations of s. 7. They are therefore illustrative of the meaning, in criminal or penal law, of "principles of fundamental justice"; they represent principles which have been recognized by the common law, the international conventions and by the very fact of entrenchment in the *Charter*, as essential elements of a system for the administration of justice which is founded upon the belief in the dignity and worth of the human person and the rule of law.

Consequently, the principles of fundamental justice are to be found in the basic tenets and principles, not only of our judicial process, but also of the other components of our legal system.

We should not be surprised to find that many of the principles of fundamental justice are procedural in nature. Our common law has largely been a law of remedies and procedures and, as Frankfurter J. wrote in *McNabb v. United States*, 318 U.S. 332 (1942), at p. 347, "the history of liberty has largely been the history of observance of procedural safeguards." This is not to say, however, that the principles of fundamental justice are limited solely to procedural guarantees. Rather, the proper approach to the determination of the principles of fundamental justice is quite simply one in which, as Professor L. Tremblay has written, "future growth will be based on historical roots" ("Section 7 of the Charter: Substantive Due Process?" (1984), 18 *U.B.C.L. Rev*. 201, at p. 254).

Whether any given principle may be said to be a principle of fundamental justice within the meaning of s. 7 will rest upon an analysis of the nature, sources, *rationale* and essential role of that principle within the judicial process and in our legal system, as it evolves.

Consequently, those words cannot be given any exhaustive content or simple enumerative definition, but will take on concrete meaning as the courts address alleged violations of s. 7.

I now turn to such an analysis of the principle of *mens rea* and absolute liability offences in order to determine the question which has been put to the Court in the present Reference.

ABSOLUTE LIABILITY AND FUNDAMENTAL JUSTICE IN PENAL LAW

It has from time immemorial been part of our system of laws that the innocent not be punished. This principle has long been recognized as an essential element of a system for the administration of justice which is founded upon a belief in the dignity and worth of the human person and on the rule of law. It is so old that its first enunciation was in Latin *actus non facit reum nisi mens sit rea*.

As Glanville Williams said:

> There is no need here to go into the remote history of *mens rea*; suffice it to say that the requirement of a guilty state of mind (at least for the more serious crimes) had been developed by the time of Coke, which is as far back as the modern lawyer needs to go. "If one shoot at any wild fowl upon a tree, and the arrow killeth any reasonable creature afar off, without any evil intent in him, this is *per infortunium*." (Glanville Williams, *Criminal Law, The General Part*, 2nd ed. (London, 1961), at p. 30)

One of the many judicial statements on the subject worth mentioning is of the highest authority, *per* Goddard C.J. in *Harding v. Price*, [1948] 1 K.B. 695, at p. 700, where he said:

> The general rule applicable to criminal cases is actus non facit reum nisi mens sit rea, and I venture to repeat what I said in *Brend v. Wood* (1946), 62 T.L.R. 462, 463: "It is of the utmost importance for the protection of the liberty of the subject that a court should always bear in mind that, unless a statute either clearly or by necessary implication rules out mens rea as a constituent part of a crime, the court should not find a man guilty of an offence against the criminal law unless he has a guilty mind."

This view has been adopted by this Court in unmistakable terms in many cases, amongst which the better known are *Beaver v. The Queen*, [1957] S.C.R. 531, and the most recent and often quoted judgment of Dickson J. writing for the Court in *R. v. City of Sault Ste. Marie*, *supra*.

This Court's decision in the latter case is predicated upon a certain number of postulates one of which, given the nature of the rules it elaborates, has to be to the effect that absolute liability in penal law offends the principles of fundamental justice. Those principles are, to use the words of Dickson J., to the effect that "there is a generally held revulsion against punishment of the morally innocent." He also stated that the argument that absolute liability "violates fundamental principles of penal liability" was the most telling argument against absolute liability and one of greater force than those advanced in support thereof.

In my view it is because absolute liability offends the principles of fundamental justice that this Court created presumptions against legislatures having intended to enact offences of a regulatory nature falling within that category. This is not to say, however, and to that extent I am in agreement with the Court of Appeal, that, as a result, absolute liability *per se* offends s. 7 of the *Charter*.

A law enacting an absolute liability offence will violate s. 7 of the *Charter* only if and to the extent that it has the potential of depriving of life, liberty, or security of the person.

Obviously, imprisonment (including probation orders) deprives persons of their liberty. An offence has that potential as of the moment it is open to the judge to impose imprisonment. There is no need that imprisonment, as in s. 94(2), be made mandatory.

I am therefore of the view that the combination of imprisonment and of absolute liability violates s. 7 of the *Charter* and can only be salvaged if the authorities demonstrate under s. 1 that such a deprivation of liberty in breach of those principles of fundamental justice is, in a free and democratic society, under the circumstances, a justified reasonable limit to one's rights under s. 7.

As no one has addressed imprisonment as an alternative to the non-payment of a fine, I prefer not to express any views in relation to s. 7 as regards that eventuality as a result of a conviction for an absolute liability offence; nor do I need to address here, given the scope of my finding and the nature of this appeal, minimum imprisonment, whether it offends the *Charter per se* or whether such violation, if any, is dependent upon whether it be for a *mens rea* or strict liability offence. Those issues were not addressed by the court below and it would be unwise to attempt to address them here. It is sufficient and desirable for this appeal to make the findings I have and no more, that is, that no imprisonment may be imposed for an absolute liability offence, and, consequently, given the question put to us, an offence punishable by imprisonment cannot be an absolute liability offence.

If imprisonment involved cannot be absolute liability → violates s.7 of C.

Administrative expediency, absolute liability's main supportive argument, will undoubtedly under s. 1 be invoked and occasionally succeed. Indeed, administrative expediency certainly has its place in administrative law. But when administrative law chooses to call in aid imprisonment through penal law, indeed sometimes criminal law and the added stigma attached to a conviction, exceptional, in my view, will be the case where the liberty or even the security of the person guaranteed under s. 7 should be sacrificed to administrative expediency. Section 1 may, for reasons of administrative expediency, successfully come to the rescue of an otherwise violation of s. 7, but only in cases arising out of exceptional conditions, such as natural disasters, the outbreak of war, epidemics, and the like.

Of course I understand the concern of many as regards corporate offences, [especially], as was mentioned by the Court of Appeal, in certain sensitive areas such as the preservation of our vital environment and our natural resources. This concern might well be dispelled were it to be decided, given the proper case, that s. 7 affords protection to human persons only and does not extend to corporations.

Even if it be decided that s. 7 does extend to corporations, I think the balancing under s. 1 of the public interest against the financial interests of a corporation would give very different results from that of balancing public interest and the liberty or security of the person of a human being.

Indeed, the public interest as regards "air and water pollution offences" requires that the guilty be dealt with firmly, but the seriousness of the offence does not in my respectful view support the proposition that the innocent *human* person be open to conviction, quite the contrary.

SECTION 94(2)

. . . .

In the final analysis, it seems that both the appellant and the respondent agree that s. 94 will impact upon the right to liberty of a limited number of morally innocent persons. It creates an absolute liability offence which effects a deprivation of liberty for a limited number of persons. To me, that is sufficient for it to be in violation of s. 7.

SECTION 1

Having found that s. 94(2) offends s. 7 of the *Charter* there remains the questions as to whether the appellants have demonstrated that the section is salvaged by the operation of s. 1 of the *Charter*. No evidence was adduced in the Court of Appeal or in this Court....

I do not take issue with the fact that it is highly desirable that "bad drivers" be kept off the road. I do not take issue either with the desirability of punishing severely bad drivers who are in contempt of prohibitions against driving. The bottom line of the question to be addressed here is: whether the Government of British Columbia has demonstrated as justifiable that the risk of imprisonment of a few innocent is, given the desirability of ridding the roads of British Columbia of bad drivers, a reasonable limit in a free and democratic society. That result is to be measured against the offence being one of strict liability open to a defence of due diligence, the success of which does nothing more than let those few who did nothing wrong remain free.

As did the Court of Appeal, I find that this demonstration has not been satisfied, indeed, not in the least. ■

The decision in *R. v. Pontes*, [1995] 3 S.C.R. 44, confirmed the constitutionality of absolute liability offences where the offence permits only a fine as a penalty, and other provincial legislation prohibits incarceration in default of payment of a fine. The Court resisted commenting on whether s. 7 would be offended if imprisonment in default of payment were a possibility. *Pontes* also confirmed a rift among the members of the Court in interpreting *Sault Ste. Marie*. This case required the Court to re-examine the same section, s. 94(1), of the B.C. *Motor Vehicle Act*. Subsection 94(2), which had stated that the offence was one of absolute liability, had been repealed after the 1985 ruling. Five members in *Pontes* ruled that the s. 94(1) offence created an absolute liability offence because of the precise language used in the section ("automatically and without notice") and because no due diligence defence was set out. Four members dissented, ruling that the scheme was a public welfare, regulatory system, and that the accused should be exculpated if they proved a reasonable belief that they had not been convicted of one of the underlying offences or had exercised due diligence in ascertaining whether this was the case.

B. STRICT LIABILITY

Strict liability has its origins in the common law, as *Sault Ste. Marie* illustrates. The fault element for strict liability is negligence, although the Crown need not prove this element. An accused instead must defend by proving, on a balance of probabilities, no negligence, based on either a reasonable mistake of fact or due diligence to avoid commission of the offence. Its use is confined, generally, to federal and provincial regulatory offences, sometimes through explicit statutory language but usually through judicial interpretation. By creating a new category of offences, *Sault Ste. Marie* has also created the possibility of a defence in many regulatory contexts where previously no defence was possible. Who are the primary beneficiaries of this legal development? Are judges well-equipped to adjudicate "due diligence" defences?

Several cases suggest a lack of understanding or possible antipathy to regulatory schemes. For example, in *R. v. Cancoil Thermal Corp.* (10 January 1985), (Ont. Dist. Ct.) [unreported] the trial judge ruled that a shearing machine whose guard had been removed and that severely injured a worker was not "unguarded" within the meaning of the statute on the basis that the foot pedal that activated the blade could be called a "guard" (reversed as an error of law: (1986), 27 C.C.C. (3d) 295 (Ont. C.A.)). In *R. v. Rio Algom Ltd.* (3 April 1987), (Ont. Prov. Ct.) [unreported] the trial judge exonerated the accused for the death of a worker using a subjective interpretation of the mistake of fact branch of the due diligence defence (reversed as an error of law: (1988), 66 O.R. (2d) 674 (C.A.)). Finally, the trial judge in *R. v. Manchester Plastics Ltd.* (28 October 1988) (Ont. Prov. Ct.) [unreported] acquitted the corporation of a strict liability offence on the basis that the Crown had not proven beyond a reasonable doubt that the corporation knew or ought to have known about the safety violation; reversed on appeal: (1989), 1 C.C.H.S.C. 25 (Ont. Dist. Ct.). For the sentencing decision in this case see Abell & Sheehy, *Cases, Context, Critique*, **Sentencing**.

The introduction of the *Charter* has provided another avenue of defence for corporations charged with strict liability offences, as *Wholesale Travel*, reproduced below, illustrates. In *Wholesale Travel*, the Court considered a *Charter* challenge, based on ss. 7 and 11(d), to the due diligence defence as enacted by the *Competition Act*, R.S.C. 1970, c. C-23 (as amended), ss. 36(1)(a), 36(5) and 37.3(2):

> **36.**(1) No person shall, for the purpose of promoting, directly or indirectly, the supply or use of a product or for the purpose of promoting, directly or indirectly, any business interest, by any means whatever,
> (a) make a representation to the public that is false or misleading in a material respect;
>
> ...
>
> (5) Any person who violates subsection (1) is guilty of an offence and is liable
> (a) on conviction on indictment, to a fine in the discretion of the court or to imprisonment for five years or to both; or
> (b) on summary conviction, to a fine of twenty-five thousand dollars or to imprisonment for one year or to both.
>
> **37.3** ...
>
> (2) No person shall be convicted of an offence under section 36 or 36.1, if he establishes that,
> (a) the act or omission giving rise to the offence with which he is charged was the result of error;
> (b) he took reasonable precautions and exercised due diligence to prevent the occurrence of such error;
> (c) he, or another person, took reasonable measures to bring the error to the attention of the class of persons likely to have been reached by the representation or testimonial; and
> (d) the measures referred to in paragraph (c), except where the representation or testimonial related to a security, were taken forthwith after the representation was made or the testimonial was published.

The Court rendered a decision in a multiplicity of judgments, summarized as follows:

1. The justices were unanimous that an offence that uses the *mens rea* component of negligence does not offend s. 7 of the *Charter*, such that s. 37.3(2)(a) and (b) is constitutional;
2. They were also unanimous that the timely retraction provisions in s. 37.3(2)(c) and (d) amount to absolute liability which, combined with the possibility of imprisonment, offend s. 7 and cannot be justified under s. 1;
3. A majority agreed that the reverse onus component of s. 37.3(2) offends s. 11(d), *per*

Lamer C.J. (joined by La Forest, Sopinka, Gonthier, McLachlin, Stevenson, and Iacobucci JJ.);

4. A majority agreed that the s. 11(d) violation was saved by s. 1, *per* Iacobucci J., joined by Gonthier and Stevenson JJ., Cory J., joined by L'Heureux-Dubé J., wrote a minority opinion on s. 11(d), finding no infringement, and would, in any event, have found any infringement justified under s. 1.
5. A minority dissented on the s. 1 analysis and would have found that the provision is not justified, *per* Lamer C.J. joined by La Forest, Sopinka, and McLachlin JJ.

R. v. Wholesale Travel Group Inc.†

[Chief Justice Lamer found that negligence is constitutionally adequate as a fault element for criminal offences.]

[LAMER C.J.:]

[T]he question to be determined here is whether the words "he establishes that" contained in s. 37.3(2) could operate so as to permit a conviction in spite of a reasonable doubt in the mind of the trier of fact as to the guilt of the accused.

... [B]oth the Crown and a number of interveners have argued that this interpretation of s. 11(d) should not apply in a regulatory setting. I can only reiterate my earlier comment that it is the fact that the state has resorted to the restriction of liberty through imprisonment for enforcement purposes which is determinative of the *Charter* analysis. A person whose liberty has been restricted by way of imprisonment has lost no *less* liberty because he or she is being punished for the commission of a regulatory offence as opposed to a criminal offence. A person whose liberty interest is imperilled is entitled to have the principles of fundamental justice fully observed. The presumption of innocence, guaranteed by s. 11(d), is clearly a principle of fundamental justice.

Given that I have determined, above, that paras. (c) and (d) of s. 37.3(2) must be held to be of no force or effect, the words "he establishes that" must be considered with respect to paras. (a) and (b) of s. 37.3(2). In this context, the words "he establishes that" place a burden on an accused to prove the two elements delineated thereafter *on a balance of probabilities* ... Thus, if an accused fails to prove either of these elements on a balance of probabilities, (assuming the Crown has proved the *actus reus*) that accused will be convicted of false/misleading advertising. The *absence* of due diligence (presence of negligence) is clearly necessary for a finding of guilt. Thus, it seems clear to me that under s. 37.3(2) an accused could be convicted of false/misleading advertising despite the existence of a reasonable doubt as to whether the accused was duly diligent and, therefore, despite the existence of a reasonable doubt as to guilt.

. . . .

Accordingly, unless this persuasive burden can be justified under s. 1 of the *Charter*, the words "he establishes that" in s. 37.3(2) must be held to be of no force or effect.

SECTION 1

Objective

As was the case under s. 7, the Crown submits that the objective of the law is to promote vigorous and fair competition. As I have indicated above, this may well be the overall objective of the *Competition Act* in general, but it is not the specific objective of placing a persuasive burden on an accused to prove due diligence (disprove negligence).

The specific objective of placing a persuasive burden on an accused via the words "he establishes that" is to ensure that all those who are guilty of false/misleading advertising are convicted and to ensure that convictions are not lost due to evidentiary problems in proving guilt. I am prepared to accept that this is a "pressing and substantial objective" for the purposes of the *Oakes* analysis.

The means chosen to achieve this objective can be characterized as follows: to facilitate convictions by removing the burden on the Crown to prove neg-

† [1991] 3 S.C.R. 154.

ligence (lack of due diligence) beyond a reasonable doubt. In other words, the means chosen to achieve the objective essentially amounts to a decision by Parliament *to convict all those who do not establish that they were duly diligent, including some accused who were duly diligent (and for whom a reasonable doubt exists in that regard) but who are unable to prove due diligence on a balance of probabilities*. This, then, is the means which must be considered under the proportionality part of the *Oakes* test.

Proportionality Test

1. Rational Connection

Convicting all those who are unable to establish due diligence on a balance of probabilities, including those who were duly diligent, is one way of ensuring that all those guilty of false/misleading advertising are convicted, and is therefore one way of ensuring that the overall goal of ensuring fair and vigorous competition is attained. While this method of achieving the objective may raise certain problems and may not be the preferred method of achieving the objective, it is nonetheless a *logical* means of achieving the desired objective.

2. As Little as Possible

While the imposition of a persuasive burden is rationally connected to the objective, it does not, in my view, infringe constitutionally protected rights as little as is reasonably possible. The Crown has not established that it is necessary to convict those who *were* duly diligent in order to "catch" those accused who were *not* duly diligent.

Parliament clearly had the option of employing a mandatory presumption of negligence (following from proof of the *actus reus*) which could be rebutted by something less than an accused's establishing due diligence on a balance of probabilities. This option was, in fact, recommended by the Ontario Law Reform Commission in its *Report on the Basis of Liability for Provincial Offences* (1990). The Commission stated (at p. 48):

> With respect to the burden of proof for strict liability offences, the Commission proposes a compromise solution that balances the fundamental rights of the accused with the need for effective law enforcement. We recommend the enactment of a mandatory presumption rather than a reverse onus. In other words, *in the absence of evidence to the contrary, negligence will be presumed. The Crown will continue to bear the burden of establishing the physical element or actus reus beyond a reasonable doubt. However, in a strict liability case, it will be necessary that evidence of conduct capable of amounting to reasonable care be adduced, either by the testimony of the accused, through the examination or cross-examination of a Crown or defence witness, or in some other way. The accused will merely have an evidentiary burden and will no longer be required to satisfy the persuasive burden of establishing, on a balance of probabilities, that he was not negligent. Where evidence of reasonable care has been adduced, thereby rebutting the presumption, in order to secure a conviction the prosecution should be required to establish the accused's negligence beyond a reasonable doubt*. [Emphasis added.]

I note that the presence of such a mandatory presumption alongside the accused's evidentiary burden would, in effect, require the accused to adduce evidence capable of amounting to evidence of due diligence, either through the testimony of the accused or that of other witnesses, including the cross-examination of Crown witnesses or by other means. It goes without saying that if the Crown has adduced such evidence, the accused can rely on it in discharge of the evidentiary burden. This will ensure that the information as to what steps, if any, were taken to avoid the occurrence of the prohibited act is in the record and will relieve the Crown of the obligation to bring forward evidence on a matter that is exclusively in the possession of the accused. On the other hand, the Crown will bear the risk of non-persuasion if the conclusions and inferences to be drawn from such information leave the trier of fact in a state of reasonable doubt on the issue of due diligence.

In view of the foregoing, this alternative would not raise the problem discussed in *R. v. Chaulk*, [[1990] 3 S.C.R. 1303], of imposing an "impossibly onerous burden" on the Crown. A requirement that the Crown prove lack of due diligence (negligence) beyond a reasonable doubt once an accused has rebutted a mandatory presumption is not akin to a requirement that the Crown prove an accused's sanity once the accused has raised a reasonable doubt about his or her sanity. In *R. v. Chaulk*, I indicated that the tremendous difficulties which would be faced by the Crown in proving sanity beyond a reasonable doubt flowed largely from the uncertainty of our scientific knowledge in this area. In my view, these difficulties are qualitatively different than the kinds of evidentiary difficulties which would be faced by the Crown in proving lack of due diligence beyond a reasonable doubt (once the accused has discharged the evidentiary burden).

. . . .

While a mandatory presumption with an evidentiary burden on the accused would be far less intrusive on s. 11(d) than would the existing persuasive burden, it must be recognized that a mandatory presumption would itself to some degree infringe the presumption of innocence. As discussed above, this Court stated in *Oakes* ... that the presumption of innocence includes both the right of an accused to be presumed innocent until proven guilty, and the right to have the *state bear the burden* of proving guilt beyond a reasonable doubt. Unless it can be said that proof of the *actus reus* of false/misleading advertising, in and of itself and in all cases, leads inexorably to the conclusion that the accused was *negligent* in carrying out that *actus reus*, a mandatory presumption of negligence leaves open the possibility that the accused will be convicted despite the fact that the Crown's evidence leaves a reasonable doubt about the accused's negligence.

. . . .

At the same time, it is my view that any such infringement of s. 11(d) would be clearly justified as a reasonable limit prescribed by law under s. 1 of the *Charter*. The objective of incorporating a mandatory presumption and evidentiary burden into s. 37.3(2) would be to avoid placing an impossible burden on the Crown. Like most public welfare offences, false/misleading advertising is of such a nature that the accused will be in the best position to garner evidence of due diligence. In the absence of *some* explanation by the accused, it will nearly always be impossible for the Crown to prove the absence of due diligence. ...

In summary, while the use of a mandatory presumption in s. 37.3(2) would also infringe s. 11(d), it constitutes a less intrusive alternative which would not violate the *Charter* (in that it would constitute a justifiable limit under s. 1). ...

[E]ven if it can be said that a mandatory presumption along with an evidentiary burden would not attain the objective *as effectively* as a persuasive burden and that the words in question therefore *do* limit *Charter* rights as little as is reasonably possible, it is my view that any marginal increase in the obtaining of the objective (via a persuasive burden on the accused) would be clearly outweighed by the detrimental effect on the presumption of innocence. In other words, if I am wrong in finding that the words in question do not pass the second branch of the proportionality test in *Oakes*, it is my view that the persuasive burden does not pass the third branch of the proportionality test in *Oakes* because the effect of the means chosen on *Charter* rights and freedoms is *not* proportional to the objective. Indeed, here we are postulating legislation enabling the imprisonment of those who were duly diligent but could not prove it on a balance of probabilities, even though there might well have existed a reasonable doubt thereof. Sending the innocent to jail is too high a price.

I also wish to point out that Parliament had the further option of maintaining the persuasive burden on the accused but removing the possibility of imprisonment. The use of a persuasive burden in circumstances where imprisonment was not a possible punishment would be far less intrusive on constitutional rights. ...

[CORY J. dissenting in part:]

The fundamental issue raised on this appeal is whether regulatory statutes which impose a regime of strict liability for breach of their provisions infringe ss. 7 and 11(*d*) of the *Canadian Charter of Rights and Freedoms*.

FACTUAL BACKGROUND AND PERTINENT LEGISLATION

The Wholesale Travel Group Inc. ("Wholesale Travel") was charged with five counts of false or misleading advertising contrary to s. 36(1)(*a*) of the *Competition Act*, R.S.C. 1970, c. C-23 (the "Act"). The charges were laid after Wholesale Travel advertised vacation packages at "wholesale prices" while at the same time charging consumers a price higher than the cost incurred by the company in supplying those vacation packages. The matter proceeded to trial in Provincial Court. Before any evidence was heard, Wholesale Travel brought a motion challenging the validity of ss. 36(1) and 37.3(2) of the Act on the basis that those sections violate ss. 7 and 11(*d*) of the *Charter* and are therefore of no force [or] effect.

. . . .

It is important to note that all four conditions must be met before the statutory defence can prevail.

Wholesale Travel contends that the statutory scheme and, in particular, the combined operation of the offence prescribed in s. 36(1)(*a*) and the statutory defence set forth in s. 37.3(2), infringes ss. 7 and 11(*d*) of the *Charter*.

. . . .

REGULATORY OFFENCES AND STRICT LIABILITY

A. The Distinction between Crimes and Regulatory Offences

The common law has long acknowledged a distinction between truly criminal conduct and conduct, otherwise lawful, which is prohibited in the public interest. Earlier, the designations *mala in se* and *mala prohibita* were utilized; today prohibited acts are generally classified as either crimes or regulatory offences.

While some regulatory legislation such as that pertaining to the content of food and drink dates back to the Middle Ages, the number and significance of regulatory offences increased greatly with the onset of the Industrial Revolution. Unfettered industrialization had led to abuses. Regulations were therefore enacted to protect the vulnerable — particularly the children, men and women who laboured long hours in dangerous and unhealthy surroundings. Without these regulations many would have died. It later became necessary to regulate the manufactured products themselves and, still later, the discharge of effluent resulting from the manufacturing process. There is no doubt that regulatory offences were originally and still are designed to protect those who are unable to protect themselves.

English courts have for many years supported and given effect to the policy objectives animating regulatory legislation. In *Sherras v. De Rutzen*, [1895] 1 Q.B. 918, at p. 922, it was held that, while the *mens rea* presumption applied to true crimes because of the fault and moral culpability which they imply, that same presumption did not apply to offences "which ... are not criminal in any real sense, but are acts which in the public interest are prohibited under a penalty." This case illustrates the essential distinction in the legal treatment of regulatory as opposed to criminal offences — namely, the removal of the *mens rea* requirement.

. . . .

R. v. City of Sault Ste. Marie, [1978] 2 S.C.R. 1299, affirmed the distinction between regulatory offences and true crimes. There, on behalf of a unanimous Court, Justice Dickson (as he then was) recognized public welfare offences as a distinct class. He held (at pp. 1302–3) that such offences, although enforced as penal laws through the machinery of the criminal law, "are in substance of a civil nature and might well be regarded as a branch of administrative law to which traditional principles of criminal law have but limited application."

The *Sault Ste. Marie* case recognized strict liability as a middle ground between full *mens rea* and absolute liability. Where the offence is one of strict liability, the Crown is required to prove neither *mens rea* nor negligence; conviction may follow merely upon proof beyond a reasonable doubt of the proscribed act. However, it is open to the defendant to avoid liability by proving on a balance of probabilities that all due care was taken. This is the hallmark of the strict liability offence: the defence of due diligence.

. . . .

THE RATIONALE FOR THE DISTINCTION

It has always been thought that there is a rational basis for distinguishing between crimes and regulatory offences. Acts or actions are criminal when they constitute conduct that is, in itself, so abhorrent to the basic values of human society that it ought to be prohibited completely. Murder, sexual assault, fraud, robbery and theft are all so repugnant to society that they are universally recognized as crimes. At the same time, some conduct is prohibited, not because it is inherently wrongful, but because unregulated activity would result in dangerous conditions being imposed upon members of society, especially those who are particularly vulnerable.

The objective of regulatory legislation is to protect the public or broad segments of the public (such as employees, consumers and motorists, to name but a few) from the potentially adverse effects of otherwise lawful activity. Regulatory legislation involves a shift of emphasis from the protection of individual interests and the deterrence and punishment of acts involving moral fault to the protection of public and societal interests. While criminal offences are usually designed to condemn and punish past, inherently wrongful conduct, regulatory measures are generally directed to the prevention of future harm through the enforcement of minimum standards of conduct and care.

It follows that regulatory offences and crimes embody different concepts of fault. Since regulatory offences are directed primarily not to conduct itself but to the consequences of conduct, conviction of a regulatory offence may be thought to import a significantly lesser degree of culpability than conviction of a true crime. The concept of fault in regulatory offences is based upon a reasonable care standard and, as such, does not imply moral blameworthiness in the same manner as criminal fault. Conviction for breach of a regulatory offence suggests nothing more than that the defendant has failed to meet a prescribed standard of care.

That is the theory but, like all theories, its application is difficult. For example, is the single mother who steals a loaf of bread to sustain her family more blameworthy than the employer who, through negligence, breaches regulations and thereby exposes his employees to dangerous working conditions, or the manufacturer who, as a result of negligence, sells dangerous products or pollutes the air and waters by its plant? At this stage it is sufficient to bear in mind that those who breach regulations may inflict serious harm on large segments of society. Therefore, the characterization of an offence as regulatory should not be thought to make light of either the potential harm to the vulnerable or the responsibility of those subject to regulation to ensure that the proscribed harm does not occur. It should also be remembered that, as social values change, the degree of moral blameworthiness attaching to certain conduct may change as well.

Nevertheless there remains, in my view, a sound basis for distinguishing between regulatory and criminal offences. The distinction has concrete theoretical and practical underpinnings and has proven to be a necessary and workable concept in our law. Since *Sault Ste. Marie*, this Court has reaffirmed the distinction. Most recently, in *Thomson Newspapers Ltd. v. Canada (Director of Investigation and Research, Restrictive Trade Practices Commission)*, [1990] 1 S.C.R. 425, at pp. 510–11, Justice La Forest adopted the following statement of the Law Reform Commission of Canada (*Criminal Responsibility for Group Action*, Working Paper 16, 1976, at p. 12):

> [The regulatory offence] is not primarily concerned with values, but with results. While values necessarily underlie all legal prescriptions, the regulatory offence really gives expression to the view that it is expedient for the protection of society and for the orderly use and sharing of society's resources that people act in a prescribed manner in prescribed situations, or that people take prescribed standards of care to avoid risks of injury. The object is to induce compliance with rules for the overall benefit of society.

The Fundamental Importance of Regulatory Offences in Canadian Society

Regulatory measures are the primary mechanisms employed by governments in Canada to implement public policy objectives. What is ultimately at stake in this appeal is the ability of federal and provincial governments to pursue social ends through the enactment and enforcement of public welfare legislation.

Some indication of the prevalence of regulatory offences in Canada is provided by a 1974 estimate by the Law Reform Commission of Canada (see "The Size of the Problem," in *Studies in Strict Liability*). The Commission estimated that there were, at that time, approximately 20,000 regulatory offences in an average province, plus an additional 20,000 regulatory offences at the federal level. By 1983, the Commission's estimate of the federal total had reached 97,000. There is every reason to believe that the number of public welfare offences at both levels of government has continued to increase.

Statistics such as these make it obvious that government policy in Canada is pursued principally through regulation. It is through regulatory legislation that the community seeks to implement its larger objectives and to govern itself and the conduct of its members. The ability of the government effectively to regulate potentially harmful conduct must be maintained.

It is difficult to think of an aspect of our lives that is not regulated for our benefit and for the protection of society as a whole. From cradle to grave, we are protected by regulations; they apply to the doctors attending our entry into this world and to the morticians present at our departure. Every day, from waking to sleeping, we profit from regulatory measures which we often take for granted. On rising, we use various forms of energy whose safe distribution and use are governed by regulation. The trains, buses and other vehicles that get us to work are regulated for our safety. The food we eat and the beverages we drink are subject to regulation for the protection of our health.

In short, regulation is absolutely essential for our protection and well being as individuals, and for the effective functioning of society. It is properly present throughout our lives. The more complex the activity, the greater the need for and the greater our reliance upon regulation and its enforcement. For example, most people would have no idea what regulations are required for air transport or how they should be enforced. Of necessity, society relies on government regulation for its safety.

THE OFFENCE IN THE PRESENT CASE

Competition Legislation Generally

The offence of misleading advertising with which Wholesale Travel is charged is found in the Act. This Act, like its predecessor, the *Combines Investi-*

gation Act, R.S.C. 1970, c. C-23, is aimed at regulating unacceptable business activity. In *General Motors of Canada Ltd. v. City National Leasing*, [1989] 1 S.C.R. 641, Dickson C.J. held that the Act embodied a complex scheme of economic regulation, the purpose of which is to eliminate activities that reduce competition in the marketplace.

The nature and purpose of the Act was considered in greater detail in *Thomson Newspapers Ltd.*, *supra*. La Forest J. pointed out that the Act is aimed at regulating the economy and business with a view to preserving competitive conditions which are crucial to the operation of a free market economy. He observed that the Act was not concerned with "real crimes" but with regulatory or public welfare offences. He put the position this way, at p. 510:

> At bottom, the Act is really aimed at the regulation of the economy and business, with a view to the preservation of the competitive conditions which are crucial to the operation of a free market economy. This goal has obvious implications for Canada's material prosperity. It also has broad political overtones in that it is aimed at preventing concentration of power.... It must be remembered that private organizations can be just as oppressive as the state when they gain such a dominant position within their sphere of operations that they can effectively force their will upon others.
>
> *The conduct regulated or prohibited by the Act is not conduct which is by its very nature morally or socially reprehensible. It is instead conduct we wish to discourage because of our desire to maintain an economic system which is at once productive and consistent with our values of individual liberty. It is, in short, not conduct which would be generally regarded as by its very nature criminal and worthy of criminal sanction. It is conduct which is only criminal in the sense that it is in fact prohibited by law.* One's view of whether it should be so proscribed is likely to be functional or utilitarian, in the sense that it will be based on an assessment of the desirability of the economic goals to which combines legislation is directed or its potential effectiveness in achieving those goals. *It is conduct which is made criminal for strictly instrumental reasons.* [Emphasis added.]

These decisions make it clear that the Act in all its aspects is regulatory in character.

The Offence of False or Misleading Advertising

Is the offence of false or misleading advertising regulatory in nature? It seems to me that the fact that the provision is located within a comprehensive regulatory framework would ordinarily be sufficient to demonstrate its regulatory nature. Several other considerations point to the same conclusion.

The offence of misleading advertising has existed in Canada since 1914. It is not without significance that it was, in 1969, transferred from the *Criminal Code* to the *Combines Investigation Act*, a step which confirms the regulatory nature of the offence. The provision was amended in 1975 to provide for a defence of due diligence, converting the offence from absolute to strict liability.

It is true that the availability of imprisonment as a sanction for breach of a statute might be taken to indicate that the provision is criminal in nature. However, this fact is not itself dispositive of the character of an offence. Rather, one must consider the conduct addressed by the legislation and the purposes for which such conduct is regulated. This view was most recently expressed by La Forest J. in *Thomson Newspapers Ltd.*, *supra*, at p. 509. He noted that many regulatory offences provide for imprisonment in order to ensure compliance with the terms of the statute and thereby achieve the regulatory goal.

The appellant has argued that conviction for the offence of false advertising carries a stigma of dishonesty, with the inference that the accused falsely advertised for the purposes of obtaining economic advantage. It is said that nothing could be more damaging to a business than the implication that it has made dishonest representations. In my view, however, the offence does not focus on dishonesty but rather on the harmful consequences of otherwise lawful conduct. Conviction suggests only that the defendant has made a representation to the public which was in fact misleading and that the defendant was unable to establish the exercise of due diligence in preventing the error. This connotes a fault element of negligence rather than one involving moral turpitude. Thus, any stigma that might flow from a conviction is very considerably diminished.

In summary, the offence of false advertising possesses the essential characteristics which distinguish regulatory offences from those which are truly criminal. Accordingly, it should be considered to be a regulatory offence rather than a crime in the ordinary sense.

A CONTEXTUAL APPROACH TO *CHARTER* INTERPRETATION

The Importance of Considering *Charter* Rights in Context

In *R. v. Big M Drug Mart Ltd.*, [1985] 1 S.C.R. 295, Dickson J. (as he then was) set out the general approach to *Charter* interpretation and the basic principles to be applied. One of his central premises was the need to consider context in order to render the rights and freedoms guaranteed in the *Charter* meaningful and relevant. He observed that the *Charter* was not enacted in a vacuum, and emphasized that its provisions had to be placed in their proper linguistic, philosophic and historical contexts.

In *Edmonton Journal v. Alberta (Attorney General)*, [1989] 2 S.C.R. 1326, Wilson J. stressed the importance of a contextual approach to *Charter* interpretation. She recognized that a particular right or freedom may have a different meaning depending upon the context in which it is asserted. She put her position this way, at pp. 1355–56:

> One virtue of the contextual appr*oach, it seems to me, is that it recognizes that a particular right or freedom may have a different value depending on the context....* The contextual approach attempts to bring into sharp relief the aspect of the right or freedom which is truly at stake in the case as well as the relevant aspects of any values in competition with it. It seems to be more sensitive to the reality of the dilemma posed by the particular facts and therefore more conducive to finding a fair and just compromise between the two competing values under s. 1.
>
> *It is my view that a right or freedom may have different meanings in different contexts....* It seems entirely probable that the value to be attached to it in different contexts for the purpose of the balancing under s. 1 might also be different. *It is for this reason that I believe that the importance of the right or freedom must be assessed in context rather than in the abstract and that its purpose must be ascertained in context.* This having been done, the right or freedom must then, in accordance with the dictates of this Court, be given a generous interpretation aimed at fulfilling that purpose and securing for the individual the full benefit of the guarantee. [Emphasis added.]

The approach articulated by Wilson J. has been cited with approval by this Court in several recent cases: see, for example, *Rocket v. Royal College of Dental Surgeons of Ontario*, [1990] 2 S.C.R. 232; *R. v. Keegstra, supra*; *Committee for the Commonwealth of Canada v. Canada*, [1991] 1 S.C.R. 139.

It is now clear that the *Charter* is to be interpreted in light of the context in which the claim arises. Context is relevant both with respect to the delineation of the meaning and scope of *Charter* rights, as well as to the determination of the balance to be struck between individual rights and the interests of society.

A contextual approach is particularly appropriate in the present case to take account of the regulatory nature of the offence and its place within a larger scheme of public welfare legislation. This approach requires that the rights asserted by the appellant be considered in light of the regulatory context in which the claim is situated, acknowledging that a *Charter* right may have different scope and implications in a regulatory context than in a truly criminal one.

Under the contextual approach, constitutional standards developed in the criminal context cannot be applied automatically to regulatory offences. Rather, the content of the *Charter* right must be determined only after an examination of all relevant factors and in light of the essential differences between the two classes of prohibited activity. This was the approach taken in *Thomson Newspapers Ltd., supra*, where La Forest J. stressed the importance of the regulatory nature of the statute in determining the scope of s. 8 of the *Charter* as applied to the *Combines Investigation Act*.

The contextual approach further requires that the appellant's claim be considered and weighed in light of the realities of a modern industrial society, where the regulation of innumerable activities is essential for the benefit of all. It is vital that the fundamentally important role of regulatory legislation in the protection of individuals and groups in Canadian society today be recognized and accepted. Canadians rely on and expect their governments to regulate and control activities which may be dangerous to others. In *McKinney v. University of Guelph*, [1990] 3 S.C.R. 229, Wilson J. noted the special role of the state in life in Canada. At page 356 of her reasons she wrote:

> Canadians recognize that government has traditionally had and continues to have an important role to play in the creation and preservation of a just Canadian society.... It is, in my view, untenable to suggest that freedom is co-extensive with the absence of government. Experience shows the contrary, that freedom has often required the intervention and protection of government against private action.

The scale and importance of public welfare legislation in Canada is such that a contextual approach must be taken to the issues raised in this appeal.

The Basis for the Differential Treatment of Regulatory Offences

In the present case, the contextual approach requires that regulatory and criminal offences be treated differently for the purposes of *Charter* review. Before proceeding to the substantive analysis, however, it is necessary to consider the justifications for differential treatment. They are two-fold: the first relates to the distinctive nature of regulatory activity, while the second acknowledges the fundamental need to protect the vulnerable through regulatory legislation.

The Licensing Justification

Those who argue against differential treatment for regulatory offences assert that there is no valid reason to distinguish between the criminal and regulatory accused. Each, it is said, is entitled in law to the same procedural and substantive protections. This view assumes equality of position between criminal and regulatory defendants; that is to say, it assumes that each starts out from a position of equal knowledge, volition and "innocence." The argument against differential treatment further suggests that differentiating between the regulatory and criminal defendants implies the subordination and sacrifice of the regulatory accused to the interests of the community at large. Such a position, it is argued, contravenes our basic concern for individual dignity and our fundamental belief in the importance of the individual. It is these assumptions which the licensing justification challenges.

Criminal law is rooted in the concepts of individual autonomy and free will and the corollary that each individual is responsible for his or her conduct. It assumes that all persons are free actors, at liberty to choose how to regulate their own actions in relation to others. The criminal law fixes the outer limits of acceptable conduct, constraining individual freedom to a limited degree in order to preserve the freedom of others. Thus, the basis of criminal responsibility is that the accused person has made a deliberate and conscious choice to engage in activity prohibited by the *Criminal Code*. The accused person who is convicted of an offence will be held responsible for his or her actions, with the result that the opprobrium of society will attach to those acts and any punishment imposed will be considered to be deserved.

The licensing argument is directed to this question of choice. Thus, while in the criminal context, the essential question to be determined is whether the accused has made the choice to act in the manner alleged in the indictment, the regulated defendant is, by virtue of the licensing argument, assumed to have made the choice to engage in the regulated activity. The question then becomes not whether the defendant chose to enter the regulated sphere but whether, having done so, the defendant has fulfilled the responsibilities attending that decision. Professor Richardson puts the position this way in "Strict Liability for Regulatory Crime: the Empirical Research," [1987] *Crim. L.R.* 295, at pp. 295–96:

> ...it can be argued that the strict liability regulatory offender is not a "blameless innocent." By indulging in the regulated activity she has voluntarily adopted the risks of regulatory infraction and her supposed "innocence" flows from the law's traditional tendency to view the criminal act "only in the context of its immediate past."

The licensing concept rests on the view that those who choose to participate in regulated activities have, in doing so, placed themselves in a responsible relationship to the public generally and must accept the consequences of that responsibility. Therefore, it is said, those who engage in regulated activity should, as part of the burden of responsible conduct attending participation in the regulated field, be deemed to have accepted certain terms and conditions applicable to those who act within the regulated sphere. Foremost among these implied terms is an undertaking that the conduct of the regulated actor will comply with and maintain a certain minimum standard of care.

The licensing justification is based not only on the idea of a conscious choice being made to enter a regulated field but also on the concept of control. The concept is that those persons who enter a regulated field are in the best position to control the harm which may result, and that they should therefore be held responsible for it. A compelling statement of this view is found in the decision of the United States Supreme Court in *Morissette v. United States*, 342 U.S. 246 (1952), where the court stated, at p. 256:

> The accused, if he does not will the violation, usually is in a position to prevent it with no more care than society might reasonably expect and no more exertion than it might reasonably exact from one who assumed his responsibilities.

The licensing justification may not apply in all circumstances to all offenders. That is, there are some cases in which the licensing argument may not apply so as to permit the imputation to an accused of choice, knowledge and implied acceptance of regulatory terms and conditions. This may occur, for instance, where the nature of the regulated conduct is so innocuous that it would not trigger in the mind of a reasonable person the possibility that the conduct was regulated.

The nature of the regulated conduct will itself go far to determining whether the licensing argument applies. It is useful to distinguish between conduct which, by virtue of its inherent danger or the risk it engenders for others, would generally alert a reasonable person to the probability that the conduct would be regulated, from that conduct which is so mundane and apparently harmless that no thought would ordinarily be given to its potentially regulated nature. In the latter circumstances, the licensing argument would not apply.

. . . .

The licensing justification finds support as well in the recent decision of this Court in *Thomson Newspapers Ltd., supra*. There, in holding that it was necessary to interpret the asserted right in light of the regulatory context in which the claim arose, La Forest J. relied on licensing-type considerations to find that there was a diminished expectation of privacy in the minds of those whose conduct was regulated. At pages 506–7 he wrote:

> ...the degree of privacy the citizen can reasonably expect may vary significantly depending upon the activity that brings him or her into contact with the state. In a modern industrial society, it is generally accepted that many activities in which individuals can engage must nevertheless to a greater or lesser extent be regulated by the state to ensure that the individual's pursuit of his or her self-interest is compatible with the community's interest in the realization of collective goals and aspirations.

By virtue of the decision to enter the regulated field, the regulated person (here the appellant) can be taken to have accepted certain terms and conditions of entry. To paraphrase La Forest J., the procedural and substantive protections a person can reasonably expect may vary depending upon the activity that brings that person into contact with the state. Thus the extent of *Charter* protection may differ depending upon whether the activity in question is regulatory or criminal in nature.

In this way, the licensing argument provides a link between the distinction between criminal and regulatory offences and the differential treatment of those two categories for the purposes of *Charter* review.

There is, as well, a second justification for differential treatment.

The Vulnerability Justification

The realities and complexities of a modern industrial society[,] coupled with the very real need to protect all of society and particularly its vulnerable members, emphasize the critical importance of regulatory offences in Canada today. Our country simply could not function without extensive regulatory legislation. The protection provided by such measures constitutes a second justification for the differential treatment, for *Charter* purposes, of regulatory and criminal offences.

This Court has on several occasions observed that the *Charter* is not an instrument to be used by the well positioned to roll back legislative protections enacted on behalf of the vulnerable. This principle was first enunciated by Dickson C.J. for the majority in *R. v. Edwards Books and Art Ltd.*, [1986] 2 S.C.R. 713. He wrote, at p. 779:

> In interpreting and applying the *Charter* I believe that the courts must be cautious to ensure that it does not simply become an instrument of better situated individuals to roll back legislation which has as its object the improvement of the condition of less advantaged persons.

The same principle has been repeated and emphasized in *Irwin Toy Ltd. v. Quebec (Attorney General)*, [1989] 1 S.C.R. 927, at p. 993, and in *Slaight Communications Inc. v. Davidson*, [1989] 1 S.C.R. 1038, at p. 1051. This principle recognizes that much government regulation is designed to protect the vulnerable. It would be unfortunate indeed if the *Charter* were used as a weapon to attack measures intended to protect the disadvantaged and comparatively powerless members of society. It is interesting to observe that in the United States, courts struck down important components of the program of regulatory legislation known as "the New Deal." This so-called "*Lochner* era" is now almost universally regarded by academic writers as a dark age in the history of the American Constitution.

Regulatory legislation is essential to the operation of our complex industrial society; it plays a legitimate and vital role in protecting those who are most vulnerable and least able to protect themselves. The extent and importance of that role has increased continuously since the onset of the Industrial Revolution. Before effective workplace legislation was enacted, labourers — including children — worked unconscionably long hours in dangerous and unhealthy surroundings that evoke visions of Dante's *Inferno*. It was regulatory legislation with its enforcement provisions which brought to an end the shameful situation that existed in mines, factories and workshops in the nineteenth century. The differential treatment of regulatory offences is justified by their common goal of protecting the vulnerable.

The importance of the vulnerability concept as a component of the contextual approach to *Charter* interpretation has been recognized in the employer/employee field in *Edwards Books*, *supra*, and *Slaight Communications Inc.*, *supra*, and in the sphere of commercial advertising in *Irwin Toy Ltd.*, *supra*. The same considerations should apply whenever regulatory legislation is subject to *Charter* challenge.

It follows that a contextual approach is required in the present case in order that the distinctive nature of regulatory offences and their fundamental importance in Canadian society may be considered. Both licensing and vulnerability considerations justify differential treatment for the purposes of *Charter* interpretation, of crimes and regulatory offences. This, then, is the basis upon which the present case must be approached.

THE CONSTITUTIONALITY OF STRICT LIABILITY

The appellant argues that strict liability violates the *Charter* on two bases. First, it is said that, at least where imprisonment is available as a sanction, s. 7 of the *Charter* requires a minimum fault element of guilty intent or wilful blindness to be proven; it is argued that, under s. 7, negligence is an insufficient degree of fault to justify a conviction. Second, the appellant alleges that the traditional requirement in strict liability offences that the defendant establish due diligence on a balance of probabilities violates the presumption of innocence guaranteed by s. 11(*d*) of the *Charter*. Let us consider these submissions.

Section 7: The *Mens Rea* Issue

Wholesale Travel contends that wherever imprisonment is available as a penalty for breach of a regulatory statute, the failure to require the Crown to prove guilty intent as an essential element of the offence violates s. 7 of the *Charter*. It is constitutionally impermissible, it is argued, to impose liability solely on the basis of lack of reasonable care. Thus, it is the appellant's position that strict liability as defined in *Sault Ste. Marie* has been superseded and rendered invalid by the *Charter*. The appellant's argument, if accepted, would eliminate any distinction between criminal and regulatory offences.

The question to be determined at this stage is what level of *mens rea* is required by s. 7 of the *Charter*. In *Re B.C. Motor Vehicle Act*, the Court considered a challenge to a provincial absolute liability offence which provided for a minimum period of imprisonment. Lamer J. (as he then was), giving the reasons of the majority of the Court, stated at p. 492:

> A law that has the potential to convict a person who has not really done anything wrong offends the principles of fundamental justice and, if imprisonment is available as a penalty, such a law then violates a person's right to liberty under s. 7....
>
> In other words, absolute liability and imprisonment cannot be combined.

At the same time, Lamer J. was careful to note that, at p. 515, absolute liability *per se* does not violate s. 7, but does so "only if and to the extent that it has the potential of depriving of life, liberty or security of the person."

In the *Vaillancourt* case, *supra*, Lamer J. expanded upon his reasons in *Re B.C. Motor Vehicle Act*. He stated at p. 652:

> ... *Re B.C. Motor Vehicle Act* acknowledges that, whenever the state resorts to the restriction of liberty, such as imprisonment, to assist in the enforcement of a law, even, as in *Re B.C. Motor Vehicle Act*, a mere provincial regulatory offence, there is, as a principle of fundamental justice, a minimum mental state which is an essential element of the offence. It thus elevated *mens rea* from a presumed element in *Sault Ste. Marie*, *supra*, to a constitutionally required element. *Re B.C. Motor Vehicle Act* did not decide what level of *mens rea* was constitutionally required for each type of offence, but inferentially decided that even for a mere provincial regulatory offence *at least* negligence was required, in that *at least* a defence of due diligence must *always* be open to an accused who risks imprisonment upon conviction. [Emphasis in original.]

It can be seen that *Vaillancourt* specifically left open the question of whether, in circumstances where imprisonment is available as a penalty, strict liability with its attenuated fault requirement of negligence constitutes an acceptable basis of liability under s. 7 of the *Charter*.

What emerges from *Re B.C. Motor Vehicle Act* and *Vaillancourt* is that the principles of fundamental justice referred to in s. 7 of the *Charter* prohibit the imposition of penal liability and punishment without proof of fault. Fault was thus elevated from a presumed element of an offence in *Sault Ste. Marie* to a constitutionally required element under the *Charter*. These cases did not, however, decide what level of fault is constitutionally required for every type of offence; rather, they make it clear that the degree of fault required will vary with the nature of the offence and the penalties available upon conviction.

Re B.C. Motor Vehicle Act does establish, however, that where imprisonment is available as a penalty, absolute liability cannot be imposed since it removes the fault element entirely and, in so doing, permits the punishment of the morally innocent.

. . . .

Does section 7 require in all cases that the Crown prove *mens rea* as an essential element of the offence? The resolution of this question requires that a contextual approach be taken to the meaning and scope of the s. 7 right. Certainly, there can be no doubt that s. 7 requires proof of some degree of fault. That fault may be demonstrated by proof of intent, whether subjective or objective, or by proof of negligent conduct, depending on the nature of the offence. While it is not necessary in this case to determine the requisite degree of fault necessary to prove the commission of particular crimes, I am of the view that with respect to regulatory offences, proof of negligence satisfies the requirement of fault demanded by s. 7. Although the element of fault may not be removed completely, the demands of s. 7 will be met in the regulatory context where liability is imposed for conduct which breaches the standard of reasonable care required of those operating in the regulated field.

It should not be forgotten that *mens rea* and negligence are both fault elements which provide a basis for the imposition of liability. *Mens rea* focuses on the mental state of the accused and requires proof of a positive state of mind such as intent, recklessness or wilful blindness. Negligence, on the other hand, measures the conduct of the accused on the basis of an objective standard, irrespective of the accused's subjective mental state. Where negligence is the basis of liability, the question is not what the accused intended but rather whether the accused exercised reasonable care. The application of the contextual approach suggests that negligence is an acceptable basis of liability in the regulatory context which fully meets the fault requirement in s. 7 of the *Charter*.

It is argued, however, that to place regulatory offences in a separate category from criminal offences, with a lower fault standard, puts the accused charged with the breach of a regulatory provision in a fundamentally unfair position. It is a violation of the principles of fundamental justice under s. 7, it is said, to allow the defendant to go to jail without having had the protection available in criminal prosecutions — that is, proof of *mens rea* by the Crown.

I cannot accept this contention. Regulatory offences provide for the protection of the public. The societal interests which they safeguard are of fundamental importance. It is absolutely essential that governments have the ability to enforce a standard of reasonable care in activities affecting public welfare. The laudable objectives served by regulatory legislation should not be thwarted by the application of principles developed in another context.

It must be remembered that regulatory offences were historically developed and recognized as a distinct category precisely for the purpose of relieving the Crown of the burden of proving *mens rea*. This is their hallmark. The tremendous importance of regulatory legislation in modern Canadian industrial society requires that courts be wary of interfering unduly with the regulatory role of government through the application of inflexible standards. Under the contextual approach, negligence is properly acceptable as the minimum fault standard required of regulatory legislation by s. 7.

What some writers have referred to as "licensing" considerations lead to the same conclusion. The regulatory actor is allowed to engage in activity which potentially may cause harm to the public. That permission is granted on the understanding that the actor accept, as a condition of entering the regulated field, the responsibility to exercise reasonable care to ensure that the proscribed harm does not come about. As a result of choosing to enter a field of activity known to be regulated, the regulated actor is taken to be aware of and to have accepted the imposition of a certain objective standard of conduct as a pre-condition to being allowed to engage in the regulated activity. In these circumstances, it misses the mark to speak in terms of the "unfairness" of an attenuated fault requirement because the standard of reasonable care has been accepted by the regulated actor upon entering the regulated sphere.

Further, from a practical point of view, it is simply impossible for the government to monitor adequately every industry so as to be able to prove actual intent or *mens rea* in each case. In order to do so, governments would have to employ armies of experts in every conceivable field. For example, it would be necessary to continuously monitor a myriad of complex activities that are potentially dangerous to members of society. Such activities include manufacturing and mining procedures, food and drug manufacturing, processing and packaging.

In our complex society, the government can, as a practical matter, do no more than demonstrate that it has set reasonable standards to be met by persons in the regulated sphere and to prove beyond a reasonable doubt that there has been a breach of those standards by the regulated defendant. The impossibility of requiring the government to prove mental culpability was recognized by Dickson J. in *Sault Ste. Marie*. He stated at p. 1311:

> Having regard to both the difficulty of proving mental culpability and the number of petty cases which daily come before the Courts, proof of fault is just too great a burden in time and money to place upon the prosecution. To require proof of each person's individual intent would allow almost every violator to escape. This, together with the glut of work entailed in proving *mens rea* in every case would clutter the docket and impede adequate enforcement as virtually to nullify the regulatory statutes.

The whole governmental regulatory scheme would be rendered meaningless if the appellant's *mens rea* argument were to succeed.

For these reasons, I conclude that the appellant's claim that strict liability offences violate s. 7 of the *Charter* cannot succeed. The requirements of s. 7 are met in the regulatory context by the imposition of liability based on a negligence standard. Therefore, no violation of s. 7 results from the imposition of strict liability.

Section 11(d): Onus and the Due Diligence Defence

Wholesale Travel argues that the placing of a persuasive burden on the accused to establish due diligence on a balance of probabilities violates the presumption of innocence as guaranteed by s. 11(*d*) of the *Charter*. As the due diligence defence is the essential characteristic of strict liability offences as defined in *Sault Ste. Marie*, the appellant's s. 11(*d*) claim represents a fundamental challenge to the entire regime of regulatory offences in Canada.

There can be no doubt since the decision of this Court in *R. v. Wigglesworth*, [1987] 2 S.C.R. 541, that the rights guaranteed by s. 11 of the *Charter* are available to all persons who are prosecuted for public offences carrying punitive sanctions. In that case, the term "offence" in s. 11 was defined so as to include criminal, *quasi*-criminal and regulatory offences, whether federal or provincial. However, there is nothing in the *Wigglesworth* decision to suggest that the content and scope of the s. 11 rights cannot vary with the nature of the offence.

. . . .

The Content of the Presumption in the Regulatory Context

Much of what has been said in regard to the validity of strict liability under s. 7 of the *Charter* is applicable as well to the s. 11(*d*) question of onus. The importance of regulatory legislation and its enforcement strongly support the use of a contextual approach in the interpretation of the s. 11(*d*) right as applied to regulatory offences.

At the outset, it is enlightening to return to the relatively recent decision of this Court in *Sault Ste. Marie*. In his reasons, Dickson J. made explicit reference to the presumption of innocence, holding (at p. 1316) that requiring an accused to establish due diligence on a balance of probabilities does not offend the basic presumption of innocence as articulated in *Woolmington v. Director of Public Prosecutions*....

. . . .

In *Sault Ste. Marie*, Dickson J. carefully considered the basic principles of criminal liability, including the presumption of innocence, and balanced them against the public goals sought to be achieved through regulatory measures. He determined that strict liability represented an appropriate compromise between the competing interests involved. This conclusion is no less valid today. The *Charter* was not enacted in a vacuum. The presumption of innocence which it guarantees had long been established and was well recognized at common law. The due diligence defence recognized in *Sault Ste. Marie* which is the target of the present challenge was itself a function of the presumption of innocence.

The reasons for ascribing a different content to the presumption of innocence in the regulatory context are persuasive and compelling. As with the *mens rea* issue, if regulatory mechanisms are to operate effectively, the Crown cannot be required to disprove due diligence beyond a reasonable doubt. Such a requirement would make it virtually impossible for the Crown to prove regulatory offences and would effectively prevent governments from seeking to implement public policy through regulatory means.

It has been suggested that requiring the Crown to prove negligence beyond a reasonable doubt, either as part of its case or after the accused adduces some evidence raising a reasonable doubt as to due diligence, would represent an acceptable compromise: it would, it is said lessen the burden on the accused while still allowing for the effective pursuit of the regulatory objective. I cannot accept this contention. While such an approach would undoubtedly be beneficial to the accused, it would effectively eviscerate the regulatory power of government by rendering the enforcement of regulatory offences impossible in practical terms. Under this approach, the Crown would be forced to prove lack of reasonable care where the accused raises a reasonable doubt as to the possibility of due diligence.

It is difficult to conceive of a situation in which a regulated accused would not be able to adduce *some* evidence giving rise to the possibility that due diligence was exercised. For instance, an environmental polluter would often be able to point to *some* measures it had adopted in order to prevent the type of harm which ultimately resulted. This might raise a reasonable doubt that it had acted with due diligence no matter how inadequate those measures were for the control of a dangerous situation. Similarly, a wholly inadequate effort to ensure that an advertisement was true might nevertheless succeed in raising a reasonable doubt as to due diligence.

To impose such a limited onus is inappropriate and insufficient in the regulatory context. Criminal offences have always required proof of guilt beyond a reasonable doubt; the accused cannot, therefore, be convicted where there is a reasonable doubt as to guilt. This is not so with regulatory offences, where a conviction will lie if the accused has failed to meet the standard of care required. Thus, the question is not whether the accused has exercised *some* care, but whether the degree of care exercised was sufficient to meet the standard imposed. If the false advertiser, the corporate polluter and the manufacturer of noxious goods are to be effectively controlled, it is necessary to require them to show on a balance of probabilities that they took reasonable precautions to avoid the harm which actually resulted. In the regulatory context, there is nothing unfair about imposing that onus; indeed, it is essential for the protection of our vulnerable society.

It must not be forgotten that the virtual impossibility of proving regulatory offences beyond a reasonable doubt was central to this Court's decision in *Sault Ste. Marie*. This consideration led the Court to conclude that the imposition of strict liability with a defence of due diligence available to the accused was both necessary and appropriate.

[He then went on to quote from Dickson J.'s judgment.]

This rationale is no less compelling today. Quite simply, the enforcement of regulatory offences would be rendered virtually impossible if the Crown were required to prove negligence beyond a reasonable doubt. The means of proof of reasonable care will be peculiarly within the knowledge and ability of the regulated accused. Only the accused will be in a position to bring forward evidence relevant to the question of due diligence.

Nor can I accept the contention that there is little practical difference between requiring the accused to prove due diligence on a balance of probabilities and requiring only that the accused raise a reasonable doubt as to the exercise of due diligence. Professor Webb, in his article, *supra*, deals with this argument in the following terms, at p. 467:

. . . .

> The "there is no difference in practice anyway" argument also fails to recognize the different quantity and quality of evidence which administrators would be forced to provide to prosecutors in preparation for a case. If an evidential rather than a persuasive burden is adopted, merely raising a reasonable doubt as to the existence of due diligence would then shift the burden of proof to the prosecutors to *prove negligence*. Prior to any case reaching the prosecution stage, administrators would be under an obligation to collect all the evidence necessary to prove negligence. In effect, prosecutors would be more likely to turn down a request from administrators for a prosecution unless proof of negligence could be established. Given the difficulty in accumulating such information, it is not unlikely that there would be a chilling effect on use of the prosecution mechanism. Once it became noticeable that less cases were reaching the courts, it is possible that regulatees would receive the signal that, in most circumstances, the offence of negligence was not enforceable. [Emphasis in original.]

I agree with these conclusions of Professor Webb. To reduce the onus on the accused would, from a practical point of view, raise insurmountable barriers for the Crown seeking to enforce a regulatory scheme.

. . . .

Nor can it be argued that other solutions would be satisfactory; there is simply no other practical solution. Both with respect to the consumption of government resources and the intrusiveness of regulatory measures, the consequences of a finding that the due diligence defence violates s. 11(*d*) of the *Charter* would be extremely severe. Governments would be forced to devote tremendous expenditure, in terms of monetary and human resources, to regulatory enforcement mechanisms. Armies of investigators and experts would be required in order to garner sufficient evidence to establish negligence or disprove due diligence beyond a reasonable doubt.

Further, a marked expansion in enforcement mechanisms by definition implies an escalation in the intrusiveness of regulatory measures. The greater the burden of proof on the Crown, the greater the likelihood that those charged with the enforcement of regulatory measures would have to resort to legislation authorizing search and surveillance in order to gather sufficient evidence to discharge that onus.

As with the s. 7 challenge, licensing considerations support the conclusion that strict liability does not violate s. 11(*d*) of the *Charter*. The licensing argument attributes to the regulated actor knowledge and acceptance, not only of the standard of reasonable care itself, but also of the responsibility to establish on a balance of probabilities the exercise of reasonable care. Acceptance of this burden is an implied term and a pre-condition of being allowed to engage in activity falling within the regulated sphere. Regulated actors are taken to understand that, should they be unable to discharge this burden, an inference of negligence will be drawn from the fact that the proscribed result has occurred.

. . . .

For these reasons, I conclude that the presumption of innocence as guaranteed in s. 11(*d*) of the *Charter* is not violated by strict liability offences as defined in *Sault Ste. Marie*. The imposition of a reverse persuasive onus on the accused to establish due diligence on a balance of probabilities does not run counter to the presumption of innocence, notwithstanding the fact that the same reversal of onus would violate s. 11(*d*) in the criminal context.

The Imprisonment Concern

Much has been made in this appeal of the potential use of imprisonment as a sanction for breach of strict liability offences. The Chief Justice considers the use of imprisonment to be determinative of the *Charter* analysis. With respect, I am unable to agree. The availability of imprisonment in no way alters my conclusion that strict liability does not violate either ss. 7 or 11(*d*) of the *Charter*.

The *Charter* does not guarantee an absolute right to liberty; rather, it guarantees the right not to be deprived of liberty except in accordance with the principles of fundamental justice. Thus, while the availability of imprisonment undoubtedly triggers *Charter* review, it does not resolve the ultimate question. What must be determined is whether, in a given case, the possibility of a sentence of imprisonment comports with the principles of fundamental justice. It is whether the principles of fundamental justice have been violated, not the availability of imprisonment, which is the determinative consideration.

In this regard, it is essential to recognize that the principles of fundamental justice are not static in meaning or application. As La Forest J. stated for the Court in *R. v. Lyons*, [1987] 2 S.C.R. 309, at p. 361:

> It is also clear that the requirements of fundamental justice are not immutable; rather, they vary according to the context in which they are invoked. Thus, certain procedural protections might be constitutionally mandated in one context but not in another.

There is quite properly a difference or variation between what the principles of fundamental justice require in regard to true crimes and what they require in the regulatory context.

The ultimate question is whether the imposition of imprisonment on the basis of strict liability comports with the principles of fundamental justice. For the reasons set out earlier concerning the underlying rationale of regulatory offences, I am of the opinion that it does.

Regulatory schemes can only be effective if they provide for significant penalties in the event of their breach. Indeed, although it may be rare that imprisonment is sought, it must be available as a sanction if there is to be effective enforcement of the regulatory measure. Nor is the imposition of imprisonment unreasonable in light of the danger that can accrue to the public from breaches of regulatory statutes. The spectre of tragedy evoked by such names as Thalidomide, Bhopal, Chernobyl and the *Exxon Valdez* can leave no doubt as to the potential human and environmental devastation which can result from the violation of regulatory measures. Strong sanctions including imprisonment are vital to the prevention of similar catastrophes. The potential for serious harm flowing from the breach of regulatory measures is too great for it to be said that imprisonment can never be imposed as a sanction.

I would only add that, in those circumstances where the imposition of imprisonment would be grossly disproportionate to the offence committed, the accused person would have a compelling claim under s. 12 of the *Charter*. However, the fact that it is possible to imagine instances where the use of imprisonment would be inappropriate should not be used to justify the conclusion that imprisonment can never be imposed in respect of strict liability offences. Imprisonment must be available to governments as a sanction if the power to regulate is to be effective.

. . . .

Section 1

In light of my conclusion regarding the appellant's ss. 7 and 11(*d*) claims, there is no need to proceed to s. 1. However, had it been necessary to consider the matter, the same reasons I have set forth in finding that neither s. 7 nor s. 11(*d*) are necessarily infringed by strict liability offences would have led me to conclude that strict liability offences can be justified under s. 1 of the *Charter*.

APPLICATION TO S. 36(1)(a) AND S. 37.3(2)

Section 36(1)(*a*) of the Act creates the offence of false or misleading advertising. Section 37.3(2) provides a statutory defence to that charge. The defence will only lie where all four conditions set out in paras. (*a*) through (*d*) are met. While paras. (*a*) and (*b*) in essence describe the common law defence of due diligence, paras. (*c*) and (*d*) create additional conditions which must be met before the defence will lie.

The Validity of Paras. (c) and (d) of s. 37.3(2)

Paragraph (*c*) of s. 37.3(2) requires an accused who has made a misleading representation to take positive steps to bring the error to the attention of those to be likely [*sic*] affected by it. Paragraph (*d*) requires this to be done promptly. The effect of these provisions is to impose an obligation on the accused to make a prompt retraction as a precondition to relying on the defence of due diligence.

The Court of Appeal unanimously held that paras. (*c*) and (*d*) of s. 37.3(2) may in some circumstances require conviction where there is no fault on the part of the accused. I agree with this conclusion. Even where an accused can establish the absence of negligence in the making of misleading representations, paras. (*c*) and (*d*) nonetheless require conviction if the accused has failed to make a prompt correction or retraction. In these circumstances, the accused would be deprived of the defence of due diligence and the offence would be tantamount to absolute liability, since liability could be imposed in the absence of fault on the part of the accused.

Such a result clearly violates s. 7 of the *Charter*. As Lamer J. stated in *Re B.C. Motor Vehicle Act*, *supra*, at p. 492:

> A law that has the potential to convict a person who has not really done anything wrong offends the principles of fundamental justice and, if imprisonment is available as a penalty, such a law then violates a person's right to liberty under s. 7 of the *Charter of Rights and Freedoms*.

Nor do I think that paras. (*c*) and (*d*) can be justified under s. 1 of the *Charter*. The Crown has filed little evidence to support its position that paras. (*c*) and (*d*) can be saved by s. 1. Perhaps this is itself a sufficient basis for finding that those paragraphs are not justifiable.

There are, however, additional grounds for reaching this conclusion. Assuming that there is a rational connection between the requirement of corrective advertising and the legislative objective of seeking to prevent the harm resulting from misleading representations, it cannot be said that the impugned provisions constitute a minimal impairment of the rights of the accused. Further, the availability of imprisonment as a sanction far outweighs the importance of the regulatory objective in correcting false advertising after the fact. In short, there is no proportionality between means and ends. Paragraphs (*c*) and (*d*) cannot then be justified under s. 1 of the *Charter*.

The Validity of Paras. (a) and (b)

These paragraphs in essence put forward the common law defence of due diligence. ... In the regulatory context, it is appropriate that fault should be imposed on the basis of negligence. There is therefore no violation of s. 7 resulting from the removal of the *mens rea* requirement in strict liability offences. It follows that paras. (*a*) and (*b*) of s. 37.3(2) do not violate s. 7 of the *Charter*.

It has been noted earlier that the s. 11(*d*) presumption of innocence has a different scope and meaning in relation to regulatory as opposed to criminal offences. In my view, the imposition in strict liability offences of a reverse persuasive onus on the accused to establish due diligence is proper and permissible and does not constitute a violation of the s. 11(*d*) presumption of innocence. I therefore conclude that paras. (*a*) and (*b*) of s. 37.3(2) do not violate s. 11(*d*) of the *Charter*.

. . . .

DISPOSITION

Since paragraphs (*c*) and (*d*) of s. 37.3(2) of the Act violate s. 7 of the *Charter* and cannot be justified under s. 1, they must be struck down and declared to be of no force or effect. What remains in s. 36(1)(*a*) and s. 37.3(2)(*a*) and (*b*) is a strict liability regulatory offence. These provisions are valid and enforceable. In the result I would dismiss the appeal and allow the Crown's appeal to the extent required to reflect this disposition.

[IACOBUCCI J. (*per* Gonthier, Stevenson, and Iacobucci JJ.):]

I have had the benefit of the reasons of the Chief Justice Lamer and of Justice Cory. I am in agreement with the conclusions of Lamer C.J. as to the standing of the appellant corporation and with both Lamer C.J. and Cory J. that paras. (c) and (d) of s. 37.3(2) of the *Competition Act* infringe s. 7 of the *Canadian Charter of Rights and Freedoms* and that such infringement is not justified under s. 1 thereof. I also share the views of Lamer C.J. that the reverse onus on the accused to establish due diligence on a balance of probabilities ... infringes s. 11(d) of the *Charter*. However, for many of the reasons given by Cory J. in the context of his s. 11(d) analysis, I arrive at a different conclusion from Lamer C.J. on the question of whether such a restriction is a reasonable and demonstrably justified limit under s. 1 of the *Charter*.

. . . .

At the outset, I would like to point out that it is now clear that a rigid or formalistic approach must be avoided when applying the various criteria of the *Oakes* analysis, and that proper consideration must be given to the circumstances and context of a particular case: *R. v. Keegstra*, [1990] 3 S.C.R. 697, at pp. 737–38, *per* Dickson C.J. speaking for the majority. In the present case, the special nature of the legislation and offence in question must be kept in mind when applying s. 1 of the *Charter*. In this respect, I agree with Cory J. that what is ultimately involved in this appeal is the ability of federal and provincial governments to pursue social ends through the enactment and enforcement of public welfare legislation. While I abstain from commenting on the dichotomy articulated by Cory J. between "true crimes" and "regulatory offences", I agree with my colleague that the offence of false or misleading advertisement may properly be characterized as a public welfare offence and that the prohibition of such offences is of fundamental importance in Canadian society.

Having said that, I will now apply the *Oakes* analysis to the case at bar. I am in agreement with the conclusions of Lamer C.J. regarding the first two requirements of the *Oakes* analysis....

However, it is with respect to the third requirement of the *Oakes* analysis, that I respectfully disagree with the conclusions of Lamer C.J. This step requires a consideration of whether the means chosen impair the right or freedom in question <u>no more than is necessary to accomplish the desired objective</u>. Lamer C.J. is of the opinion that the use of a persuasive burden in s. 37.3(2) of the *Competition Act* cannot pass this third step of the *Oakes* analysis because of the presence of an alternative means open to Parliament that would be less intrusive on s. 11(d) of the *Charter* and would "go a long way" in achieving the objective. The alternative in question is the use of a "mandatory presumption of negligence" (following from the proof of the *actus reus*) which could be rebutted by something less than an accused's establishing due diligence on a balance of probabilities, i.e., by raising a reasonable doubt as to due diligence. With respect, I cannot agree that such a means would achieve the stated objective as effectively nor would it go a long way in achieving it. Such a means would shift to the accused the burden of simply raising a reasonable doubt as to due diligence and would not thereby allow the effective pursuit of the regulatory objective. It would leave the Crown the legal burden of proving facts largely within the peculiar knowledge of the accused.

For the reasons given by Cory J. in the context of his s. 11(d) analysis, such an alternative would in practice make it virtually impossible for the Crown to prove public welfare offences such as the one in question and would effectively prevent governments from seeking to implement public policy through prosecution. It would also not provide effective inducement for those engaged in regulated activity to comply strictly with the regulatory scheme including adopting proper procedures and record keeping and might even have a contrary effect. Though such a result would be clearly advantageous to an accused, it would not be effective in avoiding the loss of convictions because the Crown could not prove facts within the particular knowledge of the accused. In sum, taking into account the particular circumstances described by Cory J. in his reasons, Parliament could not "reasonably have chosen an alternative means which would have achieved the identified objective as effectively": *R. v. Chaulk*,

[1990] 3 S.C.R. 1303, at p. 1341, *per* Lamer C.J. for the majority.

As for the final requirement of the *Oakes* analysis, I would also respectfully disagree with the conclusions of Lamer C.J. As noted by Cory J. in his reasons, regulated activity and public welfare offences are a fundamental part of Canadian society. Those who choose to participate in regulated activities must be taken to have accepted the consequential responsibilities and their penal enforcement. One of these consequences is that they should be held responsible for the harm that may result from their lack of due diligence. Unless they can prove on a balance of probabilities that they exercised due diligence, they shall be convicted and in some cases face a possible prison term. These participants are in the best position to prove due diligence since they possess in most cases the required information. Viewed in this context, and taking into account the fundamental importance of the legislative objective as stated and the fact that the means chosen impair the right guaranteed by s. 11(d) as little as is reasonably possible, the effects of the reverse onus on the presumption of innocence are proportional to the objective.

Having found that the reverse onus on the accused to establish due diligence on a balance of probabilities ... satisfies all four requirements of the *Oakes* analysis, I conclude that such an onus is saved under s. 1 of the *Charter* as a reasonable limit in a free and democratic society. Accordingly, I would dispose of the appeals in the manner suggested by Cory J.

■

Which judgment in *Wholesale Travel* do you find most persuasive on the s. 11 (d) issue: the majority judgment of Lamer C.J., or the minority opinion of Cory J.? Which do you find most compelling on the question of whether the s. 11(d) violation can be saved pursuant to s. 1: the majority opinion of Iacobucci J., or the minority judgment by Lamer C.J.? If you agree with the result in *Wholesale Travel*, whose approach to preserving the reverse onus for due diligence offences do you prefer, that of Cory J. or that of Iacobucci J.? What are the implications of these two different approaches for corporate criminal responsibility?

In light of the fact that *Wholesale Travel* struck down paras. (c) and (d) of s. 37.3, does the case actually vindicate legislative reliance on due diligence in different regulatory contexts? What forms of due diligence will survive constitutional challenge? Did the facts in this case provide an "air of reality" for a due diligence defence?

Can an offence found in the *Criminal Code* be classified as a strict liability offence? For a decision holding that s. 86(2), which forms part of the gun control legislation, creates a "quasi-regulatory" offence, see *R. v. Smillie*, [1998] B.C.J. No. 2082 (C.A.). *Smillie* held that for this offence the Crown need only prove the *actus reus* of the offence, but the accused can defend by raising a doubt as to the exercise of due diligence to avoid conviction for the crime.

C. NEGLIGENCE

There are several offences in the *Code* that use the concept of negligence as the fault element, including criminal negligence offences (ss. 219, 220, 221), failure to provide necessaries of life (s. 215), dangerous driving (s. 249), and careless handling of a weapon (s. 86(1)). As well, numerous federal and provincial offences use some concept of negligence as the fault element.

Negligence as a *mens rea* has been subjected to conflicting interpretations in the case law in terms of objective and subjective tests, in part because this mental state is used for behaviour as diverse as driving offences, medical treatment, and parental failure to provide the necessaries of life to children. The confusion has also resulted because of the use of a concept, "negligence", that is understood in tort law to be tested objectively, combined with the definition in s. 219, which requires proof of conduct that "shows wanton or reckless disregard for the lives or safety of other persons", a phrase that some argue suggests subjective awareness to risk. The *actus reus* requirement that the accused's conduct constitute a gross deviation from the standard of ordinary care serves to distinguish these offences from civil wrongs or torts.

More confusingly still, negligence as a concept is also used in the complex web of homicide offences in the *Code*. Homicide occurs where, directly or indirectly, a person causes death to a human being: s. 222(1). Homicides are classified as either culpable or non-culpable: s. 222(2). Culpable homicide may be committed as infanticide, murder, or manslaughter: s. 222(4). All other forms of homicide are non-culpable: s. 222(3). Culpable homicides under s. 222(5) require proof that death was caused by (a) an unlawful act, (b) criminal negligence, (c) threats, fear of violence, or deception, by one person that causes another person to cause their own death, or (d) in the case of a sick person or child, wilfully frightening that person. Proof of the offence under s. 222(5) without more will constitute manslaughter, as additional elements need to be proven to make out infanticide (s. 233) or murder (ss. 229, 230): s. 234 states that culpable homicide that is not murder or infanticide is manslaughter. The punishment for: manslaughter is a maximum sentence of life imprisonment or a minimum of four years imprisonment if a firearm was used in the commission of the offence (s. 236); infanticide is a maximum of five years imprisonment (s. 237); and murder is mandatory life imprisonment (s. 235), with a different period of parole ineligibility, depending on whether the offence is classified as first or second degree murder under s. 231: s. 747.

Different *actus reus* and *mens rea* elements must be proven, depending on whether the charge is murder, unlawful act manslaughter, or manslaughter by criminal negligence. What generally distinguishes murder from manslaughter is intentionality with respect to causing death. The law regarding the specific elements of proof for murder will be discussed under Intention or Knowledge, below.

Unlawful act manslaughter (s. 222(5)(a)) is made out where the prosecution proves (i) an unlawful act that is "dangerous"; (ii) a marked deviation from the standard of care that a reasonable person would exercise; (iii) foreseeability of harm as a consequence of the unlawful act; (iv) causation; and (v) death of a human being. Manslaughter by criminal negligence (s. 222(5)(b)) is indistinguishable from the offence of causing death by criminal negligence (s. 220): both require proof of criminal negligence as defined in s. 219, as well as causation and the death of a human being; both carry the identical sentence. Criminal negligence in s. 219 requires: either an act or an omission and "wanton or reckless disregard for the lives and safety of other persons". In the cases that follow, the courts discuss the nature of the fault or *mens rea* element that must be proven for manslaughter by unlawful act and by criminal negligence, as well as the impact of the *Charter* on this element.

The Supreme Court has split repeatedly on the question of whether criminal negligence offences should be tested on a subjective or objective basis, using principles of statutory interpretation and criminal law policy: *R. v. Tutton*, [1989] 1 S.C.R. 1392; *R. v. Waite*, [1989] 1 S.C.R. 1436. The Court has possibly resolved the objective/subjective debate for offences of negligence in *R. v. Creighton*, below, where the constitutionality of the objective test was squarely at issue. However, the five-four split of the Court indicates that this resolution is still unstable.

R. v. Creighton†

[McLACHLIN J.:]

This appeal considers the constitutional status of s. 222(5)(*a*) of the *Criminal Code*, R.S.C., 1985, c. C-46. In particular, the constitutional question stated by the Chief Justice asks "Does the common law definition of unlawful act manslaughter contravene s. 7 of the *Canadian Charter of Rights and Freedoms*?" The facts and judgments below have been set out by the Chief Justice. In brief, Mr. Creighton was convicted of manslaughter, arising from the death of Kimberley Ann Martin, who died as a result of an injection of

† [1993] 3 S.C.R. 3.

cocaine given by Mr. Creighton. The trial judge found that the death constituted manslaughter either on the ground that it was caused by an unlawful act, or on the ground that it was caused by criminal negligence.

I respectfully disagree with the Chief Justice on two points. The first is his conclusion that the common law offence of manslaughter is unconstitutional because it does not require foreseeability of death. The Chief Justice concludes that the offence of manslaughter must be "read up" to include this requirement in order to bring it into line with the principles of fundamental justice enshrined in s. 7 of the *Charter*, and in particular with the principle that the moral fault required for conviction be commensurate with the gravity and the stigma of the offence. In my view, the offence of unlawful act manslaughter, as defined by our courts and those in other jurisdictions for many centuries, is entirely consistent with the principles of fundamental justice. There is no need to read up its requirements; as it stands, it conforms to the *Charter*.

The second point on which I respectfully diverge is the Chief Justice's conclusion that the standard of care on the objective test in manslaughter and in crimes of negligence varies with the degree of experience, education, and other personal characteristics of the accused. This leads the Chief Justice to hold Mr. Creighton to a higher standard of care than that of the reasonable person in determining if he would have foreseen the risk in question, because of Creighton's long experience as a drug user (pp. 26–27, reasons of Chief Justice). For the reasons set out below I believe the appropriate standard to be that of the reasonable person in all the circumstances of the case. The criminal law is concerned with setting minimum standards of conduct; the standards are not to be altered because the accused possesses more or less experience than the hypothetical average reasonable person.

I will turn first to the common law test for manslaughter, and address the constitutional question as stated by the Chief Justice.

CONSTITUTIONALITY OF THE REQUIREMENT OF FORESEEABILITY OF BODILY INJURY IN MANSLAUGHTER

The *Mens Rea* of Manslaughter

The *Criminal Code* defines three general types of culpable homicide. There is murder, the intentional killing of another human being. There is infanticide, the intentional killing of a child. All other culpable homicides fall into the residual category of manslaughter (s. 234, *Criminal Code*).

Manslaughter is a crime of venerable lineage. It covers a wide variety of circumstances. Two requirements are constant: (1) conduct causing the death of another person; and (2) fault short of intention to kill. That fault may consist either in committing another unlawful act which causes the death, or in criminal negligence. The common law classification of manslaughter is reflected in the definition of culpable homicide in s. 222(5) of the *Criminal Code*:

> **222....**
>
> (5) A person commits culpable homicide when he causes the death of a human being,
>
> (*a*) by means of an unlawful act;
>
> (*b*) by criminal negligence;

The structure of the offence of manslaughter depends on a predicate offence of an unlawful act or criminal negligence, coupled with a homicide. It is now settled that the fact that an offence depends upon a predicate offence does not render it unconstitutional, provided that the predicate offence involves a dangerous act, is not an offence of absolute liability, and is not unconstitutional: *R. v. DeSousa*, [1992] 2 S.C.R. 994. But a further objection is raised in this case. It is said that the offence of manslaughter is unconstitutional because it requires only foreseeability of the risk of bodily harm and not foreseeability of death, and that the trial judge erred in requiring only foreseeability of bodily harm.

The cases establish that in addition to the *actus reus* and *mens rea* associated with the underlying act, all that is required to support a manslaughter conviction is reasonable foreseeability of the risk of bodily harm. While s. 222(5)(*a*) does not expressly require foreseeable bodily harm, it has been so interpreted: see *R. v. DeSousa, supra*. The unlawful act must be objectively dangerous, that is likely to injure another person. The law of unlawful act manslaughter has not, however, gone so far as to require foreseeability of death. The same is true for manslaughter predicated on criminal negligence; while criminal negligence, *infra*, requires a marked departure from the standards of a reasonable person in all the circumstances, it does not require foreseeability of death.

Certain early authorities suggest that foreseeability of the risk of bodily harm is not required for manslaughter. Blackstone wrote that "when an involuntary killing happens in consequence of an unlawful act ... if no more was intended than a mere trespass, it will only amount to manslaughter" (Blackstone,

Commentaries on the Laws of England (1769), Book IV, at pp. 192–93). Others disagreed. Stephen, the author of the Canadian *Criminal Code*, defined manslaughter as "unlawful homicide," which in turn he defined as requiring, at a minimum, that the act was "likely to cause death or bodily harm" (Arts. 279, 278, reprinted in G. W. Burbidge, *Digest of the Criminal Law of Canada* (1980), at pp. 216, 215).

In more recent times, the prevailing view has been that foreseeability of bodily harm is required for manslaughter. In England, it was said in *R. v. Larkin*, [1943] 1 All E.R. 217 (C.C.A.), at p. 219, that the act must be "a dangerous act, that is, an act which is likely to injure another person." In *R. v. Tennant* (1975), 23 C.C.C. (2d) 80, at p. 96, the Ontario Court of Appeal stated that the unlawful act must be "such as any reasonable person would inevitably realize must subject another to the risk of, at least, some harm, albeit not serious harm." Similarly, in *R. v. Adkins* (1987), 39 C.C.C. (3d) 346 (B.C.C.A.), at p. 348, Hutcheon J.A. wrote, "the unlawful act was such as any reasonable person would inevitably realize must subject another to the risk of at least some harm."

This Court in *R. v. DeSousa, supra*, confirmed that a conviction for manslaughter requires that the risk of bodily harm have been foreseeable. After referring to the statement in *Larkin, supra*, that a "dangerous act" is required, Sopinka J. stated that English authority has consistently held that the underlying unlawful act required for manslaughter requires "proof that the unlawful act was 'likely to injure another person' or in other words put the bodily integrity of others at risk" (p. 959). Moreover, the harm must be more than trivial or transitory. The test set out by Sopinka J. (at p. 961) for the unlawful act required by s. 269 of the *Criminal Code* is equally applicable to manslaughter:

> ...the test is one of objective foresight of bodily harm for all underlying offences. The act must be both unlawful, as described above, *and* one that is likely to subject another person to danger of harm or injury. This bodily harm must be more than merely trivial or transitory in nature and will in most cases involve an act of violence done deliberately to another person. In interpreting what constitutes an objectively dangerous act, the courts should strive to avoid attaching penal sanctions to mere inadvertence. The contention that no dangerousness requirement is required if the unlawful act is criminal should be rejected. [Emphasis in original.]

So the test for the *mens rea* of unlawful act manslaughter in Canada, as in the United Kingdom, is (in addition to the *mens rea* of the underlying offence) objective foreseeability of the risk of bodily harm which is neither trivial nor transitory, in the context of a dangerous act. Foreseeability of the risk of death is not required. The question is whether this test violates the principles of fundamental justice under s. 7 of the *Charter*.

Constitutionality of the "Foresight of Bodily Harm" Test for Manslaughter

Before venturing on analysis, I think it appropriate to introduce a note of caution. We are here concerned with a common law offence virtually as old as our system of criminal law. It has been applied in innumerable cases around the world. And it has been honed and refined over the centuries. Because of its residual nature, it may lack the logical symmetry of more modern statutory offences, but it has stood the practical test of time. Could all this be the case, one asks, if the law violates our fundamental notions of justice, themselves grounded in the history of the common law? Perhaps. Nevertheless, it must be with considerable caution that a twentieth century court approaches the invitation which has been put before us: to strike out, or alternatively, rewrite, the offence of manslaughter on the ground that this is necessary to bring the law into conformity with the principles of fundamental justice.

As I read the reasons of the Chief Justice, his conclusion that the offence of manslaughter as it stands is unconstitutional rests on two main concerns. First, it is his view that the gravity or seriousness of the offence of manslaughter, and in particular the stigma that attaches to it, requires a minimum *mens rea* of foreseeability of death. Second, considerations of symmetry between the element of mental fault and the consequences of the offence mandate this conclusion. I will deal with each concern in turn.

Gravity of the Offence

A number of concepts fall under this head. Three of them figure among the four factors relevant to determining the constitutionality of a *mens rea* requirement, as set out by this Court in *R. v. Martineau*, [1990] 2 S.C.R. 633:

1. The stigma attached to the offence, and the available penalties requiring a *mens rea* reflecting the particular nature of the crime;
2. Whether the punishment is proportionate to the moral blameworthiness of the offender; and

3. The idea that those causing harm intentionally must be punished more severely than those causing harm unintentionally.

The Chief Justice in his reasons places considerable emphasis on the first factor of stigma. He argues that "there may well be no difference between the *actus reus* of manslaughter and that of murder; arguably both give rise to the stigma of being labelled by the state and the community as responsible for the wrongful death of another" (p. 19). But later in his reasons (at p. 20) he concedes that "the stigma which attaches to a conviction for unlawful act manslaughter," while "significant ... does not approach the opprobrium reserved in our society for those who *knowingly* or *intentionally* take the life of another" (emphasis is original). The Chief Justice goes on to observe that "[i]t is for this reason that manslaughter developed as a separate offence from murder at common law." Nevertheless, in the end the Chief Justice concludes that the "constitutional imperative," taken with other factors, requires a minimum *mens rea* of foreseeability of the risk of death, suggesting that stigma may remain an important factor in his reasoning.

To the extent that stigma is relied on as requiring foreseeability of the risk of death in the offence of manslaughter, I find it unconvincing. The most important feature of the stigma of manslaughter is the stigma which is *not* attached to it. The *Criminal Code* confines manslaughter to non-intentional homicide. A person convicted of manslaughter is *not* a murderer. He or she did *not* intend to kill someone. A person has been killed through the fault of another, and that is always serious. But by the very act of calling the killing *manslaughter* the law indicates that the killing is less blameworthy than murder. It may arise from negligence, or it may arise as the unintended result of a lesser unlawful act. The conduct is blameworthy and must be punished, but its stigma does not approach that of murder.

To put it another way, the stigma attached to manslaughter is an appropriate stigma. Manslaughter is not like constructive murder, where one could say that a person who did not in fact commit murder might be inappropriately branded with the stigma of murder. The stigma associated with manslaughter is arguably exactly what it should be for an unintentional killing in circumstances where risk of bodily harm was foreseeable. There is much common sense in the following observation:

> The offender has killed, and it does not seem wrong in principle that, when he is far from blameless, he should be convicted of an offence of homicide. To some extent it must be an intuitive conclusion, but it does not seem too difficult to argue that those who kill, and who are going to be convicted of something, should be convicted of homicide. That, after all, is what they have done. (Adrian Briggs, "In Defence of Manslaughter," [1983] *Crim. L.R.* 764, at p. 765.)

It would shock the public's conscience to think that a person could be convicted of manslaughter absent any moral fault based on foreseeability of harm. Conversely, it might well shock the public's conscience to convict a person who has killed another only of aggravated assault — the result of requiring foreseeability of death — on the sole basis that the risk of death was not reasonably foreseeable. The terrible consequence of death demands more. In short, the *mens rea* requirement which the common law has adopted — foreseeability of harm — is entirely appropriate to the stigma associated with the offence of manslaughter. To change the *mens rea* requirement would be to risk the very disparity between *mens rea* and stigma of which the appellant complains.

I come then to the second factor mentioned in *Martineau*, the relationship between the punishment for the offence and the *mens rea* requirement. Here again, the offence of manslaughter stands in sharp contrast to the offence of murder. Murder entails a mandatory life sentence; manslaughter carries with it no minimum sentence. This is appropriate. Because manslaughter can occur in a wide variety of circumstances, the penalties must be flexible. An unintentional killing while committing a minor offence, for example, properly attracts a much lighter sentence than an unintentional killing where the circumstances indicate an awareness of risk of death just short of what would be required to infer the intent required for murder. The point is, the sentence can be and is tailored to suit the degree of moral fault of the offender. This Court acknowledged this in *Martineau*, at p. 647:

> The more flexible sentencing scheme under a conviction for manslaughter is in accord with the principle that punishment be meted out with regard to the level of moral blameworthiness of the offender.

It follows that the sentence attached to manslaughter does not require elevation of the degree of *mens rea* for the offence.

This brings me to the third factor relating to the gravity of the offence set out in *Martineau*, the principle that those causing harm intentionally must be punished more severely than those causing harm unintentionally. As noted, this principle is strictly observed in the case of manslaughter. It is by definition an unintentional crime. Accordingly, the penalties imposed are typically less than for its intentional counterpart, murder.

I conclude that the standard of *mens rea* required for manslaughter is appropriately tailored to the seriousness of the offence.

Symmetry Between the Element of Fault and the Consequences of the Offence

The Chief Justice correctly observes that the criminal law has traditionally aimed at symmetry between the *mens rea* and the prohibited consequences of the offence. The *actus reus* generally consists of an act bringing about a prohibited consequence, e.g. death. Criminal law theory suggests that the accompanying *mens rea* must go to the prohibited consequence. The moral fault of the accused lies in the act of bringing about that consequence. The Chief Justice reasons from this proposition that since manslaughter is an offence involving the prohibited act of killing another, a *mens rea* of foreseeability of harm is insufficient; what is required is foreseeability of death.

The conclusion that the offence of manslaughter is unconstitutional because it does not require appreciation of the consequential risk of death rests on two propositions: (1) that risk of bodily harm is appreciably different from risk of death in the context of manslaughter; and (2) that the principle of absolute symmetry between *mens rea* and each consequence of a criminal offence is not only a general rule of criminal law, but a principle of fundamental justice which sets a constitutional minimum. In my view, neither of these propositions is free from doubt.

I turn first to the distinction between appreciation of the risk of bodily harm and the risk of death in the context of manslaughter. In my view, when the risk of bodily harm is combined with the established rule that a wrongdoer must take his victim as he finds him and the fact that death did in fact occur, the distinction disappears. The accused who asserts that the risk of death was not foreseeable is in effect asserting that a normal person would not have died in these circumstances, and that he could not foresee the peculiar vulnerability of the victim. Therefore, he says, he should be convicted only of assault causing bodily harm or some lesser offence. This is to abrogate the thin-skull rule that requires that the wrong-doer take his victim as he finds him [*sic*]. Conversely, to combine the test of reasonable foreseeability of bodily harm with the thin-skull rule is to mandate that in some cases, foreseeability of the risk of bodily harm alone will properly result in a conviction for manslaughter.

What the appellant asks us to do, then, is to abandon the "thin-skull" rule. It is this rule which, on analysis, is alleged to be unjust. Such a conclusion I cannot accept. The law has consistently set its face against such a policy. It decrees that the aggressor must take his victim as he finds him [*sic*]. Lord Ellenborough C.J. discussed the principle nearly two centuries ago:

> He who deals in a perilous article must be wary how he deals, otherwise, if he observe not proper caution, he will be responsible.... [I]t [is] an universal principle, that when a man is charged with doing an act, of which the probable consequence may be highly injurious, the intention is an inference of law resulting from the doing the act.... (*R. v. Dixon* (1814), 3 M. & S. 11, 105 E.R. 516, at p. 517; approved, *per* Blackburn J., *R. v. Hicklin* (1868), L.R. 3 Q.B. 360, at p. 375, and *per* Amphlett J.A., *R. v. Aspinall* (1876), 2 Q.B.D. 48, at p. 65.)

Stephen J. illustrated the principle in similar fashion in *R. v. Serné* (1887), 16 Cox 311, at p. 313:

> ...when a person began doing wicked acts for his own base purposes, he risked his own life as well as that of others. That kind of crime does not differ in any serious degree from one committed by using a deadly weapon, such as a bludgeon, a pistol, or a knife. If a man once begins attacking the human body in such a way, he must take the consequences if he goes further than he intended when he began.

The principle that if one engages in criminal behaviour, one is responsible for any unforeseen actions stemming from the unlawful act, has been a well-established tenet for most of this century in Canada, the U.S. and the U.K.: G. A. Martin, "Case Comment on *R. v. Larkin*" (1943), 21 *Can. Bar Rev.* 503, at pp. 504–5; *Smithers v. The Queen*, [1978] 1 S.C.R. 506; *R. v. Cole* (1981), 64 C.C.C. (2d) 119, at p. 127 (Ont. C.A.) (Lacourciere J.A.); *R. v. Tennant, supra*, at pp. 96–97; *R. v. Lelievre*, [1962] O.R. 522, at p. 529 (C.A.) (Laidlaw J.A.); *R. v. Adkins, supra*, at pp. 349–56; *R. v. Cato* (1975), 62 Cr. App. R. 41 (C.A.); *Director of Public Prosecutions v. Newbury* (1976), 62 Cr. App. R. 291 (H.L.); see also *R. v. Fraser* (1984), 16 C.C.C. (3d) 250, at pp. 256–57 (N.S.C.A.) (Jones J.A.); W.R. LaFave and A.W. Scott, *Substantive Criminal Law*, vol. 2 (1986), at pp.

286–99. For the American position, see *United States v. Robertson*, 19 C.M.R. 102 (1955) (C.M.A.); *Tucker v. Commonwealth*, 303 Ky. 864 (1947); *Nelson v. State*, 58 Ga. App. 243 (1938); *Rutledge v. State*, 41 Ariz. 48 (1932).

In *Smithers v. The Queen, supra*, at pp. 521–22, Dickson J., writing for a unanimous Court, confirmed this principle:

> It is a well-recognized principle that one who assaults another must take his victim as he finds him....
>
> Although causation in civil cases differs from that in a criminal case, the "thin skulled man" may appear in the criminal law as in the civil law.... Even if the unlawful act, alone, would not have caused the death, it was still a legal cause so long as it contributed in some way to the death.

The thin-skull rule is a good and useful principle. It requires aggressors, once embarked on their dangerous course of conduct which may foreseeably injure others, to take responsibility for all the consequences that ensue, even to death. That is not, in my view, contrary to fundamental justice. Yet the consequence of adopting the amendment proposed by the Chief Justice would be to abrogate this principle in cases of manslaughter.

In fact, when manslaughter is viewed in the context of the thin-skull principle, the disparity diminishes between the *mens rea* of the offence and its consequence. The law does not posit the average victim. It says the aggressor must take the victim as he finds him [*sic*]. Wherever there is a risk of harm, there is also a practical risk that some victims may die as a result of the harm. At this point, the test of harm and death merge.

The second assumption inherent in the argument based on symmetry between *mens rea* and each consequence of the offence is that this is not only a general rule of criminal law, but a principle of fundamental justice — a basic constitutional requirement. I agree that as a general rule the *mens rea* of an offence relates to the consequences prohibited by the offence. As I stated in *R. v. Theroux*, [1993] 2 S.C.R. 5, at p. 17 "[t]ypically, *mens rea* is concerned with the consequences of the prohibited *actus reus*." Yet our criminal law contains important exceptions to this ideal of perfect symmetry. The presence of these exceptions suggests that the rule of symmetry is just that — a rule — to which there are exceptions. If this is so, then the rule cannot be elevated to the status of a principle of fundamental justice which must, by definition, have universal application.

It is important to distinguish between criminal law theory, which seeks the ideal of absolute symmetry between *actus reus* and *mens rea*, and the constitutional requirements of the *Charter*. As the Chief Justice has stated several times, "the Constitution does not always guarantee the 'ideal'" (*R. v. Lippe*, [1991] 2 S.C.R. 114, at p. 142; *R. v. Wholesale Travel Group Inc.*, [1991] 3 S.C.R. 154, at p. 186; *R. v. Finlay*, [1993] 3 S.C.R. 103, released concurrently, at p. 114).

I know of no authority for the proposition that the *mens rea* of an offence must always attach to the precise consequence which is prohibited as a matter of constitutional necessity. The relevant constitutional principles have been cast more broadly. No person can be sent to prison without *mens rea*, or a guilty mind, and the seriousness of the offence must not be disproportionate to the degree of moral fault. Provided an element of mental fault or moral culpability is present, and provided that it is proportionate to the seriousness and consequences of the offence charged, the principles of fundamental justice are satisfied.

The principles of fundamental justice, viewed thus, empower Parliament to recognize that, notwithstanding the same level of moral fault, some offences may be more or less serious, depending on the consequences of the culpable act. As Macdonald J.A. put it in *R. v. Brooks* (1988), 41 C.C.C. (3d) 157 (B.C.C.A.), at p. 161:

> Our criminal law has always recognized that the consequences of an unlawful act may affect the degree of culpability. The most noteworthy examples are attempts. They are always regarded less seriously than commission of the full offence. But the moral blameworthiness is identical. (Not absolute symmetry.)

Thus it cannot be said that the law in all circumstances insists on absolute symmetry between the *mens rea* and the consequences of the offence. Sometimes it does not insist on the consequences at all, as in crimes of attempts. Sometimes, as in unlawful act manslaughter, it elevates the crime by reason of its serious consequences while leaving the mental element the same.

Just as it would offend fundamental justice to punish a person who did not intend to kill for murder, so it would equally offend common notions of justice to acquit a person who has killed another of manslaughter and find him guilty instead of aggravated assault on the ground that death, as opposed to harm, was not foreseeable. Consequences can be important. As Sopinka J. put it in *R. v. DeSousa* (at pp. 966–67):

> No principle of fundamental justice prevents Parliament from treating crimes with certain consequences as more serious than crimes which lack those consequences.
>
> ...
>
> Conduct may fortuitously result in more or less serious consequences depending on the circumstances in which the consequences arise. The same act of assault may injure one person but not another. The implicit rationale of the law in this area is that it is acceptable to distinguish between criminal responsibility for equally reprehensible acts on the basis of the harm that is actually caused. This is reflected in the creation of higher maximum penalties for offences with more serious consequences. Courts and legislators acknowledge the harm actually caused by concluding that in otherwise equal cases a more serious consequence will dictate a more serious response.

Thus when considering the constitutionality of the requirement of foreseeability of bodily harm, the question is not whether the general rule of symmetry between *mens rea* and the consequences prohibited by the offence is met, but rather whether the fundamental principle of justice is satisfied that the gravity and blameworthiness of an offence must be commensurate with the moral fault engaged by that offence. Fundamental justice does not require absolute symmetry between moral fault and the prohibited consequences. Consequences, or the absence of consequences, can properly affect the seriousness with which Parliament treats specified conduct.

Policy Considerations

I have suggested that jurisprudential and historic considerations confirm a test for the *mens rea* of manslaughter based on foreseeability of the risk of bodily injury, rather than death. I have also argued that the considerations of the gravity of the offence and symmetry between the *mens rea* of the offence and its consequences do not entail the conclusion that the offence of manslaughter as it has been historically defined in terms of foreseeability of the risk of bodily harm is unconstitutional. It is my view that policy considerations support the same conclusion. In looking at whether a long-standing offence violates the principles of fundamental justice it is not amiss, in my view, to look at such considerations.

First, the need to deter dangerous conduct which may injure others and in fact may kill the peculiarly vulnerable supports the view that death need not be objectively foreseeable, only bodily injury. To tell people that if they embark on dangerous conduct which foreseeably may cause bodily harm which is neither trivial or transient, and which in fact results in death, they will not be held responsible for the death but only for aggravated assault, is less likely to deter such conduct than a message that they will be held responsible for the death, albeit under manslaughter not murder. Given the finality of death and the absolute unacceptability of killing another human being, it is not amiss to preserve the test which promises the greatest measure of deterrence, provided the penal consequences of the offence are not disproportionate. This is achieved by retaining the test of foreseeability of bodily harm in the offence of manslaughter.

Second, retention of the test based on foreseeability of bodily harm accords best with our sense of justice. I have earlier alluded to the view, attested to by the history of the offence of manslaughter, that causing the death of another through negligence or a dangerous unlawful act should be met by a special sanction reflecting the fact that a death occurred, even though death was not objectively foreseeable. This is supported by the sentiment that a person who engages in dangerous conduct that breaches the bodily integrity of another and puts that person at risk may properly be held responsible for an unforeseen death attributable to that person's peculiar vulnerability; the aggressor takes the victim as he finds him. The criminal law must reflect not only the concerns of the accused, but the concerns of the victim and, where the victim is killed, the concerns of society for the victim's fate. Both go into the equation of justice.

Finally, the traditional test founded on foreseeability of the risk of bodily harm provides, in my belief, a workable test which avoids troubling judges and juries about the fine distinction between foreseeability of the risk of bodily injury and foreseeability of the risk of death — a distinction which, as argued earlier, reduces to a formalistic technicality when put in the context of the thin-skull rule and the fact that death has in fact been inflicted by the accused's dangerous act. The traditional common law test permits a principled approach to the offence which meets the concerns of society, provides fairness to the accused, and facilitates a just and workable trial process.

. . . .

THE NATURE OF THE OBJECTIVE TEST

I respectfully differ from the Chief Justice on the nature of the objective test used to determine the *mens rea* for crimes of negligence. In my view, the approach advocated by the Chief Justice personalizes the objective test to the point where it devolves into a subjective test, thus eroding the minimum standard of care which Parliament has laid down by the enactment of offences of manslaughter and penal negligence.

. . . .

It is now established that a person may be held criminally responsible for negligent conduct on the objective test, and that this alone does not violate the principle of fundamental justice that the moral fault of the accused must be commensurate with the gravity of the offence and its penalty: *R. v. Hundal*, [1993] 1 S.C.R. 867.

However, as stated in *Martineau*, it is appropriate that those who cause harm intentionally should be punished more severely than those who cause harm inadvertently. Moreover, the constitutionality of crimes of negligence is also subject to the caveat that acts of ordinary negligence may not suffice to justify imprisonment: *R. v. City of Sault Ste. Marie*, [1978] 2 S.C.R. 1299; *R. v. Sansregret*, [1985] 1 S.C.R. 570. To put it in the terms used in *Hundal*, the negligence must constitute a "marked departure" from the standard of the reasonable person. The law does not lightly brand a person as criminal. For this reason, I am in agreement with the Chief Justice in *R. v. Finlay, supra*, that the word "careless" in an underlying firearms offence must be read as requiring a marked departure from the constitutional norm.

It follows from this requirement, affirmed in *Hundal*, that in an offence based on unlawful conduct, a predicate offence involving carelessness or negligence must also be read as requiring a *marked departure* from the standard of the reasonable person. As pointed out in *DeSousa*, the underlying offence must be constitutionally sound.

To this point, the Chief Justice and I are not, as I perceive it, in disagreement. The difference between our approaches turns on the extent to which personal characteristics of the accused may affect liability under the objective test. Here we enter territory in large part uncharted. To date, debate has focused on whether an objective test for *mens rea* is ever available in the criminal law; little has been said about how, assuming it is applicable, it is to be applied. In *R. v. Hundal, supra*, it was said that the *mens rea* of dangerous driving should be assessed objectively in the context of all the events surrounding the incident. But the extent to which those circumstances include personal mental or psychological frailties of the accused was not explored in depth. In these circumstances, we must begin with the fundamental principles of criminal law.

Underlying Principles

The debate about the degree to which personal characteristics should be reflected in the objective test for fault in offences of penal negligence engages two fundamental concepts of criminal law.

The first concept is the notion that the criminal law may properly hold people who engage in risky activities to a minimum standard of care, judged by what a reasonable person in all the circumstances would have done. This notion posits a uniform standard for all persons engaging in the activity, regardless of their background, education or psychological disposition.

The second concept is the principle that the morally innocent not be punished (*Re B.C. Motor Vehicle Act*, [1985] 2 S.C.R. 486, at p. 513; *R. v. Gosset*, [1993] 3 S.C.R. 76, reasons of Lamer C.J. at p. 93). This principle is the foundation of the requirement of criminal law that the accused must have a guilty mind, or *mens rea*.

I agree with the Chief Justice that the rule that the morally innocent not be punished in the context of the objective test requires that the law refrain from holding a person criminally responsible if he or she is not capable of appreciating the risk. Where I differ from the Chief Justice is in his designation of the sort of educational, experiential and so-called "habitual" factors personal to the accused which can be taken into account. The Chief Justice, while in principle advocating a uniform standard of care for all, in the result seems to contemplate a standard of care which varies with the background and predisposition of each accused. Thus an inexperienced, uneducated, young person, like the accused in *R. v. Naglik*, [1993] 3 S.C.R. 22, could be acquitted, even though she does not meet the standard of the reasonable person (reasons of the Lamer C.J., at pp. 145–46). On the other hand, a person with special experience, like Mr. Creighton in this case, or the appellant police officer in *R. v. Gosset, supra*, will be held to a higher standard than the ordinary reasonable person.

I must respectfully dissent from this extension of the objective test for criminal fault. In my view, considerations of principle and policy dictate the maintenance of a single, uniform legal standard of care for such offences, subject to one exception: incapacity to appreciate the nature of the risk which the activity in question entails.

This principle that the criminal law will not convict the morally innocent does not, in my view, require consideration of personal factors short of incapacity. The criminal law, while requiring mental fault as an element of a conviction, has steadfastly rejected the idea that a person's personal characteristics can (short of incapacity) excuse the person from meeting the standard of conduct imposed by the law.

. . . .

In summary, I can find no support in criminal theory for the conclusion that protection of the morally innocent requires a general consideration of individual excusing conditions. The principle comes into play only at the point where the person is shown to lack the capacity to appreciate the nature and quality or the consequences of his or her acts. Apart from this, we are all, rich and poor, wise and naive, held to the minimum standards of conduct prescribed by the criminal law. This conclusion is dictated by a fundamental proposition of social organization. As Justice Oliver Wendell Holmes wrote in *The Common Law* (1881), at p. 108: "when men live in society, a certain average of conduct, a sacrifice of individual peculiarities going beyond a certain point, is necessary to the general welfare."

The ambit of the principle that the morally innocent shall not be convicted has developed in large part in the context of crimes of subjective fault — crimes where the accused must be shown to have actually intended or foreseen the consequences of his or her conduct. In crimes of this type, personal characteristics of the accused have been held to be relevant only to the extent that they tend to prove or disprove an element of the offence. Since intention or knowledge of the risk is an element of such offences, personal factors can come into play. But beyond this, personal characteristics going to lack of capacity are considered under the introductory sections of the *Code* defining the conditions of criminal responsibility and have generally been regarded as irrelevant.

. . . .

I digress at this point to consider in more detail the concept of incapacity to appreciate the risk attendant on one's conduct. It may be that this is the real point of divergence between the Chief Justice's views and those which I have attempted to articulate. The Chief Justice moves from the proposition that incapacity to appreciate the risk of the activity in question should serve as a defence, which I accept, to the conclusion that the standard of care applicable in a particular case should be moved up or down, according to the educational, experiential and other "habitual" characteristics of the accused. Some of the language employed suggests that all the accused's personal characteristics — not only those related to incapacity to assess the risk — should be considered in determining whether he or she is guilty. The Chief Justice refers, for example to the test of "a reasonable person who possesses all of the accused's limitations" (p. 31), and to "the reasonable person with the accused's make-up" (p. 31). These conclusions and statements, it seems to me, go far beyond incapacity to appreciate the risk entailed by particular conduct, to suggest a broader, actor-oriented approach to criminal liability which this Court has repeatedly disavowed.

. . . .

It may be that in some cases educational deficiencies, such as illiteracy on the part of a person handling a marked bottle of nitroglycerine in the Chief Justice's example, may preclude a person from being able to appreciate the risk entailed by his or her conduct. Problems of perception may have the same effect; regardless of the care taken, the person would have been incapable of assessing the risk, and hence been acquitted. But, in practice, such cases will arise only exceptionally. The question of *mens rea* will arise only where it has been shown that the accused's conduct (the *actus reus*) constitutes a dangerous and unlawful act (as in unlawful act manslaughter), or a marked departure from the standard of care of a reasonably prudent person (as in manslaughter by criminal negligence, or penal negligence offences). This established, conflict with the prohibition against punishing the morally innocent will arise only rarely. In unregulated activities, ordinary common sense is usually sufficient to permit anyone who directs his or her mind to the risk of the danger inherent in an activity to appreciate that risk and act accordingly — be the activity bottle throwing (as in *R. v. DeSousa*) or a barroom brawl. In many licensed activities, such as driving motor vehicles, there must be a basic amount of knowledge and experience before permission to engage in that activity will be granted (see *R. v. Hundal*). Where individuals engage in activities for which they lack sufficient knowledge, experience, or physical ability, they may be properly found to be at fault, not so much for their inability to properly carry out the activity, but for their decision to attempt the activity without having accounted for their deficiencies. The law expects people embarking on hazardous activities to ask questions or seek help before they venture beyond their depth. Thus even the inexperienced defendant may be properly found to be morally blameworthy for having embarked on a dangerous venture without taking the trouble to properly inform himself or herself. The criminal law imposes a single minimum standard which must be met by all people engaging in the activity in question, provided that they enjoy the requisite capacity to appreciate the danger, and judged in all the circumstances of the case, including unforeseen events and reasonably accepted misinformation. Without a constant minimum standard, the duty imposed by the law would be eroded and the criminal sanction trivialized.

Mental disabilities short of incapacity generally do not suffice to negative criminal liability for criminal negligence. The explanations for why a person fails to advert to the risk inherent in the activity he or she is undertaking are legion. They range from simple absent-mindedness to attributes related to age, education and culture. To permit such a subjective assessment would be "co-extensive with the judgment of each individual, which would be as variable as the length of the foot of each individual" leaving "so vague a line as to afford no rule at all, the degree of judgment belonging to each individual being infinitely various": *Vaughan v. Menlove* (1837), 3 Bing. (N.C.) 468, 132 E.R. 490, at p. 475; see A.M. Linden, *Canadian Tort Law* (4th ed. 1988), at pp. 116–17. Provided the capacity to appreciate the risk is present, lack of education and psychological predispositions serve as no excuse for criminal conduct, although they may be important factors to consider in sentencing.

. . . .

The foregoing analysis suggests the following line of inquiry in cases of penal negligence. The first question is whether *actus reus* is established. This requires that the negligence constitute a marked departure from the standards of the reasonable person in all the circumstances of the case. This may consist in carrying out the activity in a dangerous fashion, or in embarking on the activity when in all the circumstances it is dangerous to do so.

The next question is whether the *mens rea* is established. As is the case with crimes of subjective *mens rea*, the *mens rea* for objective foresight of risking harm is normally inferred from the facts. The standard is that of the reasonable person in the circumstances of the accused. If a person has committed a manifestly dangerous act, it is reasonable, absent indications to the contrary, to infer that he or she failed to direct his or her mind to the risk and the need to take care. However, the normal inference may be negated by evidence raising a reasonable doubt as to lack of capacity to appreciate the risk. Thus, if a *prima facie* case for *actus reus* and *mens rea* are made out, it is necessary to ask a further question: did the accused possess the requisite capacity to appreciate the risk flowing from his conduct? If this further question is answered in the affirmative, the necessary moral fault is established and the accused is properly convicted. If not, the accused must be acquitted.

APPLICATION OF THE LAW TO THIS APPEAL

The trial judge properly found that Mr. Creighton committed the unlawful act of trafficking in cocaine. He also found that he was guilty of criminal negligence, using the standard which I view as correct, the standard of the reasonable person. The only remaining question, on the view I take of the law, was whether the reasonable person in all the circumstances would have foreseen the risk of bodily harm. I am satisfied that the answer to this question must be affirmative. At the very least, a person administering a dangerous drug like cocaine to another has a duty to inform himself as to the precise risk the injection entails and to refrain from administering it unless reasonably satisfied that there was no risk of harm. That was not the case here, as the trial judge found.

The conviction was properly entered and should not be disturbed. Like the Chief Justice, I find it unnecessary to consider the alternative ground of manslaughter by criminal negligence.

I would answer the constitutional question in the negative and dismiss the appeal.

■

Justices Lamer, Sopinka, Iacobucci, and Major dissented, arguing that, given the stigma associated with a conviction for manslaughter, it was more in keeping with the constitutional requirements of s. 7 of the *Charter* to require proof that death (as opposed to bodily harm) was a foreseeable risk of the accused's conduct. As well, they urged that the objective test be tempered by human frailties, including personal characteristics, that affected the accused's capacity to appreciate the risk created by the conduct. However, on the facts in *Creighton*, they agreed that no injustice had been done, since the accused was an experienced user of cocaine who acknowledged his own awareness of the risk of death. Justice La Forest's judgment determined the outcome in this case. Although he expressed a personal preference for subjectivizing the test, he considered the Court bound by its decision in *R. v. DeSousa*, *infra* and therefore concurred in Justice McLachlin's decision.

The Supreme Court in *R. v. Beatty*, [2008] S.C.J. No. 5, affirmed the use of the modified objective test, whereby the accused's culpability is assessed against the knowledge and conduct of a reasonably prudent person in the same circumstances faced by the accused, for penal negligence offences such as dangerous driving. Here the accused's acquittal at trial was restored by the Court because the conduct of the accused in crossing the centre line and killing three people in an oncoming vehicle did not amount to a marked departure from the reasonably prudent driver: "The trial judge appropriately focussed her analysis on Mr. Beatty's manner of driving in all the circumstances. She noted that there was no evidence of improper driving before the truck momentarily crossed the centre line and that the "few seconds of clearly negligent driving" was the only evidence about his manner of driving ... She appropriately considered the totality of the evidence in finding that "the only reasonable inference" was that "he experienced a loss of awareness" that caused him to drive straight instead of following the curve in the road ... In her view, this momentary lapse of attention was insufficient to found criminal culpability. She concluded that there was "insufficient evidence to support a finding of a marked departure from the standard of care of a prudent driver" (at para 52).

Now compare the result in *Creighton* to that achieved in *R. v. Browne* (1997), 33 O.R. (3d) 775 (C.A.). In this case the accused, 22 years old and the deceased, Audrey Greiner, 19 years old, were friends and drug dealers. At 11:30 p.m. on the night of Greiner's death, they had been searched by police, and she had swallowed a bag of cocaine to avoid detection. She was unable to regurgitate the drugs, and Browne took her to sleep at his family's home. At 2:00 a.m., when she became obviously ill, he promised to take her to a hospital. Instead of calling 911, he called a taxi. By the time she was admitted at 3:10 a.m., she was dead. At trial, Browne was convicted of criminal negligence causing death on the basis of an omission, failure to perform an undertaking, contrary to s. 217 of the *Code*. On appeal, Justice Abella wrote on behalf of the three justices and allowed the appeal and entered an acquittal. Noting that s. 215 creates duties where certain kinds of relationships exist, for example, parents and children, spouses, and dependents and their caregivers, she ruled that s. 217 requires an undertaking that is "clearly made" with "binding intent" before penal consequences can be imposed. Abella J. was unwilling to impute an implicit undertaking to care for each other in emergencies, and she found that Browne's promise to take Greiner to the hospital at 2:00 a.m. did not constitute a clear and binding undertaking. She also stated that he did fulfill his promise, and that there had been no evidence to prove that an ambulance trip would have saved her life. Do you agree with this decision? Note that while Creighton was convicted of manslaughter, Browne was acquitted. Given the similar activities engaged in by both accused, can this different treatment be justified legally or morally? See also the omissions cases discussed above, under ***Actus Reus***.

The use of the objective test and its constitutionality have been affirmed for the following offences:

- Failure to provide necessaries of life, s. 215(2)(a)(ii): In *R. v. Naglik*, [1993] 3 S.C.R. 122, the Supreme Court held that the Crown must prove that the circumstances giving rise to the duty in s. 215(2)(a)(ii) were objectively foreseeable to the reasonably prudent parent, and that while the specific circumstances facing the parent may be considered in this assessment, the accused's personal characteristics, such as youth, inexperience, or lack of education, are to be excluded unless the accused lacked the **capacity** to appreciate the risk.
- Dangerous driving, s. 249(1),(4): In *R. v. Hundal*, [1993] 1 S.C.R. 867, the Court ruled that the fault element is to be tested objectively, in the circumstances or context facing the accused, to ascertain whether the accused's conduct constituted a marked departure from the standard of care that a reasonable driver would have employed. The Court acknowledged that, for instance, an accused who experienced a sudden onset of illness or who experienced a reaction to a medication might be acquitted pursuant to this modified objective approach. In support

of the objective test, Justice Cory referred to the fact that driving is a regulated activity for which the accused is obliged to meet objective standards of safe driving, that driving is often reflexive, and not conducive to a minute examination of a driver's thought processes at a given moment, that the language of the offence suggests an objective test, and that the statistics on driving accidents suggest that it is an urgent problem requiring a realistic proof requirement for the Crown.

- Careless storage or use of a firearm, s. 86(2): In *R. v. Gosset*, [1993] 3 S.C.R. 76; *R. v. Finlay*, [1993] 3 S.C.R. 103; and *R. v. Durham* (1992), 10 O.R. (3d) 596 (C.A.), the courts concluded that the fault element of "carelessness" is to be tested objectively, but that to amount to a criminal offence, it must constitute a marked departure from the standard of care of the reasonable person. These decisions are significant in that two of them were unlawful act manslaughter prosecutions based on police misuse of their weapons: Gosset was tried on charges of unlawful act manslaughter for killing Anthony Griffin, and Durham and Stratigeas were being tried for shooting Wade Lawson (see Abell & Sheehy, *Cases, Context, Critique*, **Policing**).

D. WILFUL IGNORANCE

The mental element of wilful ignorance (or "blindness" as the judges often call it) is made out where the accused suspects that certain facts exist or that a certain consequence may ensue, but deliberately refuses to consider or acknowledge the risk. This *mens rea* is not specified in the *Code*, but may be read in by the courts as simply another form of proof of recklessness. Although theoretically it is tested subjectively, this is not necessarily the case in fact: see *R. v. Sansregret*, below, under **Mistake of Fact**. Another example of the doctrine of wilful blindness is provided by *R. v. Blondin* (1970), 2 C.C.C. (2d) 118 (B.C.C.A.) where the accused was apprehended by Customs with a scuba tank that was judged to be unusually heavy. The officers attempted to remove the valve system but had to take the tank to a dive shop, only to discover that the tank had been cut in half in order to hide 23 pounds of hashish. The accused disclosed that he was paid to bring the tank from Japan, but refused to identify either the sender or the intended recipient. He admitted that he knew that something illegal was in the tank, but claimed not to know what it was. Upon the Crown's appeal from acquittal, the court of appeal ruled that it was an error for the judge to have told the jury that they had to find that the accused had actual knowledge that he was importing hashish: "It would be sufficient to find, in relation to a narcotic, *mens rea* in the widest sense." Thus, while the accused's belief that something illegal was in the tank was insufficient to prove his *mens rea*, he could properly be found guilty at a new trial if the jury found that he "had either been reckless about what it was or wilfully shut his eyes to what it was, and then drew the inference that he suspected that it might be a narcotic."

E. RECKLESSNESS

The *mens rea* of recklessness is made out where the accused recognizes an existing circumstance or is aware that the conduct creates a certain risk, but proceeds with this knowledge. Offences in the *Code* that use this mental element include s. 433, arson ("recklessly causes damage by fire or explosion") and s. 229(a)(ii), murder ("means to cause bodily harm that he knows is likely to cause his death, and is reckless whether death ensues or not"). In addition, the Supreme Court has noted that judges may hold that proof of a reckless state of mind is sufficient to sustain a conviction for an offence that has intention or knowledge as its mental element (*Sault Ste. Marie*, *supra* at 1309), but there are offences for which the courts are unwilling to extend the *mens rea* in this manner: *R. v. Buzzanga* (1979), 25 O.R. (2d) 705 (C.A.); compare to *Re A.C.S.*, below.

Offences that employ recklessness as the *mens rea* seem to comply with the *Charter* because this mental element is tested subjectively. Challenges to s. 229(a)(ii) on the basis that it is unconstitutional to convict for murder someone who intended to cause bodily harm, while reckless as to the likelihood of death, have thus far failed in the lower courts. See, for example, *R. v. Naldzil* (1991), 68 C.C.C. (3d) 350 (B.C.C.A.). Although the Supreme Court has not yet explicitly addressed the issue, its rulings on the minimal differences between ss. 229(a)(i) and (ii), as well as its explication of the mental element in s. 229(a)(ii), suggest that such a challenge is unlikely to succeed: *R. v. Nygaard*, [1989] 2 S.C.R. 1074; *R. v. Cooper*, [1993] 1 S.C.R. 146.

F. INTENTION OR KNOWLEDGE

Many *Code* offences specify a mental element of intention or knowledge: s. 136, fabricating evidence, requires "intent to mislead"; s. 354, possession of property obtained by crime, requires knowledge that the property was obtained wholly or in part, directly or indirectly, from an offence; and s. 229(a)(i), murder, requires proof that the accused meant to cause death to another. As well, there are offences that do not specify any mental element, but for which the courts have read in intention or knowledge as the *mens rea*: *Sault Ste. Marie*, *supra* at 1309. The element of intention or knowledge is tested subjectively.

As the *Vaillancourt* decision below illustrates, there are offences for which the courts will read in a subjectively tested *mens rea* of intention or knowledge as a **constitutional** imperative.

R. v. Vaillancourt†

[LAMER J.:]

INTRODUCTION

Vaillancourt was convicted of second degree murder following a trial before a judge and jury in Montréal. He appealed to the Quebec Court of Appeal, arguing that the judge's charge to the jury on the combined operation of ss. 213(*d*) and 21(2) of the *Criminal Code*, R.S.C. 1970, c. C-34, was incorrect. His appeal was dismissed and the conviction was affirmed: (1984), 31 C.C.C. (3d) 75. Before this Court, he has challenged the constitutional validity of s. 213(*d*) alone and in combination with s. 21(2) under the *Canadian Charter of Rights and Freedoms*.

THE FACTS

For the purposes of this appeal, the Crown does not contest the following statement of the facts.

The appellant and his accomplice committed an armed robbery in a pool hall. The appellant was armed with a knife and his accomplice with a gun. During the robbery, the appellant remained near the front of the hall while the accomplice went to the back. There was a struggle between the accomplice and a client. A shot was fired and the client was killed. The accomplice managed to escape and has never been found. The appellant was arrested at the scene.

In the course of his testimony, the appellant said that he and his accomplice had agreed to commit this robbery armed only with knives. On the night of the robbery, however, the accomplice arrived at their meeting place with a gun. The appellant said that he objected because, on a previous armed robbery, his gun had discharged accidentally, and he did not want that to happen again. He insisted that the gun be unloaded. The accomplice removed three bullets from the gun and gave them to the appellant. The appellant then went to the bathroom and placed the bullets in his glove. The glove was recovered by the police at the scene of the crime and was found

† [1987] 2 S.C.R. 636.

at trial to contain three bullets. The appellant testified that, at the time of the robbery, he was certain that the gun was unloaded.

CONSTITUTIONAL QUESTIONS

Before this Court, the following constitutional questions were formulated:

1. Is section 213(*d*) of the *Criminal Code* inconsistent with the provisions of either s. 7 or s. 11(*d*) of the *Canadian Charter of Rights and Freedoms*, and therefore, of no force or effect?
2. If not, is the combination of s. 21 and s. 213(*d*) of the *Criminal Code* inconsistent with the provisions of either s. 7 or s. 11(*d*) of the *Canadian Charter of Rights and Freedoms* and is s. 21 of the *Criminal Code* therefore of no force or effect in the case of a charge under s. 213(*d*) of the *Criminal Code*?

THE LAW

Narrowing the Issue

The appellant has framed his attack on s. 213(*d*) of the *Code* in very wide terms. He has argued that the principles of fundamental justice require that, before Parliament can impose any criminal liability for causing a particular result, there must be some degree of subjective *mens rea* in respect of that result. This is a fundamental question with far reaching consequences. If this case were decided on that basis, doubt would be cast on the constitutional validity of many provisions throughout our *Criminal Code*, in particular s. 205(5)(*a*), whereby causing death by means of an unlawful act is culpable homicide, and s. 212(*c*) whereby objective foreseeability of the likelihood of death is sufficient for a murder conviction in certain circumstances.

However, the appellant was convicted under s. 213(*d*) and the constitutional question is limited to this provision. In my opinion, the validity of s. 213(*d*) can be decided on somewhat narrower grounds. In addition, the Attorney General of Canada has seen fit not to intervene to support the constitutionality of s. 213(*d*), which is clearly in jeopardy in this case, though he may have intervened to support ss. 205(5)(*a*) and 212(*c*) and other similar provisions. I will thus endeavour not to make pronouncements the effect of which will be to predispose in *obiter* of other issues more properly dealt with if and when the constitutionality of the other provisions is in issue. I do, however, find it virtually impossible to make comments as regards s. 213(*d*) that will not have some effect on the validity of the rest of s. 213 or that will not reveal to some extent my views as regards s. 212(*c*). However, the validity of those sections and of paras. (*a*) to (*c*) of s. 213 is not in issue here and I will attempt to limit my comments to s. 213(*d*).

The appellant has also challenged the combined operation of ss. 21(2) and 213(*d*). Given my decision on the validity of s. 213(*d*) and in view of the importance of s. 21(2) and the absence of the Attorney General of Canada, I do not find it necessary or advisable to deal with s. 21(2) in this appeal.

Analysis of s. 213(d)

Section 213(d) in the Context of the Murder Provisions

It is first necessary to analyze s. 213(*d*) in the context of the other murder provisions in the *Code* in order to determine its true nature and scope. Murder is defined as a culpable homicide committed in the circumstances set out at ss. 212 and 213 of the *Code*. There is a very interesting progression through s. 212 to s. 213 with respect to the mental state that must be proven.

The starting point is s. 212(*a*)(i), which provides:

> **212.** Culpable homicide is murder
>
> (*a*) where the person who causes the death of a human being
>
> (i) means to cause his death,

This clearly requires that the accused have actual subjective foresight of the likelihood of causing the death coupled with the intention to cause that death. This is the most morally blameworthy state of mind in our system.

There is a slight relaxation of this requirement in s. 212(*a*)(ii), which provides:

> **212.** Culpable homicide is murder
>
> (*a*) where the person who causes the death of a human being
>
> ...
>
> (ii) means to cause him bodily harm that he knows is likely to cause his death, and is reckless whether death ensues or not;

Here again the accused must have actual subjective foresight of the likelihood of death. However, the Crown need no longer prove that he intended to cause the death but only that he was reckless whether death ensued or not. It should also be noted that s. 212(*a*)(ii) is limited to cases where the accused intended to cause bodily harm to the victim.

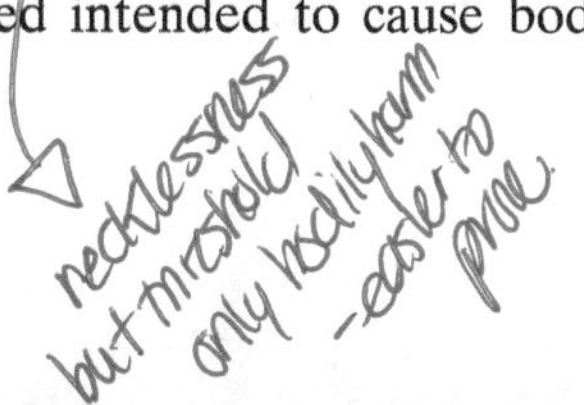

Section 212(*c*) provides:

> **212.** Culpable homicide is murder
>
> ...
>
> (*c*) where a person, for an unlawful object, does anything that he knows or ought to know is likely to cause death, and thereby causes death to a human being, notwithstanding that he desires to effect his object without causing death or bodily harm to any human being.

In part, this is simply a more general form of recklessness and thus the logical extension of s. 212(*a*)(ii), in that it applies when the accused "does *anything* that he knows ... is likely to cause death" (emphasis added). However, there is also a further relaxation of the mental element required for murder in that it is also murder where the accused "does *anything that he ... ought to know* is likely to cause death" (emphasis added). This eliminates the requirement of actual subjective foresight and replaces it with objective foreseeability or negligence.

The final relaxation in the definition of murder occurs at s. 213:

> **213.** Culpable homicide is murder where a person causes the death of a human being while committing or attempting to commit high treason or treason or an offence mentioned in section 52 (sabotage), 76 (piratical acts), 76.1 (hijacking an aircraft), 132 or subsection 133(1) or sections 134 to 136 (escape or rescue from prison or lawful custody), 143 or 145 (rape or attempt to commit rape), 149 or 156 (indecent assault), subsection 246(2) (resisting lawful arrest), 247 (kidnapping and forcible confinement), 302 (robbery), 306 (breaking and entering) or 389 or 390 (arson), whether or not the person means to cause death to any human being and whether or not he knows that death is likely to be caused to any human being, if
>
> (*a*) he means to cause bodily harm for the purpose of
>
> (i) facilitating the commission of the offence, or
>
> (ii) facilitating his flight after committing or attempting to commit the offence,
>
> and the death ensues from the bodily harm;
>
> (*b*) he administers a stupefying or overpowering thing for a purpose mentioned in paragraph (*a*), and the death ensues therefrom;
>
> (*c*) he wilfully stops, by any means, the breath of a human being for a purpose mentioned in paragraph (*a*), and the death ensues therefrom; or
>
> (*d*) he uses a weapon or has it upon his person
>
> (i) during or at the time he commits or attempts to commit the offence, or
>
> (ii) during or at the time of his flight after committing or attempting to commit the offence,
>
> and the death ensues as a consequence.

Under this provision, it is murder if the accused causes the victim's death while committing or attempting to commit one of the enumerated offences if he performs one of the acts in paras. (*a*) to (*d*). Proof that the accused performed one of the acts in paras. (*a*) to (*d*) is substituted for proof of any subjective foresight or even objective foreseeability of the likelihood of death.

I should add that there appears to be a further relaxation of the mental state when the accused is a party to the murder through s. 21(2) of the *Code* as in this case. However, as I have said, it is sufficient to deal with s. 213(*d*) in order to dispose of this appeal.

. . . .

Section 213(d) and the *Charter*

This appeal calls into play two principles of fundamental justice.

The First Principle: The Essential Elements of Certain Crimes and s. 7 of the Charter

. . . .

It has been argued that the principles of fundamental justice in s. 7 are only procedural guarantees. However, in *Re B.C. Motor Vehicle Act*, [1985] 2 S.C.R. 486, this Court rejected that argument and used s. 7 to review the substance of the legislation. As a result, while Parliament retains the power to define the elements of a crime, the courts now have the jurisdiction and, more important, the duty, when called upon to do so, to review that definition to ensure that it is in accordance with the principles of fundamental justice.

This Court's decision in *Re B.C. Motor Vehicle Act* stands for the proposition that absolute liability infringes the principles of fundamental justice, such that the combination of absolute liability and a deprivation of life, liberty or security of the person is a restriction on one's rights under s. 7 and is *prima facie* a violation thereof. In effect, *Re B.C. Motor Vehicle Act* acknowledges that, whenever the state resorts to the restriction of liberty, such as imprisonment, to assist in the enforcement of a law, even, as in *Re B.C. Motor Vehicle Act*, a mere provincial regulatory offence, there is, as a principle of fundamental justice, a minimum mental state which is an essential element of the offence. It thus elevated *mens rea* from a presumed element in *Sault Ste.*

Marie, supra, to a constitutionally required element. *Re B. C. Motor Vehicle Act* did not decide what level of *mens rea* was constitutionally required for each type of offence, but inferentially decided that even for a mere provincial regulatory offence *at least* negligence was required, in that *at least* a defence of due diligence must *always* be open to an accused who risks imprisonment upon conviction. In *Sault Ste. Marie*, Dickson J. stated at pp. 1309–10:

> Where the offence is criminal, the Crown must establish a mental element, namely, that the accused who committed the prohibited act did so intentionally or recklessly, with knowledge of the facts constituting the offence, or with wilful blindness toward them. Mere negligence is excluded from the concept of the mental element required for conviction. Within the context of a criminal prosecution a person who fails to make such enquiries as a reasonable and prudent person would make, or who fails to know facts he should have known, is innocent in the eyes of the law.

It may well be that, as a general rule, the principles of fundamental justice require proof of a subjective *mens rea* with respect to the prohibited act, in order to avoid punishing the "morally innocent." It must be remembered, however, that Dickson J. was dealing with the *mens rea* to be presumed in the absence of an express legislative disposition, and not the *mens rea* to be required in all legislation providing for a restriction on the accused's life, liberty or security of the person. In any event, this case involves criminal liability for the result of an intentional criminal act, and it is arguable that different considerations should apply to the mental element required with respect to that result. There are many provisions in the *Code* requiring only objective foreseeability of the result or even only a causal link between the act and the result. As I would prefer not to cast doubt on the validity of such provisions *in this case*, I will assume, but only for the purposes of this appeal, that something less than subjective foresight of the result may, sometimes, suffice for the imposition of criminal liability for causing that result through intentional criminal conduct.

But, whatever the minimum *mens rea* for the act or the result may be, there are, though very few in number, certain crimes where, because of the special nature of the stigma attached to a conviction therefor or the available penalties, the principles of fundamental justice require a *mens rea* reflecting the particular nature of that crime. Such is theft, where, in my view, a conviction requires proof of some dishonesty. Murder is another such offence. The punishment for murder is the most severe in our society and the stigma that attaches to a conviction for murder is similarly extreme. In addition, murder is distinguished from manslaughter only by the mental element with respect to the death. It is thus clear that there must be some special mental element with respect to the death before a culpable homicide can be treated as a murder. That special mental element gives rise to the moral blameworthiness which justifies the stigma and sentence attached to a murder conviction. I am presently of the view that it is a principle of fundamental justice that a conviction for murder cannot rest on anything less than proof beyond a reasonable doubt of subjective foresight. Given the effect of this view on part of s. 212(*c*), for the reasons I have already given for deciding this case more narrowly, I need not and will not rest my finding that s. 213(*d*) violates the *Charter* on this view, because s. 213(*d*) does not, for reasons I will set out hereinafter, even meet the lower threshold test of objective foreseeability. I will therefore, for the sole purpose of this appeal, go no further than say that it is a principle of fundamental justice that, absent proof beyond a reasonable doubt of at least objective foreseeability, there surely cannot be a murder conviction.

[The discussion of s. 11(d) of the *Charter* has been omitted.]

Application of the Principles to s. 213

The *mens rea* required for s. 213 consists of the *mens rea* for the underlying offence and the intent to commit one of the acts set forth in paras. (*a*) to (*d*) (*Swietlinski v. The Queen*, [1980] 2 S.C.R. 956). Section 213 does not impose on the accused the burden of disproving objective foreseeability. Further, it does not completely exclude the need to prove any objective foreseeability. Rather, s. 213 has substituted for proof beyond a reasonable doubt of objective foreseeability, if that is the essential element, proof beyond a reasonable doubt of certain forms of intentional dangerous conduct causing death.

The question is, therefore, can Parliament make this substitution without violating ss. 7 and 11(*d*)? As I have discussed earlier, if Parliament frames the section so that, upon proof of the conduct, it would be unreasonable for a jury not to conclude beyond a reasonable doubt that the accused ought to have known that death was likely to ensue, then I think that Parliament has enacted a crime which is tantamount to one which has objective foreseeability as an essential element, and, if objective foreseeability is sufficient, then it would not be in violation of s. 7

or s. 11(*d*) in doing so in that way. The acid test of the constitutionality of s. 213 is this ultimate question: *Would it be possible for a conviction for murder to occur under s. 213 despite the jury having a reasonable doubt as to whether the accused ought to have known that death was likely to ensue?* If the answer is yes, then the section is *prima facie* in violation of ss. 7 and 11(*d*). I should add in passing that if the answer is no, then it would be necessary to decide whether objective foreseeability is sufficient for a murder conviction. However, because in my view the answer is yes and because I do not want to pass upon the constitutionality of s. 212(*c*) in this case, I will not address that issue.

To varying degrees it can be said that in almost any case a jury satisfied beyond a reasonable doubt that an accused has done one of the prohibited acts described in paras. (*a*) to (*d*) will be satisfied beyond a reasonable doubt that the accused ought to have known that death was likely to be caused. But not always. Indeed, as a first example, drunkenness would under certain circumstances leave the jury in doubt in that regard. The rule as regards the effect of drunkenness on objective foreseeability was unanimously laid down by this Court in *R. v. Vasil*, [1981] 1 S.C.R. 469, a murder prosecution under s. 212(*c*). This Court addressed the issue at some length and then summarized its conclusion as follows, *per* Lamer J. at pp. 500–501:

> (5) Whilst the test under 212(*c*) is objective and the behaviour of the accused is to be measured by that of the reasonable man, such a test must nevertheless be applied having regard, not to the knowledge a reasonable man would have had of the surrounding circumstances that allegedly made the accused's conduct dangerous to life, but to the knowledge the accused had of those circumstances;
>
> (6) As a result, drunkenness, though not relevant in the determination of what a reasonable man, with the knowledge the accused had of those circumstances, would have anticipated, is relevant in the determination of the knowledge which the accused had of those circumstances.

It is clear to me that under s. 213 as drafted there will be cases where the effect of drunkenness on an accused's knowledge of the circumstances would leave a jury with a reasonable doubt as to whether the accused ought to have known of the likelihood of death ensuing, even though it has been proven beyond a reasonable doubt that the accused actually did one of the acts described under paras. (*a*) to (*d*).

A second example, and this case amply illustrates the point, is the accused who is brought into s. 213 not as a principal but through the operation of s. 21(2) of the *Criminal Code*. In *R. v. Trinneer*, [1970] S.C.R. 638, this Court had the opportunity to consider the combined operation of ss. 21(2) and 213 (s. 202 at the time). Cartwright C.J., delivering the judgment of the Court, stated at pp. 645–46:

> At the risk of repetition, it is my opinion that on the true construction of s. 202 and s. 21(2) as applied to the circumstances of this case it was necessary to support a verdict of guilty against the respondent that the Crown should establish (i) that it was in fact a probable consequence of the prosecution of the common purpose of the respondent and Frank to rob Mrs. Vollet that Frank for the purpose of facilitating the commission of the robbery would intentionally cause bodily harm to Mrs. Vollet, (ii) that it was known or ought to have been known to the respondent that such consequence was probable and (iii) that in fact Mrs. Vollet's death ensued from the bodily harm. *It was not necessary for the Crown to establish that the respondent knew or ought to have known that it was probable that Mrs. Vollet's death would ensue.* [Emphasis added.]

It is clear that an accused can be convicted of murder under the combined operation of ss. 21(2) and 213 in circumstances where the death was not objectively foreseeable. As section 21(2) requires proof of objective foreseeability, the culprit, in my view, must be s. 213.

These two examples suffice, in my view, for one to conclude that notwithstanding proof beyond a reasonable doubt of the matters set forth in paras. (*a*) to (*d*) a jury could reasonably be left in doubt as regards objective foreseeability of the likelihood that death be caused. In other words, s. 213 will catch an accused who performs one of the acts in paras. (*a*) to (*d*) and thereby causes a death but who otherwise would have been acquitted of murder because he did not foresee and could not reasonably have foreseen that death would be likely to result. For that reason, s. 213 *prima facie* violates ss. 7 and 11(*d*). It is thus not necessary to decide whether objective foreseeability is sufficient for murder as s. 213 does not even meet that standard. This takes us to s. 1 for the second phase of the constitutional inquiry.

Section 1

Finding that s. 213 of the *Criminal Code* infringes ss. 7 and 11(*d*) of the *Charter* does not end the inquiry on the constitutional validity of s. 213.

Any or all of paras. (*a*) to (*d*) of s. 213 can still be upheld as a reasonable limit "demonstrably justified in a free and democratic society" under s. 1 of the *Charter*.

In this case and at this stage of the inquiry, we need only consider para. (*d*) of s. 213. The criteria to be assessed under s. 1 have been set out by this Court in several cases, particularly *R. v. Big M Drug Mart Ltd.*, [1985] 1 S.C.R. 295, and *R. v. Oakes*, *supra*. First, the objective which the measures are designed to serve must be "of sufficient importance to warrant overriding a constitutionally protected right or freedom" (*Big M Drug Mart, supra*, at p. 352). Through s. 213(*d*) of the *Code*, Parliament intended to deter the use or carrying of a weapon in the commission of certain offences, because of the increased risk of death. In my view, it is clear that this objective is sufficiently important.

In addition, the measures adopted must be reasonable and demonstrably justified. The measures adopted appear to be rationally connected to the objective: indiscriminately punishing for murder all those who cause a death by using or carrying a weapon, whether the death was intentional or accidental, might well be thought to discourage the use and the carrying of weapons. I believe, however, that the measures adopted would unduly impair the rights and freedoms in question (see *Big M Drug Mart, supra*, at p. 352). It is not necessary to convict of murder persons who did not intend or foresee the death and who could not even have foreseen the death in order to deter others from using or carrying weapons. If Parliament wishes to deter the use or carrying of weapons, it should punish the use or carrying of weapons. A good example of this is the minimum imprisonment for using a firearm in the commission of an indictable offence under s. 83 of the *Criminal Code*. In any event, the conviction for manslaughter which would result instead of a conviction for murder is punishable by, from a day in jail, to confinement for life in a penitentiary. Very stiff sentences when weapons are involved in the commission of the crime of manslaughter would sufficiently deter the use or carrying of weapons in the commission of crimes. But stigmatizing the crime as murder unnecessarily impairs the *Charter* right.

In my view, therefore, s. 213(*d*) of the *Code* is not saved by s. 1.

CONCLUSION

As a result of the foregoing, I would answer the first constitutional question in the affirmative, as s. 213(*d*) violates both s. 7 and s. 11(*d*) of the *Charter*, and I would declare s. 213(*d*) of the *Criminal Code* to be of no force or effect. I would, for the reasons which I have given, decline to answer the second constitutional question. It follows that the appeal must be allowed, the appellant's conviction for murder set aside, and a new trial ordered.

[Justice McIntyre dissented; Justices Beetz and LeDain concurred with the majority opinion but expressed reservations about a minimal requirement of subjective foresight of death.]

■

Vaillancourt examined the constitutionality of *Code* s. 213(d) (since repealed) alone and in combination with *Code* s. 21(2). In subsequent decisions, *R. v. Martineau*, [1990] 2 S.C.R. 633; *R. v. J.T.J.*, [1990] 2 S.C.R. 755; *R. v. Luxton*, [1990] 2 S.C.R. 711; and *R. v. Sit*, [1991] 3 S.C.R. 124, the Court has declared other murder provisions, s. 230(a) and s. 229(c), constitutionally invalid pursuant to *Charter* s. 7, and incapable of being "saved" through s. 1. The only provisions remaining to prosecute murder are ss. 229(a)(i), whereby the Crown must prove that the accused intended to cause death; 229(a)(ii), whereby the Crown can alternatively attempt to prove intention to cause bodily harm that the accused knew was likely to cause death and was reckless as to whether death ensued; and 229(b), where the accused intended to cause death to one person or bodily harm knowing that death would be likely, and by accident or mistake caused death to another person.

The Supreme Court has, at the same time, been less inclined to insist on a *mens rea* requirement that relates strictly to the prohibited consequence of a given offence outside the context of the offence of murder. Thus, in *R. v. DeSousa*, [1992] 2 S.C.R. 944, the Court ruled that s. 269, unlawfully causing bodily harm, required proof only of intention to commit an unlawful act, which must itself be constitutionally valid as an offence, and which must be objectively dangerous, subjecting another to at least some risk of bodily harm. This decision has been applied in cases involving challenges to the constitutionality of the *mens rea* element for assault causing bodily harm, s. 268(1) (*R. v. Godin*, [1994] 2 S.C.R. 484) and the offence of unlawful act manslaughter, s. 222(5)(a) (*R. v. Creighton*, *supra*).

Rosemary Cairns Way has criticized *Vaillancourt* and *Martineau* for circular reasoning and reliance upon the unhelpful notion of "stigma" in the s. 7 analysis.

Constitutionalizing Subjectivism: Another View†

In its package of decisions released 13th September 1990 the Supreme Court of Canada had taken another giant and irreversible step in the judicial restructuring of the substantive law of homicide.

. . . .

Martineau and *Logan* invite further lengthy, complex and unpredictable litigation challenging sections of the Criminal Code on constitutional grounds, and create the potential for the judicial reformulation of the substantive criminal law. I wish to comment on two aspects of the judgments — the first being the circular reasoning about murder which underlies the majority position, and the second the continued insistence on the notion of stigma as a method of categorizing offences for constitutional purposes.

THE COURT'S REASONING

In *Martineau*, Lamer C.J.C. relies on the inaccurate picture of the homicide provisions of the Code which he painted in *Vaillancourt* — a canvas which serves to justify his characterization of the entire constructive murder provision as anomalous and thus constitutionally suspect. In *Vaillancourt*, Lamer J. (as he then was) asserted at p. 325 (C.R.) that "murder is distinguished from manslaughter only by the mental element with respect to the death." This statement about the distinction between murder and manslaughter was inaccurate. At the time when *Vaillancourt* was decided, the entirety of s. 213 [am. 1974-75-76, c. 105, s. 29; since am. 1980-81-82-83, c. 125, s. 15] of the Criminal Code, R.S.C. 1970, c. C-34 (now s. 230) as well as s. 212(*c*) (now s. 229(*c*)) required only objective foreseeability of death, making these forms of murder indistinguishable in terms of foreseeability of death from certain forms of manslaughter. Building on this false distinction, Lamer J. wrote at p. 326 (C.R.) that it is the special mental element with respect to the death which "gives rise to the moral blameworthiness which justifies the stigma and sentence attached to a murder conviction." Thus the decision in *Vaillancourt* was justified by the very result it achieved. In fact, the Code defined as murder an array of actions which resulted in death, reflecting both the risk inherent in the underlying crime and the serious harm caused by intentional, dangerous criminal activity. Clearly, in legislative terms it was not *only* the special mental element with respect to death which gave rise to the moral blameworthiness justifying the stigma and sentence. Both the longevity of the constructive homicide provisions and their existence in virtually all Western legal systems (*Martineau* at p. 154, per L'Heureux-Dubé J.) suggest that there is no obvious or inherent conflict between a commitment to moral blameworthiness as a prerequisite to conviction and provisions which characterize as murder killings which occur during the commission or attempted commission of other serious offences.

With *Vaillancourt* the court took the first step toward the restructuring of the homicide provisions to accord with the majority's paradigm. *Martineau* takes the next. As L'Heureux-Dubé J. notes at p. 145 in her dissenting opinion, the only truly subjective foresight murder provision of the Code is s. 229(*a*), which, along with s. 229(*b*), is arguably the only provision which has survived constitutional scrutiny. At p. 154 she characterizes, correctly, the introduction of a subjective foresight standard as sudden, novel and without parallel in other common law jurisdictions. The court has, by substituting its view of what murder means for that of the legislature, given itself jurisdiction to alter the legislation. For example, it is as if the court had decided that sexual assault meant only an attack by a stranger at night — and had then proceeded to declare unconstitutional all provisions which criminalized other forms of sexual assault. The result is a decision which fails to grapple with the complex issues of normative responsibility, moral innocence and social denunciation which surround any declaration that behaviour

† Rosemary Cairns Way, "Constitutionalizing Subjectivism: Another View" (1990) 79 C.R. (3d) 260 at 260–63. Reproduced with permission of the author.

resulting in death should receive the most severe sanction available in the criminal process.

STIGMA

Equally problematic is the Chief Justice's insistence on the retention of the concept of stigma in his theory of constitutionalized fault. In *Vaillancourt*, Lamer J. wrote at p. 325 (C.R.) that there are "certain crimes where, because of the special nature of the stigma attached to a conviction therefor or the available penalties, the principles of fundamental justice require a mens rea reflecting the particular nature of the crime." In *Logan*, he reasserts at p. 178 that the criteria of identification are "primarily, the stigma associated with a conviction and, as a secondary consideration, the penalties available." Indeed, he goes to great lengths to assert the importance of this consideration — reiterating at p. 178 that the sentencing range available is not conclusive and that the *crucial* consideration is the existence of a continuing serious social stigma. Lamer C.J.C. may be trying to foreclose a reading of the decisions that focuses on the mandatory minimum sentence for murder as justification for the imposition of constitutional limitations. It is clear that he does not wish to limit the potential constitutional constraints of Code provisions to those few which have mandatory minimum sentences. Although the Chief Justice tells us that only a few offences will constitutionally require a minimum degree of mens rea, the decision makes it difficult to predict what those few offences will be. Presently the most that can be said is that all provisions which result in serious continuing social stigma are constitutionally vulnerable.

The ambiguous concept of stigma is left virtually unexplained by the *Logan* decision. What precisely is meant by the term? Is sexual assault a stigmatized offence? Or common assault? Or impaired driving? Or false advertising? Surely part of the purpose of any legitimate criminal justice system is to label, and thereby stigmatize, the offender. Indeed, one of the traditional justifications for punishment is the deterrent and educative impact of a criminal conviction — in other words, the stigma which accompanies it. Lamer C.J.C. chooses the same offence to illustrate the concept of stigma that he used in *Vaillancourt*, supra — the offence of theft. In his view, theft requires, as a constitutional imperative, some degree of dishonesty. This leads to the conclusion that the stigma of a conviction, and perhaps an absolute discharge, as punishment for theft under $1000 represents a deprivation of life, liberty or security which must accord with subjectivist criteria in order to comply with the principles of fundamental justice. Yet it is difficult to conceive of how a conviction of theft results in a more serious and continuing social stigma than one of manslaughter. Presumably the court does not intend to impose subjectivist standards on the crime of manslaughter, or on any number of other Code offences which also result in stigma but include some objective aspect in the mens rea requirement.

The ambiguity of the stigma criteria creates practical difficulty which will be resolvable only through a great number of long, expensive and complicated cases. Another theoretical difficulty is the introduction of a new vague concept into the constitutional lexicon, further empowering the judiciary, through the process of interpretation, to impose and entrench their views of what behaviour should be labelled as criminal. Particularly troubling is the contingency of the idea of stigma, rooted as it must be in some kind of popular consensus. It appears to depend on both the status of the offender and the status of the crime. The serious continuing social stigma for a bank president of a fraud conviction is probably much greater than the social stigma for a repeat offender who habitually robs to support an addiction. Do we wish to afford the bank president greater constitutional protection? Notions of the relative stigma of different criminal offences change to reflect prevailing attitudes and prejudices, and in making it a constitutional criterion the court risks constitutionalizing those very same attitudes and prejudices.

■

Cairns Way's discussion of the elasticity of the stigma concept returns to the troubling issues around the gendered nature of *mens rea* doctrine and party liability for sexual assault and, indeed, femicide and homicide. It also raises questions about whether accused persons charged with lesser offences receive the benefit of *Charter* rulings.

MENS REA AND PARTY LIABILITY

Consider the application of this *mens rea* element in cases where the Crown has attempted to prosecute men who have been involved in gang rape. Given some of the legal technicalities associated with the former offence of rape, and given the problems of evidence and proof for the primary witness who may have been assaulted over a period of hours by many men, the prosecution may proceed on the alternatives that the accused was an assailant or a party under s. 21 of the *Code*. If convicted as a party, the accused is convicted of the same offence and liable to the same punishment, although judges may reduce the sentence for someone whose role was less direct. Accused persons can be made parties through either s. 21(1) or 21(2). Under s. 21(1), the Crown may prove that the accused either aided or abetted the principal perpetrator; under s. 21(2) the accused who has pursued an unlawful purpose with another perpetrator can be convicted of other offences committed by the other person if the accused "knew or ought to have known that the commission of the offence would be a probable consequence of carrying out the unlawful purpose."

Prosecutions for parties to sexual assault are problematic for the Crown in terms of both the *actus reus* and the *mens rea*. The judges have ruled that to be convicted for aiding or abetting pursuant to s. 21(1), an accused's physical presence at the scene of a group rape of a woman is not sufficiently "active" in terms of the *actus reus* to attract criminal liability, even where the accused is standing nearby with his pants down (*R. v. Salajko*, [1970] 1 O.R. 824 (C.A.)), even where the accused is "enjoying the scene" (*R. v. Clarkson*, [1971] 3 All E.R. 344 at 347 (Court Marshall App. Ct.)), and even where the witness's evidence was, in fact, that the accused was an assailant, and party liability was offered only as an alternative: *Dunlop v. R.*, [1979] 2 S.C.R. 881. In only one reported gang assault case, *R. v. Black*, [1970] 4 C.C.C. 251 (B.C.C.A.), which, interestingly, involved a gang assault by men upon another man, have the judges been willing to describe mere physical presence as a sufficient *actus reus*: "the mere presence of these accused ensured against the escape of the victim" (at 258).

With respect to the *mens rea* requirement for s. 21(1) in sexual assault cases, the judges have ruled that the Crown must prove not only actual aiding or encouragement, but intentional, or "wilful" encouragement. In *Salajko*, the court stated that "passive encouragement", or "knowingly" standing by, was insufficient; in *Clarkson*, the court stressed that it would be unjust to convict an accused whose enjoyment of the scene actually encouraged the offenders, if the accused did not intend to so encourage. Again, only in *Black* (at 265) did the court rule that non-accidental and voluntary presence at the scene of the assault, without expressing at least dissent, may give rise to an inference that the accused intended to encourage the commission of the offence.

In support of the argument that a certain politic undergirds the interpretation of the legal requirements of proof in party liability, consider the following examples where the *actus reus* and *mens rea* for aiding and abetting have been relaxed. The first example is provided by *Re A.C.S.* (1969), 7 C.R.N.S. 42 (Que. Sup. Ct.), where a youth was convicted of a delinquency for the offence of mischief, by interfering with the use of a computer centre at Sir George Williams University in Montréal. In response to counsel's argument that A.C.S. could not be convicted based on her mere physical presence, and that her intent of "wilfulness" could not fairly be inferred from that presence, without more, Judge Long ruled at 47–48:

> [I]t was the duty of A.C.S. to leave the computer area when steps were being taken to obstruct, interrupt or interfere with the lawful use, enjoyment or operation by the owners; that she could not have failed to be aware that the erection of the barricades on the inside of the area would prevent the area from being used for the purposes for which it was intended by the owners and that she was reckless whether the mischief occurred or not and is consequently deemed wilfully to have caused the mischief.

This decision was upheld by Mackay J. in (1969), 7 C.R.N.S. 51 at 60–61.

The student leaders of the protest in question were Ann Cools, Rosie Douglas, and Brenda Dash, who were representing the Black Nationalists of Canada. Their bail conditions were extraordinary: $14,000 bail for Douglas, as spokesperson for the B.N.C., and $3,000 each for the other two leaders. They were convicted by an all-white jury. Source: *Many Rivers to Cross. The African-Canadian Experience* (The National Tour, 1992–1994, Sheldon Taylor, curator).

The second example of a relaxed approach to the legal requirements for party liability can be found in *Wilcox v. Jeffrey*, [1951] 1 All E.R. 464 (K.B.), where the appellant's conviction as a party to an offence under the U.K. *Alien Order*, 1920 (S.R. & 0., 1920, No. 448), art. 18(2), was affirmed. Mr. Wilcox, owner and managing editor of *Jazz Illustrated*, was at the airport when Mr. Coleman Hawkins, described by the Lords as "a celebrated professor of the saxophone", arrived from the United States to perform in a concert.

Mr. Wilcox was present for the denial of Mr. Hawkins' application for permission to perform in England, and was aware that the musician was granted three days landing, but was prohibited from engaging in paid or unpaid employment. Wilcox was later present at a concert when Hawkins was "spotlighted" in the audience and then moved to the stage to play. Wilcox published an account and photos of the event, and was prosecuted as an aider and abettor. Although there was no evidence that Wilcox did anything to actively encourage the performance (even clapping was not alleged), his non-accidental presence, combined with the facts that he did nothing to stop or dissociate himself from the offence, and that he "made copy" from the event, were held to be sufficient to support the conviction.

Finally, for an account of the efforts by the South African government to use broad party liability to crush mass resistance to the apartheid state and of the international campaign that succeeded in securing a reprieve from the death penalty for six persons convicted of murder for their presence at a mass demonstration where a killing occurred, see Prakash Diar, *The Sharpeville Six* (Toronto: McClelland and Stewart, 1990).

In *R. v. Logan*, [1990] 2 S.C.R. 731, the Court examined the liability of parties to murder through *Code* s. 21(2), which uses an objective standard of foreseeability as the mental element linking the accused to the primary offender. It determined that this section violated s. 7 to the extent that it used an objective standard of party liability where the underlying offence requires, as a constitutional matter, subjectively tested *mens rea*. It therefore "read down" s. 21(2) for murder and attempted murder, but acknowledged that the objective component of this section should stand for party liability for manslaughter.

Yet in *R. v. Kirkness*, [1990] 3 S.C.R. 74, the accused's acquittal was upheld by a majority of the Supreme Court using a subjective test for party liability for manslaughter. All members of the Court agreed that the jury could find the accused to be a party to manslaughter where his accomplice suffocated the victim of a break-and-enter after sexually assaulting her if he were a party to the sexual assault and if he knew that the assault was likely to cause some harm short of death. The judges divided along gender lines with respect to their application of the law to the facts. Cory J. stated that there was no evidence that the appellant intended to aid or encourage the assault; there was no evidence that he knew that bodily harm short of death would result from the sexual assault; and that in any event, since he dissociated himself from his co-accused's action thereafter of suffocating the victim, he would only be responsible if her death had resulted from the sexual assault itself.

Wilson and L'Heureux-Dubé JJ. found evidence of intent to aid in a sexual assault in the accused's own admitted actions of acting as a look-out and placing a chair against a door to block it during the assault; they did not credit the accused's avowed dissociation, given that he remained in the house during the rape and murder and persisted in the robbery plan; and they would have ruled that it was open to the jury to find that the accused was aware that a sexual assault upon an 83-year-old woman would result in at least bodily harm short of death.

In a later decision, *R. v. Jackson*, [1993] 4 S.C.R. 573, in reliance upon *R. v. Logan*, and *Creighton*, McLachlin J., for the majority, stated that party liability for manslaughter requires proof only that the accused should have foreseen that the offence committed by the co-accused would cause some non-trivial bodily harm. Would Kirkness have been convicted of manslaughter pursuant to this test?

Consider party liability for other offences after *Logan*. In *R. v. E.J.* (1995), 136 Nfld. & P.E.I.R. 117 at 124 (Nfld. S.C.) the accused was convicted as a principal for theft of some meat from a store, and as a party to two assaults committed by his co-accused upon a store security guard and her husband. The basis for party liability was s. 21(2): "the evidence established that, theft having occurred, there was then a concerted plan by the parties to avoid being detained by the officer and the store employees at the entrance, and by appropriate implication, that some physical action, encompassing pushing of the security officer (constituting the alleged assault) was a foreseeable consequence of the plan." Is this a tenable analysis after *Logan*?

Section 231, which classifies murder as first or second degree, has itself been challenged using s. 7 of the *Charter*. Murder is first degree if it is "planned and deliberate" (s. 231(2)); if it is a "contract" killing (s. 231(3)); if it involves the death of persons such as police officers or prison guards acting in the course of their duties (s. 231(4)); if the victim is killed while the offender is committing or attempting to commit one of the listed offences (s. 231(5)); or if the victim was killed by someone engaged in "criminal harassment" (s. 264) of the victim, intending to cause the victim to fear for her own life or that of another (s. 231(6)).

R. v. Twigge (1996), 148 Sask. R. 254 (C.A.) examined a woman's party liability for first degree murder. The court ordered a new trial for a woman convicted of abetting first degree murder because the trial judge had failed to properly instruct the jury as to the requisite *mens rea* elements: the jury should in such cases be told that non-accidental presence at the scene of the murder may be a starting point, but they must still be satisfied that the accused possessed the necessary murderous intent and that she intended her presence to encourage the killing. The court also ruled that to render her responsible for first degree murder the Crown must prove either that she participated in a s. 231(5) offence, that she aided in the planning or deliberation of the murder, or that she intended to abet a planned and deliberate murder.

Examine the wording of s. 231: are any of these subsections vulnerable to a s. 7 challenge? Thus far, s. 231(5) has withstood challenge. Its rationale was articulated in *R. v. Paré*, [1987] 2 S.C.R. 618, as punishing the unlawful domination of the victim by the offender in circumstances where the underlying offence has been proven and there is a temporal and causal nexus between the offence and the death of the victim. In *Luxton*, *supra*, and *R. v. Arkell*, [1990] 2 S.C.R. 695, the Court upheld the section, arguing that, consistent with *Paré* and the stigma approach from *Vaillancourt*, it is justifiable to reserve the most serious penalty for offenders who have unlawfully dominated and intentionally killed their victims.

POST-CONVICTION REVIEW BASED ON *CHARTER* RULINGS

Accused persons convicted under legislation since declared invalid under the *Charter* have attempted to argue that they should receive the benefit of decisions such as *Vaillancourt*. In *Thomas v. R.*, [1990] 1 S.C.R. 713, the Supreme Court of Canada denied a request by an accused convicted under ss. 213(a) and 21(2) in 1984 because at the time of his application to the Court, he was no longer in the judicial system. The requirement that the accused be in the judicial system means that an appeal must have been launched, an application for leave have been filed, or an application to extend the time for appeal have been granted.

A similar application was launched in *R. v. Johnston*, [1988] 6 W.W.R. 465 at 468–69 (Man. C.A.), in which one of the four men who murdered Helen Betty Osborne (see Abell & Sheehy, *Cases, Context, Critique*, **Aboriginal Peoples and Criminal Law**) argued that he should receive the benefit of *Vaillancourt*:

> If s. 213 as a whole is invalid, it is so only because there was a substantial change in the law when the Charter was passed. The accused committed the crime of murder in 1971 when the valid law of Canada included s. 213 of the *Criminal Code*. As to retrospectivity, see *R. v. Stevens* (1988), 41 C.C.C. (3d) 193, 86 N.R. 85 (S.C.C.) [Ont.].
>
> ...
>
> Had there been an error of law, I would have applied the proviso to s. 613(1)(*b*)(iii). There is no doubt on the evidence, in my opinion, that the accused killed the victim and the nature of the assault shows that the accused killed in a frenzy, meaning to inflict bodily harm which he knew would result in her death. It is possible, I think, that the accused's mind was befuddled by alcohol and drugs to the extent that he did not mean to cause death, but the defence of drunkenness was adequately put before the jury and there is no reason to disturb its verdict.
>
> In this case, four young men joined in abducting a young woman and at the very least they stood by while one or more of them killed in a wanton and brutal assault. As a result of deals made by the Crown, one of those four, Menger, was not even charged with anything. A second, Colgan, had his charge stayed after agreeing to be the Crown's main witness. A third man, Houghton, who, in my opinion, surely was at least guilty of confining the accused [*sic*], was acquitted by the same jury that found the appellant guilty.
>
> It seems to me that this is a clear case which shows that Canadian law is deficient in that it is no longer an offence to conceal a felony. In my opinion, lawmakers should consider whether it is not time to reinstate the offence of misprision of felony. That would render illegal the conspiracy of silence which covered up the murder for 16 years on the advice of a lawyer.
>
> The appeal is accordingly dismissed.

Most recently, in *R. v. Sarson*, [1996] 2 S.C.R. 223, the Court ruled on an accused's application, based on *Vaillancourt*, for *habeas corpus* to secure his release from prison. He had been serving a life sentence for a conviction rendered 11 months before the judgment in *Vaillancourt* under the former s. 213(d) for a second degree murder committed in 1985. The Court refused to issue the writ because first, the common law rules governing the issuance of such writs were inapplicable. Second, the accused was "no longer in the judicial system" within the meaning of *Thomas* when *Vaillancourt* was decided since he had not launched an appeal until three and one-half years after his guilty plea and sentence and his application for an extension for that appeal had been refused. The Court refused to allow the accused to use the writ of *habeas corpus* to attempt to avoid these principles so as to secure a substantive review of the justness of his conviction. Third, while recognizing that the rules governing *habeas corpus* might be relaxed where the accused can present a serious *Charter* s. 7 claim, here there was overwhelming evidence of the accused's involvement in the murder. Since a prosecutor could have chosen, instead of s. 213(d) constructive homicide, to prove the offence by way of party liability for restraining the victim while he was killed and disposing of his body thereafter, the Court concluded that the accused had failed to establish any breach of fundamental justice under s. 7.

Authors Isabel Grant, Dorothy Chunn, and Christine Boyle suggest, in *The Law of Homicide* (Toronto: Carswell, 1996 supp.) at 4-78.3, 4-78.4 that *Sarson* opens the possibility of review of the cases of those accused convicted under s. 213(d) of first degree murder who currently could not, unlike *Sarson*, have been convicted of murder but only of manslaughter. They argue that the lengthy incarceration of such persons arguably offends s. 7 of the *Charter*, and that some sort of review process like the Self-Defence Review by Judge Ratushny (see **Self-Defence**, below) should be instigated for this group of prisoners.

G. SPECIFIC STATES OF MIND

Certain *Code* sections and other federal and provincial offences specify a very particular mental state that the accused must have possessed in order to be found guilty. For example, s. 152, invitation to sexual touching, requires a "sexual purpose", and s. 403, personation with intent, requires proof that the accused did so "fraudulently". Such mental elements are tested subjectively, and by reference to common law interpretations.

Although this *mens rea* requirement sounds as if it imposes an onerous burden upon the Crown, its relative difficulty may depend upon the offence charged, the identity of the accused, and the availability of legal representation. Triers of fact may be more willing to draw an inference of criminal intent against certain classes of accused and against racialized accused. The associations carried by the offence charged may also influence the seriousness with which the *mens rea* legal requirement is taken. Dianne Martin, after noting in "Passing the Buck: Prosecution of Welfare Fraud; Preservation of Stereotypes" (1992) 12 Windsor Y.B. Access Just. 52 that the offence of fraud requires proof of subjectively assessed intention to mislead, coupled with a dishonest intention to benefit financially from that deceit, gives a number of examples suggesting that women accused of welfare fraud may not benefit from this seemingly stringent *mens rea* requirement. She points out that many accused will not be entitled to legal aid and will, therefore, be under enormous pressure to plead guilty and "get it over with". She refers to situations where the woman's motive in non-disclosure may be to preserve her privacy or to protect herself against a partner's violence, but where conviction for fraud may nonetheless ensue; she also notes that the rules for eligibility and those governing overpayments are extremely complex, often resulting in genuine misunderstandings, but arguably barring a no *mens rea* defence because it is a "mistake of law" (at 59, note 8). Consider, by way of contrast, the creative work of the trial judge, affirmed by the court of appeal but reversed by the Supreme Court of Canada, in reading in a requirement of a "corrupt state of mind" to the offence under s. 121(1)(a) (accepting a benefit as a government official) so as to acquit the accused: *R. v. Cogger*, [1997] 2 S.C.R. 845.

4

Case Study on Corporate Homicide

Is the law of homicide, and particularly its *actus reus* and *mens rea* requirements, capable of responding to human deaths caused by corporate decisions and practices? Corporations may cause death through environmental pollution and dumping of hazardous wastes, as was illustrated by Reed Paper Company's pollution of Grassy Narrows and White Dog, described in Abell & Sheehy, *Cases, Context, Critique*, **Colonization and the Imposition of Criminal Law**. Corporations may also produce deaths by unsafe work practices and by marketing dangerous consumer products.

Corporations are frequently prosecuted under regulatory statutes (provincial and federal offences that define regulatory offences as understood by *Sault Ste. Marie* and *Wholesale Travel*) that specifically govern their conduct. Regulatory crimes are usually framed as strict liability and absolute liability offences, as discussed under ***Mens Rea***. The fault elements for these offences are objectively tested and generally place the onus on the corporation to prove due diligence. Because these offences are tested by objective standards as opposed to actual knowledge or intent, they pose little conceptual difficulty for prosecuting corporations.

However, for "true crimes", the courts have had to grapple with two main conceptual difficulties. "True crimes" (again as understood by the Court in *Sault Ste. Marie* and *Wholesale Travel*), are usually found in the *Criminal Code* and are directed at human individuals, and often (although not always) require proof of subjectively tested states of mind. For such offences, first, corporations had to be recognized as "persons" to whom the criminal law applied. Second, a doctrine needed to be developed to somehow attribute the state of mind of corporate actors to the corporation itself.

These difficulties were addressed as early as 1904 in the United States when corporations became liable to criminal prosecution as "persons" under the criminal law. The issue in Canada is addressed in s. 2 of the *Code*, which defines "every one, person, and owner" as including a corporation. With respect to the second issue of attributing *mens rea* to the corporation, Canadian courts developed the "directing mind" doctrine, which allowed the imputation of the knowledge, intention, or recklessness of a "directing mind and will" of the corporation to the corporation itself. This chapter will discuss the doctrine, the difficulties it posed to corporate prosecutions, and the legislative reform that was aimed at responding to these challenges.

A. DIRECTING MIND AND WILL DOCTRINE

The difficulties of the "directing mind" doctrine were illustrated most recently in the effort to prosecute Ontario Power Generation (OPG) for a terrible accident that occurred at Barrett Chute, on the Madawaska River, near Calabogie, Ontario on June 23, 2002 when the operator of a dam released waters onto a dry river bed, sweeping away the people who were sun bathing below. The company itself, John Tammadge, the manager whose responsibilities included Barrett Chute, and Robert Bednarek, the operator of the dam, were charged with two counts of criminal negligence causing death with respect to the death of a mother and her young son, and seven counts of criminal negligence causing bodily harm for seven others who were injured in the accident.

The prosecution against the company itself was dismissed in *R. v. Ontario Power Generation*, [2006] O.J. No. 4659 (Ct. J.) (QL), because the Crown could not identify a "directing mind and will" of OPG who was low enough in the corporate structure so as to be knowledgeable about the risks at the site. The judge summarized the principles derived from the case law, notably *R. v. Canadian Dredge and Dock Co.*, [1985] 1 S.C.R. 6627; *Rhone (The) v. Peter A.B. Widener (The)*, [1993] 1 S.C.R. 4978; and *R. v. Safety-Kleen Canada Inc.*, [1997] O.J. No. 800 (C.A.) (QL) at para. 16 of the judgment:

> [A] determination of who a person in authority is in a corporate organization requires an affirmative answer to the following questions:
> - does the individual have the power both to devise (or design) AND supervise implementation of corporate policy.
> - does the individual have governing executive authority
> - is the individual invested with full discretion to act without guidance from supervisors in relation to matters of corporate policy.

The judge then went on to describe OPG's corporate structure at paras. 22 and 23:

> OPG has (and had at the relevant time) a large, sophisticated and complex corporate structure. Just a glance at Exhibit 62 reveals its breadth and extensive stratification. The Ontario Government appoints its Chair. The executive committee, headed by the President and Chief Executive officer come next. Then, at the next lower level are the Executive Vice-Presidents and the Chief Operating Officer. Following down the chain come, in successively lower turns, the Senior Vice-President of Electricity Production, the Vice-President of Hydroelectric Production and finally the Plant Managers. Mr. Tammadge was one of 4 Plant Group Managers (along with other senior management representatives at this stratum). He managed hydroelectric production on the St Lawrence, the Ottawa and the Madawaska rivers. He was at the seventh level downward.
>
> Under Mr. Tammadge come successively the Production Manager for the Ottawa and Madawaska rivers, the First Line Manager for the Madawaska, the Trade and Maintenance Supervisors at Barrett Chute and finally the electrician/operator agents such as the co-accused Mr. Bednarek. This one-dimensional description does not do justice to the intricacies and to the interweaving of accountabilities and responsibilities within the corporate structure of OPG, but is sufficient for the purpose of these reasons.

Finally, Justice Bélanger reviewed Tammadge's job description and the evidence of other witnesses as to his function within OPG and reached the following conclusions at paras. 26, 34–36:

> While [the job specification] describes wide-ranging, complex and extensive responsibilities, it is not the language of policy making or shaping. It is language directed at the execution of policy, of stewardship, of the management of assets assigned by the policy and decision makers of the corporation. Mr. Tammadge took direction and carried out orders. Doing so no doubt required a high degree of experience, knowledge and managerial ability; it involved discretion, industry and good judgment, but these were not his directions and his orders....
>
> Mr. Tammadge, as I have said, had very significant and demanding responsibilities and accountabilities. He was in charge of the operation and maintenance of 10 hydroelectric generating stations on three river systems, with 35 dams, 65 generating units in an area extending some 500 kilometers supplying 8% of Ontario's total energy. He had a staff of approximately 276 and a budget of $60 million to effect that purpose. However, it appears to me that a determination of whether or not he was a pawn in authority does not turn on the quantitative aspects of his work. He had no power to devise or design corporate policy. He did not have governing executive authority. He was not invested with

> full discretion to act without guidance from supervisors in relation to matters of corporate policy.
>
> He was not a directing mind of OPG. The Crown specified that he was the sole directing mind through which criminal responsibility could attach to OPG. Absent evidence of a directing mind, I am forced to conclude that there is simply no case for OPG to answer and that its motion for a directed verdict must succeed. Some could, with understandable justification, find perversity in the result, particularly when there exists a substantial body of evidence pointing in the direction of a cumulative and aggregated corporate failure to ensure public safety at the site of this generating station.
>
> This case illustrates vividly why the law was changed in 2003. Clearly the same result would not obtain today but I am bound to apply the law as it existed on June 23, 2002.

The judge dismissed the charges against OPG and went on, in a separate judgment, reproduced below, to adjudicate on the remaining charges against Tammadge and Bednarek.

Justice Bélanger referred to the new law passed in 2003, which effectively abolishes the "directing mind and will" doctrine and creates new forms of responsibility for organizations. *Code* s. 2 defines "organization" as including a corporation, "representative" as including a director, partner, member, agent, contractor or employee, and "senior officer" as "a representative who plays an important role in the establishment of an organization's policies or is responsible for managing an important aspect of the organization's activities and, in the case of a body corporate, includes a director, its chief executive officer and its chief financial officer." Section 22.1 now makes a corporation party to offences of penal negligence where one or more representatives, acting within the scope of their authority, commits the offence and "the senior officer who is responsible for the aspect of the organization's activities that is relevant to the offence" breaches the criminal standard of conduct in failing to prevent the offence.

Thus, ss. 2 and 22.1 appear to resolve the "directing mind and will" problem in terms of prosecuting corporations for homicide. The rest of this chapter will examine the remaining issues for such prosecutions.

B. WHY PROSECUTE CORPORATIONS UNDER THE CRIMINAL LAW?

An article by Frank Vandall, reproduced below, lays out the arguments for and against the use of the criminal law of homicide against corporations who market dangerous products.

Criminal Prosecution of Corporations for Defective Products†

Case for the Criminal Prosecution

The purpose of this section is to evaluate both sides of the question as to whether corporations should be criminally prosecuted for the manufacture of a defective product. Essentially it will be a critique of the theory that it is efficient and, therefore, legally permissible to manufacture products that routinely cause death. The first part will respond to the argument that criminal prosecution is too costly.

The foundation of the efficiency argument is that manufacturers should not be criminally prosecuted because they face an enormous threat from civil lawsuits. The truth is just the opposite. In proportion to the amount of injury caused, product manufacturers are rarely sued. This is due to the nature of the legal system. Most suits rest on negligence and this is a very heavy burden to prove. Many plaintiffs, realising that they cannot prove neg-

---

† Frank Vandall, "Criminal Prosecution of Corporations for Defective Products". [Notes omitted.] This article first appeared in (1987) 12 ILP 66 at 67–71, published by the International Bar Association. Reproduced by permission of the author and the publisher.

ligence, never file suit. Cause in fact is another substantial hurdle. In many cases it is not clear what caused the injury. In cases involving pharmaceuticals, for example, was the drug defective, or did the person die from the pre-existing illness? In automobile crashes, was the design of the gas tank defective, or would any automobile gas tank have exploded if the car was stopped and hit from behind by a van travelling at 45 mph?

Other suits are never brought because the statute of limitations has run. For example, if there is a three-year statute of limitations, some consumers postpone their decision to sue until after the statute has run. In this situation there is no avenue of relief. Other consumers may find that they have transgressed a statute of repose. These provide that the suit fails after a given period of time, for example, nine years after the date of the sale of the product. In such cases, if the injury occurs in the eleventh year, no suit may be brought. In a large number of other suits, particularly when the cause of action rests on negligence, it is often found that the plaintiff was in fact contributorily negligent. This is a complete defence.

In evaluating Indiana's prosecution of Ford Motor Company because of the death of three young girls due to a defective gas tank, Lee Strobel stated:

> But Cosentino [the prosecutor in the Ford Pinto case] believed that huge corporations, like the Ford Motor Company, are not affected by being ordered to pay a few million dollars in one civil case, a couple of million in another, and a few hundred thousand in another. They take advantage of tax right-offs [*sic*] and return to business as usual, despite injuries to consumers. The only way to make these corporations responsible for their actions, he concluded, was to resort to criminal law.

Michael Metzger's analysis is telling:

> For, as rational manufacturers well know, "only a fraction [of those injured by defective product] will be able to identify the defect as the cause of their injuries. Fewer still will sue and ... even fewer will have the stamina and wherewithal to prosecute to judgment a difficult and expensive lawsuit." Likewise, the vagaries of litigation insure [*sic*] that some valid claims will be defeated. Compensatory damages, therefore, will not force manufacturers to bear the full social costs of marketing a defective product.

Mark Franklin reminds us that "[C]orporations and businesses treat tort liability as a cost of doing business and discount its tarnishing effect." Although we have been looking at the reasons why corporations are not sued civilly, it is important to remember why they are generally not criminally prosecuted. Nancy Franks states: "The corporate sector exercises its considerable political influence to insulate business from criminal penalties, particularly the possibility of jail sentences."

The second reason for suggesting that criminal prosecution is inefficient[ ] rests on the notion that punitive damages substantially increase the manufacturer's expected costs from civil action. This is wrong. In truth, lawsuits are rare, victories are rare, and punitive damages are very uncommon. It is the unique case that results in punitive damages. Professor Owen reported that of 1,500 claims involving MER-29, only 11 were tried to jury verdicts. Of these, seven were decided for the plaintiff. Three of the seven included punitive damages, and one of these was reversed on appeal. He concluded that—

> If this is an example of the most crushing punishment that will befall a manufacturer guilty of flagrant marketing behaviour ... then the threat of bankrupting a manufacturer with punitive damage awards in mass disaster litigation appears to be more theoretical than real.

Although it is argued that punitive damages are often crushing, in truth they are often small. In the original Ford *Pinto* case, the jury awarded over $128,500,000 in damages. $125,000,000 of this was in punitive damages. When the jury was asked why they returned such an enormous verdict, one member of the jury responded (as I remember), "All we did was take the profit that Ford Motor Company made from not remedying the defect in the Pinto gas tank and tack it to the compensatory damages as punitives." In other words, the jury awarded the $125,000,000 of punitive damages against Ford Motor Company because that is the profit that Ford made from not remedying the defect. The trial court remitted the verdict to 6.8 million dollars total ($3.5 million punitives and $3.3 million compensatory), however, because the trial court felt that the $128,500,000 verdict rested on passion.

Examination of the economics of the *Pinto* case manifests, however, that the jury was probably right and that the court was wrong. That is, Ford did, in fact, save 87.5 million dollars by failing to correct the defect in the gas tank. What the trial court did was approve Ford's conscious decision to manufacture a product that was sure to kill people, when it could have been remedied for $11 per car. If the jury verdict for $128,500,000 had been permitted to stand, it would have pronounced Ford wrong. However, the reduction of the verdict to $6.8 million stamped Ford's cost-benefit analysis as being legally permissible.

Adverse publicity may cause purchasers to shun products. One author has stated that:

> The negative publicity of a criminal conviction is a consequence most likely to deter reckless corporate conduct. A guilty verdict could threaten the fate of a corporation's entire product line by inspiring public mistrust and thereby jeopardising future revenues. Short-term cost reductions due to relaxed concern for safety would have to be discounted by the potential impact on sales revenue. Therefore, the imposition of corporate criminal penalties should deter the instigation of [inappropriate] corporate policy....

It is true that civil and criminal suits against manufacturers create adverse publicity and may negatively affect sales. But, the impact upon the manufacturer is unpredictable. For example, in the recent case involving sticking accelerator cables on Audi 5000's, sales have dropped to almost nothing and the trade-in value on a used Audi 5000 has decreased substantially since the information became widely known. But, in the case of Pinto, it is not so clear. If my memory serves me, Ford changed the name of the Pinto to the Bobcat, transferred it to the Lincoln-Mercury Division and continued selling the Bobcat for several years after the Indiana criminal prosecution. Ford has not gone out of business, just the opposite. Ford has recently had its most profitable year. It exceeded General Motors in profits for the year. Most people do not know the risks of the products they buy, nor do they know the recall history of the product. The magazine, *Consumer Reports*, is not yet in every home. The point is that the filing of criminal and civil suits will sometimes have a substantial impact on the manufacturer and the sale of its products and sometimes not.

It has even been suggested that the criminal prosecution of corporations is unnecessary because the defect in the product is likely to be detected. This is only true in regard to exploding automobile gas tanks. If we look at pharmaceuticals, for example, detection is enormously difficult. In regard to DES, it is often impossible to identify the manufacturer of the specific pill that caused the plaintiff's vaginal cancer. The same can be said in regard to Swine Flu vaccinations. Large numbers of people developed Guillain-Barre Syndrome and became very ill or died. The issue in the cases was whether the Swine Flu vaccination was the cause in fact of the injury or whether it was caused by something else. Indeed, cause in fact is almost always a difficult question in products liability cases. In the Indiana *Pinto* case, for example, one issue was whether the Pinto was moving and the van was travelling at not more than 35 mph, or was the Pinto stopped and the van moving at perhaps 45 or 50 mph. If the latter, then the design of the gas tank was not defective, because almost any automobile gas tank would have exploded when hit from behind by a van travelling at 45 or 50 mph. Charles B. Schudson concludes:

> Corporate crimes are difficult activities to detect, and their commission might continue for years without being discovered.... The world of corporate crime investigation is often considered foreign and mysterious to traditional law enforcement personnel. The language is a mixture of specialised and technical terms, and the volume of documentary evidence is often overwhelming. Frequently, the work is dull, academic, tedious, and complicated.

Malcolm Wheeler (a member of the Ford defence team) suggests that it is a simple matter to sue product manufacturers and bring them to judgment. The opposite is more accurate, once again. Large corporations will paper you to death. Crash testing cars is enormously expensive and can cost as much as $80,000. Experts are also expensive. In a major products liability case, one of the only sure things is that the trial will likely be long, complicated and expensive. Indeed, there are few small firms who can afford to litigate a products liability suit.

In the remaining portion of this section, I want to consider the costs of criminal sanctions. The argument that I will be rebutting is that prosecution of a corporation for criminal violations constitutes overdeterrence and overkill.

The first argument for not prosecuting corporation criminally is that the cost to the government will be enormous. There are two responses to this. The first is a preliminary question: is it important to prosecute corporations? Ronald Kramer argues that criminal prosecution of corporations is essential:

> The economic costs associated with corporate crime, such as consumer fraud, anti-trust and restraint of trade violations, commercial bribery, tax violations, and others simply dwarf the financial costs of commercial property crimes like robbery, burglary, and larceny. Consumers are ... victimised by corporate criminal acts. It has been estimated by the Consumer Products Safety Commission that approximately 20 million serious injuries are annually associated with unsafe and defective consumer products (unsafe food and drugs, defective autos, tires, appliances, con-

traceptive devices, and others). An estimated 110,000 of these injuries result in permanent disability, and 30,000 result in death.

These data show that corporate crimes do have enormous physical costs. After comparing these physical costs to the 22,500 murders and non-negligent manslaughters reported to police agencies in 1981, it must be concluded that "Far more persons are killed through corporate criminal activities than by individual criminal homicides."

The other response is that the government is not in a position to spend much money on prosecuting manufacturers for defective products. In the Indiana criminal prosecution of Ford Motor Company, for example, Ford spent perhaps $2,000,000 on the trial, for attorneys, testing and experts. In contrast, the prosecutor in the case spent perhaps $20,000 of the government's money and an estimated $20,000 of his own.

Strobel, author of a book on the Pinto trial, states:

> The topic at the daily press conference ... was money. "What we are seeing here in Winamac is a test of the criminal justice system, because we are talking about money," said Cosentino [the prosecutor].... "It's a test of whether a defendant can pour enough money into a case and win the case...."

Strobel continues:

> And then there was the problem of money. Surely Ford cannot be faulted for devoting whatever resources it considered necessary to present a vigorous defence against serious charges. But the disparity between Ford's outlay and Cosentino's paltry budget — even though he was aided by some free help from the state and volunteers — created a lopsided battle which hindered a full airing of the case.

Finally, Malcolm Wheeler argues that criminal sanctions against corporations are inappropriate because they result in arbitrary and unpredictable criminal stigmas. It is very difficult to find evidence of any criminal stigma, however. In the *Pinto* case, there is little evidence that the criminal prosecution had an impact. No one was fired. The father of the Pinto, Lee Iacocca, who was Ford's Executive Vice President of North American Automotive Operations and later became one of the three presidents of Ford's operation and was finally elected to sole president shortly after the Pinto's introduction, is now president of Chrysler Corporation and one of the most beloved men in America and often mentioned as a presidential candidate. Only ten years after the Indiana criminal prosecution, Ford has, for the first time ever, beaten General Motors in profits. Certainly, the record in the *Pinto* case fails to reflect a meaningful stigma. It further suggests that if there is a stigma, it has little impact on the consumer, at least in the long run. It may also suggest that if there is a stigma, it is localised. That is, the consumer attaches a stigma to the specific product involved in the criminal litigation, but does not expand it to other products produced by the manufacturer. Although people stopped buying Pintos, it is clear that they did not stop buying other automobiles manufactured by Ford.

Finally, one author suggests that the criminal prosecution should be avoided because of the extreme costliness of overdeterrence — the manufacturer's selecting of suboptimal, but safer, designs. There are no examples that we are suffering from overdeterrence in regard to products. For example, we do not have air bags, we do not have 20 mph bumpers on cars, nor do we have roll-cages, nor six-point seat belts. It is also true that we lack fire systems and gas tank bladders, that are commonly found on race cars.

Worst of all, the overdeterrence argument misses the entire point of the *Pinto* criminal prosecution. The point of the *Pinto* trial is that we will criminally prosecute manufacturers of defective products when death was clear and could have been avoided cheaply. Ford's *mens rea* came from manufacturing a car that was sure to kill 180 people when it could have been prevented for merely $11 per car. No one has suggested that all manufacturers of defective products should be subject to criminal prosecution.

Crime Pays

The conclusion is that crime pays. In regard to civil suits, the manufacturer knows that most defects will go undetected or, if detected, there will be a good chance to settle, or win at trial. If the manufacturer loses at trial, he knows he can appeal and perhaps settle. He knows that punitive damages are rare. Michael Metzger states:

> Because civil products liability actions pose significant obstacles to plaintiffs, manufacturers will never have to compensate victims fully for the injuries caused by defective products. A plaintiff's contributory behaviour may bar or reduce recovery. Consumers may be unaware that a product is defective and, therefore, may never discover or assert their right to compensation.

> The high litigation costs associated with pressing a products liability claim, whose technical and complex issues magnify the difficulties of discovery and proof, also may deter a suit.... In some cases technical rules may prevent tort law from serving its compensatory function.

In the *Pinto* case, Ford estimated that 180 persons would be burned to death and another 180 would suffer serious burn injuries. These damages to persons and vehicles came to a total of 49.5 million dollars, but Ford also knew that it would cost them $11.00 per car to prevent the gas tanks from exploding. They planned to sell 11,000,000 cars and 1.5 million light trucks and, therefore, in order to make each one safe it would cost them 137 million dollars. If you subtract 49.5 million dollars (the damages that would occur) from 137 million dollars (the costs of alternative safe designs), you find that Ford profited to the extent of 87.5 million dollars in manufacturing the Pinto in its defective condition.

For the manufacturer of criminally defective products, the chance of criminal prosecution is close to nonexistent. If prosecuted, the manufacturer knows that the government will likely be under-financed and outmanned. If a large manufacturer, he also knows that the impact of the criminal stigma will be slight and fleeting. Charles B Schudson states:

> The corporate criminal commits crime assuming that he will never get caught, prosecuted, or convicted, and certainly will never go to prison. Thus, corporate crime represents a minimum risk business, with incarceration only a very slight possibility.

In short, the unfortunate truth is that crime pays.

At this point I would like to discuss three cases where criminal prosecution of corporations for the manufacture of defective products is appropriate. The first one, of course, is the Pinto. The reason why Ford should have been prosecuted criminally is because they knew that the Pinto would cause burn deaths to 180 people and burn injuries to another 180 people and failed to modify the Pinto when it could have been done for only $11 per car.

The second case where the manufacturer should have been prosecuted criminally is *Toole v Richardson-Merrell*. In *Toole*, the plaintiff's physician prescribed the defendant's anticholesterol drug MER-29. After taking the drug, the plaintiff developed cataracts, necessitating an operation for removal of the lenses of both eyes. *Toole* should have been prosecuted criminally because the trial of the case made clear that prior to the sale of the drug Richardson-Merrell knew that MER-29 caused blindness and failed to warn of it. The manufacturer lied to the Food & Drug Administration. Richardson-Merrell reported in its New Drug Application that only four out of eight rats died during a certain study, whereas all eight rats had died. A competitor had advised the manufacturer that MER-29 caused cataracts in test animals, but this was not reported to the Food & Drug Administration. Richardson-Merrell also failed to report to the FDA that 20 out of 24 male rats had become blind during testing. They also failed to inform the FDA that of the seven dogs that survived tests, five had striations in the lens of the eyes that indicated developing cataracts. Because of their lies to the Food & Drug Administration, and failure to inform the doctors of the enormous risk of cataracts and blindness from MER-29, Richardson-Merrell should have been prosecuted criminally.

The final example is Oraflex. Eli Lilly knew of 26 deaths among overseas users of Oraflex before the Food & Drug Administration approved the arthritis medicine for sale in the United States in 1981. But Eli Lilly failed to tell the Food & Drug Administration at that time. Indeed, the Lilly organisation knew of the 26 deaths as much as 17 months before the FDA approved the drug. Up to 14 people in the United States died from Oraflex. Because of this knowledge of death and the ease of prevention through informing the FDA, Eli Lilly should have been prosecuted criminally.

Proposals

Two proposals should be considered. First the imprisonment of corporate executives and secondly, substantial criminal fines for corporations.

Imprisonment of Corporate Executives

As someone who works in an ivory tower, my first thought was to suggest that corporate executives who are responsible for criminally defective products should be imprisoned, just as we do with young persons who steal and murder. Further reflection suggests that this is unlikely to occur. There are several reasons why the imprisonment proposal is only of academic interest. First, white collar crime is wrongly thought by society to be not serious. Secondly, judges view corporate executives as equals. They will likely see the executive's decision to design the product in a certain way as a close judgment call, very similar to the one that the judge makes in many cases every day. Thirdly, the imprisonment of executives would be an easy way to protect the corporation from prosecution and substantial fines. It is very likely that most corporations would be amenable to letting their executives go to jail in order to avoid prosecution of the corporation itself. Finally, it is unlikely that in most cases corporate executives will be criminally prosecuted because it would add an enormous expense to the cost of prosecution and the prosecutor is already under-financed.

Fine the Corporation at One Per Cent of Net Profit

As we have seen, fines in the criminal prosecution of corporations are extremely small. In the *Pinto* case, the maximum fine would have been $30,000. In a case involving a nursing home in Wisconsin, that permitted a mentally disturbed patient to escape and die of exposure, the maximum fine would have been $2,500. It is clear that such small fines lack any stinging power for a major corporation. As discussed above, the criminal stigma for the prosecution of corporations for defective products is vastly overrated. Because of these considerations, I suggest that corporate defendants should be fined 1 per cent of net profit. In 1978, for example, Ford Motor Company made $4,300,000 profit each day. That amounts to 1.569 billion dollars profit each year by Ford Motor Company. Therefore, the fine in the *Pinto* case would have been approximately $16,000,000 rather than the paltry $30,000. Such a fine may have attracted Ford's attention at the design stage and with the possibility of criminal prosecution in several states, a fine of $16,000,000 might have tipped the scales and persuaded Ford to add the $11 shield package to each Pinto before they were manufactured.

Unfortunately, this proposal will require statutory changes from the legislatures. It is not likely to occur because interest groups, including large corporations, control the federal and state legislatures.

Conclusion

I disagree with the theory that the criminal prosecution of corporations is inefficient because we have adequate civil remedies, that prosecution is expensive and the stigma will lead to overdeterrence. None of these arguments are [*sic*] convincing. I conclude instead that criminal prosecution is likely to be ineffective because of the nature of the American system of justice: the judge views the executive as an equal and is very unlikely to put him behind bars, the prosecutor is likely to be under-financed, and legislative enactment of large fines is not in the cards.

■

Francis T. Cullen, William J. Maakestad, and Gray Cavender in "The Ford Pinto Case and Beyond: Corporate Crime, Moral Boundaries, and the Criminal Sanction" in Ellen Hochstedler, ed., *Corporations as Criminals* (Beverly Hills: Sage Publications, 1984) 107 at 123 comment on the difficulties faced by the prosecutor attempting to prove *mens rea* for the offence of "reckless homicide" in the Ford case:

> [The prosecutor] Cosentino felt that he had sufficient evidence to prove that Ford knew early on that the Pinto had a defective fuel tank placement. This material included internal Ford memos and documents commenting on the Pinto's safety as well as the results of crash tests on 1971 and 1972 models, conducted by Ford and the government, showing that the vehicle exploded in flames at low impact speeds. These tests would be crucial, Cosentino reasoned, because they revealed that in planning the production of the 1973 Pinto, Ford had concrete evidence of the car's defects, yet chose not to rectify them. Moreover, Cosentino did not have crash tests at low speeds for the 1973 model, and his tight budget precluded his conducting them at this stage.
>
> Recognizing the damaging nature of this evidence, [the defence lawyer] Neal moved quickly to challenge the admission of any testimony or tests that were not directly related to the 1973 Pinto, the model year of the Ulrichs' car. In a series of rulings over the course of the trial, Judge Staffeldt concurred with Neal and barred nearly all materials that predated 1973. Needless to say, this had the result of seriously undermining the state's case. In the end, only a small percentage, perhaps as low as 5 percent, of the documents the prosecution had compiled were admitted as evidence.
>
> The judge's reluctance to permit the jury to consider the totality of the prosecution's case points up the difficulty of transporting what has traditionally been a product liability case from civil into criminal court. To a large extent it appears that the rural judge was never fully comfortable in knowing how this was to be done. Indeed his grabbing onto 1973 as his evidentiary standard reveals that he either did not fully comprehend the logic of

> the prosecution's case or did not embrace the legal theory on which it was based. It seems that he wished to treat the 1973 Pinto as he would [have] any other weapon in a homicide case: Since it was this weapon that caused the crime, evidence on other weapons was irrelevant. Of course at the heart of the prosecution's case was the understanding that Ford's recklessness with regard to the 1973 Pinto was intimately contingent on what the corporation had done in its product development of the car line in the previous years. Whether rightly or wrongly, Judge Staffeldt failed to appreciate this distinction between the recklessness of corporate decision making and that involved in more traditional forms of criminality.†

Celia Wells has written extensively about the failed efforts in the U.K. to prosecute the owners and employees involved in the Zeebrugge disaster, in which nearly 200 people drowned when *The Herald of Free Enterprise* capsized just outside the harbour in March 1987 because the ferry doors had been left open. In "Corporations: Culture, Risk and Criminal Liability" [1993] Crim. L. Rev. 551, she implicates the "ideological foundation of the structure of criminal blame, that is, individualism in its various guises" for criminal law's failure to "blame" corporations (at 558). Additionally, she identifies individualism's "substantive manifestation in the form of 'recklessness' " (*ibid.*).

She describes in detail the confusion and doubt generated by the 17 defence counsel as to the appropriate test and relevant evidence regarding the *mens rea* of "recklessness". The fault element of recklessness can be proven, at least under English law, by an objective route. Thus, the prosecution can establish recklessness by demonstrating that the risk at issue was obvious and serious, yet the accused failed to give any thought to it: *R. v. Caldwell*, [1982] A.C. 341 (H.L. 1981). However, even this objective rendering of recklessness has been virtually nullified through corporate litigation. Wells notes that defence lawyers managed to persuade the judge to hear evidence on whether the risk was serious and obvious only from the owner's own captains: "It is difficult to see how such witnesses could have represented the foresight of a prudent ferry company since the company for which they worked was on trial for this very failure of foresight." She also identifies another legal hurdle as "the apparent insistence on evidence that **a particular person** had indeed had such foresight prior to the accident before the jury could consider whether a prudent ferry company would have realised the risk of open-door sailing" (at 555). [Emphasis in original.] See also Celia Wells, "The Decline and Rise of English Murder: Corporate Crime and Individual Responsibility" [1988] Crim. L. Rev. 788; Celia Wells, "Corporate Manslaughter: A Cultural and Legal Form" (1995) 6 Crim. L. Forum 45; *D.P.P. v. P. & O. European Ferries (Dover) Ltd.* (1991), 93 Crim. App. R. 73 (ruling by the Central Criminal Court that an indictment for manslaughter may lie against a corporation); and *R. v. Alcindor* (19 October 1990), (Central Crim. Ct.) [unreported] (direction to acquit employees charged in the disaster).

In the context of workplace maimings and killings, authors such as Harry Glasbeek and Susan Rowland in "Are Injuring and Killing at Work Crimes?" (1979) 17 Osgoode Hall L.J. 506 have argued for the criminal prosecution of individual corporate actors and corporate bodies for homicide. As of 2006, Canada was ranked fifth among the industrialized nations for its rate of workplace deaths. Ahead of Canada in this regard are Korea, Mexico, Portugal, and Turkey. An average of five people die every day from job-related activity in Canada, up by 18 per cent since 2004 and by 45 per cent since 1993: Centre for the Study of Living Standards, *Five Deaths a Day: Workplace Fatalities in Canada, 1993–2005* (2006).

C. CHALLENGES OF PROVING THE FAULT ELEMENT FOR HOMICIDE

Homicide prosecutions against corporations can be pursued under *Criminal Code* s. 222, manslaughter by way of unlawful act or manslaughter by way of criminal negligence, or simply s. 220, criminal negligence causing death. Recall from the chapter on ***Mens Rea*** that all these offences are tested objectively and thus should not pose insurmountable hurdles for the prosecution. In spite of the theoretical availability of the criminal law, according to Eric Tucker's research, "The Westray Mining Disaster", above, under ***Actus Reus***, Causation, in Canada there were only eight homicide prosecutions against corporations for the deaths of employees in the 20th century. Among these, only one conviction for manslaughter has withstood appeal: *R. v. Brazeau Collieries Ltd.*, [1942] 3 W.W.R. 570 (Alta. S.C.) (fine of $5000 for the deaths of 29 miners in a methane gas explosion). Homicide prosecutions against corporations have been undertaken with respect to the death of eight miners in a cave-in at Belmoral Mines in Québec in 1981 and with respect to the deaths of 26 miners in the Westray disaster in Nova Scotia in 1992.

In *A.G. Québec v. Belmoral Mines Ltée.* (1987), 55 C.R. (3d) 378, the Québec Court of Appeal ruled that the corporation should be retried on the eight manslaughter charges because the trial judge had inappropriately instructed the jury that to find criminal negligence they must find that the supervisors were aware of the risk of a cave-in created by their use of inappropriate methods, but also that they were "incompetent". The Crown declined to re-prosecute the company, even though Judge René Beaudry, head of a provincial commission into the disaster, found that the cave-in was foreseeable and that the mine had put profits before safety, because too much time had passed since the disaster (almost 10 years of legal wrangling), making effective prosecution difficult: Barrie McKenna & Patricia Poirier, "Charges dropped against mining firm" *The [Toronto] Globe and Mail* (2 February 1990) A1.

A methane gas explosion at the Westray coal mine near New Glasgow, Nova Scotia, killed 26 miners. This mine had experienced safety problems prior to the fatal explosion on May 9, 1992. On at least three occasions in 1992, the provincial mine inspectors identified serious violations of the *Occupational Health and Safety Act*, including unacceptably high levels of coal dust (which could have been the fuel for the massive methane explosion), malfunctioning methane-monitoring equipment, inadequate ventilation, and improper storage of barrels of oil. Mine inspectors had also documented that a large section of the mine's roof was collapsing in May 1991. However, despite these regulatory violations, the mine was not charged with provincial offences, and clean-up orders issued by the responsible inspectors were never enforced: CP, "N.S. report reveals mine safety flaws" *The [Toronto] Globe and Mail* (30 April 1993) A4.

Furthermore, RCMP investigations revealed that 33 minutes before the fatal explosion, an alarm went off in the surface control room, warning of high methane levels underground. Regulations under the provincial act require coal operators to cease work when methane levels reach 1.25 per cent; at 2.5 per cent the mine must be evacuated because methane becomes explosive at levels between 5 and 15 per cent. The pencilled annotations on Westray's computer records indicate that the methane level at the time of the alarm was 1.25 per cent. Westray officials claim that they did not stop work at that time because the monitoring equipment was in the process of being reconnected after being moved, and that the alarm was the result of sporadic "voltage spikes". According to Westray and the manufacturer of the computer, "voltage spikes" are insignificant but common when wiring is reconnected. Westray also claimed that subsequent computer messages assured them that the methane levels in the mine were "healthy": Peter Moon, "Alarm preceded Westray explosion" *The [Toronto] Globe and Mail* (27 March 1993) A1, A6.

Nova Scotia faced several hurdles in the effort to hold Westray accountable. First, the province laid a total of 52 charges against the company and against four of Westray's managers in October 1992 for violations of the provincial act. At the same time, a provincial inquiry into the causes of the explosion and the conduct of mine representatives, provincial safety officials, and politicians was launched. In December, the director of public prosecutions for Nova Scotia reduced the charges to 18 after his request for a delay in the hearing of the charges, in order to complete the lengthy investigation, was denied by a judge. In January 1993, the provincial inquiry was stayed by the Supreme Court of Nova Scotia pending resolution of all criminal charges because otherwise the rights of the accused to remain silent and to a fair trial could be jeopardized if they were forced to testify before the provincial inquiry. Then, in March 1993, the director of prosecutions dropped all charges under the *Occupational Health and Safety Act* against the accused because he "feared that a trial would jeopardize potential criminal charges" that might be laid by the RCMP on the same facts: Kevin Cox, "N.S. drops charges in

Westray explosion" *The [Toronto] Globe and Mail* (5 March 1993) A5.

Criminal charges of manslaughter and criminal negligence causing death were eventually laid in April 1993 against the owners of the mine and two senior officials, Gerald Phillips and Roger Parry. In May 1993, the two prosecutors withdrew from the case, stating that the government had withheld funds and thus denied them the ability to properly investigate and prosecute: CP, "Prosecutors accuse N.S. of endangering mine probe" *The [Toronto] Globe and Mail* (5 May 1993) A18. These charges were then dismissed by Provincial Court Judge Patrick Curran in July because they were said to be too vaguely worded: Kevin Cox, "Westray charges thrown out" *The [Toronto] Globe and Mail* (21 July 1993) A1, A2. Charges were re-laid several days later, with the indictments specifying 13 ways in which the conduct of Curragh Inc. showed "wanton and reckless disregard" and specifying violations of the provincial safety act.

From July 1993 until June 1995, legal wrangling continued. In September 1993, Curragh Inc. filed for bankruptcy. In October 1993, Judge Curran dismissed another effort by Curragh Inc. to quash the charges: *R. v. Curragh Inc.*, reproduced below. In December 1993, Judge Curran denied a request by Roger Parry to be tried by a judge alone rather than a judge and jury, given the size and complexity of the matter: "Westray manager can't pick mode of trial" *The Ottawa Citizen* (3 December 1993) A3. In March 1994, further inquiry into Gerald Phillips' financial means by the inquiry, which had agreed to pay his and six other mine officials' legal costs, discovered that he had agreed to buy a $500,000 retirement home in the United States: CP, "Judge rethinks legal fees deal with accused in Westray case" *The [Toronto] Globe and Mail* (26 March 1994) A3. It became public information in 1995 that Roger Parry's defence in the criminal charges was funded by Legal Aid: Steve MacLeod, "Judge halts Westray trial" *The Ottawa Citizen* (10 June 1995) A1.

When the trial commenced in February 1995, the defence started a series of motions requesting disclosure of the volumes of evidence and reports in the hands of the prosecutors, the commission of inquiry, and other provincial agencies. As a result of disagreement and criticism from the trial judge regarding the prosecution's position on disclosure, case management, and preparation for trial, the Crown asked Judge Robert Anderson to excuse himself from the case and when he refused, moved, unsuccessfully, for a mistrial in March on the basis of a reasonable apprehension of bias on the part of the trial judge: CP, "Crown asks Westray judge to quit after 'ill-advised' phone call made" *The [Toronto] Globe and Mail* (10 March 1995) A4.

After four months of legal argument and very little evidence (only 22 out 200 witnesses had testified), Judge Anderson agreed with the defence's argument that inadequate disclosure of the Crown's case had been made, in contravention of s. 7 of the *Charter*, and stayed the charges against all of the accused: *R. v. Curragh Inc.* (1995), 146 N.S.R. (2d) 163 (S.C.). Furthermore, in doing so, the judge awarded costs in the amount of $150,000 to be paid to Gerald Phillips by the Crown:

> The Court has been reminded frequently of the importance, the complexity, and difficulty of this case. It is therefore more important that the accused in such a case be treated fairly and the fundamental principles of justice be observed. This has not been the case here....

The stay of proceedings was successfully appealed by the Crown to the Nova Scotia Court of Appeal ((1995), 146 N.S.R. (2d) 161 (C.A.)) and affirmed by the Supreme Court of Canada: [1997] 1 S.C.R. 537. Gerald Phillips' appeal costs were funded by legal aid: CP, "Westray accused gets aid" *The [Toronto] Globe and Mail* (8 June 1996) A4A. The Court based its decision on the grounds of reasonable apprehension of bias as well as actual bias because the trial judge had inappropriately called a senior bureaucrat during the trial to complain about the behaviour of the prosecutor and then requested his removal from the case. Thus, Phillips and Parry were to face a new trial on the manslaughter charges, although the Court ordered that they be compensated for their legal costs.

In the summer of 1998, the Crown's office decided to stay the criminal proceedings as having "no reasonable prospect of conviction". The Honourable Fred Kaufman was asked to review the performance of the N.S. prosecution service thereafter, and he determined that a detailed analysis of the failed *Westray* prosecution was imperative. An independent report by two Halifax lawyers convinced N.S. Justice Minister Robbie Harrison to announce that he would not re-open any of the criminal charges. The *Review of the Nova Scotia Public Prosecution Service: Report on the Westray Prosecution*, by Duncan R. Beveridge and Patrick J. Duncan (Halifax, March 2000) concluded that the Crown's decision in 1998 was "not unreasonable".

The report catalogued numerous causes for the failed prosecution, including police failure to treat the mine as a crime scene and to secure the premises leading to the loss of evidence, under-resourcing of the prosecution, and systematic deficiencies in securing, cataloguing and disclosing in excess of 300,000 documents and the evidence of almost 300 witnesses. When reading the decision below, in which the charges survived an earlier challenge, consider the difficulties that would have been faced in a trial. Was the Crown's decision to stay the charges "not unreasonable"?

R. v. Curragh Inc.†

[CURRAN PROV. CT. J.:]

. . . .

The accused Curragh is charged that, between the 10th day of September 1991 and the 10th day of May 1992, at or near Plymouth, it did cause the deaths of twenty-six miners by means of an unlawful act, to wit: conducting its mine operation so that the employees were exposed to health or safety hazards of excessive accumulation of coal dust without taking systematic steps to prevent explosions of coal dust occurring, contrary to s. 9(1)(f) of the *Occupational Health and Safety Act*, R.S.N.S., 1989, c. 320, and did thereby commit manslaughter, contrary to s. 236 of the *Criminal Code*.

MANSLAUGHTER

. . . .

What is the nature of unlawful acts manslaughter based on penal negligence?

McLachlin J., on behalf of the majority in *Creighton*, *supra*, wrote at pp. 485 ...:

> ...in addition to the *actus reus* and *mens rea* associated with the underlying act, all that is required to support a manslaughter conviction is foreseeability of the risk of bodily harm.... The unlawful act must be objectively dangerous, that is likely to injure another person.

On p. 25 ... she added:

> ...in an offence based on unlawful conduct, a predicate offence involving carelessness or negligence must also be read as requiring a "marked departure" from the standard of the reasonable person.

Still further at p. 39, McLachlin J. wrote:

> The answer to the question of whether the accused took reasonable care must be founded on a consideration of all the circumstances of the case. The question is what the reasonably prudent person would have done in all the circumstances.

Can breach of a provincial statute constitute an unlawful act for purposes of s. 222(5)(a) of the *Criminal Code*?

In the case of *R. v. DeSousa* (1992), 76 C.C.C. (3d) 124, the Supreme Court of Canada decided that the term "unlawfully" in the offence of unlawfully causing bodily harm contrary to s. 269 of the *Criminal Code* included breaches of both federal and provincial offences other than those of absolute liability. In *Creighton*, *supra*, McLachlin J. held, at p. 6 ... that the test set out in *DeSousa* for the unlawful act required by s. 269 of the *Criminal Code* was equally applicable to unlawful act manslaughter. A provincial offence, therefore, can be the basis of unlawful act manslaughter.

. . . .

Can an omission constitute an unlawful act as referred to in s. 222(5)(a)?

Both Curragh and the individual accused are charged with having committed manslaughter by failing to take systematic steps to prevent the harm that resulted in the deaths from developing. Counsel for the three accused maintain that the plain meaning of the term "unlawful act" does not include omissions. If what were alleged were mere omissions, as was the case in the first set of criminal charges against the accused, I would agree. On the other hand, when what is alleged is the failure to adequately carry out a statutory duty in the course of carrying on a potentially dangerous activity, one could accurately describe the matter as either

† (1993), 125 N.S.R. (2d) 185 (Prov. Ct.).

omission or commission. Carelessness (or penal negligence) contrary to a statutory duty (to handle firearms carefully) was precisely what was involved in *Gosset*, *supra*. Without reference to whether such carelessness involved commission or omission, the Supreme Court of Canada found that such carelessness could be the basis for the offence of unlawful act manslaughter.

. . . .

... Curragh argues that the manslaughter count against it is fatally deficient in that it does not allege, in the words of s. 9(1)(f) of the *Occupational Health and Safety Act*, that Curragh "failed to take every reasonable precaution as stated in the Act." The section reads as follows:

> **9**(1) Every employer shall take every precaution that is reasonable in the circumstances to ...
> (f) conduct his undertaking so that employees are not exposed to health or safety hazards as a result of the undertaking.

As counsel for Curragh puts it, the offence is not "conducting the undertaking so that the employees were exposed to health or safety hazards" as alleged in the information, but "failing to take every reasonable precaution" against such hazards. Crown counsel, on the other hand, says the words "take every precaution" merely create a defence of due diligence.

On this issue I would disagree with the Crown ... when the charge is manslaughter. The Crown has acknowledged that the manslaughter counts are charges of penal negligence. To say the accused would have the onus of proving the absence of negligence on the balance of probability is inappropriate and wrong. It might be argued that the words "without taking systematic steps to prevent explosions of coal dust" at least impliedly adopt the "reasonable precautions" provisions of s. 9(1)(f). In any event, the Supreme Court of Canada in *Creighton*, *supra*, has made it clear that, in all unlawful act manslaughter charges based on underlying offences of penal negligence, failure by a marked degree to take the care a reasonable person would take in the circumstances is an element of the offence. Like all other elements, it is something that must be proved by the Crown. The Crown itself recognized that to be the state of the law when it said, in paragraph 62 of its brief, that "lack of reasonableness must be proved beyond a reasonable doubt". The manslaughter charge against Curragh, therefore, fails to include an essential element of the charge.

. . . .

CRIMINAL NEGLIGENCE CHARGE

The accused are charged with causing the deaths of the twenty-six miners by showing wanton or reckless disregard for their lives or safety in 13 specified ways in the operation of the Westray Coal Mine. Defence counsel argue that there is no nexus shown between the conduct alleged and the deaths of the men. Surely such a nexus or connection is at least implied in the charge and, in any event, would have to be proved beyond reasonable doubt in order for there to be a conviction. The charge need not state how the conduct caused the deaths, but if the evidence does not prove it, the accused must be acquitted.

. . . .

CONCLUSIONS

The manslaughter charges are valid, although the charge against Curragh must be read as including an allegation that the company failed to take every precaution that was reasonable in the circumstances against health or safety hazards and both charges must be read as requiring the Crown to prove a marked departure from the care that would have been taken by a reasonable person.

The criminal negligence charge is valid on its face.

The motions to quash are dismissed.

■

What additional hurdles does *Curragh Inc.* add to the prosecution's burden of proof for unlawful act manslaughter based on violations of provincial workplace safety laws, usually construed as strict liability offences? Can the Crown rely on proof that a provincial act was violated, and, in the absence of a persuasive due diligence defence, use the breach as the unlawful act? If not, what practical difficulties will homicide prosecutions face, in light of Cory J.'s comments in *Wholesale Travel* as to enforceability of regulatory regimes in the absence of strict liability?

D. LEGISLATIVE REFORM

The Westray Inquiry commenced in November of 1995 and conducted hearings through 1996. Among the items of evidence brought before the inquiry, consider the following: the testimony of numerous expert witnesses, including Westray's own chief surveyor, who spoke to the preventable nature of the explosion and the failure of management to develop a mine plan and to eliminate dangerous working conditions; the failure of the provincial government to enact a proper health and safety code and to enforce the law against Westray; testimony suggesting political pressure exerted against mining inspectors not to enforce clean up orders against the company and documenting destruction of papers related to the controversial agreement by the province to buy Westray coal (even if it was never mined) by a high level Nova Scotia official; and allegations by employees and others testifying as to the obviousness of the dangers and threats of dismissal by managers to those who complained about the conditions. The Nova Scotia government has, since the release of the report of Justice K. Peter Richard, Commr., *The Westray Story: A Predictable Path to Disaster: Report of the Westray Mine Inquiry* (Halifax: Government of Nova Scotia, 1997), apologized to the families and agreed to implement all of its 74 recommendations: Kevin Cox, "System failed Westray miners, families, N.S. says in apology" *The [Toronto] Globe and Mail* (19 December 1997) A1.

Consider again Eric Tucker's argument in "The Westray Mining Disaster" about the politics of causation, at 116–17:

> The legal process ... discourages inquiries into the systemic factors that produce the behaviour which is the subject of the prosecution. Attention will be directed to the most immediate events (thereby separating them from their social context) and the actions of particular individuals.... The process of decontextualization and individualization are driven by the need for prosecutors to focus the court's attention on the elements of the criminal offence the law requires them to prove, as well as by the ideological commitments of judges who are unlikely to sympathize with attempts to condemn as criminal conduct what they see as socially beneficial.

In fact, both the provincial and federal governments were involved in financing Westray and smoothing over safety concerns: see Harry Glasbeek & Eric Tucker, *Death by Consensus. The Westray Story* (North York, Ont.: Centre for Research on Work and Society, 1992) at 5–9; and Dean Jobb, *Calculated Risk: Greed, Politics and the Westray Tragedy* (Halifax: Nimbus, 1996).

One of the recommendations of the Westray Inquiry was that the federal government seek reforms to the *Criminal Code* that would hold corporations and corporate managers accountable for crime. The NDP brought forward Bill C-259 in 1999 in pursuit of this objective, but it only received first reading. In November 2002 the federal government published a report in which it concluded that the "directing mind" model of attaching *mens rea* to corporations does not reflect the realities of decision-making in complex organizations. However, it rejected reforms to the law as it affects the criminal responsibility of managers and directors, adoption of the doctrine of vicarious liability, and the idea of a new crime of corporate killing for workplace deaths, instead proposing to codify a duty of reasonable care for the safety of workers. It also suggested broadening the category of actors whose conduct engages corporate criminal responsibility to include those with delegated, operational authority and basing corporate responsibility for criminal negligence on the acts or omissions of corporate representatives.

The new law, *An Act to amend the Criminal Code (criminal liability of organizations)*, S.C. 2003, c. 21, was mentioned at the start of this chapter in connection with the ruling in *R. v. Ontario Power Generation*. Recall that s. 22.1 makes a corporation party to offences of penal negligence where one or more representatives, acting within the scope of their authority, commits the offence and "the senior officer who is responsible for the aspect of the organization's activities that is relevant to the offence departs ... markedly from the standard of care that, in the circumstances, could reasonably be expected to prevent a representative of the organization from being a party to the offence." To summarize, the Crown must prove that a senior officer, acting with the intent at least in part to benefit the organization and acting within the scope of their authority either (a) was a party to the offence; (b) had the mental state to be a party and directed a representative to commit the act or omission in question; or (c) knowing that a representative was about to commit the offence, failed to take all reasonable measures to stop the offence. Section 22.2 responds to crimes that use a fault element other than negligence. Finally, s. 217.1 imposes a new legal duty on those who undertake, or have the authority to direct, another person's work to "take reasonable steps to prevent bodily harm to that person, or any other person, arising from that work or task." This new section may facilitate Crown prosecutions of omissions offences like criminal negligence by corporations by specifying a legal duty owed by employers.

Will these reforms actually make it easier to prosecute corporations like Westray for homicide? Consider the work of Neil Sargent in "Law, Ideology and Corporate Crime: A Critique of Instrumentalism" (1989) 4 C.J. Law & Society 39 at 54–56:

> [I]n order to account for the failure of the criminal justice system to respond to corporate crime it is important to look not only at external factors influencing the attitudes and conduct of legislators, law enforcement officials and judges, but also at the ideological discourses underlying the form of trial and such legal conceptions as responsibility and sanctioning. In particular, it is argued that the individualist orientation of criminal law, both in its trial and sentencing moments, plays a significant ideological role in facilitating and legitimizing the preferential treatment accorded to corporate offenders by the criminal justice system.
>
> ...
>
> From a legal perspective, then, the "problem" of corporate criminal liability has always centred around the search for a theory of liability and criminal sanctioning which is consistent with the individualist model. Courts and legislators in Canada have tried to fit corporate offenders into this individualist model of liability, rather than attempting to adapt the legal system to accommodate the collective reality of large-scale corporate organization. Thus Canadian courts have remained reluctant to extend the scope of corporate criminal responsibility to include the illegal acts or omissions of a corporation's agents or employees, on the basis that vicarious liability has no place in a system of criminal law based on principles of individual responsibility.
>
> ...
>
> Consequently, the more anonymous the criminal actor (and a large diversified corporate organization is a paradigm example of an anonymous actor), and the more complex the causal link between the illegal activity and the harm which results from it, the less likely that the corporate actor and its human agents will be held criminally responsible or treated with severity by the criminal justice system.
>
> Equally significant, in terms of the effectiveness of criminal sanctions against corporate offenders, may be the internal organizational structure of the corporation itself. Given the elaborate division of management functions within large corporate structures, decisions resulting in illegal corporate behaviour may be made at various levels in the corporate hierarchy, without any one individual being ultimately responsible for the illegal activity. In such circumstances, the decentralization of management and diffusion of responsibilities typical of large corporations may promote illegal corporate behaviour, while at the same time insulating individual participants from criminal responsibility for their actions.[†]

As you read the following decision regarding the criminal responsibility of Tammadge and Bednarek for the deaths and injuries caused at Barrett Chute, note that it was rendered before the 2003 amendments came into effect.

R. v. Tammadge[‡]

[P.R. BELANGER J.:]

Ontario Power Generation (OPG), John Tammadge and Robert Bednarek were jointly charged with 2 counts of criminal negligence causing the deaths of Cynthia Marie Cadieux and of Aaron Alexander Cadieux, as well as 7 counts of criminal negligence causing bodily harm to Azelynnd Thacker, Tammy

† The Canadian Journal of Law & Society is published by University of Toronto Press Incorporated, www.utpjournals.com. Reproduced by permission of Canadian Journal of Law and Society/Revue Canadienne Droit et Société.

‡ [2006] O.J. No. 5103 (Ct. J.) (QL).

Lea Deacon, Julie Marie Breeze, Michael Cadieux, Krista Marie Kehoe, Shawn Stephen Dobec and Darren A. Umpherson.

The trial began on January 16, 2006 and continued through 2006, ending on December 1, 2006 after 75 days of trial time.

. . . .

OVERVIEW OF THE MADAWASKA RIVER SYSTEM

The Madawaska River system is located in Eastern Ontario and flows from Source Lake in Algonquin Park to Chats Lake near Arnprior, a town 55 kilometres upstream from the City of Ottawa. ...

Along this river system, Ontario Power Generation (OPG) owns and operates five separate generating stations and two control dams. ... These generating stations and dams are situated along the river in such a way that the water from one station flows into the headpond (intake area) of the next downstream station, creating what is known as a Cascading River System. ...

. . . .

BARRETT CHUTE

The Main Dam at Barrett Chute is 335 metres long and has a maximum height of 30 metres. When water reaches the main dam, it collects in a fore bay. When the generating units are operating, water is discharged from the fore bay through a man-made canal ... It then passes through the generating station and into Calabogie Lake. After the dam was constructed in 1941, the original riverbed became a spillway or a course through which water could be diverted away from the generating station. ...

. . . .

The first portion of the spillway

It is within the first portion of the spillway below the dam that the tragic events of June 23, 2002 took place.

As water trickles from the closed sluice gates, it descends on a downward gradient through that first portion into large and small ponds or basins, around rocky prominences, through crevasses and over flat, time- and water-worn rock slabs before reaching that deeper area of the spillway which doglegs to the northwest. ... Trees, brush and vegetation cover, at various points, the higher points of land in the waterway such that lines of sight from any location along its course are markedly restricted. The evidence makes it clear that from any location along the 335 metre walkway atop the dam, it was impossible, at least during the summer months, to see beyond the first of a series of pools. ...

Below the first two ponds closest to the dam, the first portion is traversed by a series of three relatively flat (but angled) rocky outcroppings around and through which trickling water snakes on its downward course. It is on the second of these outcroppings that the Cadieux family was located on the 23rd of June 2002. Their presence could not have been detected unless an observer traveled down to the southeastern bank to their location or across from their location on the northwestern bank.

. . . .

Recreational use of the Barrett Chute site

At the lower end of the spillway, opposite the generating station, persons would use the rocky point and lands immediately to the south of it for camping and fishing. Others would use the cliffs as a diving spot. ...

On the upper reaches of the spillway, people used all of the rocky outcropping areas below the dam as a place to sunbathe and picnic. Children played in the shallow pools. ...

The entire site was a popular recreational destination for people living in this part of Renfrew County and had been used for that purpose for a long time, well before construction of the dam and after its completion in 1942. ... On pleasant summer weekend days, there could be as many as 100 people in the area, according to one witness.

. . . .

Spilling water

. . . .

Prior to market opening on May 1, 2002 and of the trial periods that preceded it in March and April, spilling at Barrett Chute was a rare occurrence. Spilling water was considered a waste of a resource to be avoided if possible. ... Intentional spilling was consequently limited to raising and lowering of gates to test equipment.

. . . .

The June 23 2002 spill from the witnesses'/victims' perspective

Michael Raymond Cadieux (aged 42 at the time of trial) was the husband of the deceased Cynthia Marie Cadieux (aged 32 at the time of the incident) and the father of Aaron Alexander Cadieux (born in 1994). He and his family lived and worked in the City of Renfrew. For recreational purposes, he and his family often went to the first portion of the spillway, which he refers to as High Falls. ... There they would picnic, relax and enjoy the sunshine while the children played in the water. On June 23rd, they arrived at about 1 o'clock in the afternoon, planning to spend the afternoon.

Less than one hour after they had been there, his wife said that the water was coming up. She was closer to the middle of the rocks, 10 feet away from him. The following excerpts of the evidence describe graphically what happened next:

> *"I noticed that there was a bit more water coming over the rocks, and we just started gathering our things ... I grabbed up our things and headed off to the side. Adam (his other son) was on the side, I had a cooler, and grabbed what I could ... I put it down beside Adam, and then I heard Cyndi yell that it was coming more, and when I turned around, I went to go back to them, and I couldn't go back because I got swept down in the water. It knocked me off my feet ... Well, she wanted to come across, but when I went back, I went to grab Aaron, and I couldn't go. Like I said, I couldn't go across ... Water really started to come fast. Then you could hear the water, like a roar of water. Like I say, when I went in, turned around, the water took my feet from under me and I went down a bit. I grabbed onto a small stick standing — or coming out the side. I pulled myself up. When I stood up, I could see Adam, he was shouting, 'What's going on?' And I turned around, and Cyndi had Aaron in her arms and the water was completely around her ... I just — and I couldn't get to them. I just — the water just came too fast. I told her to stay where she was because the water was still going around, just figuring, okay, it's not going to come up anymore ... She was still hanging onto Aaron, and I told her to plant her feet. The rock came up like about a foot, and the current was pushing on her. She was still hanging onto Aaron. I had — and the water was still coming up, getting louder. I turned to Adam to make sure he was okay, and when I turned back, they were gone."*

Both Cynthia and Aaron were washed away downstream and drowned.

. . . .

ROBERT BEDNAREK

Responsibilities, training and record

Robert Bednarek began employment with OPG's predecessor, Ontario Hydro in 1990 as a probationary Power Maintenance Electrician. On June 23, 2002, he was employed (classified 1992) as a Regional Maintainer — Electric, affected to the Barrett Chute Generating Station since 1991. After 3 days of classroom training in June of 2000 conducted by Chris Tonkin (who worked in the Training and Development Centre), he was "deemed qualified" to act as an operating agent by Moreland in July of 2000.

. . . .

His training in the mechanical and safety aspects of raising and lowering sluice gates was not formalized. It was essentially on-the-job training under the supervision of more senior and experienced employees. ...

. . . .

WIP W00009 (WIP 9)
(Issue date January 25 1999)

This OPG Work Instruction and Procedure (WIP) provides direction "regarding the remote and local operation of sluice gates ... to control and minimize waterway safety hazards to employees, contractors and the public". It exists to apply corporate policy directing that "hydroelectric will manage its facilities so as to keep its employees, contractors and the public safe from any injury caused as a result of its operations".

"Local operation" is defined as follows: "Equipment which is manually operated or where visual inspection of waterway is possible **from equipment operating point**". [Emphasis in original.]

"Remote operation": "Operation where visual inspection of waterway is NOT possible from equipment operating point"

In the "Local Operation" portion of the WIP, it provides:

> Prior to opening a sluice gate ... staff must:
> - Ensure that the spillway is clear by visually inspecting the downstream spillway, waterway and shoreline.
> - Notify all employees, contractors or the public who are in areas which will or could be adversely affected by waterflow resulting from the sluice gate ... operation, to vacate these areas.

- If the public refuse to leave, notify security/police and request that they be removed from the area.
- If employees or contractors refuse to leave, notify your supervisor
- Do not operate sluice gates ... until the water safety risk to all persons has been considered

Under the "Remote Operation" caption, the WIP provides:

Staff must follow these steps:

- Lift the sluice gate 15 centimeters (6 inches) and leave it at this height for a period of 5 minutes
- After this time has elapsed, raise the sluice gate to the desired opening
- Subsequent operations may be carried out with no restriction

The new market opening in 2002

The market opening following the restructuring of Ontario's Electrical Industry is described in detail in Appendix B. ... I will not describe it in any further detail here except to say that it created great frustration for those charged with electricity production on the Madawaska River. ... Without delving into the technicalities of the market and dispatch system, it is sufficient to say ... for our purposes, spilling became a regular occurrence when it had hitherto been rare. ...

. . . .

The events of June 23, 2002 from the perspective of the OPG employees

On June 23, Bill Waite was the one of the day shift Level 1A operators at the in Chenaux Control room. At 1:01 p.m. he determined that water would have to be spilled at Barrett Chute as too much water was headed in that direction from upstream and he anticipated that water levels at Barrett Chute would have to be lowered. ...

He called Bob Bednarek at his home and requested him to go to Barrett Chute to open a sluice gate. There was some urgency to spill and he told Bednarek "we don't have time to waste". Bednarek arrived at the generating station with his binoculars around 1:39 and called Waite to confirm his arrival.

. . . .

According to his statement to police, Bednarek made an announcement over the intercom/PA system that spilling was about to occur. He then took an OPG truck and drove it to the rough river crossing to a point 3/4 of the way across. From there he looked upstream and saw no one. He looked downstream and observed about 20 people with 4-wheelers and boats in the area of the point opposite the tailrace. He advised them of the imminent spill and told them to leave. They did so. He then drove up the road on the westerly side of the spillway to the dam. He drove his truck along the base of the dam to a point just before the sluice gates discharge ramps where a wing wall prevents further progress. While driving to that location, he was looking for people but could see no one except a lone sunbather on the rocks (Mr. Brydges) and had a conversation with him that I will discuss in greater detail later on. He looked downstream with his binoculars and saw no one. He drove back to the top of the dam. According to his statement, he walked across the dam and stopped 3 or 4 times, looking downstream with his binoculars, seeing no one. ...

Bednarek raised the sluice gate about 1 metre for about 5 minutes and then raised it all the way. "Meanwhile," he says, "I had the binoculars and was looking downstream. When the gate was up to full I noticed the guy who had been below the sluice gate over by a truck. I spoke to him briefly and then went over to the shed, called Chenaux at 2:26 and told them that the sluice gate was opened all the way":

LAVIOLETTE: Chenaux George.

BEDNAREK: George.

LAVIOLETTE: Bobby.

BEDNAREK: Sluice gate number one (1) is all the way up.

...

BEDNAREK: But um ...

LAVIOLETTE: Yeah.

BEDNAREK: I'm glad I took a walk around but you know ...

LAVIOLETTE: Yeah.

BEDNAREK: You still can't see everything.

LAVIOLETTE: No you can't.

BEDNAREK: So.

LAVIOLETTE: Alright.

. . . .

At 3:28 Waite instructed Bednarek to start lowering the gate. At 3:46, in another call, he told Bednarek that he had heard that 3 children had gone missing. At 3:48, he told Bednarek to shut the gate completely. Bednarek advised that it was closed at 3:51.

. . . .

THE BRYDGES/BEDNAREK CONVERSATION

In his statement to police, Bednarek says that he walked up to Brydges. He was yelling at him, "but he did not hear me until I was closer" because, apparently, of the noise of leakage coming from under the sluice gate. Bednarek asked him to leave and asked if he had seen anyone else around the area, to which Brydges replied "no". Brydges also said that he did not hear the page on the intercom. ...

Brydges acknowledges meeting Bednarek and telling him that he had not seen anyone in the area, but says that he added that there had been people there the previous day. ...

. . . .

I accept Mr. Brydges' version that he told Bednarek there were persons using the hot rocks recreationally the previous day. Mr. Bednarek merely remembered in his statement being told that Brydges had not seen anyone there. The area was somewhat noisy because of water trickling under the gate. It may be he did not hear Brydges well. ...

BEDNAREK AND GARY CAMERON

Gary Cameron had been an employee of OPG and its predecessor for 17 years at the time of the incident and was employed at Barrett Chute as a mechanical maintainer and operating agent in training under Gary James. He had used the area of Barrett Chute as a recreational destination since adolescence and was aware of the public use of the area below the dam. ...

He stated that there was a gathering on May 1st to celebrate market opening and that "the whole plant and John Tammadge and Jim Moreland was there". He said the following in his examination in chief:

> **Q.** *And when you were told that at that gathering, what reaction, if any, did you have to that?*
>
> **A.** *I just once blurt out that you cannot just spill the water at Barrett Chute.*
>
> **Q.** *And did you explain why you can't just spill the water at Barrett Chute?*
>
> **A.** *No one reacted or sounded concerned. Jim Moreland said, "It makes good business sense, we will spill the water around it." And no one brought it up, anything further than that.*

. . . .

On a review of the preceding material as well as all of Cameron's evidence, I am unable to conclude that Bednarek heard any of Cameron's statement, whatever it may have been, in the lunchroom. ...

. . . .

Analysis relating to Robert Bednarek

On the totality of the evidence, I conclude that Robert Bednarek knew that there was an area of the spillway below the dam that he could not see on a visual inspection from the top or the foot of the dam or from the lower part of the spillway looking upstream from where the rough trail crosses the water and that he knew that that general area was used by the public for recreational purposes. He also knew that the warning water procedure was likely not effective to warn people of an impending spill; he also knew that the [PA] system at the dam could not be heard any appreciable distance away. I also conclude that he knew that spilling water from the sluice gates created a potential public hazard because of the sudden release of massive quantities of water.

. . . .

In the light of those findings, am I in a position to conclude that he was *criminally* negligent by opening of the sluice gate on June 23rd without inspecting the hidden part of the spillway?

Objectively viewed, would a reasonable person in his circumstances have foreseen the risk? I think so.

If he was negligent did his negligence constitute a "marked and substantial departure" from the standard of the reasonable person? Not every negligent act is criminal. Not *any* departure justifies conviction. ... Being aware of the existence of a risk does not lead inevitably to a finding of criminal negligence. Rather, I must find that he was wanton and reckless in his disregard for the safety of others. I must find that he was ungoverned and undisciplined and that he was heedless of consequences, headlong, irresponsible.

. . . .

After careful deliberation, I conclude that while there are negligent aspects to the conduct of Robert Bednarek on June 23, 2002, his conduct, considering the totality of the evidence, cannot be categorized as criminal. I arrive at this decision because of the following reasons:

1. While Bednarek's actions fall short of ideal, he did not open the gates without any consideration of the potential for harm. He arrived at

the site promptly after the call and made an announcement on the intercom paging system. He proceeded to the trail crossing the waterway and looked upstream with his binoculars. He attended at the point of land opposite the tail race and asked the 20 or so individuals to vacate the area. He did so with competent and polite consideration and re-examined that location when he returned to the powerhouse. When he arrived at the dam, he made a number of visual inspections with binoculars both from the foot of the dam, the road leading to the bottom of the dam and at various points along the top to see if there were individuals downstream. He did this both before and after opening the gate. He inquired of Mr. Brydges if he had seen any one in the area.

2. Whether or not Bednarek was aware of WIP 9 is unknown. There was no system in place to ensure confirmation that the staff had received the instruction. WIP 9 is ambiguous. ... Strictly speaking, Bednarek followed WIP 9 to the letter. If this was a remote operation, he not only complied with it but went beyond its exigencies by opening the gate a full metre rather than 6 inches. ...

3. There was some urgency to the situation. When he told his controlling authority that he would open the gate at one metre for 10 or 15 minutes, Laviolette demurred and told him to let it run only for 5 minutes.

4. There is no evidence that Bednarek actually *knew there were people downstream on June 23rd and that he decided to spill regardless. His post event reactions bear this out.*

5. There is no evidence that Bednarek was trained to carry out a more extensive inspection than the one he carried out. Indeed, the evidence of his co-workers and fellow operator/agents is that they did no more than Bednarek when they opened a gate. Some said they did less. ...

6. Apart from Cameron's evidence, there is no evidence that Bednarek was specifically told about the public's use of the hidden part of the spillway. ...

7. Spilling in the summer was previously a very rare event and had never led to difficulties. ... The procedure followed by Bednarek was widely thought to be a reasonable response to previously identified dangers for several decades of safe operation.

8. Bednarek enjoyed good reputation as an employee and co-worker and had a previously flawless record.

CONCLUSION

Somewhat imperfectly, Mr. Bednarek adverted to the potential risk. He followed corporate procedure. Apart from the hidden section, his inspection was competent and diligent and his warnings to the people on the point and to Mr. Brydges were timely. I am not satisfied beyond a reasonable doubt that his actions were headlong and irresponsible or that they were ungoverned or undisciplined. They were flawed, to be sure, but not so callous or grossly insensitive as to warrant criminal conviction.

In short, in all of the circumstances of this difficult case, I feel that I am not justified to find that this single instance of momentary laxity and questionable judgment in an otherwise honourable and unblemished 15-year career should burden Mr. Bednarek with the stain of a criminal conviction, despite the fact that his actions led to disastrous consequences.

He is acquitted of all charges.

JOHN TAMMADGE

Background, responsibilities and evaluations

John Tammadge, an electrical engineer, began employment with OPG's predecessors in 1976 and progressed upwards in the corporate hierarchy, assuming his present position as Plant manager for the Ottawa/St. Lawrence Plant Group in 1993.

. . . .

Analysis

Knowledge of the Barrett Chute Site

. . . .

My ruling on the motion for a directed verdict ... identified areas that should be left to the trier of fact on the issue of knowledge of the public use of Barrett chute. ... For the purpose of these reasons, I incorporate by reference the comments that I made at that time and make the following comments and findings:

1. If Tammadge was told by Cameron that people were using the hidden part of the Barrett Chute spillway, it is highly doubtful that it was heard by Tammadge ...

2. The minutes of the Lower Madawaska Stakeholders Meeting of 3 April 2002 demonstrate a generic knowledge of the dangers of spilling. ...
3. The Mary Durst letter to Tammadge demonstrates knowledge of the public use of the Barrett Chute site by the public for recreational purposes. ...
4. The background paper of 14 June 2002 to Twomey and Yap shows that Tammadge knew that public utilization of spillways had public safety repercussions. ...
5. The Tammadge/Threader conversation is evidence of knowledge that the public in significant numbers used Barrett Chute for recreational purposes.
6. Tammadge's failure to use the "safety card" is not cogent evidence of his lack of knowledge of the public safety issue at Barrett Chute. It is more likely that he underestimated the dangers associated with spilling at that site. ...

Management

The Crown refers to individual requirements of the Plant Group Manager's Role Specification ... in order to highlight Mr. Tammadge's responsibilities vis-à-vis safety:

. . . .

2. He is charged with providing advice on all Hydroelectric and Electricity Production strategic matters and decisions that have ... public health and safety ... implications.
3. He advises of any emerging issues likely to affect hydroelectric performance and/or having environmental, public health and safety ... implications.
4. He must demonstrate evidence of having managed systems in place to meet all due diligence requirements, particularly with respect to ... public safety.

. . . .

8. He must have appropriate management systems in place to meet all due diligence requirements, particularly with respect to ... public safety ...

. . . .

In addition to these general specifications, the Crown refers to WIP 10 ...

While this rambling document refers to itself as policy, it is in reality an instruction to Plant Group Managers (among others). ... It describes the governing principles for public safety at Hydroelectric and the programs required to assure the application of and compliance with its terms. In it, OPG requires its employees to

. . . .

10. Plant Groups must develop and maintain a security program to ensure compliance with the WIP
11. Plant Group Managers are to act on the recommendations of a Public Safety Needs Assessment for each site

. . . .

The Crown submits that Mr. Tammadge failed dismally in these duties and responsibilities, particularly as they pertain to public safety. It submits that Mr. Tammadge failed to effectively carry out any of these responsibilities to such an extent that he fell far short of the standard. ...

. . . .

WIP 10

. . . .

In the end, I conclude that there was only partial *de facto* compliance with WIP 10 at Barrett Chute. The most glaring departure from its directive was the Plant Group's failure to develop and maintain a security program and little monitoring of the results of its activities. The development of such a program would have permitted a re-evaluation of the 1995 hazard assessment, the identification of hazardous areas and evaluation of existing signage and barriers. That is not to say that there was total disregard for safety needs. To the contrary, in respect of each of the 13 requirements of the Public Safety Needs Assessment, there is evidence of the existence of at least some level conformity. In some cases, there is a significant level of conformity, for example, in the establishment of relations with external agencies and in advertising campaigns to alert the public to the dangers of OPG installations. ...

The security reports

. . . .

In the late 1990's and early 2000's, John Tammadge carried out his duties as Plant Group Manager in the midst of a complete restructuring of the electrical industry in Ontario. ... On May 1, 2002, the implementation of new market rules upset decades of sound water stewardship practices on the Madawaska. ...

Abiding by all of the terms of WIP 10 might well have prevented the events of June 23, but that failure to implement all of its specifics has a context that is highly relevant in a determination of the issues in this case.

. . . .

With the benefit of hindsight, it is easy to say that immediately upon the promulgation of WIP 10 Tammadge should have immediately developed a security program. However, it seems to me that the urgency for doing so at that moment in time would not have been apparent, particularly when other operational imperatives arising out of restructuring must have been competing for a senior manager's attention. ...

Barrett Chute was one of 10 generating stations in his geographically large area of responsibility. I accept that he was not familiar with the precise topographical realities of the site. And that although the evidence shows that he knew that Barrett Chute was being used recreationally and that he knew or reasonably should have know that spilling created a potential danger to users, there is no proof meeting the criminal law standard that he was aware that persons were using the hidden part of the spillway and that WIP 9 was not an effective warning method. ...

. . . .

On the state of the volume and minutiae of evidence before me at this trial, it is nearly impossible to accurately assess the nature, breadth and effectiveness of reporting mechanisms within the Plant Group by which to gauge whether delegated functions and responsibilities were effectively carried out. ...

Public safety was only one of a very large number of responsibilities and accountabilities in the management of his plant group. Production quotas, maintenance of generating and corollary equipment, physical plants, personnel issues, community relations, finances, budget management, liaison with outside agencies and ministries, advice to superiors, etc., are but a few of the daily concerns he had to attend to. ...

While public safety may not have been on his "radar screen" after market opening, there is no evidence that Tammadge was complacent. Quite the opposite, he was very busy in May and June, as his calendar shows. ... Public safety may not have been a significant concern to Tammadge, but the desired result was the same: he wanted spilling stopped and the river run as a cascading balanced whole.

Conclusion relating to John Tammadge

. . . .

John Tammadge was not aware of existence of a hidden part of the spillway at Barrett Chute. He knew that people were using parts of Barrett Chute for recreational purposes and, at the very least, should have realized that spilling water could have safety repercussions. ... When spilling increased in the spring of 2002, the urgency for the development of a security program and hazard analysis should have become apparent.

He should at least have <u>considered</u> ordering a stoppage of spilling at Barrett Chute pending the implementation of a security program and hazard analysis. He did not.

These shortcomings, however, do not exist in a vacuum. They have to be viewed against a complex contextual background that involves a chaotic corporate environment caused by a massive restructuring of the electricity industry and the sudden imposition of a radically different marketing system for electricity. ...

. . . .

That context and those circumstances lead me to the view that while John Tammadge could have done more ... his actions (or lack thereof) cannot be described as headlong, irresponsible, ungoverned and undisciplined, marked by unrestrained disregard for the safety of others, to use the language of Mr. Justice Hill in *Menezes* [[2002] O.J. No. 551]. He is one of many across the entire spectrum of this large and complex organization whose actions or inactions led to the tragedy of June 23, 2002 and who share some degree of responsibility. In my opinion, and after much reflection, if his actions are to be described as negligent, it is a negligence that is within the realm of the civil, and not the criminal law. I for one am not prepared to brand him a criminal.

He is acquitted of the charges.

■

Was the culpability of these two individuals for criminal negligence assessed on a purely objective basis? Why or why not? Would it be any easier to prosecute Tammadge as an individual under the new provisions in ss. 2, 217.1 and 22.1? If Tammadge cannot be convicted as an individual, what are the chances that OPG could be prosecuted under the new provisions relying on Tammadge as the "senior officer" whose conduct departed "markedly from the standard of care that, in the circumstances, could reasonably be expected to prevent a representative of the organization from being a party to the offence"?

Bizarro

5

Proof of Inchoate Crimes

Inchoate crimes are "incomplete" offences, such as conspiracy, attempt, and counselling another to commit an offence, where the accused is essentially prosecuted for the agreement or effort to carry through with an offence. Inchoate crimes are most likely to be charged where the *actus reus* of the offence was either not committed or is difficult to prove. For example, s. 660 of the *Code* provides that an accused can be convicted of an attempt where he or she is charged with the complete offence, but the evidence establishes only an attempt. In such situations, the *mens rea* to commit the offence will also be difficult to prove if there is no unequivocal *actus reus*. Criminal liability for inchoate crimes therefore depends on specific understandings of the *actus reus* and *mens rea*.

There is a tension between crime control and civil liberties in both the areas of attempts and conspiracy. When should the law intervene? When should we punish for intention as opposed to overt acts? Why should we punish an agreement between two or more people when the same statement of intention by one person would not attract criminal liability?

A. ATTEMPTS

Section 24 of the *Code* provides a general definition of the offence of attempting any other crime, and s. 463 of the *Code* sets out the general sentencing scheme for those convicted of attempts for most offences. The penalties for attempts vary with the offence classification, but generally attempts are punished less severely than complete offences. For example, an attempt to commit an indictable offence with a maximum penalty of 14 years of imprisonment or less renders one liable to a maximum sentence of one-half of the maximum for the complete offence: s. 463(b). As well, there are some specific attempt offences in the *Code*, such as attempted murder, s. 239, and attempted obstruction of justice, s. 139, that set out their own penalties. Section 661 provides that where the accused has been charged with attempt but the evidence establishes the full offence, the trial judge can direct that there be a trial for the complete offence (or convict the accused of attempt).

Subsection 24(1) of the *Code* defines criminal liability for attempts such that the Crown must prove an act or omission performed for the purpose of carrying out the accused's intent to commit the offence, whether or not the offence was possible under the circumstances. Subsection (2) states that the question of whether the act or omission went beyond mere preparation or was too remote is a question of law. The case that follows demonstrates the legal understanding of when actions go beyond "mere preparation" to become criminal attempts.

R. v. Sorrell†

[BY THE COURT:]

The Attorney General of Ontario appeals against the acquittal of the respondents on a charge of attempted robbery.

The respondents were tried at Kingston before His Honour Judge Campbell, sitting without a jury, on an indictment containing three counts.

Count 1 charged the respondents jointly with, on or about March 3, 1977, attempting to rob Peter Mason of Aunt Lucy's Fried Chicken store at 240 Montreal St. in Kingston. Count 2 charged the respondent Sorrell with carrying, at the time and place aforesaid, a concealed weapon, to wit: a Smith and Wesson revolver. Count 3 charged the respondent Sorrell with having in his possession, at the time and place aforesaid, a Smith and Wesson revolver, knowing the same was obtained by an offence committed in Canada punishable on indictment. The respondent Sorrell, on arraignment, pleaded guilty to the charge of carrying a concealed weapon contained in count 2; his plea of guilty was accepted by the trial Judge after the evidence was completed, and he was sentenced to imprisonment for 18 months. The trial Judge acquitted the respondent Sorrell on count 3, on the ground that the Crown had failed to prove the necessary element of guilty knowledge. The Crown does not appeal the acquittal of Sorrell on count 3, and we are not further concerned with it.

On the evening of Thursday, March 3, 1977, Miss Dawn Arbuckle was the cashier at Aunt Lucy's Fried Chicken store at 240 Montreal St. in Kingston. The store is located at the corner of Montreal and Markland Sts., the customer entrances being on Montreal St. Mr. Peter Mason was the manager of the store. The regular closing time for the store was 11:00 p.m., but on the evening in question, since almost all the chicken had been sold, the manager decided to close the store earlier, and locked the customer entrances at approximately 10:45 p.m. Around 10 minutes to 11:00 Miss Arbuckle noticed two men, wearing balaclavas, on the Markland St. side of the store; they then came to one of the customer entrances on Montreal St. The area outside the store was illuminated, and the lights normally on in the store, when open, were still on.

One of the men was wearing a blue ski jacket and the other was wearing a brown coat. The balaclavas worn by the two men were pulled down completely over their heads, and one man was also wearing sunglasses. Miss Arbuckle said that the balaclava worn by one man was blue and white in colour, and that worn by the other man was brown and white.

One of the men rapped on the door and on the window. The manager, who had been mopping the floor, turned around and said, "Sorry we are closed," and returned to his mopping. The two men turned toward each other, and made a gesture of surprise. At this time Miss Arbuckle noticed that one of the men had a silver-coloured gun in his hand. The two men then walked away on Montreal Street in the direction of Princess St.; whereupon Mr. Mason, the manager, telephoned the police. Two officers in a cruiser responded to the call, drove to the area and saw two men, whose clothing corresponded to the description that the officers had been given, walking on Montreal St. The officers drove past the two men, then made a U-turn and drove back towards them.

As the officers passed the two men, before making the U-turn, they saw one of the men throw "an article of material" towards a snow bank on the

† (1978), 41 C.C.C. (2d) 9 (Ont. C.A.).

side of the street. The two men, who proved to be the respondents, were then arrested. The respondent Sorrell had a loaded .357 Magnum revolver concealed in his waistband. The gun was loaded with six Dominion .38 shells, and another five Dominion .387 shells were removed from the respondent Sorrell's pants' pocket.

An officer conducted a search of the immediate area where the respondents had been arrested, and found a brown balaclava on a snowbank on the side of Montreal St. The point on Montreal St. where the respondents were arrested was some 411 yards from the Aunt Lucy's store, where the attempted robbery is alleged to have occurred. The officer proceeded along Montreal St. in the direction of the Aunt Lucy's store, and found a blue balaclava in the middle of the sidewalk on Montreal St. at the intersection of Raglan St.

Neither of the respondents testified in his defence.

The Crown appeals against the acquittal of the respondents on the charge of attempted robbery on the ground that the trial Judge erred in law in holding that the acts of the respondents did not go beyond mere preparation, and hence did not constitute an attempt.

Section 24 of the *Code* defines an attempt....

In order to establish the commission of the offence of attempted robbery charged, it was necessary for the Crown to prove that the respondents:

(i) Intended to do that which would in law amount to the robbery specified in the indictment (*mens rea*), and

(ii) took steps in carrying out that intent which amounted to more than mere preparation (*actus reus*).

By virtue of s. 24(2) of the *Code*, the existence of element (i) is a question of fact, but whether the steps taken are sufficient to satisfy element (ii) is a question of law.

In *R. v. Cline*, (1956), 115 C.C.C. 18 at p. 29, 4 D.L.R. (2d) 480, [1956] O.R. 539, at pp. 550–1, Laidlaw, J.A., in his much-quoted judgment, said:

> (1) There must be *mens rea* and also an *actus reus* to constitute a criminal attempt, but the criminality of misconduct lies mainly in the intention of the accused.
>
> ...
>
> (5) The *actus reus* must be more than mere preparation to commit a crime. But (6) when the preparation to commit a crime is in fact fully complete and ended, the next step done by the accused for the purpose and with the intention of committing a specific crime constitutes an *actus reus* sufficient in law to establish a criminal attempt to commit that crime.

Thus, proof of the respondents' intention to commit the robbery particularized in the indictment, which is a question of fact, was the central issue in the case. Mr. Doherty for the Crown contended before us that on the facts found by the trial Judge, he erred in law in failing to draw the legal conclusion of guilt required by the facts accepted by him as proved, and, in particular, erred in law in holding that the acts of the respondents, found by him to have been proved, had not gone beyond mere preparation. Counsel for the respondents, on the other hand, contended that the trial Judge's reasons for judgment, considered in their entirety, show that he acquitted the respondents because he entertained a reasonable doubt whether they had the intent to rob the Aunt Lucy's store, the existence of which intent was essential to constitute the attempt charged.

A detailed examination of the trial Judge's reasons for judgment is necessary in order to endeavour to ascertain the basis upon which he acquitted the respondents. The trial Judge said:

> Turning to count 1, that is the count that effects [*sic*] both Sorrel and Bondett, namely, this attempted robbery count. There are many conclusions that I have drawn from the credible evidence, beyond a reasonable doubt, and I say that those conclusions complete substantially the Crown's case subject only — and I say only — to the thorny question as to whether or not the events in question constitute an attempt within the meaning of the *Criminal Code*.

After referring to certain discrepancies in the evidence of the Crown witnesses, which he did not consider material, the trial Judge continued:

> The Crown's case on count 1 has been proved beyond a reasonable doubt in my finding on the matters of identity of the accused, the date, the place and, subject only to what I am going to be saying on the matter of attempt, as to the allegation that the attempted robbery, if there was an attempted robbery, was committed in respect of Peter Mason of Aunt Lucy's Kentucky Fried Chicken.

He then held that Mr. Mason, as the manager of the store, had the custody of the money in the store, and said:

It brings me down then to the sole remaining question, did what took place at the time and at the place, as referred to by the witnesses Arbuckle and Mason, constitute an attempt at robbery? I may say that I found the evidence of both of those witnesses to be satisfactory, credible, and my findings are based on that evidence. I as well look to the evidence at the trial as to the manner of departure from the premises — from in front of the premises — by the two accused and the actions that they were performing when seen and practically immediately apprehended by the police. I am finding that between them they rid themselves of the balaclavas which could raise the inference of guilty mind; but that, of course, raises the question: a mind having a sense of guilt of what? They may have thought that what they did at the front of the store was criminal in some way and that they should take some steps to cover up — whether they were right in that belief or not. Was what they had actually done illegal as being an attempt to rob, whether they believed it or not, that still leaves to me the question: was what they did within the ambit of an attempt to rob? The inference is pretty plain, and I think I would be naive to conclude otherwise, that they were up to no good on that occasion, that they may well have had robbery of the store in mind. But, again, I am driven back to the provisions of the *Code* that differentiate between mere preparation and the actual commencement of steps to commit the robbery.

I am obliged to counsel for their references to cases on the point, one of which endeavours to lay down tests for the assistance of the Court, and subsequent cases, but all of which have their own set of facts and circumstances with which the Court then in those cases had to deal. It is an extremely thin line, but whether thin or otherwise, if my finding is that that line had been crossed beyond mere preparation, the finding — if it were to be made — that the line had been crossed would be sufficient to bring me to a conclusion beyond a reasonable doubt. Nevertheless, the fitness of the line is a bother to me. I am conscious of the fact that the accused timed their arrival at the store such that they could expect a fund of money to be in the till, such they could expect there would likely be few if any persons there other than the store personnel, and that they had costumed themselves for the purpose of disguising their features to render subsequent identification difficult, but I am also of the view that it is important for me to consider the fact that apart from rattling the door and perhaps rattling on the window — that would be consistent with an innocent person's endeavour to get in the food store — there was no gesture of threat of violence or threat of force. The case before me is attempted robbery and not attempted break, enter and theft, or break and enter with intent, or conspiracy, or whatever. So that the endeavour to open the door would — were one of those other charges to have been before me, and I am not saying in any way that it should have been before me — what was done by way of attempt to open the door could relate more to a charge of attempted breaking rather than the charge of robbery. In brief, in my finding, the accused by virtue of I suppose good luck of not having been able to progress further in doing whatever they were going to do had not yet crossed the line between preparation and attempt. Accordingly, I am finding that count 1 as regards both accused has not been proved on that narrow ground, and I have endorsed the indictment on count 1: both accused not guilty.

It will be observed that while the trial Judge made an express finding that he was satisfied beyond a reasonable doubt that the respondents were the two men who had approached the store, and that one of them had a gun, he made no similar finding with respect to the existence of the necessary intent to rob. Mr. O'Hara, on behalf of the respondent Sorrell particularly emphasized the following passages in the trial Judge's reasons, relative to intent, which Mr. O'Hara characterized as "powerful expressions of doubt," namely: "...they may well have had robbery of the store in mind," and "...what was done by way of attempt to open the door could relate more to a charge of attempted breaking rather than the charge of robbery." In our view, the trial Judge's reasons are more consistent with a finding that the necessary intent to commit robbery was not proved beyond a reasonable doubt, than with a finding that such intent was established by the evidence. In any event, the Crown has not satisfied us that the trial Judge found the existence of an intent to rob.

The Crown's right of appeal under s. 605(1)(*a*) of the *Code* is confined to a ground of appeal that involves a question of law alone. The failure of the trial Judge to draw the appropriate inference of intent from the facts found by him, is an error of fact, and does not raise a question of law.

. . . .

If the trial Judge had found that the respondents intended to rob the store, the acts done by them clearly had advanced beyond mere preparation, and were sufficiently proximate to constitute an attempt: see *Henderson v. The King* (1948), 91 C.C.C. 97, [1949] 2 D.L.R. 121 [1948] S.C.R. 226, *per* Kerwin, J., at p. 98 C.C.C. p. 228 S.C.R., *per* Estey,

J., at pp. 114–16 C.C.C., pp. 243–6 S.C.R., *per* Locke, J., at pp. 116–17 C.C.C., p. 246 S.C.R.; *R. v. Carey* (1957), 118 C.C.C. 241, [1957] S.C.R. 266, 25 C.R. 177, *per* Kerwin, C.J.C., at pp. 246–7, *per* Rand, J., at p. 251. If the trial Judge had found that the respondents had the necessary intent his finding that the acts done by the respondents did not go beyond mere preparation did not constitute attempted robbery, would constitute an error of law that would not only warrant, but require our intervention.

Because of the doubt that he entertained that the respondents had the necessary intent to commit robbery, however, his error in law in holding that the respondents' acts did not go beyond mere preparation, could not have affected the verdict of acquittal, unless, of course, his self-misdirection with respect to what constituted mere preparation, led him into error in entertaining a reasonable doubt whether the requisite intent had been proved. This question is one of considerable difficulty. The following passage (included in those previously quoted), would tend to support the conclusion that the trial Judge was led into error with respect to the existence of the necessary intent by self-misdirection that the respondents' acts had not gone beyond mere preparation:

> It is an extremely thin line, but whether thin or otherwise, if my finding is that that line had been crossed beyond mere preparation, the finding — if it were to be made — that the line had been crossed would be sufficient to bring me to a conclusion beyond a reasonable doubt. Nevertheless, the fineness of the line is a bother to me.

The trial Judge then proceeded, however, to refer to the matters in the passages previously quoted, relating to the issue of intent, which gave him difficulty in finding that the required mental element was present. The issue of intent was basic and, the trial Judge, in our view, could not logically or appropriately make a determination whether the acts of the respondents went beyond mere preparation until he had first found the intent with which those acts were done. The issue whether the acts of the respondents went beyond mere preparation could not be decided in the abstract apart from the existence of the requisite intent.

In the present case, there was no evidence of the intent to rob other than that furnished by the acts relied on as constituting the *actus reus*. There was no extrinsic evidence in the form of statements of intention, or admissions by the respondents showing what their intention was.

The prosecution in this case was forced to rely exclusively upon the acts of the accused, not only to constitute the *actus reus*, but to supply the evidence of the necessary *mens rea*. This Court in *R. v. Cline, supra*, rejected the so-called "unequivocal act" test for determining when the stage of attempt has been reached. That test excludes resort to evidence *aliunde*, such as admissions, and holds that the stage of attempt has been reached only when the acts of the accused show unequivocally on their face the criminal intent with which the acts were performed. We are of the view that where the accused's intention is otherwise proved, acts which on their face are equivocal, may [nonetheless], be sufficiently proximate to constitute an attempt. Where, however, there is no extrinsic evidence of the intent with which the accused's acts were done, acts of the accused, which on their face are equivocal, may be insufficient to show that the acts were done with the intent to commit the crime that the accused is alleged to have attempted to commit, and hence insufficient to establish the offence of attempt.

Counsel for the respondents while conceding that the trial Judge's reasons are not free of ambiguity, submitted that they are reasonably open to the interpretation that he was searching for evidence that satisfied him beyond a reasonable doubt that the accused intended to rob the store in question, and at the end of his quest was not satisfied beyond a reasonable doubt, that the acts done by the accused supplied the necessary proof of intent.

We think that this submission accurately states the basis upon which the trial Judge acquitted the respondents, and the Crown has not satisfied us that but for the self-misdirection with respect to which complaint is made, [...] the verdict of the trial Judge would not necessarily have been the same. It is not to the point that, on the evidence, we would have reached a different conclusion with respect to the respondent's intentions.

. . . .

Appeal dismissed.

B. CONSPIRACY

No crime is committed when one person resolves or even plans to commit an offence, without more. However, if two or more persons agree or plan to commit an offence, the agreement may amount to the offence of conspiracy. Section 465 of the *Code* sets out the general framework for conspiracy offences, including penalties that depend on the classification of the offence that was the subject of the conspiracy. In addition, the *Code* contains specific conspiracy offences, such as conspiracy in restraint of trade (defined in s. 466), conspiracy to commit high treason (s. 46(2)(c)), and seditious conspiracy (s. 61).

Consider how conspiracy offences have been used historically and politically. Geoff Robertson, in *Whose Conspiracy*? (London: National Council for Civil Liberties, 1974), makes a case against the crime of conspiracy in England. In arguing that conspiracy is used to bolster the power, authority, and values of the state, Robertson provides an historical account of the ways in which conspiracy laws have been interpreted and applied by the courts. He shows that the law of conspiracy, which was enacted in 1304 as a means to punish malicious prosecutions, has been extended to agreements to commit all crimes, however trivial. The result is that the conspiracy law has been used in devastating ways against trade unions, the working class, and political and racialized minorities. It has been extended to such areas as conspiracy to intimidate, conspiracy to trespass, and has even been extended to conspiracy to interfere with the lawful rights of persons to watch a Davis Cup match against South Africa. In this case Peter Hain was convicted of conspiracy after running on the court in 1969–70 and distributing anti-apartheid leaflets. This use of the law, upheld by the U.K. Court of Appeal, effectively means that demonstrators commit a crime punishable by life imprisonment if they interfere with "public rights" using methods that are deemed "unlawful" by those in authority, even though the methods themselves are not illegal.

Robertson also argues that conspiracy law is antithetical to the rule of law: its scope is not certain, nor is it accessible or comprehensible to all citizens. For example, the wide ambit of the term "agreement" can even catch individuals who were unaware of each other's existence, such as the famous prosecution of the "Chicago Seven" in 1968. In this case, the accused were all variously involved in disrupting the 1968 Democratic Convention in Chicago in order to challenge the so-called "democratic process". They were initially charged with conspiracy and inciting riot; during their trial, several were also charged with contempt (see Abell & Sheehy, *Cases, Context, Critique*, **Powers of Prosecution**). The result is that the law has effectively been applied to make criminal anything that judges regard as morally wrong or politically or socially dangerous. The fact that the conspiracy law makes it criminal to conspire to corrupt public morals, to outrage public decency, or to pervert the course of justice, means that judges continue to have considerable power to define the public interest and use this as the marker against which to view the actions of the accused, such as Peter Hain. The proof of conspiracy is also fraught with complex and technical difficulties because numerous specific evidentiary rules have been needed to prosecute a crime that is, in many ways, so nebulous. For a discussion and attempted resolution of some of these difficulties, see J.C. Smith, "Proving Conspiracy" [1996] Crim. L. Rev. 386; and J.C. Smith, "More on Proving Conspiracy" [1997] Crim. L. Rev. 333.

Canadian courts have applied the law of conspiracy, as contained in what is now s. 465, to a conspiracy to breach a municipal by-law (*R. v. Jean Talon Fashion Centre Inc.* (1975), 22 C.C.C. (2d) 223 (Que. Q.B.)), but have refused to extend it to capture conspiracy to commit an "unlawful act" that is not the subject of a statutory prohibition (*R. v. Gralewicz*, [1980] 2 S.C.R. 493 (S.C.C.)). Furthermore, in *R. v. Dungey* (1979), 51 C.C.C. (2d) 86 (Ont. C.A.) (where the accused lawyer sought to make arrangements with a client to potentially defraud the legal aid plan), the court held at 90 that an accused cannot be convicted of an attempt at conspiracy:

> [I]f the offence of conspiracy is an auxiliary to the law which creates the crimes agreed to be committed, and if the object of making such agreements punishable is to prevent the commission of the substantive offence before it has even reached the stage of an attempt, there appears to be little justification in attaching penal sanction to an act which falls short of a conspiracy to commit the substantive offence.

In *R. v. Déry*, [2006] S.C.J. No. 53 at paras. 19–20, the Supreme Court of Canada affirmed *Dungey*:

"There is no such offence as attempt to conspire to commit a further substantive offence. The question left open by *Dungey* relates instead to offences such as conspiracy in restraint of trade and conspiracy to commit treason or seditious conspiracy, *where conspiracy is the substantive offence....*" However, as Wes Wilson points out in "The Political Use of Criminal Conspiracy" (1984) 42 U.T. Fac. L. Rev. 60, Canadian prosecutors and judges have, like their counterparts in the U.K., used conspiracy charges to contain political movements and quash resistance. See, for example, Wilson's discussion of the prosecution for seditious conspiracy of several of the leaders of the Winnipeg General Strike of 1919 (at 61–66), and the trials of the Squamish Five (at 67); see also Abell & Sheehy, *Cases, Context, Critique*, **Sentencing**.

Other infamous instances of prosecutions for seditious conspiracy (as well as seditious libel) are provided by the persecution of Jehovah's Witnesses and others who publicly challenged the authority of Premier Duplessis and the Catholic Church in Québec by their writings, speeches, and actions, such as distributing Bibles without licences. Consider the following alleged facts in another "conspiracy," as described in a seditious libel prosecution of a Jehovah's Witness, *R. v. Boucher*, [1951] S.C.R. 265 at 326:

> This [charge] was based on their having distributed in the City of Quebec a number of pamphlets with what was said to have been a seditious intention. These pamphlets included extravagant charges against the clergy, "big business" and against practically every branch of government which, it was said, was contaminated and improperly influenced, and said that there would be no peace so long as the unholy alliance of "commercial and political oppressive power with hypocritical religion" continued to exist. They contained also other statements particularly offensive to the Protestant and Roman Catholic clergy. The charges made were so sweeping that they may well have been considered as including an attack upon the manner in which justice was administered.

While *Boucher*, by a five–four majority, ruled that seditious intention cannot be manifested by criticism of the courts or statements calculated to arouse ill-will between classes of subjects without evidence of intention to incite violence, resistance, or defiance of the government, consider the context in which such an intention might be inferred. What are the constraints on the use of s. 465 to prosecute dissent?

C. COUNSELLING

Section 464 of the *Code* makes it an offence to counsel another to commit an offence, if the offence was not, in fact, committed. "Counselling" is defined in s. 22(3) as to "procure, solicit or incite". Once convicted, an accused who counselled an indictable offence has the same liability to sentence as someone who attempted the offence (s. 464(a)); an accused who counselled a summary conviction offence is liable to the punishment available for summary conviction offences (s. 464(b)). If the offence counselled was committed, the accused's criminal responsibility is determined under s. 22 of the *Code*.

For a recent example of a counselling conviction where an offender had proposed to an undercover police officer that he kill his ex-wife for a fee, see *R. v. Pereira* (1996), 83 B.C.A.C. 13 (C.A.).

6

The Trial Process

This chapter raises and discusses some of the many issues that arise for an accused in the process of a trial. The accused may have significant *Charter* rights that come into play during the trial, and many of these have been touched on in Abell & Sheehy, *Cases, Context, Critique*, **Introduction to Criminal Procedure**.

An important and basic overarching principle is that an accused must be able to understand and participate meaningfully in his or her own trial. This will of course include the right to conduct one's defence in either official language of Canada and it extends to include translation rights under s. 14 of the *Charter*. For example, in *R. v. Tran*, [1994] 2 S.C.R. 951, the Court ruled that an accused's s. 14 right to an interpreter was infringed by the interpreter's failure to provide continuous and full translation, by the fact that the translator also acted as a witness in the case, by the delay in timing of the translations that were provided, and by the translator's failure to translate exchanges between himself and the trial judge from English back into Vietnamese, the accused's language. The Court advocated a "generous and open-minded" approach to s. 14 rights, read these rights in a purposive fashion in light of ss. 7, 11(d), 15, 25, and 27 of the *Charter*, and ordered a new trial pursuant to s. 24(1) of the *Charter*.

Recall some of the issues about access to justice for Aboriginal accused and witnesses discussed in Abell & Sheehy, *Cases, Context, Critique*, **Aboriginal Peoples and the Criminal Law**. Can access to translation at trial fully solve the problems? See, for example, Susan C. Kerr, "Gratuitous justice: A review of the Queensland Criminal Justice Commission's report into aboriginal witnesses in criminal courts" (1996) 3:84 Aboriginal L. Bull. 12, for an assessment of law reform proposals emanating out of Australia that deal with changes to the law of evidence and to standard jury instructions, among other proposals.

In *R. v. Haskins* (1995), 174 A.R. 272 (C.A.) the accused, who was deaf, was also granted a new trial on the basis of the infringement of his s. 14 rights, where the interpreter for the accused was not sworn as a witness and was, therefore, unable to provide translation until after the examination-in-chief of a main Crown witness. Upon reading the appellate judgment of Côté J., who wrote alone on this point, it becomes clear that failure to provide translation also affected the accused's credibility: he was unable to answer questions regarding his past criminal record from 1956, 1963, and 1981 when, as the accused repeatedly stated, translation was not provided, and so he was unable to say with any certainty what had occurred in those proceedings. He was described by Crown counsel as "evasive", and the trial judge expressed extreme annoyance with the accused, even taking over the cross-examination of him from the Crown. As Côté J. stated at 276:

> I ... also conclude that at one point (at least) in the trial, the judge formed an adverse impression of the credibility of the accused because of what the judge thought was the accused's failure to answer simple questions straightforwardly. But it seems to me there was no such failure. I also note that was the only ground for doubting credibility which the Crown argued and I note that although no explicit reference was made to that ground by the trial judge, nevertheless the trial judge immediately after proceeded to disbelieve the accused.

Is this case only about translation, or is it also about discrimination against people with disabilities? Can ss. 14 and 15 of the *Charter* protect against such unfairness in criminal trials?

The general order of trial is as follows:

Crown election: If the offence is a hybrid, the Crown must elect to proceed summarily or by way of indictment. See discussion in Abell & Sheehy, *Cases, Context, Critique*, **Introduction to Criminal Procedure**.

Accused plea and election: The accused must enter a plea of guilty, not guilty, or a special plea: s. 606; the accused may elect the mode of trial, if applicable.

Preliminary inquiry: See discussion following.

Pre-trial conference: On application by the Crown, defence, or on its own motion, the court may hold such a conference before the court where the trial will take place, unless it is to be tried before a jury, in which case such a pre-trial is mandatory. Its purpose is "to consider such matters as may promote a fair and expeditious hearing": s. 625.1. It may result in plea negotiations.

Empanelling of jury: The jury is selected according to ss. 626–643, which permits challenges to the array, challenges for cause, and peremptory challenges for both Crown and defence. See discussion following.

Opening address: The Crown gives a description of its theory of the case and a general outline of the evidence it will present.

Crown's case: The Crown presents its evidence through witnesses who give evidence in chief, and perhaps through re-examination after cross-examination by defence counsel.

Motion for directed verdict: The defence may request that the judge direct an acquittal if, after presentation of the Crown's evidence, a properly instructed jury could not reasonably convict.

Defence case: The defence may open its case for the accused and present witnesses (s. 651). These witnesses will be open to cross-examination by the Crown, as will the accused, should he or she decide to take the witness stand.

Closing addresses: The Crown and defence each summarizes evidence and their theory of the case, defence first and Crown last, unless the defence has elected to call no evidence: s. 651.

Summing up and charge to jury: The judge summarizes the evidence but must not direct the jury regarding factual findings; the judge then directs the jury as to the law, and suggests how the legal rules might apply to the facts.

Verdict: The verdict must be returned by a unanimous jury (s. 653), without reasons, or by the judge, if the trial is by judge alone, with reasons.

Sentence: See discussion in Abell & Sheehy, *Cases, Context, Critique*, **Sentencing**.

Some of these topics are explored in further detail below.

A. DISCLOSURE

A significant aspect of preparation for trial is the gathering of evidence through witnesses and documents. Section 603 of the *Code* states that an accused is entitled to view the indictment, his or her own statement, and the "evidence and exhibits, if any" before trial. Supreme Court interpretations of s. 7 fair trial rights under the *Charter* have greatly strengthened the accused's position in obtaining disclosure before trial.

In *R. v. Stinchcombe*, [1991] 3 S.C.R. 326, the Supreme Court of Canada held that the accused, a lawyer charged with criminal breach of trust and fraud in relation to moneys held in trust, was denied s. 7 rights under the *Charter* when the Crown refused to disclose to the defence statements favourable to the accused made by a witness, and when the Crown then refused to call the witness at trial. Because the violations of the accused's right to make full answer and defence were infringed, a new trial was ordered.

The Court stated that the Crown has a general duty to disclose all material it proposes to use at trial and evidence that may assist the accused even if the Crown does not plan to adduce it. The following additional directions were given in the case: the Crown can refuse to disclose on the grounds of privilege; the Crown can exercise discretion in the timing and manner of disclosure to protect informers; in the case of potentially irrelevant material, the Crown should err on the side of disclosure; initial disclosure should take place before the accused has to elect mode of trial or to plead; and the Crown's discretion is reviewable before the trial judge in a *voir dire*.

Consider the implications of *Stinchcombe* for the prosecution of corporate criminality and sexual violence. In the context of corporate and commercial crime, the amount of time, painstaking work, and attention to detail required to prepare a prosecution is legion: Jock Ferguson, "Police engulfed in fraud cases" *The [Toronto] Globe and Mail* (2 July 1993) A5. The idea that the volumes and volumes of paper produced through investigations covering several years of police work must all be disclosed creates yet another substantial hurdle for such prosecutions, as the stay of proceedings granted (and later reversed) in the Westray case, *Curragh Inc.*, above, under **Case Study on Corporate Homicide**, well illustrates. The notion that a court might award costs against the Crown's office for breach of *Charter* rights (as was done by the Nova Scotia Supreme Court in *Curragh Inc.*) certainly makes the hurdle even more daunting.

In the context of offences of sexual violence, some judges, in their interpretations of the accused's *Charter* rights, have granted stays of proceedings where rape crisis records are no longer available and have ordered costs against record-holders who resist disclosure (*R. v. Wiseman and Beausejour*, described in Andy Morrissey, "Judge rules centre will pay for keeping case file secret" *The Chatham Daily News* (7 April 1995) 1). The *Factum of the Aboriginal Women's Council et al.* in the appeal to the Supreme Court of Archbishop Hubert Patrick O'Connor's case from the decision of the B.C. Court of Appeal ((1994), 43 B.C.A.C. 70) identifies the issues and implications of *Stinchcombe* for women, and for racialized women and children in particular: see Women's Legal Education and Action Fund, *Equality and the Charter. Ten Years of Feminist Advocacy Before the Supreme Court of Canada* (Toronto: Emond Montgomery, 1996) 451. The Aboriginal Women's Council argued that the application of disclosure rules without taking account of the impact in the context of systemic sexual and racial inequality infringes the ss. 7 and 15 rights of Aboriginal women and perpetuates that inequality. They took issue with the broad range of records identified as potentially probative and, therefore, subject to disclosure orders (e.g., employment and school records) and challenged the reliability of records created in an institutional context of cultural domination.

In *R. v. O'Connor*, [1995] 4 S.C.R. 411, the members of the Court rejected the Aboriginal Women's Council's position and widened defence access to women's therapeutic records. In a 5:4 decision, they created a new process to determine defence applications for women's records. Lamer C.J.C. and Sopinka J. wrote for the majority. Records already in the physical possession of the Crown and its agents (such as the police) are governed by *Stinchcombe* and must be disclosed to the defence, unless they are "clearly irrelevant", without regard to the privacy claims of women or confidentiality claims of therapists. When the records are in the hands of a third party, such as a rape crisis centre, although there is a constitutionally protected privacy interest under s. 7 of the *Charter*, the accused is entitled to apply for these records in writing and with a sworn affidavit setting out the specific grounds for production; notice must be given to the third party record holder and those with a privacy interest in the record; and the third party is to be subpoenaed to bring the record to court before a trial or pre-trial judge.

The judge must then determine whether the records are "likely relevant". While this sounds like a serious standard that defence must meet, the majority diluted it substantially by stating that records will be "likely relevant" where it "may be useful to the defence" because there is a "reasonable possibility" that the information sought is logically probative to a matter at issue, including the credibility of witnesses, the reliability of evidence or the competence of a witness to testify, or the possibility of a reasonably close temporal connection between the creation of the record and the date of the alleged offence, or between the creation of the record and the laying of charges. Examples given by the majority of possibly relevant evidence include: information regarding the unfolding of events, information that reveals the use of therapy that may have shaped the woman's memory of the events, or information bearing on the woman's credibility, such as the quality of her perception and memory. These justices stated that it was inappropriate to put too high an obligation upon the accused to identify in advance the specific uses of the sought after evidence, thus implicitly sanctioning "fishing expeditions" by the accused.

If the evidence is judged "likely relevant", it must be disclosed to the trial judge, who must then review the record to ascertain whether it must in turn be disclosed to the defence. At this stage, the judge is to balance the rights and interests at stake, including the need for the accused to have the record in order to make full answer and defence, the "probative value" of the record, the nature and extent of the reasonable expectation of privacy associated with the record, whether production would be premised on discriminatory beliefs or biases, and the potential prejudice to the woman's dignity, privacy, or security that would result from disclosure. The majority explicitly rejected as relevant considerations in this balancing process the effect of such disclosure on the integrity of the trial process and the impact on the reporting of sexual assaults.

The minority judgment, authored by Justice L'Heureux-Dubé, would have provided considerably more protection to women. She refrained from commenting upon the status of records in the hands of the Crown, noting that any such comments would be strictly *obiter dicta*; she required that the determination of disclosure be made at trial, rather than at a pre-trial stage; she set the initial threshold for disclosure to the judge at a standard of "likely relevance" and eschewed any dilution of this standard. She also set out a list of allegations that would be insufficient to support an order of production of the records, such as a bare assertion that the records might reveal a previous inconsistent statement or that the woman had been sexually assaulted by other men in her past. Even if the judge finds "likely relevance", the judge is to undertake a balancing process before ordering that the records be disclosed to the judge, having regard to the woman's equality and privacy rights as well as the accused's right to make full answer and defence.

If the records pass this test, then, according to the minority judgment, the judge should review the records and determine whether the records or specific parts should be disclosed to the defence in light of the considerations for balancing set out in the majority judgment, as well as the impact of disclosure upon the integrity of the trial and upon society's legitimate interests in securing women's willingness to report sexual assault to the police and to seek medical and therapeutic assistance. The standard for disclosure to the defence was stated as whether the records have "significant" probative value that is not substantially outweighed by the danger of prejudice to the administration of justice or harm to the woman's privacy rights or privileged relationship. This judgment would have also imposed additional safeguards, such as requirements that records be reviewed *in camera* and be kept sealed and in custody by the registrar, and mentioned the possibility of orders for bans on reproduction or publication and preventing counsel from discussing certain contents with the accused.

The decision was 6:3 on the issue of whether the accused was entitled to a stay of proceedings as a consequence of the Crown's non-disclosure of the women's records. The majority ruled that a stay was not an appropriate remedy, and Bishop O'Connor was sent back, finally, for a trial on the merits.

The Crown prosecutor at the original trial was very well-known for her commitment to improving the conditions under which women and children testify regarding sexual assault, and for her ability to establish a rapport and inspire the confidence of such witnesses. She resisted the trial judge's sweeping order of disclosure to the defence of all of the women's records because she was concerned that the women would be re-victimized. She was cut off and rebuked during a pre-trial hearing when she failed to meet the terms of a disclosure order and tried to argue that issues of gender bias and the implications in terms of women's equality needed to be addressed before such an order was issued:

> [CROWN]: The public perception, in reading that order, in the Crown's respectful view, would be absolutely appalled.
>
> THE COURT: At what?
>
> [CROWN]: At the fact that we have a justice system that is demanding that complainants in a trial involving a former bishop and principal of a residential school for aboriginal individuals, that those women who are coming for-

> ward with a complaint are compelled to provide full records, psychological, therapeutic, counseling [*sic*], medical, and all other records that are outlined in those order [*sic*]. It's the Crown's respectful view that if the public knew that complainants were subjected to that there would be strong reasons not to report any offences, particularly related to those of sexual assault. And the Crown says that in relation to that this is — it's tantamount to a gender bias because the statistics say that the majority of victims of sexual assault are women, that this type of —
>
> THE COURT: Excuse me, I do not know if you are now a crusade or if you are acting as Crown counsel because it seems to me that your personal views are clouding your professional integrity.
>
> [CROWN]: With respect, My Lord, it used to be that things like that could be said — but we do have a report on gender equality in the justice system. It's been published by the Law —
>
> THE COURT: I'm not hearing any more of this. Now, would you please get on with the issues in this case. And the question of gender bias is not one of them that I'm going to entertain and hear this morning on this application for a stay on the failure of the Crown to comply with an order of the Associate Chief Justice of this court.
>
> [CROWN]: Well, the Crown is concerned that there is — there are some things peculiar about this case that those records that were sought were so extensive and the order was so difficult to comply with because the —
>
> THE COURT: Are you suggesting that either [Defence Counsel] or the Associate Chief Justice are involved in some gender bias that contradicts this report? Is that what you are starting to allude to?
>
> [CROWN]: I would suggest that that is the submission of the Crown.
>
> THE COURT: I'm going to adjourn for five minutes. I have told you I've had enough of this, and I won't have any more of it. Now, I'm going to adjourn for five minutes. I'm going to come back and I want you to address the issues in this case. [Reproduced in John McInnes and Christine Boyle, "Judging Sexual Assault Law Against a Standard of Equality" (1995) 29 U.B.C.L. Rev. 341 at 344, n. 12]

Crown counsel's conduct in failing to obey the disclosure order and in resisting disclosure was criticized at the Supreme Court as "shoddy and inappropriate" (*per* La Forest, L'Heureux-Dubé, Gonthier, and McLachlin JJ. at 472) and as "extremely high-handed and thoroughly reprehensible" (*per* Cory and Iacobucci JJ. at 515). Three justices (Lamer C.J.C., Sopinka, and Major JJ.) would have stayed the prosecution on the basis of the Crown attorney's ongoing failures to fully comply with the disclosure orders.

What notions of professionalism and advocacy underlie such a reprimand? Do the societal interests in prosecuting sexual assault and women's interests and well-being warrant defence? Ultimately, the Crown attorney's judgment on the considerations that ought to be analyzed prior to ordering disclosure to the defence was vindicated by the legal framework developed by the Court in *O'Connor*. It also seems that her assessment of the relevance of the records was quite astute, given that no disclosure orders were reported as arising out of the new trial and records played no appreciable part in the reasoning of the judge who initially convicted O'Connor. Consider, in this regard, Justice L'Heureux-Dubé's rejection of a stay in this case, as set out at 473:

> [I]t must be recalled that the whole issue of disclosure in this case arose out of Campbell A.C.J.'s order requiring the Crown to "disclose" records in the hands of third parties and that the complainants authorize production of such records. This order was issued without any form of inquiry into their relevance, let alone a balancing of the privacy rights of the complainants and the accused's right to a fair trial. We all agree that this order was wrong. Although the error was compounded by the Crown's inept and ineffective efforts to have this order reviewed and modified, it is clear, at the end of the day, that the Crown was right in trying to protect the interests of justice. The fact that it did so in such a clumsy way should not result in a stay ...

Another decision was released almost concurrently with *O'Connor*, *A.(L.L.) v. B.(A.)*, [1995] 4 S.C.R. 536, wherein the Court split 4:3. The majority affirmed that *O'Connor* had established the process and criteria for the disclosure of records in the hands of third parties. Again, Justice L'Heureux-Dubé wrote the minority judgment affirming the process and criteria set out by her judgment in *O'Connor* as the appropriate one. She also reviewed the law of "privilege" for confidential communications and explained why she rejected this approach to dealing with women's therapy records. The Court agreed, however, that third parties such as record holders and the women who are the subject of such records have standing to contest the application for disclosure and to appeal such decisions to the Supreme Court of Canada before the end of trial.

While the creation of an absolute privilege for counselling and therapy records has been rejected by Canada's Supreme Court, the United States Supreme Court ruled, only seven months after the *O'Connor* decision, that psychiatrists and social workers have the absolute right to refuse to disclose confidential counselling information to any court: see *Jaffe v. Redmond*, 116 S. Ct. 1923 (1996). What are the advantages of this approach to the issue of women's records? Consider, in this regard, the legal processes and resources that will be required to determine the issues raised by the Canadian rulings.

The impact of *O'Connor* and *A.(L.L.)* on women who are willing to shoulder the burden of reporting and prosecuting their rapists is self-evident. For example, in an earlier decision, *R. v. Osolin*, discussed below, under **Mistake of Fact**, the Court suggested that a therapist's notes showing that the woman worried during counselling that the rape was her fault would be relevant evidence supporting the accused's defence that he was mistaken as to whether the woman consented, even where independent facts established that he had ripped her clothing off, driven her 40 kilometres away, shaved her pubic hair, and then left her naked on a highway. Are such self-blaming statements by women to their counsellors rare? What is the probative value of such information if survivors of trauma must work through the issues of whether somehow they are to blame or could have avoided the occurrence? Consider also the purpose of therapy and the nature of therapists' notations. Would you have any concerns as to the accuracy and reliability of such notes for the purposes of criminal litigation?

The reach of *O'Connor* and *A.(L.L.)* was further extended by the Court in *R. v. Carosella*, [1997] 1 S.C.R. 80. In another lengthy 5:4 decision marking the same lines of division among the justices, the majority ruled that a stay of proceedings was the appropriate legal result where the defence effort to subpoena the records of the Sexual Assault Crisis Centre of Windsor had failed. The centre had shredded its records, months prior to the subpoena, based on its policy of destroying all files for cases where there was police involvement, in order to protect clients' privacy and the integrity of centre services. The Court stated that the accused, pursuant to *O'Connor*, would have been entitled to disclosure of the file because there was a "reasonable possibility" that it could have contained information relevant to a matter at issue, given that the assaults allegedly occurred almost 30 years before and the crisis centre was the first place where the woman told her story (in a 105-minute interview), and because she had consented to disclosure. The accused's s. 7 right to make full answer and defence was said to have been breached by the failure to provide the record of the interview, the majority suggesting that since the centre received some government funding, it could be implicated in *Charter* violations. A stay was said to be appropriate even though the accused could not demonstrate that his defence had actually been prejudiced by the violation. The Court said the remedy is available where either no alternative remedy would cure the prejudice or where irreparable damage would be caused to the integrity of the judicial system; here both considerations were said to apply.

The dissenting justices emphasized that the duty of disclosure is one owed by the state, not private third parties such as crisis centres, where no state action is implicated. For example, the Supreme Court had ruled in *McKinney v. University of Guelph*, [1990] 3 S.C.R. 229, that universities are not state actors for the purpose of *Charter* violation, even though they too receive money from the government. The minority noted that the accused does not have the right to production of every piece of possibly relevant evidence, and must demonstrate on a balance of probabilities that denial resulted in an unfair, not an imperfect, trial. They emphasized that even if they accepted the tests established by the majority in *O'Connor*, any allegation of "relevance" was pure speculation, without any grounding. Furthermore, the dissenting justices noted that the defence had access to the police report, to the woman's statement to the police, to the transcript of the woman's cross-examination during the preliminary inquiry, as well as to other evidence.

The wide-reaching and devastating impact that these Supreme Court decisions have on individual women who have been or will be raped, on the relationships between women and their counsellors, therapists, and physicians, on feminist organizations such as rape crisis centres, on the integrity of the trial process, and on the societal interest in the reporting of sexual violence has been interrogated and documented by feminist activists, lawyers, and academics: see Marilyn MacCrimmon & Christine Boyle, "Equality, Fairness and Relevance: Disclosure of Therapists' Records in Sexual Assault

Trials" in *Filtering and Analyzing Evidence in an Age of Diversity*, edited by Marilyn T. MacCrimmon & Monique Ouelette (Montréal: Editions Themis, 1995) 81; Elizabeth Sheehy, "Legalising Justice for All Women: Canadian Women's Struggle for Democratic Rape Law Reforms" (1996) 6 Aust. Feminist L.J. 87; Andrée Côté, *Searches of the Personal and Therapeutic Files of Women Who Resist Sexual Violence* (Ottawa: Action Ontarienne contre la Violence faite aux Femmes, 1995); Bruce Feldthusen, "Access to the Private Therapeutic Records of Sexual Assault Complainants Under the *O'Connor* Guidelines" (1996) 75 Can. Bar Rev. 537; Marilyn MacCrimmon, "Trial by Ordeal" (1996) 1 Can. Crim. L. Rev. 31; Joan Gilmour, "Counselling Records: Disclosure in Sexual Assault Cases" in *The Impact of the Charter on the Criminal Justice System*, edited by Jamie Cameron (Toronto: Carswell, 1996) 239; Karen Busby, "Discriminatory Uses of Personal Records in Sexual Violence Cases" (1997) 9 C.J.W.L. 148; and Katharine D. Kelly, "'You must be crazy if you think you were raped'; Reflections on the Use of Complainants' Personal and Therapeutic Records in Sexual Assault Trials" (1997) 9 C.J.W.L. 178.

As quoted in Sheehy, *supra* at 105–106, one activist, in a consultation between women's groups and the Department of Justice about the impact of disclosure practices in April 1995, described the limitless scope of such applications:

> There's nothing that you can record about a woman's life that cannot be used to generate one of the myths that she's a liar, an idiot, a something ... There's nothing about our lives that's not gendered information. I can't entertain your name and the information that you have a child without it being gendered. I can't entertain the information that you went to a counsellor without it being gendered. There is nothing, absolutely nothing, that can be recorded about you that can't be used against you in these cases.

Busby, *supra*, notes that every imaginable record has been the subject of disclosure applications, including women's divorce, birth control, and school records, as well as women's diaries (at 149). Kelly, *supra*, reports that if women do not have records, the defence attempts to generate them by requesting psychiatric and medical evaluations of the woman (at 183–84).

MacCrimmon, *supra*, makes the point that these decisions have returned women to trial by ordeal, whereby women who are willing to prosecute their assailants must also be willing to bare their lives publicly, to be subjected to scrutiny and scorn, and to have their words tested against their records. Busby reports that some counsellors are already seeing the effects in terms of women refusing to report their rapes to police, but other effects include women withdrawing from the criminal process once a disclosure application has been made or withdrawing from therapy to protect themselves. Some clinics have changed their recording practices in order to protect their clients even though therapeutically this may not be optimal; others have been warned by police that after *O'Connor* they can no longer advertise as a "confidential" service. Sheehy notes that therapists who refuse to produce records can be criminalized through contempt charges, as indeed has happened in Australia (Margo Kingston, "Privacy issue as rape therapist jailed" *The Sydney Morning Herald* (15 December 1995) 1); those therapists who accede to disclosure demands may lose the trust of their clients and, perhaps, their practices. It has also been noted that disclosure applications can be used to intimidate women, to go on "fishing expeditions", and to delay the trial: see the further discussion of this defence tactic below under the Preliminary Inquiry, in this chapter.

Crown attorneys expressed frustration and apprehension about the precedential import of these cases, and *Carosella* in particular. That decision relaxed the requirement that the accused show actual prejudice through loss of potential evidence before the extreme remedy of a stay is ordered. It has broad implications for many cases where evidence is missing or is ostensibly missing. Crown lawyers predict an even greater explosion in disclosure motions, increased numbers of stay applications, longer trials, and further delays. Some prosecutors view the decision as aimed at punishing the centre for refusing to participate in the criminal justice system, and others put it in the context of all of the other negative Supreme Court decisions around rape law that "attack the victim": Kirk Makin, "Lawyers warn court's ruling could tie up legal system" *The [Toronto] Globe and Mail* (8 February 1997) A1.

Is the law and practice of disclosure "neutral"? In which kinds of cases are such applications for third party records likely to be made? For example, Busby notes that the overwhelming majority of cases concern sexual assault and assault charges involving women and children as complainants: *supra* at 151; see also Diane Oleskiw & Nicole Tellier, *National Association of Women and the Law Submissions on Bill C-46 to the*

Standing Committee on Justice: Proposed Legislation Governing Access to Complainants' Records in Sexual Assault Proceedings (Ottawa: NAWL, 1997). While there are some other cases and crimes where disclosure has been treated as a significant issue, such as the initial stay ordered in the prosecution of Westray officials discussed above, under **Case Study on Corporate Homicide**, counsel and courts have rarely accorded the same respect to the disclosure rights of other accused. Consider, for example, the reluctance to permit the identification of informants, discussed below, under **Entrapment**, unless the accused can show that the information is necessary to demonstrate his or her innocence: *R. v. Leipert*, [1997] 1 S.C.R. 281. As Michele Landsberg remarks in "Rock must protect privacy of Canada's rape victims" *The Toronto Star* (9 June 1996) A2: "When was the last time you heard of a defence lawyer demanding to see a police officer's personal records — his complete medical file back to childhood, for example — in order to probe for embarrassing personal details that would discredit him ... even though many, many serious cases hinge upon a police officer's credibility ...".

Compare, as well, the legal treatment of Anne-Marie Wicksted's application for a stay of proceedings of the fraud prosecution against her. Wicksted was the founder and director of the Barrie Rape Crisis Centre and was a frequent Crown witness in sexual assault prosecutions. She was charged with fraud based on allegations of misuse of the centre credit card for personal expenses, but after being exonerated by an internal investigation, she was supported by her board and centre throughout the criminal process. In her case, the investigating officer said he lost his notebook where he had recorded 10–15 hours of interviews with the Crown witness against Wicksted; then he claimed to have found it, but said there were no notes in it; then he stated that he had given the Crown a tape of the interview, but the Crown testified that this had not occurred. It then emerged at trial that the police had not disclosed that they had been investigating other members of the centre based on allegations made by the same Crown witness who had accused Wicksted, although this investigation was later abandoned.

The trial judge entered a stay, ruling that Wicksted's s. 7 rights had been breached by the police officer's actions. The Ontario Court of Appeal ruled that although her *Charter* rights to disclosure had been breached, a stay was not appropriate, and she was sent back for trial. The Supreme Court of Canada affirmed that ruling in a brief, two paragraph judgment where Sopinka J. stated: "We agree ... that ... the trial judge erred in the exercise of discretion in finding that this was one of those clearest of cases in which a stay of proceedings was the only appropriate remedy": *R. v. Wickstead* [*sic*], [1997] 1 S.C.R. 307. The Court failed to distinguish the case from *Carosella* in any way. As Michele Landsberg in "Two cases stark proof of Supreme Court gender bias" (*The Toronto Star* (23 February 1997) A2) comments, "[i]f one page of possibly irrelevant notes from a third party fatally compromised Carosella's chances of a fair trial, why did cartloads of vanished crown evidence not lead to the same result in Wicksted's case?" After comparing the impact on the public image of the judicial system of a police officer's withholding evidence, misleading the court, and being found negligent in his duties by his own force with the confidentiality practices of a rape crisis clinic, Landsberg concludes, "[t]he same legal principle, different outcomes for different genders." See also *R. v. La (H.K.)* (1997), 213 N.R. 1, where the Supreme Court distinguished that case from *Carosella* primarily on the basis that the Crown had inadvertently lost the tape of the witness's testimony.

The Supreme Court rulings on disclosure of women's records, as well as widespread defence practices, prompted public debates and campaigns to protect women's equality and privacy rights. The women's movement urged the federal government to respond with legislation and, after two years of broad consultation, drafting, and committee hearings, Bill C-46 was passed into law on the 12th of May 1997: *An Act to amend the Criminal Code (production of records in criminal proceedings)*, S.C. 1997, c. 30. It amends the *Criminal Code* by introducing new ss. 278.1–278.91 and by introducing new forms for subpoenas for documents. Its preamble grounds the legislation in ss. 7, 8, 15, and 28 of the *Charter*, and specifically refers to the rights of accused persons, as well as women and children who are victimized by sexual assault and the work of those who provide services to such women and children. It adopts the dissent of Madam Justice L'Heureux-Dubé in *O'Connor* almost entirely. The legislation applies only to disclosure in the context of sexual offence proceedings and thus, *O'Connor* and its process and principles continue to apply to disclosure applications regarding third party records for all other offences.

Sections 278.1ff adopt the process and tests set out by Justice L'Heureux-Dubé's dissent in *O'Connor* and *A.(L.L.)*. In *R. v. Mills*, [1999] 3 S.C.R. 668, the Court upheld the constitutionality of the new records legislation. However, Steve Coughlan, in his article, "Complainants' Records after *Mills*: Same As It Ever Was" (2000), 33 C.R. (5th) 300 argues that while the decision is cast in deferential language, it has actually diluted the potential of Bill C-46. Lise Gotell, "The Ideal Victim, the Hysterical Complainant, and the Disclosure of Confidential Records: The Implications of the *Charter* for Sexual Assault Law" (2002) 49 *Osgoode Hall L.J.* 251 surveys both *Mills* and the post-*Mills* case law. She concludes that in spite of the *Code* reform, women's access to privacy rights in this context are so frail that sexual assault is being re-privatized: "the systemic nature and complexities of sexual violence have been actively resisted in legal decision-making."

B. PLEA BARGAINING

Plea negotiations may take place any time. They often are undertaken closer to trial, and, often, after the preliminary inquiry, if one is to be held. Such discussions are usually conducted between the two lawyers on a "without prejudice" basis, suggesting an informal understanding that neither lawyer can use the discussions in court if negotiations break down.

Subsection 606(4) of the *Code* authorizes a judge to accept, in his or her discretion, and with the consent of the prosecutor, an accused's plea of not guilty to the offence charged, but guilty of any other offence arising out of the same transaction, whether or not it is an included offence. The provincial and territorial law societies have professional rules of conduct that govern both Crown attorneys and defence lawyers in the negotiations that precede such a plea, as Rule 4.01(3) of the Law Society of Upper Canada's *Code of Professional Conduct*† illustrates:

Duty as Prosecutor

4.01(3) When acting as a prosecutor, a lawyer shall act for the public and the administration of justice resolutely and honourably within the limits of the law while treating the tribunal with candour, fairness, courtesy, and respect.

Commentary

When engaged as a prosecutor, the lawyer's prime duty is not to seek to convict, but to see that justice is done through a fair trial on the merits. The prosecutor exercises a public function involving much discretion and power and must act fairly and dispassionately. The prosecutor should not do anything that might prevent the accused from being represented by counsel or communicating with counsel and, to the extent required by law and accepted practice, should make timely disclosure to defence counsel or directly to an unrepresented accused of all relevant and known facts and witnesses, whether tending to show guilt or innocence.

Agreement on Guilty Plea

4.01(8) Before a charge is laid or at any time after a charge is laid, a lawyer for an accused or potential accused may discuss with the prosecutor the possible disposition of the case, unless the client instructs otherwise.

4.01(9) Where, following investigation,

(a) a lawyer for an accused or potential accused advises his or her client about the prospects for an acquittal or finding of guilt;
(b) the lawyer advises the client of the implications and possible consequences of a guilty plea and particularly of the sentencing authority and discretion of the court, including the fact that the court is not bound by any agreement about a guilty plea;
(c) the client voluntarily is prepared to admit the necessary factual and mental elements of the offence charged; and
(d) the client voluntarily instructs the lawyer to enter into an agreement as to a guilty plea, the lawyer may enter into an agreement with the prosecutor about a guilty plea.

Commentary

The public interest in the proper administration of justice should not be sacrificed to expediency.

As well, Crown attorneys may be subject to guidelines produced by the relevant attorney general. See, for example, Ministry of the Attorney General, Ontario, *Crown Policy Manual* (15 January 1994), R-1, Resolution Discussions. Crown attorneys who take over files and repudiate plea agreements made by predecessors risk successful s. 7 "abuse of process" arguments: *R. v. R.M.* (2006), 83 O.R. (3d) 349 (Sup. Ct. J.). However, the Crown attorney cannot purport to bind the Attorney General who may, in rare circumstances, appeal a sentence that an individual Crown attorney found acceptable. Similarly, the Crown prosecutor cannot purport to bind the judge who passes sentence, even where the defence lawyer and Crown attorney make what is known as a "joint submission" on sentencing: *R. v. Butterworth* (1996), 84 B.C.A.C. 249 (C.A.). Many guidelines prepared by the attorneys general suggest that Crown attorneys should consult with a victim or the family of a victim before agreeing to a plea bargain, although the consent of the victim or family is not required. For example, the *Victims' Bill of Rights*, S.O. 1995, c. 6 is more about rhetoric than rights. It provides in s. 2(1) that victims "should have access to information about proposed pleas", "subject to" availability of resources, what is reasonable in the circumstances of the case, what is consistent with the law, and what is necessary to guard against delay in the criminal justice system (s. 2(2)).

Plea bargains may, very rarely, be set aside if an accused can demonstrate that the plea was not voluntary and unequivocal. One such argument succeeded, for example, in *R. v. Rajaeefard* (1996), 27 O.R. (3d) 323 (C.A.). The accused had been charged with assaulting his wife, and the Crown had elected to proceed summarily, which meant that the accused could not secure legal aid. He retained the University of Toronto's Student Legal Aid Society days before trial, and they agreed to represent him only for the purposes of securing an adjournment. At the hearing, the judge stated, out of the courtroom, that he was not prepared to grant another adjournment. He attempted to get the student to urge the client to plead guilty to the offence by indicating that he would sentence the accused to probation under a guilty plea, but to 15–20 days in jail if convicted after a trial. Although the student refused to participate in plea negotiations and adhered to the retainer agreement that the representation was for an adjournment only, he did convey the judge's words to the accused, who, as a result, decided to plead guilty. The court concluded that the trial judge's behaviour improperly pressured the accused; the plea was not, therefore, voluntary. It was set aside, and a new trial was ordered.

It will, of course, be more difficult for the represented accused whose counsel has negotiated with the Crown attorney or made representations to the judge in pre-trial conferences on their behalf to prove that their plea was not voluntary. Thus lawyers, as well as judges, are implicated in the production of guilty pleas. For example, in their searching analysis of the structural features of the American and English criminal justice systems that have resulted in the guilty plea, rather than the adversarial trial, as the primary means of case disposition, Mike McConville and Chester Mirsky identify court procedures and judicial powers used to encourage "lawyers to participate in pre-trial conferences which socialize adversaries into collaborating with one another in the hope of obtaining guilty plea dispositions" and to "authorize lawyers to instruct defendants in language which assures acquiescence": "Looking Through the Guilty Plea Glass: The Structural Features of English and American State Courts" (1993) 2 Social & Legal Stud. 173 at 176. Such an accused will also need to demonstrate that they had the ineffective assistance of counsel, which is difficult to establish: *R. v. Newman* (1993), 12 O.R. (3d) 481 (C.A.) (accused must have demonstrated a failure to appreciate the consequences of a guilty plea as a result of the flagrant incompetence of counsel).

What is the legal status of information disclosed through failed plea negotiations? Although this precise question has yet to be resolved in Canada in light of the *Charter*, the Supreme Court has ruled that the s. 10(b) right to counsel is violated where the police strike a bargain with an accused who is precluded from talking to a lawyer, and where a great deal of pressure is brought to bear upon the accused to agree to the deal. The Court therefore ruled that evidence obtained through the negotiation, which included a confession and the location of the murder weapon, was inadmissible in the ensuing trial: *R. v. Burlingham*, [1995] 2 S.C.R. 206.

C. DIVERSION

Across the country diversion programs in various forms have been experimented with in local settings through pilot projects. These projects now have a legal basis in the *Code* (s. 717). Diversion programs designed for adults constitute an exercise of prosecutorial discretion. These programs generally select appropriate cases and attempt to come up with solutions that avoid criminal prosecution by diverting the case out of the criminal courts.

Consider what factors prosecutors will assess when identifying candidates for diversion: will diversion be equally available to all accused? See, for example, Ann-Margaret Herriot, "ADR: a threat to democracy?" (1994) 19:2 Alt. L.J. 75; *R. v. Willocks* (1995), 22 O.R. (3d) 552 (Ont. Ct. J. (Gen. Div.)) (Black accused's s. 15 challenge to limited availability of diversion program and request for either a stay of proceedings or inclusion in an Aboriginal program denied). Should diversion be available for crimes of violence, such as wife assault? Note as well that the Ontario Attorney General has issued a Crown Policy Directive, #Div-1 (15 January 1994), to provide for the diversion of mentally disordered accused. What public policy concerns are met by such a directive?

D. PRELIMINARY INQUIRY

According to the *Code*, an accused charged with a s. 553 offence has no right to a preliminary inquiry. An accused charged with a s. 469 offence must have a preliminary inquiry, and those charged with s. 536 offences have the option of choosing a preliminary inquiry as part of the trial process.

The most recent amendments (S.C. 2002, c. 13) to the *Code* make the preliminary inquiry available only where the defence or prosecution requests one (s. 536(4)) and provides a statement that identifies the issues on which the defence wants evidence to be given at the preliminary inquiry and the witnesses the defence wishes to hear (s. 536.3). A judge may order a hearing before the preliminary inquiry to assist the parties in identifying the issues for the preliminary inquiry, the witnesses, and any other matters that would expedite the inquiry (s. 536.4). The judge presiding over the preliminary inquiry has the power to order the immediate cessation of abusive cross-examination (s. 537(1.1)).

The purposes of the preliminary inquiry are the following: to "determine whether there is sufficient evidence to put the accused on trial" (*Patterson v. R.*, [1970] S.C.R. 409); to prepare for trial (the defence has an opportunity to assess the Crown's case and will acquire a transcript of evidence, which can be used to cross-examine at trial); to facilitate plea bargaining; and, rarely, to preserve evidence in the event that a witness is unable to attend trial due to death or illness (s. 715).

Part XV of the *Code* governs the conduct of the preliminary inquiry. Section 535 directs the presiding justice to "inquire into the charge"; under s. 540 the Crown must call witnesses to present its case, who testify under oath and who are then subject to cross-examination by the defence counsel. The accused is afforded an opportunity to give evidence (s. 541) but is under no obligation to do so and, in fact, usually will not do so. At the close of the inquiry, s. 548 directs the justice to either discharge the accused or to order the person to stand trial if there is "sufficient evidence ... for the offence charged or any other indictable offence in respect of the same transaction." The test for committal to trial after a preliminary inquiry, where the evidence implicating the accused is direct evidence, is relatively straight-forward. It is "whether or not there is any evidence upon which a reasonable jury properly instructed could return a verdict of guilty": *United States of America v. Sheppard*, [1977] 2 S.C.R. 1067. Generally, judges presiding over preliminary inquiries are not to weigh or assess the strength of the evidence or the credibility of witnesses; it is enough if there is some evidence on all of the elements of proof that would support conviction. If the evidence pointing to the accused is circumstantial, meaning that inferences of guilt must be drawn from proven facts, the judge must go somewhat further and ask whether the inferences that the Crown relies on are reasonable ones. If competing inferences can be drawn from the same fact or facts, again the judge is barred from weighing these and must leave that task to the trier of fact at trial. According to the Supreme Court, "where more than one inference can be drawn from the evidence, only the inferences that favour the Crown are to be considered": *R. v. Sazant*, [2004] 3 S.C.R. 635. If the accused is committed for trial, the Crown will prepare an indictment under s. 574.

Even if the accused is discharged, the prosecutor or Attorney General has the power, in certain circumstances, to prefer a direct indictment against the accused: s. 577. Although the courts have generally been unwilling to describe use of the s. 577 power as violative of the accused's *Charter* rights (see *Re Patrick v. A.G. Canada* (1987), 28 C.C.C. (3d) 417 (B.C.S.C.) (A.G.'s decision reviewable by court, but no violation of ss. 7, 9, or 15); *R. v. Sterling* (1993), 113 Sask. R. 81 (C.A.) (direct indictment before preliminary inquiry did not violate the accused's rights since full disclosure was made by the prosecution)), one court has ruled that a prosecutor who offers nothing more in the subsequent prosecution than the transcript of the evidence taken at the preliminary inquiry where the accused was discharged engages in an abuse of process that triggers a *Charter* remedy of a stay of proceedings: *R. v. Parades* (1994), 35 C.R. (4th) 387 (C.Q.).

A person discharged after a preliminary inquiry who is not further pursued may nonetheless suffer enormous damage to her or his life and reputation. In this regard, consider nurse Susan Nelles, who was charged with the first degree murder of four babies in intensive care at the Sick Children's Hospital in 1982, after 43 infants died in the cardiac unit in 1981. At the time, police decided that the deaths were caused by the deliberate administration of digoxin. She was discharged at the close of her preliminary inquiry because the evidence supporting her charges was insufficient, in part because she was not even on her shift when one of the four infants died: *R. v. Nelles* (1982), 16 C.C.C. (3d) 97 (Ont. Prov. Ct.).

In spite of being cleared of all charges, Susan Nelles' name and the allegations against her made headlines for a long period of time. Susan Nelles subsequently sued the government for malicious prosecution and the courts determined that her suit against the Crown attorney and the A.G. was not barred by the immunity doctrine: *Nelles v. Ontario (A.G.)*, [1989] 2 S.C.R. 170. Ontario Premier Bob Rae announced on July 23, 1991 that Susan Nelles would receive $30,000 from the Ontario government for the grief that the wrongful accusation caused her and that the government would contribute $20,000 to a scholarship in Nelles' name at Queen's University and $10,000 to the Nelles Family Endowment Fund at Belleville General Hospital. The government also paid $225,000 in legal fees to Susan Nelles: Kevin Ward, "Nelles' grief acknowledged" *The Ottawa Citizen* (24 July 1991) A5. For further discussion of the context of the *Nelles* case, see Jacqueline Chomière, "The Grange Commission: Why Nurses are Scapegoats" (1985–86) 14 R.F.R. 11.

The police theory that a nurse or nurses were responsible for the murders has been seriously undermined by expert evidence that suggests that, in fact, *no* babies were murdered, given that digoxin is also found naturally in the body, and that the tests used in the investigation to produce the "objective" scientific evidence are now widely discredited as completely unreliable: CP, "Experts dispute '84 probe into baby deaths at Sick Kids" *The Toronto Star* (12 October 1995) A16.

Additional examples of wrongful convictions based in part "scientific" evidence that was later completely discredited are provided by the Lindy Chamberlain case, below, under The Media and the Trial Process, and the Guy Paul Morin case, discussed in Abell & Sheehy, *Cases, Context, Critique*, **Enforcement of the Law**. As a result of the testimony and evidence brought forward about the numerous failures of the "expert" evidence in the *Morin* prosecutions, the Honourable Fred Kaufman, Commr. in his report, *The Commission on Proceedings Involving Guy Paul Morin* (Toronto: Queen's Printer for Ontario, 1998) [hereinafter the *Morin Inquiry Report*] made 35 recommendations regarding the use of forensic evidence. As well, the Attorney General for Ontario prepared a new guideline for prosecutors for the full disclosure of forensic reports and governing the relationship between experts and the Crown: *Crown Policy — Physical Scientific Evidence* (13 November 1997), Appendix K.

The preliminary inquiry has been used for a different purpose than that of discovery or of testing the Crown's case in cases involving sexual assault charges. An example of these practices is provided by a talk given by Ottawa criminal defence lawyer Michael Edelson, who, at a meeting of lawyers, advised defence lawyers to "whack" the complainant at the preliminary inquiry in order to get the client discharged: Cristin Schmitz, "'Whack' Sex Assault Complainant at Preliminary Inquiry" *The Lawyers Weekly* (27

May 1988) 22. He suggests requesting disclosure of all the woman's records, hiring a private investigator to "beat the bushes", combing criminal and other court records, such as Children's Aid records, immigration records, and divorce discoveries of the complainant, establishing whether she has ever abused drugs or alcohol, and obtaining all photographs, tapes, or letters by or about the complainant: "the defence really now is slice-and-dice time for the complainant."

It is at the preliminary inquiry stage that most of the disclosure applications had been made in cases involving sexual assault charges, and, as was noted under the earlier section on Disclosure, these applications may be animated by the same motives espoused by Edelson above. As a result of defence concentration on preliminary inquiry strategies, this stage of the trial has taken on very different dimensions in sexual assault prosecutions. See, for example, the decision of Judge Romilly in *R. v. Darby*, [1994] B.C.J. No. 814 (Prov. Ct.) (QL). The new records legislation requires that disclosure applications be made to the trial judge instead of the judge presiding over the preliminary inquiry, thus preventing some of the tactics presented by Michael Edelson: see s. 278.3(1).

E. RIGHT TO SILENCE

An accused may assert the right to remain silent during pre-trial investigation or during the trial itself. What are the possible repercussions of asserting this right? For example, Susan Nelles refused to answer police questions in her investigation until she obtained access to a lawyer, which apparently convinced the police that she was guilty. Why might an accused not wish to testify at his or her own trial? Consider, for instance, the effect of s. 12 of the *Canada Evidence Act*, R.S.C. 1985, c. C-5, which permits an accused who testifies to be asked about prior convictions.

Section 7 of the *Charter* has been interpreted as guaranteeing the right to remain silent: *R. v. Hebert*, [1990] 2 S.C.R. 151. If the accused exercises the right to remain silent during pre-trial investigation or during the trial itself, this decision must not be the subject of comment by the Crown or the judge (s. 4(6) of the *Canada Evidence Act*). Furthermore, even a trial judge sitting alone must not draw an adverse inference from the accused's failure to take the stand and testify. However, counsel for the co-accused in a joint trial may make such a comment (*R. v. Crawford*, [1995] 1 S.C.R. 858) provided that the jury is not asked to view that silence as positive evidence upon which the Crown can rely as to proof of guilt. Thus, in *R. v. Noble*, [1997] 1 S.C.R. 874, the majority in a 5:4 decision ruled that an accused was entitled to a new trial because the trial judge's conviction of the accused was based, in part, on just such an inference. Only with respect to the defence of alibi may the accused's silence be used to undermine the credibility of that defence because of the ease of fabrication of an alibi and because the defence is not directly related to the accused's guilt.

In Northern Ireland, the right to silence has been severely curtailed by *The Criminal Evidence (Northern Ireland) Order*, 1988. A commentary on the impact of that new law can be found in J.D. Jackson, "Curtailing the Right of Silence: Lessons from Northern Ireland" [1991] Crim. L. Rev. 404. While an accused cannot be convicted solely on the basis of refusal to answer police questions (s. 38(4) of the *Criminal Justice and Public Order Act 1994*), s. 34 allows the drawing of adverse inferences where an accused attempts to rely on facts that he or she failed to disclose to police under questioning. Section 34 has been interpreted as permitting jurors to draw adverse inferences from an accused's failure to answer police questions even when the accused is acting on a lawyer's advice: *R. v. Condron*, [1997] 1 Cr. App. R. 185. The Court of Appeal stated that to avoid an adverse inference, the accused must explain the reasons for that advice or waive solicitor/client privilege so that the lawyer may testify on this point, to refute an inference of recent fabrication of a defence. What impact does this ruling have on the right to counsel? What might be the impact on wrongful convictions? Recall the cases of the Guildford Four and the Birmingham Six.

Consider also the implications of this law for accused who have mental disabilities. Ed Cape argues that since researchers have found that most people cannot understand the new caution that must be given by police ("You do not have to say anything. But it may harm your defence if you do not mention something which you later rely on in court. Anything you do say may be given in evidence"), people with mental disabilities will be highly at risk of failing to disclose exculpatory evidence to police, and having adverse inferences drawn against them. The law makes no provision for people with disabilities, and so this author offers concrete suggestions for lawyers who must advise and attempt to protect such clients: Ed Cape, "Mentally disordered suspects and the right to silence" (1996) 146 New L.J. 80.

F. THE JURY

ROLE OF THE JURY

The case of *R. v. Morgentaler*, [1988] 1 S.C.R. 30, discussed in more detail below, under **Necessity**, raised important and lingering questions about the role of the jury in Canadian criminal justice. In this case, after years of efforts to convict Dr. Morgentaler for violating the *Code* by performing abortions in clinics rather than through the hospital committee process, the Supreme Court ruled that the law violated s. 7 of the *Charter* and, therefore, the doctor could not be prosecuted. In making this decision, however, the Court took the opportunity to criticize the defence lawyer, who had invited the jury to disregard or "nullify" a "bad law" and acquit the doctor if they thought that the law was unjust. The Court said unequivocally that although juries cannot be called upon to account for their verdicts and thus may, in fact, disregard the law, this is not a "right" and therefore it is most improper for a lawyer to call this power to their attention.

More recently, consider the conviction of Robert Latimer, who killed his severely disabled daughter, allegedly out of compassion for her. He was not permitted to put a necessity defence to the jury, and counsel could not, pursuant to *Morgentaler*, encourage the jury to disregard the law: Sean Fine, "Jury had power to acquit farmer of murder, experts say" *The [Toronto] Globe and Mail* (18 November 1994) A6. It later became clear that the prosecution had tampered with the jury in an attempt to preclude the possibility of jury nullification. Latimer was granted a new trial by Saskatchewan Deputy Justice Minister Brent Cotter in the wake of disclosure that the RCMP interviewed prospective jurors secretly in order to ascertain their ethical beliefs regarding euthanasia. Legal commentators called the RCMP's actions "unprecedented", explaining that "the aberrations in the case attack the very backbone of the justice system." At the Supreme Court of Canada, it emerged that Crown counsel had assisted the RCMP officer in preparing a questionnaire to be used to interview prospective jurors and also failed to disclose the direct contact that the RCMP had with 30 of the prospective jurors to the trial judge, the defence, or the sheriff.

The Court ruled that the Crown's actions amounted to a flagrant interference with the administration of justice and an abuse of process; but, instead of staying the proceedings, as was ordered in *Carosella*, decided the same day by the Court, a new trial was ordered: *R. v. Latimer*, [1997] 1 S.C.R. 217. As one prosecutor commented: "In Latimer, you allegedly have a Crown and police screwing around with a jury, but it doesn't result in an acquittal ... Here you have a few women in Windsor trying to protect their clientele — and it warrants a stay": quoted in Makin, "Lawyers warn court's ruling could tie up legal system", *supra* at A5 under the discussion of *Carosella*.

Commentators on the significance of jury nullification have noted the historical function of the jury in mitigating the harshness of the criminal law and representing community-based notions of justice. *Bushnell's Case* (1670), discussed by Grant Huscroft, "The Right to Seek and Return Perverse Verdicts" (1988), 62 C.R. (3d) 123 at 123, is the source of the notion that a jury cannot be compelled to render a verdict against its conscience. The result of *Morgentaler* is that "juries are left uninformed as to both their power and any criteria which might guide them" (Huscroft at 125). While the judge has the power to declare a mistrial if a defence lawyer tells the jury that they can refuse to apply a bad law and acquit, the judge cannot direct the jury to convict. The Supreme Court has held, in *R. v. Krieger*, [2006] 2 S.C.R. 501 that a judge who directs a conviction has usurped the function of the jury and thereby denied the accused their right to trial by jury under s. 11(f) of the *Charter*.

As Huscroft points out, *Morgentaler* is representative of the conflict between judges and juries, with judges attempting to preserve the power and authority of "law" over the community, as represented by the jury: "Ironically, the jury exercised a power the court considers illegitimate to protect Dr. Morgentaler from a law which the court now finds unconstitutional. Constitutional vindication came only after passage of the *Canadian Charter of Rights and Freedoms*. However, the jury protected Dr. Morgentaler from a bad law long before the *Charter* provided a remedy" (at 126).

The tension between judges and jurors is graphically illustrated by remarks made by Manitoba's Chief Justice, Alfred Monnin, during the course of a jury trial in September 1988. He described jurors as "12 jokers" "who don't know very much", and said that the jury system can be a "lousy" one. He later apologized for his remarks, attributing them to his "impatience": Geoffrey York, "Chief Justice apologizes for remarks on jurors" *The [Toronto] Globe and Mail* (26 September 1988) A6.

Herman R

"The jury has found you not guilty, but I'm going to give you 2 years just to be on the safe side."

By Jim Urger. © LaughingStock International Inc. Reprinted with permission from LaughingStock Licensing Inc., Ottawa, Canada. All rights reserved.

JURY SELECTION PROCESS

The first step in the jury selection process involves the sheriff or other official preparing a list of those eligible for jury service under the relevant provincial or territorial legislation. From this list, panels of potential jurors are called to court. The array or panel itself may be challenged under s. 629 based on impartiality, fraud, or misconduct on the part of the sheriff or other official.

Most efforts to challenge the array, or jury panel, on the basis of representation of ancestry or gender have failed. In *R. v. Chipesia* (1991), 3 C.R. (4th) 169 (B.C.S.C.), the accused tried, without success, to challenge the array (s. 629) on the basis that no members of the panel were of Aboriginal ancestry. He failed because there was no evidence of efforts to exclude such persons from the list.

Similarly, the court in *R. v. F.(A.)* (1994), 30 C.R. (4th) 333 (Ont. Ct. J. (Gen. Div.)) ruled that neither ss. 11(d) nor 15 of the *Charter* requires that the accused be tried by a jury composed substantially of members of their own culture or race, provided that the process of jury selection is free of bias. In response to the absence of Aboriginal people in juror panels, the Manitoba Aboriginal Justice Inquiry has proposed that jurors be drawn from a 40 kilometres radius of the community where the trial is to be held, and that if a jury must be drawn from elsewhere, it should be drawn from a community "as similar as possible demographically and culturally to the community where the offence took place": Judge A.C. Hamilton & Judge C. Murray Sinclair, *Report of the Aboriginal Justice Inquiry of Manitoba* (Winnipeg: Queen's Printer, 1991) at 739.

However, in *R. v. Born With A Tooth* (1993), 81 C.C.C. (3d) 393 (Alta. Q.B.), the sheriff had attempted to ensure that Aboriginal peoples would be represented, at least in the array, and, to this end, had contacted individuals and organizations and referred to customer lists of utilities. The Crown successfully challenged the array under ss. 629 and 630 on the grounds that the array had not been prepared in a random fashion:

> Artificially skewing the composition of jury panels to accommodate the demands of any of the numerous distinct segments of Canadian society would compromise the integrity of the jury system. The effectiveness of the criminal jury system is based on widespread acceptance by the community as a fair and just method of deciding issues of criminal responsibility. (at 397)

After any challenges to the array have been resolved, there begins a process of self-disqualification, whereby prospective jurors are asked by the judge to declare any hardship or other reasonable grounds that might prevent them from serving on the jury. The presiding judge may allow these persons to be excused (s. 632) or to stand by (s. 633).

Then begins an individualized selection process: each prospective juror is called to the witness box, and both Crown and defence will have an opportunity to exclude the person by challenging for "cause" under s. 638, usually based on (b), the person "is not indifferent as between the Queen and the accused." Alternatively, if they do not have grounds to challenge for cause, the lawyers may also challenge on a peremptory basis — without providing reasons — although these challenges are limited in number, depending on the nature of the charges (see s. 634).

Historically in Canada the right to challenge for cause has been an empty right because lawyers sizing up possible jurors are not entitled to more than the name and occupation of the person and cannot freely ask further questions to probe any possible bias. However, lawyers have used the *Charter* to open up the process in some circumstances. For example, in *R. v. Parks* (1993), 15 O.R. (3d) 324 (C.A.), leave to appeal denied, (1994), 28 C.R. (4th) 403 (S.C.C.), for the first time a court permitted lawyers to ask more probing questions as part of the process of challenging for cause. The court ruled that an accused is entitled, pursuant to the *Charter* right to a fair trial (s. 7) and the right to a jury trial (s. 11(f)), to screen potential jurors for racism by asking about their ability to be impartial if the accused is African-Canadian. The court accepted at 338 the contention by the defence lawyer that "widespread anti-black racism is a grim reality in Canada and in particular in Metropolitan Toronto." *Parks* had a substantial impact upon the selection of jurors, at least in early cases, as one Toronto trial illustrates. In Thomas Claridge, "Half of would-be jurors stumble in test of impartiality" *The [Toronto] Globe and Mail* (1 October 1994) A3, it is reported that 41 out of 102 prospective jurors were disqualified in a case where two African-Canadian men were charged with firing shots at three police officers, because those questioned acknowledged that they would weigh police evidence more heavily than that of ordinary citizens.

After several initial cases from cities and regions outside of Toronto where judges denied the accused the opportunity to ask *Parks* questions in order to ground challenges for cause on the basis that racism against African-Canadian people was not a significant problem outside of Toronto, the Ontario Court of Appeal in *R. v. Wilson* (1996), 29 O.R. (3d) 97 (C.A.) rejected the notion that anti-Black racism is confined to Toronto and has, instead, said that the *Parks* questions should be available for any African-Canadian Ontario accused who is facing a jury trial. After some initial hesitation in *R. v. Ly* (1997), 32 O.R. (3d) 392 (C.A.), where the appeal court upheld a trial judge's refusal to apply *Parks* to the benefit of a Vietnamese accused because there was no evidence introduced to support the claim of widespread bias, the court instituted a new approach in *R. v. Koh* (1998), 42 O.R. (3d) 668 (C.A.). In *Koh* the court acknowledged the paucity of reliable evidence of this nature, and the insurmountable barrier such a prerequisite would pose for challenges for cause for new immigrant communities. The Ontario Court of Appeal therefore held that it is an appropriate matter for judicial notice in Ontario that reasonable persons are aware of the history of discrimination against "visible racial minorities" in Ontario, entitling accused members of these communities to challenge for cause without providing an evidentiary basis for bias in the community.

In *R. v. Musson* (1996), 3 C.R. (5th) 61 (Ont. Ct. J. (Gen. Div.)), the accused succeeded in satisfying the judge that homophobia in Canada is widespread and deeply rooted, and that, given that the accused was charged with the sexual assault of another adult male, he was likely to be viewed as a homosexual by the jury. The accused was, therefore, permitted to ask prospective jurors about their attitudes towards homosexuals.

Challenges for cause in Ontario can also be premised upon anti-poor bias. In another decision in Ontario, this time involving persons charged at the anti-poverty protest at Queen's Park in June 2000, the accused were permitted to ask prospective jurors whether their ability to judge the case without prejudice would "be affected by the fact that the people charged were participating in a demonstration on behalf of the homeless and the poor." The judge accepted the expert evidence offered that demonstrated "widespread prejudice against the poor and the homeless in the widely applied characterization that [they] are dishonest and irresponsible and that they are responsible for their own plight", which cannot, like racial prejudice, be "judicially cleansed": *R. v. Clarke* (No. 1), [2003] O.J. No. 3883 (Sup. Ct. J.) (QL).

Outside of Ontario, some courts have been reluctant to embrace the *Parks* approach. For example, the B.C. Court of Appeal upheld the trial judge's refusal to allow an Aboriginal man charged with robbery of a white person to ask prospective jurors about their biases against Aboriginal persons: *R. v. Williams* (1996), 75 B.C.A.C. 135. On appeal, the Supreme Court rejected the appeal court's decision, holding that evidence of widespread bias against Aboriginal persons on its own may, depending on the nature of that evidence and the charge against the accused, raise a realistic potential for juror partiality: *R. v. Williams*, [1998] 1 S.C.R. 1128. It is not always necessary to establish specific links between the evidence of bias and the accused's circumstances: trial judges must exercise their discretion to decide whether there is an "air of reality" to the accused's argument. On the facts, the Supreme Court held that there was ample evidence demonstrating widespread prejudice against Aboriginal accused, citing the CBA report, *Locking up Natives*, the Royal Commission on Aboriginal Peoples, *Bridging the Cultural Divide*, the *Royal Commission on the Donald Marshall, Jr. Prosecution*, and the *Report on the Cariboo-Chilcotin Justice Inquiry* (all referenced in Abell & Sheehy, *Cases, Context, Critique*, **Aboriginal Peoples and Criminal Law**). Williams therefore had no obligation to establish specific links between this evidence and the potential for bias in his own trial. He was granted a new trial in which he was entitled to raise this challenge.

Many defence lawyers have attempted to capitalize on *Parks*, by arguing that since violence against women and children is widespread and many prospective jurors have either been assaulted or know someone who has been, and since several surveys conducted by defence lawyers show widespread revulsion for perpetrators of sexual violence, the defence should be permitted to ask questions that would reveal such biases. In *R. v. B.(A.)* (1997), 33 O.R. (3d) 321 (C.A.) the trial judge had refused the defence application to question jurors along these lines. The Ontario Court of Appeal rejected the argument and dismissed the appeal against conviction and sentence for a father convicted of sexually assaulting his daughter. Moldaver J.A. wrote for the court at 336–37, 341:

> For reasons which will become apparent, I am of the view that the analogy to *Parks* is inapt and it rests upon a fundamental misperception of the principles informing that decision.
>
> *Parks* was concerned with a lack of indifference between the Crown and the accused, not a lack of indifference between the Crown and the type of offence charged. That is as it should be. Section 638(1)(b) speaks to a lack of indifference between the Crown and the accused; it says nothing about a lack of indifference between the Crown and the nature of the offence charged. While this distinction might be regarded as overly simplistic, I view it as fundamental to a proper understanding of the permissible limits within which challenges for cause based on alleged non-indifference may be brought. Moreover, it serves to place the *Parks* decision in its proper perspective.
>
> ...
>
> Racial prejudice is a form of bias directed against a particular class of accused by virtue of an identifiable immutable characteristic. There is a direct and logical connection between the prejudice asserted and the particular accused. In contrast, the prejudice asserted by the appellant involves negative views about a type of crime and not a type of person. In my opinion, there is no direct and logical connection that translates views about a particular crime into prejudice against a specific accused such that jurors would disregard their oath and render a verdict based on something other than the evidence and the legal instruction provided by the trial judge.
>
> To be more precise, I am of the view that strong attitudes about a particular crime, even when accompanied by intense feelings of hostility and resentment towards those who commit the crime, will rarely, if ever, translate into partiality in respect of the accused.

The accused also proposed a more sophisticated argument in favour of permitting the jurors to be questioned, based on a paper prepared by David Paciocco, "Challenge for Cause in Jury Selection After *R. v. Parks*: Practicalities and Limitations". This argument was described and addressed at 346–47:

> In respect of sexual offences, Professor Paciocco states that his main concern is with women, particularly those who belong to support groups and other victims' rights organizations, who view sexual assault within a larger, gendered political context in which they have a personal stake. He insists that his goal is not to exclude all feminists from juries and he acknowledges that jurors must be drawn from a spectrum of the population. Rather, he wor-

ries that there are zealots on the fringes of the victims' rights movement who subscribe to "sexist myths that would undermine the presumption of innocence," whenever the accused is male and the complainant female (at p. 24). Such myths, he argues, are so deeply held as to be subconsciously ingrained and thus are immune to the usual trial safeguards. In the end, Professor Paciocco asks rhetorically, "how much fidelity to judicial direction can be expected on the part of those who see the prosecution of sexual offenders as a battle front in a gender based war?" (at p. 25)

Unquestionably, Professor Paciocco's thesis is thought provoking. In brief, he argues that there is a realistic possibility that some prospective female jurors would not be impartial as between the Crown and males charged with sexual assault because of gender-based prejudice. By approaching the matter this way, Professor Paciocco seeks to bring the analysis in line with the reasoning in *Parks* and thereby bridge the conceptual gap between a want of indifference towards the accused and a want of indifference towards the crime.

Interesting though Professor Paciocco's analysis may be, in my view, it suffers from at least two serious defects.

First, his thesis lacks empirical data to support it. Professor Paciocco points to no studies, reports or surveys that would lend credence to his contention that there are some women likely to discriminate against a male accused charged with sexual assault simply on account of gender. Accordingly, Professor Paciocco's opinion must be rejected as merely speculative.

Second, although Professor Paciocco contends that there are potential jurors who hold sexist beliefs which undermine the presumption of innocence, it is not clear to me what those beliefs are and how they operate to undermine the presumption of innocence. In his paper, Professor Paciocco refers specifically to feminist groups and individuals who have managed to bring about changes in the law. Some of these changes include the rape shield provisions, the protection of therapeutic records, the abrogation of the doctrines of recent complaint and corroboration and the elimination of the defence of self-induced intoxication. It is this group in particular that Professor Paciocco targets as being potentially partial against males charged with sexual assault.

I think it odd that the test for partiality should somehow be linked to legitimate efforts to change the law. Surely, the test for partiality is not whether one seeks to change the law but whether one is capable of upholding the law as it currently exists.

Accordingly, I would not give effect to Professor Paciocco's thesis. At best, it strikes me as unsupported. At worst, it threatens to render the law a completely closed system, whereby those who would criticize the process are barred from participating in it.

The Manitoba Queen's Bench in *R. v. Gareau*, [1997] 2 W.W.R. 315, reached the same conclusion. The court refused to allow the defence to question prospective jurors about their attitudes about violence against women in the case of an accused charged with 18 counts of violence against a woman with whom he was involved. Judge Oliphant A.C.J. commented at 320:

> I find it interesting that notwithstanding the prevalence of charges involving break and enters and those of drinking and driving, applications to challenge each and every member of a jury panel on the basis of a perceived bias do not seem to arrive in such cases.
>
> Rather, applications of that nature seem to be confined to those cases involving charges of spousal violence and sexual violence where women are the complainants. I cannot help but wonder whether the views as to gender stereotyping held by defence counsel, most of whom are men, may have some impact on this state of affairs.
>
> ...
>
> I am not satisfied here that there exists an attitude, viewpoint, bias or prejudice which raises a reasonable prospect or possibility that a juror would not be indifferent or impartial as to the result.

In *R. v. Find*, [2001] 1 S.C.R. 863, the Supreme Court followed suit. Chief Justice McLachlin, for a unanimous Court, held that there is no evidentiary basis for the proposition that men accused of sexual assault face bias: the widespread nature of this crime and strong views about the crime do not, alone, meet the test. In the absence of evidence of widespread myths about men accused of sexual assault or "generic prejudice" against this group, judicial notice should not be invoked so as to permit a challenge for cause. The Court distinguished racial bias from the claim advanced by *Find* on several grounds.

Finally, it should be noted that there are barriers to the full participation of persons with disabilities in the jury, including s. 638(1) of the *Code*, which allows a challenge for cause on the basis that a juror cannot perform the physical functions of jury duty. See, for example, Wendy Holden, "Deaf Man's Anger at Jury Service Ban"

The [London] Daily Telegraph (27 June 1995) 12. As a result of its Consultation Paper, *Amendments to the Criminal Code and the Canada Evidence Act with Respect to Persons with Disabilities* (Ottawa: Department of Justice, 1993) at 12–14 (hereinafter *Persons with Disabilities*), the federal government, the federal government introduced Bill S-5, *An Act to amend the Canada Evidence Act, Criminal Code and Canadian Human Rights Act*, S.C. 1998, c. 9, ss. 4 and 6, which amends s. 627 of the *Criminal Code* so as to allow "a juror with a physical disability who is otherwise qualified to serve as a juror to have technical, personal, interpretive or other support devices."

G. THE MEDIA AND THE TRIAL PROCESS

This section examines the role of the media in the trial process and some of the challenges to that role. In particular, the limits on "freedom of the press" (*Charter* s. 2(b)) and the "public's right to know" are interrogated in the context of the rights of the accused and of the complainants/witnesses. Also, the selectivity of and the effects of media coverage on the characterization of individual accused and on the construction of crime are explored. There are other important issues beyond the scope of this discussion, such as the extent and impact of the concentration of corporate control of the press: James Winter, *Democracy's Oxygen: How Corporations Control the News* (Montréal: Black Rose, 1997); *Council of Canadians v. Canada (Director of Investigation and Research, Competition Act)*, [1996] F.C.J. No. 1609 (T.D.) (QL), [1997] F.C.J. No. 408 (C.A.) (QL) (the unsuccessful challenge with respect to Conrad Black's take over of the Southam newspaper chain). Writing in 1997, Winter describes how one corporate conglomerate controlled 43 per cent of daily newspaper circulation, two conglomerates controlled 55 per cent, and three controlled 66 per cent (at xxvi). More recently, deregulation and corporate and technological convergence in the news industries have arguably further narrowed the range of news available: David Skinner, James R. Compton, and Michael Gasher, ed., *Converging Media, Diverging Politics: A Political Economy of News Media in the United States and Canada* (Oxford: Lexington, 2005). As Skinner *et al.* describe, journalists continue to struggle against the redefinition of work, gag orders and imposition of control: David Skinner, James R. Compton, and Michael Gasher, "Turning the Tide" in Skinner *et al.*, *ibid.*

Limits to media coverage and orders for the exclusion of the public from the courtroom for all or part of the proceedings have been sought with respect to

- publication of the name of the complainant/witness against their wishes (see *R. v. Adams*, [1994] A.J. No. 1048 (Q.B.) (QL), rev'd [1995] 4 S.C.R. 707, and see generally s. 486; however, the Crown was unsuccessful in convicting an accused print journalist who named a complainant 10 times in an article that was published on the front page of the *Tillsonburg News*, where neither the journalist nor the newspaper was aware of the publication ban under s. 486: *R. v. Heldson* (2007), 85 O.R. (3d) 544 (C.A.).);
- testimony of witnesses;
- testimony of child witnesses;
- publication of the circumstances of the crime, where such publication would arguably prejudice the ability of the accused to receive a fair hearing (*Charter* s. 11(d)): *R. v. Joudrie*, [1996] 7 W.W.R. 438 (Alta. Q.B.) (application denied for access and authorization to duplicate and publish exhibits, until after the conclusion of any trial and appeal period);
- publication of the circumstances of the crime, where such publication would reveal the identity of the complainant/witness, or effectively re-victimize the victim: *R. v. Bernardo* (1995), 26 W.C.B. (2d) 328 (Ont. Ct. J. (Gen. Div.)); but see the restrictive interpretation of the exercise of a trial judge's discretion under s. 486(1) as to "undue hardship to the victim" when counterbalanced against s. 2(b) (freedom of the press) in *Canadian Broadcasting Corp. v. New Brunswick (A.G.)*, [1996] 3 S.C.R. 480, discussed below, this chapter;
- publication of fictionalized docudramas of the circumstances of the crime, such as the film *The Boys of St. Vincent* (Toronto: National Film

Board, 1992) where such publication would arguably prejudice the ability of the accused to receive a fair hearing (*Dagenais v. Canadian Broadcasting Corp.*, [1994] 3 S.C.R. 835);

- publication of the name of the accused: for example, in the case of a young offender, there is a prohibition against publication of any account that reports the name of the accused, or a child or young person who is a victim of the offence: *Youth Criminal Justice Act*, S.C. 2002, c. 1, ss. 110 and 111;
- publication of the name of co-perpetrators of a crime where the individuals may not necessarily have been formally charged;
- publication of parole hearings on the basis that it would interfere with the prisoner's rehabilitation (Ross Howard, "Ottawa trying to muzzle Olson: Motion seeks to stop media from seeing documents mass-murderer has filed in early parole hearing" *The [Toronto] Globe and Mail* (9 May 1997) A10;
- publication of the names of released prisoners and information as to their criminal records and whereabouts;
- publication of the names of undercover police officers (successful application by Crown for temporary one-year ban) and publication of police operational methods (unsuccessful application to oppose publication by Crown): *R. v. Mentuck*, [2001] 3 S.C.R. 442, and see discussion of the absolute importance of the protection of informer privilege in *Named Person v. Vancouver Sun*, [2007] S.C.J. No. 43 (QL), discussed below, under **Entrapment**; and
- access to information, freedom of expression and freedom of the press with respect to search warrants and informations and related documents: *Toronto Star Newspapers Ltd. v. Ontario*, [2005] 2 S.C.R. 188, and the distinction between access to information and the right to publish that information: *Ottawa Citizen Group Inc. v. Canada (A.G.)* (2005), 75 O.R. (3d) 590 (C.A.).

These demands for restrictions on publication are balanced against and tempered by the "freedom of the press", the "public's right to know", and the "duty to warn" the public about danger.

There have also been challenges with respect to the mode of coverage of trial proceedings, such as the presence of cameras in the courtroom and the filming of trials. But in most cases, these applications have been rejected: *R. v. Bernardo*, [1995] O.J. No. 585 (Ct. J. (Gen. Div.)) (QL) (application by the CBC for intervenor status to televise the trial denied). Finally, there have been challenges seeking access to the tapes, films, and sources within the knowledge and possession of reporters and media (for example, by police and defence counsel). Contempt charges and even imprisonment have resulted when reporters have refused to comply with court orders for production: *Canadian Broadcasting Corp. v. Batiot* (1996), 38 C.R.R. (2d) 96 (N.S.S.C.) (accused granted subpoenas requiring four journalists to give evidence with respect to prior interviews of complainants for a television program in a case involving a prominent Nova Scotia politician); Mike Shahin, "Journalist's arrest threat to public: TV cameramen jailed for concealing source" *The Ottawa Citizen* (20 September 1995) A1 (Hull journalist jailed for refusing to reveal a source during the preliminary inquiry of a Hull police constable charged with assault and obstruction of justice); Chris Cobb, "Lawyer asks reporter to break trust with source: Court ruling creates new search warrant, media lawyer says" *The Ottawa Citizen* (21 September 1996) B2 (defence counsel for an OPP constable charged with assault with a weapon argued for production of the journalist's notes and tape recording of an interview with a witness to the shooting). Yet, in a recent Ontario case, the Court of Appeal concluded that a journalist's right to protect their sources is anchored in the right to free speech and that the deployment of the "contempt power ... should always be tempered with a proper regard for the important values at stake": *St. Elizabeth Home Society v. Hamilton (City)*, [2008] O.J. No. 983 (at para. 40) (C.A.) (QL); Editorial, "Sources to be valued" *The [Toronto] Globe and Mail* (18 March 2008) A16.

In other jurisdictions, media has greater latitude to publish information (such as exhibits including confessions: Anthony Keller, "Who needs a trial when you can print a 'confession'?" *The [Toronto] Globe and Mail* (14 April 1997) A21, discussing the *Dallas Morning News'* publication of the alleged confession of Timothy McVeigh in the Oklahoma bombing case) and to interview witnesses (and pay them for their stories: *R. v. West*, [1996] 2 Cr. App. R. 374 (C.A.)).

The terms under which publication bans are available are defined in s. 486 of the *Code*. In some cases, the publication ban is limited to the pre-trial or trial period. In general, it is the media or the police who have tended to argue in favour of greater access to information. However, in the specific case of sexual assault, some lawyers for the accused have argued that the "protection" given to complainants/witnesses (even young children) interferes with the accused's right to a fair trial. Feminists and lawyers for complainants/witnesses have argued that public testimony and the publication of the names of complainants/witnesses are intimidating and have the effect of deterring complainants/witnesses from coming forward.

Finally, the level of support for demands for the publication of the names of accused varies depending on the crime and the accused's position in the community. An exaggerated media interest in particular crimes, especially those involving sexuality and violence, seems to shape decisions about what is "newsworthy" and what is "boring". This media distortion is demonstrated by the reporting of several law enforcement campaigns: see Thomas Fleming, "The Bawdy House 'Boys': Some Notes on Media, Sporadic Moral Crusades, and Selective Law Enforcement" (1981) 3:2 Canadian Criminology Forum 101; Banu Helvacioglu's report on the coverage of an anti-racist protest in Toronto, below; the coverage of the child abuse charges in Martensville, Saskatchewan in the 1990s (*R. v. Sterling* (1995), 137 Sask. R. 1 (C.A.); *R. v. T.S.* (1995), 131 Sask. R. 1 (C.A.); and *Popowich v. Sask.*, [1998] 8 W.W.R. 355 (Q.B.)); the Bernardo and Homolka trials in the 1990s in Ontario; and the trial of Kelly Ellard for the murder of Reena Virk in Victoria. This context and the construction of what is "normal" and "natural" — for example, the construction of motherhood and women — promote the vilification of particular accused, as Adrian Howe argues, below, happened to Lindy Chamberlain. Howe also raises provocative questions about the different ways in which witnesses are accorded credibility and expertise. As she argues, "media-drenched imagination" then enlarges this differential by glossing over the lack of scrutiny of the so-called expert evidence of scientists while discounting the expertise of other witnesses. For a discussion of another Australian case in which the media coverage was distorted to embellish and dramatize the bizarre, see: Deb Verhoeven, "Biting the hand that breeds: The trials of Tracey Wigginton" in Helen Birch, ed. *Moving Targets. Women, Murder and Representation* (Berkeley and Los Angeles: University of California Press, 1993) 95. For an exploration of media representations of, and societal attitudes towards, a number of high-profile cases of women who committed acts of violence (including Emma Humphreys, Lorena Bobbitt, and Lindy Chamberlain), see: Alice Myers & Sarah Wight, eds., *No Angels: Women Who Commit Violence* (London: Pandora/HarperCollins, 1996).

So, for example, as Karlene Faith and Yasmin Jiwani argue, women who commit acts of violence are contradictorily both demonized and cast as passive and lacking agency: "The Social Construction of 'Dangerous' Girls and Women" in Bernard Schissel & Carolyn Brooks, eds., *Marginality & Condemnation: An Introduction to Critical Criminology* (Halifax: Fernwood, 2002) 83. In the case of the killing of Reena Virk, in both the media and the trial process, the influence of racism was minimized although the narrative describes the bullying and brutal assault on a young South Asian woman who supposedly did not "fit in". The sentencing judge at first instance, Justice Morrison, is quoted as saying, "Whatever the motive for this crime, it was not racism": Faith and Jiwani at 102 citing Andy Ivens, "No apology by killer. She got the lightest sentence possible: Five years without parole" (21 April 2000) *Vancouver Province*. Since then, there have been two new trials of Kelly Ellard. At the third trial, she was found guilty of second degree murder and sentenced to life imprisonment with no eligibility for parole for seven years: *R. v. Ellard*, [2005] B.C.J. No. 2987 (B.C.S.C.) (QL). Subsequently, in *R. v. Ellard*, [2006] B.C.J. No. 2158 (C.A.), the Court of Appeal allowed an application by Ellard for the appointment of counsel (overriding the denial of legal aid by B.C. Legal Services), and on appeal the conviction was set aside and a new (fourth) trial was ordered: *R. v. Ellard*, [2008] B.C.C.A. 341. For a detailed and compelling account of the case and the background to it, see Rebecca Godfrey, *Under the Bridge* (New York: HarperCollins, 2005).

In a study of Toronto print media, Scot Wortley examines the way in which the racialization of both victim and offender shapes the media response and, in turn, skews the public perception of crime and racialized communities: "Misrepresentation or Reality? The Depiction of Race and Crime in Toronto Print Media" in Bernard Schissel & Carolyn Brooks, eds., *Marginality & Condemnation: An Introduction to Critical Criminology* (Halifax: Fernwood, 2002) 55. Wortley critically analyzes quantitatively and qualitatively the coverage and representations of race and crime in the media generally, and the coverage of interracial homicide in particular, drawing on two cases: the "Just Desserts" murder in 1994 (involving a white victim and an African-Canadian male offender) and the murder of Christine Ricketts in 1998 (involving an African-Canadian victim and a white male offender). As he demonstrates, media coverage of the two murders varied dramatically in terms of prominence and tone, choice of photos, treatment of the funeral of the victim, sympathy for the victim, and the moral panic generated by the "Just Desserts" murder compared to the treatment of the murder of Ricketts as a crime by an isolated individual. Only the "Just Desserts" case invoked widespread commentary and calls for tougher criminal sanctions. For further exploration of the representation of racial bias in Canada, see: Frances Henry & Carol Tator, *Discourses of Domination: Racial Bias in the Canadian English-Language Press* (Toronto: University of Toronto Press, 2002). For an American critique of misdirected fear, the distorted focus of that with respect to crime and race and the role of the media, see: Barry Glassner, *The Culture of Fear: Why Americans Are Afraid of the Wrong Things* (New York: Basic Books, 1999).

A longstanding area of concern in terms of media and the trial process has been the need to provide for the anonymity of rape victims to avoid what is effectively a second victimization through the public discussion of the case. The previous s. 442(3) (the precursor to s. 486) provided for a publication ban as to the name of the rape victim. However, that section was challenged by media in *Canadian Newspapers Co. v. Canada (A.G.)*, [1988] 2 S.C.R. 122. The Court held that s. 442(3) did infringe s. 2(b) of the *Charter* (freedom of the press), but not the accused's right to a fair hearing. The Court upheld the section as justified where the complainant (and not the prosecutor) was the one seeking the ban.

In *Canadian Broadcasting Corp. v. New Brunswick (A.G.)*, [1996], *supra*, the Supreme Court upheld the constitutionality of s. 486(1) but ordered access to the transcript of the portion of the sentencing proceedings that had been held *in camera*. The trial judge had exercised his discretion under s. 486(1) to protect the young female victims, on the basis of undue hardship; but Justice La Forest (writing for a unanimous Court) concluded that there was no undue hardship established here compared to that faced by other young sexual assault victims ([1996] 3 S.C.R. 480 at 504):

> While the social interest in protecting privacy is long standing, its importance has only recently been recognized by Canadian courts. Privacy does not appear to have been a significant factor in the earlier cases which established the strong presumption in favour of open courts. That approach has generally continued to this day, and this appears inherent to the nature of a criminal trial. It must be remembered that a criminal trial often involves the production of highly offensive evidence, whether salacious, violent or grotesque. Its aim is to uncover the truth, not to provide a sanitized account of facts that will be palatable to even the most sensitive of human spirits. The criminal court is an innately tough arena.

at 521:

> Most sexual assault cases involve evidence that may be characterized as "very delicate." The evidence did not establish that this case is elevated above other sexual assaults.

Thus the Court concluded that only some sexual assault victims experience sufficient "undue hardship" to bring themselves within the possible protection of s. 486(1). This uncertainty in itself will discourage complainants from coming forward. However, the more chilling aspect of the decision is the retroactive publication of a transcript of an *in camera* hearing. Thus, despite a trial judge's ruling that a portion of the process will take place *in camera*, a witness is unable to place any reliance on the privacy of their testimony or the tendering of victim impact statements. As a result of the work of a broad coalition of women's groups in the wake of *Canadian Newspapers Co. v. Canada (A.G.)*, *supra*, the *Code* has been amended, and a stronger version of s. 486 has been added to the *Code*.

In a Québec case, a judge decided to free an accused rather than allow a 17-year-old to testify in private. Thus, the outcome of the insistence on public testimony was an acquittal. The man was one of five men alleged to have raped the woman almost two years before. She had already testified four times, each time *in camera*, during the other earlier trials. The decision provoked considerable reaction from Québec women's groups. See Richard Mackie, "Groups seek new law for sex victims: Acquittal sparks demand for action" *The [Toronto] Globe and Mail* (21 August 1993) A5.

A judge may also make an order for non-publication of the name of even a convicted person. For a case in which the judge made such an order at the defence request, see: "Man guilty on sex charge, name withheld" *The Ottawa Citizen*

(18 October 1988) C2. The judge said that the anonymity would benefit the young victim of sexual assault and her younger sister, by preserving their anonymity also. However, the effect, coupled with a six-month sentence and an order for a temporary absence pass, obviously benefited the convicted man, who was allowed to keep his job in the federal public service.

In this context, some media have defied the court bans. See David Roberts, "Radio host defies ban by naming sex offender: Ruling shielded assailant, abused stepdaughter complained" *The [Toronto] Globe and Mail* (1 May 1993) A5. In *C.(P.R.) v. Canadian Newspapers Co.* (1993), 16 C.C.L.T. (2d) 275 (B.C.S.C.) in a civil lawsuit, *The [Duncan] Citizen* was ordered to pay $10,000 for printing a story that identified a sexual assault complainant/witness contrary to a court-ordered ban. See Brad Daisley, "Newspaper must pay $10,000 for identifying assault victim" *The Lawyers Weekly* (16 April 1993) 11.

In cases of prostitution, there has been a differential pattern of law enforcement, and prostitutes have been much more frequently charged than customers. (For a case that held that the particular pattern of police enforcement under s. 213 of the *Code* did not amount to a violation of s. 15 of the *Charter*, despite the fact the evidence established that five times as many women as men were being prosecuted by the Halifax police, see: *R. v. White* (1994), 136 N.S.R. (2d) 77 (C.A.), reproduced in Abell & Sheehy, *Cases, Context, Critique*, **Enforcement of the Law**.) There has also been a differential pattern as to the release of the names of those charged by police. However, in 1988, when Toronto police did release the names of customers charged, as a deterrent, Toronto's three daily newspapers declined to publish the names, saying lists alone are "boring". When Ottawa police considered releasing the names of 41 "johns" in 1988, the arguments raised included various objections, namely: that the offence carried such stigma that those charged would be deeply affected, with possible serious repercussions for them; that the police were simply attempting to use the media to harass suspects; that the media's job was to report news, not to punish lawbreakers; and that the police were not doing this as a public service but to enforce the law indirectly. For a discussion of those responses, see: Mike Blanchfield, "Group backs withholding names of accused 'johns'" *The Ottawa Citizen* (24 October 1988) B2.

Consider whether these objections to the publication of an accused's name apply to or are raised with respect to other types of offences. If so, under what circumstances? What is the impact of press coverage of any charge, where the accused is subsequently acquitted? Again, are certain charges given a broader and more damaging coverage by the media? Compare, for example, the coverage and the concerns expressed with respect to those convicted of child sexual assault to concerns expressed with respect to those convicted of unsafe labour practices. For example, Ontario's General Division Court ruled that the names of nearly 250 firms with extremely bad safety records not be released, since "the information of a safety record of a firm could be harmful, particularly in the public tendering process or in labour relations," quoted in Thomas Claridge, "Names of firms with bad safety records withheld" *The [Toronto] Globe and Mail* (12 May 1995) A5. See also *Ontario (Workers' Compensation Board) v. Ontario (Assistant Information & Privacy Commissioner)* (1995), 23 O.R. (3d) 31 (Ct. J. (Gen. Div.)). In that case, the employers' desire to suppress the information was supported by the Workers' Compensation Board and by the Attorney General. However, the decision was overturned and the information ordered released in *Ontario (Workers' Compensation Board) v. Ontario (Assistant Information & Privacy Commissioner)* (1998), 41 O.R. (3d) 464 (C.A.).

The release of names of sexual offenders by police has sometimes been advocated as a means of making communities safer. However, others have argued that this simply terrifies the community, inhibits any prospect of rehabilitation and integration, and is an attempt by police to supplant the role of the courts and the parole boards. In a case raising issues around HIV/AIDS and homophobia, Ottawa police said "it was in the public interest" to reveal the identity of a Vanier man who was suing Chief Arthur Rice and Superintendent John McCombie for malicious publication of his name and for ruining his reputation. See Tonda MacCharles, "Man ID'd in interest of public, police say" *The Ottawa Citizen* (18 October 1988) C2. In that case, the man was accused of endangering the lives, safety or health of the public by donating HIV-tainted blood. There was wide press coverage.

Consider the discourse in which HIV/AIDS is discussed, and the role of the media and the criminal justice system in perpetuating or contributing to that discourse. For example, see the prominence and tone given to the issue by the large front page headline in Dale Madill, "AIDS Fiend Strikes Again" *The [Halifax] Chronicle Herald* (19 September 1988) 1. For further examples, see "Man arraigned on charge of spreading AIDS" *The Ottawa Citizen* (27 September 1988) A5; "Halifax AIDS suspect gets bail, no-sex order" *The Ottawa Citizen* (30 September 1988) A10. Alison Young has argued that criminal justice policy marks, quarantines and banishes the HIV positive individual as the "embodiment of death": Alison Young, *Imagining Crime: Textual Outlaws and Criminal Conversations* (London: Sage, 1996) at 206. Compare the treatment of cases involving HIV/AIDS and heterosexual assault.

Consider the case of Johnson Aziga, charged with first-degree murder based on allegations that he knowingly infected sexual partners with HIV (two women he allegedly had sex with died): *R. v. Aziga*, [2005] O.J. No. 5983 (Ct. J.) (QL). The accused argued unsuccessfully that his s. 15 rights were infringed because the criminalization of HIV/AIDS amounted to the criminalization of a physical disability and/or the prosecution amounted to racial profiling: *R. v. Aziga*, [2007] O.J. No. 4965 (Sup. Ct. J.) at paras. 9–10, 15:

> ... The applicant is not being prosecuted because he is HIV Positive ...
>
> The gravamen of the offence being charged is not the fact that the accused applicant is HIV Positive, but rather that he engaged in unprotected penetrative sexual activity with the 13 named complainants, knowing he was HIV Positive and failing to disclose to them that he was HIV Positive, thereby exposing them to serious bodily harm.

In another case, Jennifer Murphy pled guilty to aggravated sexual assault for incidents of unprotected sex, in which she failed to tell her partners about her HIV infection: *R. v. Murphy*, 2005 CarswellOnt 8297 (Sup. Ct. J.) (WLeC). In October 2005, the RCMP took the unusual step of warning the public about Trevis Smith (a former CFL player) and his HIV-positive status: Anne Kyle and Rob Vanstone, "Police issue HIV alert on CFL player, Trevis L. Smith" *CanWest News Service* (29 October 2005), online: <http://www.canada.com/national/features/crime_report/>. Smith was sentenced to 5.5 years in prison: "Trevis Smith sentenced to 5½ years in prison" *CTV News* (26 February 2007), online: CTV News <http://www.ctv.ca/servlet/ArticleNews/story/CTVNews/>. See also the discussion of *R. v. Cuerrier*, below, under **Case Study on Assault**.

What legal and social policy issues does HIV/AIDS raise? What are the implications for specific groups? Does the media coverage reflect those concerns? Consider the context of homophobia, the discretion police have with respect to law enforcement, and the response of police and the criminal justice system to gay and lesbian communities generally, discussed in the materials on **Policing** in Abell & Sheehy, *Cases, Context, Critique*. Refer back to the materials there on **Law and Order** about the role of the media in the creation of moral panic and the influence of the media in describing the reality.

Shannon Bell argues that in January 1994, sex, morality, and paranoia once again coalesced to create a moral panic about child pornography and a so-called "child porn ring" in London, Ontario: Shannon Bell, "On ne peut pas voir l'image [The image cannot be seen]" in Brenda Cossman *et al.*, eds., *Bad Attitude/s on Trial: Pornography, Feminism, and the Butler Decision* (Toronto: University of Toronto Press, 1997) at 199.

Consider the ways in which Howe suggests motherhood, normalcy, credibility and expertise are constructed in the Lindy Chamberlain case following.

Chamberlain Revisited: The Case against the Media†

A bizarre chain of association links two recent, seemingly disconnected events. On October 13, 1988, the Roman Catholic Church announced that the Shroud of Turin, venerated by Christians over the centuries as the burial cloth of Jesus, could not be authentic because new scientific tests showed that

---

† Adrian Howe, "Chamberlain Revisited: The Case Against the Media" (1989) 31:2 *Refractory Girl* 2 2–8. [Notes omitted.] Reprinted by permission of the author.

the linen dates from the Middle Ages. The 'new' science — radiocarbon tests (conducted independently by three laboratories) — revealed the falsity of the claims made by the 'old' science: photographic techniques which enabled stains on a sheet to be read as the body of a man. A month earlier, on September 15, the Northern Territory Court of Criminal Appeal quashed the 1982 conviction of Alice Lynne Chamberlain for murdering her nine week old baby, Azaria, at Uluru in 1980.

The Turin Shroud and Chamberlain are both cases of missing, and subsequently mythologised, bodies. Another crucial link between them is the valorisation of science which enabled claims to be made for, and later against, both the Shroud and Lindy Chamberlain. Still another[ ] is the British forensic scientist James Cameron, who was to personify this valorisation of science at the Chamberlain trial. A key prosecution witness, Professor Cameron produced evidence based on techniques similar to the visualisation process used to verify the Shroud (in which, interestingly, Cameron also had an interest), to demonstrate the present [*sic*] of blood-stained handprints on baby Azaria's jumpsuit. How ironic that it was 'new' science — scientific investigations conducted after Chamberlain's conviction — which was used to discredit the Crown's scientific evidence against her as incompetent, unqualified and unreliable such that no judge could permit a jury to act on it.

Some people refuse to give up their belief in the Shroud and/of Lindy's guilt. This paper is not for them. It is for those, like myself, who came to believe the media-mediated scientific evidence against her and thus to condemn her. One way to exorcise this demon, this blind faith in science, this suspension of feminist political judgement, this credulity in favour of experts and the media and against the testimony of white eye-witnesses, black trackers and Lindy herself, is to re-examine the process by which we came to construct her guilt. The media's role in this process, her trial by media, was crucial.

Indeed, it has been said that the media trial of Lindy Chamberlain "read like theatre reviews" in which performance was judged "according to theatrical and dramatic conventions for tragedy": we found her guilty on the basis of a media-orchestrated 'aesthetic judgement'.

Adopting then, the role of prosecutor (in order to excoriate my guilty collusion with that judgement; my seduction by the media's lust to kill her right to be presumed innocent until proven guilty in a court of law), I propose to put the media on trial for murder. My case is this: the Australian media, aided and abetted by a large cross-section of the Australian people, murdered, killed in cold blood, the possibility of a fair trial for Lindy Chamberlain.

Some points of clarification before I begin. My concern here is not with legal technicalities but rather with examining the media's construction of the criminality of that ultra 'deviant' woman who is accused of murdering her own child. Nor am I interested in singling out particular scurrilous journalists, nor in assessing the different contributions of specific newspapers with a view to exempting those who maintained some integrity. In particular, I am not interested in specifying the sexism of certain male journalists. Unlike the Chamberlain trial, this is not a witch-hunt. One final point of clarification: the research base, the material on which my case rests, is selective. It is drawn almost entirely from Sydney-based newspapers. It may seem unfair to place the whole Australian media on trial on the basis of such an unrepresentative sample of newspapers, but this material is representative of the media's reporting of the case. The same pictures, the same photos, the same story was re-enacted in words and pictures, thereby strangling her chance of a fair trial.

The Witch Hunt

The case I wish to present against the media differs from the prosecution case against Chamberlain in several significant respects. Most crucially, we are not reduced to circumstantial evidence as the prosecution was in the Chamberlain case. While I was tempted to parody that prosecution — to say, as the prosecutor did say in that case, that the Crown does not venture to suggest any motive for the killing, that the Crown does not attempt to prove motive, nor does it invite speculation as to motive — I will resist that temptation and submit that there was a motive in this case against the media. The motive was the perception of Lindy Chamberlain as a dangerous woman: a dangerous, provoking counter-stereotypical woman who refused to play her assigned gender role; who spoke out on her behalf and on behalf of all woman, demanding her right to tell her story, her dreadful story of the death of her child, in her own way, her own defiant, non-passive way, a right which was denied her by a male-dominated media which was angered and terrified by her refusal to play the role of a properly gendered woman.

Lindy herself felt their fear when she asked "Why were they so desperate to get hold of me? Why would they be so anxious to spend millions to get me? If Jack the Ripper was running amok, you could understand it. But why me? Somebody is scared of something."

Yes, Lindy, they were afraid of you.

Chamberlain's perceived dangerousness, then supplies the motive in this case against the media. Next, the murder weapon. Unlike the Chamberlain trial, in which the prosecution was unable to supply a motive, an identifiable weapon, let alone a body, we do have a murder weapon. It was a witch-hunt, a media-orchestrated witch-hunt in which the question of Lindy's criminality and guilt was predetermined by the Australian media and many Australian people.

Finally, we have a body in this case, the sexualised body of Lindy Chamberlain, the body which, if we can believe the media, solicited criminalisation.

The media's preoccupation with Lindy's body was the first step in the creation of Lindy the Witch. The witch, a figure embodying the power and threat of female sexuality, a wild, uncontrollable sexuality which must be tamed, tamed, in this case by the objectifying gaze of the media. Lindy's sexuality became a major point of discussion among the male journalists. Hear them incriminate themselves. She was "the pert brunette" wearing a different outfit to court each day, but always looking "striking"; her "filmy apricot dress with thin straps over the shoulders" led many to ogle and tip that "she was braless beneath." The "soft roundness of her tanned shoulders" attracted their attention, and helped them formulate their opinion that "it's easy to see why Michael is a pastor and not a priest." Such views were easily formed because she looked "ravishing," her "lithe body faultlessly sun-tanned as far as could be seen." In short, she "dressed in a fairly sexy sort of way" and during the second inquest she "wore a different dress almost everyday." For these male journalists, Lindy, with her "petite frame," her "constantly changing dresses" and her "eye-catching figure," was "beautiful."

Lindy's appearance became a media obsession. It was as if the photo could tell us about her guilt, as if the media was seeking evidence which could not be used in court-evidence about her femaleness. Their photos became the evidence by which we prejudged her criminality. Sydney photographer Catherine Rogers has interrogated the 'official' photographic story of the Chamberlain case. She asks:

> What is our evidence (and I mean yours and my evidence)? It is images of HER.
>
> Does she look like a murderer?
>
> What does a murderer look like? We look at her in the newspaper and on television. The only information that we have of her, is provided for us, and comes from the radio, the newspapers, television, books and magazines. From these sources we make our assessment of her. We have judged her and found her guilty of murder.
>
> Images of HER.
>
> Camera close-ups: the camera scrutinises her body, her face and presents us with photographs of HER. An expression frozen in time. From these images we make our assessment of HER.
>
> We look into the photographic image for the recognisable facial expressions, we search for the signs of grief which we assume must be revealed in her face. We know how to recognize grief from other media images, from the movies, the one-hour television drama, the TV mini series, the midday soapie. In the absence of these recognisable signs of grief, there must be guilt.

We only knew her through the media, through media-mediated stories and photographic images, none of which were innocent of meaning. They all had definite meanings, the coded meanings produced by our 'culture' refracted through an objectifying male gaze.

The mainstream media's obsession with Lindy Chamberlain's body continued unabated through the two inquests and the trial. Innumerable male journalists became obsessed with her body, especially with its witch-like ability to change shape. Diane Johnson has noted how Lindy's ability to change her image caused concern: "On one day, said a journalist, she would look 'like a schoolgirl ...' and on the next she would look 'like a filmstar' with a black dress, red lips, shoes and handbag."

Johnson notes too how by the time of her trial Lindy's pregnancy had changed her shape again, "as if Lindy herself was pushing the contradictions of her situation to the limits." Two years later there would be more speculation about her changing body shape. While she was in Sydney in 1984 for one of her appeals, the headlines rang out: "Is Lindy pregnant again?" According to at least one report, she had put on weight and was wearing a loose-fitting smock, which "closely resembled a maternity dress." This report commented knowingly: "If she is pregnant, it will not be the first time she has been with child under such circumstances."

At the time of her trial when she was in fact pregnant one journalist described his first impressions, while waiting in the Chamberlains' driveway: "Two minutes later, our target appeared. Dressed in a bright red cardigan, knee length grey dress and brown boots, Lindy paid little attention to our appearance. She had changed since I last saw her.

She had become much bigger ... obviously having a normal, healthy pregnancy. She had changed her hairstyle, too. It had been cut short, and curled."

The pregnancy fuelled more rumours, media-instigated rumours. Was her pregnancy a play for sympathy? Who would convict a pregnant woman? More crucially, however, her pregnancy raised the vital issue of motherhood. Medical attention now focussed on her as a mother, and the assessment began of her mothering skills. In the process Lindy Chamberlain lost her status as a woman. The headlines tell the story: she became "the Guilty Mother, the "Young Mother with Far Away Eyes," the "Dingo Baby Mother." By the time of her trial in September 1982, she had been found guilty, in the media, of more than child murder: she stood condemned for violating the stereotypes and sanctity of motherhood, of transgressing the boundaries of normal, passive motherhood. Moreover, by raising the possibility of having killed her child, she became transformed into an unnatural mother and a witch.

The evidence put forward to support the witch theory took two forms. First, there was her changing body shape. Diane Johnson has observed that in the Middle Ages witches were thought to change shape and assume the shape of a beast. She traces the journalist musings: "Did Lindy purposefully change her form? None of her children were accidental, Lindy had asserted at the first inquest. Could she really have killed her clearly beloved baby? Could she have invented the dingo story? Could she indeed have been the 'two-legged dingo'?"

What were we to make of this weird 'Dingo Baby Mother'? A second body of evidence focussed on her weird, 'unnatural' non-stereotypical behaviour. Her 'unnatural' impassiveness — most crucially, she didn't cry — caught the media's attention. Moreover, it was not only the male journalists who were alert to her: women journalists shared their masculinist concerns. According to one woman: "As a mother, and a young, good-looking, eloquent woman, Lindy Chamberlain is easy for most people to identify with and difficult to picture as a murderer, especially of her own child. Yet her reaction to the loss of her child has not fitted the stereotype of the distraught mother: her composure at most times is confusing."

Furthermore, as Kerryn Goldsworthy accurately observed, hundreds of Australia [*sic*] women were convinced of Chamberlain's guilt largely on the basis of "what they saw as her flaunting, during the trial of her tanned shoulders, and her large wardrobe. The 'logic' was that a women interested in looking attractive at such a time must be a bad woman, and everyone knows that a bad woman cannot be a good mother."

While this was a generally shared perception, it was, in the first instance, a masculinist perception, one which informed the views of the male journalists reporting the trial in Darwin. We have the benefit of an account written by one of these male [journalists] of how he came to form his opinion of Lindy Chamberlain.

The Chamberlain family was, he thought, more than a little "odd" and there "just didn't seem to be the joy in the family that [a] new baby should bring." Moreover, because of their religion, they didn't smoke, drink, take drugs, eat meat, or even drink tea or coffee. That was strange enough, but Lindy herself was the weirdest of all, as he discovered when he rang their home for an interview. First she made the mistake of asking him how she could help, in a "happy, almost bubbly" voice. Then she upset all his admitted 'preconceived thoughts of a grieving mother shattered', by replying to his question about whether there was any more news: "What do you mean? Like finding bits of the body?" The journalist [was] stunned: "how could a mother ... how could anybody talk of something so horrific as findings bits of a baby's body." From then on, he would always find her "odd." Sometimes she would behave "normally," then burst into tears at mention of her "bubby Azaria," but then her "almost disturbing voice" would return. For him it was "eerie speaking to what was in effect two people in one," one whose eyes seemed "to pass through me and fix on a distant point" when he asked her if [she] had killed Azaria. Her negative reply, "with a display of absolutely no emotion, unsettled" him because she had not become angry, merely replying "in a matter-of-fact way."

The Unnatural Mother

This kind of puzzlement found its way into the press. According to one newspaper report, Lindy was enigmatic, "recovering from a crying fit within minutes, and even laughing." According to another, she responded to questions at the inquests with "words which sounded harsh coming from a supposedly loving mother's lips." She was, to them, bizarre, and for days after her trial they sought to penetrate what they called "The Private World of the 'Guilty' Mother" in order to find out: "WHO is the REAL Lindy Chamberlain? What lies behind the usually stern face which she has presented to the world?"

That she could be, according to one witness, a model wife and mother, "a perfect little mother," one minute and an impassive, dry-eyed one at the trial, was too much for the press gallery to take. Her seeming inconsistencies, her blatant contradictions, crystallised their fears, fears inherent in our conception of motherhood.

The role of ideas about motherhood in the conviction of Lindy Chamberlain has been most fully developed by Kerryn Goldsworthy. She argues that Lindy was condemned, "rightly or wrongly not for murder as such, but because of a public belief that she had violated the sanctity of motherhood." She continues: "In almost all of the millions of words spoken or written about her ... the representation of Lindy Chamberlain has been focused for good or ill on aspects of her femaleness: on her qualities as a mother, and on her sexuality." In [Goldsworthy's] view, a view published in the mainstream press in February 1986, shortly after Lindy's release, it was "public attitudes to motherhood and to female sexuality which informed and to a great degree shaped the course of Lindy Chamberlain's trial — a trial by jury, media, and by the collective unconscious of an entire nation." Furthermore, Lindy's public image, which was concentrated simultaneously on her sexuality and on her maternity, "violated the largely unconscious but deeply ingrained conviction that motherhood is good and female sexuality is not good and never the twain shall meet."

Goldsworthy concludes that "it might well have been her pregnancy, more than her determined attempts to speak for herself — to construct her own image in her own words — which turned the scales against her, simply because she represented for Australian society a disturbing and unresolvable contradiction and therefore a threat to complacently held beliefs. There is a good chance that had she not been pregnant and prettily dressed when she stood trial she never would have been in Berrima Jail."

While Goldsworthy's observations are, from feminist perspectives, plausible, they remain speculations, and unlike the prosecution in the Chamberlain case, I prefer not to speculate. After all it was speculation which characterised the media coverage of the Chamberlain case, speculation for example, that she was suffering from post-natal depression (which would explain her 'irrational' female behaviour), and, more bizarre, speculation that she was a witch. How did the media affect [*sic*] this criminalising transformation of Lindy into an evil, unnatural, witch-like killer? The steps taken were not overt. As Diane Johnson says, "the spectre of Lindy as witch was rarely articulated, yet the notion percolated just beneath the surface." But it worked: the image of Lindy as witch took hold. Clearly, however, the success of that media image could not rely on her changing body form and her alleged unnatural behaviour. To clinch the witch allegations, the press had a [*sic*] discredit her account of the baby's disappearance. They were assisted in this process by her prosecutor, who called her a "fanciful liar" and her account of a dingo taking her baby a "transparent lie." The "case against the dingo," he said, "would be laughed out of court," because it was a "transparent lie."

Headlines blazed: "Lindy's Lies," and in smaller print, "says the prosecution"; "Dingo Story a Transparent Lie"; "Lindy's Account Laughable"; "The Dingo Story an Affront." In this way, her story became "the dingo theory." Even her defence counsel referred to her account as "the dingo story." On the one hand, the media delegitimated Lindy's account, and that of witnesses, by turning it into mere theory. On the other hand, it transformed the prosecution's allegations into a factual account of the death of Azaria Chamberlain. Embellished to capture the public's imagination, this account, as retold in the press, became the account or "the sacrifice in the wilderness."

Uluru (Ayer's Rock to white tourists) provided the perfect setting for this story of the night of the great disappearance. For journalists 'the Rock' seemed to have a "brooding presence." On the night of Azaria's disappearance from the "death tent" an "eerie stillness settled over the desert." Much was made in the press of the dingo, especially of the dingo's legendary significance as a devil and the dingo spirit of Aboriginal legends. Unwittingly, Lindy contributed to the linking of the death of her child, the dingo and the devil, when she described Azaria's death as a "trial by Satan." "Dingo Baby — it's trial by Satan," blazed the headlines and the dingo became the "devil dog."

The "Sacrifice in the Wilderness" story was to become more bizarre as the press started to report that the name Azaria meant precisely that: a sacrifice. The Chamberlains could protest as much as they liked that the name meant 'Blessed of God', but the public's media-saturated imagination had already linked the Seventh Day Adventist Church to which the Chamberlain belonged, to the mystery. These "prayer warriors" who countenanced sacrifices of blood, were weird. The media propagated other stories, all of which later proved to be without foundation that the Chamberlains had dressed Azaria in sinister black ("even with black booties tied by black bows"); that she was roughly handled by her mother, that she was hurt in a fall in a supermarket; that a child's coffin was kept for her body, that the family bible opened at a page on which a passage was outlined about a woman murdering her child; that the last photo at Uluru was not of Azaria, but of an older child (to conjure up the notion that Azaria was being used for some other purpose).

As if all this wasn't bizarre enough, bold headlines, reported "Police Diggings of Mystery Objects," possibly human bones, and police tests on machetes in relation to the Azaria case — reports which prompted the Northern Territory Chief Minister to call for an end to speculation about the case. It was, he said, serving no good. It was, however, serving one cause: the police/press case against Lindy Chamberlain who was tried and convicted as a witch by the majority of the Australian people before her legal trial began.

But why did we come to believe this bizarre, media-contrived story, a story which flew in the face of witnesses' accounts and of common sense understanding of probabilities? For if Lindy killed Azaria, it must have been the fastest, cleanest throat-cutting in history. She would have had approximately ten minutes to have done the deed, cleaned everything up and presented to other campers as 'normal'.

'Expert' Guidance

The key to this puzzle lies in another crucial step which was essential to clinch the witch-craft case against her. In order to repress the knowledge of the white people who were there on the fatal night and the black trackers who found dingo tracks around the tent, the media had to find an evidential basis for the witch story which would convince those for whom the evidence of Lindy's sexualised body and 'unnatural' behaviour was not enough. They found it in the 'expert' evidence provided by forensic [scientists] such as Professor Cameron, who had worked on the Turin Shroud and who was imported by the prosecution to help construct the scenario of Azaria's throat being cut in the car.

Paradoxically, this 'expert' testimony was itself a new kind of sorcery, and as such was soundly rejected at the Morling Inquiry into the Chamberlains' convictions. Mr Justice Morling concluded that he "wouldn't hang a dog" on the crown evidence that blood was found in the car. He found that it had been established that a 4000 to 1 chance the spray pattern advanced to the trial jury in 1982 as evidence of an arterial blood spurt, was in fact sound deadener. As for Cameron's scientific discovery that there was a human handprint, a woman's handprint, on Azaria's jumpsuit, that too was totally discredited at the Inquiry. The stain turned out to be sand, the handprint a figment of the professor's over-active imagination.

Yet at the time of the trial, we were seduced by the expert evidence presented in the media as scientific fact. The forensic experts were reported to have confirmed that her death was caused by scissors which had baby's blood on the cutting edge. The car, according to reports, was awash with blood, foetal blood, and so, for that matter were the reports themselves as the experts crucified the 'dingo story'. In the small-print, dissenting scientific opinions failed to catch our eye.

My concern here is neither to reassess the scientific evidence nor to dwell, with the advantage of hindsight, on patent absurdities in the scientific evidence which passed as objective fact, but rather to reflect on the way in which the media reportage of the so-called scientific knowledge overwhelmed and submerged other knowledges. How did we allow the secondary evidence of scientists working in British laboratories far removed from the scene of the crime to take over from the primary, first-hand evidence of the witnesses, the white campers, who testified that they heard a baby cry after the time the prosecution alleged that the throat-cutting occurred? Why did we privilege the evidence of scientists, who admitted having no knowledge of dingos (but who knew about canine teeth because one of them had been bitten by a corgi)? Why did we sacrifice the common-sense understanding of witnesses to the 'higher' knowledge of experts?

We should consider too how the much-reported scientific 'facts' took over from the under-reported testimony of people of Uluru, especially of the black trackers who said they had traced dingo tracks around the Chamberlain tent. The reported scientific 'discoveries' repressed the knowledge of the trackers — knowledge which did not fully emerge until the Morling inquiry, four years after the Chamberlain trial.

Not until 1986 was an aboriginal tracker, Barbara Tjikadu, finally allowed to give evidence that she had identified tracks of a dingo carrying a baby and the places where it put the child down on the sand. Her evidence was accepted at the 1986 inquiry by Mr Justice Morling who described her as an impressive witness, with the reputation of being an excellent tracker. For her part, Barbara Tjikadu (Mrs Winmatti) was unimpressed with the white judicial proceedings. Under cross-examination, she said, in reply to repeated questions designed to get her to concede that the dingo could [*sic*] been carrying a joey: "Mr Adams, you are talking in your way using your language and you are talking about lies." Asked the same question yet again, she replied: "Was a kangaroo living in the tent?"

To the extent that the media failed to report or misrepresented the testimony of Aboriginal trackers, their construction of the criminality of Lindy Chamberlain was profoundly racist.

More broadly the Chamberlain case exemplified the tyranny of expert knowledge; the tyranny which obliterated the knowledge of the ordinary people. The media's role was crucial in this process. By presenting so-called scientific opinion as fact, they supplied the evidentiary basis (for those who still needed it) for the witch story. Lindy Chamberlain became, thanks to the media, a scientifically-proven witch.

Accessories after the Fact

If the media criminalised Lindy Chamberlain in words and pictures, thereby precluding her chance of a fair trial, the Australian people aided and abetted the media in this process. They were, in fact, accessories after the fact(s) — the incriminating facts supplied to the media by the police, facts now known to be fanciful lies. We now know that it was the Northern Territory police who, disliking the woman "with the killer eyes" as much as they disliked being criticised at the first coroner's inquiry, supplied stories of satanism to the press. Again, it was the police who passed on gossip about Lindy dressing the baby in black; not caring for her; about a doctor saying she was strange and did not love the child; that Azaria meant "sacrifice in the wilderness" — stories which found their way into the national media before the police discovered they were false. Conversely, journalists puzzled by Lindy's behaviours, such as her calm attitude immediately after her baby's disappearance passed on their suspicions to the police.

These well-documented 'special' connections between journalists and the police constitute a material factor in the miscarriage of justice which was the Chamberlain trial. Consequently, the question of a police conspiracy to subvert the course of justice is one which needs to be addressed fully. Here, however, I am concerned with the media role and, in particular, with the unequal relationship which existed between the media and the public. It was the media which created the knowledge climate about Chamberlain. We judged her through media-mediated messages which incriminated her long before the jury reached its media-contaminated verdict.

She was a Seventh day [*sic*] Adventist and therefore an easy target for a sensationalist mainstream journalism. She was a Christian woman, and therefore someone to be ignored by the Left press. Indeed, the deafening silence of the Left press must be read/can only be read as collusion with the mass media. With very few exceptions, the Left press, including the feminist press, remained silent about the witch-hunt, allowing the Right to construct a consensus that Lindy Chamberlain was guilty. Not until after she was released in February 1986 did the Left press begin to take an interest in what they now began to construct as yet another instance of injustice under capitalism. Not until after her release did [the] Left begin to ask themselves some hard questions about why they had not taken much interest in this grave miscarriage of justice. Could the answer be ideological blindness to the persecution of a middle class Christian woman who was thereby triply disqualified from a part in any Marxist morality play? Whatever the reason, the Left press defaulted to the Right on the Chamberlain case and, in their silence, aided and abetted in the mass media's [annihilation] of the possibility of a fair trial.

However, there were some pockets of resistance to our media-drenched imagination. Within a week of her conviction, people demonstrated in Brisbane (of all places) calling for her release, a gesture which prompted one leading paper to editorialise that they were trying to substitute the rule of the mob for the rule of law, and to insist that the Chamberlains were convicted in a conspicuously fair trial after due process of law. There was other resistance. From the small print we learn of a woman watching Lindy crying in the witness box. Overhearing two male journalists discussing her stress, the woman berated them: "you brutes are all the same. Whatever she does you fellows will always get it wrong."

But for the most part, we allowed the media to push and [prod] us until what we saw began to resemble what we wanted to see — an unnatural and criminal woman.

Lindy Reclaimed

In February 1986 Lindy Chamberlain was released from prison, ostensibly (reportedly) because of the discovery of the matinee jacket which, all along, she had said Azaria had been wearing. The unofficial unreported reason for her release was fear the Northern Territory newspapers were about to report that the Northern Territory government had repressed evidence pertaining to the crown's scientific evidence against her.

At least while she was in prison, she was protected from the intense media gaze. Now she was to be once more thrust into the limelight. With the tide of public opinion turning in her favour, largely due to the groundswell of public support and the publication of John Bryson's Evil Angels, it was time for the media to start decriminalising her by reclaiming her as a normal, natural woman and deconstructing the witch image. It helped that she went on national television and cried throughout the interview (although some said she cried crocodile tears). It helped undo some of the damage done by the media. A March 1987 Women's Weekly interview also helped return her to the fold of normalcy. The now almost cleared Chamberlain family appeared on the front cover. It was a happy family image, just a typical suburban family. "Everyone," the article began, "had a firmly-held belief about Lindy Chamberlain yet so little was really known about this woman at the centre of so much turmoil." The fault lay with Lindy, who "hid her feelings behind a frozen mask," showing no emotion, "to many, an indication of her guilt." But now, at last, "Lindy has let down her guard." She now shows emotion and even cries appropriately. For the Women's Weekly it was "an about-face that goes far beyond the dramatic change in her appearance." But yet another change in her appearance could not escape comment in pictures which show the pregnant witch transformed into what the words say was "a stranger: tiny, bird-like, sharp-featured, with a modified punk brushed-back hair style, trim waist, shapely legs with fashionable black and gold sandals, and a beaming smile." As Lindy now conformed to the media's notion of femininity, we could forget "the dour, some say sour, and expressionless features of the woman seen going relentlessly to courts." For Lindy had transformed herself into a woman who looked feminine and attractive, "an astonishing transformation."

Now she is even allowed a voice. She is permitted to explain that her lawyers told her to stay expressionless (it wasn't the witch in her after all), but unfortunately, "my natural expression comes over as hard." This gave the media an out: she was, they said, "her own worst enemy."

Throughout the reclamation process, the media remained obsessed with Lindy's body. According to one report, she "looked trim and taut after her months in prison" (read three years and emaciated: she had lost five stone). Two female journalists, debriefing her when she arrived home, discovered, or rather, re-discovered that "she had a lot of sex appeal." She might be a woman who "feels that everybody was against her," and she had "this sense of terrible injustice," but it was now time to "admire the way she has reacted to it."

Still, it needed to be said, as a male journalist did, that Lindy was "leathery, wrinkled and in need of a decent hair cut."

This media scrutinising was to continue during the Morling Inquiry. We were told what was important: "She wore a high-necked red and black dress, a narrow black belt, beige stockings, and black, high-heeled, ankle-strapped shoes." Moreover: "Her dark hair was teased into a bouffant style, with a lock dropping over her right eye. Her face, a little hollow-cheeked, was quite heavily made up with a red lipstick, and mascara giving a deep-set look to her eyes." But ... "What are we to make of Mrs Chamberlain? Her lips are rather turned down" and her evidence sometimes came out "as bitter and aggrieved, in an unfortunately nasal whine." And her emotions seemed to fluctuate: sometimes she appeared to be on the verge of breakdown, at others "she was capable of an amused flash of teeth." To another journalist she seemed "sharp and composed, her dark eyes smoldering, showing moments of emotion but recovering quickly to flash fire from the witness box." Whatever their impression, it has become exciting again for journalists watching Lindy Chamberlain in her new role as slick sharpshooter, firing shots as [*sic*] what she called "stupid courtroom lawyers" and telling Prosecutor Barker that she doesn't like him, his law, his legal system, "which could set anyone up for everything."

Lindy Chamberlain was pardoned by the Northern Territory Government in June 1987 following the findings of the Morling Inquiry which had established the new 'truth' about her, namely, that she was a "normal, healthy caring mother" who loved her normal healthy baby girl right until the time she disappeared. The inquiry had also determined that if the evidence now available had been given at the trial, the trial judge would have been obliged to direct the jury to acquit the Chamberlains on the ground that the evidence could not justify their convictions. Lindy Chamberlain, however, was not interested in a pardon for something she didn't do. "There was steel in her voice as she said this." But the "main impression" she gave was one of "determination and self-mastery." Had she ever felt crushed by the battle? "You always feel crushed by it," she said. "But whether you are crushed or flattened are two different things." Had she ever been flattened? "No way," came the answer. And, finally, what about nightmares? "I don't have nightmares," she said. "I have day-mares. It is reality that hurts."

■

Evil Angels, a film based on John Bryson's book about the *Chamberlain* case, was released in North America as *A Cry in the Dark*.

Lindy Chamberlain and her former husband were awarded $1.3 million in compensation from the Northern Territories government, on the basis of the report of Justice Morling: Chips Mackinoly & Malcolm Brown, "NT Govt awards Chamberlains a payment of $1.3 million" *The Sydney Morning Herald* (26 May 1992) 4; Royal Commission of the Inquiry into the Chamberlain Conviction, *Report of the Commissioner, The Hon. Mr. Justice T.R. Morling* (1987); *Re Conviction of Chamberlain* (1988), 93 F.L.R. 239.

Howe has argued that the media and police characterization of Lindy Chamberlain as a hard, unemotional, unnatural woman constructed her as "guilty". Can you suggest attributes and responses that might have been characterized as "natural" for a woman and a mother? How do these stereotypes impact on women accused and victims, and how might they be challenged? For example, consider the characterization of women as "hysterical," which may lead to the result that a woman who is not hysterical is not believed to have been in danger. As Shelley Page describes, in "Sherri Lee Guy abandoned when her life was at risk" *The Ottawa Citizen* (5 May 1995) C1, police failed to respond to the calls made by a woman whose life was threatened by an abusive husband after she had fled the relationship:

> Sherri Lee Guy called police three times to say she feared for her life, but she was not taken seriously. Police are saying it's partly because she didn't dial 911, but called the main police line.
>
> Besides, police said she didn't sound scared on the phone.
>
> How was she supposed to have sounded, this 20-year-old woman who was being threatened after fleeing an abusive relationship?
>
> Hysterical? Is that the one pitch distressed women are allowed? Maybe that was resignation in her voice. Or exhaustion. Or worthlessness. Or lifelessness ...
>
> In the end, it wasn't any of Guy's calls that brought police to her mother's Gloucester home. It was a call from a neighbour who heard her crying for help. By the time police arrived, Guy was dead on a neighbour's doorstep. She apparently screamed and pounded on several doors. None [was] opened.

For a lawsuit challenging the police response to women (and within that, the construction of women as hysterical), see *Doe v. Metropolitan Toronto (Municipality) Commissioners of Police* (1998), 39 O.R. (3d) 487 (Gen. Div.), which appears in Abell & Sheehy, *Cases, Context, Critique*, **Policing**.

In another case in which the characterization of the accused depended heavily on stereotypes (the scapegoating of nurses), the *Nelles* case discussed above, the accused was also constructed as "guilty" by police because she refused to answer questions without a lawyer. Like the *Chamberlain* prosecution, the *Nelles* prosecution was built on truth claims of scientific "experts" as well as a particular construction and hierarchy of "experts" and "expertise".

What should be the role of counsel with respect to the media? A recent Supreme Court case held that lawyers who hold press conferences to publicize the nature of lawsuits may subject themselves and their client to a libel suit: *Hill v. Church of Scientology*, [1995] 2 S.C.R. 1130, aff'g 71 O.A.C. 161. In that case, the lawyer, Morris Manning, accompanied by Church of Scientology representatives, held a news conference on the courthouse steps to announce a criminal contempt suit they were filing against a Crown attorney. The Court held that public officials have the same right to protection of their reputation as any other individual and that "it is not requiring too much of individuals that they ascertain the truth of the allegations they publish." The decision has been widely criticized by journalists and civil libertarians for the chilling effect it will have on criticism of public officials and government; others have suggested that the Church of Scientology itself has used "libel chill" to silence criticism. For a discussion of the reaction and a comparison to British and American law, see: Sean Fine, "$1.6 million libel award upheld: Supreme court defends 'importance of reputation' in Scientology decision" *The [Toronto] Globe and Mail* (21 July 1995) A1; Editorial, "Chilling effect: A Supreme Court ruling makes it less likely there will be any loosening of the libel laws as they apply to public figures" *The Ottawa Citizen* (21 July 1995) A10. In *Church of Scientology*, the libel suit protects a public official from criticism. Consider which individuals and organizations have the resources and power to launch libel suits and, thus, who is protected by "libel chill".

Kimberley Noble, a prize-winning business reporter at *The [Toronto] Globe and Mail*, documents the ways the threat of legal action has dried up sources and suppressed stories, as well as a book that she was working on about powerful individuals and corporations such as the Bronfmans and Edper group. While big newspapers such as *The [Toronto] Globe and Mail* may have the resources to fight back, individual authors and small publishers rarely do. The vast majority of libel suits are settled out of court, and the work is simply not published. Thus, she argues in *Bound and Gagged: Libel Chill and the Right to Publish* (Toronto: HarperCollins, 1992) that the libel laws need to be reformed. According to Noble, there are two constants (at 41–42):

> The first is power. There are people who are wronged in the media and who deserve the right of redress, and every writer I know wants a libel law that will provide these people with some quick and inexpensive route to a public apology or their day in court. What we are afraid of, however, and what we deal with most often instead, are people accustomed to getting their own way and to controlling those around them, who cannot accept the idea that their own views are not reflected in the community at large. When this discrepancy, this irritating gap in perceptions, makes its way into print or onto the airwaves, they are then able to use the arm of the law — which, as British espionage writer Anthony Price points out in his books, so quickly turns into the fist of the state — to exert their authority over people who cannot otherwise be coerced. And we let them do this. We Canadians have to recognize that this manipulation of power is an aspect of our society that we have to deal with, before it gets any worse.
>
> [The second constant is the use of language — legalese, accounting-speak, and lobbyists' rhetoric — to hide the facts.]

Abell & Sheehy, *Cases, Context, Critique*, **Policing**, examine the role of police, examples of racism, the construction of police violence, and, in particular, the response to the beating of Rodney King. Here, Banu Helvacioglu examines the media coverage of and the police response to anti-racist protest in Toronto in May 1992, following the acquittal of the four white police officers charged with assaulting Rodney King.

Wild in the Streets?†

On Monday, May 4, 1992, after an anti-racism rally protesting the Rodney King verdict, the police shooting of a black youth the previous weekend in Toronto and institutional racism in Canada, a small group of urban youths crashed store windows in the Yonge-Yorkville area of downtown Toronto and threw stones at the police and reporters. The next day, local media described the event as rioting, looting and hooliganism and called the youths a mob. A few days later, the "Toronto riots" became international news.

Having been at the site of the action, and afterwards having listened to both local and international accounts of the "riots," I am astounded by the processes that rapidly build political conflicts and injustices into conjecture about violence, while remaining oblivious to the collective peaceful platforms of anti-racist rallies. We are indeed living in a global village, whose main feature is not so much the globalization of communication technologies as the universalization of the village mentality.

After watching the international CNN broadcast from London, my parents called from Turkey, wanting to know if anarchy and terrorism had also spread to Canada. To their minds, anarchy is the equivalent of rioting in so far as both refer to random violence and call for the reassertion of law and order. The same week, a friend in Amsterdam called, telling me that the Toronto "riots" struck a responsive chord in Holland. The Los Angeles riots of the previous week were less of a surprise to the Dutch because racism in the U.S. is well known internationally, and violence and destruction in American cities are perceived to be mundane facts of American life. But incidents in "Toronto the Good," the big cosmopolitan city in Canada's multicultural mosaic, troubled the residents of Amsterdam, who seem to have taken the surface image of tranquil ethnic diversity in Toronto as an ideal role model.

† Banu Helvacioglu, "Wild in the Streets?" *Canadian Forum* 71:811 (July/August 1992) 5–7. Reproduced by permission of James Lorimer & Co., Publishers.

Rumours of Riot

For the inaccurate description of the Toronto incidents in early May, the main sources of information were a handful of local reporters and numerous bystanders who were primarily concerned with their own fear of attack and their own consequent anger. Coupled with this personal perception of threat, the pervasive popular views about political and legal structures also contributed to the dissemination of national and international rumours about systematic racism and urban problems. Global technology only facilitated the speedy construction of an image of Toronto as a dangerous city.

To some people living in Toronto, the rampage in early May came as a shock because they too consider the surface appearance of tranquility as a sign of peaceful, conflict-free multicultural co-existence. During the whole week following the "riots," radio, TV and newspapers solicited the views of store owners, local reporters and bystanders caught in the middle of violence. Their comments are illuminating: "I did not expect such a thing to happen here"; "Violence is increasing in the city — why don't people sit down and talk?"; "Innocent people are affected — why did [the rally] turn ugly"; "People are extremely angry, public order is broken"; "It is a nightmare; we may as well go and live in Detroit."

The sub-text of these statements is: "I am angry because I am an innocent, hard-working, law-abiding citizen." The pervasive viewpoint sees injustice only when it touches the individual, and the solutions are sought in the political and legal systems without challenging power relations embedded in the supposedly neutral and objective public order. According to this view, what occurs is not institutional racism but isolated cases of individual prejudice and discrimination. The Rodney King verdict in Los Angeles outraged most Toronto residents, but when two Toronto police officers who shot a black youth, Wade Lawson, in 1988, were acquitted in late April 1992, it did not even become headline news in the local media, let alone a topic of public discussion.

In early May, the province decided not to appeal the acquittal of the police officers, and local politicians remained silent on the issue — hoping, no doubt, that the acquittal would soon be forgotten. In the meantime, the Toronto Police department lost no time in launching a public relations campaign that portrayed its riot squad as brawl busters and police officers as genial, patient family men who were eager for the rampage to calm down so they could go home in time for supper.

Black activists' ceaseless efforts in fighting racism in the city were dismissed all too easily by the media soliciting either successful entrepreneurs or hard-working blacks who individually agreed with the collective platform of the Black Action Defence Committee, and who are proud to be Canadian citizens. In the midst of this constructed scenario, the urban youths — consisting of homeless, high-school dropouts, and/or unemployed teenagers — who could not hire an advertising agency, were described as an irresponsible, opportunistic, criminal mob. Their anger and outrage, their fear of racism and poverty, are not viewed as legitimate concerns, because they are powerless in the ongoing power play between the media, the police, the justice system, local politicians, entrepreneurs and store owners.

I work near the area where the so-called "riots" occurred and I am fearful not of physical violence but of the darkness in people's perceptions. At work, two of my colleagues are treated as if they are identical twins. They are both tall, black and male. If in a centre of knowledge two black professors are mistaken as identical twins, then the task of changing perceptions of threat and violence on the streets becomes an urgent problem.

To this day I remain sceptical about the police action and the so-called violence on that Monday night. There were more police, riot squad members and law-abiding bystanders than so-called rioters, whose total number was at most 100, probably less. Most were teenagers who were neither very unruly nor very strong physically. Since there is enough speculation about their action, I do not want to contribute to the already existing white noise. Instead, let me report what I saw and heard.

A Street Report

Throughout the course of the two anti-racist rallies held that week (May 4 and May 7), there was a strong sense of solidarity among the participants. To experience such solidarity one has to be inside the group, not on the periphery, as are all reporters and spectators. At both rallies there were agitators who made pointed remarks in favour of white supremacy, and a few times the police wanted to contain the movement of the group by specifying where protestors should stand (not on the clearly delineated property of the U.S. embassy) and where banners should be displayed (not on the second floor of City Hall which has public access via a ramp).

It was solidarity within the group that chased off the white supremacists (who could have been beaten up severely), calmed the youth who were verbally assaulted by the skinheads and defended the right of the protestors to display their banner on City Hall. The rallies were organized by the Black Action Defence Committee in solidarity and in co-operation with a number of groups, including native people, women and immigrants. As such, it was an example of a political movements whose main unifying theme was opposition to a whole series of injustices.

The anti-racist rally on Monday, May 4, started in front of the U.S. consulate at 4 p.m., proceeded to the corner of Yonge and Bloor Streets, where speeches were heard until approximately 6 p.m., and ended — peacefully — shortly after 7 p.m. in front of City Hall. When about a thousand people sat on the pavement stopping traffic at the corner of Yonge and Bloor Streets, during the late afternoon rush hour, my own subjective interpretation was: "Free at last, free at last. O mighty political awareness of the organizers, we are free at last!" The peaceful sit-in represented freedom from the daily haste of the city and the routine of work, freedom to hear through megaphones about the systemic oppression and injustices in the vicinity of the shopping malls, exclusive stores, restaurants, banks and downtown law firms. It was freedom for only 30 to 45 minutes, but nobody paid a fee to experience this brief moment and there were no restrictions on entry.

Bystanders who did not share this interpretation of freedom expressed their frustration and anger at having their routine disrupted. The next day, the *Toronto Star* described this moment as the "first spark" leading to riots, looting and violence. The front page featured quotations from Toronto Mayor June Rowlands — "It's very concerning what is happening, very concerning" — and Metro Chair Alan Tonks: "A lot of people who organized the [consulate] demonstration must be wondering ... what fury they unleashed."

The message as always was to blame the victims, not those responsible for shooting blacks, not the all-white juries acquitting police officers who beat and kill blacks. Tonks, reporters and editors do not understand the fear felt by black youths on the streets, nor the power structure in downtown Toronto where, among other things, the most basic human needs to eat and to use the washrooms are not civic rights but privileges that only money can buy.

Tonks declined black organizers' invitation to participate in the second anti-racist rally the same week (on Thursday, May 7). The Metro Chair is a typical example of those who, when it comes to expressing solidarity, always find something to hide behind. On this occasion Tonks reminded the public that his "wife and children are partly of African descent." Why do those who are concerned about looting stores continue to loot people's history in search of a custom-made, "African" suit?

As for the concerned mayor, June Rowlands, peaceful, politically aware protestors were at her doorstep on Monday, but she refused to step outside even for five minutes to express her concern publicly.

Why blame the organizers when irresponsible city officials, who were attending a council meeting in City Hall at the time, did not even attempt to acknowledge the concerns of protestors outside?

The truth is that the rally did not turn into rioting and looting. Organizers both before and during the rally tried to communicate to local politicians and the Toronto police their legitimate concerns about racism and ongoing injustices in the court system. The fact that a number of youths decided to take things into their own hands has nothing to do with the rally, its organizers, or the hundreds who peacefully protested. Toronto is not becoming a violent city, and those who compare their city with Detroit or Los Angeles do not fully appreciate what life is like either here in Toronto or there in the U.S.

On Monday night, after hearing the first radio reports of the disruption in the Yonge-Yorkville area, I made my way past broken windows outside the Eaton Centre, up Yonge St., to the scene of the "riots." As I was trying to reason with a couple of teenagers not to break windows (not out of my respect for private property but to protect them from being arrested by the approaching police officers), a bystander started yelling at me, "Why are you protecting those rapists!" The police in the area did not chase the youth but told bystanders to go home. Their exact words were: "Ladies and gentlemen, please go home; you do not need this." Hearing comments such as "Bastards!", "Opportunists!," "Look, there goes another window, yeah!," "They're crazy!" made me realize that what some of the bystanders were seeing was yet another grand spectacle, like a brawl between hockey players.

If theft had been on their minds, the urban youths did not fare well that night. There were many broken store windows, and valuable merchandise was exposed, but I saw no sign of looting. If goods were stolen earlier in the evening, their total value could not have been more than an ordinary day's shoplifting. I did not have a video camera with me to tape the scene, so it is up to you to believe my street report or not.

My perception and cognition of reality is as biased as the local reporters who covered the events that week, but their cameras and high-tech communications tools have more credibility and persuasive power. During the second anti-racist rally, City TV news informed its audience that there were about 500 people present at the rally site — Queen's Park. Since the taping of the news was taking place right in front of me, I first double-checked with my friend who also witnessed this rumour-in-the-making, then I took advantage of my non-threatening appearance to challenge the reporter. From where he was standing, he could not see the other side of the park, where there were at least 500 more people, making the total at the rally well over a thousand. The reporter refused to acknowledge my polite observation, and instead shook his head and walked away.

Missing the Message

In Canada, as in every country, national pride is promoted through individual success stories at the expense of public awareness of ongoing injustices and collective efforts to resolve misperceptions and systematic problems. It is necessary but not sufficient to criticize the media for their bias. The events concerning the anti-racist rallies and the rampage in downtown Toronto have been taken out of their political context largely by the media, with help from the police department, local politicians and bystanders/spectators. The least one can do in such circumstances is to compare the rumoured accounts with those from different sources, for the main problem lies in how one perceives power relations in one's surrounding.

In the area where vandalism took place, especially to the east of the Eaton Centre, there are homeless people, most of whom suffer from the consequences of cut-backs in federal, provincial and municipal programs. In the aftermath of the street confrontations, the general focus is not on the increasing number of homeless and mentally disturbed patients living on the streets, but on the youths hanging out in the vicinity of the Eaton Centre. The shopping mall is an attraction for both Canadian and foreign tourists who are disturbed by small groups of unemployed youth but not by large crowds of busy shoppers.

Already some institutions and stores in downtown Toronto have started tightening their private security measures for fear of "criminal youth gangs." Perception of threat, like perception of violence is subjective; it depends on one's outlook. (I know some students who are constantly harassed by the police because of their appearance and colour.)

In the meantime, public law enforcement around the Eaton Centre remains invisible, perhaps because the police, city officials and store owners do not want to spoil tourists' shopping appetites by mobilizing the riot squad daily. But it is necessary to make invisible forms of oppression visible, because what we do not see and hear continue to determine the political agenda.

A final memory illustrates this point. On Tuesday night (May 5), I was outraged to see three or four plainclothes policemen holding one teenaged boy down on his knees on Yonge Street, a couple of blocks north of the Eaton Centre. The camera crew of a local TV station was trying to get a close-up shot of the boy, who could not hide his face because his hands were tied behind his back. Nevertheless, the teenager managed to assert his power momentarily by yelling at police, "You did not read my rights, man!" It is possible that the teenager learned this lesson in democracy from watching American cop shows on TV, but I doubt that this short clip about individual rights ever made the CNN *Headline News*.

The main message of the anti-racist rallies in early May was to promote mutual understanding and solidarity against systematic problems of racism, poverty, prejudice as well as fatal police actions. To discourage this message does not make it disappear. The solidarity continues to exist.

■

For a compelling critique of the media's portrayal of the protest as a riot (using such words as "looting," "smashing," and "mayhem") and their minimization of the foundations of racial unrest, see Dionne Brand, *Bread Out of Stone* (Toronto: Coach House Press, 1994) at 154–56. Metro Toronto Police sought search warrants for the CBC, *The Globe and Mail*, and CTV with respect to video tape and photographs of that "riot" in May 1992. Counsel for the media argued unsuccessfully that the police had not established that any of the unpublished film or photographs would contain evidence that would further police investigations, and that, therefore, the warrant should not be issued. See *R. v. Canadian Broadcasting Corp.* (1992), 17 C.R. (4th) 198 (Ont. Ct. (Gen. Div.)); *Société Radio-Canada v. Québec (Procurer Général)* (1992), 52 Q.A.C. 183. For a critique of two earlier Supreme Court decisions refusing to enlarge s. 8 rights of the media to block police seizure of video footage of the vandalizing of a post office (*Canadian Broadcasting Corp. v. Lessard*, [1991] 3 S.C.R. 421) and the setting fire to a guardhouse during the course of a labour dispute (*Canadian Broadcasting Corp. v. New Brunswick (A.G.)*, [1991] 3 S.C.R. 459), see: Christie McNeil, "Search and Seizure of the Press" (1996) 34 Osgoode Hall L.J. 175.

For another example of the slant in decisions about what is "newsworthy," consider the reporting of Aboriginal issues. See, for example, Boyce Richardson, "The media's hypocrisy and Oka" *The Ottawa Citizen* (1 September 1990) B7 and Lee Maracle, "Peace" *The [Ottawa] Womanist* (Fall 1990) 9, both reproduced in Abell & Sheehy, *Cases, Context, Critique*, **Law and Order**.

II

Defending a Case

7

Case Study on Assault: An Introduction to Defences

This chapter uses the crime of assault to introduce and explore defences to crimes. Defences may be established by common law or by the *Criminal Code*. They come into play only if the prosecution can prove the *actus reus* and *mens rea* elements of the crime beyond a reasonable doubt. For most defences, the accused will need to demonstrate an evidential basis for the defence — an "air of reality" — and need only raise a reasonable doubt as to the defence. Effectively, this means that the prosecution will have to disprove a defence such as self-defence if it is fairly put at issue on the evidence. For some specific defences such as mental disorder and automatism, the accused bears a heavier onus, proof on a balance of probabilities, as discussed earlier in **Burdens of Proof**.

The offence of assault can be prosecuted as a common assault (s. 265 of the *Code*), assault with a weapon or causing bodily harm (s. 266) or aggravated assault, where the accused causes maiming, disfigures, or endangers the life of the victim (s. 267). Sexual assault relies upon the same basic definition of assault, but requires proof that the assault was "sexual". In addition, many provisions of the *Code* are devoted to specific rules that govern the prosecution and defence of this form of assault: see **Mistake of Fact**, below. Assault is also a foundational crime for homicide offences, such as manslaughter by unlawful act.

A. CONSENT

Non-consent may be defined as an element of an offence, such as assault, or it may be read in as a common law element of a crime as was done in *R. v. Lemieux*, [1967] S.C.R. 492, with respect to the crime of break and enter. Alternatively, consent can be framed as a defence to a crime, as held by the Court in *Jobidon*, reproduced below. The *Code* also contains a number of provisions that bear on consent. For example, see ss. 114, 150.1, 265(3), 286, and 273.1(2).

Jobidon is a significant case for its role in defining the scope of the crime of assault and the boundaries of "consent".

R. v. Jobidon†

[GONTHIER J. (*per* La Forest, L'Heureux-Dubé, Gonthier, Cory, and Iacobucci JJ.):]

At issue in the present appeal is the role of consent in the criminal offence of assault. More particularly, the issue is whether the absence of consent is an essential element of this offence when it relates to a fist fight where bodily harm is intentionally caused.

I. STATEMENT OF FACTS

The appellant, Jules Jobidon, was charged with manslaughter for the unlawful act of killing Rodney Haggart — through the offence of assault (alternatively, through an act of criminal negligence). The incident leading to the charge was a fist fight between the two men, in a parking lot outside a hotel near Sudbury, Ontario, on September 19, 1986. At the date of the killing, Rodney Haggart was 25 years old. He had consumed some beer. His blood alcohol level, measured a few hours after the incident, was 160 milligrams of alcohol per 100 millilitres of blood, but the trial judge found that Haggart appeared "perfectly fine" and "perfectly normal". Jobidon, a young, fit and powerful man, had also been drinking beer prior to the fight, but in the opinion of the trial judge was not inebriated.

The two men initiated their aggression in the bar of the hotel. With his brother and a few friends, Haggart was celebrating his impending marriage. He approached Jobidon, who was also in the hotel with friends, and started a fight with him. Haggart was larger than the appellant, and had previous training as a boxer. In this first encounter, Haggart was prevailing when the owner of the hotel separated the combatants and told Jobidon and his brother to leave the hotel. Jobidon and Haggart exchanged angry words in the lobby, and the trial judge found that the two men agreed the fight was not over.

Jobidon and his brother waited outside in the parking lot. When the Haggart party exited the hotel their respective older brothers began fighting at the far end of the lot. Jobidon and Haggart argued. A crowd of people, many of whom had come outside to see the fight, gathered around them.

While Haggart and Jobidon stood facing each other, Jobidon struck Haggart with his fist, hitting him with great force on the head and face. Haggart was knocked backward onto the hood of a car. The trial judge determined that Haggart was rendered unconscious by this initial punch and that he appeared to be "out cold". He was not moving and offered no resistance to the appellant.

Immediately after throwing that first punch, Jobidon continued forward. In a brief flurry lasting no more than a few seconds he struck the unconscious victim a further four to six times on the head. The trial judge found that there was no interval between Haggart's fall and the continued punching. The punches were part of "one single continuing transaction ... one fluid event, punctuated by specific blows". The judge noted that the most reliable witness testified that it all happened so quickly he thought Haggart would bounce off the hood and resume the fight.

Instead, Haggart rolled off the hood and lay limp. He was taken to the hospital in a coma, where he died of severe contusions to the head. Medical evidence showed that he had sustained extensive bruising and abrasions to the head and neck. It was determined that the cause of death was one or more of the punches he had received at the hand of the appellant in the parking lot.

The trial judge found that Jobidon did not intend to kill Haggart, nor did he intend to cause the deceased serious bodily harm. However, the possibility of injury more serious than a bruise or bloody nose, such as a broken nose, was contemplated. Jobidon intentionally hit Haggart as hard as he could, but believed he was fighting fair. He did not depart intentionally from the kind of fight that Haggart had consented to. Jobidon believed that Haggart had consented to a fair fight, the object of which was to hit the other man as hard as physically possible until that person gave up or retreated. The trial judge also found that, although mistaken, and not supported by objective facts, Jobidon honestly believed that after Haggart had been struck onto the hood of the car he was merely stunned, but still capable of fighting back, and still trying to fight.

Jobidon was tried before a judge of the Supreme Court of Ontario, and was found not guilty of manslaughter: (1987), 36 C.C.C. (3d) 340. The judge held that Haggart's consent negated assault,

† [1991] 2 S.C.R. 714.

and held further that Jobidon had not been criminally negligent. The respondent appealed the judge's holding of assault to the Ontario Court of Appeal, which allowed the appeal, set aside the acquittal, and substituted a guilty verdict on the charge of manslaughter: (1988), 45 C.C.C. (3d) 176.

. . . .

Issues on Appeal

There is one principal issue raised in this appeal; and one ancillary issue. The principal issue is whether absence of consent is a material element which must be proved by the Crown in all cases of assault or whether there are common law limitations which restrict or negate the legal effectiveness of consent in certain types of cases. A secondary issue is whether Jobidon could be convicted of manslaughter on a basis other than that of an unlawful act of assault.

. . . .

II. ANALYSIS

[The Court reviewed the evolution of the offence of assault.]

It can be seen from this brief overview that the absence of consent to intentionally applied force was a material component of the offence of assault throughout its existence in Canada. But it is also evident that consent would not be legally effective in all circumstances. For instance, it would be vitiated by fraud. Various limitations on the validity of consent have a long lineage in the history of the offence. To observe those limitations one must advert to the common law. Yet before turning to that jurisprudence it is important to note the link between the offence of assault and the offence of manslaughter, since Jobidon was convicted of the latter offence.

The connection between the two offences of assault and manslaughter is found in s. 222 (formerly s. 205) of the *Code*. That section provides a definition of manslaughter which is contingent on an unlawful act causing death.... The offence of assault is a foundation offence upon which other offences against the person are constructed. Of course assault is also unlawful. It therefore follows from s. 222 that when an assault is committed and causes the death of a person, the assailant is thereby criminally liable for manslaughter. It also follows that if consent acts as a defence to assault, it will indirectly act as a defence to a charge of manslaughter based on assault.

. . . .

We have observed from the general analysis of the *Code* and common law that, in the history of our criminal law, codification did not replace common law principles of criminal responsibility, but in fact reflected them. That history also reveals that policy-based limitations of the sort at issue here boast a lineage in the common law equally as long as the factors which vitiate involuntary consent. Since these policy-based limitations also existed before the codification of Canada's criminal law there is no reason to think they have been ousted by statutory revisions and amendments made to the *Code* along the way.

On this understanding, even if it could be concluded, contrary to my own view of the law, that s. 265(3) negated the applicability of common law rules which describe when consent to assault will be vitiated for *involuntariness*, or defects in the will underlying the apparent consent, it would not follow that those amendments erased limitations based on public policy. If Parliament had so intended, it would have stated that intention. As it is, the *Code* as amended in 1983 is entirely silent in this regard.

This view accords with the interpretation of the Law Reform Commission of Canada. In its working paper on assault it notes that, regardless of the wording of s. 265(3), not all consents will be accepted as being legally effective. Irrespective of a finding of real or implied consent, in some cases (resembling the situation in the instant appeal) "the victim's consent or non-consent is quite irrelevant." (It cites as one example at p. 6 the situation where the application of force is intended to cause death or serious bodily harm, and another when a blow is struck in the course of an illegal fight.) That irrelevance is the result of policy considerations which in some circumstances nullify the legal effectiveness of consent.

Furthermore, since s. 8(3) of the *Code* expressly confirms the common law's continued authority and provides that exculpatory defences not expressly struck down by the *Code* continue to operate to exclude criminal liability, in this appeal, where the *Code* has not erased the common law limit in fist fights, it must continue to define the scope of legally effective consent. Some may object that s. 8(3) cannot be used to support this interpretation because consent is not really a defence, but instead forms part of the offence; indeed it is the absence of consent that is relevant as an element of the offence of assault. For example, Mewett and Manning, *op. cit.*, at p. 567, write that "Real consent is therefore an essential element of assault going to the *actus reus* in the sense that if consent is present no offence can have been committed". Yet while that objection may have some relevance from a strictly formalistic perspective, it is of little consequence from a substantive point of view. Moreover it conflicts with the spirit of this Court's previously expressed understanding of s. 8(3).

Whether consent is formally categorized as part of the *actus reus* of the offence, or as a defence, its essential function remains unaltered — if consent is proved, or if absence of consent is not proved, an individual accused of assault will *generally* be able to rely on the consent of the complainant to bar a conviction. He will be able to lean on the consent as a defence to liability. This basic reality has been widely recognized. English and Canadian courts widely refer to consent as being in the nature of a defence. Leading treatises on criminal law conceive it this way. See ... G. Williams, *Textbook of Criminal Law* (2nd ed. 1983), at pp. 549 and 576–78; and Law Reform Commission of Canada, Working Paper 38, *Assault*, op. cit., at p. 24. We have also observed, in the general interpretative section above, that the law confers on s. 8(3) an open and developmental view of the common law's role. Section 8(3) strongly suggests preservation of the common law approach to consent in assault.

Assault has been given a very encompassing definition in s. 265. It arises whenever a person intentionally applies force to a person "directly or indirectly", without the other's consent. The definition says nothing about the degree of harm which must be sustained. Nor does it refer to the motives for the touching. If taken at face value, this formulation would mean that the most trivial intended touching would constitute assault. As just one of many possible examples, a father would assault his daughter if he attempted to place a scarf around her neck to protect her from the cold but she did not consent to that touching, thinking the scarf ugly or undesirable. (Even an argument for implied consent would not seem to apply in a case like this.) That absurd consequence could not have been intended by Parliament. Rather its intention must have been for the courts to explain the content of the offence, incrementally and over the course of time.

Furthermore, whereas the factors specified in s. 265(3) are readily identifiable, and are generally applicable to all sorts of situations, that is inherently not true of limitations based on policy considerations, which are fact-specific by nature. It would have been quite impractical, if not impossible, for Parliament to establish an adequate list of exceptions to apply to all situations, old and new. Policy-based limits are almost always the product of a balancing of individual autonomy (the freedom to choose to have force intentionally applied to oneself) and some larger societal interest. That balancing may be better performed in the light of actual situations, rather than in the abstract, as Parliament would be compelled to do.

With the offence of assault, that kind of balancing is a function the courts are well-suited to perform. They will continue to be faced with real situations in which complicated actions and motivations interact, as they have in the past. I do not accept the argument that by failing to enact a list of *objects* or *forms of conduct* to which one could not validly consent, Parliament intended to eliminate their role in the offence of assault and to rely only on the four factors specified in s. 265(3). Such a major departure from well-established policy calls for more than mere silence, particularly as such a list would have been unduly difficult and impractical to prescribe, and was unnecessary given their existing entrenchment in the common law. The common law is the register of the balancing function of the courts — a register Parliament has authorized the courts to administer in respect of policy-based limits on the role and scope of consent in s. 265 of the *Code*.

. . . .

[The Court reviewed decisions from English and Canadian law.]

(i) The English Position

. . . .

Attorney General's Reference (No. 6 of 1980), [1981] 2 All E.R. 1057 makes it clear that a conviction of assault will not be barred if "bodily harm is intended and/or caused". Since this test is framed in the alternative, consent could be nullified even in situations where the assailant did not intend to cause the injured person bodily harm but did so inadvertently. In Canada, however, this very broad formulation cannot strictly apply, since the definition of assault in s. 265 is explicitly restricted to intentional application of force. Any test in our law which incorporated the English perspective would of necessity have to confine itself to bodily harm intended and caused.

(ii) The Canadian Position ...

The preceding analysis reveals division in the Canadian jurisprudence. Decisions by courts of appeal in Manitoba, Ontario, Nova Scotia and (lately) Saskatchewan would nullify consent to intentionally inflicted bodily harm arising from a fist fight. [Authorities omitted.]

On the other side are decisions of appellate courts in New Brunswick, Quebec, Saskatchewan and Alberta. [authorities omitted]

Although there is certainly no crystal-clear position in the modern Canadian common law, still, when one takes into account the combined English and Canadian jurisprudence, when one keeps sight of the common law's centuries-old persistence to limit the legal effectiveness of consent to a fist fight, and when one understands that s. 265 has always incorporated that persistence, the scale tips rather heavily against the validity of a person's consent to the infliction of bodily injury in a fight.

The thrust of the English common law is particularly important in this regard because it has been consistent for many decades, indeed, centuries. It became an integral component of the Canadian common law and has remained so to this day. Many of the seemingly pivotal pro-consent decisions made by courts in the 1970s were either *obiter* or were pronounced upon insufficient consideration of the important role of the traditional common law. Moreover they were decided prior to the decision in *Attorney General's Reference*, which offered a very authoritative pronouncement of the common law position. The significance of that decision is perhaps best indicated in the instant appeal, for it provided the basis used by the Ontario Court of Appeal to overrule its decision in *R. v. Dix*. The *Attorney General's Reference* case was again observed to be pivotal in the recent decision of the Appeal Court in Saskatchewan, in *R. v. Cey*. In light of these many considerations, I am of the view that the Canadian position is not as opaque or bifurcated as one might initially think.

Notwithstanding this conclusion, given the residual indeterminacy which admittedly lingers in the recent Canadian cases, it is useful to canvass policy considerations which exert a strong influence in this appeal, for they rather decisively support the respondent, bringing down the scales even more surely in support of the decision in the court below.

Policy Considerations

Foremost among the policy considerations supporting the Crown is the social uselessness of fist fights. As the English Court of Appeal noted in the *Attorney General's Reference*, it is not in the public interest that adults should willingly cause harm to one another without a good reason. There is precious little utility in fist fights or street brawls. These events are motivated by unchecked passion. They so often result in serious injury to the participants. Here it resulted in a tragic death to a young man on his wedding day.

There was a time when pugilism was sheltered by the notion of "chivalry". Duelling was an activity not only condoned, but required by honour. Those days are fortunately long past. Our social norms no longer correlate strength of character with prowess at fisticuffs. Indeed when we pride ourselves for making positive ethical and social strides, it tends to be on the basis of our developing reason. This is particularly true of the law, where reason is cast in a privileged light. Erasing longstanding limits on consent to assault would be a regressive step, one which would retard the advance of civilised norms of conduct.

Quite apart from the valueless nature of fist fights from the combatants' perspective, it should also be recognized that consensual fights may sometimes lead to larger brawls and to serious breaches of the public peace. In the instant case, this tendency was openly observable. At the prospect of a fight between Jobidon and the deceased, in a truly macabre fashion many patrons of the hotel deliberately moved to the parking lot to witness the gruesome event. That scene easily could have erupted in more widespread aggression between allies of the respective combatants. Indeed it happened that the brothers of Jobidon and Haggart also took to each other with their fists.

Given the spontaneous, often drunken nature of many fist fights, I would not wish to push a deterrence rationale too far. Nonetheless, it seems reasonable to think that, in some cases, common law limitations on consent might serve some degree of deterrence to these sorts of activities.

Related to a deterrence rationale is the possibility that, by permitting a person to consent to force inflicted by the hand of another, in rare cases the latter may find he derives some form of pleasure from the activity, especially if he is doing so on a regular basis. It is perhaps not inconceivable that this kind of perversion could arise in a domestic or marital setting where one or more of the family members are of frail or unstable mental health. As one criminal law theorist has written:

> ...the self-destructive individual who induces another person to kill or to mutilate him implicates the latter in the violation of a significant social taboo. The person carrying out the killing or the mutilation crosses the threshold into a realm of conduct that, the second time, might be more easily carried out. And the second time, it might not be particularly significant whether the

> victim consents or not. Similarly, if someone is encouraged to inflict a sado-masochistic beating on a consenting victim, the experience of inflicting the beating might loosen the actor's inhibitions against sadism in general. (G. Fletcher, *Rethinking Criminal Law* (1978), at pp. 770–71.)

Of course this appeal does not concern sadism or intentional killing. But it comes close to mutilation. In any event, the weight of the argument could hold true for fights. If aggressive individuals are legally permitted to get into consensual fist fights, and they take advantage of that license from time to time, it may come to pass that they eventually lose all understanding that that activity *is* the subject of a powerful social taboo. They may too readily find their fists raised against a person whose consent they forgot to ascertain with full certitude. It is preferable that these sorts of omissions be strongly discouraged.

Wholly apart from deterrence, it is most unseemly from a moral point of view that the law would countenance, much less provide a backhanded sanction to the sort of interaction displayed by the facts of this appeal. The sanctity of the human body should militate against the validity of consent to bodily harm inflicted in a fight.

Some would say the offence of assault should not be concerned with these considerations. They might argue that in respect of street fights, deterrence and express disapprobation of the law is already contained in other provisions of the *Criminal Code*. For instance, Parliament has seen fit to prohibit "prize-fighting", on penalty of criminal sanction, in s. 83.

. . . .

The policy preference that people not be able to consent to intentionally inflicted harms is heard not only in the register of our common law. The *Criminal Code* also contains many examples of this propensity. As noted above, s. 14 of the *Code* vitiates the legal effectiveness of a person's consent to have death inflicted on him under any circumstances. The same policy appears to underlie ss. 150.1, 159 and 286 in respect of younger people, in the contexts of sexual offences, anal intercourse, and abduction, respectively. All this is to say that the notion of policy-based limits on the effectiveness of consent to some level of inflicted harms is not foreign. Parliament as well as the courts have been mindful of the need for such limits. Autonomy is not the only value which our law seeks to protect.

Some may see limiting the freedom of an adult to consent to applications of force in a fist fight as unduly paternalistic; a violation of individual self-rule. Yet while that view may commend itself to some, those persons cannot reasonably claim that the law does not know such limitations. All criminal law is "paternalistic" to some degree — top-down guidance is inherent in any prohibitive rule. That the common law has developed a strong resistance to recognizing the validity of consent to intentional applications of force in fist fights and brawls is merely one instance of the criminal law's concern that Canadian citizens treat each other humanely and with respect.

Finally, it must not be thought that by giving the green light to the common law, and a red light to consent to fights, this Court is thereby negating the role of consent in all situations or activities in which people willingly expose themselves to intentionally applied force. No such sweeping conclusion is entailed. The determination being made is much narrower in scope.

Conclusion

How, and to what extent is consent limited?

The law's willingness to vitiate consent on policy grounds is significantly limited. Common law cases restrict the extent to which consent may be nullified; as do the relevant policy considerations. The unique situation under examination in this case, a weaponless fist fight between two adults, provides another important boundary.

The limitation demanded by s. 265 as it applies to the circumstances of this appeal is one which *vitiates consent between adults intentionally to apply force causing serious hurt or non-trivial bodily harm to each other in the course of a fist fight or brawl.* (This test entails that a minor's apparent consent to an adult's intentional application of force in a fight would also be negated.) This is the extent of the limit which the common law requires in the factual circumstances of this appeal. It may be that further limitations will be found to apply in other circumstances. But such limits, if any, are better developed on a case by case basis, so that the unique features of the situation may exert a rational influence on the extent of the limit and on the justification for it.

Stated in this way, the policy of the common law will not affect the validity or effectiveness of freely given consent to participate in rough sporting activities, so long as the intentional applications of force to which one consents are within the customary norms and rules of the game. Unlike fist fights, sporting activities and games usually have a significant social value; they are worthwhile. In this regard

the holding of the Saskatchewan Court of Appeal in *R. v. Cey* is apposite.

The court's majority determined that some forms of intentionally applied force will clearly fall within the scope of the rules of the game, and will therefore readily ground a finding of implied consent, to which effect should be given. On the other hand, very violent forms of force which clearly extend beyond the ordinary norms of conduct will not be recognized as legitimate conduct to which one can validly consent.

There is also nothing in the preceding formulation which would prevent a person from consenting to medical treatment or appropriate surgical interventions. Nor, for example, would it necessarily nullify consent between stuntmen who agree in advance to perform risky sparring or daredevil activities in the creation of a socially valuable cultural product. A charge of assault would be barred if the Crown failed to prove absence of consent in these situations, in so far as the activities have a positive social value and the intent of the actors is to produce a social benefit for the good of the people involved, and often for a wider group of people as well. This is a far cry from the situation presented in this appeal, where Jobidon's sole objective was to strike the deceased as hard as he physically could, until his opponent either gave up or retreated. Fist fights are worlds apart from these other forms of conduct.

Finally, the preceding formulation avoids nullification of consent to intentional applications of force which cause only minor hurt or trivial bodily harm. The bodily harm contemplated by the test is essentially equivalent to that contemplated by the definition found in s. 267(2) of the *Code*, dealing with the offence of assault causing bodily harm. The section defines bodily harm as "any hurt or injury to the complainant that interferes with the health or comfort of the complainant and that is more than merely transient or trifling in nature".

On this definition, combined with the fact that the test is restricted to cases involving adults, the phenomenon of the "ordinary" schoolyard scuffle, where boys or girls immaturely seek to resolve differences with their hands, will not come within the scope of the limitation. That has never been the policy of the law and I do not intend to disrupt the status quo. However, I would leave open the question as to whether boys or girls under the age of 18 who truly intend to harm one another, and ultimately cause more than trivial bodily harm, would be afforded the protection of a defence of consent. (As was the accused in *R. v. Barron* (1985), 23 C.C.C. (3d) 544 (Ont. C.A.), in which a boy was charged with manslaughter, via assault, for pushing another boy down a flight of stairs thereby causing the boy's death. The trial judge held that the deceased boy had impliedly consented to rough-housing on the stairs as they descended.) The appropriate result will undoubtedly depend on the peculiar circumstances of each case.

. . . .

III. DISPOSITION

I would uphold the decision of the Court of Appeal. The appeal is dismissed.

[SOPINKA J. (*per* Sopinka and Stevenson JJ.):]

I have had the advantage of reading the reasons of Gonthier J. and while I agree with his disposition of the matter I am unable to agree with his reasons. This appeal involves the role that consent plays in the offence of criminal assault. Unlike my colleague I am of the view that consent cannot be read out of the offence. I come to this conclusion for two reasons: (1) consent is a fundamental element of many criminal offences, including assault, and (2) the statutory provision creating the offence of assault explicitly provides for the element of consent.

. . . .

In my view Parliament has chosen to extend this principle [requiring proof of non-consent] to all assaults save murder in the interests of making this aspect of the criminal law certain. I see no evidence in the clear and simple language of s. 265 that it intended to outlaw consensual fighting in the interests of avoiding breaches of the peace or to allow it if a judge thought that it occurred in circumstances that were socially useful. Rather, the policy reflected in s. 265 is to make the absence of consent a requirement in the definition of the offence but to restrict consent to those intentional applications of force in respect of which there is a clear and effective consent by a victim who is free of coercion or misrepresentation. Instead of reading the words "without the consent of another person" out of s. 265 I am of the opinion that the intention of Parliament is respected by close scrutiny of the scope of consent to an assault. Instead of attempting to evaluate the utility of the activity the trial judge will scrutinize the consent to determine whether it applied to the very activity which is the subject of the charge. The more serious the assault the more difficult it should be to establish consent.

. . . .

My colleague Gonthier J. concludes that on the basis of cases which applied the common law, that section should be interpreted as excluding the absence of consent as an element of the *actus reus* in respect of an assault with intent to commit intentional bodily harm. ... The issue was not finally resolved in England until the decision of the English Court of Appeal on a reference to it by the Attorney General in 1980. See *Attorney General's Reference*. Unconstrained by the expression of legislative policy, the court moulded the common law to accord with the court's view of what was in the public interest. On this basis the court discarded the absence of consent as an element in assaults in which actual bodily harm was either caused or intended. Exceptions were created for assaults that have some positive social value such as sporting events. In Canada, the criminal law has been codified and the judiciary is constrained by the wording of sections defining criminal offences. The courts' application of public policy is governed by the expression of public policy in the *Criminal Code*. If Parliament intended to adopt the public policy which the English Court of Appeal developed it used singularly inappropriate language. It made the absence of consent a specific requirement and provided that this applied to all assaults without exception. The conflict in the Canadian cases which my colleague's review discloses is largely due to the application of these two disparate strains of public policy.

In my opinion the above observations as to the appropriate use of public policy are sufficient to conclude that the absence of consent cannot be swept away by a robust application of judge-made policy. This proposition is strengthened and confirmed by the specific dictates of the *Code* with reference to the essential elements of a criminal offence. Section 9(a) of the *Code* provides that "[n]otwithstanding anything in this Act or any other Act, no person shall be convicted ... (a) of an offence at common law". The effect of my colleague's approach is to create an offence where one does not exist under the terms of the *Code* by application of the common law. The offence created is the intentional application of force with the consent of the victim. I appreciate that my colleague's approach is to interpret the section in light of the common law but, in my view, use of the common law to eliminate an element of the offence that is required by statute is more than interpretation and is contrary to not only the spirit but also the letter of s. 9(a). One of the basic reasons for s. 9(a) is the importance of certainty in determining what conduct constitutes a criminal offence. That is the reason we have codified the offences in the *Criminal Code*. An accused should not have to search the books to discover the common law in order to determine if the offence charged is indeed an offence at law. Where does one search to determine the social utility of a fight during a hockey game to take one example? There are those that would argue that it is an important part of the attraction. Judges may not agree. Is this a matter for judicial notice or does it require evidence? The problem of uncertainty which the social utility test creates is greater than searching out the common law, a problem which [led] to the prohibition in s. 9(a).

. . . .

Given the danger inherent in the violent activity in this case, the scope of the consent required careful scrutiny. The trial judge found that the consent given by Haggart did not extend to a continuation of the fight once he had lost consciousness. By striking Haggart once he was unconscious, the accused acted beyond the scope of the consent of Haggart and thus committed the *actus reus* of assault.

. . . .

In his reasons the trial judge found that the accused struck Haggart four to six times after Haggart was unconscious (p. 348). The trial judge, therefore, did not accept the testimony of the accused that he struck Haggart only twice and one is left with the admission of the accused that he realized Haggart was unconscious after the second punch. By continuing to pummel Haggart after the accused realized Haggart was unconscious, the accused acted, to his knowledge, beyond the ambit of Haggart's consent thereby committing an assault. ■

Although the majority decision purported to draw the line for consent at intentionally caused bodily harm, has it in fact succeeded in doing so? Why or why not? Which judgment do you find more persuasive? How will *Jobidon* apply to young people who fight? Compare *R. v. W.(G.)* (1994), 18 O.R. (3d) 321 (C.A.) (accused convicted) with *R. v. M.(S.)* (1995), 22 O.R. (3d) 605 (C.A.) (accused acquitted), where the severity of the bodily harm and the intention to cause bodily harm were the distinguishing facts relied upon by the court.

Now consider the defence of consent in the context of sexual assault. In *R. v. Welsch* (1995), 25 O.R. (3d) 665, the Ontario Court of Appeal applied *Jobidon* to hold that consent cannot be used to defend against charges of sexual assault causing bodily harm. After reading the chapter on **Mistake of Fact**, below, speculate as to whether a defence of mistake is available for charges of sexual assault causing bodily harm. Does its availability depend upon the interpretation given to the majority's *ratio decidendi* in *Jobidon*? The *Cuerrier* decision, reproduced below, also narrows the defence of consent.

R. v. Cuerrier†

[CORY J.:]

Is a complainant's consent to engage in unprotected sexual intercourse vitiated by fraud when her partner knows he is HIV-positive and either fails to disclose or deliberately deceives her about it? If the consent is fraudulently obtained in those circumstances can s. 268 (aggravated assault) of the *Criminal Code*, R.S.C., 1985, c. C-46, be applicable? Would the application of the *Criminal Code* endanger public health policies pertaining to the disease of AIDS? Those are the issues that must be considered on this appeal.

I. FACTUAL BACKGROUND

The respondent tested positive for HIV in August 1992. At that time a public health nurse explicitly instructed him to use condoms every time he engaged in sexual intercourse and to inform all prospective sexual partners that he was HIV-positive. The respondent angrily rejected this advice. He complained that he would never be able to have a sex life if he told anyone that he was HIV-positive.

Three weeks later, the respondent met the complainant KM and an 18-month relationship began. The couple had sexual intercourse, for the most part unprotected, at least 100 times. Near the beginning of the relationship, KM discussed sexually transmitted diseases with the respondent and although she did not specifically ask him about HIV or AIDS, he assured her that he had tested negative for HIV eight or nine months earlier. KM developed hepatitis and was advised to have an HIV test. Both she and the respondent were tested in January 1993. In February, a nurse informed KM that her test was negative but that the respondent had tested HIV-positive. KM was advised to undertake subsequent tests to determine whether she had developed the virus.

Once again, the respondent was told that he must use condoms and inform his sexual partners that he was HIV-positive. The respondent replied that in order to avoid using condoms he would wait and see if KM tested positive in a few months and, if not, he would leave her and start a relationship with an HIV-positive woman.

For several months KM continued to have unprotected sex with the respondent. This she did because she loved him and she did not want to put another woman at risk. Their relationship ended in May 1994. KM testified that if she had known that the respondent was HIV-positive she would never have engaged in unprotected sexual intercourse with him.

Upon hearing that the relationship between KM and the respondent had ended, a public health nurse delivered letters to the respondent ordering him to inform his future partners that he was HIV-positive and to use condoms. Shortly thereafter, the respondent formed a sexual relationship with BH. They had sex 10 times, on most occasions without a condom. Although BH told the respondent that she was afraid of diseases he did not inform her that he was HIV-positive. In late June BH discovered that the respondent had HIV. She confronted him and he apologized for lying. BH testified that if she had known the respondent had HIV she would never have engaged in unprotected sexual intercourse with him.

The respondent was charged with two counts of aggravated assault. At the time of trial, neither complainant had tested positive for the virus. The

† [1998] 2 S.C.R. 371.

trial judge entered a directed verdict acquitting the respondent. The Court of Appeal refused to set aside the acquittals.

. . . .

IV. ANALYSIS

The respondent was charged with two counts of aggravated assault. This charge requires the Crown to prove first that the accused's acts "endanger[ed] the life of the complainant" (s. 268(1)) and, second, that the accused intentionally applied force without the consent of the complainant (s. 265(1)(a)). Like the Court of Appeal and the trial judge I agree that the first requirement was satisfied. There can be no doubt the respondent endangered the lives of the complainants by exposing them to the risk of HIV infection through unprotected sexual intercourse. The potentially lethal consequences of infection permit no other conclusion. Further, it is not necessary to establish that the complainants were in fact infected with the virus. There is no prerequisite that any harm must actually have resulted. This first requirement of s. 268(1) is satisfied by the significant risk to the lives of the complainants occasioned by the act of unprotected intercourse.

. . . .

Up until 1983, the indecent assault provisions in the *Code* provided that consent was vitiated where it was obtained "by false and fraudulent representations as to the nature and quality of the act". The requirement that fraud relate to the "nature and quality of the act" reflected the approach to consent in sexual assault cases which has existed at common law since *R. v. Clarence* (1888), 22 Q.B.D. 23. There it was held by the majority that a husband's failure to disclose that he had gonorrhea did not vitiate his wife's consent to sexual intercourse.

. . . .

In 1983, the *Criminal Code* was amended. The rape and indecent assault provisions were replaced by the offence of sexual assault. The s. 265 assault provision was enacted in its present form, and it, by the terms of s. 265(2), applies to all forms of assault, including sexual assault.

Section 265(3)(c) simply states that no consent is obtained where the complainant submits or does not resist by reason of "fraud". There are no limitations or qualifications on the term "fraud". Nonetheless, some controversy has arisen as to whether the apparently clear language of the new section removed the requirement that fraud vitiating consent must relate to the "nature and quality of the act".

. . . .

In my opinion, both the legislative history and the plain language of the provision suggest that Parliament intended to move away from the rigidity of the common law requirement that fraud must relate to the nature and quality of the act. The repeal of statutory language imposing this requirement and its replacement by a reference simply to fraud indicates that Parliament's intention was to provide a more flexible concept of fraud in assault and sexual assault cases.

I would therefore conclude that it is no longer necessary when examining whether consent in assault or sexual assault cases was vitiated by fraud to consider whether the fraud related to the nature and quality of the act. A principled approach consistent with the plain language of the section and an appropriate approach to consent in sexual assault matters is preferable. To that end, I see no reason why, with appropriate modifications, the principles which have historically been applied in relation to fraud in criminal law cannot be used.

. . . .

In summary, it can be seen that the essential elements of fraud are dishonesty, which can include non-disclosure of important facts, and deprivation or risk of deprivation.

The deadly consequences that non-disclosure of the risk of HIV infection can have on an unknowing victim[ ] make it imperative that as a policy the broader view of fraud vitiating consent advocated in the pre-*Clarence* cases and in the U.S. decisions should be adopted. Neither can it be forgotten that the *Criminal Code* has been evolving to reflect society's attitude towards the true nature of the consent. The marital rape exemption was repealed in Canada in 1983. The defence of mistaken belief in consent was narrowed in the 1992 amendments. Section 273.2(b) eliminated consent as a defence to sexual assault in situations where the accused did not take reasonable steps to ascertain that the complainant was consenting.

In my view, it should now be taken that for the accused to conceal or fail to disclose that he is HIV-positive can constitute fraud which may vitiate consent to sexual intercourse.

Without disclosure of HIV status there cannot be a true consent. The consent cannot simply be to have sexual intercourse. Rather it must be consent to have intercourse with a partner who is HIV-positive. True consent cannot be given if there has not been a disclosure by the accused of his HIV-positive status. A consent that is not based upon knowledge of the significant relevant factors is not a valid consent. The extent of the duty to disclose will increase with the risks attendant upon the act of intercourse. To put it in the context of fraud the greater the risk of deprivation the higher the duty of disclosure. The failure to disclose HIV-positive status can lead to a devastating illness with fatal consequences. In those circumstances, there exists a positive duty to disclose. The nature and extent of the duty to disclose, if any, will always have to be considered in the context of the particular facts presented.

The second requirement of fraud is that the dishonesty result in deprivation, which may consist of actual harm or simply a risk of harm. Yet it cannot be any trivial harm or risk of harm that will satisfy this requirement in sexual assault cases where the activity would have been consensual if the consent had not been obtained by fraud. For example, the risk of minor scratches or of catching cold would not suffice to establish deprivation. What then should be required? In my view, the Crown will have to establish that the dishonest act (either falsehoods or failure to disclose) had the effect of exposing the person consenting to a significant risk of serious bodily harm. The risk of contracting AIDS as a result of engaging in unprotected intercourse would clearly meet that test. In this case the complainants were exposed to a significant risk of serious harm to their health. Indeed their very survival was placed in jeopardy. It is difficult to imagine a more significant risk or a more grievous bodily harm....

It follows that in circumstances such as those presented in this case there must be a significant risk of serious harm if the fraud resulting from non-disclosure is to vitiate the consent to the act of intercourse. For the purposes of this case, it is not necessary to consider every set of circumstances which might come within the proposed guidelines. The standard is sufficient to encompass not only the risk of HIV infection but also other sexually transmitted diseases which constitute a significant risk of serious harm. However, the test is not so broad as to trivialize a serious offence.

. . . .

The phrase "significant risk of serious harm" must be applied to the facts of each case in order to determine if the consent given in the particular circumstances was vitiated. Obviously consent can and should, in appropriate circumstances, be vitiated. Yet this should not be too readily undertaken. The phrase should be interpreted in light of the gravity of the consequences of a conviction for sexual assault and with the aim of avoiding the trivialization of the offence. It is difficult to draw clear bright lines in defining human relations particularly those of a consenting sexual nature. There must be some flexibility in the application of a test to determine if the consent to sexual acts should be vitiated. The proposed test may be helpful to courts in achieving a proper balance when considering whether on the facts presented, the consent given to the sexual act should be vitiated.

. . . .

In the result the appeal is allowed, the orders of the Court of Appeal and of the trial judge are set aside and a new trial is directed.

[L'HEUREUX-DUBÉ J.:]

... The central issue in this appeal is the interpretation to be given to the word "fraud" as it appears in s. 265(3)(c) of the *Criminal Code*, R.S.C., 1985, c. C-46. As "fraud" is not defined in the assault scheme in the *Criminal Code*, it is left to the courts to interpret its meaning as it relates to consent to the application of force. Consistent with established principles of statutory interpretation, the interpretation of "fraud" in s. 265(3)(c) must give effect to the intention of Parliament, and it must be informed by an appreciation of the context of the *Criminal Code*, its purposes, and the particular objectives of the assault scheme to which the fraud provision relates.

Contrary to McLachlin J.'s interpretation of legislative intent, I agree with Cory J.'s conclusion that the 1983 amendment to the *Criminal Code*, in which the rape and indecent assault provisions were reconstituted as the offence of sexual assault, and the words "false and fraudulent representations as to the nature and quality of the act" were removed, evidences Parliament's intention to move away from the unreasonably strict common law approach to the vitiation of consent by fraud.

. . . .

The substantial overhaul that Parliament undertook with the 1983 amendments implies that it was dissatisfied with the traditional approach to sexual offences. This approach had been informed by the common law, as well as previous statutory codifications. In this context of discontent with the law's historical treatment of victims of sexual offences, and in light of the removal of the words "false and fraudulent representations as to the nature and quality of the act", it is clear that Parliament intended to move away from the traditional approach to fraud as it relates to consent in sexual assault offences.

. . . .

As can be seen from an examination of the underlying elements of assault, which form the basis of all of the assault provisions, the *Criminal Code* prohibition against the intentional and non-consensual application of force is very broadly constructed. Any unwanted touching by another, no matter how minimal the force that is applied, is criminal. The physical acts prohibited by the assault scheme include not only a punch in the face, or forced sexual intercourse at knife-point, but also placing one's hand on the thigh of the person sitting adjacent on the bus: see *R. v. Burden* (1981), 25 C.R. (3d) 283 (B.C.C.A.). Clearly, the purpose of the assault scheme is much broader than just the protection of persons from serious physical harm. The assault scheme is aimed more generally at protecting people's physical integrity.

Relatedly, the assault scheme is also about protecting and promoting people's physical autonomy, by recognizing each individual's power to consent, or to withhold consent, to any touching. The meaningfulness of the right to consent, and thus of the right to stipulate under which conditions a person wishes to be touched, is further protected by s. 265(3). In general, s. 265(3) lists factors that have the effect of making a person's consent to the application of force meaningless. Where those factors are present, a true expression of a complainant's autonomous will cannot be obtained. Parliament has recognized with s. 265(3)[ ] that in order to maximize the protection of physical integrity and personal autonomy, only consent obtained without negating the voluntary agency of the person being touched[ ] is legally valid.

Given these objectives of the *Criminal Code* assault scheme, and the important protections inherent in the individual's power to consent or deny consent, how should "fraud" be interpreted in relation to consent in s. 265(3)(c)? When interpreting s. 265(3)(c), it is important to keep in mind that it applies to consent to all forms of assault, not, for example, just sexual assault, or assault where there is potential or actual serious physical injury. The interpretation of the fraud provision, therefore, should be based on principles that are consistent across the different assault contexts. In this respect, I must expressly disagree with the approach taken by my colleague, Cory J. In my view, his interpretation of the fraud provision is inconsistent with such a principled approach to statutory interpretation.

. . . .

Cory J. would limit its consent-vitiating effects to the traditional common law approach, and to those assault contexts where there is a "significant risk of serious bodily harm". But that which is integral to a principled interpretation of fraud is its causal effect on consent, and the objectives of the assault scheme. Accordingly, it is appropriate to define fraud in terms of its relationship to consent, as well as to any and all forms of assault, and not just in terms of the proximity and severity of the risks associated with the acts for which consent is being given.

In my view, considering the wording of s. 265(3)(c), as well as the objectives and context of the *Criminal Code* and the assault scheme, fraud is simply about whether the dishonest act in question induced another to consent to the ensuing physical act, whether or not that act was particularly risky and dangerous. The focus of the inquiry into whether fraud vitiated consent so as to make certain physical contact non-consensual should be on whether the nature and execution of the deceit deprived the complainant of the ability to exercise his or her will in relation to his or her physical integrity with respect to the activity in question. As Mewett and Manning explain at p. 789: "There must be a causal connection between the fraud and the submission" to the act. Where fraud is in issue, the Crown would be required to prove beyond a reasonable doubt that the accused acted dishonestly in a manner designed to induce the complainant to submit to a specific activity, and that absent the dishonesty, the complainant would not have submitted to the particular activity, thus considering the impugned act to be a non-consensual application of force.... The dishonesty of the submission-inducing act would be assessed based on the objective standard of the reasonable person. The Crown also would be required to prove that the accused knew, or was aware, that his or her dishonest actions would induce the complainant to submit to the particular activity. For a similar articulation of the elements of fraud, see *R. v. Théroux*, [1993] 2 S.C.R. 5, at pp. 25–26.

In considering this case, the following facts would be sufficient to establish the objective dishonesty of the accused's actions, and to infer that the accused knew that his actions induced the complainants' submission to unprotected sex: the accused knew that he was HIV-positive, he was aware of the contagious and life-threatening nature of the disease, he was advised by public health nurses to always wear a condom and inform his partners of his HIV-positive status, he expressed fears that disclosure of his status to potential partners would end his sex-life, he lied about his HIV-positive status to one of the complainants, and he failed to disclose it to the other complainant in circumstances that called for its disclosure.

. . . .

An interpretation of fraud that focuses only on the sexual assault context, and which limits it only to those situations where a "significant risk of serious bodily harm" is evident, is unjustifiably restrictive. Such a particularization and limitation is nowhere present in the assault scheme, because Parliament removed any qualifications to the fraud provision as it relates to sexual assault. It must be noted that where sexual assault is concerned, those receiving the protection of the *Criminal Code* are overwhelmingly women. Limiting the definition of fraud in the sexual assault context in the way that Cory J. proposes is to potentially fall into the same trap as those people who believe that rape in the absence of physical "violence", where the complainant just froze and did not fight back or was unconscious, is not a serious crime. The essence of the offence, as I have stated, is not the presence of physical violence or the potential for serious bodily harm, but the violation of the complainant's physical dignity in a manner contrary to her autonomous will. That violation of physical dignity and personal autonomy is what justifies criminal sanction, and always has, irrespective of the risk or degree of bodily harm involved. Why should fraud be defined more broadly in the commercial context, which is designed to protect property interests, than it is for sexual assault, which is one of the worst violations of human dignity?

Finally, my colleagues' examples of the types of trivial conduct that will be caught by this approach are grossly overstated. Cory J. downplays the limiting effect of the fact that a causal connection must be proven, to the imposing criminal standard, between the accused's dishonest act and his intention to induce the submission of the complainant. For instance, a mere misrepresentation as to a man's professional status, without proof that the man was aware that the complainant was submitting to sexual intercourse with him by reason of his lie, would not constitute sexual assault. See Mewett and Manning at pp. 789–90. Whether a complainant actually submitted to sexual intercourse by reason of an accused's fraud will necessarily depend on an examination of all of the factors, and can only be decided on a case-by-case basis.

McLachlin J.'s predictions are even more cataclysmic. Contrary to her assertion in para. 52, it is not "any deception or dishonesty" that will be criminalized by this approach. McLachlin J. argues that based on the approach to fraud that I have explained, henceforward the "implied consent inherent in the social occasion — the handshake or social buss — are transformed by fiat of judicial pen into crimes". But my approach to fraud will in no way catch such innocent conduct. The very notion of implied consent to touching that is inherent in the social occasion, and indeed, inherent in so many aspects of day to day life, is based on an understanding of social realities and a need for tolerance of a reasonable degree of incidental and trivial contact. Whether or not a man is wearing a false moustache or a woman, alluring make-up, it is inconceivable that the Crown, were it foolish enough to prosecute a case of assault by handshake or social buss, would be capable of establishing beyond a reasonable doubt both that a complainant only consented to the physical contact by reason of the deception, and that the deception was employed with the knowledge and intention of inducing the submission of the complainant. In addition, the principle of *de minimis non curat lex*, that "the law does not concern itself with trifles" might apply in such a case: see *R. v. Hinchey*, [1996] 3 S.C.R. 1128, at para. 69, *per* L'Heureux-Dubé J. Furthermore, I cannot accept McLachlin J.'s criticism that the test suffers from imprecision and uncertainty due to the fact that the dishonesty of the act is to be assessed based on an objective standard. A majority of this Court has already accepted such an approach to the assessment of the dishonesty of the act in the criminal fraud context: see *Théroux*, *supra*, at p. 16, *per* McLachlin J.

. . . .

Subject to these reasons, I agree with my colleagues' disposition to allow the appeal and order a new trial.

[McLACHLIN J. (*per* McLachlin and Gonthier JJ.):]

My colleagues L'Heureux-Dubé J. and Cory J. propose new rules which would criminalize dishonestly obtained sex in a wide variety of circumstances. I sympathize with their goals. The venereal disease of HIV and the AIDS it causes are the cause of terrible suffering and death. The wrong done to a person who is deceived into having unprotected sexual intercourse by a lie about HIV status can be inestimable. However, I respectfully find the approaches they advocate are too broad, falling outside the power of the courts to make incremental changes to the common law. I propose a narrower extension limited to failure to disclose venereal disease.

. . . .

I agree with the courts below (indeed all courts that have hitherto considered the issue since the adoption of the new definition of fraud), that the submission that Parliament intended to radically broaden the crime of assault by the 1983 amendments must be rejected. I approach the matter from the conviction that the criminalization of conduct is a serious matter. Clear language is required to create crimes. Crimes can be created by defining a new crime, or by redefining the elements of an old crime. When courts approach the definition of elements of old crimes, they must be cautious not to broaden them in a way that in effect creates a new crime. Only Parliament can create new crimes and turn lawful conduct into criminal conduct. It is permissible for courts to interpret old provisions in ways that reflect social changes, in order to ensure that Parliament's intent is carried out in the modern era. It is not permissible for courts to overrule the common law and create new crimes that Parliament never intended.

Against this background, I turn to what Parliament intended when it adopted a new definition of fraud for assault, including sexual assault, in 1983. Can the intent to radically broaden the crime of assault be inferred from the fact that Parliament omitted the old words "nature and quality of the act"? I think not.

First, the phrase "nature and quality of the act" did not state the law as it existed even before 1983. The criminal law of assault is an amalgam of the codified provisions of the *Criminal Code* and the uncodified common law. Prior to 1983, the *Code*'s reference to indecent assault described the relevant concept of fraud as fraud as to the "nature and quality of the act". It said nothing about "identity". Yet Canadian courts for over a hundred years accepted that fraud as to identity could negate consent, on the basis of the rule at common law. In 1983 Parliament removed the reference in the *Code* to the other case where the common law recognized fraud vitiating consent to sexual intercourse — fraud as to the nature and quality of the act. The reasonable inference is that Parliament supposed that just as the courts had read "identity" into the criminal law of sexual assault even though the *Code* did not mention it, so the courts would continue to read "nature and quality of the act" into the law even though it was not mentioned. To put it another way, Parliament must be supposed to have expected that the courts would continue to read the *Code* provisions on sexual assault against the background of the common law, unless it used language clearly indicating that it was altering the common law. There is nothing in s. 265 of the *Criminal Code* to indicate an intention to remove the common law limitations on fraud for assault.

. . . .

Parliament has not changed the common law definition of fraud in relation to assault. This leaves the question of whether this Court should do so.

This Court has established a rule for when it will effect changes to the common law. It will do so only where those changes are incremental developments of existing principle and where the consequences of the change are contained and predictable....

In my respectful view, the broad changes proposed by L'Heureux-Dubé J. and Cory J. do not constitute an incremental development of this common law. Rather, they amount to abandoning the common law rule and substituting new principles in its place.

. . . .

Cory J., recognizing the overbreadth of the theory upon which he founds his reasons, attempts to limit it by introducing an ad hoc qualifier: there must be a "significant risk of serious bodily harm" before consent is vitiated. This limitation, far from solving the problem, introduces new difficulties. First, it contradicts the general theory that deception coupled with risk of deprivation suffices to vitiate consent. A new theory is required to explain why some, but not all kinds of fraud, convert consensual sex into assault. Yet none is offered. Second, it introduces uncertainty. When is a risk significant enough to qualify conduct as criminal? In whose eyes is "significance" to be determined — the victim's, the accused's or the judge's? What is the ambit of "serious bodily harm"? Can a bright line be drawn between psychological harm and bodily harm, when the former may lead to depression, self-destructive behaviour and in extreme cases suicide? The criminal law must be certain. If it is uncertain, it cannot deter inappropriate conduct and loses its *raison d'être*. Equally serious, it becomes unfair. People who believe they are acting within the law may find themselves prosecuted, convicted, imprisoned and branded as criminals. Consequences as serious as these should not turn on the interpretation of vague terms like "significant" and "serious". Finally, Cory J.'s limitation of the new crime to significant and serious risk of harm amounts to making an ad hoc choice of where the line between lawful conduct and unlawful conduct should be drawn. This Court, *per* Lamer C.J., has warned that making ad hoc choices is properly the task of the legislatures, not the courts: *Schachter v. Canada*, [1992] 2 S.C.R. 679, at p. 707.

Another cause for concern is that the extension of the criminal law of assault proposed by Cory J. represents a curtailment of individual liberty sufficient to require endorsement by Parliament. The equation of non-disclosure with lack of consent oversimplifies the complex and diverse nature of consent....

The first difficulty with this [L'Heureux-Dubé J.'s] position is that it involves an assumption of Parliamentary intent to change the common law of fraud for assault that is not, as I argue earlier, valid. The second difficulty is that this approach vastly extends the offence of assault. Henceforward, any deception or dishonesty intended to induce consent to touching, sexual or non-sexual, vitiates the consent and makes the touching a crime. Social touching hitherto rendered non-criminal by the implied consent inherent in the social occasion — the handshake or social buss — are transformed by fiat of judicial pen into crimes, provided it can be shown that the accused acted dishonestly in a manner designed to induce consent, and that the contact was, viewed objectively, induced by deception. No risk need be established, nor is there any qualifier on the nature of the deception. Will alluring make-up or a false moustache suffice to render the casual social act criminal? Will the false promise of a fur coat used to induce sexual intercourse render the resultant act a crime? The examples are not frivolous, given the absence of any qualifiers on deception. A third difficulty is that this approach, like that of Cory J., suffers from imprecision and uncertainty. The test is said to be objective. Yet what constitutes deception is by its very nature highly subjective. One person's blandishment is another person's deceit, and on this theory, crime.

Not only is the proposed extension of the law sweeping, it is unprecedented. We have been told of no courts or legislatures in this or other countries that have gone so far. To the extent that Canadian law has criminalized deception, it has done so only where the deception results in actual harm or a risk of harm. The rule proposed by L'Heureux-Dubé J. would eliminate the need to show risk of harm and make deception alone the condition of criminal responsibility for sexual contact. Overbreadth on this scale cannot be cured by administrative action. Prosecutorial deference cannot compensate for overextension of the criminal law; it merely replaces overbreadth and uncertainty at the judicial level with overbreadth and uncertainty at both the prosecutorial level and the judicial level.

The theoretical difficulties with both proposals put forward by my colleagues are matched by the practical problems they would introduce. The changes proposed are of great consequence. The law does not presently make it an offence to engage in sexual contact without disclosing to one's partner possible risks, as Cory J. proposes. Nor does it make every deception inducing consent to physical contact a crime, as L'Heureux-Dubé J. proposes. What we know about the spread of HIV and other venereal diseases suggests that thousands of people engage in just such conduct every day. Henceforward, if the sweeping changes suggested are accepted, these people will be criminals, subject to investigation, prosecution and imprisonment. Literally millions of acts, which have not to date been regarded as criminal, will now be criminalized. Individual liberty will be curtailed. Police, prosecutors, the courts and the prisons will be dramatically affected. Such a change, if it is to be made, is best made by Parliament after full debate as to its ramifications and costs.

The broad extensions of the law proposed by my colleagues may also have an adverse impact on the fight to reduce the spread of HIV and other serious sexually transmitted diseases. Public health workers argue that encouraging people to come forward for testing and treatment is the key to preventing the spread of HIV and similar diseases, and that broad criminal sanctions are unlikely to be effective.... Criminalizing a broad range of HIV-related conduct will only impair such efforts. Moreover, because homosexuals, intravenous drug users, sex trade workers, prisoners, and people with disabilities are those most at risk of contracting HIV, the burden of criminal sanctions will impact most heavily on members of these already marginalized groups. The material before the Court suggests that a blanket duty to disclose may drive those with the disease underground....

I have concluded that the broad-based proposals for changing the law put forward by my colleagues go much further than the incremental change to the common law permitted to courts. However, it does not follow that all change to the law of assault is barred. It is open to courts to make incremental changes by extending the common law concepts of nature of the act and identity, provided the ramifications of the changes are not overly complex. Before the appeal can be rejected, it is necessary to consider whether this can be done.

. . . .

Against this background, I return to the conditions for court-made change. The basic precondition of such change is that it is required to bring the law into step with the changing needs of society. This established, the change must meet the condition of being an incremental development of the common law that does not possess unforeseeable and complex ramifications.

In the case at bar, I am satisfied that the current state of the law does not reflect the values of Canadian society. It is unrealistic, indeed shocking, to think that consent given to sex on the basis that one's partner is HIV-free stands unaffected by blatant deception on that matter. To put it another way, few would think the law should condone a person who has been asked whether he has HIV, lying about that fact in order to obtain consent. To say that such a person commits fraud vitiating consent, thereby rendering the contact an assault, seems right and logical.

Prior to *Clarence*, the common law recognized that deception as to sexually transmitted disease carrying a high risk of infection[ ] constituted fraud vitiating consent to sexual intercourse. Returning the law to this position would represent an incremental change to the law. If it was an increment to reverse the previous common law rule that deceit as to venereal disease could vitiate consent, it is no greater increment to reverse that decision and return to the former state of the law. The change is, moreover, consistent with Parliament's 1983 amendment of the *Criminal Code* to remove the phrase "nature and quality of the act", which suggests that Parliament, while retaining the common law of fraud in relation to consent negativing assault, did not wish to freeze the restrictive mould of *Clarence*.

. . . .

The question is whether a narrower increment is feasible that catches only harm of the sort at issue in this appeal and draws the required bright line. In my view, it is. A return to the pre-*Clarence* view of the common law would draw a clear line between criminal conduct and non-criminal conduct. As I have explained, pre-*Clarence*, the law permitted fraud to vitiate consent to contact where there was (a) a deception as to the sexual character of the act; (b) deception as to the identity of the perpetrator; or (c) deception as to the presence of a sexually transmitted disease giving rise to serious risk or probability of infecting the complainant (*Sinclair*, *supra*). This rule is clear and contained. It would catch the conduct here at issue, without permitting people to be convicted of assault for inducements like false promises of marriage or fur coats. The test for deception would be objective, focussing on whether the accused falsely represented to the complainant that he or she was disease-free when he knew or ought to have known that there was a high risk of infecting his partner. The test for inducement would be subjective, in the sense that the judge or jury must be satisfied beyond a reasonable doubt that the fraud actually induced the consent.

. . . .

With the greatest of deference to the learned judges in these cases [*Clarence*], an explanation may be suggested for why deceit as to venereal disease may vitiate consent while deceit as to other inducements, like promises of marriage or fur coats, does not. Consent to unprotected sexual intercourse is consent to sexual congress with a certain person and to the transmission of bodily fluids from that person. Where the person represents that he or she is disease-free, and consent is given on that basis, deception on that matter goes to the very act of assault. The complainant does not consent to the transmission of diseased fluid into his or her body. This deception in a very real sense goes to the nature of the sexual act, changing it from an act that has certain natural consequences (whether pleasure, pain or pregnancy), to a potential sentence of disease or death. It differs fundamentally from deception as to the consideration that will be given for consent, like marriage, money or a fur coat, in that it relates to the physical act itself. It differs, moreover, in a profoundly serious way that merits the criminal sanction.

This suffices to justify the position of the common law pre-*Clarence* that deception as to venereal disease may vitiate consent. The question of whether other categories of fraud could be logically added on the basis that deceit as to them also fundamentally alters the nature of the physical act itself, is better left for another day....

It remains to consider the argument that extending the law, even in this limited fashion, will have unforeseen, complex and undesirable ramifications. Regrettable as it is, it may be that criminalizing deceit as to sexually transmitted disease inducing consent may prevent some people from seeking testing and treatment, out of fear that if they learn about their disease they will be forced to choose between abstaining from unprotected sexual relations and becoming criminals. On the other hand, it may foster greater disclosure. The message that people must be honest about their communicable diseases is an important one. Conduct like that in the case at bar shocks the conscience and should permit of a criminal remedy. In addition, the proposed extension of the law is relatively narrow, catching only deceit as to venereal disease where it is established, beyond a reasonable doubt, that there was a high risk of infection and that the defendant knew or ought to have known that the fraud actually induced consent to unprotected sex. Finally, I note that s. 221 of the *Criminal Code* (criminal negligence causing bodily harm) already makes it a crime to engage in unprotected sexual intercourse without disclosing HIV-positive status where the sexual partner contracts HIV as a result: *R. v. Mercer* (1993), 84 C.C.C. (3d) 41 (Nfld. C.A.). There is no evidence that the application of s. 221 has had an adverse effect on testing by extending criminal responsibility to cases where the defendant's partners are unfortunate enough to have been infected. The extension I propose represents only a modest step beyond this offence. Bearing in mind all of these considerations, I am satisfied that this limited change will not have far-reaching, unforeseeable or undesirable ramifications.

I conclude that the common law should be changed to permit deceit about sexually transmitted disease that induces consent to be treated as fraud vitiating consent under s. 265 of the *Criminal Code*.

V. CONCLUSION

I would allow the appeal and order that a new trial be directed.

■

Consider the implications of the majority judgment in *Cuerrier* for women in terms of proving the element of causation. Could it mean that HIV-positive women are not entitled to as much information from potential sexual partners as are non-HIV-positive women? Does Cory J.'s approach require a focus on the woman's prior health status, sexual history, and private medical records as well as those of her other partners? In *R. v. Williams*, [2003] 2 S.C.R. 134, the Court applied *Cuerrier* to find that the accused did not commit aggravated assault against the complainant, when he had unprotected sexual intercourse with her over the course of one year and refrained from telling her beforehand that he had tested HIV-positive. The Court held that where the evidence raises a reasonable doubt that the complainant was already infected by the time the accused became aware of his HIV-positive status, the Crown must prove that the accused's behaviour posed a further significant risk to the complainant's life. In this case, there was no evidence to establish that the unprotected intercourse exposed the woman to a significant risk of bodily harm, as required by *Cuerrier*, since it was likely that Williams infected her before he was tested. Further, there was no evidence linking continued incidents of intercourse or the delay in receiving medical care with a significant risk to the complainant's life. Williams was, however, found guilty of the offence of attempted aggravated assault.

R. v. Ewanchuk[†]

[MAJOR J.:]

In the present appeal the accused was acquitted of sexual assault. The trial judge relied on the defence of implied consent. This was a mistake of law as no such defence is available in assault cases in Canada. This mistake of law is reviewable by appellate courts, and for the reasons that follow the appeal is allowed.

I. FACTS

The complainant was a 17-year-old woman living in the city of Edmonton. She met the accused respondent Ewanchuk on the afternoon of June 2, 1994, while walking through the parking lot of the Heritage Shopping Mall with her roommate. The accused, driving a red van towing a trailer, approached the two young women. He struck up a conversation with them. He related that he was in the custom wood-working business and explained that he displayed his work at retail booths in several shopping malls. He said that he was looking for staff to attend his displays, and asked whether the young women were looking for work. The complainant's friend answered that they were, at which point the accused asked to interview her friend privately. She declined, but spoke with the accused beside his van for some period of time about the sort of work he required, and eventually exchanged telephone numbers with the accused.

The following morning the accused telephoned the apartment where the complainant and her friend resided with their boyfriends. The complainant answered the phone. She told the accused that her friend was still asleep. When he learned this, the accused asked the complainant if she was interested in a job. She indicated that she was, and they met a short time later, again in the Heritage Mall parking lot. At the accused's suggestion, the interview took place in his van. In the words of the complainant, a "very business-like, polite" conversation took place. Some time later, the complainant asked if she could smoke a cigarette, and the accused suggested that they move outside since he was allergic to cigarette smoke. Once outside the van, he asked the complainant if she would like to see some of his work, which was kept inside the trailer attached to his van, and she indicated that she would. The complainant entered the trailer, purposely leaving the door open behind her. The accused followed her in, and closed the door in a way which made the complainant think that he had locked it. There is no evidence whether the door was actually locked, but the complainant stated that she became frightened at this point. Once inside the trailer, the complainant and the accused sat down side-by-side on the floor of the trailer. They spoke and looked through a portfolio of his work. This lasted 10 to 15 minutes, after which the conversation turned to more personal matters.

During the time in the trailer the accused was quite tactile with the complainant, touching her hand, arms and shoulder as he spoke. At some point the accused said that he was feeling tense and asked the complainant to give him a massage. The complainant complied, massaging the accused's shoulders for a few minutes. After she stopped, he asked her to move in front of him so that he could massage her, which she did. The accused then massaged the complainant's shoulders and arms while they continued talking. During this mutual massaging the accused repeatedly told the complainant to relax, and that she should not be afraid. As the massage progressed, the accused attempted to initiate more intimate contact. The complainant stated that, "he started to try to massage around my stomach, and he brought his hands up around — or underneath my breasts, and he started to get quite close up there, so I used my elbows to push in between, and I said, No".

The accused stopped immediately, but shortly thereafter resumed non-sexual massaging, to which the complainant also said, "No". The accused again stopped, and said, "See, I'm a nice guy. It's okay".

The accused then asked the complainant to turn and face him. She did so, and he began massaging her feet. His touching progressed from her feet up to her inner thigh and pelvic area. The complainant did not want the accused to touch her in this way, but said nothing as she said she was afraid that any resistance would prompt the accused to become violent. Although the accused never used or threatened any force, the complainant testified that she did not want to "egg [him] on". As the contact progressed,

† [1999] 1 S.C.R. 330.

the accused laid himself heavily on top of the complainant and began grinding his pelvic area against hers. The complainant testified that the accused asserted, "that he could get me so horny so that I would want it so bad, and he wouldn't give it to me because he had self-control".

The complainant did not move or reciprocate the contact. The accused asked her to put her hands across his back, but she did not; instead she lay "bone straight". After less than a minute of this the complainant asked the accused to stop. "I said, Just please stop. And so he stopped". The accused again told the complainant not to be afraid, and asked her if she trusted that he wouldn't hurt her. In her words, the complainant said, "Yes, I trust that you won't hurt me". On the stand she stated that she was afraid throughout, and only responded to the accused in this way because she was fearful that a negative answer would provoke him to use force.

After this brief exchange, the accused went to hug the complainant and, as he did so, he laid on top of her again, continuing the pelvic grinding. He also began moving his hands on the complainant's inner thigh, inside her shorts, for a short time. While still on top of her the accused began to fumble with his shorts and took out his penis. At this point the complainant again asked the accused to desist, saying, "No, stop".

Again, the accused stopped immediately, got off the complainant, smiled at her and said something to the effect of, "It's okay. See, I'm a nice guy, I stopped". At this point the accused again hugged the complainant lightly before opening up his wallet and removing a $100 bill, which he gave to the complainant. She testified that the accused said that the $100 was for the massage and that he told her not to tell anyone about it. He made some reference to another female employee with whom he also had a very close and friendly relationship, and said that he hoped to get together with the complainant again.

Shortly after the exchange of the money the complainant said that she had to go. The accused opened the door and the complainant stepped out. Some further conversation ensued outside the trailer before the complainant finally left and walked home. On her return home the complainant was emotionally distraught and contacted the police.

At some point during the encounter the accused provided the complainant with a brochure describing his woodwork and gave her his name and address, which she wrote on the brochure. The investigating officer used this information to locate the accused at his home, where he was arrested. He was subsequently charged with sexual assault and tried before a judge sitting alone.

The accused did not testify, leaving only the complainant's evidence as to what took place between them. The trial judge found her to be a credible witness and her version of events was not contradicted or disputed. In cross-examination the complainant testified that, although she was extremely afraid throughout the encounter, she had done everything possible to project a confident demeanour, in the belief that this would improve her chances of avoiding a violent assault. The following passage is illustrative of her evidence:

Q You didn't want to show any discomfort, right?
A No.
Q Okay. In fact, you wanted to project the picture that you were quite happy to be with him and everything was fine, right?
A Not that I was happy, but that I was comfortable.
Q Comfortable, all right. And relaxed?
A Yes.
Q And you did your best to do that, right?
A Yes.

Later in cross-examination, counsel for the accused again asked the complainant about the image she sought to convey to the complainant by her behaviour:

Q And you wanted to make sure that he didn't sense any fear on your part, right?
A Yes.

II. JUDICIAL HISTORY

A. Court of Queen's Bench

The trial judge made a number of findings of fact in his oral judgment. He found that the complainant was a credible witness. He found as facts: that in her mind she had not consented to any of the sexual touching which took place; that she had been fearful throughout the encounter; that she didn't want the accused to know she was afraid; and that she had actively projected a relaxed and unafraid visage. He concluded that the failure of the complainant to communicate her fear, including her active efforts to the contrary, rendered her subjective feelings irrelevant.

The trial judge then considered the question of whether the accused had raised the defence of honest but mistaken belief in consent, and concluded that he had not. The trial judge characterized the defence position as being a failure by the Crown to discharge its onus of proving "beyond a reasonable doubt that there was an absence of consent". That is, he took the defence to be asserting that the Crown had failed to prove one of the components of the *actus reus* of the offence. This led the trial judge to characterize the defence as one of *"implied consent"*. In so doing he concluded that the complainant's conduct was such that it could be *objectively* construed as constituting consent to sexual touching of the type performed by the accused.

The trial judge treated consent as a question of the complainant's behaviour in the encounter. As a result of that conclusion he found that the defence of honest but mistaken belief in consent had no application since the accused made no claims as to his mental state. On the totality of the evidence, provided solely by the Crown's witnesses, the trial judge concluded that the Crown had not proven the absence of consent beyond a reasonable doubt and acquitted the accused.

B. Alberta Court of Appeal (1998), 57 Alta. L.R. (3d) 235

Each of the three justices of the Court of Appeal issued separate reasons. McClung and Foisy JJ.A. both dismissed the appeal on the basis that it was a fact-driven acquittal from which the Crown could not properly appeal. In addition, McClung J.A. concluded that the Crown had failed to prove that the accused possessed the requisite criminal intent. He found that the Crown had failed to prove beyond a reasonable doubt that the accused had intended to commit an assault upon the complainant.

Fraser C.J. dissented. She found that the trial judge erred in a number of ways. Specifically, she found that:

- The trial judge erred in his interpretation of the term "consent" as that term is applied to the offence of sexual assault.
- There is no defence of "implied consent", independent of the provisions of ss. 273.1 and 273.2 of the *Criminal Code*.
- It was an error to employ an objective test to determine whether a complainant's "consent" was induced by fear.
- The trial judge erred in the legal effect he ascribed:
  - to the complainant's silence when subjected to sexual contact by the respondent;
  - to the complainant's non-disclosure of her fear when subjected to sexual contact by the respondent;
  - to the complainant's expressed lack of agreement to sexual contact;
  - to the fact that there was no basis for a defence of "implied consent" or "consent by conduct";
  - to the fact that there was no consent to sexual activity.
- The defence of mistake of fact had no application to the issue of 'consent' in this case.
- The trial judge erred when he failed to consider whether the respondent had been wilfully blind or reckless as to whether the complainant consented.

Fraser C.J. held that the only defence available to the accused was that of honest but mistaken belief in consent, and concluded that this defence could not be sustained on the facts as found. Accordingly, she would have allowed the appeal and substituted a verdict of guilty.

III. ANALYSIS

A. Appealable Questions of Law

The majority of the Court of Appeal dismissed the appeal on the ground that the Crown raised no question of law but sought to overturn the trial judge's finding of fact that reasonable doubt existed as to the presence or absence of consent. If the trial judge misdirected himself as to the legal meaning or definition of consent, then his conclusion is one of law, and is reviewable. See *Belyea v. The King*, [1932] S.C.R. 279, *per* Anglin C.J., at p. 296:

> The right of appeal by the Attorney-General, conferred by [the *Criminal Code*] is, no doubt, confined to "questions of law".... But we cannot regard that provision as excluding the right of the Appellate Divisional Court, where a conclusion of mixed law and fact, such as is the guilt or innocence of the accused, depends, as it does here, upon the *legal effect of certain findings of fact* made by the judge or the jury ... to enquire into the soundness of that conclusion, since we cannot regard it as anything else but a question of law, — especially where, as here, it is a clear result of misdirection of himself in law by the learned trial judge. [Emphasis added.]

It properly falls to this Court to determine whether the trial judge erred in his understanding of consent in sexual assault, and to determine whether his conclusion that the defence of "implied consent" exists in Canadian law was correct.

B. The Components of Sexual Assault

A conviction for sexual assault requires proof beyond reasonable doubt of two basic elements, that the accused committed the *actus reus* and that he had the necessary *mens rea*. The *actus reus* of assault is unwanted sexual touching. The *mens rea* is the intention to touch, knowing of, or being reckless of or wilfully blind to, a lack of consent, either by words or actions, from the person being touched.

(1) Actus Reus

The crime of sexual assault is only indirectly defined in the *Criminal Code*, R.S.C., 1985, c. C-46. The offence is comprised of an assault within any one of the definitions in s. 265(1) of the *Code*, which is committed in circumstances of a sexual nature, such that the sexual integrity of the victim is violated: see *R. v. S. (P.L.)*, [1991] 1 S.C.R. 909. ...

The *actus reus* of sexual assault is established by the proof of three elements: (i) touching, (ii) the sexual nature of the contact, and (iii) the absence of consent. The first two of these elements are objective. It is sufficient for the Crown to prove that the accused's actions were voluntary. The sexual nature of the assault is determined objectively; the Crown need not prove that the accused had any *mens rea* with respect to the sexual nature of his or her behaviour: see *R. v. Litchfield*, [1993] 4 S.C.R. 333, and *R. v. Chase*, [1987] 2 S.C.R. 293.

The absence of consent, however, is subjective and determined by reference to the complainant's subjective internal state of mind towards the touching, at the time it occurred: see *R. v. Jensen* (1996), 106 C.C.C. (3d) 430 (Ont. C.A.), at pp. 437–38, aff'd [1997] 1 S.C.R. 304, *R. v. Park*, [1995] 2 S.C.R. 836, at p. 850, *per* L'Heureux-Dubé J., and D. Stuart, *Canadian Criminal Law* (3rd ed. 1995), at p. 513.

Confusion has arisen from time to time on the meaning of consent as an element of the *actus reus* of sexual assault. Some of this confusion has been caused by the word "consent" itself. A number of commentators have observed that the notion of consent connotes active behaviour: see, for example, N. Brett, "Sexual Offenses and Consent" (1998), 11 *Can. J. Law & Jur.* 69, at p. 73. While this may be true in the general use of the word, for the purposes of determining the absence of consent as an element of the *actus reus*, the actual state of mind of the complainant is determinative. At this point, the trier of fact is only concerned with the complainant's perspective. The approach is purely subjective.

The rationale underlying the criminalization of assault explains this. Society is committed to protecting the personal integrity, both physical and psychological, of every individual. Having control over who touches one's body, and how, lies at the core of human dignity and autonomy. The inclusion of assault and sexual assault in the *Code* expresses society's determination to protect the security of the person from any non-consensual contact or threats of force. The common law has recognized for centuries that the individual's right to physical integrity is a fundamental principle, "every man's person being sacred, and no other having a right to meddle with it, in any the slightest manner": see Blackstone's *Commentaries on the Laws of England* (4th ed. 1770), Book III, at p. 120. It follows that any intentional but unwanted touching is criminal.

While the complainant's testimony is the only source of direct evidence as to her state of mind, credibility must still be assessed by the trial judge, or jury, in light of all the evidence. It is open to the accused to claim that the complainant's words and actions, before and during the incident, raise a reasonable doubt against her assertion that she, in her mind, did not want the sexual touching to take place. If, however, as occurred in this case, the trial judge believes the complainant that she subjectively did not consent, the Crown has discharged its obligation to prove the absence of consent.

The complainant's statement that she did not consent is a matter of credibility to be weighed in light of all the evidence including any ambiguous conduct. The question at this stage is purely one of credibility, and whether the totality of the complainant's conduct is consistent with her claim of non-consent. The accused's perception of the complainant's state of mind is not relevant. That perception only arises when a defence of honest but mistaken belief in consent is raised in the *mens rea* stage of the inquiry.

(A) "IMPLIED CONSENT"

Counsel for the respondent submitted that the trier of fact may believe the complainant when she says she did not consent, but still acquit the accused on the basis that her conduct raised a reasonable doubt. Both he and the trial judge refer to this as "implied consent". It follows from the foregoing, however, that the trier of fact may only come to one of two conclusions: the complainant either consented or not. There is no third option. If the trier of fact accepts the complainant's testimony that she did not consent, no matter how strongly her conduct may contradict that claim, the absence of consent is established and the third component of the *actus reus* of sexual assault is proven. The doctrine of implied consent has been recognized in our common law jurisprudence in a variety of contexts but sexual assault is not one of them. There is no defence of implied consent to sexual assault in Canadian law.

(B) APPLICATION TO THE PRESENT CASE

In this case, the trial judge accepted the evidence of the complainant that she did not consent. That being so, he then misdirected himself when he considered the actions of the complainant, and not her subjective mental state, in determining the question of consent. As a result, he disregarded his previous finding that all the accused's sexual touching was unwanted. Instead he treated what he perceived as her ambiguous conduct as a failure by the Crown to prove the absence of consent.

As previously mentioned, the trial judge accepted the complainant's testimony that she did not want the accused to touch her, but then treated her conduct as raising a reasonable doubt about consent, described by him as "implied consent". This conclusion was an error. See D. Stuart, Annotation on *R. v. Ewanchuk* (1998), 13 C.R. (5th) 330, where the author points out that consent is a matter of the state of mind of the complainant while belief in consent is, subject to s. 273.2 of the *Code*, a matter of the state of mind of the accused and may raise the defence of honest but mistaken belief in consent.

The finding that the complainant did not want or consent to the sexual touching cannot co-exist with a finding that reasonable doubt exists on the question of consent. The trial judge's acceptance of the complainant's testimony regarding her own state of mind was the end of the matter on this point.

This error was compounded somewhat by the trial judge's holding that the complainant's subjective and self-contained fear would not have changed his mind as to whether she consented. Although he needn't have considered this question, having already found that she did not in fact consent, any residual doubt raised by her ambiguous conduct was accounted for by what he accepted as an honest and pervasive fear held by the complainant.

(C) EFFECT OF THE COMPLAINANT'S FEAR

To be legally effective, consent must be freely given. Therefore, even if the complainant consented, or her conduct raises a reasonable doubt about her non-consent, circumstances may arise which call into question what factors prompted her apparent consent. The *Code* defines a series of conditions under which the law will deem an absence of consent in cases of assault, notwithstanding the complainant's ostensible consent or participation. As enumerated in s. 265(3), these include submission by reason of force, fear, threats, fraud or the exercise of authority, and codify the longstanding common law rule that consent given under fear or duress is ineffective: see G. Williams, *Textbook of Criminal Law* (2nd ed. 1983), at pp. 551–61. This section reads as follows:

> **265.** ...
>
> (3) For the purposes of this section, no consent is obtained where the complainant submits or does not resist by reason of
> (*a*) the application of force to the complainant or to a person other than the complainant;
> (*b*) threats or fear of the application of force to the complainant or to a person other than the complainant;
> (*c*) fraud; or
> (*d*) the exercise of authority.

The words of Fish J.A. in *Saint-Laurent v. Hétu*, [1994] R.J.Q. 69 (C.A.), at p. 82, aptly describe the concern which the trier of fact must bear in mind when evaluating the actions of a complainant who claims to have been under fear, fraud or duress:

> "Consent" is ... stripped of its defining characteristics when it is applied to the submission, non-resistance, non-objection, or even the apparent agreement, of a deceived, unconscious or compelled will.

In these instances the law is interested in a complainant's reasons for choosing to participate in, or ostensibly consent to, the touching in question. In practice, this translates into an examination of the choice the complainant believed she faced. The courts' concern is whether she *freely* made up her mind about the conduct in question. The relevant section of the *Code* is s. 265(3)(*b*), which states that there is no consent as a matter of law where the complainant believed that she was choosing between permitting herself to be touched sexually or risking being subject to the application of force.

The question is not whether the complainant would have preferred not to engage in the sexual activity, but whether she believed herself to have only two choices: to comply or to be harmed. If a complainant agrees to sexual activity solely because she honestly believes that she will otherwise suffer physical violence, the law deems an absence of consent, and the third component of the *actus reus* of sexual assault is established. The trier of fact has to find that the complainant did not want to be touched sexually and made her decision to permit or participate in sexual activity as a result of an honestly held fear. The complainant's fear need not be reasonable, nor must it be communicated to the accused in order for consent to be vitiated. While the plausibility of the alleged fear, and any overt expressions of it, are obviously relevant to assessing the credibility of the complainant's claim that she consented out of fear, the approach is subjective.

Section 265(3) identifies an additional set of circumstances in which the accused's conduct will be culpable. The trial judge only has to consult s. 265(3) in those cases where the complainant has actually chosen to participate in sexual activity, or her ambiguous conduct or submission has given rise to doubt as to the absence of consent. If, as in this case, the complainant's testimony establishes the absence of consent beyond a reasonable doubt, the *actus reus* analysis is complete, and the trial judge should have turned his attention to the accused's perception of the encounter and the question of whether the accused possessed the requisite *mens rea*.

. . . .

[L'HEUREUX-DUBÉ J.:]

Violence against women takes many forms: sexual assault is one of them. In Canada, one-half of all women are said to have experienced at least one incident of physical or sexual violence since the age of 16 (Statistics Canada, "The Violence Against Women Survey", *The Daily*, November 18, 1993). The statistics demonstrate that 99 percent of the offenders in sexual assault cases are men and 90 percent of the victims are women (*Gender Equality in the Canadian Justice System: Summary Document and Proposals for Action* (April 1992), at p. 13, also cited in *R. v. Osolin*, [1993] 4 S.C.R. 595, at p. 669).

Violence against women is as much a matter of equality as it is an offence against human dignity and a violation of human rights. As Cory J. wrote in *Osolin*, *supra*, at p. 669, sexual assault "is an assault upon human dignity and constitutes a denial of any concept of equality for women". These human rights are protected by ss. 7 and 15 of the *Canadian Charter of Rights and Freedoms* and their violation constitutes an offence under the assault provisions of s. 265 and under the more specific sexual assault provisions of ss. 271, 272 and 273 of the *Criminal Code*, R.S.C., 1985, c. C-46.

So pervasive is violence against women throughout the world that the international community adopted in December 18, 1979 (Res. 34/180), in addition to all other human rights instruments, the *Convention on the Elimination of All Forms of Discrimination against Women*, Can. T.S. 1982 No. 31, entered into force on September 3, 1981, to which Canada is a party, which has been described as "the definitive international legal instrument requiring respect for and observance of the human rights of women". (R. Cook, "Reservations to the Convention on the Elimination of All Forms of Discrimination Against Women" (1990), 30 *Va. J. Int'l L.* 643, at p. 643). Articles 1 and 2 of the Convention read:

ARTICLE I

For the purposes of the present Convention, the term "discrimination against women" shall mean any distinction, exclusion or restriction made on the basis of sex which has the effect or purpose of impairing or nullifying the recognition, enjoyment or exercise by women, irrespective of their marital status, on a basis of equality of men and women, of human rights and fundamental freedoms in the political, economic, social, cultural, civil or any other field.

ARTICLE II

States Parties condemn discrimination against women in all its forms, agree to pursue by all appropriate means and without delay a policy of eliminating discrimination against women and, to this end, undertake:

(a) To embody the principle of the equality of men and women in their national constitutions or other appropriate legislation if not yet incorporated therein and to ensure, through law and other appropriate means, the practical realization of this principle;
(b) *To adopt appropriate legislative and other measures*, including sanctions where appropriate, prohibiting all discrimination against women;
(c) To establish legal protection of the rights of women on an equal basis with men and to ensure through competent national tribunals and other public institutions the effective protection of women against any act of discrimination;
(d) To refrain from engaging in any act or practice of discrimination against women and to ensure that public authorities and institutions shall act in conformity with this obligation;
(e) To take all appropriate measures to eliminate discrimination against women by any person, organization or enterprise;
(f) *To take all appropriate measures, including legislation, to modify or abolish existing laws, regulations, customs and practices which constitute discrimination against women*;
(g) To repeal all national penal provisions which constitute discrimination against women. [Emphasis added.]

The Committee on the Elimination of Discrimination against Women, G.A. Res. 34/180, U.N. Doc. A/47/48 (1979), established under Article 17 of the Convention, adopted General Recommendation No. 19 (Eleventh session, 1992) on the interpretation of discrimination as it relates to violence against women:

> **6.** The Convention in article 1 defines discrimination against women. *The definition of discrimination includes* gender-based violence, that is, violence that is directed against a woman because she is a woman or that affects women disproportionately. It includes *acts that inflict physical, mental or sexual harm* or suffering, threats of such acts, coercion and other deprivations of liberty. Gender-based violence may breach specific provisions of the Convention, regardless of whether those provisions expressly mention violence.
>
> **24.** In light of these comments, the Committee on the Elimination of Discrimination against Women recommends:
>
> ...
>
> (b) States parties should ensure that laws against family violence and abuse, rape, *sexual assault and other gender-based violence give adequate protection to all women, and respect their integrity and dignity. Appropriate protective and support services should be provided for victims. Gender-sensitive training of judicial and law enforcement officers and other public officials is essential for the effective implementation of the Convention* ... [Emphasis added.]

On February 23, 1994, the U.N. General Assembly adopted the *Declaration on the Elimination of Violence against Women*, G.A. Res. 48/104, U.N. Doc. A/48/49 (1993). Although not a treaty binding states, it sets out a common international standard that U.N. members states are invited to follow. Article 4 of the Declaration provides:

> **ARTICLE 4**
>
> States should condemn violence against women and should not invoke any custom, tradition or religious consideration to avoid their obligations with respect to its elimination. States should pursue by all appropriate means and without delay a policy of eliminating violence against women and, to this end, should:
>
> ...
>
> (*i*) *Take measures to ensure that law enforcement officers and public officials responsible for implementing policies to prevent, investigate and punish violence against women receive training to sensitize them to the needs of women*;
>
> (*j*) *Adopt all appropriate measures*, especially in the field of education, to modify the social and cultural patterns of conduct of men and women and *to eliminate prejudices*, customary practices and all other practices *based on* the idea of the inferiority or superiority of either of the sexes and on *stereotyped roles for men and women*.... [Emphasis added.]

Our *Charter* is the primary vehicle through which international human rights achieve a domestic effect (see *Slaight Communications Inc. v. Davidson*, [1989] 1 S.C.R. 1038; *R. v. Keegstra*, [1990] 3 S.C.R. 697). In particular, s. 15 (the equality provision) and s. 7 (which guarantees the right to life, security and liberty of the person) embody the notion of respect of human dignity and integrity.

It is within that larger framework that, in 1983, Canada revamped the sexual assault provisions of the *Code* (S.C. 1980-81-82-83, c. 125), formerly ss. 143, 149 and 244 (R.S.C. 1970, c. C-34) which are now contained in the general assault provisions of s. 265. Together with the 1992 amendments of the *Code* (*An Act to amend the Criminal Code (sexual assault)*, S.C. 1992, c. 38), mainly ss. 273.1 and 273.2, they govern the issue of consent in the context of sexual assault. In the preamble to the 1992 Act, Parliament expressed its concern about the "prevalence of sexual assault against women and children" and stated its intention to "promote and help to ensure the full protection of the rights guaranteed under sections 7 and 15 of the *Canadian Charter of Rights and Freedoms*".

Fraser C.J., in her dissenting reasons in this case, has set out the legislative history of those provisions. In *R. v. Cuerrier*, [1998] 2 S.C.R. 371, Cory J. and I both noted the significant reform of sexual assault provisions undertaken by Parliament. (See C. Boyle, *Sexual Assault* (1984), at pp. 27–29.) I observed in *R. v. Park*, [1995] 2 S.C.R. 836, at para. 42, that:

> ... the primary concern animating and underlying the present offence of sexual assault is the belief that women have an inherent right to exercise full control over their own bodies, and to engage only in sexual activity that they wish to engage in. If this is the case, then our approach to consent must evolve accordingly, for it may be out of phase with that conceptualization of the law.

See also *R. v. Seaboyer*, [1991] 2 S.C.R. 577.

In the present case, the respondent was charged with sexual assault under s. 271 of the *Code*. The applicable notions of "assault" and "consent" are defined in ss. 265, 273.1 and 273.2 of the *Code*. ...

273.1(1) Subject to subsection (2) and subsection 265(3), "consent" means, for the purposes of sections 271, 272 and 273, the voluntary agreement of the complainant to engage in the sexual activity in question.

(2) No consent is obtained, for the purposes of sections 271, 272 and 273, where

(*a*) the agreement is expressed by the words or conduct of a person other than the complainant;

(*b*) the complainant is incapable of consenting to the activity;

(*c*) the accused induces the complainant to engage in the activity by abusing a position of trust, power or authority;

(*d*) the complainant expresses, by words or conduct, a lack of agreement to engage in the activity; or

(*e*) the complainant, having consented to engage in sexual activity, expresses, by words or conduct, a lack of agreement to continue to engage in the activity.

(3) Nothing in subsection (2) shall be construed as limiting the circumstances in which no consent is obtained.

. . . .

This case is not about consent, since none was given. It is about myths and stereotypes, which have been identified by many authors and succinctly described by D. Archard, *Sexual Consent* (1998), at p. 131:

> Myths of rape include the view that women fantasise about being rape victims; that women mean 'yes' even when they say 'no'; that any woman could successfully resist a rapist if she really wished to; that the sexually experienced do not suffer harms when raped (or at least suffer lesser harms than the sexually 'innocent'); that women often deserve to be raped on account of their conduct, dress, and demeanour; that rape by a stranger is worse than one by an acquaintance. Stereotypes of sexuality include the view of women as passive, disposed submissively to surrender to the sexual advances of active men, the view that sexual love consists in the 'possession' by a man of a woman, and that heterosexual sexual activity is paradigmatically penetrative coitus.

(For example see *Seaboyer*, *supra*, at p. 651, *per* L'Heureux-Dubé J.; M. Burt, "Rape Myths and Acquaintance Rape", in A. Parrot and L. Bechhofer, eds., *Acquaintance Rape: The Hidden Crime* (1991); N. Naffine, "Possession: Erotic Love in the Law of Rape" (1994), 57 *Mod. L. Rev.* 10; R. T. Andrias, "Rape Myths: A persistent problem in defining and prosecuting rape" (1992), 7 *Criminal Justice* 2; *Gender Equality in the Canadian Justice System: Summary Document and Proposals for Action*, *supra*; C. A. MacKinnon, *Toward a Feminist Theory of the State* (1989); E. A. Sheehy, "Canadian Judges and the Law of Rape: Should the *Charter* Insulate Bias?" (1989), 21 *Ottawa L. Rev.* 741.)

The trial judge believed the complainant and accepted her testimony that she was afraid and he acknowledged her unwillingness to engage in any sexual activity. In addition, there is no doubt that the respondent was aware that the complainant was afraid since he told her repeatedly not to be afraid. The complainant clearly articulated her absence of consent: she said no. Not only did the accused not stop, but after a brief pause, as Fraser C.J. puts it, he went on to an "increased level of sexual activity" to which twice the complainant said no. What could be clearer?

The trial judge gave no legal effect to his conclusion that the complainant submitted to sexual activity out of fear that the accused would apply force to her. Section 265(3)(*b*) states that no consent is obtained where the complainant submits by reason of threats or fear of the application of force. Therefore, s. 265(3)(*b*) applies and operates to further establish the lack of consent: see *Cuerrier*, *supra*.

I agree with Major J. that the application of s. 265(3) requires an entirely subjective test. In my opinion, as irrational as a complainant's motive might be, if she subjectively felt fear, it must lead to a legal finding of absence of consent. Accordingly, I agree with Fraser C.J. that any objective factor should be considered under the defence of honest but mistaken belief.

However, in my view, Major J. unduly restricts the application of s. 265(3) to instances where the complainant chooses "to participate in, or ostensibly consent to, the touching in question" (at para. 38; see also para. 36). Section 265(3) applies to cases where the "complainant *submits* or *does not resist*" (emphasis added) by reason of the application of force, threats or fear of the application of force, fraud or the exercise of authority. Therefore, that section should also apply to cases where the complainant is silent or passive in response to such situations.

In the circumstances of this case, it is difficult to understand how the question of implied consent even arose. Although he found the complainant credible, and accepted her evidence that she said "no" on three occasions and was afraid, the trial judge nonetheless did not take "no" to mean that the complainant did not consent. Rather, he concluded that she implicitly consented and that the Crown had failed to prove lack of consent. This was a fundamental error....

This error does not derive from the findings of fact but from mythical assumptions that when a woman says "no" she is really saying "yes", "try again", or "persuade me". To paraphrase Fraser C.J. at p. 263, it denies women's sexual autonomy and implies that women are "walking around this country in a state of constant consent to sexual activity".

In the Court of Appeal, McClung J.A. compounded the error made by the trial judge. At the outset of his opinion, he stated at p. 245 that "it must be pointed out that the complainant did not present herself to Ewanchuk or enter his trailer in a bonnet and crinolines". He noted, at pp. 245–46, that "she was the mother of a six-month-old baby and that, along with her boyfriend, she shared an apartment with another couple".

Even though McClung J.A. asserted that he had no intention of denigrating the complainant, one might wonder why he felt necessary to point out these aspects of the trial record. Could it be to express that the complainant is not a virgin? Or that she is a person of questionable moral character because she is not married and lives with her boyfriend and another couple? These comments made by an appellate judge help reinforce the myth that under such circumstances, either the complainant is less worthy of belief, she invited the sexual assault, or her sexual experience signals probable consent to further sexual activity. Based on those attributed assumptions, the implication is that if the complainant articulates her lack of consent by saying "no", she really does not mean it and even if she does, her refusal cannot be taken as seriously as if she were a girl of "good" moral character. "Inviting" sexual assault, according to those myths, lessens the guilt of the accused as Archard, *supra*, notes at p. 139:

> ... the more that a person contributes by her behaviour or negligence to bringing about the circumstances in which she is a victim of a crime, the less responsible is the criminal for the crime he commits. A crime is no less unwelcome or serious in its effects, [nor] need it be any the less deliberate or malicious in its commission, for occurring in circumstances which the victim helped to realise. Yet judges who spoke of women 'inviting' or 'provoking' a rape would go on to cite such contributory behaviour as a reason for regarding the rape as less grave or the rapist as less culpable. It adds judicial insult to criminal injury to be told that one is the part author of a crime one did not seek and which in consequence is supposed to be a lesser one.

McClung J.A. writes, at p. 247:

> There is no room to suggest that Ewanchuk knew, yet disregarded, her underlying state of mind as he furthered his *romantic intentions*. He was not aware of her true state of mind. Indeed, his ignorance about that was what she wanted. The facts, set forth by the trial judge, provide support for the overriding trial finding, couched in terms of consent by implication, that the accused had no proven preparedness to assault the complainant to get what he wanted. [Emphasis added.]

On the contrary, both the fact that Ewanchuk was aware of the complainant's state of mind, as he did indeed stop each time she expressly stated "no", and the trial judge's findings reinforce the obvious conclusion that the accused knew there was no consent. These were two strangers, a young 17-year-old woman attracted by a job offer who found herself trapped in a trailer and a man approximately twice her age and size. This is hardly a scenario one would characterize as reflective of "romantic intentions". It was nothing more than an effort by Ewanchuk to engage the complainant sexually, not romantically.

The expressions used by McClung J.A. to describe the accused's sexual assault, such as "clumsy passes" (p. 246) or "would hardly raise Ewanchuk's stature in the pantheon of chivalric behaviour" (p. 248), are plainly inappropriate in that context as they minimize the importance of the accused's conduct and the reality of sexual aggression against women.

McClung J.A. also concluded that "the sum of the evidence indicates that Ewanchuk's advances to the complainant were far less criminal than hormonal" (p. 250) having found earlier that "every advance he made to her stopped when she spoke against it" and that "[t]here was no evidence of an assault or even its threat" (p. 249). According to this analysis, a man would be free from criminal responsibility for having non-consensual sexual activity whenever he cannot control his hormonal urges. Furthermore, the fact that the accused ignored the complainant's verbal objections to any sexual activity and persisted in escalated sexual contact, grinding his pelvis against hers repeatedly, is more evidence than needed to determine that there was an assault.

Finally, McClung J.A. made this point: "In a less litigious age going too far in the boyfriend's car was better dealt with on site — a well-chosen expletive, a slap in the face or, if necessary, a well-directed knee" (p. 250). According to this stereotype, women should use physical force, not resort to courts to "deal with" sexual assaults and it is not the perpetrator's responsibility to ascertain consent, as required by s. 273.2(*b*), but the women's not only to express an unequivocal "no", but also to fight her way out of such a situation. In that sense, Susan Estrich has noted that "rape is most assuredly not the only crime in which consent is a defense; but it is the only crime that has required the victim to resist physically in order to establish nonconsent" ("Rape" (1986), 95 *Yale L.J.* 1087, at p. 1090).

Cory J. referred to the inappropriate use of rape myths by courts in *Osolin*, *supra*, at p. 670:

> A number of rape myths have in the past improperly formed the background for considering evidentiary issues in sexual assault trials. These include the false concepts that: women cannot be raped against their will; only "bad girls" are raped; anyone not clearly of "good character" is more likely to have consented.

In *Seaboyer*, *supra*, I alluded to this issue....

This case has not dispelled any of the fears I expressed in *Seaboyer*, *supra*, about the use of myths and stereotypes in dealing with sexual assault complaints (see also Bertha Wilson, "Will Women Judges Really Make a Difference?" (1990), 28 *Osgoode Hall L.J.* 507). Complainants should be able to rely on a system free from myths and stereotypes, and on a judiciary whose impartiality is not compromised by these biased assumptions. The *Code* was amended in 1983 and in 1992 to eradicate reliance on those assumptions; they should not be permitted to resurface through the stereotypes reflected in the reasons of the majority of the Court of Appeal. It is part of the role of this Court to denounce this kind of language, unfortunately still used today, which not only perpetuates archaic myths and stereotypes about the nature of sexual assaults but also ignores the law.

In "The Standard of Social Justice as a Research Process" (1997), 38 *Can. Psychology* 91, K.E. Renner, C. Alksnis and L. Park make a strong indictment of the current criminal justice process, at p. 100:

> The more general indictment of the current criminal justice process is that the law and legal doctrines concerning sexual assault have acted as the principle [*sic*] systemic mechanisms for invalidating the experiences of women and children. Given this state of affairs, the traditional view of the legal system as neutral, objective and gender-blind is not defensible. Since the system is ineffective in protecting the rights of women and children, it is necessary to re-examine the existing doctrines which reflect the cultural and social limitations that have preserved dominant male interests at the expense of women and children. [Emphasis added.]

This being said, turning to the facts of the present case, I agree with Major J. that the findings necessary to support a verdict of guilty on the charge of sexual assault have been made. ...

[McLACHLIN J.:]

I agree with the reasons of Justice Major. I also agree with Justice L'Heureux-Dubé that stereotypical assumptions lie at the heart of what went wrong in this case. The specious defence of implied consent (consent implied by law), as applied in this case, rests on the assumption that unless a woman protests or resists, she should be "deemed" to consent (see L'Heureux-Dubé J.). On appeal, the idea also surfaced that if a woman is not modestly dressed, she is deemed to consent. Such stereotypical assumptions find their roots in many cultures, including our own. They no longer, however, find a place in Canadian law.

I join my colleagues in rejecting them.

Appeal allowed.

■

The *mens rea* analysis of both the majority and the concurring judgments is reproduced below, under **Mistake of Fact**.

Justice McClung wrote a very intemperate letter to the press denouncing Justice L'Heureux-Dubé's judgment, and making inappropriate and personal remarks about her. For this he was reprimanded by the Canadian Judicial Council. For articles that discuss the backlash that was unleashed after *Ewanchuk* see: Hester Lessard, "Farce or Tragedy? Judicial Backlash and Justice McClung" (1999) 10 *Constitutional Forum* 65; Joanne Wright, "Consent and Sexual Violence in Canadian Public Discourse: Reflections on Ewanchuk" (2001) 16 C.J.L.J. 173; and Constance Backhouse, "The Chilly Climate for Women Judges: Reflections on the Backlash from the *Ewanchuk* Case" (2003) 15 C.J.W.L. 167.

Now consider the role of consent in the prosecution of assaults that occur in sports contests. What different issues and sources of information need to be considered to develop sound criminal law doctrine?

R. v. Cey†

[GERWING J.A.:]

The Crown appeals the acquittal of the accused by a Provincial Court judge on a charge of assault causing bodily harm contrary to s. 245.1(1)(b) of the *Code*. The incident which gave rise to the charge occurred in the course of a hockey game. The hockey game was between two teams in the Wild Goose Hockey League, which is composed of amateur players of the average age of 24 to 28. The league was governed by the rules of the Canadian Amateur Hockey Association.

The accused in the course of the game checked an opposing player. The incident was described by the referee, whose evidence was accepted by the trial judge, as follows:

A. My view was — total view of the whole situation. I saw the exact incident that happened. Perry was playing the puck, he had his back to the boards, approximately four feet away, three feet away from the boards. Roger came in from in front of the crease area, which is two feet past the goal line and held his stick out and checked him approximately, in the neck area. He did not make a jabbing motion, it was just he held his stick out and hit him.
Q. Let's take it back now.
A. Okay.
Q. You testified that Mr. Kingwell had his back to the boards.
A. Yes.
Q. So, he was —
A. Or, sorry, his face to the boards, his back to Roger coming in.

At the time, the victim was facing the boards attempting to retrieve the puck. His face was pushed into the boards and he suffered injuries to his mouth and nose. He had to be carried from the ice and was found at the hospital to be suffering from a concussion and a whiplash. He was in hospital for approximately three days. The accused received from the referee a five-minute penalty for cross-checking.

The complainant, although saying he had never been hit so severely before said, in examination-in-chief:

Q. If I was to ask you — or tell you that it was a fair chance that in the course of a hockey game you were going to suffer these injuries that you did sustain November 27th, would you continue to play hockey?
A. Yeah.

It is difficult to ascertain the precise ratio of the oral judgment of the Provincial Court. Though he did not expressly say so, it may be assumed the trial judge was satisfied the Crown had made out its case in relation to three of the four elements of the offence, namely that the accused had (i) intentionally (ii) applied force to the victim, thereby (iii) causing the victim bodily harm. All that remained then was the issue of consent. The trial judge appears to have addressed this issue from the perspective, first, of the accused and his intentions and, thence, from the point of view of the victim and the scope of his implied consent, having regard for the standards and rules of play.

As for the first, the remarks of the trial judge make it clear he was not satisfied the accused had intended (a) to cause injury: "It was not a deliberate attempt to injure"; or (b) to apply any greater force to the victim than was customary in the game: "There was certainly no intention on the part of Cey to do anything else than what has really been the standard of play in hockey for a long time."

As for the consent of the victim, the trial judge appears to have taken the man's expressed willingness to continue to play the game, despite the injury, as having amounted to a consent to the bodily contact which had occurred: "Would you, having suf-

† (1989), 48 C.C.C. (3d) 480 (Sask. C.A.).

fered the kind of injuries you did, continue playing hockey? The answer was yes. That's your consent. He's accepted this basic standard of play."

Having made these findings the trial judge concluded by saying:

> Well, the one other area that I wanted to mention was the CAHA rules and the application of those. We have a check that was illegal under the provisions of the CAHA rules, but it's acceptable, as a standard of play in what happens in the CAHA, say, if you check this way, this is what can happen to you. It will happen to you. It's a major and a game misconduct. That is a long cry, a far cry from saying it bears penal consequences as an infraction of the *Criminal Code of Canada*. If you make a criminal out of a person who has committed an offence in a hockey game that says he shall get a five minute major and a game misconduct, if you make a criminal out of that person and of course, maybe you can if you can find that the offence committed was one which was intended deliberately to harm the other person. To cause him bodily harm, to, in the phrase used by the Defence counsel, stop his career in hockey, cut it off. Maybe, I think that's an appropriate area where you say to the person, what you did is beyond the limits acceptable in hockey. Beyond the type of situation where all you get is a game misconduct and a five major. Where it is clearly intended that there shall be damage to the other person. But, I have not been able to come to that conclusion here and I have not been able to come to that conclusion based on the evidence given by the referee in charge of the game, by a Rosetown fan who was here and a Wilke fan who was here. So, I think that under the circumstances I don't think we can make a criminal out of this hockey player and I'm not going to and I'm going to dismiss the charge against him.

The Crown appeals suggesting that the learned judge misdirected himself. It is my view that he did in fact misdirect himself and that a new trial should be ordered.

. . . .

In this case it appears clear beyond peradventure that force was intentionally applied to the victim, causing him bodily harm. That being so, the sole remaining issue was whether the Crown had negatived consent. It might be noted that the accused did not advance the defence contemplated by s. 244(4), which is to say he did not allege that he had an honest belief in the victim having consented to the conduct that is the subject-matter of the charge. Instead he relied upon the Crown's failure to negative consent as required by s. 244(1).

Consent to the application of force may be actual or implied, and in any event its scope is limited both by circumstance ... and by law....

Intentional bodily contact in the context of an organized sporting situation requires that implied consent be considered. Decisions in this jurisdiction starting with *R. v. Langton* (unreported, October 2, 1974, Saskatchewan Court of Appeal) have contemplated that assaults in connection with hockey games may be such as to be beyond the scope of consent and hence an offence under the *Code*.

Many convictions for hockey violence such as *R. v. Gray* (1981), 24 C.R. (3d) 108, [1981] 6 W.W.R. 654 (Sask. Prov. Ct.); *R. v. Mayer* (1985), 41 Man. R. (2d) 73 (Man. Prov. Ct.); *R. v. Henderson*, [1976] 5 W.W.R. 119 (B.C. Co. Ct.), and *R. v. Watson* (1975), 26 C.C.C. (2d) 150 (Ont. Prov. Ct.), relate to incidents which occurred after play had been halted, but it is clear from other cases such as *R. v. Maki* (1970), 1 C.C.C. (2d) 333, 14 D.L.R. (3d) 164, [1970] 3 O.R. 780 (Ont. Prov. Ct.), and *R. v. Maloney* (1976), 28 C.C.C. (2d) 323 (Ont. G.S.P.), that the courts have considered assaults during the course of the game. Acquittals were entered in these cases but not expressly for that reason.

It is clear that in agreeing to play the game a hockey player consents to some forms of intentional bodily contact and to the risk of injury therefrom. Those forms sanctioned by the rules are the clearest example. Other forms, denounced by the rules but falling within the accepted standards by which the game is played, may also come within the scope of the consent.

It is equally clear that there are some actions which can take place in the course of a sporting conflict that are so violent it would be perverse to find that anyone taking part in a sporting activity had impliedly consented to subject himself to them. As the court said in *R. v. Maki*, *supra*, at p. 336:

> Thus all players, when they step onto a playing field or ice surface, assume certain risks and hazards of the sport, and in most cases the defence of consent as set out in s. 230 [now s. 244] of the *Criminal Code* would be applicable. But as stated above, there is a question of degree involved and no athlete should be presumed to accept malicious, unprovoked or overly violent attack. Bastin, J., states it this way in *Agar v. Canning* (1965), 54 W.W.R. 302 at p. 304, affirmed 55 W.W.R. 384 [Man. C.A.]:
>
>> But injuries inflicted in circumstances which show a definite resolve to cause serious injury to another, even when there is provocation and in

the heat of the game, should not fall within the scope of the implied consent.

. . . .

[The court discussed the Canadian and British authorities.]

While the *Jobidon* case dealt with a consensual fight outside a bar and while the English reference case referred to activity outside of sport, I see no reason in principle why the consent, express or implied, to assault in the context of a sporting event should not be considered similarly. That is in sporting events as well the mere fact that a type of assault occurs with some frequency does not necessarily mean that it is not of such a severe nature that consent thereto is precluded. In a sport such as hockey, however, I believe the test may be more limited than in the *Attorney General's Reference* case — that is, I think the alternate reference to "caused" to be inappropriate where actions to which there is implied consent may in extraordinary circumstances cause harm.

Thus, in summary, in my view, the Provincial Court judge ought to have directed himself to the question of whether there was express or implied consent to this type of contact and whether the contact was of such a nature that in any event no true consent could be given. Accordingly, the acquittal is set aside and the matter is returned to the Provincial Court for a new trial.

Appeal allowed; new trial ordered.

[Cameron J.A. concurred with Gerwing J.A. The dissenting judgment of Wakeling J.A. has been omitted.]

R. v. Leclerc†

[LACOURCIÈRE J.A.:]

This is an appeal by the Attorney-General of Ontario, pursuant to s. 676(1)(a) of the *Criminal Code*, against the acquittal of the respondent by a district court judge on a charge of aggravated assault, alleged to have occurred during a hockey game. The question of law raised by the appellant is whether the learned trial judge erred in his interpretation of the *mens rea* requirement of the offence charged by placing an unduly onerous burden on the prosecution, which had the effect of requiring proof of a specific intent to cause serious injury, and whether this self-misdirection had the further effect of placing an incorrect and increased burden on the Crown as to the circumstances required to be proved in order to negative implied consent.

Overview of the Facts

The aggravated assault was alleged to have taken place in the course of a semi-final play-off hockey game in the Lanark Municipal Arena between contending teams in an industrial league, The Lanark Sportsmen's Recreational League. Under C.A.H.A. rules no bodily contact is allowed. On March 3, 1989, a play-off game was held to determine the finalist team for the league championship. During the third period the respondent, who played in the forward position for the Calabogie team, pursued the complainant, James R. Conboy, a defenceman for Joe's Lake, the opposing team, who was attempting to retrieve the puck which had been shot into his own end. There was a collision on the boards as the respondent hit the complainant in the back with his hockey stick. The referee immediately blew his whistle and called a "match penalty" against the respondent for a deliberate attempt to injure. The game was halted. It was subsequently determined that the complainant had suffered a dislocation of a portion of the cervical spine: he was permanently paralyzed from the neck down.

The complainant and the Crown witnesses contended that the complainant was struck by the respondent with a cross-check to the back of his neck. The referee described the cross-check as "deliberate" and "vicious", with intent to injure. The respondent testified that he was skating fast after the puck and merely gave the complainant a push or a shove from behind to move him off the puck, which

† (1991), 67 C.C.C. (3d) 563 (Ont. C.A.).

caused the latter to lose his balance and crash head first into the boards.

The learned trial judge reserved judgment after a four-day trial, ordered a transcript of the evidence, and later delivered carefully written reasons. I quote his summary of what he described as the undisputed facts:

> Shortly after the 14-minute mark of the third period the Calabogie team dumped or snapped the puck into the Joe's Lake end. As the puck slid into the north west corner of the rink ultimately to a point very near the west end boards a few feet north of the Joe's Lake net, Jim Conboy, the Joe's Lake left defenceman pivoted from a backward skating motion to skate in pursuit. He was skating in a westerly direction toward a point just north of his own net.
>
> At approximately the same time Steven Leclerc had broken out of a pack of players outside the Joe's Lake blue line and skating at a high rate of speed was angling from the centre of the ice surface to the likely resting place of the puck just north of the Joe's Lake net. So fast was Leclerc moving that he gained some 20 to 25 feet in the approximately 75 feet he traversed as both players converged on the puck.
>
> As Conboy closed on the puck, Clifford, the goal tender, shouted "Man On!" and Conboy shifted to his right prior to his attempt to take possession and swing to his left behind the net. At that moment Leclerc's gloves and stick came in contact with Conboy's upper back, Conboy lost his balance and tumbled head first into the end boards, the top of his helmet violently contacting same a foot or two above the ice surface. His body recoiled from the boards in a twisted condition, semi-prone upon the ice. The violent contact with the end boards caused a fracture dislocation of Conboy's fourth and fifth cervical vertebrae provoking permanent paralysis.
>
> Immediately upon the contact between Leclerc and Conboy the referee, Charles Harrison, blew his whistle and assessed Leclerc a five minute match penalty for deliberate attempt to injure. Within moments he terminated the game to permit appropriate care to be given to the badly injured Conboy who remained conscious on the ice.

The learned trial judge described the disputed facts as relating to the manner, degree and the location of the force applied by the respondent's glove and stick to the upper region of the complainant's back. He then meticulously analyzed the evidence of the referee, who characterized the cross-check as deliberate and vicious, and contrasted it to that of the linesman whose evidence was that the cross-check was not vicious but had the effect of knocking the complainant off balance, face first into the boards.

The learned trial judge clearly rejected the evidence of the referee. He did not accept the respondent's version entirely, but accepted the evidence of a witness whose opinion was that the respondent shoved the complainant in the back in order to push him off and avoid more violent contact in such close proximity to the end boards. He concluded that, even in the non-contact industrial league in which the respondent and the complainant played, "in practice all players expected and accepted the risks of contact inherent in the spirited play this level of hockey traditionally produced".

he said there was an expected & accepted level

The Intent for Aggravated Assault

... The appellant does not challenge the learned trial judge's comment to the effect that the prosecution was required to establish beyond a reasonable doubt that the application of force by the respondent was without the implied consent of the complainant, and that it was deliberate and intentional in law. However, the impugned self-instruction is as follows:

> The sole issue before this court is whether the conduct of the defendant, Leclerc, in the course of play in these circumstances constituted such a malicious, egregious, vicious breach of the accepted norm as to require the sanction of the criminal law. To paraphrase the judicial pronouncement in *Agar v. Canning*, hereinbefore alluded to — Did it exhibit or display a definite resolve to cause serious injury to another?
>
> Unless this court is convinced to a moral certainty on the evidence that the response to that question must be in the affirmative, the prosecution has not met the onus of proof. And to be so convinced this court must find that that force be both of an egregious vicious nature and be intentionally applied.

The decision of *Agar v. Canning* (1965), 54 W.W.R. 302, is discussed later in these reasons.

Counsel for the appellant argued that, in this passage, the learned trial judge interpreted the *mens rea* element of the offence of aggravated assault as one of specific intent requiring, in effect, that the Crown establish that the respondent intended to wound, maim, disfigure or endanger the life of the complainant. This would be the effect of requiring the prosecution to prove "a definite resolve to cause serious injury to another".

The case-law interpreting the sections quoted makes it clear that the essential intent required for an assault, as defined, remains the same for all forms of assault, including aggravated assault. Parliament intended that the severity of the punishment should increase to reflect the more serious consequences of the assault. It never intended that, on an indictment charging "aggravated assault", the prosecution would be required to prove that the accused intended to wound, maim or disfigure the complainant or endanger his life: see *R. v. Callanan*, unreported March 6, 1985 (Ont. C.A.), leave to appeal to S.C.C. dismissed June 26, 1985....

To the extent, therefore, that the impugned wording of the self-direction quoted elevated the *mens rea* requirement to one of specific intent, it constituted an error in law. In order to determine whether the error of law influenced the findings of fact, it is necessary to examine the final conclusion of the learned trial judge:

> I hold that the push, shove or cross check was part of an instinctive reflex reaction executed by Leclerc while moving at a high rate of speed in a belated attempt to avoid more dreaded contact in such close proximity to the west end boards. It indeed violated the rules of the game but I find it lacked malicious design in that its object was not to inflict bodily harm but to minimize the prospect thereof. On all the testimony I hold it constituted an ill-fated attempt by Leclerc to extricate himself from risk self-imposed by his intemperate zeal. It bore tragic consequences but these were neither contemplated [nor] intended by him.

This passage suggests that the learned trial judge required the Crown to prove that the object of the respondent's push, shove or cross-check was to inflict bodily harm on the complainant, and that the Crown had to prove that the tragic consequences thereof were either intended or contemplated. Later, in rejecting the prosecution's contention that the conduct of the accused met the standard required for a conviction on a charge of criminal assault in the course of a hockey game, the trial judge repeated what he regarded as an essential ingredient of the charge, namely "a definite resolve to cause serious injury". This is an error of law with respect to the required *mens rea* to support a charge of aggravated assault: this court will, in the dispositive part of the judgment, consider its effect on the verdict of acquittal.

The Implied Consent Issue

As previously mentioned, the learned trial judge found that the complainant, having agreed to compete in this particular hockey league, impliedly consented to those assaults which are inherent and reasonably incidental to the normal playing of the game at this level.

Counsel for the respondent concedes that the *mens rea* for aggravated assault is in accordance with the appellant's submission and that the impugned self-direction, taken in isolation, constitutes an error. He submits, however, that the perceived error of law in the impugned passage results from the blending of the two concepts, the intentional application of force combined with the implied consent to risk inherent in the context of a hockey game. Thus, it is argued that, having regard to the earlier correct description of the requirement for assault, and to the findings of fact, no substantial wrong has occurred.

The erroneous self-direction on the question of intent was said by the learned trial judge to be a paraphrase of the judicial pronouncement in *Agar v. Canning*, *supra*. In that case, the plaintiff, a hockey player, brought an action against a member of the opposing team for damages arising from injuries sustained in a hockey game. The plaintiff had "hooked" the defendant with his stick and, in so doing, struck the defendant on the back of the neck. In retaliation therefor, the defendant turned and struck the plaintiff with the blade of his hockey stick between his nose and right eye.

The trial judge found that the game of hockey necessarily involves violent bodily contact and blows, and that persons who engage in this sport must be assumed to assume the risk of accidental harm. In other words, Bastin J. took the position that, in the normal course of a hockey match, injuries to players occur, and are not actionable, even where such injuries are a result of the "frequent infractions of the rules". He then went on to say, at p. 304:

> The conduct of a player in the heat of the game is instinctive and unpremeditated and should not be judged by standards suited to polite social intercourse.
>
> But a little reflection will establish that some limit must be placed on a player's immunity from liability. Each case must be decided on its own facts so it is difficult, if not impossible, to decide how the line is to be drawn in every circumstance. But injuries inflicted in circumstances which show a definite resolve to cause serious injury to another, even where there is provocation and in the heat of the game, should not fall within the scope of implied consent.

Bastin J., however, found that the conduct of the defendant, in striking the plaintiff in the face with his stick, went beyond the limit marking exemption from liability. In other words, the defendant's act was not the kind of "bodily contact" contemplated or impliedly consented to by the plaintiff as a participant in the hockey match.

The expression "definite resolve to cause serious injury to another", taken from the quoted language of Bastin J., was intended to show the kind of assault which falls outside the scope of "implied consent" in the context of a civil action. In my opinion, it was wrong to import that test in the present case and to elevate it to be a necessary element in considering a charge of aggravated assault causing injuries in the course of a non-contact hockey game.

. . . .

The problem that the courts face with respect to this issue is the scope of implied consent — that is, at what point does conduct in sporting activity fall outside the standards which players impliedly agree to as an acceptable part of the game? Gerwing J.A., writing for the majority, stated at p. 490:

> Ordinarily consent, being a state of mind, is a wholly subjective matter to be determined accordingly, but when it comes to implied consent in the context of a team sport such as hockey, there cannot be as many different consents as there are players on the ice, and so the scope of the implied consent, having to be uniform, must be determined by reference to objective criteria.

The conclusion that the courts should endeavour to employ objective criteria in the analysis of whether a player could be said to have impliedly consented to the conduct which is the subject of the charge does not mean, however, that such criteria should be rigidly applied. Instead, regard must be had to the whole of the conditions under which the game is played. The criteria identified by the Saskatchewan Court of Appeal [in *Cey*], which may be referred to so as to determine the scope of implied consent, include the setting of the game, the league, the age of the players, the conditions under which the game is played, the extent of the force employed, the degree of risk of injury and the probabilities of serious harm.

. . . .

In the result, the majority concluded that some forms of contact in a sports match cannot be the subject of "true consent". Wakeling J.A., dissenting, was of the view that most bodily contact is consented to merely by a decision to participate in a hockey game, except conduct intended to do bodily harm or conduct motivated by retaliation. He would have dismissed the appeal on the basis that the findings of fact of the learned trial judge negatived such exceptions.

In her reasons, Gerwing J.A. said, as well, at p. 493 that "the mere fact that a type of assault occurs with some frequency does not necessarily mean that it is not of such a severe nature that consent thereto is precluded". This is in contrast to what was said by Glanville Williams in his article Consent and Public Policy, [1962] Crim. L.R. 74 and 154. Referring to consent in "games like football" — and I would assume this would include hockey — he said at pp. 80–1:

> Games like football are not the same as fights or bouts, but they are similar in involving the use of force between the players in accordance with the rules. In these games, the consent by the players to the use of moderate force is clearly valid, and the players are even deemed to consent to an application of force that is in breach of the rules of the game, if it is the sort of thing that may be expected to happen during the game.

However, it is clear, in the context, that the learned author did not intend, in this passage, to suggest that there should be immunity from criminal liability on the basis of implied consent in cases of retaliatory conduct, conduct intended to do bodily harm or force creating a distinct probability of serious harm.

I agree with the majority judgment in *R. v. Cey*. It was quoted and applied by Corbett D.C.J. in *R. v. Ciccarelli* (1989), 54 C.C.C. (3d) 121, 9 W.C.B. (2d) 402 (Ont. Dist. Ct.), where the scope of implied consent in a team sport such as hockey is helpfully discussed. The weight of judicial authority appears to be that a player, by participating in a sport such as hockey, impliedly consents to some bodily contact necessarily incidental to the game, but not to overly violent attacks, all of which should be determined according to objective criteria: see also *R. v. Watson* (1975), 26 C.C.C. (2d) 150 (Ont. Prov. Ct.), and *R. v. Maloney* (1976), 28 C.C.C. (2d) 323 (Ont. Dist. Ct.), which were decided before *R. v. Cey*. Conduct which evinces a deliberate purpose to inflict injury will generally be held to be outside of the immunity provided by the scope of implied consent in a sports arena. This is not to be taken to mean, as the learned trial judge apparently did in the case under appeal, that in order to negative implied consent, the prosecution has the burden of proving a deliberate purpose or resolve to inflict injury.

In the present case, the Crown argued forcibly that the scope of implied consent ought to be narrowed because the alleged assault occurred in the course of a recreational industrial game in which bodily contact was not permitted by the rules, and not in a professional contact league game. However, as found by the trial judge, the ideal of non-contact rules was frequently breached in a spirited game where bumps and other contacts resulted in many penalties. While the "no contact" rule is relevant in determining the scope of implied consent, it is not by itself determinative of the issue.

In the case under appeal the ultimate question on the issue of implied consent, as in *R. v. Cey*, *supra*, is whether the cross-checking or push of the complainant across the neck in close proximity to the boards was so inherently dangerous as to be excluded from the implied consent. The question asked by the trial judge was whether the respondent's conduct exhibited or displayed a definite resolve to cause serious injury to another. In my opinion, the question of implied consent, which the Crown was required to negative, was not addressed properly in the court below. This error, together with the confusion in dealing with the *mens rea* requirement of aggravated assault, had the result of placing an inappropriate burden on the prosecution.

Disposition

The error in law does not automatically require the direction of a new trial. It becomes necessary to consider the effect of the self-misdirection in the light of the findings of fact which the learned trial judge made and which are supported by the evidence. Paraphrasing his view, the push, shove or cross-check resulted directly from the respondent's loss of balance and was part of the respondent's "instinctive reflex reaction", which had the object of minimizing the risk of bodily harm created by his high speed in close proximity to the boards. He properly rejected the alternative Crown theory that the force of the blow to the neck of the victim was sufficient to establish criminal conduct.

The Supreme Court of Canada has held in *R. v. Vezeau* (1976), 28 C.C.C. (2d) 81, 66 D.L.R. (3d) 418, [1977] 2 S.C.R. 277, and in *R. v. Morin* (1988), 44 C.C.C. (3d) 193 at p. 221, [1988] 2 S.C.R. 345, 66 C.R. (3d) 1, that where the Attorney-General appeals against an acquittal, the onus is on the Crown to satisfy an appellate court that the verdict would not necessarily have been the same had the misdirection not occurred. Having regard to the clear findings of fact made by the trial judge as to the circumstances of that particular hockey game, the Crown has not satisfied me that the verdict of acquittal would not necessarily have been the same if there had been no self-misdirection in law.

I would accordingly dismiss the Attorney-General's appeal against the acquittal.

Appeal dismissed.

In *R. v. McSorley*, [2000] B.C.J. No. 1993 (Prov. Ct.), the judge heard evidence on the unwritten code of conduct regarding slashing and fighting in NHL hockey, as well as the exercise of discretion by linemen and referees in calling penalties. In February 2000 the Canucks were leading the Bruins 4–0 in a game leading to the play-offs. With three seconds remaining and after a multitude of altercations, Marty McSorley slashed Donald Brashear in the head. According to McSorley, he intended to hit Brashear high in the body, shoulder, upper arm area; the trial judge found that he did this in order to start a fight and to lift his team's spirits. Brashear suffered a grand mal seizure and a grade three concussion. He was unable to engage in physical activity for the next month. Given that McSorley's role on the team was "policeman", and given that he was sent out to start a fight, should he have been convicted? Is this decision consistent with *Cey* and *Leclerc*? McSorley was sentenced to a conditional discharge of 18 months: [2000] B.C.J. No. 1994 (Prov. Ct.).

B. CORRECTION

Read s. 43 of the *Criminal Code* before you read the *Ogg-Moss* case. Is it surprising that this was the first occasion on which the Supreme Court considered the parameters of this defence?

Ogg-Moss v. R.†

[DICKSON J.:]

This appeal raises the issue of whether a Mental Retardation Counsellor (M.R.C.) who uses physical force on a mentally retarded adult under his supervision has the benefit of s. 43 of the *Criminal Code*, R.S.C. 1970, c. C-34....

The question of the applicability of s. 43 is basically one of statutory construction but inevitably it puts into issue two sensitive topics, namely, the status and rights of mentally retarded persons, and the limits on the disciplinary prerogatives of persons in authority over those in their charge. Despite this overlay of social concerns it is important to remember that the case before this Court is a criminal one and its resolution must be based on legal principles.

I. BACKGROUND AND FACTS

Mr. Ogg-Moss was charged with assaulting one Kent Henderson, a twenty-one year old developmentally handicapped resident of the Rideau Regional Centre, located in Smith Falls, Ontario. Mr. Ogg-Moss was employed at the Regional Centre as an M.R.C. He argues that by virtue of this position, his relationship with Mr. Henderson was that of "a person standing in the place of a parent" or of a "schoolteacher" using reasonable force to "correct" a "child" or "pupil" in his charge. He claims therefore the protection of s. 43.

Mental Retardation Counsellors are the "front-line direct care staff" in provincial facilities for the developmentally handicapped. Their duties are set out in Regulations and Directives made pursuant to the *Developmental Services Act*, R.S.O. 1980, c. 118. These duties include providing daily care for the residents of such facilities and implementing programs designed and supervised by physicians, psychologists and other more senior professional personnel.

On the day in question Mr. Ogg-Moss was supervising a group of residents in a low grade ward. The residents, including Mr. Henderson, were seated at tables awaiting lunch. Mr. Henderson was described in evidence at trial as "very low functioning" and "profoundly retarded" with an I.Q. of less than 20. He was incapable of speech and, as a result of being a "head-banger" suffered from a large haematoma on his forehead. In an apparent attempt to attract Mr. Ogg-Moss's attention, Mr. Henderson spilled his milk on the table before him, whereupon Mr. Ogg-Moss shouted "no" and struck Mr. Henderson five times on the forehead with a large metal spoon for the purpose, according to his later testimony, "of punishing him for what he did".

The incident was reported by a summer student at the Rideau Regional Centre. It was her testimony that Mr. Henderson did not cry out as a result of being struck but appeared "quite startled". She felt that had she been hit with that force she would have cried. In his evidence, in response to a question as to Mr. Henderson's reaction to the blows, Mr. Ogg-Moss replied "Kent can't speak but he gives this guttural sound and he did give a cry when I hit him". Mr. Ogg-Moss stated further that five minutes after being hit with the spoon, Mr. Henderson would be incapable of remembering the incident. He conceded he was aware that it was a contravention of hospital policy to strike residents. Previous to the incident he had certified in writing that he had read and understood Personnel Directive Number M.R. 17 of the Ministry of Social Services which specified that physical force against any resident for any reason whatsoever was strictly forbidden.

Paragraph N of the Directive reads:

> Striking of Patients: No patient is to be struck for any reason whatsoever; approved methods of necessary patient restraint specifically exclude striking and any other form of unnecessary aggression. Any employee who strikes, slaps or kicks a patient will be dismissed.

II. THE DECISIONS IN THE ONTARIO COURTS

At first instance in the Ontario Provincial Court, counsel for the Crown conceded that s. 43 was potentially available to the accused as a defence. The case was therefore argued on the issue of whether the force used by Mr. Ogg-Moss was more than "reasonable" in the circumstances. Smith Prov. Ct. J. held that it was not, and that Mr. Ogg-Moss was justified in taking the action he did to discipline the resident and to prevent the hospital from becoming a "mad house". He dismissed the charge.

† [1984] 2 S.C.R. 173.

The Crown appealed to the County Court where Matheson Co. Ct. J. took a different view of the incident and its surrounding circumstances. While acknowledging the difficult nature of the accused's job, Matheson Co. Ct. J. held that the force use was neither reasonable nor justified and substituted a conviction and a fine.

On further appeal to the Ontario Court of Appeal the applicability of s. 43 was for the first time challenged by the Crown. Since there was no evidence before them on this issue, Justices Jessup Martin and Weatherston sent the case back to the County Court for a new hearing of the appeal. At this new hearing Flanigan Co. Ct. J. held that a "child" for purposes of s. 43 included a "severely retarded" adult and that Mr. Ogg-Moss stood "in the place of a parent" to Mr. Henderson. Flanigan Co. Ct. J. then stated that in view of what he saw as the limited role of the appellate court on review, he was unwilling to draw different inferences from those drawn by the trial judge on the issue of the reasonableness of the force used by Mr. Ogg-Moss. He restored the acquittal at trial.

The appeal then returned a second time to the Ontario Court of Appeal (1981), 60 C.C.C. (2d) 127, 24 C.R. (3d) 264. In a very brief oral judgment delivered for himself and for Martin and Lacourcière JJ.A., Jessup J.A. set out the facts of the case and then held:

> However, in our opinion, the respondent was not a schoolteacher or person standing in the place of a parent and the complainant was neither a pupil or child within the meaning of s. 43. In the result we think the appeal must be allowed and the verdict of acquittal set aside and a verdict of guilty entered. By way of penalty we would impose an absolute discharge.

III. THE GROUNDS OF APPEAL

The appellant was granted leave to appeal on five grounds:

1. Whether the Ontario Court of Appeal erred in holding that a Mental Retardation Counsellor charged with the daily care of profoundly mentally retarded persons are [*sic*] not in the place of a parent vis-à-vis these persons;
2. whether the Ontario Court of Appeal erred in holding that a profoundly retarded person with the physical age of twenty-one and the mental age of five is not a "child" for the purposes of the application of Section 43 of the *Criminal Code of Canada*;
3. whether the Ontario Court of Appeal erred in holding that a Mental Retardation Counsellor charged with training mentally retarded persons in basic life skills are [*sic*] not schoolteachers and their charges not pupils in the circumstances of an institution for the mentally retarded;
4. whether the Ontario Court of Appeal erred in not ordering a new trial, having concluded that Section 43 of the *Criminal Code* had no application;
5. that the learned Justices of the Court of Appeal erred in law by basing their decision on a question of fact alone, when the jurisdiction of that Honourable Court was one of appeal restricted to questions of law alone, pursuant to Section 771(1) of the *Criminal Code*.

. . . .

Although he purports to base his reading of the terms in issue in this appeal on their "natural and ordinary meaning", the appellant's argument is essentially a functional one. He argues that the terms "person in the place of a parent" and "child", on the one hand, and "schoolteacher" and "pupil", on the other, refer to relationships. Consequently, he says, the application of s. 43 ought to be determined primarily on the basis of the nature and quality of the relationship between the "parenting person" and the "child" under his care, or between the "schoolteacher" and his "pupil", rather than on the basis of such factors as the chronological age of the "child" or "pupil".

Mr. Ogg-Moss therefore seeks to support his contention that he was "in the place of a parent" to Mr. Henderson by citing the *Province of Ontario Manual of Program Care Standards* (September 1976), from which he quotes the following passage:

> Direct-care staff shall be responsible for observing, detecting, reporting and managing usual resident illness and behaviour. They shall be trained as *surrogate parents* to handle such illness and behaviour as are commonly met in the working situation. (Emphasis added.)

He argues that the functions of an M.R.C. correspond to those of a parent and that, in fact, the M.R.C. is the only "parent" many mentally retarded persons will know. This line of argument found favour with Flanigan Co. Ct. J. who prefaced his conclusion that Mr. Ogg-Moss stood in the place of a parent to Mr. Henderson by observing:

> I can't think of any person more closely associated with this particular victim [*sic*] as a parent image than the accused.

On the basis of his contention that an M.R.C. stands in the place of a parent to a mentally retarded person, the appellant argues that the mentally retarded person is a "child" for purposes of s. 43 no matter what his chronological age may be. He contends that this reading of s. 43 is consistent with the ordinary meaning of the word "child", which, as defined by Webster's Dictionary of the English Language, includes a "childlike or childish person". The appellant cites from the decision of Flanigan Co. Ct. J.:

> When one looks at the job description that is affixed to the Appellant's Affidavit ... and when one refers to the evidence as to the condition of the victim who has been in this institution for many years, one can come to no other conclusion on any reasonable basis that [*sic*] the word "child" could not [*sic*] apply to him. Surely the very services that are applied and that this victim requires are those that we envisage being required by a child of tender years.

Finally, the appellant urges, even if Mr. Henderson was not a "child" within the meaning of s. 43, his relationship to Mr. Ogg-Moss was nevertheless that of a "pupil" to a "schoolteacher". He contends that the job description of a M.R.C. includes teaching "life skills" and that at the time of the incident in question he was teaching Mr. Henderson to eat with a spoon. In the absence of statutory definition, the terms "schoolteacher" and "pupil" should, he submits, be given a liberal interpretation so as to include this sort of instructional activity.

IV. THE PURPOSE AND THE EFFECT OF S. 43

Mr. Ogg-Moss urges a broad, functional approach to the terms in s. 43. In his submission, the purpose of s. 43 is to protect persons exercising certain parental and instructional functions and therefore its terms ought to be defined so as to further that purpose. I do not doubt that a functional reading is often more appropriate to statutory construction than a slavishly literal one and is often better suited to the attainment of legislative purposes. This appropriateness, however, depends on the accuracy with which the purpose of the enactment is identified.

I note that in the present appeal, there is something circular in the way the appellant identifies the purpose of s. 43. If he is correct, and the terms "in the place of a parent" and "child" or "schoolteacher" and "pupil" ought to be given wide interpretations, then he will also be correct that a particular result, and arguably the purpose, of s. 43 will be to protect persons exercising widely-defined "parental" or "educational" functions. But since the accuracy of this identification of the purpose of s. 43 depends on the accuracy of Mr. Ogg-Moss's "liberal" definitions of its terms, I do not see how it is possible then to turn around and use this purpose to support these very same definitions. It seems clearly true that the purpose of s. 43 and the meaning of its terms are closely intertwined, but the consequence is that neither one can be deduced from an a priori definition of the other. An abstract definition of the hypothetical purpose cannot, therefore, be the proper starting point for a consideration of the meaning of its terms.

A better starting point, in my view, is not the purpose of s. 43 but its effects. While a confident conclusion as to the purpose of s. 43 must await an accurate assessment of the meaning of its terms, the overall effects of that section are clear, no matter how its terms are defined. It exculpates the use of what would otherwise be criminal force by one group of persons against another. It protects the first group of persons, but, it should be noted, at the same time it removes the protection of the criminal law from the second. For the Attorney General of Ontario this latter effect justifies a restrictive reading of s. 43, specifically of the terms "child" and "pupil". It is his submission that:

> ... the class of persons against whom otherwise criminal force can be employed ought to be restricted, not broadened, and ... any section which authorizes otherwise illegal physical violence should be strictly construed against the actor.

There is much to be said in favour of this submission. As a statement of general principle it accords with our normal assumptions about the purpose and operation of the criminal law. One of the key rights in our society is the individual's right to be free from unconsented invasions on his or her physical security or dignity and it is a central purpose of the criminal law to protect members of society from such invasions. I agree with the Attorney General that any derogation from this right and this protection ought to be strictly construed. Where the effect of such a purported derogation is to deprive a specific individual or group of the equal protection we normally assume is offered by the criminal law, I think it appropriate to view the proffered definition with suspicion and to insist on a demonstration of the logic and rationale of the interpretation.

Finally, on this point, it should be noted that s. 43 is not necessary for the protection of persons using physical force in response to violent or dangerous behaviour or in the course of approved treatment. The former situations are already covered by, *inter alia*, ss. 34, 35, 37, 38, 39 and 41 of the *Criminal Code*. The latter are dealt with by provincial legislation such as the *Developmental Services Act*, *supra*, and the *Mental Health Act*, R.S.O. 1980, c. 262, and by regulations promulgated thereunder, as well as by the common law. Section 43 only applies to "correctional" force unrelated to treatment or to the protection of self or others.

V. IS A MENTALLY RETARDED ADULT A "CHILD" FOR PURPOSES OF S. 43?

Why in law or in policy should the word "child" be given a definition which would make a mentally retarded person over 21 subject to blows which, if directed at a mentally normal 21-year-old, would constitute an assault? In my view the proposition that a person in Mr. Henderson's position is a "child", within the meaning of s. 43, is refuted by the history of s. 43 and its common law antecedents and by the very "functional" analysis through which the proposition is articulated.

(a) "Child" in s. 43 and its common law antecedents

Both in common parlance and as a legal concept the term "child" has two primary meanings. One refers to chronological age and is the converse of the term "adult"; the other refers to lineage and is the reciprocal of the term "parent". A child in the first sense was defined at common law as a person under the age of fourteen. This definition may be modified by statutory provision: see, for example, the *Child Welfare Act*, R.S.O. 1980, c. 66, s. 19(1); the *Children's Institutions Act*, R.S.O. 1980, c. 67, s. 1(c) and the *Children's Residential Services Act*, R.S.O. 1980, c. 71, s. 1(b). No statutory modification, however, fixes an age higher than the age of majority which, in Ontario, pursuant to the *Age of Majority and Accountability Act*, R.S.O. 1980, c. 7, s. 1(1), is 18 years. A child in the second sense was defined at common law as the legitimate offspring of a parent, but in most jurisdictions this definition has been amended by statute to constitute all offspring, whether legitimate or not, as the "children" of their natural or adoptive parents: see, for example, the *Children's Law Reform Act*, R.S.O. 1980, c. 68, s. 1.

As I have indicated, according to the appellant there is a third meaning for the term "child" which focuses on the "childishness" or "childlike" behaviour of the person to whom it applies. To my knowledge this definition of child has no equivalent as a legal concept, nor — unless it succeed in the current case — has it ever successfully been urged to interpret a statutory provision. Certainly it is not the meaning of the term child in the common law antecedents of s. 43.

Like s. 43, the common law recognized a right of certain persons to use force in the correction of a "child". The "child" referred to was a child in the sense both of chronology and of lineage. This is how Blackstone in his *Commentaries on the Laws of England*, Book I, chap. 16, described the common law right:

> The power of a parent by our English laws is much more moderate [than that of the paterfamilias in Roman law]; but still sufficient to keep the child in order and obedience. *He may lawfully correct his child being under age*, in a reasonable manner; for this is for the benefit of his education ... He may also delegate part of his parental authority, during his life, to the tutor or schoolmaster of his child; who is then in *loco parentis* [in the place of a parent], and has such a portion of the power of the parent committed to his charge, *viz.* that of restraint and correction, as may be necessary to answer the purposes for which he is employed. (Emphasis added.)

I shall have occasion to return to this quote, but the underlined portion clearly indicates that the power to chastise was, at least at common law, the power of a parent (specifically the father) or of his direct delegate, to discipline his offspring until the age of majority. Blackstone is explicit on this point:

> The legal power of a father (for a mother, as such, is entitled to no power, but only to reverence and respect) the power of a father, I say, over the persons of his children ceases at the age of twenty-one: ...

I have no doubt, therefore, that at common law no chronological adult, no matter how "childish" or "childlike", was subject to corporal correction from his father or his father's delegate. History does not support the appellant's interpretation.

Given the seemingly clear restriction of the common law right of correction to a "child" under the age of majority, it seems highly unlikely that the framers of the *Criminal Code* used this same word to render a wider class of persons subject to such correction. This impression is reinforced by the fact that when a "child" is referred to elsewhere in the *Code* either explicitly or by implication, it always refers to a person chronologically younger than the age of majority: see ss. 3, 140, 146, 168(3) and 197. It should also be noted that when the *Code* does wish to refer to a person with a mental handicap it does so not metaphorically as a "child" or by reference to his purportedly "childlike" or "childish" characteristics, but rather directly, if somewhat bluntly, as a "feeble-minded person" or "an idiot" or "imbecile" or simply "insane". See, for example, ss. 2, 158(2)(b)(ii). Although somewhat disturbing to modern sensibilities the terms "feeble-minded", "idiot" and "imbecile" are, in fact, the legal equivalents to the current concepts of "mentally retarded" or "developmentally handicapped". Had the *Criminal Code* intended to include mentally retarded adults in the category of person subject to corporal punishment, these are the terms it would have used, not "child".

(b) The "functional" reading of "child"

The foregoing factors of history and statutory construction make the appellant's proposed interpretation highly unlikely. Beyond them, the scepticism which would in any event be the proper judicial response to the appellant's proposed extension of the category of persons the common law made subject to corporal correction is in no way allayed even by his "functional" reading of the term "child". The single basis cited by Mr. Ogg-Moss for his metaphorical reading of the word "child" is the purported correspondence between the dependency on a parenting figure by a severely retarded adult and by a "child". Beyond this single asserted correspondence, there are no submissions that would support a conclusion as to the "childish" or "childlike" nature of mentally retarded persons; nor do I believe that any such arguments could be successfully maintained. Certainly the description in the record of Mr. Henderson's condition affords no support for such an argument. Incapacity for speech, "headbanging" and inability to recall incidents for more than a few minutes are signs of severe physiological affliction. They do not correspond to any recognizable image of childhood. I agree with the Attorney General for Ontario that there is a qualitative difference between "immaturity", "childishness" or "childlike" behaviour and the behaviour of a mentally retarded adult, especially as in the present case, of a severely retarded adult.

A further important consideration is that chronological childhood is a transitory phase, and for a child in the chronological sense the suspension of the criminal law's protection against certain kinds of assault is a temporary phenomenon. For the mentally retarded person the definition of "childhood" proposed by the appellant is a life sentence and the consequent attenuation of his right to dignity and physical security is permanent. I cannot believe that it is the intention of the *Criminal Code* to create such a category of permanent second-class citizens on the basis of a mental or physical handicap.

If mentally retarded adults are to be considered "children" solely on the basis of their dependency on a "parenting" figure, it is difficult to see how the category of "children" would be limited to the mentally retarded. Essentially the same argument could be made with regard to the functional relationship between sufferers from senility or other cognitive disorder, or perhaps even stroke victims or other invalids, and those who take care of them. If an inability to tend to one's basic needs, or an inability, because of one's mental state, to function unassisted in society, are indices of "childishness", then the category of adults subject to correction is a very broad one indeed. I do not believe that a functional analysis of childlike dependency is appropriate in these latter cases and for similar reasons I cannot accept it with regard to mentally retarded adults.

A mentally retarded adult is not a child in fact, nor for purposes of the law in general, nor for purposes of s. 43 of the *Criminal Code* in particular.

VI. IS A MENTAL RETARDATION COUNSELLOR A "PERSON STANDING IN THE PLACE OF A PARENT" TO A MENTALLY RETARDED PERSON UNDER HIS CHARGE?

Section 43 only authorizes a "person standing in the place of a parent" to use force by way of correction of a child. Since I have concluded that a mentally-retarded adult is not a "child", it must follow that even if an M.R.C. were a person standing in the place of a parent, he would not be authorized to use force to correct a mentally retarded adult like Mr. Henderson. Even if I were wrong, however, and a mentally retarded adult could be a "child" for purposes of s. 43, I would nevertheless hold that an M.R.C. in the position of Mr. Ogg-Moss is not a "person standing in the place of a parent" within the meaning of that section.

At common law the power to use force for the correction of a child was vested in the child's parents (originally the father). Blackstone, *Commentaries on the Laws of England*, Book I, chap. 16, saw it as one of the parental rights which were the correlatives of the parental duties of support, education and protection. As the passage quoted earlier indicates, this right was conceptualized as an aid in discharging the parental duty of education and could be delegated by the parent to a schoolmaster.

It follows, then, that at common law there are two ways in which a person could put himself "in the place of a parent". The first is to assume, in the absence or default of the natural parents, the parental duties that give rise to parental rights. The second is to have that right delegated to one by the natural parent.

The first way of assuming the place of a parent is consonant with the well-known line of cases defining the legal meaning of the term *in loco parentis* or "in the place of a parent". The *locus classicus* is the decision of Jessel M.R. in *Bennet v. Bennet* (1879), 10 Ch. D. 474 (which was itself based on the decisions of Lord Eldon in *Ex parte Pye* (1811), 18 Ves. 140 and Lord Cottenham, in *Powys v. Mansfield* (1837), 3 My. & Cr. 359) wherein Jessel M.R. held at pp. 477–78:

> ... a person *in loco parentis* means a person taking upon himself the duty of a father of a child to make a provision for that child.
>
> ...
>
> In the case of a person *in loco parentis* you must prove that he took upon himself the obligation.

This line of cases has been applied in Canada, *inter alia*, in *Mitchell v. City of Toronto* (1921), 64 D.L.R. 569 (Ont. C.A.) and *Shtitz v. C.N.R.*, [1927] 1 D.L.R. 951 (Sask. C.A.) and in the United States, *inter alia*, in *Fuller v. Fuller*, 418 F. 2d 1189 (C.A.D.C. 1969), and in *Busillo v. Hetzel*, 374 N.E. 2d 1090 (Ill. App. 1978). These decisions have stressed the central necessity of taking upon oneself responsibility for the child's financial support in order to fall within the definition of a "person standing in the place of a parent". ...

I agree with these conclusions. Insofar as Mr. Ogg-Moss's claim to status of a "person standing in the place of a parent" for purposes of using force by way of correction rests on the similarity between the functions of an M.R.C. and of a parent, it cannot succeed. The parent's power of correction arises from his assumption of all the obligations of parenthood. A person does not step into the place of a parent for purposes of assuming this power unless he also assumes all these obligations. Not only does an M.R.C. have no responsibility for the pecuniary needs of the children under his temporary care, those "parental" responsibilities which he does exercise are exercised under the direction and supervision of the Minister and the senior professional staff designated by the Regulations under the *Developmental Services Act*, *supra*. He does not, by exercising these limited responsibilities become in the relevant sense, a "person standing in the place of a parent".

Even if a person does not stand "in the place of a parent" in the *Bennet v. Bennet* sense, there still remains the second way of assuming this position, that of delegation. Flanigan Co. Ct. J. found that Mr. Ogg-Moss stood *in loco parentis* to Mr. Henderson "as an agent of the Minister and an employee of the Department". With respect, I cannot agree. As the decision in *Pittard*, *supra*, clearly indicates, delegation cannot simply be inferred from the fact of placing a child in the care of another. I am willing to assume that Mr. Henderson's admission in early childhood to the Rideau Regional Centre as a voluntary patient with parental consent implies a delegation of parental powers in favour of the Minister. This, however, is not enough. For Mr. Ogg-Moss to succeed, the power must then have moved from the Minister to Mr. Ogg-Moss. On this latter point, the record in the present case goes beyond a simple absence of evidence of sub-delegation to positive evidence of non-delegation in the form of the prohibition in Personnel Directive Number M.R. 17 forbidding the striking of any resident for any reason whatsoever. Mr. Ogg-Moss was not a delegate of the Minister for purposes of exercising any right of correction that may have been delegated to the Minister; nor, as a consequence of his certification that he read and understood this directive, could he assert that he mistakenly thought that he was.

I conclude that even if a person in the position of Mr. Henderson were a child for purposes of s. 43, an M.R.C. in the position of Mr. Ogg-Moss would not be a "person standing in the place of a parent" within the meaning of the section.

VII. IS THE RELATIONSHIP BETWEEN A MENTAL RETARDATION COUNSELLOR AND A MENTALLY RETARDED ADULT UNDER HIS CARE THAT OF "SCHOOLTEACHER" AND "PUPIL"?

(a) "Pupil"

The same considerations apply to the definition of "pupil" for the purposes of s. 43 as to the definition of "child".

Blackstone, in the passage quoted earlier, makes it clear that at common law the schoolmaster's right of corporal correction only applied to a chronological child under his charge. He speaks of a parent's power to correct his underage child being delegated to the "tutor or schoolmaster of his child". A similar connotation of childhood attaches to the word "pupil" used in s. 43, which, unlike the more neutral "student", has overtones of immaturity or youthfulness. Were this not so, and were the s. 43 relationship between "schoolmaster" and "pupil" to be read as authorizing corporal correction by anyone teaching something to someone else, then anyone, no matter what his age or his mental competence, would be vulnerable to corporal correction anytime he sought instruction in any field. This would be ludicrous. It is clear that whatever else it may mean, the term "pupil" as used in s. 43 must be limited, as it was at common law, to a child taking instruction.

Since I have already concluded that a mentally retarded adult is not a child for purposes of s. 43, it follows that he is also not a "pupil" within the meaning of that section.

(b) "Schoolteacher"

Because Mr. Henderson is not a "pupil" Mr. Ogg-Moss's claim to protection by virtue of his status as "schoolteacher" would fail in any event. It also fails because an M.R.C. is not a schoolteacher.

Like its reciprocal term "pupil" which is narrower than the term "student", the term "schoolteacher" is narrower than the terms "teacher" or "instructor". Generally, it refers to a person who gives formal instruction in a children's school. I would in any event have doubt as to whether an M.R.C. could fall even within the wider definition of "teacher", since his functions are those of personal care and not, in any meaningful sense, of "teaching". *A fortiori* an M.R.C. cannot fall within the more restrictive definition of "schoolteacher". Mental Retardation Counsellors are neither qualified nor licensed as schoolteachers. Such "educational" responsibilities as they do possess (Mr. Ogg-Moss's claim rests on the fact that he was "instructing" Mr. Henderson on how to eat with a spoon) have no academic content, and the context in which they are carried out has not even a metaphorical connection with that in which a schoolteacher functions. I think counsel for Mr. Ogg-Moss was well advised at first instance to disclaim any reliance on an M.R.C.'s status as a "schoolteacher". He has none.

VIII. USING FORCE BY WAY OF CORRECTION

Even if all of the above were incorrect and an M.R.C. could be a "schoolteacher or person standing in the place of a parent" and a mentally retarded adult could be a "child" or "pupil" within the meaning of s. 43, the appeal would still fail.

Section 43 authorizes the use of force "by way of correction". As Blackstone noted, such "correction" of a child is countenanced by the law because it is "for the benefit of his education". Section 43 is, in other words, a justification. It exculpates a parent, schoolteacher or person standing in the place of a parent who uses force in the correction of a child, because it considers such an action not a wrongful, but a rightful, one. It follows that unless the force is "by way of correction", that is, for the benefit of the education of the child, the use of force will not be justified.

. . . .

Where the context does imply an educational responsibility, this same reasoning demands that the person applying the force intended it for "correction", and that the person being "corrected" be capable of learning from the correction. ...

The first prerequisite, that the force be intended for correction, has been a part of Canadian law since *Brisson v. Lafontaine* (1864), 8 L.C. Jur. 173 (S.C.) In a passage that has been quoted in almost every subsequent case on the right of correction, Loranger J. said at p. 175 that the schoolteacher's power of correction could only be exercised in "the interests of instruction" and that "any punishment ... motivated by arbitrariness, caprice, anger or bad humour constitutes an offence punishable like ordinary offences."

The second prerequisite, referring to the child's capacity, was articulated by Martin B. in *R. v. Griffin* (1869), 11 Cox C.C. 402, at p. 403: "The law as to correction has reference only to a child capable of appreciating correction." In *Griffin*, Martin B. held that a two-and-a-half year old child was not so capable. The English scholar, Professor H.K. Bevan, in his work, *The Law Relating to Children* (1973), has concluded at p. 212, footnote 11 that on this same basis "there would be no right to punish a child who was mentally disordered".

This latter conclusion could, of course, be highly relevant to the present appeal. I find it impossible and unnecessary to decide the correctness of the full breadth of Professor Bevan's categorical statement. There is no evidence before this Court to the effect that mentally retarded children either are or are not, as a class, capable of appreciating correction. I do agree, however, that insofar as a given mentally retarded child is incapable of appreciating correction, s. 43 does not, as a matter of law justify the use of force by a person standing in the place of a parent or by a schoolteacher. In the present case where the record discloses that the person being "corrected" was, to the knowledge of the person applying the force, incapable of remembering the "correction" within minutes of its application, the assault could not, as a matter of law, constitute "using force by way of correction" and the person committing it could not have recourse to s. 43.

IX. CONCLUSION

In my view the Court of Appeal was correct in each of its conclusions. An M.R.C. is neither a "person standing in the place of a parent" nor "schoolteacher" and a mentally retarded adult under his care, even if "severely" or "profoundly" retarded, is neither a "child" nor a "pupil" within the meaning of s. 43. Section 43 cannot therefore have any application to a case like the present.

. . . .

Since s. 43 does not justify the intentional application of force in a situation like the present it follows that this use of force constitutes an assault within the meaning of s. 245(1). I make no comment on the gravity of the assault nor on the appropriateness of laying criminal charges. These questions are not before us; as in the case of any other intentional application of force they are matters for prosecutorial judgment and the discretion of the sentencing court. The Court of Appeal did not err in entering a verdict of guilty.

I would dismiss the appeal.

Appeal dismissed.

■

R. v. Dupperon†

[BY THE COURT:]

The appellant was charged that on or about November 19, 1983, at the City of Saskatoon, in the Province of Saskatchewan, he did in committing an assault on Michael James Dupperon cause harm to him contrary to s. 245.1(1)(b) of the *Criminal Code* of Canada.

After a trial before a judge of the provincial court he was convicted, fined $400 and placed on probation for 18 months. He appeals against his conviction.

The evidence is that he strapped his 13-year-old son on the bare buttocks with a leather belt approximately 10 times leaving four or five bruises on the boy's left buttock which were blue and in a linear pattern. Each bruise was approximately four inches long and of a width of one-quarter to one-half an inch.

One of the grounds of appeal is based upon s. 245.1(2) which reads:

> **245.1**(2) For the purposes of this section and sections 245.3 and 246.3, "bodily harm" means any hurt or injury to the complainant that interferes with his or her health or comfort and that is more than merely transient or trifling in nature.

Counsel for the Crown agreed with the submission of counsel for the appellant that whether or not the bruises on the boy were more than "merely transient or trifling in nature" was never adequately proved by the prosecution and a conviction should not have been entered for assault causing bodily harm. It was suggested that the conviction should be set aside and a conviction for assault be entered in its place. Whether a conviction for assault should stand depends entirely upon whether the appellant is entitled to rely on s. 43 of the *Criminal Code.*

. . . .

The first ground of appeal is that the learned trial judge erred in finding that the strapping was not for the purpose of correction. He said:

† (1984), 16 C.C.C. (3d) 453 (Sask. C.A.).

> The question then remains whether the punishment represented force by way of correction, and whether it was reasonable under the circumstances. I do not view the strapping as representing correction. As stated by Mrs. Dupperon, albeit without realizing the implication, the strapping was to show his son he was "to grow up and be a man and not a bum on 20th Street". I am sure it related to an anger that was uncontrolled and without immediate cessation as the accused returned again and again I am satisfied to keep at him.

With deference to the learned trial judge, I am of the opinion that the evidence given by Michael as to why he was punished fully supports a finding that the strapping was by way of correction. In the morning on the day of the assault, Michael had been caught smoking out behind the house and for this he was "grounded". Later that morning the father, Linda Dupperon (his present wife and step-mother to Michael) and Michael were working at the Bingo Palace where the appellant had a janitorial contract. There, Michael admitted, he was "slacking off and doing things I shouldn't have"; and he also used foul language against his father. For this he was grounded for a whole week. When the appellant, Linda Dupperon and Michael returned home from work both the appellant and his wife later left the house and Michael was alone. It was then that he decided to leave home. He left a note to his father which was not produced but concerning which Michael testified: "I think I told him off. I said I wasn't going to come back to home and shit like that." He packed his clothes, radio and some food and left the house. A short time later, Linda Dupperon arrived home, saw the note and telephoned her husband. The appellant came home and about 15 minutes later the telephone rang. It was a call from Michael, who had been at a friend's home down the street, saying he was coming home.

In his evidence-in-chief, Michael testified that his father grabbed him by the hair, put him in his room, pulled down his pants and strapped him four different times for a total of about 10 strokes. When asked at trial why he ran away from home he answered: "I don't know, something to do, I guess."

Linda Dupperon testified that when Michael came home he just walked in the front door and was told by the appellant to go to his room and to take down his pants as he was going to get a strapping because "Ken said that he's going to learn to grow up to be a man and not a bum on 20th Street". She said that Michael was hit three or four times. The appellant then "started to walk out of the room and Michael lipped him off so he went back in there and strapped him another five, six times and that was it".

In the course of his judgment the learned trial judge said:

> As stated earlier anything done by the accused was placed in its most favourable light by Michael. He agreed he originally deserved punishment. For example, in cross-examination he credited his father's return to his room as "he probably came in to apologize" *and agreed that he came back only once, not four times as stated in his examination-in-chief.* Anything Michael said to make it look bad for his father on the facts was not by design. He was clearly trying to make the facts look harmless and ordinary in connection with his strapping. Therefore, when he claims he was pulled in by the hair and intermittently strapped with his stepmother intervening to stop him and his father subsequently coming back in to take up where he left off this evidence should not be taken lightly. I am satisfied that Michael when he stated this was telling the truth. Mrs. Dupperon also struck me as a witness who was deliberately trying to minimize the events and place her husband in a favourable light. I do not view her as a reliable witness. (My emphasis.)

Michael had given a statement to the police. At the trial Crown counsel obtained leave from the court under s. 9(2) of the *Canada Evidence Act*, to cross-examine on this statement which Michael agreed contained a number of outright lies, especially lies as to what his father had done, which he admitted to Crown counsel were entirely false.

The evidence shows that Michael's mother and father were divorced and that he was placed in the custody of his father. His father raised him alone until his remarriage to Linda Dupperon. There is one small child as a result of this union and Linda has three children from a previous marriage and is attempting to gain custody of them.

Howard Woods, a half-brother of the appellant testified that he arrived at the Dupperon home shortly after the strapping and took Michael to his grandparent's place at his request. In the car en route, Michael said he was very bitter towards his father and "he indicated, he said to me that he was going to fix it so that Ken and Linda would never have got Linda's kids". "When he was talking about getting Ken so that they could never get Linda's kids, he showed me this knife. And I asked him, you know, what he was going to do with it. And he said, well, I'm going to stab myself in the arm and say dad did it. He said, they'll never get Linda's kids that way".

Michael has had problems at school and in getting along with other kids. He has stolen, fought with other kids, and frequently tells lies. He is jealous of other children in the family. He has been the subject of investigation by a child protection worker and after the strapping incident he was placed in the interim custody of the Minister. He was placed in a foster home but did not get along well there and so was moved to Kilburn Hall, an institution for children with behaviour problems.

From the foregoing evidence it is clear that the strapping was by way of correction and the statement made by Mrs. Dupperon as to what the appellant said is in no way inconsistent with this purpose. In *R. v. Haberstock* (1970), 1 C.C.C. (2d) 433, the learned trial judge directed his attention to whether or not the boy had participated in the name-calling and having found that he did not, concluded that the slapping by the teacher was not for the purpose of correction and therefore found the accused guilty. In setting aside that verdict, Culliton C.J.S., on behalf of this court said at p. 435:

> With all respect, I think the approach by the learned trial Judge was too narrow. Having found that the boy did not participate in the name-calling, he should have directed his attention to the question whether there were reasonable and probable grounds upon which the appellant was justified in concluding that he did so. If there were such grounds, and the appellant administered the punishment in the honest belief that the boy had been guilty of conduct deserving punishment, then, if the punishment was reasonable, he would be excused from any criminal liability.

From the uncontradicted evidence given by Michael there were ample grounds upon which the appellant could conclude that Michael was deserving of a more severe punishment than he had already meted out to him and I am satisfied that he honestly believed that a strapping was required by way of correction. Given the weight of the evidence adduced in this respect, it was unreasonable for the learned trial judge not to have held that the strapping was for correction....

I turn now to the second ground of appeal, that the learned trial judge erred in finding that unreasonable force had been used. In the passage from his judgment which I quoted earlier he said the accused "returned again and again I'm satisfied to keep at him" and he accepted Michael's earlier evidence that his father came back four times despite Michael's admission in his cross-examination that he came back only once, which is confirmed by the evidence of Linda Dupperon. It is quite clear from both the evidence of Michael and Linda Dupperon that the first strapping consisted of only three or four strokes and that would have been the end of the strapping but for the foul language Michael then employed against his father. This resulted in a further five or six strokes. There is no dispute that the total strapping did not exceed 10 strokes. In my respectful opinion it is much more probable that the strapping took place in two stages rather than in four stages as Michael originally stated.

As Culliton C.J.S. said in *R. v. Haberstock*, *supra*, at pp. 434–5:

> Whether the force used in administering punishment was reasonable or excessive is a question of fact, to be determined in the circumstances of each case. *R. v. Robinson* (1899), 7 C.C.C. 52; *R. v. Metcalfe*, *supra*. In the determination of that question, the test is whether, at the time the punishment was administered, it was reasonable? *R. v. Gaul* (1903), 8 C.C.C. 178, 36 N.S.R. 504.

Here the learned trial judge in the course of his judgment said:

> Secondly, I do not view it at all appropriate in the circumstances to pull down a 13-year-old boy's pants and flail him with a strap on his bare buttocks to the extent of this case. It is an unnatural manner of dealing out punishment and is not justified in these circumstances and in the manner in which it was administered.

During the trial the following exchange took place between the court and counsel for the appellant:

THE COURT: You don't beat kids into being good kids. You beat them into jail and that's time and again proven.

THE COURT: When you talk about him not liking Kilburn and that's a double edged sword, he doesn't like Kilburn at all, he wants to go home with his dad. That's obvious, it's obvious in his testimony.

MR. MASON: Your Honour, the evidence, I believe, will be, if I can anticipate what the evidence will be is that at Kilburn Hall there is no physical discipline administered to Michael.

THE COURT: You mean strapping kids, nor should there be.

MR. MASON: Well ...
THE COURT: That's not the way to handle kids.
MR. MASON: Perhaps, Your Honour, but ...
THE COURT: We're not in the dark ages now, Mr. Mason, surely.
MR. MASON: Perhaps, but there is an argument to be made.
THE COURT: I'm aware that some fundamentalist sects seem to believe that spare the rod and spoil the child gives them the license to practice all kinds of brutality and sadistic practices which cause from time to time the death of the child but I didn't think we were going to argue the benefits of that kind of religiosity or morality in connection with the discipline of children.

While it appears from the above exchange and from other passages in the transcript that the learned trial judge may be opposed, in principle, to corporal punishment, that is his privilege and unless he allowed such views to interfere with his determination of whether the force applied was reasonable under the circumstances, it was not an error to express his personal view.

Put in another way, I think most people would be shocked if corporal punishment were employed in an institution such as Kilburn Hall or in any agency of government designed for the protection of abused children.

I agree with the observations of Cadsby Prov. Ct. J. in *R. v. Baptiste and Baptiste* (1980), 61 C.C.C. (2d) 438 at p. 443:

> It seems to me that a properly directed jury would apply the custom of their community. The concern of today's community for child abuse should be reflected in the standards to be applied. The maxim, "spare the rod and spoil the child" does not enjoy the universal approval it may have had at the turn of this century and indeed at the time of the various revisions of the *Criminal Code*. The formation of child abuse teams at hospitals, such as Sick Children's Hospital in Toronto reflect the distaste of our community for corporal punishment.

There is some anomaly in the fact that corporal punishment of criminals is now prohibited while corporal punishment of children is still permitted. The rationale of s. 43 of the *Criminal Code* has been explained by Dickson J. (as he then was) in the recent judgment of the Supreme Court rendered in *Ogg-Moss v. The Queen*....

In this case I have said that, in my opinion, all of the evidence supports the view that the force used was by way of correction and that the learned trial judge ought to have so found. However, when we come to the second question, namely, whether the force used exceeded what was reasonable under the circumstances, I think the evidence fully supports the finding of the trial judge.

I referred earlier to the position of the Crown that the evidence does not support a finding of assault causing bodily harm but does support a finding of assault. In making this submission counsel said in his factum:

> The respondent does not wish to be taken as suggesting that bruises alone may never be enough; in the appropriate case they may be sufficient. In this particular instance, however, such was not proven and a conviction should have been entered for assault and not assault causing bodily harm.

The only matter with which I am concerned here, therefore, is whether the force used exceeded what was reasonable under the circumstances so as to deprive the appellant of the protection afforded by s. 43 of the *Criminal Code*. In determining that question the court will consider, both from an objective and subjective standpoint, such matters as the nature of the offence calling for correction, the age and character of the child and the likely effect of the punishment on this particular child, the degree of gravity of the punishment, the circumstances under which it was inflicted, and the injuries, if any, suffered. If the child suffers injuries which may endanger life, limbs or health or is disfigured that alone would be sufficient to find that the punishment administered was unreasonable under the circumstances.

In this case counsel for the appellant argued that the bruises caused by the strapping do not in themselves prove that the force was excessive: *R. v. Metcalfe* (1927), 49 C.C.C. 260, [1927] 3 W.W.R. 194, and the judgment of McDougall J. in *Campeau v. The King* (1951), 103 C.C.C. 355 at p. 360, 14 C.R. 202 at p. 212, where he said:

> That the punishment naturally may cause pain hardly needs to be stated; otherwise its whole purpose would be lost. If in the course of the punishment the pupil should suffer bruises or contusions it does not necessarily follow that the punishment is unreasonable.

As I have indicated the injuries, if any, constitute evidence to be considered by the court.

It has been held that any punishment motivated by arbitrariness, caprice, anger or bad humour may constitute an offence and punishment for correction must never be administered with the intention of physically injuring the child. In weighing all of these matters in the context of society today, there may well be a difference of opinion as to whether the force used was reasonable or not: *Campeau v. The King*. There, in dismissing the appeal of the schoolmaster, Gagne J. (Casey and Bertrand JJ. concurring) said at p. 364 C.C.C., p. 218 C.R.:

> The learned trial judge considered that no circumstance shown by the record justified the rather severe punishment inflicted by the schoolmaster. On the question of facts, it appears to me that this Court cannot interfere. The verdict cannot be considered unreasonable.

In my opinion, the evidence in this case amply supports the finding of the trial judge. Ten strokes of a leather belt on the bare buttocks is a severe beating, particularly under the circumstances in which it was inflicted here on an emotionally disturbed boy. There is, therefore, no basis upon which this court would be justified in reversing that finding. I think the appellant now realizes that the force used in this case was excessive as is shown by the remarks of his counsel in speaking to the trial judge on the matter of sentence. He said:

> Michael suffers from very severe behavioural problems which by all accounts is highly abnormal. And he certainly does require special treatment, perhaps treatment which the parents are not skilful enough to deal with. And I think that really is the root of this problem. For whatever reason Michael is as he is, a very difficult child to control.
>
> Your Honour, I might just point out one thing. I think Ken's attitude has changed in the sense that he realizes now that in spite of what he may or may not believe the appropriate manner in dealing with Michael *he realizes now that his is conduct that is not tolerated. And I doubt very much if this type of treatment will be repeated.* (My emphasis.)

The authorities are clear that if we are to accede to the suggestion by the Crown and substitute a verdict of assault, the proper procedure is to dismiss the appeal under s. 613(1)(b)(i) of the *Criminal Code*: ...

Accordingly, the appeal is dismissed, the conviction for assault causing bodily harm is quashed and a verdict of assault is substituted pursuant to s. 613(3).

There was no appeal against sentence but I have considered the appropriateness of the sentence imposed to the substituted conviction. The appellant has a record as follows: 1967 — theft; 1968 — armed robbery; 1971 — assault causing bodily harm; 1971 — breaking and entering and assault; 1977 — theft; 1980 — obstructing peace officer. In view of this record the sentence imposed by the trial judge is appropriate to the substituted charge.

Appeal dismissed; conviction for assault substituted.

Canadian Foundation for Children, Youth and the Law v. Canada (Attorney General)†

[McLACHLIN C.J.:]

The issue in this case is the constitutionality of Parliament's decision to carve out a sphere within which children's parents and teachers may use minor corrective force in some circumstances without facing criminal sanction. The assault provision of the *Criminal Code*, R.S.C. 1985, c. C-46, s. 265, prohibits intentional, non-consensual application of force to another. Section 43 of the *Criminal Code* excludes from this crime reasonable physical correction of children by their parents and teachers.

The Canadian Foundation for Children, Youth and the Law (the "Foundation") seeks a declaration that this exemption from criminal sanction: (1) violates s. 7 of the *Canadian Charter of Rights and Freedoms* because it fails to give procedural protections to children, does not further the best interests of the child, and is both overbroad and vague; (2) violates s. 12 of the *Charter* because it constitutes cruel and

† [2004] 1 S.C.R. 76.

unusual punishment or treatment; and (3) violates s. 15(1) of the *Charter* because it denies children the legal protection against assaults that is accorded to adults.

The trial judge and the Court of Appeal rejected the Foundation's contentions and refused to issue the declaration requested. Like them, I conclude that the exemption from criminal sanction for corrective force that is "reasonable under the circumstances" does not offend the *Charter*. I say this, having carefully considered the contrary view of my colleague, Arbour J., that the defence of reasonable correction offered by s. 43 is so vague that it must be struck down as unconstitutional, leaving parents who apply corrective force to children to the mercy of the defences of necessity and "*de minimis*". I am satisfied that the substantial social consensus on what is reasonable correction, supported by comprehensive and consistent expert evidence on what is reasonable presented in this appeal, gives clear content to s. 43. I am also satisfied, with due respect to contrary views, that exempting parents and teachers from criminal sanction for reasonable correction does not violate children's equality rights. In the end, I am satisfied that this section provides a workable, constitutional standard that protects both children and parents.

I. DOES SECTION 43 OF THE *CRIMINAL CODE* OFFEND SECTION 7 OF THE *CHARTER*?

Section 7 of the *Charter* is breached by state action depriving someone of life, liberty, or security of the person contrary to a principle of fundamental justice. The burden is on the applicant to prove both the deprivation and the breach of fundamental justice. In this case the Crown concedes that s. 43 adversely affects children's security of the person, fulfilling the first requirement.

This leaves the question of whether s. 43 offends a principle of fundamental justice. The Foundation argues that three such principles have been breached: ...

A. Independent Procedural Rights for Children

It is a principle of fundamental justice that accused persons must be accorded adequate procedural safeguards in the criminal process....

Thus far, jurisprudence has not recognized procedural rights for the alleged victims of an offence. However, I need not consider that issue. Even on the assumption that alleged child victims are constitutionally entitled to procedural safeguards, the Foundation's argument fails because s. 43 provides adequate procedural safeguards to protect this interest. The child's interests are represented at trial by the Crown. The Crown's decision to prosecute and its conduct of the prosecution will necessarily reflect society's concern for the physical and mental security of the child.... I conclude that no failure of procedural safeguards has been established.

B. The Best Interests of the Child

The Foundation argues that it is a principle of fundamental justice that laws affecting children must be in their best interests, and that s. 43's exemption of reasonable corrective force from criminal sanction is not in the best interests of the child. Therefore, it argues, s. 43 violates s. 7 of the *Charter*. I disagree. While "the best interests of the child" is a recognized legal principle, this legal principle is not a principle of fundamental justice.

Jurisprudence on s. 7 has established that a "principle of fundamental justice" must fulfill three criteria.... First, it must be a legal principle. This serves two purposes. First, it "provides meaningful content for the s. 7 guarantee"; second, it avoids the "adjudication of policy matters".... Second, there must be sufficient consensus that the alleged principle is "vital or fundamental to our societal notion of justice".... Third, the alleged principle must be capable of being identified with precision and applied to situations in a manner that yields predictable results. Examples of principles of fundamental justice that meet all three requirements include the need for a guilty mind and for reasonably clear laws.

The "best interests of the child" is a legal principle, thus meeting the first requirement.... The "best interests of the child" is an established legal principle in international and domestic law.... Many Canadian statutes explicitly name the "best interests of the child" as a legal consideration: Many Canadian statutes explicitly name the "best interests of the child" as a legal consideration....

However, the "best interests of the child" fails to meet the second criterion for a principle of fundamental justice: consensus that the principle is vital or fundamental to our societal notion of justice. The "best interests of the child" is widely supported in legislation and social policy, and is an important factor for consideration in many contexts. It is not, however, a foundational requirement for the dispensation of justice.

It follows that the legal principle of the "best interests of the child" may be subordinated to other concerns in appropriate contexts. For example, a person convicted of a crime may be sentenced to prison even where it may not be in his or her child's best interests. Society does not always deem it essential that the "best interests of the child" trump all other concerns in the administration of justice....

The third requirement is that the alleged principle of fundamental justice be "capable of being identified with some precision" (*Rodriguez*, *supra*, at p. 591) and provide a justiciable standard. Here, too, the "best interests of the child" falls short. It functions as a factor considered along with others.

To conclude, "the best interests of the child" is a legal principle that carries great power in many contexts. However, it is not a principle of fundamental justice.

C. Vagueness and Overbreadth

(1) Vagueness

The Foundation argues that s. 43 is unconstitutional because first, it does not give sufficient notice as to what conduct is prohibited; and second, it fails to constrain discretion in enforcement. The concept of what is "reasonable under the circumstances" is simply too vague, it is argued, to pass muster as a criminal provision....

I conclude that s. 43, properly construed, is not unduly vague.

(A) THE STANDARD FOR "VAGUENESS"

A law is unconstitutionally vague if it "does not provide an adequate basis for legal debate" and "analysis"; "does not sufficiently delineate any area of risk"; or "is not intelligible".... Certainty is not required....

A law must set an intelligible standard both for the citizens it governs and the officials who must enforce it. The two are interconnected. A vague law prevents the citizen from realizing when he or she is entering an area of risk for criminal sanction. It similarly makes it difficult for law enforcement officers and judges to determine whether a crime has been committed....

Ad hoc discretionary decision making must be distinguished from appropriate judicial interpretation. Judicial decisions may properly add precision to a statute. Legislators can never foresee all the situations that may arise, and if they did, could not practically set them all out. It is thus in the nature of our legal system that areas of uncertainty exist and that judges clarify and augment the law on a case-by-case basis.

It follows that s. 43 of the *Criminal Code* will satisfy the constitutional requirement for precision if it delineates a risk zone for criminal sanction. This achieves the essential task of providing general guidance for citizens and law enforcement officers.

(B) DOES SECTION 43 DELINEATE A RISK ZONE FOR CRIMINAL SANCTION?

The purpose of s. 43 is to delineate a sphere of non-criminal conduct within the larger realm of common assault. It must, as we have seen, do this in a way that permits people to know when they are entering a zone of risk of criminal sanction and that avoids *ad hoc* discretionary decision making by law enforcement officials. People must be able to assess when conduct approaches the boundaries of the sphere that s. 43 provides.

To ascertain whether s. 43 meets these requirements, we must consider its words and court decisions interpreting those words. The words of the statute must be considered in context, in their grammatical and ordinary sense, and with a view to the legislative scheme's purpose and the intention of Parliament:

Section 43 delineates who may access its sphere with considerable precision. The terms "schoolteacher" and "parent" are clear. The phrase "person standing in the place of a parent" has been held by the courts to indicate an individual who has assumed "all the obligations of parenthood": *Ogg-Moss*, *supra* ...

Section 43 identifies less precisely what conduct falls within its sphere. It defines this conduct in two ways. The first is by the requirement that the force be "by way of correction". The second is by the requirement that the force be "reasonable under the circumstances". The question is whether, taken together and construed in accordance with governing principles, these phrases provide sufficient precision to delineate the zone of risk and avoid discretionary law enforcement. I turn first to the requirement that the force be "by way of correction". These words, considered in conjunction with the cases, yield two limitations on the content of the protected sphere of conduct. First, the person applying the force must have intended it to be for educative or corrective purposes: *Ogg-Moss*, *supra* ... Accordingly, s. 43 cannot exculpate outbursts of violence against a child motivated by anger or animated by frustration. It admits into its sphere of immunity only sober, reasoned uses of force that address the actual behaviour of the child and are designed to restrain, control or

express some symbolic disapproval of his or her behaviour. The purpose of the force must always be the education or discipline of the child: *Ogg-Moss*, *supra* ...

Second, the child must be capable of benefiting from the correction. This requires the capacity to learn and the possibility of successful correction. Force against children under two cannot be corrective, since on the evidence they are incapable of understanding why they are hit.... A child may also be incapable of learning from the application of force because of disability or some other contextual factor. In these cases, force will not be "corrective" and will not fall within the sphere of immunity provided by s. 43.

The second requirement of s. 43 is that the force be "reasonable under the circumstances". The Foundation argues that this term fails to sufficiently delineate the area of risk and constitutes an invitation to discretionary *ad hoc* law enforcement....

Against this argument, the law has long used reasonableness to delineate areas of risk, without incurring the dangers of vagueness. The law of negligence ... is founded upon the presumption that individuals are capable of governing their conduct in accordance with the standard of what is "reasonable".... The criminal law also relies on it. The *Criminal Code* expects that police officers will know what constitutes "reasonable grounds" for believing that an offence has been committed, such that an arrest can be made ... the criminal law is thick with the notion of "reasonableness".

The reality is that the term "reasonable" gives varying degrees of guidance, depending upon the statutory and factual context. It does not insulate a law against a charge of vagueness. Nor, however, does it automatically mean that a law is void for vagueness. In each case, the question is whether the term, considered in light of principles of statutory interpretation and decided cases, delineates an area of risk and avoids the danger of arbitrary *ad hoc* law enforcement.

Is s. 43's reliance on reasonableness, considered in this way, unconstitutionally vague? ... While the words on their face are broad, a number of implicit limitations add precision.

The first limitation arises from the behaviour for which s. 43 provides an exemption, simple non-consensual application of force. Section 43 does not exempt from criminal sanction conduct that causes harm or raises a reasonable prospect of harm. It can be invoked only in cases of non-consensual application of force that results neither in harm nor in the prospect of bodily harm. This limits its operation to the mildest forms of assault. People must know that if their conduct raises an apprehension of bodily harm they cannot rely on s. 43. Similarly, police officers and judges must know that the defence cannot be raised in such circumstances.

Within this limited area of application, further precision on what is reasonable under the circumstances may be derived from international treaty obligations. Statutes should be construed to comply with Canada's international obligations ... Canada's international commitments confirm that physical correction that either harms or degrades a child is unreasonable....

From these international obligations, it follows that what is "reasonable under the circumstances" will seek to avoid harm to the child and will never include cruel, inhuman or degrading treatment.... Section 43's ambit is further defined by the direction to consider the circumstances under which corrective force is used. National and international precedents have set out factors to be considered. Article 3 of the *European Convention on Human Rights* ... forbids inhuman and degrading treatment. The European Court of Human Rights, in determining whether parental treatment of a child was severe enough to fall within the scope of Article 3, held that assessment must take account of "all the circumstances of the case, such as the nature and context of the treatment, its duration, its physical and mental effects and, in some instances, the sex, age and state of health of the victim".... These factors properly focus on the prospective effect of the corrective force upon the child, as required by s. 43.

By contrast, it is improper to retrospectively focus on the gravity of a child's wrongdoing, which invites a punitive rather than corrective focus. "[T]he nature of the offence calling for correction", an additional factor suggested in *R. v. Dupperon* ... is thus not a relevant contextual consideration. The focus under s. 43 is on the correction of the child, not on the gravity of the precipitating event....

Determining what is "reasonable under the circumstances" in the case of child discipline is also assisted by social consensus and expert evidence on what constitutes reasonable corrective discipline.... It is wrong for caregivers or judges to apply their own subjective notions of what is reasonable; s. 43 demands an objective appraisal based on current learning and consensus. Substantial consensus, particularly when supported by expert evidence, can provide guidance and reduce the danger of arbitrary, subjective decision making.

Based on the evidence currently before the Court, there are significant areas of agreement

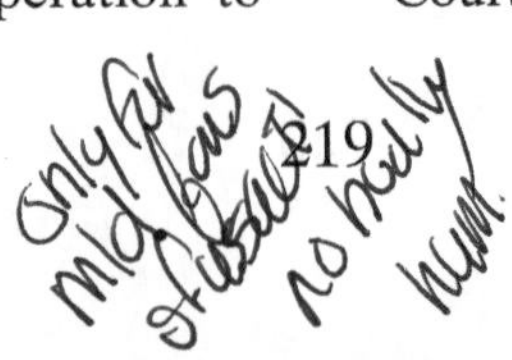

among the experts on both sides of the issue.... Corporal punishment of children under two years is harmful to them, and has no corrective value given the cognitive limitations of children under two years of age. Corporal punishment of teenagers is harmful, because it can induce aggressive or antisocial behaviour. Corporal punishment using objects, such as rulers or belts, is physically and emotionally harmful. Corporal punishment which involves slaps or blows to the head is harmful. These types of punishment, we may conclude, will not be reasonable.

Contemporary social consensus is that, while teachers may sometimes use corrective force to remove children from classrooms or secure compliance with instructions, the use of corporal punishment by teachers is not acceptable....

Finally, judicial interpretation may assist in defining "reasonable under the circumstances" under s. 43. It must be conceded at the outset that judicial decisions on s. 43 in the past have sometimes been unclear and inconsistent, sending a muddled message as to what is and is not permitted.... On occasion, judges erroneously applied their own subjective views on what constitutes reasonable discipline — views as varied as different judges' backgrounds. In addition, charges of assaultive discipline were seldom viewed as sufficiently serious to merit in-depth research and expert evidence or the appeals which might have permitted a unified national standard to emerge. However, "[t]he fact that a particular legislative term is open to varying interpretations by the courts is not fatal".... This case, and those that build on it, may permit a more uniform approach to "reasonable under the circumstances" than has prevailed in the past. Again, the issue is not whether s. 43 has provided enough guidance in the past, but whether it expresses a standard that can be given a core meaning in tune with contemporary consensus.

When these considerations are taken together, a solid core of meaning emerges for "reasonable under the circumstances", sufficient to establish a zone in which discipline risks criminal sanction. Generally, s. 43 exempts from criminal sanction only minor corrective force of a transitory and trifling nature. On the basis of current expert consensus, it does not apply to corporal punishment of children under two or teenagers. Degrading, inhuman or harmful conduct is not protected. Discipline by the use of objects or blows or slaps to the head is unreasonable. Teachers may reasonably apply force to remove a child from a classroom or secure compliance with instructions, but not merely as corporal punishment. Coupled with the requirement that the conduct be corrective, which rules out conduct stemming from the caregiver's frustration, loss of temper or abusive personality, a consistent picture emerges of the area covered by s. 43. It is wrong for law enforcement officers or judges to apply their own subjective views of what is "reasonable under the circumstances"; the test is objective. The question must be considered in context and in light of all the circumstances of the case. The gravity of the precipitating event is not relevant.

The fact that borderline cases may be anticipated is not fatal. As Gonthier J. stated in *Nova Scotia Pharmaceutical*, *supra*, at p. 639, "it is inherent to our legal system that some conduct will fall along the boundaries of the area of risk; no definite prediction can then be made. Guidance, not direction, of conduct is a more realistic objective".

Section 43 achieves this objective. It sets real boundaries and delineates a risk zone for criminal sanction. The prudent parent or teacher will refrain from conduct that approaches those boundaries, while law enforcement officers and judges will proceed with them in mind. It does not violate the principle of fundamental justice that laws must not be vague or arbitrary.

My colleague, Arbour J., by contrast, takes the view that s. 43 is unconstitutionally vague, a point of view also expressed by Deschamps J. Arbour J. argues first that the foregoing analysis amounts to an impermissible reading down of s. 43. This contention is answered by the evidence in this case, which established a solid core of meaning for s. 43; to construe terms like "reasonable under the circumstances" by reference to evidence and argument is a common and accepted function of courts interpreting the criminal law. To interpret "reasonable" in light of the evidence is not judicial amendment, but judicial interpretation. It is a common practice, given the number of criminal offences conditioned by the term "reasonable". If "it is the function of the appellate courts to rein in overly elastic interpretations" ... it is equally their function to define the scope of criminal defences.

Arbour J. also argues that unconstitutional vagueness is established by the fact that courts in the past have applied s. 43 inconsistently. Again, the inference does not follow. Vagueness is not argued on the basis of whether a provision has been interpreted consistently in the past, but whether it is capable of providing guidance for the future. Inconsistent and erroneous applications are not uncommon in criminal law, where many provisions admit of difficulty; we do not say that this makes them unconstitutional. Rather, we rely on appellate courts to clarify the meaning so that future application may be more consistent. I agree with Arbour J. that Canadians would find the decisions in many of the past cases on s. 43 to be seriously objectionable. However, the discomfort of Canadians in the face of such unwarranted acts of violence toward children merely demonstrates that it is possible to define what corrective force is reasonable in the circumstances. Finally, Arbour J. argues that parents who face criminal charges as a result of corrective force will be able to rely on the defences of necessity and "*de minimis*". The defence of necessity, I agree, is available, but only in situations where corrective force is not in issue, like saving a child from imminent danger. As for the defence of *de minimis*, it is equally or more vague and difficult in application than the reasonableness defence offered by s. 43.

(2) Overbreadth

... Section 43 does not permit force that cannot correct or is unreasonable. It follows that it is not overbroad.

II. DOES SECTION 43 OF THE *CRIMINAL CODE* OFFEND SECTION 12 OF THE *CHARTER*?

Section 12 of the *Charter* guarantees "the right not to be subjected to any cruel and unusual treatment or punishment" ...

[T]he conduct permitted by s. 43 does not in any event rise to the level of being "cruel and unusual", or "so excessive as to outrage standards of decency".... Section 43 permits only corrective force that is reasonable. Conduct cannot be at once both reasonable and an outrage to standards of decency. Corrective force that might rise to the level of "cruel and unusual" remains subject to criminal prosecution.

III. DOES SECTION 43 OF THE *CRIMINAL CODE* OFFEND SECTION 15 OF THE *CHARTER*?

Section 43 permits conduct toward children that would be criminal in the case of adult victims. The Foundation argues that this distinction violates s. 15 of the *Charter*, which provides that "[e]very individual is equal before and under the law" without discrimination. More particularly, the Foundation argues that this decriminalization discriminates against children by sending the message that a child is "less capable, or less worthy of recognition or value as a human being or as a member of Canadian society"....

The difficulty with this argument, as we shall see, is that it equates equal treatment with identical treatment, a proposition which our jurisprudence has consistently rejected.... Parliament's choice not to criminalize this conduct does not devalue or discriminate against children, but responds to the reality of their lives by addressing their need for safety and security in an age-appropriate manner.

A. The Appropriate Perspective

Section 43 makes a distinction on the basis of age, which s. 15(1) lists as a prohibited ground of discrimination. The only question is whether this distinction is discriminatory under s. 15(1) of the *Charter*.

Before turning to whether s. 43 is discriminatory, it is necessary to discuss the matter of perspective. The test is whether a reasonable person possessing the claimant's attributes and in the claimant's circumstances would conclude that the law marginalizes the claimant or treats her as less worthy on the basis of irrelevant characteristics: *Law*, *supra*. Applied to a child claimant, this test may well confront us with the fiction of the reasonable, fully apprised preschool-aged child. The best we can do is to adopt the perspective of the reasonable person acting on behalf of a child, who seriously considers and values the child's views and developmental needs....

B. Is Discrimination Made Out in This Case?

Against this backdrop, the question may be put as follows: viewed from the perspective of the reasonable person identified above, does Parliament's choice not to criminalize reasonable use of corrective force against children offend their human dignity and freedom, by marginalizing them or treating them as less worthy without regard to their actual circumstances? ...

The reality is that without s. 43, Canada's broad assault law would criminalize force falling far short of what we think of as corporal punishment, like placing an unwilling child in a chair for a five-minute "time-out". The decision not to criminalize such conduct is not grounded in devaluation of the child, but in a concern that to do so risks ruining lives and breaking up families — a burden that in large part would be borne by children and outweigh any benefit derived from applying the criminal process....

Some argue that, even if the overall effect of s. 43 is salutary, for some children the effects of s. 43 will turn out to be more detrimental than beneficial. To this, two responses lie. First, where reasonable corrective force slips into harmful, degrading or abusive conduct, the criminal law remains ready to respond. Secondly, as Iacobucci J. stated in *Law*, *supra*, compliance with s. 15(1) of the *Charter* does not require "that legislation must always correspond perfectly with social reality"....

I am satisfied that a reasonable person acting on behalf of a child, apprised of the harms of criminalization that s. 43 avoids, the presence of other governmental initiatives to reduce the use of corporal punishment, and the fact that abusive and harmful conduct is still prohibited by the criminal law, would not conclude that the child's dignity has been offended in the manner contemplated by s. 15(1). Children often feel a sense of disempowerment and vulnerability; this reality must be considered when assessing the impact of s. 43 on a child's sense of dignity. Yet, as emphasized, the force permitted is limited and must be set against the reality of a child's mother or father being charged and pulled into the criminal justice system, with its attendant rupture of the family setting, or a teacher being detained pending bail, with the inevitable harm to the child's crucial educative setting. Section 43 is not arbitrarily demeaning. It does not discriminate. Rather, it is firmly grounded in the actual needs and circumstances of children. I conclude that s. 43 does not offend s. 15(1) of the *Charter*....

I would dismiss the appeal.

■

Arbour J. concluded that s. 43 of the *Code* infringed the rights of children under s. 7 of the *Charter* and that this infringement was not reasonably justified in a free and democratic society within the meaning of s. 1 of the *Charter*. In her view, the majority's narrowing of s. 43 is "a laudable effort to take the law where it ought to be. However, s. 43 can only be so interpreted if the law, as it stands, offends the Constitution and must therefore be curtailed" (at para. 135). Do you agree? Should the majority have first found a constitutional violation before reading down s. 43?

Binnie, J., in a separate dissenting opinion, concluded that s. 43 violates children's equality rights under s. 15 of the *Charter*. However, he would have upheld the infringement as justified under s. 1 of the *Charter* as reasonable in a free and democratic society, but only in relation to parents and persons standing in the place of parents and not in relation to teachers.

Deschamps, J., in another dissenting opinion, agreed with Arbour J.'s analysis of the s. 7 issues, but concluded that s. 43 violates s. 15 of the *Charter* because it "encourages a view of children as less worthy of protection and respect for their bodily integrity based on outdated notions of their inferior personhood" (at para. 232). She found that the s. 15 violation was not saved under s. 1 because a law that permits more than only very minor applications of force, as s. 43 does, unjustifiably impairs children's rights. Like Arbour, J., she would have struck down s. 43.

C. *DE MINIMIS*

R. v. Lepage†

[McINTYRE J.:]

Guy Lepage was charged with an offence containing the following counts:

1. on or about the 12th day of December, A.D. 1988 at or near Regina, Saskatchewan did commit an assault on John Mitchell, contrary to s. 266 of the *Criminal Code*.

† (1989), 74 C.R. 3d 368 (Sask. Q.B.).

2. on or about the 12th day of December, A.D. 1988 at or near Regina, Saskatchewan did commit an assault on Leroy Fargo, contrary to s. 266 of the *Criminal Code*.

The matter came on for trial before His Honour Judge K.E. Bellerose on the 5th day of June, 1989, and at the conclusion of the hearing he found Guy Lepage guilty on count (1) and not guilty on count (2) and sentenced Mr. Lepage to pay a fine of $200.00, or in default, seven days in jail.

An appeal was launched on behalf of Mr. Lepage by notice dated the 5th of July, 1989, and on the 11th of September, 1989 an amended notice of appeal was filed containing several grounds.

The hearing of this appeal came on before me on the 20th of October, 1989, and Mr. Stoesser for the Crown, in his usual fair fashion advised that he did not object to the extra grounds set out in the amended notice of appeal and that it would be quite proper for the Court to examine the penalty imposed. It is necessary for me to examine the facts found by the learned trial judge based on the evidence before him and particularly the question of whether or not a criminal offence was committed.

Mr. Lepage operated a service station at 465 Broad Street, Regina, and among other things, he sold natural fir trees from his lot prior to Christmas. Mr. Lepage received a letter dated July 21, 1988, from R.E. Rowland, Fire Marshall of the Regina Fire Department (D-4) which reads in the first few lines:

> TO WHOM IT MAY CONCERN:
>
> INDOOR SALE OF CHRISTMAS TREES
>
> This bulletin is to inform you that the indoor sale of natural Christmas trees is prohibited.
>
> Natural Christmas trees are highly combustible and we are trying to avoid incidents such as occurred on January 1, 1980 at Chapais, Quebec where someone ignited cedar boughs used as decoration on the walls and 48 persons lost their lives.

Mr. Lepage was constructing a new cindercrete building for a car wash on the lot, and in December, 1988, he had a number of natural Christmas trees stored inside that building, but he was not selling any natural Christmas trees there.

On the 12th of December, 1988, Fire Inspector Fargo inspected the premises at 11:40 a.m. and prepared exhibit D-3, which is an order to remedy fire hazardous conditions and it states in part:

> The undersigned inspected the above property on the 12 day of December, 1988 (Time 11:40 hrs.) and has found the following conditions:
>
> Storage and Sale of Natural Christmas trees indoors.

The order went on to state:

> You are hereby ordered to:
>
> Remove all natural Christmas Trees from inside the Building by 1:00 p.m. ... on or before the 13 day of December, 1988.

This notice was signed by Inspector Fargo.

> The statement of Inspector Mitchell (D-1) was placed in evidence and he stated in part:
>
> On December 12th, 1988....
>
> At approximately 1:35 p.m. Mr. Lepage came in to the Turbo Service Station Building. At that point Inspector Fargo explained the Order to Remedy Form and how much time he had given him.
>
> He asked us into his office at the rear inside the building to discuss the matter. I went out to my vehicle to get a copy of *The Fire Prevention Act*, Chapter F-15.01. When I returned to to [*sic*] show, and explain to him the regulations it was then he turned quite belligerent, he jumped out of his chair pushing both of us aside hollering and cursing, telling us to get [the] fuck out, I don't have fucking time to talk to you. He repeated it twice so we did not discuss anything further. He proceeded to put his coat on [and] headed out the door to the newly constructed car wash building next door that is not completed, to the north that was used for the *storage* of natural Christmas trees.
>
> As we got into our vehicle to leave and in the process of starting up the vehicle, he started to remove the trees.... [My Emphasis.]

The learned trial judge considered the evidence and he found that Mr. Lepage was somewhat upset by the fact that the letter from Fire Marshall Rowland stated: "sale of natural Christmas trees is prohibited" but that the new order stated: "storage and sale of natural Christmas trees indoors" was prohibited and inasmuch as he was only storing fir trees in the cindercrete building, he was rather upset.

The learned trial judge found as follows (p. 73):

> ... As they are delivering the Order to Mr. Dalton, who appeared to be in charge of the premises at that time, Mr. Lepage enters the premises, invites Mr. Mitchell and Mr. Fargo to his little office, along the wall of the service station. I'm satisfied, there is a discussion with respect to what the City's attempting now to do and why are they changing their mind, why the

> double standard, as he describes it. I mean, he's not selling these trees, he's simply storing them and what is the particular problem.

Mr. Mitchell left the service station, went to his vehicle, and obtained a copy of *The Fire Prevention Code*. On his return [he] showed Mr. Lepage the specific section of the *Code*.

The learned trial judge then on p. 74 stated:

> ... [H]e just suddenly stands up from behind the desk, comes forward a step or two, I gather it's a very small office, pushes him on the chest area and, according to Mr. Mitchell, he may have brushed Mr. Fargo at the same time that he is pushing him, puts on his coat, goes out, starts removing Christmas trees from the particular storage shed.

Mr. Lepage in his evidence stated that he got up, went to get his coat and indicated that he did brush Mr. Fargo. He acknowledges there was contact in the sense of his clothing because the area where he had to get his coat from was so small that there would have had to be contact but he did not in the sense of intentionally applying force to him or of walking by him, bumping him intentionally and trying to make it look like an accident or anything of that nature.

The learned trial judge went on to state:

> There's, obviously, a difference between the versions of Mr. Lepage and Mr. Mitchell. Mr. Lepage denies any sort of pushing motion towards Mr. Mitchell. Mr. Lepage's version of the events is confirmed, if you will, to a certain extent by Mr. Dalton.

The learned trial judge went on to state (p. 76):

> I think, when you look at the events, I am prepared to accept the testimony of Mr. Mitchell.

He then went on to give his reasons for so stating.

On p. 78, the learned trial judge stated:

> ... I'm satisfied that, no, he waited until Mitchell came with the Fire Prevention Bylaw, probably, showed it, put it on the desk, said, "Here it is." And, I'm satisfied that he realizes at that moment, there is no talking, there is no way this Order is going to be rescinded by Mr. Mitchell or Mr. Fargo. *And, I'm satisfied, he realizes that it's suddenly out of his hands and out of their hands and he, just, says, "Oh, I might as well get this darn thing over with," and marches out. And, on the way out, I'm satisfied, Mr. Mitchell was probably standing in his way of, either, his egress to his coat or the door, one of the two, and he simply pushes him, not in the sense of, you know, striking out or anything of that nature but, more in the sense of get out of my way.* You know, you represent, the person who brings the Order, you represent bad news, you represent more problems for me, in terms of these Christmas trees, and get out of my road. And, it was in that sense that that push is administered to Mr. Mitchell. I accept Mr. Mitchell's testimony when he indicates he was pushed. [My Emphasis.]

And at p. 82:

> I think, in the end result, I am prepared to, as I indicate, accept Mr. Mitchell's statement as to how the events occurred. There was contact. There was a pushing again, *not in the sense of intending to do harm or damage to Mr. Mitchell*. Nevertheless, that push constitutes an assault under the definition within the *Criminal Code*. [My Emphasis.]

Mr. Lepage was convicted of an assault pursuant to s. 266 of the *Criminal Code* and it is noted that the Crown proceeded by way of summary conviction. The definition of assault as it relates to this case is contained in s. 265(1)....

In view of the statements made by the learned trial judge quoted earlier, I have great difficulty accepting his finding that Mr. Lepage applied force intentionally to Mr. Mitchell. I also note that the learned trial judge stated that he accepted the evidence of Mr. Mitchell, but I can't find anything in his reasons where he considered whether or not the explanation given by the accused might reasonably be true.

There is another aspect of this matter that causes me much concern, namely, the fact that if Mr. Lepage was breaching the *Fire Prevention Code*, this minor incident was used as a chance to charge him under the *Criminal Code* rather than under the *Fire Prevention Code*. It seems to me that persons in authority must carefully consider all the facts before they decide to proceed with a criminal charge.

The definition of assault in the *Criminal Code* has not changed much over the years and there are a number of cases dealing with the question of intention. A decision of the Ontario Court of Appeal in *Regina v. Starratt*, 5 C.C.C. (2d) 32 dealt with an assault causing bodily harm and the headnote is taken from the decision of Gale, C.J.O. and it reads:

> To convict of the offence of assault causing bodily harm it must be shown beyond a reasonable doubt that a person intentionally applied force. A finding by a trial Judge that a police officer applied force in the course of his duty or through carelessness is not sufficient to allow a conviction to stand in the absence of a finding

> that there was an intentional application of force in the sense of being a wrongful application of force.

Regina v. Wolfe, 20 C.C.C. (2d) 382 is another decision of the Court of Appeal for Ontario and the headnote is taken from the decision of Gale, C.J.O. and reads:

> No offence of assault causing bodily harm is committed when the accused, as a result of being struck by the complainant, strikes back in a reflex action since the element of intent, which is an essential ingredient of the offence, does not exist.

At p. 383, Chief Justice Gale stated:

> In any event, the encounter was a trifling one and we have come to the conclusion that the appeal ought to be allowed and the finding of guilt set aside, as I have already indicated.

Putting the Crown case at its highest, this incident can be described as a trifling one and it would appear that the case of *Rex v. McGibney*, 32 C.C.C. 325 is applicable.

That case was decided by Ross D.C.J. wherein McGibney was charged with an assault which was alleged to have taken place shortly after the close of the polls on the evening of the day on which the 1944 provincial election in Saskatchewan was held.

At pp. 327 and 328 it was stated:

> However, I will assume that it is established as a fact that at some stage of the argument the accused did in fact grab the appellant by the collar. The other material facts are that the accused when he detected the appellant immediately accosted him, that he addressed him in a loud voice and called him a damned liar and made other statements of a provocative character, that during this period that accused did gesticulate rather violently throwing his hands around and pointing at the appellant but I negative any finding upon the evidence of clenched fists or overt acts which might be construed as an attempt to strike if we exclude the one fact of grabbing the appellant's collar. This, however, by itself is not convincing of evidence of hostile intent. Many men in the course of an argument will involuntarily touch the person whom whey are addressing.

At p. 328 Ross D.C.J. further states:

> Now, assuming these facts to be proved, and I think I have stated the case for the prosecution as strongly as possible do these facts support a conviction for assault? I am of the opinion that in law they do not.

Judge Ross went on to quote the definition of assault which is very much the same as it is today. He stated (p. 330):

> I am of the opinion that the touching to which I have referred had no significance — if it took place it was with no intent to commit violence. The assault, if any, under these circumstances must consist of threatening actions and, while I have found that the accused's conduct was provocative and unjustified, yet I can by no process however technical find any intent to apply violence, and therefore he is not guilty.

In the case of *Rex v. Peleshaty* (1950), 9 C.R. 97, a decision of the Manitoba Court of Appeal, an accused and his wife were charged with having liquor not purchased from the Government Liquor Commission after the police made a raid on the farm premises and seized a number of bottles, some of which were empty, three of which were found among the kitchen utensils, one contained nothing but a smell, the other two contained approximately ten drops of what analysis showed to be proof spirits of 84.8 and 104.4 respectively. Each of the accused admitted knowledge of the empty bottles in the kitchen but denied that they knew the bottles contained liquor. The charge against the wife was dismissed, but the accused husband was convicted. He appealed and the Court of Appeal quashed the conviction and allowed the appeal. Adamson J.A. wrote the majority decision which was concurred in by the other four members of the Court. Although the charge was under *The Government Liquor Control Act*, 1928, R.S.M. 1940, c. 88 certain remarks made by Adamson J.A. apply with great force here and he stated at p. 106:

> The Act was not intended to be used to prosecute for having 10 drops of liquor, which is not a usable quantity. Convicting him for having 10 drops of liquor in each of two bottles is so trifling that the law should take no notice of it.
>
> Courts of justice generally do not take trifling and immaterial matters into account: *Broom's Legal Maxims*, 9th ed., p. 100.
>
> Where trifling irregularities or even infractions of the strict letter of the law are brought under the notice of the Court, the maxim *de minimis non curat lex* is of frequent practical application.... So, with reference to proceedings for an infringement of the revenue laws, Sir W. Scott observed that the Court is not bound to a strictness at once harsh and pedantic in the application of statutes. The law permits the

> qualification implied in the ancient maxim, *de minimis non curat lex*. Where there are irregularities of very slight consequence it does not intend that the infliction of penalties should be inflexibly severe ...

As I stated earlier, I have grave and serious doubts that this charge can be supported by the facts found by the learned trial judge in that there was no evidence to support a finding that there was an intentional application of force by Lepage against Mitchell in the sense of being a wrongful application of force. I am also of the view that the conduct of Mr. Lepage in this case was of such a trifling nature that the maxim, *de minimis non curat lex* should apply.

It seems to me that persons in authority should carefully assess a situation and if there is a breach of *The Fire Prevention Code*, then charge under it, and not turn a breach of a provincial statute into a criminal offence on such a trifling incident as this one.

There will be an order allowing the appeal and quashing the conviction of Guy Lepage. If the fine of $200.00 has been paid it is directed that it be returned to Mr. Lepage.

If I upheld the conviction I would have directed that Mr. Lepage receive an absolute discharge.

■

R. v. Matsuba[†]

[JONES J.:]

The accused Gregory Allan Matsuba is being tried before me on a charge that he:

> between the 27th day of April, 1992, and the 30th day of April, both dates inclusive, at or near Edmonton, Alberta, did unlawfully assault G.G., contrary to Section 266 of the *Criminal Code of Canada*.

The proceedings are by summary conviction. The charge contains some grammatical nonsense inasmuch as it talks about an assault occurring between specified dates and then purports to include those two dates. However, nothing turns on that. If found guilty, Matsuba faces possible dispositions ranging from an absolute discharge up to a fine of up to $2,000.00 plus up to six months' imprisonment.

The accused is a twenty-three-year-old Junior High School Teacher. The alleged victim is a fifteen year old girl who was a fourteen-year-old Grade IX student at the time of the alleged offence.

The incident alleged by the Crown through its witnesses clearly purports to be one that occurred in circumstances where Mr. Matsuba was acting in his professional capacity as a teacher and where G.G. was acting as a student on school property and under the direct supervision of Matsuba.

The actions of Matsuba said to constitute the assault are described as having consisted of two instances of Matsuba intentionally making physical contact by means of one of his hands or a part thereof with a portion of a leg of G.G. without her consent while he was ostensibly checking the art painting assignment which she was at the moment doing during the regular course of an art class which he was teaching and of which she was a member.

. . . .

There are two main issues requiring resolution:

(a) did the accused intentionally touch G.G. as alleged? and
(b) if he did, did he thereby commit an assault contrary to Section 266 of the *Criminal Code*?

For two reasons I choose to deal with these issues in reverse order, though more usually it would not be appropriate so to do. The first reason is because of the relatively unique and minimal impugned physical actions that the accused allegedly perpetrated against the complainant. The second is because of the rather unique relationship that can be said to exist between an adult school teacher and a teenage school student.

For the purpose of deciding whether the conduct of the accused, if proven as alleged, constitutes an assault, it is necessary to consider the allegations made against him.

The incident alleged to have given rise to the charge is said to have taken place in a classroom at

† (1993), 137 A.R. 34 (Alta. Prov. Ct. (Crim. Div.)).

a school in the City of Edmonton, Province of Alberta, known as J.H. Pickard, located on the southside of the City of Edmonton. The particular school, according to the evidence, has grades from 1 to 12. The class in question was a grade 9 class known as 9B. The particular course of study was an art course. Two photographs of what was said to be the classroom in question were entered but they are not detailed enough nor is the evidence with respect to them detailed enough to be of more than very general assistance in envisioning the setting. Each of the purported eyewitnesses aside from the complainant, G.G., testified as at the time sitting very close to or, in one case approaching the desk at which G.G. was working. Again, an examination of the evidence of each of these witnesses does not provide me with enough precise detail as to location and direction in order for me to come to positive conclusions about the vantage point that each one swore that she had. It is sufficient for me to say that I am satisfied that in all likelihood each one could have been in a position to see what she said that she saw when she gave evidence in this cause.

According to the witnesses, the incident alleged occurred during the course of an ordinary art class when the accused walked through an aisle to the point where G.G. was sitting at her desk. The particular desks were described by the witnesses as being higher than normal because they were used for art work. Each of the witnesses also stated that the students sat on stools which were higher than normal seats in classrooms. This was also the evidence of G.G. herein.

. . . .

The complainant G.G. was the fourth witness. She stated that she had been fourteen years of age during late April, 1992. She said that the accused taught religion and became their permanent art teacher part way through the year. She said that she thought the accused began teaching art during March of 1992. She said that she thought the date of the incident in question was the 29th of April, 1992 because she had looked at her calendar and concluded that that was the day on which the incident had occurred. She said that she was sitting at her desk dressed in shorts and had her legs crossed while she was painting with her legs sticking out into the aisle. She stated that the accused walked by and that first with a thumb he touched her leg at mid-shin in the front, with a brief touching that I take to have been approximately half a second to a second in terms of time, in a smudging like motion, as if he was picking up two or three grains of sand or salt from the centre of her shin, midway between her knee and her ankle. She said that her friend, A.M. came and that the accused said "when guys touch girls' legs they freak". She said that he then immediately ran his hand up her shin, and over her knee, saying "just checking to see if you shaved. She passed the test". As she had demonstrated the first alleged touching she demonstrated the second one showing the hand of the accused semi-cupped with the fingers pointed downward and basically closed, running quickly from about the centre of the front of her shin, that is to say as between her ankle and her knee, up to her knee and over the top of her knee to a point where his hand would have stopped like a cap over the knee with a little more of the hand on the part of the thigh that commences with the top of the knee than below on the shin which ends at the bottom of the knee. According to her demonstration and testimony this touching would have also been very brief, though it might well have occupied a second or perhaps two seconds in time. She said that she never consented to either of the touchings. She stated that the other three girls who were there said "that's disgusting". G.G. said repeatedly that while she didn't consent to this behaviour it was "no big deal". She did not talk to anybody in her family about it at first but she eventually received information that A.M. had told M.'s mother, who in turn had told G.G.'s mother about it. She said that eventually the principal called them all down to the office about a week after the incident and that they spoke with the principal. She then said that about two or three weeks later the principal came to class and lectured the students about having and showing respect for teachers. She said that he asked the students if they had any questions and that as a result of that they went to his office and he refused to speak with them about the matter. She said she had no discussion with her own mother about the matter before A.M.'s mother had been told and had spoken to her (G.'s) mother about the matter. Under cross-examination she stated that on the date in question there were about twenty students in the classroom and that she and the accused were both within the view of others. She said that there was no other student sitting right next to her at that desk on that day. She identified photographs of the classroom in question. She stated that H.B. was seated behind her and that N.D. was to her right. She said the A.M. was coming towards her when the incident happened. She wasn't positive which hand the accused used. G.G. stated that after the first touching A.M. said "what are you doing?" to the accused. G.G. said she didn't recall whether

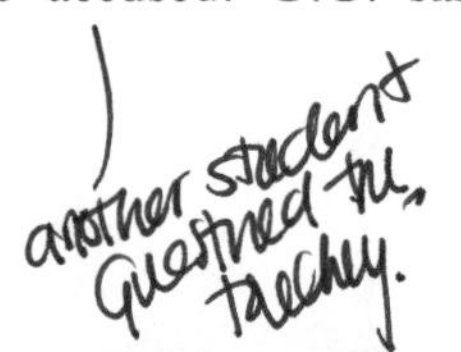

she herself said anything or if anybody else aside from A.M. said anything. She also said that they more or less collectively said to the accused "that's disgusting" upon the accused touching her the second time. At that time, she said, he made the comment about checking to see if she had shaved. She said that she then left and went to the other side of the room. Through her demonstration and testimony it was clear that the two alleged touchings took place within an interval of perhaps only at most four or five seconds. She confirmed that all of the other girls who were eyewitnesses were friends of hers. She said that she did discuss it with friends and talked with people about it but that it "was no big deal". She said that she probably said to others that it was "no big deal", although she did not agree with what had happened. G.G. confirmed that she and A. had got into trouble for painting on each other. She confirmed that the touching incident had occurred shortly after the mutual painting incident. She agreed that the Grade 9B class had a reputation for harassing teachers. At this point defence counsel, in asking G.G. about the second of three teachers to whom he had referred her with respect to the possibility that the conduct of the class had driven the particular teachers out of teaching their respective courses, asked G.G., "and there was open talk about getting rid of another teacher?" G.G.'s reply was "we didn't really plan. Like — okay — we never planned, we never said okay let's get a teacher to quit. We just did our little harassments and stuff and they quit on their own. We never actually planned to get someone to quit."

G.G., under cross-examination, also admitted that on the occasion, a few days prior, when she had been required by the accused to leave the classroom for the painting incident with A.M., she had probably had a temper tantrum, although no details were ever provided to the Court. She admitted further that she had received a lot of attention from the class for doing outrageous things. She also did admit that at one stage she talked to a friend on the soccer team about the incident although she denied that she was doing any more than telling the friend about what had happened. This conversation with the soccer friend occurred later in the summer. G.G. said that she had become somewhat annoyed with the accused at a time which she believed was about February of 1992 because he tried to act too much like he was from the same era as the students. She said that he flirted some though no specifics were asked for or given. She said that the accused annoyed several persons in the class and when she was asked more specifically about it she said that just a couple of persons here or there, not everyone in the class, became annoyed with the accused. She confirmed further that once he became a permanent teacher of the art class that he gave out more assignments, he dished out more detentions, and that he would send people out of the class if they caused difficulty in the classroom. She said that she was not aware that he ever tried to separate particular students. At one stage, under re-examination, G.G. said that the students had not allowed one of the other three teachers to teach at all. She said they would do things such as start little chants in the classroom. She said that the accused controlled the class quite well. She said that she felt a little disappointed when she found out that he was becoming their permanent teacher around the beginning of May.

G.G. also stated that she thought that the incident involving the accused was not particularly important except that in her opinion the accused should have admitted the truth about what he had done. She said that some of her friends wanted her to make an issue out of it and she said that she thought it was a lot of trouble for nothing. ...

[The court also reviewed the testimony of six other Crown witnesses: four classmates of the complainant, the complainant's parent, and the parent of one of the complainant's classmates.]

Four witnesses were called for the defence, the last of them being the accused Mr. Matsuba. The first three witnesses were school officials, the first of these being Mr. Leo Letourneau, the Principal at J.H. Pickard School at the time, the second being a Miss Anne Marie Duvoid, the Assistant Principal at the school at the time, and the third being a Dr. John Acheson, an Area Superintendent for The Edmonton Separate (Catholic) School Board, under whose jurisdiction this particular school came....

The accused, Matsuba, testified on his own behalf. He indicated that he had graduated as a teacher in 1991 with a Bachelor of Education Degree from the University of Alberta. He said that he had been engaged at J.H. Pickard School as a substitute teacher at first on behalf of The Edmonton Catholic School Board. He stated that he also substituted for art as well as religion at the School and that his art classes included class 9B. He said that the five named alleged eyewitnesses were all known to him as members of class 9B. Mr. Matsuba stated further that he was well versed in precautions with [regard] to behaviour in relation to students, even to such details such as shaking hands or patting students on the back.

Mr. Matsuba was asked specifically about the allegations made by each of the witnesses. He said in each case that he never did what the witness had described and said that it was not possible that he had done that. He specifically denied ever touching G.G. deliberately. He specifically denied ever having made the statements attributed to him by the Crown witnesses at the times of the alleged touching. Matsuba said that he would never say those things. He denied that he ever flirted with students. He also stated that he spoke to the students as an adult to students and not in some way more as a student would speak to a student. He denied that he used slang words or colloquialisms when speaking to students. The accused stated that he first heard of the accusations against him on either Wednesday or Thursday, the 5th or 6th of May, 1992, from the principal, Mr. Letourneau. The accused stated further that Letourneau had told him at that time that he, Matsuba, had been accused of running his hand up a student's thigh and that the student was G.G. The accused stated that he was utterly bewildered by the allegations. He said that he could not even remember an occasion when such an event could have occurred. He stated further that while he specifically denied ever deliberately touching the complainant it might have been possible that he had accidentally touched her while walking up what he called were rather narrow aisles between the desks, but averred further that he actually had no recollection whatsoever of even accidentally touching or coming into physical contact with the complainant G.G. at any time.

. . . .

On the assumption that I accept the general thrust of the evidence of the five eyewitnesses who testified in this case I would have no difficulty in coming to the conclusion, coupling their testimony with [regard] to what they say they saw and heard of the accused, that the accused's actions were intentional in the sense of being deliberate in causing to be done the physical contact averted to. I would also have no difficulty here in concluding, on the evidence before me, assuming that I accept its correctness, that what was done by the accused to G.G. was without her consent. Having [regard] to the particular functions which each of them [was] ostensibly carrying out at the time of the physical contact there is no way of looking at the evidence based upon which one could conclude that she somehow might have consented by implication to the physical contact. It goes without saying that there is no evidence that she had expressly consented to the physical contact.

The more serious issue that has to be dealt with in this case is, assuming the truthfulness and accuracy of the Crown [witnesses'] averments, [ ] as to whether it can be said that the accused, in this case, applied "force" as that word is used in paragraph (a) of section 265(1) of the *Criminal Code.* At this point I note that if the attendant circumstances are right the degree of force used is almost immaterial when one is talking about an assault within the meaning of the word assault in section 265(1)(a) of the *Criminal Code*. It should also be noted here that both the Crown and defence are agreed that there are no sexual connotations to be implied in respect of the touching alleged by the Crown witnesses in this case, even if the touchings in question are proven beyond a reasonable doubt. This is not a question of a possible sexual assault but simply an assault under section 266 of the *Criminal Code*, one which would have constituted a "common assault" under the *Criminal Code* before "common assault" was removed from the *Criminal Code* as a specifically separate offence by amendments made by Parliament a few years ago. Common assault as such is now essentially included among the assaults which can occur under section 266.

[The court reviewed a number of cases pertaining to the issue of force.]

It should be noted that our *Criminal Code* has included the ancient Common Law notions of "assault" and "battery" into our section 265 definitions of assault — Section 265(1)(a) essentially covers the ancient "battery". When one looks at the above noted quotation the applicable definitions, which technically relate to what is called a "battery", involve a concept which seems to go a little further than merely intentional touching to the person of the victim without that victim's consent. I refer to the fact that the two definitions which are set out above talk about the injury being committed in circumstances of anger, revengefulness, rudeness, or insolence. It is not simply enough that there be an intentional deliberate touching, without consent, but it is necessary, in order to conclude that the particular touching constitutes "force" within the meaning of the statutory provision, that there be a connotation of anger, revengefulness, rudeness, or insolence, or at least some like behaviour to the touching performed before it can be said that there is the "force" which completes the legal definition of assault. It seems to me that this must be so, otherwise any deliberate application of physical contact that exhibited nothing more than the general intent to intentionally touch the victim without the victim's consent would be actionable at the instance of the criminal law. Thus it would seem to follow that, for example, if one jostled a little bit at a bus stop in order to get on ahead of other persons in very close physical proximity, it might be argued, subject to the maxim *de minimis non curat lex* dilemma, that the person doing the jostling would be guilty of assaulting each of the other persons whom he or she had deliberately bumped in the course of the jostling no matter how gentle the bumping might be, because it would be deliberate bumping or the application of force, without the consent of each of the other persons being touched. I do not think that the criminal law can be contemplated as envisioning this in the ordinary case of such jostling although there is no doubt but that a person could be so violent during the course of committing such jostling that properly he could be charged with assault.

Coming back to the present case, it does not seem to me that taking the evidence of the Crown at its highest that there is evidence of any accompanying behaviour on the part of the accused that would disclose anger or revengefulness or rudeness or insolent behaviour, not even if one includes as one must, the words attributed to the accused with respect to girls freaking out if their legs are touched by boys or the words attributed to the accused whereby he is alleged to have said "just checking to see if you shaved, she passed the test". Assuming it is found that those words were said as well as the actions in question committed there was no indication that they were spoken and that the actions which the accused engaged in in any way showed anger or revengefulness or even rudeness or insolence. At most, if it is found that the actions and words occurred as alleged by the Crown, the most that could be said would be that they were exhibited in a lightly brief joking manner, a suggestion made by at least two of the prosecution witnesses. In the *Burden* case it was not only the matter of the accused laying his hand on the thigh of the victim for some five to ten seconds. It was the combination of that behaviour with all of the attendant circumstances, including his behaviour in getting on an almost empty bus and deliberately sitting down beside the complainant, a complete stranger, his staring at her for a short time and his then placing his hand on a portion of her body for a much more significant period of time. It seems to me that in those circumstances the Court could easily find, as the B.C. Court of Appeal seem to have found, that the behaviour of the accused was at the least rude, or insolent, or both. In my view the facts of that case are highly distinguishable from the facts in the instant case, even assuming that the Crown's allegations as to the accused's physical actions and oral statements are proven in this case.

. . . .

Consideration of the possible application of the maxim *de minimis non curat lex* presupposes, in this case, not only the proof of the facts alleged by the Crown, but also that I am wrong in concluding that the reasoning in the *Burden* case provides a complete defence for the accused Matsuba in the instant matter. Assuming that I am wrong about the effect of *Burden* in relation to the facts before me I state without hesitation that the possible application of the aforementioned maxim must be considered in relation to the facts that at this point in this judgment are assumed to have been proven. Counsel for the Crown argued that the maxim was not applicable to a criminal case and that in any event on the facts of this case the maxim should not apply. Cited in support of this argument were the decisions in *R. v. Babiak and Stefaniuk* (1974), 21 C.C.C. (2nd) 464 (Man. Crt. of Appeal), *R. v. Quigley* (1954), 111 C.C.C., 81 (Alta Supreme Court Appellate Division), and *R. v. Li* (1984), 16 C.C.C. (3d) 382 (Ont. High Court of Justice). In *R. v. Babiak and Stefaniuk* the accused had been convicted of possession of heroin in respect of traces of heroin found on a tablespoon in the house in which they lived. On appeal from the convictions the defence raised, for the first time, the possible application of the maxim *de minimis non curat lex*. The Court of Appeal of Manitoba stated at p. 468:

> Without deciding whether the defence of *de [minimis] non curat lex* does apply or does not apply in drug cases and reserving the matter for another occasion, we are satisfied that there was clear evidence, that what was in the spoon found on the kitchen counter (ex. 1) was heroin. There was ample for the analyst to identify it and that is all the law requires. The jury was amply justified in concluding that there was heroin in ex. 1.

... While the Manitoba Court of Appeal did not say so in terms I am satisfied that what the Court was implying was that if the maxim could apply to such a case it did not on the facts before it apply in that particular case. In *R. v. Quigley* the Appellate Division of the Supreme Court of Alberta had to also deal with the question of whether a very very small amount of heroin could be in the possession of the particular accused. According to the report of the case the maxim *de minimis non curat lex* was never argued before the Appeal Court and the decision allowing the Crown's appeal and convicting the accused turns on the conclusion of the Court that the small amount of the drug in question was more than a measurable quantity, and that it was found in the possession of the Respondent, the only reasonable conclusion under the circumstances being that the quantity was the remnant or residue of a larger amount. Again the case is of very limited assistance when referred to the present matter because in *Quigley* the maxim was not specifically argued and does not appear to have been specifically considered by the Court. The facts distinguish it from the case at bar.

In the case of *R. v. Li*, Mr. Justice Montgomery of the Ontario High Court of Justice was dealing with a stated case, the facts of which had involved, among other things, the acquittal of an accused who had been found in possession of a screwdriver bit which had a value of approximately $1.00. The trial judge had found that the value of the screwdriver bit, $1.00, was so little that the doctrine *de minimis non curat lex* provided a defence to the charge of theft against the accused. In stating the case to Montgomery, J., who was sitting as a Summary Conviction Appeal Court, the trial judge had also made it clear from the stated case that he had held that there is a general discretion in the Provincial Court for the Judicial District of Peel (Ont.) to set a monetary guideline of $5.00 in respect of the value of goods, below which charges may not be successfully prosecuted. It was against this factual and legal background that His Lordship, sitting as I say as an Appeal Court, adopted the statement from certain earlier cases to the effect that, and I quote him from p. 384 of the judgment as follows:

> The wealth of authority, in my view, is that the principle of *de [minimis] non curat lex* had no application to the criminal law. That certainly has been the disposition in appellate courts in Canada in drug related offences ...
>
> If the law were as conceived by the learned provincial court judge rather than inhibiting shop-lifting the law would encourage it. It would be possible for an individual to acquire items of small value from a number of stores and do a sizeable shopping [*sic*] with impunity.

The final case cited respecting the possible applicability or non-applicability of the maxim *de minimis non curat lex* is the case indexed as *R. v. G. (T)* (1990), 102 A.R. 289, Alberta Provincial Court, Youth Division, a decision of Her Honour Judge A. Russell, as she then was (recently appointed a Judge of the Court of Queen's Bench of this Province). In that case one of the issues before Judge Russell was whether the defence of *de minimis non curat lex* is available in Alberta to a young person within the meaning of the *Young Offenders Act* (Canada) charged with a municipal by-law offence. She also had to decide, assuming that the answer to the aforementioned issue was to the affirmative, as to whether the defence should be applied on the facts of that case. The accused in that case had been charged under a Municipal By-law which forbade a person from consuming food or drink on a transit vehicle. He ate some candy on a transit vehicle both before and after being warned by a transit inspector that he was not allowed to do so.

One of the major concerns that Her Honour seems to have paid quite a bit of attention to in a very carefully and well-reasoned judgment has to do with the consequences which can fall to a young person convicted of some offence other than a criminal offence and in respect of which no discharge or alternative measures were available. That had some considerable impact on her decision, as I understand it. But at p. 292 of the judgment she refers with apparent approval to certain principles set out in *Canadian Criminal Law*, Stuart (1987) p. 499, where the author urges the adoption of principles which would make it mandatory to dismiss a charge if the defendant's conduct:

> ... (1) was within a customary licence or tolerance, neither expressly negatived by the person whose interest [was] infringed nor inconsistent with the purpose of the law defining the offence; or
>
> (2) did not actually cause or threaten the harm or evil sought to be prevented by the law defining the offence or did so only to an extent too trivial to warrant the condemnation of conviction; or
>
> (3) presents such other extenuations that it cannot reasonably be regarded as envisaged by the legislature in forbidding the offence.

Her Honour then states that to the above noted should be added the requirements that the defence should only be invoked:

(a) when all other defences have been exhausted, and;
(b) where the consequences of a conviction are severe.

With respect I adopt with approval the suggestions made by Judge Russell (as she then was) in the above noted case and am prepared, at least for the purposes of the case before this Court, to apply them to the circumstances before us. It seems to me that in this case, assuming that the Crown can prove the allegations made through the five eyewitnesses in question, the circumstances meet the tests set out alternatively by Stuart in the above noted passage. In addition to that with reference to the additional requirements posed by Judge Russell it seems to me that in the instant case, on the evidence, if I did not accept the oral defence presented by the accused and did not otherwise doubt the persuasiveness of the evidence of the Crown witnesses, I would have reached the situation where there were no defences left, assuming that I had also found that the actions as proved, in their circumstances, constituted an assault. And it would not be difficult to come to the conclusion that the consequences of a conviction could be severe notwithstanding the fact that under the Criminal Law at the present time there is room for an absolute discharge to be given. Even though an absolute discharge can be said to be the most lenient disposition available, at the level of Court sanctions, known to our Criminal Law, a discharge is still given in circumstances where the Court has in fact made a finding of guilty. It can, in my view, be said that it is even more in favour of an accused to apply the maxim *de minimis non curat lex* if it is otherwise available and there is a properly founded desire to allow the accused to avoid even having a finding of guilt being made against him in the particular circumstances. It seems to me that in the case before us there is a good basis for the Court doing so even if it comes to the conclusion that the conduct of the accused is otherwise criminally actionable. The actions and words of the accused, if proven, were admittedly not made with any sexual overtones. His behaviour, if found to be as the Crown has asserted, was done in the open and in the presence of several other students in the classroom. Absolutely no physical injury was done by the brief physical contact which would be found to have been committed. The physical contact in question was brief. Surely in circumstances such as the ones in this case, assuming that this Court finds as the Crown asks it to find in terms of facts, it would tend to bring the administration of justice into disrepute to even render a verdict that the accused was in fact guilty of the offence of assault, notwithstanding the fact that the accused could possibly be thereafter considered for the granting of a discharge either conditional or even absolute. I do not hesitate to say that in the instance before me if I make findings as the Crown asks, I would not hesitate to apply the maxim *de minimis non curat lex* and find the accused not guilty by reason of the application of the maxim. This particular application of the maxim, of course, would be in relation to the particular factual circumstances of the offence. I have no doubt about the appropriateness of the applicability of the maxim in this particular case, if the same is required. Referring briefly back to a portion of the judgment of Her Honour Daniel in the *Harrison* case (*supra*) I refer briefly to a decision from Saskatchewan referred to in *Harrison*. The case is *Lepage v. R.* In that particular case the Saskatchewan Queen's Bench Judge McIntyre, J. sitting as an Appeal Court on a Summary Conviction Appeal from a conviction for a charge of assault, held that the maxim *de minimis non curat lex* applied in a case which is nevertheless a little bit clouded over by the fact that as an Appeal Court Judge he also found that there was no evidence upon which it could be found that there was an intentional application of force. When one reads the text of the judgment closely, however, it is clear from the authorities cited by McIntyre, J. and his discussion of the evidence in the case before him, that he was saying that while he was of the view that there was no evidence upon which there could be a finding against the accused that the accused had intentionally applied force, if he, McIntyre, J., was wrong about that, then in the circumstances he was prepared to find that the little push that was involved, if deliberate and intentional, should not attract the sanctions of the Criminal Law and that the maxim *de minimis non curat lex* should apply. That takes me back to the case of *R. v. Li* and the ruling of Montgomery, J. While that ruling is one of a Supreme Court of a Province and is entitled to great weight and consideration, with respect I find that I cannot follow it. It seems to me that on the facts of that case, Montgomery, J. would have been better justified in saying that the maxim had no application on the facts before him, but that it was neither necessary [nor] desirable to say that it could never apply to appropriate facts.

The resolution of what I called issue (b) above is of course enough to entitle the accused to an acquittal and dismissal of the charge against him. However, I am of the view that there are obvious reasons for attempting to also try to resolve the evidence into facts respecting whether or not the accused did in fact deliberately touch G.G. as alleged by the Crown through its witnesses. This of course involves assessment of the evidence of all of the witnesses who testified.

. . . .

I find that in the circumstances I cannot be satisfied beyond a reasonable doubt that the accused deliberately touched the complainant, G.G., as alleged. In any event if he had touched her accidentally he could not be criminally liable.... For that reason he must be acquitted.

■

Would the result have been different had the assault been characterized as a sexual assault?

R. v. Stewart†

[RENAUD J.:]

(A) The Accusation

Donald Stewart is charged that on or about September 3, 1995, in the City of Cornwall, in the Eastern Region, he did commit an assault on Gail Levere, contrary to s. 266 of the *Criminal Code*. The Crown elected to proceed by way of summary conviction and the defendant entered a plea of not guilty on July 30, 1996. The Crown called only one witness, the complainant, and no evidence was called on behalf of the defendant.

(B) The Theory of the Defence

The defence raised is two-fold: firstly, that the actions of the defendant engage the doctrine of *de minimis non curat lex* and, secondly, and in the alternative, that the defendant is not guilty of any assaultive behaviour as defined by s. 265 of the *Criminal Code*, in pushing the complainant in the manner described by her.

It will thus be of assistance to set out the factual findings of the Court in order to place the submissions of law within an appropriate context.

(C) The Testimony of the Complainant

Ms. Levere testified that she and the defendant were cohabiting at the relevant time and that they continue to be "common law" spouses. As well, that on September 3, 1995, at approximately 5:30 hours, she was in bed when the defendant entered their home. She heard him speaking on the telephone, and was advised subsequently by Mr. Stewart that he might be leaving for Pennsylvania, a remark she described as "smart". Concerned about the possibility that he might leave with their automobile, Ms. Levere inquired about its whereabouts but the defendant was not forthcoming with any information. The recitation of facts in this paragraph is not in issue and was not contested by counsel for the defendant.

The complainant testified also that as she was asking her spouse where the automobile was parked, "he pushed me back". She noted that the contact was between one of his arms and her left arm and that it caused her some momentary difficulty in maintaining her balance. She was not injured and had not touched the defendant prior to being touched and did not initiate or suggest that she was about to initiate any form of physical contact.

As a result of the defendant's actions, she stated that she had enough and wanted to contact the police but the defendant held onto the telephone situated in the same room, making it [necessary] for her to return upstairs to contact the authorities by means of another telephone. The defendant did not interfere with the complainant in this respect.

Of note, the complainant observed that the defendant had been drinking, based on the presence of an odour of an intoxicant on his breath, but she did not suggest he was drunk.

In cross-examination, Ms. Levere agreed with Mr. Sherwood's sole suggestion, that Mr. Stewart acted as he did merely to get her out of the way.

As noted, the defendant did not testify or call any witnesses on his behalf.

(D) The Submissions of Both Counsel

It was submitted by the defendant's counsel that the contact was either of such a trifling nature as to

---

† [1996] O.J. No. 2704 (Ont. Ct. J. (Prov. Div.)).

be outside of the purview of the criminal law or, in the alternative, that it falls within the type of physical exchanges that are common between spouses in the course of the normal [day-to-day] activities for which consent may be presumed, including the exchange of words in a brief discussion punctuated by physical contact for the purpose of moving to one side the other person in order to end the exchange. In other words, no suggestion was raised that the defendant pushed his spouse by reason of accident, reflex, automatism, through extreme drunkenness, mental disorder, or as a result of joking behaviour, and it was not argued that the complainant consented to the physical contact in question.

The Crown submitted briefly that the factual background satisfied the elements of an "unlawful" assault as defined at s. 265 of the *Criminal Code*. Mr. Simard emphasized the actions of the defendant in preventing the complainant from calling the police by means of the nearest telephone although no attempt was made to hinder her movements towards the other available telephone.

(E) The Factual Findings

... Firstly, that the defendant applied force intentionally to the person of the complainant, by means of a "push" on the date in question and within the judicial region described. Secondly, that the defendant did not consent to the application of force which was sufficient to interfere with her balance. Thirdly, that the defendant applied this force in order to displace her to a certain appreciable degree from the place where she was standing. Fourthly, that the defendant was able to move about freely in all other directions. Indeed, no action of the complainant impeded Mr. Stewart's freedom of movement save for the obvious fact that she was standing and occupying an area of the floor space. Fifthly, that the complainant did not initiate any contact with the defendant nor did she conduct herself in any fashion that would suggest that she was about to engage in any assaultive behaviour and thus the following sections of the *Criminal Code* are not engaged: 27, 34, 35, 37, 38, 39 and 40. And, sixthly, that the defendant's action in "interfering" with the telephone is relevant to his state of mind only to a minor degree in that it does tend to demonstrate that he was upset with the actions of the complainant. In the final analysis, however, surely it is nearly irrelevant to the proper characterization of the defendant's actions; stated otherwise, had he not seized the telephone as he did, would his actions not amount to assaultive behaviour? To state the question is to answer it.

(F) A Review of the Doctrine of *De Minimis*

A thorough and current overview of the doctrine of *de minimis non curat lex* is found in Professor Don Stuart's masterful text, *Canadian Criminal Law* (Third Edition), [1995, Carswell, Toronto], at pages 512–546.... [The court reviewed Stuart's discussion of the *Li* and *Lepage* decisions.]

In the circumstances, the decision in *R. v. Lepage* is of limited assistance as the finding of McIntyre, J., is akin to a declaration that if there was contact, it was non-intentional, consistent with an accidental push as the defendant was seeking to leave the premises "in something of a huff".

At all events, and with great respect, if the decision is cited as authority for the proposition that a "push" in such circumstances is a trifling event and without the jurisdiction of the criminal law, it cannot be applied fully to a situation involving a domestic relationship. Indeed, the Court in *R. v. Lepage* was not impressed with the apparent lack of restraint displayed by the regulatory agency involved in attempting to police a commercial activity. The policy considerations and the dynamics between "the regulators and the regulated" that are at play in a licensed activity are not the same as found in a domestic relationship. Any exposure to the administration of criminal justice suffices to impress one with a sense of admiration for the professionalism of those called upon to enforce the law, such as police officers but including parking officials and inspectors in similar positions who must "suffer" certain distasteful remarks and incidental physical contacts in order to complete their tasks with a minimum of interruption. No corresponding rationale for the easy acceptance of such "tolerance" has been identified in a family setting.

More to the point, Prof. Stuart's reference to "The Reward" includes one quite relevant passage: "If the deviation were a mere trifle, which, if continued in practice would weigh little or nothing on the public interest, it might properly be overlooked." One questions how to reconcile the easy acceptance of any form of domestic violence with a philosophy of criminal law that should be devoted to ensuring to all the opportunity to thrive in a community free of all forms of exploitation. As observed by Prof. Kent Roach in his recent book, *Criminal Law* [Irwin Law, 1996, Toronto], at page 209, "In a few cases, the *Charter* has encouraged courts to consider the effects of laws in protecting victims of crime, and in particular women and minorities that may be disproportionately [ ] the victims of certain crimes." Further, Bill C-41, "An Act to amend the Criminal Code (sentencing) and other Acts in consequence thereof", also known as Chapter 22, S.C. 1995, to be proclaimed in force on September 1, 1996, will prove of greater assistance to victims of criminal behaviour and the Court's decision in this instance must be consonant with the goals that Parliament has identified as being at the forefront of modem penal philosophy notably those set out at s. 718.2(a)(ii). That section enacts that "A court that imposes a sentence shall also take into consideration the following principles: (a) a sentence should be increased or reduced to account for any relevant aggravating or mitigating circumstances relating to the offence or the offender, and, without limiting the generality of the foregoing, ... (ii) evidence that the offender, in committing the offence, abused the offender's spouse ... shall be deemed to be aggravating circumstances".

Hence, it is difficult to reconcile the obvious desire of many commentators, such as Prof. Stuart, to temper the potential harshness of the criminal law by means of a more embracing *de minimis* doctrine, among other developments, with the day-to-day reality that domestic violence accounts for such a large percentage of trial dockets and appears to exact an overwhelming cost from those who are victimized by it, both individually and collectively.

. . . .

Prior to concluding, it will be useful to address as well the only other instance known of the doctrine being applied to a case of assault. In *R. v. McGibney*, which was influential in the conclusion reached by Mr. Justice McIntyre, Ross, D.C.J., found an individual not guilty of an assault alleged to have occurred shortly after the close of the polls in the 1944 provincial election in Saskatchewan. The relevant findings taken from pages 327–28 [C.C.C.] follow:

> However, I will assume that it is established as a fact that at some stage of the argument the accused did in fact grab the appellant by the collar. The other material facts are that the accused when he detected the appellant immediately accosted him, that he addressed him in a loud voice and called him a damned liar and made other statements of a provocative character, that during this period that accused did gesticulate rather violently throwing his hands around and pointing at the appellant but I negative any finding on the evidence of clenched fists or overt acts which might be construed as an attempt to strike if we exclude the one fact of grabbing the appellant's collar. This, however by itself is not convincing of evidence of hostile intent. Many men in the course of an argument will involuntarily touch the person whom they are addressing.

May the case not be distinguished on the basis that once again the Court was concerned with a form of accidental or involuntary blow or contact? If not, and if the clear ruling of the Court is that the grabbing of a person's collar during the course of an argument in such circumstances is not sufficient to constitute an assault, then I decline to follow the reasoning as it serves no constructive purpose. I am of the view that a finding that the action of applying force intentionally to another during the course of an argument is blameless is likely to encourage such incidents, with the obvious potential for escalation and injury. Further, in a political context, such "forbearance" may only serve to undermine the democratic process and, if taken to the domestic context which serves as the background to this case, it is feared that such an interpretation would foster a greater lack of respect as between members of a domestic relationship for the physical and emotional well-being of each partner.

In sum, and as noted, Professor Stuart advances a number of impressive arguments with a view to promoting a far more embracing doctrine "...as an ideal vehicle for judges to ensure that in some doubtful cases the criminal law can be used with total restraint, and that the accused can be given the full benefit of the doubt even if technically guilty. ... the maxim can become a vehicle for a judge invoking the social purpose rather than literal approach to statutory construction." Refer to page 545. With respect, neither the provisions of the Model Penal Code nor of the C.B.A. Task Force, set out at page 546, address satisfactorily the concerns about permitting any degree of violence within the domestic context, and it is thought that subject to the type of curial review provided by the doctrine of abuse of process, the determination of a clear case of intentional assaultive behaviour within the domestic context ought not to be influenced by the application of the doctrine of *de minimis*.

This ground is rejected.

(G) Was there implied consent?

Little authority is required to sustain the proposition that in modern life, one may be subject to all kinds of unwanted physical contact, be it the jostling for position on the subway, the unwanted "glad-handing" of politicians on the "hustle", *et cetera*. However, no persuasive argument has been advanced to sustain the submission that a spouse consents to any form of violence in the course of a domestic argument. Nothing in the decision in *R. v. Jobidon* or subsequent decisions interpreting it appear to countenance such an extension of the law.

This ground is rejected.

(H) Conclusion

For all of the foregoing reasons, the Court finds that the offence alleged has been established beyond a reasonable doubt and a finding of guilt is entered.

■

For a recent application of *Stewart* see *R. v. Downey* (2002), 208 N.S.R. (2d) 153 (Sup. Ct.). Are there any general principles that emerge from the *de minimis* case law? When, if ever, is this defence available?

Many other defences are available for assault charges, including, among others, the defence of authority available to law enforcement officers in s. 25; defence of property in ss. 38–41; self-defence in s. 34; and possibly necessity, a common law defence. Most of these defences will be canvassed in later chapters.

8

Mistake of Fact

An accused who was mistaken as to some aspect of the criminal offence may be able to argue that the mistake vitiated the *mens rea* of the offence. Although called a defence, "mistake of fact" is essentially an assertion that, due to the accused's error, the Crown is unable to prove the mental element of the offence beyond a reasonable doubt. For example, an accused who was unaware of the identity of an undercover officer was acquitted of assaulting a police officer when he hit the man to prevent him from intervening in a fight: *R. v. MacLeod* (1954), 20 C.R. 281 (B.C.C.A.).

A mistake of fact must be distinguished from a mistake of law, which, according to s. 19 of the *Code*, affords no defence to a crime (see **Mistake of Law**, below). A mistake of fact is a mistake regarding the existence of certain facts such as the identity of a person or the composition of a chemical compound. By contrast, a mistake of law is an erroneous assumption or conclusion about the legal relevance, significance, or consequence of those facts: for example, a belief that a diluted form of a chemical mixture does not constitute a prohibited drug.

A. ISSUES

The highly gendered context of sexual assault and the frequent use of mistake of fact with respect to whether the complainant consented, raise several very important issues. The three themes outlined below, whether these mistakes are really mistakes of law, how s. 15 of the *Charter* should shape the law, and whether it is appropriate to develop specific rules for the offence of sexual assault, should guide your reading of the materials in this section.

CHARACTERIZATION OF THE "MISTAKE"

Has the accused in a sexual assault prosecution who claims that he thought the complainant consented made a factual error, or should it be more accurately characterized as a mistake of law? Most accused do not argue that they misheard her "no" for "yes", or that they suffered from some other misperception but, instead, argue that they believed that failure to object amounted to legal consent, or that they were entitled to infer consent from some behaviour or language on the part of the woman or, even, some other person. These errors are more accurately described as mistakes of law, as they involve misunderstandings about the legal conclusions that can be drawn from physical facts or social interactions. Lucinda Vandervort, in "Mistake of Law and Sexual Assault: Consent and Mens Rea" (1987–88) 2 C.J.W.L. 233, elaborates upon the argument.

ROLE OF *CHARTER* SS. 15 AND 28

How should ss. 15 and 28 of the *Charter* shape the development of the law of consent and the defence of mistake of fact? The Supreme Court of Canada has recognized that sexual assault is a sex equality issue because it is a crime overwhelmingly committed by men (99 per cent of offenders) against women and girls (90 per cent of victims) and because the threat of assault constrains women in the exercise of their rights and liberties: *R. v. Conway*, [1993] 2 S.C.R. 872 at 877; *R. v. Osolin*, [1993] 4 S.C.R. 595 at 669.

Section 15 can be used to challenge discriminatory legal rules and practices in the prosecution and defence of sexual assault charges. It can also be used to support arguments for law reforms that support women's dignity, equality and liberty interests when they act as the primary witnesses in a prosecution. It is relevant to the s. 15 inquiry to identify the burdens imposed upon those who report the crime of sexual assault. Some jurisdictions have required women to submit to polygraph testing as part of the investigation ("Rape victim polygraph ban under bill" *The Austin American-Statesman* (21 February 1995) B4) and others have required women to authorize release of their psychiatric and counselling records.

Furthermore, a woman who reports the offence may find herself investigated or charged by police, particularly if she is a racialized woman: Judith Lavole, "Police slammed in rape case" *The [Victoria] Times-Colonist* (9 November 1993) A1 (Aboriginal woman who was gang raped in a park accused by police of being drunk, and of possibly having fantasized the attack); "Inuit rape victim to receive $100,000" *The [Toronto] Globe and Mail* (25 November 1993) A4 (woman handcuffed and driven to court in the same vehicle as her attacker); and "Crown drops accusations that woman faked rape" *The [Toronto] Globe and Mail* (8 March 1994) A5 (African-Canadian group home worker charged with mischief after reporting sexual assault that included broken glass inserted in her vagina by her assailant, who she believed to be connected with the Heritage Front). Racialized women may face additional insult during the trial process: see Abell & Sheehy, *Cases, Context, Critique*, **Sentencing**, and the discussion of Judge Bourassa.

Finally, the woman who proceeds to the preliminary inquiry and trial can expect a harrowing experience. Women with disabilities will have their competence to testify challenged, as well as having their credibility as witnesses undermined. See, for example, *R. v. Wyatt (F.E.)* (1997), 91 B.C.A.C. 166 (C.A.) where the sexual assault prosecution against the accused was stayed on the basis that the victim/witness' brain injury prevented her from being cross-examined "effectively", such that the accused was denied his s. 7 *Charter* right to make "full answer and defence". Additional barriers to those with disabilities are presented by the prejudicial views held by judges and jurors and by the way in which the law governing consent ignores context and imposes a burden of demonstrating non-consent upon women: see Sandra Goundry, *Women, Disability and the Law: Identifying Barriers to Equality in the Law of Non-Consensual Sterilization, Child Welfare and Sexual Assault* (Winnipeg: The Canadian Disability Rights Council, 1994) at 91–101. See also *Persons With Disabilities*, discussed above, under **The Trial Process**.

AGAINST "GENERAL RULES OF GENERAL APPLICATION"

Should the law of mistake of fact develop in specific recognition of the context and implications of sexual assault? The distortion of the mistake of fact defence in the context in which it is most frequently used raises significant questions about whether it is appropriate or just to develop "general rules of general application" rather than rules that are specific to the crime and the rights and issues it implicates. Rosemary Cairns-Way has argued, in "Bill C-49 and the Politics of Constitutionalized Fault" (1993) 42 U.N.B.L.J. 325 at 328, for a contextual approach to *mens rea*:

> Sexual assault is an area of the criminal law in which the political nature of the allocation of blame has been convincingly demonstrated by feminist and critical scholars. The doctrine of *mens rea*, understood in law as neutral and objective, has been unmasked as partial, and as privileging a particular (male) viewpoint.... [T]he development of constitutionalized prin-

> ciples of fault ... has been characterized by a failure to address either the socio-political assumptions of present substantive criminal law doctrine, or the normative implications of constitutionalizing a certain concept of culpability ... foreclos[ing] a multidimensional or contextual approach to fault.

In an article written before *Pappajohn v. R.*, reproduced below, Toni Pickard argued that alleged mistakes regarding consent to sexual contact should be tested objectively for "reasonableness". In "Culpable Mistakes and Rape: Relating *Mens Rea* to the Crime" (1980) 30 U.T.L.J. 75, she emphasized that there were no binding precedents on the test for a mistake defence and that most of the case law in fact pointed towards a "reasonableness" requirement, as did the law in most U.S. jurisdictions (Constance Backhouse & Lorna Schoenroth, "A Comparative Study of Canadian and American Rape Law" (1984) 7 Can.-U.S. L.J. 173). In addition, at 76–77† Pickard made a compelling policy argument in support of a reasonableness requirement for the offence sexual assault:

> I want now to sketch my argument that a mistaken belief in consent should be accepted as a good answer to a rape charge only if the mistake was reasonable. In developing this position, I take as given that no man can find himself unwitting in the act of intercourse — i.e., that penetration is an act which cannot be done accidentally or by mistake. Because it is the act of penetration which the offence of rape prohibits in a given context, a man about to penetrate has his mind focused necessarily on the legally relevant transaction. He is about to engage intentionally in the specific act which can itself be harmful, and whether or not the act is harmful in any particular instance cannot be determined without reference to the world outside him. That is sufficient reason to require him, as an initial matter, to inquire into consent before proceeding. No accused should be able, therefore, to defend himself successfully against a rape charge by claiming that he had no belief whatsoever about consent because he simply did not advert. He must put forward more than a claim of mere absence of knowledge of non-consent: he must assert a belief in consent. The question then is one of the quality of the belief which will be sufficient to exonerate.
>
> There can be no doubt that it is a major harm for a woman to be subjected to non-consensual intercourse notwithstanding that the man may believe he has her consent. There can be little doubt that the cost of taking reasonable care is insignificant compared with the harm which can be avoided through its exercise: indeed, the only cost I can identify is the general one of creating some pressure towards greater explicitness in sexual contexts. To accept an honest but unreasonable belief in consent as a sufficient answer in these circumstances is to countenance the doing of a major harm that could have been avoided at no appreciable cost. Therefore, in terms of simple balancing of interests, it is sound policy to require reasonable care, given the capabilities of the actor. It is true, of course, that not all sound policies can be appropriately pursued through the use of criminal law. But considering the disparate weights of the interests involved, a failure to inquire carefully into consent constitutes, in my view, such a lack of minimal concern for the bodily integrity of others that it is good criminal policy to ground liability on it.

Other authors have also argued against "general rules of general application": see Kathleen Lahey, "Implications of Feminist Theory for the Direction of Reform of the *Criminal Code*" (Ottawa: Law Reform Commission of Canada, 1984) [unpublished]; Christopher Nowlin, "Against a General Part of the Canadian *Criminal Code*" (1993) 27 U.B.C.L. Rev. 291; and Annalise Acorn, *The Defence of Mistake of Fact and the Proposed Recodification of the General Part of the Criminal Code: A Feminist Critique and Proposals for Reform* (Edmonton: The Alberta Women's and Seniors' Secretariat, 1994) [hereinafter, *A Feminist Critique*].

Are there other offences for which the argument might be made that a specific rendering of the mistake of fact defence is required in order to deal with the complexities of the offence and its context? Consider, for example, mistake of fact as a defence to trafficking in controlled drugs where the accused believes himself to be trafficking in a Schedule F drug under the *Food and Drugs Act*, which is a far less serious offence. See the result in *R. v. Kundeus*, [1976] 2 S.C.R. 272, as well as

† Toni Pickard, "Culpable Mistakes and Rape: Relating *Mens Rea* to the Crime" (1980) 30 U.T.L.J. 75 at 76–77. Reproduced by permission of University of Toronto Press Incorporated (www.utpjournals.com).

the case comment by Joseph M. Weiler, "Regina v. Kundeus. A Saga of Two Ships Passing in the Night" (1976) 14 Osgoode Hall L.J. 457. Are there any policy reasons that might support convicting such an accused despite a mistake of fact defence?

The legislature has imposed an objective rider on the mistake of fact defence in some contexts. See, for example, mistake as to age with respect to sexual abuse of a child under 14 years of age, s. 150.1(4), where the accused must show he took all reasonable steps to ascertain the age of the child. Another example is the defence of necessity for the offence of unlawfully taking a child from her parent (s. 281), set out in s. 285 of the *Code*, which provides that the abduction must be necessary to protect the child (or the accused) from the danger of imminent harm. In *R. v. Adams* (1993), 12 O.R. (3d) 248 (C.A.), the court dismissed an appeal from conviction by a common-law stepmother, her mother, her sister, and friends who together removed a six-year-old from the custody of a father who, among other things, was alleged to have disciplined his daughter through verbal abuse and by striking her hand with a belt. The court stated that while a mistake of fact defence need only be honest and not reasonable, it is limited in that case by the objective requirements in s. 285: "to be necessary within the terms of s. 285, taking Sabrina from her father, in response to a belief that she was in danger of imminent harm, must be a proportionate response, viewed objectively, but in the light of the circumstances honestly perceived by the appellants" (at 259). Could the courts read in similar riders for other mistake defences?

As you read *Pappajohn* below, consider the three themes discussed above. Was Pappajohn's alleged mistake one of fact or law in light of the fact that when asked by the interviewing police officer whether the victim/witness had resisted going to bed, Pappajohn answered: "Not violently"? See the decision at the B.C. Court of Appeal (1978), 5 C.R. (3d) 193 at 205. Can the decision be challenged on the basis of s. 15 of the *Charter*? Does *Pappajohn* represent a "general principle of general application", or does it, instead, illustrate the partiality of legal doctrine? Note, in this regard, that Dickson C.J.C.'s reference to the "virtually unanimous" scholarship in support of his position did not include the dissenting opinion of Professor Pickard, above.

Pappajohn v. R.†

[McINTYRE J. (Chouinard, Pigeon, and Beetz JJ. concurring):]

The appellant appeals his rape conviction, which was affirmed in the Court of Appeal for British Columbia with one dissent [45 C.C.C. (2d) 67, 5 C.R. (3d) 193, [1979] 1 W.W.R. 562], upon the ground that the trial Judge failed to put to the jury the defence of mistake of fact. That ground is expressed in the appellant's factum in these words:

> Did the learned trial judge err in failing to instruct the jury on the question of honest belief by the accused that the Complainant consented to intercourse and thus on the facts of this case, failed to put properly before the jury a defence, such failure being a non-direction amounting to mis-direction?

A consideration of the facts of the case is vital to a resolution of the problem it poses. The complainant was a real estate saleswoman employed by a well-known and well-established real estate firm in Vancouver. She was successful in her work. The appellant is a businessman who was anxious to sell his home in Vancouver and he had listed it for sale with the real estate firm with which the complainant was associated. She was to be responsible for the matter on her firm's behalf. On August 4, 1976, at about 1:00 p.m., she met the appellant by appointment at a downtown restaurant for lunch. The purpose of the meeting was to discuss the house sale. The lunch lasted until about 4:00 or 4:30 p.m. During this time, a good deal of liquor was consumed by both parties. The occasion became convivial, the proprietor of the restaurant and his wife joined the

† [1980] 2 S.C.R. 120.

"token" resistance.

party, and estimates of the amount of alcohol consumed varied in retrospect, as one would expect. It does seem clear, however, that while each of the parties concerned had a substantial amount to drink, each seemed capable of functioning normally.

At about 4:00 p.m., or shortly thereafter, they left the restaurant. The appellant drove the complainant's car while she sat in the front passenger seat. They went to the appellant's house, the one which was listed for sale, to further consider questions arising in that connection. Up to the time of arrival at the home, at about 4:30 or 5:00 p.m., there is no significant variation in their accounts of events. From the moment of arrival, however, there is a complete divergence. She related a story of rape completely against her will and over her protests and struggles. He spoke of an amorous interlude involving no more than a bit of coy objection on her part and several acts of intercourse with her consent. Whatever occurred in the house, there is no doubt that at about 7:30 p.m. the complainant ran out of the house naked with a man's bow tie around her neck and her hands tightly tied behind her back with a bathrobe sash. She arrived at the door of a house nearby and demanded entry and protection. The occupant of the house, a priest, admitted her. She was in an upset state and exhibited great fear and emotional stress. The police were called and these proceedings followed. More detailed reference to the facts will be made later.

When the defence closed its case and before the trial Judge commenced his charge, the jury was excluded while counsel for the appellant argued that on the facts of the case as it appeared from the evidence, the trial Judge should put the defence of mistake of fact to the jury. He contended that the appellant was entitled to have the Judge tell the jury that if the appellant entertained an honest though mistaken belief that the complainant was consenting to the acts of intercourse as they occurred, the necessary *mens rea* would not be present, and the appellant would be entitled to an acquittal. Reliance for his proposition was placed upon *Director of Public Prosecutions v. Morgan*, [1975] 2 ALL E.R. 347 (H.L.), and *R. v. Plummer and Brown*, (1975) 24 C.C.C. (2d) 497, 31 C.R.N.S. 220 (Ont. C.A.). The trial Judge refused to accede to defence counsel's request and in disposing of the motion had this to say:

> THE COURT: In this case the complainant has testified that the accused had intercourse with her during a three-hour period some five times without her consent. The accused has testified that the acts of intercourse that he had with the complainant were all with her consent and that the only resistance to his amorous advances was of a token variety, and that orally along the lines of: "Oh George, what are you doing?"
>
> There are many conflicts in the evidence during the critical period of time when the acts of sexual intercourse took place, and the jury will have to be directed to accept either the complainant's or the accused's version of the facts.
>
> The essence of the case as I see it is essentially has the Crown negatived the complainant's consent?

Later, he said, after referring to the *Morgan* case and the case of *Plummer and Brown*:

> Although the concept of mens rea underlies all criminal prosecutions I know of no obligation to instruct a jury in connection with this concept. I acknowledge and am in agreement with counsel's statements that in appropriate circumstances defences arise in favour of accused persons, even where no intent is apparent from the statute creating an offence, and these defences at a minimum are accident and mistake of fact. Although the reasoning in Director of Public Prosecutions and Morgan may have limited application to Canadian Criminal Law, I am wholly in accord with the attempt made by the learned Trial Judge in placing before the jury in that case what I conceive to be an alternative defence, namely, a mistaken view of the facts. That defence was justified in that case because three of the four accused persons pledged their oaths to the assertion that the victim's husband, also a co-accused, had told them before attending at the victim's residence that his wife was prone to put on a show of struggling but that this would only be a charade stimulating her sexual excitement.
>
> In answer to my questions during argument defence counsel has suggested that acts of familiarity prior to the time of intercourse, independently testified to by disinterested persons, and the accused's evidence where he alluded to only oral and token resistance to his advances, constituted evidence upon which I could conclude that the defence of mistake of fact should be left to the jury.
>
> In addition to that evidence, I have reviewed the evidence of the accused and I regret to say, notwithstanding the forceful submission of defence counsel, I do not recognize in the evidence any sufficient basis of fact to leave the defence of mistake of fact to this jury.

In the Court of Appeal, this ruling found support in the majority judgment of Farris, C.J.B.C., with whom Craig, J.A., agreed. The majority adopted the view that the issue emerging from the evidence was a simple one of consent or no consent. In a dissenting judgment, Lambert, J.A., was of the opinion that there was sufficient evidence to put the defence to the jury. He would have directed the jury that the accused was entitled to an acquittal if the jury found that he entertained an honest and *reasonably held* mistaken belief in the existence of consent. This is a view which I cannot share in view of the pronouncement in this Court in *Beaver v. The Queen* (1957), 118 C.C.C. 129 at pp. 136–7, [1957] S.C.R. 531 at p. 538, 26 C.R. 193.

It is well established that it is the duty of a trial Judge in giving directions to a jury to draw to their attention and to put before them fairly and completely the theory of the defence. In performing this task, it is also clear that the trial Judge must put before the jury any defences which may be open to the accused upon the evidence whether raised by the accused's counsel or not. He must give all necessary instructions on the law relating to such defences, review the relevant evidence and relate it to the law applicable. This, however, does not mean that the trial Judge becomes bound to put every defence suggested to him by counsel. Before any obligation arises to put defences, there must be in the evidence some basis upon which the defence can rest and it is only where such an evidentiary basis is present that a trial Judge must put a defence. Indeed, where it is not present he should not put a defence for to do so would only be to confuse.

What is the standard which the Judge must apply in considering this question? Ordinarily, when there is any evidence of a matter of fact, the proof of which may be relevant to the guilt or innocence of an accused, the trial Judge must leave that evidence to the jury so that they may reach their own conclusion upon it. Where, however, the trial Judge is asked to put a specific defence to the jury, he is not concerned only with the existence or non-existence of evidence of fact. He must consider, assuming that the evidence relied upon by the accused to support a defence is true, whether that evidence is sufficient to justify the putting of the defence. This question has been considered frequently in the Courts: see *Wu v. The King* (1934), 62 C.C.C. 90, [1934] 4 D.L.R. 459, [1934] S.C.R. 609, and *Kelsey v. The Queen* (1953), 105 C.C.C. 97, [1953] 1 S.C.R. 220, 16 C.R. 119. The test to be applied has, in my opinion, been set down by Fauteux, J., as he then was, in *Kelsey v. The Queen* [at p. 102 C.C.C.]:

> The allotment of any substance to an argument or of any value to a grievance resting on the omission of the trial Judge from mentioning such argument must be conditioned on the existence in the record of some evidence or matter apt to convey a sense of reality in the argument and in the grievance.

. . . .

In summary then, this was the state of evidence when the trial Judge was called upon to make his ruling. It became his task to apply the rule enunciated above. In assessing his resolution of the matter, we must consider the situation as it presented itself to him at the time. Speculation as to what the jury did, or would have done after being charged, is not relevant here.

With that thought in mind and, bearing in mind that the object of the judicial search must be evidence of a mistaken but honest belief in the consent of the complainant, one must first ask the question "Where is this evidence to be found?" It cannot be found in the evidence of the complainant. She denies actual consent and her evidence cannot provide any support for a mistaken belief in consent. Her conduct, according to her description, is that of a terrified, hysterical, non-consenting woman who resisted the appellant's advances, albeit unsuccessfully, and when able fled from his house in search of assistance. Turning then to the evidence of the appellant, it immediately becomes apparent that his evidence speaks of actual consent, even co-operation, and leaves little if any room for the suggestion that she may not have been consenting but he thought she was. The two stories are, as has been noted before, diametrically opposed on this vital issue. It is not for the trial Judge to weigh them and prefer one to the other. It is for him in this situation, however, to recognize the issue which arises on the evidence for the purpose of deciding what defences are open. In this situation the only realistic issue which can arise is the simple issue of consent or no consent. In my opinion, the trial Judge was correct in concluding that there simply was not sufficient evidence to justify the putting of the defence of mistake of fact to the jury. He left the issue of consent and that was the only one arising on the evidence.

In reaching this conclusion, I am not unmindful of the evidence of surrounding circumstances which were said to support the appellant's contention. I refer to the absence of serious injury suffered by the complainant and the absence of damage to clothing, as well as to the long period of time during which the parties remained in the bedroom. These matters may indeed be cogent on the issue of actual consent but, in my view, they cannot by themselves advance a suggestion of a mistaken belief. The finding of the clothes at the foot of the bed, the necklace and the keys in the living-room, are equally relevant on the issue of actual consent and, in my view, cannot affect the issue which was clearly framed by the opposing assertions of consent and non-consent.

It would seem to me that if it is considered necessary in this case to charge the jury on the defence of mistake of fact, it would be necessary to do so in all cases where the complainant denies consent and an accused asserts it. To require the putting of the alternative defence of mistaken belief in consent, there must be, in my opinion, some evidence beyond the mere assertion of belief in consent by counsel for the appellant. This evidence must appear from or be supported by sources other than the appellant in order to give it any air of reality. In *R. v. Plummer and Brown*, *supra*. Evans, J.A. (as he then was), speaking for the Ontario Court of Appeal, considered that there was such evidence as far as Brown was concerned and directed a new trial because the defence had not been put. In that case, the complainant had gone to Plummer's "pad" where she had been raped by Plummer. Brown entered the room where the rape occurred after Plummer had gone. Apparently, he had arrived at the house separately from Plummer. It was open on the evidence to find that he was unaware then that Plummer had threatened the complainant and terrorized her into submission. He had intercourse with her and she said that because of continuing fear from Plummer's threats, she submitted without protest. In these special circumstances, the defence was required. The facts clearly established at least an air of reality to Brown's defence. In *Morgan*, there was evidence of an invitation by the complainant's husband to have intercourse with his wife and his assurance that her show of resistance would be a sham. In other words, there was evidence explaining, however preposterous the explanation might be, a basis for the mistaken belief. In the case at bar, there is no such evidence.

Where the complainant says rape and the accused says consent, and where on the whole of the evidence, including that of the complainant, the accused, and the surrounding circumstances, there is a clear issue on this point, and where as here the accused makes no assertion of a belief in consent as opposed to an actual consent, it is unrealistic in the absence of some other circumstance or circumstances, such as are found in the *Plummer and Brown* and *Morgan* cases, to consider the Judge bound to put the mistake of fact defence. In my opinion, the trial Judge was correct in refusing to put the defence on the evidence before him.

I might add that I have had the advantage of reading the reasons of my brother Dickson, J., and, while it is apparent that I am unable to accept his view on the evidentiary question, I am in agreement with that part of his judgment dealing with the availability as a defence to a charge of rape in Canada of what is generally termed the defence of mistake of fact.

I would dismiss the appeal.

. . . .

[MARTLAND J. concurred in the result, but disagreed with the majority view that they were compelled by precedent to require that a mistake be evaluated on a purely subjective standard.]

[DICKSON J. (dissenting with Estey J.):]

. . . .

It will be convenient to identify the pivotal issues on which the appellant's case turns:

(1) What is the *mens rea* of rape?
(2) Is a mistaken belief in consent available in defence to the charge of rape?
(3) If so, does mistake afford a defence only where the mistake is one which is held both honestly *and on reasonable grounds*?
(4) Did the trial Judge err in the case at bar in ruling there was not sufficient basis of fact to justify leaving the defence of mistake of fact to the jury?

Mens Rea

There rests now, at the foundation of our system of criminal justice, the precept that a man cannot be adjudged guilty and subjected to punishment, unless the commission of the crime was voluntarily directed by a willing mind. Blackstone spoke of a "vicious act" consequent upon a "vicious will" (*Commentaries*, 15th ed., vol. IV. (1809), p. 21). Proof of the mental element is an essential and constituent step in establishing criminal responsibility. Parliament can, of course, by express words, create criminal offences for which a guilty intention is not an essential ingredient. Equally, *mens rea* is not requisite in a wide category of statutory offences which are concerned with public welfare, health and safety. Subject to these exceptions, *mens rea*, consisting of some positive state of mind, such as evil intention, or knowledge of the wrongfulness of the act, or reckless disregard of consequences, must be proved by the prosecution. The mental element may be established by inference from the nature of the act committed, or by additional evidence.

The *mens rea* which is required, and its nature and extent, will vary with the particular crime; it can only be determined by detailed examination of the *actus reus* of the offence. Speaking generally, at least where the circumstance is not "morally indifferent", the mental element must be proved with respect to all circumstances and consequences that form part of the *actus reus*. It follows that, in a case of alleged rape, where a fact or circumstance is not known to, or is misapprehended by, the accused, leading to mistaken but honest belief in the consent of the woman, his act is not culpable in relation to that element of the offence (Glanville William, *Criminal Law, The General Part*, 2nd ed. (1961), p. 141):

> [F]or if the *actus reus* includes surrounding circumstances, it cannot be said to be intentional unless *all its elements*, including those circumstances, are known. (Emphasis added.)

Taking these principles, then, what is the mental element required under s. 143 of the *Criminal Code* on a charge of rape? This crime was historically regarded as an offence of physical violence. Blackstone defined rape as "the carnal knowledge of a woman forcibly and against her will" (Commentaries, p. 210). A more comprehensive definition of rape at common law is found in *Archbold's Pleading, Evidence and Practice In Criminal Cases*, 38th ed. (1973), p. 1121, para. 2871:

> Rape consists in having unlawful sexual intercourse with a woman without her consent by force, fear or fraud: 1 East P.C. 434: and see 1 Hale 627 et seq.

Section 143 of our *Code*, in brief, defines rape as an act of sexual intercourse with a female person without her consent, or with consent if that consent is extorted by threats or fear of bodily harm. It will be seen that the statutory definition does not depart in any significant way from the common law definition. For all practical purposes, the *Criminal Code* merely codifies the common law. The essence of the crime consists in the commission of an act of sexual intercourse where a woman's consent, or genuine consent, has been withheld.

The *actus reus* of rape is complete upon (a) an act of sexual intercourse; (b) without consent. An affirmative finding as to each of these elements does not finish the inquiry, however, for, as I have indicated, the requirement that there be a guilty intention must also be satisfied. The important question then arises as to whether at common law, and under s. 143 of the *Code*, the guilty intention for rape extends to the element of consent. In principle, it would seem that it should, as intention as to consent is central to responsibility; a man should only be punished where he proceeds with an act of violation in the knowledge that consent is withheld, or in a state of recklessness as to whether willingness is present. The intention to commit the act of intercourse, and to commit that act in the absence of consent, are two separate and distinct elements of the offence.

Is the accused's perception of consent relevant to a charge under s. 143 of the *Criminal Code*? The argument against the application of *Director of Public Prosecutions v. Morgan*, [1976] A.C. 182, in Canada, is that the *Code* creates a statutory offence of rape which does not expressly advert to, or require, that there be a state of mind or intent to proceed in the absence of consent. The issue of consent as an aspect of *mens rea* for rape does not appear to have been raised directly in English authorities previous to the *Morgan* decision, although Lord Denman in *R. v. Flattery* (1877), 13 Cox C.C. 388, had occasion to say (p. 392):

> There is one case where a woman does not consent to the act of connection and yet the man may not be guilty of rape, that is where the resistance is so slight and her behaviour such that the man may *bona fide* believe that she is consenting....

The question has been topical in the Australian Courts for some time, and we have the benefit of a body of case law which deals with the mental element and honest belief as a defence of mistake. The first decision is *R. v. Hornbuckle*, [1945] V.L.R. 281 (the full Court of Victoria sitting), which established a definition of the mental element in rape, followed generally by the Australian Courts. In the course of delivering judgment, MacFarlan, J., had the following to say (at p. 287):

> To hold that knowledge that the act of intercourse was occurring sufficiently establishes the intent, because the man who knows he is committing the act must intend it, even if *prima facie* warranted, seems to us to fail to distinguish "intent to have intercourse" from "intent to have intercourse without the consent of the female".

. . . .

In *Morgan*, each of the Law Lords accepted the element of knowledge or recklessness as to consent, as a feature of the guilty intention in the crime of rape. In particular, Lord Hailsham endorsed the test formulated by the trial Judge, that the prosecution must prove that "... each defendant intended to have sexual intercourse without her consent, not merely that he intended to have sexual intercourse with her but that he intended to have intercourse without her consent" (p. 209). Lord Hailsham added the qualification, if an accused is reckless as to consent, that is equivalent, on ordinary principles, to an intent to do the prohibited act without consent. Lord Simon, though dissenting on the issue of whether a belief must be reasonably held, was succinct (p. 218):

> The *actus reus* is sexual intercourse with a woman who is not in fact consenting to such intercourse. The *mens rea* is knowledge that the woman is not consenting or recklessness as to whether she is consenting or not.

In the view of Lord Edmund-Davies, also in dissent, it is incorrect to regard rape as involving no mental element save the intention to have intercourse; knowledge by the accused of the woman's unwillingness to have intercourse is essential to the crime (p. 225): see also Lord Fraser of Tullybelton, at p. 237.

Following the *Morgan* decision, the Home Secretary commissioned an inquiry and the Report of the Advisory Group on the Law of Rape (the Heilbron Report) was soon published (1975). The mandate of the Group was to consider whether the *Morgan* decision necessitated immediate statutory reform. In the course of its report, which approved the principles elucidated in *Morgan*, the following is stated, at p. 3 para. 23:

> The mental element, which the prosecution must additionally establish [i.e., to the *actus reus*] is an intention by the defendant to have sexual intercourse with a woman either knowing that she does not consent, or recklessly not caring whether she consents or not.

Moreover, the Group agreed that a mistaken though erroneous belief is inconsistent with, and negatives, the requisite mental element. Such a belief need not be reasonably held, although the reasonableness of it is a relevant consideration for the jury. It is no longer disputed that, in England, perception of the woman's consent is an aspect of the mental element in crimes of rape.

. . . .

The law of rape was considered by this Court in *Leary v. The Queen* (1977), 33 C.C.C. (2d) 473, 74 D.L.R. (3d) 103, [1978] 1 S.C.R. 29. The appeal turned on the availability of intoxication as a defence to the charge. Mr. Justice Pigeon, although disagreeing with the contention that specific intent was required, cited the following passage from the speech of Lord Simon, in the course of his review of what had been said in *Morgan* (p. 482 C.C.C., p. 112 D.L.R., p. 58 S.C.R.):

> This brings me to the fourth question, namely whether rape is a crime of basic or ulterior intent. Does it involve an intent going beyond the *actus reus*? Smith and Hogan (Criminal Law, 3rd ed. (1973), p. 47) say No. I respectfully agree. The *actus reus* is sexual intercourse with a woman who is not in fact consenting to such intercourse. *The mens rea is knowledge that the woman is not consenting or recklessness as to whether she is consenting or not.* (Emphasis added.)

The dissenting judgment in *Leary* contained this definition of the mental element (p. 486 C.C.C., p. 116 D.L.R., p. 35 S.C.R.):

> ...the Crown must prove, beyond reasonable doubt, intercourse without consent, together with (a) an intention to force intercourse notwithstanding absence of consent, or (b) a realization that the conduct may lead to nonconsensual intercourse and a recklessness or indifference to that consequence ensuing. It will not do simply to say that because the accused committed the physical act and the woman did not consent, he must be taken to have intended to have intercourse without consent.

. . . .

It will thus be seen that the great weight of authority is in support of the view that the accused's perception of the woman's consent is an important aspect of any prosecution for the crime of rape. Counsel for the Crown in the instant appeal reviewed and compared s. 143 of the *Code* with other Part IV *Code* offences, to make the point that the subjective belief of an accused is no part of the case to be proved by the Crown. It was contended that, since reference to intention to proceed in the absence of consent is lacking in s. 143, the statutory wording prevails over case authorities which consider the mental element in terms of the common law definition. Section 148 of the *Code* was cited in comparison. This section specifies as an ingredient of the offence, knowledge or reason for belief that the female person is, by reason of her mental condition, incapable of giving a reasonable consent. Knowledge of the existence of a blood-relationship is a constituent element of the crime of incest, spelled out in s. 150 of the *Code*.

One cannot assume, on the strength of these two sections, that there is no *mens rea* element relating to consent, for crimes of rape. Parliament does not consistently employ wording which indicates express levels of intention (such as knowingly, intentionally, wilfully) for all offences which undoubtedly import a mental element. Even within Part IV, there is no consistency in the wording of the offences. I do not think the determination of the mental element for rape turns, in any way, on a comparative analysis of the wording for Part IV offences.

I refer to the statement by Lord Reid in *Sweet v. Parsley*, [1969] 1 All E.R. 347 (p. 350):

> ...for it is firmly established by a host of authorities that *mens rea* is an essential ingredient of every offence unless some reason can be found for holding that that is not necessary. It is also firmly established that the fact that other sections of the *Act* expressly require *mens rea*, for example because they contain the word "knowingly", is not in itself sufficient to justify a decision that a section which is silent as to *mens rea* creates an absolute offence.

In summary, intention or recklessness must be proved in relation to all elements of the offence, including absence of consent. This simply extends to rape the same general order of intention as in other crimes.

Mistake of Fact

Belief by an accused in a mistaken set of facts has not always afforded an answer to a criminal charge. By the early criminal law, the only real defence that could be raised was that an act had not been voluntary and, therefore, could not be imputed to the accused. Thus it was possible in some cases to excuse a man who had acted under a mistake, by the argument that his conduct was not truly voluntary (*Russell on Crime*, vol. 1, 12th ed. (1964), p. 71). In the seventeenth century, Hale wrote: "But in some cases *ignorantia facti* doth excuse, for such an ignorance many times makes the act itself morally involuntary." (1 *Pleas of the Crown* 42).

The leading English cases on mistake of fact are, of course, *R. v. Prince* (1875), 13 Cox C.C. 138, and *R. v. Tolson* (1889), 23 Q.B. 168. In the *Prince* decision (p. 152), Brett, J., cited from *Blackstone's Commentaries* by Stephen, 2nd ed., vol. 4, p. 105:

> Ignorance or mistake is another defect of will, when a man intending to do a lawful act does that which is unlawful. For here, the deed and the will, acting separately, there is not that conjunction between them which is necessary to form a criminal act....

Brett, J., held that mistake, as a defence, applies whenever facts are present, in which an accused believes and has reasonable ground to believe, which if true, would render his act innocent and not a crime. The *Tolson* case, following *Prince*, considered the extent to which a mistaken, though honest and reasonable, belief that the first spouse was dead could afford a defence to a charge of bigamy. The classic statement is that of Cave. J. (p. 181):

> At common law an honest and reasonable belief in the existence of circumstances, which, if true, would make the act for which the prisoner is indicted an innocent act has always been held to be a good defence.

An honest and reasonable mistake of fact is on the same footing as the absence of a reasoning faculty, as with infants, or impairment of the faculty, as in lunacy (*Tolson*, p. 181). Culpability rests upon commission of the offence with knowledge of the facts and circumstances comprising the crime. If, according to an accused's belief concerning the facts, his act is criminal, then he intended the offence and can be punished. If, on the other hand, his act would be innocent, according to facts as he believed them to be, he does not have the criminal mind and ought not to be punished for his act: see E.R. Keedy, "Ignorance and Mistake in the Criminal Law", 22 *Harv. L. Rev*. 75 at p. 82 (1908).

As stated by Mr. Justice Dixon, as he then was, in *Thomas v. The King* (1937), 59 C.L.R. 279 at pp. 199–300:

> States of volition are necessarily dependent upon states of fact, and a mistaken belief in the existence of circumstances cannot be separated from the manifestation of the will which it prompts ... the nature of an act of volition may be of an entirely different description if it is based on mistake of fact. The state of facts assumed must often enter into the determination of the will. It would be strange if our criminal law did not contain this principle and treat it as fundamental.

Mistake is a defence, then, where it prevents an accused from having the *mens rea* which the law requires for the very crime with which he is charged. Mistake of fact is more accurately seen as a negation of guilty intention than as the affirmation of a positive defence. It avails an accused who acts innocently, pursuant to a flawed perception of the facts, and nonetheless commits the *actus reus* of an offence. Mistake is a defence though, in the sense that it is raised as an issue by an accused. The Crown is rarely possessed of knowledge of the subjective factors which may have caused an accused to entertain a belief in a fallacious set of facts.

If I am correct that: (i) s. 143 of the *Criminal Code* imports a *mens rea* requirement, and (ii) the *mens rea* of rape includes intention, or recklessness as to non-consent of the complainant, a mistake that negatives intention or recklessness entitles the accused to an acquittal. Glanville Williams notes (*Criminal Law, The General Part*, 2nd ed. (1961), p. 173, para. 65):

> It is impossible to assert that a crime requiring intention or recklessness can be committed although the accused laboured under a mistake negativing the requisite intention or recklessness. Such an assertion carries its own refutation.

Howard (*Australian Criminal Law*, 3rd ed.), points out that rape is aimed at the protection of women from forcible subjection to non-marital sexual intercourse, but that the facts of life not infrequently impede the drawing of a clean line between consensual and non-consensual intercourse (p. 149):

> ...it is easy for a man intent upon his own desires to mistake the intentions of a woman or girl who may herself be in two minds about what to do. Even if he makes no mistake it is not unknown for a woman afterwards either to take fright or for some other reason to regret what has happened and seek to justify herself retrospectively by accusing the man of rape.

I do not think the defence of mistaken belief can be restricted to those situations in which the belief has been induced by information received from a third party. That was the situation in the *Morgan* case. In *Morgan*, the belief in consent was induced by information related by the complainant's husband, who spoke of his wife's sexual propensities. The foundation for the defence, incredible as it turned out to be, in view of the violence, was the misinformation of the husband. Had the defendants believed that information, and had the wife's overt conduct been relatively consistent with it, the defendants would have had a defence. That is the effect of the *dicta* of the House of Lords in the *Morgan* case.

In principle, the defence should avail when there is an honest belief in consent, or an absence of knowledge that consent has been withheld. Whether the mistake is rooted in an accused's mistaken perception, or is based upon objective, but incorrect, facts confided to him by another, should be of no consequence. The kind of mistaken fact pleaded by the *Morgan* defendants, however, is more likely to be believed than a bald assertion of mistaken belief during a face-to-face encounter. In any event, it is clear that the defence is available only where there is sufficient evidence presented by an accused, by his testimony or by the circumstances in which the act occurred, to found the plea.

Honest and Reasonable Mistake

The next question which must be broached is whether a defence of honest, though mistaken, belief in consent must be based on reasonable grounds. A majority of the House of Lords in *Morgan* answered the question in the negative, and that view was affirmed by the Heilbron Committee. There can be no doubt this answer is consonant with principle. As Professor Keedy has written (22 *Harv. L. Rev.* 75 at p. 88), an act is reasonable in law when it is such as a man of ordinary care would do under similar circumstances; to require that the mistake be reasonable means that, if the accused is to have a defence, he acted up to the standard of an average man, whether the accused is himself such a man or not; this is the application of an outer standard to the individual; if the accused is to be punished because his mistake is one which an average man would not make, punishment will sometimes be inflicted when the criminal mind does not exist.

In other jurisdiction, there are divergent decisions and *dicta* on the question whether mistaken belief must be based on reasonable grounds to exculpate. In the affirmative are such bigamy cases as *Tolson, supra*; *Thomas, supra*; *R. v. King*, [1963] 3 All E.R. 561; and *R. v. Gould*, [1968] 1 All E.R. 849. Non-bigamy cases are *Prince, supra*; *Bank of New South Wales v. Piper*, [1897] A.C. 383; *Warner v. Metropolitan Police Com'r*, [1969] 2 A.C. 256; and *Sweet v. Parsley, supra*. In the majority of cases in which the Courts view the mistake as a defence only if made on reasonable grounds, such as in *Tolson*, that view is not a necessary part of the *ratio decidendi*.

Among the cases in which mistaken belief was considered, and a test of reasonableness applied, are *Flannery, supra*; *R. v. Bourke* (1969), 91 W.N. (N.S.W.) 793; and *Sperotto, supra*. Cases to the contrary are: *Thorne v. Motor Trade Ass'n*, [1937] A.C. 797; *Wilson v. Inyang*, [1951] 2 All E.R. 237; *R. v. Smith*, [1974] 1 All E.R. 632; *R. v. Brown* (1975), 10 S.A.S.R. 139. Virtually unanimous rejection of the added requirement of "reasonableness" is to be found in the scholarly writings: Glanville Williams,

Criminal Law, The General Part, 2nd ed. (1961), p. 201, para. 71: "The idea that a mistake, to be a defence, must be reasonable, though lurking in some of the cases, is certainly not true as a general proposition"; Glanville Williams, *Textbook of Criminal Law* (1978), p. 100; Howard, *Australian Criminal Law*, 3rd ed. pp. 153–4; Smith & Hogan, *Criminal Law*, 4th ed. (1978), p. 182; *Russell on Crime*, 12th ed., vol. 1 (1964), p. 76; J.C. Smith, "Rape", [1975] *Crim. L. Rev.* 40; Morris and Turner, "Two Problems in the Law of Rape", 2 *U. Queensland L.J.* 247 (1952–55).

In Canada, the *Tolson* rule has already been rejected by this Court in favour of the honest belief standard. Unless this Court wishes to overrule *Beaver v. The Queen* (1957), 118 C.C.C. 129, [1957] S.C.R. 531. 26 C.R. 193, it is difficult to see how the minority in *Morgan* can decide this appeal.

In *R. v. Rees* (1956), 115 C.C.C. 1, 4 D.L.R. (2d) 406, [1956] S.C.R. 640, the issue was whether there is *mens rea* for the offence of knowingly or wilfully contributing to juvenile delinquency. Cartwright, J., set out the *Tolson* test and then held as follows (p. 11 C.C.C., p. 415 D.L.R., p. 651 S.C.R.):

> The first of the statements of Stephen J., quoted above should now be read in the light of the judgment of Lord Goddard C.J., concurred in by Lynskey and Devlin J.J., in *Wilson v. Inyang*, [1951] 2 All E.R. 237, which, in my opinion, rightly decides that the essential question is whether the belief entertained by the accused is an honest one and that the existence or non-existence of reasonable grounds for such belief is merely relevant evidence to be weighed by the tribunal of fact in determining such essential question.

One year later, in *Beaver v. The Queen*, *supra*, a narcotics case, the opinion of Mr. Justice Cartwright was accepted by a majority of the Court. He adopted the paragraph quoted above from *Rees*. *Beaver* has since been regarded as authoritative contribution to the law as to mental element, and mistaken belief, in true crimes.

It is not clear how one can properly relate reasonableness (an element in offences of negligence) to rape (a "true crime" and not an offence of negligence). To do so, one must, I think, take the view that the *mens rea* goes only to the physical act of intercourse and not to non-consent, and acquittal comes only if the mistake is reasonable. This, upon the authorities, is not a correct view, the intent in rape being not merely to have intercourse, but to have it with a nonconsenting woman. If the jury finds that mistake, whether reasonable or unreasonable, there should be no conviction. If, upon the entire record, there is evidence of mistake to cast a reasonable doubt upon the existence of a criminal mind, then the prosecution has failed to make its case. In an article by Professor Colin Howard, "The Reasonableness of Mistake in the Criminal Law", 4 *U. Queensland L.J.* 45 (1961–64), the following is offered (p. 47):

> To crimes of *mens rea*, or elements of a crime which requires *mens rea*, mistake of fact *simpliciter* is a defence; to crimes of negligence, or elements of an offence which requires only negligence, mistake of fact is a defence only if the mistake was in all the circumstances a reasonable one to make.

The same analysis is expressed by Glanville Williams, p. 202, para. 71.

In *Director of Public Prosecutions v. Morgan*, four Law Lords agreed that having accepted the mental element of knowledge as to consent, it is inconsistent to attach a standard of reasonableness to a defence of honest belief. As Lord Hailsham pointed out, the following two propositions are totally irreconcilable:

(i) each defendant must have intended to have sexual intercourse without her consent, not merely that he intended to have intercourse but that he intended to have intercourse without her consent;
(ii) it is necessary for any belief in the woman's consent to be a "reasonable belief" before the defendant is entitled to be acquitted.

The difference between the majority and minority decisions in *Morgan* turned upon the way in which each Law Lord perceived the *Tolson* precedent, as being a wide-ranging and well-established principle, or as expressing a narrow rule limited in effect to bigamy and the facts at hand.

Lambert, J.A., in his dissenting judgment in the instant case reasoned [affirmed (1978), 45 C.C.C. (2d) 67, 5 C.R. (3d) 193, [1979] 1 W.W.R. 562], on his reading of *Leary* and *Morgan*, that a defence of honest belief in consent must be based on reasonable grounds. In his view, two Law Lords in *Morgan* following *Tolson*, clearly required an honest belief to be held on reasonable grounds (Lord Simon and Lord Edmund-Davies). Two others, Lord Fraser, and Lord Hailsham, invoked general principles to conclude that an honest belief in consent need not be reasonably held. The decision of the fifth Judge, Lord Cross, turned on a distinction drawn between statutory and common law offences. Bigamy, the offence in question in *Tolson*, was a statutory offence. Rape is not. Therefore, the *Tolson* requirement that the mistake be reasonable does not apply to rape, a crime defined by common law. Were rape to be defined by statute, the defence would be available only if supported by reasonable grounds. Lambert, J.A., held that if one adapted the decision of Lord Cross to s. 143 of the *Code*, the tables would be turned, and a majority of the Lords would, for purposes of the *Criminal Code*, endorse the honest and reasonable test. If the distinction Lord Cross thought might be possible between statutory and common law offences would have the effect of giving a defence of unreasonable mistake to a person accused of a crime which, in express terms, imported *mens rea*, but would limit the defence to one of reasonable mistake to a person accused of a crime which imported *mens rea* only by implication, the justification for the distinction is not apparent. I am unable to see why the defence should be so limited. Rape is not a crime of strict or absolute liability. With respect, there is no compelling reason for extending to rape the misapprehension having its genesis in *Tolson*, and now endemic in English law, that makes bigamy a crime of negligence and would have a like effect if applied to statutory rape.

Mr. Justice Lambert recognized that while his conclusion was directed by precedent rather than logic, he also found it to be supported, in relation to rape, by policy and practical sense [at p. 85]:

> Why should a woman who is sexually violated by such a man have to defend herself by screams or blows in order to indicate her lack of consent, or have to consent through fear, for a charge of rape to be sustained? Surely a firm oral protest, sufficient to deny any reasonable grounds for belief in consent, should be a sufficient foundation in these circumstances for a charge of rape.

I am not unaware of the policy considerations advanced in support of the view that if mistake is to afford a defence to a charge of rape, it should, at the very least, be one a reasonable man might make in the circumstances. There is justifiable concern over the position of the woman who alleges she has been subjected to a non-consensual sexual act; fear is expressed that subjective orthodoxy should not enable her alleged assailant to escape accountability by advancing some cock-and-bull story. The usual response of persons accused of rape is — "she consented". Are such persons now to be acquitted, simply by saying, "even if she did not consent, I believed she consented"? The concern is legitimate and real. It must, however, be placed in the balance with other relevant considerations. First, cases in which mistake can be advanced in answer to a charge of rape must be few in number. People do not normally commit rape *per incuriam*. An evidential case must exist to support the plea. Secondly, if the woman in her own mind withholds consent, but her conduct and other circumstances lend credence to belief on the part of the accused that she was consenting, it may be that it is unjust to convict. I do not think it will do to say that in those circumstances she, in fact, consented. In fact, she did not, and it would be open to a jury to so find. Thirdly, it is unfair to the jury, and to the accused, to speak in terms of two beliefs, one entertained by the accused, the other by a reasonable man, and to ask the jury to ignore an actual belief in favour of an attributed belief. The mind with which the jury is concerned is that of the accused. By importing a standard external to the accused, there is created an incompatible mix of subjective and objective factors. If an honest lack of knowledge is shown, then the subjective element of the offence is not proved. The following passage from the Heilbron Report is, however, apposite [p. 11, para. 66]:

> 66. *Morgan*'s case did not decide, as some critics seem to have thought, that an accused person was entitled to be acquitted, however ridiculous his story might be. Nor did it decide that the reasonableness or unreasonableness of his belief was irrelevant. Furthermore it is a mistaken assumption that a man is entitled to be acquitted simply because he asserts this belief, without more.

Perpetuation of fictions does little for the jury system or the integrity of criminal justice. The ongoing debate in the Courts and learned journals as to whether mistake must be reasonable is conceptually important in the orderly development of the criminal law, but in my view, practically unimportant because the accused's statement that he was mistaken is not likely to be believed unless the mistake is, to the jury, reasonable. The jury will be concerned to consider the reasonableness of any grounds found, or asserted to be available, to support the defence of mistake. Although "reasonable grounds" is not a precondition to the availability of a plea of honest belief in consent, those grounds determine the weight to be given the defence. The reasonableness, or otherwise, of the accused's belief is only evidence for, or against, the view that the belief was actually held and the intent was, therefore, lacking.

Canadian juries, in my experience, display a high degree of common sense, and an uncanny ability to distinguish between the genuine and the specious.

The words of Dixon, J., bear repeating (*Thomas v. The King*, *supra*, at p. 309):

> ...a lack of confidence in the ability of a tribunal correctly to estimate evidence of states of mind and the like can never be sufficient ground for excluding from inquiry the most fundamental element in a rational and humane criminal code.

In *Textbook of Criminal Law*, at p. 102, Professor Glanville Williams states the view, with which I am in agreement, that it is proper for the trial Judge to tell the jury "that if they think the alleged belief was unreasonable, that may be one factor leading them to conclude that it was not really held; but they must look at the facts as a whole". It will be a rare day when a jury is satisfied as to the existence of an unreasonable belief. If the claim of mistake does not raise a reasonable doubt as to guilt, and all other elements of the crime have been proved, then the trier of fact will not give effect to the defence. But, if there is any evidence that there was such an honest belief, regardless of whether it is reasonable, the jury must be entrusted with the task of assessing the credibility of the plea.

To apply the reasonable standard in this appeal, the Court, in my view, would have to: (a) accept the minority decision in *Morgan*; (b) overrule *Beaver* or find a means of distinguishing the offence of rape; and (c) defy accepted and sound principles of criminal law.

The Plea and the Evidence

I come now to what is perhaps the most difficult part of this case, namely, whether there was an evidential base sufficient to require the trial Judge to place before the jury the defence of mistaken belief in consent....

Leaving aside the possibility of post-bondage intercourse, the jury could have reached any one of three alternative conclusions: (1) the appellant was telling the truth and the complainant did consent; or (2) he was not telling the truth, she did not consent and he was aware of that fact or reckless to it; or (3) though he did not plead mistake, he believed she was consenting, notwithstanding token resistance. His defence of consent is rejected and that of honest belief accepted. I think there was sufficient evidence to put that third alternative to the jury.

Because the case turns on evidential matters, detailed reference thereto is unavoidable....

There is circumstantial evidence supportive of a plea of belief in consent: (1) Her necklace and car keys were found in the living-room. (2) She confirmed his testimony that her blouse was neatly hung in the clothes closet. (3) Other items of folded clothing were found at the foot of the bed. (4) None of her clothes were damaged in the slightest way. (5) She was in the house for a number of hours. (6) By her version, when she entered the house the appellant said he was going to break her. She made no attempt to leave. (7) She did not leave while he undressed. (8) There was no evidence of struggle, and (9) She suffered no physical injuries, aside from three scratches.

The Heilbron Report contains the following observations which seem pertinent to the case at bar. The crime of rape involves an act — sexual intercourse — which is not, in itself, either criminal or unlawful, and can, indeed, be both desirable and pleasurable; whether it is criminal depends on complex considerations, since the mental states of both parties and the influence of each upon the other, as well as their physical interaction, have to be considered and are sometimes difficult to interpret — all the more so, since normally the act takes place in private; there can be many ambiguous situations in sexual relationships; hence, however precisely the law may be stated, it cannot always adequately resolve these problems; in the first place, there may well be circumstances where each party interprets the situation differently, and it may be quite impossible to determine with any confidence which interpretation is right.

Toy, J., gave a full, fair and accurate of the testimony by the complainant and appellant. There can be no criticism of the instructions in this respect. He did not, however, charge the jury on the defence of mistaken belief, as he earlier ruled there was not "in the evidence any sufficient basis of fact to leave the defence of mistake of fact to this jury".

In my view, with respect, the Judge erred in failing to instruct the jury (a) that as to pre-bondage intercourse, the issues were consent and belief in consent; and (b) that as to post-bondage intercourse, the issue was whether an act of intercourse occurred or not. If the answer to (b) was negative, a conviction could not be founded upon the post-bondage period. If the answer was in the affirmative, a conviction would almost, of necessity, follow, because there was admittedly no consent or belief in consent after the "bondage".

That the case gave the jury difficulty is clear from the fact that the charge was delivered about noon, on a Friday, and the verdict was not rendered until about 5.00 p.m. on Saturday.

I am mindful of the comment of Mr. Justice Pigeon in *Leary*, that consideration should be given to the plight of a complainant, who should not be subjected to the humiliation of having to testify again, unless justice makes it imperative. The possibility of a mistaken belief in consent in the pre-bondage phase was an issue that should have been placed before the jury: the Judge's failure to do so makes it imperative, in my opinion, in the interests of justice, that there be a new trial. It was open to the jury to find only token resistance prior to the "bondage" incident, which the appellant may not have perceived as a withholding of consent. The accused was convicted of that which, perhaps, he did not intend to do had he known of no consent. It does not follow that, by simply disbelieving the appellant on consent, in fact, the jury thereby found that there was no belief in consent, and that the appellant could not reasonably have believed in consent.

I would allow the appeal, set aside the judgment of the British Columbia Court of Appeal and direct a new trial.

Appeal dismissed.

■

The testimony of several of the important witnesses discussed in the media was not reproduced in the judgment of the Supreme Court. For instance, the woman who worked as a waitress testified that Pappajohn threatened to kill her during the course of the trial. He admitted doing so, claiming that he only wanted her to tell the truth: Andrea Maitland, "Accused at rape trial admits threatening to kill witness" *The Vancouver Sun* (17 August 1977) 1. As well, Dr. James Tyhurst testified on behalf of the defence to the effect that "male dominance ... facilitates male/female copulatory behaviour ... while female dominance inhibits it": Ric Dolphin, "Borderline Case" *Saturday Night* (February 1992) 42. Tyhurst was himself later convicted of indecent and sexual assault against four women patients who all asserted that he had involved them in "master/slave" relationships that included bondage, whips, and assault. His conviction was overturned on appeal on the grounds that the trial judge inadequately instructed the jury on the concept of reasonable doubt: *R. v. Tyhurst* (1992), 21 B.C.A.C. 218 (C.A.). At the new trial, only two of the women testified and the jury acquitted. On appeal, while acknowledging that the trial judge had committed several errors in conducting the trial and instructing the jurors, the court was not prepared to send the accused back for a third trial: *R. v. Tyhurst* (1996), 71 B.C.A.C. 28 (C.A.).

B. LEGACY OF *PAPPAJOHN*

The *Pappajohn* case has spawned a tremendous volume of litigation, abundant feminist criticism, and statutory law reform.

Contrary to Chief Justice Dickson's assertion, the mistake of fact defence has not been raised only rarely. Accused men have attempted "mistake of fact" defences in many cases. In *R. v. Sansregret*, [1985] 1 S.C.R. 570, the Court was faced with one of the implications of its earlier decision, which is that the defence may permit men to use high levels of violence to secure "consent".

In this case, the accused and the victim/witness had lived together and had separated, at her instance, one year prior to the assault that was the subject of the charge. The accused had raped the woman three weeks prior to the rape charged, by breaking into her home and terrorizing her. She held out some hope of reconciliation with him, in order to calm his rage, and had intercourse with him. She reported the assault to the police, but no charges were laid after his parole officer intervened, and she agreed to the discontinuance of the criminal investigation.

The accused committed essentially the same acts three weeks later. This time he also disconnected her telephone, threatened her with a weapon, struck her on the mouth, stripped her, and tied her up. Again the woman feigned reconciliation and consent in order to save her own life. She stated at trial that she thought that the accused believed her; that, in fact, her self-preservation depended on him believing her. The trial judge acquitted the accused, in accordance with the rule in *Pappajohn*; the Crown appealed the availability of the defence of mistake on these facts.

At the Supreme Court of Canada, the Court held that the trial judge had been in error in considering the defence: there was evidence from which the judge should have drawn the inference that the accused was aware that his prior act was considered non-consensual intercourse and, thus, rape. Justice McIntyre stated that the accused was wilfully ignorant regarding the impact of his violence upon the woman and, given the imputation of knowledge that this state of mind carries, the defence of honest mistake was unavailable. However, McIntyre J. emphasized the significance of the prior violence to this ruling: "If the evidence before this court were limited to the events of October 15th, it would be difficult indeed to infer wilful blindness" (at 587).

Allan Manson, in an annotation to the case, (1985), 45 C.R. (3d) 194, notes that the trial judge had, in fact, made an affirmative finding of honest belief in consent, which would preclude wilful ignorance. Although he suggests that the Court effectively and improperly reversed the trial judge's finding of fact, it seems clear that the Court was backing away from a logical but frightening application of *Pappajohn*. On the other hand, McIntyre J.'s comment quoted above suggests that accused men who use violence in this way may do so without criminal sanction at least once and, perhaps, repeatedly until it is reported to police and brought to the attention of the accused.

Further negative implications of *Pappajohn* are evident in other cases. In *R. v. Weaver* (1990), 110 A.R. 396 at 398–99 (C.A.), the court upheld a trial judge's acquittal based on mistake of fact where the victim was so intoxicated that she had vomited repeatedly, and the trial judge accepted that she did not and, in fact, could not consent:

> The Crown further urged that the trial judge had committed error in law by imposing on the victim a requirement that she resist in order to show absence of consent.... The trial judge did note that the complainant had not resisted or objected, but it seems clear that he did so in the context of determining whether Weaver's expressed belief that she was consenting was honestly held. Her failure to object or resist might, in some circumstances, be a factor on that point.
>
> ...
>
> We must observe that, on the printed record, an honest belief in consent seems a remarkable finding. But we did not see or hear the witnesses, as did the trial judge, and we must defer to his finding.

In *R. v. Letendre* (1991), 5 C.R. (4th) 159 at 173 (B.C.S.C.), the judge acquitted the accused on the basis that the woman's non-consent was not clearly and unequivocally indicated, in spite of her evidence that she had pushed the accused away and had said "no":

> The mating practice, if I may call it that, is a less than precise relationship. At times no may mean maybe, or wait awhile, the acts of one of the participants may be easily misinterpreted, a participant may change his or her mind, one way or another part way through it, and co-operation as well as enjoyment may be faked for a number of reasons.

In *R. v. Wald*, [1989] 3 W.W.R. 324 (Alta. C.A.), the court sent back for retrial three men who successfully argued the constitutional point in *Seaboyer* (see below) and who proposed to introduce evidence of the woman's sexual history to support their mistake of fact argument in a case involving sexual assault causing bodily harm. This gang rape involved not only the implicit threat of three men, but also the use of a firearm, strangulation, and a meat cleaver, making a defence of "mistake" regarding consent completely disingenuous. Worse yet, one of the judges, Harradence J., stated at 336–37:

> [E]ven if the accused did not have specific knowledge of the complainant's sexual reputation or past sexual conduct, such evidence can still be probative of the issue of honest but mistaken belief. The fact that the complainant has a reputation for participating in a specific type of conduct can strengthen the accused's testimony that he honestly believed that she was consenting notwithstanding the fact that the accused was not aware of the complainant's propensity. Such evidence enhances the credibility of the accused's assertion that he honestly but mistakenly believed that the complainant was consenting.

Does Justice Harradence fail to understand the distinction between *actus reus* and *mens rea*? Or are his beliefs showing? *Pappajohn* and the cases that have applied it have been criticized by many authors. Toni Pickard wrote another article after the decision was released, critically analyzing the legal reasoning and result in the case: "Culpable Mistakes and Rape: Harsh Words on *Pappajohn*" (1980) 30 U.T.L.J. 415. For a commentary critical of *Wald*, the use of sexual history evidence, and mistake of fact as a defence to rape, see Elizabeth Sheehy, "Canadian Judges and the Law of Rape: Should the *Charter* Insulate Bias?" (1989) 21 Ottawa L.R. 741.

Section 265(4) of the *Code* was enacted after *Pappajohn*. Does this section modify or codify *Pappajohn*? While a Department of Justice Research Section publication, *Sexual Assault Legislation in Canada: An Evaluation* (Ottawa: Communications and Consultation Branch, 1992) at 69 states that "the new law left room for courts to abandon the subjective test", the Supreme Court ignored the opening: *R. v. Robertson*, [1987] 1 S.C.R. 918. However, the rule in *Pappajohn* has now been modified by Bill C-49, s. 273.2. See the discussion, below.

C. AIR OF REALITY TEST

One way in which judges have limited the availability of the mistake of fact defence is through the evidentiary burden that must be met before any defence is put before the trier of fact: the requirement that the defence have an "air of reality". Recall that in *Pappajohn* the application of this test was what divided the majority and minority justices, and that while ruling that mistake of fact is available and is to be tested subjectively, the majority held that George Pappajohn was not entitled to the defence on the facts. Justice McIntyre stated that where the versions of the event are diametrically opposed, there must be some supporting evidence, beyond the accused's mere assertion, in sources other than the accused. As Annalise Acorn notes in *A Feminist Critique*, the air of reality test has precluded some unreasonable alleged "mistakes" from being put to the jury (at 14). See, for example, *R. v. White* (1986), 24 C.C.C. (3d) 1 (B.C.C.A.); *R. v. Robertson, supra*; *Reddick v. R.*, [1991] 1 S.C.R. 1105; *R. v. Ryan* (1993), 80 C.C.C. (3d) 514 (B.C.C.A.); *R. v. Silva* (1994), 120 Sask. R. 139 (C.A.); and *R. v. Livermore*, [1995] 4 S.C.R. 123, among others.

On the other hand, consider the examples provided by the Supreme Court where the air of reality test was said to have been met: *D.P.P. v. Morgan*, [1975] 2 All E.R. 347 (H.L.), and *R. v. Plummer* (1975), 24 C.C.C. (2d) 497 (Ont. C.A.). Do you agree? What would be the implications of such rulings? Note that the House of Lords refused to overturn the conviction in *Morgan* and send the accused back for a new trial, despite the fact that the trial judge had erroneously told the jury that the alleged mistaken belief must have been based on reasonable grounds. The Lords stated that it was clear the jury had rejected their story, which included a description of initial resistance, then enthusiastic participation, by the woman, as a "pack of lies". Would the Lords have found that the air of reality test had been met?

Consider also the application of the air of reality test to criminalized women, among others. Are such women as likely to receive any benefit from this limitation on the mistake of fact defence? For example, in *R. v. Laybourn*, [1987] 1 S.C.R. 782, the victim/witness worked as a prostitute and had agreed to sell sex to Laybourn for $80. When she entered his hotel room, she found two more men there but insisted they leave the room, one of them having arranged to buy sex from her once she had finished with the first man. Laybourn paid her the $80, but the other two re-entered the room minutes later, told her to return his money, and told her that she would have to engage in sex without payment. She stated at trial that she was afraid of the men, that she complied out of fear, and that she was not paid anything. Two of the accused testified that they accepted her story up until the time of the return of two of them to the room. They stated that she then wanted $60 each, but that they told her it was $20 each or nothing, and that she could leave if she wished. They stated that she seemed "jumpy", but that they never threatened her.

At trial they argued that she consented, and counsel for one of the accused advanced the alternative "mistake" argument. The Supreme Court ruled that the judge was correct in putting the defence of mistake to the jury, although the judge had made some errors in doing so, entitling the accused to a new trial. Justice McIntyre said that an "air of reality" was provided by a witness in an adjoining room who claimed to have overheard the woman complain about the presence of the men in the room, then the statement, "You are in a tough business, baby, and you have got to learn to take it," and by the evidence that the woman wanted $60 each but the men wanted to pay $20 each. While conceding that this evidence was equivocal, McIntyre J. ruled that it "could raise questions on the issue of whether, and to what extent, she may have consented, or to what extent the appellants may have understood her to be consenting" (at 793). Further inroads on the air of reality test will be discussed below, under The Aftermath of *Seaboyer*.

D. WOMEN'S PAST SEXUAL HISTORY

Women's past sexual history can also be used to shape a "mistake" defence as *Wald*, above, illustrates, by assisting the accused in arguing that there is an air of reality to his defence. André Marin argues, however, that "[a]ll too often, defence counsel purports to be raising this [mistake of fact] defence, when in fact he or she is merely attempting to use it as a back door to leading irrelevant but seriously prejudicial evidence against the complainant": "When is an 'Honest but Mistaken Belief in Consent' NOT an 'Honest but Mistaken Belief in Consent'?" (1995) 37 Crim. L.Q. 451 at 457.

The *Seaboyer* case set out below demonstrates the role of discriminatory myths and stereotypes in the development of the law of sexual assault, and the ways in which they support the claim that a woman's sexual past bears on a man's moral and legal culpability through the mistake of fact defence.

R. v. Seaboyer[†]

[McLACHLIN J. (Lamer C.J.C., La Forest, Sopinka, Cory, Stevenson, and Iacobucci JJ. concurring):]

DISCUSSION

1. Do ss. 276 and 277 of the *Criminal Code* Infringe ss. 7 and 11(d) of the *Charter*?

The Approach to ss. 7 and 11(d) of the Charter

Everyone, under s. 7 of the *Charter*, has the right to life, liberty and security of person and the right not to be deprived thereof except in accordance with the principles of fundamental justice.

The first branch of s. 7 need not detain us. It is not disputed that ss. 276 and 277 of the *Criminal Code* have the capacity to deprive a person of his or her liberty. A person convicted of sexual assault may be sentenced to life imprisonment. In so far as ss. 276 and 277 may affect conviction, they may deprive a person of his or her liberty.

The real issue under s. 7 is whether the potential for deprivation of liberty flowing from ss. 276 and 277 takes place in a manner that conforms to the principles of fundamental justice. The principles of fundamental justice are the fundamental tenets upon which our legal system is based. We find them in the legal principles which have historically been reflected in the law of this and other similar states: *R. v. Beare*, [1988] 2 S.C.R. 387. The sections which follow s. 7, like the right to a fair trial enshrined in s. 11(d), reflect particular principles of fundamental justice: *Re B.C. Motor Vehicle Act*, [1985] 2 S.C.R. 4867. Thus the discussion of s. 7 and s. 11(d) is inextricably intertwined.

The principles of fundamental justice reflect a spectrum of interests, from the rights of the accused to broader societal concerns. Section 7 must be construed having regard to those interests and "against the applicable principles and policies that have animated legislative and judicial practice in the field" (*Beare, supra*, at pp. 402–3 *per* La Forest J.). The ultimate question is whether the legislation, viewed

† [1991] 2 S.C.R. 577.

in a purposive way, conforms to the fundamental precepts which underlie our system of justice.

. . . .

A final point must be made on the ambit of s. 7 of the *Charter*. It has been suggested that s. 7 should be viewed as concerned with the interest of complainants as a class to security of person and to equal benefit of the law as guaranteed by ss. 15 and 28 of the *Charter*: Yola Althea Grant, "The Penetration of the Rape Shield: *R. v. Seaboyer and R. v. Gayme* in the Ontario Court of Appeal" (189–1990), 3 *C.J.W.L.* 592, at p. 600. Such an approach is consistent with the view that s. 7 reflects a variety of societal and individual interests. However, all proponents in this case concede that a measure which denies the accused the right to present a full and fair defence would violate s. 7 in any event.

The Principles Governing the Right to Call Defence Evidence

It is fundamental to our system of justice that the rules of evidence should permit the judge and jury to get at the truth and properly determine the issues. This goal is reflected in the basic tenet of relevance which underlies all our rules of evidence: see *Morris v. The Queen*, [1983] 2 S.C.R. 190, and *R. v. Corbett*, [1988] 1 S.C.R. 670. In general, nothing is to be received which is not logically probative of some matter requiring to be proved and everything which is probative should be received, unless its exclusion can be justified on some other ground. A law which prevents the trier of fact from getting at the truth by excluding relevant evidence in the absence of a clear ground of policy or law justifying the exclusion runs afoul of our fundamental conceptions of justice and what constitutes a fair trial.

The problem which arises is that a trial is a complex affair, raising many different issues. Relevance must be determined not in a vacuum, but in relation to some issue in the trial. Evidence which may be relevant to one issue may be irrelevant to another issue. What is worse, it may actually mislead the trier of fact on the second issue. Thus the same piece of evidence may have value to the trial process but bring with it the danger that it may prejudice the fact-finding process on another issue.

. . . .

The Canadian cases cited above all pertain to evidence tendered by the Crown against the accused. The question arises whether the same power to exclude exists with respect to defence evidence. Canadian courts, like courts in most common law jurisdictions, have been extremely cautious in restricting the power of the accused to call evidence in his or her defence, a reluctance founded in the fundamental tenet of our judicial system that an innocent person must not be convicted. It follows from this that the prejudice must substantially outweigh the value of the evidence before a judge can exclude evidence relevant to a defence allowed by law.

These principles and procedures are familiar to all who practise in our criminal courts. They are common sense rules based on basic notions of fairness, and as such properly lie at the heart of our trial process. In short, they form part of the principles of fundamental justice enshrined in s. 7 of the *Charter*. They may be circumscribed in some cases by other rules of evidence, but as will be discussed in more detail below, the circumstances where truly relevant and reliable evidence is excluded are few, particularly where the evidence goes to the defence. In most cases, the exclusion of relevant evidence can be justified on the ground that the potential prejudice to the trial process of admitting the evidence clearly outweighs its value.

This then is the yardstick by which ss. 276 and 277 of the *Code* are to be measured. Do they exclude evidence the probative value of which is not substantially outweighed by its potential prejudice? If so, they violate the fundamental principles upon which our justice system is predicated and infringe s. 7 of the *Charter*.

The parties, as I understand their positions, agree on this view of the principles of fundamental justice. The Attorney General for Ontario, for the respondent, does not assert that the *Charter* permits exclusion of evidence of real value to an accused's defence. Rather, he contends that any evidence which might be excluded by ss. 276 and 277 of the *Code* would be of such trifling value in relation to the prejudice that might flow from its reception that its exclusion would enhance rather than detract from the fairness of the trial. Others who defend the legislation do so on the ground that it does not exclude evidence relevant to the defence, that the exceptions contained in the provisions "encompass *all* potential situations where evidence of a complainant's sexual history with men other than the accused would be *relevant* to support a legitimate defence" (emphasis in original): see Grant, *supra*, at p. 601. It is to this issue, which I see as the crux of the case, which I now turn.

The Effect of the Legislation — What Evidence Is Excluded?

Section 277 excludes evidence of sexual reputation for the purpose of challenging or supporting the credibility of the plaintiff. The idea that a complainant's credibility might be affected by whether she has had other sexual experience is, today, universally discredited. There is no logical or practical link between a woman's sexual reputation and whether she is a truthful witness. It follows that the evidence excluded by s. 277 can serve no legitimate purpose in the trial. Section 277, by limiting the exclusion to a purpose which is clearly illegitimate, does not touch evidence which may be tendered for valid purposes, and hence does not infringe the right to a fair trial.

I turn then to s. 276. Section 276, unlike s. 277, does not condition exclusion on use of the evidence for an illegitimate purpose. Rather, it constitutes a blanket exclusion, subject to three exceptions — rebuttal evidence, evidence going to identity, and evidence relating to consent to sexual activity on the same occasion as the trial incident. The question is whether this may exclude evidence which is relevant to the defence and the probative value of which is not substantially outweighed by the potential prejudice to the trial process. To put the matter another way, can it be said *a priori*, as the Attorney General for Ontario contends, that any and all evidence excluded by s. 276 will necessarily be of such trifling weight in relation to the prejudicial effect of the evidence that it may fairly be excluded?

In my view, the answer to this question must be negative. The Canadian and American jurisprudence affords numerous examples of evidence of sexual conduct which would be excluded by s. 276 but which clearly should be received in the interests of a fair trial, notwithstanding the possibility that it may divert a jury by tempting it to improperly infer consent or lack of credibility in the complainant.

Consider the defence of honest belief. It rests on the concept that the accused may honestly but mistakenly (and not necessarily reasonably) have believed that the complainant was consenting to the sexual act. If the accused can raise a reasonable doubt as to his intention on the basis that he honestly held such a belief, he is not guilty under our law and is entitled to an acquittal. The basis of the accused's honest belief in the complainant's consent may be sexual acts performed by the complainant at some other time or place. Yet section 276 would preclude the accused leading such evidence.

Another category of evidence eliminated by s. 276 relates to the right of the defence to attack the credibility of the complainant on the ground that the complainant was biased or had motive to fabricate the evidence. In *State v. Jalo*, 557 P. 2d 1359 (Or. Ct. App. 1976), a father accused of sexual acts with his young daughter sought to present evidence that the source of the accusation was his earlier discovery of the fact that the girl and her brother were engaged in intimate relations. The defence contended that when the father stopped the relationship, the daughter, out of animus toward him, accused him of the act. The father sought to lead this evidence in support of his defence that the charges were a concoction motivated by animus. Notwithstanding its clear relevance, this evidence would be excluded by s. 276. The respondent submits that the damage caused by its exclusion would not be great, because all that would be forbidden would be evidence of the sexual activities of the children, and the father could still testify that his daughter was angry with him. But surely the father's chance of convincing the jury of the validity of his defence would be greatly diminished if he were reduced to saying, in effect, "My daughter was angry with me, but I can't say why or produce any corroborating evidence." As noted above, to deny a defendant the building blocks of his defence is often to deny him the defence itself.

Other examples abound. Evidence of sexual activity excluded by s. 276 may be relevant to explain the physical conditions on which the Crown relies to establish intercourse or the use of force, such as semen, pregnancy, injury or disease — evidence which may go to consent: see Galvin, *supra*, at pp. 818–23; J.A. Tanford and A.J. Bocchino, "Rape Victim Shield Laws and the Sixth Amendment" (1980), 128 *U. Pa. L. Rev.* 544, at pp. 584–85; D. W. Elliott, "Rape Complainants' Sexual Experience with Third Parties," [1984] *Crim. L. Rev.* 4, at p. 7; *State v. Carpenter*, 447 N.W.2d 436 (Minn. Ct. App. 1989), at pp. 440–42; *Commonwealth v. Majorana*, 470 A.2d 80 (Pa. 1983), at pp. 84–85; *People v. Mikula*, 269 N.W.2d 195 (Mich. Ct. App. 1978), at pp. 198–99; *State ex rel. Pope v. Superior Court*, 545 P.2d 946 (Ariz. 1976), at p. 953. In the case of young complainants where there may be a tendency to believe their story on the ground that the detail of their account must have come from the alleged encounter, it may be relevant to show other activity which provides an explanation for the knowledge: see *R. v. LeGallant* (1985), 47 C.R. (3d) 170 (B.C.S.C.), at pp. 175–76; *R. v. Greene* (1990), 76 C.R. (3d) 119 (Ont. Dist. Ct.), at p. 122; *State v. Pulizzano*, 456 N.W. 2d 325 (Wis. 1990), at pp. 333–35; *Commonwealth v. Black*, 487 A.2d 396 (Pa. Super. Ct. 1985), at p. 400, fn. 10; *State v. Oliveira*, 576 A.2d 111 (R.I. 1990), at pp. 113–14; *State v. Carver*, 678 P.2d 842 (Wash. Ct. App. 1984); *State v. Howard*, 426 A.2d 457 (N.H. 1981); *State v. Reinart*, 440 N.W.2d 503 (N.D. 1989); *Summitt v. State*, 697 P.2d. 1374 (Nev. 1985).

Even evidence as to pattern of conduct may on occasion be relevant. Since this use of evidence of prior sexual conduct draws upon the inference that prior conduct infers similar subsequent conduct, it closely resembles the prohibited use of the evidence and must be carefully scrutinized: *R. v. Wald* (1989), 47 C.C.C. (3d) 315 (Alta. C.A.), at pp. 339–40; *Re Seaboyer and The Queen* (1987), 61 O.R. 290 (C.A.), at p. 300; Tanford and Bocchino, *supra*, at pp. 586–89; Galvin, *supra*, at pp. 831–48; Elliott, *supra*, at pp. 7–8; A. P. Ordover, "Admissibility of Patterns of Similar Sexual Conduct: The Unlamented Death of Character for Chastity" (1977), 63 *Cornell L. Rev.* 90, at pp. 112–19; *Winfield v. Commonwealth*, 301 S.E.2d 15 (Va. 1983), at pp. 19–21; *State v. Shoffner*, 302 S.E.2d 830 (N.C. Ct. App. 1983), at pp. 832–33; *State v. Gonzalez*, 757 P.2d 925 (Wash. 1988), at pp. 929–31; *State v. Hudlow*, 659 P.2d 514 (Wash. 1983), at p. 520. Yet such evidence might be admissible in non-sexual cases under the similar fact rule. Is it fair then to deny it to an accused, merely because the trial relates to a sexual offence? Consider the example offered by Tanford and Bocchino, *supra*, at p. 588, commenting on the situation in the United States:

> A woman alleges that she was raped. The man she has accused of the act claims that she is a prostitute who agreed to sexual relations for a fee of twenty dollars, and afterwards, threatening to accuse him of rape, she demanded an additional one hundred dollars. The man refused to pay the extra amount. She had him arrested for rape, and he had her arrested for extortion. In the extortion trial, the state would be permitted to introduce evidence of the woman's previous sexual conduct — the testimony of other men that, using the same method, she had extorted money from them. When the woman is the complaining witness in the rape prosecution, however, evidence of this *modus operandi* would be excluded in most states. The facts are the same in both cases, as is the essential issue whether the woman is a rape victim or a would-be extortionist. Surely the relevance of the testimony should also be identical. If the woman's sexual history is relevant enough to be admitted against her when she is a defendant, entitled to the protections of the Constitution, then certainly it is relevant enough to be admitted in a trial at which she is merely a witness, entitled to no constitutional protection. Relevance depends on the issues that must be resolved at trial, not on the particular crime charged.

These examples leave little doubt that s. 276 has the potential to exclude evidence of critical relevance to the defence. Can it honestly be said, as the Attorney General for Ontario contends, that the value of such evidence will always be trifling when compared with its potential to mislead the jury? I think not. The examples show that the evidence may well be of great importance to getting at the truth and determining whether the accused is guilty or innocent under the law — the ultimate aim of the trial process. They demonstrate that s. 276, enacted for the purpose of helping judges and juries arrive at the proper and just verdict in the particular case, overshoots the mark, with the result that it may have the opposite effect of impeding them in discovering the truth.

The conclusion that s. 276 overreaches is supported by consideration of how it impacts on the justifications for s. 276 set out above. The first and most important justification for s. 276 is that it prevents the judge or jury from being diverted by irrelevant evidence of other sexual conduct of the complainant which will unfairly prejudice them against the complainant and thus lead to an improper verdict. Accepting that evidence that diverts the trier of fact from the real issue and prejudices the chance of a true verdict can properly be excluded even if it possesses some relevance, the fact remains that a provision which categorically excludes evidence without permitting the trial judge to engage in the exercise of whether the possible prejudicial effect of the evidence outweighs its value to the truth-finding process runs the risk of overbreadth: see Doherty, *supra*, at p. 65.

The argument based on the reporting of sexual offences similarly fails to justify the wide reach of s. 276. As Doherty points out at p. 65, it is counterproductive to encourage reporting by a rule which impairs the ability of the trier of fact to arrive at a just result and determine the truth of the report. Reporting is but the first step in the judicial process, not an end in itself. But even if it is assumed that increased reporting will result in increased convictions, the argument is persuasive. Elliott, at p. 14, discounts this justification for prohibitions of relevant evidence on the ground that it "cross[es] a hitherto uncrossed line" to rule out legitimate tactics which may help an innocent man escape conviction. To accept that persuasive evidence for the defence can be categorically excluded on the ground that it may encourage reporting and convictions is, Elliott points out, to say either (a) that we assume the defendant's guilt; or (b) that the defendant must be hampered in his defence so that genuine rapists can be put down. Neither alternative conforms to our notions of fundamental justice.

Finally, the justification of maintaining the privacy of the witness fails to support the rigid exclusionary rule embodied in s. 276 of the *Code*. First, it can be argued that important as it is to take all measures possible to ease the plight of the witness, the constitutional right to a fair trial must take precedence in case of conflict. As Doherty puts it (at p. 66):

> Every possible procedural step should be taken to minimize the encroachment on the witness's privacy, but in the end if evidence has sufficient cogency the witness must endure a degree of embarrassment and perhaps psychological trauma. This harsh reality must be accepted as part of the price to be paid to ensure that only the guilty are convicted.

Secondly, s. 276 goes further than required to protect privacy because it fails to permit an assessment of the effect on the witness of the evidence — an effect which may be great in some cases and small in others — in relation to the cogency of the evidence.

2. Is s. 276 Saved by s. 1 of the *Charter*?

Is s. 276 of the *Criminal Code* justified in a free and democratic society, notwithstanding the fact that it may lead to infringements of the *Charter*?

The first step under s. 1 is to consider whether the legislation addresses a pressing and substantial objective: *R. v. Oakes*, [1986] 1 S.C.R. 103. As already discussed, it does.

The second requirement under s. 1 is that the infringement of rights be proportionate to the pressing objective. This inquiry involves three considerations. The first — whether there exists a rational connection between the legislative measure and the objective — is arguably met; s. 276 does help to exclude unhelpful and potentially misleading evidence of the complainant's prior sexual conduct. The second consideration under proportionality is whether the legislation impairs the right as little as possible. It has been suggested that legislatures must be given some room to manoeuvre, particularly where the legislation is attempting to fix a balance between competing groups in society: *Irwin Toy Ltd. v. Quebec (Attorney General)*, [1989] 1 S.C.R. 927. Assuming that this case, although criminal and as such a contest between the state and the accused, might fall into this class, it still cannot be said that the degree of impairment effected by s. 276 is appropriately restrained. In creating exceptions to the exclusion of evidence of the sexual activity of the complainant on other occasions, Parliament correctly recognized that justice requires a measured approach, one which admits evidence which is truly relevant to the defence notwithstanding potential prejudicial effect. Yet Parliament, at the same time, excluded other evidence of sexual conduct which might be equally relevant to a legitimate defence and which appears to pose no greater danger of prejudice than the exceptions it recognizes. To the extent the section excludes relevant defence evidence whose value is not clearly outweighed by the danger it presents, the section is overbroad.

I turn finally to the third aspect of the proportionality requirement — the balance between the importance of the objective and the injurious effect of the legislation. The objective of the legislation, as discussed above, is to eradicate the erroneous inferences from evidence of other sexual encounters that the complainant is more likely to have consented to the sexual act in issue or less likely to be telling the truth. The subsidiary aims are to promote fairer trials and increased reporting of sexual offences and to minimize the invasion of the complainant's privacy. In this way the personal security of women and their right to equal benefit and protection of the law are enhanced. The effect of the legislation, on the other hand, is to exclude relevant defence evidence, the value of which outweighs its potential prejudice. As indicated in the discussion of s. 7, all parties agree that a provision which rules out probative defence evidence which is not clearly outweighed by the prejudice it may cause to the trial strikes the wrong balance between the rights of complainants and the rights of the accused. The line must be drawn short of the point where it results in an unfair trial and the possible conviction of an innocent person. Section 276 fails this test.

I conclude that s. 276 is not saved by s. 1 of the *Charter*.

. . . .

4. What Follows from Striking Down s. 276?

The first question is whether the striking down of s. 276 revives the old common law rules of evidence permitting liberal and often inappropriate reception of evidence of the complainant's sexual conduct. Some inappropriate uses of such evidence are precluded by s. 277, which I have found to be valid. But other common law rules fall outside s. 277. Does striking s. 276 revive them?

The answer to this question is no. The rules in question are common law rules. Like other common law rules of evidence, they must be adapted to conform to current reality. As all counsel on these appeals accepted, the reality in 1991 is that evidence of sexual conduct and reputation in itself cannot be regarded as logically probative of either the complainant's credibility or consent. Although they still may inform the thinking of many, the twin myths which s. 276 sought to eradicate are just that — myths — and have no place in a rational and just system of law. It follows that the old rules which permitted evidence of sexual conduct and condoned invalid inferences from it solely for these purposes have no place in our law.

. . . .

In the absence of legislation, it is open to the Court to suggest guidelines for the reception and use of sexual conduct evidence. Such guidelines should be seen for what they are — an attempt to describe the consequences of the application of the general rules of evidence governing relevance and the reception of evidence — and not as judicial legislation cast in stone.

In my view the trial judge under this new regime shoulders a dual responsibility. First, the judge must assess with a high degree of sensitivity whether the evidence proffered by the defence meets the test of demonstrating a degree of relevance which outweighs the damages and disadvantages presented by the admission of such evidence. The examples presented earlier suggest that while cases where such evidence will carry sufficient probative value will exist, they will be exceptional. The trial judge must ensure that evidence is tendered for a legitimate purpose, and that it logically supports a defence. The fishing expeditions which unfortunately did occur in the past should not be permitted. The trial judge's discretion must be exercised to ensure that neither the *in camera* procedure nor the trial become forums for demeaning and abusive conduct by defence counsel.

The trial judge's second responsibility will be to take special care to ensure that, in the exceptional case where circumstances demand that such evidence be permitted, the jury is fully and properly instructed as to its appropriate use. The jurors must be cautioned that they should not draw impermissible inferences from evidence of previous sexual activity. While such evidence may be tendered for a purpose logically probative of the defence to be presented, it may be important to remind jurors that they not allow the allegations of past sexual activity to lead them to the view that the complainant is less worthy of belief, or was more likely to have consented for that reason. It is hoped that a sensitive and responsive exercise of discretion by the judiciary will reduce and even eliminate the concerns which provoked legislation such as s. 276, while at the same time preserving the right of an accused to a fair trial.

I would summarize the applicable principles as follows:

1. On a trial for a sexual offence, evidence that the complainant has engaged in consensual sexual conduct on other occasions (including past sexual conduct with the accused) is not admissible solely to support the inference that the complainant is by reason of such conduct:
   (a) more likely to have consented to the sexual conduct at issue in the trial;
   (b) less worthy of belief as a witness.

2. Evidence of consensual sexual conduct on the part of the complainant may be admissible for purposes other than an inference relating to the consent or credibility of the complainant where it possesses probative value on an issue in the trial and where that probative value is not substantially outweighed by the danger of unfair prejudice flowing from the evidence.

   By way of illustration only and not by way of limitation, the following are examples of admissible evidence:
   (A) Evidence of specific instances of sexual conduct tending to prove that a person other than the accused caused the physical consequences of the rape alleged by the prosecution;
   (B) Evidence of sexual conduct tending to prove bias or motive to fabricate on the part of the complainant;
   (C) Evidence of prior sexual conduct, known to the accused at the time of the act charged, tending to prove that the accused believed that the complainant was consenting to the act charged (without laying down absolute rules, normally one would expect some proximity in time between the conduct that is alleged to have given rise to an honest belief and the conduct charged);

(D) Evidence of prior sexual conduct which meets the requirements for the reception of similar act evidence, bearing in mind that such evidence cannot be used illegitimately merely to show that the complainant consented or is an unreliable witness;

(E) Evidence tending to rebut proof introduced by the prosecution regarding the complainant's sexual conduct.

3. Before evidence of consensual sexual conduct on the part of a victim is received, it must be established on a *voir dire* (which may be held *in camera*) by affidavit or the testimony of the accused or third parties, that the proposed use of the evidence of other sexual conduct is legitimate.

4. Where evidence that the complainant has engaged in sexual conduct on other occasions is admitted on a jury trial, the judge should warn the jury against inferring from the evidence of the conduct itself, either that the complainant might have consented to the act alleged, or that the complainant is less worthy of credit.

CONCLUSION

I would dismiss the appeals and affirm the order of the Court of Appeal that these cases proceed to trial.

. . . .

[L'HEUREUX-DUBÉ J. (dissenting in part):]

INTRODUCTION

These two appeals are about relevance, myths and stereotypes in the context of sexual assaults. More particularly, is the prior sexual history of a complainant, in the trial of an accused charged with sexual assault, relevant and/or admissible? In that regard, the constitutionality of ss. 276 and 277 of the *Criminal Code*, R.S.C., 1985, c. C-46 (formerly ss. 246.6 and 246.7) is challenged as violating ss. 7 and 11(*d*) of the *Canadian Charter of Rights and Freedoms*.

Both appellants, Seaboyer and Gayme, were charged with sexual assault. During his preliminary inquiry, the appellant Gayme sought to adduce evidence of the complainant's prior sexual history. Since ss. 276 and 277 of the *Code* prohibit the admission of the evidence, Gayme asked the preliminary hearing judge to strike down the impugned provisions on the basis that they violated his *Charter* right to a fair trial. The judge determined that he had no jurisdiction to apply s. 52 of the *Constitution Act, 1982*, and disallowed the proposed evidence and cross-examination. The appellant Gayme was committed for trial.

The appellant Seaboyer was committed for trial after the conclusion of his preliminary inquiry. Along with the appellant Gayme, Seaboyer applied to the Supreme Court of Ontario for an order quashing his committal. The appellant Gayme also applied for declaratory relief, but this application was not addressed by the court. Galligan J. heard the appellants' applications together. He struck down ss. 276 and 277 of the *Code*, holding that they infringed ss. 7 and 11(d) of the *Charter*, and quashed the committals. He referred the cases back for a continuation of the preliminary inquiries. The appellants have yet to be tried for the offences charged.

. . . .

ANALYSIS

Of tantamount importance in answering the constitutional questions in this case is a consideration of the prevalence and impact of discriminatory beliefs on trials of sexual offences. These beliefs affect the processing of complaints, the law applied when and if the case proceeds to trial, the trial itself and the ultimate verdict. It is my view that the constitutional questions must be examined in their broader political, social and historical context in order to attempt any kind of meaningful constitutional analysis. The strength of this approach was discussed by Wilson J., in *Edmonton Journal v. Alberta (Attorney General)*, [1989] 2 S.C.R. 1326, at p. 1352. She states at p. 1355 that, "[o]ne virtue of the contextual approach, it seems to me, is that it recognizes that a particular right or freedom may have a different value depending on the context."

. . . .

SEXUAL ASSAULT

Sexual assault is not like any other crime. In the vast majority of cases the target is a woman and the perpetrator is a man (98.7 percent of those charged with sexual assault are men: *Crime Statistics 1986*, quoted in T. Dawson, "Sexual Assault Law and Past Sexual Conduct of the Primary Witness: The Construction of Relevance" (1988), 2 *C.J.W.L.* 310, at note 72, p. 326). Unlike other crimes of a violent nature, it is, for the most part, unreported. Yet, by all accounts, women are victimized at an alarming rate and there is some evidence that an already frighteningly high rate of sexual assault is on the increase. The prosecution and conviction rates for sexual assault are among the lowest for all violent crimes. Perhaps more than any other crime, the fear and constant reality of sexual assault affects how women conduct their lives and how they define their relationship with the larger society. Sexual assault is not like any other crime.

Conservative estimates inform us that, in Canada, at least one woman in five will be sexually assaulted during her lifetime (see J. Brickman and J. Briere, "Incidence of Rape and Sexual Assault in an Urban Canadian Population" (1985), 7 *Int'l J. of Women's Stud.* 195). The Report of the Committee on Sexual Offences Against Children and Youths warns that one in two females will be the victim of unwanted sexual acts (*Sexual Offences Against Children* (1984)). While social scientists agree that the incidence of sexual assault is great, they also agree that it is impossible, for a variety of reasons, to measure accurately the actual rate of victimization. However, Brickman and Briere, *supra*, report that police figures "may be multiplied anywhere from five to twenty times to correct for victim under-reporting." (See also LeGrand, "Rape and Rape Laws: Sexism in Society and Law" (1973), 61 *Calif. L. Rev.* 919, at p. 939, and L. Clark and D. Lewis, *Rape: The Price of Coercive Sexuality* (1977), at p. 57.) While there is a large gap between reported incidents and actual victimization, there is a further gap between what researchers tell us are the actual numbers and what the actual numbers are.

There are a number of reasons why women may not report their victimization: fear of reprisal, fear of a continuation of their trauma at the hands of the police and the criminal justice system, fear of a perceived loss of status and lack of desire to report due to the typical effects of sexual assault such as depression, self-blame or loss of self-esteem. Although all of the reasons for failing to report are significant and important, more relevant to the present inquiry are the numbers of victims who choose not to bring their victimization to the attention of the authorities due to their perception that the institutions with which they would have to become involved will view their victimization in a stereotypical and biased fashion. In the report of the Solicitor General of Canada, *Canadian Urban Victimization Survey: Reported and Unreported Crimes* (1984), the statistics in this regard are noted at p. 10:

> Analysis of reasons for failure to report incidents confirms many of the concerns which have already been noted by rape crisis workers — that women fear revenge from the offender (a factor in 33% of the unreported incidents) and, even more disturbingly, that they often fail to report because of their concern about the attitude of police or courts to this type of offence (43% of unreported incidents).

(See also L. Holmstrom and A. Burgess, *The Victim of Rape: Institutional Reactions* (1983), at p. 58, and P. Marshall, "Sexual Assault, The Charter and Sentencing Reform" (1988), 63 C.R. (3d) 216, at p. 217.)

The woman who comes to the attention of the authorities has her victimization measured against the current rape mythologies, i.e., who she should be in order to be recognized as having been, in the eyes of the law, raped; who her attacker must be in order to be recognized, in the eyes of the law, as a potential rapist; and how injured she must be in order to be believed. If her victimization does not fit the myths, it is unlikely that an arrest will be made or a conviction obtained. As prosecutors and police often suggest, in an attempt to excuse their application of stereotype, there is no point in directing cases toward the justice system if juries and judges will acquit on the basis of their stereotypical perceptions of the "supposed victim" and her "supposed" victimization. K. Williams, *The Prosecution of Sexual Assaults* (1978), discusses, at p. 42, the attrition rate for sexual assault cases as they progress through the system:

> ...the D.C. Task Force on Rape reported their concern that sexual assault cases did not fare well in the courts. They were not sure, however, whether this reflected normal attrition, experienced with all cases, or whether rape cases were particularly prone to dismissal. *The latter seems to be true.* In our analysis, rape cases were less likely to result in conviction than cases of robbery, burglary, and murder. The only crime with an attrition rate at all comparable was aggravated assault. There is an explanation for a large part of the attrition rate of assault cases, but it does not apply to rape. Over 60 percent of the rejections at screening and over one-half of the latter dismissals in aggravated assault cases can be attributed to the complaining witness's decision to stop cooperating with the prosecutor. The attrition that results from such a decision on the part of the victim does *not* account for the attrition in rape cases. ***Attrition in rape cases is more likely to be the result of the prosecutor's judgment that the victim's credibility is questionable.... Few cases go to trial.... Most fall out of the system before they reach that stage.*** [Emphasis added.] [Italics in original.]

More specifically, police rely, in large measure, upon popular conceptions of sexual assault in order to classify incoming cases as "founded" or "unfounded." It would appear as though most forces have developed a convenient shorthand regarding their decisions to proceed in any given case. This shorthand is composed of popular myth regarding rapists (distinguishing them from men as a whole), and stereotype about women's character and sexuality. Holmstrom and Burgess, *supra*, at pp. 174–99, conveniently set out and explain the most common of these myths and stereotypes....

. . . .

This list of stereotypical conceptions about women and sexual assault is by no means exhaustive. Like most stereotypes, they operate as a way, however flawed, of understanding the world and, like most such constructs, operate at a level of consciousness that makes it difficult to root them out and confront them directly. This mythology finds its way into the decisions of the police regarding their "founded"/"unfounded" categorization, operates in the mind of the Crown when deciding whether or not to prosecute, influences a judge's or juror's perception of guilt or innocence of the accused and the "goodness" or "badness" of the victim, and finally, has carved out a niche in both the evidentiary and substantive law governing the trial of the matter.

The effect of this filtering process is evident when one examines the end result: conviction rates. Clark and Lewis, in *Rape: The Price of Coercive Sexuality, supra*, quoted in C. Backhouse and L. Schoenroth, "A Comparative Survey of Canadian and American Rape Law" (1983), 6 *Can.-U.S. L.J.* 48, note 278, at p. 81, provide us with an estimate of the actual conviction rate in rape cases. Based upon a reporting rate of 40 percent (which is one of the highest estimates of reporting), a founding rate of 36 percent, an arrest rate of 75 percent and a conviction rate of 51 percent they concluded that only 7 percent of rapists are likely to be convicted. Although their conclusions are based upon Toronto crime statistics for 1970, their data and conclusions bring home the limited utility of statistics which use only reported cases in estimating incidence, arrest and conviction rates. Moreover, their conclusions are supported by more recent data. H. Field and L. Bienen, *Jurors and Rape* (1980), suggest, at p. 95, that, "based upon recent crime statistics, an individual who commits rape has only about 4 chances in 100 of being arrested, prosecuted, and found guilty of any offense." The conviction rates for those who are actually arrested and prosecuted are little better. Williams, *supra*, tells us at p. 19 that:

> Sexual assault cases infrequently result in a conviction. Of the arrests that had reached final disposition at the time of this analysis, 22 percent resulted in conviction — on some charge. This rate is not only low, it is much lower than the rate for other crimes, which is between 30 and 35 percent ... the conviction rates were low regardless of the age or sex of victim.

Canadian statistics are no more encouraging. Statistics Canada reports that the conviction rate for all crimes against the person in 1973 was 66.7 percent whereas the comparable rate for rape was 39.3 percent.

The previous discussion about reporting rates, rates of arrest and conviction, and the practices of the police in classifying sexual assaults, informs us as to the approximate number of women who are actually victimized. It also tells us something about the gloss that prejudicial beliefs can place on what actually happens, but it does not tell us much about a related and perhaps much larger effect. Whether or not a particular woman has been sexually assaulted, the high rate of assault works to shape the daily life of all women. The fact is that many, if not most women, live in fear of victimization. The fear can become such a constant companion that its effect remains largely unnoticed and, sadly, unremarkable. In their study of this phenomenon, M. Gordon and S. Riger, *The Female Fear* (1989), conclude that, "...women restrict their behavior — even isolate themselves — in order to avoid being harmed." The point is made dramatically at pp. 1–2 of the *Canadian Urban Victimization Survey: Female Victims of Crime, supra*:

> We now know from recent research on fear of crime that first-hand experience with victimization is only one dimension of fear.... Particularly relevant in understanding women's fear is an appreciation of the kinds of violence women are most vulnerable to, especially the experience and the impact of domestic and sexual violence. Some women live with the imminent threat of assault from someone in their own households, and many women live with the more general fear of sexual assault, concerns which rarely intrude into the lives of men.
>
> Any form of sexual aggression may feed women's fears by sensitizing them to the possibility of violent attack. Victimization surveys obviously cannot address all the subtle reminders to women of their vulnerability.
>
> While avoidance of high risk situations may well be an important element of victimization

> prevention, there are obvious limits and costs to a strategy of withdrawal.... Even moderate withdrawal in order to prevent violent victimization can diminish an individual's sense of personal autonomy and have a negative impact on the overall quality of life.

In his reasons for judgment in *R. v. Keegstra*, [1990] 3 S.C.R. 697, Dickson C.J. at pp. 746–47 discusses this phenomenon in the context of minority groups targeted by hate propaganda. His words are instructive:

> The derision, hostility and abuse encouraged by hate propaganda therefore have a severely negative impact on the individual's sense of self-worth and acceptance. This impact may cause target group members to take drastic measures in reaction, perhaps avoiding activities which bring them into contact with non-group members or adopting attitudes and postures directed towards blending in with the majority. Such consequences bear heavily in a nation that prides itself on tolerance and the fostering of human dignity....

This brings us much closer towards a recognition of the impact of societal and legal responses to the sexual victimization of women.

Forgetting about the microcosm of the criminal justice system for a moment, one must not lose sight of the fact that the individuals involved in the processing of complaints are a product of our larger society. While it is clear that those who are so involved hold and utilize stereotypical beliefs about women and rape, this should not be taken to mean that, perhaps as a result of their close association with the matter, they are unique in this respect. In a report prepared for the Ontario Women's Directorate in 1988, by Informa Inc., "Sexual Assault: Measuring the Impact of the Launch Campaign," the prevalence among Ontario residents of a number of stereotypical and discriminatory beliefs was measured. The results indicate that similar stereotypes are held by a surprising number of individuals, for example: that men who assault are not like normal men, the "mad rapist" myth; that women often provoke or precipitate sexual assault; that women are assaulted by strangers; that women often agree to have sex but later complain of rape; and the related myth that men are often convicted on the false testimony of the complainant; that women are as likely to commit sexual assault as are men and that when women say no they do not necessarily mean no. This baggage belongs to us *all*. (See also Field and Bienen, *supra*.)

Absolutely pivotal to an understanding of the nature and purpose of the provisions and constitutional questions at issue in this case is the realization of how widespread the stereotypes and myths about rape are, notwithstanding their inaccuracy.

The appellants argue that we, as a society, have become more enlightened, that prosecutors, police, judges and jurors can be trusted to perform their tasks without recourse to discriminatory views about women manifested through rape myth. Unfortunately, social science evidence suggests otherwise.

Rape myths still present formidable obstacles for complainants in their dealings with the very system charged with discovering the truth. Their experience in this regard is illustrated by the following remarks of surprisingly recent vintage:

> Women who say no do not always mean no. It is not just a question of saying no, it is a question of how she says it, how she shows and makes it clear. If she doesn't want it she has only to keep her legs shut and she would not get it without force and there would be marks of force being used.

(Judge David Wild, Cambridge Crown Court, 1982, quoted in Elizabeth Sheehy, "Canadian Judges and the Law of Rape: Should the *Charter* Insulate Bias?" (1989), 21 *Ottawa L. Rev.* 741, at p. 741.)

> Unless you have no worldly experience at all, you'll agree that women occasionally resist at first but later give in to either persuasion or their own instincts.

(Judge Frank Allen, Manitoba Provincial Court, 1984, quoted in Sheehy, *supra*, at p. 741.)

> ...it is easy for a man intent upon his own desires to mistake the intentions of a woman or girl who may herself be in two minds about what to do. Even if he makes no mistake it is not unknown for a woman afterwards either to take fright or for some other reason to regret what has happened and seek to justify herself retrospectively by accusing the man of rape.

(Howard, *Criminal Law* (3rd ed. 1977), at p. 179.)

> Modern psychiatrists have amply studied the behavior of errant young girls and women coming before the courts in all sorts of cases. Their psychic complexes are multifarious, distorted partly by inherent defects, partly by diseased derangements of abnormal instincts, partly by bad social environment, partly by temporary physiological or emotional conditions. One form taken by these complexes is that of contriving false charges of sexual offenses by men.

(Wigmore, *Evidence in Trials at Common Law*, vol. 3A (1970), at p. 736.)

Regrettably, these remarks demonstrate that many in society hold inappropriate stereotypical beliefs and apply them when the opportunity presents itself.

Field and Bienen, *supra*, write at p. 139 that, "[t]he results reported in this study confirmed what many writers and researchers studying rape have suggested: extra-evidential factors were found to influence the outcome of the rape trials." When juries are provided with certain types of information about the complainant, such as evidence regarding past sexual conduct, the weight of the evidence is that they then utilize the myths and stereotypes discussed above and focus on them in "resolving" the particular legal issues raised by the case. Though these researchers found that the effect of sexual history evidence was more complex than originally thought, they do note at pp. 118–19 that:

> Along with race of the defendant, *sexual experience of the victim proved to have important effects on juror decision making as it wds involved in four of the seven significant interactions. Support for the reformers' sentiments concerning the elimination of evidence regarding third-party sexual relations is indicated by the presence of these interactions*.
>
> In the present research, the assailant in the nonprecipitory assault was given a more severe sentence than the offender in the precipitory case indicating that the jurors appeared to attribute blame to the victim when contributory behaviour was implied. Several writers (Frederick and Luginbuhl 1976; Jones and Aronson 1973; Landy and Aronson 1969) have documented similar effects. Brooks, Doob, and Kirshenbaum (1975) found that *jurors were more likely to convict a defendant accused of raping a woman with a chaste reputation than an identical defendant charged with assaulting a prostitute. Information on the "good" or "bad" character of the victim appears to affect the decisions of the jurors, and the definitions of good or bad are likely to be broadly defined*. [Emphasis added.]

Similarly, Borgida and White, "Social Perception of Rape Victims: The Impact of Legal Reform" (1978), 2 *Law and Hum. Behav.* 339, report at p. 379 that:

> ...when specific evidence of the victim's prior sexual history is admitted in a consent defense rape case ... jurors infer victim consent, carefully and unfavourably scrutinize the victim's credibility and moral character, and tend to attribute more responsibility to the victim.... *Although defendant credibility is a consideration, perceptions of the defendant's general moral character are much less of a consideration than the victim's general moral character.*
>
> *Jurors are reluctant to convict the defendant when any testimony about prior sexual history is introduced in support of the consent defense.*
>
> *The admission of this evidence seems to enhance the likelihood that jurors make person[al] attributions and attribute more personal responsibility to the victim for the rape. Jurors also are more likely to infer victim consent from testimony about prior sexual history.* [Emphasis added.]

G. La Free, who has done extensive research on this issue, suggests that the research is consistent with respect to the conclusion that when the victim allegedly engaged in "misconduct," acquittals were more likely ("Variables Affecting Guilty Pleas and Convictions in Rape Cases: Toward a Social Theory of Rape Processing" (1980), 58 *Soc. Forces* 833). In this particular study, La Free examined all of the forcible rape cases in an American midwestern city. He defined misconduct for the purpose of his study as either sexual, i.e., the victim had illegitimate children or was sleeping with her boyfriend, or non-sexual, i.e., the victim was a runaway or drug dealer. As La Free notes, when one realizes that sexual assault cases are extensively screened prior to trial according to their conformity with mythology, it is surprising that there is much of any "deviant" behaviour left to trigger the application of stereotype and myth at trial.

In a later study conducted by La Free (G. La Free, B. Reskin and C.A. Visher, "Jurors' Responses to Victims' Behaviour and Legal Issues in Sexual Assault Trials" (1985), 32 *Soc. Prob.* 389), post-trial interviews were conducted with jurors who had served in forcible sexual assault cases. At page 392 the authors state that, "[o]ur trial observations suggest that a major avenue for challenging the complainant's victimization in consent and no-sex cases is to encourage jurors to scrutinize her 'character'." They also suggest at p. 400 that "a victim's nontraditional behaviour may act as a catalyst, causing jurors' attitudes about how women should behave to affect their judgments under certain conditions." Also relevant for our purposes are their findings at p. 397 that, where the issue at trial is whether the act occurred or whether there was consent:

> Of particular interest are the findings regarding evidence. *Although any evidence that a woman was forced to submit to a sexual act against her will (including use of a weapon or victim injury) might be expected to persuade jurors of the defen-*

> *dant's guilt, neither variable significantly affected jurors' judgments....*
>
> In contrast, jurors were influenced by a victim's "character." They were less likely to believe in a defendant's guilt when the victim had reportedly engaged in sex outside marriage, drank or used drugs, or had been acquainted with the defendant — however briefly — prior to the alleged assault. [Emphasis added.]

Although Canadian data are harder to come by, those studies that have been done support the American data. Indeed, it would be somewhat surprising to find that this was not the case. In one Canadian study (K. Catton, "Evidence Regarding the Prior Sexual History of an Alleged Rape Victim — Its Effect on the Perceived Guilt of the Accused" (1975), 33 *U.T. Fac. L. Rev.* 165), subjects were asked to read a description of a hypothetical rape case. Varied among the descriptions were the nature of the controls placed upon evidence of the complainant's sexual history. At page 173 Catton discusses the results in this fashion:

> ...when jurors heard information regarding an alleged rape victim's prior sexual history with named persons, whether this information was confirmed or denied, this information decreased their perceived guilt of the accused in comparison with the situation where no information relating to the victim's supposed past sex life was heard. *This decrease in the perceived guilt of the accused varied directly with the "amount" of negative information presented about the victim.*
>
> Although the "No information" control condition was not as successful as planned ... still the accused was seen as most guilty in this condition where no information at all about the victim's prior sexual history was given. *Any information at all implying that the victim had a prior sex history had the effect of reducing the perceived guilt of the accused regardless of whether this information was verified.* [Emphasis added.]

Importantly, she finds that even if the prior sexual history of the complainant is denied or fails to be confirmed, the perceived guilt of the accused decreases.

It is thus clear that, from the making of the initial complaint down to the determination of the issue at trial, stereotype and mythology are at work, lowering the number of reported cases, influencing police decisions to pursue the case, thereby decreasing the rates of arrest, and finally, distorting the issues at trial and necessarily, the results. Professor Catharine MacKinnon asserts that in the United States:

> It is not only that women are the principal targets of rape, which by conservative definition happens to almost half of all women at least once in their lives. It is not only that over one-third of all women are sexually molested by old trusted male family members or friends or authority figures as an early, perhaps initiatory, interpersonal sexual encounter.... All this documents the extent and terrain of abuse and the effectively unrestrained and systematic sexual aggression by less than one-half of the population against the other more than half. It suggests that it is basically allowed.

(C. MacKinnon, *Toward a Feminist Theory of the State* (1989), at pp. 142–43.)

THE LARGER LEGAL CONTEXT

My discussion to this point has primarily been concerned with the incidence of sexual assault in our society and the role of stereotype in dealing with it. What clearly emerges from this previous discussion is that myths surrounding women and sexual assault affect perceptions of the culpability of the aggressor and the moral "character" and, hence, the credibility of the complainant and, thus, shape the ultimate legal result. While all of this is relevant in a discussion of the larger context of the legislation at issue, my focus here will be on the utilization of these discriminatory beliefs in the development of legal principles applicable in trials of sexual offences and on government attempts to combat it.

The common law has always viewed victims of sexual assault with suspicion and distrust. As a result, unique evidentiary rules were developed. The complainant in a sexual assault trial was treated unlike any other. In the case of sexual offences, the common law "enshrined" prevailing mythology and stereotype by formulating rules that made it extremely difficult for the complainant to establish her credibility and fend off inquiry and speculation regarding her "morality" or "character." The matter is put succinctly by H. Galvin, "Shielding Rape Victims in the State and Federal Courts: A Proposal for the Second Decade" (1986), 70 *Minn. L. Rev.* 763, at pp. 792–93:

> Traditional ideology also maintained that unchaste women became either vindictive or susceptible to rape fantasies and inclined falsely to charge men with rape. This belief was based on the notion that extramarital sexual activity was abnormal for women.... *Distrust and contempt for the unchaste female accuser was formalized into a set of legal rules unique to rape cases.* The most prominent rule allowed the use at trial of evidence of the complainant's unchaste conduct.

These rules combined to shift the usual focus of a criminal trial from an inquiry into the conduct of the offender to that of the moral worth of the complainant. [Emphasis added.]

At common law, the prior sexual history of the complainant was admissible on two issues, one material and one collateral. It was thought that "unchasteness" was relevant to the material issue of consent and the collateral issue of credibility. In other words, women who had consensual sex outside of marriage were thought, in essence, to have a dual propensity: to consent to sexual relations at large and to lie. The *Report of the Federal/Provincial Task Force on Uniform Rules of Evidence* (1982) summarized what was admissible at common law at pp. 66–67 in this fashion:

> Evidence of the complainant's sexual history, considered at common law to be relevant to consent, consisted of (1) other acts of sexual intercourse with the accused, (2) the opinion of a witness that the complainant is a prostitute, and specific incidents of the complainant's prostitution, (3) the complainant's general reputation as a common prostitute, (4) the complainant's general reputation for unchastity or "notoriously bad character for chastity," and (5) evidence that the complainant "is in the habit of submitting her body to different men, without discrimination, whether for pay or not." The relevance of this evidence to consent was based on the moral judgment that such a woman would be more likely to have consented to the act with which the accused had been charged.

The complainant's lack of consent was an essential element of an offence of rape or indecent assault. Thus the accused, at common law, could cross-examine the complainant concerning matters deemed relevant to consent, and the complainant was required to answer. Because consent was a material issue, the trial judge had no discretion to excuse the complainant from answering such questions on the ground that they were degrading. If the complainant denied the questions, the accused person could contradict her answers, or if the complainant refused to answer, the accused could prove the matters alleged.

At common law, a witness could be cross-examined as to any matter of conduct, including sexual conduct, which was relevant to impeach the witness's credibility. At common law, it was assumed that an unchaste woman was more likely to be an untruthful witness. Thus, in a prosecution for rape or indecent assault, a complainant could be cross-examined as to her sexual history to impeach her credibility. There were two limitations on the accused's right, on the issue of credibility, to confront a complainant with her sexual history. First the trial judge had some discretion to excuse the complainant from answering degrading questions. Second, if the complainant denied the question or refused to answer, whether with the judge's approval or not, since the matter was relevant only to the collateral issue of the complainant's credibility, the accused could not call evidence on it.

Under the guise of a principled application of the legal concept of relevance, the common law allowed the accused to delve at great length into the moral character of the complainant by adducing "relevant" sexual history. The prejudicial impact of such an inquiry has already been discussed at length. The true nature and purpose of the inquiry into sexual history is revealed by the resulting prejudice and by the fact that these concepts were only applicable in respect of sexual offences and, in addition, were not deemed relevant to the credibility of the male accused.

Application of the relevance concept was not the only way in which the common law integrated stereotype and myth into trials of sexual offences. Also part of the unique body of evidentiary law surrounding sexual offences were, among other things, the doctrine of recent complaint and corroboration rules. These evidentiary concepts were also based upon stereotypes of the female complainant requiring independent evidence to support her evidence and, in addition, evidence that she raised a "hue and cry" after her assault. It is noteworthy that both recent complaint and corroboration rules formed exceptions to general rules of evidence.

Evidence of a recent complaint in sexual assault cases is an exception to the general rule that self-serving statements are inadmissible. Such evidence is described in *Cross on Evidence* (7th ed. 1990), at p. 281, as superfluous, "for the assertions of a witness are to be regarded, in general, as true, until there is some particular reason for impeaching them as false." However, in the case of sexual offences, either the absence of a recent complaint or its inadmissibility required the trier of fact to draw an adverse inference. If a recent complaint existed, the complainant had to surmount onerous requirements restricting its admissibility. If admissible, such evidence was tendered to show that the complainant's testimony was consistent but was not admitted to show the truth of its contents. The importance of the rule at common law lay not in its ability to enhance the credibility of the complainant, but rather in its ability to counter the presumption that the complainant was lying. (See *Timm v. The Queen*, [1981] 2 S.C.R. 315, wherein the principles regarding this doctrine are fully discussed.) Thus, to a large degree, the myth that complainants in sexual assault cases fabricate their allegations informed the doctrine of recent complaint.

The corroboration rules were also exceptions to traditional evidence principles. Generally, "the court may act upon the uncorroborated testimony of one witness, and such requirements as there are concerning a plurality of witnesses, or some other confirmation of individual testimony are exceptional" (*Cross, supra*, at p. 224). Certain classes of witnesses were thought to be unreliable such as children of tender years, accomplices and, interestingly, victims of sexual offences, almost always women. The requirement for corroboration may take one of two forms. In some offences corroboration was required for conviction, whereas for others, the jury had to be warned that convicting absent corroboration was dangerous. The rationale for corroboration also finds its genesis in the traditional distrust of a complainant's veracity in sexual offences. J. Hoskins, "The Rise and Fall of the Corroboration Rule in Sexual Offence Cases" (1983), 4 *Can. J. Fam. L.* 173, comes to the same conclusion and states at pp. 117–78 that "[w]hile the rule requiring corroboration or a least a prescribed warning of the danger of convicting without corroborating evidence is a relative recently development, the law has long held a deep suspicion of female complainants in sexual offence cases." The Law Reform Commission of Canada has similarly questioned the "likely false assumptions upon which our present rules of corroboration rest" (*Corroboration: A Study Paper Prepared by the Law of Evidence Project* (1975), at p. 7).

The preoccupation of the law with the credibility of the complainant in such cases and the blatant stereotyping of such complainants as untrustworthy are difficult to comprehend. As we have seen, sexual assault is the most under-reported of all violent crimes. Even after a report, the police and prosecutors filter out a significant number of the complaints based upon their congruence with rape myth and stereotype. Logically it would seem that the likelihood of false complaints is, in this context, much reduced compared to that for most crime. Indeed, there is no evidence to support the contrary.

Thus, the common law stance in respect of the admission of the past sexual history of the complainant has a larger legal context. A number of other rules were formulated that give legal voice to stereotypes both about female complainants and about the nature of sexual assault. Legislative intervention must be viewed within this larger context.

Parliament intervened on two notable occasions, both relevant to the inquiry here. In 1976, Parliament repealed the existing s. 142 of the *Criminal Code*, R.S.C. 1970, c. C-34, and enacted a provision designed to alleviate some of the problems caused by the virtually unrestricted inquiry into a complainant's previous sexual history allowed at common law (*Criminal Law Amendment Act, 1975*, S.C. 1974–75–76, c. 93, s. 8). The provision read:

> **142.**(1) Where an accused is charged with an offence under section 144 or 145 or subsection 146(1) or 149(1) no question shall be asked by or on behalf of the accused as to the sexual conduct of the complainant with a person other than the accused unless
>
> (a) reasonable notice in writing has been given to the prosecutor by or on behalf of the accused of his intention to ask such question together with particulars of the evidence sought to be adduced by such question and a copy of such notice has been filed with the clerk of the court; and
>
> (b) the judge, magistrate or justice, after holding a hearing *in camera* in the absence of the jury, if any, is satisfied that the weight of the evidence is such that to exclude it would prevent the making of a just determination of an issue of fact in the proceedings, including the credibility of the complainant.
>
> (2) The notice given under paragraph (1)(a) and the evidence taken, the information given or the representations made at a hearing referred to in paragraph (1)(b) shall not be published in any newspaper or broadcast.
>
> (3) Every one who, without lawful excuse the proof of which lies upon him, contravenes subsection (2) is guilty of an offence punishable on summary conviction.
>
> (4) In this section, "newspaper" has the same meaning as it has in section 261.
>
> (5) In this section and in section 442, "complainant" means the person against whom it is alleged that the offence was committed.

Though the motives of Parliament were commendable, judicial interpretation of the section thwarted any benefit that may have accrued to the complainant. In fact, the provision, as judicially interpreted, provided *less* protection to the complainant than that offered at common law, surely a surprising result considering the obvious mischief Parliament intended to cure in enacting it.

More specifically, in *Forsythe v. The Queen*, [1980] 2 S.C.R. 268, this Court held at p. 279 that, in order that the trial judge be able to determine whether questioning during the trial proper was necessary, the complainant was compellable at the *in camera* hearing....

. . . .

It may be argued that, not only did the Court feel a somewhat misplaced need to "balance" the "protection" of the complainant against "restrictions" placed upon the accused, it tipped the balance further in favour of the accused. This is obviously a curious result given the fact that the infirmities of the common law led Parliament to intervene. That the complainant should walk away with less than she already had is lamentable. (The same conclusion was reached by Wilson J. (dissenting) in *R. v. Konkin*, [1983] 1 S.C.R. 388, wherein she stated at p. 396 that, "[i]n effect s. 142, instead of minimizing the embarrassment to complainants, increased it.") The *Report of the Federal/Provincial Task Force on Uniform Rules of Evidence, supra*, also criticized the approach of the Court in *Forsythe, supra*, and concluded at p. 72, properly in my view, that "[t]his interpretation defeats the main purpose of the provision." The peculiar nature of the "balance" struck by the Court is commented on by C. Boyle, "Section 142 of the Criminal Code: A Trojan Horse?" (1981), 23 *Crim. L.Q.* 253, at pp. 258–59, in these words:

> This displays a regrettable and unnecessary tit-for-tat approach to judicial law-making, unnecessary because in the judge-made law prior to 1975, there was no perceived need to allow contradictory evidence and nothing has happened since to demonstrate that accused persons then were not receiving a fair trial....
>
> *There can be no equivalence between cutting out some irrelevant questions and permitting other irrelevant evidence.* [Emphasis added.]

In sum, the response of the courts to s. 142 was decidedly at odds both with a recognition of the discriminatory nature of the common law and with the larger goals of Parliament in enacting the provision. Obviously, the judicial response did not alleviate the problems with the common law, leading Parliament to try once again.

Before delving into the second legislative effort of Parliament, I will briefly discuss a reform that accompanied s. 142, as it forms part of the legal context and also provides a stronger indication of the objectives of Parliament in becoming involved in this area of the law.

Section 142, which I have discussed above, replaced the previous s. 142 which contained a discretionary warning provision. The warning provision was not reenacted. It provided that, where an accused was charged with a certain sexual offence (sexual intercourse with a female under fourteen, sexual intercourse with a female between fourteen and sixteen, rape, attempted rape, and indecent assault on a female), and the only evidence which implicated the accused was the uncorroborated testimony of the female complainant, the judge *shall* instruct the jury that it is not safe to find the accused guilty in the absence of corroboration but that they were nevertheless entitled to do so. The stereotypical vision of complainants in sexual assault cases, which informed these rules of corroboration, was discussed earlier. The question that remained was whether the repeal by Parliament of the warning requirement revived the common law rule requiring corroboration in sexual offences. Though the answer reached by most courts was no (see, *R. v. Camp* (1977), 36 C.C.C. (2d) 511 (Ont. C.A.) and *R. v. Firkins* (1977), 37 C.C.C. (2d) 227 (B.C.C.A.), leave to appeal refused, [1977] 2 S.C.R. vii), it was, nevertheless, held that the judge could still comment on the risks of relying on the evidence of a single witness. To some degree then, the objective of the legislation was not met. Repeal of the mandatory corroboration requirement, embodied in s. 139 of the *Code*, was left for a later occasion. Nevertheless, this first reform effort indicates a significant attempt on the part of Parliament to rid trials of sexual offences of certain discriminatory rules and practices.

The failure of the courts, as was indicated earlier, both to take cognizance of and to implement the objectives of Parliament in this earlier legislation, combined with further criticism of the manner in which complainants of sexual offences were treated, generated a sweeping set of reforms in 1982. The Honourable Jean Chrétien, then Minister of Justice and Attorney General of Canada, articulated the principles underlying this second, larger reform package in this manner:

> *The inequality of the present law has placed an unfair burden on female victims of sexual assault.* It has added to the trauma, stigma and embarrassment of being sexually assaulted, and has deterred many victims from reporting these serious crimes to the police.... Bill C-53 would alleviate the legal impediment which allows this to occur.
>
> ...
>
> I am pleased to note that there appears to be widespread support *for the four basic principles underlying the bill, namely the protection of the integrity of the person, the protection of children and special groups,* the safeguarding of public decency, and *the elimination of sexual discrimination*. [Emphasis added.]

(Standing Committee on Justice and Legal Affairs, *Minutes of Proceedings and Evidence*, Issue No. 77, April 22, 1982, at p. 77:29.)

Further in earlier discussion and debate, Ron Irwin, Parliamentary Secretary to the Minister of Justice and Minister of State for Social Development referred, with more particularity, to the significance of the fourth principle:

> Simple equity demands [the elimination of sexual discrimination in criminal law] ... hand in hand with the rights of the accused must go the protection of those who are victims.

(*House of Commons Debates*, July 7, 1981, at p. 11300.)

These larger reform purposes must inform any analysis of the legislation.

The *Act to amend the Criminal Code in relation to sexual offences and other offences against the person and to amend certain other Acts in relation thereto or in consequence thereof,* S.C. 1980–81–82–83, c. 125, extensively altered the law in a number of respects. To begin with, the rules relating to recent complaint were "abrogated" (s. 246.5). However, some questions remained about the scope and effect of the section; i.e., could the use of the *res gestae* and recent fabrication exceptions to the rule against narrative work to practically revive the recent complaint exception and, further, what offences are covered by the provision? In answering these questions surely some assistance can be obtained by adverting to the larger goals of Parliament in enacting s. 246.5. With these goals in mind, a narrow interpretation of this section would be anomalous. (See C. Boyle, *Sexual Assault* (1984), at p. 154.) Nevertheless, the proper interpretation of this section is not in issue here.

What is important for our purposes is the relationship of this section and its goals to those provisions directly in issue in this case. As I discussed earlier, as a significant barrier to establishing credibility, the operation of the doctrine of recent complaint worked to the disadvantage of complainants and, as the rule found its roots in stereotypes of such complainants, its repeal is in keeping with the articulated goals of Parliament.

Parliament also addressed the mandatory corroboration requirement which escaped repeal in the 1976 set of amendments. This rule, embodied in s. 139(1) of the *Code*, required corroboration for the offences of sexual intercourse with the feebleminded, incest, seduction of a female of previous chaste character between 16 and 18 years of age, seduction under promise of marriage, sexual intercourse with step-daughters, foster daughters, female wards or female employees, seduction of female passengers on vessels, and parent or guardian procuring defilement. (Note, however, that some of these offences have themselves been repealed.) In this second set of reforms, Parliament repealed s. 139 and also enacted s. 246.4 which provides that, where an accused is charged with incest, gross indecency, or one of the various forms of sexual assault, no corroboration is required for a conviction and, further, the judge *shall not* instruct the jury that, without corroboration, it would be unsafe to convict. These changes rectify the position that existed after the repeal of s. 142 referred to above, namely that a trial judge could still instruct the jury about the "perils" of relying on the uncorroborated testimony of a single witness.

Another significant step forward in respect of protecting the integrity of the person and the elimination of sexual discrimination is the change relating to the prosecution of husbands who sexually assault their wives. Section 246.8 provides that a husband or a wife may be charged with any of the sexual assault offences in respect of his or her spouse, regardless of whether or not they were living together at the time of the act. Prior to these amendments, rape was defined as occurring where "[a] male person ... has sexual intercourse with a female person who is not his wife." To give effect to the amendment, Parliament modified the *Canada Evidence Act* and removed spousal incompetence and spousal noncompellability impediments in respect of these offences. Ron Irwin, then Parliamentary Secretary to the Minister of Justice and Minister of State for Social Development, described this change as granting "[e]qual protection under the law ... to all persons" (*House of Commons Debates*, July 7, 1981, at p. 11301).

Parliament also amended pre-existing provisions which protected the identity of the complainant in sexual offences. The amendments give the complainant independent status to apply for an order directing that her identity and any information which could disclose her identity not be published and, further, require the judge to grant the order upon her application. In addition, the amendments place upon the judge a duty to inform the complainant of her right to apply for the order. (These provisions were the subject of discussion in *Canadian Newspapers Co. v. Canada (Attorney General)*, [1988] 2 S.C.R. 122, a judgment that will be discussed later in these reasons.)

Finally, this set of reforms saw the repeal of s. 142 discussed above, and the enactment of ss. 246.6 and 246.7 (now ss. 276 and 277), reproduced at the outset. I will discuss the meaning and scope of the provisions later in these reasons. For the moment, it is sufficient to note that these sections clearly also promote the larger objectives of the reform package. Notwithstanding their congruence with these larger objectives, notably the attempt to eliminate sexual discrimination, they were also viewed as effecting change on a number of other, more specific levels. A further objective of the provisions was the rationalization of trials of sexual offences through restricting the ability of the accused to adduce invasive, prejudicial evidence of sexual history and sexual reputation, except in circumstances where the evidence was sufficiently proximate to the legal issues raised. Along with, and perhaps due to, the immediate effect of the provisions at trial, they would fulfil another objective, that of increasing reporting of sexual assault. In this regard the then Minister of Justice stated:

> The reason why we want to get rid of the interminable questioning on a person's reputation is *because very often this is precisely why women refuse to make a complaint in the case of rape....* Under the bill, in the case of a charge of aggravated sexual assault or sexual assault, *the act itself will be discussed and not what may have happened in the previous years*. [Emphasis added.]

(Standing Committee on Justice and Legal Affairs, *Minutes of Proceedings and Evidence, supra*, at p. 77: 46.)

Finally, the provisions have an inestimable advantage over both the common law and the previous provision, an advantage that is especially pertinent in this area of law, that of increased certainty. Certainty in and of itself has immeasurable value in this area but it also works to ensure that the other objectives of the legislation are met.

Combined with my discussion at the outset of sexual assault, this discussion of the state of the pertinent law prior and subsequent to legislative intervention and of the legislative goals underlying the reform process provides the larger legal context for the examination of the constitutional questions stated in these cases. This contextual approach is essential, in my view, for a complete understanding of the role of the legislative provisions at issue in the present case and so that the ultimate constitutional questions may be answered with confidence.

RELEVANCE AND ADMISSIBILITY AT COMMON LAW AND UNDER THE LEGISLATIVE PROVISIONS

Like many of the other legal rules and principles that are brought to bear in trials of persons charged with sexual offences, the concept of relevance has been imbued with stereotypical notions of female complainants and sexual assault. That this is so, is plain from the common law which held that evidence of "unchasteness" was relevant to both consent and credibility. Any connection between the evidence sought to be adduced and the fact or matter of which it was supposedly probative must be bridged by stereotype (that "unchaste" women lie and "unchaste" women consent indiscriminately), otherwise the propositions make no sense. While some may think that these represent egregious examples of the use of stereotype, it is well to remember that relevancy determinations such as this are still being made, though the myth which drives the particular determination may be better obscured or, due to the entrenchment of these beliefs, more automatically made.

Traditional definitions of what is relevant include "whatever accords with common sense" (McWilliams, *Canadian Criminal Evidence* (3rd ed. 1990), at p. 3–5); "relevant" means that "any two facts to which it is applied are so related to each other that according to the common course of events one either taken by itself or in connection with other facts proves or renders probable the past, present or future existence or non-existence of the other" (Stephen's *A Digest of the Law of Evidence* (12th ed. 1946), art. 1), and finally Thayer's "logically probative" test with relevance as an affair of logic and not of law, a test adopted by this Court in *Morris, infra*.

Whatever the test, be it one of experience, common sense or logic, it is a decision particularly vulnerable to the application of private beliefs. Regardless of the definition used, the content of any relevancy decision will be filled by the particular judge's experience, common sense and/or logic. For the most part there will be general agreement as to that which is relevant and the determination will not be problematic. However, there are certain areas of inquiry where experience, common sense and logic are informed by stereotype and myth. As I have made clear, this area of the law has been particularly prone to the utilization of stereotype in determinations of relevance and again, as was demonstrated earlier, this appears to be the unfortunate concomitant of a society which, to a large measure, holds these beliefs. It would also appear that recognition of the large role that stereotype may play in such determinations has had surprisingly little impact in this area of the law. Marshall J. stated in *R. v. Oquataq* (1985), 18 C.C.C. (3d) 440 (N.W.T.S.C.), at p. 450:

> Now, then, in logic, is sexual indulgence outside of marriage or established relationships (one could perhaps still call it unchastity) logically probative of consent on a particular occasion? Does it make consent more harmonious with all the circumstances, and does it move the trier towards one preponderance of possibilities? Does it mean the girl was more likely to have consented?
>
> Or it could be put simply this way. Is the girl who indulges herself sexually outside of marriage or established relationships more likely to consent? The antithesis would be: is a girl who *does not* indulge herself outside of marriage or established relationships ever, as likely to have consented? Applying the test we use to establish judicial truth, I think the answer can only be *No. The antithesis is also logically probative, I think* — though not conclusive, of course, but logically probative.
>
> ...
>
> What offends one's sense of justice most, I think, is that relating unchastity to a likelihood of consent is unfair and also, of course, not conclusive in any individual case. *What one must realize, though, is that our test for judicial truth is based on probabilities. This is, of course, both fallible and flawed. It may also show, in a specific case, rank prejudice; but we use it*. [Italic in original.] [Emphasis added.]

It seems odd to recognize the use of stereotype in the "test for judicial truth" but nevertheless conclude that the test for "truth" is met. If the only thing that renders a determination of relevancy understandable is underlying stereotype, it would seem contradictory to conclude then that "truth" has been found. "The trier is ... trying to ascertain questions of fact, which involve truth, but which can only become fraught with untruth once unsubstantiated cultural beliefs are factored in as 'relevant' evidence" (Sheehy, *supra*, at p. 755). It is also somehow perverse to suggest that an objective application of the law of evidence mandates the admission of evidence which exhibits "rank prejudice." This seems to exclude altogether both examination of, and responsibility for, individual decision making. The sticking point is, of course, recognition that the application of "logic" and "common sense" may, in any given case, show "rank prejudice." As Dawson, *supra*, rightfully points out, at p. 316, "[legal standards] are not simply neutral mechanisms to facilitate substantive debates, but take their place in a normative structure." As such they may be used to perpetuate "rank prejudice." Though the determination of what is relevant is often represented as involving a natural standard applied objectively, both history and the magnitude of the harm done suggest otherwise:

> Definition of reality is one mechanism whereby legal systems serve to disempower and oppress non-dominant segments of a heterogeneous population. A "neutral" rule is no barrier whatsoever; if anything, it may facilitate discrimination by defusing pressure for "equal" application of the law. *Only the effects of a legal system provide significant evidence of whether it is non-discriminatory*. [Footnotes omitted.] [Emphasis added.]

(L. Vandervort, *supra*, at p. 262.)

I have discussed the effects in this area of the law in significant detail at the outset and have concluded that they do provide "significant evidence" of discrimination.

Once the mythical bases of relevancy determinations in this area of the law are revealed (discussed at greater length later in these reasons), the irrelevance of most evidence of prior sexual history is clear. Nevertheless, Parliament has provided broad avenues for its admissibility in the setting out of the exceptions to the general rule in s. 246.6 (now s. 276). Moreover, *all* evidence of the complainant's previous sexual history with the accused is *prima facie* admissible under those provisions. Evidence that is excluded by these provisions is simply, in a myth and stereotype-free decision-making context, irrelevant.

The first exception, in subs. (1)(a), has the potential for allowing the admission of a wide variety of sexual history evidence. It encompasses situations where the Crown directly or indirectly introduces, in evidence, the issue of the complainant's sexual history. If the Crown chooses to do so, the door is open for rebuttal evidence. It would allow the defence to adduce sexual history evidence to explain semen, pregnancy, injury or disease that the Crown contends was a consequence of the offence. Such evidence is, however, limited to rebutting this explicit or implicit contention of the Crown. Subsection (1)(b) allows the receipt of evidence which goes to show the identity of the person who had sexual relations with the complainant on the pertinent occasion. This subsection and subs. (1)(a) overlap, to some degree, in that rebuttal evidence regarding the physical consequences of the assault would, depending upon the circumstances of the case, be admissible under one or either subsection. Noteworthy, however, is the caveat in subs. (1)(b) that such evidence must go to establishing the identity of the person who had sexual contact with the complainant on the occasion set out in the charge. While these provisions are inherently broad, their interpretation must nevertheless remain true to the wording of the exception, otherwise they will have little effect. As for the last exception, subs. (1)(c), it allows the receipt of relevant and proximate sexual history evidence that goes to the issue of the consent the accused honestly thought he had been given. In summary, as Grange J.A. pointed out (at p. 307), for the majority of the Court of Appeal, "[t]here is nothing startling or unique about our legislation."

As to s. 246.7 (now s. 277), it merely excludes evidence of sexual reputation used to impeach or support the credibility of the complainant. The notion that reputation for "unchasteness" is relevant to credibility is insupportable and its legislative exclusion uncontentious. Furthermore, evidence of sexual reputation is inherently unreliable. Due to the nature of the activity that forms the subject matter of the reputation, the alleged reputation is often nothing more than "speculation and exaggeration" (see Galvin, *supra*, at p. 801, and A.P. Ordover, "Admissibility of Patterns of Similar Sexual Conduct: The Unlamented Death of Character for Chastity" (1977), 63 *Cornell L. Rev.* 90, at p. 105). In fact, both the appellant Seaboyer and the intervener, the Canadian Civil Liberties Association, concede that the exclusion mandated by s. 277 is uncontentious. Indeed, my colleague reaches the same conclusion at p. 612.

The literature and case law in this area abound with examples of the supposed relevant evidence that is excluded by s. 276. For the most part, however, the "relevant" evidence provided in these examples is, on a principled inquiry, irrelevant; any semblance of relevance depends, in large measure, upon acceptance of stereotype about women and rape. Much of the remainder is admissible under the provision. One hesitates, however, to construct an argument around the speculative scenarios offered. Many of the scenarios are pure fantasy and have absolutely no grounding in life or experience. Speculating in this manner depends, to some degree, upon the acceptance of stereotypes about women and sexual assault and the will to propagate them. The point is well made by Sheehy, *supra*, at pp. 755–57:

> The indeterminate exceptions [that evidence of sexual history is generally irrelevant] posed by the *Wald* case constitute an open invitation to the "pornographic imagination" with which we have all been culturally endowed. The beliefs which spring from this collective imagination are not only without empirical foundation; they also systematically deny control and credibility to those who do not belong to the dominant culture. *Even more problematic is the fact that these beliefs are insidious because they are taken for granted and are therefore almost irresistible to the trier of fact who has absorbed our culture....*
>
> *In fact, the examples used by defence counsel, academics, and judges to illustrate situations where sexual history evidence is said to be highly "relevant," resemble ... "pornographic vignettes." ... These hypotheticals play upon internalized assumptions about what women really want and male desires for specific sexual scenarios.... They evoke highly emotive reactions which bear no relationship to "truth," and they bring out the worst in us.* [Footnotes omitted.] [Emphasis added.]

I also heartily concur in the submissions at p. 17 of the factum of the intervener Women's Legal Education and Action Fund et al. on this point:

> *...in all of the hypothetical situations outlined in the Appellants' factums, evidence of sexual history and/or sexual reputation is either totally irrelevant, admissible pursuant to the exceptions provided for in s. 276, or, in the alternative, of very low probative value and highly prejudicial to the interests of the administration of justice....* [Emphasis added.]

I will, therefore resist, as much as possible, joining the discourse at this level and will restrict myself to perhaps a more general discussion of the effect of the provisions.

Many argue that the most convincing support for the argument that the provision is drawn too narrowly is provided by so-called "similar fact evidence," or "pattern of conduct evidence," i.e., that the complainant has had consensual sexual relations in circumstances that look an awful lot like those supporting the assault allegation and, hence, such evidence is probative of consent. I am of the firm opinion that such evidence is almost invariably irrelevant and, in any event, is nothing more than a prohibited propensity argument, besides being highly prejudicial to the integrity and fairness of the trial process.

Such arguments depend, for their vitality, on the notion that women consent to sex based upon such extraneous considerations as the location of the act, the race, age or profession of the alleged assaulter and/or considerations of the nature of the sexual act engaged in. Though it feels somewhat odd to have to state this next proposition explicitly, consent is to a person and not to a circumstance. The use of the words "pattern" and "similar fact" deny this reality. Such arguments are implicitly based upon the notion that women will, in the right circumstances, consent to anyone and, more fundamentally, that "unchaste" women have a propensity to consent. While my colleague suggests that this proposition is "now discredited" (at p. 604), and "[has] no place in a rational and just system of law" (at p. 630), she, nevertheless, concludes that the exclusion of "pattern" evidence is unconstitutional. In my view, the mythical bases of these arguments deny their relevance.

A second category of so-called relevant evidence is also widely set up as conclusively demonstrating the infirmity of the provision, namely evidence of mistaken belief in consent. Again, I am of the firm opinion that no relevant evidence regarding the defence of honest but mistaken belief in consent is excluded by the provision under attack here.

It is my view that, assuming that both the trier of fact and the trier of law are operating in an intellectual environment that is free of rape myth and stereotype about women, any evidence excluded by this subsection would not satisfy the "air of reality" that must accompany this defence nor would it provide reasonable grounds for the jury to consider in assessing whether the belief was honestly held. The structure of the exception provided for in s. 276(1)(c) is thus not offensive to such a defence.

Evidence of prior acts of prostitution or allegations of prostitution are properly excluded by the provision. In my opinion, this evidence is never relevant and, besides its irrelevance, is hugely prejudicial. I vehemently disagree with the assertion of the appellant Seaboyer that "a prostitute is generally more willing to consent to sexual intercourse and is less credible as a witness because of that mode of life" (at p. 21 of his factum, quoting the Federal/Provincial Task Force, *supra*). Nor do I particularly understand the phenomenon whereby many complainants in sexual assault cases are asked if they are prostitutes. (See for example, Z. Adler, "The Relevance of Sexual History Evidence in Rape: Problems of Subjective Interpretation," [1985] *Crim. L.R.* 769, at p. 778.)

Many also argue that the provision does not allow evidence going to show motive or bias. Clearly, most such alleged motives or bias will not be grounded in the complainant's past sexual history. Moreover, much of this evidence depends, for its relevance, on certain stereotypical visions of women; that they lie about sexual assault, and that women who allege sexual assault often do so in order to get back in the good graces of those who may have her sexual conduct under scrutiny. Thus, again, refutation of stereotype strikes at the heart of the argument. As to evidence that a complainant has made prior false allegations of sexual assault, such evidence is admissible under the existing provision since this evidence does not involve the admission of her previous sexual history.

As I stated at the outset, the evidence which is excluded by the provision is simply irrelevant. It is based upon discriminatory beliefs about women and sexual assault. In addition, the impugned provision provides wide avenues for the introduction of sexual history evidence that is relevant. Paradoxically, some of the exceptions may be cast overly broadly with the unfortunate result that a large body of evidence may still be improperly admitted on the basis of specious relevancy claims.

If I am wrong in concluding that no relevant sexual history evidence is excluded by the contested provision, I am of the view that such exclusion is proper due to its extremely prejudicial effect on the trial of the legal issues.

In *Morris v. The Queen*, [1983] 2 S.C.R. 190, this Court discussed the notion of relevance. Lamer J. (as he then was) discussed at p. 201 the nature of the concept and circumstances where, though relevant, evidence may nonetheless be excluded:

> Thayer's statement of the law which is still the law in Canada, was as follows:
>
> > (1) that nothing is to be received which is not logically probative of some matter requiring to be proved; and (2) *that everything which is thus probative should come in, unless a clear ground of policy or law excludes it.*
>
> *To this general statement should be added the discretionary power judges exercise to exclude logically relevant evidence ... as being of too slight a significance, or as having too conjectural and remote a connection; others, as being dangerous, in their effect on the jury, and likely to be misused or overestimated by that body; others, as being impolitic, or unsafe on public grounds*; others, on the bare ground of precedent. It is this sort of thing ... the rejection on one or another practical ground, of what is really probative, — which is the characteristic thing in the law of evidence; stamping it as the child of the jury system. [Footnotes omitted.] [Emphasis added.]

Significant for our purposes is the long-recognized discretion in the trial judge to exclude otherwise relevant evidence. Hence, a determination that something is relevant does not answer the further question whether, regardless of its relevance, there exists some rule or policy consideration that nevertheless mandates exclusion of the proffered evidence. Thus, *Cross on Evidence, supra*, at p. 60, quoting Wigmore observes that, "[a]dmissibility signifies that the particular fact is relevant and something more, — that it has also satisfied all the auxiliary tests and extrinsic policies." Indeed, highly relevant evidence that could greatly benefit the cause of the accused may, in our legal system as it presently exists, be excluded as may evidence that could assist in the judicial "search for truth." Though generally stated, more notable examples of relevant though excluded evidence include: hearsay, opinion, character, conduct on other occasions, the collateral fact rule which treats answers given by witnesses to questions involving collateral facts as final, privilege against self-incrimination, evidence obtained in a manner violating a right or freedom guaranteed by the *Canadian Charter of Rights and Freedoms*, lawyer-client privilege and other professional relationships that may, from time to time, be accorded a similar privilege (for a fuller discussion of this type of privilege see S. Schiff, *Evidence in the Litigation Process* (3rd ed. 1988), vol. 2, at p. 1010), communication between spouses, government information whose disclosure would be "injurious to the public interest," etc.

There are many reasons why relevant evidence may be excluded and such exclusions play a significant and important role in the traditional law of evidence. Some evidence is excluded in order to protect values that our society holds dear. Other evidence may be excluded because of its inherent unreliability. As well, evidence will be excluded if it distorts rather than enhances the search for truth. McCormick, *McCormick's Handbook of the Law of Evidence* (2nd ed. 1972) at pp. 439–40, quoted in J.A. Tanford and A.J. Bocchino, "Rape Victim Shield Laws and the Sixth Amendment" (1980), 128 *U. Pa. L. Rev.* 544, at p. 569, sets out four reasons for the exclusion of this latter type of "prejudicial" evidence:

> First, the danger that the facts offered may unduly arouse the jury's emotions of prejudice, hostility or sympathy. Second, the probability that the proof and the answering evidence that it provokes may create a side issue that will unduly distract the jury from the main issues. Third, the likelihood that the evidence offered and the counter proof will consume an undue amount of time. Fourth, the danger of unfair surprise to the opponent when, having no reasonable ground to anticipate this development of the proof, he would be unprepared to meet it.

Any of these four reasons would seem to encompass evidence of prior sexual activity. As La Forest J. (dissenting on other grounds) put it in *R. v. Corbett*, [1988] 1 S.C.R. 670, at p. 714:

> The organizing principles of the law of evidence may be simply stated. All relevant evidence is admissible, subject to a discretion to exclude matters that may unduly prejudice, mislead or confuse the trier of fact, take up too much time, or that should otherwise be excluded on clear grounds of law or policy.

As I discussed at the outset, this type of evidence has a significant distorting effect at trial as such evidence "arouses [the jury's] sense of horror, provokes its instinct to punish, or triggers other mainsprings of human action," J. Weinstein and M. Berger, *Weinstein's Evidence* (1976), quoted in Ordover, *supra*, at p. 108. Such evidence allows stereotype and myth to enter into the equation and sidetracks the search for the truth. Such evidence invites a result more in accord with stereotype than truth:

> Defence counsel in rape cases have also used victim history evidence in an effort to suggest that the rape victim "got what she deserved." *The truth of what happened becomes concealed by antipathy towards the victim, and belief systems which locate the "fault" in the victim, regardless of the manner in which the offence occurred. The fact that such evidence has a powerful emotional impact upon triers of fact and can result in erroneous verdicts has been well-documented and acknowledged even by judges.* [Footnotes omitted.] [Emphasis added.]

(Sheehy, *supra*, at pp. 774–75.)

Rather than negatively affecting decisions of guilt and innocence, the exclusion of evidence of sexual history rationalizes such determinations. The discussion at the outset of these reasons conclusively demonstrated that sexual history evidence preempts considered decision making. The words of Catton, *supra*, at p. 173 quoted earlier, bear repeating:

> Any information at all implying that the victim had a prior sex history had the effect of reducing the perceived guilt of the accused regardless of whether this information was verified.

The guilt or innocence determination is transformed into an assessment of whether or not the complainant should be protected by the law of sexual assault. In my view, it is indisputable that this evidence has such a prejudicial effect. Many a defence lawyer knows the effect of such evidence and thus strives to get it admitted. Indeed, during debate in the House of Commons regarding the first effort of Parliament to rationalize this area of law, one member, Mr. Jarvis, commented:

> The myth is that a "bad woman" is incapable of being raped.... We have to deal with the

> myth that the credibility of a "bad woman" is immediately in question. I *was never sure what that phrase meant. As a lawyer, all I knew was that it was of benefit to hurl as much dirt as possible in the direction of such a woman, hoping that some of it would stick and that the jury would disbelieve what she said.* [Emphasis added.]

(*House of Commons Debates*, November 19, 1975, at p. 9252.)

If, indeed, we are searching for the truth, such a result is repugnant and that which produces it properly inadmissible.

THE CONSTITUTIONAL QUESTIONS

For convenience I will reproduce the sections of the *Canadian Charter of Rights and Freedoms* relevant to the disposition of these appeals:

> **7.** Everyone has the right to life, liberty and security of the person and the right not to be deprived thereof except in accordance with the principles of fundamental justice.
>
> **11.** Any person charged with an offence has the right
>
> ...
>
> (d) to be presumed innocent until proven guilty according to law in a fair and public hearing by an independent and impartial tribunal;
>
> **15.** (1) Every individual is equal before and under the law and has the right to the equal protection and equal benefit of the law without discrimination and, in particular, without discrimination based on race, national or ethnic origin, colour, religion, sex, age or mental or physical disability.
>
> **28.** Notwithstanding anything in this Charter, the rights and freedoms referred to in it are guaranteed equally to male and female persons.

In discussing the constitutional questions I will treat s. 11(d) as a particular manifestation of s. 7 principles of fundamental justice, hence an independent analysis will be unnecessary. Moreover, since I agree with my colleague Justice McLachlin that s. 277 is constitutional, I will restrict this discussion to s. 276.

It is my view that neither "fairness" nor "the principles of fundamental justice" mandate the constitutional invalidity of s. 276. Rather, in order to achieve fairness and to conduct trials in accordance with fundamental tenets of criminal law, this provision must be upheld in all of its vigour. The words of C. Boyle, "Section 142 of the Criminal Code: A Trojan Horse?," *supra*, at p. 265, provide an appropriate introduction to these issues:

> There has been an unfortunate tendency to compare the rights of the accused and the witness and to view any amelioration in the position of the witness as needing some balance. *Yet the issue is really one of promoting convictions of guilty persons and not clouding the issue with evidence of collateral issues which may tend to prejudice the trier of fact. This is a serious matter of public interest, not a battle between feminists and defence lawyers.* [Emphasis added.]

The constitutional question posed by the present case is whether, notwithstanding the already established irrelevance and/or prejudicial nature of the evidence excluded by the impugned provision, an accused, nevertheless, has a constitutional right to adduce such evidence. On my view of the scope of these constitutional guarantees, this question must be answered with a resounding and compelling no.

It is noncontroversial to state that an accused does not have a constitutional right to adduce irrelevant evidence. To the extent that much, if not all, of the evidence excluded by the provision at issue here is irrelevant, there is no constitutional issue. Nor, in my view, does an accused have the right under the *Charter*, whether under the rubric of a right to a fair trial or the right to make full answer and defence, to adduce evidence that prejudices and distorts the fact-finding process at trial. As a corollary, neither do notions of a "fair trial" or "full answer and defence" recognize a right in the accused to adduce *any* evidence that *may* lead to an acquittal. Such propositions cast ss. 7 and 11(d) in an extremely narrow fashion and deny meaningful content to notions of "fairness" and "principles of fundamental justice." I agree with the criticism Sheehy, *supra*, at pp. 774–75, levels at such a narrow reading of the constitutional guarantees:

> *...the accused's "fairness" argument not only presumes that the evidence is objectively "relevant," but also that it can be used appropriately to ascertain the truth of what happened between the accused and the victim....* Predictably, victim vilification as a defence has had considerable success in cases where the victim history evidence can be used to invoke negative cultural stereotypes.
>
> ...
>
> ...[there is a] need for a realistic and intelligent effort to understand "fairness" as related to the concrete realities of the criminal process and the lives of the women and men implicated, rather than theoretical deprivations of *Charter* rights. [Emphasis added.]

As the provision at issue here excludes only irrelevant or prejudicial evidence, it passes constitutional muster. The accused, on any meaningful and purposive interpretation of the rights involved, has no right to adduce it. Rather than "render[ing] the ordinary rules of evidence inapplicable ... [and putting] an accused charged with sexual assault in a separate and worse position than persons charged with other serious crimes" (Brooke J.A. dissenting in part at the Court of Appeal, at pp. 310–11), the sections ensure that the ordinary rules of evidence are applied. Parliament has excluded no evidence that is not properly excluded both at common law and under the *Charter*.

Furthermore, the ss. 7 and 11(d) rights of an accused protect, in my view, not only the accused's interest in adducing all exculpatory evidence but other interests as well:

> It is true that s. 11 of the *Charter* constitutionalizes the right of an accused and not that of the state to a fair trial before an impartial tribunal. *But "fairness" implies, and in my view demands, consideration also of the interests of the state as representing the public. Likewise, the principles of fundamental justice operate to protect the integrity of the system itself, recognizing the legitimate interests not only of the accused but also of the accuser.* [Emphasis added.]

(Reasons of La Forest J. (dissenting on other grounds) in *Corbett, supra*, at p. 745.)

The proposition that s. 7 and s. 11 rights involve the consideration of interests outside of the confined interests of the accused has been endorsed by a majority of this Court in *R. v. Askov*, [1990] 2 S.C.R. 1199. In discussing the nature of the interests protected by s. 11(b) of the *Charter*, Cory J., for the majority, remarked at p. 1219:

> Although the primary aim of s. 11(b) is the protection of the individual's rights and the provision of fundamental justice for the accused, nonetheless there is, in my view, at least by inference, a community or societal interest implicit in s. 11(b).

He further stated at p. 1221:

> All members of the community are thus entitled to see that the justice system works fairly, efficiently and with reasonable dispatch.... The trial not only resolves the guilt or innocence of the individual, but acts as a reassurance to the community that serious crimes are investigated and that those implicated are brought to trial and dealt with according to the law.

Additional support for a broader analysis of the rights invoked by the appellants in this case can be found in s. 28 of the *Charter*. In the context of this case, this section would appear to mandate a constitutional inquiry that recognizes and accounts for the impact upon women of the narrow construction of ss. 7 and 11(d) advocated by the appellants.

While the exact nature of the other interests involved depends upon the nature and aspect of the right considered, it is clear from the above that the constitutional inquiry in this area is not confined to the narrow interests of the accused. (See also *R. v. Lyons*, [1987] 2 S.C.R. 309, at pp. 327–29, *R. v. Beare*, [1988] 2 S.C.R. 387, at pp. 403–7, reasons for judgment of La Forest J. in *Thomson Newspapers Ltd. v. Canada (Director of Investigation and Research Restrictive Trade Practices Commission)*, [1990] 1 S.C.R. 425, at p. 539, and *R. v. Swain*, [1991] 1 S.C.R. 933, *per* L'Heureux-Dubé J. dissenting.)

In the present case, the other interests envisaged by ss. 7 and 11(d) are not unlike those articulated by Cory J. in *Askov, supra*. The complainant, and indeed the community at large, have an interest in the reporting and prosecution of sexual offences. They also have a legitimate interest in ensuring that trials of such matters are conducted in a fashion that does not subordinate the fact-finding process to myth and stereotype. However, a discussion of the community or group interests involved is not strictly necessary as it is clear that the competing interest in this case, that of ensuring that trials and thus verdicts are based on fact and not on stereotype and myth, is not one belonging solely to any group or community but rather is an interest which adheres to the system itself; it maintains the integrity and legitimacy of the trial process. This interest is so closely intertwined with the interests of complainants and of the community that the distinction may be unimportant in reality:

> Given the social science data ... *it should be recognised that these provisions prevent bias in the judicial fact finding process, which bias specifically operates to the disadvantage of women as individual complainants and as a social group.* [Emphasis added.]

(Dawson, *supra*, at p. 333.)

The recognition and realization of the ss. 7 and 11(d) interest in maintaining the integrity of the trial process ensure the protection of these perhaps more "societal" interests as well.

Regardless of the effects of protecting this interest, it is clear that it merits consideration in the constitutional analysis. The contrary approach, the recognition of an unfettered right in the accused to adduce all relevant evidence, seriously misconstrues the phrase "principles of fundamental justice." Clearly, these principles have developed with an eye to values and interests beyond those of the accused (see the previous discussion of relevance and exclusionary rules), and thus such values and interests are pertinent in constitutional inquiries such as the one here. The contrary approach renders vacuous the fair trial and full answer and defence rights of an accused.

. . . .

> Social science research findings contradict assertions that sexual conduct evidence assists the fact-finding process or the test for "judicial truth." *Far from being relevant to ensuring a "fair" hearing or a full defence, the introduction of sexual history evidence may advantage the accused in a way that is not related to innocence. Such evidence has a non-neutral impact on the trial process.* [Emphasis added.]

(Dawson, *supra*, at p. 330.)

Unless one accepts the paradoxical assertion that an accused has the right to a biased verdict, or that the principles of fundamental justice constitutionalize the discriminatory application of the law, the provisions cannot be constitutionally impugned. In my view, interpreting the guarantees of the *Charter* in a manner that systematically excludes considerations of the harm done by the evidence sought to be elicited by the accused may, ironically, operate to undermine and trivialize notions of fairness.

SECTION 1

Although, strictly speaking, it is unnecessary for me to engage in a discussion of s. 1, I will nonetheless make some brief comments in order to make it plain that the *Code* provision, even if found to be unconstitutional in its effect, is justified.

This Court in *R. v. Oakes*, [1986] 1 S.C.R. 103, at pp. 138–39, provided the analysis to be undertaken in determining whether a limit is demonstrably justified.

Briefly stated, the party attempting to uphold the legislation must establish that: (a) the objective which the limit is designed to serve is of sufficient importance to warrant overriding a constitutionally protected right; and (b) the means chosen to attain the objective are reasonable and demonstrably justified, in that (1) the measures designed to meet the legislative objective must be rationally connected to the objective, (2) the means used should impair as little as possible the right or freedom in question, and (3) there must be a proportionality between the effects of the means chosen and the legislative objective.

As I have discussed earlier, the provision at issue in this case formed but a part of a much larger reform effort on the part of Parliament. Parliament articulated four principles that animated this package: the protection of the integrity of the person; the protection of children and special groups; the safeguarding of public decency; and the elimination of sexual discrimination. It is obvious that in respect of the provision at issue in this case, the goal of Parliament was to eliminate sexual discrimination in the trials of sexual offences through the elimination of irrelevant and/or prejudicial sexual history evidence. A further legislative goal, intimately linked to the first, is to encourage women to report their victimization. My discussion of sexual assault at the outset makes it clear that a factor that loomed large in the failure of women to report, and police to classify complaints as "founded" and in the high rate of acquittal was the admission of evidence of prior sexual history into trials of sexual offences. Such evidence triggered the application of discriminatory beliefs and stereotypes about women and about rape. Attempting to rid the law, in this area, of discrimination and attempting to increase the reporting of a crime that occurs with staggering frequency in this society are obviously sufficiently important objectives to warrant overriding a right of the accused.

While it is, in my view, clear that the objectives of Parliament in enacting this provision are sufficiently important to warrant restricting the rights of an accused, the congruence of Parliament's goals with other *Charter* values strengthens this conclusion. As Wilson J. noted in *Singh v. Minister of Employment and Immigration*, [1985] 1 S.C.R. 177, at p. 218:

> I think that in determining whether a particular limitation is a reasonable limit prescribed by law which can be "demonstrably justified in a free and democratic society" it is important to remember that the courts are conducting this inquiry in light of a commitment to uphold the rights and freedoms set out in the other sections of the *Charter*.

I have made it clear throughout these reasons that the reform of the laws of sexual assault in general and s. 276 in particular, is informed by a dedication to the goal of the eradication of sexual discrimination in the prosecution of sexual offences. Sections 15 and 28 of the *Canadian Charter of Rights and Freedoms* mirror the values which motivate the intervention of Parliament. These values have a legitimate role in shaping the s. 1 inquiry:

> ...the effects of entrenching a guarantee of equality in the *Charter* are not confined to those instances where it can be invoked by an individual against the state. In so far as it indicates our society's dedication to promoting equality, s. 15 is also relevant in assessing the aims of [the provisions] of the *Criminal Code* under s. 1.
>
> ...
>
> ...promoting equality is an undertaking essential to any free and democratic society.... The principles underlying s. 15 of the *Charter* are thus integral to the s. 1 analysis.
>
> ...
>
> In light of the *Charter* commitment to equality, and the reflection of this commitment in the framework of s. 1, the objective of the impugned legislation is enhanced in so far as it seeks to ensure the equality of all individuals in Canadian society.

(Reasons for judgment of Dickson C.J. in *R. v. Keegstra, supra*, at pp. 755–56.)

The importance of Parliament's objectives in the reform of the law of sexual assault is amplified by the nature of the harm done (discussed at length at the beginning of these reasons) and by the fact that its legislative effort gives voice to values that are paramount in a free and democratic society. In the words of McIntyre J. for the Court in *Andrews v. Law Society of British Columbia*, [1989] 1 S.C.R. 143, at p. 171:

> It is clear that the purpose of s. 15 is to ensure equality in the formulation and application of the law. The promotion of equality entails the promotion of a society in which all are secure in the knowledge that they are recognized at law as human beings equally deserving of concern, respect and consideration. It has a large remedial component.

The objectives underlying s. 276 easily satisfy the first stage of the s. 1 inquiry.

The next stage in the analysis requires an examination of the proportionality of the measures and, as the first question, asks whether the measures are rationally connected to the objective. Again, my earlier discussion of the demonstrated effect that sexual history evidence has upon triers of fact shows that the *Code* provision is rationally connected to Parliament's objective. The *Code* provision excludes evidence that promotes the invocation of stereotype about women and about sexual assault. Such evidence invites triers of fact to indulge themselves in a determination of the extent to which the complainant measures up to the current stereotypes about women and myths about rape. The fact that this happens is irrefutable. As my previous discussion demonstrates, the fact that it impacts negatively upon rates of reporting and "founded" rates and inflates rates of acquittal is also irrefutable. At all stages of the inquiry into the complaint, decisions are made about whether the complaint should proceed. The answer at all stages of the inquiry, as this earlier discussion also showed, lies in the ability of the complainant to conform to discriminatory beliefs. Often, in order to justify this screening process, reference is made to the fact that such beliefs will be applied at trial thus "justifying" decisions to ferret out all those undeserving complainants prior to trial. It is only reasonable then to conclude that any efforts on the part of Parliament to exclude sexual history evidence at trial, evidence which is largely irrelevant and nevertheless biased, are rationally connected to the stated objectives of ridding the law in this area of discriminatory beliefs and encouraging the increased reporting of such offences.

It is my view that the measures, as well as being rationally connected to the objectives, impair the rights of the accused as little as possible. The words of Dickson C.J. for the majority in *Reference re ss. 193 and 195.1 (1)(c) of the Criminal Code (Man.)*, [1990] 1 S.C.R. 1123, at pp. 1137–38, are particularly apposite:

> *It is legitimate to take into account the fact that earlier laws and considered alternatives were thought to be less effective than the legislation that is presently being challenged.* When Parliament began its examination of the subject of street soliciting, it was presented with a spectrum of views and possible approaches.... In making a choice to enact s. 195.1(1)(c) as it now reads, Parliament had to try to balance its decision to criminalize the nuisance aspects of street soliciting and its desire to take into account the policy arguments regarding the effects of criminalization of any aspect of prostitution. The legislative history of the present provision and, in general, of legislation directed to street solicitation is both long and complicated. *The legislative scheme that was eventually implemented and has now been challenged need not be the "perfect" scheme that could be imagined by this Court or any other court. Rather, it is sufficient if it is appropriately and carefully tailored in the context of the infringed right.* [Emphasis added.]

I have previously detailed the legislative efforts of Parliament in combatting discriminatory application of the law in trials of sexual offences. It has abrogated certain discriminatory doctrines developed at common law, repealed discriminatory requirements placed on complainants through legislation and attempted to align the admission of evidence of past sexual history with traditional evidentiary principles developed at common law. Resistance to legislative efforts and the continued utilization of stereotypical beliefs required the intervention of Parliament on a second occasion. This second legislative effort culminated in the provisions at issue here.

In the process of drafting legislation to replace the failed s. 142, numerous interest groups presented their views on the issue and Parliament canvassed a number of suggested changes to the legislation. Parliament did not rely solely upon external representations in order to produce alternatives but also initiated research on its own motion in an attempt to strike an appropriate balance of the interests involved. In the face of the numerous options presented, Parliament opted for this one. In the face of a previous legislative provision that was emasculated by the courts and on the heels of this, the continued application of stereotype, Parliament's measured and considered response was to codify those situations wherein sexual history evidence may be both relevant and sufficiently probative such that its admission was warranted. Parliament exhibited a marked, and justifiedly so, distrust of the ability of the courts to promote and achieve a non-discriminatory application of the law in this area. In view of the history of government attempts, the harm done when discretion is posited in trial judges and the demonstrated inability of the judiciary to change its discriminatory ways, Parliament was justified in so choosing. My attempt to illustrate the tenacity of these discriminatory beliefs and their acceptance at all levels of society clearly demonstrates that discretion in judges is antithetical to the goals of Parliament.

While some degree of latitude must be accorded to the legislative choice of Parliament due to the troubled history that informed its choice, the fact that Parliament had to choose between the interests of competing groups also requires such an approach. This is not a typical situation where the government and accused persons have squared off or where the government is "best characterized as the singular antagonist of the individual whose right has been infringed" (*Irwin Toy Ltd. v. Quebec (Attorney General), infra*, at p. 994). Rather it is plain that Parliament, in coming to its legislative decision, weighed the claims of different groups and attempted to do that which best balanced their concerns.

. . . .

Due to the concerns underlying the passage of this legislation and the extensive efforts of Parliament to assess the viability of a number of means, this is not a situation where the courts are better situated than or even as well situated as Parliament to determine whether the "least drastic means" has been chosen. The appropriate standard of review at this stage of the proportionality inquiry is thus one of reasonableness, i.e., whether the government had a reasonable basis for concluding that the legislative solution they chose impaired the right as little as possible given the government's pressing and substantial objective. It is clear from my reasons to this point that the legislative choice is, at a minimum, in the realm of the reasonable.

. . . .

In order to effectively combat sex discrimination and increase reporting, Parliament has, through this provision, attempted to eliminate the application of discriminatory beliefs at trials of sexual offences. The traditional approach, with discretion in trial judges as regards the admission of sexual history evidence, was, for good reason, rejected. As the Federal/Provincial Task Force on Uniform Rules of Evidence, *supra*, at p. 73 noted, provisions which leave discretion in the hands of trial judges are "...innocuous. They have failed to enhance the protection afforded to the complainant at common law." The point is also well put by Sheehy, *supra*, at p. 782:

> What is clear ... is that no common law system of discretion can possibly achieve the legislative objectives.... The best we can hope for will be diverse interpretations of the circumstances in which certain evidence is "relevant" and constitutes a "constitutional exemption." These interpretations will vary from trial judge to trial judge across the country. The worst we might receive are expansive interpretations of "relevance" which *will be detrimental to women both individually and collectively. This is of particular concern, given that the abysmal record of the Canadian judiciary under the common law, and under the modified common law regime of the old section 142, was the impetus for the revocation of judicial discretion by Parliament.* [Emphasis added.]

The last stage of the s. 1 analysis requires an examination of whether the effects of the measure are so deleterious that they outweigh the importance of the objective. In my view, the exclusion of largely irrelevant and highly prejudicial sexual history evidence does not significantly entrench upon an accused's right to a fair trial or an accused's right to make full answer and defence. Wide avenues of admissibility are still open to an accused under the provision to adduce evidence of sexual history that is both relevant and sufficiently probative that its admission is not outweighed by its discriminatory effect. Confining the accused to such evidence goes little distance towards the conclusion that the last stage in the proportionality inquiry is not met. Parliament has accorded more than due weight to the accused's constitutional rights in enacting s. 276. It follows that, in my view, the provision, to the extent (if any) that it is unconstitutional in its effect, is easily upheld under s. 1.

. . . .

My colleague, McLachlin J., articulates three reasons for her rejection of the "doctrine of constitutional exemption" in this case: namely, (1) it would not substantially uphold the law and the will of the legislature would become increasingly obscured; (2) applying the doctrine would be indistinguishable in result from striking down the legislation; and (3) applying the doctrine in this case would be difficult. It seems to me, however, that the same rationales highlight the infirmity of the guidelines suggested by the majority with respect to the admission of evidence of prior sexual history. More particularly, the objectives of Parliament in enacting the legislation, identified earlier in these reasons, are ill served by the guidelines. The view that the objectives of Parliament and the values of the *Charter* are better served in this fashion ignores the larger context within which the guidelines will be applied. Furthermore, as a full discussion of this context shows, any optimism that the guidelines will be effectively and consistently applied in a manner that is cognizant of both the objectives of Parliament and the infirmities of the common law is badly misplaced. My final objection to the guidelines, as my previous discussion indicates, is that they are entirely too broad and support the very stereotype and myth that they are meant to eradicate.

■

For discussion of the persistence of abuse of women's sexual history evidence, despite legislative intervention, in other common law jurisdictions, see Jennifer Temkin and Barbara Krahe, *Sexual Assault and the Justice Gap: A Question of Attitude* (Oxford: Hart Publishing, 2008); Elisabeth McDonald, "Her Sexuality as Indicative of His Innocence: The Operation of New Zealand's 'Rape Shield' Provision" (1994) 18 Crim. L.J. 321; and Department for Women, *Heroines of Fortitude: The experiences of women in court as victims of sexual assault* (Sydney, N.S.W.: Department for Women, 1996) at 223–53.

In England, for example, in spite of law reform in 2000 that attempted to stem the cross-examination of women on their sexual histories, judges have insisted on exercising their discretion to allow the tactic and admit the evidence, thus undercutting the law. Seventeen judges interviewed by Temkin and Krahe for their study acknowledged these judicial practices; one is quoted as saying: "I'm not one for being unduly fettered. I've been appointed to do a job on the basis that I have a certain amount of judgment, and to be fettered or shackled by statutory constraints I don't think helps anybody." Another study, which reported on the role of the media in reinforcing sex discriminatory myths about women and sexual assault, found that the conviction rate for rape has plummeted from what was already a comparatively low rate of 33% in 1977 to 5.7% in 2007: Natasha Marhia, *Just Representations? Press Reporting and the Reality of Rape* (London: The Lilith Project, 2008).

In the Canadian context, 90% of sexual assaults are unreported and yet of those 10% that are reported, a higher percentage of these are unfounded than are assaults of a non-sexual nature. The unfounding rate was recently studied in British Columbia, where researchers documented unfounding rates as low as 7% in Vancouver, to as high as 28% in Chilliwack (Justice Institute of British Columbia, *Police Classification of Sexual Assault Cases as Unfounded: An Exploratory Study*, by Linda Light and Gisela Ruebsaat (forthcoming)). Among that even lower percentage of cases that are actually prosecuted, the conviction rate remains well below the rate of other assaults: 54% of robberies, 52% of common assaults and 49% of major assaults result in conviction, compared to 38% of sexual assaults Statistics Canada: Canadian Centre for Justice Statistics, *Adult Criminal Court Survey 2003/2004*.

E. THE AFTERMATH OF *SEABOYER*

Seaboyer was followed by public outcry and very negative media coverage. It created a legislative vacuum in a large and significant area of criminal law. Justice McLachlin's "guidelines" did little to obviate the uncertainty: see Christine Boyle & Marilyn MacCrimmon, "*R. v. Seaboyer*: A Lost Cause?" (1991), 7 C.R. (4th) 225, and Elizabeth Sheehy, "Feminist Argumentation Before the Supreme Court of Canada in *R. v. Seaboyer*; *R. v. Gayme*: The Sound of One Hand Clapping" (1991) 18 Melb. U.L. Rev. 450. Others used the decision to illustrate how judicial ideological discourse reinforces the subordinate status of women by manufacturing "truth" through "presumptive authority" and "factitious neutrality": Michael D. Smith, "Language, Law and Social Power: *Seaboyer*; *Gayme v. R.* and a Critical Theory of "Ideology" (1993) 51 U.T. Fac. L. Rev. 118.

The suggestion in *Seaboyer* that a woman's sexual history can bolster a man's "mistake" argument and Justice McLachlin's failure to condemn the breadth of the *Wald* decision opened the door even wider to create an "air of reality" where the victim/witness can be portrayed as a woman outside the protection of the criminal law. For example, in *R. v. Osolin*, *supra*, the victim/witness went with two men, one whom she had dated before, to a third man's trailer where they drank together. She had sex with one of them in a secluded place; this man then left and two other men turned up, one of whom was Osolin. These two men, along with the owner of the trailer, went to a pub, where the owner of the trailer told them that the young woman was "easy" and that they could also have sex with her. While they were gone, the woman had sex with the second man who had remained at the trailer. Osolin and his friend returned to the trailer and barged in on the two in bed: Osolin drove the man away and his friend tried to rape the woman. When Osolin returned he threw her over his shoulder and into a car naked, having torn off her underwear. His friend drove the car 40 kilometres away and left the two alone. Osolin tied up the woman, raped her several times, and shaved her pubic hair. She was found on the highway, naked and crying, with injuries consistent with sexual assault. Her torn underwear was found near the trailer.

At trial Osolin admitted that he had overridden the woman's objections in forcing her into the car, but argued consent and characterized the woman as an enthusiastic participant in the sexual acts. He stated that she revoked consent only when he shaved her pubic area. Alternatively, his counsel tried to cross-examine the woman on the subject of her psychiatric records for the purpose of showing that her behaviour was consensual (allegedly she made self-blaming statements to her therapist), in order to support a mistake defence, although the accused did not specifically allege such a defence. The trial judge refused the proposed cross-examination and also refused to put mistake to the jury. Osolin was convicted by the jury.

The majority of the Court (Cory, Major, Sopinka, and Iacobucci JJ., and Lamer C.J.) ruled that Osolin was entitled to a new trial in order to pursue the cross-examination on the counselling records regarding both the woman's credibility and the mistake defence. On the issue of the availability of the mistake defence, the judgments broke down as follows.

Justices Cory, Major, and Iacobucci rejected the minimalist "some evidence" interpretation for the air of reality test, after reviewing the relevant authorities. They stated that the general test, applicable to all criminal defences, is whether "the evidence put forward is such that, if believed, a jury properly instructed could have acquitted." They followed *Pappajohn* and held that the defence is not available where the accused and victim/witness tell diametrically opposed versions of the facts. While they stated that there was no requirement that the evidence be found in a source other than the accused, they acknowledged that the proposed cross-examination might provide the evidence needed. They stated that the cross-examination must not be directed towards rape myths, and that generally it must not be focused on the woman's lifestyle, except "in those relatively rare cases where the complainant may be fraudulent, cruelly mischievous or maliciously mendacious." They recognized that self-blaming statements by a victim/witness may be based on shame and guilt arising from the trauma of rape rather than her outward behaviour, but said that presumably cross-examination would expose the truth.

Justice L'Heureux-Dubé would have denied the cross-examination and the availability of the defence of mistake for failure to meet the air of reality test. In this regard, she focused on the corroborative aspects of the evidence supporting the woman's story, including her ripped underwear, the bruise on her head, and her acute trauma when found on the highway.

Justice McLachlin, along with La Forest and Gonthier JJ., would have denied a new trial for the purposes of permitting cross-examination on the basis that the defence had chosen one line of defence, consent, that was inconsistent with the defence of mistake, and was not entitled to another trial to explore an alternative. They went on to state that the air of reality test may be satisfied even where the accused and the victim/witness relate diametrically opposed versions of the events. On these facts, however, they held that there was no evidence, even in the accused's own testimony, to support the defence, beyond the mere assertion of his belief, and noted the uncontroverted facts that the woman was stripped, driven some distance, and was tied up: "[N]o person, reasonable or otherwise, could **honestly** infer consent in such circumstances from the mere fact that at certain stages, the complainant may have been passively acquiescent." [Emphasis in original.] (at 651–52)

Justice Sopinka, with Lamer C.J. concurring, agreed with Cory J.'s formulation of the evidentiary burden for the air of reality test, but stated that all the accused has to do to meet it is point to "some evidence on the basis of which a reasonable jury properly instructed could acquit." They specifically agreed with McLachlin J.'s statement that the defence may be available, even if the two witnesses recount diametrically opposed versions of the facts; and, by relying on a statement quoted from another case, they suggested that all that is needed from the accused is a "credible narrative" (at 42).

Annalise Acorn, in her paper *A Feminist Critique*, *supra*, has commented at 21–22 on the implications of *Osolin*:

> Putting the defence of mistake to the jury in cases where there is uncontested evidence of resistance and force excuses the accused who a) acts in an extremely aggressive and sexually violative manner, b) believes that a woman's expression of non-consent is irrelevant to the issue of whether or not she is consenting and c) believes that a woman's reputation for promiscuity is relevant to whether she is consenting.
>
> ...
>
> Furthermore, the fact that the Court could view a case like *Osolin* as one in which the accused could have held an honest but mistaken belief in consent raises doubts as to the *bona fides* of the Court's commitment to the protection of women's sexual integrity. The concern of the justices with the possibility of moral innocence in Osolin's case reflects an understanding of morality that is deeply at odds with placing some moral responsibility on the individual to be concerned about whether his sexual partner consents to sexual activity.

The other important aspect of *Osolin* was the fact that the Court put no limits upon the disclosure of the victim/witness's counselling records and, by suggesting that her records might provide evidence for his defence, invited defence lawyers across the country to attempt to gain access to women's records. As has become plain, access to women's therapy records has provided defence lawyers with new ways to discredit women and to gain access to sexual and victimization history, effectively bypassing the *Seaboyer* guidelines and the reforms achieved in Bill C-49: see **The Trial Process**, Disclosure, and Sadie Bond, "Psychiatric Evidence of Sexual Assault Victims: The Need for Fundamental Change in the Determination of Relevance" (1993) 16 Dalhousie L.J. 416.

In *R. v. Park*, [1995] 2 S.C.R. 836, Justice L'Heureux-Dubé made it clear (at 855–56) that evidence of the woman's words or behaviour on prior occasions will not alone found an air of reality, "[a]bsent some realistic showing of how earlier events could have influenced the accused's honest perceptions of the complainant's behaviour at the time of the actual assault." In applying this analysis to the facts, the Court held that the trial judge had not erred (contrary to the view of the Alberta Court of Appeal) in refusing to put the defence to the jury based on the accused's assertion that the young woman had previously engaged in some physical contact with him, had allowed him into her apartment while she was wearing only her bathrobe, and had become passive at the moment of the assault. Will this ruling on the air of reality test affect cases such as *Osolin*? See also *R. v. Dickson*, [1994] 1 S.C.R. 153, where the Court's judgment seems to support the view that the victim/witness's prior sexual relationship with the accused was improperly admitted to support a mistake defence when, in fact, the accused testified only regarding actual consent. The Crown's appeal against acquittal was allowed, and a new trial ordered.

Some feminists saw *Seaboyer* as an opportunity to create new law and to use the gaps to shape reforms to redefine the underlying concepts themselves, such as "consent", and to create a criminal law that also serves racialized women, women with disabilities, and immigrant women: Elizabeth Shilton & Anne Derrick, "Sex Equality and Sexual Assault in the Aftermath of *Seaboyer*" [1991] Windsor Y. B. Access to Just. 107; Sheila McIntyre, "Re-Defining Reformism: The Consultations That Shaped Bill C-49" in Renate Mohr & Julian Roberts, eds., *Confronting Sexual Assault: A Decade of Social and Legal Change* (Toronto: University of Toronto Press, 1993) 293–326.

A feminist coalition worked for months on the reforms which, in spite of protest from the defence bar, culminated in the new *Code* ss. 273.1–276.5. The new legislation for the first time defines consent for the purposes of sexual assault as "the voluntary agreement of the complainant to engage in the sexual activity in question": s. 273.1(1). It also stipulates that consent cannot be legally obtained where: the agreement is expressed by a person other than the complainant; the complainant is incapable of consenting; the consent was induced by abuse of power, trust, or authority by the accused with respect to the complainant; or the complainant expressed, by words or conduct, her lack of agreement or, having consented, indicated by words or conduct that she did not wish to continue: s. 273.1(2). Subsection 273.1(3) provides that the law does not preclude the development of new categories where consent cannot be obtained.

In *R. v. Darrach*, [2000] 2 S.C.R. 443, the accused challenged the constitutionality of the new provisions on the ground that the substantive parts of the section that exclude evidence (ss. 276(1), 276(2)(c)) violate his rights to a fair trial, the presumption of innocence, and to make full answer and defence, and on the ground that the procedural parts of the section (ss. 276.1(2)(a), 276.2(2)) violate his right not to be compelled to be a witness against himself in his own trial. The Court rejected all of the defence arguments, holding that the impugned parts of the section did not offend fair trial rights as the rights of the accused were also preserved by the exclusion of misleading evidence from trials of sexual offences. As well, the presumption of innocence requires that the Crown establish all the elements of the offence. Finally, the Court refused to find that the new provisions impose upon the accused a legal compulsion to testify.

With respect to the defence of mistake of fact, s. 273.2 sets out new limits on this defence and delineates a procedure and criteria for consideration of women's sexual history evidence. Both developments and some positive preliminary assessments are described in Elizabeth Sheehy, "Legalising Justice for All Women: Canadian Women's Struggle for Democratic Rape Law Reforms" (1996) Aust. Feminist L.J. 87 at 94–104, and Christine Boyle, "Sexual Assault in Abusive Relationships: Common Sense About Sexual History" (1996), 19 Dalhousie L.J. 223.

Not all of the case law on the new limits on the mistake defence is positive for women. For example, there are several cases where accused men have successfully argued mistake with respect to consent where complainants have been asleep or "passed out" through alcohol or drug use. In *R. v. R.B.*, [1996] O.J. No. 3140 (Ct. J. (Prov. Div.)) (QL), the trial judge made the following remarks at para 100:

> So R.B. goes into his bed and finds Miss J.P. there. He did not invite her. Although he knew that she had been ill, but not the extent thereof, he could reasonably believe that she was much better having had a few hours's sleep. He tells her to move over. She does. Then she snuggles into him. He rubs her as he had done before. She moans as if to signify satisfaction or enjoyment. Is he required to shake her awake and ask if he can go further? Without seeking to claim any expertise in this area of human behaviour, I venture to say that it was not negligent of him [not] to go further and wake her. He could reasonably have taken her body language, for want of a better term, and her subliminal signals as being [knowledgeable] approval, suggesting that she was awake.

In *R. v. Osvath* (1996), 87 O.A.C. 274 (C.A.) the accused succeeded in arguing for a new trial because the trial judge had failed to seriously consider the accused's defence of "mistake" where he had proceeded to have intercourse with a woman he had never met who was passed out on a couch after a party. Abella J.A., dissenting, stated at 279–80:

> The appellant lay down on a small couch behind a woman whom he hardly knew, who was in a deep sleep. Based on the trial judge's findings of credibility, it is evident that the trial judge did not believe the accused's evidence that he asked for her consent. In any event, even if he did ask, she did not know to whom she was consenting. The complainant awoke to find herself having sexual intercourse

> with a complete stranger. She ran from the room when she realized that her sexual partner was not the man with whom she had come to the party, and with whom she was involved.
>
> ...
>
> The accused's presumptuousness could properly be characterized as wilful blindness. The appellant never asked nor took the trouble to inquire whether the complainant was consenting to sexual intercourse with him. Anyone seeking sexual activity in these circumstances could hardly fail to know that he was obliged, at a minimum, to let the person from whom permission was sought for such activity, know who was seeking the consent. Consent is not given in a vacuum, it is given or refused to a particular activity with a particular individual. The trial judge concluded, as he was entitled to do, that consent was given neither to the sexual activity nor to the individual.

In another case, the Saskatchewan Court of Appeal ordered a new trial for an accused who argued that his "mistake" defence was weakened by the trial judge's refusal to admit evidence under s. 276 that the victim/witness had, according to a friend of the accused, allegedly sat in the accused's lap at a bar several weeks prior to the assault and had touched the accused in the genital area. The majority of the appeal judges stated that this evidence, combined with the evidence that the woman had briefly sat on the accused's lap at a party on the night of the assault and had made a remark in jest to another man at the party that she would leave her door open for him that night, created an air of reality to the accused's argument of "mistake".

Lane J.A. dissented. His judgment in *R. v. Ecker* (1995), 128 Sask. R. 161 at 191 (C.A.) reads, in part:

> [T]he proposed evidence of the proposed witness would suggest that the complainant sat on the lap of the accused in a beverage room at a hotel weeks prior to the alleged assault and placed her hand on the crotch area of his jeans. One must compare the nature of this alleged previous activity to the circumstances of the assault which is the basis for the charge. The accused broke into the home of the complainant in the middle of the night, took off most of his clothes, climbed into bed with the complainant, and touched her hip awakening her and alarming her. I cannot accept the fact that the former alleged consensual activity has any real probative value with regard to the accused's alleged belief the complainant agreed he should enter her apartment in the middle of the night uninvited, remove most of his clothes, climb into bed with her and assault her.

In *R. v. Malcolm*, [2000] M.J. No. 387, a unanimous decision of the Manitoba Court of Appeal, Helper J.A. described the test under s. 273.2(b) as a "quasi-objective test", applying to the circumstances known to the accused: "The issue which arises is, if a reasonable man was aware of the same circumstances, would he take further steps before proceeding with the sexual activity? If the answer is yes, and the accused has not taken further steps, then the accused is not entitled to the defence of honest belief in consent. If the answer is no, or even maybe, then the accused would not be required to take further steps and the defence will apply." (at para. 24) In *Malcolm*, the test was not satisfied where the accused entered the complainant's bedroom while she was sleeping, during a party being held in the accused's house, with the knowledge that she was married to his close friend. The Court of Appeal found that the trial judge erred in law in not directing his mind to the issue raised under s. 273.2(b), an area of law that remains unsettled and requires written reasons for judgment. See also *R. v. Cornejo*, [2003] O.J. No. 4517 (C.A.), where the court held that the accused failed to demonstrate reasonable steps to ascertain consent from a sleeping, intoxicated woman.

The Supreme Court has had an opportunity to consider the effect of s. 273.2 in *R. v. Esau*, [1997] 2 S.C.R. 777. Justices McLachlin and L'Heureux-Dubé, in separate dissenting judgments, would have reinstated a conviction by a jury of a man who sexually assaulted his cousin. The victim/witness had no memory of the assault as she was unconscious, but stated that she would never have "consented" to a relative; the accused claimed that she had consented, and that she was not too drunk not "to be able to control what she was doing." The dissenting justices stated that the trial judge was correct in not charging the jury on an alternative defence of "mistake", because it was not asserted by the accused or his counsel, because of the obligations on the accused created through s. 273.2 on facts where a woman is unconscious, incoherent, or passive, and because of the law on putting alternative defences where the versions of the evidence are entirely incompatible. In contrast, the majority upheld the court of appeal's order for a new trial, stating that the trial judge was obliged to put the defence of "mistake" before the jury on these facts even if defence counsel did not argue the point because an "air of reality" was created by the lack of struggle, violence, or force, the accused described words and actions of which the complainant had no recollection, and the versions were not "diametrically opposed". The majority refused to apply s. 273.2 because it was not argued at trial or on appeal by Crown counsel. For a comment on the developing case law under s. 273.2(b), see Elizabeth Sheehy, "From Women's Duty to Resist to Men's Duty to Ask: How Far Have We Come?" (2000) 20 *Canadian Woman Studies* 98.

More recently, the Court returned to s. 273.2(b) in *R. v. Ewanchuk*, above, under **Case Study on Assault**, in which Justice Major for the majority said the following.

R. v. Ewanchuk (Continued)†

[MAJOR J.:]

(a) Meaning of "Consent" in the Context of an Honest But Mistaken Belief in Consent

As with the *actus reus* of the offence, consent is an integral component of the *mens rea*, only this time it is considered from the perspective of the accused. Speaking of the *mens rea* of sexual assault in *Park*, *supra*, at para. 39, L'Heureux-Dubé J. (in her concurring reasons) stated that:

> ...the *mens rea* of sexual assault is not only satisfied when it is shown that the accused knew that the complainant was essentially saying "no", but is also satisfied when it is shown that the accused knew that the complainant was essentially not saying "yes".

In order to cloak the accused's actions in moral innocence, the evidence must show that he believed that the complainant *communicated consent to engage in the sexual activity in question*. A belief by the accused that the complainant, in her own mind wanted him to touch her but did not express that desire, is not a defence. The accused's speculation as to what was going on in the complainant's mind provides no defence.

For the purposes of the *mens rea* analysis, the question is whether the accused believed that he had obtained consent. What matters is whether the accused believed that the complainant effectively said "yes" through her words and/or actions. The statutory definition added to the *Code* by Parliament in 1992 is consistent with the common law:

> **273.1**(1) Subject to subsection (2) and subsection 265(3), "consent" means, for the purposes of sections 271, 272 and 273, the voluntary agreement of the complainant to engage in the sexual activity in question.

There is a difference in the concept of "consent" as it relates to the state of mind of the complainant *vis-à-vis* the *actus reus* of the offence and the state of mind of the accused in respect of the *mens rea*. For the purposes of the *actus reus*, "consent" means that the complainant in her mind wanted the sexual touching to take place.

In the context of *mens rea* — specifically for the purposes of the honest but mistaken belief in consent — "consent" means that the complainant had affirmatively communicated by words or conduct her agreement to engage in sexual activity with the accused. This distinction should always be borne in mind and the two parts of the analysis kept separate.

(b) Limits on Honest But Mistaken Belief in Consent

Not all beliefs upon which an accused might rely will exculpate him. Consent in relation to the *mens rea* of the accused is limited by both the common law and the provisions of ss. 273.1(2) and 273.2 of the *Code* ... For instance, a belief that silence, passivity or ambiguous conduct constitutes consent is a mistake of law, and provides no defence: see *R. v. M. (M.L.)*, [1994] 2 S.C.R. 3. Similarly, an accused cannot rely upon his purported belief that the complainant's expressed lack of agreement to sexual touching in fact constituted an invitation to more persistent or aggressive contact. An accused cannot

† [1999] 1 S.C.R. 330.

say that he thought "no meant yes". As Fraser C.J. stated at p. 272 of her dissenting reasons below:

> One "No" will do to put the other person on notice that there is then a problem with "consent". *Once a woman says "No" during the course of sexual activity, the person intent on continued sexual activity with her must then obtain a clear and unequivocal "Yes" before he again touches her in a sexual manner.* [Emphasis in original.]

I take the reasons of Fraser C.J. to mean that an unequivocal "yes" may be given by either the spoken word or by conduct.

Common sense should dictate that, once the complainant has expressed her unwillingness to engage in sexual contact, the accused should make certain that she has truly changed her mind before proceeding with further intimacies. The accused cannot rely on the mere lapse of time or the complainant's silence or equivocal conduct to indicate that there has been a change of heart and that consent now exists, nor can he engage in further sexual touching to "test the waters". Continuing sexual contact after someone has said "No" is, at a minimum, reckless conduct which is not excusable. In *R. v. Esau*, [1997] 2 S.C.R. 777, at para. 79, the Court stated:

> An accused who, due to wilful blindness or recklessness, believes that a complainant ... in fact consented to the sexual activity at issue is precluded from relying on a defence of honest but mistaken belief in consent, a fact that Parliament has codified: *Criminal Code*, s. 273.2(*a*)(ii).

(c) Application to the Facts

In this appeal the accused does not submit that the complainant's clearly articulated "No's" were ambiguous or carried some other meaning. In fact, the accused places great reliance on his having stopped immediately each time the complainant said "no" in order to show that he had no intention to force himself upon her. He therefore knew that the complainant was not consenting on four separate occasions during their encounter.

The question which the trial judge ought to have considered was whether anything occurred between the communication of non-consent and the subsequent sexual touching which the accused could honestly have believed constituted consent.

The trial judge explicitly chose not to consider whether the accused had the defence of honest but mistaken belief in consent, and concluded that the defence was probably not available unless the accused testified. This conclusion ignores the right of the accused to have this defence considered solely on the Crown's case. The trial judge paid only passing interest to this defence undoubtedly because he had concluded that the defence of implied consent exonerated the accused. The accused is entitled to have all available defences founded on a proper basis considered by the court, whether he raises them or not: see *R. v. Bulmer*, [1987] 1 S.C.R. 782, at p. 789.

In *Esau*, *supra*, at para. 15, the Court stated that, "before a court should consider honest but mistaken belief or instruct a jury on it there must be some plausible evidence in support so as to give an air of reality to the defence". See also *R. v. Osolin*, [1993] 4 S.C.R. 595. All that is required is for the accused to adduce some evidence, or refer to evidence already adduced, upon which a properly instructed trier of fact could form a reasonable doubt as to his *mens rea*: see *Osolin*, *supra*, at pp. 653–54, and p. 687.

The analysis in this appeal makes no attempt to weigh the evidence. At this point we are concerned only with the facial plausibility of the defence of honest but mistaken belief and should avoid the risk of turning the air of reality test into a substantive evaluation of the merits of the defence.

As the accused did not testify, the only evidence before the Court was that of the complainant. She stated that she immediately said "NO" every time the accused touched her sexually, and that she did nothing to encourage him. Her evidence was accepted by the trial judge as credible and sincere. Indeed, the accused relies on the fact that he momentarily stopped his advances each time the complainant said "NO" as evidence of his good intentions. This demonstrates that he understood the complainant's "NO's" to mean precisely that. Therefore, there is nothing on the record to support the accused's claim that he continued to believe her to be consenting, or that he re-established consent before resuming physical contact. The accused did not raise nor does the evidence disclose an air of reality to the defence of honest but mistaken belief in consent to this sexual touching.

The trial record conclusively establishes that the accused's persistent and increasingly serious advances constituted a sexual assault for which he had no defence. But for his errors of law, the trial judge would necessarily have found the accused guilty. In this case, a new trial would not be in the interests of justice. Therefore, it is proper for this Court to exercise its discretion under s. 686(4) of the *Code* and enter a conviction: see *R. v. Cassidy*, [1989] 2 S.C.R. 345, at pp. 354–55.

In her reasons, Justice L'Heureux-Dubé makes reference to s. 273.2(*b*) of the *Code*. Whether the accused took reasonable steps is a question of fact to be determined by the trier of fact only after the air of reality test has been met. In view of the way the trial and appeal were argued, s. 273.2(*b*) did not have to be considered.

. . . .

[Justice L'Heureux-Dubé's judgment on this issue is as follows:]

I agree with Major J. that the findings necessary to support a verdict of guilty on the charge of sexual assault have been made. In particular, there is, on the record, no evidence that would give an air of reality to an honest belief in consent for any of the sexual activity which took place in this case. One cannot imply that once the complainant does not object to the massage in the context of a job interview, there is "sufficient evidence" to support that the accused could honestly believe he had permission to initiate sexual contact. This would mean that complying to receive a massage is consent to sexual touching. It would reflect the myth that women are presumptively sexually accessible until they resist. McLachlin J. has recognized in *R. v. Esau*, [1997] 2 S.C.R. 777, at para. 82, that reliance on rape myths cannot ground a defence of mistaken belief in consent:

> Care must be taken to avoid the false assumptions or "myths" that may mislead us in determining whether the conduct of the complainant affords a sufficient basis for putting the defence of honest mistake on consent to the jury. One of these is the stereotypical notion that women who resist or say no may in fact be consenting.

Furthermore, I agree with Fraser C.J. at p. 278 that there is no air of reality to a defence of mistaken belief in consent "in the face of the complainant's clearly stated verbal objections".

Moreover, s. 273.2(*b*) precludes the accused from raising the defence of belief in consent if he did not take "reasonable steps" in the circumstances known to him at the time to ascertain that the complainant was consenting. This provision and the defence of honest but mistaken belief were before the trial judge and it should have been given full effect. The trial judge erred in law by not applying s. 273.2(*b*) which was the law of the land at the time of the trial, irrespective of whether the case proceeded on that basis. As stated by McLachlin J. in *Esau*, *supra*, at para. 50, with whom I concurred:

> Major J. [for the majority] does not consider s. 273.2. This may be because it was not argued on the appeal or in the proceedings below. With respect, I do not believe that the force of s. 273.2 may be avoided on that ground. Parliament has spoken. It has set out minimum conditions for the defence of mistaken belief in consent. If those conditions are not met, the defence does not lie.

I agree entirely with Fraser C.J. that, unless and until an accused first takes reasonable steps to assure that there is consent, the defence of honest but mistaken belief does not arise (see *R. v. Daigle*, [1998] 1 S.C.R. 1220; *Esau*, *supra*, *per* McLachlin J. dissenting; and J. McInnes and C. Boyle, "Judging Sexual Assault Law Against a Standard of Equality" (1995), 29 *U.B.C. L. Rev.* 341). In this case, the accused proceeded from massaging to sexual contact without making any inquiry as to whether the complainant consented. Obviously, interpreting the fact that the complainant did not refuse the massage to mean that the accused could further his sexual intentions is not a reasonable step. The accused cannot rely on the complainant's silence or ambiguous conduct to initiate sexual contact. Moreover, where a complainant expresses non-consent, the accused has a corresponding escalating obligation to take additional steps to ascertain consent. Here, despite the complainant's repeated verbal objections, the accused did not take any step to ascertain consent, let alone reasonable ones. Instead, he increased the level of his sexual activity. Therefore, pursuant to s. 273.2(*b*) Ewanchuk was barred from relying on a belief in consent.

Major J., at para. 43, relies on this Court's decision in *Pappajohn v. The Queen*, [1980] 2 S.C.R. 120, to describe the nature of the defence of honest but mistaken belief. In *Pappajohn*, the majority held that this defence does not need to be based on reasonable grounds as long as it is honestly held. That approach has been modified by the enactment of s. 273.2(*b*) which introduced the "reasonable steps" requirement. Therefore, that decision no longer states the law on the question of honest but mistaken belief in consent.

I wish to point out that, on the facts as found at trial, s. 273.1(2) also applies to this case. Coupled with the reasonable steps requirement of s. 273.2(*b*), s. 273.1(2) restricts the circumstances in which an accused could claim that he had a mistaken belief in the complainant's agreement to engage in the impugned sexual activity. Particularly relevant to this case, s. 273.1(2)(*d*) states that no consent is obtained where "the complainant expresses, by words or conduct, a lack of agreement ...". Here, the complainant clearly expressed her lack of consent by saying "no" three times. The application of that provision acknowledges that when a woman says "no" she is communicating her non-agreement, regardless of what the accused thought it meant, and that her expression has an enforceable legal effect. It precludes the accused from claiming that he thought there was an agreement. That provision was in force at the time of trial and could not be ignored by the trial judge.

■

Which judgment is more persuasive regarding the air of reality test and s. 273.2(b)? Does the *Stone* decision (**Provocation**, below) and its discussion of the relationship between the evidentiary burden (air of reality) for defences and the substantive content of a particular defence suggest an answer?

9

Mistake of Law

A. GENERAL PRINCIPLES

Section 19 of the *Code* states that "ignorance of the law ... is not an excuse." Persons who are ignorant of the law **or** who operate under a mistake as to the law are thus **denied** a defence to charges under federal criminal legislation. A defence of mistake of law is similarly unavailable for provincial offences, either on the basis of an analogous provincial section or on the basis that s. 19 merely codifies the common law principle that is applicable to **all** offences (*R. v. MacDougall*, [1982] 2 S.C.R. 605).

In contrast, a mistake of fact offers the possibility of a defence and, where the error is one of mixed fact and law, the rules as to mistake of fact govern. However, the Supreme Court of Canada has not provided clear guidance on this distinction. For example, in responding to a defence of no knowledge by accused who were charged with driving without a valid motor licence where their licences had been automatically suspended upon prior convictions for driving with more than 80 milligrams of alcohol in their blood, the Court has characterized the mistake as one of fact where the accused was charged under federal law (*R. v. Prue*, [1979] 2 S.C.R. 547) and one of law where the accused was charged under provincial law (*R. v. MacDougall*).

The policy behind the general principle includes a number of premises:

- Everyone knows, or is capable of knowing, the law;
- Failure to apprehend the law and, thus, the community's morals is, itself, culpable;
- Citizens would, otherwise, have an incentive to remain ignorant of the law; and
- Acceptance of this defence would produce uncertainty and unfairness in the application of the criminal sanction.

For examples of what the unavailability of a defence based on mistake of law or ignorance of the law has meant historically, see the discussion of **Colonization and the Imposition of Criminal Law** in Abell & Sheehy, *Cases, Context, Critique*, and in particular the excerpt from Chief Thomas Fiddler & James R. Stevens, *Killing the Shamen*, and the discussion of Cornelia Schuh's work, "Justice on the Northern Frontier: Early Murder Trials of Native Accused".

Clearly, the rule that ignorance of the law is no defence operated harshly in the historical context of colonization. The rule also has the potential to differentially impact on particular accused in contemporary situations by ignoring, for example, language or cultural barriers. For an Australian critique of the denial of a defence of ignorance of law on the basis of culture, see: Simon Bronitt, "Cultural Blindness: Criminal Law in Multicultural Australia" (1996) 21:2 Alternative L. J. 58 (discussing the report of the Australian Law Reform Commission, *Multiculturalism and the Law* (1992)). Can you see any basis for a *Charter* challenge to s. 19 of the *Code*?

Some applications of the general principles follow. In *R. v. Aryeh* (1972), 2 O.R. 249 (C.A.), the accused's belief that the *Customs Act* permitted him to bring jewellery into Canada as household goods under his wife's name was held to be no defence to the charge of unlawful importation.

In *R. v. Campbell* (1973), 2 W.W.R. 246 (Alta. Dist. Ct.), the court held that a mistake of law defence was unavailable even where the accused's conduct was not necessarily illegal according to the judicial authority at the time of commission of the offence. Thus, the accused was wrong to rely on a lower court interpretation of the criminal law because only the Supreme Court of Canada has the authority to "discover" the law: "It is ... a mistake of law to conclude that the decision of any particular judge correctly states the law, unless that Judge speaks on behalf of the court of ultimate appeal." Consider whether this decision satisfies the policies behind the general principle of s. 19. Note also the problems created by this case for lawyers who must advise clients. Similarly, in *R. v. MacIntyre* (1983), 24 M.V.R. 67 (Ont. C.A.), the court held that reliance on an erroneous judgment of an inferior court did not constitute a reasonable excuse for the failure to provide a breath sample.

In *R. v. Potter* (1978), 39 C.C.C. (2d) 538 (P.E.I.T.D.), the defence was also unavailable even where the employer of the accused had specifically inquired of a customs official whether the activity of importing punchboards was illegal. The RCMP had monitored and, essentially, condoned the entire operation for years before arresting Potter. Is this result consistent with the policies behind the rule?

In contrast, while the ordinary citizen who makes a mistake of law has no defence, a peace officer may argue that a *bona fide* mistake of law combined with *Code* s. 25 protects him/her from prosecution. Thus, in *R. v. Devereaux* (1996), 147 Nfld. & P.E.I.R. 108 (Nfld. C.A.), a correctional officer who unlawfully applied a restraining hold and physically returned an individual to a detention cell (mistakenly concluding that he was entitled to because the individual refused to sign a property release form), was acquitted of assault on the basis of s. 25(2). The trial judge had found the allegations that excessive force had been used were not established. (The victim alleged that he had been dragged, choked, kneed, punched, and kicked by officers at the time of his arrest, and alleged that the police response was coloured by the fact that he was gay.) The effect of this decision is to excuse a mistake of law that led to an assault and the wrongful detention of an individual. Consider the wording of s. 25(2). Was Devereaux acting within the terms of that subsection, that is, "required or authorized by law to execute a process or to carry out a sentence ..."? Does this interpretation stretch the purpose envisioned by s. 25?

B. POSSIBLE EXCEPTIONS TO THE GENERAL PRINCIPLES

MISTAKE GOING TO THE *MENS REA* ELEMENT OF THE OFFENCE

For certain offences, the *mens rea* element has been interpreted as requiring that the accused know that the conduct is illegal, e.g., offences that use "knowingly" or "without colour of right" (most property offences in Part IX), **but not** offences that use the phrase "without reasonable justification or excuse". See, for example, *R. v. Howson*, [1966] 2 O.R. 63 (C.A.), where the accused tow truck operator successfully argued that he should be acquitted of theft for towing and retaining someone's car on the basis that he had an affirmative belief that he had a positive "right" to retain the car until the towing charges had been paid. In another example, *R. v. Docherty*, [1989] 2 S.C.R. 941, the Court considered the language of s. 666 of the *Code*, which creates the offence of "wilfully refusing or failing to conform" with a probation order. In this case, the accused had pleaded guilty to the offence of having care and control over a motor vehicle while intoxicated (s. 236, over .08), an offence that has a minimal *mens rea* requirement. This same accused was able to fight successfully the s. 666 charge because he did not realize that the action that constituted the s. 236 charge (merely sitting in the car) was illegal, and therefore his "mistake of law" negated the *mens rea* of "wilfully" breaching probation.

In *R. v. Jorgensen*, [1995] 4 S.C.R. 55, the accused (who owned and operated an adult video and magazine store) was charged under s. 163 of the *Code* ("knowingly, without lawful justification or excuse, sells ... any obscene ... matter") with respect to the sale of obscene videos. Justice Sopinka, writing for the majority, held that the term "knowingly" applied to all elements of the *actus reus*, and that the accused retailer must know (at 107) "that the materials being sold have the qualities or contain the specific scenes which render such materials obscene [explicitly combining sex and violence] in law." Justice Sopinka characterized the mistake as a mixed question of fact and law and held that reliance on the videos' approved rating by the Ontario Film Review Board would not necessarily negate the *mens rea* of the offence, provide an excuse as set out in s. 163(2), or form the basis for an "officially induced error". He concluded that, in the absence of any evidence that the accused had knowledge that the films in question involved the exploitation of sex, the *mens rea* requirement was not satisfied. He therefore acquitted the accused. What is the practical effect of this decision?

OFFICIALLY INDUCED ERROR OF LAW

Another exception has emerged from the case law where the accused has relied on a legal interpretation given by someone in authority charged with the administration of the law but not, it seems, a lawyer. From the earlier discussion of the policy behind s. 19, can you see what policies are served by this exception?

R. v. MacLean (1974), 46 D.L.R. (3d) 564 (N.S. Co. Ct.) appears to support this exception. Here the accused was acquitted partly on the basis that he had ascertained that his conduct was lawful through inquiries made to the Registrar of Motor Vehicles and his own employers. Convicting the accused would not have served the policy underlying s. 19. In particular, the law was not easily discoverable (even the RCMP did not know about the regulation in question); it was not "morally culpable" to be unaware of this sort of regulation; the decision would reward efforts to discover the law; and there was no unfairness generated by acquittal. However, this approach was not followed in *Campbell* (Alta. Dist. Ct., 1973), *infra*, or *R. v. Dunn* (1977), 21 N.S.R. (2d) 334 (C.A.), where lawyers had provided the erroneous advice. Is this good policy?

In *R. v. Bauman* (1994), 18 O.R. (3d) 772 (Ct. J. (Gen. Div.)), the accused had sought advice from a planner with the municipality of North York. He was told that his wife, who was a denture therapist, could lawfully open an office to work at their home, and then was subsequently charged for contravening a municipal by-law. The court held that even if zoning by-laws were absolute liability offences (which consequently have no mental or fault element, see ***Mens Rea***), a defence of officially induced error was made out on the facts of the case.

In *R. v. Cancoil Thermal Corp.* (1986), 14 O.A.C. 225 (C.A.), the offence under the *Occupational Health and Safety Act* of failing to ensure that work is carried out using protective devices was read as a strict liability offence, thus permitting the accused to raise a due diligence defence. The court directed that at the new trial, the defence of "officially induced error of law" should be available for the accused to argue that it had relied on the opinion of a safety inspector under the act. (See the discussion of this case under ***Mens Rea***, above.)

In *R. v. Johnson* (1987), 78 N.B.R. (2d) 411 (Prov. Ct.), the court accepted the defence of "officially induced error" for the offence of illegal fishing, but warned:

> Because of the inherent nature of this special defence **it will only work once**. The purse seiners of Grand Manan have had their once in a lifetime opportunity to avail themselves of this remedy.
>
> Since Grand Manan is such a small, tight-knit community and professes (according to the evidence) to have only seven purse seiners operating therefrom, I have little doubt that the remaining five captains will become aware of this judgment before even this day has ended. [Emphasis in original.]

Another recent example of successful reliance upon the "officially induced error of law" defence can be found in *R. v. Dubeau* (1993), 80 C.C.C. (3d) 54 (Ont. Ct. J. (Gen. Div.)). In that case, the accused sold guns without a licence at garage sales, relying upon the advice from a local firearms officer that it was legal to do so.

The Supreme Court of Canada has now clearly indicated that the defence of "officially induced error of law" is available as an exception to the principle that ignorance of the law is no excuse. In

Lévis (City) v. Tétreault, [2006] 1 S.C.R. 420, the Court accepted the analysis of Justice Lamer in *Jorgensen* and his identification of the constituent elements of the defence that must be established by the accused (at para. 26, citing *Jorgensen* at paras. 28–35):

> (1) that an error of law or of mixed law and fact was made;
> (2) that the person who committed the act considered the legal consequences of his or her actions;
> (3) that the advice obtained came from an appropriate official;
> (4) that the advice was reasonable;
> (5) that the advice was erroneous; and
> (6) that the person relied on the advice in committing the act

Although the Court held that the defence was not made out on the facts in *Lévis*, given the lack of diligence on the part of the accused in seeking to determine their obligations to renew a vehicle registration and a driver's licence, Justice LeBel elaborated on the factors that would be relevant to establish officially induced error (at para. 27):

> ...the efforts made by the accused to obtain information, the clarity or obscurity of the law, the position and role of the official who gave the information or opinion, and the clarity, definitiveness and reasonableness of the information or opinion [citing *Cancoil* at 303]. It is not sufficient in such cases to conduct a purely subjective analysis of the reasonableness of the information. This aspect of the question must be considered from the perspective of a reasonable person in a situation similar to that of the accused.

IMPOSSIBILITY

A final exception involves the situation where it is physically impossible for the accused to ascertain the state of the law. It has been invoked where the law has been **unpublished in any form** and the Crown has been unable to prove that the accused had actual notice of the law: *R. v. Catholique* (1979), 104 D.L.R. (3d) 161 (Y. Terr. Ct.). In that case, a new liquor regulation had been posted in two places in Snowdrift, N.W.T., but was otherwise unpublished in the *Canada Gazette*. This exception is suggested by a distinction made in *MacLean* between statutory and subordinate legislation, the latter being generally less accessible to the public. However, it should be noted that this exception does not include the situation where it is impossible to divine the law because it is still in a state of flux (*Campbell* (Alta. Dist. Ct., 1973)) or because it is difficult to keep up with newly promulgated regulations (*R. v. Molis*, [1980] 2 S.C.R. 356).

An attempted "impossibility" argument is found in *Re Unger et al. v. R.* (1990), 58 C.C.C. (3d) 518 (Ont. Dist. Ct.) where the police had placed a "designer drug" manufactured by the accused (which had not previously been listed) on Schedule H to the *Narcotics Control Act*. Because the amendment had been duly published in the *Canada Gazette* the month before, the impossibility argument was rejected, as was an effort to invoke s. 7 of the *Charter*.

The case that follows illustrates a rigid application of s. 19 to the defence of mistake of law.

R. v. Campbell (Alta. Dist. Ct., 1973)†

[KERANS D.C.J.:]

This is an appeal by Darlene Agatha Campbell from conviction and sentence on a charge before the summary conviction court that she did, between 9th February 1972 and 21st February 1972, at the City of Edmonton, in the Province of Alberta, unlawfully take part as a performer in an immoral performance at Chez Pierre's, situated at 10615 — Jasper Avenue, Edmonton, contrary to s. 163(2) of the Criminal Code, R.S.C. 1970, c. C–34.

This matter, therefore, comes before me by way of a trial de novo. That section provides, in subs. (2):

> (2) Every one commits an offence who takes part or appears as an actor, performer, or assistant in any capacity, in an immoral, indecent or obscene performance, entertainment or representation in a theatre.

The facts before me are relatively straightforward. On the dates in question, at the place in

† [1973] 2 W.W.R. 246 (Alta. Dist. Ct.).

question, the appellant danced on stage, before an audience. At the start of her performance, she was wearing some clothes. By the end of her performance, she was not wearing any clothes. The dance was described to me as a "go-go dance" which, I understand, is a violent movement of almost all parts of the body, more or less in time to strongly rhythmic music.

I have no doubt in coming to the conclusion that this is a performance within the meaning of the section, and that, in doing what she did, the appellant took part as a performer in that performance. On the question of whether or not the performance was immoral, both counsel have agreed that I am bound to follow the recent decision of the Appellate Division of the Supreme Court of Alberta in *Regina v. Johnson*, [1972] 5 W.W.R. 638, 8 C.C.C. (2d) 1. This was a stated case before Riley J., [1972] 3 W.W.R. 226, 6 C.C.C. (2d) 462, and appealed from him to the Appellate Division.

In that case McDermid J.A., speaking for the Court, said, after drawing attention to the fact that s. 170 of the Code makes it a crime for anyone to appear nude in a public place, that he understood the enactment of that offence, by the Parliament of Canada, as, and I quote, declaring "that it is a breach of a moral standard in Canada." And he goes on, "We know of no better way of establishing a moral standard than a declaration by the Parliament of Canada, and so the Provincial Court Judge was justified in accepting this as his standard and finding that the dance by the respondent in the nude was an immoral performance." I understand, therefore, that since to be nude in a public place is, itself, an offence, to perform in the nude, therefore, is an immoral performance within the meaning of the charging section. Therefore, I must conclude that the performance here was immoral within the meaning of that section.

I have been told that the decision of the Appellate Division has been appealed to the Supreme Court of Canada. In some cases it is considered appropriate to adjourn or reserve, pending the outcome of an appeal. In my view, this rule should not be followed in the case of appeals from the Appellate Division to the Supreme Court of Canada, for various reasons. One is the delay of time involved. Therefore, on this point, the position of the parties would have to be that, should the Appellate Division decision not be upheld, my decision must also be appealed.

It was argued for the appellant that the place in which this performance took place was not a theatre within the meaning of the charging section. The facts, in that respect, were these: the place in question was on the second floor of a building in downtown Edmonton; the patrons were seated; there was accommodation for approximately 200 persons; meals and soft drinks were served, but not liquor; an entrance fee was charged at the door, $3 per person. I find that there was a sign outside the front of this establishment, indicating that minors would not be allowed admission, but that all others who were prepared to pay the sum of $3 would by implication be allowed admission.

I understand that there was a practice, on the part of the management, to refuse entrance also to persons whose attendance was thought undesirable by reason of their being impaired, or unsuitably dressed. The patrons could eat, they could dance on the dance floor, and they could also, of course, watch the performance, earlier described, which was put on from time to time in the course of the evening.

[The judge went on to consider the meaning of the word "public".]

. . . .

In my view, a place is open to the public when the public, as such, are invited to come, even though certain restrictions are placed in their way, and even though certain small sections of the public are not invited. I understand the use of the word "public" here as being in distinction to the word "private." A place that is open to the public is a place that is open to persons generally, rather than open to certain specific individuals.

It is not necessary, in my view, for the application of that section, that the entire world be allowed access. Therefore, I come to the conclusion that this place was a theatre within the meaning of the Code.

The next argument raised on behalf of the appellant is that the appellant lacked the necessary *mens rea* for this offence. The facts in this respect were these: She engaged to do this performance, where, earlier, she had refused to engage to do this performance, because she relied upon the statement made to her by Pierre Couchard that he, in turn, had been informed that a Supreme Court Judge had, to use his words, because he also gave evidence, "Ruled that we could go ahead with bottomless dancing." That decision arose out of a charge in the City of Calgary of a business acquaintance of Couchard, who was the manager of the place where this performance took place. Ironically, the decision to which Couchard and the appellant referred is the decision at the Trial Division level in *Regina v. Johnson*, to which I earlier referred and, as the witnesses tell me, obtained some newspaper publicity. It was a decision then that subsequently was reversed on appeal.

Mistake of fact is a defence to a criminal charge, where it can be said that the facts believed by the accused, if true, would have afforded him a defence. It is also said that a mistake of mixed fact and law is a defence. I understand that proposition to be correct simply because, if there is a mistake of mixed fact and law, then there is a mistake of fact. In my view, there was no mistake of fact by the appellant here. What she was told happened, in fact, did happen.

Her mistake, if she made any mistake, was in concluding that a statement of law, expressed by Riley J., was the law. That is not a mistake of fact, that is a mistake of law. It is a mistake of law to misunderstand the significance of the decision of a judge, or of his reasons. It is also a mistake of law to conclude that the decision of any particular judge correctly states the law, unless that judge speaks on behalf of the court of ultimate appeal.

This is not a situation like others where a mistake of law can be a defence, not because a mistake of law is a defence, but because a mistake of law can negative a malicious intent required for that crime. Thus, for example, where the law requires that a person wilfully, or maliciously, or knowingly, do something wrong, it could conceivably be a defence as negativing intention, to show that, because of the mistake in understanding of the law, there was no wilful intent or malice. This is not one of those situations, as no such special intention is required for this offence. The only *mens rea* required here is that the appellant intended to do that which she did, and there is no suggestion, for a moment, that she lacked that *mens rea*.

. . . .

Excuse, or legal justification, is a defence at law, and I understand that defence to mean that it is a defence to a criminal charge to show that the act complained of was authorized by some other law. Section 19 says that that defence is not available, in effect, when a person has made a mistake as to whether or not this act is excused by another law or authorized by another law.

Properly understood, in my view, the section removing ignorance of the law as a defence, in criminal matters, is not a matter of justice, but a matter of policy. There will always be cases, not so complicated as this, where honest and reasonable mistakes as to the state of the law will be the explanation of the conduct of an accused. In such a circumstance one cannot help but have sympathy for the accused. But that situation, traditionally, is not a defence. It is not a defence, I think, because the first requirement of any system of justice is that it work efficiently and effectively. If the state of understanding of the law of an accused person is ever to be relevant in criminal proceedings, we would have an absurd proceeding. The issue in a criminal trial would then not be what the accused did, but whether or not the accused had a sufficiently sophisticated understanding of the law to appreciate that what he did offended against the law. There would be a premium, therefore, placed upon ignorance of the law.

. . . .

[Having ruled that ignorance of the law was no defence, the judge went on to examine the sympathetic circumstances of the accused.]

I have given some consideration as to whether or not this position varies at all, because of the unique circumstances here, where the appellant relied upon a specific judgment of a Court very immediate in terms of time and place, as opposed to a solicitor's opinion or some other understanding as to the law. There is no question that there is somewhat of an [anomaly] here. Reliance on a specific order, of a specific judge, granted at a specific time and place, seems, at first sight, not to be ignorance of the law, but knowledge of the law. If it turns out that that judge is mistaken, then, of course, the reliance on that judge's judgment is mistaken. The irony is this: people in society are expected to have a more profound knowledge of the law than are the judges. I am not the first person to have made that comment about the law, and while it is all very amusing, it is really to no point.

The principle that ignorance of the law should not be a defence in criminal matters is not justified because it is fair, it is justified because it is necessary, even though it will sometimes produce an anomalous result.

When this appellant relied on the decision of the learned trial Judge, she relied on his authority for the law. As it turns out, that reliance was misplaced, as misplaced as reliance on any statement as to the law I might make. Less so, I am sure.

. . . .

[After acknowledging that there were no authorities precisely on the point, the judge again stated that mistake of law afforded the appellant no defence.]

I have already indicated, in a quotation from Kenny, that, in this awkward situation, the matter does not afford a defence, but should certainly be considered in mitigation of sentence. Indeed, there are several cases, not as awkward as this, several cases, in the law reports, involving a person who had an honest and reasonable mistake in belief as to the law, and for whom the Courts expressed sympathy, and, in respect of whom, sentence was mitigated.

It is at this stage where the scales of justice are balanced. Clothed with very recent power to refuse to enter a conviction, I can now balance the scales of justice even more delicately. I have read a note in the English and Empire Digest, vol. 14, p. 51, of an old case, *Rex v. Bailey* (1800), Russ. & Ry. 1. In that case, the Government of England had passed a statute, making something a crime which was not previously a crime. Subsequently, the accused did the forbidden act. The Courts found that, in fact, in the district in which this crime was committed, no news had yet reached anyone of the passage of this Act, nor could any news have reached this district of the passage of this Act, and that the accused, therefore, had to be convicted of an offence which he did not know and could not have known was an offence. They said there that the proper way of dealing with the matter was to give a pardon, which I understand to be a conviction followed immediately by the wiping-out of a conviction.

I have no power to give a pardon, but I do have power to give an absolute discharge. In my view, this is the proper case.

I have considered the fact that this lady apparently also committed the crime of being nude in a public place. I say apparently, carefully, as I do not wish to accuse her of something wrongly. But it is difficult not to come to that conclusion.

However, it is not my function here to sentence her for crimes that she may have been guilty of, but with which she is not charged today, and, therefore, I do not take that into consideration. It perhaps can also be argued that no reasonable person could find, in the judgment of Riley J., justification for some of the things that lady is alleged to have done. But to argue that would be to argue that she would have to have a rather sophisticated knowledge of what he said, and the significance of what he said, and that is unreal. She understood, as she said "that some judge had said dancing bottomless is now okay," and I cannot reasonably test her understanding on that too closely. Also, I have given consideration to whether or not there ought to be a deterrent here.

■

10

Colour of Right: Mistake of Fact, Mistake of Law, or Affirmative Defence?

In the following cases, the accused are not only asserting legal justification or excuse and "colour of right" under s. 429 of the *Code*, but also contesting the definition of property that forms the basis of the offence and arguing a defence of property under s. 41(1) of the *Code*. The defence of colour of right depends on the accused's subjective, honest belief. However, there is some ambiguity with respect to the burden of proof and whether placing the onus on the accused would infringe s. 11(d) of the *Charter*. As is discussed in Abell & Sheehy, *Cases, Context, Critique*, **Colonization**, the definition of property and title with respect to Aboriginal lands continues to be contested in the courts, in the historical literature, and in the political arena. See also the discussion below, under **Broadening the Defences: Necessity, Self-Defence, and Conscience**. Both Chief Stevenson (as he then was) and Daniel Ashini are political leaders, and the issues raised are political, historical, and contested. The *Stevenson* case is further discussed below, under **Necessity**.

R. v. Stevenson†

[JEWERS J.:]

The accused are all members of the Peguis Indian Reserve in the Province of Manitoba, and they are charged that on May 6th, 1984, at the Peguis Indian Reserve, they did unlawfully commit mischief by wilfully damaging, without legal justification or excuse, and without colour of right, public property, to wit, a bridge, by burning same, which damage did exceed $50.00 contrary to s. 387(3)(a) [now s. 430] of the *Criminal Code of Canada*. They were convicted of this charge in Provincial Court on June 28th, 1985, and each accused was fined $100.00 (on default, ten days). They appeal to this court from that conviction.

The bridge forms part of Provincial Road 224, which runs through the Peguis Indian Reserve in Manitoba and is known as the Harwill Bridge. It crosses the Fisher River.

† (1986), (1987), 42 Man. R. (2d) 133 (Q.B.) 309, leave to appeal refused [1987] 1 W.W.R. 767 (C.A.).

The bridge was of wooden construction, built in 1955, with an average lifespan of 30 to 35 years. Mr. Lautens, a bridge engineer employed by the Province of Manitoba, inspected the bridge on August 27th, 1979, at the request of the Peguis Band. He noted many deficiencies, including rotting timber, rotting travelling planks, missing bridge members, lack of earth fill behind the bridge abutment, cracked main beams and broken sway braces. He recommended that a replacement structure be built, and further recommended that in the interim, the noted deficiencies be repaired and the load limit be restricted to 11,000 pounds. The learned trial judge found that the bridge was in poor condition in 1984. This finding is fully supported by the evidence.

The province did nothing with respect to the bridge from 1979 until 1984, and did not carry out the work recommended by Mr. Lautens.

The deficiencies in the bridge had been evident for some time, and as early as 1973, the band had been pressing the government to rectify the problem. By a resolution of November 8th, 1979, the Peguis Band urged that the bridge be replaced by the province. All this was to no avail. Finally, to bring matters to a head, the accused determined to take the drastic action of burning the bridge. There is evidence that they were motivated, not only by the poor condition of the bridge, but also by other conditions on the reserve including alleged overcrowded and poor housing conditions. They issued a press release to this effect. They blocked off the road with earth and burned the bridge.

The accused have raised a number of defences to the charge of mischief: that the bridge was not a public bridge, but was owned by the band; that in burning the bridge, they acted under a colour of right; and that the legal defence of necessity applied.

I reject the argument that the bridge was not public property, and was owned by the band.

The lands forming the Peguis Indian Reserve were set aside for the purpose of the reserve by virtue of an order passed by the Governor General-In-Council on July 14th, 1930. The lands were then owned by the Government of Canada, and the Order-In-Council recited that on the recommendation of the Minister of the Interior, and under and by virtue of s. 74, chap. R.S. 1927 (*The Dominion Lands Act*) the lands were withdrawn from the operation of the *Act* and set apart for the use of the Indians as Peguis Indian Reserve.

The lands then came under the operation of the *Indian Act* and by virtue of s. 18 of that *Act*, they continued to be held by Her Majesty for the use and benefit of the band. In other words, prior to and at the time of the Order-In-Council, the lands were owned by the Government of Canada and following the order, they continued to be owned by the Government of Canada pursuant to the provisions of the *Indian Act*. The lands were not owned by the band and, in my view, are not owned by the band, although they are to be held by the Government of Canada for the use and benefit of the band.

On May 1st, 1958, the Governor General-In-Council passed a second Order-In-Council pursuant to s. 35 of the *Indian Act* consenting to "the taking of a portion of the reserve lands by the Province of Manitoba, and the transferring of the lands to the administration and control of the Province of Manitoba for the purpose of creating a road through the reserve." This was the road in question which included the Harwill Bridge.

The Order-In-Council was registered in Winnipeg Land Titles Office on July 7th, 1958, as number D18219, and a document entitled "Plan of Survey of Public Road" with respect to the road in question was deposited in the Winnipeg Land Titles Office as Plan Number 6672 on December 18, 1957.

Thereafter, the road was used for general public purposes and maintained by the Province of Manitoba.

The authority for the taking of the road by the Province of Manitoba may be found in s. 35 of the *Indian Act* which reads as follows:

> Section 35(1) Where by an Act of the Parliament of Canada or a provincial legislature, Her Majesty in right of a province, a municipal or local authority or a corporation is empowered to take or to use lands or any interest therein without the consent of the owner, the power may, with the consent of the Governor in Council and subject to any terms that may be prescribed by the Governor in Council, be exercised in relation to lands in a reserve or any interest therein.
>
> (2) Unless the Governor in Council otherwise directs, all matters relating to compulsory taking or using of lands in a reserve under subs. (1) are governed by the statute by which the powers are conferred.
>
> (3) Whenever the Governor in Council has consented to the exercise by a province, authority or corporation of the powers referred to in subs. (1), the Governor in Council may, in lieu of the province, authority or corporation taking or using the lands without the consent of the owner, authorize a transfer or grant of such lands to the province, authority or corporation, subject to any terms that may be prescribed by the Governor in Council.

(4) Any amount that is agreed upon or awarded in respect of the compulsory taking or using of land under this section or that is paid for a transfer or grant of land pursuant to this section shall be paid to the Receiver General for the use and benefit of the band or for the use and benefit of any Indian who is entitled to compensation or payment as a result of the exercise of the powers referred to in subs. (1).

Under the above provision, the Governor In Council is empowered to authorize a transfer or grant of reserve lands to a province for public purposes. It was under that law which the Government of Canada purported to transfer the lands designated for the road to the Province of Manitoba.

Moreover, it is to be noted that in authorizing the transfer, the Government of Canada did not act arbitrarily. The Order-In-Council recites that the Indian locatees, whose Lands are affected by the road, have approved the transfer without payment of compensation by reason of the advantage of the road to the Peguis Band and Indian locatees. The consent of the band was evidenced by a band Council resolution dated January 20th, 1958, in which the band resolved "to transfer to the province of Manitoba, the highway through the Peguis Indian Reserve, as shown on a plan of survey ... etc."

In my opinion, the legal effect of the above actions and documents was to transfer the lands taken for road purposes from the ownership of the Government of Canada to the ownership of the Province of Manitoba. The band Council resolution itself refers to a "transfer" to the "Province of Manitoba"; the Order-in-Council makes reference to the facts that the Province of Manitoba has "applied for" the land, and recites the "transfer" referred to in the band resolutions; and further, the Order-in-Council consents to the "taking" of the lands by the Province of Manitoba and the "transfer" of the "administration and control" of the lands to the province; finally, s. 35 of the *Indian Act* enables the Government of Canada to authorize a "transfer or grant" of lands to a province for public purposes. These words and phrases all connote the notion of a transfer of ownership in the land from the Government of Canada to the Province of Manitoba.

Furthermore, in my opinion, the bridge clearly formed part of the lands. The plan filed in the Land Titles Office shows the road crossing the Fisher River. Obviously, the utility of the road would be very much reduced if there was no bridge across the river. The bridge was open to everyone, including those who did not live on the Peguis Reserve, and it was owned by a public authority, namely, the Province of Manitoba. In my view, the road, including the bridge, was public property. I am in full agreement with the learned trial judge who stated at p. 310 "In my opinion the bridge clearly is part of the roadway which was transferred to the Province and is therefore public property."

The notion that the road and bridge are not public property but band property, rests on Treaty #1 made between Her Majesty the Queen and the Chippewa and Cree Indians on August 3rd, 1871, which created the St. Peters Reserve in Manitoba. By that treaty, Her Majesty the Queen "agrees and undertakes to lay aside and reserve for the sole and exclusive use of the Indians" the lands in question. The subsequent treaties reserved to the Crown the right to acquire portions of the lands for public purposes upon paying compensation to the Indians. However, Treaty #1 contained no such clause and accordingly it may be arguable that the Crown could not legally acquire any of the lands for public purposes. The lands would forever be inalienable and remain the property of the Indians on the reserve.

In 1907 the St. Peters Reserve surrendered their lands to the Government of Canada, and between 1908 and 1912, the Indians on the reserve moved from St. Peters to their present location in the Peguis Reserve. However, the legality of this surrender was called into question by the majority of a Royal Commission appointed by the Manitoba Government in 1911. In 1914, the Attorney General of Canada laid an information in the Exchequer Court of Canada alleging that the surrender was improper and should be overturned. However, the government had second thoughts about this action and passed legislation validating the titles to the land in the former St. Peters Reserve which by then had been acquired by non-Indians. Mr. J. Gallo, a historian and former director of the Aboriginal Rights Research Centre, now manager of Treaty Land Entitlement and Claims for the Lands Branch, Department of Indian Affairs, Manitoba Region, was called as a defence witness. He referred to certain studies which had been conducted, concluding that the St. Peters surrender was illegal, and he said it was arguable that the members of the Peguis Band still retained their rights under the original Treaty #1, and by virtue of that treaty still had the exclusive right to the reserve lands, no part of which could be transferred to the Province of Manitoba, or to anybody else for that matter.

The studies to which Mr. Gallo referred were not placed before the court, and neither the trial judge nor I have had the benefit of the detailed reasoning which lead to the conclusion that the St.

Peters surrender was illegal, and that the provisions of Treaty #1 apply to the present Peguis Reserve. I am obviously not now in a position to find that the St. Peters surrender was illegal, and even if it was, it may not necessarily follow that the full provisions of the treaty, including the exclusive land rights claimed by the Indians, would apply to the lands on the Peguis Reserve. The Peguis Reserve was not created by Treaty #1, but rather by an Order-in-Council passed in 1930 affecting lands separate and distant from those in the original St. Peters Reserve. There was nothing in the Order-In-Council precluding the taking of lands for public purposes pursuant to s. 35 of the *Indian Act*. It may well be that the present members of the Peguis Reserve can maintain claims to the old lands on the St. Peters Reserve, but it may not necessarily follow that they could claim rights beyond those conferred in the *Indian Act* to the lands on which they presently reside in the Peguis Reserve.

Moreover, the point was not argued, but I raise the question: Would the granting of the "sole and exclusive use" of the reserve land for the Indians preclude the type of transfer which occurred here? As I have said, there was no attempt to arbitrarily seize the lands for the road from the Indians; in fact, they agreed to the transfer because they recognized what must have been obvious to all, that it was clearly in their best interests to have the road go through the reserve. Surely, even if they did have the exclusive use of the property, this would not prevent the Indians from agreeing to give up part of that right, particularly when they stood to gain and benefit from the transfer.

In any event, I cannot make a finding on the material before me that the band owned the bridge; all the evidence before the court points to the opposite conclusion that the bridge was public property.

Counsel for the defence submitted that the accused had acted with colour of right because they honestly believed that the bridge was band property, which they had every right to destroy. Actually, it was only Chief Stevenson who professed any such belief, and at best it could only [be] applicable in his case. His belief was based on his knowledge of the history of the St. Peters surrender and a 595 page legal opinion which was said to have supported the belief. That opinion was not put before the court, and it is not clear to what extent Mr. Stevenson had read and digested the opinion. Still, I suppose that the history of the surrender and the legal opinion might have formed the basis for an honest belief that the road, and the bridge in particular, did, indeed, belong to the Indian band. On the other hand, a person with knowledge of the history and the report might only have concluded that a reasonable argument could be made for the proposition that the band owned the bridge. Indeed, Mr. Gallo referred to the proposition as "arguable" without expressing an unshakable and firm belief that it was correct. It was for the trial judge in this case to say what the true belief and attitude of Chief Stevenson was. He dealt with the matter in this way:

> Can it be said that Stevenson had an honest belief that Peguis Band owned the bridge? He was aware of the Order-In-Council establishing the reserve on its present site. He was aware of the Order-In-Council granting the Harwill Road to the Province. He was aware of the band's request to the Province of Manitoba by letter of May 15th, 1973, and November 4th, 1980, concerning the state of the bridge. I quote from the letter of May 15th, 1973, from the band to the province of Manitoba: "Harwill Road — Plan 4018 — definitely Provincial responsibility. Roads not maintained as often as should be as school buses travelling on it. Bridge in very bad shape, dangerous."
>
> The evidence does not establish, and I am not convinced on a balance of probabilities, that Stevenson had an honest belief that the bridge was the property of the Peguis Reserve.

Counsel for the defence was critical of this passage, saying that mere awareness of the Orders-In-Council and the statement that the road was the provincial responsibility, did not lead inexorably to the conclusion that Chief Stevenson had no honest belief that the road and bridge belonged to the band. Perhaps not, but they are surely cogent factors which the learned trial judge was entitled to take into account in deciding the credibility of Chief Stevenson's statement of belief. He might very well have added the point that the band had been calling upon, and clearly expected the Provincial Government to replace the bridge. Why would they expect the government to replace a bridge which was not government, but band property? However, for my purposes, the most important consideration is that the learned trial judge had the opportunity to actually see and hear Chief Stevenson testify and to judge first hand, in the light of all of the factors pointing to public ownership, whether Chief Stevenson really held the belief which he professed to hold. The trial judge had made his finding in this regard and it would not be appropriate for me to interfere with that finding. The defence of colour of right must fail.

■

David Confronts Goliath: The Innu of Ungava versus the NATO Alliance†

THE INNU OF UNGAVA: THE CONFRONTATION

Word spread quickly around the village. The Pasteens lost no time. Hurriedly Sheshatshit's oldest couple put on their coats and rainboots. A daughter tried to dissuade them from going. It was cold and wet, the eighty-year-olds might get sick. But Mary and Michel Pasteen would not listen. Time was running out for their people.

Within a few hours Mary Pasteen was shuffling beside her nearly blind husband, clutching him for support. The Pasteens, and seventy other residents of Sheshatshit, boldly walked past a startled security guard at an entrance to the air-force base at Goose Bay. Before the guard could close the gates, the Innu were inside. Some sat down when police tried to move them. Others, like the Pasteens, stood firmly on the runway, refusing to leave until they met the NATO officials who were deciding whether to establish an $800-million Tactical Fighter Weapons Training Centre in the Innu homeland. The protestors had come to tell NATO their land is not for sale, and Canada has no right to give it away.

Hundreds of Innu have since been arrested for civil disobedience. Six times security at the base was breached.

Throughout fall 1988, tents were set up at the end of the runway and on a bombing range in western Labrador. Innu families cooked caribou, trapped, and tried to live as normally as possible as the jet bombers screamed overhead.

This did little to move the hearts and minds of government and military officials, but it increased public awareness of the issue. Canadians and people elsewhere who'd never heard of the Innu are learning how determined they are to hold on to their land and way of life. Suddenly, a people who want only to live in peace, who, until the 1950s, were living a nomadic, hunter-gatherer existence, have found themselves in the limelight, at the centre of such issues as war and peace and the rights of minority peoples to retain their cultures in the face of the military-industrial complex.

"Innu" means "human being." Perhaps at one time, many, many years ago, we thought we were the only human beings. We lived in a world dominated by animals and their spirits. The animals fed and clothed us, and we showed our gratitude by treating them with respect and honour.

Many confuse us with the Inuit; because the name is similar. It's just a coincidence that their name for "the people" is so much like ours. We are not Inuit, we are a different people, even a different race.

We are called "Montagnais-Naskapi" by French and English speakers. We were first called "Montagnais" by the French explorers because we hunted in the mountains (*les montagnes*). The "Naskapi," which conveys the meaning "uncivilized," has been incorrectly applied to those "Montagnais" who had less-frequent contact with European society.

Today there are 10,000 Innu living in thirteen villages in northeastern Quebec and Labrador. It is hard to know how many of us there were before the Europeans came. Many of our people died from diseases brought from Europe, such as measles, tuberculosis, and smallpox. Our numbers are increasing now, but collectively we are far less healthy and well-off than most Canadians, and much worse off than we were when we were running our own affairs.

"Nitassinan" is the word for "our land." It is a vast territory, stretching from the mouth of the Saguenay River to the Strait of Belle Isle, from Lac St-Jean to Ungava Bay, as far as the Atlantic coast. Our villages are called Utshimassit (Davis Inlet), Sheshatshit, Pakuat-shipu (St-Augustin), Uanaman-shipu (La Romaine), Nutashkuan, Ekuanitshu (Mingan), Pessamiu (Betsiamites), Maliotenam, Uashat (Sept-Iles), Matimekush (near Schefferville), Kawawachekamach (10 km/6 miles from Schefferville), Les Escoumins, and Quiatchouan (Pointe Bleue), near Lac St-Jean.

We are one of the last hunting-gathering cultures in North America, and just thirty years ago industrial developments on our land dealt the final blow to our nomadic way of life.

† Daniel Ashini, "David Confronts Goliath: The Innu of Ungava versus the NATO Alliance" in Boyce Richardson, ed., *Drumbeat. Anger and Renewal in Indian Country* (Toronto: Summerhill Press, 1989) 43 at 43–47, 51, 52–54, 58–68. Reproduced by permission of The Assembly of First Nations.

Despite hundreds of years of contact with the European newcomers who came to our land, we did not try to live like they did. We adapted those aspects of European society that were compatible with our own. The fur trade, for example, brought new tools to our culture, but it did not significantly change the way we lived on the land. We adopted different religions and have learned new languages, but we did not give up our valued travelling ways until our land was seized for industrial use.

For hundreds of years after the Europeans came to Nitassinan we continued to spend most of the year hunting, travelling long distances on foot and by canoe throughout the interior of our homeland. The pattern changed slightly when we started coming out to the coast each summer to visit the priests and to trade. Like clockwork, however, every fall we went back to the interior of our homeland, where southern society generally left us alone, showing little interest in our hunting way of life until they wanted our land.

Thirty years ago Nitassinan was suddenly in high demand for logging, mining, and hydroelectric development. Paper mills destroyed much of our forests. Iron-ore mining, hydroelectric projects on our rivers in Quebec, and the huge development of Churchill Falls displaced many of us from our hunting and fishing territories.

A railway was constructed at Sept-Iles to ship out the iron ore, and many airports were built, without consulting us, much less with our consent. The more territory we lost, the more difficult it was to continue hunting and fishing in the interior of Nitassinan. The only compensation we received for the theft of our land was welfare cheques and government allowances, both of which impoverished us materially and spiritually, while the Canadians who handed out these "social assistance" pittances profited greatly from our natural resources.

Dr. Hugh Grant, a political economist from the University of Toronto, estimates that, between 1975 and 1987, $14 billion was made from resource development in Nitassinan. The Innu have paid the human costs.

Our rivers are now dammed, fish-spawning grounds have been destroyed, caribou and other animals have drowned or moved away because their feeding grounds are now under water.

We are no longer nomads, but we are still Innu and continue to hunt and camp in Nitassinan's interior. We retain our language, our identity, and the values that are so dear to us. Many of us are happy only when we are living in the interior of Nitassinan, which we call "nutshimit." Our villages are plagued with social problems that vanish when we regain contact with the land.

Divided by a Stroke of the Pen

There are some who think there are two Innu territories, one in Quebec and one in Labrador. That's because, in 1927, Britain carved up its administration of Nitassinan and gave Newfoundland control of the eastern part, while Quebec got control of the rest. This imposed settlement had nothing to do with us; we are one people. With the stroke of pen on paper in England we were suddenly, and without our knowledge, administratively separated. Today our people are jailed if they stray across this border to hunt on the "other" side. The other side of what? We are one nation and will never recognize a line drawn by foreigners across our country.

The caribou, so central to our way of life, recognize no boundaries in Nitassinan. Caribou meat is the staple of our diet, the staff of our life. The other animals are important, too, but not as important as the caribou.

The caribou hunt is of immense social significance to us. Caribou brought into an Innu camp carries much prestige to the successful hunter. The meat is distributed communally, and the bone-marrow grease is eaten in a ritual during the mukushan (feast) that follows a particularly successful hunt. The caribou hunt and the rituals surrounding it reaffirm Innu values and reinvigorate the Innu spirit. Our life as a hunting people cannot be lived in the static boundaries of the village.

Every lake, river, and mountain in Nitassinan has a name in Innu-aimun, our language, but you will see few of these names on most maps. The maps have been made by the European newcomers who ignore our ownership of this land. It is heartbreaking to hear our children refer to places by these European names — foreign words plastered recently on places that have had Innu names for thousands of years. It is as if we have become strangers in our own land. We have become the foreigners. Our children learn the new names in school, and are taught to forget they are Innu. They grow up without pride in who they are, and more sadly, confused about who they should be.

You would not have to go back many years to see how happy and proud our people were in their homeland. We travelled freely to the beautiful lakes, rivers, and mountains of Nitassinan. Now, we feel like prisoners kept captive by a foreign government.

. . . .

From Cartier's time to Cabot's time, four hundred years of contact with Europeans, and we were still nomads with sovereignty over our homeland. It is only since our land and our sovereignty has been lost that the life that Cabot hoped we could maintain has been taken from us, and our existence made into a pain to be endured, or not.

. . . .

We continued our nomadic way of life, untroubled, until the middle of this century. That's when the descendants of the newcomers insisted on establishing their sovereignty over our homeland.

Now we are arrested for doing things we have done in Nitassinan for thousands of years. We are arrested if we hunt out of the seasons established by provincial laws. We are arrested for trespassing on land the settlers claim as their own. In some parts of Nitassinan, our people are even arrested if they cut firewood without permits. There is no end to the harassment we meet at the hands of those who now claim to govern Nitassinan.

. . . .

The Innu: A Classically Colonized People

What has been done to the Innu is a typical act of colonization, repeated on every continent on earth when an industrially developed society decides it has an interest in bringing "civilization" to a different culture. Sometimes the colonizers have benign goals, sometimes otherwise, but the effects are much the same.

The dictionary definition of "to colonize" is "to take possession of a relatively undeveloped country and settle one's surplus population there." We have shared our land with Europe's surplus population and were happy to do so, but we never gave them control over it. That has been taken, without treaty or land-rights agreement.

We Innu are a distinct people with a single language, a single indivisible national homeland, a single culture and national identity. This is how the United Nations defines a "people." The United Nations Covenant on Civil and Political Rights states: "All Peoples have the right to self-determination. By virtue of that right they freely determine their political status and freely pursue their economic, social and cultural development."

Canada, a signatory to this covenant, nevertheless refuses to recognize the Innu right to self-determination. It is as though Canadians don't think we are capable of running our own economic, social, and cultural institutions. This is an arrogant and racist assumption. It was well articulated by Labrador official Walter Rockwood in his 1950s report on the terms of Newfoundland's union with Canada: "Civilization is on the northward march, and for the Eskimo and Indian there is no escape ... the only course now open ... is to fit him as soon as may be to take his full place as a citizen in our society. The Indians of Labrador are still more primitive than the Eskimos ... because of less intimate contact with our civilization." He wrote this in a royal commission report about the terms of Newfoundland's union with Canada. Rockwood's arrogance indicates how little attention the rights of native people got in the transfer of Newfoundland from colony to province.

Rockwood's "northern march of civilization" has had devastating consequences for the Innu. The suicide rate for our people in Labrador and their Inuit neighbours is five times higher than that of Canadians (non-natives), and twice as high as that of other native people in Canada. The suicide rate is even higher among our young people, aged fifteen to twenty-four. The rate in northern Labrador is seventeen times the national average, and seven times higher than for native youth elsewhere. We have an exceptionally high accident rate, and many of these accidents, often fatal, are linked to alcohol addiction. We have no statistics for Innu communities on the north shore of the St. Lawrence, but we suspect they are similar.

This kind of self-destructive behaviour was unknown to the Innu until the middle of this century, when we lost control of our land and our lives. Dr. Kay Wotten presented the above figures to the Canadian Public Health Association in 1983 after two years of study on the northeast coast of Nitassinan. She concluded: "It is the plight of a people whose social framework has been gravely damaged and its fragile economy ruined leaving the young with a stultifying sense of worthlessness; a culture whose customs and traditions have been mocked."

Our customs and traditions are mocked by the colonizers, so much so that many of our own people have been convinced they are inferior. Such psychological and emotional suffering will end only when we regain our independence.

One of the greatest psychological blows to our people came when we settled into the poorly constructed houses built for us by the colonial governments in the 1950s. The Innu at Pukuatshipu hung on to their cherished tents and nomadic life-style longer than did the rest of us. They didn't move into houses until 1971, and that year all of their newborns died. Dr. Wotten says we found the transition difficult because we were "forced to live on reservations or settlements with inadequate sanitation and housing; left without [our] traditional medicine which was scorned and rejected by Whites and provided with a diet poorly suited to [our] needs."

Since we abandoned our nomadic way of life the colonial governments in Nitassinan have relentlessly worked to assimilate the Innu, and that is what is destroying us. We cannot be turned into clones of the European settlers. This is how assimilation was explained in the government's 1959–60 annual report on Labrador: "Indians must be taught the three R's, and will also need vocational training, but it would be naive to think that this will automatically solve all the problems overnight. As with Indians elsewhere there are deeply rooted psychological problems to be overcome before the process of integration is complete."

Yes, we have something deeply rooted in our psychology — we are Innu hunters and gatherers, and are proud of it. Hunting is the form of living that lies at the core of our identity as a people, that animates our social relationships, and that, for thousands of years, has breathed life into our people. We are offended by those who have categorized our hunting existence as primitive. The policies of the European newcomers in North America are racist in that they consider themselves superior to us.

. . . .

In the bush, where many Innu families spend up to half the year, our values and traditions are re-established. The beauty of Nitassinan is a source of great joy. In the autumn the country is ablaze in beautiful colours, and berries grow in profusion on the ground. The warmth of our tents and closeness of our families provides a happy refuge from the cold. We watch the spring come in all its glory, and await the honking sounds of geese returning from the south.

This is why our life in "nutshimit," the interior of our homeland, is so special to the Innu, why we have such a deep attachment to Nitassinan. This is how I expressed our aspirations to the FEARO panel on October 13, 1986: "We want to keep the door open to our children, our grandchildren, for them to be able to pursue the traditions of our ancestors in the interior of Nitassinan. The great many Innu who continue to go into the country each fall and spring will be our lifeline to the past and to the future, a lifeline that will be one of the greatest importance to us all in permitting us to pass on to future generations the great wealth of knowledge about the animals and the land that is our heritage."

The Terrifying Militarization of Nitassinan

The militarization of our homeland for jet-bomber training by the NATO air forces threatens to cut us off forever from our vital lifeline. What has been done to our homeland in the past is all bad enough. This development threatens to wipe us out.

For the past eight years Innu land has been used by an increasing number of European air forces to practise low-level flying. Jet bombers, weighing 27 tonnes (30 tons), travel 900 km/h (540 mph) just 30 m (100 feet) above the ground.

When they pass overhead, the canvas of our tents ripples, the trees sway, and animals flee in fright. The jets travel faster than the speed of sound.

Sometimes we see the huge war machines a fraction of a second before the sound roars over us. We then suffer what is known as the "startle" effect. The suddenness of the jet's arrival, and the deafening noise, take us by surprise and our hearts race as our bodies react in panic. The children cry; our elders clutch their chests in fear. This is how the colonizers now attack our peaceful life in the interior.

The Americans built the air-force base at Goose Bay in 1942 but used it as a stopover point for flights headed overseas. Their aircraft didn't fly over Innu in the bush. The British used Vulcan bombers to practise low-level flying in the 1950s, but those jets didn't fly as low or as fast as the new ones do. Few Innu families hunting in the bush ever heard or saw the Vulcans. Since 1980, however, almost every Innu family who has camped and hunted in the interior has been terrorized by British, Dutch, and German Phantoms, Tornados, and Alpha jets. The number of flights increases every year, from 3,000 sorties in 1984 to 7,000 in 1988, and a projected 40,000 in 1992.

It is hard to imagine what it is like to be overflown by one of these bombers unless you have experienced it. Here are just a few of the comments made by Innu to the FEARO panel that visited our communities in 1986. Ambroise Lalo's comment may make you smile, but try to imagine the terror he describes: "Some of our brothers from Natashquan get so afraid, in fact, that they run away. In fact, one of them was so terrified that he lost his false teeth while he was running away ... and when a man comes back from a hunting trip, he often tells us that he almost killed a caribou, but that caribou was scared by a plane flying over, and the Indian is very sad since he cannot feed his family."

Mrs. Wapistan, La Romaine: "I cannot express what I felt the first time I heard such a tremendous noise. I was so shaken up that I even forgot about my children and my husband."

George Gabriel, Schefferville: "To see them so low means that we cannot go on the water with our canoes anymore. We are afraid that they will capsize."

George Gregoire, Davis Inlet: "We do not even hear them once they are coming and suddenly a big noise hits when they are over the camp."

If you think we are overreacting because we are not used to noise, perhaps you will more readily believe a former Canadian member of parliament, Keith Penner, who was flown over by a jet bomber in Wales. His comments were quoted by Bernard Cleary at the Schefferville hearing of FEARO: "I had no warning.... I was pinned to the ground, shaking all over. It is not the sort of experience that one would like to have twice in one's lifetime."

A journalist, Marie Wadden, wrote in the *Montreal Gazette* that she was overflown while on assignment in Nitassinan: "Five minutes after the plane passed over, I was still aware of the painful pounding in my chest. I was inside a tent when the jet came."

We fear Innu families will stop going into the bush if this flight training continues. They will stop going out of fear, but also, because the animals and plant life they depend on will disappear. This is already happening, as Guy Bellefleur told FEARO: "Over the last few years the game we can catch has decreased because of the military manoeuvres of NATO.... Since these manoeuvres began the Indians have been disturbed. Their game and wildlife has been disturbed, and many other Indians will come and give testimony ... we are faced with the same problems."

James Pasteen of Davis Inlet said: "All wildlife will be driven away, lakes will be polluted, freshwater fish will not be any good to eat, there will be increased health problems."

If the Innu stop going into the bush our skills and knowledge, built up over thousands of years, will be lost.

Dr. David Suzuki, scientist and television personality, has expressed his solidarity with the Innu, and warned us at a meeting in Sheshatshit in December 1988: "If you lose your land and way of life, you will disappear. You may live in towns but you won't be Innu anymore." Many of us listened to his warning with sinking hearts. How true this is. Every day since these military activities began we have felt our land and way of life slipping farther and farther away.

Canadian Government Committed to Our Destruction

NATO's proposed $800-million Tactical Fighter Weapons Training Centre will go either to Goose Bay or to a site in Turkey. We would prefer the training site goes nowhere, for we have no wish for the Turks to suffer as we are suffering. Indeed, even if NATO chooses Turkey, Canada plans to increase the number of fighter jets training in Nitassinan through the signing of bilateral agreements with its European allies. Regardless, therefore, of the NATO decision, Canada is committed to a policy that will destroy Innu culture and lead to the death of many of our people. The military users have already carved out two large flying zones in Nitassinan, totalling 100,000 sq. km (38,000 square miles). Three-quarters of the southern zone is on the Quebec side of the colonial border, while most of the northern zone is in Newfoundland jurisdiction. We reiterate, both zones are in Nitassinan, and all Innu who camp and hunt within these flying zones are affected by this activity.

We have great concern for the health of the animals under our care in Nitassinan, especially the caribou herds that we depend on so much. We and our Inuit neighbours have been the caretakers of the largest caribou herd in the world, the George River herd, and we are afraid that low-level flying may destroy it. A workshop on caribou held in Alaska, in November 1987, was presented with evidence that the herd has been declining at a rate of 5 per cent a year since 1984, and attributes this to a decline in the females' physical condition, deterioration of the calving-ground habitat, delay in births, and several other factors. What was once thought to be a healthy herd of 600,000 animals is now estimated to be just half that.

Biologists and Innu hunters found caribou that appear to have starved to death. We know that, when caribou are frightened, they will not stop to eat, but will continue to move, day after day, until they feel safe.

At the FEARO hearings in Montreal, Alain Methot, speaking on behalf of L'Association des Pourvoyeurs du Nouveau Quebec (commercial harvesters of caribou), said the George River herd has changed its migrating habits since the low-level jets came. He says the caribou are thinner and less healthy than they used to be. Methot told the commission the caribou used to travel 8 to 15 km (5 to

10 miles) per day. Now he says they are travelling 50 and 65 km (30 and 40 miles) a day, without stopping to eat.

We are not satisfied with the scientific studies that have been carried out for governments and the Department of Defence. They have concentrated on a sedentary herd in the Red Wine Mountains, rather than on the great migratory George River herd. No cardio-vascular studies have been done to determine the physical effects low-flying jets have on the caribou. We can see, however, that serious damage is being done.

Biologists say the caribou are starving because they are too numerous and have eaten out their grazing grounds. We disagree. We believe there are other areas where the animals can graze, but they are afraid to go. Here is the testimony of a hunter, James Pasteen, in Utshimassit (Davis Inlet): "There is a good place for feeding grounds in southern Labrador but caribou will not migrate there because of the noise of the jets and the gas that has dropped on the ground."

The military says it can avoid flying over the caribou when they are mating and calving. This promise cannot be met. How can inexperienced young pilots recognize and avoid mating caribou from the cockpits of jets travelling 900 km/h? Even if certain zones are off-limits at certain times, occasionally pilots will surely stray off course.

The military also claims it can avoid Innu hunting camps. This too is impossible, since the Innu don't stay in one place when they are hunting. Innu hunter Guy Bellefleur explained this to members of the FEARO panel: "The Montagnais territory is a land without limits, without borders, so in order to survive we have to be nomads. We always have to wander and seek our subsistence and this is why we must disperse. We cannot be too numerous at a given lake or next to a given river."

The prospects of Nitassinan being turned into a theatre of war causes great anguish to our people. Father Alexis Jouveneau, a priest in La Romaine, told the FEARO panel his Innu parishioners are very concerned: "They are upset and there is a collective psychosis which is undermining the heart and way of life of Indians here on the lower north shore ... you might as well build a psychiatric clinic right here and it will soon be overfilled."

Guy Bellefleur told the panel: "The Indians cannot change their mental set-up.... Even though they have set down close to the river, they keep their mentality ... of ages past where they have travelled throughout their territory."

And Cajetan Rich of Davis Inlet told FEARO: "We were taught how to survive and live in any kind of threatening weather. We have been taught where to find food, and when to expect caribou.... We were also taught what to do in cases of emergency.... Now we see our land as a possible place where war practices are going on and that is a threat to our way of life and our culture."

Innu Land to Be Bombed

NATO planners want to establish six bombing ranges in Nitassinan, in addition to one that already exists. Four of the bombing ranges would enable NATO jets to use non-explosive concrete missiles for target practice. These kinds of missiles have already caused environmental damage on the existing bombing range in western Labrador. A young Innu hunter, Bart Penashue, and his cousin went to the bombing range in fall 1988 to see first hand what was happening to the land there and said: "Some of those bombs weigh over a thousand pounds, and they make huge craters in the ground, one we saw was over seven feet deep. They drop into rivers, and destroy beaver dams."

Three additional bombing ranges would be required by NATO for live weapons training. The bombing range at Primrose Lake in northern Alberta and Saskatchewan is 1.2 million hectares (3 million acres) in size and native people are not allowed to hunt, trap, and fish inside its boundaries.

The low-level jet flights are terrifying enough; we oppose all of the other activities that would accompany a NATO combat centre. We demand the land already seized for the existing bombing range be returned to us.

Enormous pressures will be brought to bear on the resources of Nitassinan by the visiting military personnel. It is estimated 30,000 European airforce personnel will pass through Goose Bay each year that the NATO centre is open. Already the visiting Europeans are hunting and fishing in Nitassinan, and even the residents of Goose Bay are complaining about this. What wildlife survives the low-level flying will quickly be destroyed by over-hunting and -fishing. We are also concerned about the impact 30,000 single male transients will have on the community closest to the base. Some young women in Sheshatshit are already complaining of sexual abuse from personnel at the military base.

The purpose of low-level flight training is to teach NATO pilots how to avoid enemy radar detection in wartime. More than 97 of these NATO jets (which cost an estimated $40 million each) crashed in the countries where they were training in 1988, and 100 people in West Germany lost their lives as a result of some of these accidents. In West Germany the jets are not allowed to fly below 75 metres (250 feet); yet over our land they are permitted to fly much lower. The Germans want to export the noise and danger here, and Canada has opened her arms.

Since jet training started in Nitassinan several jets have already crashed. We fear a forest fire may be started by one of these accidents. This would be ecologically disastrous since it takes 90 years for trees to grow in our scant subarctic forests.

The bombing exercises planned for the proposed NATO centre will use laser technology. The Canadian Public Health Association (CPHA), which studied the problem of fighter jet training over Nitassinan in 1987, says this is dangerous: "The output of a laser is often invisible to the eye, making accidental exposure more difficult to control. Exposure to living tissue can result in temporary or permanent damage to the tissue."

We oppose the use of lasers in our homeland, just as we oppose air-to-air combat training. During air-to-air combat, jets launched from one airport in Nitassinan play the "enemy" role, as other jets fight them at medium and high altitudes, using laser and other sophisticated technology to simulate combat and to show those on the ground which side is "winning". Nitassinan will be bombarded with sonic booms while this supersonic gamesmanship is carried out.

The CPHA concluded that sonic booms could be dangerous to animal and human health in Nitassinan as well, and recommended they be avoided until a full environmental review is completed.

The government has ignored this recommendation and supersonic air-to-air combat training, which produces sonic booms, has been permitted since February 1988.

The CPHA says the health of the Innu and Inuit in northern Quebec and Labrador has been overlooked in the planning of this development: "The Government of Canada did not adequately consider the rights and welfare of the aboriginal people of the Labrador area in any significant way when the air base was established at Goose Bay nor in its subsequent development. The aboriginal rights and welfares should have been considered in this process.... It should be recognized that it is the native people who may be at the greatest risk for bearing the costs of the development. Their cultural identity is linked to the use or abuse of the land."

Our Security Threatened by Defence Policies

Canada justifies its action under the guise of doing its part for world peace. In fact, many believe the kind of training that takes place in Nitassinan will harm the cause of peaceful relations in the world. If Canada and NATO persist in this policy, let them train over some of Canada's large national parks. We don't understand why we should be sacrificed for Canada's defence policy. We had nothing to do with any of the world's wars, and want nothing to do with any future wars. It is our security that is being threatened by the defence policies of other nations. This is unjust and immoral.

The International Federation for Human Rights sent a mission to Nitassinan and concluded in 1988 that the Innu are being denied certain internationally recognized, collective and individual human rights.

We have been totally left out of the planning and decision-making surrounding the militarization of our ancestral home-land even though it threatens irrevocably to change our lives....

. . . .

Nutshimit is our grocery store, the place we go to get our food, and it is the most nourishing food we can eat. The hard work of hunting and keeping warm in the bush is healthy for us, physically and psychologically. An Oblate priest, Father Jim Roche, described life in an Innu hunting camp to the *Montreal Gazette* on June 25, 1988: "In the bush, life is full of real struggle. It's hard to get wood and meat, but after a day of walking in snow that is soft and up to your knees, you appreciate more the simple things, like heat from the tent stove, tea, and a hot meal. In the village, that struggle is gone."

... Broken down by the policies of the colonial government, some of our people have stopped fighting against the lies and have stopped respecting our traditions because they have come to believe these practices are "primitive."

Gain for Others — Suffering for Us

The military use of our homeland cannot be justified. The people who will benefit economically are the descendants of European newcomers, and a small assimilated Métis population, who look forward to making their fortunes by serving the pilots-in-training and their military support staff.

Those who will suffer, and are already suffering the negative effects, are the 10,000 Innu and several thousand Inuit who depend on the resources of their homelands. Whose concerns are the most legitimate? At FEARO hearings in Sheshatshit, Lyla MacEachern, the wife of an Innu hunter, put it simply and eloquently:

> Whose lifestyles are more valued; who as a people are more valued? In the past, it has been quite clear that, as a people, the Innu have been the least important. My father-in-law, Matthew Ben Andrew, died several years ago. His land, his place in Nitassinan, which he considered the heritage for his children and grandchildren, was in the area flooded over and today still underwater because of the Churchill Falls hydro project. Other Innu who shared this area in Nitassinan lost canoes, traps, and other supplies because they were never even informed that this so-called development was going to happen, much less invited to take part in a process like this one [FEARO] to discuss what the outcome and mitigative measures of such a project might be.

Sixty-four-year-old Manian Michel, an Innu mother of twelve, could barely contain her anger when she spoke to the FEARO panel:

> Do you have any shame that you should come to our land and face us like you are now, requesting that we give up our land to you? You never, never stop what you are doing now, sitting in front of us trying to get our land. We will never give it up. I am very angry when I see white people, such as yourselves, looking for us to give up our birthright. I am very angry today. How many times have the Innu come to you to look for land, to look for anything?
>
> Even the Innu, in its despicable condition, in its wretched condition, never come to you for anything. Do you hate the Innu, do you want to kill the Innu?
>
> You have killed us in many respects. We have nothing. No animals, there are no animals near us, and we cannot even drink our water, we cannot get wood without a permit.

We have been accused of using this military issue to push for a generous land-claim settlement. The day a land-claim deal is signed between our people and the Canadian government will be one of the saddest days of our lives. Many Canadians think the land-claims process is a fair and just one. It is not. We will be forced to relinquish our claim to Nitassinan forever if we accept compensation for the seizure of our lands. The most we can hope for is to receive an adequate land base to continue our hunting way of life, and money to develop the few resources that will come with such a land base. We must depend on the charity of Canada, that is what it amounts to. We must go cap in hand to see what crumbs will be given to us. This reliance on charity was created by their policies and ambitions, not ours.

A lot has been said about the James Bay settlement. It has been called "just." Much of the homeland of the Cree has been flooded and more flooding will take place when other hydro projects are developed. Only time will tell if the Cree people have enough land and resources to defend and maintain their way of life. The James Bay settlement has proven, however, that we are quite capable of running our own economic and social systems.

Many of our people, the elders especially, oppose relinquishing title to Nitassinan and are highly skeptical about Canada's intention of offering us a fair settlement.

Some of our young feel we have no choice. Canada is going ahead with development on our homeland, whether or not our grievances are addressed. We have been told it will take ten to fifteen years of negotiations to resolve our land claims. What will be left of Nitassinan in ten to fifteen years' time? Will the majestic George River caribou herd be intact? Will our language and culture survive another decade of colonial domination? Will the spirit of the Innu endure that long, or will it be broken? Maybe this is what Canada is waiting for.

The Innu will continue to use civil disobedience and will continue the fight for our rights in Nitassinan. We will continue to appeal to Canadians' sense of justice. We will not simply disappear off the cultural face of this world without a fight.

■

R. v. Ashini†

[IGLOLIORTE P.C.J.:]

The four accused, Daniel Ashini, Elizabeth Penashue, Penote Benedict Michel and Peter Penashue appeared for trial last week on separate informations, all charged with an offence alleging that:

> On or about the 15th day of September 1988, A.D., at or near Happy Valley/Goose Bay, Labrador, Province of Newfoundland, did wilfully interfere with the lawful operation of property, to wit: The Canadian Forces Base Goose Bay, contrary to Section 387(1)(c) of the Criminal Code of Canada, thereby committing an offence contrary to s. 387 (4)(b) of the Criminal Code of Canada.

Thirty-four Informations, both under the *Criminal Code of Canada* for adults, and under *Young Offenders Act* for young people, have been laid against more than sixty people over a dozen different dates.

On one charge alone from September 22, 1988, forty-nine people appear on an Information.

Today, we are dealing with four charges. I will leave it to the Crown upon hearing my judgment whether they will proceed with the mass of other charges. I will not be deciding in this judgment whether to summarily dismiss or continue with any charges beyond these four.

The evidence shows that on September 15, 1988 the four people here were part of a larger group who collectively walked beyond a checkpoint gate leading [onto] the part of the Goose Bay Runway called an "apron." Since they hadn't been given permission by any airport or military authorities, they were arrested, charged and removed by the R.C.M.P.

The issue to be decided is whether the Crown has proved the constituent elements of the offence. In coming to a decision I must consider any defence allowed by Canadian law for the accused which might negate criminality.

I will, as well, refer to relevant issues raised by Crown or defence in reaching my conclusion about this criminal charge.

Since we know the present users and occupiers of the land at the Base, Crown had little difficulty presenting a *prima facie* case.

From precedent given to me to consider, the immediate question is whether the "color of right" defence put forward by Mr. Olthuis will be sufficient to be considered as satisfying the definition of "an honest belief in a state of facts, which if it existed, would be a legal justification or excuse." Creaghan, p. 453.

In my opinion, Mr. Olthuis has presented a valid defence and also a successful one. We are not dealing with any land which has been the subject of divestiture through treaties, as under the *Indian Act*, R.S.C. 1970, c. I-6. Each of these four persons based their belief of ownership on an honest belief on reasonable grounds. Through their knowledge of ancestry and kinship they have showed that none of their people ever gave away rights to the land to Canada, and this is an honest belief each person holds. The provincial and federal statutes do not include as third parties or signatories any Innu people. I am satisfied that the four believe their ancestors predate any Canadian claims to ancestry on this land.

Since the concept of land as property is a concept foreign to original people the Court must not assume that a "reasonable" belief be founded on English and hence Canadian law standards. The Innu must be allowed to express their understanding of a foreign concept on their terms, or simply express what they believe.

The Crown has presented to me recent cases such as *Baker Lake [Hamlet of Baker Lake et al. v. Min. of Indian Affairs and Nor. Dev. et al.*, [1979] 3 C.N.L.R. 17, [1980] 1 F.C. 518 (F.C.T.D.)] and *Calder* [*Calder v. A.G.B.C.* (1973), 34 D.L.R. (3d) 145 (S.C.C.)] which only emphasize the concept of land as property from an English law viewpoint. Like the I.Q. tests administered to school children some years ago which simply [reflect] the understanding of the maker of the test, not the person being tested, there is an inherent bias. For example, in *Calder*, the reference to "properly constituted authorities" is a justification of a Proclamation. It assumes that original inhabitants accepted this Proclamation and agreed that it extinguished their inter-

† [1989] 2 C.N.L.R. 119 (Nfld. Prov. Ct.).

ests as users from a time which predated the appearance of Europeans.

These four people have shown me their belief in owner's rights is unshaken by the present occupation.

All of the legal reasonings are based on the premise that somehow the Crown acquired magically by its own declaration of title to the fee a consequent fiduciary obligation to the original people. It is time this premise based on 17th century reasoning be questioned in the light of 21st century reality.

Canada is a vital part of the global village and must show its maturity not only to the segment of Canadian society that wields great power and authority to summarily affect the lives of minority groups with the flourish of a pen to yet another "agreement" or "memorandum of understanding" resulting in great social and economic benefit; but also to its most desperate people.

The forty year history of these Innu people is a glaring reminder that integration or assimilation alone will not make them a healthy community.

By declaring these Innu as criminals for crying enough the Court will be [*sic*] have been unable to recognize the fundamental right to all persons to be treated equally before the law.

Both sets of the foregoing reasons are sufficient, in my mind, to have these four acquitted of any wrongdoing under s. 387 of the *Criminal Code of Canada*.

Finally, the parties will have to negotiate answers to their problems, since the Court is unable to answer these problems for them.

■

The decision was reversed on other grounds in *R. v. Ashini* (1989), 29 Nfld. & P.E.I.R. 318 (Nfld. C.A.). Since then, protests and criminal charges have continued. Correspondingly, support for the Innu has grown. In April 1996, nine Innu supporters who occupied the British and Dutch consulates in Toronto to protest the flights were acquitted of trespassing charges on the basis of the defence of necessity to avoid a greater harm, discussed below, under **Necessity**.

In *R. v. Drainville* (1991), 5 C.R. (4th) 38 (Ont. Ct. (Prov. Div.)), the accused priest was charged with mischief for his participation in a three-minute roadblock in protest of the building of a road over land claimed by the Teme-Augama Anishnabai Nation and subject to ongoing litigation. Judge Fournier rejected a "colour of right" defence. Compare the readiness of this court to accept judicial pronouncements as proof of the law to that of the court in *Campbell* (Alta. Dist. Ct., 1973), above, under **Mistake of Law** (at 57–59):

> As noble and honourable as his motives might be, they are really irrelevant in our considerations pertaining to "colour of right." Unless it can be demonstrated to this Court that his honest belief in the existence of a state of facts, in this case title to the subject lands, is based on a mistake of fact or law, his defence cannot succeed on moral conviction alone. Moral convictions, though deeply and honestly held, cannot transform illegal actions into legal ones; only the "rule of law" must prevail.
>
> In reviewing relevant portions of Father Drainville's evidence, I note that at one point he was asked in cross-examination:
>
>> Q. And prior to attending this area on December 2nd, 1989, you were [*sic*] that Mr. Justice Steele had held the title to these lands was with the Province of Ontario? Correct?
>>
>> A. I did know that.
>
> At another point:
>
>> Q. How do you know that the Teme-Augama were not signatories to the Robinson-Huron Treaty?
>>
>> A. Because I had read documentation that indicated that.
>>
>> Q. You're aware of the fact, Sir, that Mr. Justice Steele came to the contrary conclusion?
>>
>> A. Judges make mistakes, Sir.
>>
>> Q. Right. But judges also administer the law, do you agree with that?
>>
>> A. Yes.
>>
>> Q. And that therefore, you would agree with me that in the law, at the time it was held that the Teme-Augama were signatories in the Robinson-Huron Treaty?
>>
>> A. That's what Judge Steele said.
>>
>> Q. All right. But you don't accept that?
>>
>> A. No I don't.
>>
>> Q. All right. Your opinion is a contrary opinion to the judge?
>>
>> A. Yes it is.
>
> Further on down, the line of questioning is pursued again by the Crown Attorney:

> Q. I suggested to you, your actions sprung from your belief, regardless of what the Ontario Courts had said what the law was. Isn't that exactly what you did?
>
> A. To say 'regardless' is a word which I would not use, Sir.
>
> Q. All right. Notwithstanding, then, is that a better word?
>
> A. That's a better word, yes.
>
> Q. All right. So you acted on your own personal beliefs, notwithstanding what the law was?
>
> A. Yes.

When pressed by the Crown Attorney to clarify whether his belief was that he did nothing legally wrong, as opposed to nothing morally wrong, Father Drainville purposely or inadvertently avoided a direct answer, and instead provided long and convoluted answers on a number of occasions providing, in effect, no answer on which this Court could make a valid determination; if anything, an adverse inference could have been drawn from such answers.

At another point of his cross-examination, I note the following passage:

> Q. Just prior to your arrest, Sir, you were advised that you were interfering with the property of Her Majesty the Queen in right of the Province of Ontario?
>
> A. Yes.
>
> Q. You were advised that by then there had been an injunction issued prohibiting this type of protest?
>
> A. That was indicated at the time, yeah.

When asked by the Crown Attorney whether he had made a conscious choice to participate in the blocking of the road, knowing that he would be arrested, Father Drainville again proved to be a reluctant witness and needed to be pursued quite actively by the prosecutor before he would admit finally:

> A. I knew people had been arrested. I knew also that the possibility existed that I would be.

And towards the end of his testimony, Father Drainville made the following comment to this Court:

> And in this case, the Courts have ruled in a way that they have ruled. But I see the faces of the Native People. I hear their cry. I know their claim and I stand with them. I can say no other.

It is clear on scrutiny and analysis of his evidence that Father Drainville knew what the law of the land was as it pertained to "legal" ownership of the lands in this case, but that he strongly disagreed with it. In fact he did not accept it!

In another recent Teme-Augauma case, the accused spokesperson and liaison worker (who merely pointed out the human blockade to two mineworkers) was acquitted of mischief (s. 431 (1)) and intimidation (s. 423) on the basis of colour of right: *R. v. Mallett* (1997), 25 C.E.L.R. (N.S.) 185 (Ct. J. (Prov. Div.)).

In *R. v. Manuel*, [2007] B.C.J. No. 581 (C.A.) (QL), the two accused members of the Secwepemc (Shuswap) First Nation were granted leave to appeal their conviction for participating in a roadblock on Sun Peaks Road near Kamloops. They were convicted of unlawfully obstructing a highway and mischief, contrary to ss. 423(1) and 430(a) (at paras. 3–4, 9, 13–15):

> The appellants took the position at the trial and on the summary conviction appeal that they did not have the requisite *mens rea* for conviction because they honestly believed that, in accordance with aboriginal law, they had a legal right to block Sun Peaks Road. Nicole Manuel testified that her understanding of the laws of her people, which she described as "natural laws" and "laws of the Creator", imposed a duty on her and her people to take care of and preserve the land.
>
> The trial judge accepted the sincerity of Nicole Manuel's beliefs about the ownership of the land in question, but concluded that "she was acting pursuant to a belief in a moral right under the law of the Creator".
>
> ...
>
> The appellants say that in *Pena*, *Billy*, *Pascal*, and this case, the court erred by characterizing aboriginal perspectives on aboriginal legal rights and the aboriginal legal system as a belief in morality, not law. Their counsel argued that in *R. v. Delgamuukw v. British Columbia* [*sic*], [1997] 3 S.C.R. 1010 at para. 147, and *R. v. Marshall* (1999), 138 C.C.C. (3d) 97 at para. 19 (S.C.C.), the Supreme Court of Canada recognized the aboriginal perspective of land and aboriginal legal systems as substantive, not simply as an evidentiary consideration. Appellants' counsel also cites lower court decisions from other jurisdictions as examples of recognition of aboriginal perspectives on land ownership as law [citing *R. v. Ashini*; *R. v. Potts*, [1990] O.J. No. 2567 (Ct. Just. Prov. Div.); *R. v. Wawatie*, [2002] J.Q. No. 512 (C.Q. crim. & pén.)].
>
> ...

Appellants' counsel framed the question for consideration on appeal as follows:

> Can ancestral, traditional or customary First Nations beliefs about land entitlement or ownership amount to beliefs about private law for the purpose of colour of right analyses in Canadian law?

This substantive question, in my opinion, subsumes the two errors of law raised on the application for leave to appeal: whether the trial judge erred in law by misapplying the subjective test to the colour of right defence, and by importing an irrelevant consideration into the colour of right analysis.

The Supreme Court of Canada in *R. v. Jones*, [1991] 3 S.C.R. 110, held that a "colour of right" defence is only available for offences that utilize that same concept as part of the offence definition. The defence, therefore, was unavailable for a charge of conducting bingo contrary to s. 206 of the *Code*.

Note, however, that effectively the claim of colour of right is available for an accused arguing defence of property under s. 41 of the *Code*: *R. v. Born With A Tooth* (1992), 4 Alta. L.R. (3d) 289 (C.A.)). In that case, the accused and a number of members of the Peigan Nation had made camp on Peigan lands about 200 feet from a dyke on the Oldman river. When a crew of workers accompanied by RCMP moved across the reserve toward the dyke to repair a hole that had been noticed, a confrontation took place (at 292): "About ten people, including the accused, awaited them on the dyke. They called the new arrivals trespassers, and threw rocks. When they closed to a short distance, the accused raised his rifle and shot it into the air at least twice." In allowing the appeal and ordering a new trial on charges including obstruction and assault of peace officers, the court canvassed the requirements under s. 41(1) and held that the four elements of the defence are that the accused be in possession of land; the possession be peaceable; the victim of the assault must be a trespasser; and the force used to eject the trespasser must be reasonable (at 299):

> In sum, the defence is available to an accused when the jury has at least a doubt whether the accused has a measure of control over the land, whether that assertion of control has been seriously challenged, whether the challenger has a right to come on the land, and whether, objectively speaking, the force used was reasonable in the circumstances.
>
> As regards the first two elements, and the factual content of the third element, the defence of mistake is also available. That defence requires the honest belief by the accused in a set of facts which, if true, would afford a defence: see *R. v. Pappajohn*, [1980] 2 S.C.R. 120.... An accused might, honestly but mistakenly, believe that he has a measure of control over the lands, or that his supposed control is unchallenged, or he might believe in a set of facts which, if true, makes the victim a trespasser. But honest mistake of fact appears not to be enough for the last element, because that requires that the reasonableness of the force meet an objective, not just a subjective, test: see *R. v. Scopelliti* (1981), 34 O.R. (2d) 524 (C.A.).

A reference to the composition of the jury in this case appears above, under **The Trial Process**.

In *R. v. Watson* (1999), 176 Nfld. & P.E.I.R. 263 (Nfld. C.A.) (QL) an environmental activist sought to argue colour of right as a defence to mischief charges arising from actions directed at interfering with a fishing trawler.

R. v. Watson†

[CAMERON J.A.:]

The appellant, Watson, following trial by judge and jury, was acquitted of two charges of mischief that caused actual danger to life, contrary to s. 430(2) of the *Criminal Code*. He was found guilty of mischief, for which he was sentenced to thirty days imprisonment and probation for two years. Watson appeals conviction and asks leave to appeal sentence. The Crown appeals from the acquittal of Watson on the two charges of breach of s. 430(2) and also seeks leave to appeal sentence. (For ease of reference,

† (1999), 176 Nfld. & P.E.I.R. 263 (Nfld. C.A.).

any mention of the appellant will be a reference to Watson. Any reference to the respondent is to the Crown.) ...

BACKGROUND

In his sentencing decision the trial judge described Watson as follows:

> Mr. Watson is a well-known environmental activist who, through various organizations of which he is or has been a member, has engaged in activities in different parts of the world directed against individuals, groups or organizations who he believes are acting irresponsibly with respect to the conservation of marine wildlife.

On July 28, 1993, Watson was the master of the vessel Cleveland Amory. At a point outside of the "two hundred mile limit", that is, beyond the Exclusive Economic Zone of Canada, the Cleveland Amory encountered the Rio Las Casas, a Cuban fishing trawler. The Rio Las Casas was fishing for redfish, though Watson believed, at least initially, that the Rio Las Casas was fishing for cod. There was radio contact between the Cleveland Amory and the Rio Las Casas in which Watson asked the Rio Las Casas to stop fishing and leave the area. When, ultimately, the Cubans indicated that they intended to continue fishing, Watson brought the Cleveland Amory near to the Rio Las Casas, cutting across her bow and her stern. Following a further radio exchange Watson brought the Cleveland Amory alongside the Rio Las Casas. The trial judge summarized the evidence as to what then happened as follows:

> The evidence is not consistent as to whether there was actual contact; but it can be said with certainty that at least for a short time the vessels were within a few feet of each other. At some point during this close encounter, crew members threw two one-litre glass bottles containing butyric acid, of high concentration, towards the Rio. One bottle landed in the sea; the other landed and smashed on the net retrieval deck of the Rio. The area affected by the acid effectively prevented the deployment or hauling-in of the Rio's nets without contaminating them, in fact, some of the acid seeped over to and made contact with the net exposed on the deck. There is no evidence, however, that any fish were contaminated. Butyric acid is an organic acid which in high concentration is irritating to human skin and mucus membranes. Although, even in low concentrations, it possesses a foul and noxious smell, it is not life-threatening. The crew of the Rio Las Casas were able to remove the material from the deck of the ship by washing with large amounts of water.

Watson was charged with three offences: interfering with the Rio Las Casas in such a way as to endanger the lives of the passengers or crew of the Rio Las Casas; interfering with the Rio Las Casas in such a way as to endanger the lives of the passengers or crew of the Cleveland Amory; and mischief by the throwing of Butyric acid. He was convicted only on the charge of mischief by the throwing of Butyric acid.

COLOUR OF RIGHT

One of the two grounds of appeal raised by the appellant and the cross-appeal require an examination of the nature of the defence of "colour of right" which was claimed by Watson in respect of all charges. Three sections of the *Criminal Code* are relevant to the issues before this Court.

Section 19 says:

> Ignorance of the law by a person who commits an offence is not an excuse for committing that offence.

Section 429(2) says:

> No person shall be convicted of an offence under sections 430 to 446 where he proves that he acted with legal justification or excuse and with colour of right.

Section 477.1, which was proclaimed into law on April 2, 1991, provides:

> Every person who commits an act or omission that would be an offence under a federal law if it occurred in Canada shall be deemed to have committed that act or omission in Canada if it occurred
>
> (c) outside Canada, on board or by means of a ship registered or licensed, or for which an identification number has been issued, pursuant to any Act of Parliament.

The Cleveland Amory was a registered vessel pursuant to the *Canada Shipping Act*, and, clearly, any offence committed on board or by means of the Cleveland Amory on July 28, 1993 could be prosecuted within Canada. Watson testified that he was unaware that Canadian law applied outside the 200 mile exclusive economic zone. He submits that the trial judge erred by defining too narrowly the scope of colour of right; specifically that the trial judge erred when he instructed the jury:

> ... I must tell you, that as a matter of law, which you must accept from me, that, even if you accept that the accused believed that the acts which he did were not a crime, because they were committed outside the two hundred mile limit; that cannot constitute the defence of "colour of right" because it is based on an ignorance of the law.

In other words, Watson maintains that his was an honestly held belief that Canadian law did not apply and a proper interpretation of the colour of right defence encompasses such a belief. In effect this submission is that s. 429(2) is, in all respects, an exception to the principle enunciated in s. 19.

On the other hand, the Crown argues that the trial judge defined colour of right too broadly, that if the defence of colour of right extends to mistake of law it is limited to questions regarding possessory or proprietary rights and, therefore, the trial judge erred when he instructed the jury that the defence of colour of right could be based on an honest belief by Watson that his actions vis-a-vis the Rio Las Casas were justified under the *World Charter for Nature*. The Crown further submits that s. 19 is a complete answer to the issue of the jurisdiction of the criminal law of Canada.

The parties are agreed: (1) that s. 429(2) does not place a burden of proof upon the accused but rather it is for the Crown to establish the absence of legal justification or excuse and colour of right; and (2) that the section creates two (perhaps three) separate defences "legal justification or excuse" and "colour of right." In other words the "and" which precedes the words "colour of right" is read as "or." (See: *R. v. Creaghan* (1982), 1 C.C.C. (3rd) 449 (Ont C.A.) and *R. v. Gamey* (1993), 80 C.C.C. (3d) 117 (Man C.A.).) Neither party objects to the trial judge's instructions to the jury on these points.

Parenthetically, the trial judge also instructed the jury — as a matter of law — that the *World Charter for Nature* did not constitute legal justification or excuse under s. 429(2). That instruction is not challenged in this appeal. A legal justification or excuse makes legal what would otherwise be a crime.

The most commonly used definition of colour of right is "an honest belief in a state of facts which, if it existed, would be a legal justification or excuse." (See: *R. v. Johnson* (1904), 8 C.C.C. 123 (Ont. H.C.)) As will be seen, this definition of colour of right, while accurate as far as it goes, does not really address whether colour of right extends to mistake of law which is at the heart of this appeal. However, certain characteristics of colour of right are well established and are not disputed by the parties. Those aspects are:

1. that the defence is based on the honest belief of the accused that, at the time the offence was committed, he had a colour of right (*Creaghan*).
2. that the test is a subjective one (*R. v. Howson*, [1966] 3 C.C.C. 348 (Ont. C.A.));
3. that while the belief does not have to be a reasonable one the reasonableness of the belief is a factor for consideration by the jury in determining if there is an honest belief (*R. v. Ninos and Walker*, [1964] 1 C.C.C. 326 (N.S.S.C.); see also Laskin J.A. in *Howson*); and
4. that it is not sufficient that the accused had a moral belief in a colour of right (*R. v. Hemmerly* (1976), 30 C.C.C. (2d) 141 (Ont. C.A.), *R. v. Cinq-Mars* (1989), 51 C.C.C. (3d) 248 (Que. C.A.) and *Gamey*).

There are conflicting authorities respecting whether the colour of right defence can be based on a belief respecting the law or, rather, is limited to a "state of facts" which, if it actually existed, would constitute legal justification or excuse. *R. v. Shymkowich*, [1954] S.C.R. 606; *R. v. Moore* (1981), 23 C.R. (3d) 303 (Sask. Q.B.) and *R. v. Pace*, [1965] 3 C.C.C. 55 (N.S.C.A.) are generally cited for the proposition that mistake of law is not encompassed in colour of right. *Howson*, *Gamey*, and *R. v. Pena* (1997), 148 D.L.R. (4th) 372 (B.C.S.C.) would indicate that colour of right may be based on either mistake of law or mistake of fact. In *Pena* and *Gamey* the charges were mischief. In *Howson*, the charge was theft.

While *Shymkowich* has been interpreted as holding that colour of right does not include mistake of law, only Rand J. (with Taschereau J. concurring) made such a finding. Locke J, in dissent, held that the defence of mistake of law was available to the defendant and Estey J. (with Fauteux J. concurring) indicated approval of a statement that "to prevent the taking from being felonious the claim of right must be an honest one, though it may be unfounded in law or in fact." So then, 3 of the 5 judges were of the view that colour of right included mistake of law.

R. v. DeMarco (1973), 13 C.C.C. (2d) 369 (Ont C.A.) and *Howson* are cited by the appellant as support for the position that any error in law is sufficient to ground the defence of colour of right. In

Howson the accused, a tow truck operator, towed away a car which had been left on private property contrary to "no parking" signs. The accused was convicted of theft at trial and appealed. His ground of appeal was based on his belief that he was entitled to tow cars illegally parked. Chief Justice Porter, in directing an acquittal, stated:

> If upon all the facts, the only inference which may reasonably be drawn points to an intent to steal, a conviction must follow. If the evidence shows, as in this case, that there was no legal right to withhold the vehicle and unlike this case, that there was no other evidence, there would I should think, be an irresistible inference of theft. If, however, upon consideration of all the evidence before them, a jury, properly instructed, were satisfied that the accused honestly but mistakenly believed that he had a right in law or in fact, they should acquit. The question is whether upon all the evidence the proper inference to be drawn would be that the accused did have an honest belief. This is a question for the tribunal of first instance. The weight of authority would indicate, I think, that the test for the determination of the presence of an honest belief is a subjective rather than an objective one.
>
> ...
>
> Thus there is considerable authority in the English cases culminating in the decision of the Court of Criminal Appeal in *R. v. Bernhard*, *supra*, to establish that colour of right applies equally to fact and law. I think that in England, honest mistake of either fact or law would be a defence to a charge of theft. The Canadian authorities are less clear ...
>
> In my view the word "right" should be construed broadly. The use of the word cannot be said to exclude a legal right. The word in its ordinary sense is charged with legal implications. I do not think that s. 19 affects s. 269. Section 19 only applies when there is an offence. There is no offence if there is colour of right. If upon all the evidence it may fairly be inferred that the accused acted under a genuine misconception of fact or law, there would be no offence of theft committed. The tribunal must satisfy itself that the accused has acted upon an honest, but mistaken belief that the right is based upon either fact or law, or mixed fact and law.

In *DeMarco*, Martin J.A. for the Court said at p. 372:

> The term "colour of right" generally, although not exclusively, refers to a situation where there is an assertion of a proprietary or possessory right to the thing which is the subject-matter of the alleged theft. One who is honestly asserting what he believes to be an honest claim cannot be said to act "without colour of right", even though it may be unfounded in law or in fact ... The term "colour of right" is also used to denote an honest belief in a state of facts which, if it actually existed would at law justify or excuse the act done ... The term when used in the latter sense is merely a particular application of the doctrine of mistake of fact.

Neither *DeMarco* nor *Howson* addresses the nature of the error of law which may ground the claim for colour of right, except that *DeMarco* holds it is not limited to a claim to a proprietary or possessory right.

Section 19 states the general principle, well-established long before there was a *Criminal Code*. Under such a principle, it was not an excuse that the accused did not know what he did amounted to a crime. Applying s. 19, the fact that Watson did not know that what he did outside the 200 mile limit could amount to a crime in Canada is no defence. Neither, for that matter, would his misunderstanding of the effect of the *World Charter for Nature*. Underlying the issue in this case is the question of what is the effect of s. 429(2) on the principle that ignorance of the law is no excuse. Section 429(2) makes colour of right a defence for the offence of mischief, among others. Since colour of right is not defined, we must be guided by the common law as to the meaning of the term.

While it has been the subject of some debate, the weight of the authority and logic suggest that colour of right is not limited to errors of fact but extends to errors of law. Further, contrary to the submission of the Crown, colour of right is not limited to errors of law respecting proprietary or possessory rights, though certainly most of the cases dealing with colour of right would appear to fall within that category, no doubt because of the nature of the offences to which the defence is made applicable. *DeMarco* supports both those conclusions.

However, s. 19 does apply to deny Watson a defence based on his ignorance of the fact that the *Criminal Code* was applicable to his activity on or by means of the Cleveland Amory outside the 200 mile limit. There are three reasons for this conclusion. First, and perhaps least important, this Court has not been referred to any case in which colour of right has been an answer to ignorance of the jurisdiction of the *Criminal Code*. In *R. v. Jones and Pamajewon* (1991), 66 C.C.C. (3d) 512 (S.C.C.) the accused were charged with operating an unlawful bingo on the Shawanaga reserve in Ontario. Their defence was based on a mistaken belief that the *Criminal Code* did not apply to reserves. The Court confirmed that the principle expressed in s. 19 was applicable. As to colour of right, it held that it did not apply to the crime alleged. The Crown argues that *Jones and Pamajewon* supports its position. The appellant submits that the reason colour of right was said not to apply in *Jones and Pamajewon* was that it did not apply to the offence alleged to have been committed in that case. The appellant argues that by implication that case, at least, leaves open and, at best, supports the notion that an error as to jurisdiction could ground the defence of colour of right. *Jones and Pamajewon* is unhelpful in resolving the issues in this case. It does not address colour of right except to indicate that it had no application to the offence under consideration in that case.

A consideration of the implications of this submission by the appellant militates against the acceptance of the appellant's position. If Watson were correct and any error of law (of whatever kind) can be the basis for a colour of right defence, then s. 19 has no application at all to the offences specified in s. 429(2), nor to those other offences which state an absence of colour of right as an element of the offence. The result would be that an honest belief that the law did not apply to a Canadian vessel beyond the 200 mile limit is a defence to a charge of mischief or theft but not to assault or criminal negligence causing death. There is no policy reason for such a distinction. To those who would suggest that a belief based on an honest mistake of law should be a general defence, such a declaration would nullify s. 19.

Secondly, the theory of the defence of colour of right is that it negates *mens rea*. In *R. v. Forster* (1992), 70 C.C.C. (3d) 59 (SCC), Lamer C.J.C. said at p. 64:

> This court recently reaffirmed in *R. v. Docherty* (1989), 51 C.C.C. (3d) 1 at p. 15, [1989] 2 S.C.R. 941, 72 C.R. (3d) 1, the principle that knowledge that one's actions are contrary to the law is not a component of the *mens rea* for an offence, and consequently does not operate as a defence.

It is no part of the *mens rea* of the offence of mischief that one intend to commit the crime within the jurisdiction of the *Criminal Code of Canada*.

Thirdly, the basis of the defence of colour of right as it relates to law is the misunderstanding of the law respecting private rights. For example, it is the mistake as to the ownership of property or right of possession which may be based on fact or law which generally grounds the defence. However, while the matter is clearer in the context of cases of theft, I hasten to add that a colour of right defence need not be confined to a claim to ownership or proprietary right. It may be a mere belief that the conduct was lawful. (See Glanville Williams, *Criminal Law, The General Part* (2d ed.) (1961) p. 324)

The question raised on this appeal is placed in perspective by the following passage from Stuart *Canadian Criminal Law* (3rd ed.) (1995) at p. 309:

> Mistakes grounding successful claims of right have indeed involved mistakes as to civil law or, as it has been put, mistakes of private rather than public rights. This has been suggested to be a requirement of the English law of colour of right, and there is one recent dictum to this effect in Canada. It has never been explained why this distinction should be made. It is not self-evident why a belief based on an out-of-date criminal law text that it is not stealing to take another's title deeds without permission will not ground a claim of right, whereas a belief based on a misunderstanding of the law of property that another is withholding your title deeds, will. Greater receptivity to excusing mistakes as to private law might nevertheless account for the historical tendency in England, reflected in our Code, to allow colour of right defences almost exclusively in the area of property offences.
>
> The Law Reform Commission of Canada would insert into their new *Criminal Code* a defence of mistake or ignorance of law "concerning private rights relevant to that crime". Its stated intention is to reflect the present law respecting the defence of colour of right for certain offences.

There is no attempt, in this decision, to analyse the validity of the premise upon which s. 19 is founded or to express an opinion on whether it should change. Section 19 is a part of Canadian criminal law. Whether one views colour of right as a limited exception to s. 19 or, as Porter C.J.O. did in *Howson*, not being engaged because colour of right (where it is applicable) negates *mens rea*, it does not extend to questions of jurisdiction of the criminal law. While the matter was not addressed by the parties, I see no policy reason to exclude from errors of civil law or mistakes of private rights those founded on the *World Charter for Nature*.

In summary then, colour of right is an honest belief in a state of facts or civil law which, if it existed, would negate the *mens rea* of an offence.

In this case the trial judge instructed the jury:

> ... as a matter of law again, which you must accept from me, that even if you accept that the accused believed that the acts which he did

> were not a crime, because they were committed outside the two hundred mile limit; that cannot constitute the defence of "colour of right" because it is based on an ignorance of the law.

This instruction is entirely consistent with the law as outlined above. Contrary to the position of the appellant, it does not amount to an error. As to the matter of Watson's professed belief that the *World Charter for Nature* gave him authority to do what he did, the trial judge said:

> But, on the other hand, there can be "colour of right" where an accused honestly, but incorrectly believes that he had a legal right to do something that would otherwise be a crime because he was specifically legally authorized in the particular circumstances facing him to do it. Now, let us take another example of a mistake of law which could involve the defence of colour of right. Again, we will use the umbrella example. Suppose, following his dinner the man goes to collect his umbrella from the cloak room but the attendant refuses to give him the umbrella because the man did not pay a parking fee when he arrived at the restaurant. The attendant honestly, but mistakenly believes that he has a right, in law, to withhold property of the diner until other debts are paid. The attendant, although wrong in law in withholding the umbrella might have a good defence to a charge of theft, if he honestly believed in the specific circumstances of that case that he had a lien on the umbrella or a right to retain it and hence, he had a legal right to do what he did. That would be the type of mistake of law that could constitute a colour of right. Now, in this case Mr. Watson says that, he was justified in the circumstances here, in obstructing, interrupting or interfering with the Rio Las Casas because he honestly believed he was authorized to do so by the *World Charter of Nature*. Now, I am telling you that, in principle, this could constitute a defence of "colour of right". I must emphasize however that, it is up to you to determine whether on the evidence and the facts as you find them the defence applies or not, ...

The trial judge then outlined the legal requirements for a defence of "colour of right." He said:

> Now, "colour of right" as a defence cannot apply unless a mistake is honestly held by the accused. Thus, the first step you must consider [is] whether there is evidence indicating that the accused believed that he was authorized to do what he did by the *World Charter* and that that belief was honestly held. Now, it is important for you to realize as well, that it does not matter whether the belief was reasonable; so long as it was honest. Nevertheless, when you are deciding whether the accused honestly believed that he had a legal justification or excuse, you should consider whether there were any reasonable grounds for that belief.

This instruction is also consistent with the law....

INCONSISTENT VERDICTS

The other ground of appeal raised by the appellant is that there are inconsistent verdicts in this case....

. . . .

The appellant has failed to meet the onus placed upon him in respect of inconsistent verdicts. As to the activity relating to the first charge, Watson's evidence was that neither vessel was endangered by the manoeuvring of the Cleveland Amory, that he was careful to avoid any contact with the portion of the net that was in the water and, at the relevant time, the net had not been set and the Rio Las Casas was not engaged in fishing. While there was evidence capable of supporting a conviction for mischief, on Watson's evidence there was no interference with fishing and no damage to nets or any other equipment in respect of the first count. It is possible that the jury acquitted Watson on the mischief charge not because of the *World Charter for Nature* but because they were not satisfied beyond a reasonable doubt that the charge had been proven. This is in contrast to the description of the impact on the activities of the Rio Las Casas of the throwing of the Butyric acid, which was described earlier in this decision and on the basis of which Watson was convicted of mischief.

Alternatively, even if the jury was satisfied that mischief had been proven in respect to the first count, a reasonably instructed jury could have concluded Watson's belief in the *World Charter for Nature* would allow him to interfere to the extent described in the first count but his belief did not go as far as allowing the throwing of Butyric acid.

For the reasons given the appeal of conviction and the cross-appeal are denied.

■

11

Incapacity

An incapacity defence involves an argument that the accused did not have the capacity to form the *mens rea* element of the offence. Capacity is also relevant to the question of whether the accused is fit to stand trial or instruct counsel. Consider the following bases for such arguments.

A. AGE

According to s. 13, the age of criminal responsibility in the *Code* is 12 years of age. However, the *Youth Criminal Justice Act*, S.C. 2002, c. 1 (*YCJA*), deals with the criminal responsibility of young people (defined as those between the ages of 12 and 18 years at the time of the offence) regarding federal offences, including the *Criminal Code*, but not provincial offences. This legislation replaces the *Young Offenders Act*. The new law aims to reduce the over-incarceration of young people, given that Canada had the highest rate of youth incarceration in the Western world, including the United States, by distinguishing between serious violent offences and less serious offences.

The act permits the designation of courts as "Youth Courts" for the purpose of trying all young people accused of crime. Transfer to adult court is no longer at issue, although certain young people will now be liable instead to "adult sentences" (sentencing within the *Criminal Code*) for "presumptive offences" (murder, attempted murder, manslaughter, aggravated sexual assault, or a serious violent offence for which an adult is liable to imprisonment of more than two years and the accused has already received at least two judicial determinations at different proceedings that he or she has committed a serious violent offence) if they are 14 years and over (unless the province legislates a higher minimum age of not more than 16 years). The Attorney General must apply to subject the accused to an adult sentence, based on the commission of a serious violent offence or a presumptive offence (s. 64) and the young person can also apply to be subjected to a youth sentence (s. 63). The court will consider the seriousness and circumstances of the offence, the age, maturity, character, criminal record, and background of the accused to determine whether a youth sentence would be sufficient to hold the young person accountable for the offence (s. 72).

Youth sentences generally operate to restrict the availability of imprisonment to violent offences and specific circumstances where the youth has already failed to comply with non-custodial sentences, for example, and can include a reprimand or custody and supervision of up to two years total (16 months in custody); for presumptive offences youth sentences have a three year maximum for custody and supervision (two years in custody); for second degree murder the maximum is seven years total (four in custody) and for first degree murder it is 10 years total (six in custody). This legislation also has specific provisions that deal with notification of the young person's parents, publication bans, the right to counsel, alternative measures, and judicial interim release.

Nicolas Bala, in a major study of the operation of the *YCJA* entitled *Responding to Young Offenders: Diversion, Detention & Sentencing Under Canada's YCJA* (Kingston: Queen's Faculty of Law Legal Studies Research Paper Series No. 07-10, 2007), reports that while the *YCJA* has produced only a small decline in the number of youths denied bail, it has resulted in a substantial increase in the diversion rate and in non-custodial dispositions. At the same time, he notes that there has been no increase in youth crime since the new law came into force. Further, the provisions that declare offences including manslaughter to presumptively require adult sentences have been declared unconstitutional pursuant to s. 7 of the *Charter* by the Supreme Court in a 5:4 decision. The majority in *R. v. D.B.*, [2008] S.C.J. No. 25 (QL), held that the Crown must bear the onus of persuading the judge that a youth requires an adult sentence.

B. MENTAL DISORDER

Mental disorder can become an issue in the criminal process if the accused lacks the capacity to undergo a trial, "unfit to stand trial", or if the person was arguably incapacitated from criminal responsibility at the time of the commission of the offence, "not criminally responsible". The *Charter* has had a significant impact in shaping the procedures that guide fitness and not criminally responsible determinations, as well as the outcomes that follow the findings of "unfit" and "not criminally responsible". The profession of psychiatry also has a significant impact upon these determinations. These issues will be considered in turn below.

FITNESS TO STAND TRIAL

Sections 672.11 and 672.12 provide that a court having jurisdiction over an accused may order an assessment of the accused's mental condition where it has reasonable grounds to believe such evidence is necessary to determine whether the accused is unfit to stand trial. Sections 672.22–33 provide the framework for unfitness determinations. The issue may arise at any point in the proceedings, including prior to the determination with respect to interim release. However, s. 675.25(2) provides that the court has a discretion to postpone the trial of the issue of fitness until the close of the case for the prosecution at the preliminary inquiry. Thus, *R. v. Taylor* (1992), 11 O.R. (3d) 323 (C.A.) held that a finding that the accused is not fit to stand trial should not be made in the absence of any basis to put the accused on trial. At a minimum, the trial judge should require the Crown to demonstrate that it is in a position to establish that the accused committed the acts alleged. An accused found unfit may or may not be detained (see ss. 672.45–63) and may be tried on the charges once "fit" (s. 672.33). In 2004, the Supreme Court declared unconstitutional the provisions that governed situations where there was no reasonable prospect of the accused ever becoming fit to stand trial: *R. v. Demers*, [2004] 2 S.C.R. 489. The new provision, s. 672.852, permits a court to stay the prosecution where the evidence is clear that the accused is unlikely to become fit, the accused does not present a significant risk to public safety, and a stay is in the interests of the proper administration of justice.

According to the court in *Taylor*, the standard for fitness to stand trial is a limited capacity test. It rejected a threshold "analytic capacity" test for determining fitness and held that the test was one of "limited cognitive capacity": it was not necessary that the accused be able to act in his own "best interests" in communicating with counsel. Similarly, in *R. v. Bain* (1994), 130 N.S.R. (2d) 332, the Nova Scotia Court of Appeal also held that evidence that the accused did not act in his best interest or failed to act with good judgment was not sufficient to warrant a finding of unfitness.

R. v. Brown (1993), 13 C.R.R. (2d) 341 (Ont. Ct. J. (Prov. Div.)) followed *Taylor* and set out a two-stage test for the timing of the inquiry into fitness, at 345:

> First, the Crown should call sufficient evidence either on a preliminary hearing or at a trial to satisfy the trier of fact that there is sufficient evidence against the accused to meet the test in *United States v. Sheppard*. Then the second step should be the actual hearing, and that can be either having the doctor's evidence first, or whatever evidence the Crown wishes to rely on, then the defence, if it wishes to call the accused, or whatever evidence the accused wishes to call.

In an earlier case dealing with the former provisions as to fitness to stand trial, the Québec Court of Appeal held that counsel for the accused had an obligation to raise the issue of fitness with the court. Failure to do so amounted to incompetence and formed part of the basis for allowing an appeal from conviction and ordering a new trial: *R. v. Brigham* (1992), 52 Q.A.C. 241.

NOT CRIMINALLY RESPONSIBLE

Section 16 of the *Criminal Code* sets out the parameters of the defence of mental disorder, formerly the "insanity" defence. This defence is one that must be proven on a balance of probabilities, and although the Supreme Court ruled in *R. v. Chaulk*, [1990] 3 S.C.R. 1303, discussed above, under **Burden of Proof** that this reverse onus offends s. 11(d) of the *Charter*, it was held to be saved pursuant to s. 1.

A s. 16 defence can also be raised by the Crown against the wishes of the accused. Thus, for example, in Guy Paul Morin's second trial, his counsel declined to raise the defence of insanity, but the Crown managed to convey to the jury that he had utilized this defence in his first trial, presumably to prejudicial effect: Kirk Makin, "Insanity plea carried weight with police" *The [Toronto] Globe and Mail* (17 July 1997) A5. However, a significant and successful *Charter* challenge in *R. v. Swain*, [1991] 1 S.C.R. 933, resulted in the Court ruling that this defence can only be raised by the Crown where the accused raises evidence of mental impairment that the judge finds puts the accused's mental capacity at issue. Furthermore, the Court ruled that mental disorder issues should not be permitted to taint a fair trial. Thus, the question of mental disorder should only be considered by the trier of fact after the accused has been found guilty of the crime but before the conviction is entered. In *R. v. David* (2002), 61 O.R. (3d) 1 (C.A.), the court clarified the process further. It ruled that it is preferable for the jury to be told to consider the s. 16 defence only if they are satisfied that the accused committed the *actus reus* of the offence; they should, however, consider the accused's mental disorder defence before attempting to determine whether the accused possessed the *mens rea*, since logically the accused's mental capacity will be a condition precedent to resolving the *mens rea* issue.

The defence requires proof of two elements: the accused must have suffered from a mental disorder and the disorder must have prevented the accused from appreciating the nature and quality of the act or of knowing that it was wrong. A mental disorder is defined in s. 2 of the *Code* as a "disease of the mind", a phrase that has been interpreted as a question of mixed fact and law: it is for the judge to determine whether the condition amounts in law to a disease of the mind, and it is for the trier of fact to determine whether the accused in fact experienced the condition, and whether he or she was prevented from appreciating that the act was wrong. Although experts, such a psychiatrists, may offer their opinions on these two issues, their views do not control their legal and factual resolution. For example, in *R. v. Grandbois*, [2003] O.J. No. 256 (C.A.), the jury's verdict of guilty was upheld despite the fact that the evidence of the defence's three psychiatrists was uncontradicted at trial.

The accused's ability to appreciate the nature and quality of the act must extend beyond the understanding of the ultimate physical consequences of the accused's act to include an appreciation that the act is legally or morally wrong, "according to the moral standards of society:" *R. v. Olah* (1997), 33 O.R. (3d) 385 (C.A.). Furthermore, *R. v. Oommen*, [1994] 2 S.C.R. 507, held that s. 16(1) embraces not only the intellectual ability to know right from wrong in an abstract sense, but also the ability to apply that knowledge in a rational way to the alleged criminal act. Thus, the accused should not be found guilty where a mental disorder deprived him or her of the capacity "to rationally decide whether the act is right or wrong and hence to make a rational choice about whether to do it or not" (at 518).

An accused who cannot prove that a mental disorder deprived him or her of capacity is entitled to have that same evidence considered by the jury with respect to other *mens rea* issues, such as the capacity for the planning and deliberation needed to found a first-degree-murder conviction: see *R. v. Jacquard*, [1997] 1 S.C.R. 314. However, such an accused is not necessarily entitled to insist that the judge review the evidence in detail and relate it again to these other issues.

An accused who refuses to accept counsel's advice to advance a mental disorder defence may be able to introduce fresh evidence on appeal of her mental disorder where it can be demonstrated that accused's untreated medical condition prevented counsel from adducing the evidence at trial. In *R. v. I.E.M.*, [2003] O.J. No. 953 (C.A.), the court was satisfied that counsel had not sought to gain a tactical advantage by not advancing the evidence, and substituted a finding of not criminally responsible on appeal.

Another important aspect of the Supreme Court's ruling in *Swain* was to declare unconstitutional the process that followed upon an insanity verdict pursuant to s. 16. The prior *Code* scheme mandated immediate detention under a Lieutenant Governor's warrant for an indefinite period of time. At the time of *Swain*, at least 1,000 persons were being held in institutions under warrant, some for relatively minor crimes. The new legislative scheme that was enacted is now in Part XX.1 of the *Code*. It creates Review Boards in each province, which are to be composed of at least five members appointed by the Lieutenant Governor, at least one of which must be a registered psychiatrist, and chaired by a judge, someone qualified for judicial appointment, or a retired judge. The new scheme includes the following features:

- additional remands for assessment;
- generally limited five-day assessments regarding fitness to stand trial (reduced from a previous norm of 30 days);
- a rebuttable presumption that assessments will be made out of custody;
- protection for statements made to a psychiatrist or psychologist as part of court-ordered assessment, admissible for only limited purposes: s. 672.21(2);
- mandatory review board reviews; and
- disposition hearings.

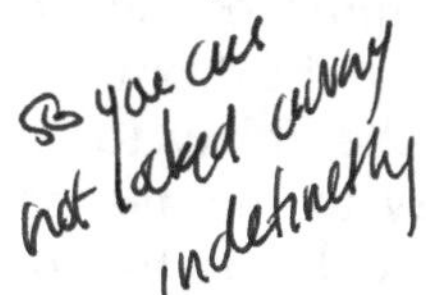

The new provisions require that upon a verdict of not criminally responsible on account of mental disorder pursuant to s. 672.34, generally the offender will receive a disposition hearing under s. 672.45 by the court. If the court fails to make a disposition order, the Review Board must, as soon as practicable but within 45 days, hold a disposition hearing (s. 672.47). The dispositions available for the offender are set out in s. 672.54: the accused can be discharged absolutely; discharged upon conditions; or retained in custody, in a hospital, subject to conditions that do not include non-consensual treatment (s. 672.55). In determining a disposition under s. 672.54 the court or Review Board must "tak[e] into consideration the need to protect the public from dangerous persons, the mental condition of the accused, the reintegration of the accused into society and the other needs of the accused", and must make the disposition that is "the least onerous and least restrictive of the accused".

In the absence of making a disposition order, a court can make a treatment disposition order for 60 days or less under s. 672.58; these orders exclude psychosurgery and electro-convulsive therapy (s. 672.61). The Review Board must review the court's disposition, unless it is an absolute discharge, before the disposition order expires but within 90 days in any event. Thereafter, appeals from dispositions are available under ss. 672.73ff. and mandatory reviews by the Review Board are required every 12 months of all dispositions except absolute discharges.

The new legislative scheme has been subject to *Charter* challenges pursuant to ss. 7 and 15. These challenges were resolved in *Winko v. British Columbia (Forensic Psychiatric Institute)*.

Winko v. British Columbia (Forensic Psychiatric Institute)†

[McLACHLIN C.J.:]

[In this case, the Court first described the structure and principles informing the disposition hearing at 667–70.]

1. The court or Review Board must consider the need to protect the public from dangerous persons, the mental condition of the NCR ["not criminally responsible"] accused, the reintegration of the NCR accused into society, and the other needs of the NCR accused. The court or Review Board is required in each case to answer the question: does the evidence disclose that the NCR accused is a "significant threat to the safety of the public"?
2. A "significant threat to the safety of the public" means a real risk of physical or psychological harm to members of the public that is serious in the sense of going beyond the merely trivial or annoying. The conduct giving rise to the harm must be criminal in nature.
3. There is no presumption that the NCR accused poses a significant threat to the safety of the public. Restrictions on his or her liberty can only be justified if, at the time of the hearing, the evidence before the court or Review Board shows that the NCR accused actually constitutes such a threat. The court or Review Board cannot avoid coming to a decision on this issue by stating, for example, that it is uncertain or cannot decide whether the NCR accused poses a significant threat to the safety of the public. If it cannot come to a decision with any certainty, then it has not found that the NCR accused poses a significant threat to the safety of the public.
4. The proceeding before the court or Review Board is not adversarial. If the parties do not present sufficient information, it is up to the court or Review Board to seek out the evidence it requires to make its decision. Where the court is considering the matter, it may find in such circumstances that it cannot readily make a disposition without delay and that it should be considered by the Review Board. Regardless of which body considers the issue, there is never any legal burden on the NCR accused to show that he or she does not pose a significant threat to the safety of the public.
5. The court or Review Board may have recourse to a broad range of evidence as it seeks to determine whether the NCR accused poses a significant threat to the safety of the public. Such evidence may include the past and expected course of the NCR accused's treatment, if any, the present state of the NCR accused's medical condition, the NCR accused's own plans for the future, the support services existing for the NCR accused in the community, and the assessments provided by experts who have examined the NCR accused. This list is not exhaustive.
6. A past offence committed while the NCR accused suffered from a mental illness is not, by itself, evidence that the NCR accused continues to pose a significant risk to the safety of the public. However, the fact that the NCR accused committed a criminal act in the past may be considered together with other circumstances where it is relevant to identifying a pattern of behaviour, and hence to the issue of whether the NCR accused presents a significant threat to public safety. The court or Review Board must at all times consider the circumstances of the individual NCR accused before it.
7. If the court or Review Board concludes that the NCR accused is not a significant threat to the safety of the public, it must order an absolute discharge.
8. If the court or Review Board concludes that the NCR accused is a significant threat to the safety of the public, it has two alternatives. It may order that the NCR accused be discharged subject to the conditions the court or Review Board considers necessary, or it may direct that the NCR accused be detained in custody in a hospital, again subject to appropriate conditions.
9. When deciding whether to make an order for a conditional discharge or for detention in a hospital, the court or Review Board must again consider the need to protect the public from

† [1999] 2 S.C.R. 625.

> dangerous persons, the mental condition of the NCR accused, the reintegration of the NCR accused into society, and the other needs of the NCR accused, and make the order that is the least onerous and least restrictive to the NCR accused.

[The Court then went on to reject the ss. 7 and 15 challenges. The Court held that s. 762.54 is not impermissibly vague because it does articulate a standard capable of legal debate; it does not shift the burden to an accused to disprove "dangerousness"; and it safeguards the accused's liberty interests by restricting the accused "no more than is necessary to protect public safety", and annual reviews and appeal rights provide a check against error. On the s. 15 claim, McLachlin C.J. for the majority ruled that although NCR accused receive differential treatment under the law compared to other accused who are convicted after trial and while mental disability is a protected ground under s. 15(1), the treatment of NCR accused is not discriminatory:]

An analysis of these provisions of the *Criminal Code* and their effect upon NCR accused reveals them to be the very antithesis of discrimination and hence not to engage the protections of s. 15(1). Part XX.1 does not reflect the application of presumed group or personal characteristics. Nor does it perpetuate or promote the view that individuals falling under its provisions are less capable or less worthy of respect and recognition. Rather than denying the dignity and worth of the mentally ill offender, Part XX.1 recognizes and enhances them.

. . . .

It is thus ... that it was not the intention of Parliament to discriminate against NCR accused in enacting Part XX.1 of the *Criminal Code*. Rather, it was Parliament's intention to combat discrimination and treat individuals who commit criminal acts which they cannot know are wrong in a way appropriate to their true situation. But good intentions, while important, are not enough to establish lack of discrimination. We must go further and ask whether in its effect Part XX.1 reflects a stereotypical application of presumed group characteristics or otherwise denies the essential dignity of NCR accused.

. . . .

The essence of stereotyping, as mentioned above, lies in making distinctions against an individual on the basis of personal characteristics attributed to that person not on the basis of his or her true situation, but on the basis of association with a group: *Andrews*, at pp. 174–75; *Law*, at para. 61. The question is whether Part XX.1 in effect operates against individual NCR accused in this way. In my view, it does not. At every stage, Part XX.1 treats the individual NCR accused on the basis of his or her actual situation, not on the basis of the group to which he or she is assigned. Before a person comes under Part XX.1, there must be an individual assessment by a trial judge based on evidence with full access to counsel and other constitutional safeguards. A person falls under Part XX.1 only if the judge is satisfied that he or she was unable to know the nature of the criminal act or that it was wrong. The assessment is based on the individual's situation. It does not admit of inferences based on group association. More importantly, the disposition of the NCR accused is similarly tailored to his or her individual situation and needs, and is subject to the overriding rule that it must always be the least restrictive avenue appropriate in the circumstances. Finally, the provision for an annual review (at a minimum) of the individual's status ensures that his or her actual situation as it exists from time to time forms the basis of how he or she is to be treated.

This individualized process is the antithesis of the logic of the stereotype, the evil of which lies in prejudging the individual's actual situation and needs on the basis of the group to which he or she is assigned. ...

. . . .

But individual treatment, by itself, cannot defeat a s. 15(1) claim: *Law*, at para. 70. A court must go further and assess the actual impact of the differential treatment on the claimant's dignity, always from the perspective of a "reasonable person, dispassionate and fully apprised of the circumstances, possessed of similar attributes to, and under similar circumstances as, the claimant" (para. 60). From this perspective, the key feature of Part XX.1 — treating every NCR accused having appropriate regard to his or her particular situation — far from being a denial of equality, constitutes the essence of equal treatment from a substantive point of view. It does not disadvantage or treat unequally the NCR accused, but rather recognizes the NCR accused's disability, incapacity and particular personal situation and, based upon that recognition, creates a system of individualized assessment and treatment that deliberately undermines the invidious stereotype of the mentally ill as dangerous. It treats NCR accused more appropriately and more equally.

Earlier in these reasons, I rejected the view that Part XX.1 perpetuates the view that all NCR are dangerous, or even presumptively dangerous. On the contrary, in neither its purpose nor its effect does the differential treatment mandated by Part XX.1 send a negative message to society about the NCR accused. Nor can it reasonably be understood to demean their dignity as individual human beings. Rather, the process it lays down and the treatment options for which it provides embody the message that every NCR accused is equally entitled to all protections available to other people, subject only to such constraints as may be required as a result of his or her illness in the interest of public safety. In its purpose and effect, it reflects the view that NCR accused are entitled to sensitive care, rehabilitation and meaningful attempts to foster their participation in the community, to the maximum extent compatible with the individual's actual situation. ...

The appellants also emphasize the "infinite" potential of supervision of an NCR accused. As alluded to earlier, this argument overlooks the fundamental distinction between the State's treatment of an NCR accused and its treatment of a convicted person. One purpose of incarcerating a convicted offender is punishment. The convicted offender is morally responsible for his or her criminal act and is told what punishment society demands for the crime. The sentence is thus finite (even if not fixed, i.e., a "life" sentence). By contrast, it has been determined that the NCR offender is not morally responsible for his or her criminal act. Punishment is morally inappropriate and ineffective in such a case because the NCR accused was incapable of making the meaningful choice upon which the punishment model is premised. Because the NCR accused's liberty is not restricted for the purpose of punishment, there is no corresponding reason for finitude. The purposes of any restriction on his or her liberty are to protect society and to allow the NCR accused to seek treatment. This requires a flexible approach that treats the length of the restriction as a function of these dual aims, and renders a mechanistic comparison of the duration of confinement inapposite.

In asserting that NCR accused must be treated "the same" as criminally responsible offenders who commit the same criminal act, the appellants assume that the infringement of their liberty is meant to serve the same function that it does for those found guilty of criminal offences. As I noted, this is mistaken. Any restrictions on the liberty of NCR accused are imposed for essentially rehabilitative and not penal purposes. In the words of Taylor J.A., unlike the sanctions faced by a convicted person, the scheme that addresses NCR accused "exacts no penalty, imposes no punishment and casts no blame": *Blackman v. British Columbia (Review Board)* (1995), 95 C.C.C. (3d) 412 (B.C.C.A.), at p. 433. Accordingly, a formalistic comparison of the "sentences" imposed on these two types of individuals belies a purposive understanding of the statutory provisions in issue.

These considerations satisfy me that Part XX.1 does not discriminate against NCR accused.

■

Two companion decisions were released by the Court with *Winko*: *R. v. LePage*, [1999] 2 S.C.R. 744, and *Orlowski v. British Columbia*, [1999] 2 S.C.R. 733 (rejecting ss. 7 and 15 challenges based on *Winko*).

Before *Swain* was decided and the new provisions enacted, 40–85 per cent of accused under warrant for a s. 16 verdict had been charged with murder or attempted murder: Isabel Grant, "Canada's New Mental Disorder Disposition Provisions: A Case Study of British Columbia Criminal Code Review Board" (1997) 20 Int. J. Law and Psychiatry 419 at 427. What new patterns of resort to s. 16 might you predict in light of the new law? What sorts of orders might you expect courts and Review Boards to impose in the typical case? One early study by Isabel Grant found that the category of offences for which mental disorder is advanced as a defence has greatly expanded. Her study of 112 cases before the B.C. Review Board found that only seven (6.25 per cent) had been charged with murder or attempted murder. The rest involved offences against the person (71.43 per cent), property crimes (19.64 per cent), and public order offences (8.93 per cent) (at 427). She also found that absolute discharges were extremely rare — one case of the 112 (at 479). Most received conditional release orders (67 per cent), but she notes that almost half of these required the accused to reside at a psychiatric facility, at the direction of the director of the facility. In the result, 37.5 per cent received true conditional release orders, leaving approximately 61.6 per cent with detention or *de facto* detention orders.

CONSTRUCTIONS OF MENTAL DISORDER

This area of criminal law makes important assumptions about "mental disorder" that deserve critical analysis. For example, at some level mental illness is constructed both by psychiatrists and by our social and political ordering of gender relations. Compare, for example, the social construction of male violence against women as individualized deviance indicative of mental illness, with the patterns that suggest that men and women are diagnosed as disordered based on deviation from class-based standards and gender role conformity in terms of sexuality, familial roles, and self-presentation. Note, for example, the following: *R. v. Sullivan* (1995), 37 C.R. (4th) 333 (B.C.C.A.) (accused "not criminally responsible" for second degree murder of his wife and sexual assault with a weapon upon her companion due to "psychogenic automatism"); *R. v. Weldon* (1995), 86 O.A.C. 362 (C.A.) (jury verdict of guilty of first degree murder of common-law wife quashed and finding of "not criminally responsible" substituted on basis that the Crown presented no contrary evidence regarding the effect of the accused's paranoid schizophrenia); and *R. v. Fraser* (1997), 33 O.R. (3d) 161 (C.A.) (accused found "not criminally responsible" for criminal harassment of former girlfriend because he was afflicted with "erotomania"). As you consider these men's and women's cases, ask whether these legal and psychiatric results are appropriate for the individual men and women, for men and women more generally, and for the larger society.

Gail Donaldson and Mark Kingwell discuss the construction of mental disorder, the psychiatric labelling of behaviour, and the influential manual *Diagnostic and Statistical Manual of Mental Disorders* (DSM), produced by the American Psychiatric Association, in "Who gets to decide who's normal?" *The [Toronto] Globe and Mail* (9 May 1993) A18. One of the examples they cite is the labelling of homosexuality as a "personality disorder" until 1969, when it was re-listed as a "disputed mental condition". For a detailed critique of the DSM, see: Paula Caplan, *They Say You're Crazy: How the World's Most Powerful Psychiatrists Decide Who's Normal* (Redding: Addison-Wesley, 1995), and Denise Russell, *Women, Madness, and Medicine* (Cambridge: Polity Press, 1995).

In a review of Russell's book, [1996] 4 Feminist Legal Stud. 249 at 250–51, Kate Diesfeld restates her arguments:

> Certain specific diagnoses are disproportionately applied to women. For example, medical researchers in North America and the United Kingdom report that alarming numbers of women suffering from multiple and borderline personality disorders have a history of child abuse. Russell does not call for a new category of disorder, but an acknowledgement of the range of *normal* reactions to abuse.
>
> Although trends in psychiatry shift, they perpetuate diagnoses which fail to locate distress in systemic oppression.
>
> ...
>
> Russell recommends that the frequency and impact of abuse must be addressed, and prevented. This requires intervention in abusive relations. Social and economic assistance is vital and children should be taught skills in the school curriculum to identify and respond to the threat of abuse.†

Consider the case of Dorothy Joudrie, above, under **The Trial Process**, and ask whether individual and broader justice was achieved. She shot her ex-husband six times at close range with a semi-automatic handgun. At her trial for attempted murder, her evidence was that she was in a robotic state and that she recalled nothing of the attack. Her testimony was supported by psychiatric evidence and legal argument to the effect that she was in a state of automatism and suffering from a mental disorder. The defence led evidence of extreme long-term mental and physical abuse by Joudrie's ex-husband, her despair about their impending divorce, and her dependency on alcohol. The jury found her not criminally responsible on the basis of mental disorder. After spending five months in a treatment facility, Joudrie was released into the community on strict conditions. For a detailed discussion of this case see Audrey Andrews, *Be Good, Sweet Maid. The Trials of Dorothy Joudrie* (Waterloo: Wilfred Laurier University Press, 1999).

Compare the effort by the authorities in British Columbia to use the mental disorder provisions to keep an HIV-positive woman who works in prostitution off the streets in *Chambers v. British*

Columbia (A.G.), [1997] B.C.J. No. 1497 (C.A.) (QL). In this case, the accused had been found not criminally responsible with respect to charges of fraudulently obtaining food and assault after she left a restaurant without paying and then bit and scratched the owner and an employee of the restaurant when they tried to detain her. Although the accused was apparently schizophrenic, she was stable at the time of the disposition hearing. Her subsequent detention order was therefore based upon her abuse of drugs and alcohol which, combined with her HIV-positive status and her work in prostitution, was said to render her a danger to herself and to others. The Court of Appeal overturned the detention order and discharged the accused because the order was, in effect, based upon her physical condition of carrying a communicable disease, rather than posing a significant threat of criminal conduct: "disinhibiting behaviour or acting on impulse when using alcohol or drugs are not in and of themselves offences under the *Criminal Code*" (at para. 24).

Questions might also be asked about structural racism, which produces particular hierarchies and then labels the reactions of those targeted by racism as mentally ill, or about the cultural bias of assessment and testing procedures. The Aboriginal Justice Inquiry of Manitoba heard testimony from Dr. Roz Wand, the medical director of the Manitoba Adolescent Treatment Centre, about the misdiagnosis and inappropriate treatment of Aboriginal youth. She cited examples of cases in which Aboriginal youth had been locked up in psychiatric facilities for months or years and subsequently found not to be mentally ill. She also described the overrepresentation of Aboriginal and Metis youth in treatment and explained it both as a result of the higher risk of disorders due to poverty and as a justifiable response to the chaos brought about when children were removed from their families. See Geoffrey York, "Natives misdiagnosed in U.S., inquiry is told" *The [Toronto] Globe and Mail* (18 November 1992) A12.

12

Intoxication and Extreme Intoxication

The following extract describes the law governing the defence of intoxication prior to the Supreme Court of Canada's decision in *R. v. Daviault*, below.

The Intoxication Defence in Canada: Why Women Should Care†

The early response of the criminal law in England to an accused's allegations that he should not be held responsible for a crime committed while intoxicated was unequivocally negative: *Reniger v. Fogossa* (1551), 1 Plow. 1 at 19, 75 E.R. 1 at 31. In England in 1920, the case of *D.P.P. v. Beard*, [1920] A.C. 479 established the "specific intent/general intent" classification that still survives in Canadian law today. This classification is anomalous in that it is only applicable to the law governing intoxication; it has no relevance to any other criminal law issue.

The effect of this classification was to make voluntary intoxication available as a defence for certain crimes, those characterized as "specific intent" offences, while still precluding intoxication as a defence for "general intent" offences. The Supreme Court of Canada has adopted, as part of Canadian common law, this understanding of the intoxication defence and the classification scheme, most notably in *R. v. George*, [1960] S.C.R. 671, *R. v. Leary*, [1978] 1 S.C.R. 79 and *R. v. Swietlinski*, [1980] 2 S.C.R. 956. The law governing the intoxication defence applies whether the accused has abused alcohol, drugs, or some combination of the two: *R. v. Curtis* (1972), 8 C.C.C. (2d) 240 (Ont. C.A.).

Specific intent offences are, with some exceptions, those offences where either the *Code* or the common law define the mental element of the offence as one that is specifically focussed on producing a particular consequence. The notion is that for such offences, extreme intoxication could impair the accused's capacity to deliberately pursue a course

† Elizabeth Sheehy, *The Intoxication Defence in Canada: Why Women Should Care* (pp. 2–3) (Ottawa: Status of Women Canada, 1995).

of action intended to result in a particular outcome. For example, the following offences have been put in the specific intent category by the judiciary: murder (requires proof of intention to cause the death of the victim: *Swietlinski, supra*), theft (requires proof of intent to deprive another permanently of their property: *George, supra*), touching a child for a sexual purpose (*R. v. Bone*, [1993] Man. J. No. 222 (C.A.) (Q.L.)), uttering a threat to cause death (*ibid.*) and using violence to overcome a victim's resistance (*R. v. J.A.R.*, [1993] O.J. No. 1566 (Ct. Just. (Gen. Div.) (Q.L.)).

General intent offences are those that have as their mental element an intent to commit the immediate act, without reference to producing any specific consequences. For these offences, it is thought that the mental element is so minimal as to only require basic voluntariness, and that no amount of alcohol or drug consumption, short of insanity, could obliterate one's capacity to intend one's immediate physical movements. Alternatively, it has been stated by judges that the mental element involved in voluntarily incapacitating oneself is sufficiently blameworthy to allow it to be substituted for the mental element for general intent offences. Such offences include manslaughter (where the required intent is simply to perform the act that ultimately causes death: *Swietlinski, supra*) assault causing bodily harm (requires proof of intent to assault, without regard to intending bodily harm: *George, supra*) and sexual assault (*Leary, supra, R. v. Bernard* (1988), 67 C.R. (3d) 113 (S.C.C.)).

For specific intent offences, the accused would be permitted to ask the jury to consider the defence of intoxication if he introduced enough evidence to convince the judge that intoxication was a real issue in the case. This means that the accused would have to show more than moderate consumption of alcohol, and may need an "expert" to testify as to the likely effect of that consumption. The jury would then be instructed that only if the intoxication was so severe that the accused was deprived of his capacity to form the intention required for the offence, could the defence be successful. If successful, the accused could still be convicted for any lesser offences, called "included offences," that were encompassed by the original charge and that were classified as "general intent" offences. For example, an accused acquitted of murder based on intoxication would still be convicted of manslaughter; an accused acquitted of robbery would still be convicted of assault.

■

R. v. Daviault†

[LAMER C.J.:]

I have read the reasons of my colleagues, Justice Sopinka and Justice Cory. My views of the matter were enunciated through my concurrence in the reasons of Dickson C.J. in *R. v. Bernard*, [1988] 2 S.C.R. 833. While I now prefer characterizing the mental element involved as relating more to the *actus reus* than *mens rea,* so that the defence clearly be available in strict liability offences, my views have not changed. I agree with my colleague Cory J.'s position on the law and, given my position in *Bernard,* which goes much further, I would of course support carving out, as he does, an exception to the rule laid down in *Leary v. The Queen,* [1978] 1 S.C.R. 29. I would accordingly allow the appeal and direct a new trial.

. . . .

[LA FOREST J.:]

In *R. v. Bernard,* [1988] 2 S.C.R. 833, as well as in *R. v. Quin*, [1988] 2 S.C.R. 825, I, along with the Chief Justice, shared the view of then Chief Justice Dickson which strongly challenged the rule in *Leary v. The Queen,* [1978] I S.C.R. 29. While the majority of the Court differed as to the specific interpretation of *Leary,* what is clear is that they rejected the view espoused by Dickson C.J. I am, therefore, left to choose between the approach set forth in McIntyre J.'s reasons in that case, developed here by Justice Sopinka, and those of Justice Wilson, developed here by Justice Cory. Of the two, I prefer the latter and accordingly (though I would be inclined to attribute

† [1994] 3 S.C.R. 63.

the mental element he describes as going to the *actus reus*) I concur in the reasons of Cory J. and would dispose of this appeal in the manner proposed by him.

[CORY J. (*per* L'Heureux-Dubé, Cory, McLachlin, and Iacobucci JJ.):]

. . . .

ISSUE

Can a state of drunkenness which is so extreme that an accused is in a condition that closely resembles automatism or a disease of the mind as defined in s. 16 of the *Criminal Code,* R.S.C., 1985, c. C-46, constitute a basis for defending a crime which requires not a specific but only a general intent? That is the troubling question that is raised on this appeal.

A review of the history of the defence of intoxication shows that, originally, intoxication was never a defence to any crime. However, with the evolution of criminal law, this rule came to be progressively relaxed and the defence of intoxication was admitted for crimes of specific intent. Although one of the justifications for this was the courts' preoccupation with the harshness of criminal liability and criminal sanctions, clearly this development was also influenced by the development of the requirements for mental elements in crimes. The defence of intoxication was based on the recognition and belief that alcohol affected mental processes and the formulation of intention (see, for example, D. McCord, "The English and American History of Voluntary Intoxication to Negate *Mens Rea*" (1990), 11 *J. Legal Hist.* 372, at p. 378). I would agree with the authors who feel that the progressive expansion of the intoxication defence has paralleled the progressive expansion of theories of the mental elements of crimes. (See, for example, T. Quigley, "A Shorn Beard" (1987), 10:3 *Dalhousie L.J.* 167.) In my view, the need for this historical expansion is justified and emphasized by the increased concern for the protection of fundamental rights enshrined in the *Charter.*

It can thus be seen that with the development of principles recognizing constituent elements of crimes, particularly the need for a mental element, there came the realization that persons who lack the requisite mental element for a crime should not be found guilty of committing that crime. For centuries it has been recognized that both the physical and the mental elements are an integral part of a criminal act. It has long been a fundamental concept of our criminal law.

This appeal is concerned with situations of intoxication that are so extreme that they are akin to automatism. Such a state would render an accused incapable of either performing a willed act or of forming the minimal intent required for a general intent offence. I will approach the issue primarily on the basis that the extreme intoxication renders an accused incapable of forming the requisite minimum intent. I have taken the reasons of Sopinka J. to have dealt with the issue on the basis of *mens rea.*

Categorization of Crimes As Requiring Either a Specific Intent or a General Intent

The distinction between crimes of specific and general intent has been acknowledged and approved by the Court on numerous occasions. (See *R. v. George*, [1960] S.C.R. 871, at p. 877 (Fauteux J.); and subsequent cases such as *Leary v. The Queen,* [1978] 1 S.C.R. 29; *Swietlinski v. The Queen,* [1980] 2 S.C.R. 956; *R. v. Chase*, [1987] 2 S.C.R. 293; *R. v. Bernard*, [1988] 2 S.C.R. 833; and *R. v. Quin*, [1988] 2 S.C.R. 825.) On this issue, I am in general agreement with Sopinka J.'s presentation. The categorization of crimes as being either specific or general intent offences and the consequences that flow from that categorization are now well established in this Court. However, as he observes, we are not dealing here with ordinary cases of intoxication but with the limited situation of very extreme intoxication and the need, under the *Charter,* to create an exception in situations where intoxication is such that the mental element is negated. Sopinka J. sees no need for such an exception. This is where I must disagree with my colleague.

[Cory J. then reviewed the law in *R. v. Leary*, [1978] 1 S.C.R. 79, and *R. v. O'Connor* (1980), 4 A. Crim. R. 348 (H.Ct. Aust.). In *Leary* a majority of the Court found that rape was a general intent offence and, as such, an offence for which the defence of self-induced intoxication was not available to the accused. The minority (Dickson J., Laskin C.J., and Spence J. concurring) took the position that drunkenness was one factor that should be put to the jury to allow them to consider whether the accused had the requisite *mens rea* for the offence such that he knew that the victim was not consenting or was reckless as to whether she was not consenting.

In contrast, in *O'Connor* the Australian High Court concluded that for all offences requiring *mens rea*, evidence of intoxication (self-induced or not) was relevant and admissible in determining whether all the required elements of the offence were present. The High Court went on to note that intoxication should be left to the jury only when the evidence shows that the accused was unconscious or that his mind was blank as a result of drunkenness at the time of the offence.]

Passage of the *Charter* and Subsequent Cases of This Court

The passage of the *Charter* makes it necessary to consider whether the decision in *Leary* contravenes s. 7 or s. 11(d) of the *Charter.* Those sections provide:

> **7.** Everyone has the right to life, liberty and security of the person and the right not to be deprived thereof except in accordance with the principles of fundamental justice.
>
> **11.** Any person charged with an offence has the right
>
> ...
>
> (*d*) to be presumed innocent until proven guilty according to law in a fair and public hearing by an independent and impartial tribunal;

There have been some statements by this Court which indicate that one aspect of the decision in *Leary* does infringe these provisions of the *Charter.* The first occurred in *R. v. Bernard, supra.* Bernard was charged with sexual assault causing bodily harm. He was tried by judge and jury and found guilty. Bernard admitted forcing the complainant to have sexual intercourse with him but stated that his drunkenness caused him to attack her. The issue was whether self-induced intoxication should be considered by the jury along with all the other relevant evidence in determining whether the prosecution had proved beyond a reasonable doubt the *mens rea* required by the offence. Bernard's appeal was dismissed by a majority of the Court. They all agreed that, as the defence of intoxication had not been made out on the evidence, s. 613(1)(b)(iii) (now s. 686(1)(b)(iii)) of the *Criminal Code* could be applied. Four sets of reasons were given.

. . . .

[McIntyre J. (Beetz J. concurring) concluded that drunkenness could not be a defence for general intent offences. They reasoned that the necessary blameworthy mental state for an accused who was so intoxicated that the voluntariness of the act committed could be in question, was established by proving that the accused consumed the alcohol voluntarily.

Wilson J. (L'Heureux-Dubé J. concurring) agreed with the conclusion reached by McIntyre J. and Beetz J. However, she argued for modification of the *Leary* rule, suggesting that evidence of intoxication could be put before a jury in general intent offences if the evidence established that the intoxication was so extreme that the accused was in a state of awareness akin to insanity or automatism.

Dickson C.J. (Lamer J. concurring) wrote a dissenting opinion. He would have found that the *Leary* rule violated the accused's *Charter* rights because it does not recognize the fundamental principles of voluntariness and fault. He reasoned that evidence of self-induced intoxication should be put to the jury to determine whether the accused had the required *mens rea* for the offence.

La Forest J. agreed with Dickson C.J.'s analysis of the law but reasoned that, since there had been no substantial wrong or miscarriage of justice as a result of the strict application of the *Leary* rule on the facts of the case, the result reached by the majority was the correct one.]

Thus it can be seen that only two judges were of the view that evidence of intoxication could not, under any circumstances, be placed before a jury for its consideration. La Forest J.'s words stressing the importance of the establishment of *mens rea* in criminal offences supply strong support for adopting the position put forward by Wilson and L'Heureux-Dubé JJ. that the *Leary* rule should be modified to permit evidence of severe intoxication, resulting in the accused being in a state akin to insanity or automatism, to be adduced.

The same position was put forward by Wilson J., again concurred in by L'Heureux-Dubé J., in *R. v. Penno,* [1990] 2 S.C.R. 865. In my view, this position has much to commend it and should be adopted.

The Alternative Options

What options are available with regard to the admissibility and significance of evidence of drunkenness as it may pertain to the mental element in general intent offences? One choice would be to continue to apply the *Leary* rule. Yet, as I will attempt to demonstrate in the next section, the rule violates the *Charter* and cannot be justified. Thus this choice is unacceptable.

Another route would be to follow the *O'Connor* decision. Evidence relating to drunkenness would then go to the jury along with all other relevant evidence in determining whether the mental element requirement had been met. It is this path that is enthusiastically recommended by the majority of writers in the field. Yet it cannot be followed. It is now well established by this Court that there are two categories of offences[: those] requiring a specific intent and others which call for nothing more than a general intent. To follow *O'Connor* would mean that all evidence of intoxication of any degree would always go to the jury in general intent offences. This, in my view, is unnecessary. Further, in *Bernard, supra,* the majority of this Court rejected this approach.

A third alternative, which I find compelling, is that proposed by Wilson J. in *Bernard.* I will examine the justifications for adopting this position in more detail shortly, but before doing that it may be helpful to review the nature of the *Charter* violations occasioned by a rigid application of the *Leary* rule.

How the *Leary* Rule Violates Sections 7 and 11(d) of the *Charter*

What then is the rule of law established by the decision in *Leary?* The conclusion of the majority in that case establishes that, even in a situation where the level of intoxication reached by the accused is sufficient to raise a reasonable doubt as to his capacity to form the minimal mental element required for a general intent offence for which he is being tried, he still cannot be acquitted. In such a situation, self-induced intoxication is substituted for the mental element of the crime. The result of the decision in *Leary,* applied to this case, is that the intentional act of the accused to voluntarily become intoxicated is substituted for the intention to commit the sexual assault or for the recklessness of the accused with regard to the assault. This is a true substitution of *mens rea.* First, it would be rare that the events transpiring from the consumption of alcohol through to the commission of the crime could be seen as one continuous series of events or as a single transaction. Secondly, the requisite mental element or *mens rea* cannot necessarily be inferred from the physical act or *actus reus* when the very voluntariness or consciousness of that act may be put in question by the extreme intoxication of the accused.

It has not been established that there is such a connection between the consumption of alcohol and the crime of assault that it can be said that drinking leads inevitably to the assault. Experience may suggest that alcohol makes it easier for violence to occur by diminishing the sense of what is acceptable behaviour. However, studies indicate that it is not in itself a cause of violence. See *Interim Report of the Commission of Inquiry into the Non-Medical Use of Drugs (1970), c. 3.; "The Le Dain Interim Report,"* referred to by S.H. Berner, in *Intoxication and Criminal Responsibility* (Law Reform Commission of Canada, 1975); Law Commission, Great Britain, *Intoxication and Criminal Liability,* Consultation Paper No. 127 (1993), at pp. 4 and 67; see also the references and additional information given in notes 14, 15, 16 and 18 at p. 4.: C.N. Mitchell, "The Intoxicated Offender — Refuting the Legal and Medical Myths" (1988), 11 *Int. J.L. & Psychiatry* 77, at p. 89; S.S. Covington, "Alcohol and Family Violence," Paper presented at the 34th International Congress on Alcoholism and Drug Dependence, at p. 24: L. Wolff and B. Reingold, "Drug Use and Crime" (1994), 14:6 *Juristat* 1, at pp. 5 to 8 and 13; and Saskatchewan Alcohol and Drug Abuse Commission, *Legal Offences in Saskatchewan: The Alcohol and Drug Connection* (Research Report, February 1989). For example, in the SADAC Research Report of 1989, the following appears at p. 8:

> While it is widely recognized that alcohol and drug abuse are associated with criminality, neither the extent of this association nor its nature has been clearly identified, (Brain, 1986: Collins, 1988; Evans, 1986; MacLatchie, 1987; Pernanen, 1976).
>
> ...
>
> ... But more research is required in order to establish with confidence the nature or extent to which such offences are drug related. However, research conducted elsewhere would suggest that, at most, 10% of violent offences in Saskatchewan are drug related (Johnson, 1986).
>
> Alcohol abuse, although it frequently accompanies violent behaviour, is not, in and of itself, a cause of violence. The standards advocated by Powers and Kotash (1982) to determine whether causal status should be accorded to alcohol abuse are adopted here. For Powers and Kotash, a factor must be both a *necessary* and a *sufficient* condition for a particular event to occur in order for it to qualify as a "cause." Consider the phenomenon of partner abuse (an all too prevalent form of assault) in this light.

In the words of Powers and Kotash:

> Alcohol and drugs are not causally related to partner abuse in terms of being necessary or sufficient conditions for the violence. Substance abuse is not a necessary condition, in that a great proportion of the violence occurs in the

> absence of alcohol or drugs. Substance abuse is not a sufficient condition, for alcohol and drugs are often used without violent occurrence (1982:42).
>
> Alcohol abuse can best be viewed as a 'facilitator' of violence. That is to say that in our culture, alcohol abuse makes it easier for violence to occur, either by blurring the boundaries between what is and what is not acceptable behaviour, or by removing conscious recognition of rules governing acceptable [behaviour] altogether (Scott, 1988; Collins, 1988).
>
> In addition, in some instances alcohol or drug abuse may serve as a conscious accompanier of violent behavior in that some offenders use alcohol or drug abuse to excuse a violent act (e.g., some instances of wife battering) (Coid, 1986; Powers and Kotash 1982). [Comment: I would note that the effects referred to in the last two paragraphs have always been held to be insufficient to deny the existence of the requisite mental element.]
>
> There is no simple causal relationship between alcohol or drug abuse and violent behavior (Brain, 1986). Patterns of violent behavior are shaped by a host of physiological, psychological, situational and socio-cultural factors. Among the various socio-cultural factors which shape patterns of substance abuse and violence, especially important are gender, age, socio-economic status and ethnicity (Coid, 1986).

In my view, the strict application of the *Leary* rule offends both ss. 7 and 11(d) of the *Charter* for a number of reasons. The mental aspect of an offence, or *mens rea,* has long been recognized as an integral part of crime. The concept is fundamental to our criminal law. That element may be minimal in general intent offences; nonetheless, it exists. In this case, the requisite mental element is simply an intention to commit the sexual assault or recklessness as to whether the actions will constitute an assault. The necessary mental element can ordinarily be inferred from the proof that the assault was committed by the accused. However, the substituted *mens rea* of an intention to become drunk cannot establish the *mens rea* to commit the assault.

R. v. Whyte, [1988] 2 S.C.R. 3, dealt with the substitution of proof of one element for proof of an essential element of an offence and emphasized the strict limitations that must be imposed on such substitutions. The position is put in this way, at pp. 18–19:

> In the passage from *Vaillancourt* quoted earlier, Lamer J. recognized that in some cases substituting proof of one element for proof of an essential element will not infringe the presumption of innocence if, upon proof of the substituted element, it would be unreasonable for the trier of fact not to be satisfied beyond a reasonable doubt of the existence of the essential element. This is another way of saying that a statutory presumption infringes the presumption of innocence if it requires the trier of fact to convict in spite of a reasonable doubt. *Only if the existence of the substituted fact leads inexorably to the conclusion that the essential element exists, with no other reasonable possibilities, will the statutory presumption be constitutionally valid.* [Emphasis added.]

The substituted *mens rea* set out in *Leary* does not meet this test. The consumption of alcohol simply cannot lead inexorably to the conclusion that the accused possessed the requisite mental element to commit a sexual assault, or any other crime. Rather, the substituted *mens rea* rule has the effect of eliminating the minimal mental element required for sexual assault. Furthermore, *mens rea* for a crime is so well recognized that to eliminate that mental element, an integral part of the crime, would be to deprive an accused of fundamental justice. See *R. v. Vaillancourt,* [1987] 2 S.C.R. 636.

In that same case it was found that s. 11(d) would be infringed in those situations where an accused could be convicted despite the existence of reasonable doubt pertaining to one of the essential elements of the offence; see *Vaillancourt, supra,* at pp. 654–56. That would be the result if the *Leary* rule was to be strictly applied. For example, an accused in an extreme state of intoxication akin to automatism or mental illness would have to be found guilty although there was reasonable doubt as to the voluntary nature of the act committed by the accused. This would clearly infringe both ss. 7 and 11(d) of the *Charter.* In my view, the mental element of voluntariness is a fundamental aspect of the crime which cannot be taken away by a judicially developed policy. It simply cannot be automatically inferred that there would be an objective foresight that the consequences of voluntary intoxication would lead to the commission of the offence. It follows that it cannot be said that a reasonable person, let alone an accused who might be a young person inexperienced with alcohol, would expect that such intoxication would lead to either a state akin to automatism, or to the commission of a sexual assault. Nor is it likely that someone can really intend to get so intoxicated that they would reach a state of insanity or automatism.

Sopinka J. refers to the common law rules of automatism in order to support his position that voluntariness is not a requirement of fundamental justice. With respect I cannot agree. The decision of this Court in *Revelle v. The Queen,* [1981] 1 S.C.R. 576, predates the *Charter.* The rule that self-induced automatism cannot be a defence has never been subjected to a *Charter* analysis. In my view, automatism raises the same concerns as those presented in this case. Thus, to state that the rule in *Leary,* which precludes the accused from negating the mental element of voluntariness on the basis of an extreme state of intoxication, does not violate the *Charter* because the same principle has been developed in the context of the defence of automatism begs the very question which is now before this Court. The presumption of innocence requires that the Crown bear the burden of establishing all elements of a crime. These elements include the mental element of voluntariness. That element cannot be eliminated without violating s. 11(d) and s. 7 of the *Charter.*

It was argued by the respondent that the "blameworthy" nature of voluntary intoxication is such that it should be determined that there can be no violation of the *Charter* if the *Leary* approach is adopted. I cannot accept that contention. Voluntary intoxication is not yet a crime. Further, it is difficult to conclude that such behaviour should always constitute a fault to which criminal sanctions should apply. However, assuming that voluntary intoxication is reprehensible it does not follow that its consequences in any given situation are either voluntary or predictable. Studies demonstrate that the consumption of alcohol is not the cause of the crime. A person intending to drink cannot be said to be intending to commit a sexual assault.

Further, self-induced intoxication cannot supply the necessary link between the minimal mental element or *mens rea* required for the offence and the *actus reus.* This must follow from reasoning in *R. v. DeSousa,* [1992] 2 S.C.R. 944, and *R. v. Théroux, supra.* Here, the question is not whether there is some symmetry between the physical act and the mental element but whether the necessary link exists between the minimal mental element and the prohibited act; that is to say that the mental element is one of intention with respect to the *actus reus* of the crime charged. As well, as Sopinka J. observes, the minimum *mens rea* for an offence should reflect the particular nature of the crime. See *R. v. Creighton,* [1993] 3 S.C.R. 3. I doubt that self-induced intoxication can, in all circumstances, meet this requirement for all crimes of general intent.

In summary, I am of the view that to deny that even a very minimal mental element is required for sexual assault offends the *Charter* in a manner that is so drastic and so contrary to the principles of fundamental justice that it cannot be justified under s. 1 of the *Charter.* The experience of other jurisdictions which have completely abandoned the *Leary* rule, coupled with the fact that under the proposed approach, the defence would be available only in the rarest of cases, demonstrate that there is no urgent policy or pressing objective which [needs] to be addressed. Studies on the relationship between intoxication and crime do not establish any rational link. Finally, as the *Leary* rule applies to all crimes of general intent, it cannot be said to be well tailored to address a particular objective and it would not meet either the proportionality or the minimum impairment requirements.

What then should be the fate of the *Leary* rule?

Approach That Should Be Taken When a Common Law Principle Is Found to Infringe the Provisions of the *Charter*

In *R. v. Swain,* [1991] 1 S.C.R. 933, Lamer C.J. (concurred in by Sopinka J. and myself) wrote on this issue. At page 978 he stated:

> Before turning to s. 1, however, I wish to point out that because this appeal involves a *Charter* challenge to a common law, judge-made rule, the *Charter* analysis involves somewhat different considerations than would apply to a challenge to a legislative provision. For example, having found that the existing common law rule limits an accused's rights under s. 7 of the *Charter,* it may not be strictly necessary to go on to consider the application of s. 1. Having come to the conclusion that the common law rule enunciated by the Ontario Court of Appeal limits an accused's right to liberty in a manner which does not accord with the principles of fundamental justice, it could, in my view, be appropriate to consider at this stage whether an alternative common law rule could be fashioned which would not be contrary to the principles of fundamental justice.
>
> If a new common law rule could be enunciated which would not interfere with an accused person's right to have control over the conduct of his or her defence, I can see no conceptual problem with the Court's simply enunciating such a rule to take the place of the old rule, without considering whether the old rule could nonetheless be upheld under s. 1 of the *Charter.* Given that the common law rule was fashioned by judges and not by Parliament or a legislature, judicial deference to elected bodies is not an issue. If it is possible to reformulate a common law rule so that it will not conflict with the prin-

> ciples of fundamental justice, such a reformulation should be undertaken.

This then is the approach that should be adopted when a common law principle is found to infringe the *Charter.* This, again, militates in favour of the adoption of a flexible application of the *Leary* rule, as was suggested by Wilson J.

Justifications for the Adoption of the Flexible Approach Suggested by Wilson J.

As I have said, the position adopted by Wilson J. in *Bernard* has much to commend it and should be adopted. Indeed, the original case which is the basis for much of our jurisprudence pertaining to intoxication seems to confirm this position. In *Director of Public Prosecutions v. Beard,* [1920] A.C. 479, Lord Birkenhead set out the three propositions which have been so frequently referred to in cases involving intoxication and criminal behaviour, at pp. 500–502:

> 1. That insanity, whether produced by drunkenness or otherwise, is a defence to the crime charged. The distinction between the defence of insanity in the true sense caused by excessive drinking, and the defence of drunkenness which produces a condition such that the drunken man's mind becomes incapable of forming a specific intention, has been preserved throughout the cases. The insane person cannot be convicted of a crime: ... but, upon a verdict of insanity, is ordered to be detained during His Majesty's pleasure. The law takes no note of the cause of the insanity. If actual insanity in fact supervenes, as the result of alcoholic excess, it furnishes as complete an answer to a criminal charge as insanity induced by any other cause....
>
> ...
>
> 2. That evidence of drunkenness which renders the accused incapable of forming the specific intent essential to constitute the crime should be taken into consideration with the other facts proved in order to determine whether or not he had this intent.
>
> 3. *That evidence of drunkenness falling short of a proved incapacity in the accused to form the intent necessary to constitute the crime, and merely establishing that his mind was affected by drink so that he more readily gave way to some violent passion, does not rebut the presumption that a man intends the natural consequences of his acts.* [Emphasis added.]

It does not appear to me that the decision was meant to create a complete bar to the defence of intoxication in the context of crimes of general intent. This appears from the subsequent statements of Lord Birkenhead found at pp. 504–5, and 507:

> I do not think that the proposition of law deduced from these earlier cases is an exceptional rule applicable only to cases in which it is necessary to prove a specific intent in order to constitute the graver crime — e.g. wounding with intent to do grievous bodily harm or with intent to kill. It is true that in such cases the specific intent must be proved to constitute the particular crime, but *this is, on ultimate analysis, only in accordance with the ordinary law applicable to crime, for, speaking generally (and apart from certain special offences), a person cannot be convicted of a crime unless the mens was rea.* Drunkenness, rendering a person incapable of the intent, would be an answer, as it is for example in a charge of attempted suicide....
>
> My Lords, *drunkenness in this case could be no defence unless it could be established that Beard at the time of committing the rape was so drunk that he was incapable of forming the intent to commit it,* which was not in fact, and manifestly, having regard to the evidence, could not be contended. For in the present case the death resulted from two acts or from a succession of acts, the rape and the act of violence causing suffocation. These acts cannot be regarded separately and independently of each other. The capacity of the mind of the prisoner to form the felonious intent which murder involves is in other words to be explored in relation to the ravishment; and not in relation merely to the violent acts which gave effect to the ravishment.
>
> ...
>
> In the present case I doubt, without reaching a conclusion, whether there was any sufficient evidence to go to the jury that the prisoner was, in the only relevant sense, drunk at all. *There was certainly no evidence that he was too drunk to form the intent of committing rape.* [Emphasis added.]

Thus, from the outset it appears to have been contemplated that evidence that the accused was too drunk to form the mental element required for a general intent offence could be presented and considered.

Further support for the modification of the *Leary* rule in favour of the more flexible rule suggested by Wilson J. comes from the fact that the decision in *Majewski, supra,* which was relied upon by the majority in *Leary,* has been the subject of severe criticism in the United Kingdom. The following extract from the Law Commission's *Intoxication and Criminal Liability, supra,* at p. 34 is an example:

> The present law is therefore objectionable on three levels. It is very complicated and difficult to explain, to the extent that it is difficult to think that it operates in practice other than by its detailed rules being substantially ignored; it purports to apply a clear social policy, of ensuring that intoxicated people who commit criminal acts do not escape criminal sanctions, but only does so in an erratic and unprincipled way; and if taken seriously it creates many difficulties of practical application. It is therefore understandable that in other jurisdictions, and under the rational scrutiny of law reformers, other solutions have been sought to the problem of protecting society from those who commit criminal acts when in a state of intoxication.

Perhaps the result in these cases arose from the understandable desire to ensure that accused persons should not escape criminal responsibility by the consumption of alcohol. A few writers have sought, rather unconvincingly in my view, to uphold these decisions on this basis. See M. T. Thornton, "Making Sense of Majewski" (1981), 23 *Crim. L.Q.* 464; E. Colvin, "A Theory of the Intoxication Defence" (1981), 59 *Can. Bar Rev,* 750; A. Dashwood, "Logic and the Lords in Majewski," [1977] *Crim. L.R.* 532, 591; and S. Gardner, "The Importance of Majewski" (1994), 14 *Oxford J. Legal Stud. 279.*

Far more writers have supported the approach advocated by Dickson J. in *Leary,* and adopted in *O'Connor.* In my view, the most vehement and cogent criticism of both *Majewski* and *Leary* is that they substitute proof of drunkenness for proof of the requisite mental element. The authors deplore the division of crimes into those requiring a specific intent and those which mandate no more than a general intent. They are also critical of the resulting presumption of recklessness, and of the loss of a requirement of a true *mens rea* for the offence. They would prefer an approach that would permit evidence of drunkenness to go to the jury together with all the other relevant evidence in determining whether the requisite *mens rea* had been established....

. . . .

I find further support for adopting the approach suggested by Wilson J. in studies pertaining to the effect of the *O'Connor* and *Kamipeli* decisions which have been undertaken in Australia and New Zealand. (Reference to these studies can be found in the English Law Commission's *Intoxication and Criminal Liability, supra,* at pp. 60–63.) One of these studies was conducted in New South Wales, by means of a survey of approximately 510 trials (see Judge G. Smith, "Footnote to O'Connor's Case," *supra).* The author, Judge George Smith, concluded, at p. 277, that:

> Those figures disclose that a "defence" of intoxication which could not have been relied upon pre-*O'Connor* was raised in eleven cases or 2.16 per cent of the total. Acquittals followed in three cases or 0.59 per cent of the total, but only in one case or 0.2 per cent of the total could it be said with any certainty that the issue of intoxication was the factor which brought about the acquittal.
>
> ...
>
> It seems to me that no one with any experience of the criminal courts should be greatly surprised at this result for the simple practical reason that any "defence" of drunkenness poses enormous difficulties in the conduct of a case. To name but one, if the accused has sufficient recollection to describe relevant events, juries will be reluctant to believe that he acted involuntarily or without intent whereas, if he claims to have no recollection, he will be unable to make any effective denial of facts alleged by the Crown.
>
> Certainly my inquiries would indicate that the decision in *O'Connor's* case, far from opening any floodgates has at most permitted an occasional drip to escape from the tap.

That study clearly indicates that the *O'Connor* decision has not had an effect of any significance on trials or on the numbers of acquittals arising from evidence of severe intoxication.

There are some who argue that Wilson J.'s suggestion favours the extremely drunk while ignoring those who are less inebriated. (See, for example, T. Quigley, in *"Bernard* on Intoxication: Principle, Policy and Points In Between — Two Comments," *supra,* at pp. 171–73.) I cannot agree with that contention. It must be remembered that those who are a "little" drunk can readily form the requisite mental element to commit the offence. The alcohol-induced relaxation of both inhibitions and socially acceptable behaviour has never been accepted as a factor or excuse in determining whether the accused possessed the requisite *mens rea.* Given the minimal nature of the mental element required for crimes of general intent, even those who are significantly drunk will usually be able to form the requisite *mens rea* and will be found to have acted voluntarily. In reality it is only those who can demonstrate that they were in such an extreme degree of intoxication that they were in a state akin to automatism or insanity that might expect to raise a reasonable doubt as to their ability to form the minimal mental element required for a general intent offence. Neither an insane person nor one in a state of automatism is capable of forming the minimum intent required for a general intent offence. Similarly, as the words themselves imply, "drunkenness akin to insanity or automatism" describes a person so severely intoxicated that he is incapable of forming even the minimal intent required of a general intent offence. The phrase refers to a person so drunk that he is an automaton. As such he may be capable of voluntary acts such as moving his arms and legs but is quite incapable of forming the most basic or simple intent required to perform the act prohibited by a general intent offence. I believe that Wilson J.'s modification of the *Leary* rule is a judge-fashioned remedy that can be adopted to remedy a judge-made law which, by eliminating the mental element of a crime, offends the *Charter.*

It is obvious that it will only be on rare occasions that evidence of such an extreme state of intoxication can be advanced and perhaps only on still rarer occasions is it likely to be successful. Nonetheless, the adoption of this alternative would avoid infringement of the *Charter.*

I would add that it is always open to Parliament to fashion a remedy which would make it a crime to commit a prohibited act while drunk.

The appellant in this case is an elderly alcoholic. It is difficult if not impossible to present him in a sympathetic light. Yet any rule on intoxication must apply to all accused, including the young and inexperienced drinker. The strict rule in *Leary* is not a minor or technical infringement but a substantial breach of the *Charter* eliminating the mental elements of crimes of general intent in situations where the accused is in an extreme state of intoxication. I would think that this judge-made rule should be applied flexibly, as suggested by Wilson J., so as to comply with the *Charter.* Such an approach would mean that except in those rare situations where the degree of intoxication is so severe it is akin to automatism, drunkenness will not be a defence to crimes of general intent.

It should not be forgotten that if the flexible "Wilson" approach is taken, the defence will only be put forward in those rare circumstances of extreme intoxication. Since that state must be shown to be akin to automatism or insanity, I would suggest that the accused should be called upon to establish it on the balance of probabilities. This Court has recognized, in *R. v. Chaulk*, [1990] 3 S.C.R. 1303, that although it constituted a violation of the accused's rights under s. 11(d) of the *Charter,* such a burden could be justified under s. 1. In this case, I feel that the burden can be justified. Drunkenness of the extreme degree required in order for it to become relevant will only occur on rare occasions. It is only the accused who can give evidence as to the amount of alcohol consumed and its effect upon him. Expert evidence would be required to confirm that the accused was probably in a state akin to automatism or insanity as a result of his drinking. Justice Grenier in his reasons ([1991] R.J.Q. 1749) properly emphasized the need for expert testimony. He stated (at p. 1797):

> [TRANSLATION] The deposition of the expert Louis Leonard is of particular importance in this matter. The testimony of an accused to the effect that he was not aware of what he was doing is unlikely, in most cases, to constitute on its own a sufficient basis to permit the court to conclude that he was unaware owing to an excessive consumption of alcohol. Scientific evidence is almost essential to support a defence of automatism attributable to an advanced degree of intoxication.

Extreme intoxication akin to automatism or insanity should, like insanity, be established by the accused on a balance of probabilities. This I take to be the position put forward by Lamer C.J. in *R. v. Penno, supra.* At pages 877–78, the following appears:

> For those reasons, I am of the view that the offence of having care or control of a motor vehicle while one's ability to drive is impaired is a general intent offence. It follows, as was decided by a majority of this Court in *Bernard,* that no defence of intoxication can negate the *mens rea* of this offence, although the question is still open as to whether intoxication giving rise to a state of insanity or automatism could achieve such a result.
>
> The trial judge found that the appellant was very intoxicated. *However, the appellant did not prove, on a balance of probabilities, that his intoxication was so great as to constitute insanity or automatism,* nor was a state of insanity or automatism found by any of the judges in the courts below. On the facts of this case, I see no need to address the issue concerning the relevance of intoxication to negate the *mens rea* where such intoxication verges on insanity or automatism. [Emphasis added.]

Thus it is appropriate to place an evidentiary and legal burden on the accused to establish, on a balance of probabilities, that he was in a state of extreme intoxication that was akin to automatism or insanity at the time he committed the offence.

Result If the Mental Element Relates Solely to the *Actus Reus* Which Requires That the Prohibited Act Be Performed Voluntarily

Should it be thought that the mental element involved relates to the *actus reus* rather than the *mens rea* then the result must be the same. The *actus reus* requires that the prohibited criminal act be performed voluntarily as a willed act. A person in a state of automatism cannot perform a voluntary willed act since the automatism has deprived the person of the ability to carry out such an act. It follows that someone in an extreme state of intoxication akin to automatism must also be deprived of that ability. Thus a fundamental aspect of the *actus reus* of the criminal act is absent. It would equally infringe s. 7 of the *Charter* if an accused who was not acting voluntarily could be convicted of a criminal offence. Here again the voluntary act of becoming intoxicated cannot be substituted for the voluntary action involved in sexual assault. To do so would violate the principle set out in *Vaillancourt, supra*. Once again to convict in the face of such a fundamental denial of natural justice could not be justified under s. 1 of the *Charter*.

[SOPINKA J. (dissenting):]

This appeal raises a single question of law: can evidence of extreme intoxication tantamount to a state of automatism negative the intent required for sexual assault, an offence which has been classified as an offence of general intent? The appellant challenges the correctness of this Court's decision in *Leary v. The Queen,* [1978] 1 S.C.R. 29, which held that voluntary intoxication can never negate the *mens rea* for an offence of general intent.

FACTS

The facts which give rise to this appeal are not in dispute. The complainant is a 65-year old woman who is partially paralysed and thus confined to a wheelchair. She knew the appellant through his wife, who was the complainant's dressmaker and ran errands for her. The complainant testified that at approximately 6:00 p.m. on May 30, 1989, at her request, the appellant arrived at her home carrying a 40-ounce bottle of brandy. The complainant drank part of a glass of brandy and then fell asleep in her wheelchair. When she awoke during the night to go to the bathroom, the appellant appeared, grabbed her chair, wheeled her into the bedroom, threw her on the bed and sexually assaulted her. The appellant left the apartment about 4:00 a.m. The complainant subsequently discovered that the bottle of brandy was empty. The trial judge found as a fact that the appellant had drunk the rest of the bottle between 6:00 p.m. and 3:00 a.m.

The appellant was a chronic alcoholic. He testified that he had spent the day at a bar where he had consumed seven or eight bottles of beer. He recalled having a glass of brandy upon his arrival at the complainant's residence but had no recollection of what occurred between then and when he awoke nude in the complainant's bed. He denied sexually assaulting her.

The defence called a pharmacologist, Louis Leonard, to testify as an expert witness. Mr. Leonard testified that the appellant's alcoholic history made him less susceptible to the effects of alcohol. He hypothesized that, if the appellant had consumed seven or eight beers during the day and then 35 ounces of brandy on the evening in question, his blood-alcohol content would have been between 400 and 600 milligrams per 100 millilitres of blood. That blood-alcohol ratio would cause death or a coma in an ordinary person. Mr. Leonard testified that an individual with this level of alcohol in his blood might suffer an episode of "l'amnésie-automatisme," also known as a "blackout." In such a state the individual loses contact with reality and the brain is temporarily dissociated from normal functioning. The individual has no awareness of his actions when he is in such a state and will likely have no memory of them the next day.

Mr. Leonard further testified that it is difficult to distinguish between a person in a blackout and someone who is simply acting under the influence of alcohol. He stated that if a person acting under the influence of alcohol behaves in a manner which requires higher cognitive functions or reflection, it is unlikely that the person is in a blackout. On the other hand, if the person departs from his normal behaviour to act in a gratuitous or violent manner, it is more likely that he is in a blackout.

The appellant was charged with one count of sexual assault. The trial judge found as a fact that the appellant had committed the offence as described by the complainant. However, he acquitted the appellant because he had a reasonable doubt about whether the appellant, by virtue of his extreme intoxication, had possessed the minimal intent necessary to commit the offence of sexual assault: [1991] R.J.Q. 1794. The Quebec Court of Appeal overturned this ruling: [1993] R.J.Q. 692, 80 C.C.C. (3d) 175, 19 C.R. (4th) 291, 54 Q.A.C. 27. The appellant now appeals to this Court as of right, pursuant to s. 691(2)(a) of the *Criminal Code,* R.S.C., 1985, c. C-46.

JUDGMENTS BELOW

Court of Québec (Grenier Q.C.J.)

After reviewing the facts, the trial judge concluded that he was left with a reasonable doubt as to whether the appellant was suffering from a blackout when he assaulted the complainant. He noted the importance of the expert evidence of Mr. Leonard, stating, [TRANSLATION] "[s]cientific evidence is almost essential to support a defence of automatism attributable to an advanced degree of intoxication" (p. 1797). The trial judge also noted that he would have convicted the appellant if he had been convinced that the appellant was conscious of what he was doing when he committed the assault.

With respect to the applicable legal principles, the trial judge began by noting that, according to the traditional rule, self-induced intoxication may only be admitted to negate the *mens rea* of offences of specific intent. It may not be admitted to negate the *mens rea* of offences of general intent, including the offence of sexual assault. He then went on to consider the judgments of this Court in *Leary v. The Queen, supra*, and *R. v. Bernard*, [1988] 2 S.C.R. 833. After canvassing the various approaches to intoxication set out in these two cases, he held that the view of the majority of the Court was represented in the reasons of Wilson J. (L'Heureux-Dubé J. concurring) in *Bernard.* Thus, he adopted Wilson J.'s view that evidence of extreme intoxication to the point of insanity or automatism may be admitted to negate the *mens rea* of an offence of general intent.

The trial judge recognized that serious problems of public protection arise under the approach condoned by Wilson J., since it prohibits the state from exercising any means of control over an individual who commits a crime while in a state of extreme self-induced intoxication. However, the trial judge identified three responses to this concern. First, he noted that it is for the legislature, and not for the courts, to create a new offence. Secondly, he noted that even under the traditional approach, self-induced intoxication may lead to an absolute acquittal in the case of offences of specific intent such as theft for which there is no lesser and included offence of general intent. Finally, he indicated that in weighing the requirements of public protection against the requirement that the prosecution prove the existence of *mens rea* beyond a reasonable doubt, he preferred to give priority to the latter.

In the trial judge's view, the evidence did not establish that the appellant was intoxicated to the point of insanity. He also held that the evidence did not support the conclusion that the appellant only suffered a loss of memory after rather than during the incident. He reiterated his conclusion that the accused had raised a reasonable doubt as to whether he had been intoxicated to the point of automatism within the meaning of Wilson J.'s judgment in *Bernard.* Accordingly, the trial judge concluded that he had a reasonable doubt as to the existence of the minimal intent required for the offence of sexual assault. He therefore acquitted the appellant.

. . . .

[Sopinka J. would have upheld the rule in *R. v. Leary* that established that intoxication is no defence for offences of general intent and reaffirmed that intoxication was not a defence for sexual assault. Justice Sopinka discussed the policy reasons for the *Leary* rule. He noted that the punishment of individuals who voluntarily render themselves so intoxicated as to pose a threat to others is consistent with the purpose of the criminal law to protect the public. He also reasoned that the *Leary* rule does not violate ss. 7 or 11(d) of the *Charter* if the definition of the offence requires that a blameworthy mental element be proved and the level of blameworthiness is proportionate to the seriousness of the offence. In this case, Justice Sopinka reasoned that the rules of fundamental justice are satisfied by showing that the accused's drunkenness was caused by his blameworthy and voluntary conduct. Sopinka J. concluded by affirming the soundness of the policy underlying the *Leary* rule and suggested that rather than rejecting the rule, the Court should explore more fully the distinction between specific and general intent offences and rectify existing problems by clearly identifying and defining the mental elements of offences.]

■

A Brief on Bill C-72†

Five accused in Canada secured acquittals using *Daviault* within nine months of the decision: *R. v. Blair*, [1994] A.J. No. 807 (Q.B.) (Q.L.) (assault upon female partner); *R. v. Compton*, reported in Gary Dimmock, "Drunk Excuse Works," *The [Saint John] Telegraph Journal* (10 November 1994) A1 (sexual assault), since sent back for re-trial, and guilty plea entered; *R.* c. *Thériault*, reported in Mike Shahin, "Cocaine high lets man beat assault charge" *The Ottawa Citizen* (18 November 1994) A1, A2 (aggravated assault and threatening death against female partner); *R. v. Misquadis*, [1995] O.J. No. 882 (Prov. Div.) (Q.L.) (assault causing bodily harm upon another man); and *R. v. Daviault* (sexual assault), the accused was acquitted at trial and sent back for retrial by the Supreme Court of Canada, but the charges were withdrawn by the prosecutor because the victim/witness had died: reported in "Law won't be derailed, experts say" *The [Toronto] Globe and Mail* (28 April 1995) A4. Five other accused had successfully used this defence, relying upon Justice Wilson's judgment in *Bernard* (described in *Daviault*) even before the Supreme Court gave the "go ahead" in *Daviault*: *R. v. Saulnier* (assault upon wife), acquittal overturned on appeal: (1992), 100 N.S.R. (2d) 58 (S. Ct.); *R. v. Edgar* (1991), 10 C.R. (4th) 67 (B.C. Prov. Ct.) (sexual assault); *R. v. Finalyson*, [1990] O.J. No. 422 (Dist. Ct.) (Q.L.) (aggravated sexual assault, break and enter); *R. v. McIntyre*, [1992] P.E.I.J. No. 85 (Sup. Ct.) (Q.L.) (assault causing bodily harm upon a woman friend); *R. v. Tom* (1992), 79 C.C.C. (3d) 84 (B.C.C.A.) (assault upon a police officer).

Women's groups in Canada raised specific and grave concerns about the implications of the case for women who are subjected to male violence:

- Canadian statistics show that significant alcohol consumption is a serious social problem; that men are heavier drinkers than women at a rate of 3:1; that intoxication is strongly related to the occurrence and severity of offences of violence, including wife assault and sexual assault; and that while this relationship is not "causal" in a direct sense, it appears that alcohol use may dis-inhibit violence by providing a "social" explanation for the offender.
- Given the disparate rates of alcohol abuse and engagement in offences of violence by men, we might expect to see an increased reliance on the *Daviault* defence in cases involving male violence against women: in fact, out of the total of ten acquittals based on "extreme intoxication," eight involved offences of violence against women.
- "Extreme intoxication" as a defence works to reinforce and excuse male violence against women by attributing the blame to alcohol, minimizing the significance of the violence, focussing on "expert" accounts of the man's alleged mental state, and claiming that pursuant to *Charter* values, someone in this state who admittedly has performed the act of physically assaulting, sexually assaulting, or even killing a woman, is "morally innocent." This defence will reinforce these men's own view that they did nothing wrong and also presents an opportunity for planned alcohol use as a defence.
- The new defence will have an impact upon the "filtering" of offences of violence against women: it will affect women's ability to identify and report violence against them because the message from the Court is that this behaviour is not "criminal" if the man is "extremely intoxicated"; it will affect police decisions as to whether to "found" an offence because they too must assess charges against the legal requirements of proof; and it will affect Crown's decisions about the pursuit of charges, given that prosecutors will need to hire their own "experts" to refute an accused's "extreme intoxication" defence.
- The end result of this filtering will be that even more violence against women will be removed from the criminal courts, thus effectively "de-criminalizing" this behaviour. Unfortunately, we will not even be able to accurately assess the ultimate impact of the *Daviault* case. It may, finally, affect the incidence and severity of violence against women in Canada.

■

† Elizabeth Sheehy, *A Brief on Bill C-72* (Ottawa: National Association of Women and the Law, 1995) at 7–10. (This is a NAWL brief.) Reproduced by permission of NAWL. Websites: www.nawl.ca and www.anfd.ca

Additional repercussions flowing from *Daviault* have emerged when intoxication as a defence is combined with other defences, such as mistake of fact, automatism (see discussion below), or *mens rea* (see the "rage" cases, discussed below, under **Provocation**). Ontario courts had prohibited an accused from arguing that his "mistake" regarding consent to sexual assault was produced by intoxication, since this would effectively evade the rule and policy barring intoxication as a defence to general intent offences: *R. v. Moreau* (1986), 15 O.A.C. 81 (C.A.). However, a B.C. Provincial Court judge reached the opposite conclusion in *R. v. Edgar* (1991), 10 C.R. (4th) 67 (B.C. Prov. Ct.), and both majority and minority opinions in *Daviault* clearly open up the possibility of combining defences in this way. What effect will s. 273.2(a)(i), which specifically prohibits this use of intoxication, have?

After considering the implications of *Daviault* for women, a group of women activists and lawyers put before the Department of Justice a law reform option. The proposal, also noted in *Why Women Should Care*, was that legislation be drafted that would specifically deny any defence of intoxication for offences involving male violence against women or girls. This bar would have extended to any offence of violence, including specific intent offences such as murder.

Bill C-72, now enacted as s. 33.1 of the *Code*, incorporates significant aspects of this proposal. Its preamble is reproduced below:

> Whereas the Parliament of Canada is gravely concerned about the incidence of violence in Canadian society;
>
> Whereas the Parliament of Canada recognizes that violence has a particularly disadvantaging impact on the equal participation of women and children in society and on the rights of women and children to security of the person and to the equal protection and benefit of the law as guaranteed by sections 7, 15 and 28, of the *Canadian Charter of Rights and Freedoms*;
>
> Whereas the Parliament of Canada recognizes that there is a close association between violence and intoxication and is concerned that self-induced intoxication may be used socially and legally to excuse violence, particularly violence against women and children;
>
> Whereas the Parliament of Canada recognizes that the potential effects of alcohol and certain drugs on human behaviour are well-known to Canadians and is aware of scientific evidence that many intoxicants, including alcohol, may not cause a person to act involuntarily;
>
> Whereas the Parliament of Canada shares with Canadians the moral view that people who, while in a state of self-induced intoxication, violate the physical integrity of others are blameworthy in relation to their harmful conduct and should be held criminally accountable for it;
>
> Whereas the Parliament of Canada desires to promote and help to ensure the full protection of the rights guaranteed under sections 7, 11, 15 and 28 of the *Canadian Charter of Rights and Freedoms* for all Canadians, including those who are or may be victims of violence;
>
> Whereas the Parliament of Canada considers it necessary to legislate a basis of criminal fault in relation to self-induced intoxication and general intent offences involving violence;
>
> Whereas the Parliament of Canada recognizes the continuing existence of a common law principle that intoxication to an extent that is less than that which would cause a person to lack the ability to form the basic intent or to have the voluntariness required to commit a criminal offence of general intent is never a defence at law;
>
> And Whereas the Parliament of Canada considers it necessary and desirable to legislate a standard of care in order to make it clear that a person who, while in a state of incapacity by reason of self-induced intoxication, commits an offence involving violence against another person, departs markedly from the standard of reasonable care that Canadians owe to each other and is thereby criminally at fault;
>
> Now, Therefore, Her Majesty, by and with the advice and consent of the Senate and House of Commons of Canada, enacts as follows....

Several authors have addressed the constitutionality of s. 33.1, including Isabel Grant, "Second Chances: Bill C-72 and the *Charter*" (1995) 33 Osgoode Hall L.J. 374; Martha Shaffer, "Criminal Responsibility and the *Charter*: The Case of *R. v. Daviault*" in Jamie Cameron, ed., *The Charter's Impact on the Criminal Justice System* (Toronto: Carswell, 1996) 313; Mark Carter, "Criminal Law, Women's Equality, and the Charter: An Analysis of the Criminal Code's Self-Induced Intoxication Provisions" in Margaret A. Jackson & N. Kathleen Sam Banks, eds., *Ten Years Later: The Charter and Equality for Women* (Vancouver: Simon Fraser University Press, 1996) 122; and Kelly Smith, "Section

33.1: Denial of the *Daviault* Defence Should be Held Constitutional" (2000) 28 C.R. 5th 350.

All of the courts that have examined the constitutionality of s. 33.1 have concluded that it offends ss. 7 and 11(d) of the *Charter*. They have split on the question of whether s. 33.1 is justified in a free and democratic society under s. 1. The following cases have held that s. 1 does not save the law: *R. v. Brenton*, [1999] N.W.T.J. No. 113 (S.Ct.) (QL), rev'd on other grounds, [2001] N.W.T.J. No. 14 (C.A.); *R. v. Lee* (1997), 35 O.R. (3d) 598 (Gen. Div.); *R. v. Dunn*, [1999] O.J. No. 5452 (Sup. Ct. J.) (QL); *R. v. Jensen*, [2000] O.J. No. 4870 (Sup. Ct. J.) (QL). The following cases have treated the law as constitutional: *R. v. Vickberg*, [1998] B.C.J. No. 1034 (S.Ct.) (QL); *R. v. Decaire*, [1999] O.J. No. 4794 (C.A.); *R. v. B.J.T.*, [2000] S.J. No. 801 (Q.B.) (QL).

Another response, this one from First Nations communities, to the problems associated with alcohol abuse has been to ban the possession of intoxicants and criminalize intoxication on reserve lands, as permitted by s. 85.1 of the *Indian Act*. Is this a legal response that could be pursued by other communities? For an unsuccessful *Charter* challenge under s. 7 to such a bylaw on a reserve, see *R. v. Campbell (G.R.)* (1996), 113 Man. R. (2d) 288 (C.A.).

Finally, in four decisions released in 1996, the Supreme Court has redefined the issue of intoxication as a defence by stating that the trier of fact must be instructed to consider the evidence of intoxication as going to the accused's actual *mens rea* as opposed to the accused's capacity to form the intention for the particular offence: *R. v. Lemky*, [1996] 1 S.C.R. 757; *R. v. Robinson*, [1996] 1 S.C.R. 683; *R. v. McMaster*, [1996] 1 S.C.R. 740; and *R. v. Seymour*, [1996] 2 S.C.R. 252. These decisions hold that the narrower focus on capacity violated *Charter* ss. 7 and 11(d).

The accused in *Robinson* and *McMaster* were granted new trials on the basis that the accused were entitled to consideration of the issue of whether their intoxication, while insufficient to meet the "no capacity" test, may have precluded them from foreseeing the consequences of their acts. *Lemky* was denied a new trial since the evidence was inadequate to provide an air of reality to support an inference that he was too drunk to appreciate the consequences of shooting his common-law partner.

On the other hand, the accused in *Seymour* was granted a new trial in part because the trial judge had focused exclusively on actual intent and had failed to leave open to the jury the possibility that his capacity to form the intent was impaired by alcohol consumption. Earlier, in *Robinson*, the Court had stated that there may be cases where it is appropriate for the judge to first address the capacity issue prior to the question of actual intent. The Court noted that where a judge has given a charge to the jury that refers to both capacity and actual intent, appellate review may be necessary to ascertain whether the issues were properly put to the jury. It outlined the relevant considerations in this regard. Seymour's case was said to be the type of situation requiring a two-step charge on intoxication because of the accused's primary reliance upon his incapacity and the use of "capacity" language by his expert witness.

13

Automatism

Automatism is both an *actus reus* and *mens rea* defence. It is classified as either "sane" or "insane", the policy distinction being whether the condition experienced by the accused is likely to recur. When the condition is classified as "insane", the accused is relegated to the Mental Disorder defence, see *Stone*, below. The effect of a successful sane automatism defence is a complete acquittal, whereas a successful mental disorder defence may result in a detention or other such order, as discussed above, under **Incapacity**.

As the law currently stands, a sane automatism defence is available for an accused who can demonstrate that he or she went into a dissociative state as a result of any number of circumstances, including blows to the head or sleepwalking. In the case of automatism caused by "psychological blow", the courts had required that the cause be "external" rather than "internal". The test to make this distinction has been whether a "reasonable" person might have also experienced dissociation as a result of the alleged shock or "blow". If not, the "cause" is said to be the accused's internal weakness, and the accused is relegated to the defence of "mental disorder". See, for example, the case of Dorothy Joudrie discussed above, under **Incapacity**.

In the leading case on this issue, *R. v. Rabey* (1977), 17 O.R. (2d) 1 (C.A.), aff'd [1980] 2 S.C.R. 513, the courts characterized a young man's rejection by a woman he was interested in as one of the "ordinary stresses and disappointments of life which are the common lot of mankind." Since a "reasonable person" would not have experienced dissociation, the court concluded that the accused was somehow psychologically frail. He was precluded from using this defence against charges for attacking and almost killing the young woman. *Stone*, noted above, followed *Rabey* in rejecting a psychological blow defence for a man who argued that he went into a dissociative state as a result of his wife's verbal abuse and stabbed her 47 times.

Who is likely to use the defence of "psychological blow" automatism? It seems to be relatively rare for a woman to advance a non-insane automatism defence. One such example is provided by *R. v. Falconer* (1989), 46 A. Crim. R. 83 (West. Aust. C.A.) where the accused was convicted of murder of her husband but granted a new trial so that the jury could consider the medical evidence and the issue of whether she was in a state of non-insane automatism. The circumstances were that following a history of marital violence, the accused discovered that the deceased had sexually assaulted her daughters and reported it to police. She feared his retaliation and, on the day in question, he had entered the house unexpectedly, made sexual advances, assaulted her, and taunted her that she and the girls would not be believed. She claimed to have no memory thereafter.

In *R. v. Parks*, [1992] 2 S.C.R. 871, the Supreme Court of Canada set out the terms on which sane automatism is to be adjudicated: the accused who wishes to introduce the defence of automatism need only meet an evidential burden before the burden of disproof shifts to the Crown; if the accused raises this defence, the Crown can raise and attempt to prove mental disorder; and mental disorder is said to be distinguishable from automatism based on the "continuing danger" test. The accused Parks had, in the middle of the night, driven 23 kilometres across Toronto, entered the home of his in-laws, hacked his mother-in-law to death with a kitchen knife, and attempted to kill his father-in-law. He then drove himself to the police station and stated:

> I just killed someone with my bare hands; Oh my God, I just killed someone; I've just killed two people; My God, I've just killed two people with my hands; My God, I've just killed two people. My hands; I just killed two people. I killed them; I just killed two people; I've just killed my mother- and father-in-law. I stabbed and beat them to death. It's all my fault.

Parks had been experiencing personal and financial difficulties: he had lost his job for stealing $30,000 from his employer and had borrowed money from his in-laws, but claimed to have had a good relationship with them. His defence of sane automatism was supported by: his demeanour at the police station; a family history of sleepwalking; the evidence of five defence experts who unanimously opined that Parks had been sleepwalking, that he was unlikely to be violent in future, and that he did not suffer from any form of mental illness; and Parks' apparent lack of motive for the attacks. The prosecution was seemingly unprepared for the defence of sane automatism and had no expert evidence with which to counter this defence, instead relying on a British case that had held that sleepwalking is a mental disorder in law because it has an "internal cause". The trial judge distinguished the British authority on the basis of the expert testimony, allowing sane automatism to be considered by the jury and refusing to charge them on insane automatism. Parks was acquitted of all charges, and his acquittal was upheld on appeal by the Supreme Court of Canada.

Authors such as Isabel Grant and Laura Spitz, "Criminal Law — Defence — Automatism — Accused Killing While Sleepwalking — Acquittal or Not Guilty by Reason of Insanity: R. v. Parks" (1993) 72 Can. Bar Rev. 224 speculated that the Court's move away from the internal/external cause test towards a continuing danger test, which focuses on whether the accused will be violent again as opposed to whether he will experience the state of automatism in the future, may expand the scope of the sane automatism by psychological blow. Others viewed *Parks* as an anomalous case whose outcome was determined by the fact that the Crown was caught by surprise and was unable to counter the expert evidence. This particular aspect of *Parks* has been dealt with by new legislation: see now *Criminal Code* s. 657.3.

In the *Stone* decision reproduced below, the Court further clarified the parameters of the defence of sane automatism.

R. v. Stone†

[BASTARACHE J.:]

The present case involves automatism, and more specifically, "psychological blow" automatism. The appellant claims that nothing more than his wife's words caused him to enter an automatistic state in which his actions, which include stabbing his wife 47 times, were involuntary. How can an accused demonstrate that mere words caused him to enter an automatistic state such that his actions were involuntary and thus do not attract criminal law sanction? This is the issue raised in this appeal.

I. FACTS

The appellant was charged with the murder of his wife, Donna Stone. At trial, the appellant admitted killing his wife. In his defence, the appellant claimed:

† [1999] 2 S.C.R. 290.

insane automatism, non-insane automatism, lack of intent, and alternatively, provocation.

The appellant met Donna Stone in the spring of 1993 and the two were married on May 8, 1993. They lived in Winfield, British Columbia, in the Okanagan Valley. This was the appellant's third marriage. He has two teenage sons from his second marriage. His sons live with their mother in Surrey, British Columbia, a suburb of Vancouver.

In March 1994, the appellant planned a business trip to Vancouver. He decided to visit his sons while in the Vancouver area. He contacted his second wife and made arrangements to take his sons out for dinner and a movie. The appellant did not tell Donna Stone of his intention to travel to Vancouver and visit his sons because she did not get along with them.

According to the appellant, Donna Stone learned of his intention to go to Vancouver. She demanded to go along with him and said she would follow him in another vehicle if he did not take her. The appellant agreed to take her with him to Vancouver.

The appellant testified that Donna Stone berated him throughout the drive to Vancouver and objected to his visit with his sons. Nevertheless, the appellant drove to the home of his second wife for the planned visit with his sons. The visit lasted only 15 minutes because Donna Stone threatened to "lay on the horn until the police come".

The appellant testified that after the brief visit with his sons, he and Donna Stone drove towards Vancouver. According to the appellant, Donna Stone asked him if he wanted a divorce. He responded that they might as well get divorced if she was not going to let him see his sons. This answer upset the victim and she again began to berate the appellant.

The appellant testified that he pulled into an empty lot and turned off the truck's engine while Donna Stone continued to yell at him:

> ... I sat there with my head down while she's still yelling at me that I'm nothing but a piece of shit and that when she had talked to the police, that she had told them lies, that I was abusing her, and that they were getting all the paperwork ready to have me arrested, and that all she had to do was phone them; and once they had me arrested, that she was going to get a court order so that I wouldn't be allowed back onto our property and that I would have to go and live with my mother and run my business from there, that she was going to quit working and she was just going to stay in the house with her children and that I would have to pay her alimony and child support.
>
> ... Well, she just continued on and she just said that she couldn't stand to listen to me whistle, that every time I touched her, she felt sick, that I was a lousy fuck and that I had a little penis and that she's never going to fuck me again, and I'm just sitting there with my head down; and by this time, she's kneeling on the seat and she's yelling this in my face....

The appellant testified that the victim's voice began to fade off. He recalls wondering why she was treating him and his children in this way. He also remembers thinking about how people in the small town in which he lived would look at him if his wife had him arrested. The appellant then remembers a "whoosh" sensation washing over him from his feet to his head. According to the appellant, when his eyes focussed again, he was staring straight ahead and felt something in his hand. He was holding a six-inch hunting knife which he kept in the truck. He looked over and saw Donna Stone slumped over on the seat. He knew she was dead. It would later be determined that Donna Stone died from loss of blood resulting from 47 stab wounds.

The appellant testified that he opened the passenger door and Donna Stone's body fell out onto the ground. After five to ten minutes, the appellant put his wife's body in a toolbox in the back of his truck. He then washed the blood from his hands in a puddle, removed his bloody clothes and put on extra clothes he kept in the truck. The appellant then pulled out of the empty lot and drove to a nearby motel where he asked for directions home and purchased a six-pack of beer to calm his nerves.

According to the appellant, he arrived home around 3:00 a.m. He did not immediately go in because the lights were on and he feared someone was still awake. The appellant parked down the road until 6:00 a.m. He then drove the truck into his garage and went into the house where he cleaned up and packed a few shirts. He left a note for his stepdaughter, the daughter of the victim:

> Sorry, Nicole, but she just wouldn't stop yelling at me. My loan to the bank, credit union has insurance on it if I die. Love Bert

The appellant testified that he checked into a hotel so he could take a shower and shave. He then collected an outstanding debt, sold a car he owned and took a cab to the airport. He flew to Mexico. While in Mexico, the appellant awoke one morning to the sensation of having his throat cut. In trying to recall his dream, he remembered stabbing Donna Stone twice in the chest *before* experiencing the "whooshing" sensation.

Donna Stone's body was found in the tool box in the appellant's truck two days after her death.

The appellant returned to Canada approximately six weeks later on May 2, 1994. The next day he spoke to a lawyer and then surrendered himself to police.

II. PSYCHIATRIC EVIDENCE

Two psychiatrists gave evidence in this case. The defence psychiatrist, Dr. Janke, interviewed the appellant on two occasions approximately 18 months after the killing. The Crown psychiatrist, Dr. Murphy, interviewed the appellant for one hour on the seventh day of the trial.

A. Evidence of Dr. Janke

Dr. Janke testified that a dissociative episode is a medical term for a circumstance in which an individual's thinking component, including his judgment and ability to know what he is doing, splits from his physical body. According to Dr. Janke, dissociation can be caused by a psychological blow and is often accompanied by partial to complete memory loss. Dr. Janke was unaware of any cases in which a violent dissociative episode had recurred.

Dr. Janke testified that the appellant's account of the facts in this case was consistent with a dissociative episode caused by a series of psychological blows. In particular, Dr. Janke noted that the following facts are consistent with dissociation: Donna Stone's words immediately prior to the killing were extreme; the appellant's second wife reported that two to three hours before the killing the appellant seemed out of character; the appellant reported experiencing a "whooshing" sensation followed by a re-awareness stage; the appellant reported decreasing concentration, difficulty following driving directions and memory loss; and the attack was of a frenzied, overkill nature.

In Dr. Janke's opinion, the appellant was in a dissociative state for at least the majority of the attack on Donna Stone. According to Dr. Janke, this state resulted from Donna Stone's extreme insults which must be viewed in the context of the stress the appellant had endured throughout the day. However, Dr. Janke qualified his opinion by noting that it was largely dependant on the accuracy and truthfulness of the appellant's account of events.

According to Dr. Janke, there was no evidence that the appellant suffered from any psychiatric or physical condition which could have been responsible for a dissociative episode. The only psychological factor the appellant possessed which may have contributed to a dissociative episode was his tendency not to be aware of his emotional state. Dr. Janke considered this factor to be within the normal range of human behaviour.

Dr. Janke agreed that the appellant told him that while he was in Mexico, he "became aware of a memory of having a knife in his hand and stabbing Donna Stone twice in the chest *before* having the 'whooshing' sensation" (emphasis added). However, Dr. Janke pointed out that an individual who has had a dissociative episode is usually unable to sequence memories of events surrounding the episode accurately and chronologically.

B. Evidence of Dr. Murphy

Dr. Murphy agreed with much of Dr. Janke's evidence about dissociation generally. For example, she accepted his explanation of what dissociation is. She also agreed that dissociation is often accompanied by memory loss and an inability to sequence memories of events surrounding the episode accurately and chronologically. Like Dr. Janke, Dr. Murphy was unaware of any cases in which a violent dissociative episode had recurred.

In relation to the appellant's claim of dissociation, Dr. Murphy testified that it is possible that the appellant was in a dissociative state when he killed Donna Stone. However, she noted that there is no scientific method of completely ruling out a claim of dissociation once it has been made. Furthermore, she opined that although it is possible, it is extremely unlikely that the appellant was in a dissociative state when he killed his wife. Dr. Murphy's scepticism was based upon several factors. First, she pointed out that the appellant's reported decrease in concentration, difficulty following driving directions and memory loss were common [phenomena] which, though consistent with dissociation, could easily be attributed to a number of other factors. In particular, the appellant's reported lack of memory in itself is not conclusive since up to 50 per cent of people who are charged with serious crimes report that they do not remember the incident. Dr. Murphy also pointed out that the frenzied, overkill nature of the attack was equally consistent with rage as with dissociation.

Dr. Murphy noted that the mind and body of a person in a dissociative state have been split. For this reason, she would expect that there would usually be no connection between the dissociated acts and the social context immediately preceding them. For example, a person who is watching television with a group of people might get up and urinate in front of the others. According to Dr. Murphy, the fact that Donna Stone was both the trigger of the dissociative episode and the victim of the appellant's dissociated violence renders the appellant's claim of dissociation suspect.

Finally, Dr. Murphy noted that Dr. Janke's opinion that the appellant had experienced a dissociative episode was based almost exclusively on the appellant's account of events. She testified that psychiatrists must view claims of dissociation with suspicion if they are made in legal contexts where the claimant has an obvious interest in a favourable disposition. In such circumstances, the evidence of bystanders who can corroborate the claimant's explanation of events and provide information about the appearance of the claimant at the time of the incident is an important element in confirming the validity of a claim of dissociation.

Dr. Murphy agreed with Dr. Janke that there was no evidence that the appellant suffered from any medically recognized psychiatric disorder which could have been responsible for a dissociative episode.

III. JUDICIAL HISTORY

A. British Columbia Supreme Court — Brenner J.

(1) Ruling on Whether to Instruct the Jury on Automatism

Brenner J. considered whether or not to put the defence of automatism to the jury in the context of a *voir dire*. He identified his first task: to determine, as a question of law, whether the defence had raised sufficient evidence of involuntariness such that the general defence of automatism was entitled to be put to the jury.

Brenner J. then turned to the definition of automatism. He cited the definition of Dickson J., as he then was, speaking in dissent in *Rabey v. The Queen*, [1980] 2 S.C.R. 513, at p. 552:

> In principle, the defence of automatism should be available whenever there is evidence of unconsciousness throughout the commission of the crime, that cannot be attributed to fault or negligence of his part.

Noting that this definition had been approved by La Forest J., speaking for the majority of this Court, in *R. v. Parks*, [1992] 2 S.C.R. 871, at p. 905, Brenner J. concluded that the defence of automatism is only available where there is evidence of unconsciousness *throughout the commission of the crime*. However, the evidence in the present case revealed that while in Mexico, the appellant recalled inflicting two of the stab wounds to Donna Stone's chest before experiencing the "whooshing" sensation. Nevertheless, since automatism had been left with juries in other British Columbia cases in which accused persons had partial recollection of the crime, Brenner J. concluded that the authorities did not exclude the availability of this defence merely because the appellant has some recollection of what happened.

Brenner J. held that in the present case there was evidence of unconsciousness throughout the commission of the crime because the only recollection of events had come to the appellant in a dream several days after he had killed Donna Stone. As a result, he found that the defence had laid the proper evidentiary foundation for the general defence of automatism. Brenner J. then correctly identified the second question before him: whether insane or non-insane automatism should be left with the jury.

Brenner J. found the case of *R. v. MacLeod* (1980), 52 C.C.C. (2d) 193 (B.C.C.A.), indistinguishable. In *MacLeod*, the British Columbia Court of Appeal applied this Court's decision in *Rabey*, *supra*, holding that where the only possible cause of the accused's dissociative state was anxiety, an internal factor, the accused must have been suffering from a disease of the mind in the legal sense and accordingly only insane automatism should be left with the jury.

Applying *MacLeod*, Brenner J. ruled that the only form of automatism available to the appellant was insane automatism. As a result, he instructed the jury on insane automatism, intention in relation to second degree murder and provocation. He then set out three possible verdicts open to the jury: not criminally responsible on account of mental disorder, guilty or not guilty of the offence of second degree murder, and guilty of the included offence of manslaughter. The jury found the appellant criminally responsible but not guilty of second degree murder. Brenner J. directed a verdict on the included offence of manslaughter.

. . . .

(3) Sentencing

A sentencing hearing was held on December 1, 1995 before Brenner J. Defence counsel argued that a sentence of one to two years was appropriate, in addition to the 18 months the appellant had already spent in custody. The Crown suggested a sentence of 15 years to life imprisonment. The Crown agreed that the 18 months the appellant had already spent in custody had to be taken into account in determining an appropriate sentence.

Brenner J. began by noting that the jury had accepted the defence of provocation, and the appellant had accordingly been convicted of manslaughter rather than second degree murder. After reviewing the circumstances of the offence and the appellant's background, he concluded that the principle concern of this sentencing was general deterrence, specifically noting in particular that this was an offence of domestic violence.

Brenner J. was of the opinion that sentencing had to be assessed in light of the jury's acceptance of the defence of provocation, while still bearing in mind the brutality of the offence. After reviewing a number of cases, two of which he found particularly relevant — *R. v. Archibald* (1992), 15 B.C.A.C. 301, and *R. v. Eklund*, [1985] B.C.J. No. 2415 (QL) (C.A.) — Brenner J. sentenced the appellant to a further four years in jail, treating the appellant's 18-month pre-trial custody as the equivalent of a three-year sentence.

B. British Columbia Court of Appeal — (1997), 86 B.C.A.C. 169 (Conviction) and (1997), 89 B.C.A.C. 139 (Sentencing)

(1) Should Non-Insane Automatism Have Been Left with the Jury?

McEachern C.J. (Cumming and Braidwood JJ.A. concurring) began by reviewing the facts. He then turned to the first ground of appeal: whether the trial judge had erred in failing to leave non-insane automatism to the jury.

. . . .

After assessing the relevant case law, McEachern C.J. was not satisfied that the trial judge erred in concluding that the internal cause theory was the best guide based on the bizarre facts of this case. Unlike *Parks*, there were no circumstances which required departure from this approach. Furthermore, there were valid reasons, including policy concerns, supporting the trial judge's decision to reject the expert evidence that the appellant was not suffering from a disease of the mind in a medical sense. There was no indication that the trial judge failed to consider these policy factors in deciding to leave only insane automatism to the jury, particularly since he had made his ruling at *nisi prius* where judges are not expected to articulate all of their reasons. To the contrary, the trial judge's reference to *Parks* indicated that he was aware of his duty to take policy considerations into account in assessing which species of automatism to leave with the jury.

McEachern C.J. concluded that the trial judge had carefully considered all of the evidence and was justified in deciding not to leave sane automatism with the jury. He thus refused to disturb that decision.

. . . .

(3) Sentencing

The Crown had two primary grounds of appeal on the sentencing issue in the Court of Appeal. First, the Crown argued that the trial judge erred in considering provocation as a mitigating factor in sentencing after s. 232 of the *Code* had reduced a verdict of murder to one of manslaughter. Second, the Crown argued that the seven-year sentence imposed by the trial judge was clearly unreasonable.

Finch J.A. (Esson and Donald JJ.A. concurring) began by reviewing the circumstances of the offence, the psychiatric evidence and the appellant's background. He then cited this Court's decisions in *R. v. Shropshire*, [1995] 4 S.C.R. 227, and *R. v. M. (C.A.)*, [1996] 1 S.C.R. 500, on the standard of appellate review of sentencing.

Finch J.A. rejected the Crown's duplication argument with respect to provocation. He found that the trial judge was correct to consider provocation as a mitigating factor when sentencing the appellant. He reasoned that the provocation evidence was probative as to the appellant's state of mind at the time of the killing and as such was relevant to the issue of moral blameworthiness. According to Finch J.A., the consideration of this evidence, among all of the other relevant evidence, did not give the appellant a second or unfair benefit.

Finch J.A. concluded that the sentence was not clearly unreasonable. It adequately reflected the gravity of the offence and the moral culpability of the appellant. It was also within the range indicated by the case law. The Crown's sentence appeal was accordingly dismissed.

. . . .

VI. ANALYSIS

1. Did the Court of Appeal err in upholding the decision of the learned trial judge to refuse to leave the "defence" of non-insane automatism to the jury?

A. The Nature of Automatism

The legal term "automatism" has been defined on many occasions by many courts. In *Rabey*, *supra*, Ritchie J., speaking for the majority of this Court, at p. 518, adopted the following definition of the Ontario High Court of Justice in *R. v. K.* (1970), 3 C.C.C. (2d) 84, at p. 84:

> Automatism is a term used to describe unconscious involuntary behaviour, the state of a person who, though capable of action, is not conscious of what he is doing. It means an unconscious, involuntary act, where the mind does not go with what is being done.

The reference to unconsciousness in the definition of automatism has been the source of some criticism. In her article "Automatism and Criminal Responsibility" (1982–83), 25 *Crim. L.Q.* 95, W. H. Holland points out that this reference to unconsciousness reveals that the law assumes that a person is necessarily either conscious or unconscious. However, the medical literature speaks of different levels of consciousness (p. 96). Indeed, the expert evidence in the present case reveals that medically speaking, "unconscious" means "flat on the floor", that is, in a comatose-type state. I therefore prefer to define automatism as a state of impaired consciousness, rather than unconsciousness, in which an individual, though capable of action, has no voluntary control over that action.

Two forms of automatism are recognized at law: insane automatism and non-insane automatism. Involuntary action which does not stem from a disease of the mind gives rise to a claim of non-insane automatism. If successful, a claim of non-insane automatism entitles the accused to an acquittal. In *Parks*, *supra*, La Forest J. cited with approval, at p. 896, the following words of Dickson J. speaking in dissent in *Rabey*, *supra*, at p. 522:

> Although the word "automatism" made its way but lately to the legal stage, it is basic principle that absence of volition in respect of the act involved is always a defence to a crime. A defence that the act is involuntary entitles the accused to a complete and unqualified acquittal. That the defence of automatism exists as a middle ground between criminal responsibility and legal insanity is beyond question.

On the other hand, involuntary action which is found, at law, to result from a disease of the mind gives rise to a claim of insane automatism. It has long been recognized that insane automatism is subsumed by the defence of mental disorder, formerly referred to as the defence of insanity. For example, in *Rabey*, *supra*, Ritchie J. adopted the reasoning of Martin J.A. of the Ontario Court of Appeal. In *R. v. Rabey* (1977), 17 O.R. (2d) 1, Martin J.A. stated, at p. 12:

> Automatism caused by disease of the mind is subsumed under the defence of insanity leading to the special verdict of not guilty on account of insanity, whereas automatism not resulting from disease of the mind leads to an absolute acquittal....

Likewise, in dissent in *Rabey* (S.C.C.), Dickson J. noted, at p. 524:

> Automatism may be subsumed in the defence of insanity in cases in which the unconscious action of an accused can be traced to, or rooted in, a disease of the mind. Where that is so, the defence of insanity prevails.

More recently, in *Parks*, *supra*, La Forest J. confirmed that insane automatism falls within the scope of the defence of mental disorder as set out in s. 16 of the *Code* when he noted that where automatism stems from a disease of the mind, the accused is entitled to a verdict of insanity rather than an acquittal (p. 896). See also *R. v. Chaulk*, [1990] 3 S.C.R. 1303, at p. 1321. This classification is consistent with the wording of s. 16, which makes no distinction between voluntary and involuntary acts. Furthermore, the inclusion of mental disorder automatism within the ambit of s. 16 provides courts with an appropriate framework for protecting the public from offenders whose involuntarily criminal acts are rooted in diseases of the mind. Courts in other commonwealth countries have also recognized that insane automatism is subsumed by the defence of mental disorder or insanity. See for example *Bratty v. Attorney-General for Northern Ireland*, [1963] A.C. 386 (H.L.), at pp. 410 and 414; *R. v. Falconer* (1990), 50 A. Crim. R. 244 (H.C.), at pp. 255–56, 265 and 273–74; *R. v. Cottle*, [1958] N.Z.L.R. 999, at p. 1007.

Accordingly, a successful claim of insane automatism will trigger s. 16 of the *Code* and result in a verdict of not criminally responsible on account of mental disorder. Thus, although courts to date have spoken of insane "automatism" and non-insane "automatism" for purposes of consistency, it is important to recognize that in actuality true "automatism" only includes involuntary behaviour which does not stem from a disease of the mind. Involuntary behaviour which results from a disease of the mind is more correctly labelled a s. 16 mental disorder rather than insane automatism. For purposes of consistency, I will continue to refer to both as "automatism". However, I believe the terms "mental disorder" automatism and "non-mental disorder" automatism rather than "insane" automatism and "non-insane" automatism more accurately reflect the recent changes to s. 16 of the *Code*, and the addition of Part XX.1 of the *Code*.

B. Establishing a Single Approach to all Cases Involving Claims of Automatism

Automatism may arise in different contexts. For example, in *Parks*, *supra*, this Court dealt with a claim of automatism attributed to a state of somnambulism. In *R. v. Daviault*, [1994] 3 S.C.R. 63, this Court addressed extreme intoxication akin to a state of automatism. In the present case, the appellant claims that nothing more than his wife's words caused him to enter an automatistic state. This type of claim has become known as "psychological blow" automatism. Automatism attributed to a psychological blow was at the centre of this Court's decision in *Rabey*, *supra*.

The application of different legal tests for automatism dependent on the context in which the alleged automatism arose is a problem because there may be cases in which the facts simply are not conducive to such strict categorization. Cases involving disputes over the cause of the alleged automatism come to mind. The solution to this problem is, of course, to develop a general test applicable to all cases involving claims of automatism. This I will do in these reasons. I therefore emphasize that the following analysis is meant to apply to all claims of automatism and not simply to cases of "psychological blow" automatism. In my opinion, the most effective general test will incorporate various elements of this Court's most recent statements on automatistic-like behaviour; see *Daviault*, *Parks* and *Rabey*.

In *Parks*, *supra*, La Forest J. set out two discrete tasks which trial judges must undertake in determining whether automatism should be left with the trier of fact. First, he or she must assess whether a proper foundation for a defence of automatism has been established. As I will explain below, establishing a proper foundation for automatism is the equivalent of satisfying the evidentiary burden for this defence. The mere assertion of involuntariness will not suffice. If a proper evidentiary foundation has been established, the trial judge must next determine whether the condition alleged by the accused is mental disorder or non-mental disorder automatism (p. 897).

In my opinion, the functionality of such a two-step framework is apparent and warrants making such an approach generally applicable to all cases involving claims of automatism. However, this framework only provides a starting point from which to develop a general legal approach to automatism. I will now clarify the particulars of the legal analysis which must be undertaken at each of the framework's two stages.

C. Step 1: Establishing a Proper Foundation for a Defence of Automatism

A review of the case law reveals that courts, including this Court, have provided little guidance about exactly what an accused must do to establish a proper foundation for a defence of automatism. Frequently, this stage of the judicial two-step analysis consists of nothing more than a remark that there is sufficient evidence on the record. By far the majority of judicial attention has concentrated on the second stage of the automatism analysis, that is, whether the defence of mental disorder or non-mental disorder automatism should be left with the trier of fact. In my opinion, this Court must provide trial judges with more detail about the required elements of a proper foundation for a defence of automatism. First, however, it is necessary to review how the proper foundation requirement fits into the general structure of our criminal law.

As mentioned above, establishing a proper foundation for automatism is the equivalent of satisfying the evidentiary burden for this defence. In *The Law of Evidence in Canada* (1992), J. Sopinka, S. Lederman and A. Bryant distinguish the evidentiary burden from the legal burden as follows, at p. 53:

> The term "burden of proof" is used to describe two distinct concepts relating to the obligation of a party to a proceeding in connection with the proof of a case. In its first sense, the term refers to the obligation imposed on a party to prove or disprove a fact or issue. In the second sense, it refers to a party's obligation to adduce evidence satisfactorily to the judge, in order to raise an issue.

The first sense of the term "burden of proof" suggested by Sopinka, Lederman and Bryant is referred to as the legal or ultimate burden, while the second is known as the evidentiary burden (p. 54). The first, or proper foundation, stage of the automatism analysis sets out what an accused must do to satisfy the evidentiary burden for automatism. As I will discuss below, this burden is directly related to the nature of the legal burden connected with automatism. Whether the accused has satisfied its evidentiary burden is a question of mixed law and fact for the trial judge. It should be noted that, until recently, this determination was considered to be a question of law: see *Canada (Director of Investigation and Research) v. Southam Inc.*, [1997] 1 S.C.R. 748, at paras. 35 and 36. In determining whether the evidentiary burden has been satisfied, the trial judge must assess the evidence before the court. According to Viscount Kilmuir in *Bratty*, *supra*, at p. 406:

> ...for a defence of automatism to be "genuinely raised in a genuine fashion", there must be evidence on which a jury could find that a state of automatism exists. By this I mean that the defence must be able to point to some evidence, whether it emanates from their own or the Crown's witnesses, from which the jury could reasonably infer that the accused acted in a state of automatism. Whether or not there is such evidence is a matter of law for the judge to decide.

D. Nature and Origin of the Burdens Applied in Cases Involving Claims of Automatism

This Court has stated on many occasions that it is a fundamental principle of criminal law that only voluntary actions will attract findings of guilt. See for example *Daviault*, *supra*, at pp. 74–75, *per* Cory J.; *Rabey* (S.C.C.), *supra*, at pp. 522 and 545, *per* Dickson J.; *Parks*, *supra*, at p. 896, *per* La Forest J.; *Rabey* (Ont. C.A.), *supra*, *per* Martin J.A., at p. 24, adopted by Ritchie J. In *R. v. Théroux*, [1993] 2 S.C.R. 5, McLachlin J. classified voluntariness as the mental element of the *actus reus* of a crime (p. 17). In *Daviault*, Cory J. also recognized that voluntariness may be linked to the *actus reus* (p. 102). See also *Chaulk*, *supra*, at p. 1321, *per* Lamer C.J.

In *Parks*, *supra*, La Forest J. classified automatism as a sub-set of the voluntariness requirement, which he too recognized as part of the *actus reus* component of criminal responsibility (p. 896). I agree and would add that voluntariness, rather than consciousness, is the key legal element of automatistic behaviour since a defence of automatism amounts to a denial of the voluntariness component of the *actus reus*.

The law presumes that people act voluntarily. Accordingly, since a defence of automatism amounts to a claim that one's actions were not voluntary, the accused must rebut the presumption of voluntariness. An evidentiary burden is thereby imposed on the accused. The nature of this evidentiary burden stems from the legal burden imposed in cases involving claims of automatism. Generally, the legal burden in such cases has been on the Crown to prove voluntariness, a component of the *actus reus*, beyond a reasonable doubt — hence Dickson J.'s contention in *Rabey* that an accused claiming automatism need only raise evidence sufficient to permit a properly instructed jury to find a reasonable doubt as to voluntariness in order to rebut the presumption of voluntariness. The Crown then has the legal burden of proving voluntariness beyond a reasonable doubt to the trier of fact. If the Crown fails to satisfy this burden, the accused will be acquitted.

My colleague, Justice Binnie, relies heavily on Dickson J.'s approach to the nature of the burdens in cases involving claims of automatism. I do not agree that the reasons of Dickson J. provide justification for the refusal to review the appropriateness of these burdens on their merits in the present appeal. Furthermore, I must respectfully disagree with my colleague regarding the treatment of Dickson J.'s views on this point by La Forest J. in *Parks*. I note that in *Parks* the appropriateness of the evidentiary burden on the defence at the proper foundation stage was not directly at issue before this Court. As a result, La Forest J. did not find it necessary to assess the precise nature of either of the burdens of proof as set out by Dickson J. in *Rabey*.

E. What Should the Burdens of Proof Associated with Automatism Be?

The relationship between the burdens associated with automatism dictates that any change in the legal burden of automatism will necessarily result in a change to the evidentiary or proper foundation burden associated with this defence. The evidentiary burden will relate either to evidence sufficient to establish voluntariness beyond a reasonable doubt, as suggested by Binnie J., or, as set out below, to evidence sufficient to establish involuntariness on a balance of probabilities. In my opinion, a review of the legal burden applicable in cases involving claims of automatism is in order. My colleague Binnie J. is of the view that this Court ought not review either the legal or the evidentiary burden set out in the dissenting reasons of Dickson J. in *Rabey*. In support of this position, Binnie J. argues that neither the respondent nor any of the intervening Attorneys General requested such a review. With respect, I disagree. In its written submissions, the respondent invited this Court to reconsider the trial judge's finding that there was a proper foundation for automatism. The respondent also requested that this Court make the proper foundation stage of the automatism analysis more stringent. As explained above, an assessment of an evidentiary or proper foundation burden cannot be undertaken without reference to the related legal burden.

In her 1993 *Proposals to amend the Criminal Code (general principles)*, the Minister of Justice recommended that the legal burden of proof in all cases of automatism be on the party that raises the issue on a balance of probabilities. This is the same legal burden that this Court applied to a claim of extreme intoxication akin to a state of automatism in *Daviault, supra*. It is also the legal burden Parliament assigned to the defence of mental disorder in s. 16 of the *Code*, which, as mentioned above, is equally applicable to voluntary and involuntary actions stemming from a disease of the mind and therefore applies to mental disorder automatism. As I explained above, different legal approaches to claims of automatism, whether based on the context in which the alleged automatism arose or on the distinction between mental disorder and non-mental disorder automatism, is problematic and should be avoided. Indeed, counsel for the appellant in the present case recognized as much in oral argument before this Court:

> No, I think that the — the conflict arises in a slightly different situation, which I'm going to come to in a moment, and that is that, when one deals with insanity, the evidentiary burden is upon the accused to establish that on the balance of probabilities.
>
> When one comes now, pursuant to this Court's decision in *Daviault*, to drunkenness akin to automatism, again, the onus is upon the accused, and the evidentiary burden as well.
>
> Whereas in non-insane automatism, the onus simply is upon the defence to raise it and for the Crown to then disprove it beyond a reasonable doubt in essence.
>
> So that is where I concede that there is a contradiction and that there may be some merit in having the same test and the same process applied to each of the different kinds of mental disorder, to use the term loosely.

An appropriate legal burden applicable to all cases involving claims of automatism must reflect the policy concerns which surround claims of automatism. The words of Schroeder J.A. in *R. v. Szymusiak*, [1972] 3 O.R. 602 (C.A.), at p. 608, come to mind:

> ...a defence which in a true and proper case may be the only one open to an honest man, but it may just as readily be the last refuge of a scoundrel.

The recognition that policy considerations are relevant is nothing new to this area of criminal law. In *Rabey* (Ont. C.A.), *supra*, Martin J.A., whose reasons were adopted by the majority of this Court, recognized that the term "disease of the mind" contains both a medical component and legal or policy component (p. 12). Dickson J., dissenting in *Rabey* (S.C.C.), noted, at p. 546, that specific policy considerations were involved in determining whether a claim of automatism should be categorized as mental disorder or non-mental disorder:

> There are undoubtedly policy considerations to be considered. Automatism as a defence is easily feigned. It is said the credibility of our criminal justice system will be severely strained if a person who has committed a violent act is allowed an absolute acquittal on a plea of automatism arising from a psychological blow. The argument is made that the success of the defence depends upon the semantic ability of psychiatrists, tracing a narrow path between the twin shoals of criminal responsibility and an insanity verdict. Added to these concerns is the *in terrorem* argument that the floodgates will be raised if psychological blow automatism is recognized in law.

Likewise, in *Parks, supra*, La Forest J. considered policy to be a relevant consideration for trial judges in distinguishing between mental disorder and non-mental disorder automatism (p. 896 and pp. 907–8).

In both *Rabey* and *Parks*, policy considerations were relegated to the second stage of the automatism analysis to determine whether the condition alleged by the accused was mental disorder or non-mental disorder automatism. In neither case is there any indication that this Court intended to preclude the consideration of policy in the determination of an appropriate legal burden for cases involving claims of automatism.

The foregoing leads me to the conclusion that the legal burden in cases involving claims of automatism must be on the defence to prove involuntariness on a balance of probabilities to the trier of fact. This is the same burden supported by Lord Goddard, dissenting in *Hill v. Baxter*, [1958] 1 Q.B. 277, at pp. 282–83, and imposed in some American jurisdictions; see for example *State v. Caddell*, 215 S.E.2d 348 (N.C. 1975); *Fulcher v. State*, 633 P.2d 142 (Wyo. 1981); *Polston v. State*, 685 P.2d 1 (Wyo. 1984); *State v. Fields*, 376 S.E.2d 740 (N.C. 1989).

In *Chaulk, supra*, and *Daviault, supra*, this Court recognized that although placing a balance of probabilities burden on the defence with respect to an element of the offence constitutes a limitation of an accused person's rights under s. 11(*d*) of the *Charter*, it can be justified under s. 1. In my opinion, the burden is also justified in the present case. The law presumes that people act voluntarily in order to avoid placing the onerous burden of proving voluntariness beyond a reasonable doubt on the Crown. Like extreme drunkenness akin to automatism, genuine cases of automatism will be extremely rare. However, because automatism is easily feigned and all knowledge of its occurrence rests with the accused, putting a legal burden on the accused to prove involuntariness on a balance of probabilities is necessary to further the objective behind the presumption of voluntariness. In contrast, saddling the Crown with the legal burden of proving voluntariness beyond a reasonable doubt actually defeats the purpose of the presumption of voluntariness. Thus, requiring that an accused bear the legal burden of proving involuntariness on a balance of probabilities is justified under s. 1. There is therefore no violation of the Constitution. On this latter point, I would note the words of Lamer C.J. in *R. v. Swain*, [1991] 1 S.C.R. 933, at pp. 996–97:

> I also wish to point out that, throughout my reasons on this issue, I have been careful to speak of the old common law rule as limiting the s. 7 *Charter* right and as violating the Constitution only after having reached the conclusion that the limitation is not justified under s. 1 of the *Charter*. This choice of language is deliberate but does not depend on the fact that this case involves a *Charter* challenge to a common law rule as opposed to a legislative provision. Whether one is speaking of a legislative provision or a common law rule it is not, in my view, correct to speak of a law violating a particular provision of the *Charter* (such as s. 7) prior to having gone through a s. 1 analysis. The *Charter* guarantees the particular rights and freedoms set out in it subject to reasonable limits which can be, under s. 1, demonstrably justified in a free and democratic society. Thus a law which limits a right set out in the *Charter* will only violate the Constitution if it is not justified under s. 1. In this instance, the law will either be struck down (to the extent of the inconsistency) under s. 52(1) or it will be reinterpreted so as not to violate the Constitution. If a law which limits a right set out in the *Charter* is justified under s. 1, that law does not violate the Constitution.

One final point on the issue of justification. My colleague Binnie J. distinguishes the s. 1 analysis in the present case from that in *Daviault* on the basis of the state of the law prior to a change established by this Court. With respect, I cannot agree that the issue of whether the previous state of the law was more or less advantageous to the accused is relevant to the justification of subsequent law. In both instances, the relevant matter is whether an *existing* infringement can be justified as a reasonable limit in a free and democratic society. The relevant subject of the s. 1 analysis is therefore the *current* state of the law rather than the comparative nature of previous law.

As explained above, what an accused must do to satisfy the evidentiary or proper foundation burden in cases involving claims of automatism is directly related to the nature of the legal burden in such cases. Accordingly, a change to the evidentiary burden associated with automatism is in order. To meet this burden, the defence must satisfy the trial judge that there is evidence upon which a properly instructed jury could find that the accused acted involuntarily on a balance of probabilities. In my opinion, this evidentiary burden is consistent with the two-step approach taken by La Forest J. in *Parks*, *supra*. As noted above, the appropriateness of the evidentiary burden on the defence at the proper foundation stage was not directly at issue before this Court in *Parks*. This explains why La Forest J. did not find it necessary to refine the burdens associated with automatism to the extent that it has been necessary for me to do in the present case. What then is the nature of the evidence which will be required to satisfy this revised proper foundation or evidentiary burden?

A review of the case law reveals that an accused must claim that he acted involuntarily at the relevant time in order to satisfy the automatism evidentiary burden. As stated earlier, a mere assertion of involuntariness will not suffice. See for example *Bratty*, *supra*, at pp. 406 and 413–14; *Rabey* (Ont. C.A.), *supra*, at pp. 24–25, *per* Martin J.A. adopted by Ritchie J.; *Parks*, *supra*, at p. 897, *per* La Forest J.; *Falconer*, *supra*, at pp. 250–51 and 266.

In addition to an assertion of involuntariness, the defence must present expert psychiatric evidence confirming its claim. See for example *Bratty*, *supra*, at p. 413; *Falconer*, *supra*, at pp. 250–57 and 266; *Daviault*, *supra*, at pp. 101 and 103; *Rabey* (S.C.C.), *supra*, at p. 552, *per* Dickson J. Even the appellant in the present case concedes that in the absence of such psychiatric evidence it is unlikely that he could satisfy his evidentiary or proper foundation burden.

The law often requires judges to make subtle and sophisticated determinations about scientific methodology and expert evidence. Cases involving claims of automatism are no exception. Yet as Breyer J. of the United States Supreme Court aptly recognized in *General Electric Co. v. Joiner*, 118 S.Ct. 512 (1997), judges are usually not scientists and thus do not have the scientific training which facilitates the making of such decisions. For this reason, when law and science intersect, judges must undertake their duties with special care (p. 520).

Although cases involving claims of automatism do not deal with complex chemical reactions or the like, they do require judges to assess confusing and often contradictory psychiatric evidence. In particular, when determining whether the evidentiary burden for automatism has been satisfied, trial judges must be careful to recognize that the weight to be given to expert evidence may vary from case to case. If the expert testimony establishes a documented history of automatistic-like dissociative states, it must be given more weight than if the expert is simply confirming that the claim of automatism is plausible. In the former case, the expert is actually providing a medical opinion about the accused. In the latter case, however, the expert is simply providing an opinion about the circumstances surrounding the allegation of automatism as they have been told to him or her by the accused. Trial judges must keep in mind that an expert opinion of this latter type is entirely dependent on the accuracy and truthfulness of the account of events given to the expert by the accused. Indeed, in the present case, Dr. Janke, the defence psychiatrist, qualified his opinion by noting that it was based almost exclusively on the accuracy and truthfulness of the appellant's account of events:

> I think that, that when, in offering the [expert psychiatric] opinion, it is, in this circumstance, it's contingent upon the person being accurate in representing what they recall from that event. There are circumstances where you do have other witnesses who can give you some supportive evidence, but in this situation, you have to rely on a person. If they're not telling the truth, then the opinion is worthless.

In order to satisfy the evidentiary or proper foundation burden, all cases will require an assertion of involuntariness and confirming psychiatric evidence. However, this burden will generally require more than an assertion of involuntariness on the part of the accused accompanied by confirming expert evidence that automatism is plausible assuming the account of events given to the expert by the accused was accurate and truthful. The recognition of Sopinka, Lederman and Bryant in *The Law of Evidence in Canada*, *supra*, at p. 129, that "[p]olicy considerations are important in determining the sufficiency of evidence that is required to satisfy [evidential burdens] in both criminal and civil proceedings" supports such an approach. I will now attempt to provide some guidance on what additional evidence is relevant to the determination of whether the defence has raised evidence which would permit a properly instructed jury to find that the accused acted involuntarily on a balance of probabilities. The factors discussed here are given only by way of example and are meant to illustrate the type of reasoning trial judges should employ when evaluating the evidence adduced at trial.

Both the majority and dissent of this Court in *Rabey*, *supra*, recognized that a "shocking" psychological blow was required before non-mental disorder, rather than mental disorder, automatism could be left with the trier of fact. Although *Rabey* dealt specifically with "psychological blow" automatism, I am of the opinion that it is appropriate in all cases for trial judges to consider the nature of the alleged automatism trigger in order to assess whether the defence has raised evidence on which a properly instructed jury could find that the accused acted involuntarily on a balance of probabilities. With reference to psychological blow automatism specifically, I agree that the defence will generally have to provide evidence of a trigger equivalent to a "shock" in order to satisfy its evidentiary burden.

The existence or non-existence of evidence which corroborates the accused's claim of automatism will also be relevant to the assessment of whether a properly instructed jury could find that the accused acted involuntarily on a balance of probabilities. Such evidence may take different forms. Two examples are worth noting here. First, evidence of a documented medical history of automatistic-like dissociative states would certainly assist the defence in satisfying a trial judge that a properly instructed jury could find that the accused acted involuntarily on a balance of probabilities. Furthermore, the more similar the historical pattern of dissociation is with the current claim of automatism, the more persuasive the evidence will be on the issue of involuntariness. For example, a documented history of dissociation in response to the particular triggering stimuli in question in the case could serve as strong evidence that the same stimuli once again triggered an involuntary response. Although I would not go so far as to make a medical history of dissociation a requirement for the defence to meet its evidentiary burden at the proper foundation stage, I would note that the lack of such evidence is also a relevant factor in determining whether this defence burden has been satisfied.

Corroborating evidence of a bystander which reveals that the accused appeared uncharacteristically glassy-eyed, unresponsive and or distant immediately before, during or after the alleged involuntary act will also be relevant to the assessment of whether the defence has raised evidence on which a properly instructed jury could find that the accused acted involuntarily on a balance of probabilities. This is confirmed by the expert evidence of Dr. Murphy, the Crown psychiatrist in the present case, as set out above. Indeed, the fact that it is common practice for judges to note specifically [witnesses'] comments about the appearance of the accused at the relevant time indicates that this may already be a factor weighed in the assessment of whether or not the defence has satisfied its evidentiary burden in cases involving claims of automatism. I would caution, however, that the evidence of bystanders must be approached very carefully since automatism and rage may often be indistinguishable to untrained bystanders.

Another factor which trial judges should consider in assessing whether the defence has raised evidence which would permit a properly instructed jury to find that the accused acted involuntarily on a balance of probabilities is motive. A motiveless act will generally lend plausibility to an accused's claim of involuntariness. Indeed, in the present case, Dr. Murphy, the Crown psychiatrist, testified that since the mind and body of a person in a dissociative state have been split, she would expect that there would usually be no connection between involuntary acts done in a state of automatism and the social context immediately preceding them. Dr. Murphy also noted that if a single person is both the trigger of the alleged automatism and the victim of the automatistic violence, the claim of involuntariness should be considered suspect. I agree that the plausibility of a claim of automatism will be reduced if the accused had a motive to commit the crime in question or if the "trigger" of the alleged automatism is also the victim. On the other hand, if the involuntary act is random and lacks motive, the plausibility of the claim of automatism will be increased. A question that trial judges should ask in assessing whether the defence has raised evidence which would permit a properly instructed jury to find that the accused acted involuntarily on a balance of probabilities is therefore whether or not the crime in question is explicable without reference to the alleged automatism. If this question can be answered in the negative, the plausibility of the accused's claim of involuntariness will be heightened. Such was the case in *Parks*, *supra*, for example, where there was no explanation for why the accused would attack his "in-laws", with whom he otherwise had a good relationship, except automatism induced by a state of somnambulism. In contrast, if this question invokes a positive response, the plausibility of the claim of involuntariness will be decreased.

To sum up, in order to satisfy the evidentiary or proper foundation burden in cases involving claims of automatism, the defence must make an assertion of involuntariness and call expert psychiatric or psychological evidence confirming that assertion. However, it is an error of law to conclude that this defence burden has been satisfied simply because the defence has met these two requirements. The burden will only be met where the trial judge concludes that there is evidence upon which a properly instructed jury could find that the accused acted involuntarily on a balance of probabilities. In reaching this conclusion, the trial judge will first examine the psychiatric or psychological evidence and inquire into the foundation and nature of the expert opinion. The trial judge will also examine all other available evidence, if any. Relevant factors are not a closed category and may, by way of example, include: the severity of the triggering stimulus, corroborating evidence of bystanders, corroborating medical history of automatistic-like dissociative states, whether there is evidence of a motive for the crime, and whether the alleged trigger of the automatism is also the victim of the automatistic violence. I point out that no single factor is meant to be determinative. Indeed, there may be cases in which the psychiatric or psychological evidence goes beyond simply corroborating the accused's version of events, for example, where it establishes a documented history of automatistic-like dissociative states. Furthermore, the ever advancing state of medical knowledge may lead to a finding that other types of evidence are also indicative of involuntariness. I leave it to the discretion and experience of trial judges to weigh all of the evidence available on a case-by-case basis and to determine whether a properly instructed jury could find that the accused acted involuntarily on a balance of probabilities.

F. Step 2: Determining Whether to Leave Mental Disorder or Non-Mental Disorder Automatism with the Trier of Fact

Only if the accused has laid a proper foundation for a defence of automatism will it be necessary for the trial judge to determine whether mental disorder or non-mental disorder automatism should be left with the trier of fact. If the trial judge concludes that a proper foundation has not been established, the presumption of voluntariness will be effective and neither automatism defence will be available to the trier of fact. In such a case, however, the accused may still claim an independent s. 16 defence of mental disorder.

The determination of whether mental disorder or non-mental disorder automatism should be left with the trier of fact must be undertaken very carefully since it will have serious ramifications for both the individual accused and society in general. As mentioned above, mental disorder automatism is subsumed by the defence of mental disorder as set out in the *Code*. Accordingly, a successful defence of mental disorder automatism will result in a verdict of not criminally responsible on account of mental disorder as dictated by s. 672.34 of the *Code*. Under s. 672.54, an accused who receives this qualified acquittal may be discharged absolutely, discharged conditionally or detained in a hospital. In contrast, a successful defence of non-mental disorder automatism will always result in an absolute acquittal.

The assessment of which form of automatism should be left with the trier of fact comes down to the question of whether or not the condition alleged by the accused is a mental disorder. Mental disorder is a legal term. It is defined in s. 2 of the *Code* as "a disease of the mind". In *Parks*, *supra*, at pp. 898–99, the majority of this Court adopted the reasons of Martin J.A. in *Rabey* (Ont. C.A.), *supra*, which included the following explanation of the term "disease of the mind", at pp. 12–13:

> Although the term "disease of the mind" is not capable of precise definition, certain propositions may, I think, be asserted with respect to it. "Disease of the mind" is a legal term, not a medical term of art; although a legal concept, it contains a substantial medical component as well as a legal or policy component.
>
> ...
>
> The evidence of medical witnesses with respect to the cause, nature and symptoms of the abnormal mental condition from which the accused is alleged to suffer, and how that condition is viewed and characterized from the medical point of view, is highly relevant to the judicial determination of whether such a condition is capable of constituting a "disease of the mind". The opinions of medical witnesses as to whether an abnormal mental state does or does not constitute a disease of the mind are not, however, determinative, since what is a disease of the mind is a legal question....

In *Rabey* (Ont. C.A.), Martin J.A. described the task of the trial judge in determining the disease of the mind issue as follows, at p. 13:

> I take the true principle to be this: It is for the Judge to determine what mental conditions are included within the term "disease of the mind", and whether there is any evidence that the accused suffered from an abnormal mental condition comprehended by that term.

Taken alone, the question of what mental conditions are included in the term "disease of the mind" is a question of law. However, the trial judge must also determine whether the condition the accused claims to have suffered from satisfies the legal test for disease of the mind. This involves an assessment of the particular evidence in the case rather than a general principle of law and is thus a question of mixed law and fact. See *Southam*, *supra*, at paras. 35 and 36. The question of whether the accused actually suffered from a disease of the mind is a question of fact to be determined by the trier of fact. See *Rabey* (S.C.C.), *supra*, at p. 519, *per* Ritchie J.; *Parks*, *supra*, at p. 897, *per* La Forest J.; and *Bratty*, *supra*, at p. 412, *per* Lord Denning.

In response to the above-mentioned proposed revisions to the *Code* regarding automatism, the Canadian Psychiatric Association submitted a Brief to the House of Commons Standing Committee on Justice and the Solicitor General. In this brief, the Association, on behalf of its 2,400 members nationwide, suggested that from a medical perspective, all automatism necessarily stems from mental disorder. Accordingly, the Association recommended that non-mental disorder automatism be eliminated and all claims of automatism be classified as mental disorders.

Since mental disorder is a legal term, the opinion of the Canadian Psychiatric Association, while relevant, is not determinative of whether two distinct forms of automatism, mental disorder and non-mental disorder, should continue to be recognized at law. In my opinion, this Court should not go so far as to eliminate the defence of non-mental disorder automatism as the Association suggests. However, I take judicial notice that it will only be in rare cases that automatism is not caused by mental disorder. Indeed, since the trial judge will have already concluded that there is evidence upon which a properly instructed jury could find that the accused acted involuntarily on a balance of probabilities, there is a serious question as to the existence of an operating mind by the time the disease of the mind issue is considered. The foregoing lends itself to a rule that trial judges start from the proposition that the condition the accused claims to have suffered from is a disease of the mind. They must then determine whether the evidence in the particular case takes the condition out of the disease of the mind category. This approach is consistent with this Court's decision in *Rabey*, *supra*.

In *Rabey*, this Court adopted the "internal cause theory" of Martin J.A. as the primary test for determining whether automatism resulting from a psychological blow stems from a disease of the mind. The following is a portion of Martin J.A.'s explanation of this approach, which was cited with approval by the majority of this Court, at p. 519:

> In general, the distinction to be drawn is between a malfunctioning of the mind arising from some cause that is primarily internal to the accused, having its source in his psychological or emotional makeup, or in some organic pathology, as opposed to a malfunctioning of the mind, which is the transient effect produced by some specific external factor such as, for example, concussion. Any malfunctioning of the mind or mental disorder having its source primarily in some subjective condition or weakness internal to the accused (whether fully understood or not) may be a 'disease of the mind' if it prevents the accused from knowing what he is doing, but transient disturbances of consciousness due to certain specific external factors do not fall within the concept of disease of the mind.

It is clear from Martin J.A.'s reasons that the internal cause theory starts from the proposition that the condition the accused claims to have suffered from is a disease of the mind. At pp. 21–22, he states:

> The malfunctioning of the mind which the respondent suffered, although temporary, is a "disease of the mind", *unless it can be considered as a transient state produced by an external cause within the meaning of the authorities*.
>
> In my view, the ordinary stresses and disappointments of life which are the common lot of mankind do not constitute an external cause constituting an explanation for a malfunctioning of the mind *which takes it out of* the category of a "disease of the mind". [Emphasis added.]

The reasons of La Forest J. in *Parks*, *supra*, are sometimes read as reversing the *Rabey* notion that the disease of the mind inquiry should begin from the proposition that the condition the accused claims to have suffered from is a disease of the mind. However, La Forest J. clearly stipulated, at p. 898, that "the approach to distinguishing between insane and non-insane automatism was settled by this Court's judgement in *Rabey*". Furthermore, in applying the second step of the automatism analysis, La Forest J. considered whether policy factors *precluded* a finding of non-mental disorder automatism (p. 908). In the end, given the fact specific approach taken by this Court in *Parks*, I would conclude that *Parks* cannot be interpreted as reversing *Rabey* on this issue.

G. Determining Whether the Condition the Accused Claims to Have Suffered from is a Disease of the Mind

In *Parks*, La Forest J. recognized that there are two distinct approaches to the disease of the mind inquiry: the internal cause theory and the continuing danger theory. He recognized the internal cause theory as the dominant approach in Canadian jurisprudence but concluded, at p. 902, that this theory "is really meant to be used only as an analytical tool, and not as an all-encompassing methodology". This conclusion stemmed from a finding that somnambulism, the alleged trigger of the automatism in *Parks*, raises unique problems which are not well-suited to analysis under the internal cause theory. I agree that the internal cause theory cannot be regarded as a universal classificatory scheme for "disease of the mind". There will be cases in which the approach is not helpful because, in the words of La Forest J., at p. 903, "the dichotomy between internal and external causes becomes blurred". Accordingly, a new approach to the disease of the mind inquiry is in order. As I will explain below, a more holistic approach, like that developed by La Forest J. in *Parks*, must be available to trial judges in dealing with the disease of the mind question. This approach must be informed by the internal cause theory, the continuing danger theory and the policy concerns raised in this Court's decisions in *Rabey* and *Parks*.

(1) The Internal Cause Theory

The internal cause theory was developed in the context of psychological blow automatism. Under the internal cause theory, the trial judge must compare the accused's automatistic reaction to the psychological blow to the way one would expect a normal person in the same circumstances to react in order to determine whether the condition the accused claims to have suffered from is a disease of the mind. As K. L. Campbell points out, at p. 354 of his article "Psychological Blow Automatism: A Narrow Defence" (1980–81), 23 *Crim. L.Q.* 342, how can abnormality be defined in any other way but by comparison to what is normal. The words of Martin J.A. in *Rabey* (Ont. C.A.), *supra*, adopted by the majority of this Court, at p. 520, highlight this comparative approach to the disease of the mind question:

> In my view, the ordinary stresses and disappointments of life which are the common lot of mankind do not constitute an external cause constituting an explanation for a malfunctioning of the mind which takes it out of the category of a "disease of the mind".... I leave aside, until it becomes necessary to decide them, cases where a dissociative state has resulted from emotional shock without physical injury, resulting from such causes, for example, as being involved in a serious accident although no physical injury has resulted; being the victim of a murderous attack with an uplifted knife, notwithstanding that the victim has managed to escape physical injury; seeing a loved one murdered or seriously assaulted, and like situations. Such extraordinary external events might reasonably be presumed to affect the average normal person without reference to the subjective makeup of the person exposed to such experience.

The nature of the alleged trigger of the automatism is at the centre of the comparison the trial judge must undertake. For example, in the context of psychological blow automatism, both the majority and dissent of this Court in *Rabey* recognized that a "shocking" psychological blow was required before non-mental disorder, rather than mental disorder, automatism could be left with the trier of fact. To this end, the majority adopted the above-quoted words of Martin J.A. In dissent, Dickson J. made the following comment, at p. 549:

> I agree with the requirement that there be a shock precipitating the state of automatism. Dissociation caused by a low stress threshold and surrender to anxiety cannot fairly be said to result from a psychological blow.

Accordingly, in *Rabey*, this Court unanimously supported the notion that there is a comparative element to the disease of the mind inquiry which involves an assessment of the nature of the trigger of the alleged automatism. In effect, the trial judge must consider the nature of the trigger and determine whether a normal person in the same circumstances might have reacted to it by entering an automatistic state as the accused claims to have done. Although I recognize that this approach will not be helpful in all cases, I believe that it remains useful in others. As such, the internal cause approach is a factor for trial judges to consider in cases in which they deem it useful. It may be helpful to provide some guidance as to how the comparison involved in the internal cause theory should be undertaken. I will do so in the context of psychological blow automatism, as I believe the internal cause approach will be most useful in cases involving automatism claims of this nature.

In his article, *supra*, Campbell points out that in assessing triggers of psychological blow automatism in *Rabey*, the majority of this Court drew the line between stressful situations and extremely shocking events. Under this approach, a finding that an alleged condition is not a disease of the mind, and consequently can support a defence of non-mental disorder automatism, is limited to cases involving triggers that normal people would find extremely shocking. Involuntariness caused by any less severe shock or mere stress is presumed to be triggered by a factor internal to the accused and as such constitutes a disease of the mind which can only give rise to a defence of mental disorder automatism (p. 357). Dickson J., in dissent, drew the line between stressful situations and mildly shocking events. Under this approach, the threshold requirement for a finding that a condition is not a disease of the mind is any shock, no matter what its severity. Only events which cannot be classified as a shock of any degree are labelled as internal, and thus diseases of the mind which can only give rise to the defence of mental disorder automatism (p. 358).

Given that the present case involves psychological blow automatism, I believe it is appropriate to express my opinion that the position of the majority in *Rabey* on this issue is preferable. The point of undertaking the comparison is to determine whether a normal person might have reacted to the alleged trigger by entering an automatistic state as the accused claims to have done. In cases involving claims of psychological blow automatism, evidence of an extremely shocking trigger will be required to establish that a normal person might have reacted to the trigger by entering an automatistic state, as the accused claims to have done.

When undertaking a comparison with a normal person, one is immediately faced with the difficulty of determining the importance of the context in which the comparison is made. I agree with the following comments of the High Court of Australia in *Falconer*, *supra*, on this issue (at p. 264):

> In determining whether the mind of an ordinary person would have malfunctioned in the face of the physical or psychological trauma to which the accused was subjected, the psychotic, neurotic or emotional state of the accused at that time is immaterial. The ordinary person is assumed to

> be a person of normal temperament and self-control. Consequently, evidence that, in the week preceding the shooting, [the accused] had demonstrated fear, depression, emotional disturbance and an apparently changed personality would not have been relevant in determining the reaction of an ordinary person. Likewise, evidence of the stress that she suffered on discovering that her husband had sexually assaulted their two daughters would not have been relevant in determining the reaction of the ordinary person to the incidents which took place on the day of the shooting. But evidence of the objective circumstances of the relationship between the parties would have been relevant to that issue, for only by considering the pertinent circumstances of that relationship could the jury determine whether an ordinary person would have succumbed to a state of dissociation similar to that which [the accused] claims overtook her on that day. Speaking generally, the issue for the jury on this aspect of the case would be whether an ordinary woman of [the accused]'s age and circumstances, who had been subjected to the history of violence which she alleged, who had recently discovered that her husband had sexually assaulted their daughters, who knew that criminal charges had been laid against her husband in respect of these matters and who was separated from her husband as a result of his relationship with another woman, would have entered a state of dissociation as the result of the incidents which occurred on the day of the shooting.

The comparison involved in the disease of the mind inquiry is thus a contextual objective test. The accused's automatistic reaction to the alleged trigger must be assessed from the perspective of a similarly situated individual. This requires that the circumstances of the case be taken into account. However, I emphasize that this is not a subjective test.

The appellant argues that the objective element of the internal cause theory violates ss. 7 and 11(*d*) of the *Charter*. According to the appellant, the *Charter* requires that the focus of the disease of the mind inquiry be on the actual, subjective response of the accused rather than that of a normal person. With respect, this argument fails to recognize that the objective inquiry into whether the condition claimed by the accused is a disease of the mind is applied only after a subjective inquiry into whether there is evidence upon which a properly instructed jury could find that the accused acted involuntarily on a balance of probabilities has been completed by the trial judge. That is, the objective standard affects only the classification of the defence rather than the assessment of whether the *actus reus* of the offence has been established. A similar objective standard was applied to the defence of provocation in *R. v. Cameron* (1992), 71 C.C.C. (3d) 272, where the Ontario Court of Appeal held that the objective standard involved in the defence of provocation does not violate ss. 7 and 11(*d*) because it does not detract from the *mens rea* required to establish murder. The point I wish to make here is that the objective component of the internal cause theory does not affect the burden of proof on the issue of whether the accused voluntarily committed the offence. Moreover, the impact of the objective comparison is limited even with regard to the disease of the mind inquiry. As noted above, I agree with La Forest J. in *Parks* that the internal cause theory is only an analytical tool. It is not being held out as the definitive answer to the disease of the mind question. In each case, the trial judge must determine whether and to what extent the theory is useful given the facts of the case. Indeed, he or she has the discretion to disregard the theory if its application would not accord with the policy concerns which underlie the disease of the mind inquiry. In this way, the internal cause approach attempts to strike an appropriate balance between the objectives of providing an exemption from criminal liability for morally innocent offenders and protecting the public. In these circumstances, the objective component of the internal cause theory does not limit either s. 7 or s. 11(*d*) of the *Charter*. I would add that consideration of the subjective psychological make-up of the accused in the internal cause theory would frustrate the very purpose of making the comparison, which is of course to determine whether the accused was suffering from a disease of the mind in a legal sense.

(2) The Continuing Danger Theory

As mentioned above, both the majority and dissenting judges of this Court in *Rabey*, as well as La Forest J. in *Parks*, recognized that policy considerations are relevant to the determination of whether a claim of automatism is the result of a disease of the mind. One policy factor which is central to the disease of the mind inquiry is the need to ensure public safety. Indeed, as mentioned above, La Forest J. recognized in *Parks* that the second dominant approach to the disease of the mind question is the continuing danger theory. This theory holds that any condition which is likely to present a recurring danger to the public should be treated as a disease of the mind. In other words, the likelihood of recurrence of violence is a factor to be considered in the disease of the mind inquiry. This approach must be qualified to recognize that while a continuing danger suggests a disease of the mind, a finding of no continuing danger does not preclude a finding of a disease of the mind. See *Rabey*, *supra*, at p. 15 (Ont. C.A.), *per* Martin J.A., and at pp. 533 and 551 (S.C.C.), *per* Dickson J.; *Parks*, *supra*, at p. 907, *per* La Forest J.

In my opinion, trial judges should continue to consider the continuing danger theory as a factor in the determination of whether a condition should be classified as a disease of the mind. However, I emphasize that the continuing danger factor should not be viewed as an alternative or mutually exclusive approach to the internal cause factor. Although different, both of these approaches are relevant factors in the disease of the mind inquiry. As such, in any given case, a trial judge may find one, the other or both of these approaches of assistance. To reflect this unified, holistic approach to the disease of the mind question, it is therefore more appropriate to refer to the internal cause factor and the continuing danger factor, rather than the internal cause theory and the continuing danger theory.

In examining the continuing danger factor, trial judges may consider any of the evidence before them in order to assess the likelihood of recurrence of violence. However, two issues will be particularly relevant to the continuing danger factor: the psychiatric history of the accused and the likelihood that the trigger alleged to have caused the automatistic episode will recur. As noted above, the defence must present expert psychiatric evidence in order to establish a proper foundation for a defence of automatism. The weight to be given to such evidence at the foundation stage will depend upon whether it establishes a documented history of automatistic-like dissociative states or simply confirms that a claim of automatism is plausible provided that the account of events given to the expert by the accused was accurate and truthful. The same distinction is again relevant when assessing the continuing danger factor in order to determine whether the condition the accused claims to have suffered from is a disease of the mind. Psychiatric evidence which reveals a documented history of automatistic-like dissociative states suggests that the condition alleged by the accused is of a recurring nature and thus increases the likelihood that automatism will recur. The likelihood of recurrence of violence is in turn heightened by the fact that at least one of the accused's automatistic episodes involved violence. In such a case, the continuing danger factor indicates that the condition the accused claims to have suffered from is likely to be classified as a disease of the mind. I would note that the absence of a history of automatistic-like dissociative states in no way indicates that there will be no recurrence of violence. In such a case, the trial judge will have to determine the recurrence of violence issue through other methods, one of which may be an assessment of the likelihood of recurrence of the alleged trigger of the automatism.

In their Case Comment on *R. v. Parks* (1993), 72 *Can. Bar Rev.* 224, I. Grant and L. Spitz point out that in assessing the likelihood of recurrence of violence, courts have been asking the wrong question. Courts have been focussing on whether the accused is likely to exhibit violent behaviour if he or she were again to encounter the alleged trigger of the current automatistic episode. According to Grant and Spitz, a more appropriate question is simply whether the alleged trigger is likely to recur. Grant and Spitz reason that there is no way of accurately predicting whether actual violence will recur. Indeed the likelihood of the initial automatistic violence would generally have been remote and thus difficult to predict. In contrast, the likelihood of recurrence of the circumstances which are alleged to have given rise to the automatism is more easily predicted (see pp. 235–36).

The logic of the reasoning of Grant and Spitz is difficult to deny. Indeed, it reveals that an assessment of the likelihood that the particular accused will again encounter the trigger alleged to have caused the current automatistic episode, or a similar one of at least equal severity, may assist a judge in assessing the continuing danger factor. The greater the anticipated frequency of the trigger in the accused's life, the greater the risk posed to the public and, consequently, the more likely it is that the condition alleged by the accused is a disease of the mind.

(3) Other Policy Factors

There may be cases in which consideration of the internal cause and continuing danger factors alone does not permit a conclusive answer to the disease of the mind question. Such will be the case, for example, where the internal cause factor is not helpful because it is impossible to classify the alleged cause of the automatism as internal or external, and the continuing danger factor is inconclusive because there is no continuing danger of violence. Accordingly, a holistic approach to disease of the mind must also permit trial judges to consider other policy concerns which underlie this inquiry. As mentioned above, in *Rabey* and *Parks*, this Court outlined some of the policy concerns which surround automatism. I have already referred to those specific policy concerns earlier in these reasons. I repeat that I do not view those policy concerns as a closed category. In any given automatism case, a trial judge may identify a policy factor which this Court has not expressly recognized. Any such valid policy concern can be considered by the trial judge in order to determine whether the condition the accused claims to have suffered from is a disease of the mind. In determining this issue, policy concerns assist trial judges in answering the fundamental question of mixed law and fact which is at the centre of the disease of the mind inquiry: whether society requires protection from the accused and, consequently, whether the accused should be subject to evaluation under the regime contained in Part XX.1 of the *Code*.

H. Available Defences Following the Determination of the Disease of the Mind Question

If the trial judge concludes that the condition the accused claims to have suffered from is not a disease of the mind, only the defence of non-mental disorder automatism will be left with the trier of fact as the trial judge will have already found that there is evidence upon which a properly instructed jury could find that the accused acted involuntarily on a balance of probabilities. The question for the trier of fact will then be whether the defence has proven that the accused acted involuntarily on a balance of probabilities. A positive answer to this question by the trier of fact will result in a successful defence of non-mental disorder automatism and, consequently, an absolute acquittal.

I would note that in his instructions to the jury on the voluntariness issue in cases of non-mental disorder automatism, the trial judge should begin by thoroughly reviewing the serious policy factors which surround automatism, including concerns about feignability and the repute of the administration of justice. It will also be helpful for the trial judge to refer specifically to evidence relevant to the issue of involuntariness, such as: the severity of the triggering stimulus, corroborating evidence of bystanders, corroborating medical history of automatistic-like dissociative states, whether there is evidence of a motive for the crime, and whether the alleged trigger of the automatism is also the victim of the automatistic violence.

On the other hand, if the trial judge concludes that the alleged condition is a disease of the mind, only mental disorder automatism will be left with the trier of fact. The case will then proceed like any other s. 16 case, leaving for the trier of fact the question of whether the defence has proven, on a balance of probabilities, that the accused suffered from a mental disorder which rendered him or her incapable of appreciating the nature and quality of the act in question. As mentioned earlier, s. 16 provides a framework within which the protection of the public will be assured when mental disorder automatism is established.

The trier of fact's determination of whether an accused has made out a successful claim of mental disorder automatism will absorb the question of whether the accused in fact acted involuntarily. That is, if the trial judge concludes that the allegation of automatism, if genuine, could only have resulted from a disease of the mind, a finding that the accused was not suffering from a mental disorder by the trier of fact necessarily extinguishes the validity of the accused's claim of involuntariness. Viscount Kilmuir L.C. put it this way in *Bratty*, *supra*, at p. 403:

> Where the possibility of an unconscious act depends on, and only on, the existence of a defect of reason from disease of the mind within the M'Naughten Rules, a rejection by the jury of this defence of insanity necessarily implies that they reject the possibility.

See also *Bratty*, *supra*, at pp. 404, 415 and 417–18; and *Rabey* (Ont. C.A.), *supra*, at pp. 24–25, *per* Martin J.A.

I. Application to the Present Case

At trial, the appellant claimed both mental disorder and non-mental disorder automatism. The learned trial judge concluded that the appellant had established a proper foundation for a defence of automatism, but that only mental disorder automatism should be left with the jury. In coming to these conclusions, the trial judge did not have the benefit of these reasons to guide him. Nevertheless, this does not warrant allowing the appeal because, as I explain below, the approach taken by the trial judge did not impair the appellant's position.

In determining whether the appellant had established a proper foundation for a defence of automatism, the trial judge stated that there must be evidence of unconsciousness throughout the commission of the crime. As I have explained above, automatism is more properly defined as impaired consciousness, rather than unconsciousness. Furthermore, lack of voluntariness, rather than consciousness, is the key legal element of automatism. Accordingly, the trial judge should have concerned himself with assessing whether there was evidence that the appellant experienced a state of impaired consciousness in which he had no voluntary control over his actions rather than whether there was evidence that the appellant was unconscious throughout the commission of the crime. Obviously, unconsciousness as defined by the trial judge supposes involuntariness. However, his finding that there was evidence of unconsciousness throughout the commission of the crime may have been based on a misunderstanding of the nature of the evidentiary burden on the accused at the proper foundation stage.

In accordance with much of the jurisprudence at the time, the trial judge may have found that a proper foundation for automatism had been established because the defence had met an evidentiary burden which amounted to no more than the appellant's claim of involuntariness and confirming expert psychiatric evidence. There is no indication that he assessed whether the defence had raised evidence on which a properly instructed jury could find that the appellant acted involuntarily on a balance of probabilities. Likewise, there is no indication that the trial judge recognized the limited weight to be accorded to the psychiatric evidence in this case, which only served to confirm that the appellant's claim of automatism was plausible provided the account of events he provided to Dr. Janke was accurate and truthful. Nor did the trial judge discuss the relevance of motive or corroborating evidence on his conclusion that a proper foundation for automatism had been established.

Turning to the disease of the mind stage of the automatism analysis, I note that the evidence in this case raised *only one alleged cause* of automatism, Donna Stone's words. Based on this evidence, the trial judge found that only mental disorder automatism should be left with the jury. This conclusion was based primarily on a finding that the present case is indistinguishable from *MacLeod*, *supra*. Such reliance on precedent fails to reveal what effect, if any, the internal cause factor, the continuing danger factor and other policy factors had on the decision to leave only mental disorder automatism with the jury. This is not in accordance with the holistic approach to the disease of the mind question set out in these reasons. However, the internal cause factor and the continuing danger factor, as well as the other policy factors set out in this Court's decisions in *Rabey* and *Parks* all support the trial judge's finding that the condition the appellant alleges to have suffered from is a disease of the mind in the legal sense. In particular, the trigger in this case was not, in the words of Martin J.A. quoted in this Court's decision in *Rabey*, at p. 520, "extraordinary external events" that would amount to an extreme shock or psychological blow that would cause a normal person, in the circumstances of the accused, to suffer a dissociation in the absence of a disease of the mind. Accordingly, I find that the trial judge nevertheless reached the correct result on the disease of the mind question. As previously noted, in such a case, only mental disorder automatism must be put to the jury. There is no reason to go beyond the facts of this case in applying the rules discussed above.

In the end, I must conclude that no substantial wrong or miscarriage of justice occurred in the present case. Even if I had found that the trial judge erred in applying the evidentiary burden at the proper foundation stage of the automatism analysis, this error could only have benefitted the appellant. Although the trial judge did not apply the holistic approach to disease of the mind established in these reasons, he reached the correct result on this issue. There is no reasonable possibility that the verdict would have been different had the errors not been made; see *R. v. Bevan*, [1993] 2 S.C.R. 599. I would therefore dismiss this ground of appeal.

. . . .

3.(a) Did the Court of Appeal err in principle in deciding that the sentencing judge was entitled to consider provocation as a mitigating factor for manslaughter where the same provocation, through the operation of s. 232 of the *Code* had already reduced the stigma and penalty of an intentional killing from murder to manslaughter?

(b) Did the Court of Appeal err in upholding a demonstrably unfit sentence that failed to reflect the gravity of the offence properly and the moral culpability of the offender?

. . . .

K. Error in Principle

(1) Provocation as a Mitigating Factor for Manslaughter

The Crown and intervening Attorney General for Ontario argue that the sentencing judge erred in principle when he considered provocation as a mitigating factor after s. 232 of the *Code* had reduced a verdict of murder to one of manslaughter. ...

As explained by Fraser C.J. in *R. v. Laberge* (1995), 165 A.R. 375 (C.A.), even for impulsive killings, there are different degrees of moral culpability. This Court has recognized that the broad sentencing range for manslaughter set out in s. 236 of the *Code* accords with the principle that punishment must be meted out with regard to the moral culpability or blameworthiness of an offender; see *R. v. Martineau*, [1990] 2 S.C.R. 633, at p. 647, *per* Lamer C.J., and *R. v. Creighton*, [1993] 3 S.C.R. 3, at pp. 48–49, *per* McLachlin J.

In reaching a sentence which accurately reflects a particular offender's moral culpability, the sentencing judge must consider all of the circumstances of the offence, including whether it involved provocation. Indeed, I agree with Finch J.A. in the court below, that to ignore the defence of provocation accepted by the jury, and the evidence upon which that defence was based, would be to ignore probative evidence of an offender's mental state at the time of the killing.

In a case involving manslaughter pursuant to s. 232 of the *Code*, however, the Crown and Attorney General for Ontario argue that provocation should not be considered in sentencing because it has already reduced the legal character of the crime from murder to manslaughter. According to this argument, considering provocation at the sentencing stage in such a case would reduce the offender's moral culpability and thereby reduce his or her sentence. This would, it is argued, give the offender a "double benefit" for the provoked nature of the killing. The Crown relies primarily on Manitoba cases in which that province's Court of Appeal refused to consider intoxication and provocation as mitigating factors when those factors had already served to reduce convictions of murder to manslaughter; see, for example, *R. v. Campbell* (1991), 70 Man. R. (2d) 158 (C.A.), and *R. v. Woermann* (1992), 81 Man. R. (2d) 255 (C.A.).

The defence of provocation applies only to the offence of murder. Historically, this limited defence was meant to guard against the unfair application of the death penalty. Even though the death penalty is no longer used as a punishment for murder, there is continued need for the limited defence of provocation. Because both first and second degree murder carry a minimum sentence of life imprisonment under s. 235 of the *Code*, judges have no discretion to consider provocation as a mitigating factor in determining appropriate sentences for these offences. Section 232 remedies this problem. In cases involving provocation, s. 232 permits a verdict of murder to be reduced to one of manslaughter, for which there is no minimum penalty unless a firearm was used in the commission of the offence (s. 236). This in turn allows for the consideration of provocation in the assessment of the offender's moral culpability and hence in the determination of an appropriate sentence. It is Parliament that has chosen to accord special attention to provocation.

It follows that an accused does not gain a "double benefit" if provocation is considered in sentencing after a verdict of manslaughter has been rendered by operation of s. 232. Rather, s. 232 provides an accused with a single benefit which can be characterized as a reduction of a verdict of murder to one of manslaughter in order to allow for the consideration of the provoked nature of the killing in the determination of an appropriate sentence. Accordingly, to give s. 232 full effect, provocation must be considered in sentencing in cases where this section of the *Code* has been invoked. The sentencing judge was therefore correct in considering provocation as a mitigating factor in the present case. The argument that the provocation factor was spent because it had already served to reduce the legal character of the crime overlooks the purpose of s. 232 and therefore must fail.

(2) Failure to Consider Appropriate Factors

The Crown and Attorneys General of Canada and for Ontario argue that the seven-year sentence imposed by the trial judge in the present case fails to reflect society's current understanding and awareness of the problem of violence against women in general, and, in particular, domestic violence. More specifically, they argue that the sentencing judge erred in failing to recognize that killing a spouse is considered an aggravating factor in sentencing in accordance with s. 718.2(*a*)(ii) of the *Code*. ...

The Attorneys General of Canada and for Ontario request that this Court specifically recognize spousal killings as an aggravating factor in sentencing under s. 718.2(*a*)(ii).

It is incumbent on the judiciary to bring the law into harmony with prevailing social values. This is also true with regard to sentencing. To this end, in *M. (C.A.)*, *supra*, Lamer C.J. stated, at para. 81:

> The objective of denunciation mandates that a sentence should also communicate society's condemnation of that particular offender's *conduct*. In short, a sentence with a denunciatory element represents a symbolic, collective statement that the offender's conduct should be punished for encroaching on our society's basic code of values as enshrined within our substantive criminal law.... Our criminal law is also a system of values. A sentence which expresses denunciation is simply the means by which these values are communicated. In short, in addition to attaching negative consequences to undesirable behaviour, judicial sentences should also be imposed in a manner which positively instills the basic set of

> communal values shared by all Canadians as expressed by the *Criminal Code*. [Emphasis in original.]

This Court's jurisprudence also indicates that the law must evolve to reflect changing social values regarding the status between men and women; see *Brooks v. Canada Safeway Ltd.*, [1989] 1 S.C.R. 1219; *R. v. Lavallee*, [1990] 1 S.C.R. 852; *R. v. Seaboyer*, [1991] 2 S.C.R. 577.

In *Weatherall v. Canada (Attorney General)*, [1993] 2 S.C.R. 872, this Court recognized the "historical trend of violence perpetrated by men against women" (p. 877). More specifically, in *Lavallee*, *supra*, at p. 872, the growing social awareness of the problem of domestic violence was recognized by this Court. In my opinion, these cases indicate that prevailing social values mandate that the moral responsibility of offenders be assessed in the context of equality between men and women in general, and spouses in particular. Clearly, spousal killings involve the breach of a socially recognized and valued trust and must be recognized as a serious aggravating factor under s. 718.2(*a*)(ii).

Turning to the present case, I would note that s. 718.2(*a*)(ii) of the *Code* did not come into force until September 3, 1996, approximately nine months *after* sentencing occurred in this case. Given that the *Code* cannot be retroactively applied to the disadvantage of an accused, the sentencing judge's treatment of the spousal nature of the killing must be assessed in light of the common law treatment of this factor prior to the implementation of s. 718.2(*a*)(ii). In my opinion, there is ample authority for the proposition that courts considered a spousal connection between offender and victim to be an aggravating factor in sentencing at common law; see *R. v. Doyle* (1991), 108 N.S.R. (2d) 1 (C.A.); *R. v. Brown* (1992), 13 C.R. (4th) 346 (Alta. C.A.); *R. v. Pitkeathly* (1994), 29 C.R. (4th) 182 (Ont. C.A.); *R. v. Jackson* (1996), 106 C.C.C. (3d) 557 (Alta. C.A.); *R. v. Edwards* (1996), 28 O.R. (3d) 54 (C.A.).

In the present case, the sentencing judge, Brenner J., had the benefit of also presiding over the trial of this matter. He could hardly have been unaware of the spousal relationship between the offender and the victim in this case. Furthermore, he heard the Crown's submissions on sentence, which specifically identified this offence as one of domestic violence. In its submissions, the Crown brought the alarming rate of domestic violence and need for general deterrence to the judge's attention. It also pointed out that women are particularly susceptible to being victims of domestic violence and that social concern surrounding this type of offence is growing. In his reasons for sentence, Brenner J. specifically identified the offence as one of domestic violence and noted that he viewed general deterrence as the principle concern in this sentencing. Furthermore, the two authorities he found most applicable, *Archibald*, *supra*, and *Eklund*, *supra*, both involved spousal manslaughter. In my opinion, the Crown has failed to establish that the sentencing judge did not properly consider the domestic nature of this offence in reaching his decision on sentence. This ground of appeal must therefore fail.

. . . .

[Lamer C.J. and Iacobucci, Major, and Binnie JJ. dissented, with the dissenting judgment written by Binnie J. Included below is Binnie J.'s summarizing conclusion regarding the issue of automatism.]

In the result, I believe the appellant was entitled to have the plea of non-mental disorder automatism left to the jury in this case in light of the trial judge's evidentiary ruling that there was evidence the appellant was unconscious throughout the commission of the offence, for the following reasons.

Firstly, I do not accept the Crown's argument that a judge-made classification of situations into mental disorder automatism and non-mental disorder automatism can relieve the Crown of the obligation to prove all of the elements of the offence, including voluntariness. As stated, such an interpretation encounters strong objections under s. 7 and s. 11(*d*) of the *Charter*, and there has been no attempt in this case to provide a s. 1 justification.

Secondly, imposition of a persuasive burden of proof on the appellant to establish "involuntariness" on a balance of probabilities, in substitution for the present evidential burden, runs into the same *Charter* problems, and no attempt has been made in the record to justify it.

Thirdly, the "internal cause" theory, on which the Crown rested its argument, cannot be used to deprive the appellant of the benefit of the jury's consideration of the voluntariness of his action, once he had met the evidential onus, without risking a violation of s. 11(*f*) of the *Charter*. *Rabey*'s treatment of the internal cause theory has to be looked at in light of the decision of this Court in *Parks*, *supra*, which signalled some serious reservations about the usefulness of the "internal cause" theory, except as an "analytical tool". *Rabey*, as clarified in *Parks*, does not impose a presumption that a lack of voluntariness must be attributed to the existence of a mental disorder any time there is no identification of a convincing external cause. Once the appellant in this case had discharged his evidential onus, he was entitled to have the issue of voluntariness go to the jury.

Fourthly, it was wrong of the courts to require the appellant to substitute for his chosen defence of involuntariness the conceptually quite different plea of insanity. One of the few points of agreement between the defence and Crown experts at trial was that the appellant did not suffer from anything that could be described medically as a disease of the mind. He was either unconscious at the time of the killing or he was not telling the truth at the time of the trial. This was a question for the jury. The statutory inquiry into whether he was "suffering from a mental disorder" that rendered him "incapable of appreciating the nature and quality of the act or omission or of knowing that it was wrong" are qualitative questions that are not really responsive to his allegation that he was not conscious of having acted at all.

Finally, the evidence established that there *are* states of automatism where perfectly sane people lose conscious control over their actions. At that point, it was up to the jury, not the judge, to decide if the appellant had brought himself within the physical and mental condition thus identified. As Dickson C.J. observed in *Bernard*, *supra*, at p. 848, the jurors were "perfectly capable of sizing the matter up".

In the result, I would have allowed the appeal, set aside the order of the British Columbia Court of Appeal and directed a new trial. Had I shared the conclusion of Bastarache J. to dismiss the appeal against conviction, I would also have concurred in the dismissal of the Crown's appeal on sentence for the reasons he gives.

■

Which opinion do you find more compelling — the majority decision by Bastarache J. or the minority decision by Binnie J.? What impact will *Stone* have on the burden of proof for other developing common law defences, such as colour of right and officially induced error of law? For the evidential burden for automatism, now see *R. v. Fontaine*, [2004] 1 S.C.R. 702.

What impact will *Stone* have on the accused's ability to get sane automatism before a jury? Consider *R. v. Luedecke*, [2005] O.J. No. 5088 (Ct. J.) (QL), where an accused who was charged with sexual assault and claimed to be in a state of "sexsomnia" was successful in a sane automatism defence. The accused had consumed approximately 12 beers and had been awake for roughly 22 hours when he fell asleep on his friend's couch at a party. The victim, who had fallen asleep on the same couch, woke up a short while later to find the accused having sex with her. The accused testified to being dazed and in a state of shock. After the incident, he drove to his parents' home, went to sleep, woke up to go to the bathroom, found himself wearing a condom and went back to sleep. When he woke up again and heard the police were investigating a sexual assault from the night before, he volunteered that he might have been responsible. At trial, the judge relied extensively on the expert testimony of Dr. Shapiro who had conducted a professional examination of the accused. According to Dr. Shapiro, the accused was suffering from "sexsomnia" — the occurrence of sexual behaviour during sleep which arises while a person is in a parasomnic state. Parasomnia was described by Dr. Shapiro at para. 10 as: "unexplained sudden arousals from sleep, where people are not aware of what they are doing. They act in ways that would not make sense otherwise." In relying on Dr. Shapiro's evidence that "sexsomnia" was not a disease of the mind, the trial judge noted that this case was one of the rare instances in which a non-insane automatism claim would be successful.

On appeal, the Ontario Court of Appeal found that the trial judge erred in law by applying the improper legal standard when characterizing the state of automatism at issue by (i) categorically ruling that somnambulism is not a disease of the mind; (ii) failing to note the hereditary nature of the condition, which suggests that is internally caused; (iii) failing to give effect to the continuing danger posed by triggers for "sexsomnia", particularly in light of the accused's record of prior acts of "sexsomnia"; and (iv) in giving too much weight to a medical opinion as to whether "sexsomnia" constitutes the legal condition of a disease of the mind. The acquittal was set aside and a new trial was ordered in which the only issue was to be whether the accused should be acquitted or found not criminally responsible on account of mental disorder, in accordance with the court of appeal's ruling on the law: *R. v. Luedecke*, [2008] O.J. No. 4049 (C.A.) (QL).

Rita Graveline was charged with the second-degree murder of her husband. Graveline's husband was over the course of their 32 year marriage, a chronic alcoholic and frequently and "continually" abusive. The accused's defence at trial was that she had acted in a state of non-insane automatism. Two experts were called by the defence, and one by the Crown. All three experts agreed that the accused had no memory of the shooting. The defence experts concluded that she was a battered wife and had acted in a state of automatism brought on shortly before the shooting by her traumatic relationship with her husband and the surrounding circumstances. The Crown's expert agreed that the accused's amnesia was genuine but concluded that it followed, rather than preceded the shooting. She was tried by a judge and jury and was acquitted of all charges. The Crown appealed the acquittal on the ground that the trial judge erred in law in his instructions to the jury by among other things putting self-defence to the jury and providing inadequate instructions with respect to the defence of non-mental disorder automatism. The Quebec Court of Appeal set aside the verdict of acquittal finding that the trial judge had erred in instructing the jury on self-defence as a possible defence to the charge: *R. c. Graveline*, [2005] Q.J. No. 7186. The Supreme Court of Canada reinstated the jury's acquittal based on a battered woman's syndrome automatism defence: *R. v. Graveline*, [2006] 1 S.C.R. 609. The Court noted that an appeal by the Crown cannot succeed on an abstract or hypothetical possibility that the accused would have been convicted but for the error of law. The Court held at paras. 17–19:

> There is no suggestion here that the errors imputed to the trial judge had any bearing, direct or indirect, on the legality of an acquittal based on the defence [of] ... non-mental disorder automatism ... The Crown argues, rather, that the jury might instead have acquitted the appellant on the ground of self-defence ... As a matter of principle, this alone does not bar a Crown appeal ... After a careful review of the record ... we have concluded that the Crown has failed to discharge its "very heavy" burden [for having the jury verdict set aside].

14

Provocation

Read s. 232 of the *Code*. Provocation is available only for murder and, if successful, is a partial defence that reduces murder to manslaughter. Briefly, the elements of the defence include: a wrongful act or insult capable of depriving an ordinary person of self-control, a resulting loss of self-control on the part of the accused, and action "on the sudden" by the accused. Section 232 utilizes a threshold "objective" test, which has thus far survived constitutional challenge: *R. v. Cameron* (1992), 7 O.R. (3d) 545 (C.A.).

However, prior to *R. v. Parent*, below, defence counsel could introduce evidence of "provocation" in other circumstances falling short of a formal "defence" of "provocation" to argue that the Crown has failed to establish the *mens rea* element of the offence or to mitigate the sentence, as discussed below, in reference to *R. v. Klassen* (18 January 1997), Whitehorse S.C. 95-01304A (Y.S.C.) [unreported], aff'd (1997), 95 B.C.A.C. (Yuk. C.A.), leave to appeal to S.C.C. refused [1997] S.C.C.A. No. 479.

As you read the materials in this section, consider the following questions:

- What are the requirements to raise a defence of provocation: objective threshold? subjective test?
- Who is the ordinary person?
- Which characteristics of the accused may be attributed to the "ordinary person"? (e.g., age, sex, culture, pugnacity, temperament, mental ability)
- Are there patterns in the circumstances for which a provocation defence is available?
- In what circumstances do men and women tend to raise the defence of provocation?
- Is the defence differentially available, for example, on the basis of gender or culture?
- What incidents are characterized as "wrongful act(s) or insult(s)"?
- What motivations and reactions are adjudged "reasonable"?
- What are the patterns in which homicide/femicide takes place?
- Does the availability of the defence meet a rational policy objective?
- What is the impact of the defence in terms of homophobic and other hate crimes, such as racist violence and femicide?
- Does the evidence led to raise (even an unsuccessful) "provocation" defence have a potential impact on judges and jurors by resonating with homophobic or misogynist assumptions?

A. CRIMES AGAINST GAYS AND LESBIANS

- What are the images of gay men presented in *D.P.P. v. Camplin* and *R. v. Hill*?
- What evidence exists in each case to support the accused's claim that he had been sexually assaulted or propositioned?

D.P.P. v. Camplin†

[LORD DIPLOCK:]

My Lords for the purpose of answering the question of law on which this appeal will turn only a brief account is needed of the facts that have given rise to it. The respondent, Camplin, who was 15 years of age, killed a middle-aged Pakistani, Mohammed Lal Khan, by splitting his skull with a chapati pan, a heavy kitchen utensil like a rimless frying pan. At the time the two of them were alone together in Khan's flat. At Camplin's trial for murder before Boreham J his only defence was that of provocation so as to reduce the offence to manslaughter. According to the story that he told in the witness box but which differed materially from that which he had told to the police, Khan had buggered him in spite of his resistance and had then laughed at him, whereupon Camplin had lost his self-control and attacked Khan fatally with the chapati pan.

In his address to the jury on the defence of provocation, counsel for Camplin had suggested to them that when they addressed their minds to the question whether the provocation relied on was enough to make a reasonable man do as Camplin had done, what they ought to consider was not the reaction of a reasonable adult but the reaction of a reasonable boy of Camplin's age. The judge thought that this was wrong in law. So in this summing-up he took pains to instruct the jury that they must consider whether —

> the provocation was sufficient to make a reasonable man in like circumstances act as the defendant did. Not a reasonable boy, as [counsel for Camplin] would have it, or a reasonable lad; it is an objective test — a reasonable man.

The jury found Camplin guilty of murder. On appeal the Court of Appeal, Criminal Division, allowed the appeal and substituted a conviction for manslaughter on the ground that the passage I have cited from the summing-up was a misdirection. The court held that —

> the proper direction to the jury is to invite the jury to consider whether the provocation was enough to have made a reasonable person of the same age as the appellant in the same circumstances do as he did.

The point of law of general public importance involved in the case has been certified as being:

> Whether, on the prosecution for murder of a boy of 15, where the issue of provocation arises, the jury should be directed to consider the question under s. 3 of the Homicide Act 1957, whether the provocation was enough to make a reasonable man do as he did by reference to a "reasonable adult" or by reference to a "reasonable boy of 15."

My Lords, the doctrine of provocation in crimes of homicide has always represented an anomaly in English law. In crimes of violence which result in injury short of death the fact that the act of violence was committed under provocation, which has caused the accused to lose his self-control, does not affect the nature of the offence of which he is guilty: it is merely a matter to be taken into consideration in determining the penalty which it is appropriate to impose: whereas in homicide provocation effects a change in the offence itself from murder, for which the penalty is fixed by law (formerly death and now imprisonment for life), to the lesser offence of manslaughter, for which the penalty is in the discretion of the judge.

The doctrine of provocation has a long history of evolution at common law. Such changes as there had been were entirely the consequence of judicial decision until Parliament first intervened by passing

† [1978] 2 All E.R. 168 A.C. 705 (H.L.). [Notes omitted.]

the Homicide Act 1957. Section 3 deals specifically with provocation and alters the law as it had been expounded in the cases, including three that had been decided comparatively recently in this House, namely *Mancini v Director of Public Prosecutions, Holmes v Director of Public Prosecutions* and *Bedder v Director of Public Prosecutions.* One of the questions in this appeal is to what extent propositions as to the law of provocation that are laid down in those cases, and in particular in *Bedder*, ought to be treated as being of undiminished authority despite the passing of the Homicide Act 1957.

For my part I find it instructive to approach this question by a brief survey of the historical development of the doctrine of provocation at common law. Its origin at a period when the penalty for murder was death is to be found, as Tindal CJ, echoing Sir Michael Foster, put in *R v Hayward*, in "the law's compassion to human infirmity." The human infirmity on which the law first took compassion in a violent age when men bore weapons for their own protection when going about their business appears to have been chance medley or a sudden falling out at which both parties had recourse to their weapons and fought on equal terms. Chance medley as a ground of provocation was extended to assault and battery committed by the deceased on the accused in circumstances other than a sudden falling out. But with two exceptions actual violence offered by the deceased to the accused remained the badge of provocation right up to the passing of the 1957 Act. The two exceptions were the discovery by a husband of his wife in the act of committing adultery and the discovery by a father of someone committing sodomy on his son; but these apart, insulting words or gestures unaccompanied by physical attack did not in law amount to provocation.

. . . .

The public policy that underlay the adoption of the "reasonable man" test in the common law doctrine of provocation was to reduce the incidence of fatal violence by preventing a person relying on his own exceptional pugnacity or excitability as an excuse for loss of self-control. The rationale of the test may not be easy to reconcile in logic with more universal propositions as to the mental element in crime. Nevertheless it has been preserved by the 1957 Act but falls to be applied now in the context of a law of provocation that is significantly different from what it was before the Act was passed.

Although it is now for the jury to apply the "reasonable man" test, it still remains for the judge to direct them what, in the new context of the section, is the meaning of this apparently inapt expression, since powers of ratiocination bear no obvious relationships to powers of self-control. Apart from this the judge is entitled, if he thinks it helpful, to suggest considerations which may influence the jury in forming their own opinions as to whether the test is satisfied; but he should make it clear that these are not instructions which they are required to follow: it is for them and no one else to decide what weight, if any, ought to be given to them.

As I have already pointed out, for the purposes of the law of provocation the "reasonable man" has never been confined to the adult male. It means an ordinary person of either sex, not exceptionally excitable or pugnacious, but possessed of such powers of self-control as everyone is entitled to expect that his fellow citizens will exercise in society as it is today. A crucial factor in the defence of provocation from earliest times has been the relationship between the gravity of provocation and the way in which the accused retaliated, both being judged by the social standards of the day. When Hale was writing in the 17th century pulling a man's nose was thought to justify retaliation with a sword: when *Mancini* was decided by this House, a blow with a fist would not justify retaliation with a deadly weapon. But so long as words unaccompanied by violence could not in common law amount to provocation the relevant proportionality between provocation and retaliation was primarily one of degrees of violence. Words spoken to the accused before the violence started were not normally to be included in the proportion sum. But now that the law has been changed so as to permit of words being treated as provocation, even though unaccompanied by any other acts, the gravity of verbal provocation may well depend on the particular characteristics or circumstances of the person to whom a taunt or insult is addressed. To taunt a person because of his race, his physical infirmities or some shameful incident in his past may well be considered by the jury to be more offensive to the person addressed, however equable his temperament, if the facts on which the taunt is founded are true than it would be if they were not. It would stultify much of the mitigation of the previous harshness of the common law in ruling out verbal provocation as capable of reducing murder to manslaughter if the jury could not take into consideration all those factors which in their opinion would affect the gravity of taunts and insults when applied to the person to whom they are addressed. So to this extent at any rate the unqualified proposition accepted by this House in *Bedder* that for the purposes of the "reasonable man" test any unusual physical characteristics of the accused must be ignored requires revision as a result of the passing of the 1957 Act.

That he was only 15 years of age at the time of the killing is the relevant characteristic of the accused in the instant case. It is a characteristic which may have its effects on temperament as well as physique. If the jury think that the same power of self-control is not to be expected in an ordinary, average or normal boy of 15 as in an older person, are they to treat the lesser powers of self-control possessed by an ordinary, average or normal boy of 15 as the standard of self-control with which the conduct of the accused is to be compared?

It may be conceded that in strict logic there is a transition between treating age as a characteristic that may be taken into account in assessing the gravity of the provocation addressed to the accused and treating it as a characteristic to be taken into account in determining what is the degree of self-control to be expected of the ordinary person with whom the accused's conduct is to be compared. But to require old heads on young shoulders is inconsistent with the law's compassion of human infirmity to which Sir Michael Foster ascribed the doctrine of provocation more than two centuries ago. The distinction as to the purpose for which it is legitimate to take the age of the accused into account involves considerations of too great nicety to warrant a place in deciding a matter of opinion, which is no longer one to be decided by a judge trained in logical reasoning but by a jury drawing on their experience of how ordinary human beings behave in real life.

There is no direct authority prior to the Act that states expressly that the age of the accused could not be taken into account in determining the standard of self-control for the purposes of the reasonable man test, unless this is implicit in the reasoning of Lord Simonds LC in *Bedder*. The Court of Appeal distinguished the instant case from that of *Bedder* on the ground that what it was there said must be ignored was an unusual characteristic that distinguished the accused from ordinary normal persons, whereas nothing could be more ordinary or normal than to be aged 15. The reasoning in *Bedder* would, I think, permit of this distinction between normal and abnormal characteristics, which may affect the powers of self-control of the accused; but for reasons that I have already mentioned the proposition stated in *Bedder* requires qualification as a consequence of changes in the law affected by the 1957 Act. To try to salve what can remain of it without conflict with the Act could in my view only lead to unnecessary and unsatisfactory complexity in a question which has now become a question for the jury alone. In my view *Bedder*, like *Mancini* and *Holmes*, ought no longer to be treated as an authority on the law of provocation.

In my opinion a proper direction to a jury on the question left to their exclusive determination by s. 3 of the 1957 Act would be on the following lines. The judge should state what the question is, using the very terms of the section. He should then explain to them that the reasonable man referred to in the question is a person having the power of self-control to be expected of an ordinary person of the sex and age of the accused, but in other respects sharing such of the accused's characteristics as they think would affect the gravity of the provocation to him, and that the question is not merely whether such a person would in like circumstances be provoked to lose his self-control but also would react to the provocation as the accused did.

I accordingly agree with the Court of Appeal that the judge ought not to have instructed the jury to pay no account to the age of the accused even though they themselves might be of opinion that the degree of self-control to be expected in a boy of that age was less than in an adult. So to direct them was to impose a fetter on the right and duty of the jury which the 1957 Act accords to them to act on their own opinion on the matter.

I would dismiss this appeal.

[LORD MORRIS OF BORTH-Y-GEST:]

My Lords, for many years past in cases where murder has been charged, it has been recognized by courts that there can be circumstances in which the accused person was so provoked that this unlawful act was held to amount to manslaughter rather than to murder. Due and sensibly [*sic*] regard to human nature and to human frailty and infirmity was being paid.

. . . .

Who then or what then was the "reasonable man"? If a reasonable man is a man who normally acts reasonably, it becomes important to consider the mind of the accused person when considering his reactions to some provocation. To consider the mind of some different person, and to consider what his reactions would have been if comparably provoked, could involve an unreal test. In the argument in *Bedder's* case the question was raised as to the position of a dwarf. If at the date of that case things said could have amounted to provocation and if grossly offensive things in relation to his stature had been said to a dwarf, had the jury to consider not whether the dwarf only acted as a reasonable dwarf might have acted in being subject to passion and in doing what he did, or must the jury consider what would have been the reactions of a man of normal physique if the things said had been said to him?

. . . .

In my view it would now be unreal to tell the jury that the notional "reasonable man" is someone without the characteristics of the accused: it would be to intrude into their province. A few examples may be given. If the accused is of particular colour or particular ethnic origin and things are said which to him are grossly insulting it would be utterly unreal if the jury had to consider whether the words would have provoked a man of different colour or ethnic origin, or to consider how such a man would have acted or reacted. The question would be whether the accused if he was provoked only reacted as even any reasonable man in his situation would or might have reacted. If the accused was ordinarily and usually a very unreasonable person, the view that on a particular occasion he acted just as a reasonable person would or might have acted would not be impossible of acceptance.

It is not disputed that the "reasonable man" in s. 3 of the 1957 Act could denote a reasonable person and so a reasonable woman. If words of grievous insult were addressed to a woman, words perhaps reflecting on her chastity or way of life, a consideration of the way in which she acted would have to take account of how other women being reasonable women would or might in like circumstances have reacted. Would or might she, if she had been a reasonable woman, have done what she did?

In the instant case the considerations to which I have been referring have application to a question of age. The accused was a young man. Sometimes in the summing-up he was called a boy or a lad. He was at the time of the events described at the trial under 16 years of age: he was accountable in law for the charge preferred against him. More generally in the summing-up he was referred to as a young man; that would appear to me to have been appropriate. In his summing-up however, the learned judge in referring to a reasonable man seemed to emphasise to the jury that the reasonable man with whom they must compare the accused could not be a young man of the age of the accused but had to be someone older and indeed had to be someone of full age and maturity. In my view that was not correct. The jury had to consider whether a young man of about the same age as the accused but placed in the same situation as that which befell the accused could, had he been a reasonable young man, have reacted as did the accused and could have done what the accused did. For the reasons which I have outlined the question so to be considered by the jury would be whether they considered that the accused, placed as he was and having regard to all the things that they find, were said, and all the things that they find were done, only acted as a reasonable young man might have acted, so that in compassion, and having regard to human frailty, he could to some extent be excused even though he had caused death.

I consider that the Court of Appeal came to the correct conclusion and agreement with what my noble and learned friend, Lord Diplock, has said as to the direction to a jury, I would dismiss the appeal.

[In his judgment, Lord Simon of Glaisdale concurred in the conclusion of Lord Diplock as to the appropriate instruction to the jury.]

Appeal dismissed.

■

R. v. Hill†

[DICKSON C.J.:]

Gordon James Elmer Hill was charged with committing first degree murder at the city of Belleville, County of Hastings, on the person of Verne Pegg, contrary to s. 218(1) of the *Criminal Code*, R.S.C. 1970, c. C-34. He was found by the jury not guilty of first degree murder but guilty of second degree mur-

† [1986] 1 S.C.R. 313.

der. He was sentenced to imprisonment for life without eligibility for parole until ten years of his sentence had been served.

Hill appealed his conviction to the Court of Appeal of Ontario. He raised many grounds of appeal, but the Court of Appeal called upon the Crown with respect to one ground only, relating to the charge on the issue of provocation. The ground of appeal was that the trial judge failed to instruct the jury properly as to the "ordinary person" in s. 215(2) of the *Criminal Code*. Section 215 of the *Code* reads in part:

> 215. (1) Culpable homicide that otherwise would be murder may be reduced to manslaughter if the person who committed it did so in the heat of passion caused by sudden provocation.
>
> (2) A wrongful act or insult that is of such a nature as to be sufficient to deprive an ordinary person of the power of self-control is provocation for the purposes of this section if the accused acted upon it on the sudden and before there was time for his passion to cool.

These two subsections, given their plain meaning, produce three sequential questions for answer by the tribunal:

1. Would an ordinary person be deprived of self-control by the act or insult?
2. Did the accused in fact act in response to those "provocative" acts; in short was he or she provoked by them whether or not an ordinary person would have been?
3. Was the accused's response sudden and before there was time for his or her passion to cool?

At this stage it is important to recall the presence of subs. (3) of s. 215 which provides:

> (3) For the purposes of this section the questions
>
> (*a*) whether a particular wrongful act or insult amounted to provocation, and
>
> (*b*) whether the accused was deprived of the power of self-control by the provocation that he alleges he received,
>
> are question of fact....

In the answering of these successive questions, the first or "ordinary person" test is clearly determined by objective standards. The second *de facto* test as to the loss of self-control by the accused is determined, like any other question of fact as revealed by the evidence, from the surrounding facts. The third test as to whether the response was sudden and before passions cooled is again a question of fact.

At the time of the killing, Hill was a male, sixteen years of age. The narrow question in this appeal is whether the trial judge erred in law in failing to instruct the jury that if they found a wrongful act or insult they should consider whether it was sufficient to deprive an ordinary person "of the age and sex of the appellant" of his power of self-control. Was it incumbent in law on the trial judge to add that gloss to the section? That is the issue.

THE FACTS

At trial both parties agreed that it was the acts of Hill which caused the death of Pegg but disagreed otherwise. The position of the Crown at trial was that Hill and Pegg were homosexual lovers and that Hill had decided to murder Pegg after a falling out between them. The Crown argued that Hill deliberately struck Pegg in the head while Pegg lay in bed. This did not kill Pegg who immediately ran from the bedroom into the bathroom to try and stop the flow of blood from his head. Realizing he had been unsuccessful, Hill took two knives from the kitchen and stabbed Pegg to death.

Hill's version of events was very different. He admitted to causing the death of Pegg but put forward two defences: self-defence and provocation. Hill testified that he had known Pegg for about a year through the latter's involvement with the "Big Brothers" organization. Hill stated that on the night in question he had been the subject of unexpected and unwelcome homosexual advances by Pegg while asleep on the couch in Peggs' apartment. Pegg pursued Hill to the bathroom and grabbed him, at which time Hill picked up a nearby hatchet and swung it at Pegg in an attempt to scare him. The hatchet struck Pegg in the head. Hill then ran from the apartment but returned shortly afterward. Upon re-entering the apartment, he was confronted by Pegg who threatened to kill him. At this point, Hill obtained two knives from the kitchen and stabbed Pegg to death.

Hill was arrested, after a car chase with the police, at the wheel of a Pontiac automobile owned by Pegg. At the scene of arrest Hill denied knowing Pegg, but later he made a statement to the police which was substantially similar to his oral testimony at trial.

THE CHARGE

. . . .

At trial, counsel for Hill objected to the instruction of the trial judge as to the objective requirement of the defence of provocation, submitting that the "ordinary person" referred to in s. 215(2) ought to have been defined as an ordinary person of the age and sex of the accused. Counsel submitted that the objective requirement would be satisfied if the judge were to recharge the jury by defining "ordinary person" as an "ordinary person in the circumstances of the accused." The judge refused to recharge the jury in those terms.

THE COURT OF APPEAL

In oral reasons Brooke J.A. (Martin and Morden JJ.A. concurring) noted that counsel for the defence, relying on *Director of Public Prosecutions v. Camplin*, [1978] A.C. 705 (H.L.), submitted that the judge should have instructed the jury to consider whether the wrongful act or insult was sufficient to deprive an "ordinary person" of the age and sex of the accused of his power of self-control. The Court of Appeal held that because the trial judge declined to do so he erred. In reaching his conclusion, Brooke J.A. stated:

> The age and sex of the appellant are not "peculiar characteristics" excluded from consideration of the "ordinary person" in the objective test in s. 215(2) (see Fauteux J. (as he then was) in *Wright v. The Queen*, [1969] 3 C.C.C. 258 at 264–5 discussing *Bedder v. D.P.P.*, [1954] 2 All E.R. 801).

He also added:

> In our respectful opinion, there is nothing in that judgment which precludes charging the jury as the defence requested. As the matter was left to the jury, the age of the appellant was only a consideration if and when the jury turned to the question of whether the wrongful act or insult deprived him of his power of self-control. The effect of the charge was that an ordinary person did not include a 16 year old or youth and may well have established as the standard an ordinary person more experienced and mature than the ordinary 16 year old or youth. If this is so, the jury may have rejected the defence judging the objective test on that basis.

In the result, the Court of Appeal held that the judge was in error and there may well have been misdirection which seriously prejudiced Hill and so the conviction could not stand. The appeal was allowed, the conviction set aside and a new trial on the charge of second degree murder ordered.

THE ISSUE

The issue in this appeal is whether the Ontario Court of Appeal erred in law in holding that the trial judge erred in law with respect to the elements of the objective test relevant to the defence of provocation in failing to direct the jury that the "ordinary person" within the meaning of that term in s. 215(2) of the *Criminal Code* was an "ordinary person of the same age and sex as the accused."

THE DEFENCE OF PROVOCATION

The defence of provocation appears to have first developed in the early 1800's. Tindal C.J. in *R. v. Hayward* (1833), 6 C. & P. 157, at p. 158, told the jury that the defence of provocation was derived from the law's "compassion to human infirmity." It acknowledged that all human beings are subject to uncontrollable outbursts of passion and anger which may lead them to do violent acts. In such instances, the law would lessen the severity of criminal liability.

Nevertheless, not all acts done in the heat of passion were to be subject to the doctrine of provocation. By the middle of the nineteenth century, it became clear that the provoking act had to be sufficient to excite an ordinary or reasonable person under the circumstances. As Keating J. stated in *R. v. Welsh* (1869), 11 Cox C.C. 336, at p. 338:

> The law is, that there must exist such an amount of provocation as would be excited by the circumstances in the mind of a reasonable man, and so as to lead the jury to ascribe the act to the influence of that passion.

The *Criminal Code* codified this approach to provocation by including under s. 215 three general requirements for the defence of provocation. First, the provoking wrongful act or insult must be of such a nature that it would deprive an ordinary person of the power of self-control. That is the initial threshold which must be surmounted. Secondly, the accused must actually have been provoked. As I have earlier indicated, these two elements are often referred to as the objective and subjective tests of provocation respectively. Thirdly, the accused must have acted on the provocation on the sudden and before there was time for his or her passion to cool.

The Objective Test of Provocation and the Ordinary Person Standard

In considering the precise meaning and application of the ordinary person standard or objective test, it is important to identify its underlying *rationale.* Lord Simon of Glaisdale has perhaps stated it most succinctly when he suggested in *Camplin*, at p. 726, that "the reason for importing into this branch of the law the concept of the reasonable man [was] ... to avoid the injustice of a man being entitled to rely on his exceptional excitability or pugnacity or ill-temper or on his drunkenness."

If there were no objective test to the defence of provocation, anomalous results could occur. A well-tempered, reasonable person would not be entitled to benefit from the provocation defence and would be guilty of culpable homicide amounting to murder, while an ill-tempered or exceptionally excitable person would find his or her culpability mitigated by provocation and would be guilty only of manslaughter. It is society's concern that reasonable and non-violent behaviour be encouraged that prompts the law to endorse the objective standard. The criminal law is concerned among other things with fixing standards for human behaviour. We seek to encourage conduct that complies with certain societal standards of reasonableness and responsibility. In doing this, the law quite logically employs the objective standard of the reasonable person.

With this general purpose in mind, we must ascertain the meaning of the ordinary person standard. What are the characteristics of the "ordinary person"? To what extent should the attributes and circumstances of the accused be ascribed to the ordinary person?

. . . .

[A review of the U.K. cases, including *Camplin*, followed:]

This Court again rejected a consideration of the drunkenness of the accused in connection with the objective test in *Salamon v. The Queen*, [1959] S.C.R. 404. Fauteux J., as he then was, endorsed the trial judge's instruction to the jury not to consider "the character, background, temperament or condition of the accused" in relation to the objective test of provocation. Similarly, Cartwright J., as he then was, (dissenting on another issue) wrote, at p. 415, that the trial judge correctly "made it plain that on this [objective] branch of the inquiry no account should be taken of the idiosyncrasies of the appellant and that the standard was that of an ordinary person."

Finally, in *Wright v. The Queen*, [1969] S.C.R. 335, a son was charged with the shooting death of his father. The evidence suggested that there had been some difficulties in their relationship. The father was said to have been a bad tempered and violent man who had mistreated his son on a number of occasions. The accused had not seen his father for a period of about five years until a few days prior to the fatal incident. On the evening of the shooting, the accused had spent most of the day drinking with his friends. In considering the objective test of provocation, the Court rejected the relevance of the quality of the accused's relationship with his father, the mentality of the accused or his possible drunkenness. Fauteux J. quoted, at p. 340, the words of Lord Simonds L.C. in *Bedder*, that the purpose of the objective test is "to invite the jury to consider the act of the accused by reference to a certain standard or norm of conduct and with this object the 'reasonable' or the 'average' or the 'normal' man is invoked." The Court went on to state, at p. 340:

> While the character, background, temperament, idiosyncrasies [*sic*] or the drunkenness of the accused are matters to be considered in the second branch of the enquiry, they are excluded from consideration in the first branch. A contrary view would denude of any sense the objective test.

Appellate courts at the provincial level have also considered the nature of the ordinary person standard of provocation. In *R. v. Clark* (1974), 22 C.C.C. (2d) 1 (Alta. C.A.), the "morbid jealousy and slight mental degeneration" suffered by the accused was held not to be relevant to the objective test. According to Clement J.A., at p. 16:

> In the first branch of the inquiry, the objective test, which in essence has to be determined as a standard of comparison is the reaction that might be expected from ordinary human nature to the wrongful act, or to the alleged insult in the present case.

In *R. v. Parnerkar* (1971), 5 C.C.C. (2d) 11, the Saskatchewan Court of Appeal held that the cultural and religious background of the accused was not relevant to the determination of the objective test. The accused, born in India, was alleged to have been provoked by, *inter alia*, the deceased's statement "I am not going to marry you because you are a black man." The Court's ruling seems to narrow unduly the conception of the ordinary person and rigidly prohibit a consideration of the physical characteristics of the accused along the lines of the *Bedder* case. I should note that *Parnerkar* was affirmed by this Court on appeal: see [1974] S.C.R. 449; however, this particular question was not addressed.

In more recent decisions, appellate courts at the provincial level appear to be moving towards the *Camplin* approach. The Ontario Court of Appeal's decision in the present appeal, *R. v. Hill* (1982), 2 C.C.C. (3d) 394, and *R. v. Daniels* (1983), 7 C.C.C. (3d) 542 (N.W.T.C.A.), reflect this trend. In the *Daniels* case, Laycraft J.A. held that in instructing the jury on the objective test of provocation, the trial judge should tell the jury to take into account all of the external events putting pressure on the accused. He stated at p. 554:

> The purpose of the objective test prescribed by s. 215 is to consider the actions of the accused in a specific case against the standard of the ordinary person. Hypothetically, the ordinary person is subjected to the same external pressures of insult by acts or words as was the accused. Only if those pressures would cause an ordinary person to lose self-control does the next question arise whether the accused did, in fact, lose self-control. In my view, the objective test lacks validity if the reaction of the hypothetical ordinary person is not tested against all of the events which put pressure on the accused.

The Appropriate Content of the Ordinary Person Standard

What lessons are to be drawn from this review of the case law? I think it is clear that there is widespread agreement that the ordinary or reasonable person has a normal temperament and level of self-control. It follows that the ordinary person is not exceptionally excitable, pugnacious or in a state of drunkenness.

In terms of other characteristics of the ordinary person, it seems to me that the "collective good sense" of the jury will naturally lead it to ascribe to the ordinary person any general characteristics relevant to the provocation in question. For example, if the provocation is a racial slur, the jury will think of an ordinary person with the racial background that forms the substance of the insult. To this extent, particular characteristics will be ascribed to the ordinary person. Indeed, it would be impossible to conceptualize a sexless or ageless ordinary person. Features such as sex, age, or race, do not detract from a person's characterization as ordinary. Thus particular characteristics that are not peculiar or idiosyncratic can be ascribed to an ordinary person without subverting the logic of the objective test of provocation. As Lord Diplock wrote in *Camplin* at pp. 716–17:

> ...the "reasonable man" has never been confined to the adult male. It means an ordinary person of either sex, not exceptionally excitable or pugnacious, but possessed of such powers of self-control as everyone is entitled to expect that his fellow citizens will exercise in society as it is today.

It is important to note that, in some instances, certain characteristics will be irrelevant. For example, the race of a person will be irrelevant if the provocation involves an insult regarding a physical disability. Similarly, the sex of an accused will be irrelevant if the provocation relates to a racial insult. Thus the central criterion is the relevance of the particular feature to the provocation in question. With this in mind, I think it is fair to conclude that age will be a relevant consideration when we are dealing with a young accused person. For a jury to assess what an ordinary person would have done if subjected to the same circumstances as the accused, the young age of an accused will be an important contextual consideration.

I should also add that my conclusion that certain attributes can be ascribed to the ordinary person is not meant to suggest that a trial judge must in each case tell the jury what specific attributes it is to ascribe to the ordinary person. The point I wish to emphasize is simply that in applying their common sense to the factual determination of the objective test, jury members will quite naturally and properly ascribe certain characteristics to the "ordinary person."

The Subjective Test and Actual Provocation

Once a jury has established that the provocation in question was sufficient to deprive an ordinary person of the power of self-control, it must still determine whether the accused was so deprived. It may well be that an ordinary person would have been provoked, but in fact the accused was not. This second test of provocation is called subjective because it involves an assessment of what actually occurred in the mind of the accused. At this stage, the jury must also consider whether the accused reacted to the provocation on the sudden and before there was time for his passion to cool.

In instructing the jury with respect to the subjective test of provocation, the trial judge must make clear to the jury that its task at this point is to ascertain whether the accused was *in fact* acting as a result of provocation. In this regard, a trial judge may wish to remind the jury members that, in determining whether an accused was actually provoked, they are entitled to take into account his or her mental state and psychological temperament.

THE VALIDITY OF THE TRIAL JUDGE'S CHARGE

To apply this statement of the law to the present appeal, we must return to the actual words of the trial judge. When instructing the jury on the objective test of provocation, he began by stating:

> First, the actual words must be such as would deprive an ordinary person of self-control. In considering this part of the Defence you are not to consider the particular mental make-up of the accused; rather the standard is that of the ordinary person. You will ask yourself would the words or acts in this case have caused an ordinary person to lose his self-control.

He later added:

> You will consider that evidence and you will decide whether the words and acts were sufficient to cause an ordinary person to lose his self-control.

In my view, this part of the charge was well-stated and correct in law. The trial judge did not err in failing to specify that the ordinary person for the purposes of the objective test of provocation, is to be deemed to be of the same age and sex as the accused. Although this type of instruction may be helpful in clarifying the application of the ordinary person standard, I do not think it wise or necessary to make this a mandatory component of all jury charges on provocation. Whenever possible, we should retain simplicity in charges to the jury and have confidence that the words of the *Criminal Code* will provide sufficient guidance to the jury. Indeed, in this area of the law, I take heed of the words of Lord Goddard C.J. in *R. v. McCarthy*, [1954] 2 Q.B. 105, at p. 112:

> No court has ever given, nor do we think ever can give, a definition of what constitutes a reasonable or average man. That must be left to the collective good sense of the jury.

It has been suggested that the instruction of the trial judge on the subjective prong of the provocation defence had the effect of misleading the jury on the appropriate content of the ordinary person standard. The charge stated:

> ...you will then secondly consider whether the accused acted on the provocation on the sudden before there was time for his passion to cool. In deciding this question you are not restricted to the standard of the ordinary person. You will take into account the mental, the emotional, the physical characteristics and the age of this accused.
>
> ...
>
> You will also ask yourselves was the provocation such that it would have led a person with the mental and physical condition and the age of the accused to respond in this way.

In my opinion, these words would not have misled the average juror with respect to the objective test, particularly when viewed in the context of the charge as a whole.

I have the greatest of confidence in the level of intelligence and plain common sense of the average Canadian jury sitting on a criminal case. Juries are perfectly capable of sizing the matter up. In my experience as a trial judge I cannot recall a single instance in which a jury returned to the courtroom to ask for further instructions on the provocation portion of a murder charge. A jury frequently seeks further guidance on the distinction between first degree murder, second degree murder and manslaughter, but rarely, if ever, on provocation. It seems to be common ground that the trial judge would not have been in error if he had simply read s. 215 of the *Code* and left it at that, without embellishment. I am loathe to complicate the task of the trial judge, in cases such as the case at bar, by requiring him or her as a matter of law to point out to the members of the jury that in applying the objective test they must conceptualize an "ordinary person" who is male and young. The accused is before them. He is male and young. I cannot conceive of a Canadian jury conjuring up the concept of an "ordinary person" who would be either female or elderly, or banishing from their minds the possibility that an "ordinary person" might be both young and male. I do not think anything said by the judge in the case at bar would have [led] the jury to such an absurdity.

[The appeal was allowed, Beetz, Estey, Chouinard, and La Forest JJ. concurring. Lamer, Wilson, and Le Dain JJ. dissented.]

■

Would the ordinary woman react with rage to a sexual advance? From a man? From a woman? Is it ever understandable or justifiable to kill another person acting in rage or under provocation, as opposed to action, for example, in self-defence or out of necessity?

Consider the context in which cases such as *Camplin* and *Hill* arise. What is the role of human rights statutes that have excluded "sexual orientation" as a prohibited ground? The following provinces have now expressly legislated against discrimination based on sexual orientation: Québec (1977), Ontario (1986), Manitoba (1987), Yukon Territory (1987), Nova Scotia (1991), New Brunswick (1992), British Columbia (1992), Saskatchewan (1993), Newfoundland (1997), and Prince Edward Island (1998). In a challenge to the Alberta *Individual Rights Protection Act*, R.S.A. 1980, c. I-2, the Supreme Court overturned the Alberta Court of Appeal and upheld the decision of the Court of Queen's Bench that ss. 7(1), 8(1) and 10 were of no force and effect because they violated s. 15 of the *Charter* by failing to include sexual orientation as a prohibited ground: *Vriend v. Alberta (Human Rights Commission)*, [1998] 1 S.C.R. 493.

What is the role of criminal law, in terms of the criminalization of specific sexual practices unless both parties are over 18 years of age and the acts occur in "private", in terms of the policing of these "crimes", and in terms of the media images of gay sexuality discussed earlier? See *R. v. C.(M.)* (1995), 23 O.R. (3d) 629 (C.A.) and *R. v. Roy* (1998), 125 C.C.C. (3d) 442 (Que. C.A.), which held that s. 159 of the *Code* was unconstitutional and of no force and effect since it violated s. 15 of the *Charter* by potentially denying individuals liberty for engaging in this form of consensual sexual conduct, on the basis of sexual orientation, age, and marital status.

Recall Cynthia Petersen's work on the prevalence and frightening intensity of anti-gay and lesbian violence, "A Queer Response to Bashing: Legislating Against Hate" in Abell & Sheehy *Cases, Context, Critique*, **Policing**. Are there any links between gay-bashing, the response of the state, and the invocation of the provocation defence? In the article that follows, Kendall Thomas critically examines a U.S. Supreme Court decision, *Bowers v. Hardwick*, 478 U.S. 186 (1986), which upheld Georgia's sodomy prohibition against constitutional challenge.

Beyond the Privacy Principle†

"Choked to Death, Burnt to Ashes": A Political Anatomy of Homophobic Violence

In October 1987, hundreds of people were arrested during the course of a demonstration against the decision in *Bowers v. Hardwick.* Those arrested had participated in a massive act of civil disobedience in which they had literally laid their bodies on the steps outside the Supreme Court building. The protest dramatically underscored the concrete corporal interests that the *Hardwick* Court ignored and evoked the tangible historical experience of gay and lesbian Americans in which the case must be situated.

Stated bluntly, that history is a story of homophobic aggression and ideology. Its central theme is the fear, hatred, stigmatization, and persecution of homosexuals and homosexuality. Over the course of American history, gay men and lesbian women have been discursively marked as "faggots" (after the pieces of kindling used to burn their bodies), "monsters," "fairies," "bull dykes," "perverts," "freaks," and "queers." Their intimate associations have been denominated "abominations," "crimes against nature," and "sins not fit to be named among Christians." Thus symbolic violence has produced and been produced by congeries of physical violence. Gay men and lesbians in America have been "condemned to death by choking, burning and drowning; ... executed, [castrated], jailed, pilloried, fined, court-martialed, prostituted, fired, framed, blackmailed, disinherited, [lobotomized, shock-treated, psychoanalyzed and] declared insane, driven to insanity, to suicide, murder, and self-hate, witch-hunted, entrapped, stereotyped, mocked, insulted, isolated ... castigated ... despised [and degraded]."

The historical roots of this violence are older than the nation itself. The 1646 Calendar of Dutch

† Kendall Thomas, "Beyond the Privacy Principle" 92 Col. L. Rev. 1431 (1992) at 1462–64, 1467, 1469, 1476, 1481, 1485, 1490. [Notes omitted.]

Historical Manuscripts reports the trial, conviction, and sentence on Manhattan Island, New Netherland Colony of one Jan Creoli, "a negro, [for] sodomy; second offense; this crime being condemned of God (Gen., c. 19; Levit., c. 18:22, 29) as an abomination, the prisoner is sentenced to be conveyed to the place of public execution, and there choked to death, and then burnt to ashes." On the same date the Calendar records the sentence of "Manuel Congo ... on whom the above abominable crime was committed," whom the Court ordered "to be carried to the place where Creoli is to be executed, tied to a stake, and faggots piled around him, for justice sake, and to be flogged; sentence executed."

The continuity between the seventeenth-century experience and homophobic violence in our own time is startling. A report issued by Community United Against Violence, an organization that monitors incidents of homophobic violence, offers a picture of the violent face of homophobia in contemporary America:

> One man's body was discovered with his face literally beaten off. Another had his jaw smashed into eight pieces by a gang of youths taunting "you'll never suck another cock, faggot!" Another had most of his lower intestine removed after suffering severe stab wounds in the abdomen. Another was stabbed 27 times in the face and upper chest with a screwdriver, which leaves a very jagged scar. Another had both lungs punctured by stab wounds, and yet another had his aorta severed.

Some months before the Supreme Court rendered its judgment in *Hardwick*, the *New York Daily News* printed the story of a homeless gay man in that city who "had his skull crushed by three men who beat him unconscious with two-by-fours while screaming anti-gay epithets"; the same article recounted an incident in which a motorist "who saw a lesbian standing on a sidewalk in [Manhattan] stopped his car, got out and beat her so badly (while shouting anti-lesbian epithets) that she suffered broken facial bones and permanent nerve damage." Two years after the *Hardwick* decision, the coordinator of a victim assistance program at a New York City hospital reported that "attacks against gay men were the most heinous and brutal I encountered." The hospital routinely treated gay male victims of homophobic violence, whose injuries "frequently involved torture, cutting, mutilation, and beating, and showed the absolute intent to rub out the human being because of his [sexual] orientation."

One would be mistaken to view these stories as aberrant, isolated instances of violence perpetrated by the psychologically imbalanced against individual gay men and women. They are not. All the evidence suggests that there are hundreds, if not thousands of such stories, most of them untold. Violence against gay men and lesbians — on the streets, in the workplace, at home — is a structural feature of life in American society. A study commissioned by the National Institute of Justice (the research arm of the U.S. Department of Justice) concluded that gay men and women "are probably the most frequent victims [of hate violence today]." We may never know the full story of the violence to which gay men and gay women are subjected. In spite of their frequency, it is estimated that a full 80% of bias violence against gay men and women is never reported to the police. This under-reporting is not surprising, since victims of anti-gay violence have reason to be fearful that the response of state and local officials may be unsympathetic or openly hostile, or that the disclosure of their sexual orientation may lead to further discrimination.

Indeed, government officials and agencies are themselves often complicit in the phenomenon of homophobic violence. Governmental involvement ranges from active instigation to acquiescent indifference. A recent survey of violence against gay men and lesbians cities a 1951 case study of police practices in which a patrolman describes his typical treatment of homosexuals:

> Now in my own cases when I catch a guy like that I just pick him up and take him into the woods and beat him until he can't crawl. I have had seventeen cases like that in the last couple of years. I tell the guy if I catch him doing that again I will take him out to the woods and I will shoot him. I tell him that I carry a second gun on me just in case I find guys like him and that I will plant it in his hand and say that he tried to kill me and that no jury will convict me.

At October 1986 hearings on homophobic violence by the House of Representatives Committee on the Judiciary, Subcommittee on Criminal Justice, the district attorney of New York County noted that "at times, [lesbians and gay men] have been, and in many areas of the country continue to be, taunted, harassed, and even physically assaulted by the very people whose job it is to protect them."

Even if we were able to document every instance of homophobic violence in America, our understanding of its effects would still be incomplete. To be sure, many men and women in the gay and lesbian communities have escaped direct physical attack by perpetrators of homophobic violence. However, the horror and sinister efficacy of homophobic violence are in many ways like those of racist violence. Like people of colour, gay men and lesbians always and everywhere have to live their lives on guard, knowing that they are vulnerable to attack at any time. As one observer has noted, "being gay means living with the reality that although you may not personally be the victim of outright homophobic attacks every day, at any moment you *could* be attacked — walking down the street, going to work, on the job, shopping, or in a restaurant." Indeed, much of the efficacy of homophobic violence lies in the message it conveys to those who are not its immediate victims.

In this respect, homophobic violence bears many of the characteristics associated with terrorism. As in the case of terrorism, much of the force of violence against gay men and lesbians lies in its randomness: individuals may know that the assertion or ascription of gay and lesbian identity marks them as potential targets of homophobic violence, but they cannot know until too late whether or when they will actually be hit. Like the terrorist, the perpetrator of homophobic violence strikes without giving warning. A second characteristic common to terrorism and homophobic violence is its utter impersonality. Like perpetrators of terrorist acts, those who attack gays and lesbians do not know, and are most often unknown to, their victims.

The terroristic dimensions of homophobic violence compel us to understand it as a mode of power. To put the point in slightly different terms, homophobic violence is a form of "institution," in the sense that John Rawls elaborates that concept. Homophobic violence is a social activity "structured by rules that define roles and positions, powers and opportunities, thereby distributing responsibility for consequences." Viewed systemically, the objective and outcome of violence against lesbians and gays is the social control of human sexuality. Homophobic violence aims to regulate the erotic economy of contemporary American society, or more specifically, to enforce the institutional and ideological imperatives of what Adrienne Rich has termed "compulsory heterosexuality." Insofar as homophobic violence functions to prevent and punish actual or imagined deviations from heterosexual acts and identities, it carries a determinate political valence and value.

I have argued that homophobic violence is an exercise of political power. I have suggested that the purpose of this violence is to terrorize the population to whom its victims belong. I have also referred to the record of state instigation of, and acquiescence in, the phenomenon of homophobic violence. I want now to explore more fully the constitutional implications of the connection between governmental instigation of and acquiescence in criminal attacks on gay men and lesbians on the one hand, and criminal statutes against homosexual sodomy on the other. It might be said that the coincidence of the law of homosexual sodomy and the lawlessness of homophobic violence by itself presents a question with which a constitutional analysis of these statutes must reckon.

However, I hope by now to have said enough to clear the ground for a somewhat stronger claim. I contend that the involvement of the state in the phenomenon of homophobic violence is in fact no coincidence at all. A close examination of the political terror directed against gay men and lesbians suggests that the relationship between homosexual sodomy law and homophobic violence is not merely coincident, but coordinate: the criminalization of homosexual sodomy and criminal attacks on gay men and lesbians work in tandem. My task, of course, is to specify the terms of their coordinal interaction. How should we think about the role the state plays in permitting, promoting or participating in homophobic violence?

. . . .

To appreciate the ways in which the relationship between homosexual sodomy law and homophobic violence presents constitutional analysis with a "political question," we might recall Seneca's claim that the body politic "can be kept unharmed only by the mutual protection" of its parts. I take this principle to mean that one of the first duties of the state is to protect the citizens from whom its powers derive against random, unchecked violence by other citizens, or by government officials.

For gay men and lesbians, the state has honored this fundamental obligation more in the breach than in the observance. As I have shown, few members of our body politic are more vulnerable to violent terrorist attack than the gay or lesbian citizen. This violence takes two forms. One form is violence at the hand of state officials such as the police. This official violence is an important part of the political history of the criminalization of homosexual sex. The second form of homophobic violence is that perpetrated by private individuals. Although this type of violence is of lower visibility than that committed by public officials, the available evidence suggests that it is even more extensive. Both involve the unlawful use of state power as a tool of law enforcement. With respect to homophobic violence perpetrated by state officials, no one would deny that a court can and should forbid a state from using terror and random violence as a standard tactic for enforcing homosexual sodomy law. Accordingly, I shall focus my discussion on the hidden constitutional dimensions of the brutal violence inflicted on gay men and lesbians at the hands of other citizens.

. . . .

Taking these theoretical lessons about state power as a point of reference, one may now specify precisely why the relationship between homosexual sodomy statutes and homophobic violence is constitutionally suspect. In assessing the constitutionality of these laws, I would argue that violence against gays and lesbians perpetrated by other citizens represents the states' constructive delegation of governmental power to these citizens. As a constitutional matter, the covert, unofficial character of this violence does not render it any less problematic than open, official attacks against gay men and lesbians. To state the point in slightly different terms, the fact that homophobic violence occurs within the context of "private" relations by no means implies that such violence is without "public" origins or consequence. The apparently private character of homophobic violence should not blind us to the reality of the state power that enables and underwrites it. The functional privatization of state power that structures the triangular relationship among victim, perpetrator, and state does not render the phenomenon of homophobic violence any less a matter of constitutional concern.

In order to see why the private lawlessness of homophobic violence is very much a problem for constitutional law, we must turn from considering *who* perpetrates this violence to considering *how* the state responds to the fact of its occurrence. The sheer difficulty of writing about the role of government in private homophobic violence may be traced in part to the insidious hidden forms state involvement takes. The political sociology of homophobic violence reveals that more often than not, the complicity of the state in private attacks on gay men and lesbians may be characterized as complicity through a consistent and calculated pattern of inaction. To paraphrase Justice Brandeis, the most important thing state governments do with respect to homophobic violence is to do nothing.

State officials seem unwilling or unable to use the criminal justice system to reach crimes of homophobic violence. In this respect, the response to private violence against gays and lesbians apparently mirrors the reaction of state governments to private violations of homosexual sodomy law. However, in the case of homophobic violence, the practical and ideological effects of government indifference are not at all the same. This difference lies in the very nature of the crime.

When political pressures or the persistence of victims have forced state officials to prosecute perpetrators of homophobic violence, those accused have often been acquitted. The relatively few individuals who have been convicted of criminal violence against gay men or lesbians have often received reduced sentences or been granted a mitigation in the degree of criminal offense. These outcomes result from the emergence of two curious defenses, which are termed "homosexual panic" and "homosexual advance." The "homosexual panic" defense permits individuals accused of attacking or murdering a gay man or lesbian to assert that their acts stemmed from a violent reaction to their own "latent" homosexual tendencies, triggered after the accused was homosexually propositioned. The "homosexual advance" defense allows the accused to claim that he was the subject of a homosexual overture. The "homosexual advance" defense differs from the "homosexual panic" defense insofar as it does not require the defendant to introduce evidence about his "latent homosexual tendencies." The critical point is that the effect of both of these defenses is to create a doctrinal space within the criminal justice system that permits the perpetrators of violence crimes against gay men and lesbians to lay the blame for their brutality at the feet of their victims.

Thus, the problem faced by those who have sought to place private violence against gay men and lesbians on the public agenda is not simply that state officials seem all too capable of either shutting their eyes to homophobic violence or looking the other way. The problem runs much deeper. Because gay men and lesbians are seen as members of a criminal class, it is almost as though state governments view prosecution of those who commit crimes of homophobic violence as an invasion of the perpetrator's rights.

The constitutional implications of this deliberate policy and practice of government indifference will likely elude us so long as we cling to the impoverished understanding of state power reflected in the regnant doctrine of state action.

. . . .

The point here is that government may effectively exercise its powers in a variety of forms, of which positive, affirmative state action is only one, and not always the most efficient means.

In the instant context, this more nuanced understanding of the combined force of the private action and state inaction that are so violently brought to bear on the bodies of gay men and lesbians clears the ground for clearer specification of the coordinal relationship between criminal laws against homosexual sodomy on one side, and criminal acts of homophobic violence perpetrated by private citizens on the other. It will be recalled that the question I posed and proposed to address was this: How ought we to think about the role state governments play in the phenomenon of homophobic violence? I believe my preceding discussion of the political sociology of power permits two inferences regarding this question, one general and one more specific. Broadly speaking, homosexual sodomy statutes express the official "theory" of homophobia; private acts of violence against gay men and lesbians "translate" that theory into brutal "practice." In other words, private homophobic violence punishes what homosexual sodomy statutes prohibit. When situated within this framework, the terms and target of my Eighth Amendment-based account of the criminal laws against homosexual sodomy become clear: one might call it an "anti-terrorist" case for judicial invalidation of homosexual sodomy laws, whose textual grounding is a *functional*, rather than *formal* interpretation of the prohibition against the infliction of cruel and unusual punishments.

. . . .

A state government's refusal to prevent, prosecute and punish the private torture, mutilation and murder of gay men and lesbians (and those to whom gay or lesbian identities are ascribed) breaches the most basic term of the social compact: the affirmative obligation of the state to use the lawful authority of government to protect citizens from lawless violence. The state's acquiescence in the "civic terrorism" directed against gays and lesbians represents the effective transfer of state power to private actors. We must view the state's inactivity with respect to crimes of homophobic violence in the context of the other mentioned forms of state inaction. Government inaction toward incidents of homophobic violence effectively accords a low visibility privilege to perpetrators of bias crimes that parallels the privilege granted to the mobs that lynched African-Americans well into this century. That is, the private citizens who commit acts of terrorist violence against gays and lesbians can be said to do so under color, or more precisely, under cover of law.

Viewed in structural terms, the "applied law" of homosexual sodomy is an important component of a broader pattern of state inaction toward homophobic violence. Functionally, the criminalization of homosexual sodomy and the effective decriminalization of violence against gays and lesbians represent a simultaneous withdrawal and exercise of state power. The complexity of the state's involvement in the institution of homophobic violence should not obscure its character. As a practical matter, the mediatory role of the state in the power relationship between perpetrator and victim inures to the benefit of the state itself. In constitutional terms, the state's deliberate indifference to the phenomenon of homophobic violence permits state governments to lend their endorsement to a brutal and barbaric arsenal of punishments on gay men and lesbians that the Eighth Amendment clearly would not allow the states themselves to inflict.

The fact that the intersection of homosexual sodomy law and homophobic violence overruns the abstract legal and political rationality of American constitutionalism ought not blind us to its real and practical effects. To be sure, as a formal matter, private violence against gays and lesbians defies conventional understandings of the concept of punishment. Formally, moreover, the modes of government power that legitimize the occurrence of homophobic violence elude standard conceptions of the unitary state and the rule of law. Strictly speaking, the fact that we cannot accommodate the terror of homophobic violence within the existing vocabulary of constitutional analysis is, strictly speaking, irrelevant. It simply means that traditional conceptual models of power and punishment no longer comport with modern realities. My project here has been to suggest a set of terms for thinking about a state of affairs which, to my mind, is cruel, unusual, and obviously unconstitutional. ■

Georgia's Attorney General Mike Bowers, who defended the state's anti-sodomy law, has also rationalized job discrimination against a lesbian by arguing that it would be confusing to the public if he did not maintain consistency with his record defending the sodomy prohibitions. He withdrew a job offer to a lesbian because of her plan to marry another woman. Thus one piece of homophobic legislation was used to bolster further discrimination. The United States Court of Appeals

(11th Circuit) rejected the claim by the woman (in a 8:4 decision), ruling that the plaintiff had no "constitutionally protected right to be 'married' to another woman" and, thus, no protection for the employment discrimination: *Shahar v. Bowers*, 120 F. 3d 630 (11th Cir. 1997). The Georgia Supreme Court has since declared the state's sodomy law unconstitutional. For further discussion of the case, see Cynthia Frank, "*Shahar v. Bowers*: That Girl Just Didn't Have Good Sense" (1997) 17 Law & Inequality 57. She argues that *Shahar v. Bowers* might be decided differently in light of that shift since there is no longer any illegality or criminality assumed as a result of the lesbian relationship. Finally, in 2003, the U.S. Supreme Court reconsidered its ruling in *Bowers v. Hardwick*, 478 U.S. 1039 (1986) and overruled the decision: *Lawrence v. Texas*, [2003] SCT-QL 144 No. 02-102 (QL). Justice Kennedy concluded for the majority at 10, that

> Bowers was not correct when it was decided, and it is not correct today. It ought not to remain binding precedent. *Bowers v. Hardwick* should be and now is overruled.
>
> ... The petitioners are entitled to respect for their private lives. The State cannot demean their existence or control their destiny by making their private sexual conduct a crime. Their right to liberty under the Due Process Clause gives them the full right to engage in their conduct without intervention of the government. "It is a promise of the Constitution that there is a realm of personal liberty which the government may not enter." [citing *Planned Parenthood of Southeastern Pa. v. Casey* 505 U.S. 833 (1992) at 847]. The Texas statute furthers no legitimate state interest which can justify its intrusion into the personal and private life of the individual.

Consider whether Kendall Thomas' argument with respect to homophobic violence is persuasive in the Canadian legal context.

For two Canadian cases in which an accused attempted unsuccessfully to argue provocation based on homosexual advances, see *R. v. Ryznar*, [1986] 6 W.W.R. 210 (Man. C.A.), and *R. v. Hansford* (1987), 55 C.R. (3d) 347 (Alta. C.A.). Compare these decisions to *Camplin* and *Hill*. As critics have noted, the "panic" in response to alleged homosexual advances might more appropriately be labelled "homophobic" or "heterosexual". Individual cases also suggest some scepticism and scrutiny of so-called homosexual panic, depending on the facts. See, for example: *R. v. Tomlinson*, [1998] S.J. No. 848 (Q.B.) (QL) (accused was significantly bigger and stronger and younger than the deceased, who was 67 years old; there had been sexual advances by the deceased farmer towards the accused farm labourer on a number of occasions, so there was no element of surprise; after the killing, the accused stole the deceased's truck and money, took the body to a wooded area, and went out drinking with his brother). Recall that the facts are generally established on the basis only of the evidence of the accused.

The cases are not always reported, particularly when the Crown accepts a plea to manslaughter based on allegations of provocation. In British Columbia, gay bashing has been described as "routine": Miro Cernetig, "Gay bashing in Vancouver routine: Politician latest victim in West End, which is enclave for gays and magnet for homophobes" *The [Toronto] Globe and Mail* (12 December 1996) A7C; Tessy Chakkalakal & Andrew Struthers, "Shields up: Legal and physical attacks put gay-bookstore employees in defence mode" *This Magazine* (September/October 1996) 4. In September 1994, in a brutal murder of a gay Aboriginal man (by slashing virtually the whole of his body and inflicting more than 60 wounds), the accused pleaded guilty to second degree murder but argued "homosexual panic". Despite the plea, the Crown reduced the charge to manslaughter, and the accused was sentenced to five years incarceration (even with a prior record of violence): *R. v. Gilroy* (1994), (B.C.S.C.) [unreported], discussed in Cindy Filipenko, "Not guilty by homosexual association" *This Magazine* (November 1995) 5. As Dennis Dahl argues (quoted in Filipenko at 5), the defence "is manipulated to try to take advantage of any homophobia by some judges or jurors, and serves to reinforce and legitimize violence against gays and lesbians by suggesting that violence may be a justifiable response by straight men to an alleged or perceived homosexual advance." He refers to two additional stabbings in which the accused sought to raise defences of homosexual panic: *R. v. Bell* (1989), (B.C.S.C.) [unreported] (the Crown accepted a plea of manslaughter on the basis of an allegation of homosexual advance) and *R. v. Moore* (1995), (B.C.S.C.) [unreported] (although provocation was not found, the defence called evidence attacking the character of the victim in an attempt to justify the violence, some 68 stab wounds). For a comment on some of these cases see N. Kathleen (Sam) Banks, "The 'Homosexual Panic' Defence in Canadian Criminal Law" (1997) 1 C.R. (5th) 371. In a recent B.C. case, the Crown accepted a plea of guilty to manslaughter from a 33-year-old accused (with an extensive criminal record for assault, break and enter, and breach of recognizance) in the beating and strangulation of a 73-year-old, partially disabled minister in his home: *R. v. G.B.T.*, [2002] B.C.J. No. 1280 (Prov. Ct.) (QL). After the killing, the accused stole money and valuables, including credit cards and a car, from the deceased. In the intervening three days before the body was discovered, the accused returned to the apartment more than once searching for additional items of value. The defence argued that the deceased had provided drug-laced beer to the accused and then attempted sexual contact with him, such that provocation and self-defence were relevant to the sentence. The court considered that an eight-year term was appropriate but sentenced the accused to four years and six months, taking into account time already served in custody.

Sometimes, the court has recognized that the hate that motivated the crime renders it more serious. In Ottawa, in 1989, a gang of six men who the judge described as a "pack of wolves" set out on a night of violent attacks motivated by homophobia, a night that even defence counsel described as "a night of abject horror and terror for the victims". Those sentenced ranged in age from 16 to 24, and the charges included murder, attempted murder, manslaughter, kidnapping, robbery, and break and enter: *R. v. D.J.M.*, [1990] O.J. No. 514 (Prov. Ct. (Youth Div.)) (QL).

On March 20, 1988, gay rights activist Joseph Rose was stabbed to death on a city bus in Montréal by a 15-year-old boy. The accused was charged with murder but pleaded guilty to manslaughter. Three other youths were charged. A week later, a 16-year-old boy stabbed another youth to death. See CP, "2 teen-agers found guilty in Montreal bus slayings" *The [Toronto] Globe and Mail* (10 July 1989) A4.

In December 1992, four boys aged 15 to 17 were charged with first degree murder in the stalking, beating, and killing of a gay man in a Montréal park. The police described the accused as neo-Nazi skinheads. As André Picard described, while the case was the most savage to date, assaults on gays had become commonplace in Montréal. Steve Pépin, of the Montréal Lesbian and Gay Community Centre, said there had been dozens of assaults on gay men, and that the attacks were believed to be part of an initiation ritual of the white supremacist group White Power Canada. He went on to say that the extent of the problem is difficult to determine since victims are often reluctant to go to the police. See André Picard, "Hate slaying of gay man stuns Montreal" *The [Toronto] Globe and Mail* (4 December 1992) A1.

By 1993, there was a series of unsolved murders of gay men in Montréal, and at least 14 men had been killed between 1989 and 1993, which attested to the level of violence faced by gay men: André Picard, "Montréal gays fear serial killer" *The [Toronto] Globe and Mail* (12 February 1993) A1, A2 and CP, "Gay slayings not serial, police say" *The [Toronto] Globe and Mail* (18 November 1993) A3. In response, the Québec Human Rights Commission launched Canada's first inquiry into discrimination and violence against gays and lesbians, with these killings as part of the context: André Picard, "Gay discrimination focus of probe: Slayings of homosexual men a backdrop to Quebec human-rights hearings" *The [Toronto] Globe and Mail* (13 November 1993) A3. In June 1994, the Québec Human Rights Commission released a report calling for the extension of benefits and rights to same sex couples and recommending steps to combat violence against gays and lesbians and to change police from adversaries to protectors. In particular, the report recommended that sexual orientation be included in the federal definition of hate crimes, and that a hate crimes registry be established and a separate record be kept of these crimes. See Richard Mackie, "Quebec urged to follow Ontario on gay benefits: Commission recommends steps to fight homophobic violence" *The [Toronto] Globe and Mail* (2 June 1994) A5; Irwin Block, "Give benefits to gay couples: Rights panel" *The [Montreal] Gazette* (2 June 1994) A1. For a discussion of the antagonistic relationship between police and the gay and lesbian community, see Matthew Hays, "The Cop Factor" *This Magazine* (February 1995) 26, where he asks (at 26) "What is the point of the federal government's hate crime bill if gays and cops can't talk?"

For a discussion of a similar pattern of the use of the defence of provocation for homophobic panic in Australia, see Jenny Morgan, *Who Kills Whom and Why: Looking Beyond Legal Categories* (Melbourne, Australia: Victorian Law Reform Commission, 2002). In one study she documents, the allegation of a homosexual advance was made in 13 of 16 gay-hate killings: Stephen Tomsen & Allen George, "The Criminal Justice Response to Gay Killings: Research Findings" (1997) 9 Current Issues in Criminal Justice 56. Stephen Tomsen interrogates models of understanding hate crime and homophobic violence through an examination of anti-homosexual killings in New South Wales from 1984–2000: Stephen Tomsen, "Homophobic Violence, Cultural Essentialism and Shifting Sexual Identities" (2006) 15(3) Social & Legal Studies 389. He argues that the sexual essentialism with respect to gay identity and heterosexuality has consequences for the response to crimes against gay men and the interpretation of that violence as a hate crime, for example. He draws out the construction of "homophobia" and "homosexual panic" and the dominant construction of gay sexuality and homophobic hate crimes to highlight the influence of these assumptions on the successful prosecution of hate crimes (for example, against openly gay men) and on the successful defence arguments about provocation (for example, for men who fit contemporary understandings of male heterosexuality).

In 1995 the federal government enacted amendments to the *Code* (Bill C-41, S.C. 1995, c. 22) that direct courts to increase sentences where the facts establish that hatred or bias about sexual orientation motivated the accused. Specific sentencing principles are given in s. 718.2:

> A court that imposes a sentence shall also take into consideration the following principles:
>
> (a) a sentence should be increased or reduced to account for any relevant aggravating or mitigating circumstances....
>
> (i) evidence that the offence was motivated by bias, prejudice or hate based on the race, national or ethnic origin, language, colour, religion, sex, age, mental or physical disability, **sexual orientation** or any other similar factor, ...
>
> shall be deemed to be aggravating circumstances.... [Emphasis added.]

How do you reconcile the continuing use of provocation as a partial defence or for mitigation of sentence with the new hate-sentencing guidelines? Are the effects inconsistent?

B. RACISM AND RACIST VIOLENCE

Consider whether the context of racism has an impact on the availability of the defence of provocation. Does the context enable the use of a "provocation" defence or, conversely, is the defence limited in its availability for the response to racism and racist violence? Can you think of an example where racist insults might amount to "provocation" to violence? Do you think the defence would succeed? Why or why not? What might be the difficulties or barriers to its availability? Should the defence have been available in *Parnerkar v. R.* (1971), 5 C.C.C. (2d) 11 (Sask. C.A.), cited in *Hill*, *supra*, or in *R. v. Smithers* (discussed above, under ***Actus Reus***)? See Camille Nelson, "(En)Raged or (En)Gaged: The Implications of Racial Context for the Provocation Defence" (2002) 35 U. Richmond L. Rev. 1007.

As we examine issues of self-defence in the next chapter, consider whether the limits placed by the "immediacy" requirement may unnecessarily restrict the availability of that defence in a context of racism and racist violence.

C. FEMICIDE

Consider another significant context in which provocation as a defence to murder is asserted: femicide. While the overall number of murders has not increased significantly in the last 20 years, there has been an increase in the number of women killed. Although men are more often the victim of murder overall, women are more often the victim of intimate murder. Also, racialized women are extremely vulnerable to such violence. Feminists have begun to document this misogynistic killing of women by men, and to develop a critique of the criminal law's bias that reflects a male reality.

For a discussion of the statistical patterns generally, see: Isabel Grant, Dorothy Chunn & Christine Boyle, *The Law of Homicide*, *supra* at 1–5; and Canadian Centre for Justice Statistics, *Family Violence in Canada: A Statistical Profile 2003* (Ottawa: Statistics Canada, 2003). Statistics indicate that the number of women murdered in spousal homicides increased significantly in 2001, that the number of incidents of spousal violence also increased from 1995 to 2001, and that there has been a significant increase in the use of shelters by women and dependent children in 2001–2002. For documentation and analysis of femicide, see: Maria Crawford & Rosemary Gartner, *Woman Killing: Intimate Femicide in Ontario, 1974–1990* (Toronto: Women We Honour Action Committee, 1992); and Maria Crawford, Rosemary Gartner & Myrna Dawson, *Intimate Femicide in Ontario, 1991–1994* (Toronto: Women We Honour Actions Committee, 1997). In their study of the patterns in femicide in Ontario in the 1990s, Crawford *et al.* found that the rate at which women are killed by their partners has increased. Also, there were clear warning signals of danger. For example, in approximately one third of the cases, the killers had criminal records involving violent crimes and police had been involved at some earlier point; in half the cases, there was evidence that the woman had been assaulted in the past. For a report on the prevalence of violence in Aboriginal families, see Ontario Native Women's Association, *Breaking Free: A Proposal for Change to Aboriginal Family Violence* (Thunder Bay: Ontario Native Women's Association, 1989). For a general discussion of the statistical patterns in homicide and femicide in Canada, see: Robert Silverman & Leslie Kennedy, *Deadly Deeds: Murder in Canada* (Scarborough: Thomson, 1993). A further troubling aspect of these cases (of men killing intimate partners) is that despite the fact that the original charge is often first or second degree murder, most convictions are for manslaughter instead. This discrepancy in result appears to be affected by the class and status of the victim (specifically, whether or not they were employed). As Grant *et al.* speculate, the lives of certain victims are valued more highly: Isabel Grant, Dorothy Chunn & Christine Boyle, *The Law of Homicide*, *supra* at 7-57–7-58.

In 2006, there was a slight decrease in the overall number of homicides in Canada and in the killing of women by their spouse or partner. Also, for violent crime generally, spousal and boyfriend/girlfriend relationships account for one quarter of all incidents, according to Geoffrey Li, "Homicide in Canada" *Juristat* (Canadian Centre for Justice Statistics: Ottawa, 2007). Shelter statistics for 2005–2006 demonstrate the extent of the continuing serious problem of abuse and violence in Canada. According to the 2005–2006 Transition Home Survey, admissions of women and children to shelters for abused women were 106,000 across Canada: Andrea Taylor-Butts, "Canada's shelters for abused women, 2005/2006" *Juristat* (Canadian Centre for Justice Statistics: Ottawa, 2007). As Taylor-Butts chronicles, abuse can take many forms (including psychological and emotional abuse, physical abuse, threats, financial abuse, harassment and sexual abuse). Although men can also be the victim of abuse, women are more often the victims and the form of abuse and the consequences are generally more serious:

> ... While spousal violence victimization rates are similar for women and men, the nature and consequences of spousal violence differ by sex. Women tend to experience more harsh forms of violence (e.g. beaten, choked, sexually assaulted), and repeated incidents of violence compared to male victims ... Additionally, women were twice as likely as men to be injured as a result of spousal violence (44% versus 19%); six times more likely to seek medical attention (13% versus 2%); twice as likely to suffer negative psychological consequences such as depression or anxiety attacks (21% versus 9%) and were three times more likely to fear for their lives (34% versus 10%) [citing Karen Mihorean, "Trends in self-reported spousal violence" in Kathy Au Coin, ed. *Family Violence in Canada: a Statistical Profile, 2005* (Statistics Canada: Ottawa, 2005).

While shelter statistics illuminate the level of violence women and children experience, the statistics do not evenly reveal the extent of that violence. For example, shelters are less available and accessible in rural areas and patterns of usage vary culturally across the country.

Critics have called for a concerted transnational response to the continuing global war on women: Brian Vallée, *The War on Women* (Key Porter: Toronto, 2007); Stephen Lewis, "Foreword" in Vallée, *ibid.*; Liz Kelly, Jo Lovett, and Linda Regan, *Violence against Women: A Briefing Document on International Issues and Responses* (London: British Council Child and Woman Abuse Studies Unit, 2006), online: <http://www.britishcouncil.org/waw.pdf>.

In *R. v. Thibert* (1995), [1996] 1 S.C.R. 37, the accused was convicted of second degree murder for the killing of his wife's lover. The Supreme Court allowed the appeal from conviction on the basis that the trial judge erred in failing to charge the jury that the Crown must prove the absence of provocation beyond a reasonable doubt. Justice Major (dissenting) reviewed the circumstances of the case in detail. What facts are characterized as a potential basis for provocation? Are there underlying assumptions about the role of women as mothers and wives that are susceptible to challenge? Who is the "ordinary person"?

Justice Major suggested that Justice Cory (and the majority) effectively relied on the events leading up to the break-up of the relationship as part of the provocation, despite Justice Cory's assertion to the contrary. How would you critically analyze the reasoning of the majority? What is the wrongful act or insult that forms the possible basis for provocation? How would you compare the significance and consequences of a conviction for murder, as opposed to manslaughter? For a discussion of *Thibert*, see generally: Edward M. Hyland, "*R. v. Thibert*: Are There Any Ordinary People Left?" (1996–97) 28 Ottawa L. Rev. 145; Wayne Gorman, "Provocation: The Jealous Husband Defence" (1999) 42 Crim. L.Q. 478; Rajvinder Sahni, "Crossing the Line: *R. v. Thibert* and The Defence of Provocation" (1997) 55 U.T. Fac. L. Rev. 143.

R. v. Thibert†

[MAJOR J. (dissenting):]

The appellant Norman Eugene Thibert was charged with first degree murder in the shooting death of his estranged wife's lover, Alan Sherren. Norman Eugene Thibert married his wife, Joan Thibert, in July 1970. The couple had two children....

The Thiberts' marriage had its share of problems. Early on in the marriage, Mr. Thibert admitted to his wife that he had had three extra-marital affairs. In September 1990, Mrs. Thibert began an intimate relationship with the deceased, a co-worker. She disclosed this relationship to her husband in April 1991. He was distraught and eventually convinced his wife to remain with him and attempt to make their marriage work.

On July 2, 1991, Mrs. Thibert decided to leave her husband. She took a hotel room rather than returning home. The appellant drove around the city that evening, unsuccessfully searching for the hotel where his wife was staying. When he returned home, he removed a rifle and a shotgun from the basement of the house to the garage. He testified that he thought about killing the deceased, his wife, or himself. He loaded the rifle, and then left the guns in a corner of the garage, having at that point abandoned his violent thoughts.

The daughter, Catrina arrived home to find her father very upset. He told her of her mother's affair. At approximately 11:00 p.m., Mrs. Thibert telephoned her husband at home to tell him of her decision to leave him. At his request, she agreed to meet him the next morning, at Smitty's Restaurant in St. Albert, a suburb of Edmonton at 7:00 a.m.

The next morning Mr. Thibert and Catrina went to the restaurant to meet Mrs. Thibert who arrived at the meeting with the deceased. The appellant attempted to persuade her to return home with him, but she refused. The meeting at Smitty's lasted approximately one hour. At the end of the meeting, Mr. Thibert promised not to bother his wife at work, and in return, she promised to think about coming home that night to again talk to him. Outside the restaurant, while waiting for Mrs. Thibert to finish talking with Catrina, the appellant told the deceased, "I hope you intend on moving back east or living under assumed names.... Because as long as I have got breath in my body I am not going to give up trying to get my wife back from you, and I will find you wherever you go."

The appellant testified that, when he returned home, he thought about killing himself, and so returned to the garage and retrieved the guns. He sawed off the barrel of the shotgun, but then discovered that the gun was inoperable since the firing pin was broken.

He telephoned his wife at work several times in an effort to persuade her to return to him.

During one afternoon call, she asked him to stop phoning her and told him that she was leaving work to make a bank deposit. The appellant then drove into the city, planning to find his wife while she was at the bank, and away from the influence of the deceased, and again attempt to convince her to give the marriage another try.

† (1995), [1996] 1 S.C.R. 37.

He put the loaded rifle in the back of his car before departing, thinking that he might have to kill the deceased. He testified that a few miles from home he abandoned that thought, but instead planned to use the rifle as a final bluff to get his wife to come with him. The police later seized a box of shells from the vehicle, although the appellant stated that he did not remember placing the ammunition in the car.

At approximately 2:45 p.m., the appellant parked across the street from his wife's place of work. When he saw Mrs. Thibert depart for the bank, he followed her. She noticed him at a stoplight, at which time he attempted to persuade her to get into his car so they could talk. The appellant followed Mrs. Thibert to the bank, and insisted that they go some place private to talk. Mrs. Thibert agreed to meet him in a vacant lot but instead, out of fear, returned to her workplace. The appellant followed her into the parking lot. The appellant again tried to persuade Mrs. Thibert to go some place with him to talk, but she continued to refuse.

The appellant told Mrs. Thibert that he had a high powered rifle in his car, but claimed that it was not loaded. He suggested that he would have to go into Mrs. Thibert's workplace and use the gun. At that time, the deceased came out of the building and began to lead Mrs. Thibert back into the office. The appellant then removed the rifle from the car.

The appellant's evidence was that the deceased began walking towards him, with his hands on Mrs. Thibert's shoulders swinging her back and forth, saying, "You want to shoot me? Go ahead and shoot me." and "Come on big fellow, shoot me. You want to shoot me? Go ahead and shoot me." At some point, Mrs. Thibert either moved, or was moved aside. The appellant testified that the deceased kept coming towards him, ignoring the appellant's instructions to stay back. The appellant testified that his eyes were closed as he tried to retreat inward and the gun discharged.

After the shot, Mrs. Thibert ran into the office building. At some point, the appellant put the gun down, entered the office building, and calmly said that he wanted to talk to his wife. He then exited the building, picked up the gun, put more ammunition in it, and said he was not going to hurt anyone. He placed the gun in his car and drove away.

While he was driving, the appellant noticed a police car following him. He pulled off onto a side road, and surrendered to the police. At the time of his arrest, Constable Baumgartner recorded that the appellant stated "It's out of me now. He was fooling around with my wife." Constable Turner recorded the appellant's statement as "For what it's worth, I was just after him. For what it's worth, it's out of me now. He was fooling around with my wife."

. . . .

The definition of insult, cited with approval by Kellock J. in *Taylor v. The King*, [1947] S.C.R. 462, at p. 475, is:

> "Insult" is defined in "The Oxford English Dictionary" *inter alia*, as
>
> > an act, or the action, of attacking or assailing; an open and sudden attack or assault without formal preparations; injuriously contemptuous speech or behaviour; scornful utterance or action intended to wound self-respect; an affront; indignity.

In my opinion, in this case there is no evidence of a wrongful act or insult sufficient to deprive an ordinary person of the power of self-control. That the deceased may have positioned Mrs. Thibert between himself and the appellant cannot constitute a wrongful act or insult. Nor can the statements "You want to shoot me? Go ahead and shoot me" and "Come on big fellow, shoot me" be considered a wrongful act or insult. Those actions are not contemptuous or scornful; they are legitimate reactions to a dangerous situation. It would be improper to require victims to respond in a certain way when faced with armed, threatening individuals. The defence claim that the wrongful act or insult came from the appellant's evidence that the deceased used Joan Thibert as a shield while taunting him to shoot is ironic. The appellant had control of the only true weapon involved in this situation, the rifle.

Further, that the deceased had a personal relationship with Mrs. Thibert is not a wrongful act or insult sufficient to cause an ordinary person to lose the power of self-control. The break-up of a marriage due to an extra-martial affair cannot constitute such a wrongful act or insult. I agree with the statement of Freeman J.A. in *R. v. Young* (1993), 78 C.C.C. (3d) 538 (N.S.C.A.), at p. 542, that:

> It would set a dangerous precedent to characterize terminating a relationship as an insult or wrong act capable of constituting provocation to kill. The appellant may have been feeling anger, frustration and a sense of loss, particularly if he was in a position of emotional dependency on the victim as his counsel asserts, but that is not provocation of a kind to reduce murder to manslaughter.

Similarly, it would be a dangerous precedent to characterize involvement in an extra-marital affair as conduct capable of grounding provocation, even when coupled with the deceased's reactions to the dangerous situation he faced. At law, no one has either an emotional or proprietary right or interest in a spouse that would justify the loss of self-control that the appellant exhibited.

In that connection, Cory J. states that the events leading to the break-up of a relationship are not factors going to provocation but I wonder whether the effect of his reasons is such that these factors have been taken into account in the context of provocation. My colleague emphasizes that the accused still wished to see his wife alone after the end of the relationship. However, in my view, she had made it clear on a number of occasions that she did not wish to be alone with him. This was a choice that Joan Thibert was free to make. The accused had no right or entitlement to speak with his wife in private. The fact that the accused believed that the deceased was preventing him from doing so is not, with respect, a fact that ought to be taken into account when considering the defence of provocation.

If I am wrong and the objective threshold test for provocation is met, the appeal would fail on the subjective element of the test. The appellant had known of the wife's involvement with the deceased for some time. He knew his wife wanted to leave him, and had seen the deceased with his wife earlier that day. It cannot be said that the appellant's mind was unprepared for the sight of his wife with the deceased such that he was taken by surprise and his passions were set aflame. There was no element of suddenness on the facts of this case.

For these reasons, I am of the opinion that neither the objective branch nor the subjective branch of the threshold test for leaving the defence of provocation with the jury has been met. There is no evidence on which a reasonable jury, acting judicially could find a wrongful act or insult sufficient to deprive the ordinary person of the power of self-control. Neither is there any evidence that the appellant acted on the sudden. The defence should not have been left with the jury. This was an error that did not prejudice the appellant.

[CORY J. (for the majority):]

[After canvassing the development of the law of provocation in Canada, Justice Cory discussed the application of the test for provocation to these circumstances.]

In summary then, the wrongful act or insult must be one which could, in light of the past history of the relationship between the accused and the deceased, deprive an ordinary person, of the same age, and sex, and sharing with the accused such other factors as would give the act or insult in question a special significance, of the power of self-control.

. . . .

Bearing in Mind the Principles Pertaining to Provocation, Was There Any Evidence Adduced in This Case Which Required the Trial Judge to Leave That Defence with the Jury?

In this case, there is no doubt that the relationship of the wife of the accused with the deceased was the dominating factor in the tragic killing. Obviously, events leading to the break-up of the marriage can never warrant taking the life of another. Affairs cannot justify murder. Yet the provocation defence section has always been and is presently a part of the *Criminal Code*. Any recognition of human frailties must take into account that these very situations may lead to insults that could give rise to provocation. Some European penal codes recognize "crimes of passion" as falling within a special category. Indeed many of the Canadian cases which have considered the applicability of the defence arise from such situations. See, for example, the cases of *Daniels* and *Conway*, *supra*. The defence of provocation does no more than recognize human frailties. Reality and the past experience of the ages recognize that this sort of situation may lead to acts of provocation. Each case must be considered in the context of its particular facts to determine if the evidence meets the requisite threshold test necessary to establish provocation.

The Objective Element of the Test

In this case, it is appropriate to take into account the history of the relationship between the accused and the deceased. The accused's wife had, on a prior occasion, planned to leave him for the deceased but he had managed to convince her to return to him. He hoped to accomplish the same result when his wife left him for the deceased on this second occasion. At the time of the shooting he was distraught and had been without sleep for some 34 hours. When he turned into the parking lot of his wife's employer he still wished to talk to her in private. Later, when the deceased held his wife by her shoulders in a proprietary and possessive manner and moved her back and forth in front of him while he taunted the accused to shoot him, a situation was created in which the accused could have believed that the deceased was mocking him and preventing him from his having the private conversation with his wife which was so vitally important to him.

Taking into account the past history between the deceased and the accused, a jury could find the actions of the deceased to be taunting and insulting. It might be found that, under the same circumstances, an ordinary person who was a married man, faced with the break-up of his marriage, would have been provoked by the actions of the deceased so as to cause him to lose his power of self-control. There was some evidence, therefore, that would satisfy the objective element of the test. Next it remains to be seen whether there was evidence that could fulfil the subjective element of the test.

The Subjective Element of the Test

It must be determined whether there was evidence that the appellant was actually provoked. Once again it is necessary to take into account the past history involving the accused, the deceased and his wife. Further, it cannot be forgotten that the accused hadn't slept for some 34 hours and that he described himself as being devastated, stressed out and suicidal. He emphasized how important it was to him to talk to his wife in private, away from the deceased. It was in this manner that he successfully persuaded his wife to stay with him on the earlier occasion. When his wife returned to her employer's parking lot and the deceased came out of the building, he testified that his thoughts were "here is the man that won't give me a half hour alone with my wife after 21 years and he has had her for 24 hours the night before."

It was when the deceased put his arm around his wife's waist and started leading her back towards the building that the appellant removed the rifle from the car. He testified that he did so as a bluff. He hoped it would make them take him more seriously and succeed in convincing his wife to accompany him so that they could talk privately. From this point, the deceased's actions could be construed as a conscious attempt to test the appellant's limits. When he saw that the appellant had a gun, he advanced towards him. The appellant's wife was in front of the deceased and the deceased had his hands on her shoulders. The appellant recalled that the deceased was swinging Mrs. Thibert from side to side like a moving target. While doing this, the deceased was laughing and grinning at the appellant. He also dared the appellant to fire and taunted him by saying "Come on big fellow, shoot me. You want to shoot me? Go ahead and shoot me." The deceased continued to approach the appellant, proceeding as fast as he could. In turn, the appellant kept backing up and told the deceased to "stay back," but the deceased continued to approach him. The appellant testified that he remembered wanting to scream because the deceased would not stop coming towards him. The appellant's eyes were tightly closed when he fired the gun. The time the appellant held the gun until he fired was not long. The events unfolded very quickly, in a matter of moments, seconds, not minutes.

The respondent submitted that "[r]ejection in the context of a romantic relationship will not constitute a basis for the provocation defence." This is correct. If the appellant had simply brooded over the unhappy situation, put a rifle in his car and gone looking for the deceased, then the history of the deceased's relationship with the wife of the accused could not be used as a basis for a defence of provocation because the necessary final act of provocation was missing. However, in this case, rejection is not the most significant or overriding factor. The appellant sought to avoid the deceased in order to talk privately with his wife. The evidence indicates that the confrontation with the deceased in the parking lot was unexpected. The appellant had gone to some lengths to avoid meeting the deceased.

In my view there was evidence upon which a reasonable jury acting judicially and properly instructed could have concluded that the defence of provocation was applicable. Next it must be considered whether the acts of the deceased were those which he had a legal right to do and thus within the exemption described in s. 232(3).

Were the Acts of the Deceased Ones Which He Had a Legal Right to Do But Which Were Nevertheless Insulting?

It will be remembered that s. 232(3) provides that "no one shall be deemed to have given provocation to another by doing anything that he had a legal right to do." In the context of the provocation defence, the phrase "legal right" has been defined as meaning a right which is sanctioned by law as distinct from something which a person may do without incurring legal liability. Thus the defence of provocation is open to someone who is "insulted." The words or act put forward as provocation need not be words or act which are specifically prohibited by the law. [Justice Cory cites *R. v. Galgay*, [1972] 2 O.R. 630 (C.A.) and *R. v. Haight* (1976), 30 C.C.C. (2d) 168 (Ont. C.A.) for this proposition.]

Thus, while the actions of the deceased in the parking lot were clearly not prohibited by law, they could nonetheless be found by a jury to constitute insulting behaviour. In light of the past history, possessive or affectionate behaviour by the deceased towards the appellant's wife coupled with his taunting remarks could be considered to be insulting. Nor can it be said that these actions really constituted self-defence. The deceased was told by the appellant's wife that the gun was unloaded and he may have believed her. In any event, he continued to advance towards the appellant and to goad him to shoot despite the request to stop. In the circumstances, the actions of the deceased could well be found not to be acts of self-defence. A jury could infer that it was the taunting of the appellant by the deceased who was preventing him from talking privately with his wife which was the last straw that led him to fire the rifle suddenly before his passion had cooled. While the deceased's conduct might not have been specifically prohibited nor susceptible to a remedy it was not sanctioned by any legal right.

In summary, there was some evidence upon which a reasonable jury acting judicially and properly instructed could find that the defence of provocation was applicable. It was appropriate for the trial judge to leave his defence with the jury. Once it was determined the defence should be left then the trial judge was required to correctly relate the principles of reasonable doubt as they applied to that defence.

. . . .

The Effect of Leaving the Defence of Provocation with the Jury

It must be remembered that to find that there was evidence which justified leaving the defence to the jury is far from concluding that jury should or would act upon that evidence. The defence is simply something that the jury will have to assess. The great good sense of jurors will undoubtedly lead them to consider all the facts, including the presence of the loaded gun in the car. Further, it must be remembered that the defence of provocation goes no farther than to reduce the conviction for murder to one of manslaughter. This is hardly an insignificant crime when it is remembered that [ ] life imprisonment can be imposed as punishment.

. . . .

[He concluded by referring to the advantageous position of the trial judge to assess the evidence and to decide whether to instruct the jury on the defence.]

Unless there is an absence of any evidence as to the objective and subjective elements of the defence such a decision of a trial judge [to leave the defence of provocation to the jury] should not be lightly interfered with by an appellate court.

. . . .

[Further, on the basis of a question pertaining to the objective element of the defence of provocation, he argued that it was apparent that the jury was seriously considering the defence.]

In the result, I would allow the appeal, set aside the decision of the Court of Appeal and direct a new trial on the charge of second degree murder. ■

Other critiques of the defence of provocation have examined the inattentiveness to culture, and the structuring of the "objective" standard as that of the "middle class ... Anglo-Saxon-Celtic [male]": Jonathan Herring, "Provocation and Ethnicity" [1996] Crim. L.R. 490, quoting the dissent in the Australian High Court in *R. v. Masciantonio*, [1995] A.J.L.R. 598. The shortcoming of many of the critiques of the ethnocentrism of the standard is that they fail to challenge the inherent malecentrism of the standard and the culture of maleness that it represents. In contrast, Sheila Galloway and Joanne St. Lewis, *Reforming the Defence of Provocation* (Toronto: Ontario Women's Directorate, 1994), responding to the Department of Justice Consultation Paper *Reforming the General Part of the Criminal Code* (Ottawa: Department of Justice, 1994), argue that evidence of "culture" regarding issues of gender roles should be barred unless it has been shaped by feminist analysis within that particular community. They argue that the defence of provocation should be eliminated or, at least, restricted and reformed. How might their critique have affected the arguments in *R. v. Humaid*, below? Which "cultural" defences should be enshrined in criminal law? Which characteristics of the accused should be imported into the "objective" standard?

Drawing on materials in Abell & Sheehy, *Cases, Context, Critique*, can you suggest ways in which the response of the criminal justice system in femicide cases could be more attentive to cultural issues? For example, in a B.C. case of mass murder, a man killed his estranged wife, her father, her mother, her brother, her four sisters, and her brother-in-law, and then killed himself. At the five-day inquest into the events, there was no examination of cultural issues and no recommendation aimed at addressing the situation confronting South Asian women, according to Mobina Jaffer (a lawyer involved in setting up Immigrant and Visible Minority Women of British Columbia): Robert Matas, "Inquest ignored culture: Lawyer: Mass murder jury focuses on rules" *The [Toronto] Globe and Mail* (30 September 1996) A1.

R. v. Humaid†

[DOHERTY J.A.:]

I. OVERVIEW

The appellant was charged with the first degree murder of his wife. At trial, he admitted that he had killed her and was guilty of manslaughter. He maintained, however, that he did not have the requisite intent for murder and, alternatively, that he had acted under provocation.

. . . .

Counsel ... argued that the trial judge misdirected the jury as to the application of the "ordinary person" component of the provocation defence by instructing the jury that the appellant's racial and cultural background were irrelevant to that component of the defence.

I would dismiss the appeal. The trial judge erred in excluding the statements made by the deceased, but that error did not occasion any substantial wrong or miscarriage of justice. If there was any misdirection in the provocation instruction, it could not have affected the outcome of the trial.

II. OVERVIEW OF THE POSITIONS AT TRIAL

The appellant and the deceased Aysar Abbas ("Aysar") were married in 1979. They lived in Dubai in the United Arab Emirates. They regularly traveled to Canada with their children on vacations in the 1990s and in 1998 the entire family became Canadian citizens, although they continued to reside in Dubai.

The Crown's position was that by the fall of 1999, the appellant's marriage had soured for various reasons, including his prior infidelity. The Crown contended that the appellant wanted out of the marriage in part because he no longer considered his wife, who was approaching middle age, sexually attractive. He also stood to gain financially by his wife's death. She controlled most of the family wealth as long as she was alive.

The Crown argued that the appellant decided to kill his wife while he was in Dubai in early October 1999. The appellant knew that his wife would be in Ottawa in mid-October 1999 with a male business associate visiting her son. He decided to travel to Ottawa without telling anyone, kill Aysar in circumstances that would cast suspicion on her male business associate, and return to Dubai before the police could suspect him.

The defence contended that the circumstances surrounding Aysar's death were entirely inconsistent with a planned and deliberate murder. It was the position of the defence that the appellant decided to travel to Ottawa in early October upon learning that his son, who had just started university in Ottawa, was using drugs. The appellant knew that his wife would be in Ottawa at the same time and arranged to meet her there so that they could discuss the problem with their son.

The appellant arrived in Ottawa on October 9. He and Aysar were getting along well during his stay in Ottawa, although the appellant did become concerned that Aysar's conduct with her male associate seemed unduly friendly and familiar. According to the defence theory, on October 14, the day the appellant was to return to Dubai, he and Aysar left the hotel intending to run some errands. They got lost, stopped their vehicle and decided to go for a walk. During the walk, the appellant and Aysar discussed her relationship with her business associate. They both became angry. Aysar made a comment that the appellant took to mean that she had engaged in sexual relations with the business associ-

† (2006), 81 O.R. (3d) 456 (C.A.).

ate. The appellant blacked out immediately after Aysar made this comment. A witness saw the appellant chasing Aysar along the side of the road and a few seconds later he saw the appellant sitting astride Aysar's prone body, flailing at her with his arms. The appellant stabbed Aysar at least 19 times.

On the defence theory, Aysar's comment, which the appellant took to be an admission of sexual infidelity, had one of two effects on the appellant. Either it amounted to a psychological blow throwing the appellant into a disassociative state in which he did not form the intent required for murder, or it caused him to lose control, fly into a rage and kill Aysar before he could regain his self-control. The defence positions were advanced through the appellant's testimony, the evidence of a psychiatrist, and the evidence of an expert in the Islamic religion and culture.

III. THE EVIDENCE

The appellant and Aysar were both engineers. She was much more successful than was the appellant. Aysar earned over $500,000 a year, while the appellant worked sporadically and was unemployed for at least a year prior to Aysar's death.

. . . .

On the morning of October 14, the appellant drove Saif to school. He returned to the hotel and convinced Aysar to accompany him on errands he had to run that morning....

The appellant testified that Aysar decided to drive shortly after they left the hotel. They intended to go to the shopping plaza where they were to meet Hussein [Aysar Abbas' colleague] later that afternoon, but got lost. They eventually found themselves parked on a relatively isolated dead end road. The appellant testified that he had no idea where they were when they parked. This road was nowhere near the shopping plaza. It was, however, on a map marked with a piece of paper in a book of maps of the Ottawa area found in the appellant's hotel room.

The appellant testified that he and Aysar sat and talked, mostly about their children. They decided to go for a walk and have a cigarette. As the appellant was about to get out of the car, Aysar reminded him that he had put a knife in the glove compartment of the rented vehicle. She told him that he should take the knife out of the glove compartment so that he would not forget it when he returned the vehicle that afternoon. The appellant testified that he had undergone extensive dental work and had a very sore mouth. He used the knife to cut fruit into small pieces so that he could eat it. The appellant testified that he removed the knife from the glove compartment and stuck it in his pocket just before he and Aysar walked away from the vehicle. The appellant used the knife, a steak knife with a 3-inch blade, to stab Aysar to death.

The appellant described how he and Aysar walked from the car arm in arm. She asked him what was bothering him and a discussion ensued about her relationship with Hussein. Aysar chided the appellant for being jealous, but acknowledged that she admired Hussein. Aysar and the appellant both became angry as they discussed Aysar's relationship with Hussein. The appellant told Aysar that he would be concerned about her fidelity if he did not know that she was having her menstrual period. The appellant did not think that Aysar would have sex while she was having her period. Aysar smirked and said that "a little pill would make a whole big difference — a little pill can make many things". The appellant understood this to be a reference to a birth control pill and that by taking a birth control pill, a woman could prevent the onset of her menstrual period. The appellant took Aysar's comment as an admission that she was having sexual relations with Hussein. The appellant testified that he blacked out immediately after Aysar made the "little pill" comment. He has no recollection of chasing Aysar along the road and repeatedly stabbing her.

A man named Kirkpatrick happened to be driving along the road where the appellant and Aysar had parked the vehicle. He saw Aysar running along the side of the road looking over her shoulder at the appellant, who was chasing her. Mr. Kirkpatrick turned his vehicle around. He saw Aysar lying on the ground. The appellant was straddling her and flaying his arms in her direction. Mr. Kirkpatrick called 911 at 11:56 a.m. He watched the appellant get up, return to his vehicle and drive away, leaving Aysar on the ground. Mr. Kirkpatrick reported the licence number to the police. The police traced the vehicle and arrested the appellant when he turned up at the car rental agency about two hours later.

The post-mortem examination revealed that Aysar had been stabbed 19 times on the right side of her neck. She had also been stabbed through the heart and suffered several defensive injuries to her hands.

. . . .

The appellant testified in great detail about the events leading up to the stabbing of Aysar, but insisted that he had no recollection of the stabbing and very little recollection of the subsequent events. He testified that he could remember certain things after he read about them in the newspaper. He described these as "dream like" recollections.

Dr. Bradford, a forensic psychiatrist, interviewed the appellant and reviewed the Crown's brief. When asked his opinion as to the appellant's state of mind when he stabbed Aysar, Dr. Bradford said:

> Assuming that the emotional impact of her statement with regards to the pill was a very emotionally charged statement so that at a psychological and emotional level with him it had a very significant psychologically traumatic impact, making those assumptions, then Mr. Humaid describes a change in his feeling. He said he can't remember, he describes feeling differently. And that type of reaction based on a psychologically traumatic event and the effect on the person subsequently, which would happen almost immediately, would — can induce, and from what he describes, is compatible with him having some type of disassociative reaction.

Dr. Bradford testified that in his opinion, the appellant underwent a change of consciousness that persisted for some time and impaired his mental functioning so that the appellant had a "diminished criminal responsibility" when he stabbed his wife.

In cross-examination, Dr. Bradford acknowledged that he had to rely on what the appellant told him in arriving at an assessment of the appellant's state of mind. His conclusion that the appellant could not remember the stabbing and had partial amnesia with respect to the subsequent events was based on the appellant telling him that he could not remember the stabbing or many of the subsequent events.

The appellant adamantly denied that he placed the knife in the car as part of a plan to kill Aysar. He said that if he had planned to kill his wife, he would have used a much bigger knife.

. . . .

V. THE PROVOCATION INSTRUCTION

(a) The nature of the provocation defence

Provocation as described in s. 232 of the *Criminal Code* is a partial defence to the charge of murder. Provocation does not negate either the act or the fault component of the crime of murder, but becomes germane only where the Crown has proved all of the elements of murder beyond a reasonable doubt. Where the Crown has proved what would otherwise be murder, provocation as described in s. 232 will reduce murder to manslaughter. When there is an evidentiary basis for the provocation defence, the Crown must prove beyond a reasonable doubt that the accused was not provoked. The provocation defence fails if the Crown proves beyond a reasonable doubt that one or more of the constituent elements of the defence does not exist....

. . . .

(b) The provocation defence at trial

In addition to the appellant's evidence describing the events culminating in Aysar's stabbing, the defence led the opinion evidence of Dr. Ayoub, an expert on the Islamic religion and culture. Dr. Ayoub testified that the Islamic culture was male-dominated and placed great significance on the concept of family honour. Infidelity, particularly infidelity by a female member of a family, was considered a very serious violation of the family's honour and worthy of harsh punishment by the male members of the family. In response to specific questions about the effect of a wife's infidelity in the Islamic culture, Dr. Ayoub said:

> It is a great stigma, infidelity. I said earlier that it is a stigma to the man and to the family and it is something that can lead to a great deal of violence, particularly if the infidelity is the infidelity of a female member of the family. There have been cases of people I know who killed, for instance, their daughters because they felt they were committing infidelity, for instance. **So it's very, very difficult, you know, in Islamic cultures; it does not tolerate the infidelity of the woman.**
>
> **There's no equality here.** I said earlier that although infidelity on the part of the man is also not condoned and supposedly not tolerated, the culture somehow tolerates it more than that of the woman. [Emphasis added.]

Dr. Ayoub acknowledged that individual Muslims would have different views on these matters, depending on their personal experiences and background.

In admitting Dr. Ayoub's evidence, the trial judge held that it was relevant to the subjective component of the provocation defence. He did not decide whether it had any relevance to the objective aspect of that defence.

The appellant is a Muslim. He described his courtship and marriage as traditional. The appellant testified that after he made his pilgrimage to Mecca in February 1997, in part to atone for his illicit affair with the family maid, he became a more devout Muslim. The appellant did not give any evidence as to whether he shared the notions of female infidelity and family honour attributed by Dr. Ayoub to Muslims in general.

The trial judge left provocation with the jury over the Crown's objection. He concluded that the appellant's evidence concerning the "little pill" comment allegedly made by Aysar could provide evidence of an insult within the meaning of s. 232. He further held that the totality of the evidence gave an air of reality to the defence.

The trial judge addressed each element of provocation in his jury instruction. He told the jury that it must first determine whether Aysar's comment as described by the appellant amounted to an "insult":

> In considering whether the alleged words or conduct meet this element, again, the whole of the circumstances must be considered, including all the characteristics of Mr. Humaid....
>
> **Thus, would the alleged conduct and words spoken in this case be construed as a wrongful act or insult by someone with Mr. Humaid's background and characteristics? It is for you to decide.** [Emphasis added.]

The trial judge then told the jury to determine whether the insult was sufficient to deprive an ordinary person of the power of self-control:

> **To apply the ordinary person test sensibly and with some sensitivity, a comparable person must be taken to be of the same age, sex, and share with Adi Humaid other factors which would give the act or insult in question special significance.** Therefore, you should also consider the relevant background circumstances, including the history of the relationship, prior insults, contacts and events of a similar nature between Mr. Humaid and his wife, Aysar Abbas.
>
> Our law adopts the standard of an "ordinary person" to fix the level or degree of self-control and restraint expected of all in Canadian society. So on this element of provocation, you need to consider whether what is alleged here as provocation is beyond the tolerance of an ordinary person. In this exercise, certain background facts pertaining to Mr. Humaid as I have just mentioned may be necessary considerations. **However, these considerations must not include peculiar, idiosyncratic traits arising from Mr. Humaid's Muslim faith or specific to his culture.** [Emphasis added.]

The trial judge next told the jury that the third component of the defence raised the question of whether Mr. Humaid was actually provoked by his wife's alleged insult. The trial judge said:

> You must determine whether or not Adi Humaid was in fact acting as a result of the provocation. **Because this is a subjective approach, you may consider all of Adi Humaid's background, including any peculiar or idiosyncratic traits which you may find he possessed arising from his culture and/or Muslim faith.** Here, again, you consider the totality of the circumstances. [Emphasis added.]

The trial judge then turned to the fourth and final element of the defence which he described as the "suddenness of the provocation". He told the jury that it must determine whether the provocation was sudden and caused the appellant to act before there was time for his passion to cool. The trial judge told the jury that in considering this component of the defence, it should consider the appellant's culture and religious beliefs.

During deliberations, the jury asked for further instructions on the "ordinary person" component of provocation. The trial judge told the jury that the "ordinary person" should be regarded as a person of the same age, sex and with the same marital background and relationship history as the appellant, but should not be taken as a person sharing the appellant's religion, culture or customs.

. . . .

(d) There was no air of reality to a provocation defence

A trial judge can only leave the defence of provocation with a jury if there is evidence upon which a properly instructed jury acting reasonably could return a verdict of manslaughter based on that defence....

The appellant testified that he took the "little pill" comment by Aysar as an admission of infidelity by her. Counsel for the appellant did not contend that an admission of infidelity in and of itself could ever amount to an insult capable of depriving an ordinary person of self-control. She submits, however, that the admission had to be placed in context and that the context could make the admission of infidelity an insult of sufficient gravity to pass the "ordinary person" inquiry. The evidence that the Muslim culture and religion regarded a wife's infidelity as a particularly serious blow to the honour of the family was relied on by counsel to give Aysar's admission of infidelity sufficient gravity to justify leaving the defence of provocation to the jury.

Assuming that an accused's religious and cultural beliefs that are antithetical to fundamental Canadian values such as the equality of men and women can ever have a role to play at the "ordinary person" phase of the provocation inquiry, the expert evidence could not assist this appellant. There was no evidence that the appellant shared the religious and cultural beliefs attributed by Dr. Ayoub to Muslims in general. It is not enough to lead evidence that Muslims, or any other group, have certain religious or cultural beliefs that could affect the gravity of the provocative conduct in issue and that the accused is a member of that group. As Dr. Ayoub candidly acknowledged, the extent to which any individual Muslim holds the views he described and would act on those views would depend on a myriad of individual factors.

I can find no evidence, either in the appellant's testimony or elsewhere in the record, from which the jury could conclude that the appellant shared the religious and cultural beliefs relating to infidelity described by Dr. Ayoub. Absent such evidence, reliance on the evidence of Dr. Ayoub in support of the provocation defence is an invitation to assign group characteristics to the appellant based on what can only be described as stereotyping. Individual free choice and individual responsibility for those choices are at the core of the Canadian notion of criminal responsibility. Verdicts that are the product of stereotyping are no less offensive because they benefit the accused.

Whatever features are to be attributed to the "ordinary person", they surely must be features possessed by the accused. Absent any evidence that the appellant shared the views described by Dr. Ayoub, the doctor's evidence could not lend any air of reality to the provocation defence. Accordingly, on the totality of the evidence, even if Aysar's comment was understood by the appellant as an admission of infidelity, that admission could not amount to an insult capable of causing an "ordinary person" to lose self-control.

I would add a second comment in respect of Dr. Ayoub's evidence. A provocation claim rests on the assertion that an accused in a state of extreme anger lost his ability to fully control his actions and acted while in that state. Provocation does not shield an accused who has not lost self-control, but has instead acted out of a sense of revenge or a culturally driven sense of the appropriate response to someone else's misconduct. An accused who acts out of a sense of retribution fuelled by a belief system that entitles a husband to punish his wife's perceived infidelity has not lost control, but has taken action that, according to his belief system, is a justified response to the situation: see *R. v. Dincer*, [1983] 1 V.R. 450 (Vic. S. Ct.), at p. 464.

The thrust of Dr. Ayoub's evidence is not that Muslim men will lose control and act in a rage when confronted with their wives' infidelities, but rather that their religious and cultural beliefs dictate that wives who are unfaithful deserve to suffer significant consequences. If an accused relies on religious and cultural beliefs like those described by Dr. Ayoub to support a provocation defence, the trial judge must carefully instruct the jury as to the distinction between a homicide committed by one who has lost control and a homicide committed by one whose cultural and religious beliefs lead him to believe that homicide is an appropriate response to the perceived misconduct of the victim. Only the former engages the defence of provocation. The latter provides a motive for murder.

(e) The verdict excludes the possibility of a successful provocation defence

Even if there was an air of reality to the provocation defence, any error in respect of the instructions on that defence could not have affected the verdict.... There was also ample evidence to support the jury's finding that the murder was planned and deliberate.

. . . .

(f) The "ordinary person" and religious and cultural characteristics

As I would hold that there is, on this evidence, no air of reality to the provocation defence and that in any event, any error in the provocation instructions could not have affected the verdict, it is unnecessary to reach the merits of the claim that the appellant's religious and cultural beliefs should have been factored into the "ordinary person" test. I think it is better to leave this difficult issue to a case where the arguments have been fully developed at trial and on appeal and the resolution of the issue is necessary to the determination of the appeal. I will, however, highlight what I consider to be the nub of the problem raised by this argument.

Hill, [1986] 1. S.C.R. 313, *supra*, and *Thibert*, *supra*, establish that the "ordinary person" inquiry is a blend of subjective and objective considerations. In some situations, there can be no doubt that the accused's religious or cultural beliefs will be attributed to the "ordinary person" to properly apply the "ordinary person" test as described in the authorities. To borrow the language of *Thibert*, one's religious and cultural beliefs can give "a special significance" to the acts or insult said to have constituted the provocation. For example, where the alleged provocative insult demeans or otherwise targets the religious or cultural beliefs of an accused, it seems beyond question that those beliefs must be factored into the "ordinary person" test to determine whether the insults were capable of causing an "ordinary person" to lose self-control.

In this case, however, the appellant's religious and cultural beliefs are not the target of the alleged insult. Rather, the appellant's religious and cultural beliefs are said to render the words spoken by Aysar highly insulting. The difficult problem, as I see it, is that the alleged beliefs which give the insult added gravity are premised on the notion that women are inferior to men and that violence against women is in some circumstances accepted, if not encouraged. These beliefs are antithetical to fundamental Canadian values, including gender equality. It is arguable that as a matter of criminal law policy, the "ordinary person" cannot be fixed with beliefs that are irreconcilable with fundamental Canadian values. Criminal law may simply not accept that a belief system which is contrary to those fundamental values should somehow provide the basis for a partial defence to murder.

The problem outlined above was not addressed in the only Canadian case to which the court was referred where beliefs similar to those of the appellant's were held to be relevant to the "ordinary person" inquiry: see *R. v. Nahar*, [2004] B.C.J. No. 278, 181 C.C.C. (3d) 449 (C.A.). Some academic commentary suggests that religious and cultural beliefs like those relied on by the appellant cannot be part of the "ordinary person" inquiry: see Christine Boyle, Dorothy Chunn and Isabelle Grant, *The Law of Homicide* (Toronto: Carswell, 1994) at pp. 6–17; Simon Bronitt and Bernadette McSherry, *Principles of Criminal Law* (Toronto: Carswell, 2001), at pp. 371–72. The resolution of this difficult issue awaits a case in which it must be resolved.

VI. CONCLUSION

I would dismiss the appeal.

■

Although, on the facts, it was not necessary for the court to determine whether the appellant's religious and cultural beliefs should be factored into the "ordinary person" test, Justice Doherty's analysis highlights the problematic aspects of that possibility and indeed the difficulties inherent in the jurisprudence on provocation which contemplates both cultural perspectives and stereotypical assumptions. As Steve Coughlan argues, the difficulty is "whether beliefs which are antithetical to fundamental Canadian values, even presuming they could be shown to be "ordinary" for some group, should ever be incorporated into the test": "Annotation" (2006), 37 C.R. (6th) 349. Those attitudes might include views about women's infidelity or uninvited sexual advances or homosexuality, for example. For an earlier case that rejected the relevance of cultural considerations to the characterization of the wrongful act or insult, see *R. v. Ly* (1987), 33 C.C.C. (3d) 31 (B.C.C.A.). Note how Justice Doherty in *Humaid* continually refers to the deceased, Aysar Abbas, by her first name only, whereas the accused is Mr. Humaid. The Supreme Court of Canada refused leave to appeal: [2006] S.C.C.A. 232.

There are many other cases in which provocation has been argued as a defence to wife murder. For an article giving examples where provocation defences have succeeded in domestic violence cases, see Jeremy Horder, "Sex, Violence, and Sentencing in Domestic Provocation Cases" [1989] Crim. L.R. 546 (citing examples of crying babies, alleged insults about male impotence, and contrasting those to the "provocation" of long-term abuse and violence); and see Graeme Coss, "'God is a Righteous Judge, Strong and Patient: and God is Provoked every Day': A Brief History of the Doctrine of Provocation in England" (1991) 13 Sydney L. Rev. 570. For a detailed examination of conjugal murder and the use of the defence of provocation in Québec, see Andrée Côté, *La Rage au Coeur* (Baie-Comeau: Regroupement des femmes de la Côte-Nord, 1991).

In *R. v. Carpenter* (1993), 14 O.R. (3d) 641 (C.A.), the specific provocation relied upon was the swinging of a vase by the deceased at the appellant's head in the context of drinking and what the court described as a history of "mutual violence" (although the injuries described indicate the husband's violence was much more serious, and the injuries the wife suffered in the past had sometimes required hospital treatment). The Court of Appeal overturned the conviction and ordered a new trial, holding that the trial judge had blurred the line between the objective and subjective components of the defence.

In *R. v. Brown* (1993), 13 O.R. (3d) 630 (C.A.), the court held that prior threats made by the accused to kill his wife tended to suggest that the killing was not provoked by the deceased's conduct. In *R. v. Young* (1993), 117 N.S.R. (2d) 166 (C.A.), leave to appeal refused, [1993] 2 S.C.R. xii, the accused's argument that his girlfriend's announcement that their relationship was over amounted to provocation was rejected by the court: "It would set a dangerous precedent to characterize terminating a relationship as an insult or wrong act capable of constituting provocation to kill" (at 170). In that case, the accused and the deceased had discussed the matter over several hours before the accused stabbed his girlfriend more than 20 times with a hunting knife.

In numerous cases, "provocation" has been raised in combination with other defences, such as "intoxication" or "self-defence". This gives rise to complicated charges that seem at times to be internally contradictory. For example, in *R. v. Taylor* (1995), 61 B.C.A.C. 186 (C.A.), the accused testified that he had been drinking heavily at an all-night stag party, and later met the 29-year-old victim (a severely mentally handicapped Aboriginal woman) on the street, engaged in what he described as consensual sexual intercourse, that she then became angry and kneed him in the groin, at which point he went berserk, picked up a stick and hit her over the head a number of times (with what the pathologist described as "very severe force") causing her death. The trial judge charged the jury ((1995), 61 B.C.A.C. 186 at (188–89) on provocation and intoxication:

> When you're considering the alleged provocation, you are to use your common sense and put that ordinary person in the position of the accused. That is, consider the ordinary person to be ... a male of the age of Dwain Taylor, in the circumstances he found himself in ... and with the background that had preceded it ... [kissing, caressing, having sex] and put your ordinary person, who is a male, a young male, in those circumstances, in a similar situation.... **That is, make that ordinary person someone who has the influences that apparently were working on him, that is he had been drinking.** And then ask yourselves whether the wrongful act, whatever you decide it was, or if there was a wrongful act, was of such a nature as to be sufficient to deprive that ordinary person, not unusually excitable or quarrelsome, or anything else — whether it was of such a nature as to deprive that ordinary person in that situation of the power of self-control.
>
> Now, it seems to me that you can say, well, even if the — this young woman did lash out — we don't really know why she did, but if she lashed out and there was no reason apparent, was that enough so that the ordinary person in that situation would commit the violence that followed? **Well, if you say no, the ordinary person has more self-control than that, you're not going to take a club and bludgeon to death somebody who you just made love to, just because for some reason you're kicked, well, that's the end of it. Provocation doesn't apply, if that's what you decide. If, on the other hand, you say, well, maybe it was such a surprise, and so unexpected, and even though the evidence is that he didn't experience any pain, the ordinary person might react in that way and grab up the nearest thing at hand and follow this girl and do what he did — well, if you find that, then you must go the further step and you must look at the evidence and ask yourselves whether in fact that is what happened with Dwain Taylor. Was he provoked?** [Emphasis added by Court of Appeal.]

The Court of Appeal allowed the appeal, set aside the murder conviction and ordered a new trial because the charge had not properly conveyed the test for intoxication with respect to specific intent offences (the trial judge had suggested that the test was whether the accused was reduced to acting like an "automaton"), and because the charge had blurred the test for provocation by suggesting that the test was whether an ordinary intoxicated man would be deprived of self-control and then act in the way the accused did (following *Carpenter*, *supra*). Consider the trial judge's charge and the circumstances of the case. What difficulties with respect to the availability of the defence of provocation does the Court of Appeal decision highlight?

A focus on the circumstances giving rise to provocation seems to promote victim-blaming rather than accountability for the accused and his "uncontrollable rage". However, another worrying development has been judicial attentiveness to the accused's state of rage, which has been deployed to create a new *mens rea* defence in circumstances in which provocation would not be available. In the cases that follow, judges have been prepared to extend a partial defence for "rage", even absent any external provocation by wrongful act or insult.

In *R. v. Listes* (1994), 66 Q.A.C. 109, the accused killed his wife and son by shooting them. The accused was a chronic alcoholic who experienced fits of uncontrolled rage, and had been diagnosed as suffering from morbid jealousy, exacerbated by alcohol, arising from his paranoid state. The psychiatrist's evidence described an explosion of rage by the accused, a "situation of crisis, confrontation, paroxysm, rage, fear" which led to an uncontrollable "climax which overwhelmed the appellant at the time of the tragedy". The court cited *R. v. Campbell* (1977), 17 O.R. (2d) 673 (C.A.) and *R. v. Wade* (1994), 69 O.A.C. 321, for the proposition that rage or anger could prevent the formation of the requisite criminal intent in the case of murder, and that such rage could exist independently of external provocation. Thus, the state of rage, and the lack of control of his impulses were seen as relevant to a possible attenuation of criminal responsibility.

In *Wade*, the Ontario Court of Appeal held that the trial judge's charge had been inadequate, allowed the appeal and ordered a new trial limited to the question of whether the accused was guilty of second degree murder or manslaughter. (The jury had already rejected the defence of automatism.) The accused appealed, and a majority of the Supreme Court (Lamer C.J. and Sopinka J. dissenting) held that, on the totality of the evidence, there was no error committed by the trial judge in not leaving with the jury manslaughter as an available verdict. Accordingly, the conviction entered by the trial judge was restored: *R. v. Wade*, [1995] 2 S.C.R. 737.

How does the defence of rage differ from other defences of mental disorder? Reconsider the cases under **Automatism**, such as *Stone* and *Rabey*, above. What is the effect of the availability of rage as a partial defence in the context of long-standing patterns of domestic violence and abuse by men of women? Is the "ordinary person" in these scenarios really male? See generally: Andrée Côté, "Stone, Provocation and the 'Nagging Wife'" (Fall 1999) 19:1 *Jurisfemme* 1. Can you make any links between the use of provocation and rage defences in cases involving alleged "gay advances" and "marital misconduct"?

In cases where a combination of defences is argued (for example, intoxication, provocation, and rage), the courts have examined "rolled up charges" (where the trial judge attempts to instruct the jury on the various possibilities). However, sometimes there is only one possible defence (such as provocation), and that is unavailable (no air of reality, no wrongful act or insult, failure to act on the sudden, etc.). The only remaining avenue for the accused, then, is an argument that the Crown has failed to prove the elements of the offence beyond a reasonable doubt: the *actus reus* (causation, etc.) or the requisite *mens rea* for first degree murder, for second degree murder, or for manslaughter (see discussion of distinction, above, under ***Mens Rea***). Thus, even if provocation is rejected as a defence to murder generally, the events and circumstances leading to the supposed "provocation" may be available to negative the deliberation required for first degree murder: *R. v. Stewart* (1995), 41 C.R. (4th) 102 (B.C.C.A.) (following *R. v. Mitchell*, [1964] 2 C.C.C. 1 (B.C.C.A.). (In *Stewart*, the "provocation" alleged was a homosexual proposition between drug dealers, but the accused did not kill the victim until a day later.)

A recent Yukon Territory Supreme Court case *R. v. Klassen*, *supra*, raises troubling questions, not only about the parameters of the defence of provocation, but also about the insidious ways in which evidence of so-called provocative conduct on the part of the victim seeps into the general *mens rea* discussion depending on the assumptions and values of judges and jurors. In *Klassen*, the trial judge declined to charge the jury on provocation. In fact, he amended his draft charge to eliminate the word "provocation" at the request of the Crown. However, in his charge, he nonetheless referred to the incidents that supposedly upset and enraged the accused. *R. v. Klassen*, *supra*, at 7–10:

> ... [F]or murder, the *Criminal Code* requires that an assailant must mean to cause death or mean to cause bodily harm that he knows is likely to cause death and be reckless whether or not death ensues....
>
> In this case the evidence of the accused was that he rolled on top of Susan Klassen [his estranged wife] and put his hands around her throat, and pressed down. He has a vague recollection of a pillowslip, or something white. He admitted that he strangled her. Whether he intended to do so is a question of fact for you to decide.
>
> In his videotaped statement to the police he said that he did not intend to kill her. In his testimony before you he swore on oath that he did not intend to kill her, nor did he intend to cause her bodily harm that he knew was likely to cause death, but conceded that he had, in fact, strangled her.
>
> ...

> The evidence of the accused was that he saw Susan Klassen building a relationship with Gordon ... that excluded him. He said that she blamed him for their inability to have children. He said that when he tried to touch her that night she said, "What is the point of making love, it is only dead sperm anyway ... besides you already know about Gord," which he testified caused a surge — like white hot metal into the back of his head, then everything went black....

The accused had left a note to his estranged wife's friend (at 8): "I went into a jealous fit of rage, the image of you and my wife together made me insane." Although the psychiatric evidence was that the accused did not have a mental disorder, the judge's charge continued on the issue of rage and *mens rea*.

> The law is that where the conduct of the deceased produces in the accused a state of excitement, anger or disturbance so intense that he may not contemplate the consequences of his act, and might not in fact intend to bring about those consequences, then you can find the accused did not have the intent to kill or cause bodily harm that he knew was likely to result in death.
>
> ...
>
> On the other hand a state of intense anger, excitement or rage could confirm the position taken by the Crown that the accused intended to do what he did.

At other points in the charge, the judge discussed the expert evidence in language very reminiscent of provocation (at 10):

> ... Dr. Lohrasbe was allowed to give his opinion on the effect on the accused of the statements [allegedly] made by Susan ... [that night]; how it would affect a person of his age, temperament, background and mental health; as well as how an overwhelming psychological blow can affect a person's memory of events....

The other evidence revealed that the strangulation was by ligature, that it would have taken several minutes for her to die, that the imagined other relationship was a creation of a jealous mind, and that the supposed insults were hardly new. The defence characterized the accused as a man with no history of violence, and used that to support the suggestion that something dramatic had to have been said or done to push him out of control that night. The jury concluded that Klassen was guilty of manslaughter but not murder. He was sentenced to five years, and the sentence was upheld on appeal: *R. v. Klassen* (1997), 95 B.C.A.C. 136 (Yuk. C.A.), leave to appeal denied, [1997] S.C.C.A. No. 479. Citing *R. v. McDonnell*, [1997] 1 S.C.R. 948, the Court of Appeal rejected the Crown's argument that they should establish a new, higher range of sentences for spousal manslaughter. Section 718.2(ii) now directs that the context of the family relationship should be considered an aggravating factor.

Trial judges in a range of cases charged juries with respect to rage or anger in ways that suggested a stand-alone defence of rage, a defence that was separate from provocation but had the same impact: to reduce murder to manslaughter. The escalating confusion about the impact of anger on the capacity to form the requisite *mens rea* was finally put to rest in *R. v. Parent*, [2001] 1 S.C.R. 761. A unanimous Court rejected the possibility that evidence of anger or rage alone could operate to negate the *mens rea*. Instead, the Court held that evidence of a state of rage or anger might assist in laying a defence of provocation or, in an extreme case, automatism, as in *R. v. Stone*, [1999] 2 S.C.R. 290, reproduced above, under **Automatism**. Nonetheless, the case leaves a number of issues unresolved as Joanne Klineberg highlights in a detailed commentary on the case and the impact of anger on intent: "Anger and Intent for Murder: The Supreme Court Decision in *R. v. Parent*" (2003) 41 Osgoode Hall L.J. 37.

R. v. Parent†

[McLACHLIN C.J.:]

On September 24, 1996, the respondent, Réjean Parent, shot and killed his estranged wife. She had initiated divorce proceedings four years earlier and they were involved in litigation over the division of their assets, some of which were held in a corpora-

† [2001] 1 S.C.R. 761.

tion. In the meantime, their financial situation deteriorated, to the point that Mr. Parent's shares were seized and put up for sale. The wife attended the sale, allegedly intending to buy the shares. Mr. Parent also attended. He carried a loaded gun with a locked security catch in his pocket. There, she suggested they speak and they retired into a nearby room. Shortly after, shots were heard.

Mr. Parent had shot his wife six times. She died from the wounds later that night. Mr. Parent was charged with first degree murder. At trial, he testified that when they proceeded to the room his wife had said, in effect: [TRANSLATION] "I told you that I would wipe you out completely." He then felt a hot flush rising and shot. He said he [TRANSLATION] "didn't know what [he] was doing any more" and was aiming in front of him. He said he did not intend to kill his wife. After doing so, he left the building and spent the afternoon in a strip club before giving himself up to police that evening.

At trial, Mr. Parent argued that the verdict should be reduced to manslaughter on the basis of lack of criminal intent or provocation. The jury found him guilty of manslaughter. He was sentenced to 16 years' imprisonment, and a lifetime prohibition on possessing firearms, ammunition and explosives: [1997] J.Q. No. 4459 (QL).

The Crown appealed the verdict of manslaughter, and Parent appealed the sentence. The Quebec Court of Appeal dismissed the appeal from the verdict without reasons, but in separate proceedings ((1999), 142 C.C.C. (3d) 82) reduced the sentence to six years' imprisonment ... In this Court, the appellant raised one point only: that the judge had erred in his instructions to the jury on the effect of anger, creating a "defence of anger" (*défense de colère*) distinct from the defence of provocation....

Two issues are raised: (1) whether the trial judge erred in his charge to the jury on intention and (2) if so, whether that error was cured by the redirection.

1. Did the Trial Judge Err in his Charge to the Jury on Intention?

... [T]he Crown suggests that the judge's directions wrongly treated anger as a matter that could negate the criminal intent or *mens rea* of the offence; wrongly suggested that negation of intent can reduce the offence to manslaughter; and wrongly left open the suggestion that anger alone can establish provocation, when in fact other requirements must be met pursuant to s. 232 of the *Criminal Code*, R.S.C. 1985, c. C-46....

The Crown objects to the portions of the jury charge in which the trial judge stated that the jury must take into account [TRANSLATION] "evidence surrounding the defence of provocation raised by the accused" in determining the accused's intent to kill. The Crown also objects to the trial judge's treatment of *mens rea* in the following passages:

> [TRANSLATION] For example, murder may be reduced to manslaughter where a person's state of mind is affected by alcohol consumption, drug consumption or where a person's state of mind is obscured or diminished by an outside force, by an incident like, for example, *a fit of anger*.
>
> ...
>
> To reduce murder to manslaughter, you must come to the conclusion that the influence of the events that occurred was *strong enough, important enough, intense enough to cause the accused to not know or not want what he was doing by reason of his state of mind, that his faculties were too diminished to fully assess the situation, or that raise a reasonable doubt in his favour, in this respect.* [Emphasis added.]

The Crown argues that this passage creates a halfway house defence of anger, between non-mental disorder automatism and provocation. I agree. This passage suggests that anger, if sufficiently serious or intense, but not amounting to the defence of provocation, may reduce murder to manslaughter. It also suggests that anger, if sufficiently intense, may negate the criminal intention for murder. These connected propositions are not legally correct. Intense anger alone is insufficient to reduce murder to manslaughter.

The passage cited overstates the effect of anger. Anger can play a role in reducing murder to manslaughter in connection with the defence of provocation. Anger is not a stand-alone defence. It may form part of the defence of provocation when all the requirements of that defence are met: (1) a wrongful act or insult that would have caused an ordinary person to be deprived of his or her self-control; (2) which is sudden and unexpected; (3) which in fact caused the accused to act in anger; (4) before having recovered his or her normal control: *R. v. Thibert*, [1996] 1 S.C.R. 37. Again, anger conceivably could, in extreme circumstances, cause someone to enter a state of automatism in which that person does not know what he or she is doing, thus negating the voluntary component of the *actus reus*: *R. v. Stone*, [1999] 2 S.C.R. 290. However, the accused did not assert this defence. In any event, the defence if successful would result in acquittal, not reduction to manslaughter.

. . . .

DID THE TRIAL JUDGE CORRECT THE ERRORS IN HIS RECHARGE TO THE JURY?

. . . .

The trial judge responded by correctly recharging the jury on provocation....

The question, however, is whether the recharge on provocation corrected the earlier misdirection suggesting that anger short of provocation might suffice to reduce murder to manslaughter by raising a doubt on the existence of the criminal intent for murder....

CONCLUSION

The trial judge erred in his charge to the jury on the effect of anger on criminal intent or *mens rea* and its relationship to manslaughter. This error was not corrected on the recharge.... It follows that the conviction for manslaughter must be set aside and a new trial directed.

As indicated earlier, the Crown in this appeal, relied solely on the trial judge's misdirections on anger and criminal intent.

It is therefore unnecessary to comment further on the applicability of the defence of provocation as it may be tendered at the new trial. It will be for the judge on the new trial to determine whether, on the evidence there presented, the defence of provocation should be put to the jury.

I would allow the appeal and direct a new trial on second degree murder.

■

At the new trial, Parent was found guilty of second degree murder and sentenced to life, without eligibility for parole for 12 years: *R. c. Parent*, [2001] J.Q. No. 6833 (Que. Sup. Ct.) (QL), aff'd. *R. c. Parent*, [2002] J.Q. no. 8294 (Que. C.A.) (QL).

Given the prevalence of homophobia and misogyny (as demonstrated by, for example, the levels of violence against women and the deeply-rooted structural inequality in Canadian society), assumptions about gender roles, sexuality and family become rationalizations for rage, loss of control, and violence and effectively serve to create different categories of victims. Justice Wilson's admonition in *Lavallee*, below, under **Self-Defence**, could usefully be applied to the area of provocation to interrogate the "popular mythology" of marital relationships, the long history of male privilege, including the privileging of male rage, the acceptance of extreme anger as "ordinary", and the notion that men do not have the responsibility to control their anger. What assumptions continue to be made about the ordinary man's concept of self-worth (its foundation and susceptibility to challenge), about supposed challenges to that self-worth (sexual jealousy, loss of possession or control of a woman as wife or partner, criticism of sexual performance or virility)? As Jeremy Horder asks in *Provocation and Responsibility* (Oxford: Clarendon, 1992) at 192:

> [Does] the doctrine of provocation under the cover of an alleged compassion for human infirmity simply [reinforce] the conditions in which men are perceived and perceive themselves as natural aggressors, and in particular *women's* natural aggressors. [Emphasis in original.]

The defence for battered women who have killed abusive and violent partners has been argued in terms of **self-defence** in Canada (discussion below), whereas in other jurisdictions, such as Britain, the defence has been argued in terms of **provocation**. In July 1995, the British Court of Appeal, in *R. v. Humphreys*, [1995] 4 All E.R. 1008 (C.A.), substituted a verdict of manslaughter for murder, ruling that cumulative abuse could amount to provocation. Emma Humphreys had already served 10 years in jail for the killing. Previously, the law restricted provocation to incidents immediately prior to the killing, and required the accused to have killed as a result of a sudden and temporary loss of control. In Britain, as in Canada, critics had argued that the old law on provocation ignored the effects of years of abuse on women, and that the required impulsiveness and overwhelming rage were more consistent with male behavioural patterns.

The background facts in *Humphreys* established a history of abuse, beatings, and rape by a jealous and possessive man. The night that Humphreys killed her boyfriend, the latter had been boasting to two friends and his 16-year-old son that they would gang-rape her. She slashed one of her wrists, and her boyfriend taunted her about her "pathetic" attempt, and removed his clothes, apparently preparing for sex.

In the judgment, Lord Justice Hirst held that the trial judge had failed to direct the jury properly on the cumulative effect on the accused of months of verbal abuse, beatings, and rapes (at 1023–24):

> This tempestuous relationship was a complex story ... of potentially provocative conduct building up until the final encounter.
>
> ... [T]here was the continuing cruelty, represented by the beatings and the continued encouragement of prostitution, and by the breakdown of the sexual relationship.

For a thoughtful examination of the characterization of Emma Humphreys, the judicial and public response to her, and the limits to the law's explanations, see Elizabeth Stanko & Anne Scully, "Retelling the Tale: The Emma Humphreys Case" in Alice Myers & Sarah Wight, eds., *No Angels: Women Who Commit Violence* (London: Pandora/HarperCollins, 1996). In particular, they identify the ways in which psychiatric evidence of her self-injury had to be converted to some other recognizable "psychological illness or disorder", such as anorexia, and how the cumulative effect of violence and abuse was only rendered relevant through the psychiatrization of her situation.

In *R. v. Thornton (No. 2)*, [1996] All E.R. 1023, the British Court of Appeal also recognized that a history of abuse and battering may be relevant to the defence of provocation, as a mental characteristic of the accused. The accused was ultimately acquitted of murdering her husband but found guilty of manslaughter, after a lengthy series of trials and appeals. As Susan Edwards and Charlotte Walsh argue, Sara Thornton should not have been subjected to the trauma of a new trial some six years after the original trial in 1990: "The justice of retrial?" (1996) 146 New L.J. 857. They also highlight a number of difficulties with the existing British law: the psychiatrization and stereotyping of battered women, the requirement of a sudden loss of control, the failure to interrogate the problematic aspects of the defence of provocation, and the mandatory sentence of life imprisonment for murder. While provocation has been differently applied in Canada, some aspects of their critique are relevant to Canadian legal doctrine.

Compare the factual basis for provocation and the receptivity of the court to those arguments in *Stone* and *R. v. Malott*, [1998] 1 S.C.R. 123. In *Malott*, the Ontario Court of Appeal upheld the trial judge's refusal to leave provocation to the jury in circumstances of severe, long-standing abuse by the deceased of the accused woman. Compare the routine evocation of provocation in the so-called "homosexual advances" cases and in the "separation anxiety" and control cases for male accused to the rarity of its consideration in the context of long-standing abusive relationships for female accused in Canada.

R. v. Malott†

[The Court of Appeal dismissed the appeal. ABELLA J.A. (dissenting in part):]

... The appellant Margaret Malott lived with the deceased Paul Malott for approximately 20 years. She had previously been married for seven years to a man who violently abused her and their five children. Shortly after she started living with Paul Malott, a man who was six feet tall and weighed 280 pounds, she discovered that he too was abusive. The violence was physical, sexual, psychological and emotional. She had tried complaining to the police, but found that since Paul Malott was a police informant on drug deals, the police told Paul Malott about her complaints, resulting in an escalation of his violence towards her. Her ongoing depression and anxiety led to two hospitalizations for nervous breakdowns and to years of taking unauthorized mixtures of prescription drugs like Halcion, Seconal and Percocet.

Four years before he left her, Paul Malott moved into his mother's home with the appellant and their two adolescent children. About four

† (1996), 30 O.R. (3d) 609 (C.A.) at 631–640.

weeks before his death, he moved into the trailer owned by his girlfriend, Carrie Sherwood. Margaret Malott and her daughter continued to live with the deceased's mother. Paul Malott visited his mother's home almost daily, usually accompanied by Carrie Sherwood. His openly affectionate behaviour with Ms. Sherwood, kissing her and having her sit on his lap, were extremely difficult for the appellant, as was the deceased's insistence that she prepare coffee or meals for him and Ms. Sherwood. The appellant made no pretence about her unhappiness at his leaving and begged him to return.

The Friday before his death, Paul Malott told the appellant to prepare dinner for him, his mother, and his girlfriend. The appellant was particularly upset that evening after her husband and Ms. Sherwood left, and took combinations of anti-depressant pills.

The deceased had arranged to pick up the appellant the next morning so she could get him some Percocet pills he needed to prepare a cocaine mixture for a drug deal to take place later that weekend. By the time Paul Malott arrived on Saturday morning, the appellant had taken three Halcion pills, some Seconal, and other medication she could not identify. She had also gone to the basement where the deceased kept his gun collection, pried open the cabinet, took a gun and a box of shells, and put them in her purse.

On the way to the medical centre, they argued over Paul Malott wanting to claim his daughter as a tax deduction rather than Margaret Malott getting mother's allowance for her. The appellant testified that the deceased threatened her in the course of the argument and choked her as she was getting out of the car upon their arrival at the medical centre.

The medical centre was locked. Walking back to the car, she said she saw the driver's door open and thought the deceased was getting out of the car to hurt her. It was her evidence that he was yelling and that she feared his reaction to her being unable to get the pills he needed. She also knew that he kept a gun in the car and had a knife on his belt that day. She shot him six times at close range, turned off the car's ignition and took a taxi to Carrie Sherwood's trailer. The taxi driver said Margaret Malott stared "straight ahead" and seemed to be in a daze. She was let into the trailer by Ms. Sherwood, they exchanged a few words, then the appellant shot Carrie Sherwood. The shot was not fatal and a violent fight between the two women took place resulting in serious injuries to both. The appellant then called 911 and told the O.P.P. that she had shot her husband, had tried to shoot Carrie Sherwood, was "pretty buzzed up on pills" and "not normal".

As a result of the death of Paul Malott and the events at Carrie Sherwood's trailer, Margaret Malott was charged with first degree murder and with attempted murder. After deliberating for three days and asking almost a dozen questions, the jury found the appellant guilty of second degree murder in connection with Paul Malott, and of the charge of the attempted murder of Carrie Sherwood. The jury also made an unsolicited recommendation that because "of the evidence of the severity of the Battered Woman Syndrome in this case", Margaret Malott receive the minimum sentence.

Dr. Peter Jaffe, an expert in domestic violence and the effects of violence on abused women, stated that of the hundreds of women he has interviewed since 1972, based on the severity and frequency of violence to which she had been subjected over a 20-year period, the appellant Margaret Malott was "one of the most severe cases" he had ever seen. Based on her medical reports and on interviews with Mrs. Malott and members of her family, Dr. Jaffe concluded that "the abuse came in every form possible that we know". He described "horrific levels of sexual violence" from the deceased Paul Malott, including:

> ...pinching of sexual organs, forcible confinement, bondage in terms of tying up with handcuffs or with rope, repeated sexual acts which in some cases included anal intercourse, use of objects during sex which included putting [ ] pop bottles into her vagina during sex, whipping during sex.

In describing the acts of physical violence, he said:

> [They] varied all the way from pushing, slapping, hitting, punching, hair pulling, hitting with a belt, hitting with a whip, choking or knife throwing. So there was a wide variety of physical acts which were designed to threaten, intimidate and harm Margaret Malott.

The emotional abuse was outlined by Dr. Jaffe as follows:

> ...chronic criticism telling her repeatedly that she's a terrible mother, that she's a terrible wife, that she's ... terrible in bed, that she's a terrible sexual partner, ... telling her repeatedly that he's going to leave her and then not leaving her or leaving her for short periods and then coming back. Being involved with other women and repeatedly telling her the other women are more attractive and more satisfying in bed than she is. ... continuous sexual putdowns. Flaunting new relationships. Bragging about new women that

> he's ... discovered. Denying parenthood. Telling her that he was not really the parent of one or both kids. Accusing her of infidelity. Exposing the children to the affairs ... [B]oth children ... were taken to meet new partners that the deceased had met and on occasion even told that the new partner would make a better mother than their own biological mother.

He also identified the following psychological abuse from Paul Malott:

> Another form of abuse which was consistent in the relationship [were] words and behaviors ... designed to threaten, intimidate, make somebody feel totally insecure, lower self esteem and also re-enforce a sense of dependency ... Threats to family members, threatening to harm. For example threats to harm Margaret's sister. Threatening to use weapons, belts, knives or guns. Restriction of movement. There were times in the relationship where Margaret would have to account for every single minute. She wasn't free to go to the corner store without trying to keep a log of how long she was gone and what she bought and then still after that being accused of being unfaithful. Reminders of past abuse. Again Margaret Malott had been abused by her previous partner and she disclosed a great deal in the early part of her relationship with Paul Malott and again he kept repeating, he kept referring back to that abuse later on, so often as he would abuse her, he would remind her of the fact that in fact she deserved or earned this because in fact other people had treated her in the same way. Again some other forms, forcible confinement.... [T]here's incidents reported where she's locked in a closet and has burning paper thrown in at her and the other thing is again part of being in the drug scene was being exposed to a number of undesirable elements in the community who ... seemed to be dangerous or having weapons. So there are a number of incidents reported where other people came to the home, made threats, fired weapons into the house.... [T]here's constant things which are meant to make you feel insecure, worry, about your own safety on a regular basis.

As for Margaret Malott's state of mind with respect to Carrie Sherwood, Dr. Jaffe made the following observations:

> ...in her own mind ... Carrie was an extension of Paul ... the two of them together were part of the abuse that she was suffering near the end because of Carrie's presence and sitting on Paul's lap and when Paul would visit Margaret and visit his mother, so she didn't describe very much in the way of anger towards Carrie. As a matter of fact what she described was that Carrie herself was a victim. That Carrie had been drawn into this relationship with Paul. That she was a lot younger and the fact that she felt badly for but in her mind she was part of, she was an extension of Paul and part of the source of the abuse at the end. What she described was more of the feeling of wanting to eliminate Carrie and then kill herself and just end everything. That's basically the pattern of what she tended to describe. She didn't describe anger, or hatred or even jealousy. It was more a sense of feeling like she was worthless, invisible and brought down to nothing and she felt she needed to eliminate the source of that.
>
> ...
>
> She saw Carrie as an extension of Paul and she felt she had to get rid of them both. She felt she couldn't take it anymore.

Dr. Jaffe stated that this quartet of abuse, physical, sexual, emotional and psychological, was linked "over and over again" so that even the emotional and psychological abuse could trigger fears of physical abuse. His synoptic conclusion about her resulting state of mind was:

> ...once someone has been severely abused as I believe Margaret Malott was over many years, you always have a sense of being in danger when you're in contact with the batterer or there's ongoing events which are in anyway linked to the previous assaultive incidents. So I think in Margaret's place, in her mind very clearly is an ongoing danger ... which fits the profile of battered women in general. ... we're not looking at a logical, rational mind. We're looking at someone in the state of crisis and great confusion. Somebody who's in a state of terror, emotionally and physically.

Analysis

The primary defence advanced at trial was self-defence. The main ground of appeal is that the trial judge's charge was a strict, literal reiteration of the components of s. 34(2), with an insufficient explanation of how being a battered woman may change the texture of her perceptions and apprehensions.

. . . .

[As Justice Abella concluded with respect to self-defence, the jury must be informed as to the relevance of the evidence of battering and its relationship to the defence of self-defence. Arguably, the relevance of the evidence of battering must similarly be related to the defence of provocation.]

The jury has to know not only what the relevant expert and other evidence is, but also why it is hearing it and what relevance it bears to the issues. As Wilson J. stated in *Lavallee*, at p. 126:

> Ultimately, it is up to the jury to decide whether, *in fact*, the accused's perceptions and actions were reasonable.... The jury is not compelled to accept the opinions proffered by the expert, about the effects of battering on the mental state of victims generally or on the mental state of the accused in particular. But fairness and the integrity of the trial process demand that the jury have an opportunity to hear them. (Emphasis in original.)

It was not, in my view, sufficient for the trial judge merely to acknowledge that the appellant was a battered woman and to reiterate that the cumulative years of abuse could have affected her perceptions. He was obliged in addition to outline to the jury how the relevant and unchallenged expert evidence of Dr. Jaffe could have explained those perceptions, and her subsequent acts. In his charge, the trial judge set out the traditional concept of self-defence using a pre-*Lavallee* approach that concentrates on the imminence of the events, that is, one that explains the act of self-defence on the basis largely of the circumstances immediately preceding the defensive act. He was also required, in my view, to show how that traditional approach to the reasonableness of an accused's perceptions might be affected when raised in a less traditional context, namely, when there has been a history of domestic violence to which the alleged act of self-defence may have been responsive.

The trial judge did not sufficiently relate the evidence, either of the expert or of the appellant, to the core issues in self-defence when raised in the context of this pattern of violence. The whole purpose of permitting this kind of expert evidence is to assist a jury in understanding how perceptions which may appear to be counter-intuitive, may nonetheless be reasonable in the mind of someone who has suffered continuous abuse. Without this link, the jury is left to try to assess on its own what potential relevance the expert evidence may have to the components of self-defence. The success of the s. 34(2) defence depended on the jury's understanding of how they were to assess the reasonableness of the appellant's apprehensions and behaviour. They did not have enough guidance from the trial judge to understand that this undertaking was to be performed from the particular perspective of someone whose perceptions on that final Saturday morning may have been shaped by her prior experiences of abuse. Nor were they adequately told how to link, if they chose to believe it, the expert evidence on the phenomenon of battered women to their task in assessing the reasonableness of the appellant's state of mind and her resulting action. The number of questions the jury asked; the fact that they did not find the appellant guilty of first degree murder, thereby concluding that the shooting was not "planned and deliberate"; and the fact that they made a voluntary request to the trial judge that the appellant receive the minimum sentence, all indicate to me that had they been properly charged, they may have come to a different verdict.

In my view, the trial judge's failure sufficiently to recite the relevant evidence and, more importantly, to relate it to the issues, was an error in law requiring a new trial.

I am not persuaded, however, that the trial judge erred when he told the jury that self-defence was not available as a defence to the charge of attempted murder in the circumstances of this case. I would not, therefore, interfere with the conviction for attempted murder.

[Only the majority considered the issue of provocation. They concluded that the accused failed to establish any evidence potentially amounting to provocation. Finlayson and Austin JJA. stated at 629–630:

> [I]t is difficult to see what acts of the deceased could be considered provocation. The argument and the choking were relatively distant in time from the shooting, which cannot be said to have followed "on the sudden". It is unlikely that the deceased's actions in opening the car door and beginning to step out would be sufficient to provoke the normal "ordinary person" mentioned in s. 232(2). Counsel for the appellant submitted that this test, like the one for self-defence, is to be applied on a modified objective standard. She argued that the trial judge failed to consider whether the ordinary person in the particular position of the appellant would have been provoked.
>
> However, even assuming that the deceased's actions could constitute provocation of the ordinary battered woman, the appellant cannot overcome the second hurdle of the provocation test. There is nothing in the appellant's evidence to suggest that she was in fact provoked within the meaning of s. 232(2). She gave no evidence that, in shooting her husband, she was acting on the sudden and shot him in a fit of passion. On the contrary, she had much earlier taken some pains to get a

> gun from locked premises, loaded it, and put it in her purse.... There is no air of reality to the theory that the appellant was provoked into action on the sudden before her passion had time to cool.

The Supreme Court dismissed the appeal: *R. v. Malott,* [1998] 1 S.C.R. 123.]

■

The public outcry after *Klassen, supra*, generated a Canada-wide petition and letter-signing campaign to abolish the defence of provocation and change the laws in cases of "wife slaughter":

> ... [A]s deeply concerned citizens we believe that the provocation defence as it is currently used in femicide/wife slaughter case inappropriately and [unjustly] changes the focus of the criminal trial from the behaviour of the accused and his intention to murder to the behaviour of the victim who from then on is identified as the one responsible for the accused's violence.
>
> Parliament's recent amendments to the *Criminal Code* in response to the *Daviault* and *Seaboyer* cases, as well as amendments to deal with stalking and harassing conduct reflect public policy underlying the law which requires males to take responsibility for their own violent behaviour towards women. The continued availability of the defence in wife slaughter cases is not consistent with this policy goal nor is it consistent with the values of our community.... More specifically, it is not consistent with the constitutional rights of women, including their right to equal protection and benefit of the law and their right to life, liberty and security.
>
> Therefore, the undersigned request that Parliament review and change relevant provisions of the *Criminal Code* to ensure that men take responsibility for their violent behaviour towards women.†

Public concern continued to mount in response to *Klassen*, *Gilroy*, and *Stone*, among other cases. Then Minister of Justice for the Yukon, Lois Moorcroft, called for a review of the defence of provocation. The federal Department of Justice acknowledged a number of the problems with the discriminatory application of the defence and released a consultation paper, *Reforming Criminal Code Defences: Provocation, Self-Defence, and Defence of Property* (Ottawa: Department of Justice, 1998). Academics and activists have continued to call for the abolition of the defence of provocation: Jeremy Horder, *Provocation and Responsibility, supra*; Joanne St. Lewis & Sheila Galloway on behalf of the Ontario Women's Directorate, *Reform of the Defence of Provocation, supra*; Andrée Côté, Diana Majury, & Elizabeth Sheehy, *Stop Excusing Violence Against Women! NAWL's Position Paper on the Defence of Provocation* (Ottawa: NAWL, 2000); Adrian Howe, "*Green v. The Queen*: The Provocation Defence: Finally Provoking Its Own Demise?" (1998) 22 Melb. U. L. Rev. 466.

Reconsider the questions posed throughout the chapter. What concerns should inform any review of the defence of provocation? What risks are attendant upon its abolition?

---

† Petition to the House of Commons in Parliament Assembled.

15

Self-Defence and Defence of Others

A. SELF-DEFENCE AGAINST UNPROVOKED ASSAULT, IN THE CASE OF AGGRESSION, AND IN PREVENTING ASSAULT

Review ss. 34, 35, and 37 of the *Code*.

Self-defence, if available, is a complete defence even, potentially, to killing. However, there are a number of pivotal criteria that the cases prior to *R. v. Lavallee*, [1990] 1 S.C.R. 852, had emphasized in determining whether or not the defence of self-defence was available to the accused. As you review individual cases, consider the interpretation given with respect to the following questions and the impact that it has on the availability of the defence:

- Was the accused faced with an unlawful assault (act or gesture, mere words insufficient)?
- Was the accused faced with an imminent attack?
- Did the accused have a reasonable apprehension of death or grievous bodily harm?
- Did the accused have a reasonable belief that no alternative was available (no excessive force, duty to retreat)?
- Which aspect of the statutory authority with respect to self-defence does the accused rely on?
- How are the elements of the defence defined?

Note the combination of objective criteria and subjective perception that the accused must meet in order to justify self-defensive violence, and the construction of those concepts. Also, for the defence to be left to the jury, the evidence must disclose an "air of reality" upon which a properly instructed jury acting reasonably might acquit: *R. v. Cinous*, [2002] 2 S.C.R. 3; *R. v. Currie* (2002), 159 O.A.C. 290 (C.A.); [2003] S.C.C.A. No. 410 (application for extension of time for leave to appeal dismissed).

An accused whose self-defence claim fails the objective criteria because the force is excessive will be convicted of the original offence, unless some other defence is available: *R. v. Faid*, [1983] 1 S.C.R. 265.

However, the interpretation of the objective element in s. 34 should be generously weighted in favour of the accused, according to *R. v. Cadwallader* (1966), 1 C.C.C. 380 (Sask. Q.B.). In that case the accused 14-year-old boy killed his father using five shots, one at close range, believing that his father was coming up the stairs to kill him (at 387):

> [I]f one believes he is in danger of life or limb he is entitled to use such force as would effectively put his assailant out of action. Where the means of defence used is not disproportionate to the severity of the assault, the plea is valid although the defender fails to measure with nicety the degree of force necessary to ward off the attack and inflicts serious injury.

Similarly, in *R. v. Bogue* (1976), 13 O.R. (2d) 272 (C.A.), the court emphasized the subjective element of self-defence in a case where the woman herself suffered injuries in her effort to protect herself, neighbours heard her screams, and she ultimately inflicted a fatal stab wound upon the deceased. The court ordered a new trial because the trial judge "should have asked whether she believed on reasonable and probable grounds that it was necessary to stab him as she did" (at 281).

The determination of reasonableness has historically imported a "reasonable man" standard, for example, on the question of the reasonable apprehension of imminent death or serious bodily injury. This has been a barrier to women who have killed in self-defence. Also, the distinction between the objective and subjective test is blurred when applied to the question of reasonable force in self-defence and depends, to some extent, on the characterizations ascribed to the comparator group of "reasonable" people (e.g., age, gender, size, capacity).

B. WIFE BATTERING AND SELF-DEFENCE

As was discussed in the chapter on **Provocation**, there has been a significant increase in femicide, the killing of women by men, in the last 20 years. Over the last 30 years, feminist activism and feminist legal strategies in Canada have dealt extensively with issues of violence against women and, specifically, wife battering and femicide.

In one example of that activism, the Ontario Association of Interval and Transition Houses (OAITH), Metropolitan Action Committee on Violence Against Women and Children (METRAC), and Women We Honour were granted standing at a "representative inquest" into the deaths of women murdered by their partners that commenced in February 1998. The inquest focused on the murder of Arlene May in Collingwood in March 1996 but was authorized to examine the systemic response of all the parties involved, the issues surrounding May's death, and their implications in other similar murders: *Inquest into the deaths of Arlene May and Ray Iles* (February 16–July 2, 1998) (Coroners Court: Toronto). The jury made 213 recommendations and emphasized the need for "zero tolerance" of the continuing violence against women and children, and for changes to the criminal justice system's response to domestic violence (including the need for victims services; more resources for shelters; public and professional education to educate and increase awareness among defence counsel, Crowns, police, and the medical profession; specialized domestic violence response units, and specialized courts; and more rigorous protocols for police and Crown Attorneys with respect to cases of domestic violence).

Horacek

By Judy Horacek. 17:5 *Alternative Law Journal*, (October 1992). © Judy Horacek. www.horacek.com.au

Violence against Women: Feminist Activism and Engagement with Law†

The history of wife battering must be understood against the backdrop of the structure of male right over women, the rights of women, the structuring of familial relations, and attitudes about gender and familial relations and the appropriateness of violence. It is evidenced, for example, by the marital regime (property law, the grounds for abandoning or dissolving marriage for men and women, the addition of cruelty to those grounds to stem some of the worst abuses, the elaboration of 'cruelty') and by the differing characterization and sanctions for marital violence depending on whether it was violence by the husband or the wife. The difficulty of pursuing remedies also limited recourse to the law.

For example, from 1351 until 1828, a woman who murdered her husband was liable to different and more serious criminal charges (petit treason) than a husband who murdered his wife. For an article which traces the legal position of married women in eighteenth century England, and the development, the particular punishments and decline of the law of petit treason, see Shelley Gavigan, "Petit Treason in Eighteenth Century England: Women's Inequality Before the Law" (1989–1990) 3 C.J.W.L. 335.

In the 1960s and 1970s, social movements challenged the family in different ways by questioning male authority, by undermining the public/private split, by critiquing the conceptualization of violence generally and the acceptability of certain forms of violence, by challenging the power of professionals to define and solve problems, and by supplanting them with self-help organizations such as battered women's shelters. By the late twentieth century, a broad level of general concern about wife battering was manifest. Demands were made that violence against women be treated as a crime, that the law be redefined, that the "law as it works" be evaluated, that shifts be made in the personnel of the criminal justice system (in police, in prosecutors, and in judges), that education be provided to encourage shifts in attitudes, and that strategies and resources be provided to enable women to escape violence (e.g. shelters, self-help groups).

There is now an increased prominence to the issue of wife battering, as a result of the work of the women's movement. However, the nature and content of that visibility is problematic. Specifically, there are difficulties with the interpretation and elaboration of the experience of women who are battered, and with the unevenness of the awareness of the extent of violence against specific groups of women. The latter point is made forcefully in a study by the Ontario Native Women's Association. Referring to an "epidemic" (at 114) and a "plague," (at 9) the study points to a horrifying incidence of "family violence" far above the statistics generally quoted. The report finds that "eight out of ten Aboriginal women have been abused or assaulted, or can expect to be abused or assaulted" (note 1, at Summary):

> It is not possible to find a First Nations or Metis woman in Ontario whose life has not been affected in some way by family violence. Either as a child witnessing spousal assault, as a child victim herself, as an adult victim of a husband or boyfriend's violence, or as a grandmother who witnesses the physical and emotional scars of her daughter or granddaughters' beatings: we are all victims of violent family situations and we want it to stop now. For too long this has been an everyday reality, whether we live in isolated Aboriginal communities, on an Indian reserve, in a rural area or a large urban centre in Ontario setting. We are tired of the beating and high statistics; we want an end to family violence; we want respect. (Ontario Native Women's Association, "Breaking Free: A Proposal for Change to Aboriginal Family Violence". (Thunder Bay: December 1989 at ii)

The report represents a very substantial articulation of Aboriginal women's concerns about family violence. The authors clearly link violence in the family to structural factors and suggest broad solutions encompassing Healing Lodges, treatment of male batterers which would draw on the resources of the Elders, alcohol and drug programmes, legal reforms (matrimonial property) and autonomous Aboriginal justice. They provide a complicated picture: a recognition of pervasive violence, an understanding of what this means for women and the community, but an insistence that the violence not

---

† Jennie Abell, "Violence against Women: Feminist Activism and Engagement with Law". (An earlier version of paper was presented at "La Violence Faite aux Femmes" session of Inter-American Law Professors Forum, San Jose, Costa Rica, November 1991.)

be individualized or attributed to individual Aboriginal men. They identify a need for protection and perhaps police; but also a long-term need for healing both at the individual and the community level.

During the 1980s, one of the important demands by feminist lawyers was for a reconceptualization and expansion of the substantive defences available to battered women who killed their batterers. The case of Jane Hurshman (Whynot) Stafford, *R. v. Whynot (Stafford)* (1983), 61 N.S.R. (2d) 33 (S.C.A.D.) had highlighted the situation confronting many battered women.

In that case, the accused, a battered woman, testified that her common-law husband had threatened to kill every member of her family if she tried to leave him. On the night in question, he threatened to burn out her neighbour and to kill her son. After he passed out intoxicated, she shot him.

She was acquitted at trial by a jury; but that acquittal was overturned on appeal.

In overturning her acquittal, the appeal court ruled (at 47) that "... no person has the right in anticipation of an assault that may or may not happen, to apply force to prevent the *imaginary assault*" (emphasis added). The ruling is problematic because it neglects the fact that the definition of assault (then section 244 of the *Code*, now section 265 of the *Code*) comprehends not merely the application of force but the threat to do so. Also, it is hardly fantastical or imaginary to assume that such threats from someone who has a long history of violence and making good on their threats would be carried out, particularly against someone at a physical disadvantage.

However, the cases had held that to amount to assault, a threat must be accompanied by a present ability to carry out the threat. The question of 'immediacy' became central to that determination.

Jane Stafford subsequently pled guilty to manslaughter and received a one year sentence of imprisonment. Her case, and reaction to it, helped to broaden the legal definition of self-defence. She became an activist and a spokesperson on issues of violence against women. In 1992, she was murdered in Halifax. As Deborah Jones reported, "A violent end to a life of abuse" *The [Toronto] Globe and Mail* (2 March 1992) A5, before she died, she received letters and phone calls threatening her to stop speaking about the abuse of women, or she would be stopped. To understand more fully the horrific extent of violence and abuse in Jane Hurshman (Stafford)'s life and her subsequent activism against violence, see: Brian Vallée, *Life with Billy* (Toronto: 1986, Seal) and *Life After Billy* (Toronto: 1995, Seal); and *Fifth Estate*, "Life with Billy" (Toronto: CBC, 1984) and "Life after Billy" (Toronto: CBC, 1992).

The Supreme Court of Canada overruled *Whynot* in *Lavallee*.

R. v. Whynot (Stafford)†

[HART J.A.:]

This is a Crown appeal from the acquittal of the respondent for the offence that she at or near Bangs Falls, in the County of Queens, Nova Scotia, on or about the 11th day of March, 1982 did unlawfully commit first degree murder upon the person of Lamont William Stafford, contrary to s. 218(1) of the *Criminal Code of Canada*. The trial took place at Liverpool before Mr. Justice C.D. Burchell with a jury.

The point of law raised by the Crown is that the trial judge misdirected the jury as to the defence of justification, pursuant to s. 37 of the *Criminal Code*, which states:

> 37.(1) Every one is justified in using force to defend himself or any one under his protection from assault, if he uses no more force than is necessary to prevent the assault or the repetition of it.
>
> (2) Nothing in this section shall be deemed to justify the wilful infliction of any hurt or mischief that is excessive, having regard to the nature of the assault that the force used was intended to prevent.

. . . .

† (1983), 61 N.S.R. (2d) 33 (S.C.(A.D.)).

The facts of the matter are not complicated and may be stated simply as follows.

In March of 1982, Jane Marie Stafford and her common-law husband, Lamont William Stafford, resided in a house in the small community of Bangs Falls, Queens County. Their son, Darren, four years of age; and Jane's son, Allan Whynot, sixteen years of age; and a boarder, Ronald Wamboldt, lived with them. Near the Stafford house there was a trailer occupied by Margaret Joudrey and a boarder, Roger Manthorne. The Mersey River flowed through Bangs Falls close to the Stafford house and the Joudrey trailer.

The evidence revealed that Billy Stafford was a very large and powerful man prone to violence, especially when drinking or under the influence of drugs. He dominated the household and exerted his authority by striking and slapping the various members and from time to time administering beatings to Jane Stafford and the others. He displayed very little respect for the law or the police, and had on occasion avoided responsibility for deer jacking by getting others to lie on his behalf. He was a great outdoorsman and had friends who shared this type of activity with him.

Billy Stafford had not been working for some time, nor had his boarder, Ronald Wamboldt, who was an alcoholic. Some animals were kept and wood cut with the assistance of Wamboldt and his stepson, Allan Whynot, but the income for the household was produced by Jane Stafford, who worked as an attendant at a nursing home. There was some suggestion that Billy Stafford may have been selling drugs to gain some income.

The Staffords got along reasonably well with their neighbours, Mrs. Joudrey and Roger Manthorne, who lived in the trailer. They played weekly games of cards and helped each other out from time to time. Mrs. Joudrey was considerably older than Jane Stafford and had become a mother figure to Jane. Billy Stafford and Mrs. Joudrey had the occasional argument over raising pigs and the location of the property line, and had exchanged some heated words the day before his death, but, as Mrs. Joudrey explained in evidence, she enjoyed an argument with Billy.

On March 11, 1982, Billy Stafford and Ronald Wamboldt had been drinking during the day at different places and when they returned home Billy demanded that Jane drive them down to Leona Anthony's home. On the way going down, she said that Billy was "very angry, hollering, saying, referring to Margaret saying the old bag sat up all night last night, he said she was worried last night, he said her light was on all night. He said won't have to worry about seeing the light shine down there no more, he said after tonight. He said he was going to burn her out. And he kept this up pretty well the whole way."

When they arrived at Anthony's they spent an hour during which Billy and Ronnie drank several beers, and Jane had one. A joint of marijuana was passed among the group. According to Jane there was no fuss while they were there, and after an hour or so Billy announced that they were going home. At that time Ronnie was in his usual state of being drunk.

Jane Stafford drove home with Billy sitting in the middle and Ronnie on the outside of the seat of the truck. Her testimony then continued:

> A. We was driving up, I was driving, the stereo, was still playing loudly. Bill's mouth was still running on about the same thing he said all the way down, he started right in again on the way back. He told me about the Mounties being out to talk to Allan. He said when he got done with Margaret he would deal with him too, might as well clean everything up in one night. This went on pretty well the whole way up the road. A little bit before we got home he passed out or went to sleep, I don't know, one or the other, he was asleep anyway. We got in the driveway, Ronny got out and went in. I had to stay in the truck, I couldn't leave as long as Bill was out. Whenever we went anywhere and we came home and he did pass out or go to sleep like that I would have to stay there until he woke up. So I just sat there and the words, everything that he had been saying just started sinking in, Margaret, Allan, what he was going to do. I just said to hell with everything, I'm just not living like this anymore. I blew the horn on the truck and Allan came to the door, and I told him to get me the gun and load it, and I got out of the truck. When he came with the gun I just held it in the window and pulled the trigger. I don't know if I put the gun down there or what I did with it. Allan came to the door and I just, I was telling him to do this and do that and do things.
>
> Q. Do you remember what you told him?
>
> A. Get me some clothes. Call my Mom. Go down to Margaret's and call my Mom. I would be back when I got there, I didn't know when or anything, I didn't know what was going to happen. I told him to take the gun down to Margaret's and Roger would go with him to get rid of it. I got in the truck and I drove away, just drove.
>
> Q. What can you remember about that drive?
>
> A. I didn't, I know the road was in bad shape. I didn't see anything. Everything was just like it

> was nothing. I just looked straight ahead and just kept on driving. I don't know if I drove the truck on the pavement or if I stopped on the gravel.

. . . .

On the day following the killing after the R.C.M.P. had found the body of Billy Stafford in the abandoned truck, Jane Stafford was arrested and charged with the first degree murder of her common-law husband, Billy Stafford....

At the trial, in addition to the facts already related, there was a great deal of evidence presented to the jury to indicate the terrible circumstances under which Jane Stafford had been living with Billy Stafford over the previous five years since the birth of their only child, Darren Stafford. This evidence was obviously admitted in an attempt to establish a certain state of mind as it related to the defence of provocation at the time Jane Stafford pulled the trigger. Whether any or all of this evidence should have been admitted will be discussed when I consider the defences raised on behalf of the respondent at her trial.

The Crown adduced certain additional evidence to show that Jane Stafford had attempted to hire a person to kill Billy Stafford a few months earlier. This evidence was, of course, properly admitted since it tended to establish premeditation on the part of the accused person.

There was also some psychiatric evidence adduced on behalf of the defence which tended to show that Jane Stafford was at her wit's end when she committed the killing. She had testified that she could not leave Billy because he had threatened to kill all of the members of her family, one at a time, should she do so, and there was no escape from her terrible plight. This evidence did not, however, establish any basis for a defence of not guilty by reason of insanity, nor was such defence raised.

The theory of the Crown as presented to the jury by the trial judge was that on the evening of March 11, 1982 at Bangs Falls, Queens County, the accused shot to death, William Lamont Stafford, her common-law husband, and that the death was planned and deliberate, and the shooting took place when the accused was aware of her act and the consequences thereof.

The theory of the defence, on the other hand, as explained to the jury was:

> that on the evening of March the 11th of 1982 the accused shot William Lamont Stafford on the sudden and before there was time for her passions to cool as a result of threats of arson to Margaret Joudrey and a threat to deal with her son Allan. Such threats in the submission for the accused amounting to provocation. It is the further theory of the defence that the accused shot Mr. Stafford in the reasonable belief that Mr. Stafford was going to assault her son Allan and that such force was necessary.

After delivering his general instructions to the jury the trial judge dealt with the specific indictment alleging that Jane Marie Stafford committed first degree murder, contrary to s. 218(1) of the *Criminal Code*. He explained s. 205 dealing with homicide, and that a person commits culpable homicide when he causes the death of a human being by means of an unlawful act. He then referred to s. 212, and told the jury that culpable homicide was murder where the person who caused the death of a human being meant to cause his death, or meant to cause him bodily harm that he knew was likely to cause his death and was reckless whether death ensued or not. He emphasized that this necessary intent had to be established beyond a reasonable doubt by the Crown in order to amount to the offence of murder. He also explained that the necessary intent could be found from the direct evidence of Mrs. Stafford or by inference from her conduct.

. . . .

Mr. Justice Burchell then explained the defence of self-defence in the following terms:

> The defence of self-defence has been raised in this case on behalf of the accused, and that, if it applies, I must tell you, would afford a complete defence to the charge against the accused. Even if it is shown, even if you're satisfied beyond a reasonable doubt that the accused would otherwise be guilty of murder, before she can be convicted you must also be satisfied to the exclusion of any reasonable doubt that she was not acting in self-defence according to law. If you conclude that she did kill Mr. Stafford in self-defence, as I shall define and explain self-defence, or if there is any reasonable doubt in your minds as to that then in either case you must find her not guilty. The term self-defence is often understood as any measure employed to preserve one's self from threatened or actual physical attack regardless of the consequences or the extent of the means used. Now that's not the legal meaning of the term, and it is, of course, only with the legal meaning of the term self-defence that we're concerned. In law self-defence is not a loose term. It's defined by the *Criminal Code*, and the conditions under which it may apply as a defence are rigidly laid down. And any defence that rests on

the theory of self-defence must come strictly within the provisions of the *Criminal Code*. Having said that, I want to emphasize that there is no burden on the accused to prove that she acted in self-defence. Instead, as in all other matters of proof, the burden is on the Crown to prove beyond a reasonable doubt that the accused did not act in self-defence as I shall explain it to you. What I've just said means that you must find the accused not guilty unless you're satisfied beyond a reasonable doubt on all the evidence that the Crown has disproved or negated self-defence.

Now the provision of the *Criminal Code* on which the defence, on which counsel for the accused relies in raising the defence of self-defence is section 37 of the *Criminal Code*. Bear with me, I thought I had it marked. 37 provides: 'Every one is justified in using force to defend himself or any one under his protection from assault, if he uses no more force than is necessary to prevent the assault or the repetition of it.' The section goes on, that provision of the Code goes on to say, 'Nothing in this section shall be deemed to justify the wilful infliction of any hurt or mischief that is excessive, having regard to the nature of the assault that the force used was intended to prevent.' Again I reassure you, I assure you that you'll have that section of the Code in the extract that's been made and you'll be able to look more closely at what I've just read to you when you retire to deliberate. But I wish to speak about the section at this stage, and I'll ask you to try to remember what I've just read to you. Now the evidence on which the defence relies relative to the defence of self-defence is the evidence of the accused that on the way to the Anthony residence and on the way back the deceased William Stafford, said that he was, in effect, that he was going to burn out Margaret Joudrey, and he also said that he would be dealing with her son Allan. I will be covering that evidence in detail later in this instruction and you will bear in mind what I'm saying now when I cover it. Those threats uttered by the deceased, William Stafford, are the basis on which the defence of self-defence is raised. The position of the defence is that the accused's appreciation of those threats was that they would be carried out; that William Stafford had the capability and disposition to carry them out, and that, in particular in relation to the son, Allan Whynot, that it was necessary to defend him from the threatened assault. As to the accused's appreciation of the necessity of defending her son you have all of the evidence to consider, and I mean in particular the evidence regarding the threats allegedly made by the deceased, and the evidence as to the character and disposition of the deceased, himself, as well as the evidence of the accused and others as to her fear of the deceased.

However, I must point out in relation to self-defence there is the aspect of that defence that mentions specifically in the section that no more force than necessary to prevent the assault, or the repetition of it, should be used, and I'll read again sub-section (2) of that section, which is, 'Nothing in this section shall be deemed to justify the wilful infliction of any hurt or mischief that is excessive, having regard to the nature of the assault that the force was intended to prevent.' Now this sets up, the language I've just read to you, sets up an objective test of what was necessary, or what was proportional force in the actual circumstances. It's therefore not a question of whether the accused thought it was necessary to shoot Mr. Stafford to defend persons under her protection in her particular state of mind at the time in question, it's a question of whether for that purpose of defending those under her protection, the killing of Mr. Stafford was objectively or actually a matter of necessity. So you must look at the means employed in self-defence and decide whether those means were necessary. In addressing that question, of course, you may take into account what you know about the character and disposition of Mr. Stafford. But it is on an objective examination of what was necessary under the circumstances not from the perspective of the accused that you must judge the question of whether the force used was excessive or not.

Now a few general and concluding remarks on the subject of self-defence. You should understand that the law of self-defence provides from necessity, from the instinctive and the intuitive necessity to preserve one's self. Under no circumstances may that defence be raised as a cloak for retaliation, or revenge. The use of force in self-defence should come as a matter of last resort. It's justified only where there are no other reasonable means to prevent the assault. If you have any reasonable doubt as to whether the accused acted in self-defence, as I've defined it, you will find the accused not guilty of murder or of any other offence because if that is your finding or if you have a doubt, a reasonable doubt as to self-defence, then the Crown will have failed to prove that the homicide was culpable, because a homicide committed in self-defence is not a culpable homicide. And it's on that logic that I said to you earlier that self-defence is a complete defence of the charge against the accused. But if you do, if you find that the defence of self-defence has not been made out and you have no reasonable doubt concerning it, then it would follow that you should find the accused guilty.

. . . .

The trial judge then went on to discuss s. 37 of the Code by saying:

> The second point that I wish to put in better prospective is that I referred throughout to the defence of self-defence as one of the defences raised, and I used that term in relation to section 37 of the Code, which I read to you. Well by description the defence under 37 is a form of self-defence defence. But the term, and this is what counsel and I agree should be pointed out to you, is somewhat misleading as the section may apply to this case, because what is involved, what was involved in the argument of counsel for the accused was not defence of the accused, herself, so the word self in self-defence is a bit misleading, but rather the prevention of assault against others under her protection, and in particular her son Allan. The heading above section 37 of the Code actually reads "Preventing assault". I find it convenient to refer to that as a defence of self-defence, and I will do so in the future, I'm sure, as I continue with these remarks. But bear in mind that for the purposes of this case the section is being relied upon by the defence in relation to measures, which it is said, were taken by the accused not to defend herself but to defend persons under her protection.

Mr. Justice Burchell then instructed the jury on the offence of manslaughter. He related manslaughter solely to a circumstance where murder is reduced to manslaughter by virtue of provocation.

. . . .

I mentioned earlier that there was a lot of evidence adduced by both the prosecution and the defence about the character of the deceased. Much of this was unnecessary and indeed inadmissible unless it was relevant to a defence that could properly be put to the jury. It served only to create sympathy for the respondent and for this reason should have been excluded.

. . . .

In my opinion there are only two possible ways the jury could have reached the verdict of not guilty in light of the evidence before them. They may have had a reasonable doubt as to whether Jane Stafford did, in fact, kill the victim, or whether the gun had been fired by her son, Allan Whynot, as had been originally alleged. This conclusion would require them to disbelieve the evidence of Jane Stafford and her son given at the trial, and such a defence was not pressed by her counsel or even referred to by the trial judge in his charge. The other route by which the jury could have arrived at its conclusion was if they understood from the judge's instructions that s. 37 of the *Criminal Code* permitted Jane Stafford to anticipate a possible assault against her son from threats made earlier in the evening, and that she used reasonable force to prevent such an assault. They had been given a copy of s. 37, isolated from the other provisions dealing with self-defence, and, in my view, after considering the overall instructions in the charge, this conclusion was left open to them. Furthermore, the legal definition of assault was not placed before them and the jury might well have understood that threats alone could amount to an assault.

The instructions given to the jury regarding s. 37 were broad enough to say that a person is justified in killing anyone who has threatened them and is likely to carry out such a threat. I do not believe that Parliament intended such an interpretation of the section.

Section 37 is grouped together with provisions relating to the defence of the person. By s. 34 a person unlawfully assaulted is entitled to repel the assault if no more force is used than is necessary to defend himself and may kill his attacker if he is under a reasonable apprehension of death or grievous bodily harm and he believes on reasonable and probable grounds that he cannot otherwise preserve himself from death. By s. 37 he is justified in defending himself or anyone under his protection from an assault from happening, and by s-s. (2) "Nothing in this section shall be deemed to justify the wilful infliction of any hurt or mischief that is excessive, having regard to the nature of the assault that the force used was intended to prevent." An assault by s. 244 of the Code is defined as follows:

> 244.(1) A person commits an assault when
> (a) Without the consent of another person or with consent, where it is obtained by fraud, he applies force intentionally to the person of the other, directly or indirectly;
> (b) he attempts or threatens, by an act or gesture, to apply force to the person of the other, if he has or causes the other to believe upon reasonable grounds that he has present ability to effect his purpose; ...
>
> A person who seeks justification for preventing an assault against himself or someone under his protection must be faced with an actual assault, something that he must defend against, before the provisions of s. 37 can be invoked, and that assault must be life threatening before he can be justified in killing in defence of his person or that of someone under his protection.

At the time that Jane Stafford said she shot and killed Billy Stafford he was passed out or sleeping in the truck. There was no assault against her and only a general statement made sometime during the evening that he would deal with Allan. Allan was the only person who could be said to have been under her protection, and there is no evidence that Billy Stafford was about to assault him at the time he was killed. The remark of Jane Stafford, after having fired the lethal shot, to the effect that "It's all over, I ain't going to have to put up with it no more", was not in reference to any need to protect her son, but that she had brought to an end the problems which she had continually faced from her association with Billy Stafford.

I do not believe that the trial judge was justified in placing s. 37 of the Code before the jury any more than he would have been justified in giving them s. 34. Under s. 34 the assault must have been underway and unprovoked, and under s. 37 the assault must be such that it is necessary to defend the person assaulted by the use of force. No more force may be used than necessary to prevent the assault or the repetition of it. In my opinion no person has the right in anticipation of an assault that may or may not happen, to apply force to prevent the imaginary assault.

. . . . .

... In my opinion the trial judge in this case should have ruled that in law there was no legal foundation in the evidence to merit a justification of the act of killing the deceased as a means of defending Jane Stafford's son from any assault by Billy Stafford. As he did with s. 34 of the Code he should have refused to place before the jury any justification of her actions under s. 37. Nobody was being assaulted at the time Billy Stafford was killed. There was no need to protect anybody from any assault. The jury should not have been permitted to consider a possible assault as a justification of her deed, and s. 37 of the Code should not have been left with them.

Since the jury was improperly instructed on the law relating to the offence alleged against the respondent, and since that improper instruction may well have permitted them to reach a conclusion that would not otherwise be open to them, I would allow the appeal, set aside the verdict of the jury and order a new trial upon the original indictment.

Appeal allowed.

■

R. v. Lavallee†

[WILSON J.:]

The narrow issue raised on this appeal is the adequacy of a trial judge's instructions to the jury regarding expert evidence. The broader issue concerns the utility of expert evidence in assisting a jury confronted by a plea of self-defence to a murder charge by a common-law wife who had been battered by the deceased.

THE FACTS

The appellant, who was 22 years old at the time, had been living with Kevin Rust for some three to four years. Their residence was the scene of a boisterous party on August 30, 1986. In the early hours of August 31st, after most of the guests had departed, the appellant and Rust had an argument in the upstairs bedroom which was used by the appellant. Rust was killed by a single shot in the back of the head from a .303 calibre rifle fired by the appellant as he was leaving the room.

The appellant did not testify but her statement made to police on the night of the shooting was put in evidence. Portions of it read as follows:

> Me and Wendy argued as usual and I ran in the house after Kevin pushed me. I was scared, I was really scared. I locked the door. Herb was downstairs with Joanne and I called for Herb but I was crying when I called him. I said, "Herb come up here please." Herb came up to the top of the stairs and I told him that Kevin was going to hit me actually beat on me again.

† [1990] 1 S.C.R. 852 at 852–60, 869–900.

> Herb said he knew and that if I was his old lady things would be different, he gave me a hug. OK, we're friends, there's nothing between us. He said "Yeah, I know" and he went outside to talk to Kevin leaving the door unlocked. I went upstairs and hid in my closet from Kevin. I was so scared.... My window was open and I could hear Kevin asking questions about what I was doing and what I was saying. Next thing I know he was coming up the stairs for me. He came in my bedroom and said "Wench, where are you?" And he turned on the light and he said "Your purse is on the floor" and he kicked it. OK then he turned and he saw me in the closet. He wanted me to come out but I didn't want to come out because I was scared. I was so scared. [The officer who took the statement then testified that the appellant started to cry at this point and stopped after a minute or two.] He grabbed me by the arm right there. There's a bruise on my face also where he slapped me. He didn't slap me right then, first he yelled at me then he pushed me and I pushed him back and he hit me twice on the right hand side of my head. I was scared. All I thought about was all the other times he used to beat me. I was scared, I was shaking as usual. The rest is a blank, all I remember is he gave me the gun and a shot was fired through my screen. This is all so fast. And then the guns were in another room and he loaded it the second shot and gave it to me. And I was going to shoot myself. I pointed it to myself, I was so upset. OK and then he went and I was sitting on the bed and he started going like this with his finger [the appellant made a shaking motion with an index finger] and said something like "You're my old lady and you do as you're told" or something like that. He said "wait till everybody leaves, you'll get it then" and he said something to the effect of "either you'll kill me or I'll get you" that was what it was. He kind of smiled and then he turned around. I shot him but I aimed out. I thought I aimed above him and a piece of his head went that way.

The relationship between the appellant and Rust was volatile and punctuated by frequent arguments and violence. They would apparently fight for two or three days at a time or several times a week. Considerable evidence was led at trial indicating that the appellant was frequently a victim of physical abuse at the hands of Rust. Between 1983 and 1986, the appellant made several trips to hospital for injuries including severe bruises, a fractured nose, multiple contusions and a black eye. One of the attending physicians, Dr. Dirks, testified that he disbelieved the appellant's explanation on one such occasion that she had sustained her injuries by falling from a horse.

A friend of the deceased, Robert Ezako, testified that he had witnessed several fights between the appellant and the deceased and that he had seen the appellant point a gun at the deceased twice and threaten to kill him if he ever touched her again. Under cross-examination Ezako admitted to seeing or hearing the deceased beat up the appellant on several occasions and, during the preliminary inquiry, described her screaming during one such incident like "a pig being butchered." He also saw the appellant with a black eye on one occasion and doubted that it was the result of an accident as she and the deceased stated at the time. Another acquaintance of the couple recalled seeing the appellant with a split lip.

At one point on the night of his death Rust chased the appellant outside the house and a mutual friend, Norman Kolish, testified that the appellant pleaded with Rust to "leave me alone" and sought Kolish's protection by trying to hide behind him. A neighbour overheard Rust and the appellant arguing and described the tone of the former as "argumentative" and the latter as "scared." Later, between the first and second gunshot, he testified that he could hear that "somebody was beating up somebody" and the screams were female. Another neighbour testified to hearing noises like gunshots and then a woman's voice sounding upset saying "Fuck. He punched me in the face. He punched me in the face." He looked out the window and saw a woman matching the description of the appellant.

Three witnesses who attended the party testified to hearing sounds of yelling, pushing, shoving and thumping coming from upstairs prior to the gunshots. It is not disputed that two shots were fired by the appellant. The first one went through a window screen. It is not clear where Rust was at the time. The appellant in her statement says that he was upstairs, while another witness places him in the basement. The second shot was the fatal one. After the second shot was fired the appellant was seen visibly shaken and upset and was heard to say "Rooster [the deceased] was beating me so I shot him" and "You know how he treated me, you've got to help me." The arresting officer testified that en route to the police station the appellant made various comments in the police car, including "He said if I didn't kill him first he would kill me. I hope he lives. I really love him," and "He told me he was gonna kill me when everyone left."

The police officer who took the appellant's statement testified to seeing a red mark on her arm where she said the deceased had grabbed her. When the coroner who performed an autopsy on the deceased was shown pictures of the appellant (who had various bruises) he testified that it was "entirely possible" that bruises on the deceased's left hand were occasioned by an assault on the appellant. Another doctor noted an injury to the appellant's pinkie finger consistent with those sustained by the adoption of a defensive stance.

The expert evidence which forms the subject-matter of the appeal came from Dr. Fred Shane, a psychiatrist with extensive professional experience in the treatment of battered wives. At the request of defence counsel Dr. Shane prepared a psychiatric assessment of the appellant. The substance of Dr. Shane's opinion was that the appellant had been terrorized by Rust to the point of feeling trapped, vulnerable, worthless and unable to escape the relationship despite the violence. At the same time, the continuing pattern of abuse put her life in danger. In Dr. Shane's opinion the appellant's shooting of the deceased was a final desperate act by a woman who sincerely believed that she would be killed that night:

> ... I think she felt, she felt in the final tragic moment that her life was on the line, that unless she defended herself, unless she reacted in a violent way that she would die. I mean he made it very explicit to her, from what she told me and from the information I have from the material that you forwarded to me, that she had, I think, to defend herself against his violence.

Dr. Shane stated that his opinion was based on four hours of formal interviews with the appellant, a police report of the incident (including the appellant's statement), hospital reports documenting eight of her visits to emergency departments between 1983 and 1985, and an interview with the appellant's mother. In the course of his testimony Dr. Shane related many things told to him by the appellant for which there was no admissible evidence. They were not in the appellant's statement to the police and she did not testify at trial. For example, Dr. Shane mentioned several episodes of abuse described by the appellant for which there were no hospital reports. He also related the appellant's disclosure to him that she had lied to doctors about the cause of her injuries. Dr. Shane testified that such fabrication was typical of battered women. The appellant also recounted to Dr. Shane occasions on which Rust would allegedly beat her, then beg her forgiveness and ply her with flowers and temporary displays of kindness. Dr. Shane was aware of the incidents described by Ezako about the appellant's pointing a gun at Rust on two occasions and explained it as "an issue for trying to defend herself. She was afraid that she would be assaulted." The appellant denied to Dr. Shane that she had homicidal fantasies about Rust and mentioned that she had smoked some marijuana on the night in question. These facts were related by Dr. Shane in the course of his testimony.

The appellant was acquitted by a jury but the verdict was overturned by a majority of the Manitoba Court of Appeal and the case sent back for retrial.

. . . .

ISSUES ON APPEAL

It should be noted that two bases for ordering a new trial are implicit in the reasons of the majority of the Court of Appeal. In finding that "absent the evidence of Dr. Shane, it is unlikely that the jury, properly instructed, would have accepted the accused's plea of self-defence" the Court of Appeal suggests that the evidence of Dr. Shane ought to have been excluded entirely. The alternative ground for allowing the Crown's appeal was that Dr. Shane's testimony was properly admitted but the trial judge's instructions with respect to it were deficient. Thus, the issues before this court are as follows:

1. Did the majority of the Manitoba Court of Appeal err in concluding that the jury should have considered the plea of self-defence absent the expert evidence of Dr. Shane?
2. Did the majority of the Manitoba Court of Appeal err in holding that the trial judge's charge to the jury with respect to Dr. Shane's expert evidence did not meet the requirements set out by this court in *Abbey*, thus warranting a new trial?

ANALYSIS

Admissibility of Expert Evidence

In *Kelliher v. Smith*, [1931] 4 D.L.R. 102 at p. 116, [1931] S.C.R. 672, this court adopted the principle that in order for expert evidence to be admissible "the subject-matter of the inquiry must be such that ordinary people are unlikely to form a correct judgment about it, if unassisted by persons with special knowledge." More recently, this court addressed the admissibility of expert psychiatric evidence in criminal cases in *R. v. Abbey, supra*. At p. 409 of the unanimous judgment Dickson J. (as he then was) stated the rule as follows:

> With respect to matters calling for special knowledge, an expert in the field may draw inferences and state his opinion. An expert's function is precisely this: to provide the judge and jury with a ready-made inference which the judge and jury, due to the technical nature of the facts, are unable to formulate. "An expert's opinion is admissible to furnish the Court with scientific information which is likely to be outside the experience and knowledge of a judge or jury. If on the proven facts a judge or jury can form their own conclusions without help, then the opinion of the expert is unnecessary": *R. v. Turner* (1974), 60 Cr. App. R. 80, at p. 83 *per* Lawton L.J.

See also *R. v. Beland* (1987), 36 C.C.C. (3d) 481 at p. 494, 43 D.L.R. (4th) 641, [1987] 2 S.C.R. 398, in which McIntyre J. speaks of an expert witness possessing "special knowledge and experience going beyond that of the trier of fact."

Where expert evidence is tendered in such fields as engineering or pathology, the paucity of the lay person's knowledge is uncontentious. The long-standing recognition that psychiatric or psychological testimony also falls within the realm of expert evidence is predicated on the realization that in some circumstances the average person may not have sufficient knowledge of or experience with human behaviour to draw an appropriate inference from the facts before him or her. An example may be found in *R. v. Lyons* (1987), 37 C.C.C. (3d) 1, 44 D.L.R. (4th) 1983, [1987] 2 S.C.R. 309, in which this court approved the use of psychiatric testimony in dangerous offender applications. At p. 48 La Forest J. remarks that "psychiatric evidence is clearly relevant to the issue whether a person is likely to behave in a certain way and, indeed, is probably relatively superior in this regard to the evidence of other clinicians and lay persons."

The need for expert evidence in these areas can, however, be obfuscated by the belief that judges and juries are thoroughly knowledgeable about "human nature" and that no more is needed. They are, so to speak, their own experts on human behaviour. This, in effect, was the primary submission of the Crown to this court.

The bare facts of this case, which I think are amply supported by the evidence, are that the appellant was repeatedly abused by the deceased but did not leave him (although she twice pointed a gun at him), and ultimately shot him in the back of the head as he was leaving her room. The Crown submits that these facts disclose all the information a jury needs in order to decide whether or not the appellant acted in self-defence. I have no hesitation in rejecting the Crown's submission.

Expert evidence on the psychological effect of battering on wives and common-law partners must, it seems to me, be both relevant and necessary in the context of the present case. How can the mental state of the appellant be appreciated without it? The average member of the public (or of the jury) can be forgiven for asking: Why would a woman put up with this kind of treatment? Why should she continue to live with such a man? How could she love a partner who beat her to the point of requiring hospitalization? We would expect the woman to pack her bags and go. Where is her self-respect? Why does she not cut loose and make a new life for herself? Such is the reaction of the average person confronted with the so-called "battered wife syndrome." We need help to understand it and help is available from trained professionals.

The gravity, indeed, the tragedy of domestic violence can hardly be overstated. Greater media attention to this phenomenon in recent years has revealed both its prevalence and its horrific impact on women from all walks of life. Far from protecting women from it the law historically sanctioned the abuse of women within marriage as an aspect of the husband's ownership of his wife and his "right" to chastise her. One need only recall the centuries-old law that a man is entitled to beat his wife with a stick "no thicker than his thumb."

Laws do not spring out of a social vacuum. The notion that a man has a right to "discipline" his wife is deeply rooted in the history of our society. The woman's duty was to serve her husband and to stay in the marriage at all costs "till death do us part" and to accept as her due any "punishment" that was meted out for failing to please her husband. One consequence of this attitude was that "wife battering" was rarely spoken of, rarely reported, rarely prosecuted, and even more rarely punished. Long after society abandoned its formal approval of spousal abuse, tolerance of it continued and continues in some circles to this day.

Fortunately, there has been a growing awareness in recent years that no man has a right to abuse any woman under any circumstances. Legislative initiatives designed to educate police, judicial officers and the public, as well as more aggressive investigation and charging policies all signal a concerted effort by the criminal justice system to take spousal abuse seriously. However, a woman who comes before a judge or jury with the claim that she has been battered and suggests that this may be a relevant factor in evaluating her subsequent actions still faces the prospect of being condemned by popular mythology about domestic violence. Either she was not as badly beaten as she claims or she would have left the man long ago. Or, if she was battered that severely, she must have stayed out of some masochistic enjoyment of it.

Expert testimony on the psychological effects of battering [has] been admitted in American courts in recent years. In *State v. Kelly*, 478 A. 2d 364 at p. 378 (1984), the New Jersey Supreme Court commended the value of expert testimony in these terms:

> It is aimed at the area where the purported common knowledge of the jury may be very much mistaken, an area where jurors' logic, drawn from their own experience, may lead to a wholly incorrect conclusion, an area where expert knowledge would enable the jurors to disregard their prior conclusions as being common myths rather than common knowledge.

The court concludes at p. 379 that the battering relationship is "subject to a large group of myths and stereotypes." As such, it is "beyond the ken of the average juror and thus is suitable for explanation through expert testimony." I share that view.

The Relevance of Expert Testimony to the Elements of Self-defence

In my view, there are two elements of the defence under s. 34(2) of the *Code* which merit scrutiny for present purposes. The first is the temporal connection in s. 34(2)(a) between the apprehension of death or grievous bodily harm and the act allegedly taken in self-defence. Was the appellant "under reasonable apprehension of death or grievous bodily harm" from Rust as he was walking out of the room? The second is the assessment in s. 34(2)(b) of the magnitude of the force used by the accused. Was the accused's belief that she could not "otherwise preserve herself from death or grievous bodily harm" except by shooting the deceased based "on reasonable grounds"?

The feature common to both para. (a) and para. (b) of s. 34(2) is the imposition of an objective standard of reasonableness on the apprehension of death and the need to repel the assault with deadly force. In *Reilly v. The Queen* (1984), 15 C.C.C. (3d) 1 at pp. 7–8, 13 D.L.R. (4th) 161, [1984] 2 S.C.R. 396, this court considered the interaction of the objective and subjective components of s. 34(2):

> [Subsection (2) of s. 34] places in issue the accused's state of mind at the time he caused death. The subsection can only afford protection to the accused if he apprehended death or grievous bodily harm from the assault he was repelling and if he believed he could not preserve himself from death or grievous bodily harm otherwise than by the force he used. None the less, his apprehension must be a *reasonable* one and his belief must *be based upon reasonable and probable grounds*. The subsection requires that the jury consider, and be guided by, what they decide on the evidence was the accused's appreciation of the situation and his belief as to the reaction it required, so long as there exists an objectively verifiable basis for his perception.
>
> Since s. 34(2) places in issue the accused's perception of the attack upon him and the response required to meet it, the accused may still be found to have acted in self-defence even if he was mistaken in his perception. Reasonable and probable grounds must still exist for this mistaken perception in the sense that the mistake must have been one which an ordinary man using ordinary care could have made in the same circumstances. (Emphasis in original.)

If it strains credulity to imagine what the "ordinary man" would do in the position of a battered spouse, it is probably because men do not typically find themselves in that situation. Some women do, however. The definition of what is reasonable must be adapted to circumstances which are, by and large, foreign to the world inhabited by the hypothetical "reasonable man."

I find the case of *State v. Wanrow*, 559 P.2d 548 (1977), helpful in illustrating how the factor of gender can be germane to the assessment of what is reasonable. In *Wanrow*, the Washington Supreme Court addressed the standard by which a jury ought to assess the reasonableness of the female appellant's use of a gun against an unarmed intruder. The court pointed out that the appellant had reason to believe that the intruder had molested her daughter in the past and was coming back for her son. The appellant was a 5 ft., 4 in. woman with a broken leg. The assailant was 6 ft., 2 in. and intoxicated. The court first observed, at p. 558, that "in society women suffer from a conspicuous lack of access to training in and the means of developing those skills necessary to effectively repel a male assailant without resorting to the use of deadly weapons." Later it found that the trial judge erred in his instructions to the jury by creating the impression that the objective standard of reasonableness to be applied to the accused was that of an altercation between two men. At p. 559, the court makes the following remarks which I find apposite to the case before us:

> The respondent was entitled to have the jury consider her actions in the light of her own perceptions of the situation, including those perceptions which were the product of our nation's "long and unfortunate history of sex discrimination." Until such time as the effects of that history are eradicated, care must be taken to assure that our self-defense instructions afford women the right to have their conduct judged in light of the individual physical handicaps which are the product of sex discrimination. To fail to do so is to deny the right of the individual woman involved to trial by the same rules which are applicable to male defendants.

I turn now to a consideration of the specific components of self-defence under s. 34(2) of the *Criminal Code.*

Reasonable Apprehension of Death

Section 34(2)(a) requires that an accused who intentionally causes death or grievous bodily harm in repelling an assault is justified if he or she does so "under reasonable apprehension of death or grievous bodily harm." In the present case, the assault precipitating the appellant's alleged defensive act was Rust's threat to kill her when everyone else had gone.

It will be observed that s. 34(2)(a) does not actually stipulate that the accused apprehend *imminent* danger when he or she acts. Case-law has, however, read that requirement into the defence: see *Reilly v. The Queen, supra*; *R. v. Baxter* (1975) 27 C.C.C. (2d) 96, 33 C.R.N.S. 22 (Ont. C.A.); *R. v. Bogue* (1976) 30 C.C.C. (2d) 403, 70 D.L.R. (3d) 603, 13 O.R. (2d) 272 (Ont. C.A.). The sense in which "imminent" is used conjures up the image of "an uplifted knife" or a pointed gun. The rationale for the imminence rule seems obvious. The law of self-defence is designed to ensure that the use of defensive force is really necessary. It justifies the act because the defender reasonably believed that he or she had no alternative but to take the attacker's life. If there is a significant time interval between the original unlawful assault and the accused's response, one tends to suspect that the accused was motivated by revenge rather than self-defence. In the paradigmatic case of a one-time bar-room brawl between two men of equal size and strength, this inference makes sense. How can one feel endangered to the point of firing a gun at an unarmed man who utters a death threat, then turns his back and walks out of the room? One cannot be certain of the gravity of the threat or his capacity to carry it out. Besides, one can always take the opportunity to flee or to call the police. If he comes back and raises his fist, one can respond in kind if need be. These are the tacit assumptions that underlie the imminence rule.

All of these assumptions were brought to bear on the respondent in *R. v. Whynot* (1983), 9 C.C.C. 449, 37 C.R. (3d) 198, 61 N.S.R. (2d) 33 (C.A.). The respondent, Jane Stafford, shot her sleeping common-law husband as he lay passed out in his truck. The evidence at trial indicated that the deceased "dominated the household and exerted his authority by striking and slapping the various members and from time to time administering beatings to Jane Stafford and the others" (at p. 452). The respondent testified that the deceased threatened to kill all of the members of her family, one by one, if she tried to leave him. On the night in question he threatened to kill her son. After he passed out the respondent got one of the many shotguns kept by her husband and shot him. The Nova Scotia Court of Appeal held that the trial judge erred in leaving s. 37 (preventing assault against oneself or anyone under one's protection) with the jury. The court stated at p. 464:

> I do not believe that the trial judge was justified in placing s. 37 of the *Code* before the jury any more than he would have been justified in giving them s. 34. Under s. 34 the assault must have been underway and unprovoked, and under s. 37 the assault must be such that it is necessary to defend the person assaulted by the use of force. No more force may be used than necessary to prevent the assault or the repetition of it. In my opinion, no person has the right in anticipation of an assault that may or may not happen, to apply force to prevent the imaginary assault.

The implication of the court's reasoning is that it is inherently unreasonable to apprehend death or grievous bodily harm unless and until the physical assault is actually in progress, at which point the victim can presumably gauge the requisite amount of force needed to repel the attack and act accordingly. In my view, expert testimony can cast doubt on these assumptions as they are applied in the context of a battered wife's efforts to repel an assault.

The situation of the appellant was not unlike that of Jane Stafford in the sense that she too was routinely beaten over the course of her relationship with the man she ultimately killed. According to the testimony of Dr. Shane these assaults were not entirely random in their occurrence. The following exchange during direct examination elicited a discernible pattern to the abuse:

> Q. How did they react during the tension that preceded the beatings? How would her ...

> A. Well, typically before a beating there's usually some verbal interchange and there are threats and typically she would feel, you know, very threatened by him and for various reasons.
>
> He didn't like the way she dressed or if she — didn't like the way she handled money or she wasn't paying him enough attention or she was looking at other men, all sorts of reasons, and she would be defending herself, trying to placate him, which was typical, saying, you know, trying to calm him down, trying to soothe him, you know, so nothing violent would happen and sometimes it would work. You know, as people's experiences indicated or as people who write about this process, if you will, have indicated.
>
> But often, as reflected by what she has told me, and the information I have from other people, such as her mother, often it would fail and she would end up being beaten and assaulted.
>
> Q. And that would be followed by this forgiveness state?
>
> A. It typically would be followed by, you know, this make-up period.

Earlier in his testimony Dr. Shane explained how this "make-up" period would be characterized by contrite and affectionate behaviour by Rust:

> In this particular case she documented many times, after he would beat her, he would send her flowers and he would beg her for forgiveness and he would love her and then the relationship would come back to a sense of equilibrium, if you will ... But then, because of the nature of the personalities, it would occur again.

The cycle described by Dr. Shane conforms to the Walker Cycle Theory of Violence named for clinical psychologist Dr. Lenore Walker, the pioneer researcher in the field of the battered-wife syndrome. Dr. Shane acknowledged his debt to Dr. Walker in the course of establishing his credentials as an expert at trial. Dr. Walker first describes the cycle in the book, *The Battered Woman*, (1979). In her 1984 book, *The Battered Woman Syndrome*, Dr. Walker reports the results of a study involving 400 battered women. Her research was designed to test empirically the theories expounded in her earlier book. At pp. 95–6 of *The Battered Woman Syndrome*, she summarizes the Cycle Theory as follows:

> A second major theory that was tested in this project is the Walker Cycle Theory of Violence (Walker, 1979). This tension reduction theory states that there are distinct phases associated in a recurring battering cycle: (1) tension building, (2) the acute battering incident, and (3) loving contrition. During the first phase, there is a gradual escalation of tension displayed by discrete acts causing increased friction such as name-calling, other mean intentional behaviors, and/or physical abuse. The batterer expresses dissatisfaction and hostility but not in an extreme or maximally explosive form. The woman attempts to placate the batterer, doing what she thinks might please him, calm him down, or at least, what will not further aggravate him. She tries not to respond to his hostile actions and uses general anger reduction techniques. Often she succeeds for a little while which reinforces her unrealistic belief that she can control this man....
>
> The tension continues to escalate and eventually she is unable to continue controlling his angry response pattern. "Exhausted from the constant stress, she usually withdraws from the batterer, fearing she will inadvertently set off an explosion. He begins to move more aggressively toward her as he observes her withdrawal.... Tension between the two becomes unbearable" (Walker, 1979, p. 59). The second phase, the acute battering incident, becomes inevitable without intervention. Sometimes, she precipitates the inevitable explosion so as to control where and when it occurs, allowing her to take better precautions to minimize her injuries and pain.
>
> "Phase two is characterized by the uncontrollable discharge of the tensions that have built up during phase one" (p. 59). The batterer typically unleashes a barrage of verbal and physical aggression that can leave the woman severely shaken and injured. In fact, when injuries do occur it usually happens during the second phase. It is also the time police become involved, if they are called at all. The acute battering phase is concluded when the batterer stops, usually bringing with its cessation a sharp physiological reduction in tension. This in itself is naturally reinforcing. Violence often succeeds because it does work.
>
> In phase three which follows, the batterer may apologize profusely, try to assist his victim, show kindness and remorse, and shower her with gifts and/or promises. The batterer himself may believe at this point that he will never allow himself to be violent again. The woman wants to believe the batterer and, early in the relationship at least, may renew her hope in his ability to change. This third phase provides the positive reinforcement for remaining in the relationship, for the woman. In fact, our results showed that phase three could be characterized by an absence of tension or violence, and no observable loving-contrition behaviour, and still be reinforcing for the woman.

Dr. Walker defines a battered woman as a woman who has gone through the battering cycle at least twice. As she explains in her introduction to

The Battered Woman, at p xv: "Any woman may find herself in an abusive relationship with a man once. If it occurs a second time, and she remains in the situation, she is defined as a battered woman."

Given the relational context in which the violence occurs, the mental state of an accused at the critical moment she pulls the trigger cannot be understood except in terms of the cumulative effect of months or years of brutality. As Dr. Shane explained in his testimony, the deterioration of the relationship between the appellant and Rust in the period immediately preceding the killing led to feelings of escalating terror on the part of the appellant:

> But their relationship some weeks to months before was definitely escalating in terms of tension and in terms of the discordant quality about it. They were sleeping in separate bedrooms. Their intimate relationship was lacking and things were building and building and to a point, I think, where it built to that particular point where she couldn't — she felt so threatened and so overwhelmed that she had to — that she reacted in a violent way because of her fear of survival and also because, I think because of her, I guess, final sense that she was — that she had to defend herself and her own sense of violence towards this man who had really desecrated her and damaged her for so long.

Another aspect of the cyclical nature of the abuse is that it begets a degree of predictability to the violence that is absent in an isolated violent encounter between two strangers. This also means that it may in fact be possible for a battered spouse to accurately predict the onset of violence before the first blow is struck, even if an outsider to the relationship cannot. Indeed, it has been suggested that a battered woman's knowledge of her partner's violence is so heightened that she is able to anticipate the nature and extent (though not the onset) of the violence by his conduct beforehand. In her article "Potential Uses for Expert Testimony: Ideas Toward the Representation of Battered Women Who Kill," 9 *Women's Rights Law Reporter* 227 (1986), psychologist Julie Blackman describes this characteristic at p. 229:

> Repeated instances of violence enable battered women to develop a continuum along which they can "rate" the tolerability or survivability of episodes of their partner's violence. Thus, signs of unusual violence are detected. For battered women, this response to the ongoing violence of their situations is a survival skill. Research shows that battered women who kill experience remarkably severe and frequent violence relative to battered women who do not kill. They know what sorts of danger are familiar and which are novel. They have had myriad opportunities to develop and hone their perceptions of their partner's violence. And, importantly, they can say what made the final episode of violence different from the others: they can name the features of the last battering that enabled them to know that this episode would result in life-threatening action by the abuser.

At p. 236, Dr. Blackman relates the role of expert testimony in cases where a battered woman kills her batterer while he is sleeping (or not actively posing a threat [to] her) and pleads self-defence:

> Perhaps the single most important idea conveyed by expert testimony in such a case pertains to the notion that a battered woman, because of her extensive experience with her abuser's violence, can detect changes or signs of novelty in the pattern of normal violence that connote increased danger. Support for this assertion must come from the woman herself, in her spontaneous, self-initiated description of the events that precede her action against the abuser. Only then can testimony from an expert offer scientific support for the idea that such a danger detection process can occur and can be expected to be as accurate as the "reasonable man" standard would imply.

Of course, Dr. Blackman points out, it is up to the jury to decide whether the distinction drawn between "typical" violence and the particular events the accused perceived as "life threatening" is compelling. According to the appellant's statement to police, Rust actually handed her a shotgun and warned her that if she did not kill him, he would kill her. I note in passing a remarkable observation made by Dr. Walker in her 1984 study, *The Battered Woman Syndrome*. Writing about the fifty battered women she interviewed who had killed their partners, she comments at p. 40:

> Most of the time the women killed the men with a gun; usually one of several that belonged to him. *Many of the men actually dared or demanded the woman use the gun on him first, or else he said he'd kill her with it.* (Emphasis added.)

Where evidence exists that an accused is in a battering relationship, expert testimony can assist the jury in determining whether the accused had a "reasonable" apprehension of death when she acted by explaining the heightened sensitivity of a battered woman to her partner's acts. Without such testimony I am skeptical that the average fact-finder would be capable of appreciating why her subjective fear may have been reasonable in the context of the relationship. After all, the hypothetical "reasonable man" observing only the final incident may have been unlikely to recognize the batterer's threat as potentially lethal. Using the case at bar as an example the "reasonable man" might have thought, as the majority of the Court of Appeal seemed to, that it was unlikely that Rust would make good on his threat to kill the appellant that night because they had guests staying overnight.

The issue is not, however, what an outsider would have reasonably perceived but what the accused reasonably perceived, given her situation and her experience.

Even accepting that a battered woman may be uniquely sensitized to danger from her batterer, it may yet be contended that the law ought to require her to wait until the knife is uplifted, the gun pointed or the fist clenched before her apprehension is deemed reasonable. This would allegedly reduce the risk that the woman is mistaken in her fear, although the law does not require her fear to be correct, only reasonable. In response to this contention, I need only point to the observation made by Huband J.A. that the evidence showed that when the appellant and Rust physically fought, the appellant "invariably got the worst of it." I do not think it is an unwarranted generalization to say that due to their size, strength, socialization and lack of training, women are typically no match for men in hand-to-hand combat. The requirement imposed in *Whynot* that a battered woman wait until the physical assault is "underway" before her apprehensions can be validated in law would, in the words of an American court, be tantamount to sentencing her to "murder by installment": *State v. Gallegos*, 719 P.2d 1268 at p. 1271 (1986) (N.M.). I share the view expressed by M.J. Willoughby in "Rendering Each Woman Her Due: Can a Battered Woman Claim Self-Defense When She Kills Her Sleeping Batterer" (1989), 38 *Kan. L. Rev.* 169 at p. 184 (1989), that "society gains nothing, except perhaps the additional risk that the battered woman will herself be killed, because she must wait until her abusive husband instigates another battering episode before she can justifiably act."

Lack of Alternatives to Self-help

Section 34(2) requires an accused who pleads self-defence to believe "on reasonable grounds" that it is not possible to otherwise preserve him or herself from death or grievous bodily harm. The obvious question is if the violence was so intolerable, why did the appellant not leave her abuser long ago? This question does not really go to whether she had an alternative to killing the deceased at the critical moment. Rather, it plays on the popular myth already referred to that a woman who says she was battered yet stayed with her batterer was either not as badly beaten as she claimed or else she liked it. Nevertheless, to the extent that her failure to leave the abusive relationship earlier may be used in support of the proposition that she was free to leave at the final moment, expert testimony can provide useful insights. Dr. Shane attempted to explain in his testimony how and why, in the case at bar, the appellant remained with Rust:

> She had stayed in this relationship, I think, because of the strange, almost unbelievable, but yet it happens, relationship that sometimes develops between people who develop this very disturbed, I think, very disturbed quality of a relationship. Trying to understand it, I think, isn't always easy and there's been a lot written about it recently, in the recent years, in psychiatric literature. But basically it involves two people who are involved in what appears to be an attachment which may have sexual or romantic or affectionate overtones.
>
> And the one individual, and it's usually the women in our society, but there have been occasions where it's been reversed, but what happens is the spouse who becomes battered, if you will, stays in the relationship probably because of a number of reasons.
>
> One is that the spouse gets beaten so badly — so badly — that he or she loses the motivation to react and becomes helpless and becomes powerless. And it's also been shown sometimes, you know, in — not that you can compare animals to human beings, but in laboratories, what you do if you shock an animal, after a while it can't respond to a threat of its life. It becomes just helpless and lies there in an amotivational state, if you will, where it feels there's no power and there's no energy to do anything.
>
> So in a sense it happens in human beings as well. It's almost like a concentration camp, if you will. You get paralyzed with fear.
>
> The other thing that happens often in these types of relationships with human beings is that the person who beats or assaults, who batters, often tries — he makes up and begs for forgiveness. And this individual, who basically has a very disturbed or damaged self-esteem, all of a sudden feels that he or she — we'll use the women in this case because it's so much more common — the spouse feels that she again can do the spouse a favour and it can make her feel needed and boost her self-esteem for a while and make her feel worthwhile and the spouse says he'll [*sic*] forgive her [*sic*] and whatnot.

Apparently, another manifestation of this victimization is a reluctance to disclose to others the fact or extent of the beatings. For example, the hospital records indicate that on each occasion the appellant attended the emergency department to be treated for various injuries she explained the cause of those injuries as accidental. Both in its address to the jury and in its written submissions before this court the Crown insisted that the appellant's injuries were as consistent with her explanations as with being battered and, therefore, in the words of Crown counsel at trial: "The myth is, in this particular case, that Miss Lavallee was a battered spouse." In his testimony Dr. Shane testified that the appellant admitted to him that she lied to hospital staff and others about the cause of her injuries. In Dr. Shane's opinion this was consistent with her over-all feeling of being trapped and helpless:

> ...she would never say that she'd been abused by the man with whom she was living and that usually happened because of this whole process. He would beg her. I mean she would tell me that on occasions he would beat her and then the police would be called by, I think, on one occasion a neighbour and he got down on his knees and he begged forgiveness and he loved her and he felt so terrible about it. And so this would be a typical scenario. Whenever she would go to the hospital, that he would attempt to, I think, attempt to have her forgive him and he would love her so much more.
>
> Again she would feel so needed and this would start the whole cycle over again.
>
> And he would also blackmail her on occasions. She had an abortion when she was in the early part of the relationship and he would blackmail her saying, "You know, I will tell your parents that you were a baby killer," et cetera.
>
> But basically the manner in which, I think, she would be prevented from telling the doctors or other people about the beatings was related to the fact that this whole process would repeat itself. He would want forgiveness and tell her he would love her and it would never happen again and she would feel grateful. She would feel a little loved. It would help her self-esteem again and she would feel a little safer for a while too. It would allow her to have a sense, a window of security for a period because she felt so trapped in this relationship.

The account given by Dr. Shane comports with that documented in the literature. Reference is often made to it as a condition of "learned helplessness," a phrase coined by Dr. Charles Seligman, the psychologist who first developed the theory by experimenting on animals in the manner described by Dr. Shane in his testimony. A related theory used to explain the failure of women to leave battering relationships is described by psychologist and lawyer, Charles Patrick Ewing, in his book, *Battered Women Who Kill*, (1987). Ewing describes a phenomenon labelled "traumatic bonding" that has been observed between hostages and captors, battered children and their parents, concentration camp prisoners and guards, and batterers and their spouses. According to the research cited by Ewing there are two features common to the social structure in each of these apparently diverse relationships. At pp. 19–20, he states:

> The first of these common features is an imbalance of power "wherein the maltreated person perceives himself or herself to be subjugated or dominated by the other." The less powerful person in the relationship — whether battered woman, hostage, abused child, cult follower, or prisoner — becomes extremely dependent upon, and may even come to identify with, the more powerful person. In many cases, the result of such dependency and identification is that the less powerful, subjugated persons become "more negative in their self-appraisal, more incapable of fending for themselves, and thus more in need of the high power person." As this "cycle of dependency and lowered self-esteem" is repeated over time, the less powerful person develops a "strong affective bond" to the more powerful person in the abusive relationship.
>
> The second feature common to the relationships between battered woman and batterer, hostage and captor, battered child and abusive parent, cult follower and leader, and prisoner and guard is the periodic nature of the abuse. In each relationship, the less powerful person is subjected to intermittent periods of abuse, which alternate with periods during which the more powerful, abusive person treats the less powerful person in a "more normal and acceptable fashion."
>
> ...
>
> Given the clear power differential between battered women and their batterers and the intermittent nature of physical and psychological abuse common to battering relationships, it seems fair to conclude ... that many battered women are psychologically unable to leave their batterers because they have developed a traumatic bond with them.

(Citations omitted.) This strong "affective bond" may be helpful in explaining not only why some battered women remain with their abusers but why they even profess to love them. Of course, as Dr. Ewing adds, environmental factors may also impair the woman's ability to leave — lack of job skills, the presence of children to care for, fear of retaliation by the man, etc., may each have a role to play in some cases.

This is not to say that in the course of a battering relationship a woman may never attempt to leave her partner or try to defend herself from assault. In *The Battered Woman Syndrome*, Dr. Walker notes at p. 30 that women may sometimes "react to men's violence against them by striking back, but their actions are generally ineffective at hurting or stopping the men. They may be effective in controlling the level of the man's violence against them." In the case at bar, Dr. Shane was aware that the appellant had pointed a gun at Rust in the past. In direct examination he stated:

> And what would also happen from time to time is that there would be moments where she would attempt to hit back to defend herself as she may take a weapon to defend herself in order to prevent herself from being harmed or even, when the underlying rage may accumulate, if you will, the feeling that she had to do something to him in order to survive, in order to defend herself.

The same psychological factors that account for a woman's inability to leave a battering relationship may also help to explain why she did not attempt to escape at the moment she perceived her life to be in danger. The following extract from Dr. Shane's testimony on direct examination elucidates this point:

> Q. Now, we understand from the evidence that on this night she went — I think you've already described it in your evidence — and hid in the closet?
>
> A. Yes.
>
> Q. Can you tell the jury why she, for instance, would stay in that house if she had this fear? Why wouldn't she so [*sic*] someplace else? Why would she have to hide in the closet in the same house?
>
> A. Well, I think this is a reflection of what I've been talking about, this ongoing psychological process, her own psychology and the relationship, that she felt trapped. There was no out for her, this learned helplessness, if you will, the fact that she felt paralyzed, she felt tyrannized. She felt, although there were obviously no steel fences around, keeping her in, there were steel fences in her mind which created for her an incredible barrier psychologically that prevented her from moving out. Although she had attempted on occasion, she came back in a magnetic sort of a way. And she felt also that she couldn't expect anything more. Not only this learned helplessness about being beaten, beaten, where her motivation is taken away, but her whole sense of herself. She felt this victim mentality, this concentration camp mentality if you will, where she could not see herself be in any other situation except being tyrannized, punished and crucified physically and psychologically.

I emphasize at this juncture that it is not for the jury to pass judgment on the fact that an accused battered woman stayed in the relationship. Still less is it entitled to conclude that she forfeited her right to self-defence for having done so. I would also point out that traditional self-defence doctrine does not require a person to retreat from her home instead of defending herself: *R. v. Antley*, [1964] 2 C.C.C. 142, [1964] 1 O.R. 545, 42 C.R. 384 (C.A.). A man's home may be his castle but it is also the woman's home even if it seems to her more like a prison in the circumstances.

If, after hearing the evidence (including the expert testimony), the jury is satisfied that the accused had a reasonable apprehension of death or grievous bodily harm and felt incapable of escape, it must ask itself what the "reasonable person" would do in such a situation. The situation of the battered woman as described by Dr. Shane strikes me as somewhat analogous to that of a hostage. If the captor tells her that he will kill her in three days' time, is it potentially reasonable for her to seize an opportunity presented on the first day to kill the captor or must she wait until he makes the attempt on the third day? I think the question the jury must ask itself is whether, given the history, circumstances and perceptions of the appellant, her belief that she could not preserve herself from being killed by Rust that night except by killing him first was reasonable. To the extent that expert evidence can assist the jury in making that determination, I would find such testimony to be both relevant and necessary.

In light of the foregoing discussion I would summarize as follows the principles upon which expert testimony is properly admitted in cases such as this:

1. Expert testimony is admissible to assist the fact-finder in drawing inferences in areas where the expert has relevant knowledge or experience beyond that of the lay person.
2. It is difficult for the lay person to comprehend the battered-wife syndrome. It is commonly thought that battered women are not really beaten as badly as they claim; otherwise they would have left the relationship. Alternatively, some believe that women enjoy being beaten, that they have a masochistic strain in them. Each of these stereotypes may adversely affect consideration of a battered woman's claim to have acted in self-defence in killing her mate.

3. Expert evidence can assist the jury in dispelling these myths.
4. Expert testimony relating to the ability of an accused to perceive danger from her mate may go to the issue of whether she "reasonably apprehended" death or grievous bodily harm on a particular occasion.
5. Expert testimony pertaining to why an accused remained in the battering relationship may be relevant in assessing the nature and extent of the alleged abuse.
6. By providing an explanation as to why an accused did not flee when she perceived her life to be in danger, expert testimony may also assist the jury in assessing the reasonableness of her belief that killing her batterer was the only way to save her own life.

Quite apart from Dr. Shane's testimony there was ample evidence on which the trial judge could conclude that the appellant was battered repeatedly and brutally by Kevin Rust over the course of their relationship. The fact that she may have exhibited aggressive behaviour on occasion or tried (unsuccessfully) to leave does not detract from a finding of systematic and relentless abuse. In my view, the trial judge did not err in admitting Dr. Shane's expert testimony in order to assist the jury in determining whether the appellant had a reasonable apprehension of death or grievous bodily harm and believed on reasonable grounds that she had no alternative but to shoot Kevin Rust on the night in question.

Obviously the fact that the appellant was a battered woman does not entitle her to an acquittal. Battered women may well kill their partners other than in self-defence. The focus is not on who the woman is, but on what she did. In "The Meaning of Equality for Battered Women Who Kill Men in Self-Defense," 8 Harv. Women's L.J. 121 at p. 149 (1985), Phyllis Crocker makes the point succinctly:

> The issue in a self-defence trial is not whether the defendant is a battered woman, but whether she justifiably killed her husband. The defendant introduces testimony to offer the jury an explanation of reasonableness that is an alternative to the prosecution's stereotypic explanations. It is not intended to earn her the status of a battered woman, as if that would make her not guilty.

The trial judge, to his credit, articulated the same principle when introducing Dr. Shane's testimony in the course of his instructions to the jury. After referring to "the so-called battered-spouse syndrome," he cautions:

> Let me say at the outset that I think it is better that we try not to attach labels to this. It doesn't matter what we call it. What is important is the evidence itself and how it impacts on the critical areas of the intent of the accused and the issue of self-defence.

Ultimately, it is up to the jury to decide whether, in fact, the accused's perceptions and actions were reasonable. Expert evidence does not and cannot usurp that function of the jury. The jury is not compelled to accept the opinions proffered by the expert about the effects of battering on the mental state of the victims generally or on the mental state of the accused in particular. But fairness and the integrity of the trial process demand that the jury have the opportunity to hear them.

Adequacy of the Trial Judge's Charge to the Jury

The second issue raised in this case is the adequacy of the trial judge's charge to the jury with respect to the expert evidence furnished by Dr. Shane. It appears that Dr. Shane relied on various sources in formulating his opinion — his series of interviews with the appellant, an interview with her mother, a police report of the incident (including information regarding her statement to the police), and hospital records documenting eight of her visits to emergency departments between 1983 and 1986. Neither the appellant nor her mother testified at trial. The contents of their statements to Dr. Shane were hearsay.

In *Abbey*, *supra*, this Court addressed the bases upon which expert evidence that relies on hearsay is admissible. The accused in that case was charged with importing cocaine and his defence was insanity. The accused did not testify. A psychiatrist gave his opinion as to the sanity of the accused and, in the course of giving the basis for his conclusions, referred to incidents and hallucinations related to him by the accused for which there was no admissible evidence. The Crown submitted before this court that the trial judge "accepted and treated as factual much of this hearsay evidence" related to the psychiatrist. Dickson J. found that the point was "well taken." This was the preliminary finding on which the case was based and I think it is fair to say that the trial judge in the case at bar clearly did not make the same mistake as did the trial judge in *Abbey*. At pp. 411–2 of his judgment Dickson J. articulated the hazards inherent in admitting expert testimony based on hearsay:

> The danger, of course, in admitting such testimony is the ever present possibility, here exemplified, that the judge or jury, without more, will accept the evidence as going to the truth of the facts stated in it. The danger is real and lies at the heart of this case. Once such testimony is admitted, a careful charge to the jury by the judge or direction to himself is essential. The problem, however, as pointed out by Fauteux J. in *Wilband* resides not in the admissibility of the testimony but rather the weight to be accorded to the opinion. Although admissible in the context of his opinion, to the extent that it is second-hand his testimony is not proof of the facts stated.
>
> ...
>
> It was appropriate for the doctors to state the basis for their opinions and in the course of doing so, to refer to what they were told not only by Abbey but by others, but it was error for the judge to accept as having been proved the facts upon which the doctors had relied in forming their opinions. While it is not questioned that medical experts are entitled to take into consideration all possible information in forming their opinions, this in no way removes from the party tendering such evidence the obligation of establishing, through properly admissible evidence, the factual basis on which such opinions are based. Before any weight can be given to an expert's opinion, the facts upon which the opinion is based must be found to exist.

For present purposes I think the ratio of *Abbey* can be distilled into the following propositions:

1. An expert opinion is admissible if relevant, even if it is based on second-hand evidence.
2. This second hand evidence (hearsay) is admissible to show the information on which the expert opinion is based, not as evidence going to the existence of the facts on which the opinion is based.
3. Where the psychiatric evidence is comprised of hearsay evidence, the problem is the weight to be attributed to the opinion.
4. Before any weight can be given to an expert's opinion, the facts upon which the opinion is based must be found to exist.

In the case at bar the trial judge was clearly of the view that Dr. Shane's evidence was relevant. He would not have admitted it otherwise. As I stated above, in light of the evidence of the battering relationship which subsisted between the appellant and the deceased, the trial judge was correct in so doing.

With respect to the second point, the trial judge warned the jury generally that they could not "decide the case on the basis of things the witnesses did not see or hear," which would seem to include those matters which Dr. Shane neither saw nor heard. He then gave the marijuana smoking and the confirmatory evidence of the appellant's mother as two sources of information which were not evidence in the case. In my opinion, it would have been preferable if the trial judge had described the interview with the appellant as a source of inadmissible evidence, the marijuana smoking being an example of inadmissible evidence from that source. Nevertheless, I think the trial judge makes his meaning clear to the jury in the subsequent passage: "In terms of the matters considered by Dr. Shane he is left, therefore, with the deceased's [*sic* — he means accused's] statement, some supplementary information from the police report and his interpretation of the hospital records." The trial judge thus eliminates the interview with the appellant and his conversation with her mother as sources of admissible evidence. Elsewhere he reinforces the rule that the jury can only consider the admissible evidence. He refers to the hospital visits made by the appellant:

> Another evidentiary caution is necessary here. Mr. Brodsky, in his remarks, said, as he did in calling some of the evidence respecting hospital attendances that this is only a representative sample. He ought not to have said that. It is not evidence and must be completely disregarded by you. The only evidence before you are the eight attendances that you heard about and nothing else — eight attendances and nothing else.

The trial judge's instructions regarding the weight attributable to Dr. Shane's opinion also emphasize his distinction between admissible evidence and hearsay:

> *If the premises upon which the information is substantially based has not been proven in evidence, it is up to you to conclude that it is not safe to attach a great deal of weight to the opinion. An opinion of an expert depends, to a large extent, on the validity of the facts assumed by the evidence of the expert.*
>
> If there are some errors and the factual assumptions aren't too important to the eventual opinion, that's one thing. *If there are errors or matters not in evidence and those matters are substantial, in your view, in terms of the impact on the expert's opinion, then you will want to look at the value and weight of that expert's opinion very carefully.* It depends on how important you think the matters were that Dr. Shane relied on that are not in evidence. (Emphasis added.)

I agree with Huband J.A. that these instructions with respect to weight conform to this court's judgment in *Abbey.* The only complaint can be with the trial judge's attempt to distinguish admissible from inadmissible evidence. The trial judge was certainly not as clear as he might have been but I have no hesitation in finding that a retrial is not warranted on this account.

Given that Dr. Shane relied extensively on his interview with the appellant, the trial judge drew particular attention to the additional element of credibility that could affect the quality of Dr. Shane's opinion: "It is the position of the Crown that Dr. Shane's opinion stands or falls on the veracity of Lyn Lavallee because he relied so heavily and extensively on what she told him and the evidence contained in the statement, Exhibit 16. That's for you to decide." Later in the charge, he elaborates:

> Undoubtably [*sic*] she was a very important source, if not the major source, of his information. Dr. Shane agreed that if what she told him was erroneous, he would have to reassess his position.
>
> On cross-examination he reiterated that in his opinion her action was spontaneous to the moment to try to defend herself. The straw that broke the camel's back was the threat, "When the others leave you're going to get it," even though similar statements had been made to her on other occasions. According to what she told him, the accused felt compelled to shoot.
>
> Based on the information he had in the interview, it was his opinion that the acts of the accused were impulsive and not premeditated. He disagreed with the Crown's suggestion that Lyn Lavallee took the opportunity when it presented itself.
>
> He conceded that patients had, on occasion, lied and misled him in the past.

The fourth proposition I have extracted from *Abbey* is that there must be admissible evidence to support the facts on which the expert relies before any weight can be attributed to the opinion. The majority of the Manitoba Court of Appeal appears to interpret this as a requirement that each and every fact relied upon by the expert must be independently proven and admitted into evidence before the entire opinion can be given any weight.

Dr. Shane referred in his testimony to various facts for which there was no admissible evidence. The information was elicited from his interviews with the appellant. It included the smoking of marijuana prior to the killing, the deterioration of the intimate relationship between the appellant and Rust, past episodes of physical and psychological abuse followed by intervals of contrition, the apparent denial of homicidal fantasies on the appellant's part, and her remorse after killing Rust.

If the majority of the Court of Appeal is suggesting that each of these specific facts must be proven in evidence before any weight could be given to Dr. Shane's opinion about the accused's mental state, I must respectfully disagree. *Abbey* does not, in my view, provide any authority for that proposition. The court's conclusion in that case was that the trial judge erred in treating as proven the facts upon which the psychiatrist relied in formulating his opinion. The solution was an appropriate charge to the jury, not an effective withdrawal of the evidence. In my view, as long as there is some admissible evidence to establish the foundation for the expert's opinion, the trial judge cannot subsequently instruct the jury to completely ignore the testimony. The judge must, of course, warn the jury that the more the expert relies on facts not proved in evidence the less weight the jury may attribute to the opinion.

On my reading of the record Dr. Shane had before him admissible evidence about the nature of the relationship between the appellant and Rust in the form of the appellant's statement to the police and the hospital records. In addition, there was substantial corroborative evidence provided at trial by Ezako, the emergency-room doctor who testified to doubting the appellant's explanation of her injuries. There was also the evidence of the witnesses on the night of the shooting who testified to the appellant's frightened appearance, tone of voice, and conduct in dealing with Rust. The evidence pointed to the image of a woman who was brutally abused, who lied about the cause of her injuries, and who was incapable of leaving her abuser. As Huband J.A. comments in dissent, if the trial judge erred at all, he was probably remiss in not mentioning the corroborative evidence of Ezako as buttressing the evidentiary foundation on which Dr. Shane premised his opinion.

The majority of the Court of Appeal attached particular significance to the absence of admissible evidence on the question whether the appellant had homicidal fantasies about Rust. As I read the evidence the appellant's alleged denial of homicidal fantasies appeared to add little to Dr. Shane's over-all opinion about her mental state on the night in question. Moreover, the evidence given by Ezako about her being an aggressor in the past and even pointing a gun at Rust were far more incriminating in terms of evincing a prior intent to kill than the presence or absence of homicidal fantasies. The gun pointing incidents were explained by Dr. Shane as not inconsistent with her victimized condition and not necessarily indicative of premeditation. Clearly, Dr. Shane's explanation was something the jury could evaluate in the context of all the evidence.

Where the factual basis of an expert's opinion is a mélange of admissible and inadmissible evidence the duty of the trial judge is to caution the jury that the weight attributable to the expert testimony is directly related to the amount and quality of admissible evidence on which it relies. The judge openly acknowledged to counsel the inherent difficulty in discharging such a duty in the case at bar. In my view, the trial judge performed his task adequately in this regard. A new trial is not warranted on the basis of the trial judge's charge to the jury.

I would accordingly allow the appeal, set aside the order of the Court of Appeal, and restore the acquittal.

[L'Heureux-Dubé, Gonthier, and MacLachlin JJ. concurred; Sopinka J. dissented in part, but concurred in the result.]

Appeal allowed; acquittal restored.

■

Violence against Women: Feminist Activism and Engagement with Law (Continued)[†]

In *Lavallee*, the Supreme Court of Canada recognized the prevalence and gravity of wife battering, the history of the way wife assault has been viewed and the way law has "historically sanctioned the abuse of women within marriage as an aspect of the husband's ownership of this wife and his 'right' to chastise her" (at 872). Madame Justice Wilson, writing for the majority, considered the effects of battering on the victim and its impact on the defence of self-defence, interpreted the defence of self-defence as necessarily gendered and pointed out that what passes for "knowledge" about the battering relationship is "subject to a large group of myths and stereotypes." Thus, according to her, "popular mythology" holds (at 873):

> Either she was not as badly beaten as she claims or she would have left the man long ago. Or, if she was battered that severely, she must have stayed out of some masochistic enjoyment of it.

Thus, Madame Justice Wilson held that expert evidence about Battered Wife Syndrome (BWS) was admissible, in the case of battered women, to rebut what she identified as "myths," these "commonsense" misapprehensions (at 873):

> Expert evidence on the psychological effect of battering on wives and common law partners must, it seems to me, be both relevant and necessary in the context of the present case. How can the mental state of the appellant be appreciated without it? The average member of the public (or of the jury) can be forgiven for asking: Why would a woman put up with this kind of treatment? Why should she continue to live with such a man? How could she love a partner who beat her to the point of requiring hospitalization? We would expect the woman to pack her bags and go. Where is her self-respect? Why does she not cut loose and make a new life for herself? Such is the reaction of the average person confronted with the so-called "battered wife syndrome." We need help to understand it and help is available from trained professionals.

As Madame Justice Wilson set out, "...subsection 34(2)(a) does not actually stipulate that the accused apprehend *imminent* danger when he or she acts" (at 877). However, courts have read in a requirement of imminence and have narrowly restricted the availability of the defence to situations that conjure up "the image of 'an uplifted knife' or a pointed gun" (at 877). Such a limitation does not make sense in the experience of battered women. These assumptions influenced the Nova Scotia Court of Appeal to deny Jane Hurshman (Whynot) Stafford the possibility of a defence under s. 37 of the *Code* (preventing assault). As Madame Justice Wilson pointed out (at 877):

† Jennie Abell, "Violence against Women: Feminist Activism and Engagement with Law". (An earlier version of paper was presented at "La Violence Faite aux Femmes" session of Inter-American Law Professors Forum, San Jose, Costa Rica, November 1991.)

> The implication of the Court's reasoning is that it is inherently unreasonable to apprehend death or grievous bodily harm unless and until the physical assault is actually in progress, at which point the victim can presumably gauge the requisite amount of force needed to repel the attack and act accordingly. In my view, expert testimony can cast doubt on these assumptions as they are applied in the context of a battered wife's efforts to repel an assault.

In referring to the history of male right, Madame Justice Wilson, referred to the oft-cited example of "the centuries old law that a man is entitled to beat his wife with a stick 'no thicker than his thumb' " (at 872).

R. v. Lavallee represents a landmark decision and an important victory in the struggle of the women's movement to establish the seriousness and prevalence of wife battering. Madame Justice Wilson's judgment provides important recognition of the pervasiveness of assumptions about women and about battering and specifically the way those "myths" shape the understanding and response of judges and juries to battered women.

However, although the decision expressly challenges certain assumptions about battering and battered women, and highlights the seriousness of the problem, there are a number of problematic aspects to the decision and to the reliance on Battered Wife Syndrome: the ideological assumptions underlying the defence, the syndromization and psychiatrization of women's experience, the need for expert witnesses to shore up women's stories and bolster women's credibility, the focus on the individual woman's psychological condition rather than on the context of male violence, and the potential disparity in the availability of the defence on the basis of culture/race and class. Some of these are not unique to self-defence, and are related to the ideological premises of criminal law (the individualization, the pathologization and the victimization).

The decision also reflects and reinforces other assumptions about women, about family, and about violence, assumptions that have been and continue to be problematic for women. The case thus has implications for other aspects of women's lives, such as family law and custody decisions. Thus, the scope of the decision, and the assumptions it challenges as well as those it leaves unchallenged, go beyond the limits of self-defence.

The recognition of the currency of these myths is extremely important because of the way these myths, and the assumptions underlying them, have shaped women's treatment as both victims and accused in various types of cases. For example, the assumption that a woman somehow enjoys or consents to the beatings has been used to deny her crime compensation, on the basis that she contributed to her own injuries or to the injuries of her child, simply because her husband or boyfriend was known to her to be violent. (See *Re A.L. (Sask. Crimes Compensation Board)* and *L.(A.) v. Saskatchewan (Crimes Compensation Board)*, [1992] 6 W.W.R. 577 (Sask. C.A.), aff'g [1991] 5 W.W.R. 315 (Sask. Q.B.))

These assumptions reappear frequently in remarks by judges on sentencing wife batterers as discussed in Abell & Sheehy, *Cases, Context, Critique*, **Sentencing**. The judges' comments, in those cases, illustrate both the assumptions about wife battering specifically and the assumption about family. Sentencing cases are important because they represent a majority of the cases dealing with wife battering. Judges have been quick to latch on to what they perceive as a woman's wish to stay as absolving the batterer. Similarly, judges do not problematize women's wishes to preserve the relationship, and continue to accept them readily as an excuse to absolve the criminal justice system of any role.

Syndromization of Women

One problematic aspect of *Lavallee* is the rigidification of the description of what amounts to battering, Battered Wife Syndrome and the "cycle of abuse." Lenore Walker's theory has been used as a formula to separate "real" battered women from supposedly less serious cases. For example, refer to the defence factum in *R. v. Inwood* (1989), 32 O.A.C. 287, reproduced in Abell & Sheehy, *Cases, Context, Critique*, **Sentencing**.

Feminists have continued to argue against the syndromization of women's experience and in favour of an expanded and reconceptualized defence of self-defence.

Why Doesn't She Leave?

Another aspect of the *Lavallee* decision which demands further analysis is the implicit assumption that if the woman involved with a violent man could overcome her individual condition of either "learned helplessness" or could find the financial security to support her decision, all would be well. This focuses on the woman rather than on the man's violence. Cases of self-defence and battering have continued to focus on the psychological and emotional power of the batterer over the victim; the women have been cast as powerless victims and they have received less sympathy where they have failed to conform to that image. That focus, however, individualizes the problem of wife battering rather than understanding it in terms of women's experience and the ideological and material reality of the family and the state. It's not simply that this context 'imprisons' women in the family, but that the effect of ideologies is contradictory. The distortion of this focus is most starkly revealed by the fact that women are at greater risk precisely when they do leave.

When women leave, separate, or divorce their abusers and batterers, a significant number report increased abuse. Their risk of serious injury or death will escalate in intensity as the man tries to reassert control through intensified violence. This phenomenon has been documented in Canada and elsewhere. For example, drawing on the statistics for New South Wales, Australia, Alison Wallace reveals that:

> ... [A] substantial number of men killed estranged wives. More than one in three (35%) of the men killed wives from whom they were separated: 47 killed legal wives from whom they were separated, 24 men killed ex-de-factos, and 4 men killed wives from whom they were divorced.... Moreover, whilst 75 wives were killed while actually separated from their husband, a further 23 women were killed while in the process of leaving their spouse (for example, while instituting divorce proceedings). Thus, altogether, in very nearly half (46%) of the wife killings, the woman had either left or was in the process of leaving her husband when she was killed ... [I]n the majority of cases it appeared that it was the woman who had taken the initiative and terminated the relationship. In the majority of these wife homicides, it was the consequences of separation that prompted the killing.

(Alison Wallace *Homicide: The Social Reality* (Sydney: New South Wales Bureau of Crime Statistics and Research, 1986), at 98–99.)

In *Battered But Not Beaten* (Ottawa: Canadian Advisory Council on the Status of Women, 1987) at 44, Linda MacLeod reports one study by Michael Smith which found that of 315 Toronto women surveyed, 18.1 per cent were experiencing abuse, but that of these, 42.6 per cent were separated or divorced, and another study in London, Ontario, by the Battered Women's Advocacy Clinic that found that two-thirds of those who were divorced for between 6 and 10 years were still being assaulted by their former partners.

Linda Gordon found in her study, *Heroes of Their Own Lives: The Politics and History of Family Violence* (New York: Viking, 1988) at 271, that threats to leave a relationship "may have been the most dangerous acts of all for women in battering relationships: much of the marital violence ... was aimed at forcing a wife to remain." She cites contemporary work corroborating this point, including the historical work of Judith Allen, "The State and Domestic Violence" (manuscript) for the point that in Australia "desertion" precipitated wife murder in 40 per cent of the cases in the 1880s, in 56 per cent of the cases in 1900–1909, 77 per cent of the cases in the 1920s, and in 81 per cent of the cases in the 1930s.

A Statistics Canada study confirmed the higher risk of violence facing women who have divorced or separated: CP, "Violence follows separated women, survey finds" *The [Toronto] Globe and Mail* (31 January 1995) A2.

As Maria Crawford and Rosemary Gartner found, in their study *Woman Killing: Intimate Femicide in Ontario, 1974 to 1990* (Women We Honour Action Committee, 1992):

> ...a woman separated from her spouse was five times more likely to be killed by her partner than women who were not. Rage over separation appeared to motivate most killers. If the woman was between 30 and 44 years old she was more likely to be murdered by her spouse than older or younger women. Women born outside Canada were no more or less likely to be killed than women born in Canada, but aboriginal women were at least six times more likely to be victims than non-aboriginals. Employed and unemployed women were slain in roughly equal numbers.

(Reported in Vivian Smith, "Vivian Smith examines a report that contains some alarming facts on the murder of women by their spouses" *The [Toronto] Globe and Mail* (22 October 1992) A20.)

While these cases don't directly relate to self-defence, the point is that the discussion of violence against women as outlined in *Lavallee* is not broad enough to encompass these realities and therefore leaves them unproblematized and unexamined.

Specificity

Finally, any reflection on specificity is absent in *Lavallee*. In the context of racism and ethnocentrism, it is reasonable to expect that the defence may be differently available to particular groups of women accused. As discussed in Abell & Sheehy, *Cases, Context, Critique*, **Prisons**, Aboriginal women and Black women are over-represented at every stage of the criminal justice system and, clearly, over-incarcerated. Within a context of racism, which women, for example, will be characterized as "helpless" or "passive"? Which men will be characterized as "violent"? The availability of the defence will also be dependent on access to counsel and the economic resources for expert witnesses. For a discussion of some of these issues, see, Joanne St. Lewis and Sheila Galloway, "Reforming the Defence of Provocation" at 24).

C. BATTERED WOMEN'S SYNDROME AND THE CASES SINCE *LAVALLEE*

There is a large body of literature addressing Battered Women's Syndrome and self-defence in the context of abusive relationships. For a further discussion of wife battering and feminist engagement with law, see Jennie Abell, *Bringing It All Back Home: Feminist Struggle, Feminist Theory and Feminist Engagement with Law, the Case of Wife Battering* (Osgoode Hall Law School, York University: Ll.M. thesis, 1991). As many feminist scholars have argued, the defence of self-defence needs to be reconceptualized. For a survey of the cases since *Lavallee* and a discussion of the importance of attending to issues of sexism and racism in reforming the law of self-defence, see: Elizabeth Sheehy, *What Would a Women's Law of Self-Defence Look Like?* (Ottawa: Status of Women Canada, 1995). For strategies and analysis from other jurisdictions, see, for example: Julie Stubbs & Julia Tolmie, "Battered Woman Syndrome in Australia: A challenge to gender bias in the law?" in Julia Stubbs, ed., *Women, Male Violence and the Law* (Sydney: Institute of Criminology, 1994) 192. For a thoughtful examination of the U.S. experience, see: Elizabeth Schneider, *Battered Women and Feminist Lawmaking* (New Haven: Yale University Press, 2000).

Consider what progressive uses for a case such as *Lavallee* there might be. Since the *Lavallee* decision, Battered Women's Syndrome (BWS) evidence has been used to defend against homicide and other charges. However, there have been very few acquittals on the basis of BWS. Some examples of cases in which BWS and a context of abuse and violence were argued follow. For a recent review of a range of cases in which BWS was raised by the defence, and a critique of the interpretations arising from *Lavallee* (for example, the syndromization, the removal of agency from the women, the stereotyping), see Martha Shaffer, "The Battered Woman Syndrome Revisited: Some Complicating Thoughts Five Years After *R. v. Lavallee*" (1997) 47 U.T.L.J. 1.

For a case in which the evidence resulted in an acquittal on murder and manslaughter, see *R. v. Kay* (1994), (Sask. Q.B.) [unreported], discussed in "Battered-woman's-syndrome defence advanced by Regina woman's acquittal" *The [Saskatoon] Star-Phoenix* (22 June 1994) C9. In *R. v. Kondejewski* (1998), (Man. Q.B.) [unreported], the accused battered woman successfully established a defence of self-defence in the context of a long history of extreme abuse (including choking, repeated acts of violence, sexual assaults and the production of pornography, threats against her, her children and her mother, constant verbal abuse, and attempts to force her to kill herself so as to collect the insurance). However, the case highlights the difficulties facing a complainant who seeks to raise self-defence (for example, establishing the evidentiary basis by forcing her children to testify). As Elizabeth Sheehy argues, the case is also problematic in terms of the Crown's decision to lay charges (initially of first degree murder) and the distortion of defences available to battered women in terms of the overlay between self-defence and defence of others (in this case, her children): "Battered Women and Mandatory Minimum Sentences" (2001) 39 Osgoode Hall L.J. 529.

In *R. v. Pétel*, [1994] 1 S.C.R. 3, the majority held that in considering the reasonable apprehension of a risk of death or bodily harm and the question of the force required, the "atmosphere of terror" and threats were relevant to the state of mind of the accused. Following *Lavallee*, which overruled *R. v. Whynot (Stafford)* (1983), 61 N.S.R. (2d) 33 (C.A.), the apprehended danger need not be imminent. A new trial was ordered on the basis of the trial judge's misdirection as to imminence, rather than on the basis of BWS.

In *R. v. Malott* (1996), 94 O.A.C. 31 (C.A.), discussed above, under **Provocation**, the accused was convicted of second degree murder of her estranged common-law husband and attempted murder of her husband's girlfriend. According to expert evidence, the accused had been physically, sexually, and emotionally abused for 20 years and suffered from "battered women's syndrome". She had been separated from her husband for four weeks but saw him daily. Prior to the killing, he had driven her to a medical clinic to pick up prescription drugs, which he required for his illegal drug trade. She was very afraid of him, so she obtained one of his guns and carried it with her in her purse. She knew that he always had a gun or a knife with him, and felt that the police would be of no assistance to her. In the past, they had advised her husband of her complaints because of his work as a drug informer. As a result, his violence had escalated. The accused and her husband had argued en route to the clinic, and he had threatened and choked her. She testified that when she found the clinic locked, she was afraid of what he would do to her because she had been unable to obtain the drugs he wanted. When he opened the car door and started to get out in what she felt was a menacing way, she shot him. She subsequently reloaded the gun and took a taxi to his girlfriend's place, where she shot her.

The majority of the Court of Appeal upheld the trial judge's charge on self-defence and concluded that he did not err in failing to leave the defence of provocation to the jury. However, Justice Abella's dissent emphasized the importance of relating the uncontradicted expert testimony on "battered women's syndrome" by Dr. Peter Jaffe, and the long history of severe abuse and violence to the circumstances of the offence [at 53–57]:

> Nowhere in this portion of his charge does he tell the jury which of the facts described by Margaret Malott could, if believed, constitute unlawful assault. Nor does he explain how her having been abused for 20 years by Paul Malott could have affected the reasonableness of her perception of the extent to which she was in danger from him.

She then went on to discuss *Lavallee* and (at 54) "the singularity of a battered woman's perceptions":

> Most apposite to this appeal, Justice Wilson, at p. 125, condensed her analysis into the following inquiry:
>
> > ... I think the question the jury must ask itself is whether, given the history, circumstances and perceptions of the appellant, her belief that she could not preserve herself from being killed ... except by killing him first was reasonable.
>
> She believed Paul Malott was all knowing and all powerful. She had no trust in the police or anyone else to help her. She was totally dependent on him and desperate to keep his love.... During the ride to the medical centre she said that he threatened her and she felt increasingly unsafe.
>
> ...
>
> Having set out some of these symptoms of her relationship ... the trial judge was obliged, in my view, to review the expert evidence relating to Margaret Malott's perceptions. Yet in his review of the expert evidence in connection with his charge on self-defence, the trial judge omits most of Dr. Jaffe's evidence, much of which was directly relevant to the key defence issue — the reasonableness of the appellant's perceptions.

She concluded that the trial judge's failure to sufficiently review the relevant evidence and relate it to the issues was an error of law. Yet she concluded that, in the circumstances, self-defence was not available as a defence. A further appeal to the Supreme Court was dismissed: *R. v. Malott*, [1998] 1 S.C.R. 123. The Court held that the charge as a whole had fairly related the expert evidence to the elements of self-defence, although it may have been desirable for the trial judge to provide more detail in the instruction to the jury. In a separate, concurring judgment Justices L'Heureux-Dubé and McLachlin JJ. noted that the principles emanating from *Lavallee* are relevant to other situations where the reasonableness of a battered woman's actions or perceptions is at issue, and they emphasized that the modification here is to the objective test itself, eschewing the proposition that *Lavallee* simply adds a "subjective" component to the objective test. They cautioned against adherence to rigid stereotypes about "battered women" as uniformly passive or dependent, and suggested a re-focusing of the inquiry for self-defence to other elements of a woman's social context — as opposed to her "personal inadequacies" or "syndrome" — such as her "need to protect her children from abuse, a fear of losing custody of her children, pressures to keep the family together, weaknesses of social and financial support for battered women, and no guarantee that the violence would cease simply because she left." Moreover, "[t]o fully accord with the spirit of *Lavallee*, where the reasonableness of a battered woman's belief is at issue in a criminal case, a judge and jury should be made to appreciate that a battered woman's experiences are both individualized, based on her own history and relationships, as well as shared with other women, within a context of a society and a legal system which has historically undervalued women's experiences." Children who have been battered may also be able to use this type of evidence to support self-defence or defence of others.

Battered Women's Syndrome (BWS) evidence has also been introduced in response to other charges where self-defence is not involved. In *R. v. Lalonde* (1995), 22 O.R. (3d) 275 (Ct. J. (Gen. Div.)), a woman accused of defrauding the welfare system (by denying that her spouse lived with her) of over $100,000 was acquitted of fraud on the basis of the vulnerability and fear she experienced because of her spouse, and the fact that there was no reasonable alternative to provide food and necessaries for her five young children: see **Necessity**, below. For a comment on the case, see: Sheila Noonan, "Lalonde: Evaluating the Relevance of BWS Evidence" (1995) 37 C.R. (4th) 110. In *R. v. Eagles*, [1991] Y.J. No. 147 (Terr. Ct.) (QL), the accused was found not guilty of uttering a threat to cause death on the basis of BWS. In another case, the Crown Attorney dropped second-degree murder charges against Roxanne Murray for her killing of Doug "Juicer" Murray after the RCMP investigation revealed a string of charges and a long history of extreme violence against the accused and others: Ken MacQueen, "Justifiable Homicide" *The Ottawa Citizen* (3 May 1991) A1.

Finally, where evidence of battering and abuse is not held to entitle the accused to a defence, it may, nonetheless, be relevant to sentencing for a manslaughter conviction. This seems to be the most frequent way in which the courts consider BWS. See *R. v. Raymond*, [1993] N.W.T.J. No. 86 (Terr. Ct.) (QL); *R. v. Tran*, [1991] O.J. No. 2052 (Ct. J. (Gen. Div.)) (QL). Disturbingly, evidence of battering may be used more frequently to negotiate plea bargains for manslaughter rather than to frame successful arguments of self-defence: Judge Lynn Ratushny, *Self-Defence Review*, *infra*.

D. CLEMENCY: REVIEWING THE PAST

In the United States, precedent-setting cases similar to *Lavallee* have resulted in reviews of the cases of women serving sentences for killing their partners, with the result that some of these women have been released: "Clemency granted to 25 women convicted for assault or murder" *The New York Times* (22 December 1990) 1. Alison Madden describes some U.S. cases in which women have been pardoned or had their sentences commuted: Alison Madden, "Clemency for Battered Women who Kill their Abusers: Finding a Just Forum" (1993) 4 Hasting's Women's L.J. 1 at footnote 14. For some insight into the conditions under which women have killed abusive and violent partners, see the film *When Women Kill* (National Film Board: Montréal, 1994).

Feminists in Canada lobbied for almost four years for a review of the cases of women imprisoned for defending themselves against abusive partners. See Stephen Bindman, "Battered Women's Syndrome: Inmates' freedom hinges on review, prior to 1990, history of abuse not considered" *The Ottawa Citizen* (14 July 1995) A3; Sheila Noonan, "Strategies of Survival: Moving Beyond the Battered Woman Syndrome" in Ellen Adelberg & Claudia Currie, eds., *In Conflict with the Law: Women and the Canadian Justice System* (Vancouver: Press Gang Publishers, 1993) 247. In October 1995, Solicitor General Herb Gray and Minister of Justice Allan Rock appointed Judge Lynn Ratushny to undertake a review of murder cases involving women convicted of killing their abusive partners, spouses, or guardians.

Terms of Reference†

In recent years, there have been developments in our understanding of the law of self-defence as it relates to battered women who have been involved in abusive relationships. There are concerns that women convicted of homicide in these circumstances may not have received the benefit of the defence of self-defence when it may have been available to them.

We also now have an increased understanding of abusive relationships and their impact upon those who have been battered, and how this might support the use of the defence. Questions have also been raised about the circumstances under which these types of offences occurred and about whether our criminal law, sentencing processes and sentencing tools are adequate to deal with these circumstances.

Accordingly, the Honourable Lynn Ratushny, a judge of the Ontario Court of Justice (Provincial Division) is appointed:

i) to review the cases of women under sentence in federal and provincial institutions who apply for a remedy and who are serving a sentence for homicide in circumstances in which the killing allegedly took place to prevent the deceased from inflicting serious bodily harm or death;

ii) to make recommendations in appropriate cases to the Government of Canada for individual women whose circumstances merit consideration for the granting of the royal prerogative of mercy;

iii) to clarify the availability and the scope of the defences available to women accused of homicide in the circumstances set out above; and

iv) to make recommendations as considered appropriate with respect to possible law reform initiatives stemming from the review.

■

Judge Ratushny tabled her report, *Self-Defence Review: First Interim Report — Women in Custody*, in early 1997, but the report was not publicly released until July 1997. Judge Ratushny expressed concerns about the delays, which caused considerable stress and hardship to women (who remained in custody) whose hopes had been raised by the review: Stephen Bindman, "Judge: Free four female killers" *The Ottawa Citizen* (3 March 1997) A1.

Judge Ratushny's final report (examining the cases of women who have already served their sentences and making law reform and policy recommendations, including the introduction of more judicial discretion in sentencing for second degree murder to allow for the possibility of leniency in exceptional circumstances) was accompanied by a letter criticizing the ways in which Justice Department officials undermined the inquiry, which she characterized as a "unique event in Canadian legal history": Stephen Bindman, "Bureaucrats 'scorned' judge's probe" *The Ottawa Citizen* (25 July 1997) A1. She described delays and refusals to provide administrative support, which amounted to a bureaucratic constraining of her ability to interpret her terms of reference, responses that "verged on scorn", an "apparent preference for the views of ... prosecutors", and prejudgment of her anticipated recommendations as untenable. For further details, see: Judge Lynn Ratushny, *Self Defence Review: Final Report* (Ottawa: Minister of Justice and Solicitor General, July 11, 1997).

Almost three months later, as a result of Judge Ratushny's recommendations, the federal government finally granted conditional pardons to two women (who had already finished serving their sentences), early release to two others (who were already on parole), and referred a fifth case (of a woman who remained in prison) to appeal. However, it rejected the recommendations to reduce the sentences of two other women who remained in prison: Anne McIlroy, "Abuse weighed in decision on women: Cases that could have used battered-syndrome defence revisited; Ottawa pardons two, cuts parole for two others" *The [Toronto] Globe and Mail* (27 September 1997) A1. Thus the recommendations were only implemented

---

† Source: "Review commissioned of murder cases involving women who allege they killed their abusers in self-defence" — News Release, Department of Justice Canada, 1995. Reproduced with the permission of the Minister of Public Works and Government Services Canada, 2008.

with respect to women previously released. The government proposed to begin consultations with judges, lawyers, and women's groups on the recommendations with respect to the reform of the law of self-defence and provocation. The government's commitment to consultation has been questioned, given the serious and rigorous consultation and inquiry in which Judge Ratushny already engaged: Canadian Association of Elizabeth Fry Societies, "Media Advisory: Justice for Battered Women — Denied, Delayed — Diminished Jails are Not the Shelters Battered Women Need" (29 September 1997). For a critical review of the *Self-Defence Review*, see: Elizabeth Sheehy, "Review of the Self-Defence Review" (2000) 12 C.J.W.L. 197.

E. OTHER DEVELOPMENTS IN THE LAW OF SELF-DEFENCE

In *R. v. McIntosh*, [1995] 1 S.C.R. 686, the Supreme Court considered whether self-defence as defined in s. 34(2) is available to initial aggressors. In the case, it had been open to the jury to find that the accused provoked the assault by threatening the deceased while the latter was armed with a knife. The majority upheld the Ontario Court of Appeal decision ordering a new trial, and concluded that provocation by the accused did not preclude resort to s. 34(2); thus, the accused who provoked an attack on himself was nonetheless entitled to the defence of self-defence where he retaliated and caused "death or grievous bodily harm". The majority held that, despite his own provocation, there was no obligation on the accused to meet the s. 35 requirement conditions of declining further conflict or retreating as far as it was feasible to do. This decision produces the absurd result that there are more onerous requirements for an accused initial aggressor who assaults the victim (s. 34(1)) than there are for a similarly situated accused who kills the victim (s. 34(2)). Even the majority recognized that the absurd interpretation calls for legislative clarification.

In contrast, the dissenting judges argued, at 714–15, that there was a requirement to retreat, and that the statutory interpretation of s. 34(2) must be attentive to the history of the section:

> Self-defence at common law rested on a fundamental distinction between cases where no fault was attributable to the killer, and cases where the killing was partly induced by some fault of the killer. Where the killer was not at fault — that is where he had not provoked the aggression — the homicide was called "justifiable homicide." Where blame could be laid on the killer, as where he had provoked the aggression, on the other hand, the homicide was called "excusable homicide"....
>
> Justifiable homicide and excusable homicide attracted different duties. In the case of justifiable homicide, or homicide in defending an unprovoked attack, the killer could stand his ground and was not obliged to retreat in order to rely on the defence of self-defence. In the case of excusable homicide, on the other hand, the killer must have retreated as far as possible in attempting to escape the threat which necessitated homicide, before he could claim self-defence. In other words, unprovoked attacks imposed no duty to retreat. Provoked attacks did impose a duty to retreat.

As Isabel Grant points out, in "Developments in Criminal Law: The 1994–95 Term" (1996) 7 Supreme Court L.R. (2d) 204, the majority never really addressed the serious policy question of whether an accused who initiates violence should then be able to use deadly force in self-defence without having to attempt retreat. This interpretation has serious consequences, particularly for vulnerable victims and those where there is a history of abuse and violence (at 19–20):

> One context where this decision is particularly problematic is in the context of domestic violence. Consider a not uncommon situation in Canada where a man assaults his spouse. If she attempts to use force to defend herself, *McIntosh* says that he may respond with deadly force if he reasonably thinks it is necessary to protect himself. He is not required even to attempt to retreat from the violence. The dissent's warning of someone deliberately provoking an attack so that he might respond with deadly force is not so far-fetched. Only the dissent in *McIntosh* meets this issue head on....

Grant suggests that Parliament should enact a duty to avail oneself of any safe means of retreat (at least for those accused who have initiated the violence). She suggests that the requirement of reasonableness (clearly necessary with respect to both the determination of the need for the use of force and the assessment of the amount of force necessary to protect oneself) be extended to encompass the evaluation of the possibility of retreat and a consequent qualified duty to retreat.

In *R. v. Trombley* (1998), 110 O.A.C. 329 (C.A.), aff'd. [1999] 1 S.C.R. 757, the Court held that the accused was not restricted to s. 34(1) but could avail herself of s. 34(2), even if the accused did not intend to cause death or bodily harm.

In a case that extends *Lavallee*, the Supreme Court considered the impact of another pattern of long-term violence, prison violence, on the vulnerability of the accused penitentiary inmates and the perceptions relevant to self-defence: *R. v. McConnell*, [1996] 1 S.C.R. 1075. The Court allowed the appeal substantially for the reasons of the dissenting judge, Conrad J. in (1995), 32 Alta. L.R. (3d) 1 (C.A.), set out below, and ordered a new trial.

R. v. McConnell†

[CONRAD J. (dissenting):]

The appellants and the deceased, Leslie Allan Casey, were prisoners in the Drumheller Penitentiary when Casey was stabbed to death in Unit 10 of the prison. Prior to the incident there had been considerable tension between McConnell and the Inmates Committee relating to the operation of the canteen. The Inmates Committee is a powerful body in the prison environment and exerts considerable influence over the constitution of the Canteen Committee.

The Inmates Committee consisted of the prisoners Marrigan, Pratt, Childs and Kreba. McConnell had had differences with Marrigan with respect to the operation of the Canteen Committee. Committee members would use income generated by the canteen to earn money for themselves either by loansharking the currency to other inmates, requiring repayment plus 50 per cent interest on the next day, or giving credit to inmates through the canteen, requiring repayment of the credit amount, plus 20 per cent interest, at the next pay period. McConnell disliked these methods of earning income, feeling that it was theft. He wanted to be on the Canteen Committee to curb its loansharking.

Casey was a member of the Canteen Committee; he was the person who kept the books for the canteen and would collect outstanding debts. In essence, he was the canteen's "heavy" or "enforcer." McConnell had never had a direct conflict with Casey before the day that Casey was killed.

. . . .

Earlier on the day of the crime, a confrontation had occurred between McConnell and Pratt and Marrigan as a result of the removal of certain posters which McConnell had placed in the gym. McConnell had placed a poster in the gym requesting participants to register for a weightlifting competition. That poster had been torn down. He then posted a new sign which stated that some "spineless individual" had torn down the previous sign. He was advised that Childs and Marrigan had torn down the poster, because they thought it was an eyesore, they didn't like it and questioned his authority to hold a competition without the committee's approval. McConnell asked Marrigan why the poster had been torn down, and Marrigan told him that they didn't like the poster, they didn't like him naming the competition without consulting them, and they didn't like him. McConnell responded by telling him that was fine, that they should each stay away from each other, and they would do good time in the prison.

. . . .

At approximately 3:30 that afternoon, Marrigan sent a message that he had wanted to see McConnell. McConnell armed himself with knuckle-dusters and went to see Marrigan in Pratt's cell, where he found both Pratt and Marrigan. Marrigan was intoxicated by drugs and started asking McConnell what authority he had to do anything without consulting the committee. McConnell's evidence was that he thought he was "all pilled up" so he just left and said, "Well, whatever, John. You

† (1995), 32 Alta. L.R. (3d) 1 (C.A.).

know whatever is whatever." And then he turned and walked out.

As he left, Pratt came tearing out of the cell, apparently wanting to fight. McConnell's reaction was to reach back for his weapon and say "Let's get at her." At this point another inmate, Steven Czupor, was preparing to hand Pratt a shank (home-made knife). Pratt seemed to have second thoughts and backed off. McConnell then heard Marrigan say: "We'll take care of this after supper. I got a lot of friends around here. We'll see how — we'll see how fucking tough you are after supper." McConnell responded by saying he would have to drain every drop of blood out of him before he fell.

Following the confrontation, McConnell testified that he believed Marrigan would put together a group of his friends to stab him or beat him up, and that he took the threat seriously. From his cell window, which faced into the courtyard, he could see Pratt, Marrigan, Childs and Czupor running around talking to people, after which the people would take off. He was of the impression they were going to obtain weapons.

McConnell did not go for supper that evening but stayed on his Range. He sent a friend, Wayne Carlson, to see Marrigan to propose a truce. Carlson returned about five minutes later to inform McConnell that Marrigan had said things had gone too far for a truce.

Another inmate and friend of McConnell's, Kevin May, a one-armed man, also attempted to ease the confrontation that was developing. He asked Pratt and Marrigan to act as a go-between, with the objective of cooling down the dispute between them and McConnell. He was struck by Casey and told to get out because if he stayed in the middle he would die in the middle.

At the preliminary inquiry, the Crown called Czupor, who testified that matters had gone too far and that "somebody had to go." That evidence was read in at discovery and confirmed the seriousness of the attack that McConnell was anticipating.

Czupor testified as to the hostility between the Inmates Committee and McConnell. He described McConnell as a loner and a man who stood his own ground. He also said that when one is alone in prison, and threats have been made, one either gets locked up or knocked off....

. . . .

He also confirmed that prisoners do "beef up" when anticipating an attack and place things under their clothes for protection. This is not done when prisoners are going out to attack someone. Czupor also testified about the loansharking and drug trafficking activities of the Inmates Committee in the prison, of which McConnell had complained. Czupor also testified that Casey was the Committee's enforcer.

Paxman, a guard, testified that he felt something was wrong when he saw Casey going down to D Range. Because the other guard on duty had gone to the bathroom, Paxman was alone. He left the bubble, locked it, and went to the area at the top of the stairs from which he could see down the range. Another guard, James Schwab, testified that he was on duty at Main Control and saw an incident in the breezeway involving May. He called the officer on duty in the bubble and warned him to be on the look-out. There was evidence that trouble was brewing and this was evidence from which a jury could conclude that the means had been assembled to carry out an attack on McConnell.

A prisoner, John Mills, was a defence witness. On a trip to the canteen with a friend he saw at least 8 or 9 inmates standing on either side of the breezeway around supper-time. Among the group was the Inmates Committee, including Marrigan, Childs and Pratt, all of whom would otherwise be running the canteen at that time. Pratt and Casey followed Mills and his friend towards the canteen and asked what they were doing, and if they had a problem. Mills responded that they were just going to the canteen and that they had no problem. On the way back from the canteen, Mills noticed the group was visibly armed with knives and appeared to be waiting for someone. The men were standing just outside of the camera range. Mills was asked for his impression on seeing the knives....

. . . .

[He responded, in part, that he had seen a group of inmates arming themselves with knives, that he was nervous about giving evidence because something might happen to him, that he was aware of threats against McConnell and May, and that he was convinced that someone would be killed that night.]

> A. *Yeah, someone was going to be getting it. It is hard to explain but you can, when you — it is like you can walk outside and you can feel it. It's like you know something is going to happen. Everybody is all tensed up and you can just feel everybody, they are just acting a lot different than they usually do.*
>
> Q. Would you say that is a result of living in the institution, you get this kind of extra instinct?

> A. Yeah. I have never felt it on the street being out. It is like you know, you know something is going to happen. It's like, it is really hard to explain. [Emphasis added.]

. . . .

In anticipation of an attack McConnell "beefed up" by placing magazines and a clipboard under his clothing for protection, putting on his winter jacket, and arming himself with knuckle-dusters and a stick. McConnell had asked Letendre and Haffter, fellow inmates, if they would stand by him. They, too, beefed up. Letendre had possession of a shank or home-made knife.

When May had tried to intervene he was struck by Casey. Once May had been struck, Czupor told Casey to get out before the guard saw him, and Czupor and Kreba then decided to take Casey to Kreba's cell, allegedly to [defuse] the situation. They headed down the range to Kreba's cell. McConnell was aware that May had been struck. He, Letendre and Haffter were standing at the top of the stairs leading to D Range. McConnell testified that when he saw Czupor, Casey and Kreba walking up the stairs past the bubble door he thought the attack was beginning. Instead, the three men did not go up toward the D Range when they entered Unit 10, but went towards Kreba's cell, away from McConnell. McConnell described the ensuing events in the following terms ...:

> ... I watched Casey go by me, and I was scared — I was pretty scared at the time, because *I thought it's coming down; it's all coming down*. I was also a little bit angry that this guy would beat up a man who has one arm, could not defend himself, and was only looking to make peace between not just one, not for me, but for everybody. And when he walked past me and he hit the top of the stairs, I said I was going to go down and give him a few punches. (Emphasis added.)

He struck Casey in the back of the head with the knuckle-dusters. Casey fell to the ground and McConnell continued to strike him in the head area. According to the Crown witness, Czupor, Letendre then "...went to his stomach with an object" which he believed was an ugly knife. Paxman had seen most of the incident and ordered McConnell, Letendre and Haffter to drop their weapons, which included brass knuckles, 2 shanks, and 2 pieces of wood crafted with protruding nails. From their clothing they removed a number of magazines, a clipboard, and weight-lifting body belts.

The pathologist's report showed that Casey had suffered superficial but severe head wounds inflicted by a heavy object such as knuckle-dusters. He sustained 6 stab wounds; the 3 fatal wounds being those which entered the heart, liver and lung. The injuries to Casey's head were not severe enough to cause death.

McConnell testified in his own defence. He said that he thought Marrigan, Pratt and Casey intended to kill him that day, and that he had no choice but to defend himself. When he saw Casey on the range, he decided to strike first. His evidence was that he was thinking that after Kevin (May) got punched out, that it had started, or that it was coming down.

He was examined as to what his alternatives were. He said he could stand and fight or he could check in. To check in at Drumheller he would have to go down to Building 3. In order to get to Building 3 he would have to go through the breezeway. With regard to that, he said "There's no way I was going outside. Forget it."

The theory of the Crown was that McConnell, Letendre and Haffter acted as parties in the killing of Casey. Because they prepared themselves in anticipation of the confrontation, the stabbing was a planned and deliberate murder. The position of the defence was that Casey had made prior threats of violence and the appellants acted under a reasonable apprehension of death or grievous bodily harm constituting self-defence within s. 34(2) of the *Code*.

Dr. Weston, a psychiatrist [who had not worked with or interviewed McConnell, Letendre, or Haffter], gave expert opinion evidence for the defence. He was qualified as an expert in the areas of the psychiatry of offenders ("inmates") and the culture of inmate population in long-term prisons. He testified that inmates have their own system of justice, which must be allowed to continue if the prison system itself is to survive.

Dr. Weston advised that an inmate whose life has been threatened may protect himself in the following ways: (1) by hiding in his cell and hoping for the best; (2) by applying for protective custody; (3) by committing a crime and being temporarily confined to "the hole"; or (4) using his friends to try and protect himself and taking the law into his own hands. Different consequences are attached to each course of action.

Dr. Weston further testified that the granting of protective custody depended upon the warden and that it is granted less frequently than in the past in federal penitentiaries. He also testified that getting protective custody or thrown in "the hole" can take some time. Inmates have to go before the warden's court, before being sent to solitary confinement and that may take 24 hours depending upon the offence and other circumstances. Under cross-examination, Dr. Weston stated that if an inmate struck an officer, a trip to the hole would quickly ensue.

When asked to draw an analogy between the situation of an inmate and the condition of a person in the larger society, Dr. Weston replied ...:

> I think in the final stages of the battered wife syndrome that you see the situation a [woman] knows she is going to be killed or kill. I think it is very similar to that. This is virtually a life or death situation. It's going to be me or I have to take some action and I think that is the similarity to it.

It was suggested to Dr. Weston in cross-examination that the final stage of the battered wife syndrome occurs when one person has assaulted one person over a length of time, usually a sufficient length of time. He replied ...:

> No. There may have been multiple assaults in that often these women, as you know, have been in previous assaulted relationships. So it is a whole series but it is the one which is the end, yes.... [All] I am saying is there is a similarity in the final thoughts of the battered wife, kill or be killed and I think that occurs.

. . . .

[Conrad J. went on to review the requisite elements of s. 34(2) and the subjective test as to the accused's belief, quoting Lamer J.'s decision in *R. v. Pétel*, [1994] 1 S.C.R. 3 at 12–13:]

> (1) the existence of an unlawful assault on the accused;
> (2) a reasonable apprehension of a risk of death or grievous bodily harm; and
> (3) a reasonable belief by the accused that it is not possible to preserve oneself from harm except by the infliction of death or grievous bodily harm on the assailant.

. . . .

The "Imminent or Immediate" Issue

In my view, the substantive issue in this appeal relates to the instruction of the trial judge in reply to questions raised by the jury and the requirement of immediacy as part of the assault charge. In order for the defence provided by s. 34(2) to apply there must be an assault. The appellants argue that the trial judge erred in his charge and recharge by equating present ability with immediacy.

[Justice Conrad then reviewed the trial judge's charge and recharge, an excerpt of which is reproduced below.]

. . . .

A person also commits assault, according to the law, when he attempts or threatens to apply force to another person, if that person who makes the attempt or threat has or causes the other person to believe on reasonable grounds that he has the present ability to carry out that purpose.

Let me give you an example. If I am standing face-to-face with Mr. Jones, and I raise my fist to him and do it in a threatening manner, that's a threat. And I'm close enough to Mr. Jones to effect my threat, I'm within striking distance, I can lash out and I can hit him, so that the mere fact of threatening in a situation where I can carry out my threat and where Mr. Jones believes that I can carry out my threat, that is an assault.

On the other hand, if I was standing over on the roof of that building out there and hollering at Mr. Jones and shaking my fist at him, that would not be an assault, because although the action is the same, I don't have the present ability. That is, at that moment I don't have the ability to carry out my threat. To get from there to here to hit Mr. Jones would take several minutes. Mr. Jones could easily be gone, and so I can't carry out my threat, so I don't have the present ability to carry out my threat.

So an assault can be a threat in circumstances where the person making the threat has the present, or immediate, ability to carry out the threat and-or, the other person believes that I have the present or immediate ability to carry out the threat. So, you needn't consider, when you are considering self-defence and looking at the word "assault," that there must be an actual physical assault. An assault can be made out by a threat where there is a present ability to carry out the threat or the other party believes, on reasonable grounds, that the person making the threat has the immediate ability to carry out the threat.

That explanation of assault is important because one of the defences in this case is obviously self-defence. Mr. McConnell testified and Dr. Weston explained the culture within a prison, and McConnell testified that he had a confrontation earlier on October 21 with Pratt, and Pratt apparently backed down, and McConnell was told that this will be dealt with after dinner, after supper, "We'll settle this another way." There were some words of a threat, some words in the nature of a threat, and that could constitute an assault. It is a question for you to decide whether, in all the circumstances, those words in the context of the prison environment constituted an assault against McConnell, the threat with what McConnell says he saw happening — some of the people huddling, talking together, according to his evidence —*whether he had the fear and reasonable ground for believing that the people who had threatened him had the present ability to carry out their threat*. (Emphasis added.)

In response to the jury's request for the trial "judge's definition of various charge definitions," the trial judge avoided using the words "imminent" or "immediate." He said only the following with respect to this issue ...:

> Are there reasonable circumstances surrounding this event from which the accused can reasonably be afraid that he would be killed or that he would have grievous bodily harm caused to him because of the violence with which the assault was originally made, that is the threats, what were perceived to be threats by Pratt earlier in the day that "We'll settle this later tonight," the question there for you is: Is this a violent assault that Pratt made and was it reasonable under the circumstances for these accused or one or more of them to feel that they were being threatened with death or grievous bodily harm?
>
> . . . .
>
> *So you have to look at the very moment when these things are happening, but it has to also be done in considering the background, because the background helps to establish the state of mind of the person*. So is there any background here that permits you to say, "Yeah, Letendre had reasonable apprehension of death or grievous bodily harm because of the violence with which he was assaulted"? That in my view would be stretching it, okay?
>
> So let's deal, then, specifically with McConnell. McConnell is the one who had the confrontation with Pratt earlier in the day; and Pratt or someone else, Marrigan, during the course of the day, I think twice there was reference made to, "We'll settle this another way" or "We'll deal with this after supper." Does that threat in your view constitute a threat of death or grievous bodily harm? Was there a threat there to kill or do grievous bodily harm, and did it set the stage? Did it put McConnell's mind in such a state where he had reason to believe when he saw what was happening with Casey—Casey was walking away from him, walking towards Kreba's cell—did he have reason to believe that it was about to happen, that he was about to get taken out? Or is it more likely that he was annoyed—I think he said he was somewhat angry because Casey attacked a one-armed man—and this was retribution, not self-defence?
>
> *So McConnell's state of mind has to be determined by not only what happened at that very moment or in those few seconds but also what happened earlier in the day*; and you have to say, "Is it reasonable for him to be in the state of mind that he was fearing death or grievous bodily harm because of the nature of the actions towards him?" ...
>
> *So while it's an immediate situation and you look at the immediate circumstances, you have to look also at the background to consider the state of mind of the individual*. (Emphasis added.)
>
> . . . .

[Justice Conrad went on to discuss a number of questions from the jury that indicated that they were obviously still grappling with the issues of imminence and immediacy.]

Appellants' Argument — An Error

Appellants' counsel states that the leading authorities have rejected the rule requiring that the apprehended danger be imminent. It is argued that the alleged rule, which does not appear anywhere in the Code, is only an assumption based on common sense. Thus, they say, the trial judge fell into error when he told the jury to consider whether the accused subjectively believed that the threat from the deceased was imminent. The appellants cite *R. v. Lavallee*, *supra*; *R.* c. *Pétel*, *supra*, and *R. v. W.(D.)*, [1991] 1 S.C.R. 742, 63 C.C.C. (3d) 397.

In *Pétel*, at pp. 14–15 (S.C.R.), Lamer C.J.C. stated the following about a trial judge's responsibility to accurately answer questions posed by a jury:

> The same is not true, however, of the answer given by the judge to the question put to him by the jury regarding the relevance of the threats immediately preceding the incident of July 21 and the threats prior to that date. The importance of adequately answering questions put by the jury should be borne in mind: *R. v. W.(D.)*, [1991] 1 S.C.R. 742, at pp. 759–60. *The question will generally relate to an important point in the jury's reasoning, so that any error the judge may make in answering it becomes all the more damaging*. It is often necessary to repeat certain aspects of the main charge in order to place the specific question in a more general context. (Emphasis added.)

Further, in *Pétel*, Lamer C.J.C. stated the following about the "alleged rule" that apprehended danger must be imminent, at pp. 13–14:

> Moreover, *Lavallee*, *supra*, *rejected the rule requiring that the apprehended danger be imminent*. This alleged rule, which does not appear anywhere in the text of the *Criminal Code*, is *in fact only a mere assumption based on common sense*. As Wilson J. noted in *Lavallee*, *this assumption*

> *undoubtedly derives from the paradigmatic case of self-defence, which is an altercation between two persons of equal strength. However, evidence may be presented (in particular expert evidence) to rebut this presumption of fact.* There is thus no formal requirement that the danger be imminent. *Imminence is only one of the factors which the jury should weigh* in determining whether the accused had a reasonable apprehension of danger and a reasonable belief that she could not extricate herself otherwise than by killing the attacker. (Emphasis added.)

It is here that the similarity between the present case and the final stages of a battered wife syndrome may be relevant, in the sense that the assault may be made by a threat, where the person reasonably believes that the person making the threat has the present ability to carry out the threat, notwithstanding that the physical aspect of the assault is not imminent or immediate. As Wilson J. stated in *Lavallee* at p. 120 [C.C.C.]: "The issue is not, however, what an outsider would have reasonably perceived but what the accused reasonably perceived, given her situation and her experience." Thus, here the appellants could reasonably believe that the threats were made, and were continuing, by persons with the present ability to carry them out, although they were not going to carry out the threat at that immediate moment.

Respondent's Argument — No Error

Respondent's counsel argues that the trial judge incorporated into the meaning of the term "imminent" all the evidence from the time of the original threat to the time of the killing itself. He was clear to include the background of threats made earlier in the day and the state of mind of the accused persons.

In any event, the respondent argues that the trial judge did not err in referring to the word "imminent," because imminence is still a factor for the jury to consider in determining the nature of the accused's apprehension involved. According to *Pétel*, the respondent argues, it is only when there is unequal bargaining strength (i.e., battered wife syndrome) that the importance of imminence declines. In other words, there is a sliding scale of importance associated with imminence. As strength between the parties equalizes, imminence becomes a greater factor. Here, the respondent argues, there was no unequal bargaining power between the parties.

Dealing with the last argument first, it is in my view that the equality of the bargaining strength is best left for the jury. McConnell was, like the others, an inmate. It is true that he was not acting entirely alone, he may have had a second assistant in Haffter. McConnell and the others attacked a group of three men — but it appeared that McConnell and Letendre were very vulnerable to a much larger group. The threatening group started with three or four members of the Inmates Committee, and expanded to eight or nine inmates, who were armed with knives and standing on either side of the breezeway. There was evidence from which it could be inferred that the group had the power to recruit other members of the inmate population, some of whom may have wished to gain favour with the Inmates Committee. There was evidence of the flurry of activity McConnell witnessed in the courtyard between the Inmates Committee and others.

In my view, the jury's final questions were the pivotal questions. They indicated that the jury was totally aware of the main issue in this case. The jury had deliberated several hours when the last questions were asked. What they really wanted to know was whether the law permitted a pre-emptive strike, or whether the actual physical component of the threatened assault had to be *immediate*. The trial judge was careful on the subjective element, and the need to have regard for the circumstances of the case, but I am satisfied he may have taken away the very defence he tried to leave with the jury when he said that the accused must believe that the threat to his life was "immediate." There is a danger the jury would think that the possibility of a pre-emptive strike, or the battered wife syndrome type defence, was not available. "Present ability" is not synonymous with "immediate."

I agree with the Crown that this trial judge communicated on many occasions that it is the subjective [belief] that must be measured. I also agree that the trial judge was correct in pointing out that the appellants' belief should be measured at the exact point of time they struck the victim. That, however, is different from saying that they must have apprehended that the physical component of the apprehended assault would have been carried out at that exact moment.

The jury's questions must be related to the facts of the case. On these facts, the three men who were part of the larger threatening group were *walking away* from the accused. It may be that they were going to get weapons with which to commit the assault they had threatened. The jury might have thought from the re-charge that the defence was not open until that point of time at which the attackers were moving towards him, notwithstanding their present ability to do the harm threatened. It is obvious if they were walking away, the assault was not going to occur at that time. The problem is that when the trial judge said: "So the simple answer to your question is yes, the accused must believe that the threat to his life was immediate," the jury may have thought it was not open for them to find self-defence because the appellants could not reasonably believe that the threats were going to be carried out at that moment. This would eliminate the possibility of a pre-emptive strike. The questions of the jury indicate that that was their very concern and, notwithstanding a careful charge, the requirement of immediacy as an element as opposed to a factor for consideration is, in my view, an error. While the appellants' state of mind must be measured at the exact point in time they struck Casey, they could be acting in self-defence to an assault by threat with present ability to carry out the threat, although the actual physical act threatened was not to be carried out at that exact moment.

I must also make reference to the respondent's argument that the battered wife syndrome arises only after a history of assaults, and that there was no such history in the case at bar. Obviously this fact situation is not identical to the battered wife syndrome, but analogous to it. It is, what I shall refer to as, "the prison environment syndrome." There was evidence from Dr. Weston about inmate behaviour and prison culture and the similarity in the environment to the battered wife syndrome. There is evidence about the environment being one in which inmates had to "kill or be killed." Thus a person could believe he or she was being assaulted (a threat with present ability) without it being immediate.

Moreover, while there is no history of assault against these particular appellants, it is not entirely accurate to say there is no history of assault in the case at bar. There was plenty of evidence that the deceased was the Committee's enforcer, that he collected on debts through force and intimidation. There was evidence that he had recently beaten the appellant's friend after the friend tried to intercede in the dispute. In summary, there was evidence in this case from which the jury could easily conclude that the strengths of the parties were unequal. Immediacy is only one factor to be considered in determining whether or not these appellants had, at the moment of striking, a reasonable belief that they were being assaulted.

. . . .

In my view there was some evidence from which a jury could conclude that an assault, as described in *Pétel*, was occurring. There was considerable evidence that a group of armed prisoners were gathering to carry out an assault on McConnell. It could be inferred from the facts that this assault would also be directed against any one who assisted him. There was evidence of the earlier verbal threat against McConnell and May, the Committee's refusal to make a truce, and McConnell's observation of the gathering of the inmates with weapons. There was evidence that Casey was part of that group, that he was the group's enforcer on certain matters and that Casey had already started the attack by striking May and telling him to stay out of it. There was evidence of Marrigan's statement that it was too late to retreat. Threats were communicated to McConnell directly and indirectly. He observed the gathering. He told Letendre, and there was evidence Letendre was with him. While Letendre did not give evidence, I cannot say the trial judge erred by leaving the defence for Letendre as well. There was evidence from which a jury could infer that the accused were subjectively of the belief, on reasonable grounds, that they were under threat of serious bodily injury by persons who had the present ability to carry out that threat. There certainly was evidence that the group had the means to carry out very serious, even fatal, injury to the accused. There was evidence that McConnell thought that the entry of Casey's group into Building D was the start of it. There was evidence from one guard that he had warned another guard in the "bubble" that trouble was brewing. Dr. Weston's evidence was also on point. He gave expert evidence on communication in the prison environment and the feeling of helplessness or the "kill or be killed" attitude that could prevail amongst the prisoners.

The trial judge felt there was a sufficient evidentiary basis to put the issues of assault, and, consequently, self-defence to the jury. I would not interfere with that decision. In saying that, I recognize the weakness of Letendre's situation, as did the trial judge. However, even if he did not testify, there was evidence from which the jury could conclude that anyone standing with McConnell would be assaulted, and could subjectively believe on reasonable grounds that he was being assaulted in the manner required by *Pétel*. The trial judge noted the weakness of Letendre's position and it may be that Letendre would more properly fit under defence of third persons, which was not raised until the appeal. However, it is my position that the earlier threats and the continuing and escalating activity with present ability to carry them out, could justify the pre-emptive strike, depending on the jury's findings.

On the whole of the evidence, the trial judge was right to leave the defence with the jury. In my view a new trial is required because I am concerned that the jury might have thought it was not open to the appellants to defend themselves unless the actual physical part of the assault was imminent or immediate.

■

For a thoughtful comment on the implications of *McConnell*, see Christine Boyle, "Annotation" (1996) 48 C.R. (4th) 200. She argues that the effect of *McConnell* is to continue the expansion of the meaning of "immediacy" and the concept of "assault". However, the decision also leaves unanswered some difficult questions about the limits on pre-emptive strikes and the amassing of weapons, whether any distinction remains between present and future danger, and the responsibility of the state to provide safety for prisoners and for women who have been battered. In the prison context, *McConnell* invites a reconsideration of *R. v. Carker (No. 2)*, discussed below, under **Duress**. As Boyle concludes, at 202, the decision is troubling:

> Any recognition that prisons are a zone of anarchy in which it is reasonable to engage in a pre-emptive strike, or in which prisoners would be seen as reasonable in arming themselves, would be a devastating indictment of our prisons, which are after all a part of the criminal justice system. They are places where people are required to be as a consequence of the operation of the criminal justice system itself.

How should the criminal law respond to these legitimate concerns? Reconsider Justice Abella's dissent in *Malott* in light of the Court's decision in *McConnell*. See also the acquittal in *R. v. Plain* (1998), 12 C.R. (5th) 373 (Ont. Ct. J. (Gen. Div.)) of a maximum security inmate in Kingston Penitentiary, a protective custody institution, for possession of a weapon and aggravated assault with a knife and upon another inmate. The assault was committed by Plain as a "pre-emptive strike" when he owed money to the victim, Alex Salmon, and the evidence was that "knives were being sharpened" as Salmon prepared for an assault against Plain. In this case, prison officials acknowledged that 90 per cent of the inmates carried knives, and the trial judge accepted the testimony of another inmate that even time in "the hole" could not have protected Plain from an attack.

In another Ontario decision, the court considered evidence of the violent character of the deceased victim, evidence of the Ojibwe community's spiritual beliefs as to the powers of the deceased "Bearwalker", and evidence of the menace felt by the individual Ojibwe accused in the face of threats, physical assault, the reputation and power of the Bearwalker, and his own spiritual beliefs: *R. v. Jacko*, [1997] O.J. No. 2472 (Ct. J. (Gen. Div.)) (QL). As one witness explained (at para. 52):

> A Bearwalker is a person who causes harm to others by the use of bad medicine. The Bearwalker can transform himself to ahimal forms such as a bear. This is known as "shake shifting [*sic*]." The Bearwalker travels as a ball of fire. The Bearwalker strikes fear into people that may result in sickness or death if not treated by good medicine.

Judge Trainor relied on *R. v. Pintar* (1996), 110 C.C.C. (3d) 402 (Ont. C.A.), *Pétel*, *supra*, and *Lavallee*, *supra* for the relevance of the victim's propensity for violence and his spiritual powers as a Bearwalker to the assessment of the reasonableness of the accused's apprehension of danger. In acquitting the accused on the basis of self-defence, Judge Trainor held (at paras. 81–83):

> [The accused's] description of himself as a warrior, who killed the Bearwalker, must be understood, not as an act of aggression but as an act of self defence, an act to protect others from an evil spirit.
>
> ...
>
> The Accused described the Victim as getting crazy when he drinks wine. The statement reflects his knowledge of the propensity of the Victim for violence, knowledge gained in part from his father. In other utterances he said words to the effect that Tab went crazy. There is no description in the evidence as to how Tab went crazy and what specific action he took. There is, however, evidence of Tab's strength compared to the accused and his reputation for violence. In addition, the Accused knew of his reputation and power as a Bearwalker, including his ability to transform himself into a bear, adding to his power and strength. That reputation and spiritual belief is not to be looked at or judged by the

> standards of non-native society. I accept the evidence about native spirituality as being sincerely held beliefs by which I must judge the reasonableness of the Accused's apprehension and belief as to the danger that he was facing when the Victim attacked the Accused.

The Nova Scotia Court of Appeal recently upheld the acquittal of an inmate (for assault with a weapon and possession of a prohibited weapon) who stabbed another inmate in a federal penitentiary. Although the accused did not testify, the trial judge left the defence of self-defence with the jury, on the basis that the subjective apprehension of the danger facing the accused and any consequent need for resort to force in self-defence could be established by other evidence including a prison videotape: *R. v. Chan*, [2005] N.S.C.A. 61. In *R. v. Kerr*, [2004] 2 S.C.R. 371, the Court upheld an acquittal for murder and set aside a conviction for possession of a weapon ("a metal knife which he had manufactured by sharpening a big spoon, and an ice pick which he had manufactured by sharpening a steel rod": para. 5) for a purpose dangerous to the public peace contrary to s. 88. While Justices Major, Bastarache, Deschamps and Fish concluded that on the specific facts the possession of the weapons was not inconsistent with the public peace, Justices LeBel and Arbour argued that the appropriate defence to the possession charge was necessity. Both cases raise troubling issues about the necessity of arming oneself in prison contexts in anticipation of self-defence or pre-emptive attacks.

While courts have been receptive to the possibility of finding an objective reasonable apprehension of death or grievous bodily harm in prison contexts, they have been more sceptical in other contexts in examining the air of reality to the objective criteria of the accused's purported perception of an imminent attack or of the apprehension of death or grievous bodily harm and of the lack of other alternatives: *R. v. Cinous*, [2002] 2 S.C.R. 3 (pre-emptive killing by shooting a criminal accomplice in the back of the head outside a well-populated service station not amounting to self-defence because alternative courses of action available even if not within contemplation of criminal subculture); *R. v. Mousseau*, [2007] Man. R. (2d) 308 (C.A.) (accused provoked response by attending at victim's residence armed with a knife and slashing the tires of the victim's wife's car); *R. v. Spidel*, [2005] B.C.C.A. 556 (no air of reality to self-defence where pre-emptive strike by accused landlord who stabbed tenant in altercation claiming the deceased was dangerous and had attacked him in the past).

In *R. v. Boucher* (2006), 42 C.R. (6th) 117 (Que. C.A.); leave to appeal refused, [2006] S.C.C.A. No. 417, the accused was convicted of murder of a police officer and armed robbery. He argued self-defence and necessity on the basis that he feared he was about to be killed by the police officer who had been pursuing him, first, in a high-speed car chase and then on foot. A unanimous court upheld the convictions. While there was an air of reality to the possibility of an unlawful act on the part of the police officer (shooting at the accused and ramming the accused's car not necessarily authorized by s. 25) and to the accused's apprehension of death or grievous bodily harm (he had heard 2 shots behind him while being pursued), there was no air of reality to the objective basis of the criterion that Boucher had no alternative to shooting the police officer (for example, surrendering). Citing Justice Binnie in *Cinous*, the court rejected the possibility of using the "rules of his criminal sub-culture ... [rather than] the values of law-abiding members of the public" (para. 40) to evaluate the reasonableness of his response.

In the converse situation, the objective basis for an officer's apprehension of the dangerousness of a situation and the need to use force is arguably more readily established.

F. THE DEFENCE OF AUTHORITY: POLICE OFFICERS AND THE USE OF FORCE

As Isabel Grant, Dorothy Chunn & Christine Boyle argue in *The Law of Homicide* (Scarborough: Carswell, 1994) at 6–88, several of the provisions of the *Code* dealing with state-authorized use of force are conceptually linked to self-defence, in that causing death is permitted or excused in the interest of physical security. They refer specifically to ss. 32, 33, and 25, and discuss the broad authority granted by the old s. 25(4) (the "fleeing felon" rule), which provided a peace officer with a defence to a murder or manslaughter charge. The new s. 25(4) is more restrictive and requires that the officer had been proceeding lawfully to arrest a person, held a reasonable belief that force is necessary to prevent imminent or future death or grievous bodily harm, and used no more force than necessary (although this latter requirement is likely to be evaluated subjectively).

In *R. v. Lines*, [1993] O.J. No. 3284 (Ct. J. (Gen. Div.)) (QL), the Crown argued successfully that the old s. 25(4) breached the suspect's rights and the rights of innocent bystanders under *Charter* ss. 7, 9, and 12. The U.S. Supreme Court, in *Tennessee v. Garner*, 105 S. Ct. 1694 (1985), had held that a similar statute was unconstitutional insofar as it authorized the use of deadly force against unarmed, non-dangerous suspects. After *Lines*, s. 25(4) was amended.

As Grant *et al.* discuss, any interrogation of police use of deadly force in these cases is more apt to take place in civil proceedings rather than in the criminal forum. They canvass some of the arguments for stricter control and scrutiny of police use of force and point out how the issue of police use of deadly force against Black and Aboriginal individuals and people with mental disabilities has become a subject of increasing concern. For documentation of some of these cases (including *Lines*), see the discussion in Abell & Sheehy, *Cases, Context, Critique*, **Policing and Enforcement of Law**. See also *Report of the Commission on Systemic Racism in the Ontario Criminal Justice System* (Toronto: Queen's Printer, 1995). Consider whether the new s. 25(4) may still be vulnerable to a s. 15 challenge. Who would have standing? What are the barriers and difficulties facing victims forced to seek civil remedies?

G. THE DEFENCE OF OTHERS

In *R. v. N.C.*, [1997] O.J. No. 2302 (QL) (Prov. Div.), the accused was found not guilty of dangerous driving and of assaulting members of the Emergency Response Team at Ipperwash. In an effort to rescue and protect another protester, Bernard George, who was being beaten and arrested by the police, he drove a bus from the parking lot at the police line. Judge Graham held that his actions were justified on the basis of the defence of others (ss. 30 and 37 of the *Code*), and that the force used was not excessive. For further discussion of the Ipperwash protest and police and government action, see Sidney Linden, Commissioner, *Report of the Ipperwash Inquiry* (Toronto: Queen's Press, 2007).

R. v. N.C.†

[GRAHAM J.:]

. . . .

The evidence of the Crown witnesses varies as to the number of natives that were scattered over the parking lot area. This court finds, however, that on the totality of the evidence there were several natives who were throwing objects at some police including sticks, stones and firebrands. Prior to the arrest of Bernard George, Sergeant Lacroix testified that a person was making a speech to the officers almost in a scripted fashion to the effect that this is the land of our forefathers and you are desecrating it. After the arrest of Bernard George he was taken to the hospital emergency room and treated by Doctor Allyson Marr. Doctor Marr testified that Bernard George has suffered 28 areas of blunt trauma as well as a cut requiring sutures, the cut being to his head.

† [1997] O.J. No. 2302 (Prov. Div.) (QL).

Bernard George testified that he was knocked to the ground backwards, started to see stars, but soon lost consciousness. He testified as to being kicked in the head, stomach and crotch and clubbed all over his body. He further testified that on several occasions he had said: "I give up." He indicated that he was endeavouring to effect a peace between the natives and the police force and his purpose in addressing the police was to engage them in dialogue.

I find Bernard George to be a credible witness and I accept his evidence.

I further find on the evidence before me that Bernard George received the injuries testified to by Doctor Marr and that he was struck 28 times with either batons, hands or feet of the officers. I do not find on the facts before me that the injuries were as a result of being struck by stones or other objects being thrown by the other natives as was suggested by the Crown in argument.

The accused, N.C., testified that he was standing in the proximity of Bernard George at the time of the beating and that he then heard someone say, "Get the bus out there" in order to rescue Bernard George. N.C. then got in a school bus which was inside the park, put it in gear and pushed a dumpster which had been put at the park entrance, out of the way and drove towards the police.

. . . .

C. testified that he was intending to rescue Bernard George and stop the beating George was receiving at the hands of the police. That evidence seems reasonable and is accepted by the court.

. . . .

On the evidence before me I find that the actions of Mr. C. were intentional, that he intended to charge at the police line and to use the school bus as the instrument for that purpose. Although Mr. C. testified that he could have stopped if need be, I find on the facts that he had no intention of stopping and had the police officers not jumped from the path of the vehicle, they would have been struck.

. . . .

[However, Judge Graham held that his actions were justified on the basis of ss. 30 and 37 of the *Code*, and that the force used was not excessive.]

The defence has argued the force was not excessive since no lesser amount of force could have been effective or reasonable in the circumstances. With that submission I agree. If the accused had ventured into the fray without the protection of the vehicle [his] actions would have been senseless, reckless and futile. ...

In another confrontation at Ipperwash Provincial Park shortly after the bus incident, the accused was convicted of criminal negligence in the operation of a motor vehicle and assault with a weapon (a car) for driving the car at a group of police officers: *R. v. George* (2000), 49 O.R. (3d) 144 (C.A.), application for leave to appeal dismissed, [2001] S.C.C. File No. 28031. The accused alleged that he did so for the purpose of assisting a different individual who had been assaulted and arrested by police. The trial judge and the Court of Appeal rejected the defence of property (s. 41 of the *Code*) on the basis that the Stoney Point members were not in "peaceable" possession of the park and that the accused had not established that he had an honest but mistaken belief in the nature of the Band members' possession of the park. The defence of justification (ss. 27 and 30 of the *Code*) was rejected in part on the basis of credibility. The trial judge disbelieved the accused as to the motivations for his actions (at para. 56):

> The difficulty with the appellant's submission [that the defence of justification should be available] is that the trial judge disbelieved the appellant's evidence that his purpose in driving the car out behind the school bus was to "help Slippery" (Cecil George) "maybe force the police away and get him into the car." He found that the appellant's purpose was to "resist, obstruct and confront any attempts by the police to enforce compliance with the law. This was his intention before Cecil George was arrested and, adopting the Crown's theory, it was his intention after Cecil George was arrested." The trial judge concluded that the defence of justification resulted from a retrospective reconstruction of events.
>
> The appellant relied on the case of *R. v. N.C*, released May 26, 1997 (Ont. Prov. Div.), the driver of the school bus that evening. He was acquitted of similar offences in a separate trial. However in his case, the trial judge found that "the only logical conclusion is that C. then entered the bus for the purposes of attempting to rescue Bernard George [Cecil

George] from the officers as futile as that action may well have, in hind sight, seem to have been."

As we have already concluded that the trial judge did not misapprehend the evidence, his finding that the appellant's purpose in driving the car in the way he did was not to assist Cecil George, distinguishes the *N.C.* case and makes the defence of justification unavailable in this case on the facts.

16

Duress

Read s. 17 and s. 8(3) of the *Code*. Section 17 codifies the defence of *compulsion* for those who personally commit the offence. Section 8 preserves defences recognized at common law in so far as they are not inconsistent with other legislation; thus the common law defence of *duress* remains available for an accused who is a party rather than a principal.

A. SECTION 17 DEFENCE

As you read the following cases, consider the impact of the restrictions in s. 17, such as "threats of **immediate** death or bodily **harm** from a person who is **present** when the offence is committed", and the restrictions at common law. What is the standard by which the harm is evaluated? Is the distinction between explicit and implicit threats important?

In *R. v. Carker (No. 2)*, [1967] S.C.R. 114, the Court denied the accused the defence of duress to a charge of mischief for damage to prison plumbing, despite the evidence that the alleged offence occurred during a widespread prison protest, on the basis that it was (at 119) "virtually inconceivable that 'immediate death' or 'bodily harm' could have come to Carker from those who were uttering the threats against him as they were locked up in separate cells." At the time, a large group of prisoners was shouting in unison from separate cells and threatening the accused that if he did not break the plumbing fixtures in his cell, he would be kicked in the head, his arm would be broken, and he would get a knife in the back at the first opportunity. Is it "virtually inconceivable" that "immediate death" or "grievous bodily harm" could have come to Carker?

R. v. Gardiner†

[HUTCHINSON J.:]

The accused is charged with eight counts in an indictment. They arise out of his sale of handguns to an undercover police officer.

The defence says that he acted under duress as defined by s. 17 [am. 1974-75-76, c. 105, s. 29] of the *Criminal Code*, R.S.C. 1970, c. C-34. There are very few reported Canadian decisions on this issue. The courts have limited the scope of this defence. The reason was put by Lord Morris of Borth-y-Gest in his speech in the House of Lords in *D.P.P. (Northern Ireland) v. Lynch*, [1975] A.C. 653, 61 Cr. App. R. 6, [1975] 1 All E.R. 913 at 918:

> In posing the case where someone is "really" threatened I use this word "really" in order to emphasise that duress must never be allowed to be the easy answer of those who can devise no other explanation of their conduct nor of those who readily could have avoided the dominance of threats nor of those who allow themselves to be at the disposal and under the sway of some gangster-tyrant. Where duress becomes an issue courts and juries will surely consider the facts with care and discernment.

Goguin approached the police with a scheme to help them get stolen handguns off the street. He spoke with Constable Presslauer, to whom he showed discharge documents to support his claim that he had been a "Green Beret" in the United States Army Intelligence. He told Constable Presslauer he would be working through an unnamed intermediary. Goguin met Constable Presslauer on a number of occasions over a three-week period and finally on 18th March 1983 the plan came to fruition. Constable Moser, posing as an arms dealer from Seattle, came to Prince Rupert and met Goguin and Constable Presslauer. Constable Moser had with him an M16 automatic rifle that he was going to exchange for the handguns. Goguin was to bring the vendor of the guns to a motel. Once the bargain was struck, Constable Presslauer and Sergeant Seefreed, who were to be in the next room, were to enter the room and arrest the vendor. The vendor turned out to be the accused and the plan was executed, so far as the police were concerned, successfully, and the accused was arrested.

This elaborate scheme had the unreal flavour of a Grade B movie. Goguin received free accommodation and meals for his family for some nights before he left Prince Rupert, but otherwise Constable Presslauer said that he was not paid. His whereabouts are now unknown.

The accused is a youth of 20 with limited education and intelligence. He boasts of connections among the criminal elements in Prince Rupert. He has no love for the police and claims to have been searched 50 times, sometimes with up to five police cars stopping him and, in his words, "with police dogs crawling all over me." He had a Smith and Wesson revolver that he knew was stolen. He was introduced to Goguin through a friend, Finnigan, who is about the same age, though even more gullible and impressionable than the accused.

Finnigan, and later the accused, were impressed by Goguin's claims of being a Green Beret, and of his working for the C.I.A. and Israeli intelligence. One night, Goguin showed Finnigan some moves that Finnigan said nearly broke his back. Goguin's story to Finnigan and the accused would have made a normal person suspicious. Finnigan and the accused were living in a world of fantasy and dreams stimulated by television and their own sense of the dramatic. Goguin persuaded them that he was working for the C.I.A. to recruit mercenaries to fight in Nicaragua and that he needed an untraceable handgun to "penetrate a dam." Goguin said pistols were scarce in Nicaragua, while semi-automatic M16s were easy to come by, he could arrange a trade. He told the accused that some M16s had been stolen from a boxcar in Prince Rupert in shipment to some other destination. First Finnigan, and then the accused, came under this modern Merlin's spell. Goguin began to terrorize the accused with threats that he would blow off the accused's head and the accused said that he was even threatened with his own revolver if he did not co-operate. Goguin said he had contacts and he had agents who were watching the accused; on one occasion he said he had people on the buildings of downtown Prince Rupert with M16s following the accused's activities. He said these agents would gun the accused down if his requests were ignored and that he personally would shoot the accused.

† (1983), 34 C.R. (3d) 237 (B.C. Co. Ct.).

I have no doubt and I accept that both Finnigan and the accused were terrified of Goguin by 18th April. This atmosphere had been built up over a period of time: both the accused and Finnigan got themselves into a situation well beyond their control. The evidence in this respect is corroborated by Constable Moser, who said the accused was very nervous and fearful when the deal was made in the motel. Goguin was outside as the look-out. Constable Moser said that Goguin told him earlier that afternoon that the accused was scared, nervous and quite afraid. Constable Moser added (I find gratuitously) that he was afraid of Constable Moser. I am satisfied on the evidence that the accused was scared, nervous and afraid of Goguin.

Finnigan was extremely nervous and anxious on the witness stand; that was brought on to some extent, I find, by his recollection of the threats that he believed in. The extent of the accused's fear would have been made plain had a tape-recording of his conversation with Constable Moser been available. The conversation of the transaction was recorded on a tape. Constable Moser made notes based on the tape and the tape was then erased. I draw the most favourable inference that I can for the accused from the failure of the police to preserve this important piece of evidence.

The defence of duress is defined by s. 17 of the *Criminal Code*:

. . . .

None of the exclusions apply to the charges against the accused, which are of being in possession of stolen property having a value over $200 and being in possession of and having in possession a restricted weapon for which there was no registration certificate, and other charges of that nature.

The difficulty in applying this defence to a case of this nature is twofold. First, the events gradually unfolded from the beginning when the accused voluntarily participated in and prepared for the crime with which he is charged, until he became involved deeply with Goguin. He later became fearful of Goguin and finally felt unable to withdraw from the scheme because of the threats posed by Goguin on him.

Second, the events were not sudden. The accused had ample opportunity to reflect, reconsider his position rationally and attempt to extricate himself from it.

I accept that the threats of Goguin at the time the sale was made to Constable Moser were immediate and Goguin was present, as defined by the words "immediate and present" in s. 17 of the *Criminal Code*. In coming to this conclusion, I have applied the test propounded in *R. v. Carker*, [1967] S.C.R. 114, 2 C.R.N.S. 16, 60 W.W.R. 365, [1967] 2 C.C.C. 190, which deals with whether there was a threat at the time the transaction came about and whether the threats immediately preceding the transaction were sufficient to bring the accused within s. 17.

I have found that the threats were immediate and present. I hold though, that the defence does not automatically succeed because of that finding. I hold that the defence is available only to a person who finds himself suddenly in the position of having to make an agonizing choice between two immediate and present evils, that is, suffer death or grievous bodily harm or commit the crime. Support for that proposition is to be found in the decision of *Lynch* supra....

. . . .

The most recent decision in this area that I could find mentioned is [a] decision from the Northern Ireland Court of Criminal Appeal, *R. v. Fitzpatrick*, 8th October 1976 (unreported), and it is referred to in Archbold, *Criminal Pleading: Evidence and Practice*, 40th ed. (1979), para, 1449d. p 979. The judgment is of Lowry L.C.J., and he says this [pp. 979–80]:

> (a) The defence of duress is not open to a man who has voluntarily joined an organization which to his knowledge might compel him to commit crimes similar to those with which he is charged;
>
> (b) the fact that he has tried to leave the organization is irrelevant. "In each case the answer is the same. If a person voluntarily exposes and submits himself ... to illegal compulsion, he cannot rely on the duress to which he has voluntarily exposed himself as an excuse either in respect of the crimes he commits against his will or in respect of his continued but unwilling association with those capable of exercising upon him the duress which he calls in evidence.' "

Application for leave to appeal was made to the House of Lords, who refused leave to appeal.

[The organization in which the accused was involved was the I.R.A. in *R. v. Fitzpatrick*, [1977] N.I. 20 (Ct. Crim. App.).]

Here, the accused, I find did voluntarily expose himself to the illegal compulsion. He voluntarily entered into an arrangement to acquire handguns and as it became more difficult he allowed himself gradually to become involved to the point that he felt he could not extricate himself in the end from Goguin's threats. The other aspect on which I find the accused does not satisfy me with respect to this defence is that the events did not arise suddenly. There was a gradual evolution and the accused was not faced with an immediate, agonizing decision as to whether to commit a crime or take some other course. He had ample opportunity to reflect on the position he was in and could have taken many alternative routes to extricate himself. He did not attempt to extricate himself and he followed in a direction that he felt was the only one that he could follow but which I find a reasonable person in his position would not have found compelling.

The distinction is put again by Lord Morris in *Lynch, supra*, at pp. 918–19, when he said this:

> Let two situations be supposed. In each let it be supposed that there is a real and effective threat of death. In one a person is required under such duress to drive a car to a place or carry a gun to a place with knowledge that at such a place it is planned that X is to be killed by those who are imposing their will. In the other situation let it be supposed that a person under such duress is told that he himself must go there and then kill X. In either situation there is a terrible agonizing choice of evils. In the former to save his life the person drives the car or carries the gun. He may cling to the hope that perhaps X will not be found at the place or that there will be a change of intention before the purpose is carried out or that in some unforeseen way the dire event of a killing will be averted. The final and fatal moment of decision has not arrived. He saves his own life at a time when the loss of another life is not a certainty. In the second (if indeed it is a situation likely to arise) the person is told that to save his life he himself must personally go there and then take an innocent life. It is for him to pull the trigger or otherwise personally do the act of killing. There, I think, before allowing duress as a defence it may be that the law will have to call a halt.

The distinction is appropriate to the facts before me. I find that the situation facing the accused leading up to this event did not put him into that agonizing choice as to which of two evils he should select. He could have followed other courses; but, having gone so far along this route before being subjected to threats, he cannot now rely on the defence of duress to excuse his conduct and his actions.

Accordingly, I find that [the] defence fails.

■

R. v. Robins†

[MAYRAND J.A. (translation):]

Tina Robins appeals against the judgment rendered on November 18, 1980, by a Judge of the Court Sessions of the Peace, District of Montreal, which found her guilty of the crime of kidnapping as set out in the following indictment:

> At Hampstead, District of Montreal, on or about May 3, 1976, Tina Robins, did illegally kidnap Hannah Alper, with intent to hold her for ransom against her will, committing thereby an indictable offence, according to Section 24(1)(c) of the *Criminal Code*.

THE FACTS

Hannah Alper was kidnapped in circumstances which she and her father, John Alper, as well as the appellant, described during their evidence.

On the morning of May 3, 1976, the appellant, calling herself Penelope, telephoned Hannah, a young girl of 20 years and asked her to participate in a fashion show for the benefit of a Jewish organization; she suggested that Hannah not speak of this to her mother in order to surprise her. The young girl accepted and agreed to meet the appellant at the corner of Glenmore and Côte St. Luc Rds. At the indicated hour, Hannah went to the rendezvous; the appellant arrived, driving the automobile of her husband, opened the door and Hannah sat in the front seat next to her. As soon as the automobile began to move, the husband of the appellant, who had hidden behind the seat, grabbed Hannah and forced her to lay [*sic*] down under the car seat after he had climbed into the front seat. He put a blindfold over her eyes and made her swallow several Valium tablets. They drove north along the Laurentian Highway to the accused's chalet

† (1982), 66 C.C.C. (2d) 550 (Que. C.A.).

in St. Sauveur. The appellant and her husband, Kevin Ogilvie, remained at the chalet for a day and a half with the victim, Hannah Alper.

Around 6:00 p.m. on the day of the kidnapping, John Alper received a telephone call. A ransom of $250,000 was demanded for the return of his daughter and he was told that he would receive instructions the following day as to the method of transferring this sum to the kidnappers. A little later, he heard his daughter speak on the telephone. She said, crying: "Daddy, help me." Alper informed the police of what had happened and procured the amount demanded. On the following day, he received another telephone call in which he was told to place the money in garbage bags and then to deposit the money at an indicated spot in Mont-Rolland in the Laurentians.

While Alper was *en route* to the arranged spot for the delivery of the money, the appellant and her husband drove the victim to a spot close to a taxi stand; the appellant took off the blindfold that the victim has been made to wear until then and Ogilvie ordered her not to turn around, to go directly to the taxi stand and to take a taxi to her house.

The appellant and Ogilvie then went into a restaurant in St-Adèle. Ogilvie then saw cars patrolling the road; he concluded that detectives had been alerted and he abandoned the scheme. Alper was informed that his daughter had been freed and he returned to his house with the ransom money.

Ten days later, the appellant recounted all she knew of the kidnapping to a member of the R.C.M.P., Brian Hunter. She then made a statement describing the circumstances of the kidnapping which she signed June 15, 1976, before Detectives Menard and Jolicoeur.

In her defence, she submitted she had been subject to compulsion and coercion. She had only acted out of fear of her husband, Kevin Ogilvie. The following facts, both prior and subsequent to the kidnapping, can enlighten us with respect to the nature of the defence of compulsion advanced by the appellant.

The appellant married Kevin Ogilvie on June 22, 1974 (J.C., p. 625). Less than one year later, on April 18, 1975, she laid an information against her husband for common assault (J.C., p. 633). The following year, she again laid an information, this time alleging that she feared that her husband would cause both herself and her daughter bodily harm as a result of threats made against them and asked that a peace bond order be rendered against him (J.C., p. 634). Subsequently, the appellant left her husband and the couple lived separately.

The appellant has known Brian Hunter, a detective sergeant of the R.C.M.P., for several years (J.C., p. 46). He was interested in the activities of Kevin Ogilvie. Hunter told the appellant that her husband, the owner of two night-clubs (J.C., p. 642), did business with criminals. Hunter suggested to the appellant that she help him find some "$3,000,000 in counterfeit money that Kevin Ogilvie had hidden" (J.C., p. 646). The appellant agreed to act as an informer (J.C., p. 67); she returned home to live with her husband approximately three months before the kidnapping of May 3, 1976 (J.C., p. 635).

Kevin Ogilvie had already demonstrated his animosity towards John Alper, who had previously employed the appellant as his secretary. He detested him "fiercely" (J.C., p. 123). Some two months before the kidnapping (J.C., pp. 444, 451 and 668) the appellant telephoned Alper and told him that she considered him as a "friend" (J.C., p. 673). She met with him and warned him that her husband was thinking of harming him in some manner (J.C., p. 45). As a result of this warning, John Alper was able to give the police the name of Kevin Ogilvie when, some time thereafter, his daughter Hannah was kidnapped (J.C., p. 452).

On Monday, May 2, 1976, Kevin Ogilvie told the appellant of his plan to kidnap Hannah Alper (J.C., p. 627). The appellant testified that she dared not reveal the plan to anyone and that she was "very afraid" of her husband (J.C., pp. 635 and 640). Ogilvie told her to call Hannah Alper and set up the rendezvous by making the victim believe that there was going to be a fashion show; Ogilvie also told her how to dress for the circumstances and told her to drive the car: "You're gonna take the wheel and do what I tell you or else." The appellant's two children were left with a Mrs. Morin in Laprairie; Ogilvie told the appellant that if she did not do as he said, she would never see her daughter again as she would be kidnapped and taken to the United States (J.C., p. 645).

One or two weeks after the kidnapping of Hannah Alper and the failed attempt at extortion, the appellant communicated with Detective Hunter and recounted to him what had happened. She explained that she had not dared telephone him sooner for fear that her husband would learn of it (J.C., p. 680). More particularly, she said that she feared communicating with any other police authority "because (if) Kevin Ogilvie had known that it was me who had betrayed him, he would have killed me" (J.C., p. 649). On June 15, 1976, at the suggestion of Detective Hunter, the appellant drew up a detailed account of the facts of the kidnapping (ex. D–1).

When asked if she had anything to add to her statement she said (J.C., p. 130):

> I didn't do it voluntarily (the kidnapping), I was extremely afraid of my husband and in addition I feared that he would kidnap my daughter through some sadistic manoeuvre because all he ever did was constantly hurt me, but I greatly regret having become mixed up in this affair; I'm sorry and I hope that God will forgive me.

REASONS FOR JUDGMENT NOW UNDER APPEAL

The fact of the kidnapping was not contested and the trial Judge rejected the defence of compulsion and coercion advanced by Tina Robins (J.C., vol. 4, pp. 879–81):

> The court finds that the accused played an important and indispensable role in the kidnapping and sequestration of Hannah Alper and that her actions can be assimilated to the co-action of a co-author of the offence.
>
> Having read the authors and books produced by the Crown, I adopt the position that section 17 of the *Criminal Code*, by referring specifically to forcible abduction, excludes the possibility of the accused advancing a defence of compulsion in the situation of a kidnapping in which the accused is "a principal in the first degree."
>
> In the circumstances of this case, and given the Court's decision with respect to the interpretation of section 17, it is impossible, except with respect to the charge of extortion, to successfully advance the codified defence in section 17 through the argument that the accused was not a party to any conspiracy or association whereby she was subjected to compulsion.
>
> Section 7(3) would have been applicable if the Court had found that Mrs. Robins was an accomplice within section 21. The *Paquette* case in the Supreme Court clearly sets out the following position, and I quote the opinion of Mr. Justice Martland:
>
>> In my opinion, the application of s. 17 is limited to cases in which the person seeking to rely upon it has himself committed an offence. If a person who actually commits the offense does so in the presence of another party who has compelled him to do the act by threats of immediate death or grievous bodily harm, then, if he believes the threats would be carried out, and is not a party to a conspiracy whereby he is subject to such compulsion, he is excused for committing the offence. The protection afforded by this section is not given in respect of the offences listed at the end of the section, which include murder and robbery.
>>
>> ...
>>
>> I have already stated my reasons for considering s. 17 to be inapplicable. That being so, the appellant is entitled, by virtue of s. 7(3) of the *Code* to rely upon any excuse or defence available to him at common law. The defence of duress to a charge of murder against a person who did not commit the murder, but who was alleged to have aided and abetted, was recently considered by the House of Lords in *Director of Public Prosecutions for Northern Ireland v. Lynch*, [1975] A.C. 653, in which the decided cases were fully reviewed.
>
> The Crown clearly set out the important facts of this case and the applicable law.
>
> Mr. Peloquin, counsel for the accused, attempted to take advantage of all the incidents involved in the drive up north in order to focus the argument on the secondary role of the accused and thereby attempted to advance a defence of duress.
>
> He saved no effort in attempting to show that the subjective criteria of compulsion and duress should apply with respect to his client.
>
> The Court is in agreement that the confession is in part exculpatory. The evidence of the accused showing compulsion or duress, however, does not in its entirety establish this thesis of duress, namely that the accused's will was overridden or affected by the actions of her husband.
>
> The Court will add that even if the defence of compulsion and duress had been open to the accused, even as the wife of Kevin Ogilvie, the Court would have been reticent, with respect to either section 17 of the *Criminal Code* or section 7(3) of the *Criminal Code*, to accept this special defence given that the objective facts are so shocking.
>
> The Court refers to the recent case *R. v. Bergstrom*, 52 C.C.C. (2d) 407, a decision of the Manitoba Court of Appeal, in which Mr. Justice Monnin expressed his views as follows:
>
>> Duress is not available to a person who has a safe avenue of escape before committing the offence, and on his own statement the accused had at least three opportunities to escape.... Finally, the threat must be one of immediate death or grievous bodily harm and in this case the threat was far from immediate, having been made on the drive from the city.

GROUNDS OF APPEAL

Reviewing the judgment under appeal and the grounds set out in the appellant's factum, the grounds of this appeal can be limited to the following three propositions:

1. the learned trial Judge erred in refusing to apply the defence of compulsion within s. 17 of the *Criminal Code*;

2. the learned trial Judge erred, even if the defence of compulsion in s. 17 were not available to the appellant, in failing to apply the defence of duress recognized at common law;
3. the learned trial Judge erred, even if the defence of compulsion within s. 17 of the common law were not available to the appellant, in failing to apply the defence of coercion which is also recognized in common law.

The Defence of Compulsion in s. 17 of the *Criminal Code*

[The judge canvassed the history behind the crimes excluded in s. 17 and concluded that "kidnapping" was not excluded although "forcible abduction" was.]

. . . .

In my view the respondent is incorrect in his argument in his factum (pp. 37–8), that forcible abduction, mentioned in the present s. 17, includes kidnapping s. 247, for the reason that kidnapping is punishable by imprisonment for life, whereas forcible abduction in s. 248 only provides a maximum term of imprisonment of 10 years. It does not seem logical to refuse the defence of compulsion to the author of a forcible abduction and to grant it to the author of a kidnapping, which is now considered to be an objectively more serious crime. But at the time when s. 12 (the present s. 17) was adopted, forcible abduction was a more serious crime. It was considered as a heinous crime because it offended social morals. Kidnapping, which was especially perpetrated in order to obtain cheap labour, was considered less scandalous. Since that period, social reprobation has decreased with respect to forcible abduction but has increased with respect to kidnapping. However, the Legislature has neglected, or has not thought it appropriate, to alter s. 17 (former s. 12).

. . . .

[T]here remains the question whether the other conditions set out in s. 17 are present in this case. One of these conditions is that the compulsion must have been exercised "by threats of immediate death or grievous bodily harm."

The trial Judge was of the view that the accused had not acted under the effect of threats of immediate death or grievous bodily harm and in any case, that she had opportunity to eliminate these threats by removing herself from the situation. This opinion follows from the citation of the reasons of Mr. Justice Monnin of the Manitoba Court of Appeal: *R. v. Bergstrom* (1980), 52 C.C.C. (2d) 407, 13 C.R. (3d) 342, [1980] 3 W.W.R. 146 (this case has since been quashed by the Supreme Court of Canada on another issue, 59 C.C.C. (2d) 481, 123 D.L.R. (3d) 584, 20 C.R. (3d) 347). The trial Judge's appreciation of the facts appears to me to conform with the evidence.

What pushed the appellant to participate in the kidnapping was undoubtedly her fear that her daughter would be kidnapped and taken to the United States where the appellant would no longer be able to see her. This is a serious threat, but not a threat of death nor of bodily harm. The appellant's husband is undoubtedly a violent man and the accused, who had already laid an information against her husband for common assault and who had already left him, might suspect some repetition of that situation when she returned to live with him. But the evidence does not reveal any assaults were perpetrated by the husband against the appellant since they began to live with each other again.

On only one occasion did she say that she feared that her husband would kill her; at that time, she had just been asked why she had waited one or two weeks before informing the police of the kidnapping (J.C., p. 635). But the trial Judge need not believe her evidence. In addition, this fear was subsequent to the kidnapping and the evidence does not show that she had acted under threats made by her husband.

In any event, the threats which may have influenced her conduct did not put her immediate security into danger. Before the perpetration of the crime and during its execution, she could have eliminated this threat by leaving her husband. In the English version of s. 17, the word "immediate" qualifies both the death and the grievous bodily harm (this is how the Supreme Court of Canada interpreted it in *R. v. Carker* (No. 2), [1967] 2 C.C.C. 190, [1967] S.C.R. 114, 2 C.R.N.S. 16). In the French version, the adjective "immediate" only applies to the word "death" which appears to me to be illogical. If the threat of death does not excuse when it is not immediate, for much greater reason, the sole threat of grievous bodily harm which is not immediate should render the perpetration of the crime even less excusable.

For these reasons, I am of the view that one of the conditions required under s. 17 of the *Criminal Code* in order that the defence of compulsion be available, was not present. It is therefore not necessary to decide if any of the other conditions required have been fulfilled, namely, that the appellant "is not a party to a conspiracy or association whereby he is subject to compulsion."

The Defence of Duress at Common Law

Section 17 of the *Criminal Code* only partially codifies the defence of compulsion. It applies only in the case where a person actually commits the crime and is not merely a party who aids the true author to commit it. This follows from the words used in the section: "A person who commits an offence ... is excused for committing the offence...." Section 21 of the *Criminal Code* distinguishes between (a) the person who "actually commits" the crime, and (b) the person who "does anything or omits to do anything for the purpose of aiding any person to commit it."

Both are parties to the offence, but only the first is the actual author and only he comes within s. 17 of the *Criminal Code*: *R. v. Paquette* (1976), 30 C.C.C. (2d) 417, 70 D.L.R. (3d) 129, [1977] 2 S.C.R. 189.

The two defences of compulsion, s. 17 of the *Criminal Code* (compulsion) and duress at common law, cannot apply at the same time. They can only be advanced in the alternative to each other.

If the appellant had actually committed the kidnapping, only the defence in s. 17 would apply. If the accused had only participated in the kidnapping as a party by aiding her husband to commit it, s. 17 is inapplicable and the defence of duress at common law may be available.

The appellant submitted that she was not the actual author of the offence. She argued that she had not actually perpetrated the kidnapping, "in that she had at no moment touched the victim" (factum, p. 12). At most, she would have "helped Ogilvie by serving as bait and by driving the vehicle" (factum, p. 14).

I find on the contrary, that the appellant, as is the case with her husband, actually effected and committed the kidnapping. Several persons can combine their actions in order to perpetrate, together, an indictable offence. The offence is their common work, because each of them "actually commits it" in the sense in which this expression is used in s. 21(1)(a).

This is what happened in the present case. The actions of the appellant, as well as those of her husband, were all essential to the perpetration of the kidnapping. Seizing a person and overpowering them does not constitute kidnapping, since this crime presumes the displacement of the victim against his will. The Ogilvie couple could have changed roles; the appellant, on the order of her husband, could have grabbed the victim and overpowered her while Ogilvie could have driven the car. In a similar case, one would not hesitate to say that the husband, as much as the wife, had actually committed the crime of kidnapping. The distribution of the essential tasks in the execution of the crime between two persons does not prevent each of them from actually committing it. The fact that only one was the directing mind and boss of the criminal operation has no importance except at the time of considering the just and appropriate sentence to be imposed. In my view, the trial Judge did not commit an error when he found that "the accused played an important and indispensable role in the kidnapping and sequestration of Hannah Alper, and that her action can be assimilated to the co-action of a co-author of the offence."

Since the appellant had participated herself in the perpetration of the kidnapping, she falls within s. 17 of the *Criminal Code* and the defence of duress at common law is not available. In addition, even if she had only been an accomplice aiding the sole author of the kidnapping, she would not have been excused unless she had been compelled by threats of death or grievous bodily harm. The defence at common law also requires that the accused had acted *pro timore mortis* or from fear of injury, the gravity of which must be proportional to the gravity of the crime committed (Smith and Hogan, *Criminal Law*, 4th ed. (1978), Butterworths, p. 203). This condition is not present in this case.

The Defence of Coercion at Common Law

Besides the defence of duress available to all citizens, a very special defence of coercion also exists at common law. This defence is only available to the married woman who commits certain crimes in the presence of her husband. The presumption that the sole presence of her husband creates compulsion can only be rebutted by evidence that the wife had taken the initiative in doing the crime, independent of her husband. The origin of this defence of coercion is explained by the former state of subjugation of the wife and her duty to obey her husband.

This defence was also a sort of equitable compensation granted to the wife, who (until 1692) could not, unlike her husband, obtain the benefit of clergy and thereby avoid the rigours of punishment then in force, which included the death penalty.

The extent of the defence of coercion has remained unsettled. It is settled however that it is not available in the case of murder or treason; but the authors are not in agreement as to whether it is available in the case of crimes such as manslaughter or robbery. The violence to which the woman who advances the defence of coercion is subjected, is simply psychological, whereas in the case of duress, the person acts out of fear of physical violence.

Does the defence of coercion at common law continue to form part of the Canadian law? Section 7 of the *Criminal Code* continues grounds of defence recognized at common law as justifications or excuses for a criminal act:

> 7(3) ... except in so far as they are altered by or are inconsistent with this Act or any other Act of the Parliament of Canada.

Section 13 of our first *Criminal Code* (1892), the equivalent of s. 18 of the present *Code*, clearly deals with the defence of coercion:

> 13. No presumption shall be made that a married woman committing an offence does so under compulsion because she commits it in the presence of her husband.

In my view, this section has had the effect of abolishing the antiquated defence of marital coercion and to place the woman on an equal footing with all other citizens (Glanville Williams, *Criminal Law*, 2nd ed. (1961), Stevens & Sons Ltd., para. 249, p. 768: "Similarly the Codes of Canada (s. 18), New Zealand and Tasmania seem to place the wife in the same position as everyone else").

The appellant refers to English and American commentators in support of her argument that this defence continues to exist. These commentators are not faced with the text of our s. 18. In England, the following text, which resembles our own but which contains an important addition, was adopted in 1925 and has caused much confusion:

> *Criminal Justice Act, 1925 (U.K.), c. 86, s. 47*
>
> 47. Any presumption of law that an offence committed by a wife in the presence of her husband is committed under the coercion of the husband is hereby abolished, but on a charge against a wife for any offence other than treason or murder, it shall be a good defence to prove that the offence was committed in the presence and under the coercion of the husband.

After the presumption on which the defence of marital coercion was based, was abolished, it was thought appropriate to recognize in the favour of the married woman, a defence which some authors attribute to the former defence of marital coercion but which others assimilate to the defence of duress. Glanville Williams commented as follows on this text of law (at pp. 764–5):

> These simple-seeming words raise an almost insoluble problem of interpretation.
>
> ...
>
> Quite obviously Parliament intended that the issue should in future be one of coercion. But "coercion" has no meaning in criminal law save as a synonym for duress. The law has never recognised any issue of moral coercion, or undue influence....
>
> The argument leads towards the conclusion that whatever the unexpressed intention of Parliament in this ill-drawn exactment, as it stands it puts the married woman in the same position as anyone else. The second sentence of the section can be explained as having been inserted *ex abundanti cautela;* the position would have been the same without it.

The survival of the defence of marital coercion is therefore both uncertain and criticized in England. On a number of occasions, its express abolition has been recommended, for no one continues to believe that the married woman, in the presence of her husband, only acts as his puppet.

In the presence of s. 18 of the *Criminal Code*, it seems to me impossible to accept the argument that a defence, based on a fiction, whose reason for its existence has since disappeared and which is incompatible with the prevailing morals and state of our law, continues to exist.

For these reasons, I find that none of the grounds of defence advanced by the appellant can be accepted. I would accordingly dismiss the appeal.

■

Does *Robins* produce a just result? When is a threat by a man with a history of violence a threat of death or bodily harm within s. 17? How relevant is the criterion of immediacy in these circumstances? Would the accused have eliminated the threat by leaving her husband, as the court suggests? Who encouraged Robins to return to her husband? By what criteria is "harm" evaluated? Do you agree with the court's conclusion that the threat to a mother by an abusive man, that he will kidnap her child and that she will never see the child again, is "not a threat of death or bodily harm"?

Now compare *Robins* to *R. v. Mena* (1987), 20 O.A.C. 50 (C.A.) where an accused convicted of robbery was granted a new trial so that duress could be put to the jury. Like Robins, Mena had performed the actions of a principal for the offence charged: he had tied and blindfolded the victim and helped to carry the goods from the store. The court on appeal said that duress may have vitiated his *mens rea* as a principal, and the evidence of the victim corroborated Mena's story, as Mena had tied his hands and the blindfold very loosely. He was therefore re-characterized as a party, entitled to the common law defence of duress. Could Robins have benefited from such a generous analysis? See now *R. v. Hibbert*, below, which may overrule *Mena* on this point.

In *R. v. Hébert*, [1989] 1 S.C.R. 233, the accused notary was denied the defence of duress when he committed perjury after being threatened with death by a man against whom he was subpoenaed to testify. Can you anticipate the reasoning? Compare *R. v. Hudson, [1971] 2 Q.B. 202 (C.A.), discussed in Mena*, above. Is the Court of Appeal decision in *Hudson* a "surprisingly indulgent decision"? Was there an "obvious and safe means of escape"?

In *R. v. Prosper* (1980), (Sask. Prov. Ct.) [unreported], the court allowed a defence of duress to a charge of unlawfully driving a motor vehicle while disqualified, where the accused testified that her abusive husband had threatened to assault her either immediately or when they got home. The readiness with which the judge accepted the defence may have been influenced by a negative perception of Aboriginal men, and the judge made gratuitous comments about the context of violence in Aboriginal communities.

There has been considerable criticism of the defence of duress by feminist scholars on the narrow construction of "imminence", the male standard of reasonableness, and the restrictive interpretation of "bodily harm". Also, the exclusion of specific offences has been challenged. For a report critiquing *Reforming the General Part of the Criminal Code* (Ottawa: Department of Justice, 1994), see: Sheila Greene, *The Impact on Women of the White Paper Proposals on the Defences of Duress and Necessity* (St. Johns: Nfld. Women's Directorate, 1994). Greene discusses several cases in which duress was argued successfully, including *R. v. Payne*, [1974] 2 W.W.R. 658 (B.C. Prov. Ct.), where a woman inmate was acquitted of escaping lawful custody because she feared for her life and safety.

The restrictions in s. 17, with respect to both immediacy and the presence of the threatener, have been challenged constitutionally on the basis that the requirements in s. 17 of the *Code* mean that an accused could be convicted although lacking "fault", thereby violating s. 7 of the *Charter*. *R. v. Parris* (1992), 11 C.R.R. (2d) 376 (Ont. Ct. (Gen. Div.)) held that the violation of s. 7 was not saved by s. 1, and therefore, the provisions in s. 17 were of no force and effect. Similarly, in *R. v. Langlois* (1993), 19 C.R. (4th) 87 (Que. C.A.), the court held that s. 17 violated s. 7, and thus, the common law defence of duress was available to the accused prison worker who smuggled drugs into a prison after numerous threatening telephone calls.

Finally, in *R. v. Ruzic*, [2001] 1 S.C.R. 687, the Court held that s. 17 was overly restrictive such that the legislation infringed s. 7 in denying the defence of duress.

R. v. Ruzic†

[LeBEL J.:]

On April 29, 1994 Marijana Ruzic, a Yugoslav citizen, landed at Pearson Airport in Toronto carrying two kilograms of heroin strapped to her body and a false Austrian passport. When the heroin was found on her, she was arrested, charged and tried for possession and use of a false passport and unlawful importation of narcotics. At trial, Ruzic successfully challenged the constitutionality of s. 17 of the *Criminal Code*, R.S.C. 1985, c. C-46, raised the common law defence of duress and was acquitted by a jury. The Crown appealed the acquittal without success to the Ontario Court of Appeal. This appeal now raises, as a core issue, the constitutional validity, under s. 7 of the *Canadian Charter of Rights and*

† [2001] 1 S.C.R. 687.

Freedoms, of s. 17 of the *Criminal Code* and more precisely of some of the conditions restricting the admissibility of the defence of duress. For reasons differing in part from those of the Court of Appeal, I will suggest that s. 17 of the *Criminal Code* be declared unconstitutional in part, that the acquittal of the respondent Ruzic be upheld and that the appeal be dismissed.

I. FACTS

The respondent Marijana Ruzic was born in Belgrade in the former Yugoslavia. She was 21 years old when she entered Canada. When heroin was discovered on her, she was charged with three offences, two of which proceeded to trial: possession and use of a false passport contrary to s. 368 of the *Criminal Code*, and unlawful importation of a narcotic contrary to s. 5(1) of the *Narcotic Control Act*, R.S.C. 1985, c. N-1.

Ms. Ruzic admitted having committed both offences but claimed that she was then acting under duress and should thus be relieved from any criminal liability. She testified that, two months before her arrival in Canada, a man named Mirko Mirkovic approached her while she was walking her dog in the streets of Belgrade, where she lived in an apartment with her mother. She described him as a "warrior" and believed he was paid to kill people in the war. An expert witness testified at trial that, in 1994, large paramilitary groups roamed Belgrade and engaged in criminal and mafia-like activities. The same expert maintained that people living in Belgrade during that period did not feel safe. They believed the police could not be trusted. There was a real sense that the rule of law had broken down.

From there began a series of encounters between Mirkovic and the respondent while she was walking her dog. Each time he approached her, he knew more about her, although she had shared no details of her life with him. He phoned her at home. He told her he knew her every move. Ms. Ruzic alleged that his behaviour became more and more intimidating, escalating to threats and acts of physical violence. On one occasion, he burned her arm with a lighter. On another, he stuck a syringe into her arm and injected her with a substance that smelled like heroin and made her nauseous. She indicated that these physical assaults were coupled with sexual harassment and finally threats against her mother.

On April 25, 1994, Mirkovic phoned the respondent and instructed her to pack a bag and meet him at a hotel in central Belgrade. Once there, he allegedly strapped three packages of heroin to her body and indicated that she was to take them to a restaurant in Toronto. He gave her the false passport, a bus ticket from Belgrade to Budapest and some money. He told her to fly from Budapest to Athens, and then from Athens to Toronto. When she protested, he warned her that, if she failed to comply, he would harm her mother.

Ms. Ruzic arrived in Budapest on April 26. Late that evening, she boarded a plane to Athens, where she arrived early the next day. She then purchased a ticket to Toronto. She missed that flight, exchanged her ticket for the next available flight, and left for Toronto two days later, on April 29.

During the two months prior to her journey to Canada, Ms. Ruzic testified that she did not tell her mother or anyone else about Mirkovic. She was afraid he would harm whoever she told. She did not seek police protection because she believed the police in Belgrade were corrupt and would do nothing to assist her. She maintained that she followed Mirkovic's instructions out of fear for her mother's safety. She made no attempt while in Budapest or Athens to seek the assistance of police or other government officials. Similarly, before her arrest, she did not ask any Canadian authorities for help. She asserted that she believed the only way she could protect her mother was to obey Mirkovic's orders.

. . . .

III JUDICIAL HISTORY

A. Ontario Court (General Division)

Ms. Ruzic was tried before Herold J. and a jury. Her main line of defence was that she acted under duress. She conceded that her claim of duress did not meet the immediacy and presence requirements of s. 17 of the *Criminal Code*. Mirkovic's threats were not of "immediate" death or bodily harm and he was not "present" when she committed the offence. Furthermore, the threats were directed at her mother. She accordingly challenged the constitutionality of s. 17 under s. 7 of the *Charter*, in order to raise the common law defence of duress that, in her mind, did not incorporate the requirements of immediacy and presence.

Herold J. accepted her submissions, holding that s. 17 of the *Criminal Code* infringes s. 7 of the *Charter* and cannot be justified under s. 1. Rather than setting out the grounds for his conclusion in any detail, he adopted the reasoning of two previous judgments in which s. 17 was found unconstitutional: *R. v. Parris* (1992), 11 C.R.R. (2d) 376 (Ont. Ct.

(Gen. Div.)), *per* Thomas J., and *R. v. Langlois*, [1993] R.J.Q. 675 (C.A.), *per* Fish J.A. He then instructed the jury on the common law defence of duress, which is preserved by virtue of s. 8(3) of the *Criminal Code*. The jury acquitted Ms. Ruzic on both charges. The Crown appealed the acquittal on the charge of importing heroin to the Court of Appeal for Ontario.

B. Ontario Court of Appeal (1998), 41 O.R. (3d) 1

Writing for the Court of Appeal, Laskin J.A. upheld the trial judge's finding that the immediacy and presence requirements in s. 17 infringe s. 7 of the *Charter*. First, he maintained that it would violate the principles of fundamental justice to convict a person whose actions are morally involuntary. He held that this Court in *Re B.C. Motor Vehicle Act*, [1985] 2 S.C.R. 486, and subsequent cases had recognized, as a principle of fundamental justice, the requirement that the morally blameless should not be punished. He likened moral voluntariness to moral blameworthiness. Those who act in a morally involuntary fashion, he stated, are not morally blameworthy for what they do. It follows that it would be contrary to s. 7 of the *Charter* to attach criminal liability to their conduct. In the alternative, he found such similarity between moral blamelessness and moral involuntariness that it would be as unfair to punish morally involuntary conduct as it would be unjust to punish morally blameless behaviour.

Second, Laskin J.A. held that the immediacy and presence restrictions in s. 17 are poor measures of moral voluntariness. They deny access to the defence to an accused who is threatened with future injury. In addition, they render the defence unavailable to persons whose family members are the target of the threatened harm. As he explained at p. 32:

> The underlying problem with the immediacy and presence restrictions is that they do not adequately capture all morally involuntary conduct. Perka and Hibbert hold that the essence of involuntary conduct is the absence of a realistic choice or a safe avenue of escape. The mother whose child is abducted, or Mr. Langlois whose family is threatened, or Ms. Ruzic who lives where the police cannot help her or her mother, or the battered spouse who cannot leave her abusive relationship, do not have a realistic choice but to commit a criminal offence, even though the threatened harm is not immediate and the threatener is not present when the offence is committed.

He concluded that the immediacy and presence requirements contravene s. 7 of the *Charter* because they permit the conviction of persons whose conduct is morally involuntary.

Laskin J.A. also endorsed an alternative basis for finding that s. 17 violates s. 7. It is that the immediacy and presence restrictions risk punishing persons contrary to the principle of fundamental justice that the deprivation of a right must not be arbitrary or unfair. In his view, these criteria conflict with Parliament's purpose in providing the defence in the first place, which is to excuse acts that are morally involuntary.

Third, Laskin J.A. held that the violation of s. 7 was not saved by s. 1. He specified three reasons for so finding: the appellant made no submissions regarding s. 1, there are no decisions of this Court in which a breach of s. 7 has been justified, and the immediacy and presence requirements in s. 17 do not satisfy the proportionality component of the s. 1 analysis. He declared s. 17 of no force or effect to the extent that it prevents an accused from relying on the common law defence of duress. He then added that this declaration applied only to those offences not listed in s. 17 as an excluded offence.

Last, Laskin J.A. concluded that ... [t]he operative test was whether the accused had a safe avenue of escape, assessed on a reasonableness standard taking into account the personal circumstances of the accused....

IV. ISSUES

Lamer C.J. stated the following constitutional questions:

1. Do the requirements in s. 17 of the *Criminal Code*, R.S.C. 1985, c. C-46, that a threat must be of immediate death or bodily harm and from a person who is present when the offence is committed infringe the rights of an accused person as guaranteed by s. 7 of the *Canadian Charter of Rights and Freedoms*?
2. If the answer to Question 1 is yes, is the said infringement of the s. 7 rights a reasonable limit that can be demonstrably justified under s. 1 of the *Canadian Charter of Rights and Freedoms*?
3. Does s. 17 of the *Criminal Code*, R.S.C. 1985, c. C-46, infringe the rights of an accused person as guaranteed by s. 7 of the *Canadian Charter of Rights and Freedoms* by precluding

access to the defence of duress where the threat is to a third party?

4. If the answer to Question 3 is yes, is the said infringement of the s. 7 rights a reasonable limit that can be demonstrably justified under s. 1 of the *Canadian Charter of Rights and Freedoms*?

The first and central question before us is thus framed in the same way that it was in the courts below: do the immediacy and presence requirements in s. 17 of the *Criminal Code* infringe s. 7 of the *Charter*, and, if so, can they be justified under s. 1? ...

. . . .

At issue also is whether s. 17 of the *Criminal Code* infringes s. 7 of the *Charter* by precluding access to the defence of duress where the threatened harm is directed not at the accused, but at a third party. The appellant puts forth a third issue, which is whether the trial judge's exposition of the common law defence of duress to the jury was defective.

Before examining each issue, it should be noted that s. 17 of the *Criminal Code* places another restriction on the defence. It lists 22 offences, ranging from murder and sexual assault to less serious crimes such as robbery and arson, which are excluded from the scope of the defence. Importation of narcotics, and possession and use of a false passport, do not appear on this list. Thus, this appeal does not concern the constitutional validity of the list of excluded offences.

V. ANALYSIS

A. Are Statutory Defences Owed Special Deference by Reviewing Courts?

The appellant argued in the Court below that statutory defences are not subject to *Charter* scrutiny. Laskin J.A. rejected this submission. The argument was recast somewhat before this Court....

It bears emphasizing that a statutory defence, like any other legislative provision, is not immune from *Charter* scrutiny. Section 24 of the *Charter* and s. 52 of the *Constitution Act*, 1982 command the judiciary to review the work of the legislature, according to the standards enshrined in those documents. As Iacobucci J. stated in *Vriend v. Alberta*, [1998] 1 S.C.R. 493, at pp. 566–67:

> Democratic values and principles under the *Charter* demand that legislators and the executive take these into account; and if they fail to do so, courts should stand ready to intervene to protect these democratic values as appropriate. As others have so forcefully stated, judges are not acting undemocratically by intervening when there are indications that a legislative or executive decision was not reached in accordance with the democratic principles mandated by the *Charter*....

Soon after the *Charter* came into force, Lamer J. (as he then was) pointed out in *Re B.C. Motor Vehicle Act*, *supra*, at pp. 496–97, that courts have not only the power but the duty to evaluate the substantive content of legislation for *Charter* compliance. In the realm of criminal law, the courts routinely review the definition of criminal offences to ensure conformity with *Charter* rights. This has included the *mens rea* element of an offence: e.g., *R. v. Vaillancourt*, [1987] 2 S.C.R. 636; *R. v. Wholesale Travel Group Inc.*, [1991] 3 S.C.R. 154. These powers and responsibilities extend equally to statutory defences. Courts would be abdicating their constitutional duty by abstaining from such a review. Defences and excuses belong to the legislative corpus that the *Charter* submits to constitutional review by the courts.

Subject to constitutional review, Parliament retains the power to restrict access to a criminal defence or to remove it altogether. As Cory J. indicated for the majority in *R. v. Finta*, [1994] 1 S.C.R. 701, a withdrawal of a criminal defence will not automatically breach s. 7 of the *Charter*. Among other things, *Finta* raised the question whether the removal of the defence of obedience to or authority of *de facto* law for war crimes and crimes against humanity infringed s. 7. Cory J. observed, at p. 865, that restricting the availability of a defence "will not generally violate s. 7 when a defence is inconsistent with the offence proscribed, in that it would excuse the very evil which the offence seeks to prohibit or punish". Likewise, in *R. v. Penno*, [1990] 2 S.C.R. 865, the removal of drunkenness as a defence to a charge of impaired driving was deemed consistent with s. 7.

The circumstances in this appeal are quite different from those in *Finta* and *Penno*. There is no suggestion that the defence of duress is inconsistent with the offences with which Ms. Ruzic was charged. Section 17 would not excuse the "very evil" that those offences seek to punish. In my view, the relevance of *Finta* and *Penno* to the present appeal is that limitations on a criminal defence may very well be consistent with s. 7 of the *Charter*. Thus, the issue is not whether the legislature may restrict or remove a criminal defence. It certainly can. The question for the courts is whether restricting the defence of duress accords with *Charter* rights.

. . . . .

B. Is it a Principle of Fundamental Justice That Only Morally Voluntary Conduct Can Attract Criminal Liability?

Whether it is a principle of fundamental justice under s. 7 of the *Charter* that morally involuntary conduct should not be punished is a novel question before this Court. We are thus called upon to canvass once more the contents of the "principles of fundamental justice", this time in the context of the defence of duress as framed by s. 17 of the *Criminal Code*.

The Court has on numerous occasions confirmed that the principles of fundamental justice "are to be found in the basic tenets of our legal system" [citing *Re B.C. Motor Vehicle Act*, *R. v. Seaboyer*, and *Rodriguez v. British Columbia*]....

The notion of moral voluntariness was first introduced in *Perka v. The Queen*, [1984] 2 S.C.R. 232, for the purpose of explaining the defence of necessity and classifying it as an excuse. It was borrowed from the American legal theorist George Fletcher's discussion of excuses in *Rethinking Criminal Law* (1978). A person acts in a morally involuntary fashion when, faced with perilous circumstances, she is deprived of a realistic choice whether to break the law. By way of illustration in *Perka*, Dickson J. evoked the situation of a lost alpinist who, on the point of freezing to death, breaks into a remote mountain cabin. The alpinist confronts a painful dilemma: freeze to death or commit a criminal offence. Yet as Dickson J. pointed out at p. 249, the alpinist's choice to break the law "is no true choice at all; it is remorselessly compelled by normal human instincts", here of self-preservation. The Court in *Perka* thus conceptualized the defence of necessity as an excuse. An excuse, Dickson J. maintained, concedes that the act was wrongful, but withholds criminal attribution to the actor because of the dire circumstances surrounding its commission....

Extending its reasoning in *Perka* to the defence of duress, the Court found in *R. v. Hibbert*, [1995] 2 S.C.R. 973, that it too rests on the notion of moral voluntariness. In the case of the defences of necessity and duress, the accused contends that he should avoid conviction because he acted in response to a threat of impending harm. The Court also confirmed in *Hibbert* that duress does not ordinarily negate the *mens rea* element of an offence. Like the defence of necessity, the Court classified the defence of duress as an excuse, like that of necessity. As such, duress operates to relieve a person of criminal liability only after he has been found to have committed the prohibited act with the relevant *mens rea*: see also *Bergstrom v. The Queen*, [1981] 1 S.C.R. 539, at p. 544 (*per* McIntyre J.).

Thus duress, like necessity, involves the concern that morally involuntary conduct not be subject to criminal liability. Can this notion of "moral voluntariness" be recognized as a principle of fundamental justice under s. 7 of the *Charter*? Let us examine possible avenues which have been put forward by the respondent towards such recognition.

1. Moral Voluntariness and Moral Blameworthiness

As we will see below, this Court has recognized on a number of occasions that "moral blameworthiness" is an essential component of criminal liability which is protected under s. 7 as a "principle of fundamental justice". The respondent in the case at bar attempts to link the principles of "moral blameworthiness" and "moral voluntariness" as a means of securing the constitutional status of the defence of duress. Laskin J.A. in the Court below has followed this line of reasoning. However, the appellant argues that "moral blamelessness" only arises in the absence of either the *actus reus* or the *mens rea* of an offence. One who acts under duress, he contends, remains a morally responsible agent whose behaviour is not blame-free. Further, the appellant submits that moral involuntariness is too vague and amorphous a concept to constitute a principle of fundamental justice.

This controversy about the concepts of moral blamelessness and moral involuntariness brings us back to the foundations of criminal responsibility. In the analysis of duress and of its relationship with the tenets of the criminal justice system, is it appropriate to equate moral blamelessness with moral involuntariness?

Even before the advent of the *Charter*, it became a basic concern of the criminal law that criminal responsibility be ascribed only to acts that resulted from the choice of a conscious mind and an autonomous will. In other words, only those persons acting in the knowledge of what they were doing, with the freedom to choose, would bear the burden and stigma of criminal responsibility. Although the element of voluntariness may sometimes overlap both *actus reus* and *mens rea* (see *R. v. Daviault*, [1994] 3 S.C.R. 63, at pp. 73–75, *per* Cory J.), the importance of *mens rea* and of the quality of voluntariness in it underscores the fact that criminal liability is founded on the premise that it will be borne only by those persons who knew what they were doing and willed it....

An example of this approach may be found in the jurisprudence on the application and interpretation of offences purporting to impose an absolute responsibility on the accused. Even before the *Charter* came into force, through the use of techniques of interpretation, the Supreme Court had sought to restrict the application of the penal provisions of statutes that imposed absolute liability. The judgment of this Court in *R. v. City of Sault Ste. Marie*, [1978] 2 S.C.R. 1299, underscores this view that absolute responsibility was inconsistent with the correct understanding of the founding principles of criminal liability. Without requiring a full *mens rea*, the Court decided that, generally speaking, absent very clear and explicit language to the contrary, at least a defence of due diligence should be available to the accused. This form of penal responsibility had to be grounded on an element of voluntariness, the choice left to the accused being at least that of acting with due diligence, to avoid convicting innocents....

It is clear from Dickson J.'s reasons in *Sault Ste. Marie* that such a regime of absolute penal responsibility was deemed to breach the most basic principle of criminal liability and criminal law, and that criminal responsibility should be attributed only to an act that is the result of the deliberation of a free and conscious mind. This principle was recognized as one of the principles of fundamental justice within the meaning of s. 7 of the *Charter* in *Re B.C. Motor Vehicle Act*, *supra*....

That decision and the Court's subsequent judgment in *Vaillancourt*, *supra*, were explained by McIntyre J. in *R. v. Bernard*, [1988] 2 S.C.R. 833, at p. 880:

> In *Re B.C. Motor Vehicle Act* ... and in *R. v. Vaillancourt* ... it was held that the requirement for a minimum mental state before the attachment of criminal liability is a principle of fundamental justice. Criminal offences, as a general rule, must have as one of their elements the requirement of a blameworthy mental state. The morally innocent ought not to be convicted.

[The Court went on to cite for support the decisions in *R. v. Vaillancourt*, *R. v. Martineau*, and *R. v. DeSousa*.]

. . . .

It should be emphasized that this Court, in cases like *Sault Ste. Marie and Re B.C. Motor Vehicle Act*, has referred to moral innocence in the context of the discussion of the mental element of an offence. *Hibbert*, on the other hand, held that the defence of duress does not normally negate *mens rea*. Rather, it operates to excuse a wrongful act once the *actus reus* and *mens rea* components of the offence have been made out. Laskin J.A. conceded this point, but countered that moral blameworthiness is a broader concept, extending beyond the traditional elements of an offence. Both Laskin J.A. and the respondent rely heavily, in this respect, on Professor Martha Shaffer's article "Scrutinizing Duress: The Constitutional Validity of Section 17 of the *Criminal Code*" (1998), 40 Crim. L.Q. 444, in making this argument.

Professor Shaffer acknowledges in her article, at pp. 453–54, that moral blameworthiness is an ambiguous concept, the meaning of which this Court has not had occasion to discuss in any significant way. I am reluctant to do so here, particularly since, in my opinion, conduct that is morally involuntary is not always intrinsically free of blame. (See also *R. v. Chaulk*, [1990] 3 S.C.R. 1303, at pp. 1396–98.) Moral involuntariness is also related to the notion that the defence of duress is an excuse.... This recognizes that there was indeed an alternative to breaking the law, although in the case of duress that choice may be even more unpalatable — to be killed or physically harmed.

... As Fletcher, *supra*, puts it ... excuses absolve the accused of personal accountability by focusing, not on the wrongful act, but on the circumstances of the act and the accused's personal capacity to avoid it. Necessity and duress are characterized as concessions to human frailty in this sense. The law is designed for the common man, not for a community of saints or heroes.

To equate moral involuntariness with moral innocence would amount to a significant departure from the reasoning in *Perka* and *Hibbert*. It would be contrary to the Court's conceptualization of duress as an excuse. Morally involuntary conduct is not always inherently blameless. Once the elements of the offence have been established, the accused can no longer be considered blameless. This Court has never taken the concept of blamelessness any further than this initial finding of guilt, nor should it in this case. The undefinable and potentially far-reaching nature of the concept of moral blamelessness prevents us from recognizing its relevance beyond an initial finding of guilt in the context of s. 7 of the *Charter*. Holding otherwise would inject an unacceptable degree of uncertainty into the law. It would not be consistent with our duty to consider as "principles of fundamental justice" only those concepts which are constrained and capable of being defined with reasonable precision. I would therefore reject this basis for finding that it is a principle of fundamental justice that morally involuntary acts should not be punished.

2. *Moral Voluntariness and Voluntariness in the Physical Sense*

The respondent's second approach, which relates moral voluntariness back to voluntariness in the physical sense, rests on firmer ground. It draws upon the fundamental principle of criminal law that, in order to attract criminal liability, an act must be voluntary. Voluntariness in this sense has ordinarily referred to the *actus reus* element of an offence. It queries whether the actor had control over the movement of her body or whether the wrongful act was the product of a conscious will. Although duress does not negate ordinarily *actus reus per se* (just as it does not ordinarily negate *mens rea* as we have just seen), the principle of voluntariness, unlike that of "moral blamelessness", can remain relevant in the context of s. 7 even after the basic elements of the offence have been established. Unlike the concept of "moral blamelessness", duress in its "voluntariness" perspective can more easily be constrained and can therefore more justifiably fall within the "principles of fundamental justice", even after the basic elements of the offence have been established.

Let us examine the notion of "voluntariness" and its interplay with duress more closely. As Dickson J. stated in *Rabey v. The Queen*, [1980] 2 S.C.R. 513, at p. 522, "it is basic principle that absence of volition in respect of the act involved is always a defence to a crime. A defence that the act is involuntary entitles the accused to a complete and unqualified acquittal." Dickson J.'s pronouncement was endorsed by the Court in *R. v. Parks*, [1992] 2 S.C.R. 871. The principle of voluntariness was given constitutional status in *Daviault*, *supra*, at pp. 102–3, where Cory J. held for the majority that it would infringe s. 7 of the *Charter* to convict an accused who was not acting voluntarily, as a fundamental aspect of the *actus reus* would be absent. More recently, in *R. v. Stone*, [1999] 2 S.C.R. 290, the crucial role of voluntariness as a condition of the attribution of criminal liability was again confirmed (at para. 1, *per* Binnie J., and paras. 155–58, *per* Bastarache J.) in an appeal concerning the defence of automatism.

In introducing the concept of moral voluntariness in *Perka*, the Court specifically linked it to the more familiar notion of physical voluntariness discussed above. Dickson J. acknowledged that the two concepts are not identical. The lost alpinist, for instance, does not act in a literally involuntary fashion; he is physically capable of avoiding the criminal act. Fletcher, *supra*, puts forth another example, more pertinent to the defence of duress. Suppose someone puts a knife in the accused's hand and forces it into the victim's chest. The accused's body is literally overpowered, as is her will. Consider next the situation of someone who gives the accused a knife and orders her to stab the victim or else be killed herself. Unlike the first scenario, moral voluntariness is not a matter of physical dimension. The accused here retains conscious control over her bodily movements. Yet, like the first actor, her will is overborne, this time by the threats of another. Her conduct is not, in a realistic way, freely chosen.

What underpins both of these conceptions of voluntariness is the critical importance of autonomy in the attribution of criminal liability: *Perka*, *supra*, at pp. 250–51; Fletcher, *supra*, at p. 805. The treatment of criminal offenders as rational, autonomous and choosing agents is a fundamental organizing principle of our criminal law. Its importance is reflected not only in the requirement that an act must be voluntary, but also in the condition that a wrongful act must be intentional to ground a conviction. *Sault Ste. Marie*, *Re B.C. Motor Vehicle Act*, and *Vaillancourt* all stand for the proposition that a guilty verdict requires intentional conduct or conduct equated to it like recklessness or gross negligence. Like voluntariness, the requirement of a guilty mind is rooted in respect for individual autonomy and free will and acknowledges the importance of those values to a free and democratic society: *Martineau*, *supra* ... Criminal liability also depends on the capacity to choose — the ability to reason right from wrong. As McLachlin J. observed in *Chaulk*, *supra*, at p. 1396, in the context of the insanity provisions of the *Criminal Code*, this assumption of the rationality and autonomy of human beings forms part of the essential premises of Canadian criminal law:

> At the heart of our criminal law system is the cardinal assumption that human beings are rational and autonomous.... This is the fundamental condition upon which criminal responsibility reposes. Individuals have the capacity to reason right from wrong, and thus to choose between right and wrong....

Punishing a person whose actions are involuntary in the physical sense is unjust because it conflicts with the assumption in criminal law that individuals are autonomous and freely choosing agents.... It is similarly unjust to penalize an individual who acted in a morally involuntary fashion. This is so because his acts cannot realistically be attributed to him, as his will was constrained by some external force....

. . . .

Although moral involuntariness does not negate the *actus reus* or *mens rea* of an offence, it is a principle which, similarly to physical involuntariness, deserves protection under s. 7 of the *Charter*. It is a principle of fundamental justice that only voluntary conduct — behaviour that is the product of a free will and controlled body, unhindered by external constraints — should attract the penalty and stigma of criminal liability. Depriving a person of liberty and branding her with the stigma of criminal liability would infringe the principles of fundamental justice if the accused did not have any realistic choice. The ensuing deprivation of liberty and stigma would have been imposed in violation of the tenets of fundamental justice and would thus infringe s. 7 of the *Charter*.

C. Do the Immediacy and Presence Requirements in Section 17 Infringe the Principle of Involuntariness in the Attribution of Criminal Responsibility?

It remains to be seen whether s. 17 respects this guiding principle of criminal justice that demands that society refrain from punishing morally involuntary action. The respondent argues that s. 17 of the *Criminal Code* does indeed infringe s. 7 of the *Charter* by reason of its underinclusiveness. The strictness of the immediacy and presence requirements in s. 17 means that individuals could be found guilty of involuntary actions.

Section 17 limits the defence of duress to a person who is compelled to commit an offence under threats of immediate death or bodily harm from a person who is present when the offence is committed. To counter the respondent's arguments, the appellant's key submission was that s. 17 is capable of being read down in a way that would make it less restrictive and more consistent with the *Charter*. The appellant argues that the immediacy and presence requirements do not dictate that the threatener be physically present at the scene of the crime. Rather, they require a temporal connection between the commission of the offence and the threatener's presence, in the sense that the threatener must be able to execute the threat immediately should the accused fail to comply. The respondent replies that the appellant's proposed interpretation would stretch the language of s. 17 beyond recognition. As counsel for one of the interveners put it during the hearing of this appeal, it would amount to construing presence as absence and immediate as sometime later.

The plain meaning of s. 17 is quite restrictive in scope. Indeed, the section seems tailor-made for the situation in which a person is compelled to commit an offence at gun point. The phrase "present when the offence is committed", coupled with the immediacy criterion, indicates that the person issuing the threat must be either at the scene of the crime or at whatever other location is necessary to make good on the threat without delay should the accused resist. Practically speaking, a threat of harm will seldom qualify as immediate if the threatener is not physically present at the scene of the crime.

The Court has in the past construed s. 17 in a narrow fashion. *R. v. Carker*, [1967] S.C.R. 114, and *Paquette v. The Queen*, [1977] 2 S.C.R. 189, are the two leading cases on the interpretation of s. 17. The accused in *Carker* was an inmate at a prison in British Columbia. He damaged the plumbing fixtures in his cell during a prison riot and was charged with public mischief. At trial, he conceded that he committed the offence, but asserted that he was acting under the compulsion of threats by other prisoners that he would be physically injured or killed if he did not participate in the riot. Ritchie J. maintained that the defence of duress was not available to Mr. Carker, as the other prisoners were not present in his cell when he committed the offence but rather locked in their own cells. In addition, Ritchie J. found the threat was of future harm, as the prisoners, who were locked in separate cells, were unable to carry out their threat immediately, had Mr. Carker resisted.

The Court's reasons in *Carker* reveal that the words "immediate" and "present" impose both temporal and spatial limitations on the defence. They indicate that the threat of harm must be contemporaneous with the commission of the offence, in the sense that it must be capable of immediate execution if the accused refuses to comply. In addition, *Carker* clearly implies that the threatener must be present at the scene of the crime.... *Paquette* appears to confirm this interpretation of s. 17 as requiring the threatener to be present both *when* and *where* the offence is committed....

. . . .

I agree with the respondent that a threat will seldom meet the immediacy criterion if the threatener is not physically present at or near the scene of the offence. The immediacy and presence requirements, taken together, clearly preclude threats of future harm.

Neither the words of s. 17 nor the Court's reasons in *Carker* and *Paquette* dictate that the target of the threatened harm must be the accused. They simply require that the threat must be made to the accused. Section 17 may thus include threats against third parties. However, as discussed above, the language of s. 17 does not appear capable of supporting a more flexible interpretation of the immediacy and presence requirements. Even if the threatened person, for example, is a family member, and not the accused person, the threatener or his accomplice must be at or near the scene of the crime in order to effect the harm immediately if the accused resists. Thus, while s. 17 may capture threats against third parties, the immediacy and presence criteria continue to impose considerable obstacles to relying on the defence in hostage or other third party situations.

Thus, by the strictness of its conditions, s. 17 breaches s. 7 of the *Charter* because it allows individuals who acted involuntarily to be declared criminally liable. Having said that, it will be interesting to see how the common law addresses the problem of duress, especially with respect to the immediacy component. In that regard, we will have the opportunity to see how the common law on duress in Canada, Great Britain, Australia, and even in some U.S. jurisdictions is often more liberal than what s. 17 provides and takes better account of the principle of voluntariness. This will confirm the view that s. 17 is overly restrictive and therefore breaches s. 7 of the *Charter*....

D. The Common Law of Duress

1. The Canadian Common Law of Duress

In Canada, the common law defence of duress has freed itself from the constraints of immediacy and presence and thus appears more consonant with the values of the *Charter*. It was never completely superseded by the provision of the *Criminal Code*. The Court held in *Paquette* and *Hibbert*, *supra*, that the common law defence remained available, notwithstanding s. 17, to parties to an offence (as opposed to persons who committed an offence as principals).

In *Hibbert*, the Court reexamined and restated the rules governing the common law defence of duress. Writing for a unanimous Court, Lamer C.J. found that the problem of the defence of duress arises when a person is subjected to an external danger, in this case, intentional threats of physical harm or of death from a person, and commits a criminal act to avoid the threatened harm. In Lamer C.J.'s view, the defence of duress constitutes an excuse that does not ordinarily negate either criminal intent or *actus reus*. When it is open to the accused, it relieves him of the penal consequences and stigma of a finding of criminal liability.

After a thorough canvassing of the jurisprudence, Lamer C.J. identified the elements of the defence of duress. But prior to that, he pointed out that in *Paquette*, *supra*, the Court had already held that the common law defence of duress remained a part of the criminal law of Canada. The adoption of s. 17 had not abrogated it and it applied to participants to a criminal act, who did not fall under s. 17. Lamer C.J. acknowledged that the law relating to duress has been plagued, nonetheless, with some uncertainties and inconsistencies since the beginning of its development. This is understandable. Duress involves the resolution of conflicts between individual rights and duties to others or obligations as a citizen. The analysis and determination of the rules governing duress should not take place in a vacuum where courts would focus only on the position and rights of the threatened party. The rights of third parties, more particularly the intended victims, may also be involved. The interest of the State or society in the preservation of public order and the proper application of laws will also be engaged.

The assessment of a defence of duress at common law may carry with it a number of practical risks and problems relating to evidence. At times, as in the case at bar, proof of the defence may rest on little more than the accused's own evidence. Verification of a spurious claim of duress may prove difficult. Hence, courts should be alive to the need to apply reasonable, but strict standards for the application of the defence. In the end, much will depend on the evaluation of the evidence and on the soundness of the instructions given to jurors during a jury trial. In *Perka, supra*, and more recently in *R. v. Latimer*, [2001] 1 S.C.R. 3, 2001 SCC 1, this Court outlined three essential elements which must be considered in assessing a defence of necessity. It held that such a defence must meet three clear and strict conditions in order to be left to a jury. These three conditions were identified as follows in *Latimer*: clear and imminent danger, absence of any reasonable legal alternative to breaking the law and proportionality between harm inflicted and harm avoided, in the sense that the harm avoided must be either comparable to or clearly greater than the harm inflicted.

Like necessity, the common law rule of duress evolved from attempts at striking a proper balance between those conflicting interests of the accused, of the victims and of society. It also sought to establish a hierarchy between them, as a full reconciliation appears problematic in this area of the law. Operating so as to avoid imposing the burden of criminal responsibility on an accused for an involuntary act, as discussed above, the defence of duress does not negate either the *mens rea* or *actus reus* of the crime, and will excuse the accused although Lamer C.J. left open, in the case of some unspecified criminal offences, that it might also negate the criminal intent or raise doubts about its existence....

This particular excuse focuses on the search for a safe avenue of escape (see *Hibbert*, *supra*, at paras. 55 and 62), but rejects a purely subjective standard, in the assessment of the threats. The courts have to use an objective-subjective standard when appreciating the gravity of the threats and the existence of an avenue of escape. The test requires that the situation be examined from the point of view of a reasonable person, but similarly situated. The courts will take into consideration the particular circumstances where the accused found himself and his ability to perceive a reasonable alternative to committing a crime, with an awareness of his background and essential characteristics. The process involves a pragmatic assessment of the position of the accused, tempered by the need to avoid negating criminal liability on the basis of a purely subjective and unverifiable excuse. A similar approach is also to be used in the application of the defence of necessity (see Latimer, *supra*, at paras. 26 ff.).

The common law of duress, as restated by this Court in *Hibbert* recognizes that an accused in a situation of duress does not only enjoy rights, but also has obligations towards others and society. As a fellow human being, the accused remains subject to a basic duty to adjust his or her conduct to the importance and nature of the threat. The law includes a requirement of proportionality between the threat and the criminal act to be executed, measured on the objective-subjective standard of the reasonable person similarly situated. The accused should be expected to demonstrate some fortitude and to put up a normal resistance to the threat. The threat must be to the personal integrity of the person. In addition, it must deprive the accused of any safe avenue of escape in the eyes of a reasonable person, similarly situated.

Lamer C.J.'s reasons in *Hibbert* followed closely the thrust of the analysis of the defence of necessity by Dickson J. in *Perka*, *supra*. Dickson J.'s comments remain particularly relevant. They emphasize the seriousness of the threat to the integrity of the person that is necessary to open the defence of necessity to an accused. In the assessment of the nature of the circumstances that may trigger the defence of necessity, while writing for the majority of the Court, Dickson J. held that in order to apply the defence of necessity, evidence should be introduced of a clear and imminent peril at the point in time where complying with the law becomes demonstrably impossible (p. 251).

According to Lamer C.J. in *Hibbert*, the defences of duress and necessity share the same juristic principles. Nevertheless, they target two different situations. In the case of necessity, the accused is a victim of circumstances. Duress finds its origin in man's wrongful acts. Moreover, Lamer C.J. drew some distinctions between the conditions of the defences of duress and of necessity. More particularly, Lamer C.J.'s reasons do not seem to have imported into the defence of duress an absolute immediacy requirement that would entirely duplicate the contents of s. 17 of the *Criminal Code*.

The analysis in *Hibbert* remains focused on the concept of a safe avenue of escape. Although the common law defence traditionally covers situations of threats susceptible of "immediate" execution by the person present and uttering threats, this immediacy requirement has been interpreted in a flexible manner by Canadian jurisprudence and also as appears from the development of the common law in other Commonwealth countries, more particularly Great Britain and Australia. In order to cover, for example, threats to a third person, the immediacy test is interpreted as a requirement of a close connection in time, between the threat and its execution in such a manner that the accused loses the ability to act freely. A threat that would not meet those conditions, because, for example, it is too far removed in time, would cast doubt on the seriousness of the threat and, more particularly, on claims of an absence of a safe avenue of escape.

A recent case on the problem of duress is *Langlois*, *supra*. Writing for the Quebec Court of Appeal, Fish J.A. interpreted the defence of duress at common law as excluding the strict requirements of immediacy and presence which form an essential part of s. 17 (p. 689). Thus, in *Langlois*, the Quebec Court of Appeal upheld an acquittal based on the defence of duress in a drug trafficking case involving a prison guard. Fish J.A. held that the common law defence was more flexible because it was not bound by the strict conditions imposed by s. 17 of the *Criminal Code* on the availability of the defence (at 689):

> ... [T]he operative test is "whether the accused failed to avail himself or herself of some opportunity to escape or render the threat ineffective."

Laskin J.A.'s reasons in the case at bar have adopted a similar approach....

[LeBel J. then reviewed the English, Australian, and American common law positions on duress.]

. . . .

5. *Summary: Rejection of the Immediacy Requirement at Common Law*

This review of the common law defence of duress confirms that, although the common law is not unanimous in the United States, a substantial consensus has grown in Canada, England and Australia to the effect that the strict criterion of immediacy is no longer a generally accepted component of the defence. A requirement that the threat be "imminent" has been interpreted and applied in a more flexible manner. The English Court of Appeal held in *Hudson* that depending on the circumstances, threats of future harm are sufficient to invoke the defence. *Hudson* remains good law in England and has been adopted by the courts in three Australian states and one territory. However, it is clear from the English cases that there must be a close temporal link between the threat of harm and the commission of the offence. The operative test in the English and Australian cases is whether the threat was effective to overbear the accused's will at the moment he committed the crime. Moreover, the safe avenue of escape test and the proportionality principle also appear to be key elements of the defence.

E. The Breach of Section 7 of the *Charter*: Conclusion in the Case at Bar

At the heart of Laskin J.A.'s decision is a concern that the immediacy and presence requirements are poor substitutes for the safe avenue of escape test at common law. In his view, their focus on an instantaneous connection between the threat and the commission of the offence misses the point in a number of special cases. He highlights two situations in particular. The first is the battered woman who is coerced by her abusive partner to break the law. Even though her partner is not present when she commits the offence and is therefore unable to execute it immediately, a battered woman may believe nonetheless that she has no safe avenue of escape. Her behaviour is morally involuntary, yet the immediacy and presence criteria, strictly construed, would preclude her from resorting to s. 17. There may also be other situations in which a person is so psychologically traumatized by the threatener that he complies with the threat, even though it was not immediate and to the objective observer, there was a legal way out. The second scenario described by Laskin J.A. is the case of a person like Ms. Ruzic, for whom effective police protection was unavailable. Do the immediacy and presence requirements demand that a person go to the authorities if he has the opportunity to do so, even when he believes it would be useless or even dangerous to do so? It should be noted that in this second scenario, a court might face a delicate task in assessing the validity of a claim that, in a foreign land, no police protection was available. It illustrates some of the difficulties in the practical implementation of a defence of duress which involves a risk of abuse through unverifiable assertions of danger and harm.

Nevertheless, s. 17's reliance on proximity as opposed to reasonable options as the measure of moral choice is problematic. It would be contrary to the principles of fundamental justice to punish an accused who is psychologically tortured to the point of seeing no reasonable alternative, or who cannot rely on the authorities for assistance. That individual is not behaving as an autonomous agent acting out of his own free will when he commits an offence under duress.

The appellant's attempts at reading down s. 17, in order to save it, would amount to amending it to bring it in line with the common law rules. This interpretation badly strains the text of the provision and may become one more argument against upholding its validity.

The underinclusiveness of s. 17 infringes s. 7 of the *Charter*, because the immediacy and presence requirements exclude threats of future harm to the accused or to third parties. It risks jeopardizing the liberty and security interests protected by the *Charter*, in violation of the basic principles of fundamental justice. It has the potential of convicting persons who have not acted voluntarily.

F. Can the Infringement Be Justified Under Section 1?

Having found that the immediacy and presence requirements infringe s. 7 of the *Charter*, I turn now to consider whether the violation is a demonstrably justifiable limit under s. 1. The government, of course, bears the burden of justifying a *Charter* infringement. Consistent with its strategy in the courts below, the appellant made no attempt before this Court to justify the immediacy and presence criteria according to the s. 1 analysis. I therefore conclude at the outset that the appellant has failed to satisfy its onus under s. 1.

Moreover, it is well established that violations of s. 7 are not easily saved by s. *1: New Brunswick (Minister of Health and Community Services) v. G. (J.)*, [1999] 3 S.C.R. 46, at para. 99. Indeed, the Court has indicated that exceptional circumstances, such as the outbreak of war or a national emergency, are necessary before such an infringement may be justified: *R. v. Heywood*, [1994] 3 S.C.R. 761, at p. 802; *Re B.C. Motor Vehicle Act, supra*. No such extraordinary conditions exist in this case. Furthermore, I am inclined to agree with Laskin J.A. that the immediacy and presence criteria would not meet the proportionality branch of the s. 1 analysis. In particular, it seems to me these requirements do not minimally impair the respondent's s. 7 rights. Given the appellant's failure to make any submissions on the issue, the higher standard of justification for a violation of s. 7, and my doubts concerning proportionality, I conclude that the immediacy and presence conditions cannot be saved by s. 1.

G. Alternatively, Do the Immediacy and Presence Requirements in Section 17 Infringe the Principle That Rights Should Not Be Restricted in a Manner That Is Arbitrary or Unfair?

Laskin J.A. found, in the alternative, that s. 17 infringes s. 7 of the *Charter* because the presence and immediacy requirements are arbitrary and inconsistent with the government's objective of excusing morally involuntary behaviour. On the view I take of the interpretation of s. 17, I need not address this argument. I prefer to ground the partial striking down of s. 17 on the fundamental principle that criminal liability should not be ascribed to physically or morally involuntary behaviour.

. . . .

VI. DISPOSITION

The appellant's submissions cannot be accepted. The immediacy and presence requirements of s. 17 of the *Criminal Code* infringe s. 7 of the *Charter*. As the infringement has not been justified under s. 1, the requirements of immediacy and presence must be struck down as unconstitutional. The Court of Appeal and the trial judge were right in allowing the common law defence of duress [to] go to the jury, and the trial judge adequately instructed the jury on the defence.

I would dismiss the appeal and confirm the acquittal of the respondent.

■

What are the limits of the concepts of immediacy and imminence? How is "moral involuntariness" elaborated upon and related to the defence of duress? How would you now argue a fact pattern similar to *Robins* in light of *Ruzic*?

In what ways does the critique of duress parallel the critique of self-defence? What are the consequences for women in abusive relationships? Is a threat more "real" or "imminent" in those circumstances? Critics have argued that the defence of duress should be available in situations where a battered woman has been coerced into criminal activity by threats made by the batterer. In *R. v. C.(T.L.)*, [2005] 3 W.W.R. 686 (Alta. Prov. Ct.), the accused battered woman was charged with uttering forged cheques and fraud when upon the instruction of her common-law partner "CK" and his friends she opened up a business bank account, deposited cheques and withdrew cash from the account. Prior to committing the offence, the accused experienced serious episodes of verbal, physical and sexual abuse from her common-law partner. In finding her not guilty on both charges, the judge commented on the combination of battered woman's syndrome and duress at para. 79: "While battered woman syndrome is now most commonly used in self-defense claims, it is equally applicable in duress defenses. It fulfills the same elements — reasonableness and imminence — in both defences. Thus, to admit it in the former and not in the latter is, at the very best, inconsistent. The legal system's recognition of battered woman syndrome as a part of self-defense should pave the way for its acceptance in the context of duress. The legal system must realize that the brutality a battered woman faces affects much more than just her relationship with her batterer. Ultimately, it affects every facet of her life."

The defence of duress continues to be narrowly constructed in other jurisdictions such as the United States, New Zealand and England. For a thoughtful critique of the U.S. courts' restrictive responses to evidence of abuse in duress cases, see: Meredith Blake, "Coerced Into Crime: The Application of Battered Woman Syndrome to the Defense of Duress" (1994) 9 Wis. Women's L.J. 67. She argues that the essential elements of self-defence and duress are fundamentally similar, and that evidence of abuse should be admissible and persuasive with respect to duress. Instead, duress has been rarely argued, and the cases resonate with many of the assumptions that have been challenged in the self-defence cases (the imminence of danger, the possibility of "escape", victim-blaming).

The codified defence of compulsion in New Zealand is limited to situations in which the threatener was present (the court interpreted this as requiring continuing presence); duress is also not available as a defence to murder. *R. v. Witika*, [1993] 2 N.Z.L.R. 424 (C.A.), highlights the barriers to invoking a defence of duress. See also Elisabeth McDonald, "Is Tania Witika Guilty? An Exploration of Battered Women's Syndrome and the Criminal Law" [1994] Women's Law Conference Papers 215.

In *R. v. Bowen*, [1996] 4 All E.R. 837, the English Court of Appeal reiterated an objective threshold test for duress. The British cases have held that "personal characteristics" (such as low intelligence in *Bowen*) are only open to consideration at the second-stage (subjective) of the test for duress. What are the implications for accused with a history of abuse and violence? See *R. v. Emery* (1993), 14 Cr. App. R. (S) 394, in which a woman (charged with cruelty in the death of her 11-month-old child for failing to obtain medical advice) argued unsuccessfully that she had lost any capacity to act independently because of the routine, prolonged, and serious abuse she and her daughter had suffered (at the hands of the co-accused father), her fear of the father, and post-traumatic stress disorder ("learned helplessness").

How realistic is it for women to raise these defences when the abusive partner is present in court, sometimes as a co-accused represented by the same counsel? Reconsider the questions raised following *R. v. Urbanovich*, above, under ***Actus Reus***, Act or Omission.

What are the implications for prisoners? Reconsider the conclusions of the Court in *R. v. McConnell* and the commentary by Christine Boyle, above, under **Self-Defence**. Should *McConnell*, *Langlois*, and *Ruzic* force a re-evaluation of situations facing prisoners such as *Carker (No. 2)*, above, by acknowledging the violent environment of prisons? How might this enhance defence arguments on behalf of abused women?

Benjamin Berger argues that the approach of "moral involuntariness" adopted by the Court in *Ruzic* is dangerous because such a mechanistic understanding of human agency hides the normative foundation of criminal law wherein judgment, understood as critical reflection on these norms, is withdrawn. Berger suggests that an idiom of "moral blameworthiness", where the moral bases of emotions is evaluated, would be preferable as it would make the law more transparent and increase its capacity to engage changing social conditions and communal norms. "[T]he defence of duress is about the quality or legitimacy of the emotions that one feels, not just their magnitude." See Benjamin L. Berger, "Emotions and the Veil of Voluntarism: The Loss of Judgment in Canadian Criminal Defences" (2006) 52 McGill L.J. 99 at 109.

B. COMMON LAW DEFENCE

The court in *Mena*, discussed above, reviewed the requirements for the common law defence of duress, noting that while it is narrower than the s. 17 defence in some respects (e.g., it requires a threat of death or serious bodily harm), in many ways it is a broader defence, as it can be based on threats of future harm and harm to third parties. There is some case law to suggest that the common law defence of duress can be relied on not only by parties, but also principals to the excluded offences under s. 17. See for example *R. v. Fraser*, [2002] N.S.J. No. 400 (Prov. Ct.)

(QL), where the court held that the excluded offence of robbery was unconstitutional and that the common law defence of duress applied. *Hibbert*, reproduced below, further develops the common law defence of duress, as discussed in *Ruzic*.

R. v. Hibbert†

[LAMER C.J.:]

[Fitzroy Cohen was shot four times with a semi-automatic handgun in his apartment lobby by Mark Bailey, having been lured downstairs by Lawrence Hibbert, a close friend of Cohen's. Cohen survived the shooting and Hibbert was charged via s. 21(1) with attempted murder. His testimony was that he had been attempting to avoid Bailey, as he owed him money for drugs, but had accidentally met him on the night of the shooting. Bailey showed him that he was armed and demanded that Hibbert take him to Cohen's building. At first he refused, but then Bailey punched him in the face several times. He feared for his life and believed that Bailey would kill him. With Bailey at his elbow he called Cohen from a telephone booth, telling him, as instructed, that "he had something for him." Once there, instead of entering the building as he usually did (through a side door that could be opened without a key in a specific way) he instead buzzed Cohen from the main door. Although he had hoped Cohen would simply come down and see Bailey through the glass in time to escape, instead Cohen buzzed him into the lobby. When Cohen stepped out of the stairwell, Bailey met him with the gun, told Hibbert to "stay where I can see you", exchanged words with Cohen, and then fired the four shots. Bailey told Hibbert he would kill him if he went to police; Hibbert called Cohen's brother and mother that night, and turned himself in to police next morning. His testimony was corroborated to some extent, although not completely, by Cohen (who said he did not hear Hibbert begging Bailey not to shoot him). Bailey was never found. At trial Hibbert was acquitted on the basis of duress, but convicted of the included offence of aggravated assault. His appeal to the Court of Appeal was dismissed.]

In *Paquette* v. *The Queen,* [1977] 2 S.C.R. 189, this Court determined that s.17 of the *Code* does not constitute an exhaustive codification of the law of duress. Rather, the Court held, s. 17 applied only to persons who commit offences as *principals*. Accordingly, it remains open to persons who are liable as *parties* to offences to invoke the common law defence of duress, which remains in existence by virtue of s. 8(3) of the *Code....*

The holding in *Paquette* that the common law defence of duress is available to persons liable as parties is clear and unambiguous, and has stood as the law in Canada for almost twenty years. The case has a second aspect, however, that is less firmly established, having given rise to differing interpretations, and having been the subject of considerable debate in the legal community. The controversy stems from certain comments made by Martland J. on the issue of the relationship between duress and the *mens rea* for party liability under s. 21(2) of the *Code.* The facts in *Paquette* were as follows. The accused had been charged as a party to non-capital murder. He had driven two acquaintances, Clermont and Simard, to a store. After Paquette had dropped them off, Clermont and Simard robbed the store, and during the course of the robbery an innocent bystander was shot and killed. Paquette was not present at the shooting, having driven away from the store once Clermont and Simard had entered. Although he circled the block and returned to the store, there was evidence that he had refused to let Clermont and Simard get back into the car. In a statement made to the police, Paquette indicated that he had driven Clermont and Simard to the scene of the crime only after Clermont had pointed a gun at him and threatened to kill him if he refused. At trial, the issue of duress had been left to the jury, which acquitted the accused. On appeal, the Ontario Court of Appeal ordered a new trial, on the grounds that the statutory defence of duress con-

† [1995] 2 S.C.R. 973.

tained in s. 17 of the *Code* could not, by the express terms of the section, be invoked as a defence to a charge of murder or robbery.

As noted above, the main holding of the Court was that s. 17 applied only to principals and not to parties, from which it followed that *Paquette* could rely on the common law defence of duress, to which the restrictions set out in s. 17 did not apply. Martland J. went on, however, to make an observation regarding duress and the mental element of party liability under s. 21(2) of the *Code,* stating (at p. 197):

> A person whose actions have been dictated by fear of death or of grievous bodily injury cannot be said to have formed a common intention to carry out an unlawful purpose with the person who has threatened him with those consequences if he fails to co-operate.

. . . .

Seen in this way, *Paquette* stands for the proposition that duress can provide a "defence" in either of two distinct ways — as an excuse, or by "negating" *mens rea*. In the present case, the appellant argues that this is a correct view of the law, and submits that the trial judge erred by not placing both alternatives before the jury. What falls to be considered, therefore, is the validity of the proposition that the *mens rea* for party liability under the *Criminal Code* can be "negated" by threats of death or bodily harm. That is, the Court is called upon to reconsider whether the second aspect of our judgment in *Paquette* reflects a correct understanding of the law of duress in Canada.

That threats of death or serious bodily harm can have an effect on a person's state of mind is indisputable. However, it is also readily apparent that a person who carries out the *actus reus* of a criminal offence in response to such threats will not necessarily lack the *mens rea* for that offence. Whether he or she does or not will depend both on what the mental element of the offence in question happens to be, and on the facts of the particular case. As a practical matter, though, situations where duress will operate to "negate" *mens rea* will be exceptional, for the simple reason that the types of mental states that are capable of being "negated" by duress are not often found in the definitions of criminal offences.

In general, a person who performs an action in response to a threat will *know* what he or she is doing, and will be aware of the probable consequences of his or her actions. Whether or not he or she *desires* the occurrence of these consequences will depend on the particular circumstances.

. . . .

To determine whether *mens rea* is "negated" in a particular case, therefore, the first question that must be asked is whether the mental element of the offence in question is defined in such a way that either an actor's motives or his or her immediate desires have any direct relevance.

. . . .

There is no requirement under s. 21(1)(b) that the person charged as a party "desire" that the victim die (that is, subjectively wish that this result come to pass), just as the principal's intent to kill is not negated even if, all other things being equal, he or she regrets the fact that he or she is killing the victim.

. . . .

I conclude that the expression "for the purpose of aiding" in s. 21(1)(*b*), properly understood, does not require that the accused actively view the commission of the offence he or she is aiding as desirable in and of itself. As a result, the *mens rea* for aiding under s. 21(1)(*b*) is not susceptible to being "negated" by duress.

. . . .

I am [also] of the view that the comments of Martland J. in *Paquette*, *supra*, on the relation between duress and *mens rea* in the context of s. 21(2) can no longer be considered the law in Canada.

[Lamer C.J. went on to discuss two other issues on appeal to do with the "safe avenue of escape" rule. The Court concluded by allowing the appeal and ordering a new trial on the basis of the error in the trial judge's instructions to the jury on duress.]

■

After *Hibbert*, for what kinds of offences might duress be said to go to the *mens rea*? For one possible example, see *Hébert*, *supra*, where a s. 17 defence was denied, but the Court stated at 235:

For there to be perjury there has to be more than a deliberate false statement. The statement must also have been made with intent to mislead. While it is true that someone who lies generally does so with the intent of being believed, it is not impossible, though it may be exceptional, for a person to deliberately lie without intending to mislead. It is always open to an accused to seek to establish such an intent by his testimony or otherwise, leaving to the trial judge the task of assessing its weight. The trial judge did not allow the accused to complete his evidence in this regard, probably because he knew he was going to acquit him on other grounds; that acquittal, however, was properly set aside on appeal.

17

Necessity

Necessity is a common law defence whose development is permitted at law by virtue of s. 8(3) of the *Code*. The defence could potentially encompass other statutory defences such as self-defence and challenge our political and economic structures. Therefore, the courts have given this defence a very narrow interpretation.

The *Morgentaler* prosecutions in Canada present the best known contemporary example of the use of the necessity defence. Dr. Morgentaler was accused of procuring a miscarriage, contrary to s. 251(1) of the *Criminal Code*. In 1975 (*R. v. Morgentaler*, [1976] 1 S.C.R. 616), Chief Justice Laskin (joined by two Justices) would have ruled that necessity was available on the facts, given that the woman patient was alone in Canada, had no medical coverage, was suffering mental and physical distress, had no guarantee that she would be granted permission for an abortion if she waited on the procedure set out in the *Code*, and would have been subjected to escalating risks the longer she waited.

Justice Dickson's majority opinion expressed doubt as to the validity of the defence in law, and reached a completely different conclusion on the same facts. He held that there was no evidentiary basis for putting the defence to the jury. He suggested that an accused must show both an urgent situation of imminent peril and that compliance with the law is demonstrably impossible; on these facts, he stated that Morgentaler had submitted no evidence as to the latter requirement. While he acknowledged there was some urgency, he concluded it did not go to establish impossibility. In canvassing the authorities, he discounted possible arguments for necessitous circumstances, saying that even a suicide threat by a pregnant woman would not necessarily be compelling. The subsequent history of the prosecutions of *Morgentaler* in some sense proved Laskin C.J. right, in that Canadian jurors have repeatedly recognized Morgentaler as operating in necessitous circumstances and acquitted him accordingly.

Some of the readers will be familiar with the background to the first series of *Morgentaler* cases (1970–1976). Dr. Morgentaler's first challenge to the federal abortion law originated in Québec and went to the Supreme Court of Canada. It began in 1970 when Dr. Morgentaler was arrested for performing abortions in his Montréal clinic. Between 1970 and 1976, Dr. Morgentaler was charged with 13 violations of Canadian law. He was tried three times, and each time was acquitted by a jury. Yet, he spent ten months in prison.

What began as a legal battle over the abortion law became a complex, precedent-setting civil rights case, a test of the judicial process, and the case that resulted in the "Morgentaler amendment" (an important modification to the *Criminal Code* that affirms the rights of Canadian citizens to be judged by a jury of their peers: s. 686(4)(b)(ii)).

As for the abortion issue, Dr. Morgentaler's 1970s challenges did not result in changes to the federal abortion law, but did affect how the law was applied. While the abortion law remained officially in force throughout the country, in Québec, as a result of *Morgentaler*, the law was considered technically unenforceable. Because of the legal ramifications of *Morgentaler* and because juries were unwilling to convict Dr. Morgentaler, the Québec government informed Ottawa that it could not enforce the federal abortion law. Ottawa did not react to Québec's decision; the federal law remained unchanged, but unenforced in Québec.

In the film *Democracy on Trial: The Morgentaler Affair* (Montréal: National Film Board, 1984), defence attorney Claude-Armand Sheppard assesses the *Morgentaler* case in terms of its significance for the Canadian judicial system. According to Sheppard, it:

- demonstrated the incredible contribution of the jury system to humanizing and changing the law;
- revealed that eventually citizens will revolt against absurd or unenforced laws; and
- proved that determined individuals, ready to make sacrifices and risk their freedom, can challenge the system and force people to face issues they do not want to face.

Dr. Morgentaler then decided to challenge the law in other provinces. These challenges led to further charges against Dr. Morgentaler and, in particular, to the Ontario case: *R. v. Morgentaler* (1988), 52 O.R. (2d) 353 (C.A.), aff'd [1988] 1 S.C.R. 30. The legal controversy created by *Morgentaler* centred not only on the availability of the necessity defence, but also on the ability of the jury to return what was called by some a "perverse" verdict, and on the role of counsel in addressing the jury, discussed above, in the chapter on **The Trial Process**.

As you read the cases in this chapter, consider the types of situations that have founded a successful defence of necessity. How do the courts assess urgency, peril, and the absence of any reasonable legal alternatives? What are the criteria used to determine the proportionality of harm? What is the importance attached to specific legal duties? What are the limitations of the metaphor of a "sudden agonizing choice"? How is "society's expectation of appropriate and normal resistance to pressure" measured?

Perka v. R.†

[DICKSON J. (as he then was):]

FACTS

The appellants are drug smugglers. At trial, they led evidence that in early 1979 three of the appellants were employed, with sixteen crew members, to deliver, by ship (*Samarkanda*) a load of cannabis (marihuana) worth $6,000,000 or $7,000,000 from a point in international waters off the coast of Colombia, South America, to a drop point in international waters 200 miles off the coast of Alaska. The ship left Tumaco, Columbia, empty with a port clearance document stating the destination to be Juneau, Alaska. For three weeks the ship remained in international waters off the coast of Colombia. While there, a DC-6 aircraft made four trips, dropping into the water shrimp nets with a total of 634 bales of cannabis which were retrieved by the ship's longboats.

A "communications" package was also dropped from a light aircraft, giving instructions for a rendezvous with another vessel, the *Julia "B"* which was to pick up the cargo of cannabis from the *Samarkanda* in international waters off the coast of Alaska. *En route*, according to the defence evidence, the vessel began to encounter a series of problems; engine breakdowns, overheating generators and malfunctioning navigation devices, aggravated by deteriorating weather. In the meantime the fourth appellant, Nelson, part owner of the illicit cargo, and three other persons left Seattle in a small boat, the *White-*

† [1984] 2 S.C.R. 232.

cap, intending to rendezvous with the *Samarkanda* at the drop point in Alaska. The problems of the *Samarkanda* intensified as fuel was consumed. The vessel became lighter, the intakes in the hull for sea water, used as a coolant, lost suction and took in air instead, causing the generators to overheat. At this point the vessel was 180 miles from the Canadian coastline. The weather worsened. There were eight-to-ten-foot swells and a rising wind. It was finally decided for the safety of ship and crew to seek refuge on the Canadian shoreline for the purpose of making temporary repairs. The *Whitecap* found a sheltered cove on the west coast of Vancouver Island, "No Name Bay." The *Samarkanda* followed the *Whitecap* into the Bay but later grounded amidships on a rock because the depth sounder was not working. The tide ran out. The vessel listed severely to starboard, to the extent that the Captain, fearing the vessel was going to capsize, ordered the men to offload the cargo. That is a brief summary of the defence evidence.

Early on the morning of May 22, 1979 police officers entered No Name Bay in a marked police boat with siren sounding. The *Samarkanda* and the *Whitecap* were arrested, as were all the appellants except Perka and Nelson, the same morning. The vessels and 33.49 tons of cannabis marihuana were seized by the police officers.

Charged with importing cannabis into Canada and with possession for the purpose of trafficking the appellants claimed they did not plan to import into Canada or to leave their cargo of cannabis in Canada. They had planned to make repairs and leave. Expert witnesses on marine matters called by the defence testified that the decision to come ashore was, in the opinion of one witness, expedient and prudent and in the opinion of another, essential. At trial, counsel for the Crown alleged that evidence of the ship's distress was a recent fabrication. Crown counsel relied on the circumstances under which the appellants were arrested to belie the "necessity" defence; when the police arrived on the scene most of the marihuana was already ashore, along with plastic ground sheets, battery operated lights, liquor, food, clothing, camp stoves, and sleeping bags. Nevertheless, the jury believed the appellants and acquitted them.

THE NECESSITY DEFENCE

History and Background

From earliest times it has been maintained that in some situations the force of circumstances makes it unrealistic and unjust to attach criminal liability to actions which, on their face, violate the law.

. . . .

In Canada the existence and the extent of a general defence of necessity was discussed by this Court in *Morgentaler v. The Queen*, [1976] 1 S.C.R. 616. As to whether or not the defence exists at all I had occasion to say at p. 678:

> On the authorities it is manifestly difficult to be categorical and state that there is a law of necessity, paramount over other laws, relieving obedience from the letter of the law. If it does exist, it can go no further than to justify non-compliance in urgent situations of clear and imminent peril when compliance with the law is demonstrably impossible.

Subsequent to *Morgentaler*, the courts appear to have assumed that a defence of necessity does exist in Canada. On the later trial of Dr. Morgentaler, the defence of necessity was again raised on a charge of procuring a miscarriage. Some admissible evidence was made in support of the plea and the case went to the jury, which rendered a verdict of not guilty. An appeal by the Crown from the acquittal failed: *R. v. Morgentaler* (1976), 33 C.R.N.S. 244. Leave to appeal to this Court was refused, [1976] 1 S.C.R. x. The defence also succeeded in four other cases: *R. v. Guenther* (1978), 8 Alta L.R. (2d) 125; *R. v. Pootlass* (1977), 1 C.R. (3d) 378; *R. v. Fry* (1977), 36 C.C.C. (2d) 396; *R. v. Morris* (1981), 61 C.C.C. (2d) 163. In a number of other cases the existence of such a defence was acknowledged but held to be unavailable on the facts. Some examples include: *R. v. Gilkes* (1978), 8 C.R. (3d) 159; *R. v. Doud* (1972), 18 M.V.R. 146; *R. v. Byng* (1977), 20 N.S.R. (2d) 125; *R. v. Walker* (1979), 48 C.C.C. (2d) 126 and *R. v. Salvador* (1981), 59 C.C.C. 521 (N.S.S.C. App. Div.), the case most nearly analogous to the one at bar, of which more anon.

In the present appeal the Crown does not challenge the appellants' claim that necessity is a common law defence preserved by *Criminal Code* s. 7(3). Rather, the Crown claims the trial judge erred in (1) instructing the jury on the defence in light of the facts and (2) imposing the burden of disproof of the defence upon the Crown, rather than imposing the burden of proof on the appellants.

The Conceptual Foundation of the Defence

In *Morgentaler*, *supra*, I characterized necessity as an "ill-defined and elusive concept." Despite the apparently growing consensus as to the existence of a defence of necessity that statement is equally true today.

This is no doubt in part because, though apparently laying down a single rule as to criminal liability, the "defence" of necessity in fact is capable of embracing two different and distinct notions. As Mr. Justice Macdonald observed succinctly but accurately in the *Salvador* case, *supra*, at p. 542:

> Generally speaking, the defence of necessity covers all cases where non-compliance with law is excused by an emergency or justified by the pursuit of some greater good.

Working Paper 29 of the Law Reform Commission of Canada at p. 93 makes this same point in somewhat more detail:

> The rationale of necessity, however, is clear. Essentially it involves two factors. One is the avoidance of greater harm or the pursuit of some greater good, the other is the difficulty of compliance with law in emergencies. From these two factors emerge two different but related principles. The first is a utilitarian principle to the effect that, within certain limits, it is justifiable in an emergency to break the letter of the law if breaking the law will avoid a greater harm than obeying it. The second is a humanitarian principle to the effect that, again within limits, it is excusable in an emergency to break the law if compliance would impose an intolerable burden on the accused.

Despite any superficial similarities, these two principles are in fact quite distinct and many of the conclusions and the difficulties in the cases (and, with respect, in academic discussions) arise from a failure to distinguish between them.

Criminal theory recognizes a distinction between "justifications" and "excuses." A "justification" challenges the wrongfulness of an action which technically constitutes a crime. The police officer who shoots the hostage-taker, the innocent object of an assault who uses force to defend himself against his assailant, the Good Samaritan who commandeers a car and breaks the speed laws to rush an accident victim to the hospital, these are all actors whose actions we consider *rightful*, not wrongful. For such actions people are often praised, as motivated by some great or noble object. The concept of punishment often seems incompatible with the social approval bestowed on the doer.

In contrast, an "excuse" concedes the wrongfulness of the action but asserts that the circumstances under which it was done are such that it ought not to be attributed to the actor. The perpetrator who is incapable, owing to a disease of the mind, of appreciating the nature and consequences of his acts, the person who labours under a mistake of fact, the drunkard, the sleepwalker: these are all actors of whose "criminal" actions we disapprove intensely, but whom, in appropriate circumstance, our law will not punish.

. . . .

With regard to this conceptualization of a residual defence of necessity, I retain the scepticism I expressed in *Morgentaler*, *supra*, at p. 678. It is still my opinion that, "[n]o system of positive law can recognize any principle which would entitle a person to violate the law because on his view the law conflicted with some higher social value." The *Criminal Code* has specified a number of identifiable situations in which an actor is justified in committing what would otherwise be a criminal offence. To go beyond that and hold that ostensibly illegal acts can be validated on the basis of their expediency, would import an undue subjectivity into the criminal law. It would invite the courts to second-guess the legislature and to assess the relative merits of social policies underlying criminal prohibitions. Neither is a role which fits well with the judicial function. Such a doctrine could well become the last resort of scoundrels and in the words of Edmund Davies L.J. in *Southwark London Borough Council v. Williams*, [1971] Ch. 734, it could "very easily become simply a mask for anarchy."

Conceptualized as an "excuse," however, the residual defence of necessity is, in my view, much less open to criticism. It rests on a realistic assessment of human weakness, recognizing that a liberal and humane criminal law cannot hold people to the strict obedience of laws in emergency situations where normal human instincts, whether of self-preservation or altruism, overwhelmingly impel disobedience. The objectivity of the criminal law is preserved; such acts are still wrongful, but in the circumstances they are excusable. Praise is indeed not bestowed, but pardon is, when one does a wrongful act under pressure which, in the words of Aristotle in the *Nicomachean Ethics*, *supra*, at p. 49, "overstrains human nature and which no one could withstand."

George Fletcher, *Rethinking Criminal Law* (1978), describes this view of necessity as "compulsion of circumstance" which description points to the conceptual link between necessity as an excuse and the familiar criminal law requirements that in order to engage criminal liability, the actions constituting the *actus reus* of an offence must be voluntary. Literally this voluntariness requirement simply refers to the need that the prohibited physical acts must have been under the conscious control of the actor. Without such control, there is, for purposes of the criminal law, no act. The excuse of necessity does not go to voluntariness in this sense. The lost alpinist who on the point of freezing to death breaks open an isolated mountain cabin is not literally behaving in an involuntary fashion. He has control over his actions to the extent of being physically capable of abstaining from the act. Realistically, however, his act is not a "voluntary" one. His "choice" to break the law is no true choice at all: it is remorselessly compelled by normal human instincts. This sort of involuntariness is often described as "moral or normative involuntariness." Its place in criminal theory is described by Fletcher at pp. 804–05 as follows:

> The notion of voluntariness adds a valuable dimension to the theory of excuses. That conduct is involuntary — even in the normative sense — explains why it cannot fairly be punished. Indeed, H.L.A. Hart builds his theory of excuses on the principle that the distribution of punishment should be reserved for those who voluntarily break the law. Of the arguments he advances for this principle of justice, the most explicit is that it is preferable to live in a society where we have the maximum opportunity to choose whether we shall become the subject of criminal liability. In addition, Hart intimates that it is ideologically desirable for the government to treat its citizens as self-actuating, choosing agents. This principle of respect for individual autonomy is implicitly confirmed whenever those who lack an adequate choice are excused for their offenses.

I agree with this formulation of the rationale for excuses in the criminal law. In my view this rationale extends beyond specific codified excuses and embraces the residual excuse known as the defence of necessity. At the heart of this defence is the perceived injustice of punishing violations of the law in circumstances in which the person had no other viable or reasonable choice available; the act was wrong but it is excused because it was realistically unavoidable.

. . . .

Limitations on the Defence

If the defence of necessity is to form a valid and consistent part of our criminal law it must, as has been universally recognized, be strictly controlled and scrupulously limited to situations that correspond to the underlying rationale. That rationale, as I have indicated, is the recognition that it is inappropriate to punish actions which are normatively "involuntary." The appropriate controls and limitations on the defence of necessity are, therefore, addressed to ensuring that the acts for which the benefit of the excuse of necessity is sought are truly "involuntary" in the requisite sense.

In *Morgentaler*, *supra*, I was of the view that any defence of necessity was restricted to instances of non-compliance "in urgent situations of clear and imminent peril when compliance with the law is demonstrably impossible." In my opinion this restriction focuses directly on the "involuntariness" of the purportedly necessitous behaviour by providing a number of tests for determining whether the wrongful act was truly the only realistic reaction open to the actor or whether he was in fact making what in fairness could be called a choice. If he was making a choice, then the wrongful act cannot have been involuntary in the relevant sense.

The requirement that the situation be urgent and the peril be imminent, tests whether it was indeed unavoidable for the actor to act at all.

. . . .

At a minimum the situation must be so emergent and the peril must be so pressing that normal human instincts cry out for action and make a counsel of patience unreasonable.

The requirement that compliance with the law be "demonstrably impossible" takes this assessment one step further. Given that the accused had to act, could he nevertheless realistically have acted to avoid the peril or prevent the harm, without breaking the law? *Was there a legal way out?* I think this is what Bracton means when he lists "necessity" as a defence, providing the wrongful act was not "avoidable." The question to be asked is whether the agent had any real choice: could he have done otherwise? If there is a reasonable legal alternative to disobeying the law, then the decision to disobey becomes a voluntary one, impelled by some consideration beyond the dictates of "necessity" and human instincts.

The importance of this requirement that there be no reasonable legal alternative cannot be overstressed.

Even if the requirements for urgency and "no legal way out" are met, there is clearly a further consideration. There must be some way of assuring proportionality. No rational criminal justice system, no matter how humane or liberal, could excuse the infliction of a greater harm to allow the actor to avert a lesser evil.

. . . .

Illegality or Contributory Fault

The Crown submits that there is an additional limitation on the availability of the defence of necessity. Citing *R. v. Salvador, supra*, it argues that because the appellants were committing a crime when their necessitous circumstances arose, they should be denied the defence of necessity as a matter of law.

In *Salvador*, Jones J.A. thought it highly relevant that the accused were engaged in an illegal venture when they were forced ashore. He would have denied the necessity defence in such circumstances.

. . . .

Were it indeed accurate that the fact of doing something illegal when the necessitous circumstances arise will deny one the benefit of the necessity defence, I would nevertheless doubt that this principle would be relevant to the present case. The accused here (as incidentally was also apparently the case in *Salvador*) were not doing any thing illegal under Canadian law when the necessity arose. They were on the high seas. They were conspiring to import marihuana into the United States, not Canada. If such a limitation on the necessity defence were to be formulated, in my view, the accused should, at a minimum, be violating some law of the forum, not just the law of a foreign state.

In any event, I have considerable doubt as to the cogency of such a limitation. If the conduct in which an accused was engaging at the time the peril arose was illegal, then it should clearly be punished, but I fail to see the relevance of its illegal character to the question of whether the accused's subsequent conduct in dealing with this emergent peril ought to be exercised on the basis of necessity. At most the illegality — or if one adopts Jones J.A.'s approach, the immorality — of the preceding conduct will colour the subsequent conduct in response to the emergency as also wrongful. But that wrongfulness is never in any doubt. Necessity goes to *excuse* conduct, not to *justify* it. ...

. . . .

In my view the better approach to the relationship of the fault to the availability of necessity as a defence is based once again on the question of whether the actions sought to be excused were truly "involuntary." If the necessitous situation was clearly foreseeable to a reasonable observer, if the actor contemplated or ought to have contemplated that his actions would likely give rise to an emergency requiring the breaking of the law, then I doubt whether what confronted the accused was in the relevant sense an emergency. His response was in that sense not "involuntary." "Contributory fault" of this nature, but only of this nature, is a relevant consideration to the availability of the defence.

. . . .

If the accused's "fault" consists of actions whose clear consequences were in the situation that actually ensued, then he was not "really" confronted with an emergency which compelled him to commit the unlawful act he now seeks to have excused. In such situations the defence is unavailable. Mere negligence, however, or the simple fact that he was engaged in illegal or immoral conduct when the emergency arose will not disentitle an individual to rely on the defence of necessity.

Onus of Proof

Although necessity is spoken of as a defence, in the sense that it is raised by the accused, the Crown always bears the burden of proving a voluntary act. The prosecution must prove every element of the crime charged. One such element is the voluntariness of the act. Normally, voluntariness can be presumed, but if the accused places before the Court, through his own witnesses or through cross-examination of Crown witnesses, evidence sufficient to raise an issue that the situation created by external forces was so emergent that failure to act could endanger life or health and upon any reasonable view of the facts, compliance with the law was impossible, then the Crown must be prepared to meet that issue. There is no onus of proof on the accused.

. . . .

Preliminary Conclusions as to the Defence of Necessity

It is now possible to summarize a number of conclusions as to the defence of necessity in terms of its nature, basis and limitations: (1) The defence of necessity could be conceptualized as either a justification or an excuse; (2) it should be recognized in Canada as an excuse, operating by virtue of s. 7(3) of the *Criminal Code*; (3) necessity as an excuse implies no vindication of the deeds of the actor; (4) the criterion is the moral involuntariness of the wrongful action; (5) this involuntariness is measured on the basis of society's expectation of appropriate and normal resistance to pressure; (6) negligence or involvement in criminal or immoral activity does not disentitle the actor to the excuse of necessity; (7) actions or circumstances which indicate that the wrongful deed was not truly involuntary do disentitle; (8) the existence of a reasonable legal alternative similarly disentitles; to be involuntary the act must be inevitable, unavoidable and afford no reasonable opportunity for an alternative course of action that does not involve a breach of the law; (9) the defence only applies in circumstances of imminent risk where the action was taken to avoid a direct and immediate peril; (10) where the accused places before the Court sufficient evidence to raise the issue, the onus is on the Crown to meet it beyond a reasonable doubt.

. . . .

In my view the trial judge was correct in concluding that on the evidence before him he should instruct the jury with regard to necessity.

. . . .

In the course of his charge on the issue of necessity the trial judge instructed the jury, using the specific words that appear in *Morgentaler*, to the effect that they must find facts which amount to an "urgent situation of clear and imminent peril when compliance with the law is demonstrably impossible" in order for the appellants' non-compliance with the law against importation and possession of cannabis to be excused. That is the correct test. It is, with respect, however, my view that in explaining the meaning and application of this test, the trial judge fell into error.

The trial judge was obliged, in my opinion, to direct the jury's attention to a number of issues pertinent to the test for necessity. Was the emergency a real one? Did it constitute an immediate threat of the harm purportedly feared? Was the response proportionate? In comparing this response to the danger that motivated it, was the danger one that society would reasonably expect the average person to withstand? Was there any reasonable legal alternative to the illegal response open to the accused? Although the trial judge did not explicitly pose each and every one of these questions in my view his charge was adequate to bring considerations underlying them to the jury's attention on every issue except the last one, the question of a reasonable alternative.

This issue was the determining obstacle to the success of the defence of necessity in a number of the cases referred to earlier, including *Gilkes*, *Doud*, *Byng* and for the present case notably, because of the similarity of its factual basis, *Salvador*. Indeed in most cases where the defence is raised this consideration will almost certainly be the most important one.

In his charge, the trial judge did ... imply that the crucial consideration was whether the accused acted reasonably in coming into shore with their load of cannabis rather than facing death at sea. That is not sufficient as a test. Even if it does deal with the reality of the peril, its imminence and the proportionality of putting into shore, it does not deal at all with the question of whether there existed any other reasonable responses to the peril that were not illegal. Indeed, aside from the initial repetition of the *Morgentaler* formula, the trial judge did not advert to this consideration at all, nor did he direct the jury's attention to the relevance of evidence indicating the possibility of such alternative course of action. In these respects I believe he erred in law. He did not properly put the question of a "legal way out" before the jury.

In my view this was a serious error and omission going to the heart of the defence of necessity. The error justifies a new trial.

I would dismiss the appeals.

[WILSON J.:]

The factual background of this case, the history of the litigation in the courts below and the grounds on which the appeal was taken in this Court are very fully set out in the reasons for judgment of Mr. Justice Dickson (as he was at the date of the hearing) and it is not necessary for me to repeat them. Indeed, inasmuch as Dickson J.'s conclusion as to the defence of necessity seems clearly correct on the facts of this case and his disposition of the appeal manifestly just in the circumstances, I am dealing in these reasons only with the proposition very forcefully advanced by Dickson J. in his reasons that the appropriate jurisprudential basis on which to premise the defence of necessity is exclusively that of excuse. My concern is that the learned Justice appears to be closing the door on justification as an appropriate jurisprudential basis in some cases and I am firmly of the view that this is a door which should be left open by the Court.

As Dickson J. points out, criminal law theory recognizes a distinction between justification and excuse. In the case of justification the wrongfulness of the alleged offensive act is challenged; in the case of excuse the wrongfulness is acknowledged but a ground for the exercise of judicial compassion for the actor is asserted. By way of illustration an act may be said to be justified when an essential element of the offence is absent, so that the defence effectively converts the accused's act from wrongful to rightful.

. . . .

On the other hand, an excuse requires the court to evaluate the presence or absence of the accused's will. In contemporary jurisprudence the most forceful champion of excuse in criminal law has been Professor George Fletcher who has advocated a trend toward individualizing the conceptual basis for culpability so that all circumstances subjectively relevant to the accused be considered by the court. As such, the jury is requested to exercise compassion for the accused's predicament in the evaluation of his claim: "I couldn't help myself" (Fletcher, "The Individualization of Excusing Conditions," (1974) 47 S. Cal. L. Rev. 1269). This type of analysis is reflected in the dissent of Seiler J. of the Supreme Court of Missouri in *State v. Green*, 470 S.W. 2d 565 (1971), in which the accused's prison escape was seen as excusable due to the intolerability of his confinement with aggressive homosexual inmates by whom he had been repeatedly victimized. The basis of the defence could not have been that of justification based on an objective balance of evils since numerous U.S. courts had already established that the evil of prison escape outweighed the evil of intolerable prison conditions (see, e.g., *People v. Whipple*, 279 P. 1008 (Cal. App. 1926); *People v. Noble*, 170 N.W. 2d 916 (Mich. App. 1969)). Rather, the issue for Seiler J. was the blamelessness of an accused in committing an act which, although admittedly wrong, was one for which any juror might have compassion. Thus, the nature of an excuse is to personalize the plea so that while justification looks to the rightness of the act, excuse speaks to the compassion of the court for the actor.

. . . .

The position in English law, by contrast, was most accurately stated in the well-known case of *R. v. Dudley and Stephens* (1884), 14 Q.B.D. 273, in which Lord Coleridge warned against allowing "compassion for the criminal to change or weaken in any manner the legal definition of the crime" (p. 288). The underlying principle here is the universality of rights, that all individuals whose actions are subjected to legal evaluation must be considered equal in standing.

. . . .

Returning to the defence of necessity as a justification, it may generally be said that an act is justified on grounds of necessity if the court can say that not only was the act a necessary one but it was rightful rather than wrongful. When grounded on the fundamental principle that a successful defence must characterize an act as one which the accused was within his rights to commit, it becomes immediately apparent that the defence does not depend on the immediacy or "normative involuntariness" of the accused's act unless, of course, the involuntariness is such as to be pertinent to the ordinary analysis of *mens rea*. The fact that one act is done out of a sense of immediacy or urgency and another after some contemplation cannot, in my view, serve to distinguish the quality of the act in terms of right or wrong. Rather, the justification must be premised on the need to fulfil a duty conflicting with the one which the accused is charged with having breached.

. . . .

... [N]ot only can the system of positive law not tolerate an individual opting to act in accordance with the dictates of his conscience in the event of a conflict with legal duties, but it cannot permit acts in violation of legal obligations to be justified on the grounds that social utility is thereby increased. In both situations the conflicting "duty" to which the defence arguments point is one which the court cannot take into account as it invokes considerations external to a judicial analysis of the rightness or wrongness of the impugned act. As Lord Colderidge succinctly put it in *Dudley and Stephens*, *supra*, at p. 287: "Who is to be the judge of this sort of necessity?"

On the other hand, in some circumstances defence counsel may be able to point to a conflicting duty which courts can and do recognize. For example, one may break the law in circumstances where it is necessary to rescue someone to whom one owes a positive duty of rescue (see *R. v. Walker* (1979), 48 C.C.C. (2d) 126 (Ont. Co. Ct.)), since failure to act in such a situation may itself constitute a culpable act or omission (see *R. v. Instan*, [1893] 1 Q.B. 450). Similarly, if one subscribes to the viewpoint articulated by Laskin C.J.C. in *Morgentaler*, *supra*, and perceives a doctor's defence to an abortion charge as his legal obligation to treat the mother rather than his alleged ethical duty to perform an unauthorized abortion, then the defence may be invoked without violating the prohibition enunciated by Dickson J. in

Morgentaler against choosing a non-legal duty over a legal one.

It must be acknowledged, however, that on the existing state of the law the defence of necessity as justification would not be available to the person who rescues a stranger since the absence of a legal duty to rescue strangers reduces such a case to a conflict of a legal with a purely ethical duty. Such an act of rescue may be one deserving of no punishment and, indeed, deserving of praise, but it is nevertheless a culpable act if the law is violated in the process of the rescue.

. . . .

In summary, it seems to me that the category of "normative involuntariness" into which an act done in the interests of self-preservation falls is characterized not by the literal voluntariness of the act but by its unpunishable nature. As such, the act may be exempted from culpability if it arose in a life-threatening situation of necessity. Where, however, a defence by way of excuse is premised on compassion for the accused or on a perceived failure to achieve a desired instrumental end of punishment, the judicial response must be to fashion an appropriate sentence but to reject the defence as such. The only conceptual premise on which necessity as an excuse could rest is the inherent impossibility of a court's responding in any way to an act which although wrongful, was the one act which any rational person would commit.

Where the defence of necessity is invoked as a justification the issue is simply whether the accused was right in pursuing the course of behaviour giving rise to the charge. Thus, where the act otherwise constitutes a criminal offence (i.e. it embodies both *mens rea* and *actus reus*) the accused must show that he operated under a conflicting legal duty which made his seemingly wrongful act right. But such justification must be premised on a right or duty recognized by law. This excludes conduct attempted to be justified on the ground of an ethical duty internal to the conscience of the accused as well as conduct sought to be justified on the basis of a perceived maximization of social utility resulting from it. Rather, the conduct must stem from the accused's duty to satisfy his legal obligations to respect the principle of the universality of rights.

I would dismiss the appeals.

■

In *R. v. Adams*, below, under **Mistake of Fact**, a battered wife attempted unsuccessfully to argue the s. 285 *Code* defence of necessity for her action in removing a five-year-old girl from her father's custody. Reconsider the case of *Lalonde*, above, under **Self-Defence**, in which a battered wife was acquitted of welfare fraud on the basis of necessity. Compare the B.C. provincial court decision to allow the defence of necessity to a charge of assault, where the accused argued that he was concerned that his pregnant girlfriend was about to harm the foetus and had slapped her in the face (causing a black eye) allegedly to prevent that harm: *R. v. Manning* (1994), 31 C.R. (4th) 54 (B.C. Prov. Ct.) at 59:

> In this case the complainant was not contemplating a conventional abortion. She was trying to inflict an injury upon both herself and her foetus. The accused was faced with an emergency. He reacted to it swiftly and **in a manner in which any right-thinking member of society would react**. [Emphasis added.]

In *Perka*, Justice Dickson confirmed the availability of the necessity defence and expanded somewhat upon the criteria that he had earlier set out in *Morgentaler*. He held that the defence is available only if the accused can frame it as an excuse, and not as a justification, that is, as circumstances that essentially deprived the accused of voluntariness or free will. Justice Dickson described this as a utilitarian form of defence and opposed its use for situations where the accused has broken a law for a higher good. Justice Wilson's dissent would have preserved the growth of the defence as a justification in those circumstances where the "higher good" is actually another legal duty, such as the duty to provide the necessaries of life or medical care. What would Justice Dickson make of the situations posed in Justice Wilson's dissent? Consider the impact of *Perka* on cases such as *Morgentaler*. What would be the result?

Now, consider the kinds of beneficiaries of the *Perka* decision. In *R. v. Stephens* (1986), 6 L.W. 615-007 (Ont. Prov. Ct.), reported in *The Lawyers Weekly* (1 August 1986) 2, a woman charged with driving while under suspension successfully argued "necessity" because she subjectively believed that the situation was one involving "urgent and imminent peril". In that case, her son had been involved in an accident about which she received no details, and she drove her vehicle to the hospital.

In *R. v. Gourlay*, [1996] A.J. No. 197 (Prov. Ct.) (QL), the impoverished accused, who suffered from severe asthma, was denied the defence of necessity to a charge of theft in obtaining his medication fraudulently. Fradsham J. rejected the accused's evidence that he had disclosed to his social worker his medical condition and his inability to afford required medications in view of her decision to deny him welfare (at para. 6–8, 19–22):

> Mr. Gourlay was denied social assistance because he had been dismissed from his previous employment and he had not made sufficient efforts to obtain new employment. He was told that he could appeal the decision and, further, that he could obtain some financial assistance if he obtained a full-time job leading to self-sufficiency.
>
> Mr. Gourlay then obtained employment delivering newspapers for the Calgary Sun. He so informed Ms. Eaton, but was told that he was not eligible for assistance because his employment would not lead to self-sufficiency. He again failed to mention to Ms. Eaton that he needed money for the purchase of asthma medication. Had he done so, there was a possibility that short-term assistance would have been provided to him.
>
> I accept Mr. Gourlay's evidence that he did not receive his earnings from the Calgary Sun until after the date of the offence.
>
> ...
>
> Was compliance with the law demonstrably unreasonable for Mr. Gourlay? I am thoroughly satisfied that the accused needed the medication that he stole. It would have been unreasonable for him not to have the medication.
>
> However, one must consider how the accused ended up in the situation he faced on September 23, 1994 (i.e., no funds with which to purchase medication that he needed for his own wellbeing). He had applied to social services for assistance and had been turned down. He was told how to obtain assistance (secure a full-time job leading to self-sufficiency) and he failed to follow that advice (he obtained a part-time job which would not lead to self-sufficiency). Knowing of the approaching medication problem, he did not consult with his social assistance contact, more importantly in my view, he did not contact his probation officer. He was on probation for the same sort of offence (obtaining his medication unlawfully). He did not inform his probation officer of the predicament in which he found himself and the likelihood of re-offending.
>
> An accused's' negligence does not necessarily deprive him or her of the benefits of the defence of necessity: *R. v. Perka, supra*. However, Dickson J. also said in *Perka* (at p. 403):
>
> > In my view, the better approach to the relationship of fault to the availability of necessity as a defence is based once again on the question of whether the actions sought to be excused were truly 'involuntary'. If the necessitous situation was clearly foreseeable to a reasonable observer, if the actor contemplated or ought to have contemplated that his actions would likely give rise to an emergency requiring the breaking of the law, then I doubt whether what confronted the accused was in the relevant sense an emergency. His response was in sense not 'involuntary'. 'Contributory fault' of this nature, but only of this nature, is a relevant consideration to the availability of the defence.
>
> This describes Mr. Gourlay's situation. On nine other occasions he had broken the law in order to obtain his medication. He was on probation for at least some of the previous offences. He had been denied social assistance and had not done that which might make him eligible. He informed neither social assistance not his probation officer of this pending predicament. [Note: The trial judge disbelieved the accused's evidence on this point to the effect that he had informed the social worker.] I am satisfied that a reasonable person in the circumstances of the accused would realize that such inaction would lead to the very emergency feared and the commission of the offence currently before the Court. Accordingly, the accused's acts in stealing the medication were not 'involuntary' as that word is used in *Perka*.

How are poverty and the failure to obtain full-time employment characterized? Would this approach ever allow poverty to be characterized as giving rise to necessity or does this analysis essentially blame the victim? In *R. v. John Doe*, [2007] B.C.A.C.. 157, the B.C. Court of Appeal set aside an acquittal on the basis that the trial judge had erred in not applying a "modified objective" test to the first two elements of the necessity defence: the existence of imminent peril or danger and the absence of any reasonable legal alternative. The accused was charged with breaking and entering and committing mischief. Prior to the incident, he had been fasting in the woods for 60 days and was apparently confused, disoriented, very hungry and possibly hypothermic. He testified he went inside the house to be warm and to eat and the trial judge accepted his evidence. However, on appeal, Justice Rowles writing for a unanimous court concluded that the appropriate test was a "modified objective" test and, also, that imminent peril "cannot apply where the peril is foreseeable and thus avoidable" [at para. 25]. In this case, the accused had fasted for lengthy periods on a number of occasions and the Crown argued that he should have been aware that such fasting would eventually cause him to lose control. A new trial was ordered to allow consideration of these issues.

Doe highlights the impact of foreseeability of risk and conduct of the accused as a barrier to satisfying the first element of imminent peril or danger. How have different courts responded to this question? Consider the way in which Justice Dickson responds to this question in *Perka* and the response in *Gourlay*.

In a recent Alberta case, *R. v. C.W.V.*, [2004] A.J. No. 786 (C.A.) (QL), the 17-year-old accused had gone to a party to retrieve a stolen keg of beer. In the process, he was assaulted and his car was surrounded by a mob of 20–40 people. In trying to escape, he hit two people and was charged with dangerous driving. The trial judge concluded that the three elements of the defence of necessity were met, but denied the defence on the basis that the accused should have know that his actions might "create a situation which might become explosive" (para. 8). The Alberta Court of Appeal overturned the conviction and ordered a new trial (at para. 10):

> ... [T]he trial judge found only that "the accused could not have proceeded to the Skinner property without some thought of a possibility of ensuing problems in retrieving the beer". He made no finding that the Appellant foresaw, or ought to have foreseen, the necessitous situation. The trial judge was entitled to take into account whether the Appellant's contributory fault deprived him of the defence of necessity. In doing so, however, the trial judge was required to apply the test articulated by Dickson, J. (as he then was) in *Perka*. The trial judge, with respect, erred in applying a lesser standard.

In *R. v. C.A.V.* (2003), 175 O.A.C. 71 (C.A.) (QL) the Court of Appeal overturned the acquittal and ordered a new trial of a mother who had argued necessity in her defence to three charges of abduction contrary to a custody order (s. 283(1) of the *Code*) on the basis that there was no "air of reality" to any of the elements of the defence (at 72–73):

> Essentially, the respondent had lost custody of the children to the father in March, 2000. The custody trial was adjourned for six months, at which time the trial judge intended to deal with whether the respondent would retain any right to access visits with her children. Fearing that the court would cut off her access completely, and that the children would thereby be deprived of any contact with their mother (herself), she cashed in her assets and prepared to abscond with the children on one of her last access visits. She hid the children in her car and drove to the United States and Panama, then returned to Mexico, where they lived for a few months until they were found and returned to Ontario.
>
> In his charge to the jury, the trial judge outlined the evidence in a manner that highlighted the situation the respondent perceived she faced. He described it as follows:
>
> > ... Turning to Ms. C.A.V.'s evidence. She described a four-year quest for pregnancy with physically intrusive long-term fertility clinic investigations and procedures with drug therapy and side effects, with donor sperm finally leading to a difficult pregnancy requiring hospitalizations culminating with two months in hospital prior to the premature birth [of triplets] by cesarean section. There was concern over the size and health of the children. There was difficulty in their care and management even with help from Neighbourlink and a baby-sitter. She badly wanted a child, she paid an exacting price.

The trial judge described her role as the primary caregiver, the respondent's leave of absence from her work as a teacher to enable her to care for the children, the difficulties that arose in the marriage, the eventual separation and the husband's application for interim custody and repeated variations of access. The husband arranged for a neighbour to care for the children and subsequently decided to marry that neighbour. As the trial judge summarized (quoted at 74):

> Ms. C.A.V.'s access had been relentlessly reduced and may have been on the verge of termination. Her view on the access issue was, "in six years, I had gone from mother to threatened zero access." She had been unsuccessful in the custody issue. She had been unsuccessful on the issue of paying child support. The momentum of the court proceeding was against her. Her fear was that the children would be cut off from all contact with their mother and from the benefits that flow from

that association. The children's total deprivation of the care, guidance, love and support of their mother was seen by Ms. C.A.V. as a danger of imminent psychological and emotional harm to the children.

From her perspective, the behaviour of the children was spiralling downward with her declining access. She was involved in a high stakes contest. At issue was a precious asset, the formative years and the welfare of their children. Ms. C.A.V. testified that she truly believed the children needed a loving mother, that she genuinely and honestly felt she had to take the children. Her testimony in part was as follows:

> Mr. Powell [for the defence] asked the question, "What did you think might be the result if you were denied access to your children in so far as your children were concerned?"
>
> Answer: Well I thought my children would be raised without a mother, that they were going to have — I just thought that they were going to come to some imminent harm, not physical harm, but psychological harm, emotional harm. I didn't think it was healthy. With what I knew and what I believed and what I felt, I didn't want my children raised without a mother. You can have caregivers, but that's not the same as a mother."
>
> ...
>
> Question [from the Crown]: Well, you were selfish and wanted the kids for yourself, not for their father and yourself?
>
> Answer: I wouldn't consider a mother's love for her children and the steps and the actions she takes in terms of that love as being selfish. I wouldn't consider that selfish at all.
>
> Question: Well you took the kids away from their stable lives. You took them away from — you took them away from their father, the one person who had been there forever for them?
>
> Answer: I took my children from a very nasty situation. They were being raised by the courts and I don't believe any judge can do a better job in raising children that their own parents. So my taking the children was not done to spite anyone. It was not done for selfish motives. It was done because I truly believed these children need a loving and good mother."
>
> ...

In making assessments of Ms. C.A.V.'s actions and motivations, bear in mind, we view these issues in calm reflection with hindsight in the sterile atmosphere of the courtroom. Ms. C.A.V. acted in developing circumstances and in a swirl of powerful emotions. T.V.'s evidence indicates the emotional force generated.

One of her friends, a neighbour and fellow multiple birth mother, described the trauma of restricted Saturday afternoon access visits for the respondent.

> ... [S]he'd go through a grieving process every time the kids would go back home. It's like she'd just cry and you know she'd come and cry on my shoulder and go on, 'I can't take this.' It's like she'd go through a bereavement every time the kids would go back home....

The trial judge continued.

> The circumstantial evidence is by fleeing with the children, her entire life and support structures were in convulsion. She sacrificed home, parents, brothers, sisters, friends, and the security of her teaching position with whatever income, health and pension benefits that may have carried. There was a finality about her actions, cashing her Retirement Savings Plan, cashing her children's educational plans, withdrawing her savings, fleeing unaccompanied by an adult into foreign countries, a fugitive with three small children. There is P.'s [one of the children] poignant description of the stealth and subterfuge, their quest for distance, losing the car, being turned back at Panama, the lack of a job, and the need to conserve money. What powerful motivation produced that result?

The trial judge suggested that the extent of investigation, assessment, intervention, and the lack of resolution over a four year period, despite a lengthy trial, might have led the respondent to conclude that (quoted at 7) "further resort to lawyers and courts was not the answer". The Court of Appeal concluded that there was no imminent harm, that there were other legal avenues (to build a record with respect to access, hire expert legal assistance instead of representing herself and, ultimately, file an appeal), and that there was no proportionality of harm between her "drastic remedy" and any imminent danger to the children (at 80):

> ... The imminence of the harm was the court date, after which she felt she would have no ability to carry out her plan to remove the children. In effect, the imminence of the harm to the children was not the perceived psychological and emotional harm that would result from being deprived of a loving mother, the effect of which would accrue over time, but the fact that after the court order, the respondent anticipated that she might no longer

> have the opportunity to exercise self-help to remove the children.
>
> ... There is neither harm, nor imminence in this situation.
>
> The defence provided by s. 285 ... is designed to deal with an emergent situation of danger, arising in circumstances that were not foreseen or contemplated by the court that granted the custody order....
>
> For the criminal court to hold that a situation deliberately created in the children's best interests by the custody court after a trial could be considered a situation of imminent harm to the children, would invite a regime of anarchy and chaos within the family law domain...
>
> ...
>
> Clearly, both the trial judge and the jury had considerable empathy for the respondent, a mother faced with the possibility of losing all access to her children, who honestly and truly believed that it was in their best interests for her to become a fugitive with them, rather than leave them with no access to their mother. The fact that the children, who were seven and a half years old, willingly went with her and co-operated in hiding from authorities without trying to contact the father, suggests that they loved and trusted their mother very much. The children's co-operative conduct could be seen as affirming the mother's perception of the situation, and in that way, as a troubling factor for the jury.
>
> Having said that, the necessity defence is not meant for situations where the parties are unhappy with custody and access decisions.... The court's orders must be respected and followed. Any other approach would lead to anarchy.

Realistically, what were the respondent's options? What was her apparent state of mind? Is there a different standard of proof in civil cases? Would it be possible to imagine a situation in which the accused could raise an "air of reality" with respect to the elements of a necessity defence in the face of an unfavourable civil decision?

In preparation for the new trial, the defence sought to challenge jurors for cause in light of the extensive ongoing publicity about the acquittal and new charges faced by the accused: *R. v. C.A.V.*, [2005] O.J. No. 1359 (Sup. Ct. J.) (QL) (at para. 9):

> ... The defence notes that the immediate publicity was intense and extended beyond the local community. A Canada-wide warrant was issued for her arrest. Ms. C.A.V. was the subject of a segment on "America's Most Wanted" television show. Interest in the case has continued after the acquittal at the first trial and the order for a new trial. An incident in Nova Scotia involving the defendant and her husband, L.F., also relating to an alleged child abduction that occurred in the spring of 2004, has kept Ms. C.A.V.'s situation in front of the public.

In the meantime, Children's Aid Society of Nova Scotia applied for permanent care and custody of a fourth child born to the mother in 2003, based on the history of previous child apprehensions and child abduction and a subsequent armed standoff with police in Nova Scotia: *Children's Aid Society of Halifax v. C.V.*, [2005] N.S.J. No. 260 (S.C. (F.D.)) (QL), aff'd. *C.V. v. Children's Aid Society of Halifax*, [2006] N.S.J. No. 2 (C.A.) (QL).

In *R. v. Stevenson* (1986), 42 Man. R. (2d) 133 (Q.B.), the accused members of an Aboriginal band were charged with mischief for destroying a bridge that was in disrepair. Their "mistake of law", "colour of right" defence was set out above, under **Colour of Right: Mistake of Fact, Mistake of Law, or Affirmative Defence**. The following extract (at 138) sets out the legal response to their necessity argument:

> It was argued that the defence of necessity applied. I reject this argument also. The defence of necessity was recently dealt with by the Supreme Court of Canada in *R. v. Perka*, [1984] 2 S.C.R. 232; 55 N.R. 1; 14 C.C.C. (3d) 385; 42 C.R. (3d) 113; 13 D.L.R. (4th) 1; [1984] 6 W.W.R. 289, and following the authority, the learned trial judge posed the question "Do the actions of the accused involuntarily, inevitably and unavoidably, offer no reasonable opportunity for an alternative course of action that does not involve a breach of the law?" See reasons for judgment, p. 314. He answered that question by saying the bridge could have been blocked off as it was on the day of the fire by dumping loads of earth at both ends, or it could have been barricaded and posted and closed off to prevent both pedestrian and vehicular traffic.
>
> The bridge was in poor condition, but it was still being used. Vehicular traffic, including school buses, was passing over it. Heavy government equipment for dragging and snow plowing went over the bridge once or twice monthly in the year prior to the burning. If the accused considered the bridge to be a danger to themselves, their alternative was not to use the bridge, and to encourage other members of the band not to do so. There were alternate routes across the river which they could have

used (and presumably did use after the bridge was burned out). The learned trial judge made the point (p. 313) in the reference to the press release that the stated purpose for burning the bridge was to bring to the attention of governmental authorities conditions on the reserve as well as the state of the bridge. The band wanted to make a point. The trial judge said they could have simply blocked off the bridge. That might have involved a breach of provincial laws respecting the placing of materials on a public highway, but at least it would have been preferable to destroying the bridge.

The defence of necessity must fail.

In the result, the evidence clearly supports the finding made by the learned trial judge. I agree with him that the various defences advanced must fail, and accordingly the appeals are dismissed.

Would the proposed alternative action also have exposed the accused to criminal charges?

Now consider a recent successful use of the necessity defence in another case involving political protest.

R. v. Langdon†

[PHILLIPS J.P.:]

The defendants were arrested and charged by the Metro Police on November 6, 1995, for the offence of Failing to Leave the Premises When Directed. The alleged offence took place at the British and Netherlands consulates in the city of Toronto. The defendants were arraigned and they pleaded not guilty to the charge. The Crown did not call the investigating police officers to the witness stand since the defence counsel, Mr. Peter Rosenthal, conceded that the defendants failed to leave the premises when directed by the police.

The trial began with the testimony of Crown witness Miss Francis Luff, vice-consul general for Britain. She testified that a group of five ladies, who are defendants before the court, arrived at the British Consulate at approximately ten thirty a.m. on November 16, 1995, and demanded a petition be sent to the British Foreign Office and Defence Secretaries in London, England. A copy of the petition was received and entered as an exhibit before the Court. The purpose of the petition was to protest against the British involvement in the low-flying exercises conducted from the military base at Goose Bay, in Labrador, jointly conducted by Canada, [Britain], The Netherlands, and Germany.

The aircraft used are powerful fighter planes, such as F-16s, F-18s and Tornados, *et cetera*. Such low-flying exercises have been going on for many years over the territory occupied by the native Innu community with a population of approximately 1,600. The Court heard [that] the thundering noise from the low-flying military fighter planes has almost destroyed the lifestyle and livelihood of the Innu people.

The petitions were received by the British Consulate staff and faxed to Britain. The defendants remained at the premises, singing and chanting, and were handing out carnations to the people around. The defendants were non-violent and peaceful throughout, and did not create any disturbance or damage to property. They wanted to remain at the Consulate office until a reply to the petition was received. The Crown witness asked the defendants individually to leave the premises, but they refused. The Crown witness, Miss Francis Luff, called in the R.C.M.P., who in turn called the Metro Police, and the protestors were forcibly removed from the Consulate office, and charged with the offence of Failing to Leave the Premises When Directed by the police.

The second Crown witness was Mr. Paul Schellekens, the Consul General for The Netherlands. The witness stated that a group of people, who are defendants before the Court, came to the Consulate office on November 16, 1995, and presented a petition to the Secretary of State for The Netherlands. This petition was similar in content to the one presented at the British Consulate on the same day, protesting the participation of The Netherlands in the low-flying exercises from the Goose Bay military base in Labrador.

A copy of the petition was entered as an exhibit before the Court. Mr. Schellekens accepted the petition from the group of defendants and faxed it to The Netherlands. The assembled group of defen-

† (9 April 1996), Toronto, (Ont. Ct. J. (Prov. Div.)) [unreported].

dants, however, refused to leave the Consulate premises when requested by the Consul General individually. Hence, police were called, and they were forcibly removed and charged with the offence of Failing to Leave the Premises When Directed by the police. The Consul General, Mr. Schellekens, stated that the defendants were very peaceful, non-violent, and they were singing and chanting without causing any disturbance or damage to property.

The Crown closed their case and the defence arguments commenced. The chief defence witness was Elizabeth Penashue, a native Innu woman, approximately 52 years of age, who is a resident of the Innu village called Sheshatshiu near Goose Bay military base in Labrador. Elizabeth Penashue came all the way from Labrador to testify in this case for the defence. Elizabeth Penashue moved to the Goose Bay when she was very young. She stated that the air force base at Goose Bay was approximately an hour's journey from her home village. She testified that the low-level flights started in 1980. She described the devastating effects of the loud thundering noise from the low-flying fighter planes as follows — and I quote: We live in a tent and also in the country. The low-flying fighter planes swoop down with a powerful bang. Everybody is nervous because of the roaring noise from the low-flying fighter planes. The terrible noise from the low-flying military aircraft interferes with our right to lead a normal life. We are deprived of our hunting and fishing privileges, which is our only livelihood, because the noise from the low-flying military aircraft scare the Caribou and other animals away. The substances from the test bombs dropped by the aircraft destroy the fish stocks.

Her son, Peter Penashue, acted as an interpreter for his mother after the Court examined and found him to be competent, as no official interpreter was available.

The next defence witness was Peter Penashue, who is the president of the Innu nation in Labrador. It is an elected position. The witness stated they are still negotiating with the government of Canada on land claims. Peter Penashue stated that the noisy fighter planes fly at a very low height of 100 feet above the ground, threatening the basic human rights of the Innu people to lead a normal life. The Court heard of numerous crashes of the low flying fighter planes over the Innu land.

The next defence witness was Mr. John Olthuis. He's a lawyer who has been deeply involved in negotiations on Labrador Innu issues since 1984. He has been actually involved in and has taken part in negotiations on land rights on the Innu nation issue with the government of Canada. Mr. Olthuis explained the damaging negative impact of the low-flying fighter planes on the Innu people. The terrible noise from the low-flying aircraft cause deafness and other physical discomforts and it violates the basic human rights of the Innu people.

The Court then heard from the defendants and supporters and the names are: Professor Mel Watkins, Lorraine Land, Father Robert Holmes, William Payne, Carolyn Langdon, Tomi Fukushima, Sandra Lang and Len Desroches.

All the above defence witnesses have worked very hard for many years to stop the destruction of the Innu people and their livelihood by the low-level flights by the military aircraft from the Goose Bay military base. They wrote letters to Members of Parliament, had interviews with the Honourable Sheila Copps and other federal ministers, had contacted the ambassadors of the participating governments, had presented briefs to all concerned parties and agencies.

It appears all their efforts over the years to have the low-flying by the military planes stopped in order to save the Innu community have failed. Their aim and objective was to save the Innu people and restore their fundamental human rights. It is very clear from the testimony that the defendants and their supporters over the Innu issue have always acted peacefully and in a non-violent fashion in their many years of committed hard work to bring justice to the oppressed Innu community.

The defendants appear to be highly motivated and dedicated people, pursuing peaceful means to restore basic human rights to the suffering Innu people in Labrador. Some of the adverse effects from the low-level flights by the powerful military aircraft over the Innu community are: heart attacks, high blood pressure, miscarriages in pregnant women, nervousness and constant fear, sleeplessness, mental agitation, anxiety, nightmares, insecure feelings, and environmental damage.

Having failed in all their peaceful non-violent efforts for many years to save the lives of the helpless Innu people, the devoted and dedicated defendants have become desperate and finally decided to present a petition to the British and Netherlands governments through their respective consuls general in Toronto. Even at the Consulate they conducted themselves in a peaceful, non-violent way. They are not at the Consulate for any personal gratification nor to gain publicity. They were not planning any forcible occupation of the Consulate. They decided to remain at the premises until they received a reply to their petition.

Under the above exceptional circumstances, taking note of the distinct possibility of the annihilation of the Innu lifestyle and the prolonged violation of the human rights by the destructive effects of the low-flying military aircraft, and the fact that the defendants have exhausted all other means of redress by peaceful, non-violent methods, is the defence of necessity available to them?

Are they justified in breaking the letter of the law for avoiding a greater harm to the Innu nation? If the defence of necessity is available to a police officer who shoots the hostage-taker, the innocent object of an assault who uses minimum force to defend him/herself against the assailant, the good Samaritan who commandeers a car and breaks the speed limit to rush an accident victim to the hospital, and if the society feels such actions are rightful and not wrongful, then such defence is equally available to the defendants.

In the *Morgentaler* case it was held that the harm inflicted must be less than the harm sought to be avoided for the admissibility of the defence of necessity. In the *Salvador* case at page 542, Mr. Justice MacDonald observed, "Generally speaking, the defence of necessity covers all cases where non-compliance with law is excused by an emergency or justified by the pursuit of some greater good." Working Paper 29 of the Law Reform Commission of Canada, *Criminal Law, the General Part, Liability and Defences* (1982), p. 93, makes the same point in the following words: "Essentially it involves two factors: one is the avoidance of greater harm or the pursuit of some greater good. The other is the difficulty of compliance with law in emergencies."

From these two factors emerge two different but related principles. The first is the utilitarian principle to the effect that within certain limits it is justifiable in an emergency to break the letter of the law if breaking the law will avoid a greater harm than obeying it. The second is a humanitarian principle to the effect that, again, within certain limits, it is excusable in an emergency to break the law if compliance would impose an intolerable burden on the accused.

In the case of *Morgentaler v. The Queen*, 1975, the trial judge instructed the jury to the effect that they must find facts which amount to an urgent situation of clear and imminent danger when compliance with the law is demonstrably impossible.

I'm prepared to hold, after hearing both sides in this case, that the defendants in this case broke the letter of the law by their non-compliance to prevent a greater evil, that is the destruction of the Innu people and their basic human rights. Further, I hold that in a limited sense that the provisions of Section 27 and Section 430 of the *Criminal Code* are applicable in this case.

For the above reasons, I find their refusal to leave the premises when directed, again, within certain limits, is a justifiable non-compliance, where the concept of punishment will be incompatible with social justice. For the reasons stated hitherto, the charges against all defendants are therefore dismissed.

■

By and large, successful necessity defences of this sort are rare. For example, in *R. v. Young* (1984), 39 C.R. (3d) 290 (Ont. Prov. Ct.) peaceful demonstrators who opposed the testing of cruise missiles in Canada by trespassing on Litton property were denied a necessity defence. Recall also the response of the legal system to the form of dissent expressed by the Squamish Five, as described in Abell & Sheehy, *Cases, Context, Critique*, **Sentencing**. See also *R. v. Bridges (No. 1)* (1989), 48 C.C.C. (3d) 535 (B.C.S.C.), where the court rejected the defence of necessity for a group of anti-abortion activists who were charged with contempt of court for breaching an injunction restraining picketing.

In another case, accused prisoners overpowered guards and escaped during the aftermath of a prison riot at Oakalla, in which they had been hosed down, locked wet in unheated cells, and either assaulted or threatened by a guard with assault. Perhaps not surprisingly, the court refused to allow the defence of necessity to even be placed before the jury on the grounds that the "air of reality" test had not been met: *R. v. McKay* (1992), 12 B.C.A.C. 234 (C.A.). Instead, the Court of Appeal minimized the harshness and dangerousness of the conditions in which the accused were held. They ruled that there was no threat of injury to be inflicted imminently so as to create a "direct and immediate peril" (because the escape took place many hours later) and that there were alternative avenues open to the accused (such as reporting the threat to other guards) (at 237):

> The evidence of the appellant White was that he feared for his life because a guard, who was not on duty at the unit but had made a

> visit there [the night before the escape], kicked his door and threatened him with a beating.... Both said they were concerned for their safety because of the conditions before, during and after the riot, which they said made them fear that anarchy reigned in the prison.... They had seen prisoners injured by the guards in the course of, or after, the riot, and one of the appellants had suffered some injury himself. They said they fled because of fear for their personal safety.
>
> ...
>
> ... The judge had to have in mind what could reasonably be considered "society's expectation of appropriate and normal resistance to pressure" in the context of the situation described by the appellants. The pressure to be considered would include that created by the wet and cold environment, the atmosphere within the prison following the riot, the conditions in which the appellants found themselves and the threat which White said had been made by the guard who he could not identify.

Compare the restrictive interpretation in the U.S. prison escape cases discussed by Justice Wilson in *Perka*, *supra*. Can you anticipate the reasoning? Would the arguments raised in *McConnell*, above, under **Self-Defence**, assist in reaching a different conclusion in *McKay*?

For a murder case in which necessity was withdrawn from the jury, see *R. v. Latimer* (1995) (Sask. C.A.), discussed above, under **The Trial Process**. The trial judge withdrew necessity from the jury because, according to him, the decision to break the law was neither unavoidable nor necessary to avert some imminent risk of peril. Instead, he held that there was a choice (cited at 38 of C.A. decision) "to persevere in the attempts to make Tracy comfortable in her life, however disagreeable those attempts might have been". Justice Tallis (for the majority of the Court of Appeal) upheld the trial judge's decision, citing the requirements according to *Perka* and *Morgentaler* (at 40–41).

> ... In this case the appellant's life was not in peril. He was concerned with Tracy's quality of life. The evidence clearly established the bleak future that faced this little girl. Although her scheduled surgery involved a long recovery period, there was the prospect of some pain alleviation.
>
> This is not a case of withholding potentially life-prolonging treatment to a seriously disabled person. It deals with the deliberate decision to terminate another's life rather than continue with the scheduled medical treatment and care. In such circumstances it is no defence for a parent to say because of a severe handicap, a child's life has such diminished value that the child should not live any longer. It does not advance the interest of the state or society to treat such a child as a person of lesser status or dignity than others.
>
> In dealing with this aspect of the case learned counsel for the Crown stressed that Tracy's medical condition was not unique. She pointed to the many families that are visited with a similar type of misfortune. Dr. Snyder testified that one in 1,000 births involve children with cerebral palsy and ten percent of that unfortunate group have severe cerebral palsy. Dr. Dzus, a specialist in orthopaedic surgery limiting her practice mainly to children, testified that in her work at the Kinsmen Children's Centre in Saskatoon, she attended to many children with multiple handicaps similar to Tracy's.
>
> Although the appellant did not testify at trial, his statement to the investigating officers indicates how he set about the termination of Tracy's life. There is no evidence that his act in terminating her life was "involuntary" within the test articulated in *Perka*.
>
> Furthermore the evidence is clear that the appellant and his family did have an option. If they could no longer bear the burden of caring for Tracy, there was the real prospect of permanent placement in a group home.
>
> Accordingly this ground of appeal must fail.

Chief Justice Bayda (dissenting) painted a compassionate picture of a father who loved his daughter too much to watch her suffer. He canvassed the cases dealing with "mercy killing" in considering the s. 12 *Charter* arguments with respect to the mandatory life sentence for murder and acknowledged the public protest generated by the harsh sentence. He concluded that a constitutional exemption to the minimum sentence was the appropriate remedy for Latimer. The appeal to the Supreme Court on other grounds was allowed and a new trial ordered: *R. v. Latimer*, [1997] 1 S.C.R. 217.

At the new trial, Latimer was found guilty of second degree murder by a jury, who nonetheless recommended a minimum one-year sentence. The trial judge held that the mandatory minimum sentence for murder (life imprisonment without eligibility for parole before 10 years) violated s. 12 of the *Charter* and would amount to cruel and unusual punishment. Accordingly, Judge Ted Noble sentenced Latimer to only one year in jail to be followed by one year confinement to his farm, concluding that the evidence clearly established a "rare act of homicide that was committed for caring and altruistic reasons" and that the principles of sentencing would not be served by a lengthy sentence: quoted in Les Perreaux, "Latimer sentenced to one year in jail" *The Ottawa Citizen* (2 December 1997) A5. The Court of Appeal affirmed the conviction but reversed the sentence, imposing the mandatory minimum sentence of life imprisonment without eligibility for parole for ten years: *R. v. Latimer*, [1999] 6 W.W.R. 118 (Sask. C.A.).

The Supreme Court dismissed the appeals against sentence and conviction, holding that the requirements for the defence of necessity had not been met (no emergency, legal alternatives, lack of proportionality): *R. v. Latimer*, [2001] 1 S.C.R. 3. Although the jury had clearly sought guidance on the likely result of a finding of guilty, the Court concluded that their confusion was not fatal, since there was no "air of reality" to the defence. Potential jury nullification was not seen as a valid factor in analyzing the fairness of the trial for the accused (at paras. 69–70):

> The appellant ... advances some right, on the part of the accused person, to a jury whose power to nullify is not undermined. He suggests the right to a fair trial under s. 7 of the *Charter* encompasses this entitlement. The appellant submits that there is a jury power to nullify, and it would be unconstitutional to undermine that power.
>
> We reject that proposition. The Appellant cannot legitimately rely on a broad right to jury nullification. In this case, the trial did not become unfair simply because the trial judge undermined the jury's *de facto* power to nullify. In most if not all cases, jury nullification will not be a valid factor in analyzing trial fairness for the accused. Guarding against jury nullification is a desirable and legitimate exercise for a trial judge; in fact a judge is required to take steps to ensure that the jury will apply the law properly. See *R. v. Shipley* (1784), 4 Dougl. 73, 99 E.R. 774 (K.B.), at p. 824, cited with approval by Dickson C.J. in *Morgentaler* (1988), at p. 78. Steps taken by a trial judge to guard against jury nullification should not, on that basis alone, prejudice the accused person.

Robert Latimer was granted day parole in February 2008 and will be eligible for full parole in 2011: Omar El Akkad, "Latimer faces uphill battle" *The [Toronto] Globe and Mail* (18 March 2008) A7. The case continues to generate considerable discussion and controversy (with respect to mandatory minimum sentencing, the defence of necessity, the exercise of prosecutorial discretion, the role of the jury, and equality rights and euthanasia, for example) as the extensive media coverage and the range of articles demonstrate: Tim Quigley, "*R. v. Latimer*: Hard Cases Make Interesting Law" (1995) 41 C.R. (4th) 89; Kent Roach, "Crime and Punishment in the Latimer Case" (2001) 64 Sask. L. Rev. 469; David Lepofsky, "The Latimer Case: Murder is Still Murder when the Victim is a Child with a Disability" (2001) 27 Queen's L.J. 319; Paul Guy, "*R. v. Latimer* and the Defence of Necessity: One Step Forward, Two Steps Back" (2003) 63 Sask. L. Rev. 485; Gary Bauslaugh, "Punishing Acts of Mercy: Robert Latimer & the Justice System" (Spring 2008) *Humanist Perspectives* 2. The *Latimer* case clearly raises equality issues with respect to disability as the intervenors' facta set out: Factum of the Intervenors, People in Equal Participation, Inc. and Factum of the Intervenors, Council of Canadians with Disabilities and Saskatchewan Voice of the Handicapped, in *R. v. Latimer* (Sask. C.A.).

The Council of Canadians with Disabilities and Voice of the Handicapped argued that five of the grounds of appeal (failing to leave necessity as an issue; failing to allow the jury to decide the case on conscience; failing to charge the jury that Latimer had the legal right to decide to commit suicide for his daughter "by virtue of her complete absence of physical and intellectual abilities"; not holding that the minimum sentence for murder violated s. 12; and not holding that the particular sentence was too harsh) "all turn either expressly or by necessary implication on the fact of Tracy Latimer's disability" (paras. 10–12) and would offend the ss. 7 and 15 *Charter* rights of disabled persons. As you read the Factum of People in Equal Participation Inc. [PEP], consider the issues generated by an analysis that is attentive to equality rights. For thoughtful critiques of the way in which the *Latimer* case has been used to support arguments for a review of mandatory minimum sentencing and the equality issues that raises, see: H. Archibald Kaiser, "*Latimer*: 'Something Ominous is Happening in the World of Disabled People...'" (2001) 39 Osgoode Hall L.J. 555; Fiona Sampson, "Mandatory Minimum Sentences and Women with Disabilities" (2001) 39 Osgoode Hall L.J. 589; and Yvonne Peters, "Reflections on the Latimer Case: The Rationale for a Disability Rights Lens" (2001) 64 Sask. L. Rev. 631.

Factum of the Intervenors, People in Equal Participation [PEP], in R. v. Latimer (Sask. C.A.)†

3. The Attorney General ... outlines evidence to demonstrate that there was quality to Tracy Latimer's life. PEP does not dispute these facts, but submits that they are irrelevant. If Tracy had been unhappy, if her prospects for living for a long time had been poor, if her pain had been unmanageable even through surgery, even if she had indicated in any way (and there is no evidence that she did) that she would prefer to be dead, the legal principle would be the same: the intentional taking of her life would be murder, and the defence of necessity would have no application. To say anything less would do a grave disservice to the cause of disabled rights in Canada, and every disabled person who was perceived to be living a miserable existence would be at risk. Such persons would be put to the ongoing obligation literally to "justify their existence." Such a principle, especially in the face of ever-declining resources for health care, would mean an ever-present prospect of doom for persons in continuing need of health care. It is crucial for this Court to state, in dismissing this ground of appeal, that not only law, but justice demands that "necessity" can never justify the murder of vulnerable persons.

4. [T]o excuse the killing of disabled persons as "necessity" would mean denying them the right to live, the right to security of their persons, and the right to equal protection of the law....

. . . .

6. Among many others, including members of Parliament, care-givers to our most vulnerable citizens will be watching the outcome, and especially the reasoning to reach that outcome in this case to understand what their options are. Please note that the Appellant ... refers to killing as an "option for pain management." Such statements must be resoundingly denounced in the judgment of this Honourable Court, if Canada's disabled citizens are to recover any sense of personal security which has so devastatingly been damaged by the public reaction to this case.

[The intervenor went on to argue that to suggest that Latimer had the legal right to decide to commit suicide for his daughter "by virtue of her complete absence of physical and intellectual abilities" is a direct attack on the s. 15 rights of disabled Canadians generally.]

7. ... The Appellant in effect concedes that a parent of an able child would not have the right to "commit suicide" on its behalf, even if the child were suffering constant extreme pains. Unlike Ground #2, here the Appellant does not plead pain as the basis for Tracy's loss of rights; under this ground of appeal, only disability denies the child the right to live. Neither s. 7 nor s. 15 of the *Charter* can countenance such a principle.

8. The Attorney General argues ... that Tracy Latimer did not, in fact, have a "complete absence of intellectual abilities." PEP submits that such a fact, while true, is absolutely irrelevant. To say otherwise would be to say that the lives of persons with no intellectual abilities do not have equal protection of the law, which would be contrary to s. 15 of the *Charter*.

9. On this issue generally, PEP draws the Court's attention to the words of McKenzie, J. in *Supt. of Family and Child Service v. R.D. and S.D.* (1983), 42 B.C.L.R. 173 at p. 184:

> "I do not think that it lies within the prerogative of any parent or of this court to look down upon a disadvantaged person and judge the quality of that person's life to be so low as not to be deserving continuance."

and at p. 187:

> "This would mean regarding the life of a handicapped child as not only less valuable than the life of a normal child, but so much less valuable that it is not worth preserving. I tremble at contemplating the consequences if the lives of disabled persons are dependent upon such judgments."

. . . .

[The intervenors discussed and distinguished *Rodriguez v. British Columbia (A.G.)*, [1993] 3 S.C.R. 519, on the basis of the lack of any consent on

† Reproduced by permission of Taylor McCaffrey, Barristers & Solicitors, Winnipeg, Manitoba.

the part of Tracy Latimer. They then went on to challenge the Appellant's arguments with respect to sentence.]

15. ... [T]he issue of sentence is as crucial as the conviction issues raised in the appeal, because if the punishment for murdering a disabled victim is less than the punishment for murdering an able victim, disabled citizens do not have equal protection of the law, as guaranteed by s. 15 of the *Charter*. One important element in the setting of any sentence is general deterrence. In general, the greater the punishment, the greater the deterrence. Crimes that are less likely to be detected, or more difficult to deter, generally attract harsher sentences, not more lenient ones. Disabled citizens can be more vulnerable to crime than others because their disability may make them physically or mentally less able to defend themselves, or to report the crime of which they are victim, and because they are seen as easy targets. When one is dependent on a care-giver, it is only made more difficult to report a crime committed by that care-giver.

16. Because of image and stereotype, there is an assumption that disabled persons suffer more pain than other persons. With this comes an assumption that they therefore value their lives less than other persons. PEP strongly urges this Court to recognize that neither of these assumptions is correct. Even where the pain is real, the only person who can decide that ending life is better than continuing life in pain is the person experiencing the pain. Any decision that considers as relevant the perception by the accused of pain in the victim as a justification for absolution or diminished responsibility in the form of a lesser sentence will rest at the top of the slipperiest, steepest and highest of slippery slopes. See Genuis and Genuis, "Living and Dying with Dignity," Journal of the Society of Obstetricians and Gynaecologists of Canada, Volume 16, Number 6 (June 1994) (Appendix A).

17. ... To consider her disability in sentence would be a direct violation of her rights, and the rights of every other disabled Canadian, under s. 15 of the *Charter.* To consider perception of pain as a sentencing factor would put even non-disabled citizens at risk, for one need not be disabled to experience pain, or to be suspected of experiencing pain! Each of these factors involves determining sentence based on an assessment of the quality of life the victim lost....

18. Would the Appellant be requesting a constitutional exemption from the statutory minimum sentence if he had murdered his ten-year-old "normal" child who was awaiting surgery to repair a painful dislocated hip? Clearly not, and equally clearly, *pain* is not the issue in this appeal — the issue is *disability*.

19. PEP disagrees profoundly with the Attorney General ... that the Appellant is a candidate for a pardon.... A pardon would amount to a statement that law dictates conviction and punishment, but that such a law is in conflict with justice. PEP urges that justice, not just law, demands the treatment of this murder as equivalent to any other murder. To suggest anything less would be to deprive disabled Canadians of equal protection of the law under s. 15 of the *Charter*.

. . . .

21. Unlike the Attorney General, PEP does not believe that the comments of the Crown counsel in his closing address to the jury were "unfortunate," or "inappropriate," or "intemperate." Stating that "it's not open season on the disabled" spoke accurately and precisely to the central issue in the trial: whether a murderer can be assigned diminished responsibility because his victim is disabled. If he can, it is, indeed, "open season on the disabled." It was important to bring home to the jury the impact of the verdict they might render, as it might affect potential future victims of "compassionate murder."

22. PEP submits that the rights of Tracy Latimer and other potential murder victims under s. 7 and s. 15 of the *Charter* must be considered in opposition to the *Charter* rights asserted by the Appellant under ss. 7 and 15 of the *Charter*.... [which] provides:

> ...*equal protection* and equal benefit *of the law* without discrimination ... based on ... *mental or physical disability*. [Emphasis added by PEP.]

. . . .

[The intervenors went on to cite, with approval, Justice McLellan's judgment in a case involving a 10-year-old girl who was severely mentally retarded and neurologically handicapped and whose parents and neurosurgeon wished to see her die rather than receive further medical treatment: *Re Minister of Health & Community Services and B. et al.* (1990), 70 D.L.R. (4th) 568 (N.B.Q.B.) at 571:]

> The neurosurgeon says that "further medical treatment will serve only to prolong (her) suffering." He is incorrect. Further medical treatment cannot prolong her suffering unless it also pro-

longs her life. That life, however low its quality, is her right.

[The final point they addressed was the Appellant's evidence of letters of support.]

. . . .

25. The Appellant has submitted through affidavit a large collection of letters he has received. The affidavit does not indicate *why* the affiant, or any of the signators [*sic*] to the petition, believe the sentence to be unjust. It is difficult to understand how these letters and petitions of support address any issue in this appeal. If anything, they demonstrate that a substantial number of Canadians do not consider a crime as serious if the victim is disabled. It would be difficult to find a better way of demonstrating the need for *Charter* protection for potential future victims of "compassionate murder" or "mercy killing".... Laura Latimer read a letter from one of these "supporters" as follows:

"Dear sir. Just a note to say how sorry I am that you are in so much trouble ... when you did something that I think was the right thing to do. The child is at peace now ... and you are sure of that. Also the rest of the family will have more rest ... and do much better. She'll be getting ... much heavier and harder to handle."

It is sentiments such as these that underline the need for this Court to render a decision that clearly states that murder is not justified because the victim is perceived as a burden. It is these grounds of support that show why PEP's members are at risk in this appeal. Letters of support are only potentially relevant for the reasons *why* support is there, not for the numbers of supporters. Furthermore, if millions of supporters write encouragement to O.J. Simpson, ought that to affect his conviction or sentence, if the evidence proves his guilt?

■

Compare the situations in *Stephens*, *Perka*, and *Manning* to *Morgentaler*, *Southwark London Borough v. Williams*, [1971] 2 All E.R. 175 (C.A.), *Adams*, *Latimer*, *Young*, and *Stevenson*. Why did the defence fail in each of the latter cases? What were the underlying political implications? Are emergencies for drug traffickers on the high seas inherently more necessitous or less foreseeable than the living conditions of poverty and homelessness? See *Southwark*, and the following analysis of the defence of necessity by Christine Boyle.

The Defence of Necessity — Who Needs It?†

Classic and harrowing instances which have been cited to illustrate the arguments both for and against [the defence of necessity] include the mother who steals food for her starving child, the shipwrecked mariners who resort to cannibalism, or throw passengers overboard to lighten a sinking lifeboat, and the more mundane case of the motorist who exceeds the speed-limit taking an injured person to hospital.

These words are from a recent judgment of Chief Justice Dickson of the Supreme Court of Canada. He was deciding whether people charged with criminal offences could argue the defence of necessity. The case in question was called *Perka v. The Queen*, and had come to the Supreme Court from the Court of Appeal of British Columbia. The accused had been found on a ship in Canadian waters with marijuana on board. They were charged with importing and possessing narcotics for the purpose of trafficking. At trial they gave evidence that they were transporting marijuana from South America to Alaska. They claimed that weather and difficulties with the ship had made it "necessary" for them to enter Canadian waters, where they encountered the police.

The Supreme Court of Canada decided that the defence of necessity was indeed available to the accused and sent the case back to the trial court for a full consideration of the issues.

† Christine Boyle, "The Defence of Necessity — Who Needs It?" [unpublished]. Reproduced by permission of the author.

This 1984 decision is important for its recognition of the defence. Until this time, it had not been entirely clear that any such defence existed. This in spite of the fact that it had convinced a number of juries in the early *Morgentaler* abortion cases.

The Supreme Court also provided some guidance on when the defence is available to people charged with criminal offences. Again in the words of Chief Justice Dickson, the defence "rests on a realistic assessment of human weakness, recognizing that a liberal and humane criminal law cannot hold people to the strict obedience of laws in emergency situations where normal human instincts, whether of self-preservation or altruism, overwhelmingly impel disobedience." Thus a humane criminal law would excuse an individual who had broken the letter of the law in an emergency situation, where there had been no reasonable legal alternative, and where the lesser of two evils had been chosen.

What has this to do with women? The question is how these high-sounding abstractions might translate into actual decisions in varying contexts.

Might courts excuse the mountain-climber who breaks into an isolated cabin to avoid freezing to death but not a homeless mother who squats in an empty office building?

Might drug smugglers have the benefit of the defence but not mothers who steal food for children who are simply hungry but not on the point of death?

Might police officers who speed to bank robberies have a defence but not women who have abortions without permission from the state?

The fact that fundamental political choices have to be made is obvious. The very way that we think about which is the lesser of two evils may cause concern that the defence of necessity will not be responsive to the reality of women's lives. To whom, as a society, using the criminal law to make a communal statement about our values, do we wish to be compassionate? Is an "emergency" something that simply presents a sudden horrifying choice or is the concept flexible enough to cover the ongoing emergencies faced by mothers without enough money to provide adequate food for their children *for an indefinite period*?

If the law recognises bad weather on the high seas as an emergency but not poverty, it then becomes relevant to ask if gender has anything to do with who is likely to be a drug smuggler and who is likely to be poor.

The scope of the defence of necessity was one of many issues addressed in *The Feminist Review of Criminal Law*, a survey of criminal law from a feminist perspective commissioned by Status of Women Canada and released early this year [Ottawa: Status of Women, 1985]. I was one of the authors of that Report, and the one responsible for the short section dealing with this issue.

While noting that feminist writing and activity had not as yet focused on this defence as such, I suggested that it could be deduced from feminist values generally that the human need for shelter, food and clothing is more important than property interests in themselves. Thus it was proposed that Parliament should indicate what interests are more important than others and that interfering with the property rights of others in order to feed, clothe or shelter oneself or one's children should be clearly covered by the defence.

While the reaction to the Report was mixed, it is certainly true to say that a common reaction was outrage, particularly on the part of the editorial writers of Canada. I was called, among other things, a "light-fingered feminist" and the proposal labelled "hare-brained," and "fatuous." The *Toronto Sun* declared the whole report to be "a socialist manifesto all gussied up in bafflegab."

There was positive reaction too. I was particularly delighted when Deidre Maultsaid of the Vancouver Rape Relief and Women's Shelter wrote to the *Vancouver Sun* publicly supporting the proposal on necessity, among other things.

I was as surprised by the negative reaction as I was warmed by the positive. Indeed, what was proposed may already represent the law. At any time, a judge in Canada could refuse to convict a woman of, say, welfare fraud, because she had no realistic alternative and what she did was the lesser of two evils.

A particularly hurtful strategy adopted by some reporters was to write that I had advocated stealing as a solution to poverty. This seemed to me to be particularly offensive to poor women and very different to the argument that we, as a community, do not have the moral authority to label as criminal people who are maintained below the poverty line and trapped in a desperate situation. Clearly the problems of poverty go far beyond questions about the scope of the criminal law. However, so long as poverty continues, it is legitimate to question the role of the criminal law in controlling people who are not passively accepting homelessness and hunger.

I have since asked myself why there was such a negative reaction. A number of ideas have occurred to me.

Firstly, I see a strong desire to deny that poverty and homelessness exist in Canada. Allied to this is ignorance or rejection of the fact that women bear a heavy and disproportionate burden of poverty. This is in spite of easily available government statistics. In 1985, Statistics Canada issued a report called *Women in Canada*. It confirms that a much higher proportion of families headed by women (45%) fall below the poverty line than do families headed by men (10%). The statistics on elderly women cause particular concern. Sixty percent of elderly unattached women fall below the poverty line. In 1982, that amounted to 335,000 Canadian women.

Secondly, I see a strong emphasis on property rights. They are often valued to the extent that they may be considered natural or even god-given, rather than as simply rights which we have because the law in our particular time and place says so. It is relevant to ask, as one asks just who is poor in our society, just who owns property. A clue can be found in the statistics on income. Again, Statistics Canada tells us that in 1982, women earned 52.85% of the amount of income earned by men.

If men have more money and more women are poor, and if the law values property rights over food and shelter rights, it is not a complex argument that women are missing the "equal protection and benefit of the law" as promised in the *Canadian Charter of Rights and Freedoms*. More important than the constitutional arguments are the moral ones. Are we being just as a society if we acknowledge interests (such as property rights) which "just happen" to be of disproportionate benefit to men, and fail to acknowledge things (such as poverty) which "just happen" to impose a disproportionate burden on women?

I identified a more complex concern with the defence of necessity. Some objectors felt that it acknowledged the situation of the accused while denying the reality of the harm to any victim. In other words someone had to be labelled a criminal to validate the loss of the victim. This concern is not unique to necessity, but is common to all similar defences. If an accused successfully argues that he drove the getaway car because a gun was being held to his head, the bank has still been robbed. If an accused person successfully argues that he thought there was consent, someone has still been sexually assaulted. There has never been a match between the fact of victimization and a finding of guilt. This is because the criminal justice system focuses on the legitimacy of punishment of the accused. As victims of crimes know from painful experience, the criminal justice system does not operate to acknowledge their pain.

This is a concern that feminists can surely share. Somehow we need a way of showing compassion to accused persons, which does not carry with it a denial of the hurt and loss of the victim.

Have I learned anything from the fuss about necessity? I have had a very practical lesson in the importance of active feminist work in the media. I also know that I would like to live in a society where a report proposing that property rights have priority over basic survival rights would be greeted with horror. The criminal justice system is a relatively unsophisticated part of our law, but it does carry some basic messages about what we value and reject in our society.

■

Recall that in *Lalonde*, discussed above, under **Self-Defence,** a battered woman charged with welfare fraud for failing to disclose that a physically and psychologically abusive man was living with her was acquitted of the offence, partly on the basis that she did not have the *mens rea* to defraud, given her mental state, and partly on the basis of necessity (at 287): "she had, in her mind no reasonable alternative and putting food on the table for her children, in her financial circumstances, was pressing." Does this case suggest that the courts are now prepared to accept the kind of necessity defence discussed by Boyle, or do you think that *Lalonde* will be narrowly construed?

18

Broadening the Defences: Necessity, Self-Defence, and Conscience

What the following cases have in common is the assertion by the accused of a different view of "necessity". Sometimes that "necessity" is seen as the imperative of conscience. Closely tied to acts of conscience, acts of resistance, and the refusal to submit to allegedly unjust laws are "criminal" acts committed as strategies to bring about political change. Also linked to criminal acts as political resistance are the potentially false charges laid against those engaged in political struggle. In some cases, the state responds to political opposition by widening the net of criminal law through redefinition to proscribe previously legal acts.

The issues of conscience or political motivation can be raised in a number of ways:

- The accused may argue a defence of conscience to justify an act such as the refusal to obey a law, or an act in defiance of the law because of the compulsion of conscience (for example, Vanunu);
- The accused may argue that the political motivation for a criminal act, done to draw attention to a political issue, should be taken into consideration as a factor to mitigate decisions about sentencing and treatment (for example, Squamish Five, Suffragettes). Conversely, the Crown may argue that the motivation should result in a harsher penalty.
- The accused may challenge the political motivation of the state in defining a particular conduct as criminal or in adopting unfair criminal procedures or practices. "Criminal acts" thus have the effect of challenging the legitimacy of the state or its laws (for example, South Africa).

Consider the following cases and materials. Should a defence be available to the accused? What are the policy considerations? How do these examples highlight the contingency of criminal law?

A. WHOSE "NECESSITY"?

As was discussed above, under ***Actus Reus***, it is important to understand the ways in which law and society fail to protect children from abuse. One very serious issue is the determination of custody and access, in the context of violence, sexual abuse, and marital breakdown. Confronted with the unwillingness of judges to interfere with fathers' "rights" to their children, even in the face of abuse, women have had to resort to remedies outside of the law. They have been called "kidnappers", "hostage takers", "fugitives", and "terrorists". Should a defence of necessity be available? Whose perspective defines "necessity"? Recall the cases of Tracie Urbanovich and Hedda Nussbaum discussed above, under ***Actus Reus***. What options did those women have?

In "Mothers and Children Seek Sanctuary" *Sojourner: The Women's Forum* (March 1988) 10, Louise Armstrong describes a war against women and the sanctuary movement of women helping women and children. She argues that women's speaking out about the past, as adult survivors of childhood assault, does not challenge the status quo. However, women acting to protect child victims in the present have obviously challenged the structure of power:

> [Women] are being vilified, pilloried, jailed by the courts, for trying to protect those children; who are, in fact, apt to lose not only custody, but all visitation with those children.
>
> ...
>
> A war has been declared against women, to preserve the right to father-rape. It is a war that feminists triggered by speaking out. If we do not join in we will have done no more than collude in what is currently a truly cruel joke.

Louise Armstrong has written extensively on this issue and cites numerous cases. See Louise Armstrong, *The Homefront: Notes from the Warzone* (New York: McGraw Hill, 1985); Louise Armstrong, *Kiss Daddy Goodnight: Ten Years Later* (New York: Pocketbooks, 1995); Louise Armstrong, *Rocking the Cradle of Sexual Politics* (Reading: Addison-Wesley, 1994). She describes how Canadian women have sought refuge in the United States. The following examples give some indication why.

In 1994, a grandmother who kept her granddaughter in hiding for almost two years was arrested and charged with kidnapping, confinement, and conspiracy to kidnap. The girl's mother had been charged several times with contempt and had been in prison for the previous 20 months because she refused to tell her former husband and the courts where her daughter was. The father had been awarded custody two years earlier. *Le Soleil (Québec)* reported that the two "fugitives" had been protected by women's groups in Ontario. See Sue Montgomery, "Bitter custody fight leads to arrest of grandmother: Held for contempt, girl's mother to be freed soon" *The Ottawa Citizen* (10 March 1994) A3.

In a B.C. case in 1988, Ethel Mansell doused herself and her two sons with gasoline and set them on fire, killing all three. The woman was described as "devastated by the knowledge her husband was a child molester". In response, the coroner's jury called for a task force to explore child abuse. In particular, they were concerned about the lack of avenues open to the woman and the delays in investigating her case, by both the Social Services Ministry and the police. Only as other children came forward, some six months later, did the police take the time to interview the children. Her husband was convicted of child sexual abuse, and it became clear that there was a history of complaints in Ontario, Manitoba, Saskatchewan, and Alberta. See CP, "B.C. deaths show need for study of child sexual abuse, jury says" *The Ottawa Citizen* (5 December 1988) A5.

In Alberta, a mother who fled to the United States with three of her children (in contravention of a judgment allowing her ex-husband unsupervised access to their son) was acquitted (of abduction charges) because she believed her children were in imminent danger of harm. Judge Heather Lamoureux held that she was acting reasonably given her history as a battered spouse, her ex-husband's conviction for molesting her daughter, and the failure of the courts to protect her and her children in the past. The mother had been arrested on a Canada-wide warrant: *R. v. A.*, [1995] A.J. No. 1304 (Q.B.) (QL).

Such examples of acquittals are rare. The difficulty of establishing the imminence of harm, or even a mistake of fact defence based on an honest belief in the danger facing a young person, is illustrated by *R. v. Adams*, discussed above, under **Mistake of Fact** and **Necessity**. In contrast to that decision, in *R. v. Sole*, [2000] J.Q. No. 1765 (QL) (Cour du Québec (Chambre criminelle)), the accused father was acquitted of abduction of his two children (to California, Haiti, and Egypt over the course of five years) on the basis of necessity where the trial judge determined that he had an honest belief that his children were in imminent danger (this despite the fact that custody had been awarded to the mother and that child welfare authorities in Québec declined to intervene because there was no evidence of potential physical risk). The trial judge indicated that he was influenced by the unrealistic potential of appeal for the father, given delays in the courts, and by the lack of alternatives for the father once he had abducted the children (for example, to negotiate with the mother) in the face of an outstanding warrant for his arrest.

B. THE DEFENCE OF CONSCIENCE

The following cases deal with individuals with specialized knowledge, as a result of their professional position, who violated the law or contravened the orders of a superior to reveal "secret" or "privileged" information. They have defended their actions on the basis of conscience and the public interest, and have paid heavy prices for their decisions.

PERRY DUNLOP

In Cornwall, Ontario, a police officer reported a priest and a probation officer, suspected of being child abusers, to the Children's Aid Society, and gave the Children's Aid Society a copy of the victim/witness statement from police files. His lawyer described the moral outrage he felt knowing that the church and the police establishment were just too reluctant to take steps. As a result, Constable Perry Dunlop was accused of misconduct and breach of confidence. When a board of inquiry stayed the charges, the Ontario Police Complaints Commission appealed the decision. The appeal was dismissed with costs: *Police Complaints Commissioner v. Dunlop* (1995), 26 O.R. (3d) 582 (Ct. J. (Gen. Div.)). He was also being sued by the victim (a former altar boy) for violating his privacy by divulging his statement, since the statement was eventually displayed during a TV broadcast. An out-of-court settlement was reached: CP, "Settlement reached in suit against Cornwall police" *The [Toronto] Globe and Mail* (4 August 1995) A1; Sean Fine, "Reported claim of sex abuse, officer under fire: A Cornwall constable acted against orders and now his career is in jeopardy" *The [Toronto] Globe and Mail* (22 July 1995) A1. The officer was on extended medical leave for stress after the charges were laid.

The Complaints Commission lawyer argued that Dunlop had contravened the direct orders of his supervising officer. The charges described the officer as acting "in a disorderly manner, or in a manner prejudicial to discipline or likely to bring discredit upon the reputation of the police force" (26 O.R. (3d) at 584).

Constable Dunlop argued that s. 72 of the Ontario *Child and Family Services Act*, R.S.O. 1990, c. C.43 obliged him to report suspected child abuse to the Children's Aid Society. The court rejected the argument that Constable Dunlop did not learn of the suspected abuse in the course of his official duties (because he was not part of the investigation) and rejected the argument that there was no "child" in need of protection (because the alleged victim was now an adult) and held (26 O.R. (3d) at 586):

> Const. Dunlop was an active duty police officer who gained information in the course of his "professional or official duties" — it does not matter that he was not the officer specifically assigned to the case — all police officers have a primary duty to prevent the commission of crime. Nor does it matter that the complainant D.S. was no longer a child as he was at the time of the alleged abuse.
>
> Constable Dunlop in September 1993 had "reasonable grounds to suspect that a child — may have suffered abuse." He had a duty, therefore, to "forthwith report the suspicion and information on which it is based to a society."

Having found that Constable Dunlop did not act maliciously or without reasonable grounds, the court concluded that s. 72(7) barred disciplinary proceedings under the *Police Services Act*, R.S.O. 1990, c. P.15. Section 72(3) sets out the duty for professionals such as police officers:

> Despite the provisions of any other Act, a person referred to in subsection (4) who, in the course of his or her professional or official duties, has reasonable grounds to suspect that a child is or may be suffering or may have suffered abuse shall forthwith report the suspicion and the information on which it is based to a society.

Were there alternatives available to Constable Dunlop? How does his duty to follow orders mesh with his professional obligations to report child abuse? How would some of the mothers described in the previous section judge his speaking out?

Compare the role of the Police Complaints Commission in this case to other cases of police misconduct discussed in Abell & Sheehy, *Cases, Context, Critique*, **Policing**. Note that the categories of professionals who owe a special duty under s. 72(4) include ss.(d) "a solicitor", as referred to above, under ***Actus Reus***, Act or Omission.

As a result of Constable Dunlop's actions and the media attention generated, new complainants came forward. Finally, in 1997, the Ontario Provincial Police announced that they were devoting a team of investigators ("Project Truth") to pursue the case involving an alleged pedophile ring in Cornwall that had operated for nearly 40 years and includes Roman Catholic priests and public officials among the 18 suspects: CP, "Police investigate Ontario pedophile ring" *The Ottawa Citizen* (26 September 1997) A8. As a result of the OPP investigation, over 100 charges against 15 men were laid in 1998; but very few charges resulted in convictions.

In April 2005, Premier Dalton McGuinty established the Cornwall Public Inquiry, with Justice Normand Glaude as Commissioner, "to inquire into and report on the events surrounding allegations of abuse of young people in Cornwall by examining the response of the justice system and other public institutions to the allegations ... [, to] make recommendations to improve the response in similar circumstances ... [and] to inquire into and report on processes, services and programs that will encourage community healing and reconciliation in Cornwall": The Cornwall Public Inquiry: www.cornwallinquiry.ca/en. The Inquiry has been running since February 2006 and is expected to continue until the fall of 2008. Dunlop has refused to testify at the Inquiry and has argued publicly that his refusal is based on a lack of faith in the justice system and the mandate of the inquiry and his feeling that he continues to be scapegoated by the process. As a result of his refusal to testify, he was charged with civil contempt and sentenced to six months in jail, which served in segregated protective custody. He was also cited for criminal contempt for his public statements challenging the integrity of the Inquiry and sentenced to a further 30 days incarceration: *Cornwall (Public Inquiry) v. Dunlop*, [2008] O.J. No. 3673 (Sup. Ct. J.) (QL).

MORDECHAI VANUNU

In 1988, an Israeli technician was convicted of treason and espionage for revealing the secrets of Israel's nuclear strength and sentenced to 18 years in prison. His capture and abduction sound like a plot for a Hollywood movie. In 1986, he was lured from England to Italy by an agent (days before his information was to be published in the *London Sunday Times*), drugged, kidnapped, and brought home illegally to stand trial in closely guarded and secret conditions. Since the trial was held *in camera*, his testimony, if there was any, remains secret.

Vanunu worked for eight years at the top secret Dimona nuclear weapons factory. (It was described as a cotton factory when it was first built in the 1960s.) Israel has maintained an ambiguous position on whether it possesses nuclear weapons; yet, with more than 200 warheads, it is the world's sixth-ranking nuclear power. It refuses to sign a non-proliferation treaty. For a detailed account of the case, including Vanunu's struggle with his conscience, his conclusion that "[t]o know is to be responsible", and his decision to speak the truth regardless of personal consequences, see: Tom Gilling & John Mcknight, *Trial and Error: Mordechai Vanunu and Israel's Nuclear Bomb* (London: HarperCollins, 1995) at 5.

Vanunu was nominated for the Nobel Peace Prize, and his lawyer presented a petition to the court (signed by 20 leading scientists, including 12 Nobel prize laureates) who described him as a "man of conscience" and wrote: "No greater regard can be shown by the court for the decent opinion of humankind than by acknowledging the lonely courage of Mordechai Vanunu."

Neither the British nor the Italian government took any action against Israel. Vanunu spent more than 12 years in solitary confinement, forbidden even to speak to the priest who brought him communion. Dedi Zucker, a member of the Knesset, argued that this isolation was calculated to destroy Vanunu's sanity. He petitioned the High Court to release Vanunu from solitary confinement. "I truly believe that the purpose of keeping Vanunu in solitary confinement all this time is to make sure that when he does get out, he will be insane and therefore nobody will pay attention to him": Uzi Mahnaimi, "Vanunu finds first backer in the Knesset" *The [London] Sunday Times* (27 July 1997) 16. Despite the brutality and hardship of solitary confinement, Vanunu remains steadfast. "I say clearly that I did what I did from a deep conviction and I would do it all again": Agence France-Presse, "Vanunu says he'd do it again: Israeli whistle-blower remains unrepentant" *The [Toronto] Globe and Mail* (20 April 1998) A8.

Support for Vanunu has continued to grow. For example, he was awarded the 1994 Sean McBride Peace Prize by the International Peace Bureau; the European Parliament has condemned Israeli actions and called for Vanunu's release; the Public Committee Against Torture in Israel has endorsed the campaign to free Vanunu; and in 1996, an international conference (organized by the campaign) was held in Israel, with such prominent participants as 1995 Nobel Peace prize winner Joseph Roblat (awarded the prize for his lifelong work in opposition to nuclear weapons after his initial involvement with the Manhattan project) and "whistle-blower" Daniel Ellsberg (who, as an act of conscience, released "classified" Pentagon papers about the U.S. role in Indochina): Mordecai Briemberg, "Vanunu's Truth" *Canadian Dimension* (March/April 1997) 37. Finally, in April 2004, after 18 years in prison, Vanunu was released from prison but subject to a range of restrictions including limits on travel and public discussion of his work: Staff, "Vanunu released after 18 years" *The [Manchester] Guardian* (21 April 2004) online. In 2007, he was arrested and sentenced to 6 months in prison for 14 parole violations including speaking to foreign journalists and attempting to travel to Bethlehem. He is appealing.

In July 1996, a divided International Court of Justice concluded that "the threat or use of nuclear weapons would generally be contrary to the rules of international law applicable in armed conflicts, and in particular the principles and rules of humanitarian law": [1996] I.C.J. Rep. 66. For a thoughtful analysis of the impact of that Advisory Opinion, see: Jenny Hatfield-Lyon, "The Legality of the Threat or Use of Nuclear Weapons: The Impact of the I.C.J.'s Advisory Opinion on International Peace and Security" in Canadian Council on International Law, *Fostering Compliance In International Law (Proceeding of the 1996 Conference of the Canadian Council on International Law* (Ottawa: Canadian Council on International Law, 1996) 69. For an example of the Canadian government's complicity in the repression of political offenders from other nations, see the discussion of the Leonard Peltier case, below, in this chapter.

CLIVE PONTING

The tensions between official secrecy in time of war and accountability to Parliament and the public are highlighted by the *Ponting* case. These tensions are further underscored by recent events in Britain. Challenges to the information provided to Parliament (with respect to the weapons capabilities of Iraq) by Prime Minister Tony Blair's government to support Britain's entry into the war against Iraq highlight the tension for civil servants and media when governments distort or misrepresent the situation. In response, the *Hutton Inquiry* into the Death of David Kelly was established in the summer of 2003 (online: huttoninquiry.org.uk). In Canada, Parliament has considered legislation to protect "whistle-blowers", but to date no such legislation has been implemented.

Clive Ponting, a senior civil servant at the defence ministry in Britain under Michael Heseltine, was charged with violating the *Official Secrets Act* by turning over embarrassing official documents to an opposition member of Parliament. The documents contradicted statements by the Conservative government to Parliament about Britain's actions during the 1982 Falklands war against Argentina, and in particular related to the sinking of the Argentine cruiser, the *General Belgrano*. Parliament was not given the information that the ship was clearly in retreat when it was sunk and was not closing in on the British.

Did Ponting have a higher duty to the truth as he knew it, when he believed that Parliament was being lied to? The *Official Secrets Act* allows for the prosecution of any government worker for the unauthorized disclosure of information. While the Act is not often invoked, it does operate as a deterrent to leaks. The judge directed the jury that the interests of the state and the interests of the government of the day were the same. Nonetheless, the jury ignored the implicit direction of the judge that they should convict and, instead, acquitted Ponting.

For further discussion of the case, see: "A verdict for Britain" and "Jury acquits Ponting of breaking Secrets Act" *The Manchester Guardian* (17 February 1985) 1, 3; John Fraser, "Belgrano affair: The trial Britain did not want" *The [Toronto] Globe and Mail* (2 February 1985) A9. In the following article, Ponting outlines his response to the criminal charges, his recognition of the importance of public support, and the consequent legal strategy adopted.

R. v. Ponting[†]

The idea behind this article is simple. It is to try and show, first, the reactions of an ordinary citizen when confronted by the majesty of the criminal law and secondly, how we decided to run a major case of crucial public importance.

The background to the *Belgrano* affair is, I hope, fairly well known by now. In this particular context all that I have space to mention is that during the early part of 1984 there were a series of long running battles within the Ministry of Defence about how to handle the two year long cover-up of the circumstances surrounding the sinking of the Argentinian warship General Belgrano by a British submarine in May 1982. In my capacity of Assistant Secretary, Head of Defence Secretariat 5, I had been asked by the then Secretary of State, Michael Heseltine, to prepare a "Top Secret" account of what had really taken place. Because of its high security information and the sensitivity of what it revealed only six copies were made and it subsequently became known as the "Crown Jewels." After a great deal of argument, in which I had strongly advocated a new policy of greater openness, I was overruled and it was decided to continue with the cover-up.

The crucial events came in July 1984 when the Foreign Affairs Committee of the House of Commons began an investigation into the events surrounding the sinking and the possible linkage with the Peruvian peace plan. The Committee asked for information which, if it had been provided by the Ministry of Defence, would have revealed the cover-up. Advice from another division within the Ministry recommended that the information should not be given to the Committee and that a misleading memorandum designed to head off the enquiry should be sent instead. After a great deal of thought I decided to send copies of two internal Ministry documents that revealed what had been going on and how the House of Commons had been consistently misled to Tam Dalyell M.P., the man who had led the campaign to unearth the truth. He quite correctly, placed the documents before the Foreign Affairs Committee.

The chairman of the Committee, Sir Anthony Kershaw, promptly returned the papers to Michael Heseltine, who then called in the Ministry of Defence police to investigate the leak. What happened when I was first interviewed by the police on 11 August 1984 became the subject of some controversy at the trial. I shall repeat what I told the jury when I was in the witness box under oath. I was told that the leak was not a matter for the Official Secrets Act and that if I were prepared to resign from the civil service that would be the end of the matter. On that basis I wrote a statement that I had sent the paper to Tam Dalyell, explaining why, and then wrote a letter of resignation which was accepted later that evening.

It was only four days later that I was told that my resignation was not accepted, that "Ministers were jumping up and down," and that they had insisted that the papers were passed to the Director of Public Prosecutions with the intention of a prosecution under section 2 of the Official Secrets Act 1911. At that stage it was a little late to start taking legal advice and I decided to wait and see what happened, but I had a clear expectation of what the outcome was likely to be. Three days later my expectations were fulfilled when I was arrested, taken to Canon Row police station in London, fingerprinted, photographed, and bailed to appear next day at Bow Street magistrates court. I spent most of the next couple of days avoiding the attentions of the media.

Since the hearing at Bow Street would only be a formal one to fix the date of the next hearing I decided to appear unrepresented and take some time finding the right solicitor for the long fight ahead. This, it seems to me, is the most difficult decision facing anybody confronted for the first time with a serious criminal charge. I knew that the average solicitor specializing in conveyancing was not going to have the qualities necessary to fight this sort of case. Where to find the right person was a different question. I was lucky in that two journalists, separately and with no ulterior motive, offered help in finding the right person and suggested several names. After some thought and consultation I chose Brian Raymond of Bindman and Partners, a well-known firm of radical but highly competent lawyers.

At our first meeting Brian and I decided on the strategy we were to use until the end of the trial. As Brian put it, "If we are to have any chance we must win the argument before we go into court. The jury

† Clive Ponting, "*R. v. Ponting*" (1987) 14 J. L. & Soc. 366 at 366–72. Reproduced by permission of Wiley-Blackwell, Oxford, U.K.

have got to know that this is a vital public trial." We were helped in this strategy at the beginning by the fact that on the day after I first appeared in court *The Observer* newspaper had printed parts of the documents involved and revealed the cover-up, so that the political arguments were already beginning. Later that week the *New Statesman* magazine published the documents in full together with more revelations about the sinking of the Belgrano. So far none of the media had been able to link my arrest with the Belgrano because of the *sub judice* rules. We decided to take a calculated risk and publish the facts ourselves in *The Observer* together with a very short statement from me about the duty of a civil servant to put the public interest above the interests of Ministers. We were completely successful and a whole new area of debate could start about the role of the civil service and the wisdom of the prosecution. The latter point was taken up again a couple of weeks later when the same newspaper discovered that Michael Heseltine had been consulted about the possibility of a prosecution and had strongly urged that one should take place.

After this flurry of activity we had time to start developing part of the legal defence, although once we had seen the police record of what had taken place within the Ministry of Defence we knew that we had an extra fight to counter what I regarded as an unrecognisable account of our conversations. Again, we were helped at the first real appearance in court by a leak in *The Guardian* newspaper that morning that Bernard Ingham, the Prime Minister's Press Secretary, had said during an internal Whitehall meeting that the government was determined to get me and that a suitable judge would have to be picked. This was glorious free publicity; even the *Sun* newspaper carried the headline "Bid to Fix Secrets Judge" and Ingham had to apologise to the Lord Chancellor for his remarks.

The next stage in the battle was to decide how to deal with the committal proceedings. We decided very early on that we would have reporting restrictions lifted, as they had been at the very first hearing at Bow Street, so that the evidence against me would be clear. Our own tactics were more difficult. We knew that there was no chance that the proceedings would be thrown out and therefore, that we would have to concentrate on preparing the ground for the full trial. Luckily, the prosecution had given us an opening in their choice of witnesses. First, Richard Hastie-Smith, who I claimed had given me the undertaking that I would not be prosecuted, was to give evidence about security matters, so we would be able to cross-examine about what had really happened. Secondly, Richard Mottram, Michael Heseltine's private secretary, was to give evidence about the return of the documents by Sir Anthony Kershaw, but we would be able to ask questions about what had happened inside the Ministry at various meetings at which both Richard and I had been present with Ministers. This would provide the springboard to ask for various internal Ministry of Defence documents that we wanted to use at the full trial. The committal proceedings must have seemed strange to those present from the media but it achieved our aims.

The next question was how to choose our Q.C. because at the committal we had relied on my brilliant junior counsel Jonathan Caplan. We knew that the choice would be crucial, that our chances at the trial would depend on the jury and, therefore, a Q.C. who could appeal to and sway the jury was vital. Many urged the selection of a political and radical Q.C. in a trial that was bound to be an attack on the record of government. Both Brian Raymond and I felt that was the wrong approach. The trial was going to be quite political enough already. Also, we had to make a crude calculation that those on the jury who were strongly opposed to the government would be sympathetic anyway; our problem was going to be the conservative members of the jury and how we could appeal to them. After a great deal of thought we chose Bruce Laughland, a jovial figure who could not have appeared less like a radical barrister, but the case brought out all his radical feelings and we never regretted the choice.

Even at this stage we were helped by the Attorney-General, Sir Michael Havers, who referred very unwisely to the fact that I had actually committed an offence. This enabled us to raise the whole question of who was protecting the *sub judice* rules and how we were to obtain a fair trial. In order to keep the issue before the public I also thought it was worthwhile to go to the hearings of the Foreign Affairs Committee when Michael Heseltine was questioned about the documents I had revealed. This produced more useful publicity, though not as much as the revelation that the log-book of H.M.S. Conqueror, the submarine that had sunk the Belgrano, had gone missing in unexplained circumstances.

We now had to settle the strategy for the trial. Much of our effort was devoted to getting out of the Ministry of Defence the documents we needed to mount a case about the cover-up. This would obviously be the centre of our evidence during my examination by Bruce Laughland. However, we knew that this would probably not be enough to sway every member of the jury. We needed to show that there were valid constitutional reasons for the action that I had taken. Our first choice of constitutional expert, Sir Henry Wade from Cambridge University, readily agreed to give evidence. Our main problem was to choose a politician who would be prepared to tell the jury that Ministers should not lie to or mislead the House of Commons, and that in the last resort it was right for a civil servant to tell Parliament the truth about what was happening. We approached a number from all three parties who refused on a variety of grounds including David Owen who agreed and then withdrew only three weeks before the start of the trial. We were lucky when we approached Merlyn Rees who had exactly the right qualifications from his ministerial experience and who readily agreed. It was an act of considerable courage since it was clear that he could expect to get no political credit from the action and many of his colleagues tried to dissuade him.

Until this point the prosecution case seemed to be simple. I had passed the documents to Tam Dalyell M.P. and confessed and that was the end of the matter. It was only a couple of weeks before the trial that the prosecution realised that I was going to admit passing the documents but argue, under the terms of section 2 of the Official Secrets Act 1911, that it was my "duty in the interests of the state" to take the action. A rapid rethink by the prosecution ensued. We know that Michael Heseltine insisted that the "Crown Jewels" should now be produced as evidence even though they were irrelevant to the cover-up. Indeed, they were so highly classified that similar information from Government Communications Headquarters at Cheltenham had never before been produced in court even at spy trials because it was regarded as too sensitive to show to the jury. Yet it was now to be done in a trial in which the prosecution had already publicly admitted that national security was not involved. Introducing the "Crown Jewels" also had the advantage for the prosecution that part of the trial could be held in camera and the jury could be vetted. The search of MI5 and Criminal Record Office files produced nothing of substance, although the prosecution may have been reluctant to challenge the Islington councillor who was selected for the jury.

We now knew that the government were playing for very high stakes in their attempt to convict me. By means of the peremptory challenge we decided to remove three middle-aged women from a strongly Tory borough in south London who we felt would tend to form a little group within the jury and who might be hard to convince. We fought the idea of introducing the "Crown Jewels" but never expected any success.

The trial opened in Court No. 2 at the Old Bailey on 28 January 1985 and lasted just over two weeks. It was certainly a strange experience sitting through the trial. Most of the time it seemed very distant and hardly as though I was on trial at all. The closely regulated procedure seemed to dull any real debate and for most of the time I felt that the trial skirted round the main issues and never really got to grips with what needed to be debated. At times I began to despair that the jury would ever be able to understand what was at stake. Our one theatrical effort inside the courtroom was to ask the judge if I could sit behind my counsel and alongside my solicitor, ostensibly to advise on security. Brian Raymond felt it was important to try and "decriminalise" the trial and leave the dock empty, which we hoped would be symbolic for the jury. As a secondary bonus it meant that I did not spend all day on my own in the dock without anybody to talk to.

The opening week was spent on the prosecution case delivered in a flat unexciting manner by Roy Amlot and which consisted mainly of reading out large chunks of Ministry of Defence documents. I was in the witness box for nearly three days and found that giving evidence was more of a strain than I expected, although in some ways I enjoyed the intellectual challenge of the cross-examination even though it was very tiring.

The crucial part of the trial came on the second Wednesday after the conclusion of the evidence when we heard the legal arguments in the absence of the jury. The prosecution argued that "duty in the interests of the state" could only mean official duty and that the interests of the state were necessarily the same as the interests of the government of the day. The judge made it clear that he accepted the prosecution views but would hear ours first before finally making up his mind. Jonathan Caplan argued that duty had to be given a wide definition — "Any old duty will do?" asked the judge — and that the interests of the state must be wider than the interests of the government. The judge said he was not impressed by our arguments and that if he accepted the prosecution arguments then there would be no scope for an acquittal, since I could not have been acting in the interests of the government (that is, Michael Heseltine) and that he would, therefore, have to direct the jury to convict me.

At this point something strange happened. The prosecution back-pedalled furiously and said that they certainly did not want a direction to convict "in this of all cases" — thereby making it clear that this was not an ordinary criminal trial — and asked for an adjournment. Reluctantly the judge agreed and the Director of Public Prosecutions, who had been present throughout the trial, rushed to the telephone — presumably to talk to the Attorney-General about whether such a direction would be acceptable. It obviously was not, because the judge came back to say that he was advised that he could not make such a ruling, and so the trial continued.

After a brilliant closing speech from Bruce Laughland, which was hobbled by the judge's rulings on the law but in which he was able to get across the real message about the issues at stake in the trial, the judge began his summing up. He told the jury that they had heard a great deal of irrelevant evidence, which according to his rulings was indeed the case since the prosecution only had to show that I had not acted in the interests of the government for me to be convicted. The judge then ignored his own rulings and launched into a long summing up devoted largely to a justification of the sinking of the Belgrano and how there had not been a cover-up. For much of the time we were all extremely annoyed at his behaviour but tried to console ourselves with the thought that it might all backfire with the jury.

When the judge sent the jury out none of us were optimistic about the result. We were surprised to be summoned back within three hours knowing that a verdict had been reached, but it seemed best to expect the worst and plan on being in gaol for a considerable time. Certainly I was staggered when the jury foreman, with a large grin on his face, announced that I was not guilty.

Why was I acquitted in the end? I think the answer lies in a number of areas. First, and obviously most important, we had a strong political case to present. There had been a cover-up. Parliament had been seriously misled and there was no way in which this could be denied. Secondly, national security was not involved and the documents had been sent not to the press but to a Member of Parliament and a Select Committee. There was, therefore, a strong foundation for mounting a case based on the "interests of the state." Thirdly, our campaign before the trial started had been successful. The trial had attracted public attention, even to the extent of nightly half hour television programmes of the highlights of the court case. This made it impossible to conduct the trial so as to leave out most of the public interest arguments. I believe that if we had not done this the trial might have been conducted from the start on the basis of the judge's rulings and all evidence not directly relevant to the question of whether I was acting in the interests of the government would have been excluded. As a corollary to this, the prosecution had had to fight on our definition as to where the public interest lay and not just on the narrow question of whether I had indeed sent the documents to Tam Dalyell. Fourthly, we had the advantage of being a small compact team united in our strategy. During the run-up to the trial we had plenty of evidence that there was not a unified view between the prosecution team, the Director of Public Prosecutions, officials in the Ministry of Defence, and Defence Ministers. The other problem for the prosecution was that although the whole trial consisted of a debate about the actions of two Ministers, Michael Heseltine and John Stanley, neither appeared to give evidence and left this task to their civil servants. On the other hand, we were able to produce a senior ex-Minister to give evidence.

What impact did all this have on the jury? I am sure that having been forced to give up two weeks of their time to sit at the Old Bailey they expected something exciting to talk about with their family and friends. Instead, they were condemned for a fortnight to listen to large extracts of civil service prose being read at them. Most of what they heard must have seemed arcane and intensely boring. Where, they must have asked, is the crime? Why are we having to read all these pieces of paper? This effect must have been compounded by the introduction of the "Crown Jewels." The jury were told that they would be shown some of the highest secrets of the British state but when they were read they must have seemed as technical and dry as dust as other government memoranda. Lastly, I am sure that the summing up by the judge, which seemed to be so biased and unrelated to what the jury had heard in the previous two weeks, must have had its effect.

The one lesson that I would draw from the experience is that in a major trial involving the government you cannot afford to play by the rules because if you do you will inevitably lose. A major trial like *R. v. Ponting* has to be conducted as a campaign using every possible resource to make the case into a public issue before the trial takes place. The courtroom is too artificial and enclosed a forum to bring out major issues of public policy. Even so, any reform of section 2 of the Official Secrets Act 1911 ought to provide for a public interest defence in some form so that these wider issues can be introduced and debated.

■

C. THE DUTY IN RESPONSE TO UNJUST LAWS

The world community and the Nürnberg Tribunal [or the Nuremberg Tribunal] affirmed, in the aftermath of the Nazi horrors, the point made by Saint Augustine in the fifth century in *City of God* (New York: Random House, 1950): "A law that is not just, seems to be no law at all. Wherefore such laws do not bind in conscience...." Individuals who acted in obedience to the laws of the Third Reich were therefore held to account for their actions, as the judgment below indicates.

The Nürnberg Tribunal†

It was submitted that international law is concerned with the actions of sovereign States, and provides no punishment for individuals; and further, that where the act in question is an act of State, those who carry it out are not personally responsible, but are protected by the doctrine of the sovereignty of the State. In the opinion of the Tribunal, both these submissions must be rejected. That international law imposes duties and liabilities upon individuals as well as upon States has long been recognized....

. . . .

Crimes against international law are committed by men, not by abstract entities, and only by punishing individuals who commit such crimes can the provisions of international law be enforced....

It was also submitted on behalf of most of these defendants that in doing what they did they were acting under the orders of Hitler, and therefore cannot be held responsible for the acts committed by them in carrying out these orders. The Charter specifically provides in Article 8:

> The fact that the Defendant acted pursuant to order of his Government or of a superior shall not free him from responsibility, but may be considered in mitigation of punishment.

The provisions of this article are in conformity with the law of all nations. That a soldier was ordered to kill or torture in violation of the international law of war has never been recognized as a defense to such acts of brutality, though, as the Charter here provides, the order may be urged in mitigation of the punishment. The true test, which is found in varying degrees in the criminal law of most nations, is not the existence of the order, but whether moral choice was in fact possible....

■

As Harvey Cox points out, the Nürnberg Tribunal confirmed and highlighted several tenets of international law:

> Three major elements of international law, which had been recognized for many years, came forcefully to the forefront as a result of the Nuremberg proceedings. The first was that governments themselves can become criminal governments. To violate international law under the color of law or for reasons of state does not exculpate a government from the guilt of its punishable actions.
>
> The second element that came into prominence at Nuremberg was that when one government becomes an outlaw, it is the duty and obligation of the other nations to protect the citizens of that nation, and of other nations that might be affected, from its criminal activity. This principle of international enforcement suggests that in such cases, intervention is not just allowable; it is obligatory. It is the equivalent of the well-established idea that if one knowingly allows a criminal action to take place when one could have done something to prevent it, one becomes a kind of accessory to the crime.
>
> The third and possibly most important idea that gained focus at Nuremberg was that every individual is responsible for the actions

† Nuremberg War Crimes Trials: (1947), 1 *Trial of the Major War Criminals* 171.

> he or she carries out. Appealing to the fact that one acted under superior orders is insufficient grounds for acquittal.[†]

In a more recent example of the prosecution of international crimes, see the discussion on the establishment of an *International Tribunal for the Prosecution of Persons Responsible for Serious Violations of International Law Humanitarian Law Committed in the Territory of the Former Yugoslavia* (1993) 32 I.L.M. 1203 in (1993) 23:4 I.L.M. 1163. The Tribunal was established in May 1993 as a result of "continuing reports of widespread violations of international humanitarian law occurring within the territory of the former Yugoslavia, including reports of mass killings and the continuation of the practice of 'ethnic cleansing'" (at 1166) and "widespread and systematic rape and other forms of sexual assault, including enforced prostitution" (at 1173). The rules of customary law, as interpreted and applied by the Nürnberg Tribunal, were cited as authority for the establishment of the Tribunal to prosecute violations of the laws or customs of war, genocide, and crimes against humanity. Once again (at 1175):

> The fact that any of the acts referred to ... was committed by a subordinate does not relieve his superior of criminal responsibility if he knew or had reason to know the subordinate was about to commit such acts or had done so and the superior failed to take the necessary and reasonable measures to prevent such acts or to punish the perpetrators thereof.
>
> ... The fact that an accused person acted pursuant to an order of a Government or of a superior shall not relieve him of criminal responsibility, but may be considered in mitigation of punishment if the International Tribunal determines that justice so requires.

The Tribunal is the first war crimes tribunal to be established since the Nürnberg and Tokyo Tribunals 50 years ago. In 1995, the International Criminal Rwandan Tribunal (ICTR) was established in response to the widespread genocide in 1994: U.N. SCOR, 3400th mtg., U.N. Doc. S/RES/935 (1994). For a critique of the limitations of the Rwandan Tribunal (for example, the inability of the tribunal to examine the role of the American government in Zaire or to challenge the role of rich and powerful countries in arming all sides), see John Philpot, "Colonialism and Injustice: The International Criminal Tribunal for Rwanda" *Canadian Dimension* (March/April 1997) 8. Justice Louise Arbour has argued that an International Criminal Court could overcome some of the limitations of *ad hoc* prosecutions of genocide and war crimes, such as those pursued in Nuremberg and Tokyo and more recently in Rwanda and the former Yugoslavia: Ron McGregor, "Making justice just: ICC needed to fill holes of ad hoc tribunals" (28 January 2002) *Law Times* 2. Consider other limitations on the availability, scope, and implementation of international prosecution of war crimes. See, for example: Christopher Hitchens, *The Trial of Henry Kissinger* (Verso: London, 2001); Peter Tatchell, "Why Milosevic, but not Kissinger?" (25 April 2002) *The [Manchester] Guardian Unlimited* (online: guardian.co.uk) (describing an unsuccessful application in the United Kingdom for an arrest warrant for Henry Kissinger in the killing, maiming, torture, and forced relocation of civilian populations in Vietnam, Laos, and Cambodia in the 1960s and 1970s).

D. THE POLITICALLY MOTIVATED "CRIMINAL"

The doctrine that political "criminals" should be treated differently and allowed more privileges than other criminals gained wide acceptance in Europe by the 1800s, yet opinion was more divided in England. Consider the treatment of one such group of "criminals", the Suffragettes.

† Harvey Cox, "Introduction" in Marlene Dixon, ed., *On Trial: Reagan's War Against Nicaragua* (San Francisco: Synthesis Press, 1985) at ii. Reproduced by permission of the author.

The Political Offender†

The doctrine that the political offender is a species apart, not to be confused in criminal law and penal practice with any other categories of criminal, and that he was therefore entitled to certain privileges, began to gain wide acceptance in Europe around the 1820s. Naturally this was a view embraced by the liberal minds of the period, such as Guizot, the eminent historian and statesman, and Rossi, the leading authority on the penal law. It was felt so deeply by many that even despotic governments no longer had the courage to repudiate it, although they had no desire to implement it. The concept was reflected, and gained considerable acknowledgement, in the vast expansion of extradition treaties, which went a long way towards exempting crimes committed for political motives.

At the turn of the century Emile Durkheim, one of the founders of modern sociology, developed the view that crime was an integral and, within certain limits, a healthy element of society. He took political crime as his prime example. The new school of criminal law and criminology, the Italian positivists, advocated drastic measures to protect society from crime, yet they too had no doubts that political offenses should stand apart. To Cesare Lombroso and Enrico Ferri the political offender was one who endeavoured to accelerate the slow rhythm of political and social evolution against the forces of *misoneism*, a strange word they forged to denote the hatred of the new. They saw political crime as a version of the *crime passionel*. The *bon delinquent politique* justified a *régime de faveur*. This concept found its place in several contemporary penal codes.

When the first Congress of the International Penitentiary Commission was convened in London in 1872, under the presidency of the Earl of Carnarvon, it reacted favourably to a resolution that "crimes of passion, not implying a great moral perversity" — which, it seemed, might include "mere political crimes" — "should not be punished ... by ordinary imprisonment, but by simple detention in a fortress or other secure place, without the cellular system, obligation of working, or confusion with those sentenced to ordinary imprisonment."

This point of view was consistently voiced whenever the subject cropped up at subsequent Congresses and at the deliberations of the International Association of Criminal Law. And whenever the idea of transportation was resurrected it was always made clear that it should not be extended to political offenders. The sinner in this respect was Imperial Russia, whose persistence in continuing the practice on a large scale gave rise to many embarrassing episodes. When legislation was evolved elsewhere at the turn of the century to deal with habitual offenders, whether through a dual-track system or a straightforward indeterminate sentence, the reservation was always made that it should not apply to recidivist political offenders.

The concept of political crime as a thing apart had obviously a long history in England. To demonstrate that, it is enough to evoke the responses to "high treason" and sedition. These were crimes, as Sheldon Amos put it "in which the general Motive, instead of being the satisfaction of some narrower Personal feeling, is rather the carrying out of some design connected more or less directly with Changes in the Constitution or in the Administration of the State." But the implications, legal and penal, were a matter of deep dispute. The matter was by no means simple. To quote Amos again:

> It may ... happen that in the course of committing these Crimes, and with a view to facilitating the commission of them, other Acts are done which, in everything but the accompanying Motive, are not distinguishable from ordinary Crimes. A question, then, may be presented whether these Acts ought to be treated as (1.) ordinary Crimes, and no more nor less, regard being had only to the Intention and not to the Motive; or (2.) as mere incidents to or aggravations of the Political Offence, regard being had to the Motive and not to the Intention; or (3.) as Acts qualified by reference both to the Intention and to the Motive, and so, as *sui generis*, being punishable on principles founded on special views of Political expediency.

The English denied that political motive or objective, as such, should secure for the offender a different mode of punishment or a different penal regime. They were emphatic that there was no provision for it in criminal law, either in common or stat-

---

 Reproduced from *The Emergence of Penal Policy in Victorian and Edwardian England*b y Leon Radzinowicz and Roger Hood (1990), pp. 401–404, 439–46, 448–51, 454–57 by permission of Oxford University Press. [Notes omitted.]

utory law. To those on the Continent it seemed strange that this attitude should prevail in England, the home of liberalism, but the English had been put to the test by three large-scale movements of vehement political discontent in the period between 1840 and 1914. The Chartists, the Fenians, and the militant Suffragists, had each raised the vexed question of the status and treatment in prison of those convicted of politically motivated crimes. It is curious that the authoritative accounts of the English penal system have been remarkably silent on the subject, a subject which remains poignantly relevant to issues we confront today both in the United Kingdom and in many other parts of the world....

. . . .

Suffragettes: Crimes as Propaganda

Demonstrations and disturbances in support of "votes for women" emerged as a political issue at the end of 1905. The militant suffragettes adopted the novel tactic of courting imprisonment. This raised at once two fundamental issues. First, were they to be regarded as political offenders and given the status of political prisoners? No one doubted that the motives of the protesters were to achieve a political objective, but they went about it not merely by voicing discontent, but primarily by committing acts which were in themselves breaches of the ordinary criminal law. They disrupted public order, maliciously damaged property, and later resorted to violence and arson. Secondly, once they had been deprived of their liberty, who was to decide the regime to which they should be subjected: the court or the Home Office?

The Prison Act of 1898 had produced a change which was potentially to the disadvantage of political offenders. Henceforth the courts were to have unfettered discretion to allocate offenders sentenced to imprisonment without hard labour to one of three divisions, according to the nature of the offence and the antecedents of the offender. The first and second divisions were to be available where there

> is evidence of good character over a considerable period of time, and when it is clear that exceptional temptation or special provocation has led to a merely temporary deviation from the paths of honesty, or to an act of violence not in consonance with the natural disposition of the defendant.

The second division was especially intended "to meet the case of persons guilty of offences not implying great moral depravity, and to a large extent the cases of persons committed to prison in default of paying a fine where the antecedents are respectable."

In practice the distinctions between the treatment of prisoners in the second and third divisions were small. Hobhouse and Brockway list them as

> (1) the separation from close contact with the (presumably) most objectionable prisoners ... (but the separation is often lax ...)
>
> (2) during the first few days an extra book or two, and a mattress; and
>
> (3) a visit and a letter after the first four, instead of after the first eight weeks. Apart from these points, prison conditions are the same for both divisions.

But the gulf between treatment in the second and treatment in the first division was enormous. The prisoners in the first division were to all intents, treated like unconvicted prisoners awaiting trial: "apart from ... severe restrictions upon their movements ... [they] are not subject to anything in the nature of 'discipline' or 'treatment.' They have merely to undergo a rather rigid form of internment, the severity of which doubtless varies very much in accordance with the dispositions of the officers who administer it." Translated into the daily regimen of prison life this meant: the provision of books and newspapers; visits once a fortnight by three friends; a letter out and in each fortnight; no requirement to work; permission, if practicable, to follow a prisoner's own trade or profession, to receive the full earnings and to pay from them for food, beer, and wine "subject to such restrictions as may be necessary to prevent luxury or waste"; permission to rent a superior and specially furnished cell, to have the use of private furniture, and to hire the help of another prisoner for relief "from the performance of unaccustomed tasks." These conditions were not unlike those obtained by some Chartists, but again were only to the advantage of those who could pay for them. The linking of *custodia honesta* with financial privilege was to lead Henry Nevinson to accuse the Government of "a determination to deal leniently with the rich, the distinguished and the highly connected; but to wreak its vengence to the full upon the poor and unknown."

Those sentenced to penal servitude for treason or treason-felony gained no advantage from the 1898 Act. An attempt to introduce a clause to allow them to associate with similar prisoners, wear their own dress, and be allowed to write and receive letters and to receive visits once a month, was defeated after a bitter debate. At first the Liberal Government adopted a lenient view towards the suffragists.

The Prime Minister, Sir Henry Campbell-Bannerman, intervened to secure the release of three women arrested for disorderly conduct in Downing Street. The Chancellor of the Exchequer asked for leniency when Miss Billington, who had been trying to see him, was arrested for slapping and kicking a policeman. Her sentence was reduced from a fine of £10 or two months' imprisonment to £5 or one month. When ten women, who had been convicted of disorderly conduct, were sent to prison for two months on failing to agree to find sureties of £10 each to keep the peace for six months, Herbert Gladstone, the Home Secretary, prompted by Keir Hardie, persuaded the magistrate to transfer them from the second to the first division. They were also set free after serving only half their sentences. In the period up to the end of March 1907, 127 women, committed by summary courts to prison under the Metropolitan Police Acts, were ordered to be treated in the first division.

The years 1908 and 1909 witnessed a growing intensity in the agitation to accord to suffragists the full status of political prisoners. Earl Russell was one of their most persuasive and eloquent supporters, insisting that "the whole object of their offence was a political object" and that to expect them to find sureties that they would keep the peace would entail giving up their right to agitate for political change." Gladstone told the Commons that the view of the courts was "that the persistence of such offences" rendered it undesirable to commit suffragettes to the first division any longer. Almost as a matter of routine the stipendiary magistrates sent them all to the second division. Again, as in the case of the Chartists and the Irish, the cry was raised that the conditions were particularly oppressive to those from good families who were acting from unselfish motives:

> these ladies, many of whom are persons of culture and refinement, have to wear a lot of old clothes brought out of the jumble store of the prison, ill-fitting clogs of some sort, not necessarily a pair; and they are served with the gruel ... in the ordinary wooden vessels and it has to be eaten with the ordinary wooden spoons.

Irish Nationalists jumped at this opportunity to reassert their conviction that "men or women who founded themselves on political motives ought to be treated on a different footing from ordinary criminals."

New precedents were drawn into the argument. The 1870 Extradition Act had laid down that "a fugitive criminal shall not be surrendered if the offence in respect of which his surrender is demanded is one of a political character." It gave no definition of what constituted a political offence. In 1891, however, the arrest of Angelo Castioni, on the requisition of the Swiss Government, for the murder of Luigi Rossi in Ticino, provided a test case. Castioni had shot Rossi to further the cause of an insurrection, apparently, without any personal spite or malice towards him. Among the three Queen's Bench judges who tried the case was Sir James Fitzjames Stephen. Although they made an attempt to define what constituted a political offence they finally admitted the impossibility of finding an exhaustive definition, suggesting that each case had to be examined on its merits as it arose. In this instance they decided that the rising had been political and the crime too had been political, being an essential part of the insurrection. When, however, the decision *Re Castioni* was raised by suffragist supporters to justify crimes committed for political motives, the Government pointed out that the Extradition Act made no reference to offences committed in this country.

Another precedent cited arose from the Jameson raid on the Transvaal in 1896. Dr. Jameson and his chief associates had been imprisoned for offences under the 1870 Foreign Establishment Act, the sentences had ranged from five to 15 months, all without hard labour. This had provoked an outcry, and a petition circulated in Parliament had been extensively signed, two of the signatories being the Irish Members John Dillon and Michael Davitt, neither of whom had been given political status when in prison. ...

Gladstone refused to agree that any of these cases were relevant to the position of suffragists. ...

. . .

... Gladstone continued to assert, however, that English law did not "recognise political motive as giving rise to any claim to special treatment in prison on the part of offenders against the ordinary law." ...

The Home Office documents reveal a persistent struggle with the problem.... [Pressure from prisoners and from outside initially led to differential treatment for the suffragettes with respect to access to visitors, books, food, clothing, and exercise. Mrs. Pankhurst, for example, argued that international custom supported their demand to be treated as political offenders rather than ordinary law-breakers. However, according to Radzinowicz, the courts began increasingly to sentence the Suffragettes to the third division, giving them less access to special treatment.]

. . . .

The prisoners began a campaign of disobedience. In February 1909 the Governor of Holloway reported that 20 suffragettes had been received and that Mrs. Emmeline Pethick-Lawrence had asked to see him to say there would be no trouble provided three points were observed: no search, exercised in two's, and the right to talk at exercise. There was fury in the Home Office. E.H.R. Blackwell, the Assistant Under-Secretary, who was consistently antagonistic to the suffragettes, declared "No doubt if this request were granted ... the next thing would be a demand ... that each prisoner should have a daily paper." Troup feared that if the authorities gave in to demands backed by threats, prison discipline would collapse. Plans were made to exercise the ring-leaders in small parties at different times. By July things had got out of hand at Holloway. All the suffragettes had demanded political status in the first division. The women refused to be searched or wear prison clothes, forcing the Home Office to abandon strip searches. Some prisoners were left covered only by a blanket. Insubordination gave way to "riot" in July 1909. The Commissioners wanted to prosecute those who had shown most violence — "biting, scratching, kicking and punching," but the Governor advised against it. Fourteen prisoners went on a hunger strike and as a consequence six had to be released on medical grounds. By September, 37 women had been discharged because of their refusal to take food and it was announced that the Government was taking action. This was forcible feeding, first carried out on nine women at Birmingham's Winson Green prison. The Prison Commissioners, with the approval of Gladstone, "instructed the medical officer to apply such ordinary medical treatment as was, in his opinion, necessary to prevent the risk of their committing suicide by starvation."

There was an enormous outcry, especially on the Labour benches. Keir Hardie exploded: "The tube is inserted in the stomach and food pumped into it — horrible outrage, beastly outrage." In fact the stomach pump was used in three of the nine cases. Disregarding condemnation by distinguished physicians and surgeons the Government spokesman, C.F.G. Masterman, insisted that it was not dangerous and that the health of those being forcibly fed was good; he used the handy euphemism "ordinary hospital treatment." To Keir Hardie, however, three or four days fast was surely enough punishment "to meet the claims of justice" where women were convicted of trivial offences. There is no doubt that both Gladstone and the Prime Minister, Mr. Asquith, were reluctant to endorse forcible feeding, and Gladstone tried to draw distinctions between prisoners like Lilian Wilcox and Theresa Grant who had been committed for assaulting wardresses at Holloway and those convicted of lesser offences. The distinction was difficult to maintain, especially in the case of those prisoners who had refused to give sureties. It seems that Miss Garnett, a Bristol, had been forcibly fed, whereas at Manchester, five suffragettes who had thrown iron balls through the windows of public halls were not, because they had been convicted of "only damage to glass." Women who persisted in refusing food had to be released when medically necessary, as did those who were unfit to be forcibly fed.

The Commissioners became uneasy and despatched their Chief Medical Officer to Bristol and Newcastle to supervise the feeding and to check the health of prisoners. Troup, noting that the Manchester prisoners on hunger strike had been released after only 60 hours detention, about half the time of those at Holloway, Leicester, Liverpool, and Exeter, commented sarcastically: "This illustrates one of the difficulties which necessarily arises when the length of detention depends on the personal qualities of the medical officer ... [others] who had better judgment or more courage" would have waited two more days before releasing them. The matter came to a head when Lady Constance Lytton was imprisoned at Newcastle in October 1909, along with another leader of the movement, Mrs. Jane Brailsford. Lady Constance had a weak heart, and Mrs. Brailsford had traces of cardiac trouble. It was decided not to forcibly feed them, and to justify this on the grounds that they were both "surety" prisoners. Gladstone ordered by telegram: "After full consideration have decided to maintain distinction between surety and other prisoners and in the case of surety prisoners not to have recourse to forcible feeding. Accordingly in the case of the two surety prisoners at Newcastle discharge if and when medical officer so advises." The ladies intended to risk death and "five days starvation" would be enough. The Home Office was well aware that its action in relation to Lady Lytton would be misconstrued, and so it was, not least by Constance Lytton herself. When she had first been arrested in 1909 she had protested at the privileged hospital treatment she had received in comparison with other prisoners: she was in the hospital ward, where her blankets were comfortable, her food good, and there was hot water in which to wash; she received a visit from her sister within a week instead of having to wait a month; her brother, Lord Lytton, a future Viceroy of India, obtained for her extra towels and flannel underclothes to wear; she was allowed to write extra letters. Even when her protests got her moved to an ordinary cell she was not allowed to clean it herself. She was particularly indignant when most of the suffragettes at Newcastle got hard labour in the third division while she, the only one actually arrested for stone-throwing, had merely been bound over to keep the peace for disorderly behaviour with the alternative of one month in the second division. Mrs. Brailsford also received this preferential treatment. Lady Constance firmly believed that their release after two days of hunger strike had more to do with their social status than their health.

Lady Constance, to prove her point, rejoined the Women's Social and Political Union (W.S.P.U.) using the name of Jane Warton and wearing a disguise of cheap clothes and badly cut hair. When arrested in Liverpool for wilful damage by stone-throwing and for insulting behaviour, she was sentenced to 14 days in the third division, with the option of a fine. The prison doctors did not give her a physical examination and, after refusing food, she was forcibly fed. Her mouth was forced open with a steel gag and food poured down a tube. Only when she had turned pale on the evening of the second day was her heart examined. Several days later she was released on medical grounds. A tremendous controversy ensued. Lady Constance had made her point: her treatment had been quite different when she had been imprisoned under her own name. Gladstone called it "A very contemptible trick which failed in its main purpose." Yet it did ensure henceforth proper medical examination for all prisoners before forcible feeding.

As far as the law was concerned, the Government's use of forcible feeding was vindicated. Mrs. Marie Leigh, who had been forcibly fed at Winson Green prison, Birmingham, sued the Home Secretary, Captain Percy Green, the Prison Governor, and Dr. Helby, the prison Medical Officer, for assault and sought an injunction to restrain repetition of the acts. Her counsel argued that Mrs. Leigh had claimed political status and refused food, therefore the forcible feeding had been imposed as a means of enforcing prison discipline.... [The jury denied the claim on the basis that prison officials were acting under a duty to preserve the health and life of the prisoner. The Government continued to be pressured to develop different standards of treatment for the Suffragettes, for example the new Rule 243A.]

. . . .

The year 1912 brought a new trial of strength. Suffragist militancy, entering a more active and destructive phase, moved from breaking windows to arson on a large scale. There were more trials and convictions on indictment and longer sentences, often to hard labour. The new Home Secretary, Reginald McKenna, attempted to take a tougher line. He ordered that hard labour prisoners were not to receive the benefits of Rule 243A, nor were those sentenced for "serious violence" at Quarter Sessions; the privileges were also to be suspended for grave breaches of prison discipline. The only concession was to allow the prisoners to keep their own clothes and not to force them to bathe. But things got worse. By March 14, 50 out of 80 prisoners awaiting trial at Sessions had forfeited Rule 243A through misconduct. In the face of hunger strikes and defiance, plans were laid to transfer such prisoners away from Holloway; "otherwise, there is a danger of insubordination ... greater than we should be easily able to control." In April, McKenna extended to all suffragette prisoners, including those sentenced to hard labour, the benefits of the Rule, "provided that they had been working and behaving well." At the same time the Rule was modified so as to make it less attractive — fewer visits and one food parcel instead of a daily ration of food from outside.

Keir Hardie's attempt, through his Prison (Political Offences) Bill, to secure treatment as first class misdemeanants both for suffragists and for syndicalist agitators was blocked by the Home Office. ...

The issues were brought to a head when Mrs. Pankhurst, Mrs. Pethick-Lawrence, and her husband (later Lord Pethick-Lawrence and Cabinet minister), were transferred, on the advice of the judge, from the second division to the first. They had been sentenced in March 1912 to nine months imprisonment in the second division and demanded greater privileges than before. Disturbances had ensued until, in June, they had given their written assurances that they would not take advantage of first division status to incite others to commit illegal acts. Although the Government claimed that the judge concerned was solely responsible for the transfer, it seems clear that considerations of prison discipline and social status had played an important part in the decision. The effect was a demand, from Labour Members of Parliament and others, for all suffragist prisoners to be transferred to the first division. The prisoners themselves protested on a massive scale; 52 out of 71 refused food and 47 had to be forcibly fed. ...

The weapon of the hunger strike forced the government yet again to seek a solution. Of the 240 suffragettes received into prison in 1912, 57 had had to be forcibly fed. Altogether 84 had been released before the expiration of their sentences, 49 of them on health grounds after refusing food. McKenna outlined the problem: these prisoners had either to be released or allowed to die and he was convinced that perhaps 30 or 40 would, if allowed, starve themselves to death. He was entirely unsympathetic with those who would let them die, asking "are you going to leave them to the penalty of death, first of all for ... window breaking, and secondly for obstinacy." The point was made by the case of Lilian Lenton who had been sent to Holloway on remand in February 1913 on a charge of setting fire to a building in Kew Gardens. She refused food and, three hours after being forcibly fed, was found in her cell seriously ill with pleurisy. Just as in the Chartist and Fenian phases, the prison medical officers claimed that she had been suffering from the condition before being forcibly fed and that it had simply become acute again. Government spokesmen vigorously denied the allegation of three physicians that her collapse had been due to food being poured into her lungs.

Faced with mounting concern from all sides for failing to control the continuing disturbances, McKenna decided on a new remedy: the Prisoners (Temporary Discharge for Ill-Health) Bill. This would give the Home Secretary power to set the women free temporarily, without remission of the sentences. Thus there would be no fear of death, no objectionable forcible feeding, and no surrender by the State. At first he had wanted to add a clause depriving temporarily released prisoners of civil rights, but this was withdrawn to make the conditions "mere machinery — not punitive," because, from the outset, the Home Office recognised "that whatever conditions are inserted they will not be obeyed." Nevertheless the Bill was vigorously opposed by Labour members and a few back bench Liberals and Conservatives. Atherley-Jones declared it a "new departure ... in ... penology," giving too much power to prison officials and the Home Secretary to impose conditions for temporary licences. Punishment would no longer be certain and the result of judicial proceedings. [However, the conduct of those released under this measure continued to be scrutinized. If there was evidence of continued political activity, they were likely to be arrested and re-imprisoned. Therefore, as Radzinowicz argues, the measures, while compassionate in part, also enabled greater surveillance and control of political dissidents.]

E. SILENCING DISSENT: THE POLITICAL MOTIVATION OF THE STATE

SOUTH AFRICA

In defending themselves against criminal charges stemming from political struggle, sometimes the accused and outside observers have reacted with outrage to the particular charges of the criminal process. Often, the accused has refused to recognize the authority or legitimacy of the courts or the "justice" system. For example, the following statements were made during political trials in South Africa that took place during the 1960s. They are taken from a collection of statements, *The Sun Will Rise*, edited by Mary Benson, made from the prisoners' dock by Southern African political prisoners.

As Mary Benson says in her introduction, at 4–5:†

> Nelson Mandela's powerful statement in Pretoria's Palace of Justice on 20 April 1964, when he and other members of the African National Congress and the Congress Alliance were in the dock in the Rivonia Trial, has become an historic document. Two years later Bram Fischer Q.C., the advocate who had led the Rivonia defence, was himself on trial in the same court.... This was the period immediately after the ANC and the PAC were outlawed. The liberation movement's long-maintained policy of non-violence was finally abandoned for sabotage and armed struggle. Wide-spread arrests and 90-day detention, involving solitary confinement and torture, culminated in major trials as a result of which many of the top leadership of the ANC were swept away to life imprisonment. From innumerable small trials,

† Mary Benson, ed., *The Sun Will Rise* (London: International Defence and Aid Fund for Southern Africa, 1981). Reproduced by permission of the University of Cape Robben Island Museum Mayibuye Archives.

> particularly in the Eastern Cape, hundreds of political prisoners were taken to Robben Island or mainland jails.

In the 1970s, guerilla activity increased, and the leaders of the Black Consciousness movement were brought to trial under the *Terrorism Act*. In June 1976, the schoolchildren of Soweto rose in protest. In the next 16 months, hundreds of children died, mainly shot by police. Hundreds more were taken into detention. Some disappeared, and most were charged with offences such as public violence and arson. There are few statements from these "trials", since many were held *in camera*, some even in police stations.

Nelson Mandela

Mandela studied law in Johannesburg, and joined other young African nationalists in moving the African National Congress into militant action. He was active in the Defiance Campaign in 1952, and was one of the 156 accused in the Treason Trial of 1956–1960, leading the defence at one point. He continued his political activities underground. He evaded an intensive police search for two years, making a secret tour of Africa and going to London, where he met with heads of state and politicians. Soon after his return, he was captured and charged with inciting to strike and leaving the country without a valid travel document. Addressing the court in Pretoria, he said:

> I feel oppressed by the atmosphere of white domination that lurks all around in this courtroom. Somehow this atmosphere calls to mind the inhuman injustices caused to my people outside this courtroom by this same white domination.
>
> ...
>
> South Africa and the world know that during the last thirteen years your government has subjected us to merciless and arbitrary rule. Hundreds of our people have been banned and confined to certain areas. Scores have been banished to remote parts of the country, and many arrested and jailed for a multitude of offences. It has become extremely difficult to hold meetings, and freedom of speech has been drastically curtailed. During the last twelve months we have gone through a period of grim dictatorship, during which seventy-five people were killed and hundreds injured while peacefully demonstrating against passes.
>
> Political organizations were declared unlawful and thousands flung into jail without trial. [Benson at 10–11]

He went on to describe the history of African protest and his role within that:

> I regard it as a duty which I owed, not just to my people, but also to my profession, to the practice of law, and to justice for all mankind, to cry out against this discrimination which is essentially unjust.... I believed that in taking up a stand against this injustice I was upholding the dignity of what should be an honourable profession.... The law as it is applied, the law as it has been developed over a long period of history, and especially the law as it is written and designed by the nationalist government, is a law which, in our view, is **immoral**, **unjust**, and **intolerable**. Our consciences dictate that we must protest against it, that we must oppose it, and that we must attempt to alter it. [Benson at 11]

Mandela reminded the court that peaceful protest, such as the stay-at-home strike in 1961, was treated by the Government as though it was a preparation for civil war:

> The Government set out from the beginning of this campaign, not to treat with us, not to heed us, not to talk to us, but rather to present us as wild dangerous revolutionaries, intent on disorder and riot, incapable of being dealt with in any way save by mustering an overwhelming force against us and the implementation of every possible forcible means, legal and illegal, to suppress us.... We have been conditioned by the history of white governments in this country to accept the fact that Africans, when they make their demands strongly and powerfully enough to have some chance of success, will be met by force and terror on the part of the Government. This is not something we have taught the African people, this is something the African people have learned from their own bitter experience. We learned it from each successive government. [Benson at 11]

As he described to the court, he had been forced to go underground to continue his work:

> I was made, by the law, a criminal, not because of what I had done, but because of what I stood for, because of what I thought, because of my conscience.... It has not been easy for me ... to separate myself from my wife and children, to say goodbye to the good old days when, at the end of a strenuous day at an office, I could look forward to joining my family at the dinner-table, and instead to take up the life of a man hunted continuously by the police, living separated from those who

> are closest to me, in my own country, facing continually the hazards of detection and of arrest.... No man in his right senses would voluntarily choose such a life ... but there comes a time, as it came in my life, when a man is denied the right to live a normal life, when he can only live the life of an outlaw because the government has so decreed....
>
> I am prepared to pay the penalty even though I know how bitter and desperate is the situation of an African in the prisons of this country. I have been in these prisons and I know how gross is the discrimination, even behind the prison walls, against Africans, how much worse is the treatment meted out to African prisoners than that accorded to whites....
>
> When my sentence has been completed, I will still be moved as men are always moved, by their consciences; I will still be moved by my dislike of the race discrimination against my people when I come out from serving my sentence, to take up again, as best I can, the struggle for the removal of those injustices until they are finally abolished once and for all.
>
> ...
>
> I have done my duty to my people and to South Africa. I have no doubt that posterity will pronounce that I was innocent and that the criminals who should have been brought before this Court are the members of the Verwoerd government. [Benson at 11–12]

Mandela was sentenced to three years imprisonment for incitement to strike and two years for leaving the country without a valid permit. Subsequently, while he was in Pretoria Central Prison he was again brought to trial along with eight other accused on charges of sabotage. This was the Rivonia Trial. On 20 April 1964, in Pretoria's Palace of Justice, Nelson Mandela made a statement from the dock:

> In my youth in the Transkei, I listened to the elders of my tribe telling stories of the old days. Amongst the tales they related to me were those of wars fought by our ancestors in defence of the fatherland. The names of Dingane and Bambata, Hintsa and Makana, Squngthi and Dalasile, Moshoeshoe and Sekhukhuni, were praised as the glory of the entire African nation. I hoped that life might offer me the opportunity to serve my people and make my own humble contribution to their freedom struggle. This is what has motivated me in all I have done in relation to the charges made against me in this case....
>
> ... Some of the things so far told to the Court are true and some are untrue. I do not, however, deny that I planned sabotage. I did not plan it in a spirit of recklessness, nor because I have any love of violence. I planned it as a result of a calm and sober assessment of the political situation that had arisen after many years of tyranny, exploitation and oppression of my people by the whites.
>
> I admit immediately that I was one of the persons who helped to form Umkhonto We Sizwe, and that I played a prominent role in its affairs until I was arrested in August 1962. [Benson at 13]

Robert Sobukwe

Sobukwe was a leader in founding the Pan Africanist Congress (PAC) and, in 1959, was elected its President. He was a lecturer in African languages at the University of Witwatersrand, but resigned to lead the anti-pass laws protest in 1960. Sobukwe was arrested in Orlando with 22 others and charged with inciting the destruction of reference books. In conducting his defence in Johannesburg Regional Court, he explained that he and the other accused had refused to enter a plea because the law under which they were charged was made exclusively by and for the white man and therefore they did not expect justice:

> The chief aims of the PAC are the complete overthrow of white domination and the establishment of a non-racial democracy in South Africa as well as throughout the whole of Africa....
>
> ...
>
> It will be remembered that we refused to plead to the charges against us.
>
> We felt we had no moral obligation to obey the laws made by a white minority. Without wishing to impugn the personal honour and integrity of the magistrate, an unjust law cannot be applied justly.
>
> We have said we believe in the human race and that alone. The history of the human race has been a struggle for the removal of mental, moral and spiritual oppression, and we would have failed had we not made our contribution to the struggle. We are glad we made it.
>
> If we are sent to jail there will always be others to take our place. We are not afraid to face the consequence of our actions and it is not our intention to plead for mercy. [Benson at 8–9]

He was sentenced to three years imprisonment in 1960 and, upon release, detained a further six years on Robben Island. He died in 1978.

Bram Fischer

Fischer was a Rhodes Scholar at Oxford and a Queen's Counsel who practised law in Johannesburg where he was elected to the Bar Council and, for some years, was its chair. He led the defence in a number of political trials, including the Treason Trial of 1956–1960 and the Rivonia Trial in 1963–1964. In 1964, he was arrested and charged under the *Suppression of Communism Act*. Released briefly on bail, he went underground. He evaded capture for almost a year, and then was brought to trial under the *Sabotage Act* and the *Suppression of Communism Act*. In Pretoria, on 28 March 1966, he addressed the court:

> I am on trial for my political beliefs and for the conduct to which those beliefs drove me. Whatever labels may be attached to the fifteen charges brought against me, they all arise from my having been a member of the Communist Party and from my activities as a member. I engaged upon those activities because I believed that, in the dangerous circumstances which have been created in South Africa, it was my duty to do so.
>
> When a man is on trial for his political beliefs and actions, two courses are open to him. He can either confess to his transgressions and plead for mercy or he can justify his beliefs and explain why he acted as he did. Were I to ask forgiveness today I would betray my cause. That course is not open to me. I believe that what I did was right....
>
> My belief, moreover, is one reason why I have pleaded not guilty to all the charges brought against me. Though I shall deny a number of important allegations made, this Court is aware of the fact that there is much in the State case which has not been contested. Yet, if I am to explain my motives and my actions as clearly as I am able, then this Court was entitled to have had before it the witnesses who testified in chief and under cross-examination against me. Some of these, I believe, were fine and loyal persons who have now turned traitors to their cause and to their country because of the methods used against them by the State — vicious and inhuman methods. Their evidence may, therefore, in important respects be unreliable.
>
> There is another and more compelling reason for my plea and why I persist in it. I accept the general rule that for the protection of a society laws should be obeyed. But when laws themselves become immoral and require the citizen to take part in an organised system of oppression — if only by his silence or apathy — then I believe that a higher duty arises. This compels one to refuse to recognize such laws. The laws under which I am being prosecuted were enacted by a wholly unrepresentative body, a body in which three-quarters of the people of this country have no voice whatever. These laws were enacted, not to prevent the spread of communism, but for the purpose of silencing the opposition of the large majority of our citizens to a Government intent upon depriving them, solely on account of their colour, of the most elementary human rights: of the right to freedom and happiness, the right to live together with their families wherever they might choose, to earn their livelihoods to the best of their abilities, to rear and educate their children in a civilized fashion, to take part in the administration of their country and obtain a fair share of the wealth they produce; in short, to live as human beings. [Benson at 35–36]
>
> ...
>
> I cannot address any argument to this court. What I can do is to give the court certain facts regarding the manner in which the criminal law has come to be administered in political cases in this country. It presents a picture which is horrifying to those brought up with traditional ideas about justice.
>
> In July of 1964 I was detained for three days under the ninety-day law and was twice interrogated. There was nothing fair or impartial about the interrogation.... As for solitary confinement, I can only say that every South African voter should try it on himself. He can do so by locking himself up for a week-end in one small unfurnished room with no window through which he can see, by allowing himself to be taken out twice a day only, by a stranger, to walk around an enclosed yard for half an hour and for the rest to see no one at all, except the stranger who brings him food three times a day. One week-end would be sufficient to convince him of its callous inhumanity — of why, in wiser days its application was strictly limited by the law.
>
> For the past four and a half months I have also been held in conditions which in some ways amounted to solitary confinement. I was interrogated once only though an extremely unfair method was used to try and extract information from me. And though I was the accused it was suggested that by giving this information I could obtain the release of an elderly person in poor health who was then being detained.
>
> Compared with others, I have not suffered. During these four and a half months I have twice a week been allowed to see my children. I have also been allowed to consult with my legal advisers and to obtain reading

> matter. Nevertheless on the majority of days I have, sleeping and working, had to kill twenty-three hours a day by myself and I can only state that, if under such conditions pressure had really been applied to me — if I had been made to stand in one spot for twenty or thirty or even sixty hours at a time with batteries of trained men firing questions at me — the "statue" method as it is known — if under those conditions I had given information it could only have been information of a most unreliable character. Solitary confinement in itself is a vicious and inhuman form of treatment....
>
> I cannot testify to the extreme forms which this "treatment" has taken. But there are facts of which the State knows, and some of which have come before our courts which establish what their consequences have been apart from twisting and distorting human personalities like those of Beyleveld and Hlapane. These methods have already produced three suicides, one of them by an Indian who was a close friend of mine, a man no one could ever have dreamed would take his own life. They have also produced two serious attempts at suicide by two other close friends. The first was by Mrs. Slovo, the mother of three small daughters, a courageous woman if ever there was one. The other, by Mr. Heymann, also a person of outstanding character and courage.
>
> These facts which all should know ... bring shame to our country. Few whites recognize them. Most accept the application of the 180-day law as a normal procedure. But the facts remain and they are the result of an attempt to use the criminal law in order to suppress political beliefs. In such circumstances the administration of criminal law ... ceases to have integrity. It becomes an inquisition instead. It leads to the total extinction of freedom. It adds immeasurably to the deep race hatred. [Benson at 48–49]

Fischer was sentenced to life imprisonment. His health began to fail, and he was diagnosed with cancer. The Government refused to release him until death was imminent. When he died, in May 1975, the Government refused to release his ashes to the family.

While the names of Nelson Mandela, Robert Sobukwe, and Bram Fischer are well known, there were many others accused and convicted, and still more who were detained and tortured without trial. For one account of the way women were targeted by the South African state (for example, for protesting the wanton murders of their children) see: Sindiswa Gwazela, "The Female Target: Behind Prison Bars in South Africa" in Jennie Abell & Gloria Geller, eds., "Women and the Criminal Justice System" 14:4 (1985) Resources for Feminist Research 23.

For a detailed and thoughtful examination of the engagement with law to challenge the legalized racism of the former apartheid system in South Africa, see: Richard Abel, *Politics by Other Means: Law in the Struggle Against Apartheid, 1980–1994* (New York: Routledge, 1994). Abel documents 10 major campaigns (including, for example, the treason trials, the challenges to the pass law, and Black trade union demands for recognition) and the ways in which a small group of lawyers was able to use law strategically on behalf of opponents of apartheid. While recognizing that law was not the most important forum of struggle, he argues that legal victories were important both in de-legitimating the regime and in strengthening the commitment of the post-apartheid polity to legality.

FIRST NATIONS AND CANADA

Lubicon

Closer to home, consider the situation of the Lubicons, who were charged with contempt of court for blockading four roads in northern Alberta in October 1988 to press their longstanding claim for a reserve in northwestern Alberta. After five days of the blockade, a force of 50 RCMP officers arrived. They smashed the barricades and arrested 27 people. Two days after the arrests, Chief Bernard Ominayak and Alberta premier Don Getty agreed on the establishment of a 250-square kilometre reserve. For a detailed history and analysis of the issues, see Boyce Richardson, "The Lubicon of Northern Alberta" in Boyce Richardson, ed., *Drumbeat: Anger and Renewal in Indian Country* (Toronto: Summerhill Press, 1989) 229; and Ward Churchill, "Last Stand at Lubicon Lake: An Assertion of Indigenous Sovereignty in North America" in Ward Churchill, *Struggle for the Land: Indigenous Resistance to Genocide, Ecocide and Expropriation in Contemporary North America* (Toronto: Between the Lines, 1992) 217. Churchill quotes Chief Bernard Ominayak in 1989, at 217: "We've been pushed as far as we can go. This is where we make our stand."

The Attorney General's department offered to drop the contempt of court charges if the accused would apologize. The Lubicons, however, contested the court's authority to pass judgment on them, since they have never been conquered and have never ceded territory to Canada. In protest, the accused and their lawyer remained silent throughout the proceedings. As Frederic Lennarson, a band adviser who was charged, said: "We acknowledge the power of the police state troopers to drag us before the court, but we don't recognize the court's jurisdiction" (quoted in Matthew Fisher, "Lubicons challenge judge's authority" *The [Toronto] Globe and Mail* (9 November 1988) A1). The judge concluded that, while he was mindful "of a long-standing dispute between the Lubicon Lake Indians and the governments of Alberta and Canada, ... to allow court orders to be disobeyed is to tread the road to anarchy" (quoted in "Lubicon gives no defence as he is fined for contempt" *The [Toronto] Globe and Mail* (10 November 1988) A2).

Consider what your professional responsibility and role might be as a lawyer in this situation. James O'Reilly, a lawyer, was one of those arrested at Little Buffalo. He described his commitment and practice (quoted in Laurie Ridsdel, "Native rights lawyer wants justice — no more, no less" *The National* (November 1988) 8): "I can see why I'm branded as being an activist ... but if I expect the Indians to stand up for their rights I can do no less than stand up with them. I am committed or I am not." He explained why he thinks the Lubicon case is perceived as such a threat:

> The Lubicon are a tiny band and Indian nation that have questioned the conventional wisdom that the federal government can decide who is an Indian and who is not an Indian and why, without having to account for the logic and without having to bear the baggage of the justice of the treatment. In challenging the status quo of the legal system and in questioning the political legislation relating to Indians, the Lubicon have created a direct confrontation between minority rights and very powerful interests essentially preoccupied with money and political jurisdictions.

Reflecting on his own role, he said that he was guided by two principles:

> The first is to ask if, in my conscience, I feel that what I am doing is right. The answer is Yes. Overwhelmingly right. The second is to ask what the reaction is of the Indian peoples for whom I am working. I think again it has been unanimously very supportive of what I am trying to do. So, in my role of working with the Indian peoples I must be doing something right.
>
> ...
>
> I think more lawyers should be guided by what is just and far less by what is convenient or simply what will be a good monetary result. If a lawyer can't in a sincere way say that they have considered it to be an advance to the cause of justice then how can they be satisfied with their professional life?
>
> ...
>
> For me the law should be the means of attaining justice and if, somehow you're not considered to be carrying out your responsibilities as a lawyer as directed by the conventional bar, which is a relatively self-interested group, then the fact that one might be rejected by these people is not something that particularly concerns me. In other words, I will do what I think is right as long as it falls within the fundamental criteria recognized by international law.... The fact that a particular bar or something decides that I'm not properly upholding the dignity of the profession is not a judgment that is particularly relevant. Who are they to judge me?†

The escalation of oil sands development is only the latest assault on the boreal forest and the homeland of the Lubicon Nation. Genovali describes the development as the "biggest oil development scheme in the history of North America": Christopher Genovali, "Alberta's Black Gold Rush" (March/April 1997) *Canadian Dimension* 24 at 24.

Meanwhile, in Ontario, the giant paper products firm Daishowa Inc. (who has been given access to log Lubicon land by the Alberta government, despite outstanding land claims) applied for a permanent injunction to halt the successful seven-year consumer boycott campaign by Toronto-based Friends of the Lubicon. Justice MacPherson denied Daishowa a permanent injunction against the picket and boycott campaign (which has cost Daishowa $14 million in sales) on the basis of freedom of expression. However, he enjoined the defendants from using the word "genocide" in any of their communications in their campaign and from asserting that Daishowa and the Lubicon Cree Nation had reached an agreement in March 1988: *Daishowa Inc. v. Friends of*

† Laurie Ridsdel, "Native rights lawyer wants justice — no more, no less". This paper was originally published in *National* magazine (vol. 15, no. 10), a publication of the Canadian Bar Association. For more information on the CBA, please visit www.cba.org.

the Lubicon, [1998] O.J. No. 1429 (Ct. J. (Gen. Div.)) (QL).

The Lubicon land claim remains unsettled. In 2003, Amnesty International called on the Canadian government to respect the rights of the Lubicon Cree and to reach a long-overdue settlement: Amnesty International, *"Time is Wasting": Respect for the land rights of the Lubicon Cree long overdue* (Amnesty International: Ottawa, April 2003) (online: www.amnesty.ca):

> It has now been more than 100 years since the Lubicon were overlooked in the Alberta treaty process, more than 60 years since they were first promised recognition of a secure land base, more than a quarter century since the first negotiations began with the federal government, and more than a decade since the United Nations called on Canada to stop the violation of the Lubicon's human rights. To say that justice is overdue is an understatement.

Leonard Peltier, AIM, and the Canadian State

In 1976, a Canadian court ordered Leonard Peltier, a leader of the American Indian Movement (AIM), extradited based on fraudulent evidence: *Re Peltier*, [1977] 1 F.C. 118. (For example, one of the key witnesses, Myrtle Poor Bear, later admitted that she lied and that she was a paid worker for the FBI.) At the time, Peltier's lawyers in Canada argued that the offences were of a political nature and, therefore, he could not be surrendered under the terms of the *Canadian Extradition Act*. Peltier asked for political asylum. In his statement, set out in "U.S. Prosecutors Move Against Peltier" *Akwesasne Notes* (Mid-Winter 1989) 12 (republication of (1976) 8:3 *Akwesasne Notes*), he described the charges against him as:

> [A] continuation of past North American government policy of oppressing Indians by using the court system against our people....
>
> When colonial white society invades and occupies our territories, these are not called criminal acts. But when the native people stand up and resist, those acts are considered criminal. But these are not crimes — these are political acts in which our people stand for their rights of self-determination, self-dignity, and self-respect against the cruel and oppressive might of another nation.

Akwesasne Notes describes how the presiding judge delivered his judgment in a closed court after having more than 40 spectators forcibly removed. The crowd had responded with cheers and salutes to Peltier's entry into the courtroom, but refused to stand for the entrance of the judge. When Peltier stood up to hear the judgment, the entire gallery rose with clenched fists held high. When the police were clearing the courtroom, one officer grabbed a little girl from her mother, saying: "Give her to me! What kind of a mother are you to allow your child to see this?" (quoted at 12).

The following excerpt provides a brief background to the *Peltier* case, written by one of his lawyers.

The Oglala Shootout†

For at least a decade there has been a virtual reign of terror on South Dakota's Pine Ridge Indian Reservation. Bands of vigilantes, referred to as "goon squads," under the control of a tyrannical tribal chairman as well as Bureau of Indian Affairs (BIA) police officers, according to many observers, have been responsible for hundreds of unsolved murders on the reservation. Since the occupation of Wounded Knee in 1973, the FBI has been widely regarded by Pine Ridge residents as the modern-day equivalent of the United States Cavalry units which, among other things, massacred entire native villages on the Great Plains during the latter half of the nineteenth century.

On June 26, 1975, Ronald A. Williams and Jack R. Coler, two FBI agents who, without advance warning, had approached an American Indian Movement (AIM) enclave on the reservation, and a young

† William M. Kunstler, *Trials and Tribulations* (New York: Grove Press Inc., 1985) 40–43.

Indian, Joseph Stuntz, were killed during a fire fight that eventually involved hundreds of federal agents and BIA officers. Although they were completely surrounded, the handful of besieged Indians managed to escape by following the trail of an eagle, which one of them later claimed had led their way to safety. Subsequently, the four oldest Indian males thought by the Bureau to have been present at the scene — Robert E. Robideau, Darelle Dean Butler, James T. Eagle, and Leonard Peltier — were indicted jointly for the murders of the agents. No one was ever charged with Stuntz's death.

During the summer of 1976, Butler and Robideau, who had pleaded self-defence, were tried together in Cedar Rapids, Iowa, where their case had been transferred because of anti-Indian prejudice in South Dakota. During their trial in which I represented Butler, a small army of witnesses, including an associate of the United States Civil Rights Commission, testified to the intense fear of unannounced visitors felt by many reservation Indians. Convinced that the defendants had fired at the agents in order to protect themselves, the jury acquitted them both.

Following the verdicts, the government dropped the charges against Eagle "so that the full prosecutive weight of the Federal Government could be directed against Leonard Peltier." After his indictment, the latter had fled to Canada and was shortly to be extradited by that country on the basis of three affidavits obtained by the FBI from Myrtle Poor Bear, who swore that she had seen him shooting the agents. The government was later forced to admit publicly that all of these documents were false, a concession that led one federal appellate court to characterize their use as "a clear abuse of the investigative process by the FBI."

On April 18, 1977, Peltier was convicted by a jury in Fargo, North Dakota, where his case had been mysteriously shifted, of the murders of the agents, and eventually sentenced to two consecutive terms of life imprisonment. Upon appeal, his convictions were affirmed with the reviewing court finding that although "[T]he evidence against [him] was primarily circumstantial," the "critical evidence" was the testimony of Evan Hodge, a Washington-based FBI firearms identification specialist. Agent Hodge had told the jury that a .223-caliber shell casing found in the open trunk of Coler's car, just a few feet from his body, was extracted from an AR-15 rifle attributed to Peltier. Since the pathologists who had conducted the autopsies on the victims opined that they had each been killed by a high-velocity, small-caliber weapon, such as an AR-15, fired at close and point blank range, Hodge's testimony was extremely damaging to Peltier, and was characterized by the prosecutor in his summation as "the most important piece of evidence in this case."

Long years after the trial Peltier obtained, through the Freedom of Information Act (FOIA), a number of documents relating to the FBI's ballistics examination. On October 2, 1975, a teletype from Hodge to the FBI resident agency at Rapid City, South Dakota, the field officer in charge of the overall investigation, stated that a comparison between the .223 casings found at the shootout scene, referred to in FBIese as RESMURS, and Peltier's AR-15, had revealed that the weapon contained "a different firing pin than that in [the] rifle used at [the] RESMURS scene." On the strength of this report an appellate court last April ordered the Fargo judge to conduct a hearing on "the meaning of the October 2, 1975, teletype and its relation to the ballistics evidence introduced at Peltier's trial."

This hearing, at which I, along with John Privitera, Lewis Gurwitz, and Bruce Ellison, represented Peltier, took place in Bismarck, North Dakota on October 1 to October 3, 1984. Hodge, the only witness produced by the government, testified that by the time of the teletype of October 2, he had only been able to examine seven of the 136 or so .223 RESMURS casings submitted to him for comparison. In fact, he hadn't gotten around to looking at the key casing, which he had received on July 24, 1975, until late December or early January of 1976. However, he freely admitted that he was constantly being importuned by Rapid City to test every .223 casing forwarded to him against any AR-15 associated with the incident of June 26, and that any found near the bodies of the agents should have been examined on a priority basis, given the pathologists' opinion as to the cause of their death. His failure to do so promptly, he explained, was due to a number of factors — the large volume of work associated with the RESMURS investigation, his necessary absences from Washington in connection with other FBI business, and the fact that only he and one assistant were available for firearms identification purposes.

While Hodge was on the stand, we were given an opportunity, for the first time, to look at the handwritten notes of his RESMURS work. In doing so, we noticed that his key report — the one stating that the extractor marks on the .223 casing matched Peltier's AR-15 — contained what looked like a far different handwriting than that of either Hodge or his assistant. Accordingly, just before the hearing's end, I asked him whether a third person had worked on the RESMURS ballistics, and he replied that none had. He also insisted that the writing on the report in question was that of his assistant.

We then sought permission to have all of Hodge's notes examined by a handwriting expert. Despite strenuous objections by government counsel, who claimed that this request was "ridiculous," our motion was granted. The original notes were to be examined by an expert selected by us at the FBI Laboratory in Washington, D.C., in the presence of a representative of the government, and the results made part of the hearing record.

An hour after the hearing ended, we were suddenly asked to return to the courtroom. At that time the government, claiming that it had "stubbed its toe," recalled Agent Hodge, who testified that after leaving the stand, he had shown the report in question to his assistant who, unknown to us, had been brought to Bismarck and had been informed by him that the handwriting was not his. Hodge further said that he did not know the identity of the person who had written the document.

The judge, visibly affected by these disclosures, then ordered the government to turn over to the defense counsel copies of all of the RESMURS ballistics notes. He also directed that it attempt to determine just who had written the report at issue Finally, he adjourned the hearing, pending whatever additional evidence developed from the new turn of events. The FBI then forwarded copies of the ballistics notes to us, as well as the name of William Albrecht, Jr., the laboratory trainee who wrote the key report about the matching of the crucial .223 casing and the AR-15. It also disclosed that there were several other such trainees who had assisted Hodge.

On January 7, 1985, Albrecht's deposition was taken in Washington, D.C. He testified that Hodge had been "ecstatic" and "even hugged me" when he said that he had written the key report about the matching of the .223 casing and Peltier's weapon. He also stated that a fourth agent, one Reedman, had also been involved in the RESMURS investigation. It was his opinion that the deaths of two FBI agents would have "high priority" in the firearms unit, and would be "of personal interest since it is a fellow agent."

In the light of these developments we asked Judge Benson to open the hearing so that Agents Tardowski and Reedman could be examined by us. He declined to do so, and directed all parties to submit their final briefs. On May 22, 1985, he refused to grant Peltier a new trial [holding that no "constitutional error" had been shown], and the case will soon be returned to the appellate court for review.

On June 25, 1984, three months before the Bismarck hearing, four Soviet Nobel Prize winners, physicists Pavel A. Cherenkov, Nikolai G. Basov, Aleksandr M. Prokhorov, and mathematical economist Leonid V. Kantorovich, signed an appeal to President Reagan on Peltier's behalf. In it they cited his case as "a typical example of politically motivated persecution of Americans who are fighting for human rights...." Putting aside their rhetoric, the laureates, on the face of the record in Peltier's prosecution, shared the appellate court's expressed concern with "the truth and accuracy of Hodge's testimony." If anything, the hearing, with its startling conclusion, raised the specter of a tragic miscarriage of American justice. ■

In June 1989, the Supreme Court of Canada refused to reopen Peltier's 13-year-old extradition case: *United States of America v. Peltier*, [1989] S.C.C.A. No. 207 (QL). In the applicant's memorandum of argument to the Supreme Court of Canada, Peltier's lawyers documented the inadequacy of the evidence at the extradition hearing and asserted the complicity of agents of the American government in knowingly obtaining and presenting false material. They argued that the extradition judge lacked jurisdiction because of the fraud, that leave to appeal should be granted and that, on appeal, the extradition order should be quashed.

Efforts to secure the release of Leonard Peltier continue. In 1993, the U.S. Eighth Circuit Court of Appeal again turned down an appeal on behalf of Peltier. Fifty-five Canadian Parliamentarians intervened as *amicus curiae* in the U.S. case in which former U.S. Attorney-General Ramsay Clark presented the litany of legal errors and prosecutorial misconduct to the court. The main arguments were all dismissed, and the court refused to consider the wrongful extradition as part of a pattern of prosecutorial misconduct. Peltier has now been in prison for 30 years, serving two life-term sentences for the murder of two FBI agents. The Leonard Peltier Defense Committee continues the Canadian campaign.

In a speech made only a few months before his death in 1995, Kunstler compared the fabrication of evidence and dirty tricks in Peltier's case to the miscarriage of justice in the case of the Birmingham Six (portrayed in the movie *In the Name of the Father*): William Kunstler, "Remarks on the Leonard Peltier Case" (1995) 20 Am. Indian L. Rev. 281. Kunstler described both the ongoing campaign and his lack of hope that Peltier, "a political prisoner in a land that says we have no political prisoners" (at 282), would ever be released. For a tribute to Kunstler's activism, see: Randall Coyne, "Defending the Despised: William Moses Kunstler" (1995) Am. Indian L. Rev. 257.

For a thorough study of the background to the case and the context of what Dee Brown (the author of *Bury My Heart at Wounded Knee*) calls "the U.S. government's renewed assault upon American Indians that began in the 1970's", see: Peter Matthiessen, *In the Spirit of Crazy Horse* (New York: Viking, 1983). Although the book was first published in 1983, it was effectively suppressed, and all subsequent editions were blocked for eight years by libel suits filed in three states. Among those who filed suit were South Dakota Governor William Janklow and FBI Special Agent David Price. Although the legal proceedings were ultimately unsuccessful (probably in part because of the reputation of the author and the publisher), they cost Matthiessen and Viking substantial sums. What is clear from the case is that the cost and harassment of extensive litigation can effectively suppress the expression of ideas critical of powerful government officials and institutions. For a summary of that litigation, see Martin Garbus, "Afterword" in Peter Matthiessen, *In the Spirit of Crazy Horse* (New York: Penguin, 1992) at 593. The film, *Incident at Oglala: The Leonard Peltier Story* (1992) provocatively depicts the legal case and prompts many questions about the handling of the case and the differential enforcement of the law.

Also, Mary Crow Dog writes movingly about her life, the origins of AIM, her work within the movement and, specifically, the 71-day siege of Wounded Knee in 1973: Mary Crow Dog, *Lakota Woman* (New York: Harper, 1990). The book illuminates the long struggle taking place.

Anna Mae Aquash, a Micmac woman from Canada who was to have been a witness for the defence in the Butler-Robideau trial, was killed in February 1976. Her frozen body was found in February 1976. In a macabre move, FBI agents ordered her hands cut off and sent to Washington for identification. The doctor who conducted the first autopsy ruled that she had died of exposure. A second autopsy showed that she had been shot in the back of the head with a .38 calibre gun. The doctor claimed to have "inadvertently overlooked" the bullet wound! The case was buried. See Johanna Brandt, *The Life and Death of Anna Mae Aquash* (Toronto: J. Lorimer, 1978). In February 2004, Arlo Looking Cloud was convicted of her murder. Another former member of the American Indian Movement (AIM), John Graham, was also indicted and extradited from Canada to the United States to face trial for her murder: *Graham v. United States of America*, [2007] S.C.C.A. No. 467.

Ipperwash

In the summer of 1995, Chippewa protesters at Ipperwash Provincial Park protested the desecration of burial grounds and demanded the return of adjacent land that had been arbitrarily appropriated for use as a military training facility and base in 1942. For further background, see discussion in Abell & Sheehy, *Cases, Context, Critique*, **Colonization and the Imposition of Criminal Law**, and **Policing**. Anthony (Dudley) George was killed in that protest, and OPP Sergeant Kenneth Deane was convicted of criminal negligence causing death: Michael Grange, "Officer guilty in Ipperwash killing: Judge rejects testimony about events leading up to shooting of native protester" *The [Toronto] Globe and Mail* (29 April 1997) A1. However, Deane was given a conditional sentence of two years less a day to be served in the community. The sentence required Deane to perform 180 hours of community service and prohibited him from the use of firearms for two years less a day (rather than the 10-year prohibition sought by the Crown). Dudley George's sister, Carolyn, is quoted as saying that the sentence means "it's OK to go out and kill a native": Pearce Bannon, "Officer who shot native can walk free, judge rules" *The Ottawa Citizen* (4 July 1997) A3. Deane unsuccessfully appealed the conviction: *R. v. Deane* (2000), 129 O.A.C. 335 (C.A.), aff'd [2001] 1 S.C.R. 279.

The George family commenced a lawsuit against then Ontario Premier, Mike Harris, several former cabinet ministers (including Charles Harnick, Robert Runciman), and others: *George v. Harris*, Court File No. 96-CU-99569 (April 1996) (Ont. Ct. J. (Gen. Div.)). Demands for a public inquiry to investigate the level of participation of the provincial government in the policing decisions taken at Ipperwash were made with considerable support in the wake of Deane's conviction: Jim

Coyle, "Ipperwash whitewash" *The Ottawa Citizen* (2 April 1997) A10; Editorial, "Investigate Ipperwash" *The Ottawa Citizen* (30 April 1997) A12. One of the groups that called for a full public inquiry is Amnesty International, whose Annual Report for 1996 referred to Dudley George's shooting as having taken place "in circumstances suggesting he may have been extrajudicially executed." The Conservative government delayed and obstructed requests for access to information: Ann Rees, "Tories used bogus delay tactics" *The [Toronto] Star* (21 September 2003) A1. Public Safety Minister Robert Runciman succeeded in having the wrongful death lawsuit delayed until after the October 2 provincial election: Harold Levy & Peter Edwards, "Ipperwash trial delay approved" *The [Toronto] Star* (19 September 2003) A23. In October 2003, the family of Dudley George accepted a settlement of $100,000 in anticipation of a new Liberal government and a promised judicial inquiry: Joseph Brean, "Dudley George's family agrees to settlement" *The Ottawa Citizen* (3 October 2003) A7.

In November 2003, Justice Linden was appointed to lead a public inquiry into events surrounding the death of Dudley George, an unarmed peaceful protester, at Ipperwash: Sidney B. Linden, Cmmr., *Report of the Ipperwash Inquiry* (Toronto: Queen's Printer, 2007). Commissioner Linden concluded that

> Ipperwash has always been controversial. Questions about the death of Dudley George were raised almost immediately: How could an apparently peaceful occupation and protest turn violent? What was the urgency in taking action? What was the role of the Premier and other senior government officials? What was the role of the federal government? Was racism or cultural insensitivity a factor? These and other questions about Ipperwash have been answered in this report ...
>
> ... [at a cabinet meeting to discuss the provincial government's response to the occupation, the] former Attorney General [Charles Harnick] testified that he heard Premier Harris say "I want the [expletive] Indians out of the park". This is the same meeting at which former Deputy Solicitor General Todres testified that she heard former Minister of Natural Resources Hodgsosn say, "Get the [expletive] Indians out of my park." Both denied making these comments ... **I have found that the statements were made and that they were racist, whether intended or not.** [Emphasis added.]
>
> ... [B]oth the Attorney General Charles Harnick and Premier Harris misled the Legislature about the "dining room meeting" with the result that it took a public inquiry for the public to learn the details of this key event.

Linden also concluded that the manner in which the OPP Crowd Management Unit (CMU) and the Tactics and Rescue Unit (TRU) operated "increased the potential for violence" (*Report: Volume I* at 682) and was an "offensive not a defensive strategy" (*ibid.* at 682). Finally, the Inquiry found evidence of "cultural insensitivity and racism on the part of some of the OPP officers involved ... both before and after Dudley George's death" (*ibid.* at 683) and on the part of the community [who produced coffee mugs and t-shirts to commemorate the OPP actions]. The Inquiry concluded that the "cultural insensitivity and racism ... may have contributed to the lack of a timely and peaceful resolution of the occupation" and called on the federal government to resolve the long-standing neglect of the claims of the Kettle and Stony Point First Nation.

MORE DANGEROUS DESPERADOS

Those involved in demonstrations and protests are often charged with "mischief" (s. 430), "obstruction" (s. 129), and/or "causing a disturbance" (s. 175). A condition required for interim release and a term of sentence is that the accused refrain from such conduct in the future. Failure to do so may result in a "contempt" (s. 127) or "breach of probation" (s. 740) charge.

Military testing, armaments buildup, and nuclear technology have provoked considerable protest. While there are many groups active in the protest movement, the Greenham Common peace camp in Britain was one of the best known. For a discussion of the media representation of the protest activities, see Alison Young, *Femininity in Dissent* (London: Routledge, 1990).

There has been considerable activism in Canada. For an example, see the discussion of *Ashini*, above, under **Colour of Right: Mistake of Fact, Mistake of Law, or Affirmative Defence**. For another example, Ottawa police arrested more than 160 peace activists in 1989. They were charged for their sit-down blockade of entry into Lansdowne Park, the site of an arms technology bazaar, what then Liberal leader John Turner called a "shopping centre for human rights violators" and New Democrat MP Howard McCurdy described as a "military fleamarket". See Carey French, "160 protesters charged at arms technology show" *The [Toronto] Globe and Mail* (23 May 1989) A1. ARMX was the largest arms technology bazaar ever staged in Canada. Those charged were held in custody to await bail hearings if they refused to sign a document agreeing to stay away from the area. In another case, a British court acquitted four women charged with causing $3.1 million damage to a British Aerospace military jet on the basis that their actions were morally justified because they alleged the jet would be used by Indonesia against East Timorese rebels: Reuters, "Women acquitted of 'disarming' jet" *The [Toronto] Globe and Mail* (31 July 1996) A8.

Rights activists have also been charged with criminal offences and incarcerated for their protests. In 1988, a group of 20 disability rights activists in wheelchairs blocked escalators and elevators at the American Public Transit Association Convention and were convicted of mischief and sent to jail for three days: "20 handicapped jailed for protest" *The [Toronto] Globe and Mail* (4 October 1988) A4. In 1997, five animal rights activists were convicted with break and enter, theft, and mischief in connection with their alleged role in freeing more than 1,500 minks from a fur farm near Chatham, Ontario. The accused, Gary Yourofsky, argued that his actions were justified, that he freed the animals in the interests of truth and justice and freedom for animals and that, ultimately, the struggle for justice would triumph, just as it did in the struggles of Gandhi and the slave abolitionists: *R. v. Yourofsky*, [1999] O.J. No. 1901 (Sup. Ct. J.) (QL). In another example, anti-poverty activists were charged with participation in a riot and counselling to assault police in Toronto for a protest at Queen's Park at which about 1,500 people participated. The charges against John Clarke, a leader of the Ontario Coalition Against Poverty (OCAP), were finally stayed by the judge after more than three years of legal proceedings, based on unconstitutional delay: *R. v. Clarke* (No. 2), [2003] O.J. No. 4706 (Sup. Ct. J.) (QL).

Another huge area of continuing protest involves environmental issues and attempts to resolve land claims. On Vancouver Island, the fight for Clayoquot Sound is perhaps one of the best known of those struggles. Clayoquot Sound encompasses one of the last intact stands of the great coastal temperate rainforests that once bordered North America from Alaska to northern California. The fight for the forest has been going on for over 14 years.

In April 1988, Friends of Clayoquot Sound announced that they were preparing to act to block the construction of a logging road into the wilderness area. In June, they held a blockade "picnic" in their boats. The logging company, Fletcher Challenge, was granted an *ex parte* injunction against anyone blockading the road or the work. A second strong injunction authorized the police to arrest anyone if they were identified by the company. See The Friends of Clayoquot Sound, "The Battle for Clayoquot Sound" *Canadian Dimension* (July/August 1989) 27:

> Soon, many people found themselves flying to Vancouver in handcuffs to appear before a judge, being denied any opportunity to speak, and having court dates set. As part of the conditions of bail, those charged could not go within three miles of Sulphur Pass. Some individuals who weren't even blockading were also arrested. Children watched as their mothers and fathers were flown away by police.
>
> The bail conditions meant that charter boat and whale-spotter tour-boat operators were out of business until the three-mile limit was lifted, since they couldn't get to the northern half of Clayoquot Sound without passing Sulphur Pass on inside waters. Some people were jailed for up to 45 days after returning to the site. The vice-president of the chamber of commerce and a local doctor were fined and thrown in jail, the doctor for 30 days.
>
> One young man who had hung a hammock 80 feet up in two trees above the blast site for three days was shot at with an air gun. He was finally chopped down in the middle of the night by a gang of loggers, but, by some miracle, the trees in which he was suspended fell to the side, hanging him up in a nearby cedar, preventing his injury or death. No charges have been laid, even though photographs and video tapes had been taken of the loggers involved.†

Since then, hundreds of people have been arrested.

In April 1993, the B.C. government announced that logging of the old-growth timber would be permitted in over 70 per cent of the area. MacMillan Bloedel obtained an injunction, targeting the public at large, in a private civil lawsuit. The Sierra Legal Defence Fund challenged the

† Reproduced by permission of Friends of Clayoquot Sound and Canadian Dimension.

breadth of the injunction, but the injunction was upheld at the B.C. Court of Appeal: *MacMillan Bloedel v. Simpson* (1993), 106 D.L.R. (4th) 556, aff'd (1994), 96 B.C.L.R. (2d) 201 (C.A.), aff'd [1996] 2 S.C.R. 1048. Subsequently, many protesters were arrested and charged with "contempt of court". See *Sierra Legal Defence Fund Newsletter* (November 1993) 1.

On August 9, 1993 police charged more than 250 protesters. Deborah Wilson, "Mass arrests in logging protest: RCMP round up more than 250 men, women and children in B.C." *The [Toronto] Globe and Mail* (10 August 1993) A1, reported that it was the largest mass arrest in B.C. history. Fifty children were taken into custody, although the RCMP said that none would be charged. Those adults who refused to promise to appear in court or to obey an injunction against blockades were imprisoned. All were charged with "contempt of court" (for defying the injunction).

In another environmental case, an environmentalist protesting the Alberta-Pacific pulp mill was charged with causing a public disturbance for giving several Alberta politicians a middle-finger salute and yelling "f— you." He was put on probation for 18 months. See Stephen Bindman, "Environmentalist wants right to express himself in public" *The Ottawa Citizen* (13 October 1993) A4. See also *R. v. Lawrence* (1993), 9 Alta L.R. (3d) 347 (C.A.), leave refused [1993] 3 S.C.R. vii.

Some critics have suggested that environmental activists do not pay sufficient attention to the preponderance of problems facing racialized communities, given that racialization is the most significant predictor of the location of pollution sources. For a documentation of some of those issues and protest actions, see: Robert D. Bullard, ed., *Unequal Protection: Environmental Justice and Communities of Color* (San Francisco: Sierra Club, 1994). Can you suggest Canadian examples that support this analysis? In what ways is the Canadian state implicated in those instances, for example, through the enforcement of criminal law?

Groups recognize that protest strategies can backfire in terms of public support. That is, they can generate public hostility as well as legal resistance. As that happens, government may toughen its stance, as B.C.'s [then] NDP government threatened to do in the face of numerous blockades throughout B.C. For a discussion of the extensive media campaigns waged on behalf of the industry, see Joyce Nelson, "Pulp and Propaganda" *Canadian Forum* (July/August 1994) 14.

For a brief historical review of direct action, including road and rail blockades, by First Nations in British Columbia, see Nicholas Blomley, "First Nations blockades in British Columbia" *Canadian Law & Society Association Bulletin* (Fall 1995) 4. The irony is that direct action becomes necessary through the inaction of the government and the unwillingness to negotiate. While direct action then sometimes generates a hostile and overbearing response from the state (for example, the use of police and military powers, criminal charges), the state continues to refuse to negotiate legitimate and longstanding grievances and, indeed, expends huge resources to avoid any settlement. For example, when the government intervened in a 31-day standoff at Gustafsen Lake, British Columbia, in the summer of 1995, it did not intervene to mandate some arbitration or resolution of the dispute. Instead, the government intervened to prevent any resolution and to escalate the confrontation using criminal law powers, which led to 60 charges (ranging from attempted murder to mischief causing danger to life and mischief to property) against 18 people. Prior to the escalated intervention, Aboriginal RCMP constables had been negotiating with the Sundancers and were attempting to resolve the dispute. Instead, the RCMP sent in 400 police officers (complete with helicopters, armoured personnel carriers, and thousands of shots fired) and mounted what has been described as "the biggest RCMP operation in B.C. history and manipulated the media to make camp occupants look like terrorists": Kim Pemberton, "Mixed verdicts in B.C. over Gustafsen Lake" *The Ottawa Citizen* (21 May 1997) A3; Kim Pemberton, "Trial itself was a long ordeal, for everyone" *The Ottawa Citizen* (21 May 1997) A3. After a 10-month jury trial (one of the longest and most expensive trials in B.C. history), many of the charges were dismissed: Robert Matas, "Gustafsen rebels guilty of trespassing: Leader acquitted of attempted murder" *The [Toronto] Globe and Mail* (21 May 1997) A1. Bruce Clark, a lawyer acting for the accused, was charged and convicted of contempt of court: *R. v. Clark (B.)* (1997), 88 B.C.A.C. 216 (C.A.). The RCMP's costs were estimated at $5.5 million, according to Pemberton, and the trial was estimated to cost another $5 million, according to Matas.

At the other end of the country, Katie Rich, the former chief of Davis Inlet, was jailed for contempt of court when she told a Newfoundland judge he was not welcome in Davis Inlet because of the way the Canadian justice system unfairly penalized Aboriginal people: *Newfoundland (A.G.) v. Rich* (1995), 133 Nfld. & P.E.I.R. 1 (Nfld. C.A.), discussed in Abell & Sheehy, *Cases, Context, Critique*, **Powers of Prosecution**. She has been an activist on many important issues facing her community, including opposing the low-level military flights over the Innu (which she describes as genocide), raising the profile of pressing social issues, such as poverty and substance abuse, pressuring for promises to be kept about relocation, and demanding consultation about economic and resource development in the area. In 1995, she was awarded the "Woman of Courage" annual award from the National Action Committee on the Status of Women. As she said, "I'm just a regular Innu person.... I'm just trying to do the job and fight for what we believe in": David Pugliese, "Innu leader from Davis Inlet gets Woman of Courage award" *The Ottawa Citizen* (12 June 1995) A4.

Recently, Chief Donny Morris and five band council members of Kitchenuhmaykoosib Inninuwug (KI) First Nation were sentenced to jail for six months for contempt of court for violating an order to allow a mining company (Platinex) entry onto their land to do exploratory drilling on treaty land: Rachel Ariss, "Are the KI Six outlaws or prisoners of conscience?" *The [Toronto] Globe and Mail* (20 March 2008) A17; Murray Campbell, "Six jailed leaders in land dispute deserve better" *The [Toronto] Globe and Mail* (12 April 2008) A11. In February, Bob Lovelace, a member of the Ardoch Algonquin First Nation, was sentenced to six months in jail for contempt for protesting mining exploration on that community's traditional lands: *ibid*. The cases highlight tensions between First Nations claims, environmental concerns and mining legislation that allow broad intrusions onto Crown, First Nations' and private land at a time when governments continue to neglect to fulfill treaty obligations.

Can you think of other examples of political actions and acts of conscience that have been characterized as crimes? Recall the charges laid in Ontario against student and labour protesters (for example, "intimidating the legislature") in February 1996 and the use of state powers at Kanehsatake in 1990, and in Québec city in April 2001, as discussed in Abell & Sheehy, *Cases, Context, Critique*, **Law and Order**.

Recall the excerpt from Radzinowicz discussing the different treatment of political "criminals", and then consider the response of the legal system to some of the cases outlined. What impact does the defendant's political motivation appear to have on sentence? For a particularly egregious example, consider the Australian case of *Neal v. R.*, [1982] 149 C.L.R. (High Ct.). In that case, an Aboriginal activist who was convicted of unlawful entry onto property and assault for swearing and spitting at a store manager, who he told to leave the reserve, was sentenced initially to two months with hard labour. The Court of Criminal Appeal increased the sentence to six months with hard labour. In allowing the appeal and substituting a sentence of a fine of $130, the High Court acknowledged the pervasive racism and commented on the deep sense of grievance felt by Neal and other members of the community and on the right to political activism and, specifically, emphasized the inappropriateness of considering the advocacy of change to be an aggravating factor in sentencing (at 316–17):

> That Mr. Neal was an "agitator" or stirrer in the magistrate's view obviously contributed to the severe penalty. If he is an agitator, he is in good company. Many of the great religious and political figures of history have been agitators, and human progress owes much to the efforts of these and the many who are unknown. As Wilde aptly pointed out in *The Soul of Man under Socialism*, "Agitators are a set of interfering, meddling people, who come down to some perfectly contented class of the community and sow the seeds of discontent amongst them. That is the reason why agitators are so absolutely necessary. Without them, in our incomplete state, there would be no advance towards civilisation." Mr. Neal is entitled to be an agitator.

19

Entrapment

The doctrine of entrapment provides a remedy (stay of proceedings) where the conduct of police or their agents has been found to amount to an abuse of process. Entrapment was sketched out in several early Supreme Court decisions, *R. v. Amato*, [1982] 2 S.C.R. 418, and *R. v. Jewitt*, [1985] 2 S.C.R. 128, but it was not until *R. v. Mack*, [1988] 2 S.C.R. 903, reproduced below, that its underlying rationale and legal requirements were laid out more definitively by the Court. The materials that follow raise issues about the relationship between police and informers, the propriety of "random virtue testing" of citizens, the use of rewards for informers, the relevance of the informer's criminal activity, and the doctrine of informer privilege. How should the law of entrapment respond to these issues?

A. THE POLICE/INFORMER RELATIONSHIP

George Wool, a retired staff sergeant with the RCMP, draws on his own knowledge and experience of police practice to challenge the lack of judicial intervention in scrutinizing the police-informer relationship. As he points out, the judiciary has repeatedly protected informants. It is only relatively recently that police practices in this area, including illegal activities by police and agents, have come to light. See, for example, the *Commission of Inquiry Concerning Certain Activities of the Royal Canadian Mounted Police* (Canada: August 1981, Commr. Mr. Justice D.C. McDonald); and the *Keable Commission* (Québec: 1977), established under the *Public Inquiry Commissions Act*, R.S.Q., 1977, c. C-37, both of which investigated the recruitment of informers by illegal or reprehensible means.

Police Informants in Canada: Law and Reality†

INTRODUCTION

Despite advances in crime detection and control, Canadian governments and courts continue to defend the police-informer privilege rule that was upheld in *Bisaillon v. Keable et al. per* Beetz J. Conceptually, that rule has not changed since *Marks v. Beyfus* where it was founded in public prosecutions "on grounds of public policy." Remarkably, many Canadian jurists dogmatically repeat the rule without any apparent understanding of contemporary underlying issues. This paper proposes to critically examine the law surrounding police informers. It will be argued that the law in Canada has not kept up to informant and policing realities.

Public inquiries and some reported case law are now exposing incidents of police misconduct. The judicial response has often been cosmetic. Stays of proceeding have been ordered, but in most cases judges refuse to investigate the *modus operandi* used to ensnare the alleged criminal. *R. v. Wray*[ ] illustrates the Canadian judicial attitude, where the Supreme Court of Canada, *per* Martland J., enunciated the standard that it was not the concern of the court how or by what means evidence was obtained. Even the *Charter of Rights and Freedoms* is not *prima faci* [*sic*] violated by police methodology. To date, courts responsible for protecting individual rights and freedoms have not clearly addressed themselves to police informant tactics such as "calculated entrapment," "reverse stings," and "offers of immunity from prosecution."

It is the author's opinion that judicial reluctance to face these issues has led the law concerning police informers into a state of confusion and uncertainty. Police officers are often left to determine a course of action without any guidance or control. Politicians and members of the public seemingly pressure the police with demands for investigative results to crime while other segments of society abhor the methodology used, *i.e.*, informants, to obtain those results.

The courts have shown a reluctance to investigating or discussing the issues. Who is a police informant? Is it hypocritical for a court to condone and to punish illegality arising out of the same set of facts? What controls do the police have over informants? Do informants have a right to protection? These are just some of the informant issues that currently vex the law. This paper offers a realistic view of the criminal justice system and shows how the law and courts are failing to cope with what is happening in it. Hopefully the discussion will spark some judicial and legislative re-thinking.

HISTORICAL JUSTIFICATION FOR THE USE OF INFORMERS

. . . .

In *Marks v. Beyfus* the rule regarding informants was formulated as it now stands to hold the proposition that the Crown, in a public prosecution, is entitled to refuse disclosure of the informant's identity and additionally the nature of the information received, except if the disclosure is necessary to prove the accused innocent. The circumstances were that Beyfus, and others, conspired to prosecute Marks, who was later acquitted of fraud. Marks brought a civil action against Beyfus and called the Director of Public Prosecutions as a witness to determine the identity of those who had given information to the Director. The Director refused on the grounds that this was a public prosecution based on a public object and as matter of "public policy" ought not to be disclosed. ...

. . . .

CONTEMPORARY SCOPE OF INFORMANT PROTECTION

The Law in Canada

The judiciary has repeatedly protected informants. In the 1960's and 70's, Canadian courts were passive towards notions of informant illegality, entrapment, or the strategies of criminal detection by police. Theoretically, trial judges were to be impartial and seen as passive arbitrators who only responded to the evidence before them. It was easy for the judiciary to state the rule in *Marks v. Beyfus*. If the defendant suggested identity was necessary, the point was often dismissed on the basis that identity was:

† George Wool, "Police Informants in Canada: Law and Reality" (1985–86) 50 Sask. L. Rev. 249 at 249–56, 261–69. [Notes omitted.]

i) irrelevant;
ii) illegally obtained evidence was [admissible]; and
iii) judicial investigation was confined to the trial process and had nothing to do with substantive police investigations. That thinking was clearly stated in *The Queen v. Wray* by Martland J. when he wrote:

> The test to be applied in considering whether evidence is admissible is whether it is relevant to the matters in issue. If it is, it is admissible and *the Court is not concerned with how the evidence was obtained.* [Emphasis added.]

Martland J. was repeating a long line of Anglo-Canadian jurisprudence. Courts in Canada were often insensitive to defendants who raised issues of informant conduct or identity. Stated bluntly, courts had no interest in controlling police or informant behaviour. Conceptually, this broadened the protection for police informers from what it was held to be in *Richardson*. Despite the burden of the Crown having to prove its case beyond a reasonable doubt, the defendant was still faced with the threshold of first having to convince the court that the identity of the informant was relevant to the issue and secondly, that such disclosure would prove the defendant's innocence. If the judges were not prepared to investigate the defendant's innocence, who was? The short answer, in practical terms, is nobody. The cases support that conclusion.

. . . .

In *R. v. Johnston*, Holland J. in the Ontario High Court[ ] rejected the accused's application for mandamus. At issue was the accused's assertion that drugs had been planted in his apartment. To defend himself at the preliminary hearing the accused wanted to know the identity of the police informant. Holland J. held "the rule (police-informant privilege) as stated is one which has its application at the trial and *not at a preliminary inquiry* ..." [emphasis added]. He continued:

> ... [I]f I were to accede to the request of the applicant here, I believe that this would largely do away with the rule of public policy expressed by Lord Esher. I do not consider that disclosure of the name of the informant here is necessary or right in order to show the prisoner's innocence. The same argument as advanced here could be advanced in almost any criminal proceeding in which the prosecution has obtained evidence from informants.

Were drugs "planted" in the apartment? The question was not answered and it is difficult to reconcile this reasoning with the exception to the rule that "an innocent man is not to be condemned when his innocence can be proved." If Johnston could not discover the identity of the informant, how could he prove his innocence?

Johnston illustrates a strict application of the rule and the practical difficulty of an accused asserting innocence. Here the presiding judge implicitly places an onus on the accused to prove innocence. That, in reality, would be a [formidable] task. What if a paid police informant had in fact "planted" drugs for a reward from the police?

The courts in *Blain* and *Johnston* failed to investigate the police-informant relationship; the allegation was not seen as an issue. But in fairness to those courts, the concept of paid informers was then not well developed or even known to the judiciary until *Palmer and Palmer* when the Supreme Court of Canada endorsed the police practice of paying informers. In 1981 the McDonald Commission which was investigating police-informer practises found incidents of apparent illegality. In a number of detailed situations McDonald J. concluded that either the police or the informant working with them "may have been guilty of conspiracy to traffic" in drugs. But the conclusions of McDonald J. raised profound disagreement. In response, the Federal Government said that:

> ...with one possible exception, the Commission did not report any facts or evidence which would have justified the institution by the Attorney General of Canada of criminal prosecutions against any particular individual.

To [understand] this disparity between McDonald J. and the Federal Government one has to turn to *R. v. Kirzner* where the Supreme Court left open the question of whether entrapment by an informant, if established, should be a defense. As McDonald J. noted, the R.C.M.P. interpreted *Kirzner* to mean that entrapment *per se* was permissible and that there is language in *Kirzner* which specifically approves of informers as "an inevitable requirement for detection of consensual crimes and of discouraging their commission." In *Kirzner* the accused was an R.C.M.P. paid informant who had, from time to time, been used to buy drugs for information purposes. The entrapment and the appeal was disallowed by the Supreme Court of Canada. The dicta of Laskin C.J. is instructive in terms of giving scope to the role of the court and to informant practices:

> **1. Role of the Court**
>
> Courts are concerned with the proper interpretation and application of the criminal law invoked against accused persons, with the propriety of the conduct of the prosecution and of the defence, especially in the light of the fundamental principle of the presumption of innocence and, in this connection, with the behaviour of the police authorities in respect of their dealings with an arrested or about-to-be arrested accused.... There is, of course, a balance to be struck [ ] giving reasonable latitude to the police in the employment of stratagems to control the spread of crime, especially in the case of the illegal drug traffic.
>
> **2. Informant Practices**
>
> The police, if they are to respond to the public disapprobation of such offenses as reflected in existing law, *must take some initiatives*. They may, for example, use a spy, either a policeman or another person, to obtain information about a consensual offence by infiltration; they *may make arrangements with informers who may be parties to offences* on which they report to the police to enable the other parties to be apprehended; or the police may use decoys [ ] to enable the other parties to be apprehended; or the police may use decoys or themselves act under cover to provide others with the opportunity to commit a consensual offence or to *encourage its commission*. Going one step further, the police may use members of their force or *other persons to instigate the commission of an offence, planning and designing it ab initio to ensnare others*. [Emphasis added.]

If the R.C.M.P., as McDonald J. discovered, gave Laskin C.J.'s dicta a broad interpretation, then it stands to reason that police-informant strategies quickly developed, McDonald J. noted:

> ... [I]t became clear that the informants were not always under control of their handler ... it is at least arguable that the informant (in a particular drug trafficking case) was in effect given a license to commit crimes while in the employ of the R.C.M.P.

How could that situation develop? Another look at *Kirzner* is helpful. The Court failed to limit or explain what it meant by police "initiatives," "arrangements with informers," or "to instigate." As did McDonald J., academics and judges[ ] might interpret such language to be used in the context of organized crime or sophisticated networks of drug trafficking. But Kirzner was not a sophisticated criminal. In fact he was a drug addict and obviously susceptible to pressures and coercions associated with people caught by drug addiction. He was operating at the lower end of the victim scale in the hierarchy of a drug world. Unfortunately, Laskin C.J. gave no recognition to that fact. The result was that the R.C.M.P., without any *mala fide* intent, concluded that the means used to suppress drug trafficking *per se* justified the end result. Notably Laskin C.J. did not limit his dicta to drug trafficking. The use of the phrase "consensual crime" theoretically covers many facets of crime ranging from conspiracies such as trafficking in arms for an unlawful purpose, to offences of a moral nature. Again, that kind of broad conceptualization leaves it open for the police to interpret what they perceive to be a "consensual crime" at a particular time and place, such as the police establishing a second-hand store and using informers, as agents provocateur, to induce youths and petty criminals to deliver stolen property to the store. In *Lemieux v. R.* an informer was working under police instructions. The informer induced the accused to break into a home using a key the police had obtained through the home-owner's cooperation. Judson J. said:

> Had Lemieux in fact committed the offence with which he was charged, the circumstance that he had done the forbidden act at the solicitation of an agent provocateur *would have been irrelevant to the question of his guilt or innocence.* [Emphasis added.]

It was open for a court to acquit Lemieux on a finding that there was no *actus reus*. The home-owner had given consent. What is instructive is the judicial attitude taken in this case. The solicitation by the informant of the accused was not reprehensible in the eyes of the court. Thus it may be difficult to draw a line[ ] with any certainty as to when a court will be moved to strike down police instigation or entrapment by informers. It is not intended in this paper to thoroughly deal with entrapment except to point out the close connection between the police-informer privilege rule and entrapment. Often, both arise from the same facts. However if the rule is advanced by the court, the prosecutor, the police, or the witness, there is a danger that even before the merits of the defendant's claim [are] considered, a court acting under the rubric of protecting the informant will decide, as in *Johnston*, that the informant's identity and communications will not be disclosed. Another judicial attitude is that what the informant did or said is not relevant to the accused's conduct. In terms of defending an accused and attempting to discover details of what an informant did, timing and raising the defense either as entrapment or attempting to identify the informer to prove innocence under the *Richardson* exception may be crucial. It is important to stress that in the late 1970's judicial attitude was clearly weighted in favour of non-disclosure.

The cases illustrate how courts avoided the informer-privilege rule by refusing defense counsel to even raise questions on the issue of identity or the transaction. In *R. v. Auger*, the Provincial Court Judge disallowed any questioning on the relevance of entrapment as a defense to drug trafficking. At the Court of Appeal the issue was shifted to an error in law by the judge in the exercise of jurisdiction. It was held that what the judge did was not enough to lose jurisdiction on the ground of procedural defect. Despite that reasoning, no judicial effort was made to investigate the defense complaint.

. . . .

By the late 1970's anyone who communicated with the police was *prima facie* an informant. W. and N. Kelly, in their book *Policing in Canada*, advance this proposition. In *Reference Re: Legislative Privilege*, Lacourciere J.A. distinguished police informants and concluded that evidence going to the identity of informants in "criminal proceedings" should be *prima facie* excluded from "forensic investigation." Hence, raising a defense of entrapment or attempting to prove innocence became rather remote. Against the backdrop of judicial rigidity, two significant cases went to the Supreme Court. [Wool goes on to demonstrate how both cases, *Solicitor General of Canada et al. v. Royal Comm. of Inquiry into the confidentiality of Health Records in Ont. et al.* (1981), 23 C.R. (3d) 338 and *Bisaillon v. Keable et al.*, (1983), 2 D.L.R. (4th) 193 (SCC), strengthened the scope of informant protection.]

. . . .

Bisaillon v. Keable et al.

The Keable Commission was to investigate and report on allegations of police forces in Quebec committing illegalities [arising out of the 1970 FLQ crisis] that included the recruitment of informers by reprehensible means. During the inquiry the Commissioner identified a police informer. A police officer was called as a witness to confirm the Commissioner's suspicion about the identity of the informer. The officer refused disclosure and sought a writ of evocation on several grounds including that the Commissioner had exceeded his jurisdiction in requiring this disclosure. The police officer's application was dismissed by the Quebec Supreme Court as was an appeal to the Quebec Court of Appeal.

Supreme Court of Canada

The unanimous judgement of the court was delivered by Beetz J. (Laskin C.J.C., Ritchie, Dickson, Beetz, Estey, Chouinard and Lamar JJ.) In allowing the appeal, Beetz J. quoted Martland J. extensively, with approval, in the *Health Records Case*.

The police-informer privilege, as a rule, was put this way:

> The rule is subject to only one exception, imposed by the need to *demonstrate* the innocence of an accused person. There are no exceptions in proceedings other than criminal. Its application *does not* depend on the judge's discretion, as it is a legal rule of public order by which the judge is bound.... It should also be mentioned that its application is not subject to any formal requirement and, if no one raises it, the court must apply it of its own motion. [Emphasis added.]

Beetz J. followed *Marks v. Beyfus* where it was said that "if the Director of Public Prosecutions had been willing to answer the questions put to him the judge ought not to have allowed him to do so" and *Rogers v. Home Secretary*, where Simon L.J. said:

> It is true that the public interest which demands that the evidence be withheld has to be weighed against the public interest in the administration of justice that courts should have the fullest possible access to all relevant material, but once the former public interest is held to outweigh the latter, the evidence cannot in any circumstances be admitted. *It is not a privilege which may be waived by the Crown or by anyone else*. [Emphasis added.]

From that position, Beetz J. then turned to informer's consent, the scope of the police officer's duty and the distinction between the police-informer rule and Crown Privilege.

INFORMER'S CONSENT

The police-informer rule exists in the public interest. It is not given to the informer, and it does not depend on the informer's misconduct. The privilege is the Crown's based on an exchange of information "under an assurance of secrecy." The Crown cannot waive the informant's consent for disclosure because the rule is not in the "interests of police informers, but in fact protects each of them." Even the informant cannot waive the rule that protects him or her.

The argument had been that if the informer revealed his identity the rule would be waived. Wigmore said: "If the identity of the informer is admitted ... then there is no reason for pretended concealment of his identity." This was not the situation, according to Beetz J., before the *Keable Commission* and in any case Wigmore's approach was not viewed favourably because it "would mean weakening a rule which should remain firm." The Commissioner's attempt to have the police confirm the informer's identity was seen by Beetz J. as a contravention of the rule of secrecy.

POLICE OFFICER'S DUTY

The police-informer privilege imposes duties on police officers [as Beetz J. identified:]

> i) The duty not to disclose "an informer's identity in judicial proceedings." This is based on the public interest, "superior to that of the *administration of justice by the court.*" [Emphasis added.]
>
> ii) The duty to maintain confidentiality "outside of any judicial proceedings, when the administration of justice by the courts is not in issue."

Beetz J. admitted no precedent on this point, but by analogy reasoned that if a peace officer disclosed identities of informers to the media, "severe disciplinary action," liability for damages or even a charge of "obstructing justice under s. 127(2) of the *Criminal Code*" would be possible. This places a positive duty on a peace officer not to disclose an informer's identity.

Yet this reasoning regarding police duties towards informers lacks direction or guidance. While confidentiality is important, the controls and limits of informant conduct must also by considered. The assumption that police are comfortable with unlimited discretion or that they enjoy the responsibility of controlling informants is naive or idealistic. What Beetz J. said assumes informers will not commit offenses or will not be exposed, as in the *Kirzner* case. The problem remains then, "What does a police officer do about informer illegality?" At least with the Judges Rules regarding confessions, wiretaps, surreptitious entry, searches and arrest there is some judicial predictability which gives rise to police conformity in procedures and practises. Why should the law be silent about informers? Unfortunately Beetz J. does not give us any indication on [as to] what the limits should be on informer illegality or to what extent police should condone or cooperate in illegality under the rubric of a police duty to maintain confidentiality. In the writer's view the police duty to maintain confidentiality coupled with judicial reluctance to investigate[ ] creates uncertainty and a potential for abuse.

CROWN PRIVILEGE AND THE INFORMANT RULE

Beetz J. begins by saying the police informer rule regarding identity "has been confused with Crown Privilege." There are similarities but the differences are in application and procedure. Crown privilege has a procedure. The informant rules does [*sic*] not. Under Crown privilege documents are usually at issue and the Executive makes the initial decision to invoke it. This is done by affidavit or sworn statement and the judge then balances the interests and may even review the information in deciding disclosure. That procedure does not apply to the police informer rule. In this situation there is no executive or court decision or any balancing of public interests because the public interest is to keep informer information secret. Beetz J. then extends the rule to say "this interest will prevail over the need to ensure the highest possible standard of justice."

The common law made "a special system (for informants) with its own rules which differ from those applicable to Crown privilege." It seems remarkable that control of informers, with the dangers of entrapment, illegality, instigation and trickery is left to police discretion without at least some judicial direction. This gives the police a free hand to decide who is, or who is not, an informant and whatever transpires between the police and the informant is, in practical terms, not open to judicial discretion. In the writer's view this is an untenable situation which is deteriorating. The gap between the informer rule law and reality is growing. To make some sense of that situation requires a look at the realities.

THE REALITIES

In most cases police officers will preface their evidence with the phrase "as the result of confidential information received, I searched the accused, etc." Any effort to question or identify the source or substance of that information, as we have seen, will prove futile. Judges will not actively investigate what transpired between the informer and the police and judicially it is easy to mouth the rule, as noted above.

Do judges understand informer status, informer motivation and other underlying factors? In the writer's opinion, many do not. An explanation requires a look at what informers are, what they are doing and how the traditional justifications and arguments are breaking down.

Informants

The definition of a police informant is expansive. As illustrated in the *Health Records* case it includes those who may not even consider themselves to be informants. Kelly says: "Anyone who gives information to the police is a police informant." At first blush that doesn't make sense because a great deal of public and police communication is not premised on the citizen being an informant. But the *Health Records* case and *Bisaillon* indicate that it is for the police to decide who is, or is not, an informant. That being so, the police also decide the legality of the informer and their conduct, even before prosecutorial review. In reality no legal regulation requires police officers to report incidents of wrongdoing. The result can mean the manipulation of witnesses and evidence under the rubric of informant protection. From a sociological perspective, Skolnick notes that informants are permitted to commit offenses. McDonald J. found several incidents where R.C.M.P. members allowed informers to commit crimes, with no intention of charging the informer or exposing the situation. Thus, the line between offenders, informers and witnesses is blurred. Unfortunately, this can result in abuses which by and large are uncontrolled by judicial review.

Furthermore, there is a lack of judicial effort in correctly determining the nature and extent of the informant's relationship to the police. There are gradations of police informants. Finally important factors such as motivation and reliability of information are often overlooked by the courts.

Informer Motivation

What motivates informants has not been definitively researched. The police-informer rule has traditionally shielded any notion of testing the information or evidence that arises from informants through the police. The arguments are usually expressed this way:

i) Informers may be subject to reprisal if their identity were made known.
ii) The information will "dry up and the police would be hindered in their duty of preventing and detecting crime."

If the informant gives information for some altruistic or community-spirited reason, the two arguments are valid but both arguments are vulnerable to other factors. For instance, if the informant is paid or given some consideration the reprisal and "dry up" arguments start breaking down. What emerges is a bargain between the police and informant where the risks of reprisal and detection are weighed against cost benefits. The informant becomes a willing participant, but not because of purist thinking. The informant is treating the transaction as a business venture if the price is right. Thus the argument is made that money or other considerations[ ] motivate informants to provide information but such reasoning is not realistic when the gain of money outweighs other risks.

Until *Palmer and Palmer v. R.*, the notion of police money payments to people was not well known. There were occasional references to paid informers, as in *Kirzner* but there was no judicial analysis of how these payments were negotiated or administered.

In *Palmer and Palmer* several convictions arose out of a conspiracy to traffic in heroin. Following the trial, a material witness for the Crown, one Ford, alleged his evidence was untrue and among other things he said he was induced to give evidence on the promise of being paid $60,000. Ford was an admitted drug trafficker who participated in the conspiracy to the extent of handling and delivering heroin for the Palmers. The arrangement Ford had with the R.C.M.P. was for a payment of $60,000, to be made after the trial. In April of 1976 the trial concluded with convictions. In the following month, Ford was paid $25,000 by the R.C.M.P. in lieu of protection and relocation expenses that had been originally bargained for between Ford and the police.

The appeal to adduce fresh evidence was dismissed. McIntyre J. saw nothing wrong with the payment of $25,000. Since it was done openly by cheque it negated improper motives on the part of the police. The use of the words "services rendered" and "services" on the receipt had no sinister significance. The judgment goes on to say that "unfavourable inferences against the Crown by reason only of this expenditure of public funds" should not be made.

McIntyre J.'s reasoning is not convincing. The fact that the payment was made by cheque is not relevant to the issue of proper motive because the cheque and receipt were used simply to account for public funds; McIntyre's reasoning that this method of paying Ford negates improper motive is without force. McIntyre J. seems to have overlooked the obvious question: "How are informants who assist the police paid?"

It should be remembered that from a police perspective Ford's credibility was in doubt. Some indicia of payment was necessary to avoid the possibility of Ford claiming police corruption (the police record shows $25,000 paid but Ford claims receiving a lesser amount). McIntyre J. gave no indication of understanding that possibility. The arrangement to pay was made before the trial. Why was it necessary to change the initial arrangements? It suggests the police were prepared to negotiate and pay a large sum of money, not before, but after Ford gave his evidence. The inference is that if Ford had not given the evidence he did, then presumably the payment would have been withheld. In other words, if there was nothing secret about the payment, as relocation or protection expenses, why wasn't it paid before the trial? McIntyre J. did not investigate. He stated: "This figure would presumably have replaced all payments for maintenance, moving and relocation expenses...." This is a presumption and not a fact that McIntyre J. is referring to. What makes it even more suspect is the so-called receipt for $25,000 that had the words: "Payments in full for services rendered" crossed out and the words "Payment for services" written in. What services did Ford provide? These R.C.M.P. officers may not have been legally trained to draft contracts and settlements, but is it not strange that Ford received payment "for services" when the documentation should have reflected a settlement of $25,000 for relocation expenses[?] Again, there was no judicial investigation and the court proceeded on the assumption that the payment was for relocation. The receipt from Ford was not for relocation. With the ambiguous wording on the cheque, an argument could be made that the "services" referred to Ford's giving evidence against Palmer. One might also query why the [arrangement] to pay $60,000 and an actual payment of $25,000 after the trial was kept secret from Crown counsel. It was only because of Ford's complaint that he had not received the balance ($35,000) that the matter came to the attention of the Crown. Surely, all these alternative interpretations should have prompted judicial suspicion and moved the court to explore what motivated Ford to change a proper and understandable arrangement — living and relocation expenses — to a lump sum payment of $25,000. Why would the police even entertain that kind of negotiation one month before the trial? Who was controlling the situation — the police or Ford? It was obviously Ford and that fact opens up all kinds of unanswered questions.

Methods of recruiting, handling, negotiating and payments to informers were not well known to judges at the time of *Palmer*. It wasn't until the *McDonald Commission* that many of these underlying factors about police relationships with informers came to light. When some of these practices were uncovered, it became evident that informer motivations were often intertwined with payments or other important considerations such as being given permission to traffic drugs, charges being withdrawn, etc. In *Palmer* there was no proactive attempt by McIntyre J. to understand those possibilities.

McDonald J. investigated R.C.M.P. informant policies. Among other things, McDonald J. found incidents of informers being given a license "to commit crimes while in the employ of the R.C.M.P.," promoting and instigating offenses and committing acts of vandalism. The guidelines and policies, designed to control informers, were violated in many cases. Even R.C.M.P. witnesses admitted inabilities to control informants, particularly in the area of drug enforcement. The Commission made this observation:

> We feel that the R.C.M.P. and other drug enforcement agencies should not be left to struggle alone with such questions of *law and policy*, as these problems are not solely the concern of the Force, nor can they be dealt with in a manner that makes the Force for all practical purposes unresponsive to governmental and Parliamentary control unless some external scrutiny of the decisions taken is undertaken.... While making the decision may be difficult, even more troubling is the absence of external guidance and the apparent absence of requests for governmental guidance in regard to these sensitive problems. [Emphasis added.]

The reality is that informant motivation, ranging from money payment to plea bargains, has now developed to the extent that even the police are uncomfortable about the situation. In the writer's view, the police are often under pressure to solve crimes, and in the circumstances it is unrealistic for them to conceptually adhere to legality when no legal guidelines have been given. Courts have simply left the informant problem as a matter of police discretion.

... [T]he inflexibility of the analysis of Beetz J. [in *Bisaillon*] has left the law in a state of conceptual rigidity which prohibits any non-police investigation of an informant's motivation. In light of what the *MacDonald Commission* uncovered, one wonders whether this is a comfortable situation. As McDonald J. suggests, "external scrutiny" is necessary. Surely this means some judicial activism is warranted, especially in determining the motivation of the informant in the circumstances.

At least two questions[ ] in the writer's view are relevant whenever the informer rule surfaces:

i) Was the informer promised or given any payment or consideration in connection with the charge?
ii) What controls, if any, were on the informant?

The answers will dictate the amount of judicial scrutiny or suspicion necessary in the circumstances. If it turns out that there was no consideration involved and there was no reason for the police to impose controls on the informant, then it follows that there should be minimal concern about ulterior or illegal conduct that might have motivated the informant. But if payment or other considerations were involved, then the rights of the accused and the integrity of the court should prompt further questioning. The balancing point is the informant's conduct relative to the accused's offence. If the informant was motivated to create the offence by threats, perhaps "planting" drugs or other forms of coercion then surely a court would be moved to scrutinize and, if necessary, remedy the charge against the accused.

Reliability

Akin to what motivates informers is the reliability of the information itself. The information provided by the informer triggers police action. In a proper situation the information, gathered by the informant, is tested by corroboration. This usually means that conversations the informant has with the suspect will be controlled by recording or observation. Modern technology makes such control possible. The *Criminal Code*, s. 178.18(2)(d) gives recognition to these situations. Informants by authorization "of a licence issued by the Solicitor General of Canada" are permitted to possess recording devices. Again, in a proper situation there will be an effort made to have the informant's information confirmed using the available techniques.

As the seriousness of the crime increases, so should the effort to confirm or establish the accuracy of the information. For example if the charge is murder then the credibility and accuracy of the information should be carefully checked out. There is always the risk of fraud on the police by the use of false or manufactured information. More importantly, if the motivation of the informant is unknown, the reliability of the information becomes critical and deserves strict scrutiny as he might be motivated out of revenge, etc. Judicial scrutiny in this areas has been scarce and the realities indicate that the police actually take an opposite approach. The police wilfully avoid testing the reliability of the information provided. The so-called "need to know" principle illustrates the problem.

The "need to know" principles came to the attention of McDonald J. in the context of misconduct by members of the R.C.M.P. and the frustration that the Commission was experiencing in that "not one serving member of the Force has come directly to us to volunteer information about incidents or practices that may have been unlawful." A senior R.C.M.P. officer, testifying to the McDonald Commission, referred to the "need to know" principle in the context of R.C.M.P. management practices and the reason he did not know about the questionable activity of his own subordinates:

> ... [I]t is part of the police tradition, of esprit de corps and professional secrecy, that as long as people do not break these codes, as long as they do not rat on each other, that police groups are tolerant of the existence among them, of individuals of this kind.... A number of people in the Section knew it, but they knew intuitively that the last thing they could do was let that knowledge get to the level of a person who would have to act on it....

McDonald J. didn't explore the rationale or scope of the principle, even though it was often invoked to explain a lack of awareness by officers. Had McDonald J. pursued the point beyond managerial and administrative matters in the Force, the "need to know" principle would have surfaced in terms of criminal investigations and the handling of informants. It came to the attention of Hogarth J. in *R. v. Ross*.

In *Ross* the R.C.M.P. recruited a known drug addict, Ms. Woodside, to work as an informant on a fee basis. She worked with an undercover R.C.M.P. officer to make purchases of drugs. She was given assurances of not having to testify and at the time of trial she was not available. Hogarth J. entered a stay of proceedings, in the circumstances, and commented on the instructions Woodside and the undercover officer were required to follow:

> He (Cst. Lahaye) was directed, as was Ms. Woodside that they were not to discuss their separate activities each with the other and that each would keep in touch with Corporal Board, who was in charge of the day-to-day functioning of the operation. The arrangement and directions given to Ms. Woodside and Constable Lahaye

> clearly left something to be desired, as, to apply the old adage, "the right hand did not know what the left hand was doing" or, for that matter, had done.

Instead of attempting to determine what transpired between the accused who was charged with trafficking in heroin and the informant, the police purposefully shielded the undercover officer from details relevant to trafficking. Whatever happened between the informant and the accused was not determined. There was some inconsistent evidence and an inference of instigation was raised. Thus the reliability of Ms. Woodside's information became suspect and Hogarth J. said:

> There are several reasons why I have a great deal of concern with respect to the arrangement made with Ms. Woodside, some of which are as follows: First, the bounty to be paid to her was a direct inducement for her to be extremely persuasive to bring about a sale of drugs to Lahaye whether same might ordinarily take place or not. Secondly, Constable Lahaye was deliberately deprived of any knowledge of what she said and did and thus observations of his that might well form the basis of meaningful evidence for the defence could well have been overlooked.

The reality is that uncontrolled informant information is dangerous and of dubious reliability, for the reasons indicated in *Ross* and the *McDonald Commission*. In *Ross* had it not been for counsel's "strong plea to enforce her (Ms. Woodside's) presence" and Hogarth J.'s direction "to provide to Mr. Gable all information that the police had on hand with respect to the whereabouts of the informant" an injustice would probably have resulted.

Ross illustrates the reality that surrounds informants and demonstrates what is occurring, as opposed to what the Supreme Court of Canada in *The Health Records Case* and *Bisaillon* seems to believe is occurring. Conceptually what is being suggested here is a difference in perception of reality, where honest opinions differ and as a result it may be that senior judges have not understood or appreciated the problem in the light of contemporary informant developments. With all due respect, the Supreme Court of Canada must educate itself with [regard] to informants and their motivation so that they might better understand the basis of the information that is so often being advanced in courtrooms. The type of prying and investigation, initiated by Laskin C.J. in the *Health Records Case* is certainly a starting point. The concerns expressed by Dubin J.A. concerning the impairment of justice that could affect public confidence in the long term is a sufficient reason to justify that sort of judicial suspicion and investigation. ...

[Wool concludes with a call for greater judicial scrutiny of informer information and informer motivations to ensure that rights and freedoms and the integrity of the court are not compromised.]

■

As you read *R. v. Mack* below, and the case notes following, consider whether the pre-*Charter* issues raised by Wool have been resolved by the courts.

R. v. Mack†

[LAMER J.:]

The appellant was charged with unlawful possession of a narcotic for the purpose of trafficking. He testified at trial and, at the close of the case for the defence, brought an application for a stay of proceedings on the basis of entrapment. The application was refused and a conviction entered by Wetmore Co. Ct. J., sitting without a jury, in written reasons reported 34 C.R. (3d) 228.

. . . .

It is appropriate to reproduce in its entirety the summary of the evidence provided in the reasons for judgment of Wetmore Co. Ct. J. (at pp. 234–37):

† [1988] 2 S.C.R. 903.

Through information obtained from an officer of the Ontario Provincial Police, one Momotiuk was brought to British Columbia. This man had apparently been dealing in narcotics in Kenora, Ontario. He was placed under police "handlers" in Vancouver, he visited the accused on a number of occasions, and eventually a transaction was set up whereby the accused would deliver cocaine to Momotiuk.

The accused testified. He first met Momotiuk in 1979 in Montreal where the accused was visiting one Franks. The accused understood Franks and Momotiuk to be associated in some clothing franchise.

The accused at this time was attempting to develop some property for sale near De Roche, British Columbia, and told Franks and Momotiuk of this and both expressed some interest in buying. Both arrived in British Columbia in October 1979. In the course of this visit the accused says that Momotiuk told him he was a drug trafficker in Kenora and wanted some "Thai pot". The accused says he had no interest.

Momotiuk, according to the accused, called later still wanting to make drug deals, and the accused told him he was interested only in real estate deals.

The accused again went to a yoga retreat near Montreal in December 1979. Franks and Momotiuk visited him there. Momotiuk produced some cocaine, which he and Franks used, and again asked the accused to become a supplier. A few days later they met again. At this time conversation was directed to show Momotiuk as an importer of drugs on a large scale, and again the accused was invited to join in and refused.

In January and February there were approximately seven telephone calls from Momotiuk to the accused soliciting his involvement. The accused says he refused.

In mid-February 1980 Momotiuk visited the accused again, asking him to supply drugs. The accused says he told Momotiuk he was not interested and asked to be left alone. Momotiuk continued to visit two or three times and also telephoned.

In March the accused says Momotiuk arrived again. They went for a [walk] in the woods. Momotiuk produced a pistol and was going to show the accused his marksmanship. He was dissuaded because of the probability of startling the horses nearby. The accused says that at this remote area Momotiuk said, "A person could get lost." This the accused says was a threat. He says the matter of drugs was again raised and the accused says he was adamant that he had no knowledge of drug sources.

The accused was asked to phone him twice and did not. One Matheson attended at the accused's residence on 13th March with a message that Momotiuk was very excited and wanted to see him at the Biltmore Hotel. The accused says he wanted nothing to do with Momotiuk but was terrified of him and agreed to go into town to the Biltmore. He also says that Matheson told him Momotiuk had some friends with him. This the accused took to be other members of this illegal syndicate.

While en route to the city he twice noted a car which seemed to be following him. This was probably so, because undercover police officers were doing a surveillance at the time.

On arrival at the hotel he met Momotiuk. Again he was informed of the syndicate. He was asked then if he wished to see the buying power. The accused agreed. He was directed to a car outside the hotel. In this car was an open briefcase with $50,000 exposed. The custodian, unknown to the accused, was an undercover policeman.

The accused returned to the hotel, Momotiuk asked him to get a sample and gave him $50 for this purpose.

The accused left and went to a supplier he had known of from years back. This supplier, one Goldsmith, now dead, heard the accused's story and agreed to supply "in order to get Doug (Momotiuk) off me". He obtained the sample and delivered it to Momotiuk, who tested it and said to get as much as he could. He returned to the supplier and offered $35,000 to $40,000 for a pound.

At the meeting the following day the accused had still not acquired the drugs and he says that at this point he was told to get his act together, in a threatening way.

I need not detail the accused's evidence of the following two days. He obtained 12 ounces of cocaine, and was to pay $27,000 for it. The credit, he says, was extended to him by Goldsmith on the basis of payment when delivered to Momotiuk. It was in the course of this delivery that he was arrested.

It is on the basis of this testimony that the accused says he was entrapped. Momotiuk, Matheson and Franks did not testify. Neither did "Bonnie", the accused's former wife, who was apparently present at one of the Montreal meetings, where cocaine was produced and some discussion took place.

The accused has drug convictions in 1972 and 1976, two in 1978 and one in 1979. Those in 1976, one in 1978 and one in 1979 involved cocaine. He says his former use of drugs arose to relieve back pain, but in 1978 he discovered relief from yoga and gave up the use of narcotics. The offence in 1979 was a fall from grace when he met up with old friends.

. . . .

It is essential to identify why we do not accept police strategy that amounts to entrapment. ... One reason is that the state does not have unlimited power to intrude into our personal lives or to randomly test the virtue of individuals. Another is the concern that entrapment techniques may result in the commission of crimes by people who would not otherwise have become involved in criminal conduct. There is perhaps a sense that the police should not themselves commit crimes or engage in unlawful activity solely for the purpose of entrapping others, as this seems to militate against the principle of the rule of law. ... Ultimately, we may be saying that there are inherent limits on the power of the state to manipulate people and events for the purpose of attaining the specific objective of obtaining convictions. ...

The competing social interest is in the repression of criminal activity. Further, our dependence on the police to actively protect us from the immense social and personal cost of crime must be acknowledged. There will be differing views as to the appropriate balance between the concepts of fairness and justice and the need for protection from crime, but it is my opinion that it is universally recognized that some balance is absolutely essential to our conception of civilized society. ...

It must be stressed, however, that the central issue is not the power of a court to *discipline* police or prosecutorial conduct but, as stated by Estey J. in *Amato* (at p. 461), "the avoidance of the improper invocation by the state of the judicial process and its powers". In the entrapment context, the court's sense of justice is offended by the spectacle of an accused being convicted of an offence which is the work of the state (*Amato*, at p. 447). The court is, in effect, saying it cannot condone or be seen to lend a stamp of approval to behaviour which transcends what our society perceives to be acceptable on the part of the state. The stay of the prosecution of the accused is the manifestation of the court's disapproval of the state's conduct. The issuance of the stay obviously benefits the accused but the court is primarily concerned with a larger issue: the maintenance of public confidence in the legal and judicial process.

. . . .

The next and more difficult issue to be considered is: What is the appropriate method of determining whether police conduct has exceeded permissible limits such that allowing a trial to proceed would constitute an abuse of process?

. . . .

For ease of reference I will paraphrase the essential elements of the defence as stated by Estey J. in *Amato*, at p. 446:

1. (a) The offence must be instigated, originated or brought about by the police; and
   (b) the accused must be ensnared into the commission of the offence by the police conduct.
2. The purpose of the scheme must be to gain evidence for the prosecution of the accused for the very crime which has been so instigated.
3. The inducement may include, among other things, deceit, fraud, trickery or reward and will usually, although not necessarily, consist of calculated inveigling and persistent importuning.
4. The character of the initiative taken by the police is unaffected by the fact that the law enforcement agency is represented by a member of a police force or an undercover or other agent, paid or unpaid, but operating under the control of the police.
5. In the result the scheme must be considered, in all the circumstances, so shocking and outrageous as to bring the administration of justice into disrepute.
6. In examining the character in law of the police conduct, for example persistent importuning, the existence of reasonable suspicion on behalf of the police that the accused would commit the offence without inducement is relevant.
7. By itself and without more the predisposition in fact of the accused is not relevant to the availability of the defence.

It is evident to me that Justice Estey's criteria have nothing to do with a determination of whether the particular accused should be excused from the commission of the crime. The question is whether the conduct of the police has exceeded acceptable limits. The issue is whether this conduct should be evaluated in light of the *particular accused* or whether the analysis should be more detached and focus on police conduct with accused persons generally. I have come to the conclusion that it is the latter method of analysis which is the most consistent with the reasons for recognizing the doctrine of entrapment, and which best achieves the objective of ensuring that the administration of justice commands the respect of the community.

. . . .

[T]he police are entitled to provide opportunities for the commission of offences where they have reasonable suspicion to believe that the individuals in question are already engaged in criminal conduct.

. . . .

The past criminal conduct of an individual is relevant only if it can be linked to other factors leading the police to a reasonable suspicion that the individual is engaged in a criminal activity. Furthermore, the mere fact that a person was involved in a criminal activity sometime in the past is not a sufficient ground for "reasonable suspicion". But when such suspicion exists, the police may provide that person with an opportunity to commit an offence. Obviously, there must be some rational connection and proportionality between the crime for which police have this reasonable suspicion and the crime which the police provide the accused with the opportunity to commit. For example, if an individual is suspected of being involved in the drug trade, this fact alone will not justify the police providing the person with an opportunity to commit a totally unrelated offence. In addition, the sole fact that a person is suspected of being frequently in possession of marijuana does not alone justify the police providing him or her with the opportunity to commit a much more serious offence, such as importing narcotics, although other facts may justify them doing so.

There should also be a sufficient temporal connection. If the reasonable suspicions of the police arise by virtue of the individual's conduct, then this conduct must not be too remote in time. I would note, however, that the reasonable suspicions of the police could be based on many factors and that it is not necessary for one of these factors to be a prior conviction. ... I do not think the requirement that the police act on reasonable suspicion is unduly onerous; from a common sense viewpoint it is likely that the police would not waste valuable resources attempting to attract unknown individuals into the commission of offences.

. . . .

There is, therefore, entrapment when (a) the authorities provide an opportunity to persons to commit an offence without reasonable suspicion or acting mala fides [based on "dubious motives"], as explained earlier, or (b) having a reasonable suspicion or acting in the course of a *bona fide* inquiry, they go beyond providing an opportunity and induce the commission of an offence. As I have already mentioned, the first form of entrapment is not likely to occur. ...

As regards the latter form of entrapment, to determine whether police conduct gives rise to this concern, it is useful to consider whether the conduct of the police would have induced the average person in the position of the accused, i.e., a person with both strengths and weaknesses, into committing the crime. I believe such a test is useful not only as an analytical mechanism that is consistent with objective analysis, but also because it corresponds to one of the reasons why the defence is thought desirable. In other words, it may be inevitable that when apprised of the factual context of an entrapment case, members of the community will put themselves in the position of the accused; if a common response would be that anyone could have been induced by such conduct, this is a valuable sign that the police have exceeded the bounds of propriety. The reasoning does not go so far as to imply that the accused is therefore less blameworthy; rather, it suggests that the state is involved in the *manufacture* as opposed to the detection of crime.

. . . .

I remain in agreement with Estey J.'s statement that "the inducement may be but is not limited to deceit, fraud, trickery or reward, and ordinarily but not necessarily will consist of calculated inveigling and persistent importuning" (p. 446), but there is no magic number of requests made on behalf of the police to the accused that will trigger the defence. I would also agree that the scheme must have been for the purpose Justice Estey indicated and that the state's responsibility extends to those people who operate on its behalf in an entrapment situation. It is also necessary for the offence to be "instigated, originated or brought about by the police", but this is clearly a minimum standard since, in cases where the police merely provide a person with the opportunity to commit an offence, it could be said that the same requirement will be met. Similarly it can be said that, in any offence instigated by the police, the offence would not have been committed without their involvement. Taken alone, these requirements are insufficient to determine when police conduct goes beyond what is generally thought to be acceptable in protecting society from crime.

In certain cases the police conduct will be offensive because it exploits human characteristics that as a society we feel should be respected. As I noted earlier, if the law enforcement officer or agent appeals to [the] person's instincts of compassion, sympathy and friendship and uses these qualities of a person to effect the commission of a crime, we may say this is not permissible conduct because it violates individual privacy and the dignity of interpersonal relationships, and condemns behaviour that we want to encourage. (Such appeals generally indicate that more than a mere opportunity is being provided, although it must be recalled that the police or agents will in the detection of certain crimes have to infiltrate criminal organizations, and thus gain the confidence of the people involved.) Along the same lines, if the police appear to exploit a particular vulnerability of an individual, such as by encouraging one who suffers from a mental handicap to commit a crime, this too may strike us as patently offensive because such a person is in need of protection and not abuse. Similarly, the inducement of those attempting to recover from drug or alcohol addiction into committing offences relating to those substances may not be proper, since the result will be to retard, as opposed to advance, the interest of society in reducing the personal and social costs of drug and alcohol abuse.

In some cases we may find that the degree of police involvement is disproportionate to the crime committed by the accused insofar as it causes more harm than it seeks to catch. In addition, we may be offended by disproportionality in the role played by the police in the criminal activity, as compared with the role played by the person being targeted. In assessing this, the timing of the police involvement, and whether the criminal activity is ongoing, should be considered. Whether the police or their agents themselves commit crimes in the course of efforts to induce another is relevant, but I am not willing to lay down an absolute rule prohibiting the involvement of the state in illegal conduct.

Earlier I noted that one indication of impermissible action on the part of the state would be the existence of any threats, implied or express, made to the individual being targeted by inducement techniques. If the strategy used carried the risk of potential harm to third parties, this too should be considered and, absent exceptional circumstances, condemned. A further consideration, if the facts so warrant, would be the extent to which the conduct of the police is directed at undermining other constitutional values, such as legitimate exercises of freedom of thought, belief, opinion and association.

The above description of activity is not intended to be exhaustive in terms of possible situations, or conclusive in the assessment of propriety. It is meant only to illustrate that, in any number of situations, the reason why something is "improper" may vary. It cannot be stated that only one reason will be compelling or determinative. The issue of permissibility of police conduct must be considered in light of the totality of the circumstances. ...

. . . .

Both the appellant and the respondent agree that objective entrapment, involving police misconduct and not the accused's state of mind, is a question to be decided by the trial judge and that the proper remedy is a stay of proceedings. I too am of this view. The question of unlawful involvement by the state in the instigation of criminal conduct is one of law, or mixed law and fact.

. . . .

Finally, I am of the view that before a judge considers whether a stay of proceedings lies because of entrapment, it must be absolutely clear that the Crown had discharged its burden of proving beyond a reasonable doubt that the accused had committed all the essential elements of the offence. If this is not clear and there is a jury, the guilt or innocence of the accused must be determined apart from evidence which is relevant only to the issue of entrapment. This protects the right of an accused to an acquittal where the circumstances so warrant. If the jury decides that the accused has committed all of the elements of the crime, it is then open to the judge to stay the proceedings because of entrapment by refusing to register a conviction. ... Because the guilt or innocence of the accused is *not* in issue at the time an entrapment claim is to be decided, the right of an accused to the benefit of a jury trial in s. 11(f) of the *Charter* is in no way infringed.

. . . .

I have come to the conclusion that it is not inconsistent with the requirement that the Crown prove the guilt of the accused beyond a reasonable doubt to place the onus on the accused to prove on a balance of probabilities that the conduct of the state is an abuse of process because of entrapment. I repeat: The guilt or innocence of the accused is not in issue. The accused has done nothing that entitles him or her to an acquittal; the Crown has engaged in conduct, however, that disentitles it to a conviction.

. . . .

It is obvious to me that requiring an accused to raise only a reasonable doubt is entirely inconsistent with a rule which permits a stay in only the "clearest of cases". More fundamentally, the claim of entrapment is a very serious allegation against the state. The state must be given substantial room to develop techniques which assist it in its fight against crime in society. It is only when the police and their agents engage in a conduct which offends basic values of the community that the doctrine of entrapment can apply. To place a lighter onus on the accused would have the result of unnecessarily hampering state action against crime. ... I would also note that this is consistent with the rules governing s. 24(2) applications ... where the general issue is similar to that raised in entrapment cases: Would the administration of justice be brought into disrepute?

[Lamer J. concluded that a stay of proceedings should be entered because although police had a "reasonable suspicion" that Mack was involved in criminal conduct, the actions of their agent went beyond providing an opportunity, given the persistent and threatening requests, and amounted to entrapment, particularly because there was no evidence of an ongoing criminal transaction.]

B. RANDOM VIRTUE TESTING

The Supreme Court of Canada rejected an entrapment argument where the police engaged in "random virtue testing" in the Granville Mall in Vancouver in a "buy-and-bust" operation, where they had reason to believe a healthy drug trade was flourishing: *R. v. Barnes*, [1991] 1 S.C.R. 449, rev'g (1990), 54 C.C.C. (3d) 368 (B.C.C.A.). The officer did not have a reasonable suspicion that the accused was likely to traffic in illicit drugs. However, the Court held that the police were engaged in a *bona fide* inquiry. Chief Justice Lamer cited *Mack* for the authority that the police conduct, therefore, did not amount to entrapment.

In a lower court decision on "random virtue tests", Chief Judge Pierre Lalonde, of the Laval Municipal Court, wrote that "Police do not have a right to test at random, the virtue of citizens": André Picard, "Jurist insists virtue tests aren't work for police" *The [Toronto] Globe and Mail* (23 November 1993) A7. In that case, an undercover police officer solicited sex from the accused (at A7):

> These police officers masqueraded as prostitutes to sexually provoke men and entice them to commit a crime they otherwise would not have committed.

In an earlier case, Judge Lalonde had acquitted six dancers of charges of public indecency "because [of] police 'evidence-gathering' techniques consisting of hanging around strip clubs, drinking a lot, fondling the dancers and urging them to perform sexual acts" (A7). In both cases, the police had consulted the Crown attorney, who had approved the undercover operations.

How should the law of entrapment apply in the context of regulatory crimes, in light of the licensing justification articulated in *Wholesale Travel*, above? In one case involving the use of an underage test shopper to buy cigarettes, the court stayed the proceedings on the basis that the investigatory practice essentially amounted to "random virtue testing" of various shops: *R. v. Myers*, [1999] S.J. No. 671 (Prov. Ct.) (QL). *Myers* has not been followed in subsequent cases, either because the provincial statute specifically contemplates test purchases for the purposes of enforcement (*R. v. Sobeys*, [2000] N.S.J. No. 32 (S. Ct.) (QL); *R. v. Reid*, [2001] N.J. No. 149 (Prov. Ct.) (QL)) or because the regulatory context leads to the conclusion that the community would not be shocked by the practice of using test shoppers (*Reid*, *supra*; *R. v. Huebner*, [2003] M.J. No. 76 (Prov. Ct.) (QL)).

C. REWARDS TO INFORMERS

In *R. v. Showman*, [1988] 2 S.C.R. 893, a case decided at the same time as *Mack*, the police used the services of a friend of the accused (Wade Kirkus), in exchange for consideration with respect to a "potential" narcotics charge against Kirkus. The Supreme Court held that the police acted on reasonable suspicion, and that the pressure of the number of telephone calls made by the friend to bring about the drug sale was not significant.

The use of a paid agent was allowed in *R. v. Dikah* (1994), 70 O.A.C. 214 (C.A.), aff'd [1994] 3 S.C.R. 1020, and held not to violate the accused's rights. In that case, the agent was to receive a cash payment of $10,000 if the RCMP was able, through his assistance, "to successfully investigate" the accused. The trial judge held that the inducement offered to the agent "tainted the legal process" and constituted an abuse of process and a violation of the accused's s. 7 *Charter* rights. She held that such payments would encourage "falsification of evidence and misrepresentations to the court" and ordered a stay. See Stephen Bindman, "Cash for conviction approved by top court" *The Ottawa Citizen* (10 December 1994) C2; and Stephen Bindman, "Supreme Court to decide if RCMP can pay informants more if charges stick" *The Ottawa Citizen* (24 May 1994) A5, citing Justice Lynn Ratushny:

> It prejudices the informant from the beginning by inviting him to put a spin on his evidence, to blur, shade and fabricate it so that charges can be laid and he can pocket more money.

On appeal, the Ontario Court of Appeal held that the payment did not render the evidence inadmissible, but only went to the weight to be attached to it.

In June 2007, a senior officer acknowledged that the RCMP were "duped" into paying more than $100,000 for evidence manufactured by a police agent who then went on to kill someone once he entered the witness protection program: Greg McArthur "Mounties 'duped' by police agent, officer testifies" *The [Toronto] Globe and Mail* (8 June 2007) A7. The RCMP fought hard against revealing the agent's name who was allowed to remain in the witness protection program. Their argument was that revealing that agent's name would be illegal under the *Witness Protection Program Act*, S.C. 1996, c. 15 and that it would scare off potential witnesses in other cases. Greg McArthur and Thu Thanh Ha, "Coming clean on witness protection" *The [Toronto] Globe and Mail* (5 June 2007) A5.

D. CRIMINAL ACTIVITY OF POLICE AND INFORMANTS

In *R. v. Elzein* (1993), 53 Q.A.C. 99, leave refused [1993] 4 S.C.R. v, the Court of Appeal held that police were conducting a *bona fide* investigation and only presented the opportunity to commit the offence to anyone in the area, albeit through their agent who had performed (at 476):

> an impressive number of things, some of which were obviously criminal (importation of hashish, providing false identity papers, possession of narcotics) and others [which] were inducements to commit offences (proposition to deal in gold, in jewellery and in counterfeit money and to receive stolen automobiles). It is important to remember, however that the initiatives in question were undertaken to the knowledge and with the agreement of the R.C.M.P. and that they essentially formed part of the plan of action....
>
> ... I am of the view that the R.C.M.P., through their agent, only set a trap for the appellant after having had serious grounds for suspecting that he was already involved in a criminal activity. In order to put an end to it they used the classic weapon that one finds in almost all investigations of this type, that is infiltration of the milieu. The fact that they entrusted the execution of their plan to an individual whose general morality was far from being without reproach and who knew this milieu well, is not condemnable nor unusual in itself. Finally, and above all, neither the R.C.M.P., by its officers nor its undercover agent, went beyond the confines of its role which was to provide the appellant with an opportunity to commit the offences which he was found guilty of.

For a case that reached a similar conclusion and dismissed an application for a stay in the face of illegal police actions (a "reverse sting"), see *R. v. Matthiessen* (1996), 41 Alta. L.R. (3d) 201 (Q.B.). However, in *R. v. Wolfe*, [1995] 10 W.W.R. 44, the Saskatchewan Court of Appeal stayed proceedings under the *Wildlife Act*, S.S. 1979, c. W-13.1 on the basis of illegal activities by the undercover conservation officer (specifically, the importation of alcohol onto a dry reserve), discussed in Abell & Sheehy, *Cases, Context, Critique*, **Policing**.

R. v. Campbell (S.C.C., 1999)[†]

[The RCMP were alleged to have violated the *Narcotic Control Act* by selling a large quantity of hashish to senior "executives" in a drug trafficking organization as part of a reverse sting operation. The appellants, as purchasers, were charged with conspiracy to traffic in cannabis resin and conspiracy to possess cannabis resin for that purpose. The trial judge found the appellants guilty as charged but, before sentencing, heard their motion for a stay of any further steps in the proceeding. The appellants argued that the reverse sting constituted illegal police conduct, which "shocks the conscience of the community and is so detrimental to the proper administration of justice that it warrants judicial intervention". The stay was refused by the courts below.

As part of their case for a stay, the appellants sought, but were denied, access to the legal advice provided to the police by the Department of Justice, on which the police claimed to have placed good faith reliance. The Crown's position implied that the RCMP acted in accordance with legal advice.

At issue here is the effect, in the context of the "war on drugs", of alleged police illegality on the grant of a judicial stay of proceedings, and related issues regarding the solicitor-client privilege invoked by the RCMP and pre-trial disclosure of solicitor-client communications to which privilege has been waived.]

[BINNIE J.:]

In this appeal the Court is asked to consider some implications of the constitutional principle that everyone from the highest officers of the state to the constable on the beat is subject to the ordinary law of the land. Here the police were alleged to have violated the *Narcotic Control Act*, R.S.C., 1985, c. N-1, by selling a large quantity of hashish (cannabis resin) to senior "executives" in a drug trafficking organization as part of what counsel called a "reverse sting" operation. The appellants, as purchasers, were charged with conspiracy to traffic in cannabis resin and conspiracy to possess cannabis resin for that purpose. The trial judge found the appellants guilty as charged but, before sentencing, heard the appellants' motion for a stay of any further steps in the proceeding. The appellants argued that the reverse sting constituted illegal police conduct which "shocks the conscience of the community and is so detrimental to the proper administration of justice that it warrants judicial intervention" (see *R. v. Power*, [1994] 1 S.C.R. 601, at p. 615). The stay was refused by the courts below.

As part of their case for a stay the appellants sought, but were denied, access to the legal advice provided to the police by the Department of Justice on which the police claimed to have placed good faith reliance. The Crown indicated that the undisclosed advice assured the police, rightly or wrongly, that sale of cannabis resin in the circumstances of a reverse sting was lawful. The appellants argue that the truth of this assertion can only be tested by a review of the otherwise privileged communications.

We are therefore required to consider in the context of the "war on drugs", the effect of alleged police illegality on the grant of a judicial stay of proceedings, and related issues regarding the solicitor-client privilege invoked by the RCMP and pre-trial disclosure of solicitor-client communications to which privilege has been waived.

. . . .

Court of Appeal for Ontario (1997), 32 O.R. (3d) 181

Carthy J.A. disagreed with the conclusion of the trial judge that it was not necessary to determine the legality of the police conduct. Also basing himself on the judgment of Lamer J. in *Mack*, *supra*, Carthy J.A. considered that police illegality was an important factor to be weighed in evaluating an accused's claim of abuse of process and, indeed, he considered that illegality may in certain instances be determinative.

After setting out the relevant portions of the *Narcotic Control Act*, Carthy J.A. noted that the *Narcotic Control Regulations*, C.R.C., c. 1041, s. 3(1), saves the police harmless where possession of a narcotic results from sting operations. There is no corresponding regulation giving the police immunity when they are offering to sell a narcotic. Carthy J.A. concluded that the RCMP's offer to sell a narcotic

† [1999] 1 S.C.R. 565.

to the appellants constituted trafficking, and that it was irrelevant that the RCMP had no intention of completing the sale. Therefore, on the face of the statute, the conduct of the RCMP in this case was, in Carthy J.A.'s view, illegal.

Carthy J.A. then considered the Crown's arguments about extending public interest immunity to the RCMP and concluded that the Crown does not exercise sufficient de jure control over the activities of RCMP members to justify such immunity from prosecution for breach of the criminal law as it relates to narcotics. As to the related concept of immunity derived from Crown agency, Carthy J.A. considered that, while members of the RCMP are entitled to seek out criminality through a variety of different methods, this mandate does not extend to methods that would be illegal if done by any other person. Carthy J.A. examined *R. v. Eldorado Nuclear Ltd.*, [1983] 2 S.C.R. 551. When Crown agents act within the scope of the public purposes they are statutorily empowered to pursue, they may be entitled to claim Crown immunity, he held, but in this case the RCMP officers had stepped outside the scope of any agency relationship that may have existed.

Carthy J.A. agreed with the trial judge that there was no entrapment. He went on, however, to consider whether the RCMP conduct amounted to an abuse of process for reasons other than entrapment. He noted that the illegal conduct of the RCMP did not involve a trifling amount of drugs. Further, he noted that the illegal conduct was authorized at all levels of the RCMP. He was prepared to infer that the reverse sting was considered lawful by the Department of Justice, and he treated this as an aggravating factor because "the full might of the Crown resources were set upon the task of illegal conduct" (p. 197). Carthy J.A. noted an alternate possibility that the police were acting on their own as "mavericks" contrary to legal advice. While he doubted that this was in fact the case, Carthy J.A. at p. 197 considered this would be

> ...an aggravating factor against the Crown of about equal weight to the first assumption [i.e., of equal weight to the assumption that the RCMP did follow the legal advice].

A third possibility, he considered, was that the RCMP had been advised that the reverse sting would be legal provided no drugs were passed to the appellants as part of a "sale". If so, the RCMP had complied with the advice rendered, even though failure to complete the transaction did not change its illegality. Carthy J.A. recognized that all three scenarios were necessarily speculative on his part. He said, at p. 200, that had he been the trial judge he "would have directed production of the documents and evidence of the Crown law officer". However, while "[i]t obviously would have been better if the [Department of Justice] information had been conveyed [to the appellants] at trial" (p. 200), no miscarriage of justice occurred because even assuming "the worst" against the Crown no stay could be justified in the circumstances of this case. It was not one of the clearest cases, nor did it involve conduct that would cause the public conscience to be shocked if the convictions were permitted to stand. He concluded, at pp. 198–99, that "[h]aving condemned the actions of the R.C.M.P. and having held up [his] hand against repetition, it would, in [his] view, be sanctimonious to say that the rule of law ha[d] been eroded by these convictions and sentences". The Court of Appeal dismissed the other grounds of appeal, save for the technical variation in the order for forfeiture previously mentioned.

ANALYSIS

Reverse Sting Operations

There is a general recognition that "[i]f the struggle against crime is to be won, the ingenuity of criminals must be matched by that of the police" (*Mack*, *supra*, *per* Lamer J., at p. 916). In a "sting" operation, the police pose as willing purchasers of narcotics to obtain evidence against traffickers. The *Narcotic Control Regulations* accept the legitimacy of this technique by deeming police possession in these circumstances to be authorized under that Act. The problem is that traffickers caught by ordinary "sting" purchases are generally minor street level personnel whose conviction has little deterrence effect on the day-to-day operations of the drug organization as a whole. As pointed out by Cpl. Reynolds in this case, the "executives" up the chain of command of large-scale drug organizations are able to insulate themselves from sting operations. The street level pushers apprehended by the police are easily sacrificed and easily replaced. For the purpose of more effective law enforcement, the police therefore devised what counsel referred to as "reverse sting" operations whereby the police became vendors rather than purchasers, i.e., the roles of vendor and purchaser were reversed within the sting operation. Because of the amount and value of drugs involved, reverse sting operations brought the police "vendors" into direct contact with the executive purchasers in the large drug organizations. It has proved to be an effective technique. It also, however, brought the police into conflict with the very law that they were attempting to enforce. Neither the *Narcotic Control Act* nor its regulations authorize the police to sell drugs. The appellants, as stated, purport to be shocked at the illegality of police conduct, and ask the Court to hold that the conduct so violates the community's fundamental sense of decency and values that it should result in a stay of proceedings against them.

. . . .

The Rule of Law

It is one of the proud accomplishments of the common law that everybody is subject to the ordinary law of the land regardless of public prominence or governmental status. As we explained in *Reference re Secession of Quebec*, [1998] 2 S.C.R. 217, at p. 240, the rule of law is one of the "fundamental and organizing principles of the Constitution", and at p. 258, it was further emphasized that a crucial element of the rule of law is that "[t]here is ... one law for all". Thus a provincial premier was held to have no immunity against a claim in damages when he caused injury to a private citizen through wrongful interference with the exercise of statutory powers by a provincial liquor commission: *Roncarelli v. Duplessis*, [1959] S.C.R. 121. Professor F. R. Scott, who was counsel for the successful plaintiff, Roncarelli, in that case, subsequently observed in *Civil Liberties & Canadian Federalism* (1959), at p. 48:

> ...it is always a triumph for the law to show that it is applied equally to all without fear or favour. This is what we mean when we say that all are equal before the law.

The principle was famously enunciated by Professor A.V. Dicey in Introduction to the Study of the *Law of the Constitution* (8th ed. 1927) as the second aspect of the "rule of law". This principle was noted with approval in *Attorney General of Canada v. Lavell*, [1974] S.C.R. 1349, at p. 1366:

> It means again equality before the law or the equal subjection of all classes to the ordinary law of the land administered by the ordinary courts; the 'rule of law' in this sense excludes the idea of any exemption of officials or others from the duty of obedience to the law which governs other citizens or from the jurisdiction of the ordinary courts.

The argument of the appellants is that not only are the police subject to prosecution for their participation in the very transaction that gave rise to the charges on which the appellants have been found guilty, but (more importantly from their perspective) police illegality should deprive the state of the benefit of a conviction against them. It is relevant that in s. 37 of the *Royal Canadian Mounted Police Act*, R.S.C., 1985, c. R-10, Parliament has specifically imposed on RCMP officers the duty to stay within the law, as follows:

> **37.** It is incumbent on every member
> (a) to respect the rights of all persons;
> (b) to maintain *the integrity of the law*, law enforcement and the administration of justice;
> (c) to perform the member's duties promptly, impartially and diligently, *in accordance with the law* and without abusing the member's authority;
>
> ...
>
> (e) to ensure that any improper or *unlawful* conduct of any member is not concealed or permitted to continue.... [Emphasis added.]

It is recognized, of course, that police officers gain nothing personally from conduct committed in good faith efforts to suppress crime that incidentally violates the law the police are attempting to enforce. Nevertheless, the seeming paradox of breaking a law in order to better enforce it has important ramifications for the rule of law.

Test for Abuse of Process

In *R. v. Jewitt*, [1985] 2 S.C.R. 128, the Court set down what has since become the standard formulation of the test for abuse of process, *per* Dickson C.J., at pp. 136–37:

> I would adopt the conclusion of the Ontario Court of Appeal in *R. v. Young* [(1984), 40 C.R. (3d) 289], and affirm that "there is a residual discretion in a trial court judge to stay proceedings where compelling an accused to stand trial would violate those fundamental principles of justice which underlie the community's sense of fair play and decency and to prevent the abuse of a court's process through oppressive or vexatious proceedings". I would also adopt the caveat added by the Court in *Young* that this is a power which can be exercised only in the "clearest of cases".

. . . .

Entrapment is simply an application of the abuse of process doctrine. Lamer J., in *Mack*, *supra*, set out the applicable test as follows, at pp. 964–65:

> ...there is entrapment when,
> (a) the authorities provide a person with an opportunity to commit an offence without acting on a reasonable suspicion that this

person is already engaged in criminal activity or pursuant to a *bona fide* inquiry;
(b) although having such a reasonable suspicion or acting in the course of a *bona fide* inquiry, they go beyond providing an opportunity and induce the commission of an offence.

The trial judge concluded that she was "satisfied that the police acted on reasonable suspicion. That being so, the police were fully entitled to provide both accused with opportunities to commit the offences". There was ample evidence to support her finding. She also found that the police had not crossed the boundary line from providing opportunity to commit the offence into the forbidden territory of inducing commission of the offence. The appellants needed no inducement. Once the opportunity presented itself, they, not the police, were the driving force behind the making of the deal.

In the absence of any plausible case for entrapment, the appellants can only succeed on the more general ground of a serious violation of "[the community's sense of] fair play and decency ... disproportionate to the societal interest in the effective prosecution of criminal cases" (*Conway*, *supra*, at p. 1667). In this regard, the centrepiece of the appellants' argument, as stated, is the allegation of police illegality, and the refusal of the courts below to order disclosure of what the appellants consider to be relevant communications between Cpl. Reynolds and Mr. Leising of the Department of Justice relied on by the police to establish their "good faith".

The Issue of Police Illegality

The allegation that the police have put themselves above the law is very serious, with constitutional ramifications beyond the boundaries of the criminal law. This was not a trivial breach. In the end, the transaction was for 50 kilograms, but at the outset the police were trying to organize the sale of over a ton of cannabis resin. The failure of the police to make a deal on that scale was not for want of trying.

The effect of police illegality on an application for a stay of proceedings depends very much on the facts of a particular case. This case-by-case approach is dictated by the requirement to balance factors which are specific to each fact situation. The problem confronting the police was well described by the Alberta Court of Appeal in *R. v. Bond* (1993), 135 A.R. 329 (leave to appeal refused, [1993] 3 S.C.R. v), at p. 333:

> Illegal conduct by the police during an investigation, while wholly relevant to the issue of abuse of the court's processes, is not *per se* fatal to prosecutions which may follow: *Mack*; *supra* at 558. Frequently it will be, but situational police illegality happens. Police involve themselves in high speed chases, travelling beyond posted speed limits. Police pose as prostitutes and communicate for that purpose in order to gather evidence. Police buy, possess, and transport illegal drugs on a daily basis during undercover operations. In a perfect world this would not be necessary but, patently illegal drug commerce is neither successfully investigated, nor resisted, by uniformed police peering through hotelroom transoms and keyholes or waiting patiently at police headquarters to receive the confessions of penitent drug-traffickers.

The Crown contends, as it did in the courts below, that the police did not violate the *Narcotic Control Act* which at the time the reverse sting was initiated provided in s. 4 as follows:

> **4.**(1) No person shall traffic in a narcotic or any substance represented or held out by the person to be a narcotic.
>
> (2) No person shall have in his possession any narcotic for the purpose of trafficking.
>
> (3) Every person who contravenes subsection (1) or (2) is guilty of an indictable offence and liable to imprisonment for life.

"Traffic" is defined in the *Narcotic Control Act* as follows:

> **2.** In this Act,
>
> ...
>
> "traffic" means
> (a) to manufacture, sell, give, administer, transport, send, deliver or distribute, or
> (b) to offer to do anything referred to in paragraph (a) otherwise than under the authority of this Act or the regulations. [Emphasis added.]

The conclusion that the RCMP acted in a manner facially prohibited by the Act is inescapable. Their motive in doing so does not matter because, while motive may be relevant for some purposes, it is intent, not motive, that is an element of a full *mens rea* offence: see *Lewis v. The Queen*, [1979] 2 S.C.R. 821, at p. 831. The *actus reus* of the offence of trafficking is the making of an offer, and when accompanied by intent to do so, the necessary *mens rea* is made out: see *R. v. Mancuso* (1989), 51 C.C.C. (3d) 380 (Que. C.A.), at p. 390, leave to appeal refused, [1990] 2 S.C.R. viii. There is no need to prove both the intent to make the offer to sell and the intent to carry out the offer: see *R. v. Mamchur*, [1978] 4 W.W.R. 481 (Sask. C.A.). See also, e.g., *R. v. Sherman* (1977), 36 C.C.C. (2d) 207 (B.C.C.A.), at p. 208, upholding a conviction where there was evidence that the accused had offered to sell heroin to a person he knew was an undercover police officer, with a view to "rip off" the officer and not complete the sale. Sherman was later followed on this point in *Mancuso*, *supra*, at pp. 389–90, where the accused argued unsuccessfully that he did not intend actually to sell narcotics to a police informer, but really wished to steal his money.

Public Interest Immunity

The Crown submits that even if the conduct of the RCMP was facially prohibited by the terms of the *Narcotic Control Act*, no offence was committed because members of the RCMP are either part of the Crown or are agents of the Crown and as such partake of the Crown's public interest immunity. Such an argument is difficult to square with s. 3(1) of the *Narcotic Control Regulations* which authorizes the police to possess narcotics that come to them from "sting" operations:

> **3.**(1) A person is authorized to have a narcotic in his possession where that person has obtained the narcotic pursuant to these Regulations and
>
> ...
>
> (g) is employed as an inspector, a member of the Royal Canadian Mounted Police, a police constable, [or] peace officer ... and such possession is for the purposes of and in connection with such employment....

Even though the authority is contained in a regulation rather than the Act itself, it is clear that the Regulation would be entirely unnecessary and superfluous if the Act did not apply to the police in the first place.

The Status of the Police

The Crown's attempt to identify the RCMP with the Crown for immunity purposes misconceives the relationship between the police and the executive government when the police are engaged in law enforcement. A police officer investigating a crime is not acting as a government functionary or as an agent of anybody. He or she occupies a public office initially defined by the common law and subsequently set out in various statutes. In the case of the RCMP, one of the relevant statutes is now the *Royal Canadian Mounted Police Act*, R.S.C., 1985, c. R-10.

Under the authority of that Act, it is true, RCMP officers perform a myriad of functions apart from the investigation of crimes. These include, by way of examples, purely ceremonial duties, the protection of Canadian dignitaries and foreign diplomats and activities associated with crime prevention. Some of these functions bring the RCMP into a closer relationship to the Crown than others. The *Department of the Solicitor General Act*, R.S.C., 1985, c. S-13, provides that the Solicitor General's powers, duties and functions extend to matters relating to the RCMP over which Parliament has jurisdiction, and that have not been assigned to another department. Section 5 of the *Royal Canadian Mounted Police Act* provides for the governance of the RCMP as follows:

> **5.**(1) The Governor in Council may appoint an officer, to be known as the Commissioner of the Royal Canadian Mounted Police, who, under the direction of the [Solicitor General], has the control and management of the Force and all matters connected therewith.

It is therefore possible that in one or other of its roles the RCMP could be acting in an agency relationship with the Crown. In this appeal, however, we are concerned only with the status of an RCMP officer in the course of a criminal investigation, and in that regard the police are independent of the control of the executive government. The importance of this principle, which itself underpins the rule of law, was recognized by this Court in relation to municipal forces as long ago as *McCleave v. City of Moncton* (1902), 32 S.C.R. 106. That was a civil case, having to do with potential municipal liability for police negligence, but in the course of his judgment Strong C.J. cited with approval the following proposition, at pp. 108–9:

> Police officers can in no respect be regarded as agents or officers of the city. Their duties are of a public nature. Their appointment is devolved on cities and towns by the legislature as a convenient mode of exercising a function of government, but this does not render them liable for their unlawful or negligent acts. The detection and arrest of offenders, the preservation of the public peace, the enforcement of the laws, and other similar powers and duties with which police officers and constables are entrusted are derived from the law, and not from the city or town under which they hold their appointment.

At about the same time, the High Court of Australia rejected the notion that a police constable was an agent of the Crown so as to enjoy immunity against a civil action for wrongful arrest. Griffith C.J. had this to say in *Enever v. The King* (1906), 3 C.L.R. 969, at p. 977:

> Now, the powers of a constable, quâ peace officer, whether conferred by common or statute law, are exercised by him by virtue of his office, and cannot be exercised on the responsibility of any person but himself. If he arrests on suspicion of felony, the suspicion must be his suspicion, and must be reasonable to him. If he arrests in a case in which the arrest may be made on view, the view must be his view, not that of someone else. ... A constable, therefore, when acting as a peace officer, is not exercising a delegated authority, but an original authority, and the general law of agency has no application.

Over 70 years later, Laskin C.J. in *Nicholson v. Haldimand-Norfolk Regional Board of Commissioners of Police*, [1979] 1 S.C.R. 311, at p. 322, speaking with reference to the status of a probationary police constable, affirmed that "we are dealing with the holder of a public office, engaged in duties connected with the maintenance of public order and preservation of the peace, important values in any society" (emphasis added). See also *Ridge v. Baldwin*, [1964] A.C. 40 (H.L.), at p. 65.

Similar sentiments were expressed by the Judicial Committee of the Privy Council in *Attorney-General for New South Wales v. Perpetual Trustee Co.*, [1955] A.C. 457 (P.C.), another civil case dealing with the vicarious liability of the Crown, in which Viscount Simonds stated, at pp. 489–90:

> [A constable's] authority is original, not delegated, and is exercised at his own discretion by virtue of his office: he is a ministerial officer exercising statutory rights independently of contract. The essential difference is recognized in the fact that his relationship to the Government is not in ordinary parlance described as that of servant and master.

While for certain purposes the Commissioner of the RCMP reports to the Solicitor General, the Commissioner is not to be considered a servant or agent of the government while engaged in a criminal investigation. The Commissioner is not subject to political direction. Like every other police officer similarly engaged, he is answerable to the law and, no doubt, to his conscience. As Lord Denning put it in relation to the Commissioner of Police in *R. v. Metropolitan Police Comr., Ex parte Blackburn*, [1968] 1 All E.R. 763 (C.A.), at p. 769:

> I have no hesitation, however, in holding that, like every constable in the land, he [the Commissioner of Police] should be, and is, independent of the executive. He is not subject to the orders of the Secretary of State, save that under the *Police Act 1964* the Secretary of State can call on him to give a report, or to retire in the interests of efficiency. I hold it to be the duty of the Commissioner of Police, as it is of every chief constable, to enforce the law of the land. He must take steps so to post his men that crimes may be detected; and that honest citizens may go about their affairs in peace. He must decide whether or not suspected persons are to be prosecuted; and, if need be, bring the prosecution or see that it is brought; but in all these things he is not the servant of anyone, save of the law itself. No Minister of the Crown can tell him that he must, or must not, keep observation on this place or that; or that he must, or must not, prosecute this man or that one. Nor can any police authority tell him so. The responsibility for law enforcement lies on him. He is answerable to the law and to the law alone. [Emphasis added.]

To the same effect, see the more recent Canadian cases of *R. v. Creswell*, [1998] B.C.J. No. 1090 (QL) (S.C.), which involves facts closer to those in the present appeal; *Doe v. Metropolitan Toronto (Municipality) Commissioners of Police* (1989), 58 D.L.R. (4th) 396 (Ont. H.C.), affirmed (1990), 74 O.R. (2d) 225 (Div. Ct.); and *Perrier v. Sorgat* (1979), 25 O.R. (2d) 645 (Co. Ct.). A contrary conclusion was reached by Bielby J. of the Alberta Court of Queen's Bench in *Rutherford v. Swanson*, [1993] 6 W.W.R. 126, but her decision, I think, suffers from the frailty of failing to differentiate the different functions the RCMP perform, and the potentially different relationship of the RCMP to the Crown in the exercise of those different functions.

While these cases generally examine the relationship between the police and various governments in terms of civil liability, the statements made are of much broader import. It would make no sense in either law or policy to hold the police to be agents of the Crown for the purposes of allowing the Crown to shelter the police under its immunity in criminal matters, but to hold the police not to be Crown agents in civil matters to enable the government to resile from liability for police misconduct. The Crown cannot have it both ways.

Parenthetically, it should be noted that Parliament has provided in the *Crown Liability and Proceedings Act*, R.S.C., 1985, c. C-50, s. 36, that:

> **36.** For the purposes of determining liability in any proceedings by or against the Crown, a person who was at any time a member of the Cana-

> dian Forces or of the Royal Canadian Mounted Police shall be deemed to have been at that time a servant of the Crown. [Emphasis added.]

A "deeming" section would not be necessary if it were the case that, at law, an RCMP officer was in any event a Crown servant for all purposes.

The Limitations on Crown Agency Expressed in *R. v. Eldorado Nuclear Ltd.*

Even if the police could be considered agents of the Crown for some purposes, and even if the Crown itself were not bound by the *Narcotic Control Act*, I agree with the Ontario Court of Appeal that in this case the police stepped outside the lawful ambit of their agency, and whatever immunity was associated with that agency was lost. This principle was elaborated upon by this Court in two cases decided in 1983, namely *Eldorado Nuclear*, *supra*, and *Canadian Broadcasting Corp. v. The Queen*, [1983] 1 S.C.R. 339. In the latter case, the CBC, which by its enabling statute is expressly constituted a Crown corporation, was nevertheless held subject to prosecution for broadcasting an obscene film. This Court held that the CBC's conduct put it outside the scope of its agency, *per* Estey J., at p. 351:

> ...even if Crown immunity may be attributed to the appellant [CBC] in some circumstances, and the actions of the appellant in such circumstances attributed to the Crown, it does not necessarily follow that the immunities attendant upon the status of Crown agency will flow through to the benefit and protection of the appellant in all circumstances.

In *Eldorado Nuclear*, on the other hand, the Court concluded that two Crown corporations, namely Eldorado Nuclear Limited and Uranium Canada Limited, who were accused of being parties to an unlawful uranium cartel, could not be prosecuted under the *Combines Investigation Act*. They were acting pursuant to their corporate objects set out by Parliament in their respective constitutive statutes, and, in respect of acts done in furtherance of their statutory objects, the *Combines Investigation Act* had no application to them.

While it may be convenient and expeditious for the police to enforce the *Narcotic Control Act* by breaking it themselves under "controlled circumstances", such a strategy in the present case was not necessary to accomplish the RCMP's statutory mandate (*Eldorado Nuclear, supra*, at p. 568). Parliament made it clear in s. 37 of the *Royal Canadian Mounted Police Act*, that the RCMP must act "in accordance with the law". Parliament has made it clear that illegality by the RCMP is neither part of any valid public purpose nor necessarily "incidental" to its achievement. If some form of public interest immunity is to be extended to the police to assist in the "war on drugs", it should be left to Parliament to delineate the nature and scope of the immunity and the circumstances in which it is available, as indeed was done in 1996, after the events in question here, in s. 8 of the *Controlled Drugs and Substances Act*, S.C. 1996, c. 19.

The respondent raises one further argument concerning the legality of the RCMP's conduct in engaging in the reverse sting operation. This argument consists of the bald assertion that the police have available to them a so-called "necessity" justification or defence as that term was used in *R. v. Salvador* (1981), 59 C.C.C. (2d) 521 (N.S.C.A.), *per* Macdonald J.A., at p. 542:

> Generally speaking, the defence of necessity covers all cases where non-compliance with law is excused by an emergency or justified by the pursuit of some greater good.

It is not alleged that the RCMP conduct is such that it could be said to fall within one of the established "justification" defences (e.g., self-defence or defence of third parties) and the Crown offers no authority for the proposition that there exists (or should exist) in Canada a so-called "law enforcement" justification defence generally. The United States experience is mixed: see G. Greaney, "Crossing the Constitutional Line: Due Process and the Law Enforcement Justification" (1992), 67 Notre Dame L. Rev. 745. In any event, the author points out that the law justification defence "only applies if the 'conduct is within the reasonable exercise of the policeman's duty ...'" (p. 784) and "...courts also look to an officer's adherence to state and federal laws when examining the reasonableness of the officer's conduct" (p. 787). The law enforcement justification is frequently raised in the United States in the context of federal law enforcement activity that complies with federal laws but breaches state laws. In such cases, the United States Supreme Court held in *In re Neagle*, 135 U.S. 1 (1890), *per* Miller J., at p. 68 and following, that the officer claiming the law enforcement justification must be performing an act that he or she is authorized by federal law to perform as part of police duties and that actions in violation of state law must be carefully circumscribed so as to do no more than is necessary and proper. See *Baucom v. Martin*, 677 F.2d 1346 (11th Cir. 1982), *per* Wood J., at p. 1350. It would therefore appear that in the

United States a police officer would not be entitled to the law enforcement justification where, as here, the constitutive statute of the police force imposes on its members the duty to act "in accordance with the law" (*Royal Canadian Mounted Police Act*, s. 37).

In this country, it is accepted that it is for Parliament to determine when in the context of law enforcement the end justifies means that would otherwise be unlawful. As Dickson J. (as he then was) put it in *Perka v. The Queen*, [1984] 2 S.C.R. 232, at p. 248:

> The *Criminal Code* has specified a number of identifiable situations in which an actor is justified in committing what would otherwise be a criminal offence. To go beyond that and hold that ostensibly illegal acts can be validated on the basis of their expediency, would import an undue subjectivity into the criminal law. It would invite the courts to second-guess the legislature and to assess the relative merits of social policies underlying criminal prohibitions. Neither is a role which fits well with the judicial function.

While it is true that Dickson J. was not addressing the issue of police illegality in that case, a general "law enforcement justification" would run counter to the fundamental constitutional principles outlined earlier. It should be emphasized that the police in this case were not acting in an emergency or other exigent circumstances. This was a premeditated, carefully planned attempt to sell a ton of hashish. If the Crown wishes to argue for specific relief against criminal or civil liability of the police in emergency or other exigent circumstances in a future case on facts where the argument fairly arises, the issue will be more fully addressed at that time. Such arguments have no application here.

Evidence of Police "Good Faith"

The conclusion that the police conduct in undertaking a reverse sting is, on the facts of this case, illegal does not of itself amount to an abuse of process or, to take it a step further, entitle the appellants to a stay. The legality of police action is but a factor, albeit an important factor, to be considered in the determination of whether an abuse of process has taken place: see *R. v. Lore* (1997), 116 C.C.C. (3d) 255 (Que. C.A.), at p. 271; *R. v. Matthiessen* (1995), 172 A.R. 196 (Q.B.), at pp. 209–10; and *Bond*, *supra*, at p. 333. Where the courts have found that the illegality or other misconduct amounts to an abuse of process, it has by no means followed that a stay of proceedings was considered the appropriate remedy. In *R. v. Xenos* (1991), 70 C.C.C. (3d) 362 (Que. C.A.), for example, a stay was refused despite the finding that the police had participated in conduct that was said to be totally unacceptable, *per* Brossard J.A., at p. 371.

I should make it clear that even if it should turn out here that the police acted contrary to the legal advice provided by the Department of Justice (and we have no reason at this stage to believe this to be the case), there would still be no right to an automatic stay. Apart from everything else, the trial judge would still have to consider any other information or explanatory circumstances that emerge during the inquiry into whether the police or prosecutorial conduct "shocks the conscience of the community". In *Mack*, *supra*, Lamer J. considered that the need to grant some leeway to law enforcement officials to combat consensual criminal offences such as drug trafficking must be weighed against the courts' concern about law enforcement techniques that involve conduct that the citizenry would not tolerate. The underlying rationale of the doctrine of abuse of process is to protect the integrity of the courts' process and the administration of justice from disrepute: see *Mack*, at pp. 938 and 940. Lamer J. stated, at p. 939, that "the doctrine of abuse of process draws on the notion that the state is limited in the way it may deal with its citizens".

Relevance of Legislative Change

It was considered in the court below, and by the Quebec Court of Appeal in *Lore*, *supra*, at p. 271, that the immunity provisions of the new *Controlled Drugs and Substances Act* should be seen as confirmation that the use of reverse stings would not shock the conscience of the community in such a way as to constitute an abuse of process. The fact that Parliament has now enacted specific legislation permitting (in defined circumstances) the police to engage lawfully in the type of conduct at issue in this appeal confirms that the police conduct was not considered lawful by Parliament prior to the amendments' being made. The *Interpretation Act*, R.S.C., 1985, c. I-21, s. 10, provides that "[t]he law [is] always speaking", and Parliament's view at the relevant time was embodied in its then existing enactments. At the material time, Parliament had enacted that conduct otherwise illegal could be done lawfully "under the authority of this Act or the regulations", and under the regulations the police were authorized to possess but not to sell controlled drugs. Judicial notice can certainly be taken of continuing public concern about the drug trade, and in a general way of the difficulties of successfully employing traditional police techniques against large-scale crime organizations. There is little need in this case to resort for evidence of public concern to legislative amendments that were not made until two years after the trial. Nevertheless, given that the test in *Mack* calls for a broad inquiry into the balance of public interests, I would not want to exclude the possibility that after-the-fact legislation may throw some light on community acceptance of a reverse sting operation. It was but a short step from the existing regulatory authority to possess drugs as a result of a sting to the desired regulatory authority to sell drugs in the context of a reverse sting. One of the purposes of the balancing exercise discussed by L'Heureux-Dubé J. in *O'Connor*, *supra*, at paras. 129–30, is to put misconduct by the authorities, worrisome as it may be, in a larger societal perspective.

The point here, however, is slightly different. Superadded to the issue of illegal conduct is the possibility of a police operation planned and executed contrary to the advice (if this turns out to be true) of the Department of Justice. The suggestion is that the RCMP, after securing the relevant legal advice, nevertheless put itself above the law in its pursuit of the appellants. The community view of the police misconduct would, I think, be influenced by knowing whether or not the police were told in advance by their legal advisers that the reverse sting was illegal. Standing by itself, therefore, the subsequent 1996 enactment addresses only part of the issue.

The Assertion of Police Good Faith Was Based in Part on Advice Received from the Department of Justice

Counsel for the Crown has invited the Court to evaluate the police conduct throughout the reverse sting and submits their actions do not constitute an abuse of process. One of the issues is good faith, as discussed in A. Choo, *Abuse of Process and Judicial Stays of Criminal Proceedings* (1993), at pp. 107–118. As evidence of the fact that the reverse sting was undertaken "with the purest of motives", the Crown has pointed out that the reverse sting proposal went through between 9 and 14 stages of approval before finally being authorized. The reverse sting operation was carefully planned, narrowly targeted, and ensured that no hashish actually changed hands, and thus never entered the criminal black market. Most importantly for present purposes is the fact that the Crown emphasized the good faith reliance of the police on legal advice. In the factum prepared for the Ontario Court of Appeal, for example, the argument was put as follows:

> **26.** The conduct of the R.C.M.P. in the present case falls far short of conduct that has hitherto received the courts' seal of approval. In the case at bar, as in the aforementioned case law, there has been no abuse of process or any conduct by the police that could "shock the conscience of the community". In particular, regard must be had to the following considerations:
>
> ...
>
> (f) The R.C.M.P. based, at least in part, the legality of there [*sic*] investigatory techniques on valid case law (*R. v. Lore*, unreported, Quebec Superior Court, 26 February, 1991, Pinard, J.S.C.) and consulted with the Department of Justice with regard to any problems of illegality. [Emphasis added.]

The RCMP's reliance on legal advice was thus invoked as part of its "good faith" argument. The privilege belonged to the client, and the RCMP joined with the Crown to put forward that position. While not explicitly stated in so many words, the plain implication sought to be conveyed to the appellants and to the courts was that the RCMP accepted the legal advice they were given by the Department of Justice and acted in accordance with it. The credibility of a highly experienced departmental lawyer was invoked to assist the RCMP position in the abuse of process proceedings.

The Crown now says that the content of communications between the police and the Department of Justice could not affect the issue as to whether the conduct of the RCMP gave rise to an abuse of process. The Crown says it does not matter what the RCMP were told as to the legality of the reverse sting operation the RCMP planned. Assuming the worst, the Crown says, no stay is warranted. On this point they rely on the analysis of the Court of Appeal, already quoted at para. 13, that if it were shown that the RCMP "moved ahead on their own as mavericks" (p. 197) despite legal advice to the contrary, it would be "of about equal weight" to a situation where the RCMP acted on a positive legal opinion that what they proposed to do would be lawful. With respect, I do not agree. A police force that chooses to operate outside the law is not the same thing as a police force that made an honest mistake on the basis of erroneous advice. We have no reason to think the RCMP ignored the advice it was given, but as the RCMP did make an issue of the legal advice it received in response to the stay applications, the appellants were entitled to have the bottom line of that advice corroborated.

It appears, therefore, that the only satisfactory way to resolve the issue of good faith is to order disclosure of the content of the relevant advice. This should be done (for the reasons to be discussed) on the basis of waiver by the RCMP of the solicitor-client privilege. ...

Waiver of Solicitor-Client Privilege

The record is clear that the RCMP put in issue Cpl. Reynolds' good faith belief in the legality of the reverse sting, and asserted its reliance upon his consultations with the Department of Justice to buttress that position. The RCMP factum in the Ontario Court of Appeal has already been quoted in para. 46. In my view, the RCMP waived the right to shelter behind solicitor-client privilege the contents of the advice thus exposed and relied upon.

. . . .

It is convenient to recall at this point that at the time of the original disclosure motions, the position of the appellants was clear, i.e., disclose the communications or forswear reliance upon them. Notwithstanding this caution, the RCMP and their legal counsel chose to rely upon the communications to support their argument of good faith reliance. In doing so, the privilege was waived.

. . . .

Disclosure Direction

The relevant legal advice received by Cpl. Reynolds should be disclosed to the appellants. This is not an "open file" order in respect of the RCMP's solicitor and client communications. The only legal advice that has to be disclosed is the specific advice relating to the following matters identified by Cpl. Reynolds:

1. The legality of the police posing as sellers of drugs to persons believed to be distributors of drugs.
2. The legality of the police offering drugs for sale to persons believed to be distributors of drugs.
3. The possible consequences to the members of the RCMP who engaged in one or both of the above, including the likelihood of prosecution.

While Cpl. Reynolds also sought advice from Mr. Leising about other matters, including the legality of any release of a sample of hashish to potential buyers, advice in these respects need not be disclosed as they do not relate to a live issue at this stage of the case. If the relevant advice is documented, those portions of the documents that deal with extraneous matters or that describe police methods of criminal investigation may be masked. All that is required is disclosure to the appellants of the bottom line advice to confirm or otherwise the truth of what the courts were advised about the legal opinions provided by the Department of Justice. If there is a dispute concerning the adequacy of disclosure, the disputed documents or information should be provided by the Crown to the trial judge for an initial determination whether this direction has been complied with. The trial judge should then determine what, if any, additional disclosure should be made to the appellants.

If it turns out that Mr. Leising simply erred in connection with this particular opinion, disclosure will support the RCMP officers' claim that they acted in good faith on legal advice, and the application for a stay of proceedings will have to be dealt with on that basis.

Nature of the New Trial

Even if it is established that the RCMP proceeded with the reverse sting contrary to the legal advice from the Department of Justice, the result would not automatically be a stay of proceedings. The test in *Mack* would still apply. The RCMP used its alleged good faith reliance on the Department of Justice legal advice to neutralize or at least blunt any finding of police illegality. If it were determined that the police did not rely on Department of Justice advice, the result would be a finding of police illegality without extenuating circumstances. As discussed in paras. 42 and 43, police illegality does not automatically give rise to a stay of proceedings.

If it should turn out that the reverse sting was launched despite legal advice to the contrary, I think this would be an aggravating factor. However, to repeat, it will be up to the trial judge to determine whether or not a stay is warranted in light of all the circumstances, including the countervailing consideration that police conduct did not lead to any serious infringement of the accused's rights, the RCMP was careful to keep control of the drugs and ensure that none went on the market, and the acknowledged difficulty of combatting drug rings using traditional police methods.

In *R. v. Pearson*, [1998] 3 S.C.R. 620, this Court accepted that in entrapment applications where the innocence of the accused is no longer a live issue, a new trial may be limited to the stay of proceedings application. ...

As entrapment is simply one form of abuse of process, the same approach should be adopted in the present case.

Conclusion

The appeal is allowed in part, a new trial is ordered limited to the issue of whether a stay of proceedings should be granted for abuse of process. The respondent is ordered to disclose to the appellants the materials referred to in para. 74 of these reasons in advance of the retrial.

■

In 2000 the Department of Justice released its *White Paper on Criminal Liability and Law Enforcement* in which it stated that law reform was necessary because *Campbell* (S.C.C., 1999) "changed the law" by taking away police power to break the law in order to enforce the law. Do you agree that this decision changed the law in light of the findings of the McDonald Commission in its 1981 reports? The new law, contained in ss. 25.1 ff. of the *Criminal Code*, sets out the following principle:

> s. 25.1(2) It is in the public interest to ensure that police officers may effectively carry out their law enforcement duties in accordance with the rule of law and, to that end, to expressly recognize in law a justification for public officers and other persons acting at their direction to commit acts or omissions that would otherwise constitute offences.

Read the new provisions carefully. What are the limits that the provisions place on this new justification? What safeguards does it include to protect citizens against police criminality and to promote democratic principles such as public accountability? For criticisms of the new criminal immunities for police: see Kenneth Swan, *A Response to Government of Canada White Paper on Law Enforcement and Criminal Liability* (Toronto: Canadian Civil Liberties Union, 2000); British Columbia Civil Liberties Association (BCCLA), *Submission regarding White Paper on proposed amendments to section 25* (Vancouver: BCCLA, 2000); Elizabeth Sheehy, "Twelve Good Reasons to Oppose Granting Criminal Immunity to Police" (2001) 20:1 Jurisfemme 19; and Grégoire Webber, "Legal Lawlessness and the Rule of Law: A Critique of Section 25.1 of the Criminal Code" (2005) 31 Queen's L.J. 121.

E. INFORMER PRIVILEGE

As Wool establishes, police and the judiciary have actively protected information revealing the identity of informers. Some recent cases have challenged that protection. In *R. v. Khela*, [1995] 4 S.C.R. 201, the Court held, following *R. v. Stinchcombe*, above, under **The Trial Process**, that the disclosure of the identity and whereabouts of the informer was material to the ability of the defence to make full answer and defence. The Crown had refused to divulge the identity of the informer (in an alleged conspiracy to commit murder of persons aboard an aircraft), but had arranged for a meeting at the courthouse between defence counsel and a recalcitrant and hooded "Billy Joe", who was accompanied by two large men. The Court held that this was not sufficient disclosure, and that if disclosure was difficult to comply with, or if there was any new evidence to suggest that the safety of the informer was in jeopardy, the onus was on the Crown to apply to the court to vary the disclosure order.

In contrast, in *R. v. Leipert*, discussed above, under **The Trial Process**, the Court declined to create any new exception to the protection given by the informer privilege on the basis of the right to disclosure and the *Charter* right to make full answer and defence. The Court ruled that the only possible exception to informer privilege arose where there was an evidentiary basis to conclude that the information was necessary to demonstrate the accused's innocence. In *Leipert*, a Crime Stoppers' tip (that drugs were being grown in the accused's house) formed part of the basis for the search warrant, and the accused had unsuccessfully sought disclosure of the source.

More recently, in *Named Person v. Vancouver Sun*, [2007] S.C.J. No. 43 (QL), the Supreme Court of Canada confirmed the absolute importance of protecting informer privilege. The Court considered the proper approach to be employed in a case where informer privilege competes with the open court principle. Justice Bastarache for the majority stated at paras. 16, 19 and 30:

> The law has ... long recognized that those who choose to act as confidential informers must be protected from the possibility of retribution. The law's protection has been provided in the form of the informer privilege rule, which protects from revelation in public or in court the identity of those who give information related to criminal matters in confidence. This protection in turn encourages cooperation with the criminal justice system for future potential informers ... This general protection is so important that it renders informer privilege a matter beyond the discretion of a trial judge... .Informer privilege is of such importance that once found, **courts are not entitled to balance the benefit enuring from the privilege against countervailing considerations** ... Once a trial judge is satisfied that the privilege exists, a complete and total bar on any disclosure of the informer's identity applies. Outside the innocence at stake exception, the rule's protection is absolute. No case-by-case weighing of the justification for the privilege is permitted. All information which might tend to identify the informer is protected by the privilege, and neither the Crown nor the court has any discretion to disclose this information in any proceeding, at any time. [Emphasis in original.]

Finally, as Wool argues, the relationship between police and informers can be quite close. For example, in February 1993, the former head of the RCMP drug squad in Montréal, staff sergeant Paul Sauvé, was convicted and sentenced to jail for possession for the purposes of trafficking and conspiracy to traffic. One of his prized informers was also convicted and sentenced to jail: André Picard, "Former head of drug squad off to jail" *The [Toronto] Globe and Mail* (12 February 1993) A4.

Questions have been raised about the types of people used as informers (their backgrounds, criminal records, reliability, credibility), the activities in which they are engaged (for example, crime), the police support they receive, the rewards and payments they are given, and the investigations in which they are involved. So, who are these informers?

One such RCMP informer was Carney Nerland, the white supremacist who killed Leo LaChance. (See discussion in Abell & Sheehy, *Cases, Context, Critique*, **Enforcement of the Law**.) Police sought to suppress information revealing the identity of their informer to the LaChance/Nerland Commission of Inquiry in Saskatchewan (appointed under the *Public Inquiries Act*, R.S.S. 1978, C-38, to inquire "into certain matters relating to the January 28, 1991, shooting of Leo LaChance at Prince Albert and the consequent conviction of Carney Milton Nerland"). They argued for a police informer privilege: *RCMP v. Saskatchewan (Commission of Inquiry into the death of Leo LaChance*, [1992] 6 W.W.R. 62 (Sask. C.A.)). Even in the face of the clear public interest that had prompted the inquiry, the court held that there was a police informer privilege to be protected. The inquiry had been prompted by protests by Aboriginal and human rights groups that Nerland had been too leniently treated and that he should have been charged with murder, not manslaughter. The RCMP resistance to revealing the identity of the informer prompted the question whether Nerland himself might have been their informer, which was revealed to be the case. After the Supreme Court of Canada refused to hear an appeal, the Prince Albert Tribal Council publicly identified the informant as Carney Nerland himself: CP, "Cree's killer named as police informant" *The [Toronto] Globe and Mail* (13 November 1992) A5.

In December 1993, the month following the report of the inquiry, Carney Nerland was released from jail into the RCMP witness protection program. As Alphonse Bird, Chief of the Prince Albert Grand Council said, "Aboriginal peoples, minorities, Jews — they're all victims in this case, and they're not being protected. It's the perpetrator who's being protected now" (cited in Warren Kinsella, "Provost, and two men who were there" in *Web of Hate: Inside Canada's Far Right Network* (Toronto: HarperCollins, 1994) at 186).

In contrast to the great lengths to which the RCMP went to protect Nerland, they abandoned their promise to protect a battered woman who informed for the RCMP against her husband. She was subsequently denied the promised protection and relocation for herself and her four children and sued the RCMP. See Rudy Platiel, "Closed hearing sought for lawsuit: Woman alleges negligence regarding witness program" *The [Toronto] Globe and Mail* (22 September 1993) A14; Rudy Platiel, "RCMP's closed-hearing request refused: Woman alleges negligence regarding witness program" *The [Toronto] Globe and Mail* (23 September 1993) A2B; and Rudy Platiel, "Relocated witness living in limbo: RCMP sued by woman" *The [Toronto] Globe and Mail* (18 November 1993) A6. Recall the treatment of *Robins*, above, under **Duress**. She had returned to live with her abusive partner at the suggestion of the police and had agreed to inform on him. Not only did she not receive police protection, but she also ended up facing criminal charges herself. Is entrapment available to such a woman as a defence? Meanwhile, some efforts have been made to allow battered women informants to receive new social insurance numbers so as to enable them to adopt a new identity: Debra Huron, "Battered women get chance to start over with new SIN: Government records won't link number to old one" *The [Toronto] Globe and Mail* (7 October 1996) A4.

Police use of questionable informers, such as cellmates, has been the subject of controversy. Critics have advocated the creation of guidelines on the use of informers. The reliance on informers was examined during the Morin Inquiry: Rick Westhead, "The problem with rats, snitches and stoolies: Inquiry to examine use of informants" *Law Times* (4–10 November 1996) 1. One of the witnesses against Guy Paul Morin, above, under **The Trial Process**, was a cellmate who had an outstanding assault charge dropped in exchange for his testimony against Morin. Another inmate was admitted to the temporary absence program in exchange for his testimony. See also the discussion of Morin's wrongful conviction in Abell & Sheehy, *Cases, Context, Critique*, **Enforcement of the Law**. The *Morin Inquiry Report* (**The Trial Process**, above) made 33 recommendations regarding the use of jailhouse informants, calling for numerous limitations upon the use of such informants, restrictions upon the benefits promised or conferred, prohibitions upon benefits conditional upon conviction, and broader disclosure obligations, among many others.

In *White Hoods: Canada's Ku Klux Klan* (Vancouver: New Star Books, 1983) Julian Sher has raised questions about the types of organizations and activities identified as meriting investigation and targeted for infiltration. See particularly the discussion in "Inside the Invisible Empire", at 119–24, where he describes both the extent of police involvement in extreme right organizations and the lack of effective prosecution of those organizations (at 119):

> It was widely suspected by anti-racism activists that the Klan was heavily infiltrated by the police. Certainly, the American experience supported such suspicions. In the mid-sixties, for example, it was estimated that the FBI had informers in the top levels of seven of the fourteen different Klans then in existence; of the estimated 10,000 active Klansmen, 2,000 were reportedly relaying information to the government. The morality, let alone the legality, of the actions of FBI informers was highly questionable.†

Sher discusses the case of Robert Toope in Canada, who was paid by the RCMP for his Western Guard activities and was never prosecuted for any of his illegal activities. Sher suggests that William Richardson was probably also an informer on the RCMP payroll for his work in the Klan. The difficulty of determining the extent of the practice of paying informers to work with extreme right groups is bolstered by police secrecy and denial (at 123):

> ... The RCMP admitted to the McDonald Commission that the use of informers was the "bread and butter" of its security service. For the authorities, the employment of informers within groups like the KKK was justified by the fact that it allowed them to keep tabs on the organization and to catch criminal elements it attracted.
>
> Such reasoning might have been acceptable had the police forces' inside information on the Klan led to prosecutions, but the law enforcement bodies proved to be extremely slow in moving against the Klan in any way. More importantly, the use of police informers within the Klan posed serious legal and ethical questions. "A paid informant may think he has a license to commit any offense in order to gain the desired result," warned the McDonald Commission. "The nature of his task and the environment in which he must work often create considerable pressure on him to commit unlawful acts." The nagging questions remained: how many Klansmen were getting paid by the police while they were carrying out various activities of racial harassment and violence?

As he concludes (at 208):

> While governments fail to take action against the Klan and racism, law enforcement agencies are equally unwilling or unable to act. Various police forces play a dubious role in countering the Klan and its fellow racial extremist groups, paying informers who commit acts of racial violence while never really bringing the full force of the law down on the Klan. Fighting

---

† Reproduced from *White Hoods: Canada's Ku Klux Klan* by Julian Sher, (1983), published by New Star Books, with permission of the author (www.juliansher.com).

> the KKK, for some policemen at least, appears to be a big joke. In October, 1982, several black Ontario Provincial Police officers found KKK application forms in their lockers; O.P.P. officials dismissed the incident as a prank. Police forces in general have shown little readiness to clean up their own house when it comes to institutionalized racism.

In 1994, it came to light that Grant Bristow, a founder of the racist Heritage Front, was likely a paid informant for CSIS. He was reported to have passed on money and information to the violent American neo-Nazi group, White Aryan Resistance; passed on information about a CBC investigation into racism in the military; and infiltrated the Reform party. See Stephen Bindman, "MPs to probe role of CSIS 'spy': Heritage Front founder focus of hearings" *The Ottawa Citizen* (9 June 1994) A9. In December 1994, a 100-page report (on CSIS and the Grant Bristow affair) written by the Security Intelligence Review Committee was completed, essentially vindicating Bristow while acknowledging that he "tested the limits of appropriate behaviour of someone acting on behalf of the government": Tu Thanh Ha, "Gray reviewing CSIS report: Proposals to change handling of informants expected" *The [Toronto] Globe and Mail* (10 December 1994) A6; Donn Downey, "Judge rejects bid for Bristow to testify: CSIS informant is 'vital' to defence, lawyer for white supremacist argues" *The [Toronto] Globe and Mail* (21 February 1995) A3. In the latter article, Downey points out that the arguments made by counsel for Wolfgang Droege and Peter Mitrevski contradict the conclusions of the report, and suggest that Bristow was much more than a "passive mole" and was, in fact, an instigator and a mastermind. As counsel for Mitrevski argued, Bristow is probably being protected by the federal government under some sort of witness-protection program.

The information about Bristow became available because of a leak by Brian McInnis, a former aide to former Solicitor-General Douglas Lewis. Recall the cases of other "whistle blowers" (government workers who have breached confidentiality), discussed above, under **Broadening the Defences**. It was only in July 1995, a year later, that Federal Justice Minister Allan Rock decided that McInnis would not be charged under the *Official Secrets Act*: CP, "Rock drops case against Tory aide: Man who leaked CSIS files won't face Official Secrets Act charge" *The [Toronto] Globe and Mail* (20 July 1995) A4. McInnis admitted that he might have broken the law by releasing the document that detailed a CBC investigation of racism in the Canadian Forces. The report documented links between some soldiers serving in Somalia and the Heritage Front.

On the other hand, police have used informants to infiltrate Aboriginal organizations and communities. In 1989, CSIS investigated the Labrador Innu community, as part of a larger investigation of Aboriginal groups, to gather information as to whether political violence was likely: Richard Cleroux, "CSIS probed Labrador Innu and other native groups" *The [Toronto] Globe and Mail* (1 June 1989) A1. For an example of the way undercover resources are (ab)used, consider "Operation Rainbow", a five-year investigation (the largest undercover operation ever undertaken by the Ministry of Natural Resources). In 1990, that undercover operation on Manitoulin Island led to illegal hunting charges against 35 people, most of them Aboriginal. By 1995, the United Chiefs and Councils of Manitoulin (U.C.C.M.) applied for an adjournment to raise money. They argued that the years of legal manoeuvring had drained their defence fund dry. See CP, "Natives want trial delayed" *The [Toronto] Globe and Mail* (18 April 1995) A4.

In August 1996, the Chiefs adopted a proposal that they hoped would lead to a negotiated settlement of the outstanding charges. They offered to enter guilty pleas on the "purely safety-related matters" if the remaining hunting and fishing charges were withdrawn and a negotiation process established: "UCCM offers Operation Rainbow settlement to provincial government" *Manitoulin Expositor* (21 August 1996) 9. In the meantime, the conservation officer (who has been referred to as the architect of the prosecution in Operation Rainbow) was named "Wildlife Officer of the Year" by the North American Wildlife Enforcement Officers Association. In a statement by the Chiefs, they expressed "puzzlement and anger" (reproduced in Chief Glen Hare, "Letter to the Editor" *Manitoulin Expositor* (7 August 1996) 4):

> The occasion of this award highlights the fact that the Anishnabe continue to be viewed as outcasts and poachers when it comes to fish and wildlife. It shows us that we still have a long way to go before we are recognized as human beings and stakeholders by enforcement agencies and the sports hunters that they serve. And it also underscores the reality that fish and wildlife management in North America

continues to be dominated by white people for the benefit of white people. These comments may seem harsh to some, but they reflect the reality that we deal with every day.

According to a report published by the Manitoulin Recorder, Officer Anderson was praised by the Association for his dedication to "community involvement." This is news to us. He certainly hasn't been involved in any positive way with our communities, unless targeting and prosecuting Indians is regarded as a public service. The Recorder also observed that Officer Anderson had to meet nine criteria to get the award, including "professionalism." We suppose that using alcohol to encourage infractions (as officers were instructed to do in Operation Rainbow) and seeking the authority to break laws in order to facilitate a prosecution (again, Operation Rainbow) is a sign of professionalism among the CO elite.

... No one noted that out of the 170 charges which were laid against the 19 UCCM defendants in 1990, only six convictions have resulted — the remaining 100+ charges have either been withdrawn or are still outstanding. Is this the basis of a success story?

... If Operation Rainbow and it's [*sic*] architects deserve any awards, it's for sowing the seeds of conflict, wasting taxpayers [*sic*] money [almost $1 million], and promoting an open season on Indians. We don't think that's anything to write home about."[†]

† Courtesy of the *Manitoulin Expositor.*

Index of Cases

P

R

S

T

U–W